INTERNATIONAL POLITICAL ECONOMY

Conflict and Cooperation in the Global System

INTERNATIONAL POLITICAL ECONOMY

Conflict and Cooperation in the Global System

Frederic S. Pearson
Center for Peace and Conflict Studies
Department of Political Science
Wayne State University
Detroit, Michigan

Simon Payaslian
Department of History
UCLA
Los Angeles, California

Boston Burr Ridge, IL Dubuque, IA Madison, WI New York San Francisco St. Louis
Bankok Bogotá Caracas Lisbon London Madrid
Mexico City Milan New Delhi Seoul Singapore Sydney Taipei Toronto

McGraw-Hill College

A Division of The ***McGraw-Hill*** *Companies*

INTERNATIONAL POLITICAL ECONOMY: CONFLICT AND COOPERATION IN THE GLOBAL SYSTEM

This book is printed on acid-free paper.

1 2 3 4 5 6 7 8 9 0 QPF/QPF 9 3 2 1 0 9 8

ISBN 0-07-049082-1

Editorial director: *Jane E. Vaicunas*
Sponsoring editor: *Monica Eckman*
Editorial assistant: *Hannah Glover*
Senior marketing manager: *Suzanne Daghlian*
Project manager: *Mary Lee Harms*
Production supervisor: *Laura Fuller*
Designer: *K. Wayne Harms*
Senior photo research coordinator: *Lori Hancock*
Compositor: *GAC Indianapolis*
Typeface: *10/12 Garamond*
Printer: *Quebecor Printing Book Group/Dubuque, IA*

Cover design: *Jamie O'Neal*
Cover image: *© Phil Banko/Tony Stone Images*

Library of Congress Cataloging-in-Publication Data

Pearson, Frederic S.
International political economy: conflict and cooperation it the global system / Frederic S. Pearson, Simon Payaslian. — 1st ed.
Includes bibliographical references and index.
ISBN 0-07-049082-1
1. International economic relations. 2. International economic integration. 3. International trade. 4. Regionalism.
I. Payaslian, Simon. II. Title.
HF1359.P4 1999
337—dc21 98-45017
CIP

www.mhhe.com

ABOUT THE AUTHORS

FREDERIC S. PEARSON (Ph.D., University of Michigan) studies international military intervention, international conflict, and the arms trade and its connection to the international political economy. Among his recent publications is the fourth edition of *International Relations: The Global Condition in the Twenty-first Century* with J. M. Rochester. Dr. Pearson also has two books on the international arms trade: *The Global Spread of Arms: Political Economy of International Security* (1994) and *Arms and Warfare,* with Michael Brzoska (1994) on the effect of arms transfers during war. Dr. Pearson directs the Center for Peace and Conflict Studies and the Detroit Council for World Affiars, and he is professor of political science at Wayne State University in Detroit. His teaching interests include the causes of war, international theory, the roots of social conflict, and Middle East politics.

SIMON PAYASLIAN holds a Ph.D. in political science (Wayne State University, 1992) and is currently working toward a Ph.D. in history at the University of California, Los Angeles (UCLA). He has taught courses on international relations, U.S. foreign policy, American government, public opinion and propaganda, developing countries, the Middle East, the former Soviet Union, and Latin America at Wayne State University, the University of Michigan–Dearborn, Eastern Michigan University, and the University of Windsor, Canada. He is the author of *U.S. Foreign Economic and Military Aid: The Reagan and Bush Administrations* (1996), as well as articles on international human rights, the United Nations, peace and conflict studies, the former Soviet republics, and U. S. foreign policy.

To The Coming Generations

BRIEF CONTENTS

CONTENTS

PART 3

IPE IN A DIVIDED GLOBAL SYSTEM

LIST OF REVIEWERS

Dr. John H. Oneal, University of Alabama

Dr. Dirk C. van Raemdonck, Lafayette College

Cynthia A. Hody, University of Maryland Baltimore County

Dr. Curtis Peet, Bowling Green State University

Dr. Dimitris Stevis, Colorado State University

Dr. Herman Schwartz, University of Virginia

Dr. Lev S. Gonick, California State University at Pomona

Dr. Birol Yesilada, University of Missouri

Dr. Michael Mastanduno, Darmouth College

Dr. Robert Hunt, Illinois State University

Dr. Jongryn Mo, University of Texas at Austin

Dr. Walter Arnold, Miami University

Dr. Harrison Wagner, University of Texas

PREFACE

Trends toward interdependence and globalization through greater integration and expansion of world markets have provided opportunities for international cooperation, but occasions for increased conflict as well. The "shrinking and linking" of the world through technological and political breakthroughs raises some old problems seen in earlier centuries, as well as some new and unprecedented ones. Globalization has been praised and pilloried by interest groups and national leaders, as well as by academic analysts. On the one hand, it is seen as a benefit to humanity, bringing unprecedented prosperity and, in some estimations, peace; on the other hand, it is seen by some as a driving force of exploitative capitalism and by others as the stacking of a house of cards, in which severe economic crises in one region will drag down states in other regions. At the very least, while the United States and Russia still remain the preeminent military powers, even before the end of the Cold War in 1989 competition was switching from the military/strategic to the economic realm. This does not negate "realpolitik" as a hallmark of international relations, but it elevates a new set of issues to the strategic calculus—seen, for example, in the shift of intelligence agencies to include issues of commercial spying.

These shifts have implications for various facets of the international political economy. For example, since the 1940s, multilateral and bilateral aid programs have reflected major powers' Cold War political and geo-strategic priorities. More recently, with diminished disposable budgets, aid policies have reflected efforts to bypass potentially corrupt governments and directly reach needy populations with more effective, project-oriented assistance, and even "micro-loans" giving to individuals. After decades of experimentation with various economic development and industrialization schemes, and with the reduction of the strategic Cold War aid impetus and strong reform pressures from the West, in the late 1980s and 1990s some developing countries opted for greater economic liberalization. Whether these trends prove sufficient to weather storms of currency and stock market collapse (witnessed in the supposedly dynamic East Asia at century's end), of debt and default, of endemic poverty, and of growing trade rivalry and protectionism remains to be seen.

Clearly, however, such questions constitute a rich agenda for analysis and a good reason for a fresh look at the global economy.

It is now necessary to take stock of the changes and continuities of the international political economy and to do so with more attention to political interests, forces, and consequences. This means first that we should understand the history of the international political economy, as well as how it has evolved over the centuries. Then we must attend to the sociopolitical consequences of market forces and economic policies. One of our economist colleagues used to lament trends toward "celestial" economic analysis, in which real policy questions and choices were obscured in a maze of models and equations. While models and data are indespensible in taking stock of which directions things are going and likely to go, as well as the costs and benefits of moving in those directions, there is no substitute for political and philosophical analysis to determine what is worth the price. As in local economies, the everyday impacts of social choices on people and groups and the contention between political interests are really what drive the global economy.

In this book, we seek to relate the basic theories, or "paradigms," of international economic analysis to likely social and political outcomes in the new century. We cannot lose sight of the fact that multinational corporations, development policies, conditions of inequality and dependency, arms production, wars, and the growing reality of informal economies directly and indirectly shape the lives of millions around the world. We recall one study that noted the choices of destitute parents in India: knowing that they cannot afford all three, should they spend scarce resources on cooking fuel to boil water (and thereby avoid cholera), on mosquito netting to ward off malaria, or on shoes to avoid parasites? Economics is not just statistics and figures; the impact of production, the distribution of capital, the availability of jobs, and the quality of the environment have real and varied meanings for people in certain stations of life and in certain regions.

The intriguing part of the international political economy is that it is populated by financial speculators, corporate moguls, technological wizards, power brokers, smugglers, warriors, refugees, shift workers, protest groups—by everyone who takes part in the movement of capital or labor. We all have a role, and those roles are complicated and changing. How do governments and private individuals or interest groups relate in the emerging economy? We are only now discovering the complexity of both mapping global economic exchanges and evaluating them in terms of policy wisdom, efficacy, and ethics. This book can help equip readers to make such judgments.

We present a general overview of the international economic system since the mid-seventeenth century, its evolution and dominant features, and the current issues of contention. The text, which includes tables, illustrative boxes, and a glossary, is meant to be readable and to combine theory with examples and insights. At the end of each chapter is a *Summary* of some of the major issues covered, as well as *Points of Contention* derived from the material presented to facilitate class discussion and critical thinking. We try to encourage and suggest further reading and research, in part through the text's *Suggested Readings.*

Equally as important, and by way of acknowledgment, the references in the chapter *Notes* and in the *Suggested Readings* signify more than the conventional practice of attribution; we express our appreciation for the many contributions and observations of IPE scholars. We also owe much gratitude to Marie Olson for her diligent research assistance and to Barbara Betcher for her assistance with the manuscript. We also would like to thank the McGraw-Hill editors for their patience and kind assistance, despite the delays that sometimes attended our creations. Finally, we thank our families for constant encouragement and each other for a durable and remarkable long-distance friendship and collaboration.

Frederic S. Pearson
Simon Payaslian

PART ONE

INTRODUCTION TO INTERNATIONAL POLITICAL ECONOMY

Queen Elizabeth II of Great Britian and former French President Francois Mitterand dedicate the Channel Tunnel, or "Chunnel," commerical symbol of the emerging European Union. (AP/Wide World Photos)

CHAPTER ONE

INTRODUCTION

Between the time of the **Group of Seven (G-7)** jobs conference in Detroit in March 1994 and the May 1998 annual summit of the **Group of Eight (G-8)** in Birmingham, England, symbolically and actually much had changed in the international economic system, yet much also had remained the same, reflecting basic economic challenges and processes going back a century or more in the industrial era. Beyond the fact that an important country, Russia, had been added to the G-7, the international economy had experienced transformations in economic and political relations in a process labeled "globalization," and the transformations seemed to be coming ever faster. Early in the 1990s, the world economy began adjusting to the end of the Cold War competition between the United States and the former Soviet Union, which had lasted nearly forty-five years. By 1994, it was clear, and subsequent years made it even clearer, that, in an era of instantaneous communications and networks of international financial investors and currency traders, no Japanese prime minister or American president could introduce economic policies without considering their global dimensions and impacts.[1]

The globalization process has created serious dilemmas for citizens and governments alike in the industrialized and developing countries. The 1994 conference, taking place in one of America's hardest hit industrial cities, was meant to confront a serious crisis in lost jobs and chronic unemployment in many parts of the world. In the early 1990s, an estimated 120 million registered unemployed (excluding those who had not registered or were no longer seeking employment), many who were victims of "corporate downsizing," constituted a massive political and social problem, reflected, for example, in growing ethnic violence and tension among resentful neighbors in many regions—including France and Germany in Western Europe. It was also estimated that at least 700 million people were "underemployed" in low-paying jobs with little opportunity for a decent living.[2] Of particular concern to the G-7 leaders was the unemployment rate for people between the ages of sixteen and twenty-five. In 1993, for example, youth unemployment levels in Italy were about 30 percent, in France 25 percent, in Canada and Britain 17 percent, in the United States 13 percent, and in Japan and western Germany 5 percent. This represented hopelessness for the next generation.[3]

By 1998, however, the Detroit area and most of the United States were enjoying record low unemployment, even as joblessness remained at disturbingly high levels in most U.S. inner cities and in Europe and grew alarmingly in Japan and much of East Asia. New crises emerged, beginning in 1997, with Japan and its seemingly prosperous Asian neighbors suffering tremendous and unexpected economic setbacks related to poor banking, taxation, and investment decisions and, in some cases, to political and economic corruption. The crisis extended to the shaky Russian economy and to Latin America in 1998. Meanwhile, Europe was frantically preparing for the introduction of a common "Euro" currency, while still suffering the shocks and costs of a reunited Germany and investment in the former Soviet bloc to the east.[4] The European Union (EU) countries (see Map 1.1) have about 372 million people, conduct approximately $4 trillion worth of business per year, and account for nearly 30 percent of the world's total gross domestic product (GDP). Additional European states, ranging from prosperous Scandinavia to the struggling Balkans, have applied to join.[5]

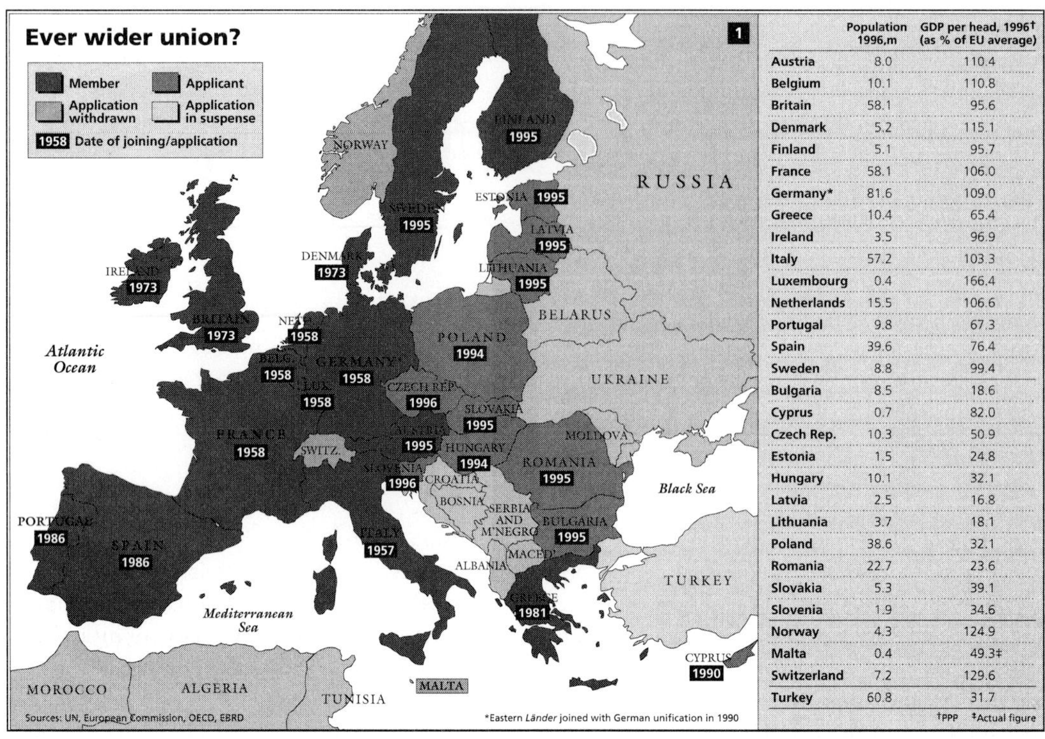

	Population 1996,m	GDP per head, 1996† (as % of EU average)
Austria	8.0	110.4
Belgium	10.1	110.8
Britain	58.1	95.6
Denmark	5.2	115.1
Finland	5.1	95.7
France	58.1	106.0
Germany*	81.6	109.0
Greece	10.4	65.4
Ireland	3.5	96.9
Italy	57.2	103.3
Luxembourg	0.4	166.4
Netherlands	15.5	106.6
Portugal	9.8	67.3
Spain	39.6	76.4
Sweden	8.8	99.4
Bulgaria	8.5	18.6
Cyprus	0.7	82.0
Czech Rep.	10.3	50.9
Estonia	1.5	24.8
Hungary	10.1	32.1
Latvia	2.5	16.8
Lithuania	3.7	18.1
Poland	38.6	32.1
Romania	22.7	23.6
Slovakia	5.3	39.1
Slovenia	1.9	34.6
Norway	4.3	124.9
Malta	0.4	49.3‡
Switzerland	7.2	129.6
Turkey	60.8	31.7

†PPP ‡Actual figure

MAP 1.1
Source: "European Union" [survey], *The Economist,* May 31, 1997, p. 5.

Many facets of the international economy are illustrated by these twists and turns in global developments. International institutions and agreements—that is, "regimes"—meant to stabilize the world economy attempted to meet the trade, currency, and unemployment crises of the 1990s. The **International Monetary Fund (IMF)**, which gives loans to countries suffering from shortages or weakness in their currencies, swung into action during the Asian crisis. This crisis, however, one of a series of dilemmas affecting various regions such as Central America, the former Soviet Union, and Africa over the course of the past two decades, led to a loss of faith in such key institutions by many citizens and politicians. The IMF was criticized for being too intrusive into the policies of specific "sovereign" countries and for being too dependent on the wealthier western powers, such as the United States—that is, for failing to heed the right of specific governments to set their own economic policies and budget priorities. In Indonesia, for example, IMF pressure and resentment at the scandal-ridden and inflexible government of President Suharto led to severe rioting and bloody military crackdowns as prices of everyday goods and services skyrocketed. However, most economists continued to support the role of the IMF as a fund of last resort to keep economies afloat.

The jobs conference also took place immediately after the highly controversial **North American Free Trade Agreement (NAFTA)** went into effect in January 1994. Like the 1992 Maastricht Treaty setting up the **European Union,** NAFTA was an effort to *integrate* more closely the Canadian, U.S., and Mexican economies through freer trade. NAFTA supporters, including both Republicans and the Clinton administration, argued that its reduced tariff (tax) barriers to imports would reinvigorate the North American economies, seemingly threatened by foreign competitors from across the Atlantic and Pacific. NAFTA would generate greater markets for U.S. goods, and job opportunities in Mexico would stem the tide of illegal immigrants seeking entry into the United States. Whether NAFTA indeed led to the improved employment scene of 1998 is debatable; to opponents, including trade union leaders, some business leaders, and some politicians from both the left and right (such as independent presidential candidates Ross Perot and Pat Buchanan), the agreement threatened the U.S. economy and jobs (the famous "loud sucking sound" of jobs leaving

TABLE 1.1
NAFTA and Jobs

Study	Net U.S. Job Gain/Loss
Stanford	−91,974
Almon	+44,000
DRI/McGraw-Hill	+221,000
Hufbauer, Schott[a]	+171,000
Economic Strategy Institute	−32,000 to −220,000

Source: Christian Science Monitor, Dave Herring/© The Christian Science Monitor. November 12, 1993, p. 8.
[a]Study often cited by President Clinton

the country). Outside observers viewed NAFTA as a last-ditch effort by Washington to halt the gradual decline of U.S political and economic dominance, or **hegemony,** so successfully established after the Second World War. NAFTA, they noted, "would take the United States down a road trod by the Dutch and British Empires in their days of decline when financiers shifted investment abroad to more promising frontiers."[6] As shown in Table 1.1, NAFTA's job creation potential is still subject to much heated debate. According to studies by Almon, DRI/McGraw-Hill, and Hufbauer and Schott, the agreement was expected to generate between 44,000 and 221,000 jobs in the United States. Other studies, however, estimated that it would cost between 32,000 and 220,000 jobs.[7]

Economic agreements in other regions paralleled both NAFTA and the EU. These included the proposed Free Trade Area of the Americas (meant to integrate North and South America into a giant trading sphere), several separate free trade areas in South America and Africa, and the Asia-Pacific Economic Cooperation (APEC) linking East Asia and North America. States in all of these "multilateral" organizations hoped for the benefits of forming larger economic markets within which to buy and sell products or to develop opportunities for labor. In the case of the EU, there was also the prospect of competing with the United States as the world's largest and most advanced economy, with the potential of the world's leading currency as well. For the United States, therefore, the "Pacific community" provides not only critical markets for its products but also a vehicle to balance the potentially negative impact of the EU's exclusionary market practices, such as a single tariff against non-European states. This illustrates the range and mixture of economic and political motives in the global economy—indeed, the reason the subject of this book is referred to as **"international political economy."** States compete and collaborate to increase both their wealth and their influence over how policies are made and over who benefits the most. The results can range from prosperity to violence, as seen in the streets of Jakarta Indonesia.

While no trade liberalization agreements similar to NAFTA have yet included such countries as Australia, China, and Malaysia, they all are members, or would-be members, of the **General Agreement on Tariffs and Trade (GATT),** a system of periodic, *multilateral* meetings designed to reduce tariffs and set workable rules for freeing up trade. GATT has now been reinforced by the **World Trade Organization (WTO),** a body to adjust those rules and settle conflicts arising over their interpretation.

In order to provide a better understanding of such political and economic developments, this chapter introduces some of the key principles and concepts of international political economy (IPE). Much of the way the international economy operates is directly related to politics, as interest groups such as corporations and unions pressure governments for favorable economic policies, both at home and abroad. Some of the more pressing problems in the political economy, especially those arising within the context of post-Cold War trade and political rivalries, are reviewed in the following sections and in subsequent chapters.

THE PRINCIPLES OF INTERNATIONAL ECONOMIC RELATIONS

International political economy is the relationship between political and economic changes and their impact on global and domestic political, market, and production activities. It covers a wide range of issues among countries, as well as public and private institutions in both domestic and global arenas. It is concerned with such issues as power and security, cooperation and conflict in international trade and financial relations. It also concerns the role of **multinational corporations (MNCs)** in, and their impact on, the economies and politics of parent and host countries, the nature of technological changes and their impact on the globalization of industrial and information networks, the rapidly changing international political and economic context of employment, international inequalities, military expenditures, foreign debt and dependency, informal economic activities, environmental degradation, and the use and misuse of our global natural resources, to name but a few.[8]

A basic premise of this book is that rapid globalization and related transformations in the international political economy inevitably cause conflicts but also create opportunities for cooperation among countries. For example, in order to prevent a repetition of the financial chaos experienced after the First World War, the post–World War II leaders in the West, primarily under the auspices of the United States, created the International Monetary Fund, the **World Bank,** and the General Agreement on Tariffs and Trade to maintain global financial stability and to develop international standards for and lower barriers to trade. Over the years, other such international regimes were formed to address various problems, such as environmental degradation, proliferation of nuclear weapons and nuclear technology, fishing rights, deep sea mining, and food production and distribution.[9] Despite their shortcomings, these efforts to promote cooperation have been at least partially successful, although at times such multilateral arrangements have come under attack from various groups in both developing and industrial countries. Critics argue that the United States and the international institutions it created have dominated international economic relations and have intentionally or unintentionally rendered other states' economies both dependent on the whims of decision makers in New York and Washington and vulnerable to the vicissitudes of foreign markets in the more advanced Northern Hemisphere. Islamic societies, such as Iran, viewed such multilateral organizations as mere extensions of centuries of Western political and economic domination, imposing Western precepts and undermining local customs and institutions. The globalization of political economy may provide opportunities to enable societies to overcome such difficulties, but it may also exacerbate existing tensions when domestic economic conditions deteriorate, people feel financially less secure, and governments find themselves unable to address various and increasingly interrelated international and domestic social and economic issues.

Two key ingredients of international economic relations particularly subject to political pressures are international trade and international finance (Chapters 4 and 5, respectively).

International Trade

A traditional, classical liberal conception of trade has been that a country exchanges goods with others primarily to obtain cash or foreign exchange earnings, to acquire needed goods at reasonable prices and to compensate for its deficiencies in natural resources or human skills in the labor force. The unequal distribution of natural resources across the globe, climatic conditions, geographical location (for example, whether landlocked or accessible via major waterways), terrain, and population size compel a country to enter into trade agreements with other countries for various commercial and industrial goods, sometimes even at the risk of diplomatic difficulties. One aspect of Japan's foreign policy illustrates the relationship between politics and foreign trade. Japan is nearly completely lacking in natural resources. Prior to the Arab-Israeli Yom Kippur War in 1973 and the oil embargo by the **Organization of Arab Petroleum Exporting Countries (OAPEC)** against supporters of Israel, Japan's policy vis-a-vis Israel was quite favorable. However, Japan also imported more than 85 percent of its oil from OAPEC countries at the time. In response to the oil embargo, Japan and some Western European countries dependent on Middle Eastern oil modified their positions toward the region in favor of Arab governments. Thereafter, Japan's foreign policy toward the Middle East became more sensitive to its dependence on Middle Eastern oil, while adopting "diversification" strategies, such as the development of nuclear power, so that during the Gulf War of 1990–1991 Japan's oil imports from the region dropped to about 70 percent. Clearly, not all trade relations are as complicated and vital as the Japanese case, yet all trade relations involve a good deal of domestic and bilateral political considerations.

International Finance

International trade would not occur without some form of international financing, and it certainly would not occur as easily as it does today if no mechanisms were available to transfer and exchange one country's currency (for example, the U.S. dollar) for another (such as the Japanese yen). In the absence of such arrangements, bartering—that is, the exchange of goods—would be the main mode of international trade. Generally, international finance is related to banking and is dependent on two components: foreign exchange rates and balance of payments.

Foreign Exchange Rates Foreign exchange is used to make international payments, and the exchange rate is the price an individual pays for one currency to purchase another currency. Instruments of foreign exchange include a country's currency, checks, drafts, and bills of exchange.[10] For example, individuals, businesses, and governments involved in international trade and related financial transactions obtain U.S. dollars and exchange them for Japanese yen. They purchase and sell foreign exchange in international markets through foreign exchange dealers or local commercial banks, just as they buy and sell stocks, bonds, and commodities. Some of the major international foreign exchange centers are located in Brussels, Hong Kong,

London, New York, Paris, Tokyo, and Zurich. Ultimately, the principal function of foreign exchange markets is to facilitate the transfer of "purchasing power from one country to another and from one currency to another."[11] In so doing, the exchange rate influences not only capital flows and the cost of borrowing money but also competition between countries and their standard of living, unemployment rate, consumers' purchasing power, and so forth. These factors will be discussed in greater depth in Chapter 5.

Balance of Payments A country's balance of payments consists of the value of all transactions, including imports and exports of goods and services and transfer of investments, currency, gold, and so on, between that country and others. Such transactions constitute a fundamental element in a country's financial standing in the global economic system. Its economic strength is largely based on the ability to maintain a healthy equilibrium between capital inflows and outflows. Very much as a company's quarterly or annual reports of its balance sheet reflect its financial condition, so does a country's "balance sheet" reflect its financial position—that is, the status of its currency, goods, services, and policies—in the international economy.

Thus, international trade and monetary relations are subject to international market forces of supply and demand, just as domestic markets are; just as in domestic markets, international competition exerts a great influence on corporate production priorities and government import and export decisions. Nevertheless, there are a number of distinctions between the domestic and international environments in which market forces operate. Although these distinctions have considerably blurred over the past twenty years or so, they have three significant political implications for the nature and role of international trade relations. First, while a domestic market operates under a single government, international trade and financial transactions involve two or more governments or multilateral institutions, such as the World Bank. Second, a domestic market, at least a healthy one, is based on a single currency. International exchange, on the other hand, consists of various currencies, some of which—such as the British pound before the Second World War, the U.S. dollar since then, increasingly the DMark and the Japanese yen, and perhaps in the future the Euro—belong to a more prestigious group than others, based on the size and economic vitality of their home countries. Third, it is easier to transfer labor and capital from one area to another within the domestic economy than across international borders. In international trade, such transfers involve greater financial and even political costs and risks,[12] though unprecedented changes in technology in general and communications technology in particular enable multinational corporations and financiers to challenge the state as the historically central actor in international trade and financial relations.

THE PRINCIPAL COMPONENTS OF INTERNATIONAL POLITICAL ECONOMY

In addition to trade and finance as two major elements of international economic relations, certain key components, such as a country's economic and political resources, form the principal determinants of its foreign policy toward others in the international political economy. Such resources include, for example, skilled population, land, infrastrtural development, technological advancements, and military capabilities. No country is completely self-sufficient; uneven distribution of wealth and resources across the globe has allowed some countries to be far better off than others. Economic and political resources form the very essence of a country's relations with others. A country's foreign policy reflects its international standing and reputation based on its resources, which can be translated into economic but also political and military power and influence in international relations. These three forms of power—economic, political, and military—constitute the basic foreign policy instruments in bilateral and multilateral relations, and fluctuations in these resources and capabilities play a crucial role in determining the rise and decline of major powers.[13]

Thus, two fundamental concepts, states and markets, constitute the core, and often colliding, components of international political economy. The state is predicated on principles of juridical and administrative unity, territorial integrity, territorially defined national identity and loyalty, and legitimate authority in relations with subjects within its jurisdiction. State **sovereignty** refers to the supremacy of state authority in all domestic matters, as well as in relations with all other entities at home and abroad—for example, other theoretically equally sovereign states and international organizations. The market is a more fluid concept, however. It primarily involves production and commercial activities transcending national boundaries, identities, and loyalties. Operating within and across the confines of individual states, the market is, nevertheless, an intricate web of interdependent transactions reflecting and shaping prices, technological advances, and consumer tastes. The pull and push between state sovereignty and market forces often create frictions between the two. As Robert Gilpin has stated aptly, "For the state, territorial boundaries are a necessary basis of national autonomy and political unity. For the market, the elimination of all political and other obstacles to the operation of the price mechanism is imperative."[14]

The globalization of international political economy in the late twentieth century, however, is expected to lead to greater similarities between state and market functions. The wave of privatization of previously state-owned enterprises in the 1980s and 1990s may be indicative of this convergence, as the interests of markets and of states coincide. This does not necessarily mean that the state "retreats," as some observers have argued, but that the state begins to adopt values and principles previously held by those in the market. However, there are also certain factors in domestic and international politics that hinder such homogenization. The following sections focus on the economic and political resources that lend power and influence to individual nation–states and that form the bases of international economic relations among nation–states.

Before discussing specific components of state power, it is useful to identify, following Susan Strange, two general types of power in international political economy: relational power and structural power.[15] *Relational power* is the ability of one actor to compel another to behave in a way that the latter otherwise would not.[16] The influence OAPEC exerted on Tokyo's foreign policy toward Israel and its Arab neighbors, as previously mentioned, is an example of relational power. A more visible example of this is the defeat and withdrawal of Iraqi forces from oil-rich Kuwait during the Persian Gulf War of 1991. Strange has defined *structural power* as "the power to shape and determine the structure of the global political economy within which other states, their political institutions, their economic enterprises and (not least) their scientists and other professional people have to operate."[17] Accordingly, primary power structures consist of four key ingredients: structure of security (physical, national), structure of production (private and state enterprises, MNCs), structure of finance (credit and money), and structure of knowledge (information, science and technology).[18]

These structures are closely intertwined, involving both state and market, political and economic actors. Those in control of structures of security, such as armies, easily and directly influence structures of production, and vice versa, and are in turn influenced by people in control of credit and information. The exercise of control in the primary power structures also rests on the exercise of control on secondary power structures involving more specific policy issue-areas, such as control over energy and natural resources, transportation, trade, and welfare.[19] A country is said to emerge as a world power—that is, one that controls world structures of power—as it first produces and develops its own national economic resources (including natural resources, population, education and training, infrastructural development, currency, and gold reserves) and then widens and maintains, for a long period of time, its transnational control over such resources across borders and continents. A hegemon's political resources, such as the ability to exercise power and influence in international organizations as well as its military capability, reflect and complement its economic strength. The emergence of the United States as a world hegemonic power after the Second World War was based first on the government's and corporations' ability—in the nineteenth century, especially after the Civil War—to develop the vast economic resources in the country and then to translate, through political and military strength, that economic strength into an internationalist policy and structural power in the twentieth century.

Economic Resources

Land and Natural Resources Since time immemorial, the size and quality of land and the geoclimatic position of civilizations have shaped their productive capabilities. Given basic human needs, such as for food, one important aspect of a people's territory is the amount of available arable land. Less than half of the earth's land surface is suitable for agricultural production. Since the quality of cultivable land varies from one country to another, from one region to another, some countries are endowed with greater agricultural "carrying capacity"—that is, a higher "maximum population that could be fed a minimum daily diet, given the particular soils and climate."[20]

In developing countries, about 70 to 80 percent of the labor force works in the agricultural sector, which accounts for 35 to 45 percent of their **gross domestic product (GDP).** In the more industrialized countries, less than 7 percent of the labor force is involved in agricultural production, accounting for about 3 percent of GDP. However, because of technological efficiencies, the more industrialized countries, including Australia, Canada, and the United States, are the biggest food producers and exporters (for example, grains). Such disparities in carrying capacities have led to grave disparities in the global distribution of food, and well over 300 million people, mostly in developing countries, suffer from malnourishment. As Knox and Agnew have pointed out, however, it is toosimple to conclude that hunger is due exclusively tofood shortages; distribution problems and peoples' inability to afford the purchase of food are other severe complications.[21]

In addition to arable land, energy resources, including industry-related fuels such as coal, oil, and natural gas, also constitute an important ingredient of power in the international political economy. Although most industrialized countries are fairly well endowed with such resources (a conspicuous exception being Japan), they nevertheless rely on vast quantities of imported raw materials, with oil alone comprising over 13 percent of the total value of world trade.[22] The uneven distribution of land and raw materials has been a key factor in trade, at times leading countries into either intense competition or cooperation, as the Persian Gulf War of 1990–1991 demonstrated (the violence and conflict of Iraq's attack on Kuwait, the cooperation of states coming to Kuwait's defense, and the devastating violence they in turn unleashed on Iraq) (see Box 1.1 on the political economy of oil).

Population At the global and domestic levels, population and demographic patterns, such as urbanization, immigration or emigration, and infant mortality, are directly related to economic and political circumstances, such as the level of unemployment, political instability, or civil war. Currently, world population is over 5 billion, and it is estimated that it will increase to over 6.5 billion by the year 2000. About 90 percent of the growth in world population is in developing countries. Annual population growth in the industrialized countries, on the other hand, has been between 0 and 0.5 percent.[23] Theorists speculate that when people become more prosperous, they naturally have fewer children.

In economic and political terms, the size of a country's population can be both a blessing and a curse. Human resources are a vital element in a country's productive and military capabilities. While a sufficient population base, in proportion with a country's territorial and resource endowments, is necessary for the normal workings of its economy, a large population and unsustainable population growth also can prove to be a burden on its financial and political institutions. Unsustainable population growth can particularly pose serious challenges as a society evolves from an agriculture-based economy to an industry- or a **service-based economy** (see Figure 1.1). During this evolutionary phase, a substantial percentage of the rural population migrates to cities where factories and jobs are located, placing enormous burdens on available services and infrastructure (roads, housing, sewers, and so on).

Today, nearly 70 percent of the U.S. workforce is in the service sector, including telecommunications, insurance, banks, education, medicine, law, and consultant firms in various areas of the economy. In the early 1950s, the service sector, including activities ranging from medicine and law to insurance and restaurants, accounted for about 55 percent of **gross national product (GNP);** by the mid-1980s, it had increased to more than 70 percent, whilethe industrial sector fell from 30 percent to 21 percent.[24] Changes of such magnitude, from labor-intensive to capital and information-intensive economies, require a proportionately well-educated and skilled population and can exacerbate unemployment problems. MNCs compete for labor as they compete for resources, and in recent years their efforts have led to the weakening of organized labor, in part by intensifying international labor competition and stressing the search for skilled workers. In 1994 a survey of 510 U.S. and Canadian companies indicated that about two out of five companies were understaffed because of shortages of skilled employees.[25]

Education, Training, and Technology An important factor in improving the living standard of a society and the ability to remain competitive in the global political economy, therefore, is the quality and level of education obtained by a large percentage of its population. Emphasis on education and training for purposes of modernization is not without its pitfalls, however. In the post-Mao period in China, for example, while the Communist Party maintained its hold on the educational system, the government emphasized progress in science and technology and introduced major reforms in academic standards throughout the 1980s, including openness to education abroad. As a result, by 1991 more than 70,000 Chinese students were attending graduate schools in Japan and the United States.[26] However, changes in the education policy created a new generation of university students who could not live by technological modernization alone; they also demanded political rights and reforms. The Tiananmen Square pro-democracy movement in 1989 was a manifestation of the underlying tensions between the new demands placed on the political institutions to create a competitive China in the global economy and the demands by a new generation of students who are the very products of the globalized environment.

Infrastructural Development is the spatial development of a country through communication and

BOX 1.1

OIL ROLLS OVER

The market's verdict was scathing. When, on March 27th, ministers of the Organisation of Petroleum Exporting Countries (OPEC) decided to "roll over" the cartel's existing production quota of 24.5m barrels a day until the end of the year, the price of a barrel of North Sea Brent oil fell to $13.20, 70 cents down on the previous trading day and near to a five-year low. And despite OPEC'S perennial springtime prediction of higher demand towards the end of the year, prices could drift still lower.

Thanks to OPEC's persistently prodigious output, the price of oil has fallen by almost a third since mid-1992. Saudi Arabia, which has long dominated OPEC and produces a third of its oil, has refused to cut its output despite appeals from the cartel's smaller members. This is hardly surprising: a small cut in output would have little effect on prices, whereas a large cut might not boost Saudi Arabia's profits from each barrel by enough to offset the lost production. And when the kingdom refuses to lead, other cartel members are stuck.

Nobody knows when this pattern will break. While growth in demand remains sluggish—and non-OPEC production in areas such as the North Sea continues to break records—there is unlikely to be any change. But one reason to think prices will eventually shift is that companies are scaling down their plans for investment in oil exploration and the development of wells. "Cutbacks are on everybody's mind," says Dillard Spriggs, an oil analyst based in New York.

If prices stay this low, even the existing amount of exploration may have to be reduced. Irene Himona, an analyst with Société Générale Strauss Turnbull, a securities house, says that only those companies which have low borrowings, and which are more involved with oil refining than production, have enough money to maintain spending.

Among the handful of oil-rich countries in OPEC the situation is no better. No sooner did Saudi Arabia expand two offshore fields than there were rumours that it would mothball them to save money. Far from investing in new production, Iran and Nigeria may not even be able to fill their OPEC quotas. And Venezuela, unable to pay for its oil-development plans out of its own pockets, is looking for international partners.

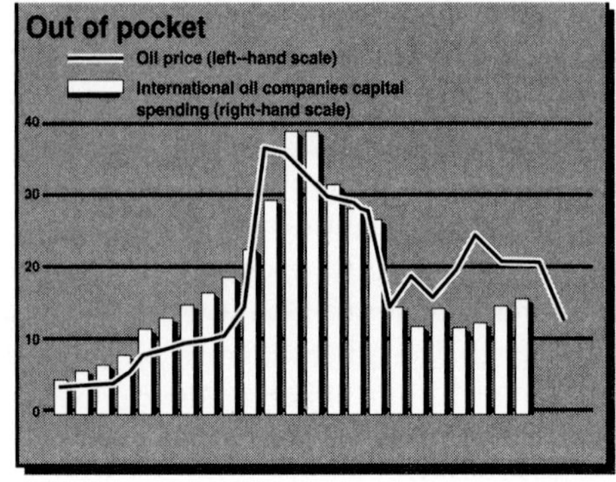

Anecdotes are supported by statistics, which show that global investment in the industry has long been following the oil price downwards (see chart). Moreover, there are now plenty of other oil-industry activities sucking in capital that might have gone to finding new oil. These include large-scale privatisation, massive energy-infrastructure projects in developing countries and the former Soviet Union, and the costs of adapting refineries in Europe and America to new environmental regulations.

Which leaves the oil industry in a bind. New technology and cost-cutting continue to make oil cheaper to produce. But how long can such productivity be a substitute for a higher oil price?

Source: The Economist, April 2, 1994, p. 65.

transportation networks. It facilitates the integration of peoples, international commerce, investment, and production capabilities through the transfer of goods and services. The process of industrialization, for example, requires construction of ports of access, waterways, railroads, highways, bridges, airports, telegraph and telephone systems, and electrification. In the case of the United States, the construction of vast railway networks was an integral part of the industrial boom after the Civil War. During the Civil War, approximately 4,000 miles of rail lines were constructed, and, in the subsequent two decades, more than 30,000 miles of new track were built, most of them in the industrial East and the Midwest, and later in the Mississippi Valley.[27] By the early twentieth century, when the United States had emerged as a major industrial power, the country had an enormous railroad system from the Atlantic to the Pacific, totaling about 170,000 miles.

In developing countries, the extent of such developments varied, based on the investment and mining

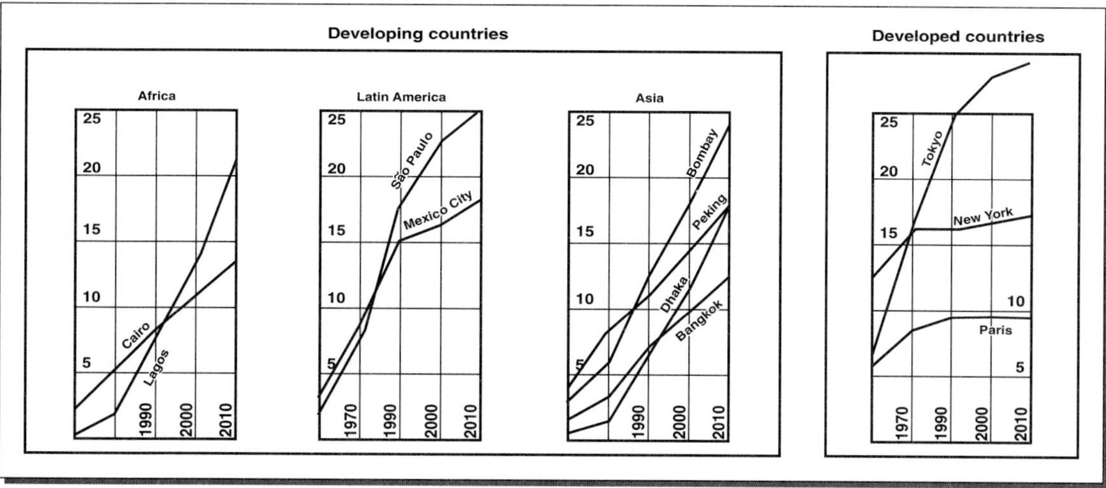

FIGURE 1.1 Population growth in selected cities, 1950–2010 (millions of inhabitants).
Source: World Urbanization Prospects 1992, United Nations, New York, 1993.

objectives of the colonial countries and the capabilities of newly independent states. In most African, Latin American, and Asian countries, relatively basic railroad systems were constructed solely to move raw materials, such as coal, from the interior to coastal ports of access and on to Europe and North America. In other countries, such as India, however, railroads were more than mere hoppers to transfer raw materials. They were also instrumental in the development of highly interconnected networks of administrative units between the more "privileged" economic and political decision-making centers and locations of production. While in 1868 the British railway system in India totaled 1,588 miles, by 1881 it had increased to 9,891 miles, and by 1900 to 24,760 miles.[28] The colonial tendency to concentrate resources and financial wealth in one or two centers (often port cities) while extracting raw materials and even human beings for the slave trade from the countryside resulted in the development of "dual societies," in which the countryside remained economically poor and politically powerless.[29]

Similar infrastructural developments occurred in the globalization of national economies. Transnational development based on land-, sea-, and air-lines as well as telecommunications networks included vast air travel facilities and inter-oceanic waterlanes, such as the Suez and Panama Canals, which entailed considerable political intrigue and manipulation, such as the creation of the Republic of Panama by the Theodore Roosevelt administration. The Suez and Panama Canals, for example, enabled the colonial traders to take "shorter and less hazardous routes between 'home ports' in Europe and North America and colonial destinations."[30]

In the coming age of telecommunications, the most important development is expected to be the computerized *information superhighway.* During the past decade or so, telecommunication highways, such as electronic mail and Internet web service via computer, phone, and satellite, have gained a prominent place in international economic relations and, in fact, have become equally as important as, if not more important than, traditional transportation and communication structures of the globalized political economy.[31] "Informatics"—that is, the merger of telecommunication technologies, such as satellite and microwave transmission systems, with computer technologies—facilitate instantaneous, worldwide transmission of information. Texas Instruments, for instance, uses a satellite-based communication system connecting 8,000 computer terminals in nineteen countries for purposes of "production, planning, cost accounting, finance, marketing, customer service, and personnel management."[32] The enormity of such transboundary information flows in stock markets, banks, and insurance companies has rendered manual processing facilities obsolete.[33] As the construction of railroad networks was indispensable to the development of industrial economy, so is the construction of telecommunications networks indispensable to the development of a "postindustrial" service economy.

Such technologies also pose a serious challenge to the territorial *sovereignty* of nation–states and their governments. It is commonly believed that television, radio, audio and video cassette and compact disc players, computers, and fax machines, by penetrating national borders, played a major role in the revolutionary and prodemocracy movements that exploded in Eastern Europe and China during the late 1980s. In China, the leadership of the Tiananmen Movement of 1989 relied extensively on fax communications with the outside world.[34] In Iran's "cassette revolution" of 1979, tapes of Ayatollah R. Khomeini's fiery speeches were smuggled in for the masses hoping to overthrow the Shah.[35]

Corporations and their parent governments have expended enormous resources to develop their telecommunications infrastructural base, and this development itself has become one of the major areas of international competition. For example, since the mid-1960s, the French government has extended financial support to prominent companies (even those with joint U.S. ownership), such as the Compagnie Internationale Pour l'Informatique Honeywell Bell (CIIHB), and, through major investments, the government has strengthened the French information industry to be more competitive with the United States and Japan. In the early 1980s, the French government adopted a $24 billion plan for investment in telecommunications and computer technologies and took part in establishing joint satellite systems with Canada and Germany. Similarly, the European Community created the EUTELSAT in an effort to capture at least one-third of the global telecommunications market and network system. The following statement by the former magistrate with the French Ministry of Justice, Louis Joinet, at a symposium on Transborder Data Flows and Protection of Privacy, best captures the essence of the issue:

> Information is power and economic information is economic power. Information has an economic value, and the ability to store and process certain types of data may well give one country political and technological advantage over other countries. This, in time, leads to a loss of national sovereignty through supranational data flows.[36]

The lagging task of infrastructural development in developing countries also involves construction of new transportation networks and information and energy production capabilities. At least before their economic downturn in the late 1990s, Asian governments reportedly were planning to spend more than $1 trillion on improvements to power stations and phone lines. Given the lack of indigenous technology, however, much of the business in this initiative would go to firms from the G-8 industrial countries. Companies such as General Electric and Mitsui have joined to invest more than $5 billion for infrastructural projects in the region. In the early 1990s, for instance, the Indonesian government signed an agreement with such an international consortium to construct the Paiton project, the country's largest private coal-fired power station at a cost of over $2 billion, to add 1,220 megawatts to its current 9,700 megawatts. The government's own estimate suggested that Indonesia will need a capacity of well over 25,000 megawatts by the year 2003, and it was considering additional plans to build Paiton 2. Similarly, Malaysia's current capacity of 5,500 megawatts will have to be increased to at least 12,000 megawatts by 2000. China is planning on adding 15,000 megawatts every year during the next decade, and India is estimated to need over 6,000 megawatts a year for the next five years.[37] These plans, of course, have potentially great negative side effects for global energy fuel supplies and for the environment.

International Currency and Gold Reserves Another important ingredient in a country's economic and political strength and its foreign contacts is its currency and gold reserves. The global economy is comprised of nearly as many currencies as there are countries. However, a number of currencies are linked by formal or informal agreements, "pegged" in exchange rate terms within certain limits. Due to economic and political circumstances, only a very few national currencies emerge dominant as "international currencies" for some period of time and facilitate exchanges in the international economy. Such currencies are known as *reserve currencies.* The U.S. dollar, Japanese yen, and German DMark, for example, are reserve currencies held by governments, businesses, and individuals. The reserve holdings strengthen the holder's financial standing as well as the value of the reserve currency for purposes of investments, trading, lending, and so on. To be accepted as a reserve currency, the economy of the issuing country must be considered "solid" (that is, not subject to decay or destruction in warfare) and sufficiently large to provide foreign exchange to many other states (through imports or foreign aid). Changes in global power configurations can weaken the position of the leading international currency, however, and can even replace it with a stronger and more stable one.[38]

Throughout the nineteenth century, the British pound sterling enjoyed the status of the lead international currency, especially through the vast colonial sterling currency area. At the turn of this century, however, a number of rising powers, including Germany, Japan, and the United States, gradually began to expand their own currency areas and challenged the British position in the international economy. By the close of the Second World War, only the United States, almost intact from the ravages of the war and with a massive industrial base, emerged as a major global economic power, willing and able to support and sustain an international reserve currency of unparalleled credibility and prestige around the world. As one testament to this role, the Truman administration launched an unprecedented aid program in 1947, the Marshall Plan, dispensing dollars to prevent the growth of communism in war-ravaged Europe. Very much like the challenges that weakened the position of the British pound during the early decades of this century, however, a similar competition by other rising economies and currencies, such as the German Dmark and Japanese yen, has challenged the position of the dollar during the past decade or so; yet other competitors lack the overall size and volume of the U.S. economy, leaving the question open as to whether the United States or any other single country can continue to play the role of "world banker" or economic hegemon in the future.

Historically, gold has been one of the most revered monetary and industrial metals and a basis for solid reserve currencies. It is difficult to be precise regarding the value and size of gold reserves governments currently hold, since they place different value on their reserves. Some governments value their holdings at about $42 per ounce (the value set in February 1973); others set it at 75 percent of market values; still others follow the market price (about $380 per ounce in May 1994). Traditional gold reserves have been replaced by more modern and flexible reserves consisting of gold, international credits such as **Special Drawing Rights (SDR),** and other combinations, or "baskets," of international currencies. Unlike the simpler gold hoarding practices of the past, under the current international financial system, decision making requires far greater sophistication and faster information collection mechanisms. Countries and blocs of states in possession of vast quantities of international reserves and well equipped with modern information technologies will certainly have an advantage over others lacking in such amenities.

Economic power, then, is based on the absolute and comparative economic advantages a country has in its relations with others. It consists of productive output of goods and services, which influences bilateral trade relations and status in multilateral trade regimes, investment capabilities, international currency reserves, and distribution of capital and foreign assistance.[39] Through such coercive measures as protectionist policies (for example, tariffs), embargoes, prohibition of foreign investments or loans at home or by domestic companies in the target country or **international governmental organizations (IGOs**—through a state's proportional voting power), termination of economic assistance, or seizure of foreign assets,[40] an economically powerful state can coerce another into altering its domestic and foreign policy behavior. More positive inducements consist of "most favored nations" trade status, foreign assistance, loan guarantees, and joint international ventures. Through such instruments, a state can reward or punish friends or enemies. In this respect, and allowing for the fact that influence sometimes fails, the state, despite challenges to its sovereignty, remains the central actor in international political economy.

Political Resources

Power and Influence The availability of a country's economic resources sets the foundations for its economic, military, and political power in the international arena. Power is said to be a form of international political currency that governments and other international actors use to achieve their domestic and foreign policy objectives.[41] While there is no agreement on the precise definition of power, most analysts agree that it is a reflection of a state's resources and the ability to control others through inducements, rewards, sanctions, and punishments. Robert Gilpin, for example, emphasizes resources as related "to the military, economic and technological capabilities of states."[42] It is worth pointing out, however, that, regardless of the variations in definitions, power traditionally has been almost exclusively defined in terms of the state as the dominant actor; little effort has been made to integrate other actors, such as MNCs, IGOs, and **NGOs (non-governmental organizations)** in the international power calculus. A valid synthesis based on the various definitions offered by observers leads us to define *power as the military, economic, and technological capabilities of states and other international actors to control various targets or targets' environments and to change political outcomes.*

Such a definition underscores how the availability and impact of resources can shape a state's or an international actor's behavior in bilateral and multilateral relations. MNCs' political involvement in efforts to control a target country's domestic environment include, for example, Western oil companies' efforts to overthrow the nationalistic Mossadegh government in Iran in 1953, the United Fruit Company's campaign to overthrow the reformist Arbenz government in Guatemala in 1954, and ITT's

(International Telegraph and Telephone) and other MNCs' role in the overthrow of the Allende government in Chile in 1973, to prevent nationalization of their properties. In all these cases, a combination of government (sometimes using clandestine intelligence services) and corporate power was used to shape the political outcomes.

Power and influence are used in multilateral organizations as well. State members in IGOs, such as the **North Atlantic Treaty Organization (NATO),** the International Monetary Fund, the World Bank, and the United Nations, use their influence variously to maintain international security, to manage international trade, and to transfer capital to and from developed and less developed countries (LDCs). Other forms of transnational organizations, such as NGOs, consisting of private profit- or public-oriented groups, such as General Motors and Amnesty International, also use capital and other resources, such as moral suasion and publicity, to influence others in the international system.[43]

Military power largely reflects a country's ability to increase military expenditures, to mobilize sufficient personnel for military purposes at home and abroad, and to deploy ground, naval, and air forces for the conduct of war and diplomacy, as required by circumstances. In times of conflict or crisis, when the use of power is most essential, a country's military power ultimately can determine whether it maintains and sustains its reputation, maintains its nominal independence, and controls the international environment. Military power can be used to acquire territory, to create a buffer zone between one's core territory and an adversary, and to gain access to resources needed to compete effectively in the international system.[44] As numerous wars (from Napoleon's campaign to conquer Europe to Saddam Hussein's campaign to conquer Kuwait) have demonstrated, however, mismanaged military power can lead to political and economic disasters and to enormous human suffering, rather than enhanced national security.

The industrial revolution and nineteenth century wars (for example, the Franco–Prussian War) have shown the link between industrial output and military power—that is, the ability to produce and use military equipment. Japan's military success in the Russo–Japanese War in 1905 suggested that such efforts would have to be continued to strengthen Japan's regional position. Accordingly, in the 1930s the Japanese military government enunciated the Greater East Asian Co–Prosperity Sphere doctrine, whose primary objective was to conquer the vast territories from Manchuria to littoral China to Vietnam and to the Philippines, not only to acquire territories *per se* but also to acquire essential raw materials, such as oil and rubber, for further industrialization and militarization. These moves were considered illegitimate by opposing powers, such as the United States and the Soviet Union, and led to countermoves and war, which ultimately brought down the Japanese state.

Political and military power also consists of various intangible properties, including political culture, political will, domestic stability, leadership in multilateral arenas, and influence through overt and covert operations used to reward or punish others. These can involve the allocation of funds and economic assets and may include such activities as psychological warfare via propaganda; support of opposition parties, labor unions, or revolutionary movements to instigate political unrest; and the bribing of officials and leaders.[45] Political power is most effective when the relationship between the two actors is "asymmetrical," or unequal, whereby the initiator can penetrate the target country's domestic arena. Nevertheless, established relations—as between Israel and the United States, for example—can allow "reverse influence" by the weaker partner on the stronger, as well.

Interdependence and Asymmetrical Interdependence

Interdependence in the international political economy refers to conditions of mutual dependence among states, characterized by reciprocal influences among countries or other international actors. It consists of various transactions involving transfer of currencies, goods and services, transportation of people, and communications. As Keohane and Nye have pointed out, however, mere interconnectedness in and of itself does not constitute interdependence. The latter implies that such transactions involve certain "reciprocal (although not necessarily symmetrical)" constraints and costs, or, as some would term it, mutual "fate control,"[46] i.e., the ability of each state materially to affect the fate of the other.

The political economy of interdependence, therefore, is most successfully managed by a country when political and corporate leaders can maintain a healthy equilibrium between the costs of transactions and the potential consequences of terminating such transactions. Persistent failure to maintain that equilibrium because of economic, political, and military circumstances leads to asymmetrical interdependence, whereby the less dependent entity can use "the interdependent relationship as a source of power in bargaining over an issue and perhaps to affect other issues." [47] Over the years, U.S. allies and friendly governments, such as France and the Philippines, have used such uneven relations to boost their negotiating power, as when the United States desires to use their air space for military operations or to renew rights to use military bases on their territory. While some observers have viewed interdependence as creating new opportunities for international cooperation and a mechanism to prevent wars, the fact that it also limits a country's sovereignty in the domestic and international arenas has been a source of much tension in bilateral and multilateral relations, especially in North–South relations—that is, relations between developed and developing economies.

THE NORTH–SOUTH DIVIDE: THE SEARCH FOR A GLOBAL PROGRAM

In 1980, an international commission headed by Willy Brandt, former mayor of West Berlin and later chancellor of the Federal Republic of Germany, published the controversial Brandt Commission report entitled *North–South: A Program for Survival.* A decade later, the South Commission, headed by Julius Nyerere, the former president of Tanzania, published its report, entitled *The Challenge to the South.* Both reports identified various economic, political, and social problems plaguing the international system in general and "North–South divide" in particular. Among these problems were the role and responsibilities of international organizations (for example, the United Nations, the International Monetary Fund, and the World Bank) and the role of multinational corporations in alleviating the economic difficulties in developing countries; **dependent development,** unemployment, poverty, and hunger; and the impact of armament spending, energy consumption, technological changes, and environmental degradation on the global economy. Both commissions also made a number of recommendations to combat these problems. In the areas of armament and development, for example, the Brandt Commission Report, on the assumption that arms are wasteful to struggling economies, advocated a system of international taxation on military expenditures and arms sales to generate revenues for economic development. In doing so, the commission argued, all parties concerned could move beyond the strict sense of "national security" and provide "basic conditions for peaceful relations between nations, and solving not only the military but also the non-military problems which threaten them."[48]

To prevent marginalization of the South, the Brandt Commission reiterated the need for a "New International Economic Order" (NIEO), with increased global assistance and trade preference to LDCs, and proposed the creation of a World Development Fund, comprised of lenders and borrowers, for the purpose of administering development aid transfers and international taxation. This global institution, the Brandt Commission argued, would seek to rectify the structural deficiencies in the international financing system and "ultimately . . . serve as a channel for such resources as may be raised on a universal and automatic basis."[49] This in turn would enable developing countries to improve their industrial and technological base by strengthening their own technological capacities.

A decade later, the Nyerere Commission argued that, instead of improving living standards in the South, as the Brandt Commission had hoped, since the late 1970s the globalization of the world economy had further marginalized the developing countries. As the wealthier countries in the North managed to establish strong regional groups, such as the European Community, the South remained on the periphery, unable to exert much influence on such developments and unable to take advantage of the technological advancements taking place within these communities.[50] By 1990, the NIEO idea had been rejected in the North, with piecemeal attempts at debt relief and bank lending stressed instead, along with open market reforms.

The controversy with which the Brandt Commission report itself was received illustrated the controversial nature of international economic issues and solutions, as viewed from different quarters. Susan Strange has summarized the controversy surrounding the report, and it is worth briefly repeating some of the arguments here. One view argued that, despite its concern, the Brandt Commission failed to address the "evident paradox" of the developing countries, where people in greatest need of help "either cannot (or will not) use it effectively," while actual recipients "do not need it because the banks and the corporations are only too ready to join in their development." On this score, note the differences in "Southern" states indicated by the sample in Boxes 1.2–1.4. Another perspective noted that the implementation of the Brandt Commission's recommendations would result in the "moneyed lenders" benefiting more than the "moneyless poor." "The reason is that the economic crisis and its solution lie not in northern technology downgrading to low-wage consumer goods in the South but in northern industrial upgrading to more advanced technology in the capital good and technology-producing industries." Finally, a third group criticized the redistribution-oriented nature of the commission's recommendations and noted that "large-scale transfers of resources from the West to the South cannot achieve their declared objectives and in fact obstruct the achievement of those objectives. Damaging the interests of the West, they serve those of the rulers but not the people of the South." In the case of Tanzania, for example, "food aid plus social experimentation with village cooperatives were in fact followed by a major decline in national food output."[51] However, the problems addressed by the Brandt Commission persist, as reflected by criticism of the 1998 G-8 conference for failing to move toward widespread debt forgiveness for the poorest states.

This discussion of international economic, political, and military power and the problems identified in the Brandt and Nyerere Commissions' reports underscores a number of key characteristics of the contemporary international environment—as it has evolved since the rise of the nation–state, the Industrial Revolution, and particularly the Second World War (as discussed in Chapter 3). The economic potential and plight of individual LDCs are illustrated in Boxes 1.2–1.4. These countries have been selected to show the variety of cases and problems confronting LDCs and to indicate that such states do not conform to any single stereotype. The international system currently consists of more than 190 nation–states, each with its own economic, political, and security concerns.

THE POLITICAL ECONOMY OF INTERNATIONAL RIVALRY: POST–COLD WAR DILEMMAS

In addition to the North–South divide, the end of the Cold War catapulted heretofore less salient, if not invisible, issues and rivalries to the forefront of global politics and created what some have called the new "geopolitical cartography" of international cooperation and conflict.[52] The end of the ideological rivalry between the two superpowers, it was hoped, would permit greater opportunities

BOX 1.2

THE VARIETY OF "SOUTHERN" STATES: BRAZIL

FACTS

Population: 158 million
Ethnic groups: Portuguese, Africans, mullatoes, native Indians, Italians, Germans, Japanese, Jews
Religion: Roman Catholic (89%)
Area 3,286,470 sq. mi.
Industries: steel, autos, ships, appliances, petrochemicals
Chief crops: coffee, cotton, sugar, fruits
Defense: 2.6% of GDP
Literacy: 81%
Foreign debt: $49 bln (1994)
Monetary unit: Cruzeiro (3,059 = $1 U.S.)
Gross domestic product: $388 bln
Per capita GDP: $2,540
Imports: $23 bln; partners: U.S. 21%, EU 23%
Exports: $36 bln; partners: U.S. 26%, EU 27%
Transport: railroads 18,721 mi.; passenger cars 14 mln
Communication: TV 1 per 5 persons; radios 1 per 2.5 persons; telephones 1 per 10 persons
Major IGOs: UN (and most of its specialized agencies), Oganization of American States

BACKGROUND

Over the years, Brazil has become one of the most dynamic economies in Latin America. With 158 million people, Brazil alone accounts for nearly 40 percent of production in Latin America (well above Mexico's 18 percent and Argentina's 11 percent). More than 60 percent of Latin America's largest corporations and 50 percent of the foreign investments in Latin America are located in Brazil. Currently, its gross domestic product is about $390 billion, with a per capita GDP of $2,540. However, despite its enormous size and human and natural resources, Brazil remains divided into two societies. The wealthier one-third of the population, including professionals and large business and commercial farming leaders, reside in the rapidly developing regions of the country, while the rest are in another and much poorer Brazil, mired in unemployment, crime, and illiteracy. Annual per capita income in the wealthier regions, such as São Paulo, is over $4,000; in the poorer regions it barely reaches $600.

Brazil was under military regime for twenty years (1964–1985). The generals seized power during a period of economic chaos and promised to improve conditions and Brazil's standing in the international economy. To that end, they brought the country's best trained technocrats to administrative management and economic policy-making positions. They established a highly repressive regime and outlawed all political parties and union strikes. Only a strong government, they believed, could control inflation and regain public confidence. The government could then encourage foreign and domestic companies to invest in Brazil and to extract and export its abundant natural resources. Subsequently, the country registered 11 percent annual growth in its national product and the generals claimed to have worked a "Brazilian miracle." That miracle, however, for cooperation, as the threat of a nuclear holocaust receded and both superpowers' strategies for mutual attrition through proxy wars, support for military coups, transnational psychological warfare, to name but a few, ceased. Subsequently, billions of dollars would be converted from military expenses to "peace dividends" in the form of social welfare, education, and employment programs. The end of the Cold War, it was also hoped, would remove the superpower rivalry that had paralyzed multilateral institutions, such as the United Nations, and would integrate the former Communist bloc countries into the major global financial and trade regimes, such as the IMF, the World Bank, and the GATT. Global interdependence had underscored increasing international cooperation via economic transactions, the proliferation of multinational corporations, and the globalization of communications technology.[53]

However, this new "geopolitical cartography" also contained traditional problems and highlighted numerous present and potential arenas of international rivalries, which replaced the ideological rivalry of the previous decades. These include political, ethnonational rivalries, with all of their components, such as conflict over territory, religion, and cultural integrity, as well as terrorism, economic rivalries, such as trade, financial, and resource rivalries.[54] Intelligence agencies, in some cases, switched from spying on governments to spying on companies for the latest trade secrets. Thus, the peace dividend did not materialize, as military and peacekeeping preparations continued and, in some cases, increased, while efforts to lessen budgetary deficits mounted. Before concluding this chapter, a brief discussion of some of key issues concerning international cooperation and conflict in the post–Cold War period is in order.

BOX 1.2 (concluded)

THE VARIETY OF "SOUTHERN" STATES: BRAZIL

was short-lived. Following OAPEC's oil embargo in 1973, the price of imports increased by 120 percent, and Brazil was forced to borrow heavily from international banks in order to continue to finance the economic expansion. By 1979, Brazil had borrowed more than $40 billion, 85 percent in loans. The military invested extensively in the areas of steel, arms production, petrochemicals, hydroelectric power facilities, and communications systems, with the hopes of generating lucrative rates of return in the future. However, oil prices increased again in 1979, and interest rates on the billions of borrowed dollars skyrocketed. Oil importing economies entered a recessionary period. Consumption of oil dropped, as did prices on Brazilian exports. Desperate, the Brazilian military borrowed even more, increasing the debt to nearly $100 billion in three years. By the early 1980s, the military could no longer maintain its authoritarian regime, and in 1985 it simply gave up on the "Brazilian miracle" and returned power to civilian government.

Recently, Brazil embarked on an economic stabilization plan to strengthen its business environment and encourage domestic and foreign investment. Foreigners invested more than $6.5 billion in Brazilian shares in 1993, and by early 1994 they owned nearly $11 billion worth of Brazilian equities, accounting for 15 percent of daily trading, averaging about $300 million, an increase from only $50 million in 1990. Foreign banks and companies continued to pay close attention to the economic situation and its political implications for the future of the country and its investment environment. In an effort to regain international confidence, in April 1994, Brazil, the largest debtor among the developing countries, concluded an agreement with 750 banks in New York to reduce its foreign debt from $49 billion to $45 billion, to lower interest rates, and to establish new long-term loans. The results appear to be positive, though Brazil was threatened by global economic downturns in the late 1990's. In the early 1990s, for example, despite hyperinflation and chronic corruption, production in the auto industry increased by about 30 percent to 1.39 million units in 1993, making Brazil the tenth largest auto producer in the world, surpassing its closest competitors, Italy and Mexico. Pierre-Alain de Smedt, the president of Autolatina, a Volkswagen AG–Ford Motor Company joint venture, has reportedly stated that Brazil will be "a car market of five million units by 2015"—boosting international confidence in the future of Brazil.

Sources: See Gary W. Wynia, *The Politics of Latin American Development,* 3d ed. (Cambridge: Cambridge University Press, 1990), 217; Thomas E. Skidmore and Peter H. Smith, *Modern Latin America,* 3d ed. (Oxford: Oxford University Press, 1992); *The Economist,* April 2, 1994, pp. 39, 75; *The New York Times,* April 17, 1994, p. A8; *Wall Street Journal,* April 20, 1994, p. A1. Data for "Facts" section are from *The World Almanac,* 1994.

BOX 1.3

THE VARIETY OF "SOUTHERN" STATES: SYRIA

FACTS

Population: 13,730,000
Ethnic groups: Arabs 90%, Armenians, Jews, Kurds
Religion: Sunni Muslim 74%, other Muslim 16%, Christian 10%
Area: 71,498 sq. mi.
Industries: oil products, textiles, tobacco, glassware
Chief crops: cotton, grain, olives, fruits
Defense: 10.9% of GDP
Literacy: 64%
Monetary unit: Pound (March 1993: 11.22 = $1 U.S.)
Gross domestic product: $30 bln
Per capita GDP: $2,300
Imports: $2.7 bln; partners EU 42%
Exports: $3.6 bln; partners E. Europe 42%, EU 31%
Transport: railroads 948 mi.; passenger cars 117,000
Communication: TV 1 per 17 persons; radio 1 per 4.1 persons; telephones 1 per 17 persons
Major IGOs: UN (IMF, WHO, FAO), Arab League

BACKGROUND

Syria gained independence from the French Mandate in 1946. Although the post-WWII period was politically highly unstable (in 1949 alone three military coups occurred), during the next decade or so both the industrial and agricultural sectors grew and the political system stabilized. Since the Baath Party revolution in 1963, Syria increasingly relied on foreign capital. In the 1970s, the government of Hafez al-Asad granted permission to create joint ventures in the tourist and transportation industries but maintained a small percentage of the shares. In the meantime, the government adopted new development policies to eliminate the traditional Baathist socialist-oriented, hands-on management style and to encourage domestic and foreign enterprises. The government, however, remained the provider of last resort. After the 1973 October War with Israel, a new class of entrepreneurs emerged in close business-government, patron-client symbiotic relations in trade and contracting. As in Brazil, Nigeria, and elsewhere, the informal sector expanded, and corruption permeated various aspects of society.

In the late 1970s and the 1980s, Asad's government established joint ventures with Western companies, such as the Spanish-Syrian tractor company in Aleppo and a fairly successful Dutch-U.S.-German consortium of oil companies developing the oil fields near Deir al-Zor on the Euphrates River. By the early 1990s, production in these relatively new fields had already exceeded the output of Syria's older fields, and profits from such operations have been shared between the companies and the Syrian government. During this period, the Lebanese Civil War, though highly disruptive, enhanced Syria's economy in a number of ways. After 1976, neighboring Arab countries, especially Saudi Arabia, paid most of the expenses for the Arab Deployment Force (Syrian army in Lebanon). The war also

International Cooperation

A number of scholars have examined patterns of international transactions in the form of communications (for example, mail), trade, and mobility (for instance, tourism, student exchange) and have contended that, in general, greater transactions facilitate the development of wider and faster communication networks, as well as national and human tendencies toward greater international integration and cooperation.[55] One example of such integration has been the European Community (now European Union, EU), as first established after the Second World War, and its gradual and sporadic evolution toward a single European entity with transboundary financial and institutional arrangements. David Mitrany, Karl Deutsch, Ernst Haas, and Amitai Etzioni, among others in the *functionalist* (and *neo-functionalist*) school of thought, looked at the growing importance of the technical and routine everyday transactions leading to international cooperation.[56] They maintained that international transactions create opportunities for technical collaboration in functionally specific sectors, such as the European Coal and Steel Community of 1952. Further, and perhaps more significantly, the very presence of one such technical sector, they believed, generates "ramifications" or "spill-over" effects whereby related transactions develop comparable, collaborative patterns of institutional behavior in other technical sectors (for ex-ample, the development of international transportation systems, international financial arrangements, and coordination of monetary and fiscal policies). Ultimately, expanding collaboration would lead to regional and global peace in a closely interdependent world.

As anticipated by the functionalist school, during the past twenty years or so, the most distinctive characteristic of the international political economy has been the globalization of economic activities. For most of the history of international

BOX 1.3 (concluded)

THE VARIETY OF "SOUTHERN" STATES: SYRIA

improved Syria's tourist industry. Foreign tourists who normally would have traveled to Lebanon instead visited Syria. Also, large sums of Syrian capital that had been transferred to Lebanon over the years returned to Syria's relatively safe banks. Finally, the war caused most of the naval, land, and air traffic to shift their routes from Beirut's ports and airport to the ports of Latakia and the airport of Damascus.

A critical factor in Syria's domestic and foreign affairs has been the regional power configuration, especially the decades of hostility toward Israel. Since his rise to power in 1970, Asad's regional ambitions have ranged from the establishment of "Greater Syria" to the consolidation of direct and indirect dominance over the region. After the 1990–1991 Gulf War, however, it was obvious that he could not achieve such objectives. His failure to have an independent foreign policy vis-a-vis Iraq indicated that Asad could not elevate Syria to the status of a regional power, especially after the collapse of the Soviet Union, its greatest benefactor. However, negotiations with Israel under U.S. auspices may provide an opportunity for better Syria-Israel relations, particularly in resolving the Golan Heights issue.

At home, the Asad government faced a serious legitimacy crisis. The 1980s and early 1990s witnessed unprecedented levels of inequalities. The civilian and military institutions and the new and old commercial sectors closely associated with them reaped enormous financial and political benefits from government policies in the formal and informal arenas. However, since most of the public had been excluded from the patron-client loops, they were left without such benefits, if not in abject poverty. Moreover, Asad's authoritarian regime prevented the economically marginalized groups from playing a meaningful role within the political system. In a way, political stability in Asad's Syria is similar to the political stability in Tito's Yugoslavia. Asad was able to maintain the balance of power among competing factions and ethnic groups through cooptation and coercion, as in the cases of the Hama and Homs massacres against political opponents. It is doubtful that his successors will so deftly balance the scales. For most, the economic future inspires little optimism. As long as economic privatization and liberalization continue without political liberalization, Syria's political future might be only a repetition of the Lebanese civil war.

Sources: See Volker Perthes, "The Syrian Economy in the 1980s," *Middle East Journal* 46, 1 (Winter 1992); Derek Hopwood, *Syria 1945–1986: Politics and Society* (London: Unwin Hyman, 1988); Patrick Seale, *Asad: The Struggle for the Middle East* (Berkeley: University of California Press, 1988); Ilya Harik and Denis J. Sullivan, eds., *Privatization and Liberalization in the Middle East* (Bloomington: Indiana University Press, 1992). Data for "Facts" section are from *The World Almanac,* 1994.

economic relations, a country's principal production base was confined to its territory.[57] The globalization of production has led to integrated "circulation activities," such as banking, insurance, advertising, communications, and related services. The worldwide restructuring of production and management in the private sector has particularly relied on telecommunications and transportation technologies (for example, containerized shipping and more sophisticated air cargo systems).[58] In addition, governments in developing countries have established a legal environment—export processing zones, limited regulation—conducive to greater foreign investment and mobility. Nevertheless, globalization does not mean the dissolution of the nation–state; the persistence of individual states' nationalism has interfered with "spillover." For example, the British, Danes, and others have resisted the formation of a single Euro currency and a central bank. In addition, nationalism has caused some nation–states, such as Czechoslovakia, to break up into smaller entities rather than form bigger entities.

Multinational corporations (MNCs) have been a primary factor in the globalization of the international political economy. Their basic characteristics include ownership of production facilities and intra- and inter-industry transactions across international borders, access to various geographical and geopolitical "factor endowments," and intra-industry flexibility whereby human and material resources as well as operations are easily transferred from one country to another.[59] As a result, MNCs can exert considerable influence on the global economy as they increase or terminate their operations in a country or region, with economically, environmentally, and politically significant consequences for the communities involved, in both the formal and informal economic sectors.[60]

Although MNCs have been a part of international political economy for centuries, since WWII the global scene has witnessed a dramatic increase in their numbers. Currently, more than 10,000 MNCs around the world own and operate more than 90,000 subsidiaries. In the early 1990s, the

BOX 1.4

THE VARIETY OF "SOUTHERN" STATES: CHINA

FACTS

Population: 1,169,619,000
Ethnic groups: Han Chinese 94%, Mongols, Manchus, Tibetans
Religion: officially atheist; Confucianism, Buddhism, Taoism
Area: 3,696,100 sq. mi.
Industries: iron and steel, textiles, agriculture, trucks
Chief crops: grain, rice, cotton, tea
Defense: 3.0% of GNP
Literacy: 70%
Monetary unit: Yuan (July 1993: 5.71 = $1 U.S.)
Gross national product: $393 bln
Per capita GNP: $360
Imports: $76.3 bln; partners: Japan 20%, HK 20%
Exports: $80.5 bln; partners: HK 38%, Japan 16%
Transport: railroads 41,973 mi.; passenger cars 4.1 mln
Communication: TV 1 per 8 persons; radio 1 per 9.1 persons; telephones 1 per 89 persons
Major IGOs: UN (IMF, FAO, WHO)

BACKGROUND

With over 1.1 billion people, the People's Republic of China (PRC) is the world's most populous country. Despite its recent remarkable economic progress, China is a predominantly poor country. Its annual per capita income is no more than $360, among the lowest in the world. After the Communist revolution in 1949, the Communist Party, under the leadership of Mao Tse-tung, instituted a Soviet-style command economy. In his efforts to create a self-sufficient Chinese economy wholly independent of foreign, especially Western, financial and political influences (as experienced in the nineteenth century), Mao refused to engage in any form of "open door" policy and consequently refused to be involved in international aid or loans programs. In the meantime, China failed to develop modern communications and transportation systems, failed to produce quality consumer products, and remained mired in bureaucratic bottlenecks. To a large extent, these problems could be attributed directly to Mao's authoritarian regime and ideological dogmatism. His emphasis on ideological loyalty to "Mao Tse-tung thought" rather than professional merit to fill positions in bureaucracies, for example, resulted in huge shortages of competent managers.

During the 1980s, Deng Xiaoping's leadership emphasized liberalization with regard to private property and production of consumer goods and services based on market economy, including profit incentives. The economy grew nearly 5 percent and reached 10 percent a year in the early 1990s, while industrial output increased 12.5 percent. While reforms led to economic successes, there were also problems. Inflation reached 20 percent in 1989 and continued to rise thereafter. Also, liberalization raised a host of questions regarding the legitimacy of the regime, especially after the Tiananmen Square massacres in

United States was the home-base for the 500 largest industrial corporations, followed by Japan (111), Great Britain (43), and Germany (32).[61] As such, MNCs provide transboundary, integrative mechanisms facilitating greater international cooperation between and among peoples and MNCs afford their "home" governments greater opportunities for influence abroad (Map 1.2).

In addition to MNCs, *international regimes* constitute another form of cooperation in international political economy. The concept of international regimes, which has gained much scholarly attention since the early 1970s, refers to "principles, norms, rules, and decision-making procedures around which actor expectations converge in a given issue area."[62] As such, they are manifestations of international cooperation among various political and economic actors whose mutually acceptable institutional arrangements govern their collaboration and coordination. Since the Second World War, numerous such arrangements have been established to enable governments and corporations to manage specific aspects of transboundary issues through their diplomatic and commercial relations in the absence of a global government. For example, immediately after the war, the major powers created a trade regime under GATT for the purposes of better management and liberalization of international trade relations. Recently, this has been extended to a new World Trade Organization (WTO), with equalized voting power for member states.

Similarly, since the 1950s, an international food regime has emerged,consisting of two specialized agencies of the United Nations, the Food and Agriculture Organization (FAO) and the World Food Program (WFP). The food regime also includes the International Wheat Council (IWC), the International Fund for Agricultural Develop-ment, and the Consultative Group on International Agricultural Research, to "help to manage the world food systems and uphold norms of the regime." Some

BOX 1.4 (concluded)

THE VARIETY OF "SOUTHERN" STATES: CHINA

1989 and the collapse of the Soviet regime. In the early 1980s, no more than 1,500 private businesses operated in China. That number reached nearly 400,000 in the early 1990s. To encourage foreign trade and investments, the government opened four Special Economic Zones (SEZs) in 1979, giving foreign investors preferential tax rates and other financial incentives. In 1984, fourteen additional cities and Hainan Island were designated as SEZs. The 1980s and 1990s also witnessed the proliferation of joint ventures in various industries ranging from textiles to toys, totaling about $40 billion. Hong Kong's return to China in 1997 is expected to further raise such totals. Currently, foreign companies and joint ventures account for nearly 7 percent of China's GNP. More than 50 percent of the investment capital is by investors in Hong Kong and Macao, 10 percent from Taiwan and South Korea, and 5 percent from the United States. China's biggest trade partneris Japan, accounting for $20 billion in the late 1980s. In1993, China's trade surplus with the United States exceeded $22 billion.

Inflation poses a major challenge to economic growth and stability. While the national economy grew by 13 percent in 1993, inflation was about 22 percent, and, in January of 1994, the cost of living in the major cities was over 23 percent higher than in 1993. Although the government is committed to economic liberalization and rapid growth, it also wants to avoid inflationary pressures that may lead to another "1989." Indeed, in an address to parliament, Prime Minister Li Peng placed heavy emphasis on "economic reform" and "stability."

Human rights issues remained a problem in the 1990s. During his visit in 1994, U.S. Secretary of State Warren Christopher accomplished no more than cosmetic promises by Beijing regarding human rights. The latter insisted that China's domestic problems are not subject to foreign intervention and that such efforts infringes on its sovereignty. At the same time, a politically charged issue such as human rights can also jeopardize U.S. business interests, who would rather expand and protect their investments in the Chinese market than see tensions between Washington and Beijing weaken their position vis-a-vis Europe and Japan. Beijing is concerned about China's world reputation because it seeks a greater role in IGOs, such as the UN Security Council, IMF, and GATT. Beijing has sought readmission to GATT in order to be among the founding members of the World Trade Organization. However, Beijing's readmission to the GATT is contingent on its willingness to expand liberalization.

Sources: See Charles Hauss, *Comparative Politics: Domestic Responses to Global Challenges* (Minneapolis/St. Paul: West Publishing, 1994), 286; Harry Harding, *China's Second Revolution: Reform After Mao* (Washington, DC: The Brookings Institution, 1988); *The Economist,* January 8, 1994, p. 74; *The Economist,* March 19, 1994, p. 37. Data for "Facts" section are from *The World Almanac,* 1994.

international regimes' principles and rules are "codified in treaties, agreements, and conventions such as the FAO Charter, the International Grains Agreement, and the Food Aid Convention."[64] Other examples of such regimes include the International Coffee Agreement, the International Civil Aviation Organization, and the International Seabed Authority. Other regimes, such as MTCR, the Missile Technology Control Regime (created in 1987 to regulate the potentially destabilizing trade in missiles), are informal and consultative rather than treaty-based.

These vertically and horizontally functional "integrationist forces" in the global political economy can provide the basis for greater cooperation between major and minor powers, between industrialized countries in the North and developing countries in the South, to coordinate their domestic policies and international activities to deal with the problems mentioned by the Brandt and Nyerere Commissions. However, a number of emerging issues potentially can destabilize such cooperative mechanisms and render them impotent. These include, for example, the resurgence of ethnonationalism and its more virulent derivatives, such as neo-Nazism and neo-fascism in Europe; the disintegration of political units, as in Yugoslavia, the Soviet Union, and potentially Rwanda, Zaire, and Sudan; resource and financial rivalries; economic crises; and trade rivalries.

International Conflicts

Theories of international conflict encompass a wide variety of ingredients, ranging from religion to sociobiological or genetic factors to economic and historical forces to **balance of power** geo-politics. No effort will be made here to explicate fully such theories of conflict; rather, this chapter will concentrate on four types of conflict—territory and natural resources, international labor competition, trade wars, and financial rivalries—that may become more salient during the post–Cold War decades and early

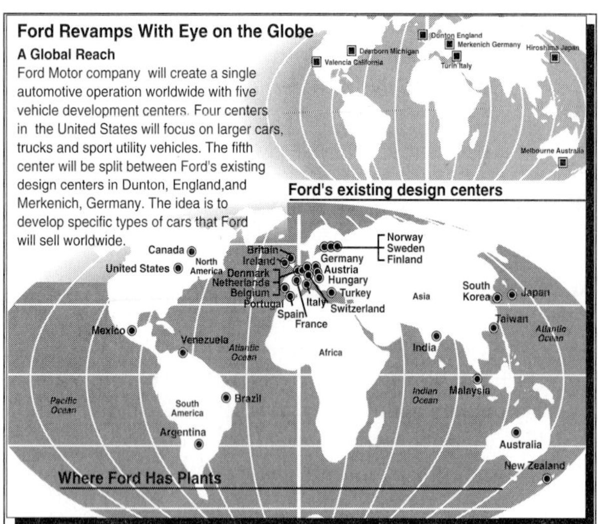

MAP 1.2. The modern MNC—Ford Motor Company. *Source: The New York Times,* Friday, April 22, 1994, C1.

twenty-first century and that, in certain circumstances, could lead to violence.

Territory and Natural Resources Competition over borders and for resources is one of the oldest causes of international conflict. In the early twenty-first century, as more and more developing countries grow disillusioned with their efforts to compete with technologically advanced Western countries, the developing countries may compete for natural resources, even including freshwater, within their immediate neighborhoods, either through cooperation or coercion (see Box 1.5). Internally, as ethnic and social groups compete over control of "home" territory, leaders of rapidly expanding or midlevel industrialized countries come under constant pressure to secure the required raw materials for the survival of their economies.[65]

The African and Asian countries that gained independence during the Cold War years appear to be most vulnerable to such conflicts, along with ethnically diverse and economically underdeveloped former Soviet bloc countries. During the Cold War, their leaders generally relied on either the West or the East for economic and military support to maintain power, and their efforts to achieve higher levels of industrialization and economic modernization took place within the global context of the East–West ideological competition; the two sides could be played off for aid and financing. As devastating as the Cold War was for the developing countries, with the collapse of the Soviet Union they also lost the Cold War. Those relying on Soviet support could no longer expect similar (if any) amounts of economic support from post–Communist Russia. Others relying on the United States and Western Europe realized that Western governments and corporations preferred to invest in the newly opening markets and labor forcesof Eastern Europe and Russia or in "big emergingmarkets"—that is, populous developing states, such as Brazil and Indonesia—rather than in smaller developing countries. As a result, some LDCs sought close tieswith key Western powers or with each other through the development of free trade organizations and preferential agreements.

International Labor Competition In addition to competition over raw materials, competition for cheap labor also is a salient characteristic of post–Cold War international political economy. Currently, it is estimated that the potential size of the working-age labor force in developing countries is three times that available in most industrialized countries. In the 1980s, competition from low-wage workers in developing countries also led to competition between workers in the North and the South to attract more jobs or to hold on to their current ones. This in turn increasingly resulted in northern workers settling for "third-world working conditions," lower wages, and relatively high unemployment levels,[66] while, in the South, as in the maquiladoras in the U.S.-Mexican border region, new plants provided new jobs but at relatively low wages, perpetuating illegal immigration into the United States.[67] Among the wealthiest industrialized countries, Germany's labor costs $24.90 an hour and, in the United States, France, Britain and Japan, about $15–$17 an hour. Hourly labor costs in less developed countries, however, are more than 50 percent lower, at about $2.00 in Mexico and less than $1.00 in China, Haiti, and Thailand, offering sufficient incentives for labor-intensive industries to move to these countries (Figure 1.2), as discussed in Chapter 7.[68] (Of course, such relocation decisions depend on other factors as well, such as transportation costs, population skills, and political stability.)

While cheaper production can benefit consumers through lower-priced imported goods, international labor competition and declining living standards fuel economic nationalism in the form of protectionism and xenophobia in the industrialized countries, as increasing imports and foreign or immigrant workers are blamed for social and economic ills. The resurgence of neo-Nazi, "skin head,"and neo-fascist movements in European countries, particularly in Germany, France, and Italy, and in the U.S., is the ominous manifestation of this international labor

BOX 1.5

RESOURCES AND INTERNATIONAL CONFLICT

Nigeria and Cameroon have been in a border dispute over the Bakassi peninsula, an area rich in oil. Although governed from Nigeria during colonial years and French and Nigerian oil companies have initiated exploration projects, Cameroon claims it. In early March 1994, the French government transported a small number of paratroops and helicopters as a demonstration of French support for Cameroon's claim. The Nigerian foreign minister, Baba Gana Kingibe, charged that this move by the French government does nothing but escalate the conflict. Nigerians are ready to "defend every inch of territory," he declared.

Nigeria produces 2 million barrels of oil per day, with proven reserves of over 25 billion barrels. Plummeting oil prices in the 1980s and 1990s have jeopardized the country's economic viability, and there has been a mounting pressure on the government to solve the problem. Cameroon, on the other hand, produces about 120,000 barrels a day, and, according to one estimate, without new exploration even that production could end by the year 2005. A 1913 Anglo-German treaty included the Bakassi peninsula within Cameroon's territory. According to Cameroonians, Nigeria's former president, Yakubu Gowon, had accepted the colonial boundaries because of Cameroon's support during the Biafran War. The French government's support for Cameroon is expected to prevent any Nigerian military attacks, and former Nigerian leader General Sani Abacha initiated negotiations with his neighbor, Cameroon's President Paul Biya. The latter, however, insisted that he would personally go to the negotiating table only after Nigeria "removes its troops from Cameroonian territory—i.e., Bakassi."

A similar conflict over oil is also developing in the South China Sea region. In this case, the countries involved include China, Vietnam, Singapore, Malaysia, Thailand, Indonesia, the Philippines, and Brunei. Their claims to overlapping maritime boundaries is one of the most troubling sources of security problems in that region. Two closely interrelated issues are at the core of the dispute: the maritime boundaries of each country's exclusive economic zones and jurisdiction over a huge seabed area with billions of barrels of reserves ready for offshore drilling. As noted by Vatikiotis, Thailand disputes Malaysia's claims; Malaysia disputes Brunei's, Indonesia's, and Singapore's claims; Vietnam disputes China's claims; and China claims all of the South China Sea. The countries in the region view China as a threat to their regional security and would prefer to include Beijing in their plans for regional economic development. Although Beijing has promised to play a leading role in negotiationsfor regional development, the region's leaders, nevertheless, are worried about the potential "Tibetization" of the South China Sea.

Sources: See Michael Vatikiotis, "Trouble on the Horizon," *Far Eastern Economic Review*, September 23, 1993, p. 26; *The Economist*, March 12, 1994, p. 50.

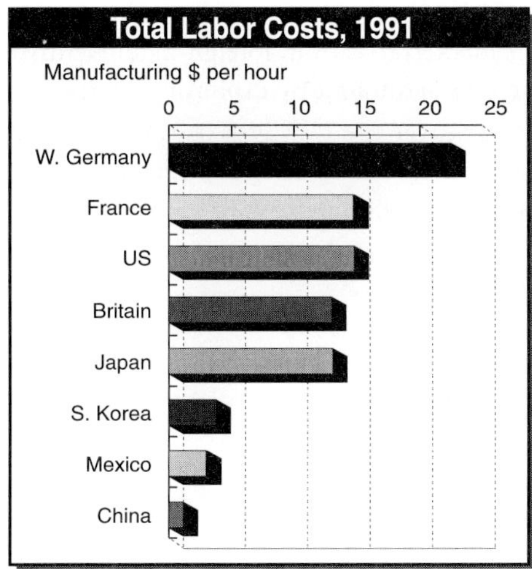

FIGURE 1.2
Source: The Economist, November 21, 1992.

competition. On the positive side, increasing international trade during the past two decades has certainly connected North-South labor markets. Lower trade barriers and transportation and telecommunications costs have further strengthened the structural linkages. In addition, the South's share of exported manufactured goods increased appreciably from 10 percent in the early 1980s to more than 20 percent in the early 1990s.[69]

Changes in labor structures and standards of living have serious implications for the new generation in the industrialized economies. In the United States, for example, there has been a widening gap between the wages received by skilled workers and the wages of unskilled workers. In the 1980s, wages for the highest 10 percent of male skilled workers rose by 20 percent relative to the lowest 10 percent of unskilled workers. Wages for low-skilled jobs among the bottom 10 percent of male workers actually dropped by13 percent. Also, male college graduates' wages increased by nearly 30 percent relative to those with fewer than twelve years of education, while those with the lowest levels of education constituted the highest percentage of the unemployed. The wage gap similarly widened in twelve of seventeen industrial countries.[70]

Economists disagree about whether the North–South international labor competition has been the primary factor contributing to the constant widening of the wage gap and chronic unemployment levels in industrialized economies. Adrian Wood, for example, blames ever increasing imports from the developing countries for these outcomes. He argues that, during the past two decades, but especially in the 1980s, increasing trade with developing countries caused a 20 percent reduction in the demand for unskilled labor in the North. Richard Freeman, however, contends that competition from low-wage economies does not in and of itself cause the decline in wages for low-skilled workers in the United States, because imports from developing countries constitute no more than 3 percent of U.S. GDP—"not much higher than the equivalent figure of 2% in 1960, when Japan and some European countries were then counted as low-wage economies."[71] Also, rising U.S. exports to developing countries create new manufacturing jobs in U.S. industries, and lower-cost products become available to U.S. consumers.

It would perhaps be safe to say that the primary cause of the declining demand for unskilled workers, and therefore declining wages, in industrialized countries has been the profit motive enhanced by the technological transformations and stockholder interests in the previously labor-intensive industries. Automation, computers, and related technological developments have changed the labor environment, and the influx of women into the workforce has tended to increase job competition.[72]

Trade Wars Another area of conflict in the post–Cold War period expected to continue well into the early twenty-first century involves international "trade wars" among countries—that is, trade **sanctions,** or penalties, resulting in a series of retaliatory countersanctions. As previously noted, although interconnected through financial and trade transactions, and although they remain political allies, the most competitive industrialized states—the United States, Germany, and Japan—remain highly competitive with each other, and their governments, through various policy instruments and in various degrees, are encouraging home industries to be more competitive in the world economy to improve their trade and payment balances (Table 1.2). Thus, even in the midst of greater cooperation and integration of economies, trade rivalries and the structural symptoms underlying such rivalries persist.[73]

The trade "wars" of the late 1970s, 1980s, and 1990s have had a significant impact on the global economy, as well as on the bilateral relationships between the competing countries. Like the superpower rivalry and the Cold War nuclear arms race, even the appearance of being involved in such a rivalry puts considerable political pressure on policymakers to "win the war." Many hope that the conflict resolution mechanisms of the WTO can prevent or lessen destructive trade wars.

As previously discussed, the primary factor contributing to the potential escalation of trade rivalry among the industrialized economies is *trade disequilibrium.* During the 1980s, bilateral trade deficits between the United States and Japan, for example, ranged from $15.8 billion in 1981 to $56.3 billion in 1987, and the 1990s have seen little improvement in this area. The United States accused Japan of unfair trade practices and violations of free trade principles by closing its markets to various foreign-manufactured products, on the one hand, and by exploiting its trading

TABLE 1.2

G-7 Trade Balances, 1960–1997 ($ Billions)

Country	1960	1970	1980	1985	1990	1995	1997
Britain	−2.0	−2.0	−5	−8	−38	22	34
Canada	−0.3	3.0	5	10	4	−15	−24
France	0.6	−1.0	−19	−7	−18	12	14
Germany	1.0	4.0	−98	25	64	69	82
Italy	−1.0	−2.0	−66	−11	−12	44	53
Japan	−0.4	0.4	−11	47	52	132	102
United States	3	0.3	−31	−135	−123	−174	−151

Source: UNCTAD, *Handbook of International Trade and Development Statistics,* 1994; *OECD Economic Outlook,* Copyright OECD (June 1996).

partners' more open borders to capture large shares of the market on the other. In fact, as Stephen Cohen has noted, "The more rabid critics of Japan accuse it of continuing to fight World War II through economic means."[74] Whether a more "open" Japan can guarantee any increase in U.S. exports to Japan is not so obvious, however. As one observer has pointed out, the U.S. auto companies could sell no more than 20,000 cars in Japan in 1993, largely because they did not have established dealer networks there. Ford, for example, has arranged to sell its cars through Toyota and Nissan dealers.[75] Japan, on the other hand, has pointed to its own low tariffs as well as U.S. trade barriers, such as quotas, as well as U.S. corporations' ineffective marketing strategies, their inefficient and overpaid corporate management systems, and their inability to introduce innovative techniques for industrial production as the primary causes of their loss of the world market. The real issue, the Japanese have argued, is not a U.S. bilateral trade deficit with Japan but, rather, Washington's multilateral trade disequilibrium.[76]

Financial Rivalries As with trade, financial rivalries are also an important part of the global political economy. By the early 1990s, the volume of international financial transactions had surpassed the volume of international trade in value, and governments and businesses had become as concerned about the impact of financial arrangements (for example, repatriation of profits by MNCs) as they had been with trade. Financial rivalries include issues related to international taxation, international financial services and investments, and the nature and role of international public and private finance. While these will be discussed in Chapter 4, this section will focus on one aspect of international taxation as an example of international financial rivalry.

During the past twenty-five years, California has levied a controversial state "unitary tax system" on foreign corporations with operations in that state. In early 1994, Britain's Barclays Bank challenged this tax in the U.S. Supreme Court. The state had adopted the "unitary" tax to prevent foreign companies from avoiding the full amount of taxes by lowering prices for various transactions; accordingly, California taxed foreign companies, including their subsidiaries, in the state. As a result of this system, foreign companies that have even a single subsidiary in the state pay taxes on their incomes from global operations, even when the California subsidiary shows no profits.[77] In 1988, the Reagan administration pressured California into providing an alternative to the "unitary" system, and in October 1993 the state terminated the system, in its stead adopting a more palatable policy of taxing subsidiaries as independent entities. Barclays, however, continued with its case for compensation, contending that California's tax on companies' profits abroad violated the federal government's exclusive authority to regulate international commerce and that the state's "unitary" tax system imposed "double taxation."[78] In a highly interdependent global world economy, such issues may lead to retaliatory and counterretaliatory measures, with serious repercussions for industrialized and developing economies.

THE IMPORTANCE OF INTERNATIONAL POLITICAL ECONOMY

As demonstrated in this chapter, international political economy is inextricably connected to forces shaping domestic political and economic conditions.[79] It would be misleading, therefore, to focus on international political economy premised on the assumption that transactions at the international level are generated in isolation and independently of political and economic activities within the domestic realm. As former Speaker of the U.S. House of Representatives Tip O'Neill used to say, "All politics is local," and that "local" is rich in ideologies, values, and religions, in histories of economic growth and decline, in technological progress for peace and war, and in formaland informal relationships. International political economy is concerned with how the globalization of trade and finance, production, and telecommunications in world markets has globalized the very "localness" of domestic political economies; the latter in turn affects the pace of globalization.

The chapters presented in this volume emphasize the point that international political economy inherently contains the seeds of international conflict and cooperation. Chapter 2 discusses the theoretical foundations of international political economy and focuses on a number of political economy paradigms. Classical liberal theory, for example, holds that greater international economic transactions create greater opportunities for cooperation among nations, governments, and corporations and can eventually lead to a more peaceful world. Marxists, on the other hand, view international political economy as being dominated primarily by corporate interests at the expense of the laboring masses and poorer sectors of societies around the world. Structural "asymmetries" predicated on exploitative social class relationships lead to struggles between the wealthy and the poor.

Chapter 3 provides a history of modern international economic relations from the 1600s to the emergence of the modern international political economy. It examines the role of the industrial and related technological revolutions in international relations, the evolution of the post–WWII East–West and North–South relations, and the international environment in the aftermath of the Cold War. Chapters 4 and 5 focus on the politics of international trade and financial relations, respectively. Chapter 4 identifies the principal characteristics of contemporary international trade relations. It examines the traditional and modern versions of "comparative advantage," strategic trade policy, and the role of multilateral institutions, such as GATT and the World Trade Organization, in post–Cold War international political economy. In a similar vein, Chapter 5 identifies the principal characteristics of international finance and its various components, such as exchange rates and Special Drawing Rights (SDRs) and the role of institutions such as the IMF. Chapter 6 discusses efforts toward regional integration as facilitated particularly by trade and financial relations.

Chapter 7 deals with the politics of MNCs and the nature and impact of their capital transactions. It discusses the emergence of MNCs as powerful players in the international and domestic arenas, the controversies surrounding such issues as international taxation and the politics of government regulation and nationalization of corporations. Chapter 8 focuses on the politics and globalization of science and technology. Special attention is paid to such cases as postindustrial technologies (for example, semiconductors), international industrial espionage, and the problems associated with the "brain drain" phenomenon. Chapters 9 and 10 consider international political economy within a global system on the one hand divided between the industrialized countries of the North and the developing countries of the South, and among the industrialized economies and less developed economies themselves.

Chapter 11 examines the political economy of multilateral and bilateral development assistance and the impact of such assistance on the politics and economies of both donor and recipient countries. Chapter 12 considers international *informal* economies as mechanisms for cooperation and causes of conflicts, including issues related to migration, labor, state corruption, and narco-businesses. Chapter 13 highlights various avenues toward a new political and economic order and hegemonic stability, and it concludes this book by reviewing the major future issues in international political economy (IPE), such as the changing nature of "human security," arms technology and transfers, energy resources, ecological protection, and their implications for international cooperation and conflict in international political economy in the 1990s and early twenty-first century.

Chapter Summary

International political economy is the relationship between political and economic activities at the global and domestic levels. It covers a wide range of issues and actors, such as the role of international public and private institutions in both domestic and global arenas, the nature of power politics, and international cooperation and conflict.

Technological changes during the past twenty years have led to the globalization of industrial and information production systems and employment opportunities, but also to greater structural inequalities among states.

The globalization of economic activities has created serious dilemmas for citizens and governments in the industrialized and developing countries, especially in the areas of military expenditures, foreign debt and dependency, employment and immigration policies, informal economic activities, the use of natural resources, and environmental degradation.

Key components of international economic relations include international trade and international finance. The main purpose of trade is to acquire needed goods at reasonable prices and to compensate for deficiencies in natural resources or human skills in the labor force. International finance involves foreign exchange rates and balance of payments. The former is used to make international payments, while the latter is the total value of all transactions including imports and exports of goods and services between a country and its partners.

A country's economic and political resources—including population, land, infrastructure, technological advancements, and military capabilities—constitute the basis and means of its relations with others in the international political economy. Governments and other international actors use economic, political, and military power, as a form of international political currency, to achieve domestic and foreign policy objectives. A country that is well endowed with resources can establish a reputation as being wealthy and, in so doing, create the perception that it is economically, politically, and potentially militarily powerful—that is, able to get its way.

Interdependence in the international political economy refers to conditions of mutual dependence, characterized by reciprocal influences between and among countries or other international actors. Dependence or interdependence can arise from various transactions involving transfer of currencies, exchange of goods and services, transportation of people, and communications.

One critical area of international political economy is the North–South relationship involving various economic, political, and social problems including dependent development, unemployment, poverty, hunger, armament, energy consumption, technological changes, and environmental degradation, as well as the roles and responsibilities of international organizations such as the United Nations, the International Monetary Fund, the World Bank, and MNCs in developing countries.

It was expected that the end of the Cold War and the ideological rivalry between the two superpowers would eliminate the threat of a nuclear holocaust and end proxy wars, support for military coups, and psychological warfare, leading to greater international cooperation. Subsequently, billions of dollars would be converted from military expenses to peace dividends. However, actual changes have fallen short of expectations. Certain types of conflicts persist, including territorial, resource, and financial rivalries; international labor competition; and trade wars.

International political economy is inextricably connected to forces shaping domestic political and economic conditions. IPE is concerned with how international trade and finance, production, labor, and telecommunications in the world market have globalized domestic economies and politics and how the latter in turn have shaped the international political economy.

Points of Contention

What are some of the major issues in the 1990s that illustrate the close relationship between politics and economics at the national, regional, and global levels?

Can multilateral meetings, such as the Detroit job conference, be a useful approach to address unemployment and related problems? What, if any, impact did the meeting have in your community?

Can issues such as military expenditures, foreign debt, immigration, and environmental degradation be best addressed at the national, regional, or global level?

Does military expenditure help or hurt an economy?

Can you identify ten resources in your community that may be considered essential for the economic development and well-being of your country? How many of these are imported from other countries?

What dilemmas has the globalization of international economic relations created for citizens and governments in the industrialized and developing countries?

It has been argued that technological advancements and globalization have led to greater socioeconomic inequalities. Can you identify some examples in your community?

To what extent should a government intervene in companies' foreign trade disputes?

How do other nations perceive the role of the United States as a hegemonic leader in world politics?

Should governments control multinational corporations' involvement in domestic and foreign political and economic affairs? How?

It was expected that the end of the Cold War would free billions of dollars from national security expenditures for the "peace dividend"— that is, for domestic and international social and health purposes. To what extent were such expectations realistic? Can governments maintain a balance between the two objectives?

To what extent is interdependence within the context of North–South relations conducive to economic development in the developing countries?

What evidence is there to support the argument that international organizations such as the United Nations, the International Monetary Fund, and the World Bank pose a serious threat to national sovereignty? Should such organizations be eliminated?

Can you find any examples in your community in which telecommunications technologies, tourism, immigration, and migrant labor have encouraged greater international integration? Are such changes desirable? Have they led to greater cooperation or conflict in your community?

Does economic or military power constitute the best form of "international political currency"?

NOTES

1. As part of his domestic economic policy, about a week before the summit, U.S. President Bill Clinton had introduced a Reemployment Act, aimed at providing $3.4 billion to support two years of training programs for workers who had lost their jobs as a result of defense cuts, corporate restructure, or trade liberalization policies, including jobs

transferred abroad. *Christian Science Monitor,* March 17, 1994, p. 9; *The Economist,* March 12, 1994, p. 19.

2. UNCTAD, *World Investment Report 1994* (New York: United Nations, 1994), pp. 164-165.
3. *The Economist,* March 19, 1994, p. 27.
4. By 1991, it had become clear that western Germany would have to spend up to $100 billion, or approximately 6 percent of its gross national product a year for the next ten years to modernize eastern Germany's economy and clean up its pollution. Industrial production in the east was down by 70 percent, and 3.5 million workers out of a total labor force of 8.8 million were unemployed due to the east's noncompetitive industries. See Charles Hauss, *Comparative Politics: Domestic Responses to Global Challenges* (Minneapolis/St. Paul: West, 1994), pp. 161–166.
5. *The Economist,* March 26, 1994, p. 58.
6. *Christian Science Monitor,* November 10, 1993, pp. 1, 4.
7. *Christian Science Monitor,* November 12, 1993, p. 8.
8. Dietrich Fischer, *Nonmilitary Aspects of Security: A Systems Approach* (Aldershot, U.K.: Dartmouth Publishing and U.N. Institute for Disarmament Research, 1993).
9. Robert O. Keohane and Joseph S. Nye, *Power and Interdependence* (Boston: Little, Brown, 1977); Stephen D. Krasner, ed., *International Regimes* (Ithaca: Cornell University Press, 1983); Robert D. Putman and Nicholas Bayne, *Hanging Together: Cooperation and Conflict in the Seven-Power Summits* (Cambridge: Harvard University Press, 1987).
10. William J. Baumol and Alan S. Blinder, *Economics: Principles and Policy,* 2d ed. (San Diego, CA: Harcourt Brace, 1982), p. 730.
11. *Ibid.,* p. 576.
12. *Ibid.,* pp. 710–711.
13. Robert Gilpin, *The Political Economy of International Relations* (Princeton: Princeton University Press, 1987). See also his *War and Change in World Politics* (Cambridge: Cambridge University Press, 1981); Paul Kennedy, *The Rise and Fall of Major Powers* (New York: Random House, 1987).
14. Gilpin, *The Political Economy of International Relations,* pp. 10–11.
15. Susan Strange, *States and Markets,* 2d ed. (London: Pinter, 1994).
16. Strange, States and Markets, p. 24. For a wider discussion on power and influence, see John M. Rothgeb, Jr., *Defining Power: Influence and Force in the Contemporary International System* (New York: St. Martin's Press, 1993); Thomas C. Schelling, *Arms and Influence* (New Haven: Yale University Press, 1966).
17. Strange, *States and Markets,* pp. 24–25.
18. *Ibid.,* pp. 45–138, *passim.*
19. *Ibid.,* pp. 138–227, *passim.*
20. Knox and Agnew, *Geography of the World Economy,* pp. 22–24; Lester Brown, *State of the World* (New York: Norton), volumes 1987–1995.
21. Knox and Agnew, *Geography of the World Economy,* p. 25.
22. *Ibid.,* p. 19.
23. Brown, *State of the World* [various years].
24. Jean-Claude Derian, *America's Struggle for Leadership in Technology,* trans. Severen Schaffer (Cambridge: MIT Press, 1990), 154–55; Dennis Pirages, *Global Technopolitics* (Pacific Grove, CA: Brooks/Cole, 1989).
25. *Christian Science Monitor,* April 20, 1994, p. 8. While in 1993 most of the businesses surveyed reported *budget constraints* as the primary cause of understaffing, in 1994 about 50 percent cited shortages of *skilled personnel,* rather than budget constraints, as the cause.
26. Gabriel A. Almond and G. Bingham Powell, *Comparative Politics Today: A World View,* 5th ed. (New York: HarperCollins, 1992), p. 439.
27. William Miller, *A New History of the United States* (New York: Dell, 1958), pp. 294–295, 297.
28. Knox and Agnew, *Geography of the World Economy,* p. 249; R.C. Dutt, *An Economic History of India in the Victorian Age* (1904), p. 548, discussed in Bernard Porter, *The Lion's Share: A Short History of British Imperialism, 1850-1995,* 3d. ed. (London: Addison Wesley Longman, 1996), pp. 41–42.
29. See Stephan Haggard, *Pathways from the Periphery* (Ithaca: Cornell University Press, 1990); Michael Lipton, *Why Poor People Stay Poor: The Urban Bias in World Development* (Cambridge: Harvard University Press, 1977).
30. Knox and Agnew, *Geography of the World Economy,* p. 246.
31. Anthony Smith, *The Geopolitics of Information* (New York: Oxford University Press, 1980), p. 111.
32. Laurie J. Wilson and Ibrahim Al-Muhanna, "The Political Economy of Information," *Journal of Peace Research* 22, 4 (1985): p. 293.
33. Derian, *America's Struggle for Leadership in Technology,* pp. 154–155.
34. Thomas B. Rosentiel, "TV, VCRs Fan Fire of Revolution," *Los Angeles Times,* January 18, 1990, pp. A1, A14, A15.
35. This was first reported by Anthony Sampson, *New York Times,* May 6, 1979, p. 2.
36. Wilson and Al-Muhanna, "The Political Economy of Information," p. 296.
37. *The Economist,* February 26, 1994, p. 66.
38. Tim S. Campbell and William A. Kracaw, *Financial Institutions and Capital Markets* (New York: HarperCollins, 1994); Dilip K. Das, ed., *International Finance: Contemporary Issues* (London: Routledge, 1993); Richard E. Caves, Jeffrey A. Frankel, and Ronald W. Jones, *World Trade and Payments,* 6th ed. (New York: HarperCollins, 1993).
39. Klaus Knorr, *The Power of Nations: The Political Economy of International Relations* (New York: Basic Books, 1975), pp. 6–7.

40. *Ibid.,* pp. 20–21.
41. Rothgeb, *Defining Power,* pp. 13–29. See also Michael P. Sullivan, *Power in Contemporary International Politics* (Columbia: University of South Carolina Press, 1990).
42. Gilpin, *War and Change in World Politics,* p. 13.
43. Rothgeb, *Defining Power,* p. 22.
44. *Ibid.,* p. 60.
45. Knorr, *The Power of Nations,* p. 6.
46. Robert O. Keohane and Joseph S. Nye, *Power and Interdependence* (Boston: Little, Brown, 1977), p. 9.
47. *Ibid.,* pp. 10–11.
48. North-South: *A Program for Survival. Report of the Independent Commission on International Development Issues* (Cambridge: MIT Press, 1980), p. 124. [hereinafter referred to as Brandt Commission Report]. For some years now, there has been an extensive debate on the question of whether military expenditure harms development. See, for example, Robert E. Harkavy and Stephanie G. Neuman, eds., *The Arms Trade: Problems and Prospects in the Post–Cold War World* 535 (The Annals of the American Academy of Political and Social Science, September 1994).
49. *Brandt Commission Report,* pp. 139, 291. As Strange has correctly pointed out, the *Brandt Commission Report* was far more controversial in European policymaking and intellectual circles and far more visible in Europe than in the United States. Because 1980 was an election year in the United States amidst the Iranian hostage crisis, and because the conservative administration of Ronald Reagan won the election, the *Brandt Commission Report* simply could not have received as much coverage as it deserved. The *Nyerere Commission* report largely went unnoticed in Europe and the United States. See Susan Strange, "Reaction to Brandt: Popular Acclaim and Academic Attack," *International Studies Quarterly* 25, 2 (June 1981): pp. 328–342.
50. *Challenge to the South: The Report of the South Commission* (Oxford: Oxford University Press, 1990) [hereinafter referred to as the *Nyerere Commission Report*].
51. Strange, "Reaction to Brandt," pp. 335–339. See also the Brandt Commission's second report, *Common Crisis: North-South, Co-operation for World Recovery* (Cambridge: MIT Press, 1983).
52. John Lewis Gaddis, "Toward the Post–Cold War World," *Foreign Affairs* (Spring 1991) p. 103.
53. Martin Carnoy, Manuel Castells, Stephen S. Cohen, and Fernando Henrique Cardoso, *The New Global Economy in the Information Age: Reflections on Our Changing World* (University Park: Pennsylvania State University Press, 1993); James N. Rosenau, *Turbulence in World Politics: A Theory of Change and Continuity* (Princeton: Princeton University Press, 1990); Nathan Rosenberg, Ralph Landau, and David C. Mowery, eds., *Technology and the Wealth of Nations* (Stanford: Stanford University Press, 1992); Richard J. Barnett and Ronald E. Muller, *Global Reach* (New York: Simon and Schuster, 1975).
54. Gaddis, "Toward the Post–Cold War World," p. 103.
55. Roger W. Cobb and Charles Elder, *International Community: A Regional and Global Study* (New York: Holt, Rinehart and Winston, 1970), p. 19. See also Oran R. Young, *International Cooperation: Building Regimes for Natural Resources and the Environment* (Ithaca: Cornell University Press, 1989).
56. James E. Dougherty and Robert L. Pfaltzgraff, *Contending Theories of International Relations,* 3d ed. (New York: Harper and Row, 1990).
57. Peter Dicken, *Global Shift: The Internationalization of Economic Activity,* 2d ed. (New York: The Guilford Press, 1992), p. 3.
58. *Ibid.,* p. 5; Jeffrey Henderson, *The Globalization of High Technology Production* (London: Routledge, 1989).
59. Dicken, *Global Shift,* p. 47.
60. See Barnett and Muller, *Global Reach;* Forest L. Grieves, ed., *Transnationalism in World Politics and Business* (New York: Pergamon Press, 1979); George Modelski, ed., *Transnational Corporations and World Order* (San Francisco: W.H. Freeman, 1979); Raymond Vernon, *Sovereignty at Bay* (New York: Basic Books, 1971); Richard Robinson, *The Internationalization of Business* (New York: Dryden Press, 1984); Alejandro Portes, Manuel Castells, and Lauren A. Benton, eds., *The Informal Economy* (Baltimore: Johns Hopkins University Press, 1989); J.J. Thomas, *Informal Economic Activity* (Ann Arbor: University of Michigan Press, 1992).
61. Frederic S. Pearson and J. Martin Rochester, *International Relations: The Global Condition in the Late Twentieth Century,* 3d ed. (New York: McGraw-Hill, 1992), p. 468.
62. Stephen D. Krasner, ed., *International Regimes* (Ithaca: Cornell University Press, 1983), p. 1.
63. Donald J. Puchala and Raymond F. Hopkins, "International Regimes: Lessons from Inductive Analysis," in *International Regimes,* ed. Krasner, p. 76.
64. *Ibid.*
65. Arthur H. Westing, ed., *Global Resources and International Conflict* (Oxford: Oxford University Press, 1986); Albert O. Hirschman, *National Power and the Structure of Foreign Trade* (Berkeley: University of California Press, 1969).
66. *The Economist,* April 2, 1994, p. 69.
67. Steven E. Sanderson, ed., *The Americas in the New International Division of Labor* (New York: Holmes and Meier, 1984); Manuel Castells, "High Technology and the New International Division of Labor," *International Labor Review* (October 1989).
68. *The Economist,* April 2, 1994, p. 69.
69. *Ibid.,* pp. 69–70.
70. *Ibid.*
71. *Ibid.*
72. *Ibid.,* p. 70.

73. Harry Harding and Edward J. Lincoln, "Rivals or Partners? Prospects for U.S.-Japan Cooperation in the Asian-Pacific Region," *The Brookings Review* (Summer 1993): pp. 7–11.
74. Stephen D. Cohen, "United States-Japan Trade Relations," *Political Science Quarterly* 37, 4 (1990) p. 124.
75. *The Economist,* March 12, 1994, pp. 72–73.
76. Cohen, "United States-Japan Trade Relations," pp. 122–125; Laura D'Andrea Tyson, *Who's Bashing Whom: Trade Conflicts in High Technology Industries* (Washington DC: Institute for International Economics, 1992); Kozo Yamamura and Yasukichi Yasuba, eds., *The Political Economy of Japan: The Domestic Transformation,* vol. 1 (Stanford: Stanford University Press, 1987); Takashi Inoguchi and Daniel I. Okimoto, eds., *The Political Economy of Japan: The Changing International Context,* vol. 2. (Stanford: Stanford University Press, 1988).
77. *The Economist,* April 2, 1994, p. 74. On international taxation in general, see Assaf Razin and Joel Slemrod, *Taxation in the Global Economy* (Chicago: University of Chicago Press, 1990).
78. *The Economist,* April 2, 1994, p. 74.
79. See also Martin Staniland, *What Is Political Economy?* (New Haven: Yale University Press, 1985).

CHAPTER TWO

THE THEORETICAL FOUNDATIONS OF INTERNATIONAL POLITICAL ECONOMY

Most of the issues presented in Chapter 1 have long been one way or another subject to much theoretical debate regarding the nature of international political economy, the role of government, and the major factors that contribute to a nation's success or failure. The ancient "riverine," or "hydraulic," civilizations in China, India, Egypt, Mesopotamia, and pre-Columbian America required efficient irrigation systems, internal stability, sophisticated communications and transportation systems, and trade relations. Each civilization developed its own bureaucracies, methods of operation, and degree of centralization of authority deemed essential for effective self-preservation. Despite the differences in institutional arrangements, each sought territorial security, domestic control, and the enrichment of the imperial treasury, deemed essential for the maintenance of sufficient military capability against external threats and domestic subversion. Military strength, in turn, was necessary for further territorial conquests and acquisition of greater wealth; security and treasury considerations remained inextricably intertwined through the ages. Since the sixteenth and seventeenth centuries, the rise of strong nation-states and their constant competition to control essential resources and territories, the rise of the middle class in commercial and manufacturing enterprises, and various scientific and technological advancements have exerted a considerable impact on the nature and evolution of international political economy. The nation-state and the private interests it sought to promote and protect have shaped the structure of the world economy, yet even today it is a truism to state that a country's national security considerations cannot be detached from its economic considerations—domestic and foreign.[1]

Also, since the sixteenth and seventeenth centuries, a number of major **paradigms** or "grand theories," of political economy have emerged, attempting to explain the essence of domestic and foreign economic relations on the one hand and to provide certain theoretical guidelines to policymakers on the other. Each paradigm emerged in reaction to what its proponents considered to be deficiencies in previous paradigms and policy objectives, and it underscored the gap between theory and practice. Thus, for example, the **classical liberalism** of Adam Smith and David Ricardo in the eighteenth and nineteenth centuries challenged the **theory of mercantilism,** which had dominated political and economic thought throughout Europe during the previous centuries; **socialism** and **Marxism,** in turn, challenged classical liberalism throughout the nineteenth and twentieth centuries. In addition, each paradigm identified certain structural aspects of national and international political economy purportedly conducive either to cooperation or to conflict. Mercantilists saw international relations as a competition for power and wealth, therefore requiring states with sufficient economic and military power to integrate and direct domestic energies toward securing the nation's territorial sovereignty and survival. **Laissez-faire** liberals emphasized the market as an arena for cooperation, and international trade and finance as an extension of the cooperative relations in the domestic market. Marxists viewed **capitalism** in terms of domestic power structure as determined by exploitative modes of production, divided between owners of production and workers, which was said to be the basis for class struggles inevitably leading to revolution.

Various macro- and micro-level explanatory theories sprang from each paradigm, each claiming to hold the key to a better understanding of international political economy and therefore to a policy blueprint for a better world (see Table 2.1). Mercantilism led to modern **Realism (or Realpolitik)** and **economic nationalism** and subsequently to theories of **hegemonic stability**. Classical liberalism led to Wilsonian Idealism, **Keynesianism,** and the school of **functionalism**. Marxism led to **Marxism-Leninist,** Maoist, liberation theology, Gramscian, **dependencia,** and **world system** theories.[2]

In the 1970s, Islamic Revolution in Iran signaled the resurgence of Islam as a potent religious force in modern political economy throughout the Muslim world, stretching from western Africa to Southeast Asia. Concurrently, dissatisfied with the male-dominated theorizing in international political economy, feminism, in various philosophical predilections, charged that all of the previously mentioned paradigms are essentially products of androcentric (or male-centric) worldviews excesssively concerned with male, rather than human, well-being.

Recent developments in communications and transportation technologies and the resultant globalization of economic activity also have signaled the potential need for theories dealing with *globalization.* While some scholars consider globalization and interdependence as an extension of the liberal school, interdependence is distinct from globalization. Following the liberal school, interdependence is inherently a state-centric theory; it holds that nation-states become interdependent in their economic sphere. Globalization theory, on the other hand, consists of national but *equally important* extra-national and even supra-national properties in which economic activities, such as the production and coordination of market arrangements and the international division of labor, are viewed as occurring in a global society far more independently of the state than assumed by the other theories. Unlike in mercantilism, accumulation of wealth is not solely for the interest of the state, but, unlike in laissez-faire liberalism, the state is not a passive observer. MNCs and powerful international organizations have eroded the political and economic space of the nation-state. Also, while mercantilist-, liberal-, and Marxist-oriented theories view international political economy as *either* cooperative or conflictual, globalization theory underscores the point that both cooperation *and* conflict are the essential ingredients of international political economy. As such, globalization, analytically speaking, is neither inherently liberal, mercantilist, nor Marxist in orientation. This chapter presents an overview of some of these main IPE theories, which have influenced both scholarly analyses and government policies. The next chapters demonstrate the force of these competing paradigms as they have shaped the modern international political economy. This and the following chapters should provide sufficient information for the reader to decide which paradigm holds the key to successful performance in the global political economy in the twenty-first century.

CLASSICAL MERCANTILISM AND ECONOMIC NATIONALISM

Economic activities in the Western world, as well as in some Asian and African societies, during the late Middle Ages, from about the twelfth to the fifteenth centuries, revolved around the farming, or feudal, economy on the one hand and the town, or market, economy on the other. In the agricultural sector, peasants produced agricultural products first for their own consumption, second to pay their rent to the feudal lord, and third to sell their surplus at the market in the nearby town. Town economies were comprised of small industries of "guild handicrafts" and "master craftsmen" who owned a small shop and employed a number of apprentices.[3] By the late fifteenth century, however, the Western feudal economy was in the process of major transformation as it gave way to merchant capitalism based on a broad national economy. This epoch of merchant capitalism, or early mercantilism, during the sixteenth and seventeenth centuries witnessed rapid transformations in European economies, with the rise of seafaring trade and commercial capitalism.[4] The state, the predominant actor in mercantilist theory, encouraged expansion of trade as a means to fill the state's coffers with wealth and resources, thereby strengthening the national economy.

The Mercantilist State

Mercantilist practice dates back to the accession of Charles V to the Spanish throne in 1516 and his retaliatory financial and trade policies against the commercial monopoly held by Venice. This period also corresponded to the early phases of the emergence of the nation-state and the gradual development of national economy, particularly in the aftermath of the Treaty of Westphalia in 1648.[5] Meanwhile, the transition to a national economy required the abandonment of the loosely organized feudal monarchy in favor of more complex and highly centralized government institutions consisting of more sophisticated civilian and military bureaucracies. At least out of sheer self-interest,

TABLE 2.1

Paradigms of International Political Economy: Principal Tenets

	Mercantilism	Liberalism	Marxism	Globalization	Islam
Nature of relationship between economics and politics	Politics determines economic policy	Totally separate	Economics determines politics	Cannot be separated	Religion determines both
Nature of international political economy	Struggle for power	Cooperation	Struggle between rich and poor	Conflict and cooperation	Conflict and cooperation
Role of international institutions	Minimal to nonexistent	Facilitate cooperation	Instrument of capitalist control	Functional regimes facilitate limited cooperation	Facilitate cooperation
Extent of conflict in international political economy	High	Minimal to nonexistent	High	Varies, depending on issues and actors	Varies, depending on issues and actors
Nature of the market	Imperfect	Perfect	Imperfect	Imperfect	Imperfect
Distribution of resources	Minimal to nonexistent	Minimal to nonexistent	Redistribution from rich to poor necessary	Minimal	Essential for well-being of individual and community of believers (umma)
Role of the state	Maximum	Minimal to nonexistent	Instrument of the capitalist class	Mixed; competing with corporations	Maximum
Ownership	State or state-guided	Private individuals	Capitalist class; means of production should be socialized	Mixed; state and private	State or state-guided
Economic action motive	State aggrandizement	Individual profit	Close the rich-poor gap	Individual profit and state aggrandizement	Improvement of individual and society (the umma)
Economic power	State	Individual	Should be shifted from capitalist class to community	Individual and state	State

Sources: See John E. Elliott, *Comparative Economic Systems,* 2d ed. (Belmont: Wadsworth, 1985), 27; and *The Politics of Global Economic Relations,* 4th ed by Walters/Blake, ©1992. Adapted by permission of Prentice-Hall, Inc., Upper Saddle River, NJ. 7.

governments strongly supported and were actively involved in this transition from a feudal to a capitalist economy, since with the growing centralization of *national* political authority they could also benefit directly from the increasing economic power of merchant capital.[6] At the same time, however, the state lacked the sophisticated fiscal and monetary policy instruments that are so familiar today. Instead, the mercantilist state relied on the simpler notion of balances between inflows and outflows of precious metals as the ultimate measure of economic well-being. Surplus capital inflows indicated a strong economy.[7]

Thus, the initial objectives of early financial mercantilist policies as developed in Europe were primarily to strengthen the financial base of the government and to enhance its revenue-raising capabilities. This is referred to as the mercantilist **balance of trade** system. To that effect, the government imposed heavy taxes on its subjects and made every effort to import precious metals, such as gold and silver, into the country, and to prevent such resources from leaving the country. The government actively encouraged exports of manufactured products but heavily regulated trade activities and closely supervised all financial transactions to maximize the inflow of precious metals.[8] Two fundamental characteristics of mercantilism, therefore, were the government's active involvement in the development of newly emerging national industries and trade and its heavy reliance on protectionist policies to safeguard domestic industries against foreign competitors. Mercantilism also emphasized thrift to minimize the need for foreign goods and to maximize productive surplus for export.[9]

As capitalists and merchants became financially and politically more powerful, the state's fiscal and trade policies reflected their priorities through state subsidies and tax incentives for domestic production and export on the one hand and protectionist policies to regulate imports on the other. In its mature form, mercantilism was centered on both protectionism, in which the state imposed strict trade or customs regulations to encourage and protect local industries and keep out foreign competitors, and export expansion. Mercantilism, however, involved more than protectionism and encouragement in trade. In 1664, Thomas Mun, the father of mercantilism who also served on the committee of the East India Company,[10] wrote

> The ordinary means . . . to encrease our wealth and treasure is by Forraign (*sic*) Trade. . . . This ought to be encouraged, for upon it hangs the great revenue of the king, the honor of the kingdom, the noble profession of the merchant, the school of our arts, the supply of our poor, the improvement of our lands, the nursery of our mariners, the walls of the kingdom, the means of our treasure, the sinews of our wars, the terror of our enemies. . . .[11]

Mercantilism entailed state-building and the formation of national economies through state intervention in various aspects of economic activities, including wage and price controls, subsidies, and tax concessions to businesses to strengthen both production and trade. Moreover, in order to increase the pool of available labor, mercantilists advocated various policies, such as freedom of religions, to attract foreign labor. In the mid-sixteenth century, French mercantilist and the father of the modern philosophy of national sovereignty, Jean Bodin, insisted that the state maintain absolute sovereignty for territorial security but also that it encourage economic development and accumulation of wealth for purposes of war. Since such priorities required workers, Bodin advocated the elimination of "witches," considered responsible for abortion and other forms of birth control.[12]

Mercantilism and Realism

Concomitantly, in part reflecting the internal power configurations between the landed aristocrats and the rising merchant classes and in part reflecting the rapidly changing international system as viewed from the perspectives of European states, competition among existing (Portuguese and Spanish) and emerging (Dutch, British, French) empires for precious metals and territorial conquests deeply instilled a Realpolitik conception of international relations. The health and wealth of national economies were viewed as heavily relying on each state's ability to "struggle for power." As previously noted, the Realist school of thought regards world politics as a constant struggle for power in a hostile, "anarchic" international system, in which nations struggle to survive and in which the strong dominate the weak. In such a system, the mercantilist state placed a premium on geostrategic military balance of power considerations, often through selective foreign alliances, for the protection of its territorial sovereignty and wealth.[13]

Throughout the nineteenth and twentieth centuries, governments in both democratic and totalitarian, developed and developing countries also emphasized industrial mercantilism and regarded its spillover effects as indispensable for overall economic development and, more important, as the basis for economic *autarky*, or political autonomy, and ultimately for military power.[14]

The U.S. experience is a good example. In the closing decades of the eighteenth century, for example, the most famous mercantilist theorist in U.S. economic thought was Alexander Hamilton. The national debate raging between the competing Jeffersonian and Hamiltonian philosophies regarding the nature and role of the national government in its transition from the Articles of Confederation to the federalist Constitution best exemplified the conflict between the proponents of agricultural supremacy and the proponents of manufacturing supremacy. This conflict was ultimately and irrevocably resolved in favor of the latter by the conclusion of the Civil War. However, long before the 1860s, *national* economic thought had already become a powerful philosophy in the country. In fact, the adoption of the federal Constitution itself, as supported by leading Federalists, such as Hamilton, was the most important first step toward that end.

As the leading proponent of economic nationalism, Hamilton's arguments focused on two key issues to strengthen the national economy: (1) the creation of a central Bank of the United States and (2) the importance of manufacturing over agricultural priorities.[15] Hamilton's *Report on Manufactures,* submitted to the House of Representatives on December 5, 1791, to date stands as perhaps the most important document in the history of U.S. economic thought. The primary purpose of the report was to promote industrial or manufacturing development in a well-integrated national economy. Echoing mercantilists in Europe, Hamilton argued that although agricultural employment and production were necessary for the sustenance of the population, they alone could not provide a strong basis for a productive industrial economy.[16] Like the German *kameralists* (see Box 2.1), Hamilton asserted that "not only the wealth but the independence and security of a country appear to be materially connected to the prosperity of manufactures."[17]

CLASSICAL LIBERALISM

Adam Smith & Classical Liberalism

Classical liberalism emerged in the late eighteenth century in reaction to mercantilism, as the latter increasingly came under challenge by proponents of limited government and free enterprise. Since then, despite significant variations in liberal theories of political economy (such as Keynesianism, monetarism, and "rational choice"), a number of fundamental liberal propositions have remained with a strong commitment to free market operations both at home and

BOX 2.1

GERMAN KAMERALISM & ECONOMIC NATIONALISM

From the second half of the seventeenth century and well into the eighteenth, the Prussian state directly governed and guided the Prussian economy. The term *kamer* referred to the royal treasure chamber, kameral to the economy of the prince, and kameralism to the administration of the royal income, and such matters as pertaining to property, income, taxation, and the development of finance. Between the years of Charles V (1519–1556) and the Thirty Years' War (1618–1648), Germany was in political turmoil, caught between "princely and burgher economies." After years of internal tensions and military and trade conflicts with the Ottoman Empire, France, Holland, and England, German leaders sought to establish some sense of political and economic stability after the Treaty of Westphalia. In reaction to this turbulent situation, German kameralism emerged as a fairly developed school of thought in political economy in university studies. It emphasized extraction of natural resources, especially gold and silver; the use of physical labor to maximize industrial production and production of raw material to meet the immediate needs of the national economy; and consumption of domestic rather than foreign goods, which, kameralists argued, should not be imported if such goods could be produced domestically, even when foreign products may be purchased at prices lower than those of domestic goods. Unlike their English counterparts, who were mainly concerned with finance and trade, German kameralists particularly stressed administrative efficiency for maintaining and increasing the state's treasury. Nevertheless kameralist objectives were the same as mercantilism in England, France, and elsewhere: mercantilist economic theory met the economic expectations of the commercial classes. In twentieth century Germany, economic nationalism appeared in its most virulent manifestation under the Third Reich.

Sources: See Lewis H. Haney, *History of Economic Thought* (New York: Macmillan, 1911), 96, 119–20; Isaac Ilych Rubin, *A History of Economic Thought,* trans. and ed. by Donald Filtzer (London. Ink Links. 1979) 34.

Adam Smith (1723–1790)
NorthWind Picture Archives.

in international economic relations.[18] With the emergence of the middle class, classical liberalism sought to replace the traditional landed aristocracy and mercantilist views by liberating individual economic activity. Classical liberal economic thought, including Adam Smith's *The Wealth of Nations,* David Ricardo's *The Principles of Political Economy and Taxation,* John Stuart Mill's *Principles of Political Economy,* and their descendants, advocated minimum government interference in human affairs. In essence, classical liberalism sought to eliminate "artificial" (that is, government imposed) barriers to economic freedoms in production, consumption, competition, trade, and economic activity in general. These theorists stressed the role of the market free of government constraints and viewed certain economic rights, such as the right of property and the right to trade (sell and buy), as inherent in individuals' "inalienable rights."[19]

Free from government intervention, each individual can best determine and pursue his or her interests. In doing so, the cumulative result of individual freedom and competition will further society's common good in part by preventing excessive accumulations of power by individuals or groups. Very much influenced by the mechanical universe of Newtonian physics, classical liberals argued that providence and the **invisible hand** have created a society in which the natural order of things is "so carefully balanced that the benefit of one could not conflict with the good of all."[20] Given this supposedly balanced natural order of things, classical liberals argued that government interference in human affairs would introduce economic distortions and imbalances, and should be limited to the protection of property, national defense against external threats, and the administration of justice and public services.[21]

Whereas mercantilists had sought sources of wealth in accumulation of precious metals and resources and through foreign trade, classical liberalism found sources of wealth in labor. At its core, it is constant labor, Adam Smith argued, that supplies nations all that they consume and attain as wealth.[22] He opened his "Introduction" to *The Wealth of Nations* by stating that

> The annual labour of every nation is the fund which originally supplies it with all the necessaries and conveniences of life which it annually consumes and which consist always either in the immediate produce of that labour, or in what is purchased with that produce from other nations.[23]

Based on "contractual relations" in the market, the individual pursues his or her self-interest in buying and selling, borrowing or lending, hiring laborers, and seeking employment. The market reflects the competition in the supply and demand for goods and ultimately determines prices.[24] Regarding the individual operating in the market, the classical *homo economicus,* classical liberalism assumed that humans operating as economic beings are well informed, have complete information with which to select the best course of action, and behave rationally—hence, the concept of "rational choice." People attempt to maximize or satisfy certain values at the least possible cost. Therefore, liberalism viewed human behavior as predicated on "individualistic and rationalistic assumptions,"[25] and it emphasized individualism, free market, and private property in an open system. The open market also allows new competitors to enter freely and unsuccessful ones to exit easily, as consumers' demands and producers' supplies meet freely. Furthermore, classical liberalism assumed that political and economic spheres are separate, with political interference and state intervention kept to a minimum, and reserved for extreme cases of market failure.[26]

David Ricardo and Comparative Advantage

Ricardo, as did liberals in general, did not attribute the causes of market failures to any inherent shortcomings in the liberal economic system. Rather, liberals viewed such events as mere aberrations in an otherwise inherently stable economic system.[27] According to liberals, free market economy based on private interests ultimately benefits the public good because markets "naturally" regulate themselves, and, under "natural" or normal conditions without government interference, a self-regulating market ensures the maximum and efficient use of a community's resources. Government regulation, tariffs, and similar interventions, they argued, usually involve political motives not related to profitability; therefore, they distort the market and investment decisions and obstruct the market's tendencies toward the general common good.[28]

As with the domestic economy, liberals believed that the international economy operates according to the principles of *allocative equilibrium.* Classical liberal conceptions of international trade and international economic relations in general posited that nations engage in trade primarily to compensate for their deficiencies in natural resources or labor, as well as to gain access to the most efficiently produced goods. Contrary to mercantilism, liberals did not view the state as owing primary loyalty to select domestic producers. Rather, the unequal distribution of natural resources across the globe compels a state to enter into trade agreements with others for various commercial and industrial goods. Given the situation of inequitable distribution of natural resources and division of labor, classical liberals, Ricardo in particular, introduced the principle of **comparative advantage**. Briefly, **absolute advantage** "exists when each country, due to natural or acquired endowments, can provide the other with a good or service for less than it would pay to produce the product at home."[29] For example, England imports beef from Argentina, Argentina imports oil from Mexico, and Mexico imports corn from the United States. Comparative advantage, on the other hand, exists when one country produces one set of goods more efficiently than another and, hence, concentrates on its most efficient production and trades excess production for higher value abroad. According to the principle of comparative advantage, what ultimately determines which products a country specializes in producing is the relative efficiency and lower costs of production. To quote Spencer,

> The *law of comparative advantage* states that if one nation can produce each of two products more efficiently than another nation, and if the former can produce one of these commodities with comparatively greater efficiency than the other commodity, it should specialize in production of the product in which it is most efficient and leave production of the alternative product to the other country. The two nations will then have more of both goods by engaging in trade.[30]

The following hypothetical example illustrates the point. Let us assume that two countries, China and Canada, produce two products, textiles and wheat, and that the price of each good is determined solely by its labor, as expected by the labor theory of value. As the hypothetical case in Table 2.2 shows, workers in Canada produce more wheat and textiles in *absolute* terms per week than do workers in China. However, the principle of comparative advantage highlights the fact that Canada does not have an equal degree of advantage in both sectors. It has a 3 to 1 advantage in wheat but only a 2 to 1 advantage in textiles. Comparative advantage theory suggests that Canada possesses a greater advantage in wheat, and China has a comparative advantage in textiles, and thus that Canada should devote its labor to produce wheat and use trade receipts to buy its textiles from China; in turn, China should produce textiles and purchase wheat from Canada. Both countries would have access to more total goods produced each week. The logical conclusion of the principle of comparative advantage is that free trade leads to international specialization, encouraging maximum *efficiency* in allocation of goods produced around the world.[31]

Trade relationships on a such simple basis, needless to say, rarely exist in our more complex world. Countries, especially the advanced industrialized societies, trade numerous products. The advent of globalization of trade relations in the twentieth century has introduced a number of new properties, including the globalization of multinational production, the relocation of production abroad for cheaper labor, and the rise of information telecommunications technologies. The traditional commodity-, labor-, and territory-oriented conception of comparative advantage must be modified to take into account the technology-related comparative advantages, including, for example, the

TABLE 2.2

Comparative Advantage (Weekly Production per Person)

	Wheat (Bushels)	Textiles (Yards)
Canada	300	400
China	100	200

role of telecommunications technologies that enhance a multinational corporation's synchronization of material and component deliveries and production capabilities.

More specifically regarding international political economy, classical liberals believed that trade and international economic relations can be instrumental in promoting greater cooperation and peaceful relations among nations, based on mutual benefits derived from such relations, as well as increasing *interdependence.* As such, a liberal international economy is said to exert a positive influence on international politics through networks of mutual interests.[32] In terms of security, though, one need only note the complication for comparative advantage and free trade theory if, in Table 2.2, the two commodities being traded were guns and butter. Would leaders be willing to depend totally on another country for military or food supplies?

Proponents of free trade praised the theory of comparative advantage as conducive to the promotion of mutual interests and peace among trading countries. By the mid-nineteenth century, however, with the rapid growth of industrialization and urbanization, enormous problems had already appeared in all aspects of society. Gradually, general public discontent regarding the living and working conditions they faced daily gave rise to alternative philosophies of political economy, some of them quite speculative, challenging classical liberalism and its notions of harmony (for example, see Box 2.2). Liberalism's opponents—first Marxists and later the dependencia school, for example—argued that, as expected by the theory, in practice free trade and comparative advantage lead to commodity specialization, as well as to commodity and market dependence and conflict in relations between industrialized and developing countries. Commodity specialization leaves the developing economies dependent on the economic well-being of markets in the North. Given the fact that raw materials are labor-intensive commodities and therefore cheaper than

BOX 2.2

FAR OUT THEORIES OF INTERNATIONAL POLITICAL ECONOMY:

"The Solar Influence on Commerce" William Stanley Jevons (1878)

The recent and present condition of industry in Great Britain imperatively demands the careful attention of economists and men of science. A vast calamity has to be investigated, and its recurrence as far as possible provided against. Artizans have been thrown out of employment by tens of thousands, if not by hundreds of thousands. Through no fault of their own, they find themselves suddenly reduced to pauperism, with families which can only be saved from starvation by public or private charity. . . .

The state of things is not equally bad in all parts of the country; it chiefly affects Lancashire & Yorkshire where industry depends much upon foreign trade. No doubt, too, the destitution will be very temporary. . . .

The most casual inquirer can hardly fail to be struck by the fact that these epochs of distress are periodic. The crisis or collapse of credit which ushers in a period of destitution is more definite in date than the interval of destitution itself, and if we remember that there was, especially in the United States, a collapse in 1837, another in 1847, another in England in 1857, & again in 1866, and now a most distinct one in 1878, we may be tempted to carry out thoughts still further back to 1825–6 when there was likewise a most fully developed crisis followed by depression of industry. These events have thus occurred at intervals successively of say 12, 10, 9 and 12 years, and the approximation to an average period of about 10½ years is so remarkable, that no one who really contemplates the facts can fail to be struck by the fact. But many who have been forced to admit the periodic character of these events have shown a strange unwillingness to enter upon any scientific examination of its causes. They say that they do not want mere theory; it is to facts, and to daily experience they look; to mention the sun or planets to them is only to call forth a denunciation of astrological speculations. . . . I need not inform my readers that a series of eminent astronomers, meteorologists, and physicists of different ranks & branches of science, have gradually established the fact that the sun is a variable star, having a period variation of somewhere between ten and twelve years, as Professor Loomis states the fact in his newest work on astronomy. An eminent meteorologist, Mr. J.A. Broun, lately the Director of the Magnetic Observatory at Trivandrum in the Madras Presidency estimates the period, as we shall see, precisely at 10.45 years, and this period so closely agrees with the commercial period already pointed out, that a strong presumption of causal connection at once arises. . . .

Source: R.D.Collison Black, ed., *Papers and Correspondence of William Stanley Jevons,* vol. 7 (London: The Macmillan Press, 1981), 90–98.

assembled products, it is far more difficult for developing countries to develop technologically advanced and competitive industries already dominated by the North. (Others—Marxists and non-Marxists—have pointed to the informal economy as an integral component of political economy, but one often ignored by the liberal theory. The informal economy is discussed in Chapter 12.)

Liberalism and Keynesianism

In the 1830s, amid the near breakdown of the capitalist system, Great Depression, and rampant unemployment, the extent to which the government should expand its role to rectify systemic deficiencies became the subject of intense debate in industrialized societies. The emergence of Keynesian economics as a palatable antidote to such economic failures greatly widened the acceptable parameters of government involvement, leading to the reformulation of terminology regarding "liberals" and "conservatives."[33] This was a crucial turning point because classical liberals, especially their descendants of the modern era, see no necessary causal connection between economics and politics, between the process of economic growth and political development and crises, such as wars and revolutions. As Roll has pointed out, although Ricardo had witnessed the Napoleonic wars and the political and economic problems of his time, he nevertheless devoted no more than a brief chapter, entitled "On Sudden Changes in the Channels of Trade," to a discussion of these problems. Gilpin adds that liberals see no causal relationship between "the advance of capitalism in the late 19th century and the upheavals of **imperialism** after 1870 and the outbreak of WWI."[34]

However, the Great Depression posed a serious threat to political stability and undermined public confidence in laissez-faire capitalism. The most influential British economist at the time, John Maynard Keynes, criticized classical liberalism as being inherently incapable of preventing cyclical trends and of addressing the social and economic problems caused by the depression. Liberals would expect that there would be winners and losers in the workings of capitalism and free markets. However, rather than passively relying on market forces, Keynes argued, governments would considerably enhance the workings of the market by becoming, through fiscal and monetary instruments, actively engaged in steering the economy. Keynes prescribed a more direct government management of economy to remedy imbalances between productive output (supply) and market consumption (demand). He proposed deficit financing through increased public expenditures—for example, in the form of public works—to provide employment in times of economic downturn, recessions, and depressions as well as tax increases in times of economic growth, to curb inflationary pressures.[35]

Keynes, however, was preoccupied strictly with the *policy* aspect of economic cycles and recovery from the depression. During the same time, Europeans were concerned not only with the economic depression but also with the destruction wrought by the First World War and the rise of Nazism and fascism, which threatened the region's peace again shortly after the conclusion of the peace treaty in 1919. Led principally by David Mitrany, the *functionalists* drew attention to the need for nonpolitical regional *institutions* that would be built on consensual proclivities of states and would eventually develop an integrated, region-wide system of economic and political stability.

Liberalism & Functionalism

For centuries after the Peace of Westphalia, political theorists were confronted with the twin forces of the rise of the powerful nation-state and its implications for political freedoms on the one hand and the need to develop specific arrangements to prevent wars on the other.[36] Montesquieu, Voltaire, Rousseau, Locke, and Smith attacked repressive governments; and their antimercantilist, liberal values stressed natural rights derived from natural law and the importance of economic liberalization. At the same time, however, as Falk has noted, the nation-state system and the "logic of Westphalia" had led to a fragmented and an inhospitable world for the internationalization of these values.[37] Thus, some proposals were made for European regional order to eliminate war and to create an environment conducive to the development of natural rights. These included, for example, the works of seventeenth- and eighteenth-century giants, such as Emeric Cruce's *Le Nouveau Cynée,* William Penn's *Essay Towards the Present and Future Peace of Europe,* John Bellers' *Some Reasons for a European State,* and the Abbe de Saint-Pierre's *Project of Perpetual Peace.*[38]

This intellectual tradition provided the foundation for the *functionalist* school of thought, especially as it developed in reaction to the horrific consequences of the First and Second World Wars. Functionalism contended that international cooperation can be achieved through the piecemeal, incremental processes of structural adjustments and readjustments as required by the technically complicated and technologically varied functions which must be performed for the benefit of citizens and firms. David Mitrany, the father of functionalism, argued that, as societies and government responsibilities become more complex, government institutions require a greater number of technical (nonpolitical) experts to solve daily problems, ranging from public health to facilitating communication. Given the fact that many of the issues facing modern societies are not confined within national boundaries, international cooperation among technicians, as opposed to politicians, from different countries becomes indispensable. Functionalists believed that the creation of international organizations as mechanisms for technical collaboration would eventually grant greater powers to technicians while limiting politicians' involvement in international affairs, thereby preventing the escalation of conflicts into wars.

Moreover, Mitrany added that functional cooperation leads to the **ramification** effect, or what political scientist Ernst Haas has called the **spill-over** effect—that is, functional collaboration in one area necessitates cooperation in other areas as well.[39] As functional international organizations proliferate throughout the world, the mercantilist propensities of the nation-state diminish. Interdependent networks of organizations increasingly become a system of technical collaboration and coordination of international activities and **regimes,** facilitating nonpolitical and, hence, nonmilitary resolutions of conflicts.

The functionalist school, and its descendants in "neofunctionalist" and *interdependence theories,* believed that a principal objective of domestic and international economic activity is to maximize the efficient use of global resources, thereby maximizing global welfare.[40] As such, and in sharp contrast to the mercantilist view that international economic relations are a *zero-sum* "win-lose" affair, functionalist and interdependence theorists maintain that international economic relations can be a positive-sum game, whereby all members of the community gain a share of the benefits accrued from such cooperative relationships. It is, therefore, they argue, absolutely essential that governments refrain from interventions in such activities and allow free market operations and the "invisible hand" of global competition to propel the immense international economic machine toward its natural equilibrium. In such a self-equilibrating system, the international division of labor and distribution of wealth lead to greater harmony and prosperity, and authority and loyalties are automatically, if gradually, transferred from the local level to the national, then to the regional and unto the supranational.[41]

Western states adopted "Keynesianism," if not necessarily as presented by Keynes,[42] and functionalist policies after the Second World War. The Marshall Plan to rebuild European economies and the creation of the International Monetary Fund and the World Bank were the products of Keynesian economic theory. Neofunctionalism in Europe led to the creation of regionally based institutions, such as the European Coal and Steel Community (ESCE), which expanded ("spilled over") to become what is known today as the European Union (EU). In geopolitical terms, Keynesianism and functionalism proved acceptable to Western policymakers because they, especially Keynesianism, proposed solutions within the overall theoretical framework of liberal capitalism. In fact, Keynesianism was credited for saving capitalism at a time when the Bolshevik Revolution in Russia had launched its communist experiment, and Western political and economic elites feared that the economic depression and massive unemployment would instigate similar revolutions in Europe and, to some extent, in the United States.

MARXISM, DEPENDENCY, AND THE CAPITALIST WORLD-ECONOMY

The advent and spread of industrialization in the nineteenth century, while providing jobs on an unprecedented scale, also created miserable working and living conditions wherever factories were built. Masses of people with limited financial means did not have the luxury of avoiding the drudgery of factory life, while a small group of wealthy landowners, financiers, and industrialists escaped such difficulties and controlled both capital and political power. For the masses, conditions deteriorated over the years; for the elite, accumulation of wealth meant greater economic and political influence.[43] These conditions led Karl Marx, the most influential socialist theorist of political economy in the nineteenth century, to criticize capitalism and to

Karl Marx (1818–1883)
Historical Pictures

develop his own "scientific" theory of political economy to explain the changes taking place in the newly industrializing Europe.[44] His theory was predicated on the notion of class struggle between the *proletariat* (workers) and the bourgeoisie (owners of the means of production).

Marxism, Lenin, and Class Conflict

Central to Marx's theory was class conflict. Marx argued that capitalism and capitalist production, though clear improvements over the prior feudal system, are fundamentally doomed by excess reliance on private property and competition for profit. A key feature of capitalist production in the newly emerging industrial economies, he argued, was the division of society between the capitalists who owned the means of production—for example, factories—and the workers, who had nothing but their physical labor. According to this theory, the capitalist seeks to maximize profits from the market and employs, or "exploits," others' labor to do so. In the process of production, the owner of the means of production pays the worker no more than subsistence wage, while the worker produces a value that far exceeds the wages he or she receives.[45] Marx predicted

> continuous struggle between capital and labor, the capitalist constantly tending to reduce wages to their physical minimum, and to extend the working day the opposite direction. . . . The very development of modern industry . . . must progressively turn the scale in favor of the capitalist against the working man, and . . . consequently the general tendency of capitalistic production is not to raise, but to sink the average standard of wages, or to push the *value of labor* more or less to its *minimum limit.*[46]

According to Marx, real profit in a capitalist economy is derived from the difference between the amount of wages paid to the worker and the value produced by the worker—that is, *surplus value,* accumulated by the capitalist. The principal cause of conflict in capitalist societies, Marx held, is not only the mode and means of production but also the mode and means of distribution of that surplus capital.[47]

Marx rejected the idea of a tendency in the market toward equilibrium and maintained that capitalist economies contain an inherent contradiction between capitalists' capacity to produce goods and consumers' capacity to purchase them. The widening gap between production and consumption in the market causes economic fluctuations and depressions, and the severity of such economic crises intensify and eventually "impel the suffering proletariat to rebel against the system."[48] Therefore, Marx argued, in capitalism structural factors create an environment more conducive to class struggle than to economic and political harmony and cooperation.

Furthermore, in sharp contrast to the classical liberal view of economics and politics as analytically distinct concepts and separated in the workings of the market, Marx's formulation rested on the proposition that the two cannot be separated and that the political is not at all independent of the economic factors shaping society. Both the political and economic aspects of the market economy are central to issues of class-based distribution of capital, and distribution derived from the market cannot analytically or practically be separated from the society within which they operate. The political constructs of authority—that is, the state—dominate the institutions erected for purposes of control and the extraction of resources from society. Religion acts as an "opiate" to blind people to these disparities. These processes and policies, Marx argued, are directly shaped by and in service to the class forces operating in the economic substructure.[49]

Marx and his contemporary socialists believed that, in the nineteenth century, capitalism and the rapid internationalization of the capitalist market economy, propelled by profit and accumulation of wealth, would soon but inescapably cause a worldwide "proletarian revolution" and lead to the demise of capitalism. Indeed, Marx did not believe that a political movement would be necessary to achieve this; rather, it would occur according to the economic laws he had discovered. In their famous *Manifesto of the Communist Party* (first published in 1848), Marx and Engels stated,

> The history of all hitherto existing society is the history of class struggles. Freeman and slave, patricians and plebeians, lord and serf, guild-master and journeyman, in a word, oppressor and oppressed, stood in constant opposition to one another, carried on an uninterrupted, now hidden, now open fight, a fight that each time ended, either in a revolutionary reconstitution of society at large, or in the common ruin of the contending classes.[50]

There were clear indications that future events would prove otherwise, however, and nationalism was certainly one of them. According to Marx, since the real cause of conflict was class struggle between the proletariat and the bourgeoisie, workers would transcend international boundaries to join together in their struggle against capitalist domination, yet not only did capitalism not disappear by the end of the nineteenth century, but, perhaps even more important, the First World War demonstrated that workers, and even socialist parties in capitalist societies, were more nationalists than proletariat and would fight against, rather than unite with, workers of enemy countries.

Besides the issue of proletariat solidarity against capitalism, early twentieth-century Marxists and socialists, Vladimir I. Lenin being the most influential among them, regarded the First World War as a struggle among capitalists for colonial territories, resources, and markets. Viewed from this perspective, nationalism and imperialism led socialists to modify Marxist theory to incorporate it into a theory of international political economy. This found its full expression in Lenin's *Imperialism: The Highest Stage of Capitalism,* first published in 1917; Lenin transformed Marx's theory of domestic political economy into a theory of *international* political economy.[51]

By the first decade of this century, capitalism had emerged technologically far more advanced, far more resilient, and far more globally oriented than Marx and nineteenth-century socialists had imagined. The expanding consumer production (typified by Henry Ford's production line and willingness to pay line workers $5 per day), as well as trade and capital transactions among capitalists and between capitalists and developing countries by way of colonization and empire-building, had transformed the global economy, dominated by large and powerful industrial and financial monopolies and trusts. Lenin theorized that monopoly capitalism and imperialism are predicated on two fundamental conditions: the emergence of monopolistic operations, such as cartels and trusts in industry and finance concentrated in a few hands, and the worldwide competition for raw materials, which inevitably leads to international military conflicts and "struggle for spheres of economic interest in which the richer and the more powerful nations exploit the weaker ones."[52] This mode of imperialism, Lenin wrote, is the highest stage of capitalism, whereby capitalist societies would seek to alleviate domestic economic tensions by expanding abroad. As capitalist monopolies eliminate competition in the domestic market and win over consumer-laborers, so does imperialism attempt to eliminate competition in the global market.

Vladimir Ilyich Lenin (1870–1924)
(Corbis-Bettmann)

The following quote from Cecil Rhodes, the British financial tycoon who led the colonization of southern Africa in the late nineteenth century, illustrates the imperial mindset:

> I was in the West End of London yesterday and attended a meeting of the unemployed. I listened to the wild speeches, which were just a cry for "bread! bread!" and on my way home I pondered over the scene and I became more than ever convinced of the importance of imperialism. . . . My cherished idea is a solution for the social problem, i.e., in order to save the 40,000,000 inhabitants of the United Kingdom from a bloody civil war, we colonial statesmen must acquire new lands to settle the surplus population, to provide new markets for the goods produced in the factories and mines. The Empire, as I have always said, is a bread and butter question. If you want to avoid civil war, you must become imperialists.[53]

The First World War, Lenin argued, was the clearest manifestation of the competition and conflict among imperialist powers, as they divided the colonial territories among themselves. Lenin believed that the capitalist international competition turned into international war because the constant "scramble" for colonies gradually limited resourceful territories available for colonization. Economic rivalries among rising and declining capitalist states could not be resolved peacefully and, therefore, would inevitably lead to war, such as the First World War.[54] Thus, Lenin argued that capitalism contains within itself its own "seeds of destruction," the inherent contradiction that as it develops the global economy it also develops technological and industrial capabilities around the world, giving rise to new competing forces. As Gilpin has noted, Lenin "asserted that this had been the fate of the British-centered liberal world economy of the nineteenth century. Today he would undoubtedly argue that, as the U.S. economy declines, a similar fate threatens the twentieth-century liberal world economy, centered in the United States."[55]

Not all Marxists agreed with Lenin, however. Karl Kautsky, for example, contended that capitalism does not automatically lead to conflict. Instead, capitalism can evolve through different phases, in which capitalist powers maintain their ideological and economic alignments for a long time and develop into a broader *ultra-imperialism.*[56] According to Kautsky, cooperation among capitalist states is possible, and capitalist domination of the world system does not necessarily lead to wars. Imperial war is *not* inevitable. While the First and perhaps even the Second World War might have seemed to support Lenin's thesis, U.S. hegemony after the Second World War and the cooperation the United States received from Western European countries lent greater credibility to Kautsky's prediction.

The successful Bolshevik Revolution (Lenin believed—unlike Marx—that a "vanguard" political party, the Bolshevik Party, was necessary to ignite and lead the revolution) and the creation of the Soviet Union appeared to legitimize Lenin's theory of imperialism as the "orthodox" Marxist theory of international political economy. Other revolutionary leaders subsequently adopted Marxist-Leninist theories to explain the historical development of their own countries and regions. In doing so, they also made their own contributions to this radical philosophy (see Box 2.3, for example, on Mao Tse-tung's sinification of Marxism as he led the Communist revolution against Chiang Kai-shek's Nationalist government).

Dependencia Theory

In addition to the Leninist and Maoist transformations of Marxism, a plethora of neo-Marxist or Marxist-oriented literature during the second half of the twentieth century made major contributions to the theory of imperialism. *Dependencia* theory has been one of the most influential recent schools of thought in IPE as developed in the works of Raoul Prebisch, Andre Gunder Frank, Samir Amin, Arghiri Emmanuel, and Immanuel Wallerstein, to name but a few, since the early 1960s. A variant of Marxist-Leninist structural thought, dependencia theory attempts to explain the wide discrepancies between the industrialized, wealthy countries of the North and the poorer, less developed countries in the South. Its primary thesis is that in North-South relations the wealthy countries (the "core") have historically relegated the developing countries (the "periphery") to a subordinate position through exploitation and extraction of resources, including human beings (even slaves) and raw materials.[57] Besides their exploitative relationship, the North often simply ignores the South economically.

The North-South dialogue became an important issue in international relations, as developing countries in Africa and Asia formally gained independence from colonial rule after the Second World War. The urgency of the situation, according to dependencia theorists, is largely attributable to the fact that, while Western capitalist countries evolved gradually from agricultural to mature industrial and modern societies over a period of more than a century, on independence neither the leaders nor the institutions in developing countries could command sufficient political or economic influence to accelerate economic development and modernization at the desired pace. And, when some tried, as in the case of Iranian Premier Mohammed Mossadegh's nationalization of foreign oil companies in 1951, colonial capitalist powers—the United States and Britain—reacted with sanctions (oil boycott) and subversion. The CIA orchestrated the overthrow of the Mossadegh government and returned the pro-West Shah to power in 1953.[58]

North-South tensions were exacerbated by the fact that the emerging countries were entering an international system that was caught amid an intense ideological and power struggle between capitalism (U.S.) and communism (USSR). Moreover, the international economic scene did not prove to be very hospitable to newly independent states, as the North had already established its supremacy over all key international organizations and definitions of law, and the developing countries had no choice but to operate within them. Consequently, because of domestic and foreign policy considerations, the leaders of developing countries were under enormous domestic and international pressure to modernize quickly.

Dependencia theory has gained much support among Latin American intellectuals because even Latin American countries, which gained independence in the early decades of the nineteenth century, have not been able to achieve the level of technological modernization of their northern neighbors, the United States and Canada, and remain in a dependent relationship with them, as the foreign debt crises since the 1980s have demonstrated. The Latin American case suggests that the period when a country or region gains independence is not necessarily as crucial to its development potential as the historical "development of underdevelopment" supposedly imposed on it by dominant powers before and after independence. Thus, from Africa and Asia to Latin America, most developing countries are faced with enormous difficulties in both domestic and international arenas, ranging from abject poverty, socioeconomic inequities, weak political institutions, political and economic instability, and chronic corruption to unequal trade partnerships with foreign states and multinational corporations and financially debilitating foreign debt and finance crises.

BOX 2.3

MAO TSE-TUNG AND THE SINIFICATION OF MARXISM

Following the Opium Wars in the nineteenth century, China was repeatedly subjected to invasions and interventions by Western powers, such as Great Britain and the United States, as well as by its immediate neighbors, Japan and Russia. Marxism and Leninism provided the Chinese Communists the philosophical basis that corresponded to the problems in China and their struggle against the "foreign devils." Thus, in contrast to the Marxist analyses of industrial Europe's "class struggles" between the proletariat and the bourgeoisie (which did not include a foreign factor), in China the foreign factor, along with the role of the peasantry, had to be an integral part of any analysis of any struggle. A theory of revolution, if it were to have any applicability to China, would necessarily have to be a theory of the concrete practice of revolution because, Mao Tse-tung argued, what was needed in China was a concrete revolution and not an abstract theory. For Mao and his generation, Marxism without sinification would have been irrelevant to China. Analysis of Chinese exploitation could not simply be separated from Chinese nationalism and the revolutionary movements. The overthrow of the foreign-supported elite necessarily required the overthrow of foreigners; the overthrow of foreigners necessarily required the overthrow of the ruling elite. Mao's contributions to Marxism included shifting the locus of revolution from the urban centers to the rural areas, and he emphasized protracted military conflict based on peasant guerrilla warfare. According to the Marxist theoretical scheme of things, the peasant has no significant role to play in the events leading to the proletarian revolution. Peasants, according to Marx, are ill-equipped as a class to lead the revolution against the capitalists. Marx, the consummate theoretician, had not developed any theory for guerrilla warfare. Mao, the consummate practitioner, emphasized the need for an organized revolutionary military force as the most effective vehicle to achieve a concrete revolution.

In China, the very low degree of industrialization created no basis for an interpretation similar to Marx's Eurocentric analysis of the more exploitative nature of the industrial, capitalist mode of social relations. It required first and foremost the philosophy of revolutionary nationalism through mass mobilization against the social, economic, and political status quo, including the centuries-old Confucian tradition. In his earlier years (1920s), Mao had emphasized the role of the urban workers and merchants as most capable of carrying on the revolution in China. Mao had repeatedly stated that the Chinese people were both revolutionaries and nationalists. By early 1927, as his *Hunan Report* revealed, Mao had become aware of the "importance of the peasant uprisings and identified wholeheartedly with them." Mao clearly stated his position regarding the role of the peasantry in China's revolution:

> A rural revolution is a revolution in which the peasantry overthrows the authority of the feudal landlord class. If the

Dependencia theorists point out the role of Western governments and multinational corporations and the adverse consequences of their operations for most of the population in developing countries. They note that the governments and multinational corporations of the industrialized North dominate the developing countries' political and economic institutions through bribery and cooptation of local elites and capital, while perpetuating dependency relationships through investments in extractive industries, low-technology production facilities, and cheap labor. It is this mode of "exploitative" relationship, according to dependencia theorists, that has enabled the West to achieve a high degree of modernization and affluence while leaving the less developed regions in poverty and dependent on the North's capital and technology.

Critics of dependencia theory note, however, that the disadvantages of LDCs at the time of their independence cannot be continually blamed for their current problems. Economic mismanagement by national leaders and banking interests, they argue, plays a larger role in the South's distress and debt burdens. Supporters of free trade contend that the benefits of increasing trade and wages, and plentiful consumer goods will gradually filter down to LDCs on the open market, just as they did within nations in the North.

Dependencia theorists, however, have raised serious questions regarding the viability of the classical liberals' most fundamental assumption that trade benefits all equally, and that international free trade relationships, by way of "comparative advantage" create international harmony and cooperation. They have stressed that the capitalist world system is essentially based on asymmetrical relationships, whereby the wealthier capitalist countries subordinate, if not actually oppress, the poorer, underdeveloped countries. According to dependencia theory, then, the primary cause of dependency and the numerous problems associated with it in the developing countries is the

BOX 2.3 (concluded)

MAO TSE-TUNG AND THE SINIFICATION OF MARXISM

> peasants do not use the maximum of their strength, they can never overthrow the deeply rooted, age-old authority of the landlords. The rural areas must experience a great, fervent revolutionary upsurge, which alone can arouse hundreds and thousands of the people to form a great force.

And the concrete peculiarity of China was above all the numerical predominance of the peasantry in the countryside, without whose mobilization the revolution could not succeed. In his *Hunan Report* (1927) Mao wrote,

> Being the most revolutionary, the poor peasants (*particularly the poorest ones*) have won the leadership in the peasant association. . . . This leadership of the poor peasants is extremely necessary. Without the poor peasants there can be no revolution. To reject them is to reject the revolution. To attack them is to attack the revolution.

In October 1938, Mao's report to the Central Committee stated that "we must not study the *letter* of Marxism and Leninism, but the *viewpoint* and *methodology* of its creators, with which they observed and solved problems." He stated,

> There is no such thing as abstract Marxism, but only concrete Marxism. What we call concrete Marxism is Marxism that has taken on a national form, that is, Marxism applied to the concrete struggle in the concrete conditions prevailing in China, and not Marxism abstractly used . . . the Sinification of Marxism [is to make] certain that in all of its manifestations it is imbued with Chinese peculiarities, using it according to these peculiarities.

In China, while the peasants had clear numerical superiority over the workers, Mao could not ignore the fact that, without the urban workers, the revolution could not be completed. In the struggle against Japan, Mao had no choice but to give equal weight to both rural and urban forces, if for no other reason than the reality that Japan was in control of the major urban financial and urban centers of China littoral. Furthermore, Mao's "class struggle" did not mean a mere struggle between the proletariat and the bourgeoisie; it meant that a revolution, a society's transformation from one stage to the other, required the "transformation of the people's minds through [permanent] ideological purification and rebirth."

Sources: See M. Rajai, *Mao Tse-tung on Revolution and War* (Garden City NJ: Anchor Books, 1970); George Thomson, *From Marx to Mao Tse-tung* (London: China Policy Study Group, 1971); Stuart R. Schram, *The Political Thought of Mao Tse-tung* (New York: Praeger Publishers, 1969); James Chieh Hsiung, *Ideology and Practice: The Evolution of Chinese Communism* (New York: Praeger Publishers, 1970); and James R. Ozinga, *Communism: The Story of the Idea and Its Implementation* (Englewoods Cliffs, NJ Prentice Hall, 1987).

globally integrated capitalist world-economy as developed under Western industrialized powers.

Capitalist World-Economy Model

Primarily an offshoot of Marxism and predicated largely on views advanced by the dependencia theory, the major premise of the capitalist world-economy approach is that the nature and issues of the contemporary world economy can be best understood within the context of the historical evolution of capitalism and the origins of the modern economic system dating back to the sixteenth century.[59] Over the centuries, the modern "world system" has been transformed from geographically isolated and predominantly agricultural societies to industrialized and technologically complex networks of trade and financial institutions and production facilities dominated by major capitalist powers. According to this view, changes taking place in the international economic system during the late twentieth century do not in and of themselves constitute totally new phenomena but a continuation of the single capitalist world system, with its own uniform laws of expansion and exploitation. Thus, contrary to the view that the current system is totally different from previous epochs, the world-economy model holds that it is only a change in the degree of the structural complexity involved. The world-economic system has been inherently capitalist in its orientation since the sixteenth century and remains as such without any interruptions to this day.[60]

According to Immanuel Wallerstein, the capitalist world-economy, as it has developed over the past three centuries or so, is comprised of a number of fundamental ingredients, including a single global market; a small number of major, powerful capitalist countries (each with its own state-corporate complexes) that dominate the global market; and the division of the world system into "core" and "periphery" countries. The core countries consist of the original and now highly advanced capitalist states of Western Europe, Japan, and North America; the peripheral countries are the developing countries of Latin America, Africa, and Asia. In the tradition of the literature on imperialism, Wallerstein holds that the relationship between the core and peripheral countries is exploitative in nature, whereby the core, having created the structural foundations of modern world economy in their own image, dominate and mold the direction of economic and political developments in the periphery. Their primary objective is to ensure, through multi-lateral and bilateral trade and financial arrangements and military force, if necessary, the preservation of the status quo and their privileged status within the system. Those in the periphery, on the other hand, seek to overturn this system. As Wallerstein has stated,

> The capitalist world economy as a totality—its structure, its historical evolution, its contradictions—is the arena of social action. The fundamental political reality of that world economy is a class struggle which however takes constantly changing forms: overt class consciousness versus ethno-national consciousness, classes within nations versus classes across nations.[61]

Hegemonic Stability Theory

Unlike the Marxist orientation of the "capitalist world-economy" theory, hegemonic stability theory is derived from the *Realist* and *neo-Realist* schools. As previously noted, Realism views international politics as a struggle for power and domination. For neo-Realists, such as Kenneth Waltz, the international struggle for power is a central component as well, but they contend that neither the struggle nor power is random; instead, a specific set of world systemic—that is, *structural*—factors determines the nature of both.[62] The structural characteristics of the modern international system, for example, include its "anarchic" nature and the development of **"balance of power"** (*bipolar* or *multipolar*) politics; the number of hegemons competing for world domination; and the unequal distribution of economic and military power among individual nation-states. The behavior of nation-states is determined by the structure of the world system.

Hegemonic stability theory holds that, at any given period in the history of the world system, the global economic system—including trade relations, banking and financial arrangements, and the multinational corporations' production operations, as well as the supportive political and military constructs—can be dominated by a single hegemonic power, with both positive and negative results. On its emergence, the new hegemon takes measures to consolidate its position of hegemonic preponderance and to avert its demise in the future. Such measures include taking control over raw materials, sources of capital, markets, competitive advantages in production, comparative advantages in strategic goods, and sufficient military capability and ideological alignments to support its position of hegemony. The hegemon gains access to such resources either by exercising direct control over vast territories or through proxy governments that—based on explicit agreements, such as treaties or tacit "understandings"—ensure the hegemon easy access to and control over territory and resources. The hegemon establishes a new international economic, political, and military system according to its own domestic needs.[63]

The hegemon becomes the principal actor in the international system but, rather than "exploiting" it unfairly, also assumes certain financial and political responsibilities to strengthen and maintain the new order. In the modern world system since the sixteenth century, a number of hegemons have successively dominated the world following the demise of the Spanish and Portuguese empires—the United Provinces of the Netherlands in the seventeenth and eighteenth centuries, the British in the eighteenth and nineteenth centuries, and the United States in the twentieth century (the UN and Bretton Woods system).[64] During each period, the hegemon supposedly has acted as the stabilizing force within an otherwise "anarchic international society,"[65] and its position of leadership in multilateral international organizations and in bilateral relations has permitted wide latitude to bring pressure on others to act according to its own "rules of the game." Immediately after the Soviet invasion of Afghanistan in December 1979, for example, the Carter administration enunciated the "Carter Doctrine," warning the Soviet Union that if it continued territorial expansionist aggression toward the Persian Gulf region and threatened the global flow of oil, the United States would use military means, if necessary, to protect the region.

In multilateral financial regimes, such as the International Monetary Fund and the World Bank, the hegemon dominates through voting and financing. In bilateral relations, it dominates through various financial arrangements, credits, loans, and economic and military assistance. As the hegemon, it can also deny these privileges to its enemies or those who refuse to cooperate with the system. Over the years, as part of its containment policy, the United States gave large sums of economic and military assistance to countries, such as Iran and Turkey, deemed strategically significant, since they shared borders with the Soviet Union, but it denied such aid to Marxist-oriented governments, such as Cuba and Vietnam, while offering aid to some Marxists opposed to Moscow, such as President Tito of Yugoslavia. More recently, in 1998, Washington briefly tried economic sanctions to penalize India and Pakistan for setting off underground nuclear weapons tests.

Some analysts, such as Kindleberger, Gilpin, and Krasner, have considered the presence of a hegemonic power as desirable.[66] Given the anarchic nature of the international system, they have argued, a hegemonic stabilizer is essential for the effective functioning of the world financial system, and for maintenance of peace. In its absence or during a transitional phase in which the hegemon is in decline, usually caused by what Kennedy referred to as "imperial overstretch,"[67] the international system cannot for long sustain a healthy sense of economic and political equilibrium. For example, in *The World in Depression,* Kindleberger's thesis was that the depression of the 1930s occurred precisely because the British empire, in gradual decline since the 1880s, was no longer willing and able to maintain the control over the global financial system it had managed for more than a century. With the rise of rival industrial and capitalist powers, especially the United States after the Spanish-American War, the British failed to compete, and the international system collapsed.

This line of argument, however, assumes that the hegemon functions in the interest of the international system. A number of scholars and national leaders have challenged that assumption and have argued that the hegemon, and particularly the elite within its domestic power structure, regardless of the rhetoric used, is exclusively interested in its own well-being, usually at the expense of others. Nor are its concerns abroad always related to national or international security proper. Rather, critics contend, for example, since the Second World War, the United States has been an imperialist hegemon, and U.S. foreign policy has been preoccupied with more than mere national security objectives, serving instead to protect corporations' investments abroad.[68] According to this view, on assuming the role of hegemonic leadership after the Second World War, the United States did not act as a "benevolent hegemon," as Kindleberger and others would have expected. Instead, immediately after the war, under the Truman administration it inaugurated its hegemony through the implementation of the containment policies of the Truman Doctrine and the Marshall Plan against Soviet power and communism.

Concomitantly, the United States supported the creation of multilateral organizations such as the United Nations and the Bretton Woods system, GATT, IMF and so on as instruments for domination of world trade and financial relations. Even in the area of trade, despite Washington's rhetoric regarding the virtues of free trade, it instituted protectionist policies and never completely opened its own market to foreign imports. Instead, as a hegemonic power, the United States used international institutions, such as GATT, to justify its own protectionist policies for the benefit of a number of domestic industries in the 1970s—for example, "in the early 1960s, when the cotton industry was in trouble, subsequently in the 1970s, when the problem had extended to man-made fiber, and lastly in the 1980s, when other natural fibers were brought under discriminatory restrictions."[69]

Such a conception of hegemonic stability, however, assumes that Realpolitik designs totally shape a country's foreign policy objectives. Was the Marshall Plan's unprecedently large-scale aid to Europe a "benefit America" ploy or a hegemon's sacrifice in funds to keep the world trade system going? Or was it both? Is it desirable, even imperative, that under conditions of international competition a single hegemonic power impose certain rules of conduct among nations to ensure a more stable and secure international system, and agree to purchase large amounts of foreign goods to keep foreign exchange flowing?

According to the functionalist school, nations often have great opportunities for cooperation, and world political economy does not necessarily entail "struggles for power." Indeed, according to Robert Keohane, an international system based on cooperation through international regimes of transnational functional units would even eliminate the need for a hegemon. Contrary to the dependencia theorists, Keohane has argued that, in the case of U.S. hegemony, its economic and political preponderance was already in the process of erosion by the mid-1960s, and international regimes came under enormous pressures. He has noted, however, that

> the changes in these regimes did not always correspond to the shift in power, and the decline of American hegemony did not lead uniformly to the collapse of regimes. Cooperation persists and, on some issues, has increased. Current patterns of discord and cooperation reflect interacting forces: the remaining elements of American hegemony as well as the effects of

> erosion, the current mixture of shared and conflicting interests, and the international economic regimes that represent an institutional legacy of hegemony.[70]

Keohane has challenged the major premise of the hegemonic stability theory that international stability requires a hegemonic leader. Such a conception of hegemony presupposes constant international conflict and struggles. However, according to Keohane, this view, although valid to some extent, is too simplistic. There is more frequent cooperation than wars in the world political economy, and one also needs to explore why states defer to the hegemon's leadership. Thus, as Keohane has pointed out, following Kautsky's theory of ultra-imperialism based on cooperation among capitalist powers, "the common interests of the leading capitalist states, bolstered by the effects of existing international regimes (mostly created during a period of American hegemony), are strong enough to make sustained cooperation possible, though not inevitable."[71] This is similar to what Keohane and Nye have called "complex interdependence," referring to the functioning of the international system "with multiple issues, multiple channels for contact among societies, and inefficacy of military force for most policy objectives."[72]

Keohane's and others' emphasis on cooperation and interdependence, as valid and as sophisticated as their arguments are, have not convinced Marxists in and out of the developing countries that the international system so dominated by the North is conducive to cooperation. From their perspective, the international system needs major structural changes, a New International Economic Order, to eliminate "structural violence" and "structural conflicts." Non-Marxists, as well, have underscored the intensification of competition among different "capitalisms" as an essential structural feature of the capitalist world economy in the late twentieth century.

ALTERNATIVE MODELS OF CAPITALISM IN THE LATE TWENTIETH CENTURY

After the collapse of the Soviet Union and the end of the Cold War ideological conflict between capitalism and communism, a number of scholars argued that, although capitalism is no longer facing any serious competition, the new competition is now within capitalism itself. Michel Albert, for example, has identified two distinct models of capitalism: the Anglo-Saxon or Anglo-American model and the Rhine model. Others have added the East Asian–Japanese, model. The following sections briefly review these models individually and highlight some of their central characteristics.

Anglo-American Model

The Anglo-American model is the closest to traditional classical liberalism, with its emphasis on limited government intervention in the economic affairs of the community in particular. The Anglo-American model reasserted itself with a vengeance in the late 1970s and throughout the 1980s under the conservative, laissez-faire-oriented governments of Margaret Thatcher and Ronald Reagan. The revival of this model reflected conservatives' discontent with the welfare state as it had emerged with Keynesianism during the Great Depression. In the case of the United States, for instance, the Roosevelt administration's New Deal and the Johnson administration's Great Society policies increasingly came to be viewed as burdensome on the taxpayers and the government itself too encumbered by bureaucratic priorities to facilitate efficient provision of goods and services for the "truly needy." In addition to domestic economic difficulties, this discontent was also fueled by foreign policy failures after the Vietnam War. Thus, the combination of foreign and domestic policy problems, such as the Iran hostage crisis and high inflation, brought Reaganomics to the White House. Reaganomics consisted of two key elements: deregulation and "supply-side economics." Deregulation sought to repeal regulatory policies that the administration found unnecessary financial and legal burdens on corporations. Supply-side economics meant, in part, providing tax incentives for corporations as a way of stimulating new investments and renovations of plants. Both strategies were, the administration argued, necessary to reinvigorate the economy. At its core, at least philosophically speaking, Reaganomics was fairly close to classical liberalism's laissez-faire capitalism and was politically conservative, although the federal government rang up record deficits during the Reagan administration due mainly to massive military spending to regain public confidence. In the 1990s, the "Contract with America," as adopted by the Republicans in Congress, and President Bill Clinton's own brand of Democratic reform promised further dismantling of federal regulations and spending, and the budget debates between Congress and the Clinton administration reaffirmed the ideological and policy priorities as identified by the Anglo-American model of capitalism.

Rhine Model

The Rhine model, according to Albert, encompasses northern and western European countries and to some extent Japan. Like its Anglo-American rival, it is capitalism emphasizing private property and free enterprise. The Rhine model, however, differs from the Anglo-American model in its economic organization and general political structure and culture, assigning a greater role to the state. Immediately after the Second World War, neither Germany nor Japan, for obvious historical reasons, favored a strong, authoritarian government imposing central planning. In Germany for example, the West German government opted for "liberal capitalism known as the social market economy (*Sozialmarktwirtschaft*)." It consisted of a number of key components, including the welfare state with extensive social security and health care programs, state protection for domestic industries, and coresponsibility (*Mitbestimmung*), whereby employers and employees shared the responsibilities of management.[73] Government involvement in various social programs and regulations to maintain healthy standards of life and work complemented semiprotectionist policies for domestic industries. Thus, unlike the Anglo-American model, and despite a basically conservative fiscal policy, the Rhine model is inherently more statist in its orientation, with greater emphasis on social welfare and protectionism.

Further, the Rhine model is largely bank-driven instead of revolving around the stock market, as in the Anglo-American model. According to Albert,

> It is the strength and vigor of German banks that explain this situation. While everyone has heard of the Deutsche Bank, with its commanding position in the German economy, and of others such as the Dresdner Bank or the Commerz Bank, few suspect how very powerful they are. Crucially, they may (unlike American banks) conduct all types of business; no regulations restrict them to a single activity or sector. German banks are 'universal' institutions: they make ordinary loans and have ordinary depositors; they deal in stocks and bonds, and manage company treasuries; they also operate as commercial banks, providing investment advice and carrying out acquisitions and mergers. And finally, they maintain whole networks of economic, financial, business and industrial information for the benefit of client companies. The result is a special relationship between bankers and their customers in which mutual cooperation is constantly reinforced.
>
> Above all, German banks have assumed the role of company financiers, which elsewhere has been taken over by the stock markets. Most firms have their 'house bank' to whom matters of finance are entrusted; one can almost imagine the German banker telling his client, the company president: 'You just take care of improving production and increasing sales, and leave the financial problems to us!' In Japan . . . the symbiosis of industry and banking is even more pronounced, with many industrial groups owning their own banks. It is almost possible to reverse the equation and say that the Japanese banks (and insurance companies) own their own industrial groups.[74]

The Deutsche Bank, for example, owns 25 percent of the shares in Daimler Benz, a German car company that merged with (bought out) Chrysler Corporation in 1998; in Philipp Holzmann, a major construction company; and in Karstadt, a trading giant. In turn, these enterprises are the bank's largest shareholders.

Operating within symbiotic networks of institutions, the Rhine model supposedly possesses important advantages over Wall Street, Albert adds; the former tends to be much more long-term-oriented in its business outlook and is therefore based on commitment, while the Anglo-American model is primarily geared toward immediate profitability. Moreover, unlike the Anglo-American model, the Rhine model places special emphasis on company loyalty and mutual trust between employer and employees. While in the Anglo-American model a corporation (like any other commodity) and employee wages are "subject to the prevailing winds of the market at any given moment,"[75] and therefore negotiable, in the Rhine model a corporation is a *community* rather than a commodity. German employees are among the highest paid, they enjoy longer vacations, their wages (as determined by "qualification, seniority and nationally agreed pay scales")[76] are more stable, and the wage gap between the highest- and lowest-paid employee is narrower than employees' in most industrialized societies. Companies' long-term interests are served well by cultivating a strong sense of trust, as well as by training and retraining for purposes of promotion. However, states in the Rhine model also have sustained chronically high unemployment rates in the past decade, have proved highly vulnerable to failed bank investments (Germans in Russia, Japanese in Asia and North America), and they have not clearly surpassed the United States in levels of technological development.

East Asian–Japanese Model

Some of the characteristics found in the Rhine model are also present in the East Asian–Japanese model, a third form of modern capitalism. Primarily statist in orientation, as one scholar has pointed out, a central element in Japanese cultural tradition, worldview, and organization of political economy is the "*ie* genotype" (ie originally meant household) or, in some cases the *mura* ('village') variant."[77] The Japanese culture places great emphasis on collective goals and the long-term survival of the immediate and intertwined community of family and corporation. As in the Rhine model, long-term commitment is essential for employee-employer relationships, and wages are relatively stable, but the networks of suppliers and producers are much more extensive, traditional, and geographically localized than in Europe.

While in the Anglo-American model the philosophy of laissez-faire advocates separation of the economy from politics, the East Asian–Japanese model recognizes no such separation. Nevertheless, it is important to point out that, unlike the Communist planned economies of the former Soviet Union, in which the state controlled all corporations and properties, the East Asian–Japanese model allows corporations to own vast properties in multiple industries and to keep their profits. Japan's cultural tradition and community-driven values, however, have culminated in far greater governmental involvement in the economic affairs of the country than in Britain or the United States, and the relationship between the Japanese state and traditional *zaibetsu* (major corporate conglomerates) arrangements is closer than in the Anglo-American model. A prime example of this is the Ministry of International Trade and Industry's (MITI) close relationship with the major corporations.[78]

One observer has identified key areas, including promotional policies, entry controls, and investment guidance, as dominated by MITI. In the 1950s, a number of laws, such as the Firm Rationalization Promotion Act (1952), authorized MITI to use various strategies—for example, tariffs, tax exemptions, distribution of government financial assistance, and contracts—to promote certain industries deemed essential by the government. MITI also controlled new entries into the market by major industries (automobiles, steel, petrochemicals), and it became more selective as the economy grew during the 1960s and 1970s, with emphasis on production for export and with strict discriminatory policies against foreign firms.[79] MITI also controls corporate investment through its own quota system and investment guidelines.

Some Japanese are concerned about the implications of the *zaibetsu*-style and the political domination and extensive economic control by the bank-driven *keiretsu* networks of companies. As in the German experience, they perceive the potential development of pre-WWII military-industrial complexes as a threat to efforts for long-term political and economic stability, and especially for greater democratization. Economic crises, such as those of the late 1990s, as well as natural disasters, such as the earthquake in Kobe in January 1995, are likely to lead to greater state intervention and regulatory reforms. Cultural traditions in the economy, as well as the structure of supply networks, tend to be barriers to foreign penetration, even when formally protectionist policies are dropped.

The Japanese government also has been intent on opening foreign trade and investment opportunities to foster dependencies on Japan and reduce Japanese dependence on foreign sources of raw materials. Variations on these themes can be seen in China as well, and in the "Asian tigers," the export-oriented economies of Singapore, Taiwan, and South Korea, which also have encountered crises related to weak currencies and failed investments in the 1990s. The expansion of these Asian economies and their interests in world markets has led to intense market competition worldwide since the early 1980s. Expanding trade relations signify greater international cooperation, as liberal theorists would argue, but the rapid intensification of international market competition in time of economic difficulties, as in the 1980s and 1990s, also has led to international rivalries, with serious implications for international relations at global and regional levels and for inter-cultural relations at home. The Clinton administration came into direct and open conflict with Tokyo in the 1990s, pressing Japan to open its markets, increase government spending, lower taxes, increase consumption, and lay off excess workers, policies reminiscent of the Anglo-American model previously outlined.

Neo-Statism, Neo-Mercantilism

As noted earlier, faced with intense trade competition in the global economy during the past decade or so, the world economy has witnessed a growing trend, especially among the highly industrialized countries, toward more statist policies to mollify public demands for greater protection of national industries, borders, and sovereignty. Some countries, including France, Germany, the United States, and Japan, appear to have opted for a statist-oriented political economy, at least for the sake of economic and political, if not military, power. The rapidly changing circumstances in international political economy have increased public interest in statist or mercantilist, or neo-mercantilist, thought. While during the industrial revolution industrial mercantilists emphasized the supremacy of manufacturing over agriculture, during the past two decades neo-mercantilist priorities have emphasized advanced technology, "the desire for national control over the 'commanding heights' of the modern economy."[80] Under the current circumstances, we might expect to witness economic nationalism again manifest itself through various forms of economic competition and warfare. Similar to the United States in the nineteenth century, but affected by Marxism-Leninism, neo-mercantilism has resurfaced in developed and developing countries largely because of the maldistribution of economic resources and political power between the industrialized and developing countries. The latter have continued to express concerns regarding the vulnerability of their domestic economies to foreign influences.

In the ever increasingly competitive global market, neo-mercantilists regard their own state's "relative gains to be more important than mutual gain," as each state struggles to enhance its position, not only in terms of trade but also in international organizations and regimes "to benefit themselves disproportionately with respect to other economic powers."[81] While liberalism underscored the mutual benefits of trade, and Marxists viewed such relations as primarily based on class relations and conflict, neo-mercantilists, like their predecessors in the sixteenth and seventeenth centuries, have focused on the centrality of government, its political, economic, and military demands and policies. For neo-mercantilists, economics, like politics, is a struggle among states for power.[82]

The new state-centric mercantilism is very similar to classical mercantilism in emphasizing the role of the state as an agent of economic development, independent of market and class motives. Politics and security considerations remain key components of international economic relations. It is politics more than anything else, as practiced by major domestic and international institutions, that delineates the contours of economic activity. Gilpin has observed that

> throughout history each successive hegemonic power has organized economic space in terms of its own interests and purposes. [Therefore,] transnational actors and processes are dependent upon peculiar patterns of interstate relations. Whether one is talking about the merchant adventurers of the 16th century, 19th century finance capitalism, or 20th century multinational corporations, transnational actors have been able to play an important role in world affairs because it has been in the interest of the predominant power(s) for them to do so.[83]

Thus, contrary to some scholars' predictions that the state as an important player in international relations will "wither away" or will be replaced by MNCs, and despite moves to lower government spending and regulations, neo-mercantilists maintain that such predictions are at best premature. They find no indications in the global system to conclude that the state will disappear from the political and economic scene anytime soon. Rather, MNCs' impact on international political economy, they argue, is similar to influences exerted by pressure groups in domestic politics, and the nation-state continues to function as the most potent economic and political force in international relations. Circumstances that have led to interdependence in the late twentieth century also have led to greater state involvement in world economic activities,[84] reflecting public demands for a greater share of public goods, including economic protection and security.

GLOBALIST THEORIES

In addition to the theories of international political economy previously discussed, a number of theories with wider implications for international relations and concerning more diverse ideas of what is or should be valued have gained or, as in the case of Islam, have regained relevance. For example, scholars used to pay more attention to the relationship between religion and political economy. One of the most influential German sociologists and political economists, Max Weber, devoted a number of studies to this topic (for example, *The Protestant Ethic and the Spirit of Capitalism, Ancient Judaism, The Religion of India, The Religion of China*),[85] as did Tawney and others.[86] Despite the worldwide spread of secularization, the resurgence of religious "fundamentalisms" suggests that religion-based theories remain relevant in the post-WWII IPE literature. The three theories discussed in the following sections—globalization, Islamic, and feminist—are like Orthodox Marxism, globalist in essence, in that with some variation they claim universal applicability, transcending territorially based conceptions of international political economy.

Globalization Theory

The newest of the three theories, globalization theory, emphasizes the transnational interconnectedness of public and private economic activities. This model entails more than mere interdependence in international relations; it focuses on the new globalization of international structures, patterns, and processes in the world political economy. However, it is also worth emphasizing that, contrary to popular understanding of the concept of globalization, the term does not mean the creation of a "world government," nor does it refer to a single entity dominating the world economic system, as held by the hegemonic stability theory. Rather, its primary focus is the increasingly and closely intertwined economic activities, such as production, management, communications, and transportation. Internationalization of economic activities certainly is not unique to the twentieth century. Improvements in navigation technology and the subsequent expansion of trade relations in the sixteenth through eighteenth centuries set the stage for the fundamental changes taking place in the late twentieth century. Indeed, internationalization already existed during the times of ancient civilizations and empires as they traded goods and slaves. Nor are issue specific "international regimes" the exclusive products of this century. However, the second half of the twentieth century, especially since the 1970s, witnessed unprecedented transformations in transnational trade and financial activities that qualitatively and quantitatively differ from traditional patterns.

While theories of political economy, such as mercantilism, classical liberalism, Marxism, and their ideological derivatives and updates, remain relevant to certain aspects of international political economy, each places primary emphasis on either cooperation or conflict. A major premise of the globalization theory, on the other hand, is that international relations involve both cooperation and conflict and that relations among governments, among corporations, and between the two are too complex to premise one's analysis on such simplistic conceptions of political economy as "interdependence leads to cooperation" or "the history of all hitherto existing society is the history of class struggles."

Globalization theory holds that, in recent decades, corporate operations have become so vastly encompassing in geographical and structural terms that the nation-state no longer performs the pivotal role assumed by the traditional theories or even by world-system theorists. Nor can the nation-state or hegemon constrain transnational activities, as assumed by mercantilist and hegemonic stability theory. The globalization of political economy, through geographical dispersion of corporate activities, production, and information channels, demands ever greater bargaining flexibility on the part of decision makers at different levels and locations. Products are no longer produced with any degree of geographical specificity as pertaining to a nation-state. In some sectors, such as the automobile industry, it is no longer clear what constitutes an American, a Japanese, or a German product. The traditional national symbolism behind "Made in X" is no longer meaningful for many goods found at the malls.[87] Thus, according to Robert Reich, Secretary of Labor during the Clinton administration,

> The central question for a nation competing in the international economy is not who owns the factories within its borders, but how efficient those factories are. Prospering in today's global economy requires an educated, skilled work-force and sufficient capital investment. If capital and other types of investment enhance the efficiency of a nation's workforce, it makes no difference which investor—foreign or national—provided the capital, only that it was provided.[88]

Trends toward globalization have added a new dimension, a new layer in the structure of governance; an individual government alone can no longer address major issues, such as employment, inflation, social welfare, and national security. For an increasing majority of people worldwide, in the large and wealthy economies of the North and the smaller and poorer economies in the South, decisions made by national governments are directly influenced by decisions made in other capitals, international organizations, and corporate headquarters continents away. How Paris responds to inflationary pressures at home depends on decisions made in the halls of treasury ministries and central banks in Tokyo, London, Bonn, and Washington. Corporate decisions pertaining to auto assemblies and production levels in São Paulo are directly related to decisions made in Detroit, Lisbon, Singapore, Toyota, and Vancouver. As a result, national channels—political parties and local interest groups—for citizen participation in national policymaking processes become less relevant.[89] Globalization theory contends that in the late twentieth century the traditional significance attached to the state and the domestic arena for promotion and protection of fundamental human values such as *liberté, égalité, fraternité* diminished considerably, as global networks of corporations and other entities gained in prominence.

Thus, a central dilemma in globalization theory is the organizational arrangement of the MNCs. MNC managers have to choose between various tradeoffs in terms of location of production facilities, costs, marketing and so forth. Conceptually, these choices are made between the two extreme poles of *firm-specific advantages* on the one hand and *country-specific advantages* on the other. Such a conceptual framework is useful to explain corporate decisions regarding management, production, and marketing, as well as the advantages available under different economic, political, and cultural conditions across the world. The first model, emphasizing firm-specific advantages, holds that a multinational firm can maximize its profits and minimize expenditures through centralization of corporate structure and *standardization* of production and products as the most efficient means of operation. The second model stresses country-specific advantages where the multinational firm is decentralized along national lines. Instead of standardization, through decentralization the firm "tailors the attributes of the product, the packaging, the promotion, and the distribution to the preferences of consumers in each country."[90]

In the global economy, the theory of firm-specific advantages implies production and marketing of goods across the globe, regardless of differences in national economies; distribution of wealth and income within each country; and consumers' habits and culture-bound preferences and tastes. Whether the MNC is selling cars, shirts, soft drinks, or home appliances, the product remains the same in all countries. The main advantage in this firm-specific model is that, because the firm maintains standardization at the global level, economies of scale keep its operation costs low.

In the country-specific model, however, managers pay close attention to national and cultural tastes in each country. An MNC produces a product or a style of the product for France, another for Saudi Arabia, and another for India or Japan. This model implies that national borders are still an important factor in corporate decisions regarding production and marketing, and differences in countries are taken into consideration. In this case, the costs of highly fragmented production and packaging may be higher than in the more centralized system, although profits might be higher as well. Unlike the traditional view of corporations operating on the principles of comparative advantage, MNC managers are now confronted with a number of strategic choices with respect to research and development (R&D), production, and marketing priorities.

A combination of both models would suggest a new international division of the market. MNCs would be more inclined to produce specifically tailored products for wealthier countries, since a larger pool of the population can afford more expensive goods. Standardized and therefore less expensive products, on the other hand, would be marketed primarily in the poorer countries, where the market for "tailored goods" is limited and a larger percentage of the population could not afford them, further widening the gap between the developed and developing economies, as well as between rich and poor within each country.

The globalization of MNC operations also has important implications for the international division of labor. Contrary to traditional classical liberalism and Marxism, which saw firms as immobile, globalization theory holds that firms, having developed global manufacturing networks, are not necessarily bound to a specific, predetermined territory but can transfer their operations from one country to another with relative ease, assisted by modern telecommunication technologies. Highly competitive world markets require lower costs of production and of labor. Firms search for cheap labor in political and economic environments with minimum regulatory constraints, as in the 1980s and 1990s, when an increasing number of companies in the United States moved from highly unionized industrial cities in the north to the nonunionized regions in the south and across the border to Mexico, Honduras, and Guatemala. Thus, the international division of labor through integration of cheaper labor had, by the mid-1990s, significantly weakened the labor unions, with serious consequences for "job security," full-time employment, and employment benefits.

It should be noted, however, that, while MNCs are the most important factor influencing events in the global 1st political economy, it would be an exaggeration to view them as omnipotent and omnipresent actors dictating their commands to helplessly submissive government officials. On the contrary, the nation-state is hardly on the verge of disappearing from the maps. Indeed, the disintegration of the Soviet Union and the "rebirth" of Eastern European countries are testimony to the persistent strength of nationalism, which some globalists, along with liberals and Marxists, expected to disappear with the advent of industrialization and modernization. Today, the nation-state is the most vivid manifestation of various aspects of nationalism—territorial, economic, religious, and so on—commanding strong followings among their respective populace.

Relations between MNCs and host governments frequently involve multifarious bargaining processes and strategies, both seeking to maximize potential advantages presented by the opportunities of international relations in finance, foreign direct investments (FDI), and trade. In fact, one of the new features of the global political economy is the increasing interconnection between FDI and trade, as MNCs expand their operations through strategic alliances and joint ventures, which in turn result in growing intra-firm trade. The ability of an MNC to create global networks of production and supportive service facilities from one country to another is itself the product of each government's willingness to negotiate and manage the terms of corporate operations within its boundaries.[91] Contrary to the traditional theories, the global political economy and international activities, then, are not seen as the exclusive domain of either nation-states or MNCs. They are the culmination of conflicts and cooperation in MNC government relations.[92]

The MNC search for cheap labor is also exaggerated as a globalizing factor. In the rapidly modernizing East Asian economies, in Japan, Malaysia, Singapore, South Korea, and Taiwan, corporations have not moved *en masse* to other regions for cheap labor. Rather, they have kept unions relatively weak and wages comparatively low (with exceptions, such as in Japan), and East Asian governments, through coercive measures, have played a direct role in controlling labor. Further, contrary to claims that globalization of international trade and finance has led to the "end of geography," the nation-state continues its traditional role in economic management and national security—the difference now being that it has to share its political and economic space with other powerful entities, such as multinational corporations. Despite some of its theoretical shortcomings, then, globalization theory has underscored the need for global economic management, especially since "existing international institutions were designed to coordinate a system of nation-states in which each state was supposed to be sovereign over its domain."[93]

Islam and International Political Economy

Some Western observers hold the view, repeatedly reinforced by the mass media, that Islam, deeply rooted in the traditional tenets of the **Quran,** is incompatible with the technological changes in the modern global economy. They point to the Islamic societies' supposed inability to achieve economic development along Western standards in the twentieth century as directly attributable to the failure of Islam to adapt to modern conditions. Alternatively, they present the leaders of the OAPEC countries as conniving, duplicitous, oil-rich sheikhs who successfully manipulate Western markets and finance terrorist organizations. Others, particularly Muslim scholars more closely familiar with Islam and Islamic cultures, in turn argue that nothing inherent in Islam (as nothing inherent in Christianity, Judaism, Hinduism, and so forth) obstructs technological and economic development and modernization (see Box 2.4).[94] Islamic countries in the Middle East, Africa, and Asia have lagged behind Western industrial economies largely because of historical circumstances rather than religious or cultural proclivities. Muslim countries' current underdeveloped status and their inability to modernize like the West is attributable to the long period of Western colonization at a critical juncture in world history, when the industrial revolution catapulted the West toward technological and military superiority and subsequently toward colonization throughout the nineteenth and twentieth centuries. Otherwise, as in most parts of the world, international commerce and cooperation, geopolitics and conflicts, have been as much a part of daily life in relations between Islamic and Christian societies as between other regions and religions and have contributed as much to the globalization of world political economy.[95] Contrary to misperceptions in the West, Islamic governments have instituted economic policies that combine Western and Islamic and secular and religious principles of international trade and finance, dating back to the Middle Ages, when growing commerce between merchants from Asia and Europe influenced each others' financial and trade techniques and methods.[96] The resurgence of Islam, in conjunction with Arab nationalism, in the twentieth century is in part an effort to modernize after centuries of European and Ottoman imperial rule.[97]

Not only does Islam not impede international economic progress, but it was founded and gained strength in one of the most important trading areas of the world, the Middle East, which for millennia has served as a commercial corridor between Asia and Europe. While in pre-Islamic Arabia the region consisted mainly of loosely organized tribal communities, the rise of Islam in the seventh century served as a powerful unifying force, eventually mobilized for the expansion and conquest that culminated in the empire stretching from the Indus River (in India) to the Iberian Peninsula on the Atlantic.[98] Islam provided a new religion and a comprehensive philosophy of life that, like most other major religions, survived and shaped millions of people's lives for centuries, despite the divisions between *sunni* and *shi'a* (and other) Muslims. Some of humanity's greatest scientific and technological breakthroughs (for example in mathematics and astronomy) came in lands under Islamic rule.

Today, the Islamic world is not confined to the Arab world or to the Middle East, as is often incorrectly presented in the West. A large majority of the world's nearly 1 billion Muslims live in non-Arab countries as diverse as Senegal, Indonesia, and the United States. There are twenty-four countries whose official religion is Islam. As with classical liberal and Marxist economic theories (as with most theoretical constructs, for that matter), however, in practice Islamic economic systems do not necessarily or completely reflect the principles and classical teachings of the Quran. It is said that economic Islam worked "ideally

BOX 2.4

RELIGION AND INTERNATIONAL ECONOMY

The resurgence of religious movements around the world since the mid-1970s has had a considerable impact on international political economy. Whether it is Christian fundamentalism, Islamic resurgence, Orthodox Judaism, or *Hindutva* (Hinduness), religions role in world politics is expected to increase with both negative and positive consequences. With minor variations, the major world religions promote similar social, political and economic values. While secular philosophies of political economy emphasize material factors in society, such as the state, the market, or class structure, as determinants of political and economic behavior, religious philosophies emphasize communal and spiritual factors. Secular philosophies are almost exclusively concerned with rational economic behavior, while religious philosophies presume a sense of moral guardianship of human welfare in the religious community. Some of the key principles commonly found in religions include social justice, international peace, and political realism. The principle of social justice is predicated on *equitable distribution* of resources and *mutual obligations* between ruler and ruled, the community and its members, producer and consumer, and employer and employee. While *classical liberal* economics emphasizes market utility, maximization of profit, and free competition, *Buddhist* economics, for example, emphasizes generosity, perseverance, patience, and cooperation. Secular and religious political economic thoughts, however, are not necessarily mutually exclusive. For example, *liberation theology*, as developed in Latin American Catholicism, has integrated both *Judeo-Christian* thought and *Marxism-socialism* as a way of addressing social and economic problems. Led by local clergy, liberation theology has demanded a greater role on the part of the Catholic Church in various social and economic developmental programs, such as literacy, social justice, economic equality, and promotion of human rights and democratization. During the past two decades, liberation theology has found a large following not only in Latin America but throughout the developing world.

Religions are related to international political economy through issues of war and peace as well. In the sixth century b.c., Lao Tse of China, founder of *Taoism,* held that military force is not compatible with human values, the *Tao* (the *Way*). Similarly, Confucius (ca. 550 b.c.), a younger contemporary of Lao Tse and the founder of *Confucianism,* believed that the primary objective of creating an orderly society is to achieve universal harmony and stability based on *jen* (empathy). During the Vietnam War, a number of Buddhist monks through self-immolation expressed their opposition to the government and the war's killing and destruction. In the *Judeo-Christian* tradition also there is a strong commitment to peace. In the Old Testament, God prohibits killing. He commanded, "Thou shalt not kill" and urged people to "turn from evil and do good, seek peace and pursue it" (Ps. 34.14), to end all wars so that "they shall beat their swords into mattocks and their spears into pruning-knives" (Isa. 2.4, Mic. 4.3). For centuries, both the Old and New Testaments have served as the bases for Judeo-Christian pacifism.

However, political realism (that is, power politics) and war-crusades are also integral components of religions, and they have created ambiguities between religious principles of pacifism and exhortations for religious crusades. In *Hinduism,* Arjuna, the God of War, urged his followers to fight and to sacrifice themselves for the community. India has named many of its modern weapons after Hindu gods. The Old Testament God commanded, "When the Lord your God has given them over to you, and you defeat them, then you must utterly destroy them, you shall make no covenant with them, and show no mercy to them." (Deut. 20) "Christian realism" holds that Christian participation in war is necessitated by the violence caused by evil people—hence, the "Just War" doctrine. In his *Moral Man and Immoral Society,* Reinhold Niebuhr, a Christian theologist, argued that, although individuals are essentially good and yearn for peace, the world of sovereign nations has created an international community in which security requires power and preparedness for war. Fourteen-hundred years ago Islam rode to world prominence through a series of military conquests.

The ideal international political economy as envisioned by these religions never had an opportunity to materialize. However, technological advancements in the area of telecommunications, the *information superhighway* (for example, the Internet), like the rapid transportation systems before them, have already created Judeo-Christian, Islamic, and Buddhist *religious telecommunities.* While the full potential and impact of such telecommunities are subject to debate, they certainly provide forums for greater international cooperation and confrontation.

Sources: See Glen Alexandrin, "Elements of Buddhist Economics," *International Journal of Social Economics* 20, 2 (1993): 3–11; Archie J. Bahm, *The World's Living Religions* (Berkeley: Asian Humanities Press, 1992); David P. Barash, *Introduction to Peace Studies* (Belmont: Wadsworth, 1991), 6–7; Alexandra David-Neel, *Buddhism: Its Doctrines and Its Methods* (New York: St. Martin's, 1977); and Glenn Tinder, *The Political Meaning of Christianity* (San Francisco: HarperCollins, 1991).

during the Prophet's lifetime and subsequently during the tenure between A.D. 632 and 661 of the four 'rightly-guided' caliphs, but that system began to fall ever shorter of the ideal thereafter."[99] Here we shall focus on some of the key concepts in Islamic political economic thought as they relate to modern international political economy.

Islamic political economic thought differs from Western secular notions of positivism and rationalism in that, while Western nations purport to deal exclusively with material aspects of society for objective understanding of social, economic, and political phenomena, Islamic political economy explicitly rejects any claims to such "nonvalue-oriented" epistemology and seeks to bridge the gap between the material life of the present and the spiritual life of the hereafter. As John O'Brien has pointed out, those who insist on a "strictly rigorous value-free approach" to the science of political economy would obviously reject the Islamic approach and its methodologies "on the grounds that it deal[s] with pseudo-scientific knowledge."[100] Islamic economists view Islamic political economy as a social but also a "beneficial" science concerned with relations between individuals and between communities. Therefore, they contend, it cannot, nor is it its purpose to, remain only scientific—that is, positivist, empiricist, value-free, and impartial. Islamic political economy is "religious-based, valuation-oriented, morality-judged, and spiritually-bound."[101] As in Christianity and Orthodox Judaism, it is both positive and normative, it integrates both spiritual and material worlds into a coherent whole, and it seeks to force its interpretations into the domain of politics and law. Islamic political economic thought springs from the Quran, **Sunna** (which consists of Prophet Mohammed's words and deeds), **Shari'a** (the "true path," Muslim law, and Islamic way of life), and **ijma** (leading Muslim theologians' consensus on issues not clarified in the Quran and the Sunna).[102]

Thus, contrary to the Western liberal view, which emphasizes the rationality of the market, in Islamic economic thought the market is not completely devoid of psychological and spiritual factors. In classical liberalism an individual's primary motivating factor is self-interest. Marxist economic determinism is an inherently and explicitly atheistic philosophy and views religion as the "opiate of the people," serving the ruling class. However, in Islam, by definition religion is an integral component of the principles of political economy. The Quranic human being, constantly "exhorted to do right instead of wrong, good instead of evil," acts based on Quranic principles, the "divine law of the universe," and the *Sunna.* These principles, or laws, are all-pervasive, embodying all aspects of life through the Islamic community's consensus, *ijma.* Unlike the market-rational individual in classical liberalism, therefore, individuals in the Quran are human beings "with all the foibles of human beings, and capable of error."[103] Islamic political economy replaces the classical economists' *homo economicus* with the Quran's *homo Islamicus,* who submits to divine authority.

Islamic political economy has an explicitly defined goal, "an ultimate end," as decreed in the Quran,[104] and emphasizes economic prosperity as a "good thing and among God's favors on mankind."[105] The fundamental obligations and practices to receive God's favors are based on the five *faraidh* (duties) or the "five pillars" of Islam: *shahadah,* the profession of faith; *salat,* daily prayer; payment of the **zakat** (charity-tax); *sawm,* fasting during the month of Ramadan; and the *haj,* the pilgrimage to Mecca.[106] For example, in economic policy, *zakat* is considered the basis of Islamic fiscal policy. Hence, economic aid by wealthier states, such as Saudi Arabia, to other states can be viewed as fulfilling the will of Allah. Realists and Marxists, however, would reject this religious and moralist view as mere justification for geopolitically and economically driven policies. A related Quranic principle, the prohibition of *riba* (interest), is also a central feature of Islamic monetary policy, although many banks in the Middle East and other Islamic societies do charge forms of interest. Islamic economists place great emphasis on this "trio—the norms, *zakat,* and zero interest," as the pillars of Islamic economics.[107]

Islam believes in the creation of an egalitarian community through the equitable distribution of resources, a community in which exploitation is not permissible and equality of opportunity and equality of results are emphasized. According to S.M. Hasan-uz-Zaman, "Islamic economics is the knowledge of application of inductions and rules of the Shariah [Shari'a] that stop injustices in the acquisition and disposition of material resources in order to provide satisfaction to individuals and enable them to perform their obligations to Allah and the society."[108] Workers work for their own benefit but also for the benefit of the community. The Quran also contains certain principles of ecological well-being. Since land, agriculture, and vegetation are sacred, created by Allah, they are to be enjoyed by humans and require proper cultivation to maximize human welfare. As such, certain principles of Quranic economic thought are similar to today's explicitly environmentalist perspectives. Ibn Khaldun (1332–1406), a historian and leading proponent of political Realism, considered political economy as the "desire for food and other requirements and efforts to obtain them; further, a science which deals with management of households and city (economy) in accordance with dictates of reason as well as ethics so that masses may be directed towards a behavior that leads to the preservation and performance of their species."[109]

The Islamic conception of welfare rests on the generation of income from production of commodities deemed beneficial to society,[110] hence the principle of *israf,* the avoidance of waste in production and consumption. While sometimes violated in practice, Islam explicitly opposes concentration of wealth in the hands of a small circle of political and economic elites, and insists on a more equitable distribution of wealth, rendering it "unlawful for a Muslim to possess wealth beyond essential needs of his family."[111] Similarly, production expenditures and investment in production facilities must be allocated not only for profits *perse,* but also for the benefit of the community. The market system is not simply an arena for competition but also a "divine opportunity" to generate capital for the promotion of social justice, which, according to Islam, can be obtained only if certain restrictions are applied on *israf* and conspicuous consumption. Conspicuous consumption leads to socioeconomic and class differences and incurs losses on the majority of the population.

The same principles apply at the international level. As with laissez-faire classical liberalism, the Islamic theory of international economic relations stresses freedom of commerce, based on assumptions of straightforwardness, reliability, and honesty, and envisions a harmonious universe without divisions between rich and poor as the ultimate goal of international relations. According to the Quran, nations rise and decline based on their deeds and loyalty to Allah. Disobedience to Allah results in annihilation.[112] Islamic prescriptions for international cooperation and economic development call for well-integrated programs based on equity- and efficiency-oriented considerations to improve employment and general standards of living. The central idea of the *umma,* the Muslim community of believers, has been institutionalized by a number of transnational organizations, such as the Organization of Islamic Conferences created in 1973. Under its aegis, the Islamabad Declaration, for example, advocated the adoption of various programs in the 1980s and 1990s, including joint venture projects for economic development to benefit the *umma,* rather than each country's national interests. As Choudhury has noted, in this "crusade of principles" the Islamic institutions of the South attempt to play an important role in North-South and South-South relations,[113] and individual national boundaries have come to mean less than the *umma.*

After the 1973 Arab oil embargo, the oil-producing countries accumulated enormous wealth and subsequently increased their foreign aid contributions to Islamic and other, less developed countries (see Chapter 11). For example, the government of the United Arab Emirates was one of the most generous foreign aid donors. In the mid-1970s, about 20 percent of Abu Dhabi oil revenues were disbursed in aid to neighboring Arab states.[114] Stressing his government's humanitarian objectives, reflecting Quranic principles, Shaikh Zayad ibn Sultan Al Nahayan stated that "this wealth is not for us alone; it must be shared. . . ." The then Minister of Petroleum and Mineral Resources, Mana Al Otaiba, agreed that "no country, no matter how secluded, can hope to exist prosperously for long when its neighbors are poor."[115] In addition to bilateral arrangements, the transfer of *zakat* funds increasingly requires international coordination through new or existing institutions, including, for example, the Islamic Development Bank, the Organization of Islamic Conferences, and the Muslim World League.[116] Skeptics have noted, however, that such aid bought for the small wealthy states the toleration of poorer but larger neighbors; large wealth discrepancies continue to exist within the *umma.*

Islam and the State Two interpretations of the Quranic principles regarding the role and nature of political leadership and political community appear in the literature: the "benevolent state" and the authoritarian ruler. According to the first view of Quranic political economy, the state has a relatively limited role in society in issues related to law and order, and its main function is to "prevent violations of the norms." In the ideal-typical Quranic world, government officials, as leaders of their immediate communities and the *umma*—the worldwide community of Muslim believers—are expected to internalize the Islamic values, to abstain from self-promoting practices, and to refrain from abusing power at the expense of the community. Their actions are expected to benefit the Islamic society and the *umma.* The Quran thus encourages the state to exploit and administer all natural resources for the benefit of the community according to ethical standards of welfare in consumption and production.[117] The leader strengthens the political legitimacy of the state institutions through promotion and protection of Islamic values and through patronage for the arts, education, sciences, employment, and so forth. The state is thus viewed as a benevolent state and the leader as a charismatic, benevolent ruler,[118] whose instruments of power and patronage maintain order and sustain social institutions.[119]

The second, authoritarian, view holds that the Islamic state is founded on the belief that ultimate sovereignty and the source of legitimacy rest with Allah, who alone "delegate[s] certain powers to people for legislation and absolute control over administration."[120] Accordingly, Islamic state authority is not derived from secular democratic and pluralistic principles but, rather, from long traditions of dynastic and military rule and imperial geopolitical conflicts. As a result, the modern Islamic states, despite their constitutions and elections, rest on highly authoritarian structures. The authoritarian nature of the structures of political power and economy is similar to that of the statist and mercantilist East Asian systems, but with a greater emphasis on the centrality of the personal ruler. The authoritarian state enables the leader to develop personal rule, governing through a mercantilist state with its own political and economic interests in domestic and foreign affairs—in some cases, as in Saudi Arabia and Jordan, as traditional absolute monarchs. It is within this type of system that Al-Hariri defined Islamic political economy in the eleventh century as "the making of living through political power, trade, agriculture and industry."[121]

Today, all Muslim countries have elements of Islamic values, classical liberalism, socialism, and mercantilism, combined with pragmatism, modernism, traditionalism, and fundamentalism.[122] As Choudhury has noted, no Muslim country "can claim itself Islamic in the true spirit of the word . . . governed under the legal and politico-economic system of Islam."[123] Some countries are comprised of a strong majority of Muslim population, although of various sects—for example *Sunni* and *Shi'ite*—and are governed by leaders based on different adaptations of Islamic principles. Almost all Muslim countries, however, have legal, political, and economic systems founded on a combination of Islamic traditions, Western laissez-faire liberalism, and socialist philosophies (as was shown in Table 2.1).[124] For example, after Malaysia gained independence from British colonial rule in 1957, its founders, including the first prime minister, Tunku Abdul Rahman, integrated into the new constitution both Islamic principles and the legal codes developed under British colonialism.[125] Since Malaysia's independence, government economic policies have stressed industrialization and modernization along the lines of statist-capitalism and in close cooperation with Western and Japanese MNCs. At the same time, the government has also allowed the establishment of an Islamic Bank, an Islamic insurance company, and the Pilgrims' Savings Fund, which operate on both Islamic and secular principles.

As Nagata has observed, however, development and modernization objectives at times collide with Islamic values and the priorities of religious groups. Malaysian development and modernization projects (most notably, Prime Minister Mahathir Mohamad's famous and ubiquitous slogan, "Vision 2020"), supported by private banks and state bureaucracies, often must convince Muslim religious groups and the political opposition that the replacement of "religiously-endowed *wakaf* land, donated by Muslim benefactors for mosques and Muslim welfare," by industrial projects can equally benefit both religious and secular interests as the country works toward full modernization by the year 2020.[126] Despite such tensions, and despite the fact that Malaysia is an Islamic country, it is host to 350 high-technology plants producing semiconductors and electronics products.[127] Petroliam Nasional Bhd. (Petronas) is the twenty-fourth largest oil company and the eleventh largest gas company in the world, with an annual net profit in the early 1990s of $3.4 billion, and with investments throughout Asia and the Middle East.[128]

Islam and Realism Along with its idealism, political Realism—that is, power politics—also has become an important component of Islamic political economic thought, although the Quran does not explicitly formulate a specific theory of international relations.[129] Islamic political theory views the world as divided between *dar al-Islam,* Islamic and non-Islamic regions under Islamic sovereignty, and *dar al-harb* (the "land of war"), territories beyond the Islamic domain. *Dar al-Islam* is at the heart of the Muslim community, the *umma,* inclusive of other communities of believers (Christians, Jews, and other Peoples of the Book) but under Islamic hegemony, where all are expected to obey the laws of Muslim authority.[130] *Dar al-harb,* on the other hand, is viewed as subject to Muslim conquest and integration into *Pax Islamica,* the envisioned aim of Islamic globalization. As Khadurri has noted, however, some Muslim legal scholars—for example, the *Shafi'i* school—also consider a third alternative, "*dar al-sulh* (territory of peaceful arrangement) or *dar al-ahd* (territory of covenant), giving qualified recognition to non-Islamic communities if they entered into treaty relations with Islam, on conditions agreed upon between the two parties (provided Islam was paid an annual tribute)."[131]

Islamic Realpolitik considers the protection of Muslim territories, especially such holy places as Mecca, Medina, and Jerusalem, as a religious duty. In the Middle Eastern countries, independence from Turkish and Western colonial rule during the first four decades of this century forged new religious and nationalist sentiments against external enemies. Both antiforeign and inter-Arab conflicts and wars were justified on religious grounds. Westerners are familiar with the concept of *jihad*—"holy war," or, more accurately, "crusade," as in Christian terminology. During such wars, seldom as they may be declared, Muslim soldiers killed on the battlefield are believed to secure entrance into heaven. They are required to make such sacrifices especially when fighting to protect Muslim lands against non-Muslims (such as the medieval Christian crusaders who invaded the Middle East from Europe). Concerning the Palestinian question, for example, Shaikh Abd al-Aziz Ben Baz, the leading Saudi religious scholar, has reportedly written that "the Palestinian problem is an Islamic problem first and last," and Muslims "must fight an Islamic *jihad* against the Jews until the land returns to its owners."[132]

During the 1990–1991 Persian Gulf War, as the conflict escalated into a full- fledged war, Saddam Hussein stated that, like the Israeli occupation of Palestine, so have the holy cities of Mecca and Medina fallen hostages of the Americans, and, despite his socialist secular political leanings, he called for a *jihad* to liberate them. As Piscatori has pointed out, "The response in the Muslim world to this call for *jihad* was not hesitant. . . . Even among Muslims as far away from the Arab world as China, some believed that the dispatch of Western troops to Saudi Arabia had violated the integrity of Muslim territory."[133] However, senior religious officials in Saudi Arabia issued a *fatwa* (ruling) endorsing the king's defense decision based on the *Shari'a.* The king as a Muslim ruler, they asserted, is required to be prepared to defend Muslim land even if he has to seek military assistance from non-Muslim states with the power and capability to undertake the mission. A similar *fatwa* in January 1991 approved the use of military force against Iraq and declared that war a *jihad.*[134] The Gulf War, like the Iran-Iraq war of the 1980s, suggested that Islam and Realism are not confined to struggles of power solely against non-Muslims. In the Iran-Iraq War, the Iranian theocrats, engaged in a territorial struggle with neighboring Iraq, also claimed to be fighting the Iraqi leadership, whose policies they considered to be too closely aligned with Islam's archenemies, such as the United States and USSR.

Religious purity sometimes gives way to perceived national interest, just as in the Western or the socialist world. Whether Islam will be a religious, political, and economic force for greater international cooperation, or for greater polarization across cultural lines remains to be seen. It will depend in part on the extent to which Western and Islamic states and groups respond to each other's initiatives and seek mutual accommodation. There certainly are ample opportunities for cooperation in the international political economy, if only to overcome a "clash of civilizations"[135] and to prevent potential local and worldwide military conflicts and bloodshed. The current theocratic leadership in Tehran views itself as the true spiritual center of the Muslim world, especially in competition with the Saudi monarchy. As such, since the rise of Ayatollah Rouhollah Khomeini and the Islamic Revolution against the Shah in the late 1970s, Tehran has denounced Western secularism and imperialism.[136] Washington, in turn, views itself as the leader of the "free world," and, as such, since the Islamic Revolution and the hostage crisis, despite occasional cooperation with Tehran, has taken an anti-Iranian military stance and has denounced regressive and repressive policies, such as the imposition of wearing of the veil for women. Such policies have been misperceived by the West, however, as Islam's condoning of repression and violence against women. In fact, a Quranic verse states,

> O you who believe! You are forbidden to inherit women against their will. Nor should you treat them with harshness, that you may take away part of their dower you have given them, except where they have been guilty of open lewdness; On the contrary, live with them on a footing of kindness and equity.[137]

Be that as it may, the 1997 election of President Mohammad Khatami, who represented the more moderate wing of the clergy in Iran, may lead to normalization of relations with the West, especially if even more radical religious regimes emerge in places like nearby Afghanistan.

Western and Muslim, but especially feminist, critics see such policies as restricting women's public economic and social roles as reinforcing inter-cultural boundaries and heightening tensions between the two cultures. Specifically, feminists contend that the wearing of the veil reinforces male-dominated social structures, and that "the Quranic, Islamic law, and the moral attitudes carried by the 'ulama' have favored a moral and social climate leading to subordination" of women.[138] Feminist criticism of male-dominated institutions and customs is not limited to Islamic societies, however.

Feminism and International Political Economy

The feminist perspective has come mainly in reaction to the traditional, male-dominated conception of political economy. Feminist scholars of various philosophical leanings argue that, while women make enormous contributions to the global economy, the theoretical and statistical literature on this subject, as well as economic reward systems, have failed to reflect that reality. Women constitute a strong majority of employment in the service sectors and perform "servicing" work—for example, caretaking and homemaking—often without financial compensation.[139] "Servicing" labor does not appear in official statistical tables; consequently, it is neither regarded as an important contribution to domestic and global economies nor integrated in scholarly theories on political economy. Given the fact that "androcentric" theorizing has historically neglected the central roles performed by women in the economies of their respective countries, such theoretical constructs as classical liberalism, and Marxism fail to present an accurate view of the workings of the domestic and international community. Feminist scholars contend that the mercantilist, classical liberal, Marxism, and Islamic theories of political economy are predicated on androcentric conceptualizations of society, value, production, consumption, and employment, and they remain limited to male experiences within male-dominated domestic and international economic activities. The mercantilists focused on the state, liberals on the market, Marxists on class relations, and Islam on the Quran, and each in its own way neglected gender-related division of labor, especially as it relates to the valuation of production and reproduction. The dominance of these androcentric theories have led to or have encouraged government policies that fail to meet the daily needs, rights, and demands of women and children. Thus, the central objective of feminist writings has been to bring women and their concerns into the theoretical and analytical realm of political economy.

During the closing decades of the eighteenth century, when the leaders of the American Revolution were writing the Declaration of Independence and the leaders of the French Revolution the Declaration of the Rights of Man, Judith Sargent Murray published her "On the Equality of Sexes," and Mary Wollstonecraft her *A Vindication of the Rights of Woman,* the first significant exposition of feminist theory, while in France Olympe de Gouges wrote her *Les Droits de la Femmes (The Rights of Woman).*[140] Peterson and Runyan have identified three major feminist theories: liberal feminism, radical feminism, and socialist feminism.[141] In the 1970s and 1980s, "ecofeminist" theory, a derivative of the last two, also contributed significantly to international political economy, with a focus on the environment in relation to women.

Liberal feminism has its philosophical roots in the first phase of the feminist movement as expressed in the writings of Wollstonecraft, her contemporaries, and their descendants. Like their male counterparts, they are heavily influenced by the philosophical revolutions of the Age of Enlightenment, including the Newtonian paradigm. The Newtonian paradigm, which dominated classical liberal theories of "natural" rights and political economy, viewed the physical—and, by extension, the social and economic universe—as operating mechanically and rationally according to specific rational and natural laws. Adam Smith's liberal theory of the market and its tendency toward equilibrium was a major work reflecting these views.[142] Accordingly, liberal feminists stress the necessity of social equilibrium and "sameness" and advocate equal rights for women. They maintain that women should be treated as the equals of men because women are "essentially the same as men in regard to capacities for aggression, ambition, strength, and rationality."[143]

AFSC

Equality between men and women, therefore, they argue, should mean the elimination of masculine-feminine, superior-inferior dichotomies in our conceptualization of society and economic roles, as well as in political and economic behavior and values.

Operating from these premises, some liberal feminists also emphasize the importance of the state, at both the domestic and international levels. According to Mona Harrington, for example, the state under the social contract performs the central function of mediating among competing groups within society. The political arena, rather than class, still remains the most viable vehicle for the pursuit of equality between the sexes. Harrington argues that the "liberal state is a suitable, even elegant, agent to advance a feminist agenda, in both domestic and international relations."[144] The liberal state, she asserts, need not be abandoned, as feminists generally advocate but, rather, it can be reformulated based on liberal principles of justice to promote and protect "both public and private spheres," whereby the public sector assumes greater responsibilities for various programs, such as day care and parental leave.[145]

Liberal feminists emphasize reforms in structures of international political economy, whereby men and women bridge their cultural gaps across gender and international borders. Contrary to the traditional liberal assumption of harmonious international relations, however, liberal feminists believe that structural reforms to promote gender equality would lead to a highly pluralistic international environment in which "no visible hand would assume smooth, mutually beneficial transaction flowing around the globe."[146]

Radical feminism gained momentum in the 1960s and early 1970s, largely in reaction to the condescending attitudes toward the "contemptuous treatment" of women by male activists in the "New Left" during the civil rights and anti–Vietnam War movements.[147] Rather than advocating equality of the sexes along liberal lines, radical feminists, regard "masculinity, with its emphasis on aggression and violence directed by men against women and men, as the problem, not the solution for liberating women and other subordinated groups."[148] Radical feminists stress the politics of sexuality, in which women are viewed as oppressed by male-dominated structural and institutional arrangements, such as property laws and division of labor, that perpetuate androcentricity in philosophy and in practice.[149]

Radical feminist theory holds that, since issues related to political economy, such as division of labor, equality, peace, and security, have been traditionally defined by men in male-dominated institutions, one consequence has been the perpetuation of male supremacy and the subjugation of women. Radical feminists stress that neither liberal nor Marxist theories take into consideration male domination as a source of women's oppression. According to Roxanne Dunbar, for example, the current international system is an "international caste system, at the top of which is the Western white male ruling class, at the very bottom of which is the female of the non-white colonized world."[150] Contrary to the Marxist-Leninist conception of imperialism as rooted in class domination, Dunbar maintains that Western imperialism is based on male domination as well. In their struggles for independence from Western colonial rule in developing countries, male revolutionaries were not particularly concerned with women's rights and viewed their revolutionary movements primarily through male lenses.

Regarding the Algerian independence movement against French colonialism for example, some feminists have noted that revolutionary writer Franz Fanon's reference to Arab women's veils as symbolizing ethnic Arab culture confused "male culture with ethnic culture; the veil in fact symbolizes female oppression."[151] Similarly, in her *Sexual Politics,* Kate Millett asserted that the state rules through force as well as through ideology, socializing women to serve male-dominated institutions and to accept women's subservient position.[152] "Torture," wrote Millett in her *The Politics of Cruelty,* "is based upon traditional ideas of domination: patriarchical order and masculine rank."[153] Radical feminists insist that it is the overthrow of this oppression of women that should be the basis of a revolution against male-domination and the basis for a new society.

Radical feminists also argue that the liberal "masculine" conception of interdependence should be redefined and revalued within the context of the relationships not only among countries, as commonly done by scholars, but also, and more important, between men and women, between people and nature. Taking *that* interdependence seriously, they argue, is "essential for human and planetary survival."[154]

Socialist Feminism To a great extent **socialist feminism** agrees with the general premises of both liberal and radical feminism. However, socialist feminists place greater emphasis on the economic than on the cultural dimensions of male-dominated society. Socialist feminists are primarily concerned with the relationship among production, reproduction, and the oppression of women. They emphasize a number of key essential facts, including domestic labor, the subjugation of women in the workplace as wage earners, women and class, the role of women in the family, and ideological socialization. During the formation of the androcratic state, the very process of the institutionalization and centralization of political authority, as under mercantilism, necessitated the accumulation and concentration of resources. That process, however, occurred through the labor of women, prisoners of wars, and slaves. The state increasingly defined citizenship and requirements for military conscription, and it formulated the legal bases for labor and its mobility through emigration and immigration laws. Through laws of contract, the state regulated extraction of resources, as well as definitions of property. In the process, socialist feminists argue, women became more and more marginalized and subjected to the male-dominated order.[155]

Socialist feminists agree that the rise of industrialization created capitalism in societies with divisions between commodity production and housework, transforming workers into commodities. In doing so, it separated "life" from "work" and led to the *proletarianization* of human existence and the division of values along sex lines. With the advent of industrialization and industrial capital, productive labor as real work became the central component of the male-dominated economy as "the industrialization process removed labor and resources from the household, and the site of 'production' shifted to the factory."[156] In the process, reproductive labor and housework were marginalized and relegated to the *secondary economy* of the "second sex." Society was thus divided between the personal sphere (the home) and economic production sphere (the workplace), based on sexual division of labor, whereby women were identified with the former.[157]

Contrary to the liberal theory of value derived from labor and production, socialist feminists argue that the distinction between productive and reproductive labor and the higher value given to the former has been a product of capitalism. States' calculations of the gross domestic product exclude women's reproductive labor, as well as the informal, home-based economy. Little attention has been paid to the miserable working conditions of women, whose labor nevertheless contributes immensely to the general well-being of societies. Calculating their domestic contributions to the national economy as part of the gross domestic product, feminists argue, would "expose the costs to society extracted by capitalist reliance upon women's cheap or free labor to make a profit."[158] In her "Political Economy of Women's Liberation," Margaret Benston has argued that analyses of national economic patterns and behavior must include domestic labor—that is, housework—and that such factors must not be "relegated to a marginal or non-existent status."[159] Under capitalism, Benston wrote, one's value is determined by money. Women who are not paid for their domestic work are viewed as performing valueless daily housework chores; therefore, their contributions to society are not deemed as important as men's, whose work is almost always compensated with money.[160]

Socialist feminists argue that, since employers are not required to pay for the reproductive work women perform at home, corporations are able to keep wages artificially low and to accumulate wealth. They emphasize that major structural changes are necessary to improve the very nature of corporate organizational and instrumentalist culture. Wages will have to be improved, and governments must compensate for reproductive labor. Thus, welfare programs

> would no longer be a system of meager handouts but a societal priority to increase all people's productivity in equitable, healthful, mutually respectful, and life-affirming ways. . . . This can be accomplished best by a societal and global redistribution of power, as opposed to placing their hopes in the empowering capacity of feminine traits. As a result, socialist feminists are most active in socialist revolutions and women's economic movements, organizing around such issues as women on welfare, women in development, and women in the "global factory."[161]

Ecofeminism Closely related to the radical and socialist feminist theories is Francois **ecofeminism,** a term coined by Francois d'Eaubonne in 1974. Ecofeminists hold that male domination of women and of nature constitutes a critical component of male social power. While environmentalists blame humans in general for the current ecological crises around the globe, ecofeminists blame men exclusively and their androcentric worldview. As a result, ecofeminists advocate the promotion of women to top decision-making positions in corporations or, more radically, the dissolution of all forms of male-dominated institutions.[162] Ecofeminist theory is especially pertinent to the ecological crisis caused by industrialization and deforestation in developing countries; it holds that the women-nature connection is more emphatically threatened in countries in which the preservation of the natural world is necessary for their livelihood and, in some regions, for local religious, traditional observances. For example, the Indian ecofeminist Vandana Shiva notes that, in the Indian Chipko (or "Embrace the Tree") movement, Indian women attempted to protect nature against destructive development plans, by using Gandhian tactics of nonviolent resistance—hugging the trees in endangered forests.[163] Shiva writes,

> Since the ecological crises threaten survival irrespective of the industrial status of societies, the philosophical significance of redirecting development onto an ecologically sustainable path relates to the industrialized north as much as to countries of the south. . . [T]he ecological strategy of Chipko finds new application in the people's movement in European countries such as Switzerland, Germany and Holland. . . The ecological world-view of Chipko, which is a civilisational response of India, provides a strategy for survival not only for tiny villages in the Garhwal Himalaya, but for all human societies threatened by environmental disasters.[164]

Overall, then, feminists contend that the male-dominated conceptualization of the state cannot adequately, if at all, address the problems of economic and political injustices toward women, global maladjustments and maldevelopments, and environmental degradation. Indeed, feminists argue, men's emphasis on the state and national security has led to "women's systemic insecurity" in the global androcentric and androcratic political economy.[165]

CONCLUSION

For more than three centuries, the nation-state has been viewed as the most important player in international political economy. Each state has claimed total sovereignty (even if this concept was always something of a myth) and control of its national economy, seeking maximum security and self-sufficiency. During the sixteenth and seventeenth centuries, mercantilism was the dominant theory of political economy and, of the theories presented in this chapter, is the most state-centric. However, even under classical liberalism, which challenged the mercantilist state's role in political economy, the nation-state continued to be assumed as the exclusively dominant player in international relations. Marxism envisioned a world in which, after a general, world proletarian revolution against the bourgeois classes, the proletariat would gain control over the means of production, and the state would wither away. International political economy, therefore, would become classless and thus stateless. Lenin's theory of imperialism and Mao's brand of communism reverted to the assumption that the nation-state is central to the functioning of international political economy. Despite the differences between these two major paradigms, they viewed international economic relations as either fundamentally and exclusively harmonious (classical liberalism) or contentious (mercantilism, Marxism-Leninism).

The globalization theory presented in this chapter has argued that the technological changes in communications and transportation have radically transformed the nature of international political economy from being strictly international to a virtually globalized system of networks. Under such a system, international political economy is comprised not only of nation-states but also of MNCs and transnational actors as the dominant players and international political economy as a combination of competition and cooperation among nation-states and MNCs in international and domestic arenas. Thus, globalization theory does not see the nation-state as disappearing, but the nation-state can no longer claim the international arena as its exclusive domain. Islamic international political economy also emphasizes competition and cooperation among states but with reference to leaders of the global Islamic umma. The nation-state is the building block for the formation of the Islamic imperial state, although in this case the imperial state is viewed as the deputy of God. Feminism has challenged all of these paradigms as perpetuating male dominance over women. Some feminists have demanded gender equality, while others have advocated the total dissolution of male-dominated institutions to build anew. As in Islam and Marxism, feminism, too, seeks unity across national borders, as well as the imposition of more humane values.

A central issue examined in the following chapters is the extent to which each of these theories explains the likely changes taking place in the late twentieth century and which theory, if any, can best serve as a guide for policies in the early decades of the twenty-first century. Most of the theories presented were the products of, or were in reaction to, the age of laissez-faire capitalism and the industrial revolution. The telecommunications revolution experienced since the 1980s may render classical economic theories irrelevant to current issues in international political economy and ultimately may be replaced by the more globally oriented theories reviewed in this chapter, or by other approaches yet to be articulated.

Chapter Summary

Paradigms, or "grand theories," of international political economy are intellectual tools used to explain the nature of domestic and foreign economic relations, as well as to provide guidelines to policymakers. Theories include the mercantilist theory of the sixteenth and seventeenth centuries, classical liberalism of the eighteenth and nineteenth centuries, and socialism and Marxism of the nineteenth and twentieth centuries.

Mercantilism and merchant capitalism date back to the sixteenth and seventeenth centuries, as Europe was experiencing rapid economic and political transformations. Not accidentally, this period also witnessed the emergence of the nation-state. The absolutist state controlled resources within its territory as a means to greater power and wealth.

Proponents of classical liberalism advocated limited government and free enterprise,and claimed this would lead to peace and harmony. Despite significant variations in liberal theories of political economy, a number of fundamental propositions have remained, with a strong commitment to free market operations both at home and in international economic relations.

According to the principle of comparative advantage, each nation produces what it can, relatively more efficiently and less expensively than another nation. Theoretically, an advantage of the principle of comparative advantage is that free trade leads to international specialization, encouraging maximum allocation efficiency of goods produced around the world. With the advent of globalization of international economic relations in recent years, views on comparative advantage need to consider new properties, including globalization of multinational production, relocation of production abroad for cheaper labor, public-private trade and financial strategic alliances, transnational intra-industry trade, and the rise of information telecommunications technologies.

The spread of industrialization in the nineteenth century created miserable working and living conditions for most people involved in factory life. These conditions led Karl Marx to criticize the situation and develop his own theory of political economy. Central to his theory was the notion of class struggle between the proletariat (workers) and the bourgeoisie (owners of the means of production). Unlike the capitalist notion of market equilibrium, Marx held that the widening gap between production and consumption in the market causes economic fluctuations and depressions. As the severity of such economic crises intensifies, the suffering proletariat take arms and rebel against the capitalist system. According to Marx, structural factors in capitalism create an environment more conducive to class struggle than to economic and political harmony and cooperation.

Lenin adapted Marx's theory of domestic political economy to develop his theory of international political economy. Colonization and empire-building, he argued, had transformed the global economy, dominated by large and powerful industrial and financial monopolies and trusts. The emergence of monopolistic operations and the worldwide competition for raw materials inevitably lead to international military conflicts and struggles for spheres of economic and geopolitical influence—that is, imperialism.

Pointing to recent developments in telecommunications and transportation technologies and the globalization of economic activities, globalist theory holds that international political economy consists of extra-national and even supra-national properties whereby economic activities, such as the production and coordination of market arrangements, are viewed as occurring in a global society beyond the traditional, territorially based state.

Islam provides a comprehensive philosophy of political economy that has survived and shaped millions of people's lives for centuries. Islamic thought on international political economy envisions a harmonious universe without divisions between rich and poor. The Quran stresses freedom of commerce, straightforwardness, reliability, and honesty. According to the Quran, nations rise and decline based on their deeds and loyalty to Allah (God). As with other paradigms, there is a discrepancy between theory and practice.

The feminist perspective on international political economy has been mainly a reaction to the traditional, male-dominated conception of political economy. Feminist scholars maintain that, while women have contributed immensely to the development and workings of the global economy, the scholarship on this subject fails to take into account their contributions. Major feminist theories include liberal feminism, radical feminism, and socialist feminism, as well as ecofeminism.

Due to the changing circumstances in international political economy and the ever increasingly competitive global market, during the past decade or so there has been a growing interest in mercantilist thought. Neo-mercantilists give top priority to their own national gains at the expense of mutual gains. In the process, the state continues to enhance its political power and position in international political economy.

Points of Contention

What role, if any, should value and moral considerations have in IPE analyses?

How was mercantilism related to the rise of the nation-state?

Why did early mercantilist thought emphasize monetary balance?

How are Alexander Hamilton's and Adam Smith's views expressed in today's political debate?

How was classical liberalism related to industrial capitalism?

Can you find any examples in which labor determines the value of goods purchased?

Under what circumstances should government intervene in economic affairs?

What are some of the advantages and disadvantages of the principle of comparative advantage?

To what extent are the criticisms by the dependencia school valid?

Why do Marxists reject the notion of "market equilibrium"?

What were Marx's views on national identity? How would he analyze the ethnic conflicts in the former Soviet republics and Yugoslavia?

According to Lenin, what factors contribute to imperialism? Is his theory of imperialism valid today?

What were some of the consequences of colonialism in the developing world?

How is the theory of "capitalist world economy" related to Marxism?

Distinguish between the classical view of *homo economicus* and *homo Islamicus.* What role, if any, should religious values have in the workings of international political economy?

Is international stability under a single hegemon desirable? If yes, under what conditions?

How is the functionalist concept of ramifications (or spill-over) related to the globalist theories?

Does the globalization of international relations as experienced during the past two decades promote international peace as envisioned by the liberal or functionalist school?

What aspects of the feminist theories support the traditional, androcentric theories of international political economy? What aspects are most critical of them? What would be the ramifications of fully valuing women's work?

How would you support the argument that each of the modern models of capitalism is both conducive to international cooperation and prone to conflict?

Notes

1. Robert Gilpin, *The Political Economy of International Relations* (Princeton: Princeton University Press, 1987), p. 32. See also John M. Rothgeb, Jr., *Defining Power: Influence and Force in the Contemporary International System* (New York: St. Martin's Press, 1993); Dennis Pirages, *Global Technopolitics* (Pacific Grove, CA: Brooks/Cole, 1989); George Modelski, ed., *Transnational Corporations and World Order* (San Francisco: W.H. Freeman, 1979).
2. We would like to thank the anonymous reviewers for pointing out the need to stress these points.
3. Isaac Ilych Rubin, *A History of Economic Thought,* trans. and ed. by Donald Filtzer (London: Ink Links, 1979), p. 19.
4. *Ibid.*
5. Lewis H. Haney, *History of Economic Thought* (New York: Macmillan, 1911), p. 88.
6. During this first phase, mercantilism also became "the age of absolute monarchy" and the age of fiscal mercantilism as emphasis was placed on the *monetary balance system* (Rubin, *A History of Economic Thought,* pp. 25–26). A major premise of the mercantilist school of thought at this time was that economic activities should be directed toward nation- but particularly state-building efforts, should cater to the financial and political needs of the state, and should ultimately serve the state's demands for maximum military capabilities for purposes of national security. As Gilpin, Knorr, and others have argued, mercantilists regarded accumulation of national wealth in the hands of the state as "an absolutely essential means to power," which in turn would enable the state to acquire greater wealth. Wealth and power were the principal objectives of domestic and foreign policy. Economic strength, therefore, would be translated into political and military strength for the state as an independent entity capable of surviving both at home and in the international arena (Gilpin, *Political Economy,* pp. 31–32). Gilpin discusses "malevolent" mercantilism in reference to the extreme form of mercantilism as experienced, for example, in Nazi Germany during the 1930s under Economic Minister Hjalmar Schacht's economic policies toward Eastern Europe. Nationalists emphasize the geographic location and the distribution of economic activities in the global political and economic scheme of things (Ibid., p. 34). As a result, Haney reminds us, the management of warfare, for instance, had drastically changed. While before the conduct and management of warfare "had been a hasty expedition, a pitched battle, and the issue was settled by courage," by the end of the sixteenth century "the whole art of war seemed, in a manner, reduced to money, and that prince who could best find money to feed, clothe, and pay his army, not he who had the most valiant troops, was surest of success and conquest" (Haney, *History of Economic Thought,* p. 90).
7. John Maynard Keynes, *The General Theory of Employment, Interest, and Money* (San Diego: Harcourt Brace Jovanovich, 1953), pp. 333–371.

8. Rubin, *A History of Economic Thought,* pp. 25–29; Mark Blaug, *Economic Theory in Retrospect,* 4th ed. (Cambridge: Cambridge University Press, 1992), pp. 10–11.
9. Haney, *History of Economic Thought,* p. 96.
10. Joseph A. Schumpeter, *History of Economic Analysis* (London: George Allen and Unwin, 1954), p. 356.
11. Thomas Mun, *England's Treasure by Forraign Trade,* quoted in Haney, *History of Economic Thought,* p. 93.
12. J. Ann Tickner, "On the Fringes of the World Economy: A Feminist Perspective," in Craig N. Murphy and Roger Tooze. eds., *The New International Political Economy* (Boulder, CO: Lynne Rienner, 1991), p. 197.
13. Peter J. Taylor, *Political Geography: World-Economy, Nation-State and Locality,* 3d ed. (London: Longman, 1993), pp. 158–159.
14. Gilpin, *Political Economy,* p. 32.
15. Regarding the constitutionality of establishing a central bank, President Washington had transmitted to Hamilton, the Secretary of the Treasury, Thomas Jefferson's (Secretary of State) and Edmund Randolph's (Attorney General) objections to the creation of such a bank. In his reply, Hamilton stated,

    > Accordingly, such only are the regulations to be found in the laws of the United States, whose objects are to give encouragement to the enterprises of our own merchants, and to advance our navigation and manufactures. And it is in reference to these general relations of commerce that an establishment which furnishes facilities to circulation, and a convenient medium of exchange . . . is to be regarded as a regulation of trade. . . . The relation of a bank to the execution of the powers that concern the common defence has been anticipated. . . . Such an institution is essential to the measures to be pursued for the protection of our frontiers. [Alexander Hamilton, *Papers on Public Credit, Commerce, and Finance* (New York: Liberal Arts Press, 1957), p. 128.]

16. *Ibid.,* p. 183; see also pp. 204–5; 224–28; 234–49 on his eleven points on government policy.
17. *Ibid.,* p. 227. Hamilton continues: "Every nation . . . ought to endeavor to possess within itself, all the essentials of national supply. These comprise the means of subsistence, habitation, clothing, and defence. The possession of these is necessary to the perfection of the body politic; to the safety as well as to the welfare of the society."
18. Gilpin, *Political Economy,* p. 27.
19. Roy C. Macridis, *Contemporary Political Ideologies,* 3d ed. (Boston: Little, Brown, 1986), p. 25; Maurice Dobb, *Theory of Value and Distribution Since Adam Smith* (Cambridge: Cambridge University Press, 1973).
20. Eric Roll, *A History of Economic Thought,* 5th ed. (London: Faber and Faber, 1992), p. 146.
21. Roll, *History of Economic Thought,* p. 147; Adam Smith, *An Inquiry into the Nature of Causes of the Wealth of Nations,* ed. Edwin Cannan (Chicago: University of Chicago Press, 1976), Bk IV, vol. ix, pp. 208–9. See also Blaug, *Economic Theory in Retrospect.*
22. Roll, *History of Economic Thought,* p. 154; William O. Thweatt, ed., *Classical Political Economy: A Survey of Recent Literature* (Boston: Kluwer Academic Publishers, 1988).
23. Smith, *Wealth of Nations,* p. 1.
24. Macridis, *Contemporary Political Ideologies,* p. 26; Dobb, *Theory of Value and Distribution.*
25. Gilpin, *Political Economy,* p. 28; Blaug, *Economic Theory in Retrospect.*
26. Macridis, *Contemporary Political Ideologies,* pp. 26–28.
27. Roll, *A History of Economic Thought,* pp. 188–89; Gavin C. Reid, *Classical Economic Growth: An Analysis in the Tradition of Adam Smith* (New York: Basil Blackwell, 1989), pp. 16, 19–21. While Adam Smith found the notion of equilibrium useful, contrary to the conventionally held views of Smith's as well as others' views of equilibrium, Smith had serious reservations regarding the use of equilibrium models based on Newtonian automaticity in political economy. Gilpin, *Political Economy,* pp. 28–30. See also Terence W. Hutchison, *On Revolutions and Progress in Economic Knowledge* (Cambridge: Cambridge University Press, 1978); Charles E. Staley, *A History of Economic Thought: From Aristotle to Arrow* (Cambridge: Blackwell, 1989); Richard D. Wolff and Stephen A. Resnick, *Economics: Marxian Versus Neoclassical* (Baltimore: Johns Hopkins University Press, 1987).
28. James A. Caporaso and David P. Levine, *Theories of Political Economy* (Cambridge: Cambridge University Press, 1992), pp. 42–43.
29. Milton H. Spencer, *Contemporary Economics,* 2d ed. (New York: Worth, 1974).
30. *Ibid.,* p. 566.
31. *Ibid.*
32. Gilpin, *Political Economy,* p. 31; Roll, *History of Economic Thought,* p. 149.
33. Keynes' *General Theory* extended classical liberalism to twentieth-century political economy without undermining the foundations of classical liberalism. He argued that government had to regulate the excesses of capitalism and had a responsibility, through controls on the money supply and through government spending, to keep the economy stable and vibrant. John Maynard Keynes, *The General Theory of Employment, Interest, and Money* (San Diego: Harcourt Brace Jovanovich, 1953). See also W.W. Rostow, *Theories of Economic Growth from David Hume to the Present* (New York: Oxford University Press, 1990); Joseph Schumpeter, *History of Economic Analysis* (London: George Allen and Unwin, 1954); Lionel Robbins, *Theory of Economic Policy* (London: Macmillan, 1952).

34. Gilpin, *Political Economy,* p. 30.
35. See, for example, Blaug, *Economic Theory in Retrospect,* pp. 668–678.
36. Burns Weston and Richard Claude, eds., *Human Rights in the World Community* (Philadelphia: University of Pennsylvania Press, 1989), pp. 12–15.
37. Richard Falk, *A Study of Future Worlds* (New York: Free Press, 1975), pp. 59–69.
38. Seyom Brown, *The Causes and Prevention of War* (New York: St. Martin's Press, 1987).
39. For some of the essential works in the area of functionalism, see David Mitrany, *A Working Peace System* (Chicago: Quadrangle Books, 1966); Mitrany, *The Functional Theory of Politics* (New York: St. Martin's Press, 1977); Ernst B. Haas, *Beyond the Nation-State* (Stanford: Stanford University Press, 1964); Haas, *The Uniting of Europe* (Stanford: Stanford University Press, 1958); Claude Ake, *A Theory of Political Integration* (Homewood, ILL: Dorsey Press, 1967); Karl Deutsch, *The Nerves of Government* (New York: Free Press, 1966); Amitai Etzioni, *Political Unification* (New York: Holt, Rinehart, 1965); Leon N. Lindberg, *The Political Dynamics of European Economic Integration* (Stanford: Stanford University Press, 1963); A.J.R. Groom and Paul Taylor, eds., *Functionalism: Theory and Practice in International Relations* (New York: Crane, Russak, 1975).
40. Gilpin in Robert J. Art and Robert Jervis, eds., *International Politics: Enduring Concepts and Contemporary Issues,* 3d ed. (New York: HarperCollins, 1992), p. 242.
41. Amitai Etzioni, *International Political Communities* (New York: Doubleday, 1966), p. 147. in Art and Jervis, eds., *International Politics,* p. 243, fn 15.
42. See Joseph A. Schumpeter's discussion on European economists (for example, Erik Lundberg, *Studies in the Theory of Economic Expansion,* and Carl Föhl, *Geldschöpfung und Wirtschaftskreislauf,* both published in 1937) who held views similar to those of Keynes. Schumpeter, *History of Economic Analysis,* pp. 1173–1174.
43. Macridis, *Contemporary Political Ideologies,* p. 101; James E. Dougherty and Robert L. Pfaltzgraff, *Contending Theories of International Relations,* 3d ed. (New York: Harper and Row, 1990), p. 225.
44. Marx sought a "scientific" theory. "Scientific" meant analyzing the root (or "objective") causes of economic conditions and class conflict.
45. Macridis, *Contemporary Political Ideologies,* p. 102.
46. Quoted in Samuel Hollander, *Classical Economics* (New York: Basil Blackwell, 1987), p. 380.
47. Macridis, *Contemporary Political Ideologies,* p. 102.
48. Gilpin, *Political Economy,* p. 36.
49. Caporaso and Levine, *Theories of Political Economy,* pp. 53-54.
50. Robert C. Tucker, ed., *The Marx-Engels Reader,* 2d ed. (New York: W.W. Norton, 1978), p. 474.
51. Gilpin, *Political Economy,* pp. 37–38.
52. Dougherty and Pfaltzgraff, *Contending Theories of International Relations,* p. 229.
53. Quoted in William I. Robinson, *Promoting Polyarchy: Globalization, US Intervention, and Hegemony* (Cambridge: Cambridge University Press, 1996), pp. 346–347.
54. Gilpin, *Political Economy,* p. 40.
55. *Ibid.,* pp. 40–41.
56. See Robert O. Keohane, *After Hegemony* (Princeton: Princeton University Press, 1984).
57. See Paul Sweezy, *The Theory of Economic Development* (London: Dennis Dobson, 1946); J.A. Hobson, *Imperialism: A Study* (Ann Arbor: University of Michigan Press, 1972); J.M. Blaut, *The Colonizer's Model of the World* (New York: The Guilford Press, 1993); Anthony Brewer, *Marxist Theories of Imperialism* (London: Routledge, 1980); Richard A. Higgott, *Political Development Theory: The Contemporary Debate* (London: Croom Helm, 1983).
58. Fred Halliday, *Iran: Dictatorship and Development* (Middlesex, England: Penguin Books, 1979), p. 25.
59. Immanuel Wallerstein, *The Modern World System I* (New York: Academic Press, 1974); *Wallerstein, The Modern World System II* (New York: Academic Press, 1980); Wallerstein, *The Capitalist World Economy* (Cambridge: Cambridge University Press, 1979).
60. Gerald Epstein, Julie Graham, and Jessica Nembhard, eds., *Creating a New World Economy: Forces of Change and Plans for Action* (Philadelphia: Temple University Press, 1993); Stephen D. Krasner, *Structural Conflict: The Third World against Global Liberalism* (Berkeley: University of California Press, 1985); Susan Strange, ed., *Paths to International Political Economy* (London: Allen and Unwin, 1984).
61. Immanuel Wallerstein, "Class-Formation in the Capitalist World-Economy," *Politics and Society* 5, 3 (1975): p. 375. See also Ronald H. Chilcote, *Theories of Comparative Politics* (Boulder, CO: Westview Press, 1981).
62. Kenneth N. Waltz, *Theory of International Politics* (Reading: Addison-Wesley, 1979).
63. Robert Gilpin, *War and Change in World Politics* (Cambridge: Cambridge University Press, 1981); Robert O. Keohane, "Theory of World Politics: Structural Realism and Beyond," in Robert O. Keohane, ed., *Neorealism and Its Critics* (New York: Columbia University Press, 1986), pp. 158–203; Keohane, *After Hegemony.*
64. Immanuel Wallerstein, "The Three Instances of Hegemony in the History of the Capitalist World-Economy," in George T. Crane and Abla Amawi, eds., *The Theoretical Foundations of International Political Economy: A Reader* (New York: Oxford University Press, 1991), pp. 238–240.
65. Hedley Bull, *The Anarchical Society: A Study of Order in World Politics* (New York: Columbia University Press, 1977).

66. Charles P. Kindleberger, *The World in Depression, 1929–1939* (Berkeley: University of California Press, 1973); Stephen D. Krasner, *Structural Conflict: The Third World against Global Liberalism* (Berkeley: University of California Press, 1985); and Gilpin, *War and Change in World Politics, passim.*
67. Paul Kennedy, *The Rise and Fall of Major Powers* (New York: Random House, 1987).
68. Dougherty and Pfaltzgraff, *Contending Theories,* p. 242.
69. Diana Tussie notes that "the major difference between the trading order under the hegemony of the United Kingdom and that under the U.S. primacy was that Britain had reduced tariffs unilaterally and sustained not only a free export policy, but also a free import policy." Diana Tussie, "Trading in Fear? U.S. Hegemony and the Open World Economy in Perspective," in Craig N. Murphy and Roger Tooze, eds., *The New International Political Economy,* pp. 82–83.
70. Keohane, *After Hegemony,* pp. 8–15.
71. *Ibid.,* pp. 39, 43.
72. *Ibid.,* p. 40. Robert O. Keohane and Joseph S. Nye, *Power and Interdependence* (Boston: Little, Brown, 1977), especially Ch. 2.
73. Michel Albert, *Capitalism vs. Capitalism* (New York: Four Wall Eight Windows, 1993), pp. 100, 118.
74. *Ibid.,* p. 107.
75. *Ibid.,* pp. 102–3.
76. *Ibid.*
77. Yasusuke Murakami, "The Japanese Model of Political Economy," in Kozo Yamamura and Yasukichi Yasuba, eds., *The Political Economy of Japan: The Domestic Transformation* (Stanford: Stanford University Press, 1987), p. 35.
78. Chalmers Johnson, *MITI and the Japanese Miracle: The Growth of Industrial Policy* (Stanford: Stanford University Press, 1982).
79. Murakami, "Japanese Model of Political Economy," p. 49.
80. Gilpin, *Political Economy,* p. 34.
81. *Ibid.,* p. 33.
82. *Ibid.,* p. 34.
83. Robert Gilpin, "The Politics of Transnational Economic Relations," in Modelski, ed., *Transnational Corporations,* p. 70.
84. *Ibid., passim.*
85. Max Weber, *The Protestant Ethic and the Spirit of Capitalism* (New York: Charles Scribner's Sons 1958); M. Weber, *The Religion of China* (Glencoe, Il: Free Press, 1951); M. Weber, *Ancient Judaism* (Glencoe, Il: Free Press, 1952); M. Weber, *The Religion of India* (Glencoe, Il: Free Press, 1958). In his "Introduction" to *The Protestant Ethic,* Anthony Giddens notes that Weber "also planned, but did not complete, a full-scale study of Islam." See also Bryan S. Turner, *Weber and Islam* (London and Boston: Routledge and Kegan Paul, 1974).
86. Richard H. Tawney, *Religion and the Rise of Capitalism* (New York: Harcourt, Brace and Co., 1926).
87. Peter Dicken, *Global Shift: The Internationalization of Economic Activity,* 2d ed. (New York: The Guilford Press, 1992), pp. 3–4.
88. Robert B. Reich, "Who Is Us?" in Art and Jervis, eds., *International Politics,* p. 236.
89. For analyses of the impact of globalization on various aspects of domestic and international political economy, see Stephen Gill, ed., *Globalization, Democratization, and Multilateralism* (Tokyo: United Nations University Press, 1997); Keith Griffin, *Studies in Globalization and Economic Transitions* (Houndmills, UK: Macmillan, 1996); Evans Luard, *The Globalization of Politics: The Changed Focus of Political Action in the Modern World* (Houndmills, UK: Macmillan, 1990).
90. Robert Z. Aliber, *The Multinational Paradigm* (Cambridge: MIT Press, 1993), p. 11.
91. Dicken, *Global Shift,* pp. 95–96.
92. *Ibid.,* pp. 95–96. See also Aliber, *The Multinational Paradigm;* Peter F. Drucker, *The New Realities* (New York: Harper and Row, 1989).
93. James H. Mittelman, "Restructuring the Global Division of Labour: Old Theories and New Realities," in Gill, ed., *Globalization, Democratization, and Multilateralism,* p. 89.
94. Muhammad Abdul-Rauf, *A Muslim's Reflections on Democratic Capitalism* (Washington, DC: American Enterprise, 1984); Maxine Rodinson, *Islam and Capitalism* (New York: Pantheon Books, 1974); Mir Zohair Husain, *Global Islamic Politics* (New York: HarperCollins, 1995).
95. See Akbar S. Ahmed and Hastings Donnan, *Islam in the Age of Postmodernity,* in Akbar S. Ahmed and Hastings Donnan, eds., *Islam, Globalization and Postmodernity* (London: Routledge, 1994); Husain, *Global Islamic Politics, passim.*
96. See Peter M. Holt, ed., *The Eastern Mediterranean Lands in the Period of the Crusades* (Warminster, UK: Aris and Phillips, 1977); P.M. Holt, *The Age of the Crusades: The Near East from the Eleventh Century to 1517* (London: Longman, 1986). For a brief but useful summary of Islam and finance, see Zamir Iqbal, "Islamic Financial Systems," *Finance & Development* (June 1997): pp. 42–45.
97. Zeine N. Zeine, *The Emergence of Arab Nationalism: With a Background Study of Arab-Turkish Relations in the Near East* (Delmar, NY: Caravan Books, 1973).
98. Stephan Viljoen, *Economic Systems in World History* (New York: Longman, 1974), p. 95; Ira M. Lapidus, *A History of Islamic Societies* (Cambridge: Cambridge University Press, 1988).
99. Timur Kuran, "The Economic System in Contemporary Economic Thought: Interpretation and Assessment,"

International Journal of Middle Eastern Studies 38 (May 1986) p. 141; Seyyed Vali Reza Nasr, "Islamic Economics: Novel Perspectives," *Middle Eastern Studies* 25, 4 (October 1989) pp. 516–30; Farhad Nomani and Ali Rahnema, *Islamic Economic Systems* (London: Zed Books, 1994).

100. John C. O'Brien, "Introduction," in Masudul Alam Choudhury, ed. *The Principles of Islamic Political Economy* (New York: St. Martin's Press, 1992), p. xvii.
101. Muhammad Nawaz Khan, Islamic and Other Economic Systems (Lahore, Pakistan: Islamic Book Service, 1989), p. 22.
102. O'Brien, "Introduction," p. xvii; Nazih N. Ayubi, *Political Islam: Religion and Politics in the Arab World* (London: Routledge, 1991); Allan M. Findlay, *The Arab World* (London: Routledge, 1994); Ira M. Lapidus, *A History of Islamic Societies.*
103. O'Brien, "Introduction," in Choudhury, ed., *Principles of Islamic Political Economy,* pp. xvii–xviii.
104. *Ibid.,* p. xix.
105. Khan, *Islamic and Other Economic Systems,* p. xv.
106. Kuran, "Economic System in Contemporary Islamic Thought," p. 135.
107. *Ibid.*
108. Khan, *Islamic and Other Economic Systems,* pp. 2–4.
109. *Ibid.,* p. 2.
110. *Ibid.,* p. 335.
111. *Ibid.,* pp. 21, 335, 357; Nomani and Rahnema, *Islamic Economic Systems,* pp. 24–37.
112. *Ibid.,* p. 323.
113. Masudul Alam Choudhury, *Islamic Economic Co-operation,* (New York: St. Martin's Press, 1989), pp. 370–371.
114. Quoted in Andre Simmons, *Arab Foreign Aid* (London: Associated University Presses, 1981), 68.
115. *Ibid.,* pp. 68–69.
116. Masudul Alam Choudhury and Uzir Abdul Malik, *The Foundations of Islamic Political Economy* (Houndmills, UK: Macmillan, 1992), pp. 315–316.
117. Khan, *Islamic and Other Economic Systems,* pp. 21–22.
118. Kuran, "Economic System in Contemporary Islamic Thought," p. 141.
119. John Renard, *Seven Doors to Islam: Spirituality and the Religious Life of Muslims* (Berkeley: University of California Press, 1996), pp. 145–146, 164–180, *passim.*
120. Khan, *Islamic and Other Economic Systems,* p. 341.
121. *Ibid.,* p. 2.
122. Husain, *Global Islamic Politics,* pp. 152–157.
123. Choudhury, *Islamic Economic Co-operation,* p. 389.
124. *Ibid.*
125. Judith Nagata, "How to Be Islamic Without Being an Islamic State," in Akbar S. Ahmed and Hastings Donnan, eds., *Islam, Globalization and Postmodernity* (London: Routledge, 1994), pp. 66–67.
126. *Ibid.*
127. Michael Richardson, "Malaysia Hit by Hard Times: Chip Glut Batters Penang's Silicon Valley," *International Herald Tribune,* September 20, 1996, p. 17.
128. "Petronas Aims to Join World's Oil Majors," *International Herald Tribune,* September 20, 1996, p. 17.
129. Majid Khadduri, "The Islamic Theory of International Relations and Its Contemporary Relevance," in J. Harris Proctor, ed., *Islam and International Relations* (New York: Frederick A. Praeger, 1965), pp. 25–26.
130. *Ibid.*
131. *Ibid.*
132. James Piscatori, "Religion and Realpolitik: Islamic Responses to the Gulf War," in James Piscatori, ed., *Islamic Fundamentalisms and the Gulf Crisis* (Chicago: American Academy of Arts and Sciences, 1991), p. 6. See also R.H. Dekmejian, *Islam in Revolution: Fundamentalism in the Arab World* (Syracuse: Syracuse University Press, 1985).
133. Piscatori, "Religion and Realpolitik," p. 6.
134. *Ibid.,* p. 9.
135. Samuel P. Huntington, "Clash of Civilizations?" *Foreign Affairs* 72, 3 (Summer 1993) pp. 22–49.
136. Michael C. Hudson, "Islam and Political Development," in John L. Esposito, ed., *Islam and Development: Religion and Sociopolitical Change* (Syracuse: Syracuse University Press, 1980), pp. 1–2. See also William R. Polk, *The Arab World Today* (Cambridge: Harvard University Press, 1991); Don Peretz, *The Middle East Today,* 5th ed. (New York: Praeger, 1988).
137. Quoted in Husain, *Global Islamic Politics,* p. 35.
138. Ira M. Lapidus, *A History of Islamic Societies,* p. 898.
139. Simone de Beauvoir, *The Second Sex,* trans. and ed. H.M. Parshley (New York: Vintage Books, 1952); Cynthia Enloe, *Bananas, Beaches and Bases: Making Feminist Sense of International Politics* (Berkeley: University of California Press, 1990); Sue Ellen Charlton, Jane Everett, and Kathleen Staudt, eds., *Women, the State, and Development* (Albany: State University of New York Press, 1989); Rachael Kamel, *The Global Factory: Analysis and Action for a New Economic Era* (Philadelphia: American Friends Service Committee, 1990); V. Spike Peterson and Anne Sisson Runyan, *Global Gender Issues* (Boulder, CO: Westview Press, 1993); V. Spike Peterson, ed., *Gendered States: Feminist (Re)Visions of International Relations Theory* (Boulder, CO: Lynne Rienner, 1992); Rae Lesser Blumberg, *Women, Development, and the Wealth of Nations: Making the Case for the Gender Variable* (Boulder, CO: Westview Press, 1992).
140. Josephine Donovan, *Feminist Theory,* expanded ed. (New York: Continuum, 1992), 1. See also Marilyn Frye, *The Politics of Reality: Essays in Feminist Theory* (Trumansburg, NY: Crossing Press, 1983).
141. Peterson and Runyan, *Global Gender Issues,* p. 117.
142. Donovan, *Feminist Theory,* pp. 2-4.

143. Peterson and Runyan, *Global Gender Issues,* p. 117.
144. Despite her argument in favor of a "liberal state," Harrington's proposed state is closer to the mercantilist view. She contends that the state "must be explicitly protectionist" in using its political power to protect "from harm the positions of its own most vulnerable people." Mona Harrington, "What Exactly Is Wrong with the Liberal State as an Agent of Change?" in Peterson, ed., *Gendered States,* pp. 65, 73–74.
145. *Ibid.,* p. 65.
146. *Ibid.*
147. Donovan, *Feminist Theory,* p. 141.
148. Peterson and Runyan, *Global Gender Issues,* p. 117.
149. *Ibid.,* p. 118.
150. Roxanne Dunbar, "Female Liberation as the Basis for Social Revolution" in Robin Morgan, ed., *Sisterhood Is Powerful: An Anthology of Writings from the Women's Liberation Movement,* (New York: Vintage Books, 1970), p. 481.
151. Peterson and Runyan, *Global Gender Issues,* p. 144.
152. Kate Millett, *Sexual Politics* (Garden City, NY: Doubleday, 1970).
153. Kate Millett, *The Politics of Cruelty* (New York: W.W. Norton, 1994), pp. 34–35.
154. Peterson and Runyan, *Global Gender Issues,* p. 118.
155. V. Spike Peterson, "Security and Sovereign States: What Is at Stake in Taking Feminism Seriously?" in Peterson, ed., *Gendered States,* p. 34; June Nash and Maria Patricia Fernandez-Kelly, eds., *Women, Men and the International Division of Labor* (Albany: State University of New York Press, 1983); Sneja Gunew and Anna Yeatman, eds., *Feminism and the Politics of Difference* (Boulder, CO: Westview Press, 1993).
156. Peterson, "Security and Sovereign States," p. 43.
157. Donovan, *Feminist Theory,* p. 78.
158. Peterson and Runyan, *Global Gender Issues,* p. 119.
159. Margaret Benson, "Political Economy of Women's Liberation," *Monthly Review,* 2d, no. 4 (September 1996), p. 15, as discussed by Donovan, *Feminist Theory,* p. 76.
160. *Ibid.,* pp. 76–77.
161. Peterson and Runyan, *Global Gender Issues,* p. 120.
162. Donovan, *Feminist Theory,* p. 206; see also Mary Mellor, *Feminism and Ecology* (New York: New York University Press, 1997), ch. 3, pp. 44–70 *passim.*
163. Vandana Shiva, *Chipko: India's Civilisational Response to the Forest Crisis* (New Delhi: INTACH, 1986), pp. 2–11.
164. *Ibid.,* p. 21.
165. Peterson, "Security and Sovereign States," p. 32.

CHAPTER THREE

THE HISTORY OF MODERN INTERNATIONAL POLITICAL ECONOMY

Prior to the advent of the modern international political economy in the seventeenth and eighteenth centuries, the economic world was divided into a number of fairly developed zones. The Mediterranean zone consisted of the major Italian trading cities of Venice and Genoa in the Middle Ages, the Byzantine empire from the fourth to the fifteenth centuries, followed by the Muslim Ottoman Empire, and the Muslim eastern Mediterranean and North Africa, the Maghrib, after the rise and expansion of Islam between the seventh and tenth centuries. Closely related to the North African Maghrib economy were the sea and overland trade routes linking the kingdom of Ethiopia on the east with the South Asian zone, including the Moghul empire in India, the Indian Ocean. The East African Red Sea zone was connected to the trade zone on the western coast of Africa, first centered on the empire of Ghana (not to be confused with today's Ghana), followed by the empire of Mali and its successor, the Songhay. The trans-Saharan trade network for millennia had connected northern and western African trade routes with central and southern Africa, before the arrival of the Portuguese on the west coast in the fifteenth century and the European colonization of the continent in subsequent centuries. The Indian Ocean trade zone was linked with the trade zone in the South China Sea, dominated by the Chinese empire well into the late eighteenth century, which in turn was connected to central Asian silk and caravan routes, extending from Mongolia to Russia, especially after the Mongolian invasions in the thirteenth and fourteenth centuries, which in turn was linked with the trade zone in the Baltic region.[1] Isolated from these international trade networks at the time were the Amerindian empires, including the Mayans, the Aztecs, and the Incas, to name a few, with their own financial arrangements and trade relations.

The economic zones, with their expanding networks of regional and interregional trade relations, were the descendants of ancient civilizations, often developed on the banks of major river networks, such as the Tigris, the Euphrates, the Nile, the Indus, the Yellow, and the Mississippi rivers. Each region had witnessed various inventions and their economic and political consequences for the future of local and global political economy. For example, China's gunpowder, printing press, paper, and compass proved to be particularly critical to the expansion of Western commerce and the sophistication of navigation and military technology.[2]

From the eleventh century onward, European exploration campaigns included, inter alia, Marco Polo's to East Asia in the 1270s–1290s, the Crusades to the Middle East in 1095–1396, Christopher Columbus' "discovery" of the Americas in 1492, Vasco de Gama's arrival in Calicut on the western shores of southern India, Hernando Cortes' conquests of the Aztec Empire under Montezuma in Mexico between 1519 and 1521, and Francisco Pizarro's conquest of the Inca Empire under Atahualpa in Peru by 1533. They enabled Europeans to expand their influence and acquire access to raw materials and precious metals. Relations were frequently characterized by the parallel forces of commerce, conquests, and cultural clashes, as when European merchants followed the Crusades between the late eleventh and late fourteenth centuries from France, Britain, Germany, and Italy to the Middle East and India.[3] They engaged in import-export relations, trading lemons, rice, melons, apricots, sugar, textiles, spices, cotton, and rugs from China, India, and Persia over the years, accumulating enormous capital for further expansion.

The opening of the Americas for competition after 1492 provided an opportunity for greater wealth than ever before imaginable. Gold and silver were used to purchase consumer goods that otherwise would not have been accessible to most Europeans. This in turn stimulated rapid production and economic growth and the "Golden Age" of prosperity throughout Europe in the sixteenth and early seventeenth centuries, gradually shifting the balance of power from the Muslim Mediterranean region dominated by the Ottoman Empire to the emerging Atlantic zone to the west.[4] With unprecedented pace Europeans stretched their commercial and military reach from the Atlantic-Mediterranean region to the Indian Ocean and the Pacific.[5] Europe's expansion abroad was a great turning point in world political economy. It marked the beginning of the modern age of global integration dominated by European powers up to the early twentieth century.

This chapter presents an historical overview of the modern international political economy from the mid-1600s to the present. Four distinct stages are identified: the first phase from the mid-1600s, the industrial revolution to European consolidation of the world political economy by the mid-1800s; the second between the 1860s and WWII, involving the spread of industrialization and escalation of trade and empire-building to new regions; the third between the 1940s and 1970s, an international system shaped by three decades of U.S. hegemonic leadership; and the fourth encompassing the emergence of a potentially new international political economy in the 1980s and 1990s.[6] The following sections review each of these phases.

THE ORIGINS OF THE MODERN INTERNATIONAL POLITICAL ECONOMY: THE 1600s–1860s

During the five-centuries-long evolution of the world political economy from the time of the Portuguese hegemony in the sixteenth century to the rise of the United States in the mid-twentieth, five major periods, or hegemonic cycles, can be identified, each characterized by intense competition for power and for world hegemonic leadership. As presented in Box 3.1, eight major European powers competed for hegemonic power, and four were successful. Their competition shaped the modern world political economy, and, in each hegemonic cycle, the hegemon first imitated earlier imperial strategies and then developed its own structures of domination.

The most significant turning points in the world political economy during the past millennium were the concurrent decline and disintegration, in the fourteenth and fifteenth centuries, of the Arab-Muslim empire on the Iberian Peninsula (A.D. 711–1492) and of the Byzantine empire centered at Constantinople (A.D. 324–1453). These two events signaled seismic transformations in world political economy and changed global power configurations, shaping the course of modern world history. During the first centuries of Arab-Muslim rule, Spain witnessed enormous economic development and prosperity, and a dynamic Hispanic-Arab culture emerged through conversion and assimilation. Soon, however, internal conflicts, financial mismanagement, and corruption fueled the *Reconquista* movements headed by the Christian kings and supported by the local population against Muslim domination. After three centuries of Christian-Muslim holy wars on the peninsula, the Crown of Castile, under Ferdinand and Isabella, was established, launching one of the earliest and most expansive empires in modern history.

In the meantime, the Byzantine empire was experiencing similar internal political and financial difficulties, when the Ottoman Turks, forced westward from Central Asia by Mongolian invasions toward Asia Minor and the Middle East, sought land and booty on the eastern frontiers of Byzantium.[7] The latter, mired in repeated financial and military disasters and the catastrophic consequences of the Black Death plague of 1348, failed to defend its territories from the Muslim Turkish onslaught. By the early 1400s, the Turks had captured large portions of Byzantine territories, and in 1422 they launched their first siege of Constantinople (today's Istanbul), followed by their successful capture of that geostrategically significant and much coveted city on the Bosphorus in 1453. The decaying Byzantine defenses could not withstand the numerically superior manpower of Turkish forces and their highly advanced bronze cannons and siege machinery, nor could European monarchs, divided among themselves, provide sufficient military assistance to prevent the fall of Constantinople.[8]

The Turkish capture of Constantinople, which had been the center of Byzantine Christianity (as the "Second Rome") for centuries, shocked Europe. One Cardinal Bessarion to Francesco Foscari of Venice lamented that "a city which was so flourishing, with such a great empire, so prosperous, the head of all Greece, the splendour and glory of the East, the school of best arts, the refuge of all good things, has been captured, despoiled, ravaged, and

BOX 3.1

HEGEMONIC LEADERSHIP CYCLE

Period:	ca. 1500 —	1600 —	1700 —	1790 —	1940 —	?
Hegemonic power:	Portugal	Netherlands	Britain I	Britain II	United States	
Failed aspirants:		Spain	France	France	Germany	USSR

Source: Joshua S. Goldstein, *Long Cycles: Prosperity and War in the Modern Age* (New Haven: Yale University Press, 1988), 127.

completely sacked by the most inhuman barbarians and the most savage enemies of the Christian faith. . . ." He warned that "much danger threatens Italy not to mention other lands, if the violent assaults of the most ferocious barbarians are not checked."[9] The Turkish successes against Byzantium caused Christians in Spain to redouble their efforts against the Muslims.

Subsequent conquests of the Balkans by the Turks and the rapid consolidation of power over the geostrategically important territory from Eastern Europe to Asia Minor disrupted European commercial ties with Asia. As a result, it has been argued that, in the second half of the fifteenth century, when modern European colonialism began, European monarchs and merchants searched for alternative trade routes to Asian markets and spices and expanded their naval operations along the coast of West Africa to the Cape of Good Hope en route to the Indian Ocean and on to India and southeastern Asia. A small number of sea adventurers even sought a new route to India westward across the Atlantic Ocean (hence, the naming of American "Indians").

European expansion and conquests, which combined both military and commercial interests, could not have been successful without the requisite superior military technology. By the early fifteenth century, Europeans had sufficiently developed artillery technology, especially bronze guns, that could easily demolish city walls of the older empires. European bronze casting technology was already advanced, as craftsmen were "well acquainted with the process because of the early and widespread demand for church bells"[10]—one of the earliest examples of dual technology (discussed in Chapter 7) in modern political economy. Portugal and Spain (after eight centuries of Arab-Muslim rule) became particularly interested in acquiring such technology as their empires expanded across continents. Unable to meet increasing demand, Portugal imported copper and cannons from other European countries, such as Germany, paid for by Portuguese trade in West African gold and ivory, as well as in spices from East Asia.[11]

The combination of effective military capability and commercial zeal enabled the Portuguese, throughout the sixteenth century, to acquire vast territories and wealth in the New World, Africa, and Asia. The Portuguese initially used Crusade-style religious reconquista invasions against the Muslims from the west coast of Africa to the Indian Ocean and to China in order to gain access to gold, slaves, and spices. Portuguese colonization of the African west coast began in the early 1440s, and, by the end of that century, colonization had led to the development of forts, trading posts, and plantations from Sierra Leone to the Cape of Good Hope. African slaves were bought in Senegal and Gambia and sold on plantations in Spain and Portugal, a trade that soon expanded to the New World (especially Brazil) and continued well into the nineteenth century.[12] Subsequently, the Portuguese empire expanded to India and Southeast Asia. In the process, Portuguese ships bombarded into submission islands and port towns and seized control over trade on the Indian Ocean.[13]

The Portuguese empire declined as domestic finances and the overall imperial political economy became unsustainable. Moreover, local industries in the colonies developed and emulated Portuguese navigation and military technologies, intensifying competition in trade. By the early decades of the 1600s, Muslim counterattacks in the Persian Gulf region on the one hand and declining imperial revenues from trade on the other ended Portuguese hegemonic leadership (although, even in 1998, while the former British colony Hong Kong was returned to China, Macao technically remained in Portuguese hands, de-spite Beijing's public refusal to recognize it as a colony).

Despite its growing wealth accumulated in American gold and silver, the Spanish empire never attained the same degree of military capability as its Portuguese competitor. Its initial phase of imperial expansion was driven largely by the need to secure Spain's home territory against the potential return of Muslims; accordingly, the Castilians enthusiastically supported expansion from the Islamic domain in North Africa further south. There was no effort on the part of Ferdinand and Isabella, Charles V, and Philip II, however, to institutionalize an extensive Spanish dominion in Africa. Instead, the Castilians began to pay greater attention to the potential financial and political support its representatives, such as Columbus, could garner in the "East" against the Turkish-Islamic threat.[14]

The conquest of the Americas by the Spanish *conquistadores* generated considerable wealth for Castilian Spain, but there was a military advantage as well. Contrary to its European empire, which required constant vigilance, in the safer realms of the Americas, where its military guaranteed clear superiority over Amerindian resistance, the Spanish empire increasingly became an Atlantic-American empire and shunned Africa and much of Asia (with the exception of the Philippines and nearby islands), where commercial and military competition would require highly advanced military and communications capabilities. It is believed that Cortes conquered the Aztec kingdom of Montezuma with no more than 600 soldiers and sixteen horses, and Pizarro crushed the Inca empire with 180 soldiers and thirty-seven horses[15]—conquests that, if true, could not as easily be replicated in Asia and Africa.

Having conquered the Americas, the Spaniards began the task of building communities. By the 1520s and 1530s, educational institutions, including universities in Mexico City and Lima, were established, as were schools for Indians and girls. In 1539, the Spaniards took the first printing press to Mexico, and mining, commerce, hunting, cattleraising, and agriculture constituted the principal components of economic activities.[16] Officials serving in the imperial bureaucracies were required, by law, to take their wives with them to the new land, and—contrary to the conventional view that the conquests were undertaken only by men—women participated in the conquests and contributed to the economic development of the Spanish empire in the Americas. Queen Isabella herself was the prime example of a woman's involvement in the decision-making process in Spain, while in the Americas women owned properties, worked as interpreters, managed farms, managed their husbands' financial affairs, and inherited political and administrative posts after the death of their fathers and husbands.[17] At the same time, however, the imperial expansion transplanted the *machismo* (that is, manifestation of masculine power) culture, as developed along the tradition of knighthood, to the Americas. On the one hand, women were seen as the *marianismo,* based on cultural images of the Virgin Mary, possessing saintly qualities, with the moral and spiritual fortitude to protect the family honor; while the husbands worked away from home, they often served as the family matrons. On the other hand, women were also employed as domestic servants and slaves, catering to the familial and physical needs of their masters. This cultural bifurcation between man's work and woman's housework is best captured by the old Spanish adage "El hombre está hecho para la calle y la mujer para la casa" (men are made for the street and women for the home).[18]

Despite extraordinary successes, the opening of the Americas for Spain caused serious domestic problems. Those who had no opportunity to improve their fortunes at home risked the hazards of the ocean for better opportunities in the New World. The aristocrats, however, resented the loss of labor; more significantly, they resented the increasing centralization of political authority. The Spanish Crown instituted highly centralized civilian and military bureaucracies, built on a doctrine of "permanent war," as the Ottoman threat expanded across the Mediterranean (including the Turkish conquest of Egypt in 1517). At the same time, the Crown cultivated closer ties with the emerging merchant classes, whose mercantile activities abroad and the capital they imported were deemed essential for government finances.[19] This was the age of "absolute monarchy" and the age of mercantilism, which insisted that mercantile and all economic activities cater to the financial and military needs of the state.[20]

By the mid-1600s, Spain had imported an estimated 16 million kilograms of silver and 185,000 kilograms of gold from the Americas, tripling the supply of silver available for Europe and increasing the supply of gold by one-fifth.[21] The bureaucracy made sure that approximately 25 percent of the wealth remained in the hands of the Crown, while the rest went to the private sector—merchants, banks, and so on.[22] In turn, the spread of colonies in the Americas, inhabited by nearly 118,000 people by the 1570s, opened opportunities for Spanish merchants and producers to export their goods, complementing the expanding markets in Europe. Profiting from this expansion was the textile industry, followed by the agricultural sector, exporting wine, corn, olives, oil, and so forth. In fact, to ensure expansion of domestic production, the Crown even ordered "the destruction of the newly planted Peruvian vineyards and olive groves, for fear of their competing with the wine and oil exports of Andalusia."[23] This colonial export pattern would be repeated by other powers, including most notably, Britain.

The vast Spanish colonial administration placed enormous fiscal pressures on the Crown treasury, compounded by constant problems of mismanagement and corruption.[24] For example, the *Casa de Contratación,* created in 1503 to maintain absolute control over trade with the Americas, was severely criticized by European governments, especially by the German banks, whose financial support for the Crown was essential for investments at home and abroad. Moreover, by the mid-1500s, while the inflow of silver increased and public confidence in the economy and the Crown rose, demand for foreign goods increased, as did inflation. The mercantilist priorities of the state and the need to secure the economic dynamism sustained by the local and foreign merchants collided.[25] While its administrative mechanism was highly centralized, the Crown nevertheless failed to produce a coherent, rational economic program. Its finances were increasingly determined by foreign banks, and the empire, confronted by one crisis after another, finally faced total bankruptcy during the last years of the reign of Philip II in 1596.

Neither could Spain maintain sufficient military strength to combat naval competitors. In 1588, the struggle to defeat Protestantism, as against England, resulted in the defeat of the Spanish Armada. The Roman Catholic Church tried to wage its holy war against England, and Protestants in general, but after 1588, despite Spain's rapid recovery of ships and war matériel, imperial designs for further expansion and domination were finally defeated, as public disillusionment and economic discontent mounted. Anti-Spain rebellions in European lands, especially the Dutch declaration of independence in 1581, had signaled the demise of the Spanish empire by the mid-seventeenth century.

Imperial envy was contagious, and during the sixteenth and seventeenth centuries the Spanish and Portuguese empires were challenged first by Holland, then by England and France in the eighteenth century. The military and technological requirements for the conduct of their wars with Spain necessitated expansive trade networks with other European countries, such as German princely states and Sweden, and additional resources from overseas. By the early seventeenth century, the Dutch first imported their military hardware, such as cast-iron artillery from England, but soon developed their own local industries, as in Amsterdam, Maastricht, The Hague, and Utrecht, with supplies, such as tin and copper, imported from England, Germany, and Japan.[26] The Dutch demand for military hardware fueled manufacturing production in other European countries—where, even after the mass destruction of human lives and infrastructure by wars, especially the Thirty Years' War, production operations recovered and expanded in conjunction with further advancements in military and navigation technology.

Particularly significant was the transition from the great galley of the "long ship," dependent on oarsmen, to sophisticated sailing vessels that enhanced European naval power relative to empires in other regions. The new ships had easy maneuvering capability and could carry greater military weight (e.g., artillery). The Portuguese and Spanish empires had begun improvements in navigation technology, and the Dutch, French, and English further developed it. As one historian has noted, "Supremacy was gained by those nations which shifted more completely to guns and sails. The era of human energy was over and the era of the machine was beginning to open up."[27]

Unlike the Spanish and Portuguese colonizers, who had conquered in the name of God and the Crown and had relied on the military organizations for the conduct of trade, the newly emerging European empires encouraged private enterprises to be actively involved in and to lead the colonial expansion. One such arrangement, for example, was the creation of giant corporate conglomerates, such as the Dutch East India Company, the English East India Company, and the Massachusetts Bay Colony. The state, for its part, extended civilian administrative and bureaucratic support as promoter of domestic enterprises at home and abroad, while, for purposes of greater efficiency, the role of the military was reserved for conquests and protection. This was the early phase of the emergence of international corporate entities into the modern international political economy.

France and England were quick to react to the Spanish and Portuguese expansion. Both sought access to the Americas and their abundant natural resources—precious metals, fur, and so forth. England sent its first explorer, Italian navigator John Cabot, to North America as early as 1497, immediately after Columbus' arrival. Cabot's followers, such as Sir Martin Frobisher in 1576, sought to secure waterways for navigation into the hinterland but limited their explorations mainly to the east coast. The French financed explorations of littoral North America by an Italian sea captain, Giovanni de Verrazano, in 1524, followed by the explorations by Jacques Cartier on the St. Lawrence River in 1534–1535, Jacques Marquette and Louis Joliet on the northern part of the Mississippi in

1673, and southward to the Gulf of Mexico by Robert Cavalierde la Salle in 1682. The French claim to this river network afforded the new empire control over the vast interior of the North American landmass, the New France, divided into the two provinces: Canada and Louisiana. Each province was governed by an *intendant,* or governor, appointed by and loyal to the king. The major administrative and trade centers included Quebec, Niagara Falls, Detroit, Green Bay, Cahokia/St. Louis, and New Orleans.

In the early 1600s, as English colonies became more stable, King James I granted the first charter to the London Company (1607) to establish an English colony in North America. Having failed in the pursuit of major gold deposits, tobacco plantations in the Virginia colony became the first significant economy in North America. By 1617, Virginia's tobacco export to the England had increased from a mere 20,000 pounds to 500,000 pounds. Increased production required a larger pool of workers, initially supplied by the immigration of indentured servants—that is, the poor who sought better opportunities in the New World but could not pay for their journey and therefore agreed to work for a number of years for their benefactor. Among the indentured servants were women, subjected to various "bastardy legislation"—rules and regulations with respect to marriage and childbirth. During the period of servitude, they could not marry without permission and were discouraged from doing so for fear that the responsibilities of marriage and childrearing would take away working hands from the master's farm. A Virginia law even "allowed a master who fathered his servant's child to demand compensation from her for her bastardy in the form of extra service."[28] In 1672, a law required that, on expiration of indenture, the servant be sold by the church for employment in the parish for an additional number of years.

The African slave trade experienced a dramatic increase to meet the needs of the expanding plantation operations. The geographical conditions in the southern colonies—the climate, rivers, rainfall, and soil—were conducive to large-scale agricultural production, while, in the north, despite the rivers, the land was arid and the winters too long and too severe. Thus, while the south maintained a lucrative agricultural economy, the north turned to lumbering, mining, and manufacturing, as shipbuilding became one of the major industries. London was content to allow the colonies to carry on their daily life and economic activities freely, as long as they paid their taxes.

Economic growth in the colonies fueled two triangular trade relations. The first involved the export of lumber, grain, and fish to the West Indies in exchange for molasses, fruit, and sugar, which were then traded in England for manufactured goods to be sold in the North American colonies. The second consisted of the export of rum to the western coasts of Africa, in exchange for slaves, who were transported to the West Indies in exchange for gold, silver, and molasses. The molasses was sold to the distilleries in the North American colonies for rum, which was then transported to Africa. By the time the slave trade was terminated in the 1880s, an estimated 12 million Africans had been sold into slavery, although some historians contend that the consideration of unrecorded trade would double that number.[29]

A number of factors contributed to the slave trade. On the demand side, as previously noted, European imperial expansion and trade required sufficient, cheap labor to sustain production on the plantations. On the supply side, wars between local African kingdoms produced captives, who in turn were sold to the Europeans, or to Arab Muslim traders. As in other parts of the world, these wars were often caused by struggles for power and by aspirations for territorial and economic expansion, as in the case of the Oyo, Dahomey, and Asante kingdoms. It has also been argued that some wars were premeditated schemes by the more powerful African kings to generate captives for the lucrative trade. As a result, in some cases, the primary objective of war was the total destruction of the enemy's society. Whether viewed from the demand or the supply perspective, the sheer magnitude of human misery (a fact mirrored in some twentieth century events) devastated what previously were prosperous societies, each with its own kings, social institutions, customs, and traditions. While prior to European colonialism such captives would be confined to forced labor for a number of years and then would be granted freedom to return to their homeland or to work in the new society, the slave trade "totally removed [them] from African society, with a short life-expectancy in harsh conditions and no hope for return."[30] The centuries of forced migrations of the African populace *en masse* led to declining agricultural production, economic bankruptcy, and famine. By the time the slave trade ended, African economies had become dependent on European manufactured goods, their local industries were stifled by European mercantile practices, and their social and political institutions were subjugated to European domination and decision making in European capitals.

Further, the cumulative effect of these changes in military and navigation technologies and the European gravitation to the Atlantic and the Western Hemisphere proved to be a major turning point in favor of the emerging northern European empires, while the Mediterranean and Asian powers, from Italy to China, fell behind.[31] The highly sophisticated Chinese civilization had produced various technologies initially not found in other parts of the world. The primary examples include the gunpowder and fireworks used to drive evil spirits and foreign enemies away, the compass for navigation purposes, and the printing press for use by the "scholar gentry," or *literati*, classes.[32] For centuries, Confucianism had served the Chinese emperors well in providing principles of authority and order, and well into the fifteenth century there was an overall parity in military and navigation capabilities between the western and eastern civilizations. Unlike the European monarchs, however, the Imperial Courts of the Ming (1368–1644) and Ch'ing (Manchus, 1644–1912) dynasties, always vigilant with respect to internal subversion, did not possess a zeal for militarization of the economy and the spread of military know-how.

Although culture as well as military and naval technologies spread from China to neighboring countries in Asia, the Chinese imperial bureaucracy, for fear of foreign and domestic enemies, neither officially sanctioned nor privately encouraged the sale of military technology abroad, nor did the Imperial Court support overseas explorations for colonial conquest and trade. Viewing himself as the "Son of Heaven" and his imperial domain as the "celestial empire," the Chinese emperor found no need to engage in expansionist projects. Even in later centuries, when the expansionist Europeans had already used their military forces to enter Canton and other littoral cities, Emperor Ch'ien-lung could write to King George III that "our celestial empire possesses all things in prolific abundance and lacks no product within its own borders. There is therefore no need to import the manufactures of outside barbarians."[33] Further, the Chinese generally viewed the mercantile classes, among the lowest in the social hierarchy, as parasitic in pursuit of commerce and capital, and as those whose growing wealth in capital and land increasingly encroached on traditional imperial prerogatives. Accordingly, the Imperial State maintained a monopoly on virtually all natural resources and agricultural production, and it closely supervised and taxed related transactions.[34] By about the latter half of the fifteenth and early sixteenth centuries, however, the balance of technological power had tilted in favor of the West. For centuries thereafter, Asian societies, particularly Japan, pursued strategies to adopt Western methods and technologies in order to counter western military and increasing economic superiority.

Prior to the emergence of the Ottoman empire in the fifteenth century, and particularly during the "Golden Age" of Islam from the eighth to the twelfth century, the Middle East also witnessed a proliferation of scientific works, ranging from the science of language and logic to mathematics, physics, and astronomy to chemistry, mineralogy, medicine, and military technology.[35] The scientific developments in the Middle East were influenced by and in turn influenced European, especially Greek and Spanish, scientific thought, but with greater emphasis on empiricism, experimentation, and observation.[36] Similar to their Chinese counterparts, however, Islamic and Jewish scientific developments remained the exclusive reserves of the elites for mercantilist purposes, and they never achieved the degree of commercialization experienced in the West in the later centuries of laissez-faire capitalism. The Muslim Ummayad (661–750) and its successor, the Abbasid (750–1258) caliphates, used civilian and military technologies for the aggrandizement of their empires and for the extension of vast systems of patronage for political support. Internal instability, religious factionalism and divisions, however, soon created opportunities for external invaders—the Seljuks, the European Crusades, the Mongols, and the Ottoman Turks—and obstructed future scientific developments in the Arab and Persian societies.[37]

By the late 1600s and early 1700s, the effective use of commercial and military technologies by the West had rendered the traditional empires greatly vulnerable to European mercantilist objectives and worldwide competition, particularly enhanced by Europe's wealth from the Americas and Africa. As European monarchs consolidated their power and sealed their borders against foreign import, the economies of the old Mediterranean trade centers, mostly under the Ottoman empire, stagnated and fell further behind in commercial development. European monarchs used their newly found wealth to strengthen their "national" armies and navies, while economic and political conditions in the old empires deteriorated from the Mediterranean to the Indian Ocean to the South China Sea.[38]

Historians view the Treaty of Westphalia, which concluded the Thirty Years' War in 1648, as the origin of the modern international system, because this treaty resulted in the emergence of a new political unit, the nation-state, as the principal actor in the international—but increasingly *Atlantic*—system. Each nation-state as a juridical entity consisted of a single national and *sovereign* government over a legally delineated territory. The emerging sovereign nation-state put an end to the highly fragmented, independent authority of various feudal lords, city-states, and principalities. In their stead, each national kingdom consolidated power within a single government and unified the various political groups within its territory as a single political unit.[39] Monarchs successfully centralized and consolidated power against fragmented feudalism because of a number of factors: the accumulation of wealth in their central treasuries from, for example, explorations in the Americas; advances in military technology, as in artillery, rendering castles and walled cities defenseless; greater efficiency in central administration; and incessant religious conflicts that "enhanced the legitimacy of secular authority."[40] Each monarch jealously guarded its sovereignty against foreign political interference in domestic affairs and against foreign economic competition, as the very survival of national economy depended on its ability to secure strong military and financial bases for the country.[41]

In the meantime, the growing merchant and trading groups began to replace the feudal system and developed merchant capitalism, in which merchants played a central role in providing the capital needed to expand trade beyond the town markets. As merchant capitalism grew and expanded, so did trade, enhancing the financial and political position of merchants, producers, and financiers. The growth in trade, in turn, encouraged the development of major urban centers and growing consumerism. While the old trading relationships continued in the traditional commercial centers, such as Venice, Florence, and the Hanseatic League (comprised of Bremen, Hamburg, Lubeck, Rostock, and Danzig), with the rise of merchant capitalism similar centers proliferated across Europe, with waterways and roadways connecting them together.[42]

Europeans used advanced navigation and military technologies to explore and colonize, and their traditional religious (Catholic, Protestant) and emergent secular European conceptions of *Imperium Romanum,* the Holy Roman Empire, the Germanic *sacrum imperium, Respublica Christiana, Empire François* and the British Empire, clashed with the Islamic community of the Ottoman Empire and competing forces in the region.[43] As in the Americas earlier, European competition for power and wealth eventually led to the disruption and destruction of trade and shipping in the Mediterranean, African and Asian regions.[44]

Mercantilism at this time depended on a constant supply of precious metals (gold and silver) and new and exotic products to encourage demand and growth of trade to compensate for trade imbalances. Thus, mercantilist policies encouraged the colonization of far away territories in pursuit of wealth, with resources brought back for the production of finished goods in local European factories. By the eighteenth century, Europeans were dominating the world political economy, having established a number of farflung administrative and military headquarters, including trading stations, entrepots, and ports for colonial economic and political control.[45] These included cities such as Canton in China, Madras in India, Rio de Janeiro in Brazil, Georgetown in British Guinea, Port of Spain in Trinidad, Lagos in Nigeria, Jamestown, Boston, Newport, New York, Philadelphia, and so on. In areas where sufficient manpower did not exist, as on the plantations, Europeans transferred slaves from one community to another to meet consumer demands back home.[46]

The first blow to this system—seen as relatively minor at the time—occurred when the British empire lost the thirteen colonies, named the United States of America, as a result of the anti-British revolution for independence, formalized by the Treaty of Paris in 1783. London acceded to "complete commercial reciprocity" with the new nation,[47] hence the end of the "British empire I" (as was shown in Box 3.1). In agreeing to relax restrictions on the north Atlantic commerce, the British hoped to win U.S. alliance against the French. Accordingly, they allowed U.S. ships to visit British ports to deliver various goods, such as lumber, flour, grain, and vegetables, and to transport British goods, such as sugar, rum, coffee, and nuts. In order to protect certain domestic economic sectors, however, London refused the importation of U.S. dairy, produce, meat, and fish and insisted on maintaining a monopoly over British shipping for the empire.[48] The loss of the thirteen colonies inevitably raised a host of questions in London with respect to the political economy of imperial governance, but, by then, the British had developed the most powerful navy in the world, and were not discouraged by such failures.

Efforts to apply principles of "responsible government," while successful to some extent in Canada, failed miserably in other parts of the empire.[49] The purportedly anti-imperialist movement, known as "Little Englanders," believed that the burdens of imperial rule could be eliminated if London, following the doctrine of "free trade," granted independence to its colonial holdings. However, in fact, the ideological dualism of responsible government and free trade, as developed in the early nineteenth century and as applied to Australia, Africa, Asia, and Latin America, served as mere justification for imperial expansion and control following the age-old dictum of *divide et impera* in the form of both formal and informal empire.[50] Canada was divided into Upper and Lower Canadas, a division that has persisted in the form of English- and French-speaking Canadas, respectively. During the 1840s and 1870s, Britain gained direct or indirect control over numerous Asian and African territories, including Basutoland, Berar, British Columbia, Burma, the Gold Coast, Griqualand, Hong Kong, Labuan, Lagos, Natal, Punjab, Sind, New Zealand, Queensland, and the Transvaal.[51] In the process, Britain, ruling mainly indirectly, often playing local political groups and leaders against each other, continued to export capital, industry, language, and ideology across continents with diverse indigenous cultures and traditions. By the late nineteenth century, the U.K. had become the most powerful among the major European powers, and it had become the largest Muslim empire.[52]

Led by the British experience, the major European powers also devised a number of transnational mechanisms for greater cooperation and management of the international system: the principle of balance of power; international law; major-power congresses; and the establishment of permanent embassies, and conventions on key regulations, all of which facilitated and protected European commerce.[53] Through the balance of power system, often described as the systematic practice of anti-hegemonialism, the major powers claimed to maintain international order based on a rough political and military equilibrium in order to prevent any one state from threatening other sovereign states. Maintaining the power-equilibrium, or at least keeping foes from gaining complete control of regions, became especially crucial, as expanding powers could no longer be content with the distribution of power on the European continent itself; with industrialization, the colonial struggle for greater power and wealth became a necessity for national economic and political survival.[54]

Modern international law, first enunciated by Dutch scholars (most prominently, Hugo Grotius), sought to regulate state practices in trade and navigation in times of war and peace in order to create a more orderly international system and more predictable state behavior in an otherwise anarchic and chaotic arena of self-interested independent states. International law, however, soon became the preserve of European powers and was increasingly used to support and protect their colonial interests against challenges by competing and colonized states. For example, in the name of "Free Trade," the British imposed treaties on Persia in 1836, 1841, and 1857; on Turkey in 1838 and 1861; on China in 1842 and 1860 (Nanking and Tientsin, respectively, in the aftermath of the Opium Wars); on Thailand in 1855; on Morocco in 1856; and on Japan in 1858. These treaties established legal precedents and standards in international law, as European powers forced the weaker states to reduce or eliminate internal barriers to trade and instituted extra-territorial jurisdiction and privileges.[55]

In addition, major-power congresses were held to address various political crises, such as the Congress of Vienna in 1815 concluding the Napoleonic Wars, the Congress of Berlin in 1878, and the later conference of Berlin (1884–1885), which led to Europe's partition of Africa. Such congresses were the exclusive clubs of European powers; non-Europeans were seldom invited.

Finally, new diplomatic institutions, such as permanent embassies, were created to keep communication open among sovereign states and to facilitate the orderly conduct of trade and political negotiations. Increasingly, "higher diplomacy" became entangled with capital in the form of loans to governments in need and foreign direct investments in public utilities (for example, railways, waterways), government stocks, banking, and insurance companies.[56] Capital exports were primarily linked to industrialization, however, and were available mostly in the more advanced countries, granting them greater control over the economic development of less industrialized countries. Transfer of capital and competition for resources raised the stakes in the domestic affairs of recipient governments, leading nation-states to covert and overt political and military interventions in each others' affairs.[57]

The advent of the industrial revolution (see Box 3.2) during the eighteenth and early nineteenth centuries transformed the nature of economic activity from merchant capitalism to industrial capitalism. The latter was essentially characterized by the need to expand, the development of new technologies to improve production and surpass competitors, the development of new markets at home and abroad, and the pursuit of cheaper labor and raw materials abroad.[58] Inventions in various technologies, including the spinning jenny (1765), the machine loom (1787), and the steam engine (1782) created the foundations for the rapid spread of industrialization. Technologies were used to develop heavy industries and consumer goods for new and expanding domestic and international markets. Factories were built based on the principles of functional specialization (or division of labor) and economies of scale, and they attracted large numbers of workers from the rural areas to the cities, as well as immigrants from abroad.[59]

Industrialization created opportunities for work in factories, mills, and mines, but it also led to inhumane exploitative practices for men and women. While it is difficult to generalize, some women went looking for opportunities to gain greater financial independence from their

BOX 3.2

GREAT BRITAIN: THE BIRTHPLACE OF THE INDUSTRIAL REVOLUTION

Industrialization first occurred in Britain for a number of reasons. By the eighteenth century, Britain already possessed a commercial and industrial base and a labor force using highly advanced industrial processes available in various locations. The availability of resources (especially coal), water power, and local canal systems facilitated the development of manufacturing. Transport technology facilitated the transfer of raw materials, such as coal, tin, copper, and iron, from their sources to the industrial and trading centers of Liverpool, Bristol, and Glasgow. The transition from an agricultural to an industrial society took place gradually but almost freely. The government imposed little constraints on the movement of labor and capital from one sector to the other. The free entrepreneurial environment was conducive to structural adjustments as various enterprises, especially those in the area of wool and cotton production, developed new technologies. As a result of economies of scale, the costs of production and therefore prices dropped, considerably augmenting the pool of consumers, as industrial regions spread their influence throughout the economy and, in the process, undermined the agricultural sectors.

The birth of industrialization in Britain underscored the "interplay of history and geography," of resources and technology, and of policy and power; of course, the Crown and the government played an important role. As the agricultural sector declined, protective policies, such as the Corn Laws, were challenged by manufacturers as too restrictive and expensive. They lobbied for lower trade barriers for agricultural goods; however, they advocated stronger protectionist policies for **infant industries**—that is, newly emerging domestic industries. During the mercantilist era, the British government, in an attempt to guard its technology against falling into foreign hands, passed numerous laws prohibiting the transfer of industrial blueprints and machinery, as well as the emigration of skilled labor. By the late 1840s, the government had repealed several key protectionist policies, including the Navigation Laws and the Corn Laws. The government's support for liberal, free trade policies encouraged the expansion of British foreign trade and financial relations. Moreover, the government's and manufacturers' demands for luxury and military goods led to the development of dockyards and military-industrial complexes. The British took advantage of their early industrialization and for a while attempted to prevent the rise of competitors in other countries. The Great International Exhibition of 1851 at London's Crystal Palace was celebrated as the triumph of British industrial progress, represented by more than 14,000 firms.

Later industrialists in Europe, the United States, and elsewhere had to compete in international markets already dominated by Britain. Nevertheless, technical-scientific literature, industrial spies, and employment abroad resulted in the transfer of technology to the Continent and the Americas. By the mid- to late nineteenth century, Belgium, Germany, the Netherlands, Scandinavia, Austria, and the United States had acquired and developed their own industrial technologies in various forms, had become industrialized societies, had embraced industrial capitalism, and had even begun to challenge British economic and political dominance around the world.

Sources: See Eric J. Hobsbawm, *The Age of Revolution, 1789–1848* (New York: Mentor Book, 1962); Eric J. Hobsbawm, *Age of Capital,* 1848–1875 (New York: Meridian Book, 1979), p. 31; Sidney Pollard, *Peaceful Conquest: The Industrialization of Europe 1760–1970* (Oxford: Oxford University Press, 1981); Paul Knox and John Agnew, *The Geography of the World Economy* (London: Hodder and Stoughton, 1989), p. 132; Andrew Tylecote, *The Long Wave in the World Economy* (London: Routledge, 1991); Robert L. Reynolds, *Europe Emerges: Transition toward an Industrial Worldwide Society* (Madison: University of Wisconsin Press, 1961); A.G. Kenwood and A.L. Lougheed, *The Growth of the International Economy, 1820–1990* (London: Routledge, 1992).

families; others sought employment out of necessity. Women were employed in mines along with male workers, but many were harassed and raped by their employers and male co-workers. For some factory managers and supervisors, the factory was their workplace and harem.[60] In Whitehaven, England, conditions in one coal mine became so intolerable that in 1827 the company decided not to employ women. In Chester, a judge observed that the employment and rapes of young girls had become "an all too common vice . . . above all, in this manufacturing country, where the females were, at a tender age, placed away from the control of their parents, to work at the factories."[61] Increasingly, protection of women employees became a major concern, and laws were instituted to regulate working conditions. The British Parliament passed a number of factory acts to regulate child labor, working hours, and working conditions in factories. In the mill towns of northeastern United States, stricter housing rules were introduced to separate women from men at night. In Japan, factories were surrounded by dormitories built exclusively for women. However, abuse, sexual and otherwise, continued.

The internationalization of industrial capitalism gradually challenged nationalist, state-centric, mercantilist controls of the economy. The rise of industrialization and the entrepreneurial environment within which it occurred gave rise to antimercantilist views, especially among the capital-owning sectors of society. The latter became the torch-bearers for liberalism, advocating the liberalization of economic activities independently of state controls. Classical liberals favored economic development to enhance individual profits rather than to enrich the state's treasury. In the 1820s and 1830s, responding to such pressures, governments began to repeal some of the protectionist policies, except tariffs, instituted by absolutist sovereigns during the previous century. During the nineteenth century, free trade replaced mercantilism as the preferred means to encourage economic growth, national power, and security. Mercantilism was now viewed as too restrictive in the face of rapid changes in the flow of technology, capital, and goods.[62] The shift reflected the rise of the capitalist middle class, demanding its own political and economic share in the transition from agricultural to industrial society.

In Britain, for example, the Reform Act of 1832 began the long process of expanding the franchise to increase the proportion of citizens eligible to vote. In the end, Britain was more successful than most other Western societies in securing a relatively stable transition from agricultural to industrial economy. The United States, for instance, failed in that transition, as forces of manufacturing in the northeast and agricultural interests in the south collided, culminating in the Civil War in the 1860s. The victorious northeast, having resolved the issue, catapulted the economy toward rapid industrialization and in so doing, posed a serious challenge to European competitors. The collision of the two forces of agricultural conservativism and manufacturing modernization has plagued societies, old and new, for centuries.

INDUSTRY, TECHNOLOGY, AND EMPIRES: THE 1870s–WWII

The period between the 1870s and the Second World War included phases of industrial growth and prosperity, depression, reconstruction, phases of peace and turbulence, and wars. While previously industrialization was confined mainly to a small region of the world, primarily Britain and parts of the European continent (especially Belgium, France, and Germany) and to limited regions within each country, now industrial expansion spread to previously agricultural regions and to a number of non-European countries as well, most prominently the United States and Japan. As Table 3.1 indicates, by the 1870s, the United States had surpassed Britain and the major European powers in technological inventions, discoveries, and innovations—a sure sign of a rising economic power. Britain, however, retained its dominant position as the financial center of the world economy, providing financial, trading, and shipping services to British and foreign international businesses.[63]

Contrary to the laissez-faire liberal theory, however, the state directly contributed to the development of specific industries and to the proliferation of industrialization. Responding to various domestic and international pressures, governments in Western societies closely cooperated

TABLE 3.1
Major Inventions, Discoveries, and Innovations by Country, 1750–1950 (as a Percentage of Total)

	Total	Britain %	France %	Germany %	USA %	Others %
1750–1775	30	46.7	16.7	3.3	10.0	23.3
1776–1800	68	42.6	32.4	5.9	13.2	5.9
1801–1825	95	44.2	22.1	10.5	12.6	10.5
1826–1850	129	28.7	22.5	17.8	22.5	8.5
1851–1875	163	17.8	20.9	23.9	25.2	12.3
1876–1900	204	14.2	17.2	19.1	37.7	11.8
1901–1914	87	16.1	8.0	17.2	46.0	12.7
1915–1939	146	13.0	4.1	13.0	58.6	11.3
1940–1950	34	2.9	0.0	6.7	82.4	8.8

Source: John H. Dunning, *Explaining International Production* (London: Unwin Hyman, 1988), 90.

with businesses, directly and indirectly subsidized industries and infrastructural development, introduced land policies, and instituted protective tariffs; in some respects, state-business relations resembled practices found in the age of mercantilism. In the United States, companies engaged in expansive international trade supported the creation of a modern navy to secure the protection of investments abroad. After the depression of the 1890s, Charles Conant, economist and adviser at the State Department, stated that

> the United States have actually reached, or are approaching, the economic state where . . . outlets are required outside their own boundaries, in order to prevent business depression, idleness, and suffering at home. Such outlets might be found with the exercise of political and military power, if commercial freedom was the policy of all nations. As such a policy has not been adopted by more than one important power of western Europe, and as the opportunities for the sale of products of American labor . . . under conditions of equality of opportunity are seriously threatened by the policy of some of these powers, the United States are compelled, by the instinct of self-preservation, to enter, however, reluctantly, upon the field of international politics.[64]

Foreign policy ventures such as the opening of the Panama Canal by the United States in 1901–1905, as had the opening of the Suez Canal by Britain and France in the 1860s, clearly demonstrated the close relationship between government and business. The Pan-American Congress of 1889, the Open Door policy opposing exclusive trade zones in China, the McKinley Tariff Act of 1890, the creation of the Bureau of Foreign Commerce within the State Department in 1897, the Platt Amendment of 1901 with respect to Cuban independence, and the Payne-Aldrich Tariff Act of 1909 all were examples of the U.S. government's support for American businesses at home and abroad.[65]

As societies industrialized and manufacturing and mass production gained momentum, working and living conditions changed rapidly. Preindustrial economies gave way to manufacturing plants, where unskilled workers labored for long hours away from their homes and families and became dependent on factory owners and managers to secure their living. Working conditions were poor, safety precautions were virtually nonexistent, and daily working hours were as long as fifteen or eighteen hours or more. Those who could maintain their physical condition continued to work; those who could not lost their jobs. Emphasis was placed on generating mass-based consumption of mass-produced products. As companies scrambled for markets and consumer loyalty, a new phenomenon at the time, expenses that accrued from the marketing and distribution of company products, from corporate corruption, and from sheer greed kept employee wages low and prices high.

The operation of industrial capitalism involved increasing concentration of capital in the form of monopolies and "big business." This was the age of giant corporations, run by shareholders and hired managers, replacing small, family-owned businesses.[66] The expansion of industry required new methods of management and industrial operation. One major development was "scientific, management." Its founder, Frederick Winslow Taylor (1856–1915), sought to improve industrial organization and production through rational, or scientific, methods. Since then, Taylorism has become synonymous with industrial management and production techniques. It consisted of a number of key elements, including; the isolation of individual workers on the assembly line and control of the work process by the management; "a systematic breakdown of each process into timed component elements with the use of time and motion studies;" and piece work as a system of "wage payment which would give the worker an incentive to produce more."[67]

While providing economic opportunity, especially for unskilled labor, and new products, industrialization rendered people greatly dependent on the factory owners, managers, and foremen for their livelihood; piece-work as a system frequently proved exploitative. Particularly vulnerable were immigrant workers and women, who worked for lower wages and with little protection from abuses. Immigrants provided not merely surplus labor but cheap surplus labor to maintain low wages.[68] Both men and women were engaged in labor strikes against these conditions, but women's complaints involved sexual harassment as well. In 1893, for instance, Russian workers went on strike against the Egorov factory in Riazan to protest "the tyranny of foremen," who had been given total authority to do as they pleased with women under their supervision. "If one refused to submit to his bestial desires," an inspector reported, "she would be unceremoniously fired. And not just she, but her entire family would be kicked out of the factory."[69] In 1912, women employees went on strike, organized by the International Ladies Garment Union, against the Kalamazoo Corset Company, in Michigan, to protest against "the tyranny of foremen" who engaged in sexual harassment and who made decisions based on sexual favors.[70] In 1925, Chinese women workers in a Japanese plant in China struck the company, complaining that "the

Japanese are immoral and rude. They make advances toward the women workers. The clever ones flirt with them; the less clever ones reject their advances and scorn them, so that sometimes they are forced to quit."[71] Such examples can fill volumes, but suffice it to say that exploitative and poor working conditions led to labor strikes, boycotts, rioting, and eventually to the creation of well-organized labor unions by the last decades of the nineteenth century.

Organized labor movements first appeared in Europe and then were adopted by other industrialized countries. Their primary goal was to secure improved working conditions and standards of living. At first ridiculed and resisted by company owners for their demands and by governments for their anarchism and "radicalism," trade unions and the principle of collective bargaining gradually gained formal and legal recognition in Britain in the 1870s, in France in the 1880s, in Germany in the 1890s, and in the United States in the 1930s. The emergence of labor organizations was soon accompanied by labor-oriented, socialist political parties. In the process, classical liberal parties, such as the British Liberal Party, tended to decline in popular support as they failed to meet the challenges of urbanization and industrialization.

In addition to organized labor, women's suffrage movements demanded greater and direct participation in the political arena to reflect women's growing economic independence and as a just compensation for their contributions to economic development. In this case as well, after much resistance and ridicule, women gained the right to vote in the 1910s and 1920s in most of Europe, with some variation in specific laws and regulations. In developing societies, changes were slower. In Latin America, for example, Ecuador was the first (1929) to grant women the right to vote, followed by Brazil and Uruguay in 1932, and Cuba in 1934. Seven Latin American countries extended the right to vote to women in the 1940s, an equal number in the following decade, and Paraguay in 1961.[72]

Industrial expansion and internationalization encouraged and were facilitated by the expansion of communications technologies in transcontinental and transoceanic cables, radio, news services, motion pictures, and aviation.[73] Technological revolutions and information exchange in transportation and communication meant that, by the early decades of the twentieth century, the world political economy was already global. The steamship and railroad networks had established connections among vital trading centers around the world and had shortened travel time with unparalleled speed. Thousands of miles of railway networks, such as the Trans-Siberian Railway completed in 1904; the electric telegraph; and networks of port cities and waterways, such as the Suez and Panama Canals meant faster communication and transportation systems transmitting information and moving people across the globe with unprecedented pace and facility (see Table 3.2).[74]

In the process, new conglomerates challenged established competitors. Britain had long established monopoly over international cable lines from the Atlantic to Latin America and to East Asia. In the late nineteenth century, however, the U.S. All-America Cables (the predecessor of International Telephone and Telegraph, ITT), headed by James A. Scrymser and financed by the J. P. Morgan bank, challenged the British monopoly under Western Telegraph. By the late 1890s, with the political support of the State Department in Washington and Latin American capitals, All-America Cables had linked the United States via Mexico with Central and South America. Commercial Cable and Western Union launched extensive lobbying campaigns in Congress to subsidize a Pacific cable between the United States and East Asia, where they were competing against British cables.[75]

Changes in technology and the spread of industrialization by the closing decades of the nineteenth century were accompanied by greater integration of the global financial system. The establishment of the international gold standard was one such system, whereby countries pegged their currencies to gold as a mechanism to maintain fixed exchange rates, and governments held gold reserves to settle trade deficits. Britain was the first to adopt the gold standard as early as 1821, while most countries used either bimetallic (silver and gold) or silver standards. With the expansion of commercial relations and growing complexities of, and therefore growing uncertainties in, international

TABLE 3.2

Railway Route Mileage, 1840–1910 (Thousand Miles)

	1840	1870	1910
Europe	2.6	65.4	212.1
North America	2.8	55.4	265.8
Latin America	0.1	2.4	60.7
Asia	—	5.1	59.5
Africa	—	1.1	23.0
Oceania	—	1.1	19.3
World	5.5	130.5	640.4

Source: A. G. Kenwood and A. L. Lougheed, *The Growth of the International Economy, 1820–1990* (London: Routledge, 1992), 13.

transactions, it became necessary for governments and businesses to maintain a stable monetary system.[76]

Parallel with efforts to improve management in the private sector, Western governments adopted new measures, such as the Civil Service (Pendleton) Act of 1883 in the United States, to improve their bureaucracies. At the international level, governments also became involved in multilateral arrangements for greater international cooperation, such as the international conferences in the 1860s and 1870s leading to the creation of the World Postal Union in 1878. Similar integrative arrangements continued and, as one historian has noted, by the mid-1910s,

> there had been 9 collective international agreements on postal matters, 10 on telegraphs, 5 on underwater cables, 1 on wireless, 7 on railway-goods transport, 3 on the technical unification of railways, 2 on the Danube, 1 on the Suez Canal, besides 3 on the law of the sea and the Safety at Sea Conference of 1913.
>
> Another important area for international conferences and lasting agreements and supervisory institutions was the attempt to prevent the spread of epidemic diseases, both human and plant, like phylloxera. There were 7 conferences on copyright, 1 on bills of exchange, 6 on coinage, 12 on sugar. There were also agreements on fishing, on labour protection, on anti-slavery, on fighting 'anarchism,' on prisoners of war, and hospital ships in times of war. At the first Hague Conference in 1899, 26 countries were represented in an attempt to find means of international arbitration, and the Hague Court was set up in 1907. Altogether, 12 such collective international agreements have been counted in the period 1815–1851, 45 in 1852–1880, and 129 in 1881–1910.[77]

Not all government efforts were geared toward cooperation. Rather, as Pollard has observed, policies during these years were schizophrenic: they encouraged multilateral economic cooperation, while at the same time instituting mercantilist policies reasserting national priorities to counter international integrative trends. In the late nineteenth century, domestic considerations in times of economic difficulties led to protectionist trade policies at home. With the exception of Britain, the industrialized countries, including Germany, France, and the United States, imposed protective tariffs on various agricultural and manufactured products.[78] These mercantilist policies led to economic warfare among the major economic powers, which later exploded as the First World War.

Mercantilist policies manifested themselves in many forms, and foreign workers were one of the most obvious targets. In the 1880s, the Prussian government, for example, sealed off the Silesian border and commenced a policy of expulsion of all non-Prussian Poles; it also imposed stricter controls on foreign landownership. In a similar vein, France and Switzerland restricted the mobility of foreign, especially Italian, workers. In the 1920s in the United States, the "land of opportunities" for thousands of immigrants coming through Ellis Island and the Golden Gate to fill the demand for cheap industrial labor, stricter quota systems were introduced, targeting southern and Eastern Europeans as the primary source of immigration. "Discrimination against the foreigner became the order of the day: higher harbour dues for foreign ships, veterinary laws to keep out foreign cattle, or laws to limit the numbers or drive out altogether foreign directors of joint-stock companies, though their money was still welcome."[79] In the first half of this century, the Armenian Genocide by Ottoman Turkey during the First World War, and the rise of Nazism and fascism in Europe in the 1920s and 1930s, culminating in the Jewish Holocaust during the Second World War, were the ultimate manifestations of the inhumanity of nationalist political economy pushed to its extremes.[80]

Another area of conflict during these transitions was the escalation in colonization and empire-building throughout the developing world. Japan became the first non-European power to compete in this league, signaling its new status with the defeat of Russia in the Russo-Japanese War of 1905. Industrial and technological advantages easily translated into military power to dominate the less industrialized countries (see Box 3.3). Even the former major colonial powers Spain and Portugal, having failed the competition toward industrialization, also failed to compete in the new scramble for colonies. The United States, for example, easily ousted the Spanish empire from Cuba, Puerto Rico, and the Philippines during the Spanish-American War (1899).[81]

Imperialism, while greeted with much enthusiasm and nationalist fervor in the industrialized economies, created deep resentment among the conquered in developing countries. Commercial and humanitarian (for example, missionary) interests welcomed the opportunity to expand their operations beyond national borders. In strictly economic terms, as seen in the World System approach, one of the most significant consequences was the development of an unequal, asymmetrically interdependent relationship between a handful of "core" industrial countries and the "periphery"—a situation that has only begun to change in the twentieth century. The economics of the periphery, based precariously on commodity specialization, such as sugar in the Caribbean Islands, directly and adversely affected the general economic well-being of their

BOX 3.3

THE ROOTS OF IMPERIALISM

Whether the rise of imperialism during this period was related to domestic economic challenges confronting the major powers has been the subject of lively debates. There appears to be little doubt, however, that the search for lucrative investments and markets contributed to colonialist, expansionist policies. "Territorial expansion," one U.S. State Department official stated in 1900, "is but the by-product of the extension of commerce." Investors with surplus cash sought opportunities to invest in lucrative projects in mining, construction, and so forth. Western foreign direct investments in developing countries experienced enormous increases. In Latin America, for example, railway construction more than doubled. In turn, iron production between 1870 and 1890 in the industrialized North increased from 11 to 23 million tons, while steel production increased from half a million to 11 million tons. The industrialized countries competed for the steady supplies of raw materials, such as oil and rubber, to fuel the machines of industry. Initially, the United States and Russia were among the primary sources of oil, but gradually the Middle East became the central theater of much European colonial diplomatic maneuvering, at times with calamitous political and social consequences. The sources of rubber included the rain forests of the Amazon and Malaysia, with even greater catastrophes for the natives. Copper, increasingly in much demand, was found mainly in developing countries, such as Zaire, Chile, Peru, and Zambia. Precious metals were found in South Africa. In all such countries, colonial powers established their control over drilling and mining, created the necessary infrastructure for communication and transportation, and politically and economically dominated the lives of the local population. As one historian has put it regarding a colonial war, "whatever the ideology, the motive for the Boer War was gold." The colonial scramble for investment opportunities and for markets led to territorial partitions throughout the developing countries, especially Africa, where national boundaries were drawn and redrawn according to colonial interests.

Domestic political and economic considerations, such as the emergence of labor movements and gradual democratization for mass participation, also played a significant role in imperial expansionism. Cecil Rhodes, for example, one of the key leaders of colonial conquests in Africa in the 1890s, stated that "if one wanted to avoid civil wars [at home] one must become imperialist." Sometimes referred to as "social imperialism," such expansionism is said to have been used by government and corporate elites to diffuse tensions at home by creating new opportunities in new lands for the discontented masses while at the same time serving the financial interests of the investors and companies. The Cornish miners, for instance, "left the declining tin-mines of their peninsula en masse for the goldfields of South Africa, where they earned a great deal of money. . . ."

Equally important in domestic politics was the political leaders' drive to bring national glory to their voters. Raising the national flag over a colonial territory meant enhancing the colonizer's prestige in global power politics. Germans, for example, are said to have "deeply resented the fact that so powerful and dynamic a nation as themselves should own so notably smaller a share of colonial territory than the British and the French, though their colonies were of little economic and less strategic interest." Each major power sought to create its own sphere of influence and to maintain a favorable balance of power vis-a-vis the other competing powers, even if it meant inheriting distant territories with little apparent rationale, as in Italy's conquests of Ethiopia and Libya.

Another significant factor is, of course, geo-strategic considerations that complement economic concerns. In the case of the British empire, for example, India was the keystone of British strategy. Its geographic location necessitated British control over vast areas of land and sea-lanes from the Atlantic to the Indian Ocean. Conquering new territories and populations of "dervishes" and "heathens" in the short run enhanced the British government's chances for reelection and in the long run strengthened the voters' identification with the nation-state, which in turn strengthened the legitimacy of the government.

Sources: See Eric J. Hobsbawm, *The Age of Empire, 1875–1914* (New York: Vintage Books, 1987), 45, 63–69; Franz Ansprenger, *The Dissolution of the Colonial Empires* (London: Routledge, 1981).

populations.[82] What happens to such states when the market for their export crops falls, or when several of their neighbors produce the same crop for export? Although global commerical networks made the world appear geographically smaller, the world was also becoming more and more divided between rich and poor countries, those highly dependent and those with diverse economies. Technology—industrial, communications, and military—contributed considerably to this widening gap. This is not to say, however, that there were no industries in the developing countries. Some already had rapidly developing financial centers with prospering elites and relatively small white-collar sectors. This was true, for example, in Argentina, Brazil, Uruguay, and New Zealand, where, in addition to infrastructural development and mining, colonial economies also included textile and food processing, as well as iron and steel industries. However, none paralleled the modern industrial machinery in the developed countries, with their centers of production and banking.[83] Where economic diplomacy failed, gunboat diplomacy tilted the balance of power in favor of the Western industrialized states. One country, however, Japan, sought systematically to counteract and offset dependency on other powers (see Box 3.4).

By the turn of the twentieth century, the number of industrial countries increased, and their economies grew at a rapid pace. With industrialization also came expansion of the middle class and, thus, a wider consumer base for their products, particularly in larger countries, such as the United States. These developments made the industrialists far more confident than they were in the 1870s and gave them an optimism about science, technology, and "human progress" that was put on display at gala "world's fairs" and expositions in Europe and the United States. According to one estimate, the Western industrialized countries alone "constituted 80 per cent of the international market.[84] By 1913, both the United States and Germany had become the leading producers of industrial goods and mining, providing 46 percent and 23.5 percent, respectively, of the four major industrial economies, surpassing Britain (19.5 percent) and France (11 percent).[85] Symbolically, however, neither country was yet recognized as the world leader—a status retained by Britain, at least until the U.S. intervention in the First World War in 1917.

No longer did the Latin American, African, and Asian countries export most of their products to Britain alone. While London remained "the switchboard" for the world's international business transactions, including financial, trading, and shipping services, the other industrialized countries imported in constantly growing volume from the developing world. Britain's enormous foreign investments and merchant shipping, nevertheless, kept it at the center of the international capital market. In 1914, Britain still maintained 44 percent of the world's foreign investments.[86]

The period between the First and Second World Wars was a major turning point in world economic and political history. It was the beginning of the dissolution of the European empires. At the closing of WWI, the traditional global power configurations as dominated by Europe began to shift, and the United States and Japan emerged as economic, political, and military powers. The former had the advantage of being both a Pacific and an Atlantic power, while the latter moved to dominate East Asia. The British never regained their pre-WWI naval supremacy, and the other powers never successfully reasserted their dominion over colonial subjects.[87] In the meantime, Woodrow Wilson's attention to "self-determination" inspired anti-colonial movements seeking independence throughout the colonies. The global economic collapse during the Great Depression, shortly after the First World War, caused financial havoc and compelled Europeans to pay greater attention to their economies at home.[88] Consequently, as colonial territories demanded independence, Europeans were hardly in a position to continue to impose their rule.

While the relative significance of the causes and consequences of the Great Depression are debated to this day, a brief summary is in order to underscore some of the structural and policy problems, with an eye toward drawing lessons for the future. The First World War provided the opportunity for economies outside Europe, particularly for the United States, to increase their domestic agricultural and manufacturing production to supply consumer goods to the European markets. After the war, as Europe recovered and resumed full production, its products challenged the competitors, especially the U.S. farmers, who had made significant wartime gains in international markets. Europe's return to commercial production added deflationary pressures to the world economy, further complicated by the European war debts, particularly the $4.7 billion and $4 billion Britain and France, respectively, owed to the United States, as well as Germany's failure to pay the heavy war reparations as required under the Versailles Treaty.[89] London and particularly Paris were reluctant to pay their war debts to the United States as long as Germany failed to pay its war reparations, estimated by the Reparations Commission to be at about 132 billion gold marks (or about $31.4 billion) in April 1921.[90] To address the economic and political difficulties surrounding these financial issues, in September 1924 the United States introduced the Dawes Plan, whereby it would lend money to Germany so that it could pay the reparations, and so that Britain and France, in turn, could pay their debts, with interest. It was significant that under this plan the United States acquired the right to appoint half of the board members of the German Reichsbank, which gave the bank greater autonomy at home but caused resentment on the part of the French who, fearing German military expansionism, would have preferred to keep Germany in a weaker position. Thus, a complex set of factors—including declining investments in new production capabilities, high interest rates, a

BOX 3.4

THE EMERGENCE OF JAPAN AS A WORLD POWER

The emergence of Japan as an industrial power dates back to the late 1860s. For more than two centuries the Tokugawa government had promoted and protected the dominant traditional feudal society. After a period of cultural imports from China, the Tokugawa shoguns discouraged commercial businesses and insulated Japan from nearly all external forces, including restricting of Christianity and closing the country's ports to foreign ships. In 1853, however, the arrival of U.S. Admiral Perry at Tokyo (then Edo) Bay, with his fleet of "black ships," was perceived by the Japanese as a profound shock, affront, and threat to their country. Admiral Perry demanded the opening of Japan's ports for trade and for U.S. port operations on the way to China. The Japanese, however, were already familiar with Western colonial conquests throughout East Asia, especially British involvements in China and the Opium Wars. As a result, they were determined not to allow foreign powers to gain control over their political economy. They reacted to U.S. demands with strong nationalism and determined to introduce reforms, which in turn led to internal turmoil, the collapse of the Tokugawa government, the restoration of the emperor, and a crash program in adopting Western technology.

During the Meiji Restoration, beginning in 1868, massive industrialization projects were launched to maintain political and economic independence from foreign powers. Unlike Western capitalism, however, Japan's model of industrialization was not premised on laissez-faire philosophy; rather, the government played a central role as the primary force behind industrialization. The country's political and economic leadership closely cooperated to strengthen the country economically and militarily against any future foreign threats. In sharp contrast to the expanding role of the U.S. government in regulating corporate behavior to prevent monopolies (as in the case of the Sherman Antitrust Act, for example), the Japanese government intervened to encourage industrial development and expansion through large conglomerates (*zaibatsu*) or monopolies.

In the case of Japan, the purpose of industrialization was not only to make a profit and to compete effectively in the international market. As with the mercantilist policies of European kings and princes in the fifteenth and sixteenth centuries, the purpose of industrialization also was to strengthen the state and national security against foreign enemies. To this end, Japan emphasized the production of iron and steel, armaments, and shipbuilding. The state spent enormous sums on the construction of ports, railways, highways, and educational institutions to modernize the economy.

Finally, Japan, with almost no natural resources, embarked on a number of patently aggressive military ventures. It defeated China in the 1894–1895 war, and Russia in the 1904–1905 war, and it annexed Korea and the island of Taiwan in 1910. Indeed, Japan was the nation most often at war during the first half of the twentieth century. These wars further expanded industries related to the military, including shipbuilding and technological development and modernization, and gained needed resources.

By the end of the First World War, with the state's guidance, Japan's industrialization had advanced so far as to make the country one of the major suppliers of textiles, weapons, and industrial machinery on the world market. During the depression years, the Japanese responded to economic pressures with further militarization and aggression. Under the doctrine of the Greater East Asian Co-Prosperity Sphere, Japan invaded Manchuria in 1931 and China proper in 1937; by the early 1940s, Japan was in possession of vast territories throughout East Asia, including European colonies. Economic sanctions (boycotts and embargoes) against Japan by the United States and the League of Nations failed to dissuade Tokyo from this policy of power aggrandizement. Japan styled itself as Asia's hope against a decadent, dominant, and racist West.

The Second World War signaled the final demise of the old European colonial empires. The French military was in ruins as it was quickly overrun by the Nazi army. Britain fared better than France, but it, too, hardly recovered from the damages. Belgium, the Netherlands, Spain, and Portugal were in no position either economically or militarily to maintain their control for long. After Hiroshima and Nagasaki, Japan surrendered its claim to the Greater East Asian Co-Prosperity Sphere, but it was to achieve even greater prosperity and foreign influence through peaceful competition.

Sources: See Edwin O. Reischauer, *The Japanese* (Cambridge: Harvard University Press, 1981), 78–86, 95–102; Paul Knox and John Agnew, *The Geography of the World Economy* (London: Edward Arnold, Hodder and Stoughton, 1989) 149–152; Bruce Cummings, "The Origins and Development of the Northeast Asian Political Economy: Industrial Sectors, Product Cycles, and Political Consequences," in Frederic C. Deyo, ed., *The Political Economy of the New Asian Industrialism* (Ithaca: Cornell University Press, 1987), 44–83.

sudden drop in public confidence, economic populism and mercantilism, shortages of gold in the world economy, the absence of international financial organizations and of a hegemonic center powerful enough to maintain financial stability in world markets—is said to have led to the depression.[91]

The United States, where the Great Depression first exploded in the form of the stock market crash in October 1929, was one of the major economic powers in the world. Its manufacturing production comprised 42.5 percent of total world production, Germany's 11.5 percent, Britain's 9.5 percent, and France's 6.6 percent. U.S. exports constituted 5 percent of its total GNP, while the other three industrialized countries were more trade dependent at 14 percent.[92] After World War I, the world economy experienced rapid, though not necessarily even, growth, and U.S. and European banks made capital easily accessible. Among the major borrowers from the U.S. and British banks in the 1920s were the Central (including Germany) and Eastern European countries, most of them successors of the Austro-Hungarian empire; economic ties with Germany had rendered these states vulnerable to Berlin's economic ill health. German hyperinflation, caused by government efforts to rebuild the economy, pay reparations, and expedite the postwar recovery well into the late 1920s, did not appear to threaten the world economy as long as international loans were available to meet the German demand. Confidence in the expanding German economy, therefore, remained high as production continued to increase. In 1928 and 1929, however, the U.S. banks recalled their credit to Eastern Europe in order to finance loans for stock speculations in New York. In 1930, after the stock market crashed, the Austrian Creditanstalt lost $20 million, setting investors and the public into panic. This was followed by the collapse of the German economy in mid-1931, which in turn exacerbated the financial crisis in Eastern Europe, already in financial paralysis.[93]

It has been argued that, at this crucial moment, better-informed monetary and fiscal policies could have averted the world economic meltdown, but the panic was not confined to the investors and to the public. Policymakers also panicked. Rather than loosen trade barriers to encourage easy access to markets, governments reacted by immediately raising tariffs. Particularly debilitating were, on the one hand, the Federal Reserve Board's decision to tighten the money supply, when in fact it should have increased it to stimulate demand, and, on the other, the Hawley-Smoot Act in 1930, which elicited retaliatory measures from foreign governments and led to a sharp decline in U.S. exports.[94]

There were a number of contributing factors when the depression first hit the United States. About 50 percent of the American population still lived in rural areas. The rapid industrialization of the previous decades had skewed the nation's income distribution in favor of the top 5 percent of the population, and the absence of a sufficiently large middle class and consumer market meant lack of a sufficiently large pool of capital for consumption, while the wealthy engaged in speculation. The corporate structure was another factor. Consumption levels of major manufactured goods—for example, cars—and housing construction reached their saturation point in 1926–1928 and began to decline thereafter. Reduction in consumption led to reduction in production and in corporate investments in new production facilities, while the major corporations, as economic historian John Kenneth Galbraith put it, "had opened [their] hospitable arms to an exceptional number of promoters, grafters, swindlers, imposters, and frauds. This, in the long history of such activities, was a kind of flood tide of corporate larceny."[95] Holding companies and large investment trusts borrowed heavily and defaulted on bonds, which led to total bankruptcy.

The flawed banking structure also contributed to the depression. The banking system consisted of independent entities, which not only made management of national finances difficult but also made it virtually impossible to control the downturn trend once public confidence in banks dropped and general panic set in. Moreover, since the government banking system, headed by the Federal Reserve Board, did not control the stock market, companies preferred to purchase and merge existing factories to show profits to their shareholders, which in turn encouraged massive stock speculation—the value of shares traded in 1925 was $27 billion, which rose to $87 billion in 1929.[96] Rather than stabilize the market, the Federal Reserve in fact chose to reduce the money supply and, in doing so, further contributed to the deflationary pressures. In 1930, reflecting public sentiment in favor of mercantilist-protectionist policies to protect industries and jobs at home, the Hoover administration and Congress succumbed to economic populism and passed the Smoot-Hawley Act, raising tariff barriers on imports.

These structural and policy problems were compounded by a financial crisis in foreign economic relations and reckless lending practices of U.S. commercial banks. By the First World War, the United States had emerged as a major international creditor, and the postwar reconstruction and rising levels of speculation encouraged easy credit to governments in need, especially in Europe and Latin America. Major U.S. commercial banks were more than willing to extend credit for the asking, and some even "convinced," through much bribery, foreign governments to seal deals despite the potential risks involved. Galbraith has noted, for example, the deal involving a $50 million loan secured by J. and W. Seligman and Company and the National City Company of the National City Bank for Peru. In 1927, they paid $450,000 to Juan Leguía, son of Peruvian President Augusto B. Leguía (1919–1930), "for not blocking the deal."[97]

Unemployment increased dramatically immediately after the market collapse. In the United States, between 1921 and 1925, the annual average unemployment rate was about 4.3 percent, which dropped to 3.2 percent during the period 1926–1929. In 1930, that figure rose to 8.9 percent, in 1931 to 16.3 percent, in 1932 to 24.1 percent, and in 1934 to 25.2 percent, its highest level.[98] Indeed, unemployment hovered around 18–19 percent until the U.S. entered the Second World War in 1941. This pattern, with some variation in magnitude, was repeated in industrialized and developing economies.

As previously noted, by the late 1920s, Central and Eastern European countries, including Germany, were in debt to British and American banks. In 1931, the German economy collapsed, and in 1932 it stopped paying the war reparation; Adolf Hitler rose to power shortly after. The economies of Latin American countries also collapsed, and one after another they defaulted on their loans.[99] The collapse of the German and Latin American economies exacerbated domestic financial imbalances, and political difficulties in the United States and Britain led to a domino effect, with enormous implications for the global political economy. In 1934, Britain and France defaulted on their war debts.[100]

Thus, the Great Depression was a global phenomenon, and its devastating impact was not limited to the industrialized economies. In the developing countries, as in the industrialized ones, it led to financial disasters and to political instability, and it unleashed a chain of events that dramatically altered their history. The collapse of the European and U.S. markets caused a sharp drop in demand for Latin America's principal export products, such as coffee, sugar, meat, and metals. The total value of Latin American exports declined by 48 percent in the 1930–1934 period.[101] The economic pressure of the depression, as in the industrialized economies, led to economic populism, extremism, and political instability. In a large number of Latin American countries—for example, Argentina, Brazil, Chile, Guatemala, Honduras, and Peru—the military ousted the constitutionally elected civilian leaders, whose economic policies were discredited. The military in some countries, such as Argentina, despite their ideological tilt to European fascism, responded with moderation and a willingness to negotiate certain conditions for trade, so as not to further jeopardize their markets abroad.

Elsewhere, repressive colonial policies fueled peasant rebellions and intensified revolutionary movements against colonial rule. In the Belgian Congo, for example, rebellions were quelled ruthlessly, albeit temporarily. In southern Nigeria, when the British colonial administration, seeking to compensate for losses in Europe, instituted the poll tax in 1927 and as news of a planned extension of taxes (as "hut taxes") to women spread, peasant rebellions led to the "War of the Ibo Women" (referred to by the Ibo as *ogu umanwayi*) in December 1929; and the bloodshed compelled the administration to lower the tax.[102] In Kenya, where the "hut tax" on women was added to the poll tax on men, the tensions led to the Mau-Mau revolutionary movement, which lasted right up to independence in the 1960s. Peasants had tolerated the poll tax and exploitation before the depression, as long as they could afford to pay with their labor, but the increases during the depression proved too excessive. Some peasants left cash crop production for jobs in the cities, which possessed an even smaller industrial base than their Latin American counterparts and, therefore, were hardly in a position to absorb newcomers. While on the whole Africa had less to lose in the depression than did Latin America, this situation exacerbated conditions in both rural and urban areas.

Middle Eastern and Asian societies were equally affected by the Great Depression. In the aftermath of the First World War, most of the Middle East—with the exception of Egypt, Persia (Iran), Saudi Arabia, and Yemen—were British and French mandates. The four states were sovereign in their domestic and foreign affairs, but the mandatory powers exercised direct and indirect influence on their economies as well. The British mandate included Iraq, Transjordan, and Palestine, but London maintained control over Egypt's finances, the Suez Canal, and Persia's oil fields. The British not only were interested in Middle Eastern resources but also thought it geopolitically essential to maintain control over communications and trade with India. The French controlled Syria and Lebanon as mandates but also dominated the North African Maghrib, and these territories were integrated into the French franc bloc.[103] Egypt, ruled under a local monarchy with British colonial tutelage,suffered the most during the depression, primarily because of its heavy dependence on exports, especially cotton (80 percent). As the nation's trade balance deteriorated, state intervention in the economy increased, but Egypt's industrial and financial programs, supported by theprivately owned Bank Misr, advanced the interests mostly of industrialists and landlords.[104] Due to gold reserves,the state budget was not as severely affected as in other countries, but the government failed to introduce policies to address some of the country's fundamental problems, such as population increase, abject poverty and hunger,and illiteracy.[105]

As in other parts of the developing world, the economic and political problems during the depression, particularly under the burdens of colonial rule, led to the emergence of popular organizations in Egypt that channeled public discontent and provided public services in the absence of government initiatives.[106] The Muslim Brotherhood, founded by Hasan al-Banna in 1928, developed into a major public-service organization, encompassing 500 branches and tens of thousands of members throughout the country. Its leadership believed that Western economic and cultural penetration was the primary cause of Egypt's economic and social malaise and that rectification of the situation required revival of Islam and the *shari'a,* whose implementation, Banna argued, would lead to greater social and economic equality and political stability. Accordingly, the Muslim Brotherhood, in cooperation with proponents of labor unions, advocated unemployment benefits, welfare programs, land reform, and national self-sufficiency. It established soup kitchens, free hospitals, and schools for technical and religious training.[107]

In the mandated territories, Britain and France paid little attention to the needs of the local population, while unemployment and declining purchasing power intensified political, economic, and religious tensions, as nationalist movements for independence caused deep divisions among the various ethnic and religious communities. Particularly troubling was the mandatory powers' emphasis placed on free trade, when in fact they had introduced protectionist tariffs for their own domestic economies at home. One newspaper, *Le Commerce du Levant,* protested in 1935: "No Member-State of the League of Nations Assembly in Geneva does, in fact, stick to free trade. But all the members of this Assembly demand the application of this system to Syria and Lebanon."[108] In Lebanon, between 1931 and 1933 alone, 118 local industries declared bankruptcy.[109] Added to these pressures was the British and French insistence that the local economies, as successors to the Ottoman empire, contribute to the repayment of the Ottoman debt, which led to increases in taxes, further aggravating conditions.

In India, as elsewhere, colonial policy—in this case, exclusively British—was primarily concerned with using the local economy to satisfy creditors and to sustain finances in London. In the post-WWI period, the declining prices of silver (India's main coin in circulation), rice, and textiles led to serious trade imbalances for the economy and fiscal imbalances for the colonial administration. The colonial administration reduced the circulation of silver by nearly 30 percent (from 3.1 to 2.2 billion rupees) between 1927 and 1931, and by 1938 the currency (coins and notes) in circulation was reduced by 40 percent.[110] At a time when agricultural prices for what peasants produced were dropping and their debt was rising, the British decision in 1931 to abandon the gold standard led to increases in gold prices as well. In order to service their debts, peasants were virtually pressured to "sell their wives' gold ornaments or sell some of their land to richer neighbors and money lenders."[111] It is worth quoting Rothermund's description of the situation:

> The enormous stream of 'distress gold' which flowed out of India in this way helped to support the sterling bloc. The British had not expected this flood, and [Sir George] Schuster [of the colonial administration] was amazed when he saw the piles of beautiful gold ornaments in the government of India's currency office. But once the stream of gold was there, the British did everything to perpetuate it. The officers of the government of India used to state in public that this stream was simply due to the fact that the Indians sold their gold because they got a good price for it, but in secret files they admitted that deflation and indebtedness made the peasants part with their gold. . . . The edifice of British Indian finance now had a solid foundation, built on the distress of India's indebted peasants.[112]

By the time agricultural prices recovered in 1937,[113] peasant rebellions had spread throughout India, and the Indian National Congress, headed by Mahatma Gandhi and Jawaharlal Nehru, gained momentum and emerged as the leading organization for the national liberation movement. The British retaliated with repressive measures, while promising constitutional reforms. During the Second World War, the contributions by Indian industries and nearly 2 million soldiers to the British economy and military exceeded the debt the colony owed to London; since London purchased Indian goods on credit, by the end of the war London was in fact indebted to India. After the war, "it proved to be much easier to grant independence to a creditor than to a debtor."[114]

In China, the Republican Revolution of 1911–1912 had overthrown the Ch'ing (Manchu) dynasty, which had ruled the empire since 1644, but the republican euphoria soon evaporated as the new government failed to establish political and economic stability. Regional divisions under "warlordism" and the inability of the national leadership to unite the country led to a chaotic political and financial situation. Moreover, despite the revolution, China still remained under British semicolonial rule, as it had been since the Opium Wars, and its finances were closely tied to events and decisions in the British empire, although, since the turn of the century "Open Door" policy, the United States had gained a prominent role as well. When the New York stock market crashed in 1929 and the depression hit the world economy in the early 1930s, China was in the midst of internal political and economic crisis—a situation made worse by the Japanese invasion of Manchuria in 1931, followed by the proliferation of Japanese industries behind China's tariff walls and the Japanese invasion of China proper in 1937. As in India, the British and increasingly the United States supported the Chinese financial system, as long as it served their interests, and, as in India, China's finances (the tael silver-based currency) depended heavily on the value of silver in world markets. Falling silver prices wreaked havoc on the Chinese economy. The government abandoned the tael in 1933 and replaced it with the yuan and gold.

The leading, quasi-fascist Kuomintang Party, under the leadership of nationalist Chiang Kai-shek and the banking magnate families, such as the Soongs, instituted protectionist policies and encouraged **import-substitution** industries, which at first, albeit briefly, appeared to strengthen the economy. Nevertheless, such policies failed to protect the economy against the depression, which hit China hard in 1933, exacerbating existing political tensions; as in Africa, Latin America, and India, peasants and, increasingly, urban dwellers were drawn to revolutionary movements against the Kuomintang, a process that led to the protracted civil war and culminated in the Communist Revolution in 1949.

Japan was politically more stable than China, but it could not, as hard as it tried, insulate its economy from external pressures. Japan relied on its gold and dollar reserves to support the yen, and it appeared to have a fairly well-managed monetary policy in the mid-1920s. The earthquake of 1923 foreshadowed the impending crisis. As the reconstruction required enormous capital, the value of the yen depreciated rapidly. On the positive side, this made Japanese exports—silk, for example—attractive in foreign markets. Inflationary pressures, however, led to the hemorrhage of Japan's gold reserves, and, although the value of the yen was enhanced, domestic prices fell sharply well into the early 1930s. As in Latin America, the economic crisis gave rise to a military government to protect the nation against what it perceived as incompetent civilian leaders, and, as in Germany and Italy, the military set the country on an expansionist course to resolve domestic problems. The military invaded Manchuria in 1931 in violation of the Japanese constitution, while at home it launched a campaign of terror against its opponents and former civilian leaders, including the murder of finance ministers Inouye and Takahashi and Baron Dan, the head of the Mitsui Corporation.[115] The military adopted import-substitution industrialization and rearmament programs, which strengthened the *zaibatsu,* major corporate conglomerates, including Mitsubishi, Sumitomo, and Nissan, built on a pyramid of subcontractors and suppliers run by small family shops. This rapid industrialization campaign rested primarily on the ruthless exploitation of urban and peasant workers. Particularly vulnerable were the young girls in the workforce, who lived in the factory towns near the textile mills and factories. Under the deteriorating financial conditions, the poor were confronted with the dilemma of selling their daughters either to the factories or to prostitution.[116] Unlike in Latin America, Africa, and India, no significant peasant-based rebellious movements emerged in Japan.

In the final analysis, Kindleberger has argued, when all explanations of the depression are considered, a central deficiency in the international economic system during the inter-war period must be emphasized as a fundamental cause of the depression:

> [T]he 1929 depression was so wide, so deep, and so long because the international economic system was rendered unstable by British inability and U.S. unwillingness to assume responsibility for stabilizing it by discharging five functions:
> 1) maintaining a relatively open market for distress goods;
> 2) providing countercyclical, or at least stable, long-term lending;
> 3) policing a relatively stable system of exchange rates;
> 4) ensuring the coordination of macroeconomic policies;
> 5) acting as a lender of last resort by discounting or otherwise providing liquidity in financial crisis.[117]

"These functions," he maintained, "must be organized and carried out by a single country that assumes responsibility for the system."[118]

Neither were there any multilateral financial organizations to arrest the world decline to economic depression. Instead, the preferred mechanism was international conferences to address the problems of rising trade barriers and financial difficulties stemming from war debts and German war reparations. These included the conference at Brussels in 1920, Portorose in 1921, and Genoa in 1922, followed by the World Economic Conference sponsored by the League of Nations in Geneva in 1927. None of the countries, however, showed any inclination to reduce trade barriers.[119] The World Economic Conference, thus, demonstrated not only the impotence of the League of Nations but also the inability of the international system to transcend national priorities in order to address crises that were clearly transnational in scope—a condition underscored by the outbreak of the Second World War.

THE EAST-WEST AND NORTH-SOUTH DIVIDE

The United States emerged from the Second World War with its colossal industrial base intact, while the other industrial countries were devastated. In fact, while certain regions of Europe, Asia, and Africa were witnessing the wholesale destruction of their economies, between 1941 and 1944 the U.S. gross national product increased by 72 percent. During the immediate postwar years, the U.S. economy accounted for about 50 percent the world's total GNP.[120] With its economic strength and unprecedented military capabilities, the United States led the post-WWII reconstruction and redesign of the global financial, trade, and military multilateral arrangements that shaped international political and economic relations during the next four decades.

Two major considerations guided the policymakers in Washington. One was to prevent another Great Depression like that experienced after the First World War. That meant that global and regional trade would have to be stimulated with a heavy emphasis on free trade theory. Another and equally potent factor was the perceived threat of communism and Soviet power. The Truman administration sought to build international economic and military systems based on multilateral regimes that would implement the policy of containment and prevent the expansion of Soviet/Communist ideology and power around the world.[121] These two objectives led the United States, still styling itself as anticolonial, into areas previously controlled by nineteenth-century colonial powers Great Britain and France, especially in the Middle East and Southeast Asia.

In the meantime, Washington saw a tremendous growth in its financial and trade relations abroad. For instance, although from the late 1920s to 1946 U.S. foreign direct investments had dropped from $7.9 billion to $7.2 billion, between the late 1940s and early 1960s they increased from about $19 billion to $65 billion, with a net capital return of $16 billion.[122] About 2,800 U.S. corporations had foreign operations, especially manufacturing industries whose foreign investments reached 17 percent of domestic investments and accounted for over 20 percent of the net profits of manufacturing firms in 1965. Net returns on foreign oil and mining investments alone in developing countries ranged from 57 percent in the Middle East to 17 percent in Venezuela in 1966.[123]

During the 1950s and 1960s, as the world economy grew at a rapid pace, so did MNC **foreign direct investments (FDIs).** The number of new manufacturing MNC subsidiaries around the world increased from about 100 each year in the late 1940s to 700 in the late 1960s.[124] The rapid growth in MNCs immediately after the Second World War was led predominantly by U.S. corporations. By 1960, U.S. firms held about 48 percent of all foreign direct investments in the world economy, while their nearest competitors, the British, held about 16 percent (see Table 3.3). In the manufacturing sector, for example, U.S. foreign direct investment increased from about seventy new subsidiaries per year in the early 1950s to more than 300 in the late 1960s. During the same period, British investment increased from thirty subsidiaries to about 150 per year, while Japanese investments rose from two to thirty per year.[125] This was the period of U.S. hegemony and unprecedented prosperity. The question was, could it last?

THE BRETTON WOODS SYSTEM

International Finance

Even before the Second World War had ended, delegates from more than forty countries met in Bretton Woods, New Hampshire, in July 1944 under the auspices of the United States to establish a new and more manageable international economic system than had been possible just after the First World War. From the Roosevelt administration's perspective, the economic collapse during the inter-war years had occurred because of Washington's unwillingness to play a leading role in international economic relations. The U.S. delegation was convinced that, in view of the general economic conditions in Europe, it would be in the United States' interest to lead the major

TABLE 3.3

Estimated Stock of Accumulated Foregin Direct Investment by Country of Origin, 1914–1983

	1914		1938		1960		1973		1983	
	$m	**%**	**$m**	**%**	**$bn**	**%**	**$bn**	**%**	**$bn**	**%**
Developed countries	14302	100.0	26350	100.0	62.9	99.0	204.4	97.1	555.2	97.4
North America										
USA	2652	18.5	7300	27.7	31.9	48.3	101.3	48.1	227.0	39.6
Canada	150	1.0	700	2.7	2.5	3.8	7.8	3.7	29.1	5.1
Western Europe										
UK	6500	45.5	10500	39.8	10.8	16.3	26.9	12.8	95.4	16.7
Germany	1500	10.5	350	1.3	0.8	1.2	11.9	5.7	40.3	7.0
France	1750	12.2	2500	9.5	4.1	6.2	8.8	4.2	29.9	5.2
Belgium					1.3	2.0	2.2	1.0	6.7	1.2
Italy					1.1	1.7	3.2	1.5	9.8	1.7
Netherlands	1250	8.7	3500	13.3	7.0	10.6	15.8	7.5	36.5	6.4
Sweden					0.4	0.6	3.0	1.4	10.1	1.8
Switzerland					2.3	3.5	7.2	3.4	19.8	3.5
Other developed countries										
Russia	300	2.1	450	1.7	neg.[a]	neg.	neg.	neg.	neg.	neg.
Japan	200	0.1	750	2.8	0.5	0.8	10.3	4.9	32.2	5.6
Australia					0.2	0.3	0.5	0.2	3.0	0.4
New Zealand	180	1.3	300	1.1	n.a.	n.a.	n.a.	n.a.	n.a.	n.a.
South Africa					n.a.[b]	n.a.	2.1	1.0	6.5	1.1
Other	neg.	neg.	neg.	neg.	2.5	3.8	3.4	1.6	9.0	1.2
Developing countries	neg.	neg.	neg.	neg.	0.7	1.1	6.1	2.9	17.6	2.6
TOTAL	14482	100.0	26350	100.0	66.1	100.0	210.5	100.0	572.8	100.0

Source: John H. Dunning, *Explaining International Production* (London: Unwin Hyman, 1988), 74.
[a]negligible
[b]not available

powers' construction of the postwar international economic order.[126] Washington sought to create a new system based on laissez-faire, liberal principles of free trade. An international economic system predicated on such principles, it was believed, would lead to greater prosperity and international cooperation.

The Bretton Woods conference created two bedrock multilateral financial institutions: the International Monetary Fund (IMF) and the World Bank (the International Bank for Reconstruction and Development, IRBD). The former would give loans of hard currencies to countries when their trade was imbalanced and currency reserves were depleted, and the latter would give loans for development projects. Their primary purpose was to buttress free trade and economic recovery through the effective management of international economic relations and the expansion of foreign exchange currency holdings. The United States expended enormous efforts to strengthen both organizations, and Washington enjoyed great influence through a weighted voting system based on the level of contributions to the joint funds. Under the Bretton Woods system, the U.S. dollar dominated international currency values and was the principal currency of exchange, since the currencies of most countries were pegged to it, and in turn the dollar was convertible to gold—$35 per ounce of gold.

International Trade

In addition to the financial arrangements under the IMF and the World Bank, the United States and Western allies also hoped to prevent a resurgence of economic nationalism and protectionist policies believed to have been largely responsible for the collapse of the international economic order after WWI and for leading to political extremism in Germany and Japan. In 1947, again under U.S. leadership, the General Agreement on Tariffs and Trade (GATT) was established in Geneva. Its primary purpose was to reduce trade barriers in order to encourage liberal international trade practices based on international law, liberal international norms, and certain codified rules and procedures for trade negotiations. In doing so, member states were expected to "settle grievances in a manner designed to minimize further restriction of international trade."[127] It was reasoned that all states would prosper under such a system, and that the United States would benefit greatly if foreign states were in a sound and stable political and economic order and able to buy U.S. goods.

Containment and Economic Strategies

Given the war-torn conditions in Europe, the Truman administration adopted a number of policies to improve the economic situation as a way of strengthening the U.S. position in the postwar global political economy. Prosperity and security were seen to go hand in hand. In addition to the multilateral arrangements in the area of finance and trade, the administration adopted the policy of **containment** to combat communism. Thus, in addition to the creation of the Bretton Woods system, the Truman administration also introduced the Marshall Plan, extending $17 billion in economic assistance to Western European countries, even offering it to the Soviet Union. Of particular concern was the popularity of Communist parties in both France and Italy, as the party that most staunchly resisted wartime fascism. Behind the scenes, American economic aid also was sent to the Italian Catholic Church-oriented Christian Democratic Party, after an earlier plan to allow southern Italy to be ruled at least temporarily by American *mafia* leaders fell through.

In the interest of allied recovery, the administration even encouraged Western Europe and Japan to adopt discriminatory policies against U.S. exports and the dollar. The Western European countries subsequently created the multilateral European Payment Union and the Organization of European Economic Development (later the Organization of Economic Cooperation and Development, or OECD) to promote trade relations and manage U.S. aid efficiently. The primary purpose of such U.S. policies was to make European and Japanese industries competitive in the international markets as a way of rebuilding their economies and to develop stable, absorptive, and non-Communist markets for future U.S. exports. Finally, these policies were also intended to create international liquidity (reserve currency) based on the dollar.[128]

Suspicious of U.S. strategy, the Soviet Union established Communist governments in Eastern Europe and rival East bloc economic institutions; ultimately, Moscow also became heavily involved in supporting anti-West, anticolonial "liberation" movements throughout the developing world. Neither the British nor the French, however, could muster sufficient financial and military capability to maintain their pre-WWII colonial status and prevent nationalist or socialist revolutions against their colonial regimes. While European security was the Truman administration's main concern, events in Asia, such as the Communist revolution in China and the Korean War, drew Washington's economic and political commitments eastward. In places like the former Belgian Congo and Portuguese ruled African colonies, Washington also was sometimes embarrassed by its NATO connections to hated colonial rulers.

Massive U.S. involvement, such as the Korean and Vietnam wars and NATO in Europe, however, required huge expenditures, which in turn resulted in the transfusion of U.S. dollars into the international economy. Given the fact that the United States alone had the financial, political, and military capability to assume such a responsibility against Soviet "expansionism," both the European allies and Japan readily acquiesced to U.S. leadership while keeping their defense budgets down.[129] The massive—and, some would say, excessive—implementation of containment cost the United States enormous sums, as billions of dollars left for other countries in the form of economic and military assistance and the maintenance of a strong military presence on bases throughout the world. As early as the mid-1950s, events around the world had begun to challenge U.S. hegemonic leadership (see Box 3.5).[130]

The Erosion of the Bretton Woods System While during the European reconstruction period after the Second World War the question was how to expand dollar liquidity, in the 1960s the question was how to stop the hemorrhage. The dollar glut had considerably weakened its value, and people were less willing to use it as reserve currency. This adverse situation was largely due to the enormous expenditures in maintaining military bases around the world, foreign economic and military assistance, and private foreign investments abroad, leading to balance-of-payments deficits.[131] In addition, U.S. gold reserves declined in proportion to dollars held abroad, which further diminished confidence in the dollar and the U.S. economy. Indeed, French President Charles de Gaulle "insisted on exchanging dollars for gold, albeit in part for reasons related more to French nationalism than the value of the dollar."[132]

BOX 3.5

CHALLENGES TO U.S. HEGEMONIC LEADERSHIP: THE SUEZ CRISIS AND THE HUNGARIAN REBELLION, 1956

Gamal Abdel Nasser, the nationalist president of Egypt, was intensely opposed to European colonial involvement in Egypt and Arab countries. He viewed British control over the Suez Canal as a humiliating effort to maintain British colonial status in the region. After the British established the Baghdad Pact anti-Communist alliance in early 1955, Nasser grew even more suspicious of British and U.S. designs in the Middle East. Later that year, he responded by establishing closer relations and secured an arms deal with the Soviet Union. Less than a year later, faced with disagreements with the Eisenhower administration and the latter's withdrawal of support for the construction of the Aswan Dam, Nasser nationalized the Suez Canal and turned to the Soviet Union for support.

In turn, after much diplomatic maneuvering, the British and the French, with Israel's support, responded with military force to Nasser's nationalization. The Eisenhower administration not only refused to take part in but actually condemned the invasion and proposed—*with the Soviet Union and a Soviet-supported government* in—a cease-fire resolution in the U.N. Security Council. Here, for the first time since the beginning of the Cold War, U.S. leadership was questioned not only because the United States did not support the invasion but, more important, because it opposed its own NATO allies. But the Eisenhower administration went a step further. By "freezing" British assets in U.S. banks, the administration forced the Bank of England "to draw down its gold and dollar reserves by some 15 percent to meet the demands for gold and dollars from holders of sterling—more than $250 million. Much of the large-block selling was taking place in New York, and there was speculation that it was being initiated by the Treasury Department at Eisenhower's direction." The British economy was on the verge of collapse, and the Eisenhower administration insisted on an immediate cease-fire as a condition for further financial support. The cease-fire occurred on November 6, 1956. Washington had demonstrated the diplomatic value of economic muscle. The lesson was not lost on the French, who subsequently led the resistance to U.S. (and British) economic penetration of Europe.

During the same weeks, another crisis was developing in Budapest, Hungary. On October 23, an anti-Communist demonstration spread throughout the capital. The Soviet Red Army intervened and crushed the demonstrations. Unlike the Berlin airlift of 1948, however, this time there was no response from the United States. According to most accounts, the Eisenhower administration had refrained from taking action because it feared such a military conflict would lead to WWIII. Regardless of Eisenhower's domestic election-year considerations, Eastern and Western Europeans looked at the U.S. inability or unwillingness to actively support the prodemocracy movement as a sign of weakness in commitment and leadership. Thus, by the late 1950s and early 1960s, confidence in U.S. leadership within NATO and around the world was already beginning to deteriorate, even as U.S. power remained paramount.

Source: See James A. Nathan and James K. Oliver, *United States Foreign Policy and World Order,* 3d ed. (Boston: Little, Brown and Company, 1985), 199–203.

As Western European and Japanese economies recovered, they were no longer so inclined to support dollar hegemony, and Washington began to rethink the wisdom of encouraging partners, such as Japan, to maintain artificially low exchange values for their currencies, thereby reducing the prices of their products and expanding exports. Disagreements over economic and military policies in Asia, the Middle East, and Africa grew more vocal and visible to the public. While the Cold War and the presence of a common enemy in the Soviet Union continued to keep the Western alliance together, neither European nor Japanese allies were willing to acquiesce readily to U.S. policy priorities. U.S. involvement in Vietnam proved to be one such policy, as few allies were willing to join the fight. The U.S. defeat in the Vietnam War particularly exacerbated the situation and considerably weakened world confidence in its position in the global political economy.[133]

By the late-1950s the European and Japanese economies had recovered from World War II. At the same time, as their reserves increased, U.S. gold holdings dropped from $24.4 billion in 1948 to $19.5 billion in 1959. The amount of dollars in circulation abroad increased from $7.3 billion to $19.4 billion, respectively, and, for the first time, in 1960, U.S. dollars held abroad exceeded U.S. gold holdings. Throughout the second half of the 1960s, "the export of dollars directly attributable to military spending increase[d] to more than $3.2 billion annually."[134] After

1966, the U.S. balance of payment deficit increased to more than $2 billion. In addition, in the absence of offsetting tax increases, the Johnson administration's war spending and Great Society programs led to inflationary pressures, causing a further drop in international confidence in the dollar.[135]

As inflationary pressures, trade deficits, and rising unemployment levels boosted political pressures, the Nixon administration, in August 1971, the administration responded by unilaterally terminating the dollar-gold convertibility that had been the financial keystone for the stability of the Bretton Woods system. Nixon's surprise announcement shocked the world, and at the time it was believed that the shock had irrevocably shaken public confidence in the U.S. dollar. With the advantage of hindsight, however, it seems more realistic to argue that, although the dollar was devalued and public confidence was shaken throughout the 1970s, the dollar did not lose its international status in financial markets in the long run. The U.S. economy was not falling apart; the economy was still the world's largest, with the largest trade volume, and the United States still had considerable military power. The most significant adverse consequence of this "Nixon shock" was that for the first time since WWII the country began to experience a relative decline in its economic and political/military status.[136]

The post-WWII international economic order had been predicated on Western principles of liberalism, with emphasis on free trade and laissez-faire capitalism, which in many respects proved to be an unrealistic guide for the future of the developing world. During the 1950s and 1960s, the developing countries experienced turbulent phases of decolonization, with accompanying losses of foreign investment capital, followed by efforts to achieve rapid economic development, nation- and state-building. Under such conditions, liberalism not only appeared irrelevant but, more important, a Western neo-colonial strategy to continue exploitation, easy trade, and repression of former colonial subjects. After the Second World War, at least three anticolonial umbrella movements—Pan-Islamism/Pan-Arabism, Pan-Africanism, and communism/socialism—seriously challenged European colonial rule. These movements called for total independence based on national economic, political, and military power, for preferential trade policies to protect infant industries, and for nation-building and state-building by way of industrialization and modernization (see Box 3.6).

Instead of embracing liberalism, the movements opted for national and collective strategies to rectify what they perceived as structural deficiencies and economic disparities within the international system, including global trade issues (see Table 3.4). Individually, some adopted import-substitution industrialization (ISI) to produce at-home products previously imported from abroad. This, they hoped, would lead to greater economic independence and to sustainable economic development and growth. A small number of developing countries, most notably China and Tanzania, insisted on a strategy of maximum self-reliance and pursued a more isolationist (China) or regionalist (Tanzania) course.

In the Middle East, for example, anticolonialism and nationalism in the 1950s and 1960s led to the nationalization of the former British- and French-owned banks and the development of new ones with local capital. In Egypt, Gamal Abdel Nasser nationalized, in addition to the Suez Canal, British and French holdings, including the British Barclay's, renamed the Bank of Alexandria, the National Bank of Egypt, the French Banque du Caire, and all private holdings in the Bank Misr. In Syria, foreign banks were consolidated under the new government-owned Commercial Bank of Syria; in Iraq the government-owned Raifidain Bank controlled all internal and foreign financial transactions, as did the Algerian government under the Banque Nationale d'Algérie and the Crédit Populaire d'Algérie. These policies were justified on grounds of national self-determination but also on grounds of liberating Islamic banking and finance from Western influences. In fact, they were more nationalist than Islamic in orientation. In Saudi Arabia, however, because of greater sensitivity to Islamic principles of finance and credit, particularly with respect to the *riba,* the monarchy resisted the development of central banking, instead preferring to rely on monetary agencies. However, financial difficulties in the 1960s and pressures to exercise greater independence from foreign operations led the Saudi government to nationalize foreign holdings, such as Citibank, and to establish the Saudi American Bank, whereby Saudis would retain 60 percent of the bank's capital, and Citibank the rest. This shift in policy led to the creation of Saudi-European banks, such as the Saudi British and the Saudi French banks.[137]

In general, the process of economic development and patterns of employment particularly affected the division of labor along gender lines, and modernization both hurt and improved women's position in society.[138] Despite new opportunities and increased education, women tended to be subordinated in processes of production and assembly. As governments encouraged urbanization and industrialization,

BOX 3.6

THREE MOVEMENTS

Pan-Arabism and Pan-Islam emerged during the second half of the nineteenth century and gained considerable momentum at the turn of the century. While the two movements were to some extent distinct, they nevertheless originated in the Middle East in reaction to European colonialism. Among their leaders were Jemal al-Din al-Afghani, Muhammed Abdu, Chekib Arslane, Amin el-Husseini, and Saad Zaghlul, who sought to strengthen Arab nationalism through unity against colonial powers, as well as to modernize Arab countries. In December 1931, el-Husseini organized the World Islamic Congress, and in 1945 the League of Arab States was founded. Since then a number of Arab leaders have sought unification based on pan-Arabism and pan-Islam as a counterforce against Western economic and military superiority and dominance. Examples include Nasser's Pan-Arabism throughout the 1950s and 1960s and Khomeini's Pan-Islamism in the 1980s. In general, though, despite their temporary successes in mobilizing mass public support, they have failed in their efforts to achieve a united pan-Arabic or pan-Islamic community.

Pan-Africanism, led by Marcus Aurelius Garvey of Jamaica and W.E.B. DuBois of the United States along with a host of African leaders, such as Kwame Nkrumrah of Ghana, Jomo Kenyatta of Kenya, Julius K. Nyerere of Tanzania, and Sekou Toure of Guinea, had an even more difficult task at unification and modernization. Like their Arab counterparts, while they agreed in principle that European colonization would have to end, they were divided as to the means of achieving nation-building and development after independence and generally were more dependent on former colonial rulers than were their Middle Eastern counterparts.

Finally, communism and socialism also attracted many nationalists fighting against Western colonialism. While communism and its variants made some inroads in the Middle East and Africa, its full force as a nationalist revolutionary ideology was seen in Asia, particularly in China under Mao Tse-tung and in Vietnam under Ho Chi Minh. In both countries, initially the primary targets were the British (in China) and the French (in Vietnam), gradually replaced by the United States and the local ruling elites they supported. The collapse of the Soviet Union for all practical purposes has rendered Communist movements far less legitimate and attractive than they were historically. However, the IMF's demands that developing countries dismantle socialist institutions and nationalized industries as a condition for its loans continue to make Marxist critiques of capitalism appealing to those who oppose such Western influences in their domestic political economy.

Source: See Franz Ansprenger, *The Dissolution of the Colonial Empires* (London: Routledge, 1981), 125–41.

usually at the expense of agriculture, young girls and women mostly from poor families moved from the farms to the cities to find jobs.[139] Those entering the labor market in factories operating in the formal sector received lower wages than their male counterparts, while those who failed to secure such employment relied increasingly on the "informal economy" and took even more poorly paid jobs in sweatshops and the service sector.[140] Repressive state and corporate

TABLE 3.4
World Exports by Major Areas, 1963–1987 (% of Total)

Exporting Region	1963	1973	1979	1987
Industrial area[a]	64.3	68.2	63.4	68.2
Australasia, South Africa	2.8	2.7	2.1	1.7
Developing countries[b]	20.7	19.2	25.3	19.7
Centrally planned economies	12.1	9.9	9.3	10.4
Total	100.0	100.0	100.0	100.0

Source: A.G. Kenwood and A.L. Lougheed, *The Growth of the International Economy, 1820–1990* (London: Routledge, 1992), 287, citing General Agreement on Tariffs and Trade, *International Trade,* 1987–88, Vol. 2, Table AA10.
Note: Discrepancies due to rounding.
[a]Includes all Western Europe, United States, Canada, and Japan.
[b]Of which the oil-exporting countries recorded 5.9%, 7.3%, and 12.8% in 1963, 1973, and 1979, respectively.

BOX 3.7

THE NONALIGNMENT MOVEMENT

The Nonalignment Movement was primarily concerned with international economic inequalities and maldistribution of resources between the Western industrialized countries and the developing countries. The latter argued that the post-WWII international economic system was the product of the colonial legacy and that, while its members gained formal independence from colonial powers, their economies continued to suffer. Also, the movement was labeled "nonaligned" because its members viewed the Cold War as destructive and wasteful, depleting much needed resources on armaments that otherwise could have been used for economic growth in developing countries. Singham and Hune have identified five fundamental principles reflecting the common concerns of the nonaligned members:

1. Peace and disarmament, especially the reduction of tensions between the major powers
2. Independence, including the right of self-determination of all colonial peoples and the right of equality among all races
3. Economic equality, with an emphasis on restructuring the existing international economic order, particularly with respect to the growing and persistent inequality between rich and poor nations
4. Cultural equality, with an emphasis on restructuring the world information and communications order, and opposition to cultural imperialism and the Western monopoly on information systems
5. Universalism and multilateralism through strong support for the United Nations system—whose principles are also nonaligned principles—as the most appropriate body to deal with all global issues. Consequently, the Movement resisted efforts within its own organization to create alternative structures at the expense of the UN.

Source: See A.W. Singham and Shirley Hune, *Non-Alignment in an Age of Alignments* (London: Zed Books, 1986), 14–15.

policies, combined with the traditional constraints of patriarchal family structure, contributed to the persistence of women's subordinate position in society.[141]

Collectively, the developing countries pursued two closely interrelated strategies to combat dependence on the North: the Nonalignment Movement and the creation of the Group of 77 (G-77). The **Nonalignment Movement** was founded at the Bandung Conference in 1955 by more than twenty developing countries as an alternative to the East-West conflict, and, by the mid-1980s, its membership had increased to more than 100 states, although not all of them were neutral in the Cold War. Among its most famous leaders were Josip Broz Tito of Yugoslavia, Jawaharlal Nehru of India, Gamal Abdel Nasser of Egypt, Kwame Nkrumah of Ghana, Mohammed Ben Bell of Algeria, and Fidel Castro of Cuba (see Box 3.7). Further, as Asian and African countries gained independence in the 1950s and 1960s, their numbers at the United Nations grew and fundamentally altered the composition of the organization. To capitalize on their numerical strength, the second strategy the developing countries pursued was the creation of the Group of 77 (G-77) in 1964 at the UN Conference on Trade and Development (UNCTAD). This organization provided the developing countries a global forum to express their grievances and demands. The relationship between UNCTAD and the Nonalignment Movement was strengthened in the early 1970s, and in 1974 the UN General Assembly adopted the Declaration on the Establishment of a New International Economic Order (NIEO), reiterating the five principles of the Nonalignment Movement.

In addition, Muslim states joined together to create the Organization of the Islamic Conference (OIC) in 1969 (today it consists of fifty-four countries). The principal goals of the OIC include promoting Islamic solidarity and cooperation in various aspects of international political economy, strengthening consultation among Muslim states in international organizations and cooperation between member and nonmember states, eliminating all vestiges of Western colonialism, and supporting the Palestinian people in their conflict with Israel.[142] It was in this context of intensifying North-South conflict that OAPEC (Organization of Arab Petroleum Exporting Countries) raised the price of oil from \$3 to \$12 per barrel and imposed an oil embargo on the United States and the Netherlands in retaliation for their support for Israel during the 1973 Arab-Israeli war. Another "oil shock" occurred in the late 1970s during the political turmoil in Iran, causing a decade of global inflation. As a result, throughout the 1970s, huge sums of dollars (a record \$40 billion in 1977 and \$74 billion in 1980) went abroad to import energy resources, causing further loss of confidence in the value of the dollar as it declined on foreign exchange markets.[143] High oil prices led to high levels of inflation and unemployment, stagnanting economies, and trade deficits. At the same time, taking advantage of the oil revenues, Islamic banking proliferated in the Arab oil-producing countries. In 1975 the Dubai Islamic Bank was created, in 1977 the Kuwait Finance House, in 1979 the Bahrain Islamic Bank, and in 1982 the Qatar Islamic Bank.[144] International banks scurried to lend out excess "petro-dollars" circulating in the world economy, fueling a global debt crisis when many less developed countries could no longer export enough to pay the interest to foreign lenders.

Leaders of various industrial, labor, and agricultural sectors in the United States and other industrialized countries called for protectionist policies to fend off foreign economic competitors. Europe's and Japan's growing share of global trade was viewed as the direct cause of U.S. economic malaise and decline in general. For the first time in the post-World War II boom period, real (inflation-adjusted) income of American workers failed to keep pace with the cost of living. Throughout the 1960s and 1970s, the United States also had higher unemployment than the other G-7 countries (in the late 1980s, that changed).[145]

Despite adversities, the U.S. economy as a whole fared better than most other industrialized economies. Although high interest rates, driven by inflation in the United States, added to the financial burden of the debtor developing countries, they also enhanced the value of the dollar and the attraction of investing in U.S. financial institutions and securities (stocks and bonds). Greater demands for dollars pushed the exchange rate even higher. Gradually, the U.S. economy recovered, inflation subsided, unemployment eased, and public confidence restrengthened the dollar.

THE EMERGING INTERNATIONAL POLITICAL ECONOMY: THE 1980s, 1990s, AND BEYOND

The stronger dollar brought advantages and disadvantages for the U.S. economy. It meant lower costs for imported goods, but it also meant higher prices for American products abroad. As a result, foreign demand for U.S. goods dropped, while imports from foreign countries increased. The U.S. *trade deficit* reached $122 billion in 1985, $145 billion in 1986, and $160 billion in 1987, and in the process tens of thousands of American jobs were lost.[146] In 1985, in response to the weakening of the United States trade competitiveness in foreign markets, largely because of

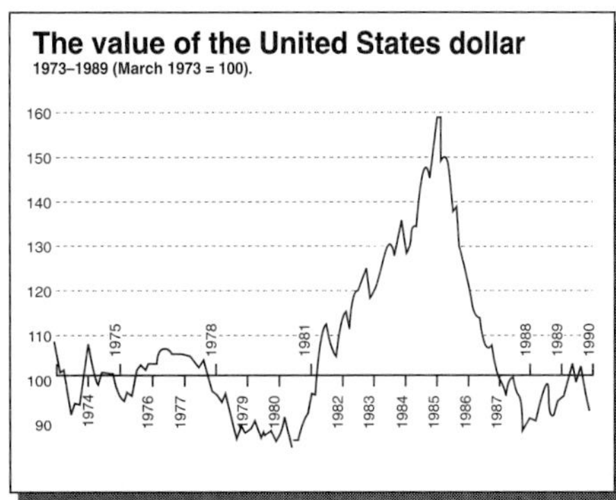

FIGURE 3.1
Source: Copyright © 1991. by St. Martin's Press, Inc. *From American Foreign Policy: Patterns and Processes,* 4E. by Kegley, et. al. Reprinted with permission of St. Martin's Press.

the overvalued dollar (see Figure 3.1), the Group of Five—the United States, Britain, France, Japan, and West Germany—met secretly at the Plaza Hotel in New York in an effort to develop an agreement to lower the dollar's value. The Plaza conference failed to produce significantly positive results, and, in 1987, representatives of the G-5 countries met in Paris at the Louvre to strengthen their exchange rate stabilization and financial management strategies.[147] As U.S. competitiveness in the global market was increasingly challenged by European and Japanese firms (for example, see Table 3.5), the United States consistently registered trade deficits, and the budget deficit, driven by revived military spending, averaged about $150 billion during the 1980s, a sharp increase from $60 billion before Ronald Reagan's election in 1980.[148] The budget deficit was covered largely by foreign money invested in U.S. markets at relatively high interest rates.

In addition to multilateral approaches through G-5 and G-7 conferences, which proved ineffective, Washington adopted unilateral quasi-protectionist policies. Under Section 301 of the 1974 Trade Act and the 1988 omnibus trade act, also known as "Super 301," Congress mandated the president with authority "to identify countries engaged in unfair trade practices with a view toward negotiations to seek remedies or face U.S. retaliation." Although it did not specifically mention target countries, "Super 301" was obviously aimed largely at Japan and the export-oriented so-called Asian tigers—Hong Kong, Singapore, South Korea, and Taiwan.[149] In 1989, U.S. imports from Japan, its second leading trade partner for decades, reached $97 billion, while the United States' exports to Japan totaled

TABLE 3.5
Distribution of the Export Trade of Major Industrial Countries, 1937–1987 (% of total)

Country	1937	1950	1960	1973	1979	1987
United Kingdom	20	20	14	9	10	9
United States	23	32	28	20	20	17
France	7	10	9	11	11	10
Germany[a]	16	6	15	19	19	20
Other Western Europe[b]	20	20	21	23	24	23
Canada	8	9	7	7	6	7
Japan	6	3	5	11	11	15
Total	100	100	100	100	100	100

Source: A.G. Kenwood and A.L. Lougheed, *The Growth of the International Economy, 1820–1990* (London: Routledge, 1992), 289.
[a]Germany experienced a reduction in geographical size between 1937 and 1950; only West German trade is considered after 1945.
[b]Includes Belgium–Luxembourg, Netherlands, Italy, and Sweden.

$45 billion. The Bush administration was not very supportive of such protectionist policies, however, and, despite the trade imbalance, in April 1990 it exempted Japan from "Super 301" and even allowed "Super 301" to expire. In early 1994, the Clinton administration revived "Super 301," but by then, in many ways, as Kegley and Wittkopf have noted, the United States had become "a more 'ordinary' power. . . ."[150]

In the late 1980s, on the heels of record foreign investment in the United States, for the first time in more than fifty years the country, once the world's biggest creditor, became a debtor country (in fact, the largest debtor). By 1989, its assets abroad were $1.4 trillion, while foreign holdings in the United States had reached well over $2 trillion—a net debt of about $663.7 billion.[151] Of course, this type of investment debt is different from that of countries simply unable to pay their bills. Although countries still flocked to "invest in America," the United States had receded somewhat from its post-World War II preeminence. Prior to that war, Washington's share of global economic exchange was about what it was in the mid-1990s. The period of controlling well over 50 percent of the world's wealth was probably abnormal and transitory. The U.S. position in the global political economy declined as foreign direct investments—85 percent of which were by Western Europe, Canada, and Japan—since 1988 surpassed U.S. foreign direct investments abroad.[152] Although the U.S. dollar still enjoyed the status of being the most important international currency, it has been argued that a new monetary order, such as the European Monetary System or an internationalized yen, could threaten its status in the future. The challenge then was for the United States, its leaders, and the public to adjust to a role of prominence but not necessarily dominance.

The multilateral institutions created under the Bretton Woods system under U.S. leadership facilitated further globalization of production by multinational corporations and set the foundations for the globalization of finance through international public and private banks and institutions. In addition to the emergence and reemergence of major and new competing centers of power, such as Germany, Japan, and the European Union, the 1980s and 1990s witnessed the further globalization of international economic activities as another factor contributing to the relative U.S. decline. However, a number of fundamental elements in the international system also impede this process of globalization, and, if the history of the nation-state is a guide to the future of the international political economy, there is little to suggest that the nation-state will disappear anytime soon. The next section briefly discusses globalization of the international political economy in the late twentieth century, focusing on two central ingredients in the development of globalism: multinational corporations and international finance. Next we examine three factors challenging globalism: the persistence of the nation-state, nationalism, and protectionism.

Consolidation of Globalism

Multinational Corporations and Globalization MNCs are corporations that extend their productive operations beyond the boundaries of a single country. Because of their transboundary nature, they become directly and indirectly involved in various countries' international and domestic economic and political affairs. Historically, corporations had been involved in trade and extraction activities outside of their home country, but the production of industrial goods was seldom undertaken away from "home." Largely due to lack of technology, they could not establish complex networks of international production systems. Although by WWI overseas manufacturing had already been developed, rapid growth in the globalization of production began to take place in the 1960s and 1970s because of developments in technologies of "circulation," or service, activities to build global infrastructures.[153]

While only a small number (about 5 percent) of MNCs are truly global, their size and economic activities give them enormous power in national economies. Multinational corporations, such as General Motors and IBM (U.S.), Toyota (Japan), Daimler-Benz (Germany)—now Daimler-Chrysler (Germany-U.S.)—and Unilever (the Netherlands), comprise more than half of the 100 largest economic units in the world, nation-states constituting the other half.[154] MNCs have been involved in international economic activities for centuries, but they became a particularly significant force in international relations during the twentieth century, especially after the Second World War.

The 1970s and 1980s, however, proved to be a turning point in the power configurations within the global market. While U.S. multinational firms remained predominant, by the early 1970s German and Japanese investments were growing rapidly relative to the U.S. and Britain. Japan's share of foreign direct investment consistently increased from 0.7 percent to 5.7 percent to 11.7 percent, and West Germany's from 1.2 percent to 6.5 percent to 8.4 percent between 1960 and 1985. By the mid-1980s, Japan had become the third largest holder of foreign direct investments, and by the early 1990s for the first time it ranked first in the amount of dollars expended annually in foreign investments.[155] Indeed, many economists noted that poor planning led Japanese banks to some very unwise foreign investments, especially in real estate, leading to failed loans and near banking failures in the 1990s.

In addition to the major industrialized powers, the 1970s and 1980s also witnessed the emergence of MNCs from a small group of developing countries, most notably East Asia's newly industrializing countries (NICs)—South Korea, Taiwan, Singapore, and Hong Kong.[156] Predominantly export-oriented economies, the governments and enterprises adopted aggressive, strategic industrial and exporting policies, such as *industrial targeting,* and worked closely together to expand their new industries. Industrial targeting involved the promotion of "winning industries," as well as various incentives for technology-intensive corporations. In the early 1980s, South Korea and Taiwan began to discourage light industries and adopted industrialization policies for further development of their industrial base through their heavy shipbuilding, steel, cars, and chemical industries. These policies entailed greater government involvement in the coordination of and support for production and export-import relations in key sectors of the economy, and they led to financial overcommitments, which eventually weakened their economies and currencies.[157]

The expansion of MNC operations across continents and the transnational integration of their subsidiaries through various communications and capital networks have propelled world economic activities toward globalization. Governments that promise lower taxes or various tax incentives attract MNCs to invest in their countries. Governments also provide certain *public goods* and services, such as a well-maintained infrastructure, including roads, port cities, railroads, airports, communications systems (mail, fax, phone lines), waste collection, and sufficient protection for property. Sometimes an MNC enters the host country not to compete but instead to establish a monopoly with the local suppliers and with the available pool of joint production partners, including the host government. Pepsi-Cola's efforts in China's interior during recent years and AT&T's contracts with some of the former Soviet republics are examples of such attempts. They offer certain location-specific or firm-specific services and products with an eye toward controlling a sector of industry. Not surprisingly, MNCs resist pressures to share control over investments and profits but increasingly have agreed to regulations and taxes by host governments, as well as to partnership with entrepreneurs in host countries interested in and required to purchase a share of the corporation, including the creation of joint ventures.

Strategic management and **alliances,** formed by MNCs to take advantage of foreign markets and local business familiarity with cultures, regulatory policies, customs and practices, involve various forms of ownership and collaboration among companies and governments. They have increasingly led to monopolistic and *oligopolistic* tendencies at home and abroad. Semiconductor producers in Japan, for example, have a near monopoly in the home market. However, while they cooperate to maintain high prices in the domestic market, in foreign markets their prices and products are subject to greater competition from foreign MNCs. In this sense, then, "these producers act jointly as a monopoly at home but as oligopolists in external markets. . . ."[158]

MNCs are involved in a considerable share of employment and production around the world, accounting for over 25 percent of total world output.[159] Transboundary and industrial divisions have created a global political economic environment of intense international competition for labor. In the 1980s and 1990s, the available labor force in developing countries was three times larger than that of most industrialized countries. Given the fact that workers in developing countries receive lower wages, North-South labor competition has intensified as countries try to attract more jobs.[160] Also, contrary to the Marxist theory, in such a competitive economic environment, workers are less likely to organize radical political movements. As a result, more companies have relocated their operations to these regions, leading to loss of jobs and lower standards of living, particularly among low- and semi-skilled workers in the industrialized regions, and to demands for greater protectionist policies and newer technologies. In the past two decades, growing trade with developing countries has been linked to an approximately 20 percent drop in the demand for unskilled labor in the North.

International Finance and Globalization International financial networks have expanded with corporate international activities and trade and the growing worldwide integration; hence, the globalization of financial institutions has facilitated the rapid transfer of funds for purposes of savings and investments. Investors acquire holdings in many stock markets throughout the world; "global assets" mutual funds move money rapidly around the globe sometimes to the displeasure of particular governments. By the late 1970s and early 1980s, the globalization of international financial and commodity markets was already in the process of consolidation, facilitated by the advent of worldwide networks of computerized information and telecommunications systems. For example, telecommunications technology eliminated the intermediaries in investment houses, establishing direct links between financial institutions and their clients and gave stock markets instantaneous knowledge of each other's transactions, while widening the scope of international financial activities and reducing their costs.[161]

Following WWII, U.S.-based multinational banks had dominated international banking and lending. While, in the late 1950s, eight U.S. banks had foreign branches abroad with total assets of approximately $3.5 billion, in the mid-1970s more than 125 U.S. banks had established branches abroad with total assets of well over $180 billion. During the early 1970s, thirteen U.S. banks held over two-thirds of all U.S. banking activities abroad, and their international earnings represented over 95 percent of total earnings. By the late 1980s, however, private lending had become truly globalized, as illustrated by the decline of the U.S. position in international lending to developing countries from 50 percent to 10 percent.[162] In part, of course, these patterns also reflect growing caution and alarm about over-lending, rising global debts, and possible loan defaults in many developing countries, such as Mexico.

As we shall see in later chapters, the concept of Eurodollars—that is, dollars on deposit in or borrowed by European financial institutions abroad and in the United States—is a prime example of truly globalized international finance and markets. Eurocurrency deposits have increased rapidly since the 1960s, and currently they account for well over 80 percent of foreign deposits in the United States. Eurodollars have also facilitated the worldwide creation of Eurocenters, including small, developing countries, such as the Bahamas, where governments impose minimum regulations on foreign banks.[163]

During the 1980s, the emergence of stock markets in a number of developing countries, particularly Brazil, Indonesia, South Korea, Malaysia, Mexico, and Taiwan, and international lending by wealthier countries to developing countries also contributed to the globalization of international finance and led to the further consolidation of the global economy. Since a considerable number of emerging stock markets are in export-oriented economies, international liberalization and privatization in the 1980s resulted in rapid economic growth in Latin America and East Asia.

This growth led observers to argue that the post-WWII dichotomous view of the international political economy as being divided between "North" and "South" is no longer appropriate. As the North was never a single, monolithic entity, neither was the South, particularly as measured by the expansion of their production capabilities and trade activities (as discussed in later chapters). Accordingly, the international politica]l economy in the last decade of the twentieth century can perhaps be best seen as divided between the *first industrialized economies (FIEs)* comprised of the older, some would say postindustrial economies of Western Europe, the United States, and Japan; the *advanced industrializing economies (AIEs)* comprised of the emerging but still troubled markets of Argentina, Brazil, Chile, Singapore, South Korea, South Africa, Malaysia, Israel, China, Mexico, and Taiwan; and the *less developed economies (LDEs)* comprised of the less developed countries—thus replacing the monolithic label "South."[164] This classification takes into consideration the economic, technological, and military advantages FIEs have over other regions because of their early industrialization. The trend toward globalization of markets whereby lesser developed economies become more deeply integrated with the world economy through diffusion of technologies and commercialization is most likely to continue in the early part of the twenty-first century. Whether these changes will lead to a structural transformation of the world political economy remains to be seen.

As an increasing number of industrialized and developing countries shifted some of their economic sectors to **privatization** and liberalized trade policies, international investors and *currency speculators* became more involved in international market activities to expand their pool of foreign assets. Rather rapidly, the virtual integration of various international markets, particularly stock markets, as well as international financial institutions led to the development of the "global market" of the 1990s. Despite the fluctuations in market activities in recent years, the global market—in terms of financial, commodity, and various service transactions—grew more integrated among different market sectors and among international public and private institutions. The global market also meant that economic problems in one key region, such as East Asia, would reverberate throughout the world.

Challenges to Globalism

Despite the development of the globalized MNC operations and international finance by way of worldwide telecommunications networks, certain factors in the international system mitigate against further integration and globalization. Three closely interrelated elements are the persistence and power of the nation-state, nationalism, and protectionist sentiments frequently surfacing, especially in times of economic hardship.

The Nation-State The most significant ingredient in the international system that inherently hinders globalization is the nation-state. Both leaders and citizens are loath to surrender the sovereignty of their country to external forces. The nation-state has come to represent more than merely a territorial entity; it has also become an economic, legal, social, cultural, and psychological construct for individuals and collectivities. Despite the diminishing significance of international borders, the nation-state continues to function as the principal unit providing public goods and services—for example, welfare, education, stability, and defense—for citizens within its administrative jurisdiction. Within this system of nation-states, governments assume civic responsibilities, but consistent failure in governmental performance also leads to public discontent, to political instability (as in the former Zaire in the 1990s), and in extreme cases to revolutions to create a new political order, as in Iran and Nicaragua in the late 1970s, or to recreate old national units, as in the disintegration of the Soviet Union in the late 1980s.

Although recently the nation-state has increasingly been compelled to share its traditional "political space" with international actors such as multinational corporations and international organizations (for example, the United Nations and the IMF), the nation-state remains the fundamental unit in the international system, which in fact has witnessed a substantial increase in the number of nation-states—from 21 in the 1770s, to 53 in 1917, to 68 in the mid-1940s, and to 185 (after the collapse of the Soviet Union) in the early 1990s.[165] It is true that MNC operations encompass vast geographical areas, with integrated structures for production, management, and communications and transportation facilities; however, the nation-state continues to perform a pivotal role it had traditionally assumed, and nation-states still enjoy the "sovereign right to arm."[166]

Moreover, although MNCs are usually regarded as private enterprises, a large proportion of them have a significant percentage of their shares held by governments, thus maintaining traditional strong ties between government and enterprise. The French government, for example, held about 94.5 percent of Renault Motors shares in the 1970s. During the same period, the British government held 51 percent of British Petroleum. Company ownership with large bank shareholding includes German companies such as Daimler-Chysler, 30 percent of which was owned by Deutsche Bank, and Japan's Nippon Steel and Mitsubishi Heavy Industries.[167] In general, state-ownership, itself a reflection of the persistence of nationalism, is often deemed necessary to maintain national control over production and profits.

Nationalism The collapse of the Soviet Union signaled the reemergence of one of the most potent social forces that for centuries has shaped and reshaped international relations—namely, nationalism, i.e., the search by cultural groups for political autonomy. Nationalism in its various forms and degrees of intensity has resurfaced with enormous consequences for international political economy. The recent resurgence of nationalism is largely attributable to both domestic and international failures in political and economic performance of governments and various public and private institutions, particularly in the area of national and international economic development. By some counts, there are more than 5,000 ethnic groups in the world, and many of these groups view themselves as oppressed minorities. Some groups style themselves as "nations" and demand greater political and economic equality, some degree of autonomy (as in the case of Quebec), or complete self-determination and independence (as in the case of the former Soviet bloc countries).[168] Most nationalist movements manifest strong attachments to a specific historically defined territory as their homeland, and they demand greater autonomy from the central government or ultimately self-determination and independence (like the Palestinians).

In recent years, an increasing number of scholars have argued that a government can no longer assume that ethnic groups within its jurisdiction will automatically accept its authority.[169] Observers of nationalist movements agree that nationalism and the "crisis of nationality" were among the main contributing factors to the disintegration of the Soviet Union, Czechoslovakia, and Yugoslavia.[170] Russia continues to struggle with this issue in its own vast domain, as does India (Kashmir), China (Tibet), and to an extent, the United States (Puerto Rico).

The resurgence of nationalism, however, has both negative and positive consequences for international political economy and globalization. On the *negative* side, nationalist movements, whose target usually is a dominant government, cause domestic political and economic instability and, in extreme cases, destruction of human lives and property, as in the conflict between Russia and Chechnya, and in Bosnia. Political and economic instability, even of limited magnitude, can divert resources; can hinder economic development, production, and growth; and can dissuade potential investors from considering the country. For proponents of global economic integration and coordination, nationalism jeopardizes opportunities for greater international cooperation and enlarged markets.

On the other hand, nationalism can also be viewed as a *positive* force. In the twentieth century, for example, nationalism challenged and at times destroyed old empires and governments with long histories of tyrannical rule. When successful in establishing a new order, nationalism at least created opportunities for experimentation with democratization, egalitarianism, and modernization, as in the cases of the American Revolution against the British empire and the former Soviet countries against the Soviet empire. Such opportunities for modernization accelerate international economic activities, increase foreign investments, and integrate new national economies into the global political economy.

Protectionism A challenge closely related to globalism that also exemplifies both forces of nationalism and the nation-state is **protectionism**—that is, regulation or taxation imposed on foreign goods and services to restrict their importation into a country. Protectionist measures include **non-tariff barriers (NTBs),** antidumping regulations (which prohibit the sale of foreign goods for lower prices abroad than at home), restrictions on the quality and quantity (that is, quotas) of foreign goods, *orderly market arrangements (OMAs), voluntary export restraints (VERs)* agreements (that is, quotas), safety as well as health regulations, intellectual property rights, and government subsidies for domestic producers.[171] Some regulations are multilateral, while others, such as VERs, are bilateral agreements aimed at promoting "fair trade" relations (in this context, two-way balanced trade), as in the case of U.S.-Japanese agreements during the 1980s.

Since the mid-1970s, there has been a dramatic rise in neo-mercantilist policies designed by states to weaken or limit foreign competitors. In 1974, for example, the Long-Term Arrangement Regarding International Trade in Textiles was increasingly accompanied by a host of OMAs and VERs in various industries, including automobiles, motorcycles, consumer electronics, steel, and footwear. During the second half of the 1970s, protectionist regulations increased especially in the industrialized countries, undermining GATT's principles for trade liberalization. As some observers have pointed out, during the first half of the 1980s, for example, the European Community and at least seven countries initiated more than 1,500 antidumping cases against cheap foreign exports.[172]

Of particular significance in this regard has been the role of the United States. After the Second World War, the United States played a leading role in the construction of the liberal world economic order, largely because it stood to gain most from free trade relations. As corporate and government interests converged, the liberal world order reflected U.S. priorities as the United States consolidated its political and economic hegemony. In the 1960s and 1970s, revived European and Japanese economies, however, began to challenge that hegemony. The worldwide economic stagnation, recession, and unemployment in the 1970s and 1980s, as well as the accelerating trends toward globalization, put enormous pressures on policymakers to negotiate various bilateral and multilateral agreements with trading partners while introducing protectionist policies to preserve jobs at home.

THE END OF HEGEMONISM?

In recent years, scholars and practitioners have engaged in heated debates concerning the future of the U.S. role and position in the rapidly changing global political economy.[173] *Declinists* argue that the 1970s and 1980s witnessed the closing of the "American Century." They hold that during the 1970s the United States' military failure in Vietnam, the oil crisis, inflation, and the subsequent chronic deficits and economic difficulties in the 1980s weakened its position as a hegemon. According to this view, the U.S. decline is similar to the crumbling of previous major empires. As an expanding power attempts to protect its geostrategic interests, it expends enormous resources on its military capabilities to dominate the world. Inevitably, however, the cumulative costs of maintaining the empire become too burdensome on the domestic economy, and the hegemon's power begins to erode. In the meantime, another economically and militarily expanding power emerges and establishes its own hegemonic rule over the international system. This inevitable fate, referred to as "imperial overstretch," has been experienced by all empires. The implication of this argument is that the United States is no exception, and its demise has already begun since the 1970s.[174]

Revivalists, on the other hand, maintain that the weakening of the United States' position in world politics does not necessarily mean the end of U.S. hegemonic leadership. While during the 1970s the United States certainly experienced a decline from its post-WWII commanding political, military, and economic status, they contend, its current position can be best characterized as reaching a plateau as the other pre-WWII industrial powers again compete and challenge the United States.[175] Revivalists also note that the United States has recovered economically and has brought its domestic budget deficits under control, even while still running chronic trade deficits. In a sense, hegemons might be called on to import vast amounts in order to provide foreign exchange ("hard currencies"), so that other countries can continue purchasing the hegemon's goods.

Perhaps an equally important question is whether the international system will see hegemonism in any form under any single leadership in the future. If the declinists are correct, then Lester Thurow's statement is revealing: "Rome lasted a thousand years, the British Empire 200 years, why are we slipping after about 50 years?"[176] It is possible that rapid technological changes in communications and transportation make it impossible for a single economic-military power to maintain its position long enough to consolidate its hegemonic order around the world. As Seyom Brown has argued, instead of a hegemonic hierarchy, the future of the international system might be characterized as **polyarchy:** "a situation of many communities, spheres of influence, hegemonic imperiums, interdependencies, trans-state loyalties—some of which overlap, some of which are concentric, some of which are substantially incongruent—that exhibits no clearly dominant axis of alignment and antagonism and has no central steering group or agency."[177]

The argument that a single hegemon can no longer manage the global political economy is further supported by the emergence of *regional communities,* leading to a *multipolar* world without a single hegemonic player. The European Union (EU), North American Free Trade Agreement (NAFTA), and Asia-Pacific Economic Community (APEC) are examples of such regional blocs, or communities, likely to have ample opportunities to expand and to become more inclusive in the future. According to this view, the EU will eventually include the former Warsaw Pact countries of Central and Eastern Europe, especially Poland, the Czech Republic, and Hungary. NAFTA will become a hemispheric bloc to include not only North Americans but also Central and South American countries, especially the "ABC countries" (Argentina, Brazil, and Chile). Japan and China are most likely to dominate any future regional arrangements in East Asia. The Casablanca Conference may lead to a Middle Eastern–North African or even a Mediterranean zone, perhaps gradually extending to most of Africa and southern Europe, while southern Africa could gravitate around South Africa and West Africa around Nigeria (if political stability is reestablished). Thus, the emergence of regional communities, it has been argued, would preclude the rise of a single hegemonic power. In fact, they supposedly emerge precisely because of the hegemon's failure to "manage" the world political economy.

It may be said that the future of the international economy is very much "up for grabs," as discussed in Chapter 13. Indeed, when economic crises emerge, as in a crumbling Russian economy in 1998, who but the United States has the clout to call together and organize an international response? By focusing more clearly on various sectors of today's economy, we can begin to assess the most valid predictions of the future. We adopt such a sectoral focus in Part Two.

Chapter Summary

Prior to the rise of modern international political economy, the world was divided into a number of economic zones, including the Mediterranean and African zones, the Chinese empire, the Amerindians, Central Asia, the South Asian zone, and the Baltic region.

By the mid-1500s, the Europeans' zeal for exploration abroad, commerce, and conquest, had expanded their influence throughout most of the world. In 1648, after the Treaty of Westphalia concluded the Thirty Years' War, the modern international system emerged, comprised of new political units, the nation-states, each with its own juridical entity as a sovereign and national government.

During the age of mercantilism, governments protected their sovereignty against external political and economic competition. The survival of their national economy was viewed as being heavily dependent on the states' ability to secure a strong economic base. Mercantilism also gave rise to enormous expansion in international trade and related activities, as bankers, insurance companies, and other service industries ventured abroad for profits.

By the early seventeenth century, particularly because of superior navigation and military technology, Europeans had become the dominant powers in the world political economy. In order to make their expanding political and economic affairs more manageable, Europeans advocated balance of power strategies, adherence to international legal principles, major-power congresses, and the creation of permanent embassies in economically and geopolitically important countries.

In the late eighteenth century, the industrial revolution first occurred in Britain, and in the nineteenth century it spread throughout Europe and North America and reached other parts of the world—most prominently, Japan. In the process, the second half of the nineteenth century saw major technological achievements in transportation and communications, enabling the more advanced countries to have greater control over the world economy. The primary means of extending their influence over vast regions of the world was imperialism, as they colonized and divided new territories among themselves throughout the developing world.

At the turn of the twentieth century, the world economy was integrated, as governments engaged in numerous multilateral regimes for international cooperation. However, governments also introduced various protectionist measures against foreign competition and, at various times, immigration.

After the Second World War, the prewar major European powers were in no position to return and reconsolidate their colonial dominance in the developing world; the United States emerged as the most powerful country, the new hegemonic leader of the world political economy. The United States led the creation of the Bretton Woods system to better manage the world economy. It included the International Monetary Fund and the World Bank. GATT was also established to maintain national trade barriers as low as possible.

The United States also introduced the containment policy to prevent Soviet-Communist expansion around the world. This policy consisted of economic strategies, such as the Marshall Plan, as well as military-geopolitical strategies, such as the North Atlantic Treaty Organization and a number of bilateral and multilateral mutual security arrangements encircling the Soviet Union. These policies, and particularly the Vietnam War, however, resulted in massive exports of the U.S. dollar, causing a precipitous decline in its value. In response, the Nixon administration terminated certain parts of the Bretton Woods system, thus indicating the decline of the United States as the hegemonic leader of the world political economy. Furthermore, in the 1960s and 1970s, the developing countries, as well as Europe and Japan, sought to rectify economic disparities in world economy and to strengthen their position in world politics. To that end, LDCs demanded a New International Economic Order and organized the Nonalignment Movement and the Group of 77.

Despite the economic hardship caused by the Arab oil embargo in the 1970s, industrialized countries, especially the United States, had recovered a decade later. However, as in the late 1880s and 1890s, because of intensification of trade competition during the late 1980s and early 1990s, industrialized nations tried to impose more protectionist policies against foreign competition and immigration.

Concomitantly, primarily due to technological developments, there has been far greater global trade and financial integration than ever before. Technological changes in communications and transportation radically transformed the nature of international political economy, from being strictly inter-national to a virtually globalized system of production networks. Under such a system, international political economy can no longer be said to be comprised solely of nation-states; MNCs, NGOs, and IGOs also are prominent.

Nevertheless, a number of factors—such as the persistence of the nation-state, a resurgence of nationalism and regionalism, and growing demands for protectionist policies—mitigate against global consolidation of economic and political power. In fact, the reemergence of Germany and Japan, and potentially of China, may suggest that it is no longer possible for a single major power to maintain hegemonic leadership in the new international political economy. Some scholars also argue that, in the closing decades of this century, international competition will be primarily among variants of capitalism itself. Three general models are identified: the Anglo-American model, the Rhine model, and the East Asian–Japanese model.

Points of Contention

Why did mercantilism lead to colonization? What was the role of technology? What were the consequences for the developing world?

What impact did the "discovery" of the Americas have on European power politics? on Africa? on the Mediterranean and Asian economies?

What are the advantages and disadvantages of industrialization? How has industrialization influenced your community?

What were the structural characteristics of empires for the management of the world political economy? How did the U.S. hegemonic system after the Second World War differ from them? How was it similar?

What factors contributed to industrialization in Britain? in Japan?

What domestic considerations led to protectionism in the late nineteenth century? to imperialism?

What impact did (1) World War I and (2) the Great Depression have on the world economy? on the developing world?

What were the advantages of the Bretton Woods system? the disadvantages?

What was the relationship between the U.S. policy of containment and foreign economic assistance, such as the Marshall Plan?

Why did the Nixon administration terminate the gold standard? Did the decline of the Bretton Woods system also signal the decline of the United States as a hegemonic power?

How did the world economy recover from the Arab oil embargo of 1973? Did all countries recover equally? Why or why not?

What was the nature of the relationship between the U.S. (or Japanese, or German) domestic economy and the international political economy in the 1970s and 1980s?

Why does nationalism present an obstacle to globalism? Is it possible that, in the future, divisive nationalist movements will weaken the nation-states?

How valid is the argument that the 1990s were a transitional phase from hegemonism to a polyarchical international system?

Notes

1. Paul Knox and John Agnew, *The Geography of the World Economy* (London: Hodder and Stoughton, 1989), p. 112; Immanuel Wallerstein, *The Modern World System I* (New York: Academic Press, 1974); Wallerstein, *The Modern World System II* (New York: Academic Press, 1980).
2. See, for example, F. C. Lane, "The Economic Meaning of the Invention of the Compass," *The American Historical Review* 68 (1963): pp. 605–617.
3. Aziz S. Atiya, *Crusade, Commerce, and Culture* (Bloomington: Indiana University Press, 1962); Atiya, *The Crusade in the Later Middle Ages* (London: Matheun, 1938); Atiya, "The Crusades: Old Ideas and New Conceptions," *Journal of World History* 2, 2 (1954): pp. 469–475; René Grousset, *Histoire des Croisades et du Royaume Franc de Jérusalem,* 3 vols. (Paris: Plon, 1934); Steven Runciman, *History of the Crusades,* (Cambridge: Cambridge University Press, 1951); Leften S. Staviranos, et al., eds., *Readings in World History* (Boston: Allyn and Bacon, 1970); Stephan Viljoen, *Economic Systems in World History* (New York: Longman, 1974).
4. See, for example, Palmira Brummett, *Ottoman Seapower and the Levantine Diplomacy in the Age of Discovery* (Albany: State University of New York Press, 1988).
5. Paul Kennedy, *The Rise and Fall of Major Powers* (New York: Random House, 1987).
6. Andrew Tylecote, *The Long Wave in the World Economy* (London: Routledge, 1991).
7. George Ostrogorsky Press, *History of the Byzantine State,* rev. ed. (New Brunswick, NJ: Rutgers University Press, 1969), pp. 490–492; Robert Browning, *The Byzantine Empire,* rev. ed. (Washington, DC: Catholic University of America Press, 1992), pp. 240–248; A. A. Vasiliev, *History of the Byzantine Empire,* vol. 2 (Madison: University of Wisconsin Press, 1952 [1971]), pp. 621–637.

8. Browning, *Byzantine Empire,* p. 250; Vasiliev, *History of the Byzantine Empire,* p. 650.
9. Quoted in Carlo M. Cipolla, *Guns, Sails, and Empires: Technological Innovation and the Early Phases of European Expansion* (New York: Minerva Press, 1965), p. 15.
10. *Ibid.,* p. 23.
11. *Ibid.,* p. 32.
12. For an excellent introduction to the history of Africa, see Kevin Shillington, *History of Africa* (London: Macmillan, 1989).
13. The Portuguese empire relied heavily on military forces, and its "comparative advantage was in the deployment of force, not in trading per se." The empire functioned through its military institutions, such as the *Carreira da India,* which controlled the transportation of products to Portugal, and the *Estado da India,* which controlled trade networks (forts and trading posts). The purposes of both were to eliminate competition and to maintain control over geostrategic areas (especially sea-lanes). The Portuguese never consolidated power over production of resources and their distribution in Europe, however. Further, the Portuguese empire remained primarily an Asian empire. Its extension to Brazil—unlike Spain's enormous deposits of gold and silver in the Americas—did not produce sufficient wealth to defray expenses incurred in the overall imperial scheme of things, particularly as imperial trade increasingly but consistently produced unfavorable balances with respect to the administrative and military costs maintaining the empire. By the mid-1500s, the empire had increasingly grown dependent on Spanish silver to finance its operations at home and abroad. In the 1570s and 1580s, amid national economic bankruptcy and political instability, the Portuguese political and economic elite acceded to the demands by the Spanish Crown, King Philip II, for Portugal's annexation with Spain (which lasted sixty years) but with the condition that the Portuguese colonies would remain in Portuguese hands. See Herman M. Schwartz, *State versus Markets: History, Geography, and the Development of International Political Economy* (New York: St. Martin's Press, 1994), 34; John H. Elliott, *Imperial Spain, 1469–1716* (London: Penguin Books, 1990), pp. 271–274.
14. *Ibid.,* pp. 59–60.
15. *Ibid.,* p. 63.
16. Juan Francisco Maura, *Women in the Conquest of the Americas,* trans. John F. Deredita (New York: Peter Lang, 1997), p. 10.
17. *Ibid.,* pp. 7–30, *passim.*
18. Quoted in Helen I. Safa, "Gender Inequality and Women's Wage Labour: A Theoretical and Empirical Analysis," in Valentine M. Moghadam, ed., *Patriarchy and Economic Development: Women's Positions at the End of the Twentieth Century* (Oxford: Clarendon Press, 1996), p. 194.
19. Rubin, *A History of Economic Thought,* pp. 25–26.
20. John Maynard Keynes, *The General Theory of Employment, Interest, and Money* (San Diego: Harcourt Brace Jovanovich, 1953), pp. 333–371.
21. Elliott, *Imperial Spain,* p. 183.
22. Earl J. Hamilton, *American Treasure and the Price Revolution in Spain, 1501–1650* (Cambridge: Harvard University Press, 1934), 34; Elliott, *Imperial Spain,* p. 183, Table 4.
23. Elliott, *Imperial Spain,* p. 199.
24. Imperial expansion and domestic centralization of political and economic power required the reorganization of the bureaucracies, which included reforms in the Council of Castile, in addition to, for example, the creation of the *Casa de Contratación,* the Council of Finance, the Council for the Indies, the Council of Italy, the Council of Portugal, and the Council of Flanders, all directly accountable to the Crown. The two viceroyalties (governors) of New Spain and Peru came under the direction of the Council of the Indies as the supreme authority, thus increasing the number of viceroyalties to nine: the two in the Americas, Aragon, Catalonia, Valencia, Navarre, Sardinia, Sicily, and Naples. This vast organizational machinery was predicated on specific administrative and judicial authority granted to local administrators, whose powers were controlled by the Crown through an intricate network of checks and balances. Centralization also aimed at facilitating direct communication with the Crown, although the long time required for the transmission of despatches over long distances (nearly eight months between Peru and Spain) was never resolved because of the lack of technologies. Elliott, *Imperial Spain,* pp. 171–82.
25. *Ibid.,* pp. 197–98.
26. *Cipolla, Guns, Sails, and Empires,* pp. 48–51.
27. *Ibid.,* pp. 88–89.
28. Kerry Segrave, *The Sexual Harassment of Women in the Workplace, 1600 to 1993* (Jefferson, NC: McFarland and Company, 1994), pp. 12–13.
29. Shillington, *History of Africa,* p. 174.
30. *Ibid.,* p. 175.
31. Cipolla, *Guns, Sails, and Empires,* pp. 80–84.
32. John K. Fairbank, *The United States and China,* 4th ed. (Cambridge: Harvard University Press, 1979).
33. *Ibid.,* p. 8.
34. *Ibid.,* pp. 47–49.
35. C.A. Qadir, *Philosophy and Science in the Islamic World* (London: Routledge, 1988), pp. 104–121; Ahmad Yousif al-Hassan, "Chemical Technology in Arabic Military Treatises," *Annals of the New York Academy of Sciences,* vol. 500: *From Deferent to Equant: A Volume of Studies in the History of Science in the Ancient and Medieval Near East in Honor of E.S. Kennedy,* David A. King and George Saliba, eds. (New York: New York Academy of Sciences, 1987) pp. 153–166.

36. D. L. E. O'Leary, *How Greek Science Passed to the Arabs* (London: Routledge, 1949); F. E. Peters, *Aristotle and the Arabs* (New York: New York University Press, 1968); Seyyed Hossein Nasr, *Science and Civilization in Islam* (Cambridge: Harvard University Press, 1968).
37. The literature on these issues is enormous. For example, see Ira M. Lapidus, *A History of Islamic Societies* (Cambridge: Cambridge University Press, 1988); A. L. Udovitch, ed., *The Islamic Middle East, 700–1900: Studies in Economic and Social History* (Princeton: Princeton University Press, 1981).
38. See Ömer Lutfi Barkan, "The Price Revolution of the Sixteenth Century: A Turning Point in the Economic History of the Near East," trans. Justin McCarthy, *International Journal of Middle East Studies* 6 (1975) pp. 3–28.
39. Charles Tilly, *Coercion, Capital, and European States, AD 990–1992* (Cambridge: Blackwell, 1992).
40. Donald J. Puchala, *International Politics Today* (New York: Harper and Row, 1971), 30. See also Tilly, *Coercion, Capital, and European States, passim.*
41. Peter J. Taylor, *Political Geography: World-Economy, Nation-State and Locality,* 3d ed. (London: Longman, 1993); Nathan Rosenberg and L. E. Birdzell, *How the West Grew Rich: The Economic Transformation of the Industrial World* (New York: Basic Books, 1986); E. L. Jones, *The European Miracle: Environments, Economics, and Geopolitics in the History of Europe and Asia* (Cambridge: Cambridge University Press, 1981); Paul Sweezy, et al., *The Transition from Feudalism to Capitalism* (New York: Science and Society, 1963)
42. Knox and Agnew, *The Geography of the World Economy,* p. 119.
43. George Lichtheim, *Imperialism* (New York: Praeger, 1971).
44. Jeremy Black, *A Military Revolution? Military Change and European Society, 1550–1800* (Atlantic High-lands, NJ: Humanities Press International, 1991).
45. Knox and Agnew, *The Geography of the World Economy,* pp. 119–121.
46. *Ibid.*, p. 122.
47. A. L. Burt, *The British Empire and Commonwealth* (Boston: D. C. Heath, 1956), p. 44.
48. *Ibid.*, pp. 48–49.
49. Robert A. Huttenback, *The British Imperial Experience* (New York: Harper and Row, 1966), pp. 20–37.
50. John Gallagher and Ronald Robinson, "The Imperialism of Free Trade," *Economic History Review,* 2d ser., 6, 1 (1953) pp. 1–15.
51. *Ibid.*, pp. 2–3.
52. Bernard Porter, *The Lion's Share: A Short History of British Imperialism, 1850–1995,* 3d. ed. (London: Longman, 1996); Ronald Hyam, *Britain's Imperial Century, 1815–1914,* 2d ed. (London: Macmillan, 1993).
53. Adam Watson, "European International Society and Its Expansion," in Hedley Bull and Adam Watson, eds., *The Expansion of International Society* (Oxford: Clarendon Press, 1985), 24. See also R. Reynolds, *Europe Emerges: Transition Toward an Industrial Worldwide Society* (Madison: University of Wisconsin Press, 1961).
54. See, for example, A. J. P. Taylor, *The Struggle for Mastery in Europe, 1848–1918* (Oxford: Oxford University Press, 1954).
55. Hyam, *Britain's Imperial Century,* pp. 117–27, *passim.*
56. See Sidney Pollard, *Peaceful Conquest: The Industrialization of Europe, 1760–1970* (Oxford: Oxford University Press, 1981), p. 156.
57. *Ibid.*, p. 156.
58. Knox and Agnew, *Geography of the World Economy,* p. 131.
59. Eric J. Hobsbawm, *The Age of Revolution, 1789–1848* (New York: Mentor Books, 1962); Fernand Braudel, *Capitalism and Material Life, 1400–1800* (New York: Harper and Row, 1967).
60. Frederich Engels, *The Conditions of the Working Class in England* (Stanford: Stanford University Press, 1968), p. 168.
61. Segrave, *Sexual Harassment of Women in the Workplace,* pp. 40–41.
62. Pollard, *Peaceful Conquest.* See also Richard Rosecrance, *The Rise of the Trading State: Commerce and Conquest in the Modern World* (New York: Basic Books, 1986).
63. A.G. Kenwood and A.L. Lougheed, *The Growth of the International Economy, 1820–1990* (London: Routledge, 1992).
64. Quoted in Emily S. Rosenberg, *Spreading the American Dream: American Economic and Cultural Expansion, 1890–1945* (New York: Hill and Wang, 1982), p. 50.
65. *Ibid.*, pp. 50–56. See also Walter LaFeber, *The American Age: U.S. Foreign Policy at Home and Abroad, 1750 to the Present,* 2d ed. (New York: W. W. Norton, 1994), pp. 210–211.
66. Eric J. Hobsbawm, *The Age of Empire, 1875–1914* (New York: Vintage Books, 1987), p. 10.
67. *Ibid.*, p. 45.
68. Alejandro Portes and John Walton, *Labor, Class, and the International System* (New York: Academic Press, 1981), pp. 49–59.
69. Rose L. Glickman, *Russian Factory Women: Workplace and Society, 1880–1914* (Berkeley: University of California Press, 1984), 166; Segrave, *Sexual Harassment of Women in the Workplace,* p. 58.
70. Segrave, *Sexual Harassment of Women in the Workplace,* pp. 52–54.
71. *Ibid.*, p. 60. Kazuko Ono, *Chinese Women in a Century of Revolution, 1850–1950* (Stanford: Stanford University Press, 1978), p. 119.

72. Elsa M. Chaney, *Supermadre: Women in Politics in Latin America* (Austin: University of Texas Press, 1979), p. 169. Note that women's suffrage came even later in Switzerland.
73. Rosenberg, *Spreading the American Dream,* pp. 87–107, *passim.*
74. Knox and Agnew, *The Geography of the World Economy.*
75. Rosenberg, *Spreading the American Dream,* pp. 89–91.
76. Countries trading with Britain would remain at a disadvantage if they continued to conduct their trade in silver, since European countries' commercial relations with each other and other regions were being financed through or directly by Britain. To strengthen the monetary system, Europeans held the Paris international monetary congress in 1867, when they agreed to the formal creation of a universal gold standard, and during the next two decades, a growing number of countries adopted the gold standard. Germany adopted a new currency unit, the mark, based on the gold standard in 1872. Two years later, Holland adopted a gold standard, followed by Norway, Sweden, Denmark, and France by 1879. Russia and Japan adopted the gold standard in 1897. The United States had shifted from bimetallism to gold by 1900, and by 1910 a number of developing countries, including Siam, India, Argentina, Mexico, and Peru, had adopted the gold standard. Nevertheless, with London's commercial centers, merchants, banks, insurance companies, and related financial institutions, Britain remained the financial hub of international trade, and the pound sterling, convertible to gold, dominated the world political economy well into the 1920s. Expanding international trade meant "increased use of sterling as an international currency," since Britain maintained the convertibility of sterling into gold. "Sterling was as good as gold." A key factor contributing to the development of the gold standard was the discovery of large gold deposits in California and Australia in the 1850s, as the value of silver depreciated. See Kenwood and Lougheed, *The Growth of the International Economy, 1820–1990,* pp. 108–110.
77. Pollard, *Peaceful Conquest,* p. 271.
78. *Ibid.*
79. *Ibid.*, p. 275.
80. Robert Melson, *Revolution and Genocide: On the Origins of the Armenian Genocide and the Holocaust* (Chicago: University of Chicago Press, 1992); Leo Kuper, Genocide: *Its Political Use in the Twentieth Century* (New Haven: Yale University Press, 1981).
81. Kennedy, *Rise and Fall of Major Powers.* See also Harry Magdoff, *The Age of Imperialism* (New York: Monthly Review Press, 1969); Michael Mandlebaum, *The Fate of Nations: The Search for National Security in the Nineteenth and Twentieth Centuries* (New York: Cambridge University Press, 1988).
82. P. T. Bauer, "The Economics of Resentment: Colonialism and Underdevelopment," *The Journal of Contemporary History* 4 (1969): pp. 56–59; Walter Rodney, *How Europe Underdeveloped Africa* (Washington, DC: Howard University Press, 1982); Johan Galtung, "Structural Theory of Imperialism," *Journal of Peace Research* 13, 2 (1971), pp. 81–117; Immanuel Wallerstein, *The Modern World System II* (New York: Academic Press, 1980); Wallerstein, *The Capitalist World Economy* (Cambridge: Cambridge University Press, 1979); Franz Fanon, *Wretched of the Earth* (New York: Grove Press, 1963); Andre Gunder Frank, *Capitalism and Underdevelopment in Latin America* (New York: Monthly Review Press, 1969); Frank, "The Development of Underdevelopment," *Monthly Review* 18, 4 (1966), pp. 17–36; Samir Amin, *Imperialism and Unequal Development* (Sussex, U.K.: Harvester Press, 1978); Amin, *Unequal Development: An Essay on the Social Formation of Peripheral Capitalism* (Sussex, U.K.: Harvester Press, 1976).
83. Frank, *Capitalism and Underdevelopment in Latin America;* Frank, "The Development of Underdevelopment"; Amin, *Imperialism and Unequal Development;* and Amir, *Unequal Development.*
84. Hobsbawm, *The Age of Empire,* p. 50.
85. *Ibid.*, p. 51.
86. *Ibid.*
87. Ansprenger, *The Dissolution of the Colonial Empires,* p. 34.
88. Charles P. Kindleberger, *The World in Depression, 1929–1939* (Berkeley: University of California Press, 1973); Kindleberger, *A Financial History of Western Europe,* 2d ed. (New York: Oxford University Press, 1993).
89. Dietmar Rothermund, *The Global Impact of the Great Depression,* 1929–1939 (London: Routledge, 1996), pp. 32–33.
90. Kindleberger, *World in Depression,* p. 19.
91. *Ibid.*, pp. 288–291. See also Herman van der Wee, ed., *The Great Depression Revisited* (The Hague: Martinus Nijhoff, 1972); Christian Saint-Etienne, *The Great Depression, 1929–1938: Lessons for the 1980s* (Standford, CA: Hoover Institution Press, 1984); Peter Temin, *Did Monetary Forces Cause the Great Depression?* (New York: Norton, 1976).
92. Saint-Etienne, *Great Depression,* pp. xiv, 18.
93. *Ibid.*, pp. 8, 16–17.
94. *Ibid.*, pp. 18–21.
95. John Kenneth Galbraith, *The Great Crash, 1929* (Boston: Houghton Mifflin, 1988), 178.
96. Rothermund, *Global Impact of the Great Depression,* p. 50.
97. Similarly, the Chase, through Cuban President Gerardo Machado Morales' (1925–1933) son-in-law, an employee of Chase at the time, secured loan packages from Chase for the Machado government, one of the most corrupt and dictatorial regimes in Latin America. The deal also included

$200,000 personally for Machado. *Stock Exchange Practices,* Report, 1934, pp. 220–221, mentioned in Galbraith, *The Great Crash,* p. 181.

98. U.S. Department of Commerce, *Historical Statistics of the United States, Colonial Times to 1970* (Washington, DC: U.S. Government Printing Office, 1975).
99. In April 1931, Peru suspended its debt payments, followed by Chile in July. In August, Brazil issued a "temporary moratorium" on its debt payments, as did Mexico in January 1932. By the end of 1932, virtually all the Latin American governments had defaulted on their loans. Saint-Etienne, *Great Depression,* p. xiv.
100. Rothermund, *Global Impact of the Great Depression,* p. 67.
101. Thomas E. Skidmore and Peter H. Smith, *Modern Latin America* (New York: Oxford University Press, 1984), p. 53.
102. J. Van Allen, "'Aba Riots' or Igbo Women's War? Ideology, Stratification, and the Invisibility of Women," in N. Hafkin and E. Bay, eds., *Women in Africa: Studies in Social and Economic Change* (Stanford: Stanford University Press, 1976).
103. Rodney Wilson, *Economic Development in the Middle East* (London: Routledge, 1995), pp. 82–83.
104. Marius Deeb, "Bank Misr and the Emergence of the Local Bourgeoisie in Egypt," in Elie Kedourie, ed., *The Middle Eastern Economy: Studies in Economics and Economic History* (London: Frank Cass and Co., 1976), pp. 69–86; Hershlag, *Modern Economic History of the Middle East,* pp. 208–213.
105. One organization advocating greater democratization, for example, was the Egyptian Feminist Union, founded in 1923. Led mostly by upper-class women and proponents of Western liberalism, the union advocated women's suffrage, equality in education, abolition of the veil, and reforms in marriage laws. William L. Cleveland, *A History of the Middle East* (Boulder, CO: Westview, 1994), p. 186.
106. Rothermund, *Global Impact of the Great Depression,* pp. 74–79.
107. See Richard P. Mitchell, *The Society of the Muslim Brotherhood* (London: Oxford University Press, 1969); Eric Davis, *Challenging Colonialism: Bank Misr and Egyptian Industrialization, 1920–1941* (Princeton: Princeton University Press, 1983); Joel Beinin and Zachary Lockman, *Workers on the Nile: Nationalism, Communism, Islam, and the Egyptian Working Class, 1882–1954* (Princeton: Princeton University Press, 1987).
108. Quoted in Z. Y. Hershlag, *Introduction to the Modern Economic History of the Middle East* (Leiden, Netherlands: E. J. Brill, 1964), p. 231.
109. *Ibid.*, p. 233.
110. Rothermund, *Global Impact of the Great Depression,* p. 90.
111. *Ibid.*
112. *Ibid.*, p. 91.
113. *Ibid.* In 1931, British gold reserves totaled £130 million (or about 1.7 billion rupees), but that figure jumped to £825 million (or 11 billion rupees) in 1932.
114. *Ibid.*, pp. 96–97.
115. *Ibid.*, pp. 115–116.
116. *Ibid.*
117. Kindleberger, *World in Depression,* p. 289.
118. *Ibid.*
119. *Ibid.*, pp. 63–67.
120. Charles W. Kegley, Jr., and Eugene R. Wittkopf, *American Foreign Policy: Pattern and Process,* 4th ed. (New York: St. Martin's Press, 1991), pp. 142–143. See also James A. Nathan and James K. Oliver, *United States Foreign Policy and World Order,* 3d ed. (Boston: Little, Brown and Company, 1985).
121. Nathan and Oliver, *United States Foreign Policy and World Order;* Richard Smoke, *National Security and the Nuclear Dilemma* (Reading: Addison-Wesley, 1984); William H. Becker and Samuel F. Wells, Jr., eds., *Economics and World Power: An Assessment of American Diplomacy Since 1789* (New York: Columbia University Press, 1984), especially Ch. 7, Robert A. Pollard and Samuel F. Wells, Jr., "1945–1960: The Era of American Economic Hegemony," pp. 333–390.
122. David Horowitz, ed., *Corporations and the Cold War* (New York: Bertrand Russell Peace Foundation and Monthly Review Press, 1969), pp. 17–19, 135. See also Joan Edelman Spero, *The Politics of International Economic Relations* (New York: St. Martin's Press, 1990).
123. William Appleman Williams, "The Large Corporations and American Foreign Policy," in Horowitz, *Corporations and the Cold War,* pp. 97–98; Joseph D. Phillips, "Economic Effects of the Cold War," in the same volume, p. 188.
124. The latter is particularly crucial to the operations of corporations because today a large portion (over 50 percent) of total world trade in the manufacturing sector is intra-corporate rather than international. See Peter Dicken, *Global Shift: The Internationalization of Economic Activity,* 2d ed. (New York: The Guilford Press, 1992), pp. 48–52.
125. Dicken, *Global Shift,* pp. 52–53.
126. Spero, *The Politics of International Economic Relations,* p. 31.
127. David H. Blake and Robert S. Walters, *The Politics of Global Economic Relations* (Englewood Cliffs, NJ: Prentice-Hall, 1992), pp. 14–15.
128. Kegley and Wittkopf, *American Foreign Policy,* p. 188.
129. Spero, The Politics of *International Economic Relations,* pp. 36–37. In the 1950s, the Eisenhower administration expanded the parameters of containment even further as it sought the institutionalization of containment through globalwide networks of mutual defense alliances, including the Central Treaty Organization (CENTO, the successor of the Baghdad Pact) covering the Middle East, and the Southeast Asia Treaty Organization (SEATO) for Southeast

Asia. Mutual defense treaties were also signed with a host of countries, including Japan, South Korea, and Taiwan. The United States had created the Rio Pact in 1947 for the Western Hemisphere, and ANZUS with Australia and New Zealand in 1951. Thus, at least in terms of defense treaties, containment had been implemented to the fullest extent possible, encircling the Soviet Union, China, and North Korea. U.S. leadership was demonstrated in other areas as well. One important field was the telecommunications industry. U.S. communications corporations, which had concentrated their resources primarily in the domestic market, increased their activities abroad, and for a while U.S. technological superiority dominated the telecommunications industry. After WWII, the proliferation of U.S. telecommunications networks complemented other U.S. firms' activities in foreign economies as well as in military communications systems. The "space age," with built-in U.S.-Soviet competition after the latter launched its first *Sputnik* satellite in 1957, underscored the need for the use of communications satellites in the international arena. Such technological developments led to multilateral agreements, such as at the 1963 Extraordinary Administrative Radio Conference to Allocate Frequency Bands for Space Radio Communication of the International Telecommunication Union. On the domestic front, in 1962, Congress passed the Communications Satellite Act and approved plans to establish the Communication Satellite Corporation. Subsequently, the Department of Defense created the first global space communications system. The four largest industry stockholders—AT&T, ITT, General Telephone, and RCA—held 45.5 percent of the total stock issued. The 1963 Geneva Conference was followed by the 1964 agreements at the European Conference on Satellite Communication to strengthen Europe's competition against the United States. Nevertheless, by then U.S.-based corporations had become quite powerful and visible in the global political economy, and European companies were not in a position to compete with them. Phillips, "Economic Effects of the Cold War," pp. 193–197.

130. David P. Calleo, "Since 1961: American Power in a New World Economy," in Becker and Wells, eds., *Economics and World Power,* pp. 391–457.
131. Kegley and Wittkopf, *American Foreign Policy,* p. 190.
132. *Ibid.*
133. The United States replaced the French in 1954 after the latter's military was decimated at Dien Bien Phu by the nationalist-Communist North Vietnamese. While the Eisenhower administration supported the South Vietnamese government, the first phase of the expansion of the U.S. role took place under the Kennedy administration as the number of U.S. "advisors" increased from about 500 to more than 10,000. On the passage of the Gulf of Tonkin Resolution in August 1964, which granted the president the power to protect U.S. personnel in Southeast Asia, the Johnson administration escalated the conflict into a full-fledged war. Nathan and Oliver, *United States Foreign Policy and World Order,* pp. 306–313.
134. Nathan and Oliver, *United States Foreign Policy and World Order,* p. 298.
135. Spero, *Politics of International Economic Relations,* pp. 37–38. In the 1960s, confidence in the dollar gradually declined as the amount of dollars ($80 billion) in circulation around the world far exceeded U.S. gold reserves ($10 billion). As its goods became more expensive, the United States registered its first trade deficit (about $2 billion in 1971) in the twentieth century.
136. During the 1970s, the sluggish world economy and recession caused a drop in corporate activities, but, even then, FDIs continued to increase. In the 1980s, FDIs grew even more rapidly. While in 1960 total worldwide foreign direct investment was about $70 billion, that number reached about $800 billion in the mid-1980s. Dicken, *Global Shift,* p. 51; DeAnne Julius, *Global Companies and Public Policy: The Growing Challenge of Foreign Direct Investment* (London: Pinter, 1990), p. 60. Just as with trade, however, a large portion (about 65 percent) of worldwide foreign direct investments occurred among Western industrialized countries, while FDIs in developing countries remained at about 30 percent or so in the late 1960s and early 1970s, although the second half of the 1970s witnessed a rise in the average annual rate of FDI in developing countries, from $6.0 billion in 1973–1975 to $10.0 billion in 1976–1978, to $12.8 billion in 1979–1981. Stephen D. Krasner, *Structural Conflict: The Third World Against Global Liberalism* (Berkeley: University of California Press, 1985).
137. Wilson, *Economic Development in the Middle East,* p. 93.
138. Ester Boserup, *Women's Role in Economic Development* (New York: St. Martin's Press, 1970).
139. See V. Spike Peterson and Anne Sisson Runyan, *Global Gender Issues* (Boulder, CO: Westview Press, 1993); Sue Ellen M. Charlton, Jana Everett, and Kathleen Staudt, eds., *Women, the State, and Development* (Albany: State University of New York Press, 1989); Valentine M. Moghadam, ed., *Patriarchy and Economic Development: Women's Positions at the End of the Twentieth Century* (Oxford: Clarendon Press, 1996).
140. Kathryn Ward, ed., *Women Workers and Global Restructuring* (Ithaca: Cornell University Press, 1990).
141. Diane L. Wolf, "Daughters, Decisions and Domination: An Empirical and Conceptual Critique of Household Strategies," *Development and Change* 21 (1990) pp. 43–74. In Latin America, between 1950 and 1980, it is estimated

that the proportion of women in the workforce increased from 18 percent to 26 percent, most of whom were between the ages of twenty and twenty-nine and whose pay was nearly 60 percent lower than that of their male co-workers. Domestic servants constituted 20 percent of active women in the region's labor force. Safa, "Gender Inequality," pp. 195–196; Mary Turner, "Women and Development: The Caribbean and Latin America," in Jane L. Parpart, ed., *Women and Development in Africa: Comparative Perspectives* (Lanham, MD: University Press of America, 1989), pp. 103–114. On experiences in East Asia, see Rita S. Gallin, "Women and the Export Industry in Taiwan: The Muting of Class Consciousness," in Ward, ed., *Women Workers and Global Restructuring,* pp. 179–192.

142. Mir Zohair Husain, *Global Islamic Politics* (New York: HarperCollins, 1995), p. 20.
143. Kegley and Wittkopf, *American Foreign Policy,* pp. 192–194. Some Japanese and German leaders felt that the U.S. benefited from these developments, since higher global oil prices slowed mainly the European and Japanese economies, which were far more dependent on foreign oil supplies than the United States was at that time.
144. Wilson, *Economic Development in the Middle East,* p. 119.
145. During the recession of the early 1980s, the unemployment rate in the United States was about 9 percent, while in the G-7 countries it was about 7 percent.
146. *Ibid.*, pp. 192–195.
147. Kegley and Wittkopf, *American Foreign Policy,* p. 197. Whether such multilateral initiatives can in the long run create a more stable international financial system remains to be seen, but a number of observers, dissatisfied with its chaotic nature, have advocated reconstruction of some form of a gold standard. See Judy Shelton, *Money Meltdown: Restoring Order in the Global Currency System* (New York: Free Press, 1994).
148. The problems associated with the budget deficit were exacerbated by the Savings and Loans (S&L) scandal. While it is well beyond the purview of this chapter to discuss the S&L scandal in detail, suffice it to say that it involved such prominent names as the "Keating Five"—Senators Alan Cranston, Dennis DeConcini, John Glenn, John McCain, and Don Riegle (so named because of their close association with Charles Keating, the head of Arizona's Lincoln Savings and Loan)—at the highest levels of the U.S. government, including Neil Bush, President George Bush's son. It is estimated that during the next decade the scandal cost the taxpayers between $300 and $500 billion, approximately $15,000 per taxpayer or about the cost of the Korean War. Budget deficits and such budgetary "crises" have serious consequences for the U.S. economy at home but also for its ability to remain competitive in the global political economy. Michael Waldman, *Who Robbed America?* (New York: Random House, 1990), pp. 3, 95.
149. Kegley and Wittkopf, *American Foreign Policy,* pp. 207–208.
150. *Ibid.*, pp. 192, 208.
151. *Ibid.*, p. 195.
152. *Ibid.*, pp. 195–196.
153. Dicken, *Global Shift,* p. 5.
154. I. Benson and J. Lloyd, *New Technology and Industrial Change* (London: Kogan Page, 1983), p. 77.
155. *Ibid.*, pp. 52–53.
156. Roy Hofheinz, Jr., and Kent E. Calder, *The Eastasia Edge* (New York: Basic Books, 1982); Frederic C. Deyo, ed., *The Political Economy of the New Asian Industrialism* (Ithaca: Cornell University Press, 1987).
157. Stephan Haggard and Tun-jen Cheng, "State and Foreign Capital in the East Asian NICs," in Deyo, ed., *The Political Economy of the New Asian Industrialism,* pp. 118–119.
158. Edward M. Graham, "Strategic Management and Transnational Firm Behavior: A Formal Approach," in Christos N. Pitelis and Roger Sugden, eds., *The Nature of the Transnational Firm* (London: Routledge, 1991), pp. 160–161.
159. Dicken, *Global Shift,* p. 48.
160. *The Economist,* April 2, 1994, p. 69.
161. Dilip K. Das, "Contemporary Trends in the International Capital Markets," in Dilip K. Das, ed., *International Finance* (London: Routledge, 1993), p. 16. In the case of U.S. corporations, as investment activities increased abroad, so did their financial needs increase accordingly. As a growing number of U.S. corporations expanded their foreign operations, U.S. banks followed their customers and became international to provide the needed financial services. Their operations included the so-called Edge Act corporations (which were subsidiaries of U.S. banks authorized by the Edge Act of 1919 to operate as international banking under the Federal Reserve's supervision) and the establishment of representative offices abroad, IBFs (International Banking Facilities, as authorized by the Federal Reserve in 1981), and full-service branches. Acting as intermediaries, banks developed various financial services to cater to MNCs' needs, including short- and long-term debt services and markets for foreign currencies. Tim S. Campbell and William A. Kracaw, *Financial Institutions and Capital Markets* (New York: Harper-Collins, 1994), pp. 213–215.
162. Stephany Griffith-Jones and Osvaldo Sunkel, *Debt and Development Crises in Latin America: The End of an Illusion* (Oxford: Clarendon Press, 1986), pp. 68–69, 76–77.
163. Rudi Weisweiller, *How the Foreign Exchange Market Works* (New York: New York Institute of Finance 1990), p. 132.
164. This classification differs somewhat from the *World Bank Atlas* method, which is based on income (GNP per capita). Thus, for example, while the World Bank classifies

Singapore among the high-income group, that country would be considered among the AIEs, rather than FIEs, according to our categories. Some countries, such as Russia and China, may be more difficult to classify. The World Bank lists Russia, also referred to as one of the former Soviet "transitional economies," in the lower middle-income group (countries with a GNP per capita of $695–$2,785), while China is listed in the low-income group (countries with less than $695 GNP per capita). See *World Tables 1995,* pp. 763–764.

165. Gabriel A. Almond and G. Bingham Powell, Jr., eds., *Comparative Politics Today: A World View,* 6th ed. (New York: HarperCollins, 1995), Fig. 1.1, p. 4.
166. See Gilles Paquet, ed., *The Multinational Firm and the Nation-State* (Don Mills, Ontario: Collier-Macmillan Canada, 1972); Jon P. Gunnemann, ed., *The Nation-State and Transnational Corporations in Conflict, with Special Reference to Latin America* (New York: Praeger, 1975).
167. George Modelski, ed., *Transnational Corporations and World Order* (San Francisco: W. H. Freeman, 1979), pp. 57–58.
168. Stephen Ryan, *Ethnic Conflict in International Relations* (Brookfield, VT: Dartmouth, 1990), pp. 26–27; Rodoflo Stavenhagen, *The Ethnic Question: Conflict, Development, and Human Rights* (Tokyo: United Nations University Press, 1990); Daniel Patrick Moynihan, *Pandaemonium: Ethnicity in International Politics* (Oxford University Press, 1993); Ted R. Gurr, *Minorities at Risk: A Global View of Ethnopolitical Conflicts* (Washington, DC: United States Institute of Peace Press, 1993). Problems associated with rapid industrialization, such as urbanization, widening socioeconomic gaps, persistent maldistribution of political and economic resources, ecological degradation, and dangerous health conditions, exacerbate ethnic conflicts and give rise to nationalist movements. In the case of the former Soviet Union, for example, misconceived and mismanaged policies—such as the use of defoliants, chemical weed and pest killers supposedly to improve cotton production—left vast regions poisoned. Kumar Rupesinghe, Peter King, and Olga Vorkunova, eds., *Ethnicity and Conflict in a Post-Communist World: The Soviet Union, Eastern Europe and China* (New York: St. Martin's Press, 1992), pp. 108, 144–145, 176.
169. Stavenhagen, *The Ethnic Question.*
170. Rupesinghe, King, and Vorkunova, eds., *Ethnicity and Conflict in a Post-Communist World,* p. 2; Bohdan Nahaylo and Victor Swoboda, *Soviet Disunion: A History of the Nationalities Problem in the USSR* (New York: Free Press, 1990).
171. Kegley and Wittkopf, *American Foreign Policy,* p. 205.
172. J. M. Finger and J. Nogues, "International Control of Subsidies and Countervailing Duties," *World Bank Economic Review* 1 (1987) p. 707.
173. Samuel P. Huntington, "The U.S.—Decline or Renewal?" *Foreign Affairs* 67 (Winter 1988/1989), pp. 76–96; Susan Strange, "The Future of the American Empire," *Journal of International Affairs* 42 (Fall 1988) pp. 1–17; David P. Calleo, *Beyond American Hegemony* (New York: Basic Books, 1987).
174. Kennedy, *The Rise and Fall of Great Powers.* However, see Murray L. Weidenbaum, *Military Spending and the Myth of Global Overstretch* (Washington, DC: Center for Strategic and International Studies, 1989).
175. Joseph S. Nye, *Bound to Lead: The Changing Nature of American Power* (New York: Basic Books, 1990), p. 237.
176. Quoted in *Ibid.*, p. 2.
177. Seyom Brown, *New Forces, Old Forces, and the Future of World Politics* (Glenview, IL: Scott, Forseman, 1988), p. 242.

PART TWO

THE POLITICS OF INTERNATIONAL MONETARY AND TRADE RELATIONS

Reprinted with permission AP/Wide World Photos

CHAPTER FOUR

THE POLITICS OF INTERNATIONAL MONETARY RELATIONS

One of the major concerns for policymakers and businesses in the developed and developing countries, as the twentieth century drew to a close, was the volatility of major currencies. Public confidence in the dollar dropped as its value dropped 10 percent against the yen and 12 percent against the DMark between December 1994 and March 1995.[1] Such a drop, *The Wall Street Journal* cautioned, "might set off a full-blown global currency crisis that could drag down stock and bond markets around the world, disrupt trade and depress the economies of half-a-dozen countries."[2] Equally critical was the drop in other currencies. The British pound, French franc, Spanish peseta, Portuguese escudo, Swedish krone, and Norwegian krone also declined, as measured against the German DMark. In August 1995, representatives from a number of central banks met to discuss how to stabilize the international financial system, and they decided to take steps to raise the value of the dollar by 2.8 percent and 3.4 percent against the DMark and the yen, respectively.

Just three years later, it was the yen, the Russian ruble, and several Asian currencies that plummeted against a resurgent dollar. Whether it was the 1995 agreement or, more likely, the relative stability of the U.S. economy as compared with the crisis-ridden Asian region that made the difference, the quick turnaround again illustrated the speedy pace of global economic developments at the dawn of the twenty-first century. Overall, as shown in the previous chapter, international economic relations follow a long-term pattern, which began developing more than three centuries ago, and today's world—including its multinational enterprises and competing economic philosophies—still bears a resemblance to the world of the nineteenth century. However, short-term changes and cycles in the midst of these trends make a remarkable difference and, as seen in the 1930s and World War II, can cause tremendous damage and hardship.

Many short-term economic ups and downs profoundly affect investor confidence and, thereby, the value of national currencies. A number of factors, aside from general economic slowdowns, contribute to these fluctuations. In the case of the mid-1990s, dollar value slippage, for example, the 1995 U.S. aid package for Mexico, totaling $50 billion, led central bankers and edgy investors to fear that much more might be needed to stabilize Mexico's economy, which would in turn put more pressure on the American and European economies.[3] Another factor weakening the dollar was the inability of the White House and Congress to balance the federal budget in their partisan bickering. Subsequently, the Republicans and Democrats did agree on effective measures to wipe out the federal deficit, although a chronic trade deficit still clouded the picture. The budget agreement and continued economic growth without inflation led to a rebounding of dollar values.

Such difficult issues and their impact on national economies leave little doubt that business leaders and students of international political economy have to be far more knowledgeable about international finance in today's competitive and rapidly changing global environment than in previous generations. Twenty-first-century international business and finance take place in an interconnected global market, and what ails one economy profoundly impacts on others.

INTERNATIONAL FINANCIAL RELATIONS: SOME CONCEPTS AND CONSIDERATIONS

The financial structure of the world political economy as we know it today is the cumulative result of centuries of historical evolution.[4] As Susan Strange has pointed out, political and economic power in the international political economy consists largely of the power to dominate the international monetary system and the power of governments and banks to create credit. Strange defines a *financial structure* as "the sum of all the arrangements governing the availability of credit plus all the factors determining the terms on which currencies are exchanged for one another."[5] The trend toward globalization of the financial structure has created an intertwined network of centers of capital dominated by the wealthier, first industrialized economies (FIEs)—that is, Western Europe, the United States, and Japan—whose economic strength enables them to exert disproportionate political power over the international monetary system and credit creation beyond their national borders. Because of historical factors noted in Chapter 3, the industrializing economies (IEs), such as Argentina, Brazil, South Korea, and Taiwan, and the preindustrial economies (PIEs), become financially integrated into that globalized system through their relations with the dominant governments and banks for credit and investments. Thus, this financial structure is based on inequalities between the more affluent and technologically advanced FIEs, as the sources of money and credit, and developing economies, whose financial well-being depends on decisions made by the governments and banks of the FIEs.

Money and Its Functions

Money is a standardized, universally accepted means of transaction between two entities. It consists of a variety of assets, including coins, paper currency, and bank deposits—for example, checks. As an asset, money's *liquidity*—that is, its facility for the exchange of goods and services—makes it the most useful medium of exchange. It is worth noting, as Paul Einzig did in the 1940s, that "money does not exist in a vacuum. It is not a mere lifeless object, but a social institution."[6] In primitive times, before the emergence of coins and paper currency, money consisted of various "currencies" as determined by local cultures and the value attached to scarce resources. According to anthropological studies, such currencies included whales' teeth, fur, shells, beads, animals, tin ingots, grain, and even tea. Bartering constituted the primary means of exchange, but such a system was useful only in economies with limited trade activities and where taxation was limited to extraction of labor and goods labor produced.[7] To be sure, bartering was not a characteristic of primitive economies only. During and immediately after the Second World War, the so-called cigarette standard emerged in parts of European and Asian economies devastated by the war, whereby cigarettes were used for barter.[8]

Money developed to facilitate increasingly complex domestic and foreign commercial transactions, but, in addition to its economic significance, the origins of money had religious and political dimensions as well. In some instances, religious practices and supernatural qualities more than economic factors contributed to the evolution of systems of barter into money systems. Bernhard Laum contended that sacrifices to gods were in fact a form of barter between humans and gods, a "payment for blessings already received, or more often in anticipation of blessings requested, or in an effort to conciliate the offended gods."[9] Objects considered sacred in ancestor worship and offerings to gods assumed qualities of money for purposes of exchange.

Money is also political power.[10] The political origins of money involved the payment of tributes and taxes by tribe members to their leaders, surplus wealth accumulated from booty, as well as blood money, ransom, and compensation. The state determined the value of such payments, and in doing so also determined the direction of labor by its subjects. As economies advanced, it became customary for monarchs to mint coins as a confirmation of their sovereignty, and money became an integral component of political power. The feudal lord directed the labors of his serfs by demanding a certain quantity of wine or poultry from them. The transition to taxation based on money allowed the serfs greater latitude in the choice of employment, as long as they met their financial obligations to the lord.[11] Monarchs, for their part, distributed part of their wealth for patronage and economic development. Susan Strange has summarized the political significance of money:

> In political terms, money is a substitute for force as a means to economic growth and as an instrument to provide collective goods. The Incas and the Pharaohs could organize great public works programmes (chosen by themselves, naturally) without money. But political systems where power was more dispersed or more constricted were unable to invest (and thus to increase wealth) until they developed their monetary systems. Money is thus a necessary adjunct to liberty if a society wishes to enjoy *both* freedom *and* wealth.[12]

The smooth functioning of national and international economy requires the effective state management of international finance;[13] the failure to do so leads to economic and political crises, as demonstrated by the experience of the Great Depression, discussed in Chapter 3. To a great extent, a government's legitimacy rests on its ability to secure an economic environment conducive to individual and national economic growth. The Indonesian financial crisis in 1998, which led to the resignation of President Suharto, the collapse of the Soviet Union in the late 1980s and early 1990s, and the Chiapas peasant movement in Mexico in the second half of the 1990s are only recent demonstrations of the significance of the relationship between the management, or mismanagement, of money—or, more particularly, the distribution of wealth—and political power. Equally important, the power of the world hegemon rests on its ability to manage the international financial system while maintaining its house in order, as the former empires from Rome to Spain to England witnessed.

Economists identify three general functions money performs in modern economy. First, it serves as a *medium of exchange,* whereby, as a means of payment, it is exchanged for goods and services. Money facilitates transactions that otherwise would be inordinately difficult through painstaking barter.[14] Money also functions as a *unit of account,* as a measure of value. The value of personal, corporate, and government assets, goods, and services is expressed in terms of their price in a given market or economy, and that price is in turn expressed in monetary units. The value of goods and services expressed in terms of money enormously "simplifies economic calculations by making it easy to compare the prices of different commodities."[15] Commodities assume a certain standardized value as determined by national and international markets, and as a unit of account money reflects the value of exchange—that is, *exchange rates*—across countries. Although there are still ambiguities, as in the American CIA's long debate on how to count or value Cold War Soviet defense spending, the absence of money to indicate the value of goods and services would render international trade and transactions extremely difficult and costly. Finally, money serves as a *store of value.* Money, as an expression of value and as a medium of exchange, is a contract promising to retain its value in the future. This is indicated by the value and promises printed on the currency itself. Without such an explicit promise, it would possess little credibility, and people would refuse to use it as a medium of exchange for their goods and services. As discussed in the following section, an economy experiencing inflation and hyperinflation, as some Latin American countries did in the 1980s,[16] sees the value of its currency drop, which leads to declining public confidence in the credibility of the currency and even the government—that is, the contract that today's $1 dollar bill will retain its purchasing power tomorrow. Examples of governments seeking foreign capital to regenerate financial credibility at home are the former Soviet bloc countries in Eastern Europe, the Caucasus, and Central Asia, each struggling to establish a nationally credible and internationally **convertible currency** in the process of transformation to market economy, as well as efforts to rebuild finances after years of civil war in Lebanon.[17]

Exchange Rates and International Currencies

The concept of exchange rates refers to the value of a currency's convertibility to another. While the post-WWII international financial system was based on **fixed exchange rates,** pegged to exact ratios in relation to the cost of gold, the current system is based on **floating exchange rates.**[18] In the case of the latter, the values of the currencies "float," or appreciate (or depreciate) as their exchange values in terms of other currencies increases (or decreases) as determined by the supply-and-demand forces operating freely in the foreign exchange markets; that is, the supply and demand for a currency determine its international market value, or exchange rate.[19] A currency is said to be strong on the foreign exchange market when increasing demand for it raises its exchange value and the parent country maintains a surplus of payments; conversely, a currency is said to be weak when demand for it drops and the parent country has a balance of payment deficit. Thus, a currency's exchange rate is, as a matter of course, automatically affected by the economic environment in the parent country, as well as in other trading countries.[20]

However, in addition to supply-and-demand forces per se, other factors, some domestic and some foreign, also influence a currency's exchange rate, including interest rates, prices, a trading country's competitive edge, levels of income, and the advance "betting" on future values indulged in by "currency speculators" on the international financial markets.[21] As Kreinin reminds us, "The entire constellation of economic circumstances exerts its influence on the exchange rates through its effects on internationally traded items."[22]

Theory of Exchange Rate Determination When the original Bretton Woods system (see Chapter 3) ended in March 1973, it was replaced with a modified international currency system based on a combination of fixed and floating exchange rates. Table 4.1 presents selected currency exchange rates in 1995 and 1998. Note the range of variation in the value of the currencies in relation to the U.S. dollar and the British pound. In some cases, such as Argentina's austral and Brazil's novo crusado, the currency value is almost on par with the U.S. dollar, while in others, such as Indonesia, Italy, Russia, and Turkey, the value of their currencies is substantially low. In almost all cases, the value of the dollar and the pound increased during the three years, indicating their relative strength. In general, three main factors determine confidence in and the supply and demand for foreign currencies: a country's "real income relative to foreign incomes, its rate of inflation to relative inflation abroad, and its rate of interest relative to rates abroad."[23]

TABLE 4.1

Exchange Rates, 1995 and 1998

	Currency Unit Value, 1995		*Currency Unit Value, 1998*	
Country (Currency)	**Per $**	**Per £**	**Per $**	**Per £**
Argentina (austral)	1.00	1.60	1.00	1.63
Australia (dollar)	1.38	2.21	1.59	2.60
Austria(schilling)	9.79	15.70	12.50	20.40
Belgium (franc)	28.60	45.90	36.70	59.90
Brazil (novo crusado)	0.92	1.47	1.15	1.87
Britain (pound)	0.62	———	0.61	———
Canada (dollar)	1.38	2.21	1.44	2.36
Chile (peso)	373.00	598.00	453.00	741.00
China (yuan)	8.30	13.30	8.28	13.50
Czech Republic (koruna)	26.30	42.10	32.70	53.50
Denmark (krone)	5.44	8.73	6.77	11.06
France (franc)	4.89	7.83	5.96	9.74
Germany (deutsche mark)	1.39	2.23	1.78	2.90
Greece (drachma)	225.00	361.00	308.00	504.00
Hong Kong (dollar)	7.74	12.40	7.75	12.70
Hungary (forint)	125.00	201.00	210.00	343.00
India (rupee)	31.40	50.30	39.80	65.00
Indonesia (rupiah)	2,228.00	3,573.00	11,400.00	18,625.00
Israel (new shekel)	2.97	4.76	3.66	5.98
Italy (lira)	1,640.00	2,629.00	1,753.00	2,864.00
Japan (yen)	84.50	136.00	134.00	219.00
Malaysia (ringgit)	2.44	3.91	3.88	6.34
Mexico (peso)	6.25	10.00	8.52	13.90
Netherlands (guilder)	1.56	2.50	2.00	3.27
Philippines (peso)	25.70	41.20	39.60	64.60
Poland (zloti)	2.38	3.82	3.41	5.58
Portugal (escudo)	147.00	235.00	182.00	298.00
Russia (ruble)	4,546.00	7,290.00	6.00	9.80
Singapore (dollar)	1.40	2.24	1.66	2.71
South Africa (rand)	3.66	5.88	5.08	8.30
South Korea (won)	760.00	1,219.00	1,418.00	2,316.00
Spain (peseta)	121.00	194.00	151.00	247.00
Sweden (krona)	7.26	11.60	7.68	12.60
Switzerland (franc)	1.16	1.85	1.48	2.41
Taiwan (dollar)	25.90	41.50	33.40	54.60
Thailand (baht)	24.70	39.50	39.00	63.70
Turkey (lira)	43,162.00	62,910.00	252,575.00	412,657.00
United States (dollar)	———	1.60	———	1.63
Venezuela (bolivar)	170.00	272.00	536.00	876.00

Source: The Economist, June 24, 1995, pp. 99–100; May 16, 1998, pp. 113–114.

Financial changes taking place in a country's domestic economy are affected by the financial changes taking place around the world. The greater the level of a country's income—measured in terms of GNP, for example—the greater the value of the goods and services its population can purchase and the more it can spend on imports; the larger the volume of imports, the greater the foreign currency demand in that country, which may lead to depreciation of the domestic currency's exchange value. When a country's inflation rate rises, the prices of its goods and services increase at home and abroad; as a result, foreign demand for its products drops, while domestic demand for less expensive foreign imports increases. This situation leads to increases in domestic demands for foreign currencies on the one hand and to lower foreign currency reserves on the other. Thus, the foreign exchange value of a domestic currency depreciates as the level of inflation increases. Further, higher interest rates attract greater volume of foreign funds, increasing foreign demands for one's currency, which in turn leads to appreciation of the domestic currency's exchange value in the world economy. Appreciated currency, in turn, makes foreign goods less expensive, thus further increasing imports.[24]

Moreover, ingredients not directly visible in economic transactions exert considerable influence on a currency's foreign exchange value. Psychological factors, as in times of political disturbances with unpredictable outcomes, rumors of scandals and national security breaches, public expectations with respect to the country's economic performance, and so on, all influence foreign exchange value (see Box 4.1). A country's foreign exchange and trade position also is influenced by technological discoveries, changes in consumer tastes in international markets, and changes in the quality and design of products. In fact, as one observer has put it, "[P]ractically any economic change—such as the lengthening of workers' coffee breaks or an increase in the price of fuels—would affect exchange rates through its impact on costs, prices, interest rates, and income, which in turn influence inpayments and outpayments."[25] It is commonly and often mistakenly assumed that depreciation of a country's foreign exchange value is necessarily unacceptable or that its appreciation is necessarily desirable. In reality, analysis should take into consideration the actual causes and effects of exchange rate fluctuations.

Under a *fixed exchange rate,* governments agree to set the official exchange rate at a specified level until such time as deemed necessary to readjust it. For example, the German government agrees to set, or fix, the foreign exchange value for its DMark at 1DMark = $0.50. For various reasons, however, the German government may decide to decrease the value of the fixed currency rate of the DMark—say, from 1 DMark = $0.50 to 1 DMark = $0.30, thus making German goods effectively cheaper to holders of dollars. This is known as *devaluation,* cheapening one's own currency in relation to others'. Conversely, it may decide to increase the value of the deutsche mark from 1DMark = $0.50 to 1 DMark = $0.70, in effect, making foreign goods cheaper to Germans. This is known as *revaluation.* Such government intervention to change the domestic currency's foreign exchange value, however, does not occur frequently, nor are fixed exchange rates allowed to fluctuate freely on the market in response to daily changes in demand and supply. Rather, the government intentionally sets the foreign exchange value of the domestic currency, unlike the minor daily fluctuations under the *floating exchange rate* system.[26]

Governments in most of the developing countries have pegged their domestic currencies to one of the major internationally acceptable floating currencies, such as the U.S. dollar and the French franc. A few have pegged their currencies to what is referred to as a "weighted basket" of major currencies, such as IMF's Special Drawing Rights (SDRs,) based on a weighted average of the five major currencies, including the U.S. dollar, the DMark, the French franc, the Japanese yen, and the British pound sterling. Major international currencies, such as the U.S. dollar and the British pound sterling, acquire international status for a number of reasons. In the twentieth century, economic vitality and hegemonic leadership have been the most important factors.

In addition, regarding balance of payments, the free (or clean) float holds that, in a global political and economic environment where, at least in theory, governments maintain a hands-off policy toward foreign exchange market fluctuations—official reserve holdings would remain stable and no deficit or surplus would occur in the balance of payments. That theory, however, is unrealistic, because governments and their central banks have to contend with imbalances, and they directly and indirectly intervene in foreign currency markets (buying or selling currency) to push their currency's exchange value in the desired direction. The foreign exchange market based on such government intervention is referred to as a managed (or dirty) float; presently all currencies of the industrialized economies operate under a managed float system. Thus, under a fixed exchange rate system, external deficits and surpluses produce fluctuations in a country's international reserves. Under a

BOX 4.1

THE TRANSNATIONAL PRICE OF DOMESTIC POLITICS

FROM THE HOUSE OF DINI . . .

Political uncertainties in Italy infected financial markets across Europe today, sending the dollar sharply lower and driving down stock and bond prices. Investors, jittery about the economic outlook in Italy if the current Government fails to survive a vote of confidence in Parliament this week, sold Italian lire and purchased German marks. The mark, a traditional safe haven for European investors, then strengthened against other currencies, including the dollar. Canadian markets were also shaken today by political forces. Stock and bond prices plummeted after a poll showed Quebec separatists gaining an upper hand in a referendum next week. . . . The rise in the mark raised fears in Germany that exporters, already hit hard by the strong currency in recent months, would see their profits come under more intense pressure. A strong mark makes German goods more expensive abroad. . . . Analysts said the dollar, rather than suffering from any new fundamental problem, simply became caught in the European crossfire and was driven down as traders bought German marks and sold lire, French franc and other European currencies. Some of these transactions also involve the dollar; a trader, for example, may sell lire for dollars and then sell the dollars to buy marks. The dollar also fell against the Japanese yen in European trading. The dollar was at 99.60 yen late in the day, down from 100.18 on Friday. Late in the day, the dollar was trading 1.3821 marks, down from 1.3975 on Friday. The dollar traded as low as 1.3812 marks during the day, its lowest level in nearly three months. Later in New York, the dollar recovered a bit, trading at 99.96 yen and 1.3882 marks. But the dollar was still down from Friday's levels in New York, when it was trading at 103.35 yen and 1.3977 marks.

The rocky performance of the markets today came against the background of political and economic problems across Europe. The Italian Government of Prime Minister Lamberto Dini appeared likely to lose a vote of confidence in the lower house of Parliament. If the Government falls, its budget proposals would probably be doomed. At the same time, the French Government is struggling with the value of the franc while trying to address a stubborn unemployment problem. And doubts are growing in many countries about the ability of the European Union to meet its goal of a single currency by the end of the decade. . . . In that atmosphere, the mark has proved even more attractive than usual. The trend was strengthened last week by higher-than-expected money supply figures for September that cast some doubt on the ability of the Bundesbank, the central bank of Germany, to cut interest rates any time soon.

The currency markets were also unsettled by reports in France that prosecutors had been asked to investigate whether President Jacques Chirac had used his influence while Mayor of Paris to insure that he could keep living in an apartment he rented from a city-subsidized real estate company. The French currency plunged briefly after the report and then recovered somewhat.[a]

. . . TO THE HOUSE OF JUPPÉ AND CHIRAC

After his Prime Minister had to leave his city-owned apartment or face prosecution for conflict of interest, President Jacques Chirac is being confronted with the possibility of prosecution on a similar charge. The President, who was Mayor of Paris for 18 years, stayed in his Left Bank apartment when a corporation that was indirectly and partly controlled by the city took over the building in 1989. He still lives in the apartment. Mr. Chirac's critics say the corporation was formed just to keep his rent from rising when the previous owners put the building up for sale. Mr. Chirac's rent was frozen in 1990 at $2,440 a month, including monthly maintenance charges. The 2,035-square-foot apartment has a nearly 7,000-square-foot private garden and is on the Rue du Bac in one of the most desirable quarters of Paris. Traders on international currency markets, already nervous about the plummeting popularity ratings of Mr. Chirac's Government in public opinion polls, sold francs heavily for a while today when the news came out that a French lawyer had taken formal action against Mr. Chirac.[b]

Sources: [a]Richard W. Stevenson, "Italy's Political Turmoil Hurts European Stocks and the Dollar," *The New York Times,* October 24, 1995, pp. D1, D23; [b] Craig R. Whitney, "As Juppé Moves Out, Chirac Rues a Rent Deal," *The New York Times,* October 24, 1995, p. A3.

free-float system, depreciation of a country's currency reflects its external deficit, and appreciation of a currency reflects its external surplus. Under a managed float system, such as the one now basically in operation, external deficits result in both changes in exchange rates and in a country's international reserves.[27]

International Currencies An international currency performs a number of functions in international economic relations. As discussed earlier in this chapter, an international currency serves as a medium of exchange, whereby investors, traders and central banks use that currency—for years, the British pound sterling; since WWII, the U.S. dollar—to conduct their foreign financial transactions and to finance balance of payments. An international currency also functions as a unit of account, used to invoice imports and exports, as well as to determine currency exchange rate values. Finally, an international currency serves as a store of value, held as reserve capital assets by public and private financial agents.[28]

In order for a currency to become an international currency, traders and central banks must have a high degree of confidence in it and the economic status of its home country, usually one of the major industrialized countries or a hegemonic power. A currency, such as the British pound, captures the coveted status of an *international currency* as its parent economy makes strong technological and industrial advances that enable that country to develop expansive trade networks, facilitating the use of its national currency around the world. This, in turn, enhances the international prestige of the parent country. In the process, the parent country usually develops sophisticated financial institutions, such as banks, to accommodate the needs and demands for various financial services for banking and trading constituents at home and abroad. Traditionally, as well, the country enjoying international currency status tacitly agrees to be a consuming society, buying foreign goods and making foreign payments with sufficient regularity and in sufficient quantities to facilitate transnational diffusion of its currency abroad, in turn, to facilitate smooth commercial transactions. A key expectation, however, is that the parent country successfully manages its domestic economy so as to avoid excessive depreciation of the international currency, since everyone holds and depends on it. The parent country must be able to control inflationary pressures and address imbalances in trade and the national budget. The requirements of controlling inflation and remaining a consumer society can, however, conflict unless carefully managed. Failure to do so leads to erosion of public confidence in and use of the currency in international trade and financial transactions. Thus, the management of the international currency involves purely economic but also political considerations.

POLITICAL CONSIDERATIONS

Domestic Pressures

In increasingly globalized markets and finance, governments must balance domestic and international economic policies. While international finance and related problems at the international level appear removed from most people's daily lives, domestic economic problems do not. People see first-hand their income levels rise or decline, jobs—and the type of jobs—created or lost, fluctuations in food and energy prices, houses built or destroyed in their neighborhoods, the overall economic condition of their communities, and so forth. Inflation, recession, and unemployment directly influence their living standards, and governments come under increasing pressure to improve conditions. As previously noted, government inability to address such problems can have serious ramifications for the political system. In the United States, as the Nixon, Ford, and Carter administrations struggled to rescue the dollar's value in foreign markets, the Federal Reserve Board (the Fed) adopted stringent monetary policy to strengthen the dollar, as well as to check the inflation. The Fed raised the discount rate, the interest rate on money borrowed by commercial banks, from 5.25 percent in 1976 to 11.0 percent in 1979, and to 14.0 percent in 1981, the highest level in the past two decades.[29] This had drastic effects on American consumers and on foreign investors attracted by the lucrative returns.[30]

Given that the dollar is an international, or the hegemonic, currency, decisions made to maintain its value can contribute to economic dislocations, especially among developing economies. This is also true of regionally dominant currencies, such as the Japanese yen. Some economies are virtually based on the dollar instead of on their local currencies, particularly for business transactions. The increasing *dollarization* of their economies (as in Russia, for example) has made them more dependent on decisions by U.S. banks, such as Citicorp and Chase Manhattan; the U.S. government; and international financial organizations—most prominently, the International Monetary Fund. It has also deepened socioeconomic divisions between those who can earn or accumulate dollars through legitimate or corrupt business practices and those who cannot. In a given country, businesses borrow dollars to operate and trade; however, since most consumers use the local currency, in order to repay their loans businesses "must 1) raise prices, thus necessarily spurring inflation locally, and 2) reduce wages in order to compensate for the higher cost of borrowing in their total costs." [31] The poorer the population, the larger the pool of employees willing to work for lower wages in the formal and informal sectors, and businesses can pit poor employees against each other while exporting raw materials and semifinished goods for dollars.[32]

Since a nation's budget deficit weakens its currency value and its economic position in the world economy, its government must be able to manage its expenditures and revenues, while addressing a host of economic issues, including inflation, national debt, declining production, and unemployment. As the 1980s demonstrated, the national debt of an advanced economy can be financed through attracting foreign currencies (higher interest rates), but production and exports must expand sufficiently to service the debt.[33] The Reagan administration's failure to balance its expenditures for the military and its failure to balance imports and exports resulted in turning the world's largest creditor country into the largest debtor (see Ch. 3). Attracting investment to a basically poor country experiencing high foreign debt can be nearly impossible, unless international lending agencies come to the rescue.

National Sovereignty The current international system, as developed since the mid-1600s, is essentially based on the sovereignty principle, but the globalization of international financial markets and multilateral institutional arrangements, such as the World Bank and IMF, as well as European Union (EU) and North American (NAFTA) regional integration, gave rise to popular suspicions regarding the "true" intentions of such institutions and of policymakers who cooperate with them. In the case of developing countries, governments accept, for lack of viable alternatives, international deals and obligations, such as IMF **conditionality,** to inject much needed capital into their otherwise unsustainable economies. Thus, a government's control over its macroeconomic policy has diminished due to international financial arrangements and the impact of MNCs able to move cash and operations from country to country.

HISTORY OF INTERNATIONAL FINANCE AND THE GOLD STANDARD

While it is difficult to date precisely the origins of international financial relations, developed monetary systems operated throughout various regions of the ancient world. Ancient African, American Indian, Chinese, Egyptian, Persian, Greek, and Roman civilizations had devised their "monetary order" to encourage internal control and trade relations with nearby and distant neighbors. The Roman financial system based on Julius Caesar's "gold standard" and later Byzantium's gold solidus shaped the Western international financial world for more than twelve centuries. In the seventh century, a newly emerging silver bloc based on the Muslim dinar, which emerged with the rise of Islam in the Middle East, began to expand toward and compete with the Roman system in the West.[34] The latter totally collapsed with the Ottoman conquest of Constantinople (now Istanbul) in 1453.[35] During the next five centuries, various key currencies, including the Florentine fiorino, the Venetian ducato, the Spanish reale, and the Dutch florin, dominated the international financial system of fluctuating exchange rates.[36]

In the meantime, banking developed from goldsmiths and expansion of foreign trade, as an increasing number of major trade merchants—for example, the French *négociant* and the German *Kaufmann*—chose to trade in bills of exchange rather than in goods.[37] Bills of exchange as a medium of exchange used in domestic economy, however, initially were not acceptable universally in other parts of the world for purposes of trade. As Kindleberger has pointed out, what served as a bill of exchange in England was not redeemable as currency for trade with the Hanseatic League, with the Middle East, or with the Far East. Governments and merchants preferred to rely on precious metals, such as gold and silver. In the Middle Ages, this led to persistent outflow of the silver and gold from Western Europe to the east for various imports, including food, and resulted in currency shortages. European governments reacted to this hemorrhage in precious metals by means of monetary mercantilism in the seventeenth and eighteenth centuries and heavily regulated international financial transactions, as well as movements of goods across city- and nation-states.[38]

Concomitantly, major public banks emerged to coordinate trade and finance. These included the Casa di San Giorgio (Bank of St. George) in Genoa; the Taula de Canvi of Barcelona and the Taula de Valencia in the 1400s; Il Banco della Piazza del Rialto (Bank of Venice) in the sixteenth century; its successor, the Banco del Giro, a century later; and the Bank of Amsterdam (the Wesselbank), the Bank of England, the Bank of Hamburg, and the Bank of Nuremburg in the seventeenth century. Competition, trade, and financial conflicts among the emerging European markets and financial centers intensified. Each emerging nation-state created a strong, centralized banking system to maintain greater control over its domestic financial situation, to enhance its competitive edge with others, to finance wars and manufacture of military hardware, and to stimulate foreign trade.[39] As foreign trade expanded, mercantilism came under severe criticism by proponents of classical liberalism, while the industrial revolution catapulted the British pound sterling to global prominence, signaling the demise of the fiorino, the ducato, the reale, and the florin in international monetary relations.[40]

Along with competition and conquests, international efforts for cooperation were not uncommon, as each country sought avenues to address its domestic financial difficulties. At an 1865 international convention, for example, France, Belgium, Switzerland, and Italy created the Latin Monetary Union (LMU) to coordinate their financial policies and to maintain the value of currencies. A financial crisis in Italy and disagreements concerning adoption of a gold standard or bimetallism rendered the LMU inoperative and led to its dissolution. The International Monetary Conference, held in Paris during the Universal Exhibition in 1867, proposed to extend the principle of the LMU to international finance in general in order to establish a universal money. Such a currency, the delegates believed, would facilitate the interchangeability of coins in trade transactions among nations and would simplify exchange rate calculations and international monetary coordination. The conference agreed to establish a gold standard.[41]

In the history of international finance, gold and silver (but particularly gold) have been the most important and universally accepted commodity standards. Over the years, there have been various gold standards. Under a *gold coin standard,* central banks and government-run mints used gold coins, following prescribed standards as set by law, accepting these coins as legal tender. The *gold bullion standard* was based on the convertibility of paper money, as bank notes into gold bullion. However, since a gold bullion bar consisted of a substantially greater volume of gold and was physically heavier than a coin, the use of bullion was unsuitable for purposes of daily purchases and market transactions. Conversion from gold bullion into paper money and vice versa also was a very expensive and cumbersome process, discouraging gold-money conversions. Nevertheless, since gold bullion and convertibility facilitated the standardization of payments and trade between countries, some countries adopted this standard after WWI, while they attempted to shelter their gold reserves.[42]

In the domestic economy, the gold standard operated on the principle that each government restricts its money supply to the value of the gold reserves held by its central bank. Accordingly, the nation's currency in circulation would be based on at least a fraction of its gold reserves, and the central bank would be required to purchase and sell gold at a set price, thus maintaining some currency-gold convertibility. To proponents of the gold standard, this system placed checks on the supply of money in circulation and on inflationary pressures.[43] Based on the gold standard before WWI, the foreign exchange value of currencies was fixed in terms of gold, and central banks purchased and sold various quantities of gold at a set price in their own currencies. When the supply of gold exceeded demand, the central banks retained gold reserves in vaults for the future. Alternatively, when demand for gold exceeded supply, the central banks alleviated that shortage by releasing the reserves. This system led to enormous losses in reserves, however. Central banks preferred to maintain substantial levels of reserves.[44] When a central bank purchased gold with its own currency, the nation's money supply in circulation increased; when a central bank sold gold for its own currency, the nation's money supply in circulation declined. In addition, governments used gold, as a universally acceptable denomination against which national currencies were pegged, to maintain fixed-exchange ratios among the currencies (for example, see Box 4.2).

The classical gold standard, which came to a crashing end in 1914 (but which was revived after WWI and retained in modified form until 1973), had two principal

BOX 4.2

GOLD AND CURRENCY EXCHANGE RATES

If an ounce of gold is worth	The exchange rate is fixed at
£10	£1
$20	$2
40DM	4DM
80FF	8FF
¥800	¥80

That is, £1 = $2 = 4DM = 8FF = ¥80
$1 = £0.5 = 2DM = 4FF = ¥40
1DM = £0.25 = $0.5 = 2FF = ¥20
1FF = £0.125 = $0.25 = 0.5DM = ¥10
¥1 = £0.0125 = $0.025 = 0.05DM = 0.10FF

characteristics. In order to be on the gold standard, a country's central bank agreed "to buy and sell gold (and only gold) freely at a fixed price in terms of the home currency" and permitted "its private residents [to] export or import gold freely."[45] These two elements determined the exchange rate and balance-of-payments system. The primacy of the gold standard began to weaken the position of silver as reserve asset by the 1870s, and the British pound became the most sought after national currency during this period, while the French franc, the German mark, and the U.S. dollar emerged as potential competitors. The outbreak of WWI caused all nations on the gold standard, concerned with protecting their gold reserves, to suspend convertibility of their currencies and to prohibit gold exports. As a result, the classical gold standard ended, as gold could no longer be sold to foreign markets.[46]

The Great Depression of the 1930s and the accompanying banking crises led to the withdrawal of gold coins and the suspension of the gold bullion standard in many countries, although the United States and the "gold bloc" of France, Belgium, the Netherlands, Switzerland, and Italy continued to cooperate.[47] The largest currency bloc was the sterling bloc, centered on Britain. It included a number of independent states and colonial territories, except Canada, which was already within the U.S. dollar bloc. Others, such as Germany and Eastern European countries, dissolved all convertibility arrangements and opted for more mercantilist financial and trade policies, widening the mercantilist economic warfare, as each state fended for itself. Unpredictable fluctuations of exchange rates resulted in loss of public confidence in the major currencies, as governments intentionally depreciated or devalued their currencies to alleviate balance-of-payments and unemployment problems—trying to make their goods cheaper for export (though customers were scarce). In 1936, Britain, France, and the United States signed the Tripartite Agreement, promising greater cooperation and currency coordination and stabilization, but this failed to restore international financial order and regain public confidence.

Analysts have offered a number of explanations for the international financial crisis in the 1930s, and they are worth discussing here briefly. One explanation is that governments terminated their laissez-faire policies because domestic social and political conditions had experienced enormous changes, including the transformation from agricultural to industrial economies, which brought with it unprecedented urban problems. Equally as important, on the international front, the Bolshevik Revolution in Russia and the rise of socialism in Europe were perceived as a threat to the existing capitalist order of things. Governments feared that economic instability, caused by wide fluctuations in prices and incomes, not only could fail to sustain currency convertibility but also could lead to political instability and the spread of Bolshevik revolutions in Europe. More directly, the possible spread of civil wars, such as the Spanish Civil War, throughout European countries, along with Germany's disastrous inflation of the late 1920s and early 1930s, haunted political and economic leaders, and domestic stability became the order of the day—sometimes even at the price of trade and crushed democracies.[48]

National banks could not maintain the gold standard at the expense of domestic interests. Contrary to price flexibility and fixed exchange rates for automatic adjustments, as required under the gold standard, governments imposed massive protectionist policies and froze prices and wages, while introducing major social welfare policies. By the time the major powers reintroduced the gold standard, the domestic social, political, and economic environments had changed so radically as to render the new gold standard inoperative, premised on unrealistic assumptions of national and international financial and political stability.[49]

Charles Kindleberger has argued that the principal flaw in the international financial system during the inter-war years was the absence of a single, dominant center.[50] The emergence of rival financial blocs by 1931 weakened British hegemony, yet the competing industrial and financial centers, as in France and the United States, while successful in challenging British financial hegemony, failed to provide effective economic and financial leadership, resulting in worldwide financial instability and chaos.[51] In fact, the primary purpose of developing international currency standards, such as the gold standard, has been to maintain stable currency exchange rates and, hence, stable international economic relations. After the Second World War, the major powers adopted a new exchange rate system based on the U.S. dollar, and all countries adopted a paper currency standard.[52]

PRINCIPAL CHARACTERISTICS OF THE CONTEMPORARY INTERNATIONAL FINANCIAL SYSTEM

Management of the international monetary system requires international cooperation and mutual confidence to coordinate multilateral economic arrangements and to facilitate transfers of public and private capital. It may involve various mechanisms of exchange rate and the management of balance of payments and interest rates, as well as multilateral international financial institutions for the distribution of international loans and credits. In order for the international monetary system to operate, however, mutual confidence is necessary, the lack of which would lead to nationalist mercantilist financial policies and eventually to international financial instability and chaos. Contrary to the principles of laissez-faire liberalism, a greater role for governments is called for, as they routinely intervene to adjust and readjust their national and international finances. The leading proponents of the post-WWII multilateral institutions under the Bretton Woods system were fundamentally capitalists, believing in a Keynesian approach to managed capitalist international order premised on international cooperation and consensus.

Disagreements among the major theories of international political economy, however, hardly provide a basis for consensus. Laissez-faire liberals, on the nineteenth century model, for example, contend that the free flow of capital is essential for the workings of international finance, even if it requires multilateral arrangements, such as the World Bank and the International Monetary Fund, to ensure the effective management of international economic relations. Marxist-socialist critics of the Bretton Woods system, on the other hand, argue that international capital flows are not "free" but controlled by the Western industrialized governments and MNCs, while institutions such as the World Bank and IMF serve as mere instruments of domination, created by the West to control the economies of the poorer, developing countries. Although by the 1970s and 1980s Western-oriented financial institutions had integrated into the Middle Eastern regional system, in the 1950s and 1960s Muslim and secular leaders in the newly decolonizing Middle Eastern countries saw these institutions as an effort by Western powers to maintain colonial control over the region, even after decolonization. To feminist theorists, international flows of capital and related multilateral institutions are instruments of male domination as well, whereby governments and MNCs show little regard for the *just* distribution of resources, especially between genders. Disagreements about these issues abound. The global financial structure, however, since the Second World War has been clearly dominated by the multilateral—that is, inter-governmental—institutions created under the Bretton Woods system, bearing both advantages and disadvantages.

MULTILATERALISM & INTERNATIONAL FINANCIAL INSTITUTIONS THE BRETTON WOODS SYSTEM, 1944–1973

After WWII, most countries continued to maintain a certain percentage of their currency reserves in gold, but the major powers, led by the United States, made specific efforts to reconstitute the international financial system, with the explicit purpose of avoiding a repeat of 1930s financial chaos. After decades of war, destruction, and chaos, the Western powers insisted that a stable and managed international financial system was necessary for world economic order and global cooperation in financial and trade relations. In 1944, the UN Monetary and Financial Conference met at Bretton Woods, New Hampshire, to create the General Agreement on Tariffs and Trade (GATT), the World Bank (or the International Bank for Reconstruction and Development), and the International Monetary Fund (IMF) and a new gold exchange standard system based on the U.S. dollar as the international standard for currency value.

The International Monetary Fund

The Bretton Woods system established the IMF, today consisting of more than 150 member states, "as the central instrument to develop and oversee the ground rules of an international financial system."[53] The IMF consists of two major departments: the General Department and the Special Drawing Rights (SDRs) Department. The former administers each member's general resource account (GRA) quotas of contributions as determined by the IMF, while the latter oversees the distribution of SDRs as international reserve assets. The principal objectives of the IMF include the development of specific rules and procedures for the conduct of international financial relations, the institutionalization of consultative instruments to advance financial and trade cooperation among nations, and the provision of financial assistance to governments with foreign deficits. While the World Bank focuses mainly on long-term development projects, the IMF deals with immediate currency-related issues.

In essence, the IMF is comprised of nations pooling their financial resources to address national and international economic problems, particularly balance of payments deficits. The IMF provides a mechanism for the distribution of internationally acceptable reserves, such as

TABLE 4.2

IMF Quotas (Million SDRs)

Member		Member		Member	
Alghanistan, Islamic State of	120.4	China	3,385.2	Guyana	67.2
Albania	35.3	Columbia	561.3	Haiti	60.7
Algeria	914.4	Comoros	6.5	Honduras	95.0
Angola	207.3	Congo	57.9	Hungary	754.8
Antigua and Barbuda	8.5	Costa Rica	19.0	Iceland	85.3
Argentina	1,537.1	Cõte d'lvoire	238.2	India	3,055.5
Armenia	7.5	Croatia	261.6	Indonesia	1,497.6
Australia	2,333.2	Cyprus	100.0	Iran, Islamic Republic of	1,078.5
Austria	1,188.3	Czech Republic	589.6	Iraq	504.0
Azerbaijan	117.0	Denmark	1,069.9	Ireland	525.0
Bahamas, The	94.9	Djibouti	11.5	Israel	666.2
Bahrain	82.8	Dominica	8.0	Italy	4,590.7
Bangladesh	392.5	Dominican Republic	158.8	Jamaica	200.9
Barbados	48.9	Ecuador	219.2	Japan	8,241.5
Belarus	280.4	Egypt	678.4	Jordan	121.7
Belgium	3,102.3	El Salvador	125.6	Kazakhstan	247.5
Beliz	13.5	Equatorial Guinea	24.3	Kenya	199.4
Benin	45.3	Eritrea	11.5	Kiribati	4.0
Bhutan	4.5	Estonia	46.5	Korea	799.6
Bolivia	126.2	Ethiopia	98.3	Kuwait	995.2
Botswana	36.6	Fiji	51.1	Kyrgyz Republic	64.5
Brazil	2,170.8	Finland	861.8	Lao People's Dem. Rep.	39.1
Bulgaria	464.9	France	7,414.6	Latvia	91.5
Burkina Faso	44.2	Gabon	110.3	Lebanon	146.0
Burundi	57.2	Gambia, The	22.9	Lesotho	23.9
Cambodia	65.0	Georgia	111.0	Liberia	71.3
Cameroon	135.1	Germany	8,241.5	Libya	817.6
Canada	4,320.3	Ghana	274.0	Lithuania	103.5
Cape Verde	7.0	Greece	587.6	Luxembourg	135.5
Central African Republic	41.2	Grenada	8.5	Macedonia, former Yugoslav Republic of	49.6
Chad	41.3	Guatemala	153.8	Madagascar	90.4
Chile	621.7	Guinea	78.7		
		Guinea-Bissau	10.5		

continued

the U.S. dollar, to countries lacking sufficient resources. In this respect, the IMF functions as a mechanism for a more stable adjustment of deficits and exchange rates than would have been possible otherwise. The IMF charter originally required members to set the official par value of their currency as the exchange rate and to maintain their currency value within a "narrow band around that par value (1 percent or below), called a 'tunnel.'"[54] Under this system, each government purchased and sold dollars at fixed rates based on a gold exchange standard.[55] Under the U.S. leadership, gold-dollar convertibility was maintained for member countries; accordingly, governments pegged their currencies to the U.S. dollar, with 1 ounce of gold equivalent to $35.

Two sources—quotas and loans—provide the IMF its own resources for the distribution of financial assistance. Quotas, the most important source, are funds (or subscriptions) derived from member states, based on each country's economic and financial position in the global political economy (see Table 4.2). Thus, the greater a country's importance in the world economy, the larger its IMF quota, and the more votes it gets on IMF policies. The IMF tends, thereby, to reflect the political and economic importance and priorities of its primary donors. The IMF also borrows from financially strong countries under various interest rates, usually to be repaid within five years or so.[56]

Based on its Articles of Agreement, the IMF has over the years been involved in financial policies to promote

TABLE 4.2 (concluded)
IMF Quotas (Million SDRs)

Member		Member		Member	
Malawi	50.9	Peru	466.1	Swaziland	36.5
Malaysia	832.7	Philippines	633.4	Sweden	1,614,0
Maldives	5.5	Poland	988.5	Switzerland	2,470.4
Mali	68.9	Portugal	557.6	Syrian Arab Republic	209.9
Malta	67.5	Qatar	190.5	Tajikistan	60.0
Marshall Islands	2.5	Romania	754.1	Tanzania	146.9
Mauritania	47.5	Russia	4,313.1	Thailand	573.9
Mauritius	73.3	Rwanda	59.5	Togo	54.3
Mexico	1,753.3	St. Kitts and Nevis	6.5	Tonga	5.0
Micronesia	3.5	St.Lucia	11.0	Trinidad and Tobago	246.8
Moldova	90.0	St.Vincent and the		Tunisia	206.0
Mongolia	37.1	Grenadines	6.0	Turkey	642.0
Morocco	427.7	San Marino	10.0	Turkmenistan	48.0
Mozambique	84.0	São Tomé and Principe	5.5	Uganda	133.9
Myanmar	184.9	Saudi Arabia	5,130.6	Ukraine	997.3
Namibia	99.6	Senegal	118.9	United Arab Emirates	392.1
Nepal	52.0	Seychelles	6.0	United Kingdom	7,414.6
Netherlands	3,444.2	Sierra Leone	77.2	United States	26,526.8
New Zealand	650.1	Singapore	357.6	Uruguay	225.3
Nicaragua	96.1	Slovak Republic	257.4	Uzbekistan	199.5
Niger	48.3	Slovenia	150.5	Vanuatu	12.5
Nigeria	1,281.6	Solomon Islands	7.5	Venezuela	1,951.3
Norway	1,104.6	Somalia	44.2	Vietnam	241.6
Oman	119.4	South Africa	1,365.4	Western Samoa	8.5
Pakistan	758.2	Spain	1,935.4	Yeman, Republic of	176.5
Panama	149.6	Sri Lanka	303.6	Zaire	291.0
Papua New Guinea	95.3	Sudan	169.7	Zambia	270.3
Paraguay	72.1	Suriname	67.6	Zimbabwe	261.3

Source: IMF Survey, September 1995, p. 5.

[a]Quotas are those in effect as of September 1, 1995. As of that date, six members had not yet paid for their quota increases under the Ninth General Review of Quotas. The quotas listed for these members are those determinded under the Eighth General Review. These members (with their Ninth Review quotas, in millions of SDRs, appearing in parentheses) are as follows: Iraq (864.8), Liberia (96.2), Somalia (60.9), Sudan (233.1), Zaire (394.8), and Zambia (363.5).

international trade and the efficient use of development resources. To achieve these objectives, it has primarily concentrated on balance-of-payments problems. As previously noted, imbalances in a country's payments occur because of international factors—for example, unfavorable terms of trade or rising interest rates—or national economic policies and political circumstances. To finance their balance-of-payment deficits, member states borrow major currencies, such as the U.S. dollar, or SDRs from the IMF, using their own currencies as a form of collateral, then repay their loans by repurchasing their currencies.

Special Drawing Rights (SDRs) constitute a system of international reserve assets, under the International Monetary Fund, to supplement gold and the dollar in international financial transactions and trade. At least in theory, the principal purpose of establishing the SDR system was to increase international liquidity, making use of the power of various European and Asian currencies to add to the dollar.[57] The IMF adopted the proposal and created the SDR system in 1970, and today IMF accounts are in SDRs. Referred to as "paper gold," SDRs are paper "coupons" distributed to each IMF member state, allowing it to borrow from another member for a specified period of time and interest, to enable the borrower to balance its payments.

The IMF allocates SDRs in proportion to each member's quota, and it increases or decreases outstanding SDRs according to changes in the world economy. Accordingly, the principal recipients of SDRs are the United States (entitled to nearly 25 percent of the total), the European Union members (entitled to about 60 percent of the total allocation), and the industrialized Asian countries.[58] In the 1990s, the total amount of IMF quotas was 145 billion SDRs, each SDR worth about $1.47. Under a special agreement, the IMF may borrow as much as 17 billion SDRs from the major industrialized countries and about 1.5 billion SDRs from Saudi Arabia. The IMF also holds 104 million ounces of gold in reserve, worth over $42 billion.[59] Table 4.3 shows SDRs value as the weighted average of the five most important currencies.

A country may borrow SDRs through IMF arrangements and may use SDRs for a number of reasons. First, it may use SDRs to secure foreign currencies to settle balance-of-payment accounts. Under the IMF's supervision, a country transfers SDRs to another country, which is usually financially strong, in exchange for that country's currency. A country may also use SDRs to obtain its own currency held by another country. Finally, a country may use SDRs to pay its financial charges owed to the IMF, as well as to repurchase its own currency from the IMF.[60]

IMF loans are subject to conditions. A subject of increasing controversy in world politics, IMF *conditionality* frequently requires loan recipients to adopt austerity, or *structural adjustment,* measures to reduce government expenditures and to adjust restrictions on imports. These conditions are directed primarily toward improving investor confidence by correcting the borrower's balance-of-payments deficits while averting inflation and balancing the domestic budget. The IMF thus reflects a dominant Western philosophy of holding down consumption in order to foster savings and investments, reduce inflation, and correct imbalances.

TABLE 4.3

SDRs' Value as the Weighted Average of the Five Major Currencies: 1981, 1990, and 1996

	Weight (%)		
Currency	**1981**	**1990**	**1996**
U.S. dollar	42	40	39
Deutsche mark	19	21	21
Japanese yen	13	17	18
French franc	13	11	11
Pound sterling	13	11	11

Table from International Economics: A Policy Approach, 4th ed. by Mordechai E. Kreinin, copyright © 1983 by Harcourt Brace & Company, reproduced by permission of the publisher. International Monetary Fund, *IMF Survey,* October 9, 1995, p. 308.

However, in the process of budget cutting, borrowing governments also run the risk of provoking popular unrest, when they can no longer subsidize food, housing, and jobs, for example.

The IMF also maintains special programs to extend credits to member states. For example, between 1974 and 1977, the IMF operated a 7 billion SDR *oil facility* to assist IMF members to supplement the rapidly rising cost of oil. In addition, the IMF created an 8.7 billion SDR *supplementary financing facility* in 1977 to help members with excessively large budget deficits.[61] In the early 1990s, the IMF used its *systemic transformation facility* to distribute millions of SDRs to facilitate the former Soviet bloc countries' transition from centrally planned to market economies. In 1995, the IMF also committed $17.8 billion to save Mexico's economy.[62] Experts agree, however, that the IMF is not in a financial position to rescue many more Mexicos and Russias.[63] Further, its critics charge that IMF decisions to support an economy are politically and economically driven, reflecting the interests of the United States and the European powers, as in the case of securing the Mexican and Russian governments' survival against their domestic opponents. The fund also tends to dribble out its aid as it waits to see if the recipient government adopts effective economic reforms, with delays often adding to political tensions and involving continuous negotiations.

Responding to the worldwide recession and the debt crises since the 1970s, the IMF has emphasized reforms in three structural areas of economic policies as a way of addressing economic difficulties (for example, see Box 4.3). These areas include trade reforms, agricultural pricing reforms, and financial reforms. In each instance, the IMF has pressed for liberalization and privatization policies, limiting the role of the public sector in the economy. With respect to trade, this means the elimination of quantitative and tariff barriers, which for some states means less protection for "infant industries" that now advanced powers, such as the United States, once enjoyed. In the area of large farm and food subsidies, the IMF has advocated an end to government-set prices and to large farm subsidies. IMF experts have argued that the practice of lowering prices on agricultural products to sell in world markets lowers export-based income levels, causes financial problems for the government and producers, and "creates disincentives to both production and exports and can increase imports and smuggling."[64]

Indeed, for decades a key issue in international financial and trade relations has been the extent to which IMF rules and regulations should govern foreign exchange markets and related transactions.[65] The governments of most

BOX 4.3

THE IMF AND MOZAMBIQUE

Here is another small war in Africa. But this one is different. It is a war of words between the International Monetary Fund and the local representatives of the governments of rich countries. Usually they are all on the same side. Not now in the Mozambican capital, Maputo.

The row—for it has reached that level—is over what is to be done to revive the country, supposedly recovering after decades of civil war, but in practice all-but lifeless. The IMF argues that only more budget cuts will squeeze inflation out of the system and gives warning that Mozambique's structural adjustment may soon be "off track"—a term of art, well understood in aid circles, that means "get back on track, or else." On the other side, aid-giving governments argue that if the IMF goes on squeezing there will be nothing left to adjust. Mozambique, they point out, already has the lowest annual income per head in the world, $90. More cuts, say the aid donors, and this will be a corpse.

The issue came to a head this month when the Mozambican government agreed to increase the minimum wage—the equivalent of less than $14 a month, for those lucky enough to have a job—by 37.5%. This could hardly be a nationwide license to spend: over 95,000 of Mozambique's 7m adults are formally employed, not least because structural adjustment has cost 30,000 jobs. But it would hit the government's budget, and it was too much for Sergio Leite, the IMF representative, who took the unusual step of calling a press conference and denouncing the deal as "excessive and unacceptable."

Three days later, Mr. Leite met the ambassadors of Mozambique's donors and lectured on the virtues of more budget cuts. Health and education spending had already been severely cut back, but the adjustment program was not working and prices had already risen by 21% in the first six months of the year. Mr. Leite wanted annual inflation to be kept to 24% and demanded more cuts.

Normally aid-giving governments fall in with the IMF's analyses and withhold funds until its medicine has been swallowed by the government concerned. This time they rebelled. "Leite has no interest in the lives of ordinary people, he only cares about monetary targets," commented one western ambassador.

After several meetings, the ambassadors ganged up and wrote a stiff letter to IMF headquarters in Washington. They complained that Mr. Leite's obsession with monetary targets was unbalanced, and urged instead more investment. Mozambique, they said, had made "great efforts" to follow all the IMF demands and had done all that could be expected of it. This was not the soft-hearted pleading of Scandinavian aid workers. It was signed by almost all the western ambassadors including the man from the United States, Dennis Jett, whose government usually takes a hard line. Only Britain and Denmark declined to sign. The British usually follow the IMF in Africa; the Danes thought the letter not strong enough.

More astonishing still, the World Bank's representative in Maputo, Roberto Chavez, has come out openly against his sister organization, arguing that more cuts would make any development, even World Bank projects, exceedingly difficult. On Mozambique, it seems, the Fund no longer consults the Bank.

The IMF has a powerful weapon in its armory: to declare a country "off track" means that both IMF and World Bank funds are frozen. Several other donors have made it a rule not to finance countries that are "off track." Mozambique's aid donors were determined that it should be saved from this fate.

So far their letter has been a success. The Mozambican government, heartened by their support, confirmed the rise in the minimum wage. Officials who spent two weeks arguing with the IMF in Washington returned last week with no agreement; Mozambique remains in a kind of limbo, with no prospect of a new agreement with the Fund before February [1996], at the earliest. But at least the IMF, though breathing fire, has not actually condemned it.

Source: The Economist, October 28, 1995, p. 46.

developing countries, because of domestic economic and political conditions, heavily regulate their financial systems, and their first priority is to distribute financial credits to major state-owned institutions as a form of patronage and as a way of managing and governing their countries. At least two important consequences follow from such practices. First, smaller enterprises continuously experience shortages in capital, which in turn may lead to lower levels of production and employment. Second, the major beneficiaries of state support are usually inefficient and even foreign operations, further draining much needed capital for more productive purposes.[66]

With this in mind, the current debate concerning the IMF's role in the world economy, especially after its commitment of huge sums to rescue Mexico, revolves around the issue of whether the fund should be viewed as the international lender of last resort. Proponents of a more expansive IMF role contend that, given the globalized nature of international economy, one country's financial crisis is all countries' financial crisis. The repercussions of an economic collapse in one region, such as East Asia or Russia, cannot be contained in that region alone and can have deleterious consequences for the world economy as a whole. Accordingly, they argue, the IMF is the only international financial institution created to deal with such problems, and it should. Opponents, on the other hand, maintain that countries should not rely on any "international lender of last resort" or "international bureaucracy" to put their house in order.

While rescuing one country may not totally exhaust IMF resources, the institution is not prepared to cope with such problems—unless, of course, countries are willing to increase their contributions to its budget.[67] Rather than the IMF becoming mired in national financial difficulties or adopting a completely laissez-faire approach, Michel Camdessus, managing director of the IMF, in 1995 proposed the creation of a special facility to strengthen public confidence in economies, so as to prevent a regional or global "domino effect," in case a state, such as Mexico, experiences a financial disaster. Such a facility could also develop an early-warning system to avert economic crises.[68]

A major concern regarding IMF support and conditionality has been whether IMF-government arrangements are practical and can successfully restore economic and financial stability and stimulate growth. Most analysts are rather pessimistic. One empirically based study found that "fiscal targets were achieved in about half the cases, but 'by 1977 and 1978, expenditures were contained as planned in less than 20 percent of the programs, compared with over 50 percent in 1969 and 1970. . . .' Governments were not generally successful in meeting targets with respect to the composition of expenditure between current and capital outlays."[69] Economist Jeffrey Sachs has stated that the "[u]nsuccessful implementation of IMF recipes has been the norm in Latin America, not the exception."[70] A large number of IMF programs have failed to improve government finance and domestic credits, and where improvements have occurred they are more "attributable to chance" than to IMF programs. "The obvious conclusion," Sachs writes,

> is that economic, social, and political impact of IMF programs has been overstated. To describe the IMF as a 'poverty broker. . . or to charge the Fund with undermining democracy is to engage in hyperbole. The power of the IMF remains a useful myth for governments seeking a scapegoat to explain difficult economic conditions associated with severe balance of payments disequilibria, but the ability of the IMF to impose programs from the outside is distinctly limited.[71]

Unlike the IMF, governments have domestic constituents and are daily confronted with various social and political forces operating within a context of centuries-old histories, religions, cultures, and institutions.

In the second half of the 1980s Egypt faced a serious economic crisis as its GDP fell by nearly 2 percent, investments dropped from 31 percent of GDP in 1982 to 20 percent in 1986, the trade deficit was nearly $8 billion, its foreign debt reached $50 billion, unemployment rose to about 20 percent, and inflation rose as high as 40 percent, while the population in the major cities increased at a rapid pace (in Cairo, from 8 million in the 1970s to 9.8 million a decade later).[72] In addition, the U.S. government threatened to terminate its security-driven annual aid of over $2 billion to Cairo. To avert a total systemic collapse, in 1985–1987 the Egyptian government negotiated with the IMF for assistance. The IMF insisted on major structural adjustment and austerity measures, especially substantial reductions in agricultural subsidies, as a prerequisite for loans. After initial resistance, the government of Hosni Mubarak finally, in 1987, accepted the IMF conditions and received a $325 million loan for the next year or so. The government introduced policies to reduce the budget deficit—for example, raising prices on agricultural goods—and to establish partial foreign exchange liberalization.[73] The IMF agreement improved Cairo's credit with Western creditors (known as the "Paris Club"), and the Mubarak government was successful in arranging to reschedule $10 billion of its debt.[74]

On the Egyptian domestic front, however, this proved to be disastrous. The economy failed to perform as expected in 1987, and the financial crisis continued unabated. In 1988, the IMF demanded additional and stricter austerity plans, including further reduction in the budget deficit, further cuts in subsidies, and increases in the interest rate and prices—within eighteen months. Cairo, for its part, insisted on less draconian measures and a longer scheduling for improvement. Specifically, the Mubarak government argued that it could no longer cut subsidies as demanded by the IMF. Egypt's major newspaper, *al-Ahram,* criticized IMF's conditions: "The fund considers it from a purely economic point of view . . . while we look at it as a political and social, not merely economic matter."[75] The government's austerity measures led to even higher prices, expansion of the informal economy, labor strikes, food riots, and other violent clashes, including terrorism, between opposition groups and the police. These difficulties created opportunities for the parliamentary opposition parties, including the Muslim Brotherhood, to expand their political base. They called for greater emphasis on Islamic values than on IMF conditions in national economic policies, especially since the country's constitution proclaims Islam as the official state religion. In 1989, for example, the Socialist Labor Party (SLP) passed a resolution demanding a "comprehensive reform by Islamic standards."[76]

In addition to such difficulties in the developing countries, in recent years another major challenge for the IMF in the post–Cold War era has been the economic situation in the former Soviet bloc countries. The transition from centrally planned to market economies requires economic stability, while pursuing privatization and market liberalization reforms. However, domestic fiscal pressures, as well as the politically sensitive issues of unemployment, inflation, and rising crime, present obstacles to a successful transition to stable market systems. As Massimo Russo, director of the IMF's European I Department, noted at an IMF conference, large fiscal imbalances impede the implementation of effective monetary policies. Obsolete industrial structures, while they continue to provide employment, cannot be relied on for long-term trade objectives demanding greater competitive capacity in global markets.[77]

Table 4.4 shows the amount of SDRs the former Soviet bloc countries had borrowed as of 1995. The amount of SDRs drawn as a percentage of quotas by each country is perhaps indicative of the great need for capital resources and of the economic difficulties experienced due to capital shortages. Ukraine and Russia, for example, negotiated to borrow $1.5 billion and $6.5 billion, respectively, from the IMF.[78] John Odling-Smee, director of the IMF's European II Department, has pointed out that the transition is far more difficult in Russia and the inner Soviet republics than in the Baltic states and Eastern European countries because the former have been "isolated from mainstream developments in the world economy" for a longer period of time than their European counterparts.[79]

Critics over the years have argued that the IMF is essentially the creation of the global financial powers, particularly the United States, to exert maximum influence on the international financial system and financial arrangements between the industrialized and developing countries. For example, some years ago, the government of the Philippines began negotiations with the IMF for loans and changes in foreign exchange taxes to finance industrial imports, and initially the IMF responded favorably to the proposal. However, soon reports came from the U.S. State Department that Washington did not support the IMF's position. One government official representing the Philippines in the negotiations reported:

> When we discussed the matter with the Fund's Managing Director, this official would have supported the plan had not the American member of the Fund informed him that the US government did not think the Philippines government could re-impose a foreign exchange tax . . . . I was furnished a copy

TABLE 4.4

IMF SDRs Drawn Under STF by the Former Soviet Republics (as of December 31, 1995)

Member	IMF Quotas (million SDRs)	Amount Drawn	Percentage of Quota	Date of Drawings
Armenia	67.5	33.75	50	Dec. 19, '94; July 3, '95
Azerbaijan	117.0	58.50	50	Apr. 24, '95; Nov. 22, '95
Belarus	280.4	140.20	50	Aug. 2, '93; Feb. 2, '95
Estonia	46.5	23.25	50	Nov. 1, '94; Jan. 12, '95
Georgia	111.0	55.50	50	Dec. 20, '94; July 3, '95
Kazakhstan	247.5	123.75	50	July 28, '93; Jan. 31, '94
Kyrgyz Republic	64.5	32.25	50	May 17, '93; Sep. 23, '93
Latvia	91.5	45.75	50	Dec. 20, '93; July 20, '94
Lithuania	103.5	51.75	50	Oct. 27, '93; Apr. 13, '94
Moldova	90.0	45.00	50	Sep. 21, '93; Dec. 22, '93
Russia	4,313.1	2,156.55	50	July 6, '93; Apr. 25, '94
Tajikistan	60.0	NA		
Turkmenistan	48.0	NA		
Ukraine	997.3	498.65	50	Oct. 31, '94; Apr. 12, '95
Uzbekistan	199.5	99.75	50	Jan. 30, '95; Dec. 21, '95

Source: IMF, *IMF Survey,* February 5, 1996, p. 48. Percentage of quota (50 percent) is the maximum amount per eligible member under the systemic transformation facility (STF).

of an opinion to this effect written by a clerk of the State Department.

When the Managing Director of the Fund learned of the views of the State Department, he refused to discuss the matter further with us . . . I felt very deeply the refusal of Managing Director Per Jacobsson to have his staff discuss our stabilization programme with our mission when he learned that the State department did not favour it. I thought it was not good policy for an international organization such as the International Monetary Fund to allow itself to be influenced by any member country.[80]

Similar experiences have involved other developing countries, including Nehru's India in the 1950s, Quadros' and Goulart's Brazil in the 1950s and 1960s, Allende's Chile in the early 1970s,[81] and Abache's Nigeria in the 1980s and early 1990s, to name but a few.

The IMF (and the World Bank) also has been criticized for alleged disregard for family, community, and human life in developing countries. Women particularly in rural sectors from Latin America to Southeast Asia to Africa argue that the IMF's financial adjustment and stabilization programs do not consider contributions their agricultural and related productive work makes to society. Such neglect, they argue, directly and indirectly causes serious damage to the economic and ecological well-being of their local communities.[82] A UNICEF report stated that, in the 1980s, as an increasing number of heavily indebted African countries accepted the World Bank's structural adjustment and the IMF stabilization programs,

the common aim of these programs [was] to stabilize the balance-of-payments, extinguish the debt and reduce inflation. National objectives such as the creation and protection of jobs, guarantees for a minimum family income, and the provision of basic public services become secondary.[83]

IMF defenders, however, would note that governments that overextend themselves financially also cannot hope to safeguard their people's health and welfare over the long term and that failure to rationalize and reform their economies simply perpetuates long-term stagnation and misery. In other words, "tough love" is necessary.

The World Bank The World Bank (also referred to as the IBRD) was another of the key multilateral institutions created at the Bretton Woods Conference in 1944. Membership in the IMF is required for membership in the World Bank, and the IMF and the World Bank usually conduct their annual meetings together. The bank's principal purpose is to encourage economic development and growth in the developing countries, and the Articles of Agreement stipulate a number of specific purposes for the bank's loans. Immediately on its creation, its programs were meant to facilitate stable "transition from a wartime to a peacetime economy."[84] Since the post-WWII period, the bank has supported various development projects to stimulate economic growth and to increase productivity in developing countries. Accordingly, its lending programs seek to stimulate private foreign investments in those countries and to promote long-term growth in international trade, while raising the standard of living, increasing productivity, and improving labor conditions.[85]

The bank lends approximately $24 billion per year to more than 100 countries in the developing world for various economic development projects and programs in specific areas, including agricultural and urban development, transportation, and energy. The bank's loans may be repaid within fifteen to twenty years, generally at prevailing commercial interest rates (loans usually are resold to private Western banks). Voting on bank policies is, as with the IMF, weighted according to financial contribution, with advanced Western states dominant. With respect to the sectoral distribution of the bank's loans, in recent years agriculture and rural development have accounted for 23.7 percent (the greatest share) of its commitments; energy 19.7 percent; transportation and telecommunications 13.3 percent; urban public services 9.6 percent; development finance companies 9.1 percent; industry 6.1 percent; education 4.5 percent; small enterprises 2.8 percent; population, health and nutrition 1.3 percent; public management 0.4 percent; and nonproject loans 8.8 percent.[86]

The process of obtaining a loan from the bank requires from two to four years, and the formulation and implementation of a project requires a six-step "project cycle." This process, however, is extremely political, as major contractors, local bureaucracies, and international agencies compete for a share of the pie.

In the first stage of the loan process, the applicant country *identifies* the project to be financed. This stage is critical, since projects defined as suitable for finance can have a significant impact not only on local and national economies but also on domestic politics in general.[87]

In the second stage, the borrowing country and the bank *prepare* the project by conducting numerous analyses delineating its technical, social, and financial aspects. The bank may, through its technical assistance loans programs, invite other international agencies to lend their expertise and financial support for particular areas of the project. Such agencies include the Food and Agricultural Organization (FAO), the

UN Educational, Scientific, and Cultural Organization (UNESCO), the UN Industrial Development Organization (UNIDO), the UN Development Program (UNDP), and the World Health Organization (WHO).[88]

The third stage involves project appraisals and, if needed, instructions for plan modifications. Bank staff review the technical, economic, and institutional aspects of the proposed project and submit their report with recommendations to bank headquarters for further cost-benefit analysis. In the fourth stage, the borrowing country and the bank engage in formal and informal *negotiations* with respect to the terms of the loan agreement. After further appraisal, the bank's executive directors approve the project and sign the agreement with the borrowing country.

The fifth stage is the *implementation* stage, in which the borrowing country, under the supervision of and with some assistance from the bank, sets the project in motion. The final stage is project evaluation. After the project is completed, the bank's Operations Evaluation Department compares the initially proposed budget with the actual budget results.[89] One expert, who had worked for the World Bank, stated that

> Cost-benefit analysis becomes "cosmetic analysis" as the projects are of course chosen a priori on purely political grounds . . . (the complexity of methods offering sufficient freedom of interpretation to the experts so that they can produce the high rate of return which will give a good conscience to the decision makers on both sides).[90]

The bank does not operate by itself; it is the umbrella organization for the so-called World Bank Group, comprised of four other associated agencies. The World Bank created the *International Finance Corporation (IFC)* in 1956 to disburse loans to private enterprises. Such loans were prohibited under the original Articles of Agreement. The IFC's principal objectives are to provide long-term loans to private enterprises that cannot otherwise accumulate funds for further investments, as well as to facilitate the distribution of funds from wealthier countries to developing countries by way of international financial institutions and markets. The IFC provides legal and financial support to governments for stable and healthy, market-oriented domestic and international economy. IFC operations have continuously expanded, by an average of about 20 percent per year since the mid-1980s, and its membership includes more than 130 countries. By fiscal year 1990, the total amount of its approved investments had reached about $9.7 billion, 16 percent higher than in 1989.[91]

In 1960, the World Bank established the *International Development Association (IDA),* as a mechanism to lend without interest (only a small service fee is charged) and under more flexible repayment schedules. While IBRD members are assessed for regular support payments, the wealthier members contribute on a voluntary basis to IDA funds, and, while normal bank loans are distributed to more creditworthy countries, IDA loans support *least developed,* poorer, and risk-prone countries. Also, unlike repayment in most international financial organizations requiring "hard" currency (for example, the U.S. dollar), countries may repay their IDA loans in their domestic "soft" currency. Membership in the IDA is also more than 130 countries, and its capital resources are about $15.5 billion. In addition, the bank and IDA manage and administer a number of trust funds totaling about $2.4 billion.[92]

A third agency is the *International Center for Settlement of Investment Disputes (ICSID).* Founded in 1966, it is the only nonfinancial agency within the group, and its major purposes include the promotion of private foreign investment and the prompt and orderly settlement of disputes between foreign investors and contracting host governments.[93] In addition to the International Chamber of Commerce, the ICSID has emerged as one of the most important forums for international litigation and arbitration in the area of international financial and commercial disputes.

A fourth and more recent organization, the *Multilateral Investment Guarantee Agency (MIGA),* has been in operation since 1988. The only worldwide nongovernmental organization in its area, it provides insurance for foreign investments in the developing world against noncommercial, political risks.[94] In doing so, it seeks to provide a more secure and favorable environment for foreign investments in developing countries. Its Guarantee Program for investments against political risks makes it attractive for foreign investors who otherwise would not engage in long-term commitments in potentially unstable regions. With a ceiling of $50 million per coverage, the Guarantee Program includes protection against risks of expropriation, war, revolution, and other forms of civil disturbances, as well as risks in currency transfers and breach of contract. Within a year after its creation, nearly seventy applications for international insurance coverage were submitted to MIGA.[95]

With respect to the World Bank's performance, it can be argued that, since the end of the Second World War, developing countries in general have improved their living standards. Between the 1960s and 1980s, the share of world

GDP by countries with an annual GDP of $6,000 or lower rose from 16 percent to 21 percent, and the volume of their manufacturing exports rose from 11 percent to 13 percent. They also registered improvements in their infrastructural development, level of life expectancy, rate of infant mortality, level of literacy and educational attainment, and consumption levels. During those two decades, for example, official poverty in Indonesia dropped from 60 percent to 20 percent. Infrastructural development was the best in oil-producing Arab countries, and manufacturing rapidly expanded in East Asian countries. Over the years, some former borrowers "graduated" from the World Bank, as consumption per capita rose by 70 percent, life expectancy from fifty-one to sixty-two years, and enrollment in primary education from 73 percent to 84 percent. In the 1980s and 1990s, however, conditions deteriorated somewhat. In Latin America, Africa, and the Middle East, living standards in a large number of countries worsened, dropping to the levels of the late 1960s and early 1970s, as prices for oil and other commodities dropped. Concomitantly, developing countries' export profits declined, in many cases to levels at which those countries could no longer sustain production, forcing them to borrow heavily from international banks. Between 1980 and 1989, their cumulative foreign debt increased from $649 billion to $1.3 trillion, over 60 percent of it owed to commercial banks.[96]

As with the IMF, whether the World Bank has been successful in meeting the challenges of the 1980s and 1990s remains an important question. Its reports suggest that it has made efforts to cope with the difficulties by concentrating on the needs of the borrowing countries. Investment lending has accounted for over 66 percent of its operations since 1980. Loans for *structural adjustment*—that is, policy reforms for more market-oriented arrangements, including privatization—totaled about 17.5 percent, and the rest, approximately 16 percent, were used for technical assistance. Very little was used, however, for the explicit purpose of reducing developing countries' debt burden. In the early part of the 1990s, the World Bank began to expand the volume of its operations from $16.4 billion in FY1989 to $54 billion in FY1991; IDA support increased from $4.9 billion to $17.7 billion, respectively. *Adjustment lending,* lending to reduce a country's balance-of-payments deficit and to implement reform policies required by the bank, has remained stable at between 17 and 20 percent.[97]

The bank has continued to emphasize privatization of industries as the best strategy for economic development. It has stressed market-oriented reforms and the restructuring of the public sector for greater efficiency and financial stability. Such a strategy, however, may not be very realistic if poverty and unemployment levels in developing countries increase. At the end of the 1990s, 20 to 25 percent of the world population continue to live in abject poverty, and, in some regions, such as Sub-Saharan Africa, the level of poverty is expected to *increase.*[98] Population growth in the developing world will further weaken governments' ability to more effectively address the problems of poverty and declining standards of living.

Critics charge that, contrary to its rhetoric, the World Bank does not promote "economic development" and improvements in living standards equally for the general population in developing countries. Rather, they argue, the bank is highly elitist in its ideological and operational orientation, and it promotes and protects the interests of the international banking industry and multinational corporations first and foremost.[99] Despite rises in IDA outlays, critics also note the relative scarcity of low-interest loans to the neediest countries. The bank also supports local civilian and military leaders willing to cooperate and implement structural adjustment reforms—that is, the privatization of previously state-owned industries and the lowering of barriers to trade for greater liberalization—in return for greater financial support.[100]

The bank, however, has responded to criticism that it shows little concern for the impact of development projects on the social and environmental well-being or on the democratic institutions of the countries involved. It has attempted to monitor programs more thoroughly and to aim assistance at small business development and "microenterprises" for the poorest areas. It also advises governments on achieving environmentally "sustainable development."[101] Still, disastrous social, economic, and environmental consequences have been attributed to some World Bank–supported projects in the 1980s and 1990s, including the Pak Mun dam project on the Mun River, the Khor Chor Kor land development projects in Thailand, the Kedung Ombo dam in Indonesia, the Narmada River Sardar Sarovar dam in India, and the Polonoroeste and Carajás infrastructural development projects in Brazil's Amazon region.[102]

In the case of Thailand's Khor Chor Kor land development project, the bank was instrumental in proposing the multilateral forestry program called the Tropical Forestry Action Plan (TFAP). The project involved major companies, such as the Royal Dutch Shell, and the Thai government agreed to resettle and if necessary forcibly evict more than 1.25 million people from their homes in an area of

1.5 million hectares between 1991 and 1995. The land would be used for industrial development and eucalyptus plantations to produce paper pulp for export by foreign and domestic investors and joint ventures. The government, especially the Thai Royal Forest Department, tried to convince the public that this mega-project was needed for purposes of reforestation and agricultural development. The villagers, however, protested because eucalyptus plantations were poisonous and could destroy surrounding soil and water tables. The number of protestors increased, including Thai and foreign academic and environmental activists, Buddhist priests, and villagers throughout the region. The military reportedly terrorized those who refused to leave and threatened to burn their houses.[103] The Thai population also complained that the government's economic growth programs had resulted in the growth of the prostitution economy as well, making Bangkok "the planet's brothel." Development projects implemented by the Thai government and international organizations such as the World Bank widened the gap between rich and poor. The poor migrated from the rural areas to find jobs in Bangkok. Women working in factories earned about $0.80 to $2.00 per hour, while those working as waitresses earned up to $60 a month. Prostitutes, on the other hand, earn from $400 to $800 a month.[104] In the long series of interconnected developments, the rise in prostitution also led to a rapid increase in cases of AIDS in Thailand.

Some would argue that considerations such as the environment and urban migration are necessarily secondary in the face of the overwhelming need for jobs in places such as Thailand. Others, however, would call for sustainable development strategies, emphasizing food production first, along with planned socially and environmentally sound projects. Some within the bank's bureaucracy, in fact, have advocated greater care and attention to environmental and ethical concerns.[105]

The Bank for International Settlements (BIS)

An international commercial bank, the BIS was founded in 1930 as an international agency for the immediate purpose of administering the German war reparations. Before the First World War, no international financial organization existed to facilitate the coordination of financial policies among central banks. Reconstruction efforts after the war necessitated greater cooperation to stabilize the major currencies and to minimize the adverse consequences of the financial chaos. However, the close relationship between the BIS and Nazi Germany in the 1930s and numerous suspicious transactions in gold transfers—according to one estimate, totaling 3,740 kilograms worth $4.2 million ($48 million at today's value)—undermined its role as a credible international bank. In fact, after WWII the United States recommended closing the BIS, but Europeans refused.[106] The current BIS membership is comprised of twenty-eight shareholding central banks. Its original members included the central banks of Belgium, France, Germany, Great Britain, Italy, and Japan, while the United States was represented by a consortium of banks, including J. P. Morgan, First National Bank of New York, and First National Bank of Chicago. Five countries—Belgium, France, Germany, Italy, and Great Britain—now hold 50 percent of the shares. The United States is represented by Citibank of New York; although the Federal Reserve is not officially a member, it holds a seat on a number of BIS committees.[107]

The BIS has a number of powers with the long-term objective of promoting greater coordination of international financial relations among national central banks. It can purchase and sell gold, currencies, and securities under its own and central banks' accounts. It can lend to and borrow from central banks. It can accept deposit accounts for central banks within international settlements, and it provides related services for them. BIS members meet ten times a year to settle issues regarding international currency values, money supplies, and interest rates. The minutes of the meetings are not public documents but, rather, remain on the basis of "gentlemen's agreements," mutual confidentiality and anonymity. Its daily operations are conducted by BIS officers communicating with central banks through a network of telephones, faxes, and computers. As a commercial bank, in theory premised on principles of classical liberalism, the BIS was expected to avoid political considerations,[108] but it is doubtful whether the BIS, or any international bank, for that matter, can in practice insulate itself from politics.

During the early 1980s, for example, along with the IMF and the World Bank, the BIS also became involved in international efforts to rescue the Mexican economy, and it provided $1.85 billion to the Mexican government to avert a major financial and economic collapse. Over $920 million of the funds came from the U.S. Federal Reserve, and the central banks of Germany, Switzerland, Britain, Italy, and Japan paid the rest.[109] In 1995, the BIS contributed about $10 billion to the international rescue package for Mexico.[110] The BIS was instrumental in preventing a financial disaster, which could have had serious consequences for the other central banks. As one analyst has noted, "A crisis for the central banker in one country is a crisis for all of them."[111] Be that as it may, from the standpoint of Mexican political parties and groups opposing the *Partido Revolucionario Institucional's (PRI)* monopoly over the nation for the past seventy years, such assistance from the first industrialized economies (FIEs) must have been viewed as an effort to prevent not merely an economic crisis but also to guarantee for FIE investments. PRI officials at different levels welcomed outside support as a reaffirmation of the PRI's legitimacy in the international community. Translated into financial and political support, such assistance would, in practice, mean the distribution of resources through employment and bribery in the formal and informal sectors to reaffirm public loyalty to the PRI and to PRI officials.

Despite its claims to the contrary, therefore, the BIS, like the IMF and the World Bank, has become directly involved in economic programs with political objectives and ramifications. Marxists, dependencia, and radical and socialist feminists would argue that, in fact, the BIS is no more than another institutional mechanism to perpetuate imperialism and the status-quo.

Whether one agrees with the laissez-faire or its critics' views, there is sufficient cause to believe that the worldwide repercussions of an economic chaos in Mexico, if unchecked, would further jeopardize the international status of the U.S. dollar as the hegemonic currency, caught amid emerging competitors—the German DMark and the Japanese yen—a situation resembling the diminishing hegemonic status of the British pound sterling in the early decades of this century, when the rising U.S. dollar replaced it after the devastating 1930s and 1940s. As then, it is possible that, in the absence of a hegemonic dollar, neither the DMark nor the yen, regardless of its increasing internationalization, would be able to stabilize the international financial system.

GLOBALIZATION AND THE ROLE OF HEGEMONIC CURRENCY

Globalization of International Finance

The 1970s and 1980s were a period of rapid transition toward a more globally integrated international financial system, as facilitated by information technologies—computers, telecommunications, satellites, and so forth. Globalization has changed the financial landscape from a traditionally institution-based system to a predominantly telecommunications-based system. Despite continued mystifying delays in how long it takes an individual's checks to clear his or her bank, the telecommunications technology allows investors around the world direct and instantaneous access to capital markets regardless of their geographic location.[112] In fact, one scholar has claimed, albeit perhaps overstating a bit, that the 1980s and 1990s witnessed "the end of geography."[113] Technology has made it easier for major banking institutions to store an enormous amount of information in their consumer databases, to more efficiently target lucrative markets and link their products with appropriate customers, and to operate in many locations at once. The ability to combine technology, products, and consumers is said to have been one of the principal market advantages Citicorp and Travelers sought through their merger in April 1998. Renamed Citigroup, it has subsidiaries in more than 100 countries, making it a virtual "global financial supermarket."[114]

Globalization of international finance and integration of financial markets also have resulted in financial confusion and frustration for investors, speculators, and governments. Massive international capital flows have eroded national economic sovereignty, and governments can no longer fully manage their national economies and protect their economic interests. Currently, foreign-exchange trading—that is, currency speculation—is sixty times larger than foreign trade.[115] The NASDAQ (National Association of Securities Dealers Automated Quotation) stock market in the United States, for example, founded in the early 1970s, was among the first globalized market trading centers based on computerized information regarding prices and investments for thousands of large and small companies around the world. Since the early 1990s, the PORTAL (Private Offerings, Resales, and Trading Through Automated Linkages) system likewise has stimulated worldwide trading in securities. Such globalized markets systems have developed telecommunications systems, instantaneously connecting major stock exchanges from trading centers in one part of the world to those in another. James Carville, one of President Bill Clinton's campaign strategists, has put it most aptly: "I used to think that if there was reincarnation, I wanted to come back as the president or the pope. But now I want to be the bond market: you can intimidate everybody."[116]

No longer can a government rely solely on such traditional economic instruments as fiscal policy (taxation, government spending), monetary policy (interest rates, printing money), and exchange rates to manage its economy. Indeed, with increasing privatization and budget-cutting priorities, fiscal policy itself has been shelved by many leading governments. Since the early 1980s, government decentralization and deregulation of domestic financial institutions, mergers, acquisitions, and international financial transactions, along with the expansive role of the computers and telecommunications systems, have created a dynamic global environment, but they have also led to financial insecurity for individuals and nations; governments hardly appear to be in a position to reassert their role as managers of domestic economy in financial relations.[117] Mexico's and Asia's financial and currency crises in 1994–1995 and 1997–1998, respectively, have raised serious questions regarding the advantages of the global financial system for individual countries and even regions.[118] It is hoped that, as consumer information in electronic databases has become so readily available for corporate use, so will information on transactions between governments and banks become available for better informed decisions in order to prevent future financial crises of such magnitude.

Despite the rapid changes in telecommunications technology, however, governments continue to play an important role in transboundary financial arrangements and economic policies, including various forms of regulatory policies. Telecommunications technology places heavy demands on governments for greater flexibility, as transnational trading systems and international financial institutions create global networks. Governments remain an important factor through regulation and standardization of financial relations. The U.S. Federal Reserve and the German Bundesbank continue to set interest rates to address economic imbalances, such as inflation. It would perhaps be more accurate to say that the globalization of international finance has made the economic management job for governments and their central banks in the industrialized and developing countries much more difficult. Because of deregulation and the rapid pace of transnational financial transactions, it is more difficult for governments to measure the supply of money in the domestic economy and the domestic-foreign flow of national capital. "Central banks can therefore no longer set policy simply by their monetary compass; they now have to look at a wider range of economic and financial indicators, exercise more judgment."[119] Financial arrangements from commercial banks to NYSE and NASDAQ have to obtain government's support and willingness to negotiate the terms of operations within national boundaries. The globalization of political economy has not become the exclusive preserve of international financial institutions and trading MNCs and individuals, but it involves transboundary foreign investments, as well as public-private competing and cooperative networks of relationships.[120]

In the face of globalization, such relationships become particularly critical for domestic employment issues and fiscal policy priorities.[121] Through public and private international financial policy integration and coordination, governments' policies and management capabilities can exert a considerable influence on human resources and the balanced use of natural resources in both industrialized and developing countries.[122]

For example, access to global financial markets enables governments to borrow on relatively inexpensive terms. As one observer put it,

> On a world scale, bigger budget deficits will still push up real interest rates, but the domestic penalty is now smaller. It is surely no coincidence that public sector debt in industrial countries has increased sharply, and real interest rates have risen, as the international capital market has become more integrated over the past two decades. In the 30 years to 1974, total net public-sector debt as a proportion of GDP in the OECD economies fell steadily. Since then it has risen from 15% to 40% of GDP. Under the Bretton Woods system, fixed exchange rates and restricted capital flows meant that current-account deficits had to be financed out of official reserves. That made it impossible for governments to run big deficits.[123]

The globalization of international finance also has put forth challenges perhaps requiring an expansive role for international financial institutions, such as the International Monetary Fund and the World Bank, despite the controversies previously noted. In a speech delivered at the Wharton School of the University of Pennsylvania in April 1995, Camdessus, head of the IMF, identified at least two general goals. He stated that, since globalization has linked different regions of various levels of economic development into a closer international community, more than ever it is necessary for international organizations to provide the institutional framework for adjustments and to prevent future misadjustments. To this end, the IMF's first objective is to expand its role "through the policy advice it provides to its member countries in the course of its surveillance activities . . . [to] achieve progress and avoid policy mistakes."[124] This requires closer consultation, collaboration, and coordination of national and international policies. Closer ties between national governments and international institutions, he stated, also enables the IMF to achieve its second objective: to cure financial disequilibria and macroeconomic maladjustments, as experienced in Mexico and to be accomplished in Russia. He concluded,

> Over the past fifty years, the IMF has adapted its lending facilities in many ways to meet the changing needs of its growing membership. We are now considering carefully whether the IMF's financial resources are adequate for it to continue playing its essential role of providing financial support for stabilization, adjustment, and reform in the new environment of our globalized world economy.
>
> Our globalized world economy has opened up new opportunities and increased the scope for economic progress in the world. Globalization is something we must embrace. But it has also brought increased risks, and increased the importance of vigilance and discipline in economic policies, of strengthened adjustment and reform efforts and of active international economic cooperation. The IMF is well aware of its increased responsibilities in this environment . . . .[125]

Thus, the globalization of the world economy has facilitated greater international integration of international finance and markets, providing opportunities for economic growth. However, globalization also poses serious challenges for the general public, who fear that rapid changes in international realm will leave them poorer at home.[126] Industrialized countries view globalization as a threat to their jobs and economic security, as well as to their ability to tax or regulate MNCs; developing economies unable to be integrated into the world economy—due to lack of technological capability or leadership expertise—face the threat of marginalization and further decline in standard of living while others advance at a rapid pace.[127]

The Rise and Fall of the Dollar Under the Bretton Woods system, the U.S. dollar became the standard measure for international terms of currencies, gold, and international reserves. Until August 1971, the United States agreed to exchange dollars for gold, at $35 an ounce, at home and abroad, with no comparable commitment from other foreign central banks. This system, based on the dollar-gold convertibility, was called the *gold exchange standard*.[128] During the post-WWII period, the world economy witnessed serious "dollar shortages" as most, especially European, countries devastated by the war were in the process of reconstruction, which required huge sums of money for materials and equipment. Since the United States was the only major industrial and financially sound country that had escaped such wartime devastation, domestic and international public confidence in the U.S. dollar was high, and there was enormous need for it to finance the reconstruction of economies.[129]

One of the most attractive features of the U.S. dollar was the fact that, reflecting U.S. traditional laissez-faire capitalism, it was not heavily controlled by the government, while being supported by the most powerful economy in the world. Moreover, the United States had been a net creditor in the area of long-term investment accounts, and U.S. investments abroad far exceeded foreign investments at home. Another advantage the United States enjoyed was its substantially diverse domestic capital and product markets; foreign central banks benefited from "a variety of liquid, low-risk financial instruments (such as U.S. Treasury bills) in which to invest their dollar reserves."[130] Yet another advantage the U.S. economy had was that, well into the 1960s, inflation was appreciably lower than in other countries.

The central role assumed by the dollar under the Bretton Woods system placed the United States in a powerful position as the central banker in the world political economy.[131] Confident that the value of the dollar was protected by gold, foreign central banks held dollars as a universally admissible currency to discharge international financial imbalances. By the late 1960s, however, international confidence began to erode as U.S. balance-of-payment and then balance-of-trade deficits led to diminishing U.S. gold reserves, while the volume of dollars held by foreign central banks continued to increase.[132]

By the early 1970s, the system of dollar-gold convertibility as established since the Second World War was no longer sustainable. In August 1971, the Nixon administration suspended it. In December, the Group of 10 (G-10) countries—Belgium, Canada, France, Germany, Italy, Japan, the Netherlands, Switzerland (associate member), the United Kingdom, and the United States—accepted the Smithsonian Agreement, which inaugurated the "dollar standard" as based on a paper currency standard not convertible to gold. The other G-10 countries revalued their currencies vis-a-vis the U.S. dollar, while they permitted the Canadian dollar to float—that is, to not be pegged to the U.S. dollar. The Smithsonian Agreement thus lowered the value of the dollar in relation to other currencies and raised the price of gold from $35 an ounce to $38. The Smithsonian Agreement, in fact, was the initial phase of the decline of "dollar hegemony" as established under the Bretton Woods system.[133]

The Reagan administration responded to rebounding U.S. dollar values but declining exports in the 1980s by making an effort to prevent further increases in the dollar; in September 1985, Secretary of the Treasury James Baker, along with the other finance ministers of the Group of Five (Britain, France, Japan, United States, West Germany), met in New York to negotiate a readjustment in the dollar's exchange rate. In the Plaza Accord, they agreed to increase the value of their currencies relative to the dollar, although they set no specific exchange value. The G-5 ministers met again in February 1987, in Paris, and adopted the Louvre Agreement, which set the dollar at DM1.8512 and Y153.5.[134]

Budget and trade deficits continued to plague the U.S. economy, and by the late 1980s the value of the dollar once more had plummeted, by about 60 percent relative to the DMark and 70 percent against the yen[135] (see Figure 4.1). This trend continued into the 1990s, as the government sought to balance its domestic deficits by attracting huge foreign investments through high interest rates. Finally, these rates were lowered to stimulate the economy, and the question of budget deficits was addressed.[136] The dollar again rebounded in the late 1990s with the Asian and Russian financial skids. It became clear that an international currency cannot maintain its hegemonic status and remain a world reserve currency under severe domestic and international pressures.[137]

In the world economy, the U.S. dollar constitutes 60 percent of all foreign-exchange reserves and 50 percent of the world's private financial wealth, while the United States contributes no more than 20 percent of world total output and 14 percent of total trade. However, observers note that the dollar no longer serves as *the* international reserve currency. The transition from a hegemonic-currency system to a multipolar-currency system requires a sufficient period of time; however, a precipitous drop in public confidence in the dollar and the international financial system could cause financial earthquakes, sending shockwaves throughout the global political economy. While central banks are interested in supporting a major international currency, it also is clear that they are diversifying their currency reserves and holdings.[138] Future political economists and historians will determine whether the current relative decline of the U.S. dollar's hegemonic status is similar to that experienced by the British sterling; this transition from unipolar hegemonic currency to a multipolar system, if mismanaged, may lead to similarly pernicious consequences.[139]

FIGURE 4.1 Declining Dollar Values Through the Mid–1990s
Source: The Economist, August 19, 1995, p 69.

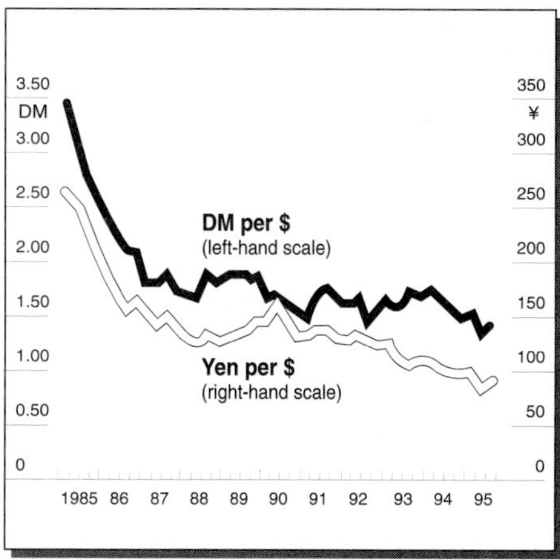

The European Union and the Euro In the twentieth century, the most important case of removing international barriers to capital mobility has been the creation of a Single European Market within the European Union (EU).[140] Built on principles of functionalism (see Chapter 2) and the promise of spillover ramifications—that is, the gradual integration of technical functions of economic management into the regional economy—the Treaty of Rome (1957) created the European Economic Community (EEC) following from the prior European Coal and Steel Community, consisting of Belgium, France, Italy, Luxembourg, the Netherlands, and Germany, to coordinate financial policies to protect their mutual interests and to take advantage of a vastly enlarged joint trading market. In 1967, the EEC merged with the European Coal and Steel Community and the European Atomic Energy Community in order to create the European Community (EC).[141]

The European Union, successor to the EC, thus has had a checkered history. France vetoed British entry, as a slap at London's close dealings with Washington, until 1972. France and Italy twice withdrew and rejoined the community. Despite pessimistic assessments of the comunity's potential to achieve greater integration, the second half of the 1980s witnessed accelerated efforts to move forward as a way of addressing problems of unemployment and inflation. By the late 1970s, Denmark, Ireland, and Britain had already become EC members. Greece joined in 1981, and Portugal and Spain, having shed their dictatorial governments, followed in 1985, raising the number of members to twelve. By May 1998, the number stood at fifteen, including former neutrals Austria, Finland, and Sweden, with a number of former Soviet bloc countries and Turkey still applying for membership. Cultural and political concerns were raised by the European Union, which turned a cold shoulder to Turkey, a prime Greek opponent and potential source of Islamic immigrants, as compared with the former East bloc states.

In March 1979, the EC established the European Monetary System (EMS) and Exchange Rate Mechanism (ERM), whereby ERM members agreed to realign exchange rate fluctuations of their currencies, within a 2.25 percent band—that is, of its value in terms of the *European Currency Unit (ECU),* a combined basket of currencies.[142] Significantly, this required ERM members to intervene in markets in unspecified amounts to readjust the value of their currencies in line with that of the community's.[143] The ECU was comprised of member currencies, whose share is based on their GNPs. As a monetary unit, governments have used the ECU for various financial transactions, including settling debts and claims. Member central banks are required to maintain exchange rates within specified terms of ECUs. Under the ECU system, erratic fluctuations in exchange rates and other economic indicators would warn the ECU Council and trigger intervention to address the imbalances as indicated by fluctuations in a member's currency rate. In 1985, the EC Commission proposed a number of initiatives to strengthen the ECU in the world economy and to integrate EC markets. The proposals included liberalization of capital mobility, elimination of border restrictions on financial transactions and services, and elimination of restrictions to transborder transfers of goods and services. EC members adopted the Single European Act in 1986 to begin the implementation of these proposals, a process to be completed on January 1, 1999, by the full implementation of the European Monetary Union, when member currencies are expected to be converted into the single European currency, the Euro. One Euro is set to equal one ECU.[144]

Following a traditional pattern of spillover from one agreement to the next, as expected by the neo-functionalist theory,[145] in 1988, the European Council, in an effort to prepare for the establishment of a unified European currency, created the Delors Committee, named after its chair, Jacques Delors, the then finance minister of France and the president of the European Commission. In 1989, the European Council accepted the Delors Committee Report, which proposed a conversion scheme to a unified currency, based on three phases. The first phase required close coordination of the Exchange Rate Mechanism (ERM). The second phase required that the central banks of EC countries widen their coordination of monetary policy and set up a European Central Bank (ECB). Finally, in the third phase, the ECB would assume full responsibility of managing European monetary policy, and a single European currency would replace existing national currencies.[146] By the end of 1990, when the first phase was supposed to have been completed, British membership in the ERM had just come into effect, and London, concerned with surrendering monetary sovereignty, showed no interest in greater monetary integration. The process of integration continued, however, and central banks began to accept the ECU, and ECU-denominated bonds, as national and international ECU-issues already had increased to 15 billion ECUs.[147]

A number of problems had to be overcome before further integration could be accomplished. Greater integration, some feared, would mean diminishing national sovereignty with respect to issues involving national monetary policy, but particularly employment, taxation, and social security. In 1992, Danish voters rejected a referendum on the Maastricht Treaty, maintaining EU membership but rejecting economic unification and the common currency. Moreover, economic difficulties in German reunification, including concerns over a spiraling inflation and rising unemployment in both western and especially in eastern Germany; the failure of Britain and Italy to meet ERM requirements for currency convergence; the necessary readjustments in Spain's, Portugal's, and Ireland's currencies; and France's and Italy's level of budgetary deficits raised doubts regarding the future of the EMU. These problems were exacerbated by rising unemployment levels in most of the EU countries, as discussed in Chapter 1, and instability in foreign exchange rates.[148] However, by the time of the May 1998 EU summit at Brussels, leaders had cleared the way toward implementation of the Euro, even with possibly delayed participation by Britain, Denmark, and Sweden.[149]

Despite the difficulties, EU economic integration moved forward, and financial transactions and services are expected to be streamlined, so that, for example, a business license issued by a member country will be acceptable throughout the EU. As Box 4.4 shows, a similar traumatic process occurred in the history of the United States as the new republic moved from the Articles of Confederation to the new federal Constitution and established an integrated currency system. In the process of EMU development there also were periods of dissension, as in divisions between a DMark bloc (including Germany, Benelux, and Austria) and a franc bloc (including France, Spain, Britain, and Italy).[150]

What, then, can be said regarding the future prospects for European financial integration as formulated under the EMU? First, as Eichengreen and Frieden correctly note, it is worth stressing that the EMU is a political as well as a

BOX 4.4

THE DEVELOPMENT OF A SINGLE U.S. CURRENCY: A CASE OF MONETARY UNION

The United States did not create its modern central banking system, the Federal Reserve, until 1913. A number of financial crises eventually convinced the political and economic leaders that a central banking system was required to maintain financial stability based on sound monetary policy. Among the industrialized countries, however, the United States was a relatively latecomer to such a system. England had created its central banking system in the 1840s, Germany in the 1870s under Bismarck, and Japan in the 1880s as a result of the Meiji Restoration. Under the Articles of Confederation (1780–1789), the "League of Friendship" reserved total financial sovereignty for the states, while the national government remained powerless in economic matters. Prior to the integration of the national financial system, state banks issued bank notes, circulated as currency convertible to gold or silver and held as bank assets. The United States did not have a nationally integrated, uniform currency, and each state bank issued its own notes, with widely different market values. States struggled against each other for more economic power and territory—for example, Connecticut–New York skirmished to control parts of Vermont. These conditions were exacerbated by the chaotic currency situation as the Continental paper money virtually lost its value, while the states' currencies depreciated in various degrees. Under such unstable and unpredictable conditions, it was not surprising that investors had little incentive to invest and risk their capital. Created in 1781 as a private financial institution, the Bank of North America was the first national bank in the United States. Its primary goal was to finance the Continental Army, but it ceased its operation in 1791 after the ratification of the Constitution. The adoption of the Constitution sought to create a stronger national government and to promote greater financial integration and stability.

As the first Secretary of the Treasury (1789–1795), *federalist* Alexander Hamilton insisted that a strong national banking system was necessary in order to develop a strong national economy based on manufacturing. In opposition, however, the *antifederalists* led by Thomas Jefferson emphasized the agricultural economy and advocated state rights and self-reliance, rather than a nationally integrated banking system under a strong national government. George Washington, however, with federalist leanings supported Hamilton, and the U.S. government granted its first twenty-year charter of the First Bank of the United States in 1791. The new national currency, which had already been in place since the Confederation, was adopted by Congress in 1792 at $1 = 24.75 grains of gold, following the value of the Spanish milled dollar, based on the decimal system (silver $1 = 371.25 grains of silver—hence, the original U.S. bimetallic standard). The adoption of the Constitution, thus, paved the way for centralization of the national economy and currency and allowed greater freedom for transboundary movement of goods across states within the new republic. The Constitution created a "dollar zone" in the new republic and a free, internal common market, while protecting domestic infant industries against foreign competitors—steel and paper mills in Pennsylvania, iron in New England, brewers in New York, and so forth. The two crucial decisions by ultra-federalist Chief Justice John Marshall in *McCulloch v. Maryland* (1819) and *Osborn v. United States Bank* (1824) strengthened the position of Congress with respect to the creation of a national banking system vis-a-vis the states.

The First Bank of the United States issued paper currency, and individuals and businesses deposited their accounts with and borrowed loans from it. The country's largest bank, it had branches in major cities—for example, Boston, New York and Chicago—and became the vehicle for the federal government's monetary policy, as state banks could not meet the developmental needs of the nation. In the late 1790s, no more than five banks operated; by 1811 about 250 banks were in operation. However, the need for a national currency remained unmet, and states resisted greater integration of the national banking system.

The federal government accumulated a considerable national debt during the War of 1812, and the state banks failed to meet that challenge as well. In order to address the national debt and stabilize the economy, the federal government created the Second Bank of the United States in 1816 and sought to formalize a national currency and a uniform monetary system. In 1834, it changed the coinage system to paper money. Like its predecessor, the Second Bank failed to have wide public support, particularly because of jurisdictional disputes with the states. The opposition included national leaders among its ranks as well. President Andrew Jackson (1829–1837) viewed the Second Bank as being dominated by the northeastern banking and emerging manufacturing establishment. In 1833, the Treasury redeposited funds into state banks, and the Second Bank's charter expired in 1836. The collapse of the national banking system led to the "free banking era" (1836–1863), with little national regulation of banking throughout the country. *The Independent Treasury System (ITS)* was introduced in 1846, with federal reserve branches in major cities. This system, however, proved to be highly unstable due to erratic reserves fluctuations and

BOX 4.4 (concluded)

THE DEVELOPMENT OF A SINGLE U.S. CURRENCY: A CASE OF MONETARY UNION

cumbersome organizational arrangements involving *reserve cities* and *central reserve cities.* Under the ITS, one growing difficulty was that national economic development was occurring mostly in regions other than the Northeast, but it remained the national banking center. As a result, the national banking system did not appear to be meeting the local financial needs of developing regions.

By the time the National Bank Act was passed in 1863, there were 1,000 national and 600 state banks issuing their own bank notes as IOUs. Banks and the public continued to accept gold and silver coins as legal tender, even when the banks did not possess sufficient reserves for convertibility. Many banks failed. During the Civil War, the Lincoln administration suspended state banks' currency-gold convertibility and instead issued *greenbacks,* federal national paper currency not supported by gold. In the meantime, the national government functioned without an officially established central bank, leaving the Treasury Department to conduct the national government's financial operations. The national government discontinued the greenbacks and returned to gold convertibility.

By the 1870s, the number of state banks declined, and Congress precipitated the elimination of state bank notes by imposing a 10 percent tax on them, which soon led to the disappearance of state bank notes. Deposit funds and checks became the mainstay of state banking, and, since state banking laws were more accommodative of local needs and interests than were federal laws, the number of state banks rose. As public confidence in the national economy improved, so did the position of banks. Between 1900 and 1920, the number of national and state banks increased from 12,427 to over 30,000.

During the late 1800s, however, chronic financial panics had underscored the need for a politically independent central bank to manage the circulation of currency and credits, and, in the first decade of this century, Congress and the White House created the National Monetary Commission to examine and propose a comprehensive national banking plan without relying on a highly centralized system. Their proposals led to the passage of the Federal Reserve Act in 1913, creating a new national banking system comprised of twelve regional banks, each operating as "bankers' bank." The Federal Reserve is institutionally and legally independent of the political institutions. Decentralized in their organization, the regional banks regulate banking operations within their respective regions under the auspices of the Federal Reserve Board in Washington, DC. The board does not operate a central bank per se; rather, it makes monetary policy for the nation and directs lower-level banks to expand or contract the supply of money in the economy. The principal objective of the Federal Reserve was to maintain financial stability and to avoid financial panics experienced in previous decades. The board adjusts the interest rate and securities transactions in money markets. Under the Federal Reserve, the United States became a "single bank country," with an integrated national economy and financial system.

Sources: See Hazel J. Johnson, *Financial Institutions and Markets: A Global Perspective* (New York: McGraw-Hill, 1993); Charles Manfred Thompson and Fred Mitchell Jones, *Economic Development of the United States* (New York: Macmillan, 1939); Harold Underwood Faulkner, *American Economic History* (New York: Harper and Brothers, 1924); Ross M. Robertson, *History of the American Economy* (New York: Harcourt, Brace and Company, 1955); and John J. Klein, *Money and the Economy,* 2d ed. (New York: Harcourt, Brace and World, 1970).

financial arrangement, and analyses focusing exclusively on its financial aspects can prove misleading.[151] Moreover, the EMU operates in a global political economy, having been stimulated by a sense of North American and Asian competition in advanced technologies. Events on other continents can exert an enormous impact on the EMU's internal affairs. As an advantage of unification, the EMU is expected to provide a cushion against inflationary and recessionary pressures. As economies converge, so will their trade and budgetary policies. As the inflation in the 1970s and 1980s made the idea of pegging national currencies to the DMark politically more palatable for EMU member countries, so might the Euro function as an effective tool against a regionwide inflation. At issue in this respect is whether the European Central Bank (ECB) and its Governing Council, comprised of the governors of national central banks, will be able to remain politically independent, so as to respond to inflationary pressures effectively. Despite being more committed to EMU than Britain, even German officials and citizens have expressed qualms about handing over responsibility for monetary policy to a multilateral central bank. Although the Maastricht Treaty explicitly prohibits the ECB from rescuing national governments and their banks, debt levels and public spending in countries such as France and Italy traditionally have been far greater than those in Germany.[152] Eichengreen and Frieden contend that, while in theory central bank independence may be desirable, in practice it may not be possible to insulate the ECB from national political pressures to the extent necessary.[153] Whether the ECB succeeds in establishing its political independence remains to be seen, but the credibility of the Euro, as the region's money, will hinge on the credibility of the bank, its manager.

Clearly, further financial integration would not be possible without the removal of national restrictions on capital mobility across borders. Conversion to a single regional currency would eliminate wide fluctuations in exchange rates and, in so doing, would remove fears of financial collapse, for whatever reasons, of national currencies.[154] The EMU structure would provide a safety net for exchange-rate stability. Such an arrangement is expected to prove crucial in times of economic difficulties, when the tendency for each nation, as experienced during the Great Depression, would be, for economic and political reasons, to rely on mercantilist policies favoring its national currency, industries, and employment.

The principal disadvantage associated with the EMU is the diminution of national monetary sovereignty. This remains central in all scenarios for the future of the EMU. While in times of economic growth and prosperity national sovereignty may not pose a serious problem to the European unification scheme, in hard times "asymmetric shocks"—that is, economic difficulties (inflation, unemployment) affecting different regions differently—may increase resentment toward EMU partners and national policymakers, not only for their inability to rectify the economic situation but now also for their failure to provide sufficient shock absorbers between the EMU and the national economy. Greater freedom for worker mobility across borders within the region is also likely to pose a serious adjustment problem, as the unemployed in one country seek employment in another. Further, it is necessary to establish a viable mechanism for the redistribution of fiscal resources from one region experiencing economic growth to another in decline. Despite the move toward integration, structural, cultural, and linguistic differences still exist and may cause political difficulties when economies slow down.[155]

Besides the advantages and disadvantages, it is necessary to add that the EMU does not exist in a vacuum. It is very much a part of the global system, and its internal financial situation affects, and is directly influenced by, that system. In this regard, one question is which economy among the EU members is most likely to maintain strong leverage in international finance and, hence, in the EU itself. In the 1980s, the German DMark clearly established itself as a leading regional and international currency, directly challenging the U.S. dollar and yen, as Germany emerged as one of the largest exporters in the world.[156] Increases in German trade enhanced the international status of the DMark, as more countries used it for trade purposes. As shown in Table 4.5, in 1996, about 14 percent of the world's total official reserves were in DMarks, while nearly 63 percent were in U.S. dollars.[157] The U.S. dollar dropped by 11 percent against the DMark in 1994, and it continued to fluctuate between \$1.37 in 1995 and \$1.70 in 1997. European currencies met a similar fate.[158] It remains to be seen the extent to which Germany will be able to translate its global status into regional hegemonism through the Euro.

The Euro is expected to enjoy considerable weight as an international currency, although the U.S. dollar continues to dominate the international financial scene. The Euro's relative strength will depend on the economic situation in the EU and on the EU's competitiveness in world markets. As discussed in Chapter 5, the EU's position is clearly stronger than pessimistic evaluations would suggest, and the Euro, based on the vast market it represents, is likely to emerge as the dollar's primary competitor for world hegemony. An international crisis, such as the Great Depression in the 1920s and 1930s, could catapult the

TABLE 4.5
Composition of World Official Reserves (excluding gold)

	1980 %	1996 %
Dollar	68.6	62.7
DMark	14.9	14.1
Yen	4.4	7.0
Sterling	2.9	3.2
FFr	1.7	1.7
ECU	—	1.7
Other	7.5	9.6

Source: "EMU," *The Economist* (April 11, 1998), [survey], p.17, quoting the International Monetary Fund.

Euro into a position of world hegemony, as the U.S. dollar replaced the British pound sterling in the 1930s and 1940s. On the negative side, however, if the EU experiences a political, military, or economic crisis, similar to the Asian economic crisis during the late 1990s, its impact on the international monetary system could be calamitous.

How well the European financial unification scheme can respond to international economic crises, such as the Asian crisis, after the conversion to a single currency in January 1999 is another question. In the second half of the 1990s, after the Asian economies began to collapse, serious questions were raised concerning the health of major European banks, which stood to lose billions of dollars in Asian investments. Standard & Poor's (S&P), the international credit agency, estimated that European banks would lose nearly $20 billion in Asian loans.[159] More optimistic observers noted that the Asian crisis was not likely to jeopardize European banking and the financial situation. In fact, the Asian crisis was seen by some in both North America and Europe as providing opportunities for banking and other industry expansion to Asian markets. In 1998, the Banque National de Paris (BNP) announced its acquisition of the Peregrine's Greater China and BNP's plan to merge PrimEast, a brokerage firm in Singapore it had purchased in 1997, with the Peregrine group.[160]

Finally, another set of issues is worth considering. This involves the question of EU leadership and international representation. As of this writing, it is not clear, for example, who will represent the EU in multilateral institutions, such as the International Monetary Fund and the World Bank, not to mention the UN Security Council (where two of the five permanent members are Britain and France). Will the United States and Japan accept representation by individual EU countries at the G-8 summit meetings, or will they insist on one representative for the EU?[161] Political union may not necessarily follow monetary union, but the reality that these issues may cause serious difficulties is obvious.

East Asia and Yen Diplomacy The decade of the 1980s proved a major transition period for Japan's status in the international trading and financial system, as the world economy experienced structural changes in various sectors. By the end of the decade, Japan had emerged as the world's largest lender, with a total net asset of $240 billion, and Japanese banks began to function as global financial centers—to the extent that some observers began to draw similarities between Japan's position as international financier and that enjoyed by the British in the nineteenth and early twentieth centuries, and by the United States for three decades after the Second World War.[162] Thus, as the decline of the U.S. dollar in the 1970s and 1980s bore similarities to that of the British, so the position of the Japanese yen seemed similar to that of the U.S. dollar in the 1930s and 1940s. Nevertheless, Japan's economy is probably not large enough to supply enough yen to the world economy to make the yen the hegemonic currency in the twenty-first century, nor, as the Asian economic crisis of 1997–1998 suggests, do the Japanese banks and the economy in general appear to be on as strong a footing as some Western experts believed in the 1980s and early 1990s.

While no one expects an EMU-style integration in East Asia, the expansive role of Japanese trade and financial relations has strengthened the yen's role in that region, and the yen is in a similar position as the DMark in Europe, although the DMark's credibility remains stronger. The strength of the Japanese yen stems largely from the balance-of-payments and trade surpluses Japan has registered consistently since the early 1980s. Further, during the Cold War, the security umbrella provided by the United States freed large sums of Japan's national budget for corporate innovations and advancements, many of which were geared to providing secure employment to Japanese workers and a steady flow of Japanese exports.

While by the mid-1980s public opinion began to exert some influence on the U.S. government to deal with trade imbalances, it was not until the Cold War neared its end that the dollar-yen rivalry intensified. In 1984, U.S. banks were still the leading lenders in the world economy, their holdings totaling 27 percent of international assets markets. Japan's share was about 23 percent (second highest), and France, Britain, and West Germany about 5 to 10 percent. In terms of the composition of world official reserves, in 1980 the yen's share was 4.4 percent, which increased to 7.0 percent by 1996 (see Table 4.5). The dollar's share declined from 68.6 percent to 62.7 percent for the same period. Thus, while the U.S. dollar continues to dominate the hierarchy of international currencies, the Japanese yen has secured significant gains. As Table 4.6 shows, however, the position of the U.S. banks declined as the Japanese banks began a surge of expansion, by early 1985 equaling that of the U.S. banks' and by late 1985 surpassing them.[163] Soon, Japan became the leading creditor in the world economy, in large part because of its surpluses in balance of payments. Among these five major economies, only the United States exhibited a continuous decline in bank holdings by over ten percentage points, in

TABLE 4.6

International Positions by Nationality of Ownership of International Assets, 1985–1990 (Billions of U.S. Dollars)

Country	September 1985	December 1985	December 1986	December 1987	December 1988	December 1989	December 1990
Japan	639.6	706.2	1,119.3	1,553.9	1,765.4	1,967.4	2,071.5
	(25.7)	(26.3)	(32.4)	(35.4)	(38.2)	(37.9)	(36.0)
USA	580.2	589.4	600.3	649.4	666.8	727.7	687.9
	(23.3)	(21.9)	(17.4)	(14.8)	(14.4)	(14.0)	(11.9)
France	221.0	233.7	288.7	376.6	384.1	432.9	524.8
	(8.8)	(8.7)	(8.4)	(8.6)	(8.3)	(8.4)	(9.1)
Germany	165.1	191.2	279.1	346.9	354.0	435.6	551.2
	(6.6)	(7.1)	(7.8)	(7.9)	(7.7)	(8.4)	(9.5)
UK	181.7	191.8	211.5	253.9	239.1	247.1	267.2
	(7.3)	(7.1)	(6.1)	(5.7)	(5.2)	(4.8)	(4.6)

Source: BIS, *International Banking and Financial Market Developments,* Basle, various issues.
Note: Figures in the parentheses stand for the proportional share of the total international assets market (in percent).

direct proportion to Japan's increase by ten percentage points.[164]

In the early 1990s, one of the major debates concerned not only whether the yen had been sufficiently internationalized to replace the dollar and the DMark, but also whether a new *yen zone* was emerging in the newly industrializing East Asia. One of the implications of Japan's growing economic power in international financial relations has been its expanding (or reasserting) and, some would say, increasingly "burdensome" influence on Asian countries' financial situation, as in the case of Indonesia (see Figure 4.2). Faced with resentments in the industrialized countries, especially in the United States, toward its growing wealth and economic power in the world economy, Japan witnessed the intensification of *kenbei* ("dislike of the United States") at home and public demands to "return to Asia."[165] The subsequent Asian economic crisis, however, underscored a dilemma for the countries in the region. While they resented Japanese economic penetration of their national economies, the withdrawal of the Japanese banks and companies also raised the specter of total economic collapse without the safety net these banks and companies could provide.

During the past two decades, Japanese banks have used their leverage in East Asia through credit-creation by financing vast public and private development projects. By one estimate, in the mid-1990s Japanese banks financed between 40 and 60 percent of investments in the region's projects. In fact, after the early 1980s, the total volume of Japanese investments in East Asia exceeded U.S. investments by a wide margin. Moreover, Japan's foreign aid programs for Asian countries also have surpassed those of the United States. According to one estimate, Japan's official development aid (ODA) to the region has increased by about 5.7 percent per year since the early 1980s, while the U.S. ODA increased by 2.2 percent. Japan contributed over 50 percent of ODA to the members of the **Association of Southeast Asian Nations (ASEAN)** and to China, while U.S. contributions were about 11 percent.[166] Nevertheless, despite the expanding trade and financial

FIGURE 4.2 Indonesia's Long-Term Debt by Currency, 1993
Source: The Economist, March 25, 1995, p. 40.

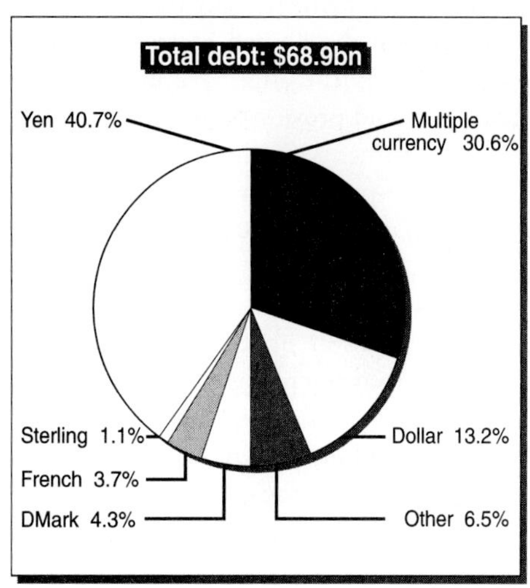

relations between Japan and the other countries in the region, nearly 80 percent of intra-Asia trade is still conducted in U.S. dollars.[167] During the Asian economic crisis in 1997–1998, however, public officials and private investors in East Asia expressed concern that, as the yen declined in value, Japanese banks were no longer inclined to provide the investment loans needed for growth.[168]

The first signs of trouble were Japanese banking failures caused by overzealous, poorly judged investments in U.S. properties during the 1980s. There followed an even worse set of shocks, as other Asian economies, stock markets, and currencies nose-dived in the late 1990s. The reasons for these disruptions ranged from poor local banking practices, to bad local investments, to government corruption. Japan, highly committed financially throughout the Asian region, shared in these stock and economic slumps.

Despite the economic growth of the 1980s, the Asian financial crisis compelled observers to reevaluate their analyses of East Asia's economic robustness. This crisis perhaps underscores structural deficiencies in East Asian political economy. It is argued that "Asian capitalism" suffers from a *zaibetsu*-style symbiotic relationship between policymakers and corporate conglomerates dominated by bank-driven *keiretsu* companies, as pointed out in Chapter 2. In such a system, especially in the case of Japan, the close relationship between policymakers and banks, who are also the major shareholders in the major corporations, effectively insulated their decisions from market pressures and accorded highest priority to increases in cross-shareholding and political calculations.[169] Culture and tradition also dictated that banks "cover" for their best customers wherever possible when loans could not be repaid. Japanese banks themselves suffered heavy blows when their own overcommitments to risky foreign investments (as in real estate), in the United States, Thailand, and elsewhere, fell apart. In the aftermath of the crisis, complete restructuring would prove very costly; it is likely that the East Asian governments would opt for intervention, such as massive pump-priming through public works, and regulatory reforms to revive their economies and political fortunes.[170]

After the demise of the Soviet Union and the gradual weakening of the U.S. position in the region after the Vietnam War, China emerged as a major regional competitor, but one with which Japan and the United States also have sought collaboration and investment opportunities, as demonstrated by President Clinton's visit to China in 1998. Some countries in the region tend to prefer closer ties with Japan and to distance themselves from the United States. Others remember bitter wartime experiences at the hands of the Japanese, or conflictual ethnic experiences with the Chinese. In fact, as **Asia Pacific Economic Cooperation (APEC)** was being organized in the early 1990s, Malaysia's prime minister, Mohamed Mahathir, proposed the creation of an East Asian Economic Group (EAEG) to further strengthen trade and financial links in the region. If such a plan does materialize, it would most likely develop a yen bloc, centering on Japan. The Mahathir proposal, however, was rejected by some in the region and most vociferously by the United States, because the plan would exclude North America and Australia, founding members of APEC.[171]

More significantly, countries in the region are apprehensive about any potential *regionalist* geo-economic and geo-political designs Japan might yet envision. They still remember the devastation and suffering Japan's military expansionist binge caused in the 1920s and 1930s. In an effort to address their concerns, during his tour of Southeast Asian countries in August 1977, Japan's Prime Minister Takeo Fukuda enunciated what became known as the *Fukuda Doctrine,* encompassing three key principles of Japan's future foreign policy toward the region (1) Japan's decision not to use military force in the region; (2) emphasis on "heart-to-heart" understanding between Japan and its neighbors to expand regional cooperation in areas of economic, cultural, and social relations; and (3) the extension of development assistance to the region to strengthen bilateral and multilateral relations.[172] Nevertheless, a visit by the Japanese emperor to Southeast Asia in October 1991 and to China a year later still elicited massive criticism of Japan's historical regional role. Japan has yet to apologize formally for its aggressive military policy, and it is not clear whether its promises not to use military force in the future assuage the neighbors' fears.[173] Accordingly, most countries prefer to maintain an equidistant policy toward both the United States and Japan: to expand economic ties with Japan, while counting on the United States as the Pacific "power balancer" for purposes of national security.[174]

Thus, while Japan has become the world's largest creditor, because of its high capital concentration in Asia, it is safe to say that the yen has yet to replace the DMark as the second competitor international currency;[175] despite its sometimes weak position, the dollar remains the international currency. The speed with which Japan can recover from the Asian economic crisis will affect the yen's value relative to the Euro at the turn of the millennium. The industrialized countries, and those in transition, such as the former Soviet Union, continue to favor the dollar (to be precise, in Russia's case, $100 bills, redesigned to better prevent counterfeit) and the DMark over the yen. To be sure, the purpose of this discussion of currency multipolarity is not to suggest that the U.S. dollar as an international currency is dead. Despite the advances made by the DMark and the yen, central banks are interested in maintaining strong dollars to assure financial stability and liquidity for their own economies,[176] yet it is also obvious that the dollar no longer commands the heights of international finance, and central banks will choose other currencies if necessary.

The Islamic Development Bank In addition to the European Monetary Union and Japan, which already have emerged as major actors in international finance, Islamic societies also have the potential of developing a financial system, centered on the Islamic Development Bank (IDB).[177] Founded in 1974 by member states of the Organization of Islamic Conference (OIC), the creation of the IDB was a part of the general movement among the developing countries in the 1960s and 1970s to create multilateral institutions counterbalancing Western economic domination. Although the IDB thus far has not met the expectations of its founders, its operations during its first decades have expanded substantially, encompassing a wide variety of financial activities.

The Bank's principal objectives include, *inter alia,* forging closer cooperation among Muslim countries to develop international banking structures based on Islamic principles of the *Shari'a* (such as "interest-free" banking), encouraging economic development and improvements in social and related programs, and promoting saving and investments in Muslim countries and throughout the *umma.*[178] The IDB finances economic development and promotes trade among Islamic countries. By one estimate, trade represents 80 percent of its operations through a network of Islamic multilateral institutions, such as the Import Trade Financing Operations (ITFO), the Islamic Banks' Portfolio (IBP), the Longer-Term Trade Financing Scheme (LTTFS), the Islamic Co-operation for the Insurance of Investment and Export Credit, the Unit Investment Fund (UIF), and the Islamic Trade Company (ITC), the last two established in 1990. Income from trade transactions represent between 30 and 40 percent of IDB revenues. The combined assets among Islamic banks total nearly $50 billion, and the IDB has expanded its operations to include various derivative contracts—for example, future commodity contracts, stock options, currency options—operating within the global financial system.[179]

The IDB has been successful in integrating its operations among Muslim states, such as Iran, Malaysia, Pakistan, and Sudan, whose finances adhere quite strictly to Islamic principles, into other Muslim countries that have maintained a combination of Islamic and Western-style finances, such as in Egypt, Indonesia, and Jordan. One of the principal characteristics of the financial system developed under the IDB is the absence of a single dominant country. Unlike the case of the EMU, in which Germany is the dominant economy, or East Asia, where Japan has reigned supreme, no single country commands a clear primary position in the Islamic financial system. Saudi Arabia holds a prominent position in Islam because Mecca, the holy city for pilgrimage, and Medina, also significant in the history of Islam, are located there and because of vast "petro-dollar" holdings, but its limited population base and close ties with the West have precluded it from playing a preeminent role in Islamic finance. In addition, there is no indigenous reserve currency among the Islamic states to compete with the dollar or yen in their commercial relations. However, Islamic banking, based largely on dollars, has spread throughout the world, from London and Copenhagen to South Africa and Southeast Asia. The IDB is positioned to propel Islamic finance toward greater global integration in the next century, if not toward the type of hegemony that comes from issuing a reserve currency.

Globalization and Financial Crises

It was previously noted that globalization places a premium on the effective management of national and international economy. The inability to do so can lead to economic and political crises emanating from the epicenter of the crisis to the neighboring economies, to the region, and to the world economy, as experienced during the Great Depression, and during Asian and Russian crises of the late 1990s. Such a crisis would undermine the legitimacy of the governments involved and—if Kindleberger's analysis is valid—would further undermine the leadership capabilities of a declining hegemonic power. In fact, Kindleberger's thesis would stress that financial crises as experienced in Mexico, Russia, and Asia are symptomatic of a world financial system that lacks a clear leader, a world financial "balancer."

The previous discussion suggests that, under trying circumstances, globalization of finance can have serious disadvantages but also some advantages. The primary disadvantage is that the structure of the global political economy, as founded on telecommunications technologies, can instantaneously transmit repercussions of an economic catastrophe in one region of the world to another. It is incumbent on decisionmakers in public and private milieus, therefore, to respond with sufficient pace and wisdom to contain financial crises. The principal advantage of financial globalization is that there are national and international mechanisms that, despite their shortcomings, and given sufficient political will, can respond quickly with the requisite international support. The quick international response to the Mexican crisis in 1994–1995, driven by the vast implications of a peso collapse for U.S. banks, firms, and Wall Street investors, may have alleviated the total collapse of that economy. That was certainly the hope of the multilateral IMF intervention to shore up Asian economies and Brazil during the 1990s as well. As noted with respect to money generally, globalization of international finance *and* international responses to financial crises do not operate independently of politics and political interests.[180]

The question of leadership entails a combination of both political and economic consequences. The collapse of the Mexican peso, if unchecked, would wreak havoc on the U.S. banking system and on Wall Street, which in turn could potentially be perceived by the international community as a manifestation of U.S. hegemonic decline. Further, in 1995, it was estimated that nearly 770,000 jobs in the United States depended on exports to Mexico, and the number of Mexican jobs affected by the collapse would certainly be at least twice as much. For the state of Texas alone, the collapse of the peso would cost from nearly $2.5 billion to as much as $7 billion in exports. In addition, further deterioration of economic conditions in Mexico would increase illegal immigration to the United States—a politically unpalatable picture a year before the 1996 elections. Therefore, from the perspectives of the Clinton administration and of companies in the first industrialized economies (FIEs), it was imperative to save the Mexican economy even in the face of Congressional opposition. In the early 1990s, foreign companies held portfolio investments worth well over $60 billion in Mexico. A total collapse of the Mexican economy would mean the lossof corporate and public confidence and an enormous loss of investments by the FIEs, followed by another round of defaults on debts, as experienced in the 1980s, with equally serious repercussions for the rest of Latin America.

As in Mexico, the East Asian financial crisis also underscored serious structural problems, such as the prodigal corporate monopolies Indonesian President Suharto's family and associates held, which had heretofore remained less visible, as the economies in the region registered startling economic growth in the 1980s and early 1990s. The international response was not as uniform with respect to the East Asian countries, however, and the Clinton administration proved less forthcoming than in the Mexican case. In the case of Indonesia, for example, the administration promised nearly $20 billion, although it initially attempted to block the transfer of additional IMF dollars, when the agency, in late 1997, had issued $3 billion of its overall bailout package totaling $40 billion. The Clinton administration insisted that the Indonesian government had failed to meet IMF requirements for structural reforms, and therefore would not qualify for the rest of the IMF aid.[181] Prior to his resignation, President Suharto had promised to dissolve some of the monopolies.[182] As was seen in Table 4.1, the fact that the value of the Indonesian rupiah had dropped from 2,228.00 rupiah for $1 (or 3,573.00 rupiah for £1) in 1995 to 11,400.00 rupiah for $1 (or 18,625.00 rupiah for £1) in 1998 would give sufficient cause for serious concern with respect to the credibility of that vast country's currency. The crisis undermined the leadership in every East Asian country from Japan to the Philippines. Thus, Washington could assume that a joint regional approach would emerge, rather than a mainly unilateral U.S. bailout attempt.

When such international rescues are mounted, it is not entirely clear how much major powers, such as the United States, seek to preserve and enhance regional economies, as opposed to expanding and extending the powers' own influence and profits in those economies. American advice to lower barriers to foreign investment and banking in Asia, for example, stands to advantage American financial interests. When President Clinton ignored diplomatic and cultural protocol by lecturing the Japanese publicly in 1998 about putting their own economic house in order, lowering taxes, stimulating the economy, and so forth, he was in a sense both acting out of concern over possible Japanese instability and advocating remedies that would stand to benefit U.S. exporters, a fact not lost on the Japanese.[183]

CONCLUSION

International finance and monetary policies constitute an essential component of international political economy.

Changes in technology and international financial institutions during the past several decades have underscored the globalization of financial relations and the advantages and challenges for governments in the industrialized and developing countries. The need to become more competitive has strengthened trends toward greater regional monetary unions, as in the case of the European Union, while international financial institutions such as the World Bank and the International Monetary Fund have been instrumental in globalization. Either way, nationalist politicians and large sectors of the public view regional integration and globalization as a direct challenge to national sovereignty.

While such changes may create the impression that we are moving toward a more unified world economy, in reality nothing can be further from the truth; interdependence is not the same as unity. Deep economic disparities and inequalities due to regional historical evolution and current international financial arrangements have resulted in the inequitable distribution of financial resources so that, even if and when organizations such as the World Bank are engaged in development projects, they are, rightly or wrongly, viewed as instruments of multinational corporate and national elite interests. The fact that the international financial system has been dominated by the major powers' currencies—for example, the British pound, U.S. dollar, the German DMark, and the Japanese yen—lends credence to claims that the international system is biased in favor of the wealthy FIEs.

However, the economically advanced FIE region itself is not a monolithic entity. While after the Second World War the U.S. dollar was the principal currency, the past decade has seen the emergence of other contenders. Currency multipolarity poses serious challenges to individual governments and the international financial order, especially if no state or states assume the role of financial leader. Some observers believe that multipolarity will lead to global financial chaos and collapse, as experienced in the 1930s and 1940s. Whether greater financial integration and globalization via telecommunications technologies can enable central banks and investors to make the transition from the U.S. hegemony to a well coordinated multipolar system remains to be seen. The globalization of finance has certain advantages and disadvantages, depending on circumstances and one's perspective. The Mexican and Asian economic crises indicate that a hegemon may still be essential for the functioning of the world economy, and despite criticisms of the United States as a hegemon, at least its currency—and its influence remain paramount. Of course, this also affects global trade, as we shall see in the next chapter.

Chapter Summary

The globalization of the international financial system requires wider knowledge and greater sophistication on the part of business leaders and students of international political economy. As international business and financial arrangements have created a single global market, the high degree of interdependence developed in the late twentieth century has made national economies more vulnerable to financial crises in faraway countries.

The world economy, however, remains divided between the historically major financial powers and the newly emerging markets. While there are equal opportunities for international cooperation and for conflict in financial matters, there is little doubt that, with globalization, the world economy has, for better or worse, achieved greater financial integration. Historically, major powers have introduced various international financial arrangements—the classic gold standard, for example, under *Pax Britannica*—to strengthen their hegemonic position in the world economy.

After the Second World War, the Bretton Woods system established two major multilateral financial institutions: the International Monetary Fund (IMF) and the World Bank. The former has developed international rules and standards in efforts to maintain stability in the international financial system. In 1970, the IMF established Special Drawing Rights (SDRs) as an additional mechanism to promote stability and economic growth. The World Bank was created specifically to enable war-torn countries to rebuild their economies and then to encourage economic development in developing countries.

Also, under the Bretton Woods system the international financial system was based on fixed exchange rates, in which currencies were pegged to the cost of gold and the U.S. dollar. After the collapse of that system, countries adopted the system of floating exchange rates, whereby the value of a currency appreciates or depreciates in relation to other currencies, as determined by the free market dynamics of supply and demand.

Several factors influence the foreign exchange value of a currency: the financial changes taking place around the world and their impact on the currency, the level of a country's income, its GNP, the level and value of imports, and the level of inflation. Further, social-psychological factors, political scandals, national security crises, public perceptions and expectations, technological discoveries, and changes in consumer tastes all influence a currency's foreign exchange value.

After the Second World War, the U.S. dollar was the hegemonic international currency, and international financial and trade transactions were conducted primarily in dollars. By the late 1960s, however, public confidence in the dollar had eroded. Although the dollar gradually recovered its strength, by then at least two major and potentially international currencies had emerged—the German DMark and the Japanese yen. The former is strong in the European Union where a Euro currency is emerging, while the latter may develop its own "yen zone" in East Asia. The end of the Cold War has certainly provided the international political and economic environment for competing currencies to emerge, although the U.S. dollar continues to be the dominant international currency.

Points of Contention

Based on the material presented in the chapter, to what extent would you say the newly emerging stock markets in places such as China and Russia will be able to compete with the more established markets? Will the newly emerging markets contribute to international financial stability or lead to instability?

Should the world economy be based on a system of fixed exchange rates or floating exchange rates? Should a gold standard be renewed?

Should the IMF and the World Bank have any role in further strengthening the current international financial system?

In your opinion, how successful was the Bretton Woods system?

Would you support the creation of a *universal money?* Should the IMF create a universal currency to replace all national currencies? Are SDRs such a currency?

Should the IMF continue to maintain its principle of conditionality when giving out loans to states?

Should voting in the World Bank and the IMF be weighted according to financial contribution, population, economic need, or some other criteria?

Is the U.S. dollar in the process of decline as an international currency? If yes, will the German DMark or the Japanese yen emerge as the next hegemonic currency? What are the implications of the Asian economic crisis of 1997–1998 for the yen as an international currency?

How successful has the European Currency Unit (ECU) been in integrating EU markets? What are some of the similarities and differences in the history of U.S. and EU financial integration and unification?

How do Japan's neighbors perceive its role as a major economic power in the region? Should Japan formally apologize for its past misdeeds?

What factors would enable the Islamic Development Bank to emerge as a major international banking system in the next century?

What is the impact of the globalization of international finance on national economic sovereignty? What is its impact on government management of national economies? What is your overall assessment of the globalization of finance and the functions of money?

Notes

1. *The Wall Street Journal,* March 8, 1995, p. A1.
2. *Ibid.*
3. *The Economist,* February 4, 1995, p. 65.
4. Susan Strange, *States and Markets,* 2d ed. (London: Pinter, 1994).
5. *Ibid.,* p. 90.
6. Paul Einzig, *Primitive Money in Its Ethnological, Historical and Economic Aspects* (London: Eyre and Spottiswoode, 1949), p. 25.
7. *Ibid.,* pp. 340–64, and passim. See also Strange, *States and Markets,* p. 95.
8. Einzig, *Primitive Money,* p. 25.
9. As discussed in Einzig, *Primitive Money,* p. 381.
10. See Henry L. Bretton, *The Power of Money: A Political-Economic Analysis with Special Emphasis on the American Political System* (Albany: State University of New York Press, 1980).
11. Georg Simmel, *The Philosophy of Money,* ed. David Frisby, trans. Tom Bottomore and David Frisby, 2d enl. ed. (London: Routledge, 1990), p. 286.
12. Strange, *States and Markets,* p. 95. Italics in original.
13. Ethan B. Kapstein, *Governing the Global Economy: International Finance and the State* (Cambridge: Harvard University Press, 1994). See also reviews by Benjamin Cohen, in *World Politics* 48, 2 (January 1996) pp. 268–297; Gerard Caprio, Jr., in *Journal of Economic Literature* 34, 1 (March 1996) pp. 144–146.
14. See Paul R. Krugman and Maurice Obstfeld, *International Economics: Theory and Policy,* 2d ed. (New York: HarperCollins, 1991), pp. 350–351.

15. *Ibid.*, p. 350.
16. See, for example, Manuel Pastor, Jr., *Inflation, Stabilization, and Debt: Macroeconomic Experiments in Peru and Bolivia* (Boulder, CO: Westview Press, 1992).
17. Hansjörg Herr, Silke Tober, and Andreas Westphal, eds., *Macroeconomic Problems of Transformation: Stabilization Policies and Economic Reconstructuring* (Aldershot UK: Edward Elgar, 1994). See also Elmar Murtazayev and Anna Baneva, "Finance," *Current Digest of the Post-Soviet Press,* June 14, 1995, p. 24; Equally critical to financial credibility after wars. See Josh Martin, "Lebanon Lures International Finance to Pay for Reconstruction," *Middle East* (July–August 1995): pp. 18–20.
18. Mordechai E. Kreinin, *International Economics: A Policy Approach,* 4th ed. (San Diego: Harcourt Brace Jovanovich, 1983), p. 26.
19. For an experimental analysis of exchange rate determination, see Charles N. Noussair, Charles R. Plott, and Raymond G. Riezman, "The Principles of Exchange Rate Determination in an International Finance Experiment," *Journal of Political Economy* 105, 4 (August 1997): pp. 822–62.
20. See, for example, Paul R. Krugman and Maurice Obstfeld, *International Economics: Theory and Policy,* 2d ed. (New York: HarperCollins, 1991); Robert J. Carbaugh, *International Economics,* 3d ed. (Belmont: Wadsworth, 1989).
21. For a discussion on derivatives, see Andrew Cornford, "Some Recent Innovations in International Finance: Different Faces of Risk Management and Control," *Journal of Economic Issues* 30, 2 (June 1996): pp. 493–509.
22. Kreinin, *International Economics,* p. 30.
23. *Ibid.*
24. Each country's central bank intervenes in the foreign exchange market by buying and selling currencies or setting pegged exchange rates to maintain stable currencies and to avoid erratic exchange rate fluctuations, especially in the undesirable direction. When the exchange value of a currency increases, the central bank sells its currency and purchases foreign currencies to restrain the level of increase. When a country's currency outflow presses its exchange value downward, the central bank purchases its domestic currency and sells foreign currencies to restrain the decline. In the case of the United States, for example, the Federal Reserve intervened a number of times in the 1970s to strengthen the dollar by selling German marks. Steven Husted and Michael Melvin, *International Economics,* 2d ed. (New York: HarperCollins, 1993); Kreinin, *International Economics,* pp. 56–57.
25. *Ibid.*, p. 35.
26. *Ibid.*, pp. 43–46.
27. Krugman and Obstfeld, *International Economics,* p. 469; Kreinin, *International Economics,* pp. 36, 57; Andrew Walter, *World Power and World Money: The Role of Hegemony and International Monetary Order* (New York: Harvester Wheatsheaf, 1991).
28. George S. Tavlas, "The Deutsche Mark as an International Currency," in Dilip K. Das, ed., *International Finance: Contemporary Issues* (London: Routledge, 1993), pp. 566–568.
29. Board of Governors of the Federal Reserve System, *Federal Reserve Bulletin* and *Annual Statistical Digest* (various years).
30. As the economy recovered in the mid-1980s, the Fed lowered the discount rate to 9.0 percent in 1984 and to 5.0 percent in 1991. The recession of 1990–1992 forced the discount rate to about 3.5 percent, which rose to 5.0 percent in 1994–95 as the economy showed signs of improvement. In the meantime, popular movements known as "taxpayers' revolts" gained momentum, demanding limits on government taxation and spending. At the state and local levels, such movements led to the passage of referenda, as in the case of California's Proposition 13 in 1978, setting limits on property taxes. In 1981, the Economic Recovery Tax Act was adopted to reduce taxes at the national level, and, in the 1990s, the Republican Party adopted the "Contract with America" for similar objectives, but, by then, the federal budget deficit had increased from $53.6 billion in 1977 to $203 billion in 1994, the national debt from $709.1 billion to $4.6 trillion, and the interest paid by the federal government on the public debt from about $75 billion (12 percent of federal outlays) to $296 billion (20 percent). Tavlas, "The Deutsche Mark as an International Currency," in Das, ed., *International Finance,* pp. 566–68; U.S. Office of Management and Budget, *Budget of the U.S. Government* (various years); U.S. Department of the Treasury, *Statistical Appendix to the Report of the Secretary of the Treasury on the State of the Finances;* and U.S. Department of the Treasury, *Monthly Statement of the Public Debt of the United States.*
31. Susan George, *A Fate Worse Than Debt: The World Financial Crisis and the Poor,* rev. ed. (New York: Grove Weidenfield, 1990), p. 122.
32. See Steven M. Rubin, Jonathan Shatz, and Colleen Deegan, "International Conservation Finance: Using Debt Swaps and Trust Funds to Foster Conservation of Biodiversity," *Journal of Social, Political and Economic Studies* 19, 1 (Spring 1994) pp. 21–44; See also Eric S. Hardy, "Going Global," *Forbes* (July 28, 1997), pp. 178–198; Hazel J. Johnson, *Financial Institutions and Markets: A Global Perspective* (New York: McGraw-Hill, 1993), p. 175; Jeff Madura, *International Financial Management,* 2d ed. (St. Paul: West, 1989).
33. Johnson, *Financial Institutions and Markets,* p. 175.
34. See Benjamin J. Cohen, "A Brief History of International Monetary Relations," in Jeffry A. Frieden and David A. Lake, eds., *International Political Economy: Perspectives on*

Global Power and Wealth, 3d ed. (New York: St. Martin's Press, 1995), p. 210.

35. Palmira Brummett, *Ottoman Seapower and Levantine Diplomacy in the Age of Discovery* (Albany: State University of New York, 1994), pp. 5–7.
36. Cohen, "A Brief History of International Monetary Relations," p. 210.
37. Charles P. Kindleberger, *A Financial History of Western Europe,* 2d ed. (New York: Oxford University Press, 1993), p. 37.
38. *Ibid.,* p. 33. See also Charles Tilly, *Coercion, Capital, and European States, AD 990–1992* (Cambridge: Blackwell, 1992); Herman M. Schwartz, *States Versus Markets: History, Geography, and the Development of International Political Economy* (New York: St. Martin's Press, 1994).
39. As the Bank of Amsterdam was created immediately after the founding of Dutch Republic by the Union of Utrecht in 1579, so did Germany consolidate its banking system under the Reichsbank in the newly unified Germany three centuries later. The latter integrated the *Zollverin* (customs union), formed in 1818, among the Prussian states, and some years later the Prussian bank notes from twenty different *Länder* as part of German unification in the 1870s. Kindleberger, *Financial History of Western Europe,* pp. 119–122. The Prussian *thaler* (from which—and from the Spanish *thaler*—the word *dollar* is derived) became the deutsche mark.
40. Cohen, "A Brief History of International Monetary Relations," p. 210.
41. In 1878, the United States, to promote its silver in world trade, called for another International Monetary Conference to return to bimetallism. No other country agreed, however. European countries were in the transitional process to adopt the gold standard, while some developing countries, such as Mexico and China, maintained their silver standard. Formally, the gold standard, generally under the leadership of the British imperial scheme of things, became the universal standard in 1880 and functioned reasonably well until the outbreak of WWI. In the late nineteenth century, however, the British monopoly over international finance began to falter, and the newly rising U.S. dollar began to challenge the British pound. The U.S. dollar emerged as the dominant international currency after the final collapse of the British international financial system during the Great Depression and the war years of the 1930s and 1940s. Angela Redish, "The Latin Monetary Union and the Emergence of the International Gold Standard," in Michael Bordo and Forrest Capie, *Monetary Regimes in Transition* (Cambridge: Cambridge University Press, 1994), pp. 68–82; A.G. Kenwood and A.L. Lougheed, *The Growth of the International Economy, 1820–1990* (London: Routledge, 1992); L. Yeager, *International Monetary Relations: Theory, History and Policy* (New York: Harper and Row, 1976).
42. Under a gold exchange standard, a country's paper money is accepted as legal tender (its *par value*), and is convertible into "gold drafts" payable in the currency of another country using either the gold coin or gold bullion standard. Governments, however, are not obligated to adopt gold-to-money convertibility. A country on a gold exchange standard holds the currency in gold-bullion reserves and may use them to purchase additional gold reserves from foreign countries on the gold bullion standard. The purpose of using "gold drafts" instead of gold bullion in daily transactions under the gold exchange standard is to avoid expensive transfers and processing of gold bullion. A silver standard would operate on the same principles as a gold standard. While over the years some governments have experimented with silver standards as well as both silver and gold standards (bimetallism), the silver standard has lost public support because its market value dropped relative to that of gold's. See Johnson, *Financial Institutions and Markets,* pp. 21–22.
43. Kreinin, *International Economics,* p. 46.
44. *Ibid.*
45. Cohen, "A Brief History of International Monetary Relations," pp. 210–211.
46. The silver vs. gold debate became a key political conflict in the United States at the turn of the century. The "silver faction" saw gold as bolstering British control over the U.S. economy. Walter, *World Power and World Money,* pp. 116–144.
47. Johnson, *Financial Institutions and Markets,* p. 22.
48. Cohen, "A Brief History of International Monetary Relations," pp. 215–216.
49. Also, international debt after WWI further exacerbated domestic economic conditions in the 1920s. The United States emerged as the major creditor to finance the Allied powers' loans and the defeated Germany's reparations, the biggest debtor. Since after WWI most countries could not quickly rebuild their economies and produce sufficient account surpluses, they, including Germany, depended on U.S. capital to reinvigorate their economies. Germany paid its reparations largely with capital from the United States, and, as U.S. foreign investments abroad ended immediately after the stock market crashed in 1929, so did German reparations and Allied debt payments. *Ibid.,* pp. 216–217.
50. Charles P. Kindleberger, *The World in Depression, 1929–1939* (Berkeley: University of California Press, 1973).
51. Indeed, some analysts go so far as to argue that all nations should have confidence in a single hegemonic leader that can, as the vortex of the global financial order, manage and lead the system. During the inter-war period, for example,

they argue, Britain lost its hegemonic position, yet neither France nor the United States seemed prepared to assume that pivotal role. At the same time, however, the three powers entered the ring to accumulate as much wealth (in gold and resources) as possible. The result was lack of coordination of the gold standard system and eventually its total collapse, leading to the Great Depression. Cohen, "A Brief History of International Monetary Relations," pp. 217–218.

52. A noncommodity standard can be either an inconvertible or a controlled paper standard. In the former case, a government prohibits currency conversion into gold. Governments allow conversion into foreign currencies, however, if other governments do not restrict such conversion. Although a controlled paper standard permits some conversion into gold or silver, it has historically limited international trade, added to inflationary pressures, and led to expansion of black market or informal foreign currency exchange operations. Johnson, *Financial Institutions and Markets,* p. 22.
53. Kreinin, *International Economics,* p. 48.
54. Johnson, *Financial Institutions and Markets,* p. 22.
55. Kreinin, *International Economics,* pp. 48-49.
56. Carbaugh, *International Economics,* p. 323.
57. In the mid-1960s, the IMF created a committee, under the chairmanship of Otmar Emminger of Germany, to examine the issue of world liquidity shortages. The committee proposed to create SDRs to increase international reserves and expand international trade. Kreinin, *International Economics,* p. 67.
58. *Ibid.*, pp. 65–66.
59. *The Economist,* "The IMF's Sums," February 11, 1995, p. 67.
60. SDRs could conceivably be used for such purposes if commercial banks began to use SDRs in conjunction with the major currencies. Over the years, the SDR system, as international reserves, has become universally accepted as a mechanism to correct imbalances among countries. However, SDRs are reserves held by central banks only, and they cannot be used by central banks to intervene through pegging currencies' values. See Kreinin, *International Economics,* p. 67.
61. *Ibid.*
62. *IMF Survey,* February 6, 1995, p. 1; *The Economist,* "The Fund's Sums," February 11, 1995, p. 67.
63. *The Economist,* "The Fund's Sums," February 11, 1995, p. 67.
64. Jacob A. Frankel and Mohsin S. Khan, "The International Monetary Fund's Adjustment Policies and Economic Development," in Das, ed., *International Finance,* pp. 86–92.
65. Kreinin, *International Economics,* p. 57.
66. Frankel and Khan, "The International Monetary Fund's Adjustment Policies and Economic Development," p. 91.
67. Jeffrey D. Sachs, "Conditionality, Debt Relief, and the Developing Country Debt Crisis," in Jeffrey D. Sachs, ed., *Developing Country Debt and the World Economy* (Chicago: The University of Chicago Press, 1989), pp. 275–277.
68. After the Mexican financial crisis, the G-7 leaders meeting in Halifax, Nova Scotia, agreed to expand the IMF's surveillance responsibilities to obligate member countries to make public in a timely fashion reliable economic information to prevent mismanagement of international capital markets and investments. *The Economist,* February 11, 1995, pp. 19–20; *The Economist,* "The World Economy," [survey] October 7, 1995, p. 37.
69. According to another study, "of the thirty adjustment programs launched under the auspices of the Extended Fund Facility, twenty-four were renegotiated, or had payments interrupted, or were quietly allowed to lapse. Of these twenty-four, sixteen were formally cancelled by the IMF, virtually for non-compliance." Sachs, "Conditionality," p. 280.
70. *Ibid.*
71. *Ibid.*
72. Ami Ayalon, "The Arab Republic of Egypt," *Middle East Contemporary Survey* 11 (1987) pp. 332–335; Ayalon, "Egypt," *Middle East Contemporary Survey* 14 (1990) pp. 316–322.
73. Ayalon, "The Arab Republic of Egypt," pp. 332–335; Ayalon, "Egypt," pp. 316–322.
74. Ayalon, "The Arab Republic of Egypt," pp. 332–335; Ayalon, "Egypt," pp. 316–322.
75. *Ibid.,* p. 296.
76. *Ibid.*, p. 303.
77. *IMF Survey,* October 9, 1995, pp. 309–310.
78. *The Economist,* March 18, 1995, p. 51.
79. *IMF Survey,* January 9, 1995, p. 2; *IMF Survey,* February 6, 1995, pp. 40–42. To meet such challenges around the world, the IMF decided to increase lending from SDR 5.3 billion (or $7.7 billion) in 1993 to SDR 5.9 billion (or $8.6 billion) in 1994. Loans under the IMF's concessional facilities, which include structural adjustment facility (SAF) and the enhanced structural adjustment facility (ESAF), increased substantially from SDR 271.7 million (or $394.0 million) in 1993 to SDR 910.5 million (or $1.3 billion) in 1994. Systemic transformation facility (STF) accounts rose as well from SDR 1.4 billion (or $2.0 billion) to SDR 1.9 billion (or $2.8 billion). The IMF created the STF account in April 1993 to assist member countries in addressing serious balance-of-payments difficulties due to transition from centrally planned economies and their nonmarket trade prices to market-based prices.
80. Quoted in Cheryl Payer, *The Debt Trap: The International Monetary Fund and the Third World* (New York: Monthly Review Press, 1974), pp. 59–60.

81. *Ibid.*, pp. 143–206, *passim.*
82. Mariarosa Dalla Costa and Giovanna F. Dalla Costa, eds., *Paying the Price: Women and the Politics of International Economic Strategy* (London: Zed Books, 1993).
83. UNICEF, as quoted in Andrée Michel, "African Women, Development and the North-South Relationship," in *Ibid.*, pp. 62, 65–67. Since the IMF- and World Bank-imposed "reform" programs took effect in the early 1980s in sub-Saharan countries, for example, health services deteriorated and educational institutions declined. As a result, maternal mortality reached its highest levels, infant mortality rates rose, and literacy rates dropped, leading to the virtual "deschooling" of Africa, from Ethiopia to Tanzania to Burkina Faso to Malawi and Angola.
84. Johnson, *Financial Institutions and Markets,* p. 338.
85. *Ibid.*
86. *World Bank Annual Report 1982–1989.* See also Ibrahim F.I. Shihata, "The World Bank in the 1990s," in Das, ed., *International Finance,* pp. 78–80.
87. See, for example, Escott Reid, "McNamara's World Bank," *Foreign Affairs* (July 1973).
88. Cheryl Payer, *The World Bank: A Critical Analysis* (New York: Monthly Review Press, 1982), pp. 73–74.
89. The rationale for his evaluation is that each project provides the bank and the borrowing country valuable lessons to use in identification, preparation, and appraisal of future projects. Payer, *World Bank,* pp. 84–85; Johnson, *Financial Institutions and Markets,* p. 339.
90. Jacques Berthelot, "Développement du Tiers Monde et Methodes de Selection des Projets," *Mondes en Developpement* 31 (1980), as quoted in Payer, *World Bank,* p. 80.
91. The IFC was instrumental in the creation of the so-called developing country funds, as well as the development of capital market programs for developing countries. International banking experts have proposed to increase IFC's capital to $2.6 billion to stimulate more funding for productive programs. *Ibid.,* pp. 72–78.
92. Shihata, "The World Bank in the 1990s," p. 73.
93. John H. Jackson and William J. Davey, *Legal Problems of International Economic Relations,* 2d ed. (St. Paul: West, 1986), p. 280.
94. *Ibid.*, p. 387.
95. Since its establishment, the World Bank has approved over $189 billion worth of loans for 106 countries. In the late 1980s and early 1990s, the group's average annual operations have totaled $21.8 billion in commitments, and $242.1 billion in trust funds and facilities administered by the group. According to the 1989 balance sheet, the World Bank's assets totaled $108 billion, about $78 billion, or 70 percent, of which disbursed as loans to member states. State securities and deposits totaled about 10 percent each. Bank capital accounted for approximately 16 percent of total capital and liabilities, and medium- and long-term borrowings about 70 percent. In 1990, the total resources of the bank, including its associated agencies, were about $242 billion. The IDA's operations since its creation have totaled $58.2 billion for eighty-eight countries, and the IFC's operations $9.7 billion for ninety-four countries. Shihata, "The World Bank in the 1990s," p. 73; Johnson, *Financial Institutions and Markets,* pp. 338–41.
96. Shihata, "The World Bank in the 1990s," pp. 73–74.
97. *Ibid.*, pp. 78–80.
98. *Ibid.*, p. 83.
99. Payer, *World Bank.*
100. Aart van de Laar, *The World Bank and the Poor* (The Hague: Martinus Nijhoff, 1980).
101. The World Bank Group, "Your Business Partner in Emerging Economies," Washington DC, 1998.
102. See also Bruce Rich, *Mortgaging the Earth: The World Bank, Environmental Impoverishment, and the Crisis of Development* (Boston: Beacon Press, 1994), pp. 26–29; Jacques Attali, *Millennium: Winners and Losers in the Coming World Order* (New York: Times Books, 1991); Edward S. Mason and Robert E. Asher, *The World Bank Since Bretton Woods* (Washington, DC: Brookings Institution, 1973); Paul Handley, "The Land Wars," *Far Eastern Economic Review* October 31, 1991, pp. 15–16; Linda Greenbaum, "The Failure to Protect Tribal Peoples: The Polonoroeste Case in Brazil," *Cultural Survival Quarterly* 8 (December 1984): 76–77; George Monbiot, *Poisoned Arrows* (London: Michael Joseph, 1989).
103. Rich, *Mortgaging the Earth,* pp. 15–17.
104. *Ibid.*, pp. 17–18.
105. Rich writes, "The Bank's attempts to respond to international pressures for environmental reform exposed a whole series of paradoxes that up through the early 1980s had been unarticulated. The crystal palace of global economic development, whose mission seemed so certain in earlier years, had become a castle of contradictions by the early 1990s. Internally, the Bank was at war with itself, showing signs of acute bureaucratic schizophrenia. . . . Those . . . responsible for pushing through debacles like Polonoroeste, Indonesia Transmigration, and Narmada Sardar Sarovar suffered no consequences to their careers. On the other hand, . . . [those] who opposed or delayed proposed projects on policy and even ethical grounds have suffered the wrath of irate country department directors. . . ." Rich, *Mortgaging the Earth,* pp. 182–83.
106. Johnson, *Financial Institutions and Markets,* pp. 334-335.
107. The other member central banks are Australia, Austria, Bulgaria, Canada, the Czech Republic, Denmark, Finland, Greece, Hungary, Iceland, Ireland, the Netherlands, Norway, Poland, Portugal, Romania, South

Africa, Spain, Sweden, Turkey, and the former Yugoslavia. *Ibid.,* p. 334.

108. Headquartered in Basil, Switzerland, the BIS, as a commercial bank, operates based on a Swiss license, but an international treaty protects its legal status from political pressures as an independent agent. See Johnson, *Financial Institutions and Markets,* pp. 334–35; Fred Hirsch, *Money International: Economics and Politics of World Money* (New York: Doubleday and Company, 1969).
109. Johnson, *Financial Institutions and Markets,* p. 335.
110. *The Economist,* February 4, 1995, p. 65.
111. Johnson, *Financial Institutions and Markets,* p. 335.
112. Das, "Contemporary Trends in the International Capital Markets," in Das, ed., *International Finance,* p. 16.
113. Richard O'Brien, *Global Financial Integration: The End of Geography* (London: The Royal Institute of International Affairs, 1992).
114. *The Economist,* April 11, 1998, p. 55.
115. *The Economist,* "The World Economy," [survey] October 7, 1995, p. 29.
116. Quoted in O'Brien, *Global Financial Integration,* p. 1.
117. With respect to financial market deals, the early 1990s witnessed serious difficulties by some European governments to protect their finances against the "evil brain [of international benefactor and financial marketeer] George Soros, whose Quantum fund made $1 billion on Black Wednesday by helping to push the sterling out of the ERM" (Exchange Rate Mechanism). *Ibid.,* p. 4.
118. See Edwin M. Truman, "The Mexican Peso Crisis: Implications for International Finance," *Federal Reserve Bulletin* 82, 3 (March 1996): pp. 199–210.
119. *The Economist,* "The World Economy," [survey] October 7, 1995, p. 11.
120. Peter Dicken, *Global Shift: The Internationalization of Economic Activity,* 2d ed. (New York: Guilford Press, 1992) pp. 95–96.
121. See, for example, Alejandro Lichauco, *Nationalist Economics: History, Theory and Practice* (Quezon City, Philippines: SPES Institute, 1988).
122. See Dicken, Global Shift, pp. 197–198, 224–225; Robert Z. Aliber, *The Multinational Paradigm* (Cambridge: MIT Press, 1993); John H. Dunning, *Explaining International Production* (London: Unwin Hyman, 1988), pp. 277–279; Martin Carnoy, Manuel Castells, Stephen S. Cohen, and Fernando Henrique Cardoso, *The New Global Economy in the Information Age: Reflections on Our Changing World* (University Park: Pennsylvania State University, 1993); Gerald Epstein, Julie Graham, and Jessica Nembhard, eds., *Creating a New World Economy: Forces of Change and Plans for Action* (Philadelphia: Temple University Press, 1993).
123. *The Economist,* "The World Economy," [survey] October 7, 1995, p. 15.
124. *IMF Survey,* April 17, 1995, p. 119.
125. *Ibid.*
126. *IMF Survey,* March 20, 1995, pp. 85–86.
127. On fluctuation in stock markets in the developing economies, see, for example, Graeme Littler and Ziad Maaouf, "Emerging Stock Markets in 1995: Decline Followed by Year-end Upturn," *Finance and Development* 33, 1 (March 1996): pp. 27–30.
128. Kreinin, *International Economics,* p. 48.
129. In fact, between the dollar and gold, governments chose the former because they saw no need to accumulate gold. Transactions in dollars were far less expensive and more efficient than dealing in gold. The formal internationalization of the dollar made the American market more accessible. Equally significantly, the U.S. dollar as a reserve asset earned interest, but gold did not. Soon, public and private international financial and trade transactions between countries were being conducted in dollars, which greatly benefited the U.S. economy as the dollars found their way home to purchase U.S. goods—goods unavailable at that time elsewhere in the world. *Ibid.,* pp. 52–53.
130. *Ibid.,* p. 55.
131. William H. Becker and Samuels F. Wells, Jr., eds., *Economics and World Power: An Assessment of American Diplomacy Since 1789* (New York: Columbia University Press, 1984).
132. During the first decade, foreign holdings of U.S. dollars rose from $4.8 billion to $13 billion. As most observers agree, since U.S. gold reserves at the time were approximately $22 billion, large sums of dollars held by foreign central banks did not appear to hazard the U.S. reserves and economy. However, by the late 1950s, Western European governments had so accelerated the "dollarization" of European financial markets that they developed Eurodollar markets (that is, trading in U.S. dollars). Within a single year in 1958, Eurodollar markets drew $2.3 billion in gold from U.S. reserves. The United States, in fact, attempted to prevent further outflow, but the hemorrhage persisted during the next decade. David P. Calleo, "American Power in a New World Economy Since 1961," in Becker and Wells, *Economics and World Power,* pp. 410–411; Loukas Tsoukalis, *The Politics and Economics of European Monetary Integration* (London: Allen and Unwin, 1977). For an earlier assessment, see Robert Triffin, *Gold and the Dollar Crisis: The Future of Convertibility* (New Haven: Yale University Press, 1960); Johnson, *Financial Institutions and Markets,* pp. 22–23; Kreinin, *International Economics,* p. 56.
133. Kreinin, *International Economics,* p. 56.
134. Harold James, *International Monetary Cooperation Since Bretton Woods* (Washington, DC: International Monetary Fund; and New York: Oxford University Press, 1996), pp. 433–466; Diane B. Kunz, *Butter and Guns: America's*

Cold War Economic Diplomacy (New York: Free Press, 1997), pp. 312–313.

135. *The Economist,* August 19, 1995, p. 69; *The Economist,* "The World Economy," [survey] October 7, 1995, p. 18.
136. In 1994, the U.S. dollar dropped by a further 11 percent against the DMark and the yen, and in early 1995 it dropped 2.5 percent against the DMark and 3 percent against the yen. While in 1980 about 34.5 percent of world exports were in U.S. dollars, by the late 1980s that figure had dropped to about 24.8 percent, a decline of 10 percentage points. Tavlas, "The Deutsche Mark as an International Currency," in Das, ed., *International Finance,* pp. 571–572. *The Wall Street Journal,* March 8, 1995, p. A1. *The Economist,* February 25, 1995, p. 17.
137. Currently, they hold about 3 percent of their total financial assets in foreign currencies; in comparison, 25 percent of British investors and over 10 percent of Germans and Japanese hold their total financial assets in foreign currencies. *The Economist,* February 25, 1995, p. 18.
138. *The Economist,* "The World Economy," [survey] October 7, 1995, p. 23.
139. Like the debate whether a bipolar or a multipolar system is more conducive to world stability, scholars have been waging a similar debate in recent years with respect to the transition from a hegemonic currency system to a multipolar currency system. Bergsten and Williamson, for example, argue that a multipolar currency system might lead to financial instability. Others, on the other hand, contend that a multicurrency system will "promote exchange rate stability if accompanied by policy co-ordination among the reserve currency countries." During the Cold War, the U.S. dollar provided a shelter for currencies in the industrialized and developing world; with the ending of the Cold War, governments and private investors feel safer to use other currencies that for short- and long-term purposes promise greater returns. They believe a strong bank and investment opportunities are now as important as military capability. C.F. Bergsten and J. Williamson, *The Multiple Reserve Currency System: Evolution, Consequences, and Alternatives* (Washington, DC: Institute for International Economics, 1983), p. 564; T. Gyooten, "Internationalization of the Yen: Its Implications for the U.S.-Japan Relationship," in Hugh T. Patrick and Ryuichiro Tachi, eds., *Japan and the United States Today: Exchange Rates, Macroeconomic Policies, and Financial Market Innovations* (New York: Center on Japanese Economy and Business, Columbia University, 1986); *The Economist,* February 25, 1995, p. 78.
140. John Pinder, *European Community: The Building of a Union* (Oxford: Oxford University Press, 1991); Hans J. Michelmann and Panayotis Soldatos, eds., *European Integration: Theories and Approaches* (Lanham, MD: University Press of America, 1994); Paul Michael Lützler, ed., *Europe After Maastricht: American and European Perspectives* (Providence: Berghahn Books, 1994); Paolo Guerrieri and Pier Carlo Paoan, eds., *The Political Economy of European Integration: States, Markets and Institutions* (New York: Harvester Weatsheaf, 1989).
141. Since then, their goal has been to achieve greater monetary integration. Following the Werner Report in 1969, which proposed specific plans for monetary integration in 1980, European Community members sought to integrate their reserves and to maintain specific agreed-upon limits on currency exchange rates, to find means of resolving issues within the region so as not to jeopardize exchange-rate stability, and eventually to replace the members' national currencies by a single EC currency. These plans failed to materialize at the time, however, rendered inoperable by the collapse of the Bretton Woods system. They were further frustrated by the oil crises in the 1970s. Johnson, *Financial Institutions and Markets,* pp. 130–131; Barry Eichengreen and Jeffrey A. Frieden, "The Political Economy of European Monetary Unification: An Analytical Introduction," in Jeffry A. Frieden and David A. Lake, eds., *International Political Economy: Perspectives on Global Power and Wealth,* 3d ed. (New York: St. Martin's Press, 1995), p. 268.
142. *Ibid.*, p. 268.
143. Johnson, *Financial Institutions and Markets,* pp. 131–32.
144. *The Economist,* April 11, 1998 [survey], p. 4. Loukas Tsoukalis, *The New European Economy: The Politics and Economics of Integration,* rev. 2d ed. (Oxford: Oxford University Press, 1993), pp. 61–65.
145. On the theory of integration and the spillover effect, see Ernst B. Haas, "International Integration: The European and the Universal Process," *International Organization* 15 (Autumn 1961); Haas, *Beyond the Nation-State* (Stanford: Stanford University Press, 1964); Leon N. Lindberg, *The Political Dynamics of European Economic Integration* (Stanford: Stanford University Press, 1963); Philippe C. Schmitter, "A Revised Theory of Regional Integration," *International Organization* 24, 4 (1970).
146. Johnson, *Financial Institutions and Markets,* p. 132. See also, D. Barry, ed., *Toward a North American Community?* (Boulder, CO: Westview Press, 1995), p. 236.
147. *Ibid.*, p. 133.
148. Eichengreen and Frieden, "The Political Economy of European Monetary Unification," p. 270.
149. *The Economist,* April 11, 1998 [survey], p. 1.
150. *The Economist,* "A Funny New EMU," March 4, 1995, p. 49.
151. Eichengreen and Frieden, "The Political Economy of European Monetary Unification," pp. 270–271.
152. *The Economist,* April 11, 1998 [survey], p. 9.
153. Eichengreen and Frieden, "The Political Economy of European Monetary Unification," p. 271.

154. *Ibid.*
155. *The Economist,* April 11, 1998 [survey], pp. 5–6. The French will hardly welcome unemployed Kurds and Germans from Germany, nor will Germany welcome unemployed Algerians and French from France. Transfer of fiscal resources from one country to another for the sake of maintaining regional financial stability is likely to be resented by people who assign greater priority to national and personal economic well-being than to assisting other countries. It would be unrealistic to expect that the EMU will in the foreseeable future eliminate national political considerations and even outright conflicts within the region. Martin Feldstein, "The Euro and War," *Foreign Affairs,* November/December 1997).
156. Germany's share of exports in manufacturing goods as a percentage of its total exports increased from 38 percent to 47 percent. In comparison, the share of manufactured goods in U.S. exports increased from 32 percent to 44 percent, and Japan's from 52 percent to 71 percent. In the 1980s, a larger proportion of Germany's own trade accounts were held in DMarks. While in 1980 43.0 percent of German imports were denominated in DMarks, in 1988 52.6 percent were—an increase of about ten percentage points. As one expert has noted, this increase occurred "mainly at the expense of U.S.-dollar-denominated imports." A growing number of EC countries have used the DMark for trade purposes and in various international financial transactions, and to a large extent it is the use of the DMark in European markets that has strengthened its position as an international currency. Tavlas, "The Deutsche Mark as an International Currency," in Das, ed., *International Finance,* p. 570.
157. *The Economist,* April 11, 1998 [survey], p. 17.
158. *The Economist,* February 25, 1995, p. 77.
159. According to S&P's estimates, European banks, including such giants as the French Société Generale and Credit Lyonnais and the German Deutsche Bank and Commerzbank, are likely to lose 30 percent of their loans to Thailand and as much as 50 percent in the case of Indonesia. Shada Islam, "No Pain, No Gain: European Banks Brace for Asian Fallout—but Sit Tight," *Far Eastern Economic Review,* February 12, 1998, pp. 60–61.
160. Other European banks, such as Spain's Banco Santander, the Union Bank of Switzerland, and the Swiss Bank Corp., are also expected to seize the opportunity provided by the Asian crisis to seek cheaper investments than would have been possible in times of Asian economic growth. Alkman Granitsas, "Clearance Sale: European Banks See Opportunities Amidst Turmoil," *Far Eastern Economic Review,* February 12, 1998, p. 62.
161. See *The Economist,* April 11, 1998 [survey], pp. 20–21.
162. Stanley W. Black, "The International Use of Currencies," in Das, ed., *International Finance,* p. 553.
163. Dilip K. Das, "The Internationalization of the Yen," in Das, ed., *International Finance,* pp. 580–581.
164. Another factor in these totals was the substantially lower savings rates in the United States compared with those in Japan and Germany. *Ibid.*
165. Bernard K. Gordon, "Japan: Searching Once Again," in James C. Hsiung, ed., *Asia Pacific in the New World Politics* (Boulder, CO: Lynne Rienner, 1993), p. 62.
166. Jong H. Park, "International Perspectives: Japan and the United States in Pacific Rim Trade and Economic Cooperation," *Business Economics* (October 1992): p. 49.
167. Japan's relations with the ASEAN are an important dimension of its leadership role in the region. Japan's foreign assistance programs under the auspices of the Asian Industries Development (AID), which include transfer of investment capital and direct loans, as well as technology transfers, have enhanced the status of the yen as an international currency. Alan Rix, "Japan and the Region: Leading from Behind," in Richard Higgott, Richard Leaver, and John Ravenhill, eds., *Pacific Economic Relations in the 1990s: Cooperation or Conflict?* (Boulder, CO: Lynne Rienner, 1993), pp. 68–69.
168. Henny Sender, "Out of Asia: Japanese Banks and Companies Head Home," *Far Eastern Economic Review,* April 16, 1998, pp. 12–13.
169. *The Economist,* April 11, 1998, pp. 15–17; *Far Eastern Economic Review,* February 12, 1998, pp. 56–59.
170. *Far Eastern Economic Review,* February 12, 1998, pp. 62–63.
171. Andrew J. MacIntyre, "Indonesia, Thailand and the Northeast Asian Connection," in Higgott, et al., eds., *Pacific Economic Relations in the 1990s,* p. 265.
172. Charles E. Morrison, "Japan and the ASEAN Countries: The Evolution of Japan's Regional Role," in Takashi Inoguchi and Daniel I. Okimoto, eds., *The Political Economy of Japan: The Changing International Context,* vol. 2 (Stanford: Stanford University Press, 1988), pp. 421–422.
173. MacIntyre, "Indonesia, Thailand and the Northeast Asian Connection," in Higgott, et al., eds., *Pacific Economic Relations in the 1990s,* p. 265.
174. Specifically within the context of international aid worldwide, observers agree that, while Japan currently has greater leverage in the International Monetary Fund and the World Bank than before, it has not emerged as a "world leader" in the development aid circles. Its foreign aid ties with African and Latin American countries remain limited. There has been little domestic and international debate regarding the role of Japanese foreign aid beyond East Asia, and Japan does not appear to be posed for an international leadership role in the near future. This limited role by implication also limits the Japanese yen's role as a truly international currency. Rix, "Japan and the Region," in Higgott, et al., eds., *Pacific Economic Relations in the 1990s,* pp. 75–76.

175. Das, "Internationalization of the Yen," in Das, ed., *International Finance,* p. 583.
176. *The Economist,* August 19, 1995, p. 69.
177. See Fuad Al-Omar and Mohammed Abdel-Haq, *Islamic Banking: Theory, Practice and Challenges* (Karachi, Pakistan: Oxford University Press, and London: Zed Books, 1996), pp. 88–95.
178. *Ibid.*, pp. 88–89.
179. *Ibid.*, pp. 90–91.
180. *The Economist,* February 4, 1995, pp. 24–25, 65.
181. *The New York Times,* May 1, 1998, p. A1.
182. The crucial question, however, as in the Mexican case, was not whether Suharto would keep his promise but whether the aid package would restore corporate and public confidence in the Indonesian economy.
183. Indonesia's economic significance is not limited to its market and labor potential as the fourth populous nation in the world; the archipelago has enormous geo-political/geo-economic significance as well. As the *Far Eastern Economic Review* has noted, approximately 40 percent of the total world shipping pass through its four key straits: Lombok, Malacca, Ombai-Savu, and Sunda. Nearly 80 percent of Japan's and 70 percent of South Korea's oil imports use these straits, as does 20 percent of Australia's trade. Australia finds itself in the same situation as the United States with respect to influx of immigrants. Political instability throughout the Indonesian islands would pose a serious threat to these strategic waterlanes but may also escalate emigration to the neighboring countries. John McBeth and Deborah Lutterbeck, "Neighbours in Need: Security Concerns Underpin Support for Suharto," *Far Eastern Economic Review,* April 16, 1998, p. 20.

CHAPTER FIVE

THE POLITICS OF INTERNATIONAL TRADE RELATIONS

The twelve members of the European Community (EC) signed the Single European Act in 1985 and agreed to eliminate all barriers to free trade and free movement of goods, services, people, and capital. They sought to create a single European economy and a single common market, the largest economic area in the world, comprised of nearly 320 million producers and consumers. This was to culminate a process begun in the 1950s with the signing of the Coal and Steel Community and the common market agreements. Business and political leaders believed that such a united trade front was necessary to make Europe successful and competitive in international markets and to link old rivals, such as Germany and France, in peaceful interdependence. The elimination of barriers to free trade involved the removal of physical barriers (such as customs checks), technical barriers (such as national regulatory policies and standards), and fiscal barriers (such as customs duties), yet member states were slow to complete the process. They did not immediately implement a common currency, nor were they willing to eliminate all restrictions on internal trade. Italy and France, for example, maintained their quotas on cars. Most such trade barriers were particularly aimed at Japanese imports. Italy and France argued that some British-made Nissans should be counted as Japanese until 80 percent of their content become European in origin. Neither was there a consensus with respect to the free movement of people across borders—that is, an immigration policy. France stressed the need for uniform personal identity cards, which Britain refused to support. EC members agreed, however, that certain border checks were required to prevent the free flow of drugs. The idea of European economic integration found sufficient support because of the advantages such economic unity would create. Some estimates hold that the formation of a fully integrated European market would increase the EC's gross domestic product (GDP) by 4.5 percent, would reduce market prices by over 6 percent, and would reduce unemployment—a chronic problem in European economies since the early 1970s—by 1.5 percent.[1] Regional integration as a global phenomenon is discussed in the next chapter; here, we focus on questions related to trade liberalization.

In dollar values, the total volume of world trade increased from $126 billion in 1950, to about $4 trillion in 1980, and to $7 trillion in the mid-1990s, signifying a strong basis for international cooperation.[2] However, for most of the twentieth century, there has been little consensus regarding the precise nature of cooperation attainable through international trade relations. To some, particularly in the liberal school, cooperation based on "mutual advantages" means a stable, albeit competitive, international environment unencumbered by government restrictions; therefore, they view cooperation as conducive to trade and investment growth.[3] International trade widens the choices available to consumers, whose tastes and consumption would otherwise be limited to goods produced in their own countries.[4] Proponents of laissez-faire international economics contend that in the modern interdependent world trade system, in which the survival of one's domestic economy depends on its ability to secure access to imports of foreign goods and services, especially raw materials, such protectionist policies as tariffs and various customs controls restricting free transportation of goods and resources are counterproductive and even dangerous (for political and security reasons).[5]

Others see mutual advantages as mostly limited to wealthier trading partners, with little benefit for the poor.

Marxist-socialist critics of laisse-faire contend that free trade creates an *asymmetrically* interdependent system, whereby the poorer economies grow more dependent on foreign capital and technology, a situation worsened by the globalization of highly advanced telecommunications technologies. Structural transformations in the global economy and trade, they argue, involve more than the "invisible hand" of market competition; they also involve power relations among the major industrialized economies and between them and the developing countries. The international trade structure solidifies inequalities in the international and national structural division of labor not only between center and periphery countries but also within societies, whereby the poorer countries and the poorer sectors (classes) within each society are economically and politically marginalized.[6]

Proponents of globalization theory view the recent acceleration in trade activities as a part of the broader structural transformations taking place in the late twentieth century and as being somewhat similar to other periods of transformation in the history of human civilization, such as the demise of the Roman empire in the fourth and fifth centuries, the impact of printing in the fifteenth century, and the Renaissance in Europe in the fourteenth and fifteenth centuries. However, the pace of the changes taking place today in communications technologies and international transactions capabilities is so fast that they are "literally reshaping the world within the lifetime of a single generation."[7] Regardless of these changes, however, the nation-state remains the legitimate source of the laws, rules, and regulations shaping the political and economic behavior of the individuals and institutions under its jurisdiction. As one observer has put it, "The basic unit is going to remain the nation-state. Nothing else can govern whole societies without toppling, one way, into the infranationalist error of tribalism or, the other way, into the supranationalist sterility of rule by bureaucrats."[8]

Many critics see in the emerging global trade economy a threat to individual workers. Corporate downsizing and searches for cheaper labor have tended to produce chronic unemployment problems and the erosion of real incomes in many industrialized countries. The state's ability to promote welfare and opportunities for its citizens while joining in global collaboration is the crucial political and economic challenge for the twenty-first century. As in international finance, discussed in Chapter 4, the effective management of international trade is a necessary condition for international cooperation.

PRINCIPAL CHARACTERISTICS OF CONTEMPORARY INTERNATIONAL TRADE RELATIONS

International Trade: Cooperation and Conflict Among Sovereigns

As noted in Chapter 2, laissez-faire classical liberalism in the late eighteenth century viewed political economy and trade as a means to acquire needed goods, capital, and services, and it stressed limited government and free enterprise. Following that intellectual tradition, one of the principal characteristics of contemporary international trade has been the emphasis by some countries, particularly Britain and the United States, on free trade as a way to promote economic growth. Contrary to mercantilist and Marxist-Leninist views, sovereign nations are said to enter into multilateral and bilateral trade negotiations to eliminate tariff and non-tariff barriers and, thus, to free market activities of artificial distortions.[9] Freed from such obstacles, businesses pursue their economic interests without government interference and thereby contribute to international cooperation as the transnational transfer of goods and services increases in volume and variety.[10]

Contemporary trade relations, however, are far more complicated than international trade relations envisioned by classical liberalism, as the proliferation of multinational production and intra-industry trade facilities (e.g., in raw materials or parts) around the world, trade and financial strategic alliances, and the information telecommunications technologies constantly introduce new factors into market activities. No longer can such trade advantages be defined or accounted for purely based on commodity, labor, and land. They must also take into account technology-based advantages, including the role of telecommunications and services that facilitate multinational corporations' far flung production and component-delivery capabilities. As discussed in Chapter 12, they must also account for the expanding informal economy and the increasing informalization of domestic and international economic activities. Such developments challenge the traditional assumption of trade advantages in the "perfect market." The imperfect economy also requires government intervention to manage the economy through regulation of trade and protection of key industries or interest groups, such as farmers.

International trade also can cause economic and political conflicts. At the height of classical mercantilism, the state attached great importance to the relationship between management of power and management of trade. As the review of the history of international political economy demonstrated in Chapter 3, that relationship is still relevant today. The unequal distribution of various resources requires countries to enter into trade agreements, but, contrary to laissez-faire assumptions, with little guarantee of market growth and financial stability. As a result, those endowed with advantages such as arable land, capital, technology, roads, and so forth are in a better position to absorb economic setbacks and set the terms of trade than are their poorer partners specializing in the production of a specific commodity or product.

In all countries, issues of **balance of trade**—a country's total value of products exported minus imports—and **balance of payments**—a country's total value of imports and exports of goods and services, as well as transfer of investments, currency, gold, and so on, with other countries—are crucial for effective economic management. Management, however, is a highly political process, and it becomes even more politicized in difficult economic times. Some among the public and policymakers, especially those negatively affected by unemployment, view government interference in trade relations as necessary and even desirable to maintain a healthy balance of trade and balance of payments. Local industries, labor unions, and politicians allied with them often cite balance of trade deficit to advocate stricter protectionist limits on foreign imports. Industries harmed by such competition stress that the balance of trade deficit signifies the threat foreign competitors pose to the national economy and even to national security, making the balance of trade a politically sensitive issue.[11]

Further, a country's balance of payments and balance of trade are thought to reflect its economic health at home and its financial standing in the world political economy. A country is said to be economically strong if it maintains a healthy overall balance-of-payments equilibrium on its national accounting "balance sheet"—that is, between its *credits* (exports, or money coming in) and debits (imports, or money going out). A country's balance sheet reflects its financial position and can be one of the determining factors in whether the international community accepts its currency, goods, and services. As the line of demarcation between domestic and international political economy becomes increasingly blurred, issues related to balance of trade and balance of payments wield greater influence on issues of employment and public programs, further exacerbating problems associated with the national budget deficit, as in the case of the United States during recent decades. "Approximately 24,000 American jobs are lost for each $1 billion in the U.S. trade deficit."[12] If valid, the trade deficit of $139 billion in 1993, for example, is said to have resulted in the loss of about 3 million jobs.[13] Governments possess policy tools to address such issues. The question is whether policymakers—presidents, prime ministers, legislators, and bureaucrats—have the political will to use available instruments of policy. As statist theorists would point out, how *policymakers' own political interests* figure in the calculus of domestic and foreign policies can be a determining factor in policy decisions favoring one instrument over another.

Instruments of Trade Policy

Governments possess a number of policy instruments to check trade imbalances. One such instrument is the tariff. **Tariffs** are taxes levied on imported products, either *ad valorem*—that is, percentage of the value of the imported product—or according to the category of products. Governments impose tariffs for a number of reasons. Historically, they used tariffs to raise revenues for the state, and some governments in developing countries still rely on tariffs for this purpose. In more modern times, however, tariffs are used for not only economic but also for political objectives. A government levies tariffs on certain imported products to make them more expensive than equivalents produced by domestic industries. In so doing, the government hopes to protect favored industries and to reduce balance of payments deficits, while satisfying interest group demands (for example, from trade unions and chambers of commerce).

A government also uses tariffs to retaliate against a trading partner's trade restrictions and practices, such as **dumping**—the practice of selling a product in a foreign market at prices lower than those of the home market. Although GATT regulations prohibit dumping, governments have at times permitted and even encouraged it for a number of reasons, including competition to capture foreign markets and to export surplus products so as to prevent domestic prices from falling and diminishing industry's profits and income. Tariffs are also used to protect infant industries at home from foreign competition or, similarly, to protect certain strategic industries for purposes of national security.

There are non-tariff barriers (NTBs) to trade as well. **Quotas,** for example, are limits on the quantity of specific products imported. Another policy instrument to check trade imbalances includes regulatory restrictions. For example, government regulatory policies for purposes of environmental or consumer protection may directly or totally prohibit the sale of a product in the domestic market or may increase its price so as to discourage domestic consumption. Governments also *subsidize* home industries in specific sectors, such as agriculture, so as to maintain lower prices against foreign competitors. In France, for example, as the transition from coal to oil as the primary source of energy was completed in the 1960s, the French government introduced various forms of indirect restrictions (indirect taxes on petroleum and petroleum products) to protect the declining coal industry, while subsidizing research and development (R&D) for the emerging nuclear industry to limit the country's dependence on imported oil.[14]

The extent to which a government uses these policy instruments is highly political. Rather than acting as neutral managers for the national economy, policymakers choose trade policies that reflect their national and local interests. Like most policies, trade policies are determined by the close (sometimes even illegal) relationship among presidents and prime ministers, legislators, interest groups, and bureaucracies. Policymakers view subsidies, for example, as the distribution of public goods to enhance the welfare of specific and powerful interest groups.[15] In Europe, the United States, and Japan, corporations and farmers are among the most powerful groups, and they lobby heavily, and often make campaign contributions, in favor of government R&D and farm subsidies. While tariff levels have declined since the Second World War, according to one estimate, between the mid-1960s and the 1980s, NTBs by the industrialized countries rose—in the case of the United States from about 36 to 45 percent, in Europe from 21 to 54 percent, and in Japan from a little over 31 percent to 44 percent.[16] Such policies, however, extend beyond mere political interests per se. They are also social welfare policies, the means to maintain the standards of living for constituents through the distribution of subsidies and to maintain politically acceptable employment levels.

According to the laissez-faire theory, governments are expected to refrain from engaging in such policies. Critics argue that subsidies harm international trade relations, as well as national economic interests. From one government's perspective, its trade partners might see such subsidies as distorting market competition, hence requiring countervailing measures to protect their own domestic interests. This moves us close to what are termed "trade wars"—that is, tit-for-tat retaliation.

Comparative Advantages and Strategic Policies

The theory of laissez-faire free trade is premised on the principle of allocative equilibrium, whereby nations trade to compensate for their deficiencies in resources and goods. Thus, traders can have absolute and comparative advantages, as discussed in Chapter 2. Absolute advantage occurs when a country offers certain resources or products to other countries at lower prices than if produced in those countries. According to the principle of comparative advantage, on the other hand, a country concentrates its energies on manufacturing and exporting those goods it produces relatively *most* efficiently, even foregoing the production of other goods for which it might still have an advantage over other countries.[17] Instead, it imports those goods from abroad, focusing all its production on its very best industries on the assumption that, in that way, it can generate more income with which to purchase what it needs. Comparative advantage theory, thus, stresses that trade relations are driven by product specialization—that is, the production of goods and services relatively most efficiently with minimum expenditures.[18]

The globalization of trade relations especially in the twentieth century, however, has been characterized by a new set of properties. These involve, for example, globalization and relocation of production in search for cheaper labor, various trade and financial strategic alliances, and transnational intra-industry trade, all facilitated by the advent of information telecommunications technologies. These changes have led some scholars to advocate *strategic trade theories.*[19]

Strategic trade and dependencia theorists contend that free trade based on the principle of comparative advantage not only leads to commodity specialization in such products as timber, cocoa, bananas, and sugar, and commodity and market dependence, but also results in conflictual relations between industrialized and developing countries. Less developed countries produce raw materials, such as copper, oil, gold, and bauxite, and are the primary source for cheap labor and labor-intensive commodities; they also are famous for"one crop" economies, such as bananas, coffee, or sugar. Commodity specialization in these sectors is cheaper; therefore, it is far more difficult for developing countries—already dominated by the first industrialized economies (FIES)—to develop technologically advanced and competitive industries.[20]

Strategic trade theorists note that free trade is desirable in ideal theoretical models in which "free trade can be shown be perfectly efficient."[21] Economies with a strong market share in a commodity or product, as with Saudi oil, can limit exports to increase prices in world markets. Much of world trade, however, cannot be so simply explained by supply and demand analysis. Rather, international trade requires explanations accounting for "economies of scale, learning curves, and the dynamics of innovation—all phenomena incompatible with the kind of idealizations under which free trade is always the best policy"—that is, "market imperfections."[22] As one observer has noted, "Nobody would suggest that Saudi Arabia would be richer with free trade."[23] Some countries face geographical or political problems that impede their free trade; the former Soviet republic of Turkmenistan, for example, is the 11th leading natural gas producer but has great difficulty bringing its gas to market; it is cross pressured by Russia, Iran, the U.S., and Shell Oil to choose pipelines through potentially hostile territories. The changing trade environment in the late twentieth century has rendered the traditional comparative advantage theory questionable, if not unworkable. Trade, Krugman has argued,

> now seems to arise because of the advantages of large-scale production, the advantages of cumulative experience, and transitory advantages resulting from innovation. In industries where these factors are important, we are not going to see the kind of atomistic competition between many small firms that is necessary for "perfect" competition to be a good description of the world. Major U.S. exporters like Boeing or Caterpillar, and many smaller firms as well, are in a different kind of competition from that facing wheat farmers or garment manufacturers. They face a few identifiable rivals, they have some direct ability to affect prices, and they make *strategic* moves designed to affect their rivals' actions.[24]

Analysts have come to view the international market as being "imperfectly competitive" and, therefore, far more complicated than understood in simplified versions of world supply and demand. The theory of strategic trade concentrates on the strategic choices businesses make, which in turn shape and are shaped by domestic and multinational industries.[25] In strategic trade policy, the government is expected to play an active role in promoting competitive industries through various forms of subsidies—for example, subsidies for research and development (R&D) in the software industry—while allowing less competitive industries to exit the market.

Such strategic policies, however, can easily force governments and the resources at their disposal to become trapped into supporting large, multinational industries because of their sheer size and political clout in policymaking circles.[26] At its core, strategic trade theory seeks to restrict a share of a market to identified enterprises in order to encourage their expansion into other markets. Thus, the domestic market needs protection from foreign competitors, while domestic businesses are protected at home and in foreign markets. Profits from export markets strengthen not only the enterprise involved but also the domestic economy (via employment and revenues) and national security. Of particular concern here is advanced communications technology and its domestic and foreign markets. Because such technology is essential for both commercial and military purposes, governments strictly regulate its export and import, and in the process they provide the necessary protection to domestic companies (discussed in greater detail in Chapter 8).[27] Such policies, however, increase the government's stake in company activities and can lead to restrictions and regulations. A U.S. satellite firm, Loral Inc., was first assisted in and then investigated for providing sensitive missile technology upgrades to China in 1997–1998. The company wished to protect its investment in having its communications satellites reliably and cheaply launched on Chinese rockets. The U.S. government, and particularly Congress, objected to possible security trade violations that might also improve China's nuclear weapons delivery capabilities on similar rockets. Such collaborating and conflicting government-company interests are but one example of the decision-making complications in strategic trade analysis.

Protectionist policies also become controversial when, for example, companies buy and sell to themselves across borders. AT&T, for example, used to produce telecommunications equipment through its Western Electric subsidiary; it also was "the principal buyer through its operating companies."[28] Equally as important, strategic theory takes into consideration corporate learning as an essential ingredient in global trade competitiveness. Learning reduces the cost of production as the process of production becomes more efficient. In theory, protection of the domestic market encourages more production as domestic businesses learn to produce efficiently, which in turn enhances their ability to compete in foreign markets—hence the difference between traditional liberal and strategic trade theories: the latter is premised on more realistic but more complicated assumptions regarding the nature and dynamics of international and domestic markets and the role and impact of businesses. Unlike liberal trade theory, it does not assume perfect competition, but it does consider such factors as institutional learning, technological changes, economies of scale, trade barriers, and R&D competitions.[29]

It should be pointed out, however, that government involvement in trade policies, such as protectionist tariffs, to promote domestic industries and markets can intentionally or unintentionally jeopardize the strategic advantages of trading partners and can instigate retaliatory measures, such as competing subsidies or non-tariff barriers.[30] Retaliation and counterretaliation usually leave both trading partners, as well as the international economy, in a worse condition than before. Trade cooperation is said to be mutually beneficial, but unilateral action "self-defeating." However, in times of economic recession and high unemployment, policymakers feel compelled to expand industrial targeting—that is, favoring key leading exporters—and strategic protectionist policies, even if they cause otherwise cooperative trade partners to retaliate. Retaliatory and counterretaliatory measures, whether introduced to mollify domestic public opinion pressures or as a strategic industrial policy, may lead to negotiations and renewed cooperation, but they may also lead to trade wars, as each side tries to protect its political and economic interests.[31]

Patterns of International Trade Relations

As previously noted, international trade has experienced substantial expansion during the second half of the twentieth century, and this pattern is expected to continue well into the twenty-first.[32] In the process, a number of factors influencing trade patterns have become visible, including geographic distribution, the composition of commodities traded, and the impact of technological development. One of the most apparent patterns of international trade evolving over the twentieth century is the geographic concentration of commerce among the first industrialized economies (FIEs)—the European Union, the United States, and Japan. Trade among them is discussed in greater detail later in this chapter; suffice it to say here that a substantial portion of world trade—ranging from 60 percent in the 1950s and 1960s to well over 70 percent in the mid-1990s—has been among the FIEs. This unequal distribution reflects a number of conditions in the international trade structure, but the primary contributing factor is the concentration of wealth and, hence, purchasing power in the FIEs.

Concentration of purchasing power in the wealthier societies means that international trade activities revolve around their markets, tastes, habits of consumption, and market fluctuations. Rising standards of living and consumerism have created comparable markets for a vast array of products in various price ranges and for people of varied socioeconomic status. Market compatibility among the FIEs has intensified international competition, as producers in one country can offer their goods (whether Nike, Coca-Cola, computers, TV sets, or cars) to consumers in other countries with relative ease.

Changing patterns of purchasing power and the expansion of world trade have influenced the composition of commodities traded. The period between 1948 and 1978 witnessed a ten-fold growth in the trade of manufactured goods, while trade in raw materials and food products increased only roughly four times.[33] These changes have resulted in tensions between the developed and developing countries, as the economic and earnings gap between them widened (see Chapter 10). While in the early twentieth century developing countries exported nearly 40 percent of the primary goods in world trade, their share declined to 28 percent in the 1970s and to 20 percent in the 1980s and 1990s. By the late 1970s, developed countries were the major producers of primary products, as well as manufactured goods. Developing countries, on the other hand, had to export more of their primary products in order to be able to purchase manufactured goods from the developed countries.[34]

Since the 1980s, international trade composition has witnessed another change—namely, the expansion of trade in commercial services (banking, communications, insurance, and so forth). Between 1995 and 1997 alone, exports of commercial services rose from $1.2 trillion to $1.3 trillion.[35] The United States is the leading service exporter, in 1997 accounting for nearly 18 percent of total world trade in service, followed by Britain (6.5 percent), France (6.3), and Germany (5.6 percent).[36] In the meantime, trade in agriculture has declined. In the case of the United States, for example, while in 1980 exports of services totaled $48 billion (or 18 percent of total U.S. exports), in 1996 that figure had increased to $237 billion (or 28 percent). While U.S. exports of agricultural products have increased in absolute dollar value from $42 billion to $61 billion, they have declined as a percentage of total U.S. exports from 15 percent to 7 percent for the same years.[37]

The expansion in the trade of services also underscores the role of technological changes. Technology has been the basis for modern, or post-modern, industries, and its international diffusion has created vast new markets for sophisticated computers and software, telecommunications, and related products, such as toys. Technology also has affected the international structure of trade, as in the case of commerce between FIEs and developing countries, enabling the former to replace primary commodities previously imported from the developing countries with synthetic products, thereby diminishing or even eliminating the markets for producers from developing countries in FIEs. One of the earliest examples foreshadowing this change concerned Chile's nitrate industry. In the late nineteenth century, Chilean landowners and European (mostly British) investors competed for control over the nitrate fields, but Chileans maintained control over at least 50 percent of the revenues until the 1920s, causing much aggravation for their European trade partners. By the 1930s, however, Europe was producing synthetic nitrate, and the Chilean nitrate industry collapsed.[38] Technological development and the changing structure of international trade also have affected the domestic structure of labor in the developed countries, as demands for competitiveness and corporate profits have placed a premium on automation, replacing employees in labor-intensive jobs.

Finally, another development among the patterns of international trade has been the increase in intra-industry trade—that is, exchanges within a single sector, such as in automobiles. A large portion of world trade is within industries, mostly in the area of technologically advanced manufactured products—autos, electronic office equipment, chemicals, and pharmaceuticals. For the United States, for example, 57 percent of trade in 1996 was in intra-industry trade.[39] Intra-industry trade is based on economies of scale and the production of differentiated goods, rather than based on comparative advantages; therefore, patterns of intra-industry trade, as influenced by consumer tastes, are less predictable than are those of inter-industry trade. Like trade in general, intra-industry trade occurs primarily among the developed countries, whose markets, labor, and levels of overall economic development and wealth are similar, while trade between developed and developing countries remains largely in the area of inter-industry trade (for example, Canadian grain for Cuban cigars).[40]

INTERNATIONAL TRADE: TRIADS AND TRIBULATIONS

United States–Europe–Japan: A Trade Triad

The three major economic centers of the world economy today—the United States, Europe, and Japan—experienced enormous economic growth and prosperity in the second half of the twentieth century, and international trade relations increased accordingly. The United States, Europe, and Japan long have been among the largest partners, but trade among them became particularly contentious because of widening trade imbalances after the 1970s. With the ending of the Cold War, the absence of a common enemy (such as the Soviet Union) allowed economic tensions to surface, as trade competition among the three intensified. Trade, as a percentage of GDP, also increased in importance, or policy *salience,* for the United States, as compared with Europe and Japan (see Figure 5.1).[41]

Among the industrialized countries, the United States has had the largest trade deficit, totaling about $125 billion in 1990, and an average deficit of $140 billion during the 1991–1995 period, reaching nearly $198 billion in 1997.[42] Britain has consistently had a trade deficit since the 1950s; its average annual deficit was $38 billion in 1987–1989 and about $28 billion for the 1991–1995 period. Two countries with substantial surpluses, however, have been Japan and Germany. Well into the late 1970s (with the exception of 1969–1971), Japan ran trade deficits of up to $3.3 billion (1979–1981). Thereafter, its trade balance improved, and its surplus increased from $55 billion in 1984–1986 to $65 billion in 1990; for 1991–1995, its average annual surplus was $106 billion. Germany's balance-of-trade gain also was impressive. Its trade surplus rose from $1.4 billion in 1959–1961 to $16 billion in 1974–1976, and to $70 billion in 1987–1989;[43] for the 1991–1995 period, its average annual surplus was $43 billion.[44]

FIGURE 5.1

Source: Loukas Tsoukalis, *The New European Economy: The Politics and Economics of Intergration,* rev. 2nd ed. (Oxford: Oxford University Press, 1993).

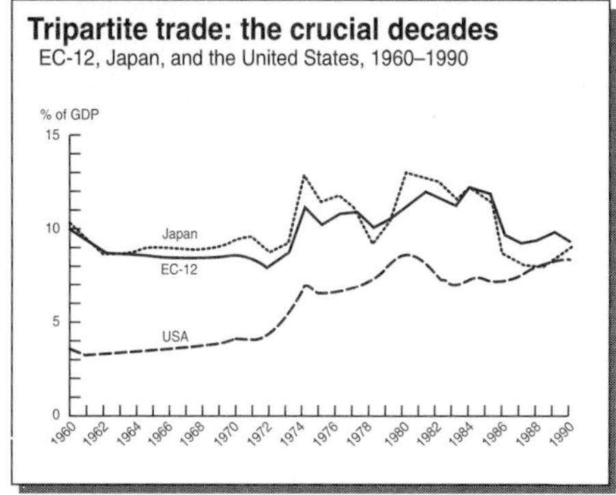

The U.S. trade balance with the European Union indeed registered some surplus in the early 1990s, as Europe's markets for U.S. products grew stronger, but by the mid-1990s its Euro-trade deficit recurred. Canada remains the United States' largest trade partner, exchanging a vast array of products, ranging from agriculture to highly advanced technologies. In 1994, for example, U.S. exports of civilian aircraft, mostly to Canada, rose by $661 million to $1.5 billion, as did exports of cars by $920 million to $5.2 billion.[45] Nevertheless, the U.S. trade deficit with Canada has begun to look chronic, increasing from $7.1 billion in 1991 to nearly $20 billion in 1997.[46]

For more than a decade since the early 1980s, the bilateral U.S. trade deficit with Japan increased from $15.8 billion in 1981, to $42 billion in 1992, to $67.3 billion in 1994,[47] due largely to the popularity of Japanese products in the United States and the relatively restricted sales of U.S. consumer and agricultural products in Japan.[48] In its overall trade relations, Japan registered a trade surplus of $123 billion and $78 billion in 1996 and 1997, respectively, the highest among the industrialized economies, followed by Germany's trade surplus of $65.2 billion.[49]

As a result, U.S. public and industry demands for protectionist policies became quite vocal. Since the mid-1980s, policymakers have responded by implementing various forms of trade restrictions, and U.S. trade restrictions imposed on the percentage of imports have increased from 25 percent to 40 percent. For example, in 1983 the Reagan administration increased tariffs on Japanese motorcycles by 1,000 percent to protect the U.S.-made Harley-Davidson. The United States also demanded greater access to foreign markets, particularly in Japan.[50]

The U.S. trade deficit with Japan is likely to remain a major source of controversy in U.S.-Japan relations (for example, see Table 5.1), and the balance of trade has been a serious issue with other Asian countries as well, especially China, involving equally powerful issues, such as intellectual property rights. The levels of U.S. trade are highest with the industrialized economies, although the trade deficit remains a problem with AIEs and LDEs. American tactics for addressing these issues appear to have shifted. The early Clinton administration, for example, concentrated on heavy-handed trade demands and numerical targets, especially in auto parts exports, in bilateral negotiations with Tokyo. While Japan made vague commitments to improve the balance, few concrete improvements materialized. Ultimately, Washington had to decide whether it preferred a stable Japanese government, economy, and stock market or forced trade concessions, especially as the Asian financial crisis of 1997 threatened the banking and securities industries. The United States appeared to opt for efforts to stabilize the yen and to move toward more multilateral consultation, even as it kept up public pressure for Japanese economic liberalization. American leaders hoped to open Japanese markets in fields such as banks and mutual funds and to head off a flood of relatively cheap Japanese exports by stabilizing the yen.

Europe's share of Asian markets has been declining as well. In the late 1960s and early 1970s, about 25 percent of total Asian imports were European products. By the mid-1990s, that figure had dropped to nearly 15 percent. Europe's share of Asia's imports fell, largely due to the rise in intra-Asian trade; however, in *absolute* terms, Europe's trade with Asia has increased rather quickly. European products did relatively well, although Japanese and U.S. products tended to dominate the emerging Asian markets—that is, Asia excluding Japan. By 1995, the total value of Europe's trade with the so-called emerging Asia was about $212 billion, more than double the volume of trade since the mid-1980s.[51]

Europe also enjoys better balanced trade relations with non-Japan Asia than do the United States and Japan. While the total value of U.S. trade with emerging Asia is higher than Europe's total, the volume of Europe's exports is higher. In 1994, the United States exported $91.8 billion worth of products, while European exports totaled $99 billion. The United States also maintains a large trade deficit with non-Japan Asia. In fact, the U.S. trade deficit with non-Japan Asia (mainly China) has been far larger than its deficit with Japan. At least until Asia's economic slowdown of the late 1990s, Japan had a huge trade surplus with the rest of the region.[52]

While production and export shares of the industrialized economies are discussed in Chapter 8, their export and import structures are indicative of the trends in trade competition. For example, the U.S. share of total world exports in agricultural products was 15.3 percent in 1980 and increased slightly to 15.9 percent in 1992. The European Union's share, on the other hand, rose from 17 percent to 23.2 percent during the same period.[53] The United States has at times attributed its declining share in this sector to EU members' subsidies and protectionist policies (they, in turn, point to America's long tradition of agricultural subsidies). As in the case of the "wine war" with France in the early 1990s, Washington has accused the EU of maintaining trade barriers, such as the Common Agricultural Policy

TABLE 5.1
U.S. Total Trade and Trade Balance, 1996 (in Millions of Dollars)

	Total Trade	Trade Balance
Top Five Trade Partners: First Industrialized Economies (FIEs)		
Britain	60,620	1,220
Canada	292,330	−27,160
France	33,627	−4,760
Germany	63,463	−16,520
Japan	185,499	−50,427
Top Five Trade Partners: Advanced Industrializing Economies (AIEs)		
Brazil	21,996	3,402
Malaysia	26,852	−9,810
Mexico	130,873	−17,350
Singapore	37,334	−3,962
South Korea	49,880	3,286
Top Five Trade Partners: Less Developed Economies (LDEs)		
China (and Hong Kong)	90,605	−38,737
Egypt	3,860	2,432
Honduras	3,541	−259
India	9,864	−3,210
Nigeria	6,988	−5,356

Source: IMF, *Direction of Trade Statistics Quarterly,* March 1998, pp. 217–218.
[a]Negatives in this column indicate U.S. trade deficit.

(CAP), despite the EU countries' claimed commitment to trade liberalization.[54]

The intensification of trade competition among the industrialized economies during the past two decades is, of course, the result of their relative equality in economic, industrial, and technological capabilities. Clearly, because these states are also political and military allies in most cases, their trade competition also is limited or muted; they would not like to destroy each other's economies. As noted earlier, however, not all regions are equally developed and not all have such common political interests. Trade relations between unequal partners, as between countries in the industrialized North and those in the developing South, are quantitatively and qualitatively different from those between comparable partners. The following section looks at some of the issues involved in that relationship.

FIE–AIE/LDE Trade

There is a wide gap in economic terms between the industrialized countries of the northern first industrialized economies (FIEs) and the less developed AIE and LDE countries. In 1994, the world real gross domestic product (GDP) per capita in terms of purchasing power parity (PPP) was $5,798; that figure for the FIEs was $15,986, while it was $2,904 for all of the developing countries ($965 for LDEs).[55] The developing economies are either primarily agriculture-based or have not developed major industrial capabilities. This is not to suggest, however, that the North and the South are two monoliths with no differences among themselves. As noted in Chapter 1, both the FIEs and the developing countries are diverse groups of nations, with various levels of development and modernization. In the North, for example, in 1990, Portugal's GNP per capita was about $5,000, while Spain's was $11,000, Sweden's $24,000, and Japan's $26,100. Similarly, major differences appear in the South. In Latin America, in 1990, Argentina's GNP per capita was $3,290, placing it among the advanced industrializing economies (AIEs), while Peru's was $1,000 and Haiti's $420, one of the lowest among the less developed economies (LDEs). Among African countries, South Africa's GNP per capita for the same year was $2,530, Nigeria's $350, and Mozambique's $90. In Asia, India's GNP per capita in 1990 was $370, China's $410, but South Korea's was $5,770, and Singapore's $12,740.[56] Trade and economic-political power relations between the North and the South reflect these disparities, and since the Second World War the chasm between the two has grown wider. The South has relied on the North mainly for its industrial, military, and consumer imports, while the North has found the South useful as a source of raw materials and cheap labor.[57]

While the Bretton Woods system can be credited to some extent for the economic growth and stability of the industrialized Western countries, the results were not the same for developing states. The founders of the Bretton Woods system—mostly the United States—were preoccupied primarily with the general well-being of their own economies and paid scant attention to remote marginal economies. In fact, most of the developing countries in Africa and Asia had not even gained independence from colonial rule in the late 1940s. The post-WWII international economic order, which stressed free trade and laissez-faire capitalism, could not stimulate economic growth in developing countries. The 1950s and 1960s were decades of political upheaval, as many LDEs fought for and gained independence from colonization; this period saw declining foreign investments in southern economies and subsequent southern efforts to achieve economic independence and development. Further, the burdens of nation- and state-building exacerbated their economic difficulties, allowing little room for the free play of market economics as anticipated by liberalism. Developing countries tended to view their situation as the product of Western colonialism, and their inability to gain economic freedom from the world economic system as devised under the Bretton Woods as a "neo-colonial" strategy to continue exploitation through international financial and trade relations and such institutions as the World Bank. As a result, many LDE leaders opted for strong statist economic policies to move their societies toward industrialization as a means to challenge northern dominance, sometimes resorting to such extreme measures as nationalizing productive or revenue-generating facilities (discussed in Chapter 7).

Southern states demanded complete economic and political independence and introduced policies accordingly, including discriminatory trade policies to protect domestic infant industries and to stimulate industrialization and modernization. Such strategies, they hoped, would produce national economic, political, and military power. They resorted to collective measures as well, establishing the Group of 77 (G-77) in 1964 at a UN Conference on Trade and Development (UNCTAD) as an international forum for collective negotiations. As previously noted, in 1974 they adopted the Declaration on the Establishment of a New International Economic Order (NIEO), demanding a more equitable distribution of resources and wealth.[58]

In the 1970s, the two "oil shocks" exacerbated the worldwide recession and inflation (or stagflation), unemployment, and trade deficits. During this period, banks scrambled to lend the ever expanding pool of available excess "petro-dollars," which in turn led to the global debt crisis throughout the developing world in the 1980s.[59] LDEs simply lacked sufficient economic resources—in trade, capital, and industrial capacity—to produce and export enough to pay the interest to foreign lenders. In the early 1970s, the FIEs' share of the total world exports was over 70 percent, with the developing countries' share only 19 percent. By the late 1970s, the latter's share increased to nearly 30 percent, but, in the 1980s and early 1990s, the gap widened again, as the FIEs' share increased to 72 percent, and the developing countries' share dropped to about 25 percent in the mid-1990s.[60] Even as the 1980s and 1990s witnessed expanding international trade relations and closer North-South relations, of the $3.7 trillion in world exports, only about 25 percent were exports from the South[61] (see Figure 5.2).

Nevertheless, expanding North-South trade has begun to cost jobs for the developed countries and has been accompanied by a 20 percent reduction in unskilled labor. Analysts and politicians have debated whether expanding trade and competition from low-wage economies caused this decline. In the case of the United States, for example, in the early 1990s imports from developing countries were not even 4 percent of GDP.[62] The ability to export remains particularly critical for smaller developing countries

FIGURE 5.2
Source: Nyerere Commission Report, *Challenege to the South: The Report of the South Commission* (Oxford: Oxford University.Press, 1990), p. 154.

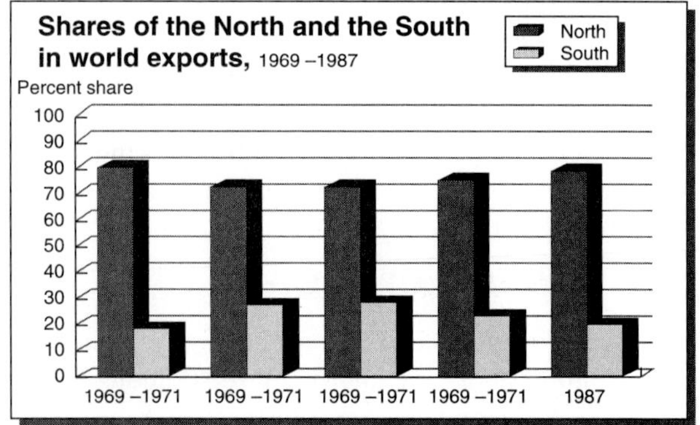

because they possess limited domestic market absorption capacity. What they produce, therefore, must be sold in foreign markets of the North, which in turn requires commodity specialization and leads to dependence on the world economic system and the health of foreign markets. For many developing countries, export diversification and greater development of manufacturing and service sectors remain major objectives (see Box 5.1). At the same time, just as common political interests sometimes soften major powers' own trade competition, major powers' interests in "stability" for the developing regions also have tended to improve chances for economic assistance, more favorable trade concessions, and the formation of organizations presumably beneficial to the South, such as the World Trade Organization (discussed below).

Trade Among AIEs and LDEs

Relatively little trade takes place among developing countries. In the early 1990s, trade among AIEs and LDEs accounted for less than 10 percent of total world trade, leaving them highly dependent on trade earnings from the

BOX 5.1

A PROGRAM OF PRIORITY ACTION FOR SOUTH-SOUTH COOPERATION: THE NYERERE COMMISSION

South-South co-operation will be of very great importance to developing countries in the years ahead. Its scope is vast and it has to be pursued as a long-term undertaking. The set-backs of the 1980s now require that immediate efforts should be made to impart a fresh momentum to the South's collective work. These should start with action in a few key areas, progress in which could have catalytic effects and help to put South-South co-operation on a more secure path for the future.

As a prerequisite for the priority action programme, we wish to underline the importance of three matters for the future of South-South co-operation and of the South as a group:

- The proposal to establish the South Secretariat requires immediate action. We believe that the secretariat could act as a vital pillar of the South's efforts to expand co-operation within the South and to secure a fairer system of global relationships through negotiations with the North.
- The participation of heads of state or government in regular institutionalized consultations is a very important step towards the South's improved organization. Therefore the [Nyerere] Commission welcomes the decision by a group of heads of state or government of developing countries to set up a Summit Level Group for South-South Consultations and Co-operation.
- The attitude of the North towards South-South co-operation has ranged from lukewarm support to benign neglect, to veiled discouragement, down to overt opposition. There are some quarters in the North that see South-South co-operation as a threat and also resist any attempt by the South to organize itself to promote its interests. We believe that the North's attitude is a matter that should be raised with the North at the highest level and that the South should seek a clear policy commitment of support for its efforts to help itself through South-South co-operation. The South should endeavor to have it accepted widely within the world community that diversified links and cooperation among developing countries are desirable as a contribution to peace, to the well-being of all, and to the successful functioning of the world economy.

The programme of priority action we propose [is] a call to action to the governments and peoples of the South:

- The success of the South-South co-operation is dependent on supportive national policies and, ultimately, on the support of the people of the South. Each developing country should reflect in its development plans and national policies an explicit commitment to South-South co-operation. It should give to one government ministry or department responsibility for coordinating action within the country arising from the commitment to South-South co-operation. In addition, each country should set up a national committee to advise the government, to mobilize public opinion in support of South-South co-operation, and to promote people-to-people contacts in the South.
- As part of the efforts to develop the South's human resources, fuller use should be made of the South's educational institutions in meeting the needs of countries with inadequate facilities of their own. Priority should be given to the identification and development of selected Centres of Educational Excellence, particularly in the fields of basic sciences, engineering, medicine, management, and public administration. It is equally necessary to create a Foundation for South Fellowships to facilitate the movement of students, teachers, researchers, and other technical personnel among developing countries.
- The proposal to establish a South Bank should be implemented. A start should be made with a narrower range of functions than originally planned. A broad group

BOX 5.1 (concluded)

A PROGRAM OF PRIORITY ACTION FOR SOUTH-SOUTH COOPERATION: THE NYERERE COMMISSION

of developing countries whose association with the project would give it international credibility should take the initiative in establishing the bank, but its membership should be open to all developing countries.

- The framework for facilitating and promoting all forms of South-South trade created by the Global System of Trade Preferences should be purposefully used . . . .
- With a view to improving their position in world markets through supply management or other means, commodity producers within the South should urgently consider reinforcing existing producers' associations and setting up new ones. In particular, producers of the three tropical beverages—tea, coffee, cocoa—should work out a comprehensive programme of co-operation among them. The Group of 77 and the Non-Alignment Movement should provide strong support to these initiatives.
- Co-operation among business enterprises of the South should be promoted at the bilateral, sub-regional, regional, and interregional levels. All developing countries should introduce legal, technical, and fiscal measures that encourage joint ventures and the conclusion of agreements for the transfer of technology among Southern enterprises. They should give preferential treatment to investment and technology flows from other developing countries. A code for the operation of Southern multinational enterprises and for the transfer of technology should be adopted, setting out the rights and obligations of all parties. Business and industry in the South should be brought into the mainstream of South-South co-operation; the establishment and effective functioning of the Association of Third World Chambers of Commerce and Industry should be made a priority. The Group of 77 and the Non-Aligned Movement should set up a Standing Committee consisting of government representatives as well as businessmen to keep enterprise co-operation under regular review . . . .
- The South should develop a strategy for scientific cooperation focused on issues of major concern in which research and innovation could offer tangible benefits through the pooling of resources. The Center for Science and Technology of the Non-Aligned and Other Developing Countries should be invited to draw up, in cooperation with the Third World Academy of Sciences and other scientific institutions in the South, a programme for co-ordinating scientific and technological research in the South in . . . key areas of high technology such as biotechnology, informatics, and material sciences. Southern institutions with a high level of research and facilities should be identified for training scientists, engineers, and technicians from other countries in the South under programmes for co-operation.
- Measures should be taken to make schemes for subregional and regional co-operation more effective. The existing preferential trading ar-rangements should be strengthened and new ones created. Controls on trade and foreign exchange, and non-tariff barriers removed. Clearing and payments arrangements should be revitalized. These initiatives should be complemented by the regional planning of investment in selected areas. Each regional and subregional group should critically examine its options and draw up a more up-to-date agenda of action, identifying immediate priorities and targets to the year 2000, as well as a longer-term plan extending to the year 2020.

We believe that the conditions for South-South co-operation have become more favorable and that the need for such cooperation has become more compelling. We are convinced that if the South takes up the challenge seriously . . . South South co-operation can add an important dimension of international political and economic relations by the end of this decade.

Source: *Challenge to the South: The Report of the South Commission* (Oxford: Oxford University Press, 1990), pp. 206–210.

FIEs. Regional and inter-regional efforts to promote trade and economic integration have to some extent been successful in raising the level of "the South's consciousness," but, with the exception of a brief improvement in the 1970s, the AIEs and LDEs have not been able to rectify the imbalances in their trade and power relations with the FIEs. During the 1970s, as developing countries experienced increases in trade and capital transactions, they expected their economies to grow and to develop sufficient and stable bases for a more technologically advanced, financially sound, and diversified market and production capabilities. Further, they hoped that rapid economic development would stimulate greater financial and trade cooperation among themselves and decrease their dependence on the markets and financial institutions of the North.[63] Accordingly, they advocated widening the scope of intra-regional trade and the creation of additional forums for regional and subregional economic cooperation.

Figure 5.3 presents intra-regional trade levels in Africa, Asia, and Latin America. As the figures indicate, in the mid-1960s, about 6 percent of Africa's total trade occurred within the region; the levels for Asia's and Latin America's trade were nearly 25 percent and 17 percent, respectively. Intra-regional trade in both Africa and Asia dropped in the early 1970s, but Latin America's increased slightly. While Asia saw no major changes in the early 1980s, its intra-regional trade increased from 23 percent of its total world trade in 1980 to about 30 percent in 1987. By 1995, that figure had reached nearly 40 percent.[64] Japan was by far the largest contributor (33 percent) to the Asian trade, followed by Hong Kong (21 percent), while mainland China's share was about 16 percent. Other economically dynamic countries with a large share in intra-Asia trade included South Korea, Malaysia, Singapore, Indonesia, and Thailand. These countries, however, are confronted with the problem of potentially being dominated by the two regional giants: Japan and China. The reunification of Hong Kong with China, if no political upheavals or military conflicts cause disruptions in trade, will raise their combined share to about 38 percent.

FIGURE 5.3

Source: Nyerere Commission Report, *Challenge to the South: The Report of the South Commission* (Oxford: Oxford University Press, 1990), p. 175.

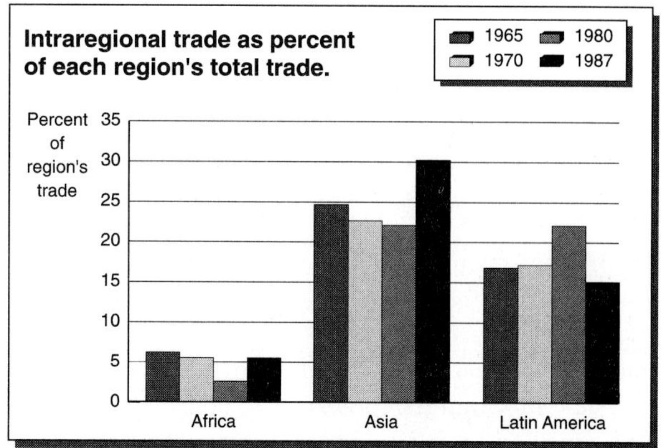

Unlike Asia, intra-regional trade in the other developing regions was limited. Latin American intra-regional trade increased from about 17 percent in 1970 to about 22 percent in 1980 but dropped to near 16 percent in 1987 and recovered somewhat to 19 percent in 1995; over 70 percent of Latin American trade remained with the industrialized countries.[65] In the case of Africa, intra-regional trade as a percentage of the region's total trade dropped from just above 5 percent in 1970 to about 3 percent in 1980, rising to nearly 6 percent in 1987. The figures improved in the 1990s, but the highest level was about 10 percent in 1995, while 65 percent of total African world trade was with the industrialized economies.[66]

The Middle East was in a similar situation. Although trade figures may be skewed due to oil revenues, in the late 1980s, the share of intra-regional trade was 8.7 percent of the region's trade, but it fell to 7.5 percent in 1991 and dropped again to 6.3 percent in 1995. Unlike Africa and Latin America, and because of the large oil sector, however, the distribution of Middle Eastern trade was more balanced between the industrialized and developing economies. In 1995, 52 percent of total Middle Eastern exports were with the North, 38 percent with the South.[67] Particularly worth noting is the recent expansion of trade relations between Middle Eastern and African countries. The long tradition of Islamic relations is seen as providing opportunities for trade among the countries in the two regions. In the 1990s, for example, Arab countries (among them Bahrain, Morocco, Yemen, Iran, Saudi Arabia, Jordan, and Egypt) and South Africa signed a number of trade agreements. Trade relations between Arab and African countries include oil and gas, agricultural products, and arms, and each sees the other's market as an opportunity to promote economic diversification. In the early 1990s, South Africa's Prosper Cutlery established a plant in Dubai's Jebel Ali free zone, while South Africa's Armscor has sold arms to Abu Dhabi. Sheikh Saleh Kamel, head of the Saudi Albaraka banking group, has stressed the need to develop closer relations with "two million-strong Muslim community in South Africa" and to improve its socio-economic situation through Islamic banking and joint ventures.[68]

Leaders of developing countries attempted to strengthen South-South trade and cooperation through the Global System of Trade Preferences (GSTP), effective since April 1989. The GSTP includes general rules for reciprocity with respect to tariff and non-tariff policies for commodities and manufactured products, as well as provisions for greater trade liberalization. Most observers, however, agree, and the trade figures for developing countries indicate, that since its creation the GSTP has at best acquired a symbolic value with little direct and effective means to enhance South-South cooperation and trade. Given the opportunity, it may potentially become a powerful unifying force and develop well-coordinated inter-regional strategies for economic relations and development. However, such expectations have yet to materialize, as discussed in the next chapter.

INTERNATIONAL TRADE AND DOMESTIC PRESSURES

The previous discussion underscores at least two key issues in international trade. First, why would governments opt for *free trade?* Second, what factors contribute to protectionism? International trade, like international finance, must be seen within the context of its global, national, and local structural properties encompassing state and corporate powers, preferences, policies, and profits.[69] The choice between free trade and protectionism manifests more than merely ideological predilections; it also entails domestic competition to define national economic and political priorities.[70] This section discusses the reasons a state chooses trade liberalization or protectionism.

As noted in Chapter 2, globalization theory holds that any analysis of international financial and trade relations must take into consideration the role of both state and nonstate actors. Various groups (corporations, unions) and even individuals lobby governments to introduce policies for the protection and promotion of their respective interests, but it is still the government—whether in Argentina, Brazil, Burma, Germany, Japan, Mozambique, the United States, or Zambia, whether in the industrialized or the developing countries—that formulates and implements trade policies. As noted by Behboodi, trade policy is, in fact, *trade politics,*[71] the *relative* "retreat of the state" in recent years notwithstanding.[72]

Why Free Trade?

In addition to the strictly economic principles such as comparative advantage, states pursue free trade policies for political reasons as well. In his now classic article, Stephen Krasner argued that the structure of international trade is the product of the power and interests of states.[73] He identified four fundamental interests that determine the "degree of openness" states allow for trade: aggregate national income, economic growth, political power, and social stability. The degree of openness a state permits is based on the relative size and level of its economic development. As postulated by the liberal laissez-faire theory, Krasner noted, "the greater the degree of openness in the international trading system, the greater the level of aggregate economic income,"[74] and, the smaller the size of a country, the larger the benefits from open trade, as the share of national income derived from trade is potentially greater in smaller states seeking larger foreign markets. At the same time, larger and economically more developed states might encourage open or liberalized trade because of the political advantages accrued as expansive international economic activities accord them greater political power and export income in relations with other states.

With respect to the relationship between distribution of power and trade structure in the world economy, Krasner further theorized that an international trade structure with multiple economic centers is likely to be a relatively open system, while a structure comprised of "unequally developed states" is likely to be relatively closed. The greater the openness of the international trade system, the greater the political vulnerability of the less developed economies, which lack the degree of domestic structural (including production) flexibilities necessary to absorb international and national economic shocks.[75]

In an international trade structure dominated by a hegemonic power, Krasner maintained, the hegemon opts for an open trade system. An open system provides greater opportunities for the hegemon's own economic growth and, hence, increases in its aggregate national income. Such a trade structure also increases the hegemon's political power, since international trade relations constitute a greater proportion of national income for the smaller, especially less developed, states. In fact, the hegemon is likely to use unilateral and multilateral policy instruments, including foreign aid and military force, to realign the trade position of smaller states deviating from the open system. Unlike the smaller states, however, the hegemon's economic and technological advancement facilitates greater distribution and mobility of resources across industries and regions at home, thereby absorbing internationally induced shocks to the domestic structures. The international trade system experiences greater openness when the "hegemonic state is in its ascendancy . . . [and] has the interest and the resources to create a structure characterized by lower tariffs, rising trade proportions, and less regionalism."[76]

Thus, Krasner identified five periods since the early nineteenth century alternating between openness and closure. The period 1820–1879 was characterized by openness, as Britain lowered trade barriers, such as the repeal of the Corn Laws in 1846, followed by France, Belgium, Portugal, Spain and other European countries, a process culminating in the British-French Cobden-Chevalier Treaty of 1860. The period 1879–1900 witnessed rising trade barriers, as in Austria–Hungary in 1876 and 1878, Italy in 1878, and Germany and France during the next decade. The United States, as advocated by Alexander Hamilton, remained a protectionist country for most of the nineteenth century. Between 1900 and 1913, prior to the First World War, the international trade system opened somewhat, and trade levels increased. This period was soon followed, however, by a period of sharp increases in tariffs and protectionism in general amid economic difficulties and the Great Depression, as discussed in Chapter 3. The fifth period, 1945–1970, experienced increasing openness as trade barriers were lowered under the GATT and trade activities expanded rapidly.[77]

The paradox witnessed in the international structure since the 1970s is that there has been both a (some would say, declining) hegemon and spreading regionalism amid the convergence of multiple factors in the overall world political economy. These factors have included near "trade wars" among the United States, Japan, and Europe; expanding trade; economic liberalization in some developing countries; regional trade integration; and continued U.S. hegemonism, especially after the collapse of the Soviet Union. As globalization theory suggests, these varied patterns may be due to the strengthened role of the MNCs relative to the state, particularly relative to the smaller economies, while the United States—because of its considerably absorptive market capacity, because it is home to some of the most powerful MNCs, and because of its military capabilities—has retained its hegemonic position through its financial, diplomatic, and military power.

Krasner held that openness to trade renders the domestic economy vulnerable to world market fluctuations and may lead to conflicts in society—especially in smaller states, since a larger proportion of their economies is likely to be affected by international trade relations. In the case of developed economies, both major and minor, Krasner argued, the negative impact of openness, which otherwise would lead to instability, tends to be compensated for by the advantages of economic growth derived from open trade.[78] However, when societies experience economic hardships, as in periods of rising unemployment, public and business pressures on policymakers grow, demanding some government intervention to ameliorate the situation.

Protection of Domestic Industries

Demands for government intervention usually emphasize greater protectionist policies for domestic purposes. These policies can be categorized according to the following areas: (1) reciprocity, (2) employment protection, (3) wage protection, (4) infant industries, (5) national security considerations, (6) diversified economy, and (7) revenue raising.[79] This section discusses each of these policies.

Reciprocity In international trade, as in most international bilateral and multilateral legal arrangements, trading partners base their relations on the promise to conduct trade and related transactions governed by specific terms of agreed-upon contracts signed in good faith. The parties enter into such contracts largely based on expectations of *mutually* beneficial financial gains. However, while trade agreements may have the quality of permanence, domestic political and economic conditions do not. The latter are dynamic and at times change very rapidly, as indicated by the situation in China during the Tiananmen Square prodemocracy movement in 1989, the reunification of Hong Kong with China in 1997, and the Mexican and Asian financial crises in 1994–1995 and 1997–1998, respectively. As a country's economic condition changes, its political and business leaders propose or even demand corresponding changes in trade relations with their partners. They may propose a renegotiation of existing or new trade agreements for greater liberalization or protectionism as necessitated by the new economic circumstances. Such changes—or the threat to change—cause frictions and even trade wars among trade partners.

The recent literature on international political economy and trade has identified two types of reciprocity: aggressive reciprocity and passive reciprocity. *Aggressive reciprocity* involves the actual or potential threat of retaliation "for breach of or defection from" a trade agreement. One controversial type of aggressive reciprocity involves a country's threat of or actual withdrawal of trade concessions to its trading partner, "in the hope that this (or the threat thereof) will induce the breaching country to fulfill its prior commitments."[80] Another type of aggressive reciprocity is the imposition of rigid trade restrictions, aimed at communicating a country's displeasure toward its trading partner. One much publicized contemporary example of aggressive reciprocity was the United States' retaliatory measures adopted by the United States under the Omnibus Trade and Competitiveness Act of 1988 (also known as "Super 301"). The purpose of "Super 301" was to retaliate by restricting trade with countries that systematically discriminate against U.S. companies; it was applied—not totally successfully—against Japan in 1995. *Passive reciprocity,* on the other hand, entails a country's refusal to lower trade barriers "until its trading partners agree to reduce some of their trade restrictions." Laissez-faire theorists note that such threatening policies limit "trade liberalization and lead to inefficient outcome in which everyone is worse off."[81] Proponents (for example, labor unions), however, contend that some trade barriers are necessary to protect domestic jobs.

Employment Protection Advocates of protectionism maintain that tariffs and quotas are needed to minimize imports in favor of promoting domestic industries, exports, or both. Nations prefer relatively higher levels of exports not only because they bring higher levels of income but also because increases in foreign sales provide new employment opportunities. In times of economic difficulties and higher levels of unemployment, therefore, public pressure for protectionist policies intensifies.

Critics, on the other hand, contend that higher incomes and profits derived from protectionism can have only short-term benefits. Trade partners eventually, if not immediately, will retaliate to protect their own industries. Also, tariffs and quotas barring cheaper foreign goods lead to increases in prices in the domestic market, while protecting inefficient industries and encouraging inefficiency ând waste. Higher consumer prices for domestic production can be a heavy burden on the average wage earner. In the final analysis, the critics argue, protectionism restricts trade and, in doing so, diminishes the margin of gross income and net profit.[82]

Wage Protectionism Since wages in some industrialized societies are higher than in others, some analysts and corporate and union leaders contend that protectionist policies, such as tariffs and quotas, are required to shield high-wage-earning workers from imported goods produced by cheap labor—sometimes, it is contended, even by forced or slave labor—in foreign countries. Protection from foreign cheap labor is necessary, it is argued, to enable producers in industrialized, high-wage economies to compete in their own domestic as well as global markets. Opponents of protectionism, however, note that this contention is false, simply because the products of many high-wage, industrialized countries continue to compete effectively in foreign markets. Labor is relatively more important in labor-intensive production, usually found in developing countries, than it is in the more automated production in the industrialized countries, and free trade can give hope and jobs to destitute families in developing countries.[83]

Infant Industries Infant industries are newly emerging enterprises that supposedly need government protection in order to survive foreign competition. They first grow stronger in the domestic market and then expand their operations abroad. Tariffs and quotas may be necessary, at least temporarily, to shield such industries, to "develop technological efficiency and economies of scale which will enable them to compete with foreign industries."[84]

Observers, however, have identified a number of problems with the protectionist theory for infant industry. First, protective policies become the captives of political and corporate interests, who depend heavily on relations with their constituents and grow reluctant to terminate them. Second, some infant industries, even when protected, fail to mature and to compete effectively with older and larger industries at home and abroad. Finally, protective measures such as tariffs and quotas invariably lead to domestic price increases. Some economists believe, therefore, that subsidies rather than tariffs are preferable as a means to protect infant industries from international competition, because subsidies inject capital into the firm to increase production while reducing costs and prices.[85]

National Security Considerations Often, mercantilists or statists argue, protection for domestic industries is necessary for protection of national security because of the close relationship between national industrial strength and national security capabilities. A strong domestic industrial base is necessary in times of war, international crises,and trade disruptions affecting imports of strategic supplies and products. In a similar vein, trade restrictions are advocated on exports of certain products deemed "strategically sensitive," such as dual technology computers—that is, technology used for civilian and military purposes—especially if they can potentially be sold to "enemy" countries via third parties or can fall into "the wrong hands."

Business and political leaders frequently advocate protection for domestic industries from foreign competition in the name of national security. For example, Spencer notes,

> In one of his many pleas for increased protection, Robert Blough, when he was chairman of the board of the U.S. Steel Corporation, asked a congressional committee in the 1960s: "Can we be assured of the strong industrial base in steel we need for modern defense if one-quarter or more of the steel we require were imported from countries lying uncomfortably close to the Soviet Union or China?"[86]

Such arguments emphasizing national security as justification for more government protection or subsidies for domestic industries are effective in convincing not only the government but also the media and public opinion because of national security concerns. Protection for domestic industries and self-sufficiency become symbols for national strength and national defense, although at times such considerations are ignored in favor of profits and political expediency. The United States has been known to restrict imports of foreign weapons to protect domestic defense industries, while calling for NATO partners to open their markets to import U.S. weapons.

Another dimension of national security considerations opposing free trade is the actual or perceived impact of international trade on political sovereignty. Populist political leaders sometimes view trade treaties as restricting national sovereignty through contractual obligations with trading partners, especially in times of political and economic difficulties.

Critics of protectionism, however, point out that economic policies should not be based on ephemeral popular sentiments but, rather, on sound strategic reasoning. Neither should political and military considerations be allowed to distort business- and trade-related policies. Further, while some industries are essential for national defense and may need protection, not all industries that claim to serve security purposes actually do.

Diversified Economy While greater protection of domestic industries may at times be necessary, most economists agree that the best form of protection is diversification of the industrial base; this is particularly true in developing and transitional economies, such as those of the former Soviet bloc. Protectionist policies may be necessary to develop different industries and to offset the "one-crop" or single raw material economy. Through diversification, however, highly specialized economic sectors and even a country's basic national economy—such as Bolivia's "tin economy" or Chile's "copper economy"—becomes more immune to market fluctuations and foreign decision making.[87]

Diversification, however, has its problems as well.[88] First, for highly diversified economies, as in the case of the United States, further diversification obviously would not be a particularly useful policy, although some cities are required to diversify and adjust to changing market structures, as Detroit and nearby cities such as Flint, Michigan, attempted to become less dependent on the auto industry in the 1980s. Second, since developing countries do not possess sufficient capital, industrial base, and market capacity, diversification has meant "decentralization" of the public sector through privatization of state-owned enterprises. As discussed in Chapter 6, while privatization encourages foreign direct investments, it does not necessarily address the social and economic problems—for example, unemployment and poverty—that make diversification a pressing concern in the first place. Governments may diversify their responsibilities by shifting blame for social and economic problems to the private sector and, in doing so, may minimize the burden of public accountability.

Revenue Raising Some trade-based government policies, such as customs duties to raise revenues for the state, also pose obstacles to free trade. Historically, before the introduction of the income tax, governments relied heavily on customs duties and export taxes to finance their operations. While no longer a significant portion of government revenues in the industrialized economies, customs duties and similar trade taxes constitute a large share of government revenues in developing countries, since they can be fairly efficiently collected.[89] In some societies, such as Nigeria, where the informal economy is relatively large, such revenues are crucial to sustain the economy.

MANAGEMENT OF INTERNATIONAL TRADE: GATT AND WTO

To foster international cooperation and trade, governments increasingly engage in multilateral arrangements, such as the Group of Eight (or G-8)[90] summits and General Agreement on Tariffs and Trade (GATT)/World Trade Organization (WTO) negotiations. Multilateral institutions specifically related to international trade, such as GATT and WTO, have established formal rules and norms of economic behavior. The Group of Eight, on the other hand, has no legally distinct institutional framework. It holds annual summit meetings to discuss the main issues of international political economy. The G-8 summit conferences, often attended by other states as well, gained prominence in recent years because of the globalization of employment and industrial issues and greater interdependence among the industrialized economies. In addition, since the collapse of the Soviet Union, the G-8 countries have expanded G-8's geographical scope as well as the issues it has to address—for example, transition from planned to market economy, instability in Asia, and wars and dislocation in the Balkans.

Multilateral cooperation becomes particularly crucial in an international system that, comprised of more than 185 sovereign nation-states of varying military power, economic wealth, and political leverage, lacks central authority to enforce law and order among nations. Even violence and rebellions become economic concerns because of the potential threat to orderly markets and public welfare. As each state seeks to maximize national security and to compensate for uneven distribution of resources and capabilities, various bilateral and multilateral mechanisms are needed for mutual consultation and coordination of economic policies. One of the most important functions of multilateral institutions is the establishment of formal rules and standards to mitigate the adverse impact the anarchic nature of the international system may have on international economic relations. Ultimately, the purposes of rules and standards are to engender and institutionalize routine trade engagements and to render them more stable and predictable.

Immediately after WWII, the Allied powers, led by the United States, created GATT as a major step toward liberalization of world trade. In 1994, GATT was succeeded by the World Trade Organization, which maintained the same fundamental objective. An international agreement signed in 1947 by twenty-three countries, GATT sought to prevent economic nationalism and trade wars as experienced in the late nineteenth and early twentieth centuries. It currently consists of more than 120 member states controlling nearly 90 percent of world trade.[91] As a multilateral institution, GATT provides a forum with periodic meetings, or "rounds," to facilitate trade relations among nations in a multilaterally managed global system. Following laissez-faire principles of free trade, and reflecting the economic and geopolitical priorities of the United States as the leading economic power since the Second World War, GATT's principal objective has been to liberalize trade through the reduction or elimination of tariff and non-tariff barriers. Specific rules and norms (expectations) were devised and retained under WTO to regulate trade relations.

GATT is based on a number of key principles.[92] The first is the principle of nondiscrimination. Article I of GATT requires that any benefits granted to a contracting party be similarly granted to all other signatories. Referred to as the **most-favored-nation (MFN)** status, over the years nations have used the practice of granting the most-favored-nation status to other countries to normalize trade relations and strengthen diplomatic ties, as the Clinton administration did to strengthen U.S. trade relations with China.[93] Furthermore, GATT Article III requires parties not to discriminate against foreign products in favor of domestic goods regarding domestic taxation, transportation regulations and fees, and legal requirements in general.[94]

The second principle is *prohibition against non-tariff barriers* (NTBs) to trade. Article XI requires that "no restrictions other than duties" be imposed on imported products. For policymakers stressing sovereignty in economic matters, however, this rule appears to be too restrictive. Recently, for example, the U.S. Marine Mammal Protection Act required catching tuna without killing dolphins, and it prohibited the importation of tuna fished by means that also kill dolphins. This act also extended the ban on imports of "all fish products if, presumably, the offending country does not change its practices." This led to a trade dispute with the Mexican fisheries industry and government, which argued that saving the dolphins "served as a rationale for a ban on imports of tuna from Mexico."[95] The United States contended that GATT rules, specifically Article III, obliged nondiscriminatory policies toward foreign products. Mexico, on the other hand, maintained that Article XI prohibits all trade restrictions, with the exception of tariffs. In 1991, GATT formally decided that the restrictions under the Marine Mammal Protection Act violated the United States' legal obligations to Mexico under Article XI.[96] Both countries viewed the issue in terms of the relationship between national sovereignty and international obligations. Policymakers often bypass GATT regulations in favor of negotiating bilateral "voluntary export restraints" (VERs) with their trading partners and avoid the economic and political burdens of such obligations, especially when a country's domestic economic climate increases public pressure to limit foreign imports.

The third principle is *reciprocity* in trade practices. Article XVIII requires that states negotiate trade policies "on a reciprocal and mutually advantageous basis . . . directed to the substantial reduction of tariffs" to expand international trade as freely as possible. Immediately after GATT was created, this principle of reciprocity inspired confidence among the signatories in the newly emerging international economic system as they eliminated much of the protectionist policies in place since the early years of the century. They could reassure domestic interest groups that trade agreements would be balanced. However, over the years numerous issues have challenged this principle, especially those involving trade relations between economically unequal (for example, developing and industrialized) partners. The reciprocity principle has been enshrined in GATT and World Trade Organization rules concerning "symmetry" in trade negotiations, whereby reduction of trade barriers among parties is expected to be approximately balanced and proportionally equal, no matter what the power or relative trade advantages one side enjoys.[97]

Another principle involves *safeguards*. The founding members adopted this strategy as a pragmatic means to ensure that periodic protections for certain industries would not jeopardize the principal objective of trade liberalization and would not lead to the total dissolution of GATT itself. Article XIX permits a country to temporarily suspend its obligation to reduce tariffs when changes are needed in the market to adapt to changing circumstances in the domestic or world political economy.[98] In practice, nations have refrained from using safeguards because they must be nondiscriminatory—that is, not target a specific country—and instead have relied on mechanisms such as VERs to sidestep GATT restrictions. Some observers have argued that such bilateral agreements as VERs can have a corrosive effect on GATT's multilateralist framework. Others, however, have regarded the safeguard provision as a pragmatic approach to reconciling domestic political considerations and multilateral objectives. They, however, have pointed out that GATT's guiding philosophy of free-market liberalism is worth pursuing, despite some of its shortcomings now that the post–Cold War international system is moving toward greater globalization.

The augmented membership and complex nature of the trade agenda have led to intra-GATT coalitions independent of the traditional North-South and East-West groupings developed during the Cold War. Agricultural trade issues, for example, led to the formation of the Cairns Group (G-13) of farm exporters, frequently allying with the United States. On the other hand, the EU and Lomé South countries, many from Africa, formed coalitions on NTBs, while Japan and some developing countries formed coalitions on issues related to the service sectors and intellectual property. These changes may be viewed as signifying fundamental transformations in the nature of the traditional Cold War era global division with respect to North-South trade issues, and the post–Cold War period intensification of trade disputes may further erode intra-North relations among FIEs and intra-South alliances among AIEs and LDEs. Since the 1980s, an increasing number of AIE and LDE countries have gravitated toward open-market policies and privatization, rendering the GATT-based trade liberalization negotiations directly relevant to their economic future.

Since its creation, GATT has held eight rounds of multilateral trade negotiations (see Table 5.2), but, as Conklin has noted, "the consistent need to extend the length of sessions reflects the increased difficulty and complexity of international trade negotiations."[99] The first five rounds (1947–1962) sought to institutionalize trade liberalization and tariff reductions, and, since during this period the United States clearly was the hegemonic power, GATT's objectives reflected U.S. post-WWII economic and geopolitical goals. The United States encouraged Europe's rapid recovery from the destruction of the war to ensure international economic stability, as well as protection against the threat of communism in Europe. The United States also promoted greater integration among European nations and closer trans-Atlantic ties. In the process, U.S. hegemonic leadership was established through multilateral institutions, such as GATT and IMF, but also through the emergence of the U.S. dollar as the international currency.

European consensus generally supported the U.S. leadership in trade issues, and, during the optimistic years of the 1950s and 1960s, GATT's objectives partially began to materialize as tariff barriers on manufactured products dropped. Average U.S. tariffs, for example, fell from

TABLE 5.2
GATT Trade Negotiation Rounds

Round	Years	Participating Countries
1. Geneva, Switzerland	1947–1948	23
2. Annecy, France	1948–1949	33
3. Torquay, England	1950–1951	34
4. Geneva, Switzerland	1955–1956	22
5. Geneva, "Dillon Round"	1960–1962	45
6. Geneva, "Kennedy Round"	1964–1967	48
7. Geneva, "Tokyo Round"	1973–1979	99
8. Punta del Este, "Uruguay Round"	1986–1994	125

Sources: John H. Jackson and William J. Davey, *Legal Problems of International Economic Relations,* 2d ed. (St. Paul, MN: West, 1986), pp. 324–325; John G. Conklin, "From GATT to the World Trade Organization: Prospects for a Rule-Integrity Regime," in C. Roe Goddard, John T. Passé-Smith, and John G. Conklin, eds., *International Political Economy: State-Market Relations in the Changing Global Order* (Boulder, CO: Lynne Rienner, 1996), pp. 384–385.

36 percent in 1940 to 25 percent in 1946, 13 percent in 1950, and 10 percent in 1970.[100] These multilateral rounds, however, largely for domestic reasons excluded some economic sectors, most prominently in the agricultural and service areas. The communist states also were excluded.

The three decades after the Second World War proved to be a critical turning point in the global political economy. The European Community eventually became the largest trading unit in the world economy.[101] In the meantime, the developing countries sought to heighten the international community's awareness of their economic and political predicament and their demands to remedy structural disparities between FIEs and the developing world.[102] The latter's growing strength in the UN General Assembly, as demonstrated by the adoption of the Declaration on the Granting of Independence to Colonial Countries and Peoples, in December 1960,[103] was indicative of its collective effort, through multilateral organizations such as the United Nations, the Nonalignment Movement, the *UN Conference on Trade and Development (UNCTAD),* and the Group of 77 (G-77), to effectively influence the global political economy. In 1974 the U.N. adopted the *Charter of Economic Rights and Duties of States*[104] and the Sixth Special Session of the UN General Assembly adopted the *Declaration on the Establishment of a New International Economic Order (NIEO)*[105]—both of which focused on economic inequalities between the industrialized and the developing countries.[106] With the exception of a few provisions in its rules (for example, Article XVIII), GATT did not differentiate between developed and developing countries.[107] In contrast to GATT objectives, most developing countries relied on high-tariff protectionist policies buttressing their import-substitution industrialization strategies for rapid development.

The *Tokyo Round* (1973–1979) of multilateral trade negotiations (MTNs) began at a time of considerable economic turbulence. Unlike the earlier rounds, when most countries involved enjoyed reconstruction and expanding economies, in the 1970s they experienced oil crises, inflation, recession, rising unemployment, and protectionism. Despite these difficulties, however, the Tokyo Round extended beyond the initial phase of trade liberalization on manufactured goods to cover NTBs to trade, such as subsidies and countervailing duties, antidumping duties, procurement, customs evaluation, and previously unregulated sectors, such as agriculture and trade in civil aircraft.[108] Moreover, while prior to the Tokyo Round developing countries were largely excluded from the negotiations, by the mid–1970s their membership and influence had increased, and the Tokyo Round codes included specific provisions for them, as in the case of the Lomé Convention between the European Community and a number of African, Caribbean, and Pacific countries.[109]

The Tokyo Round negotiations were concluded in 1979 with some impressive results. Most importantly, reflecting international and domestic difficulties at the time, they institutionalized *managed trade,* as opposed to the original GATT *freer trade* approach.[110] In addition to more reciprocity, managed trade involved the introduction of a number of new NTB codes to broaden multilateral management of international trade. The Code on Subsidies and Countervailing Duties, for example, defined subsidies on manufactured goods as NTBs. The Code on Government Procurement established rules granting equal treatment to domestic and foreign companies bidding for government contracts. Similar provisions created mechanisms for surveillance and trade dispute settlement.[111] Issues related to agriculture, however, proved to be divisive, and the Tokyo Round failed to achieve major agreements in this area,[112] left to be resolved by future rounds of negotiations.

The principal failure of the Tokyo Round, however, rested in the international economic system's failure to recover quickly from the economic difficulties of the 1970s. The world economic recession, mixed with inflation, and rising unemployment levels could hardly create an environment conducive to further cooperation and liberalization. Trade tensions and protectionist policies provided little opportunity for the implementation of the agreements negotiated. For the developed FIE economies, GATT rules proved too restrictive, as governments sought specific solutions for particular industries. Accordingly, they largely ignored GATT and opted for bilateral negotiations and agreements, as in tough U.S.-Japan bargaining whereby the latter agreed to introduce voluntary export restraints on auto exports.[113] Many developing AIE and LDE countries, especially those mired in the debt crisis and already skeptical of Western-dominated schemes, found no viable mechanisms in GATT to address their economic grievances, preferring to ignore the system. Western countries, and particularly the United States, in turn argued that the flaws in GATT were amplified by the fact that the developing economies were not sufficiently prepared for membership, since they were allowed to retain high levels of trade restrictions. Moreover, some Asian countries, particularly the "newly industrializing countries" (NICs)—Hong Kong, South Korea, Taiwan, and Singapore—had become successful exporters and no longer seemed to need preferential treatment.[114] By the mid-1980s, it was amply apparent to both developed and developing countries that a new round of negotiations was needed. As a symbolic gesture for greater trade cooperation between the developed and developing countries, a new GATT Preparatory Committee decided to hold the next round in Uruguay.[115]

The *Uruguay Round* (1986–1994) focused on non-tariff barriers to trade, as well as agricultural and service issues, involving 125 participating countries.[116] The inaugural meeting was held on September 14, 1986, perhaps appropriately in the casino of a hotel in the seaside resort town of Punta del Este. Rather than approach the new negotiations with a "global vision," the delegates, now including a large number of developing countries, tended to stress *national* interests. Agreements on lower tariffs required consideration of national priorities for economic growth, unemployment, and protection of domestic industries. Even before the meeting, a number of these issues proved controversial. Some agricultural exporting countries insisted on including agriculture on the agenda. The Reagan administration insisted that the new round must consider intellectual property, such as patents, books, art, software and music, and investment. Despite their differences, after a week of negotiations, the delegates adopted the Punta del Este Declaration, promising

> to halt and reverse protectionism and to remove distortions to trade . . . to preserve the basic principles and to further the objectives of GATT . . . [and] to develop a more open, viable and durable multilateral trading system . . . convinced that such action would promote growth and development. . . .[117]

While the post-WWII GATT negotiations were concerned primarily with lowering quantitative barriers (such as quotas), the Uruguay Round, reflecting the complexities of a globalized political economy, involved a variety of closely interrelated issue-areas. Tariffs and non-tariff measures (NTMs) were grouped with issues related to natural resources and natural-based products. Delegates interested in the textile and clothing negotiations sought to terminate the Multifibre Arrangement, which had resulted in a host of bilateral trade restrictions, while others advocated a specific set of rules to penalize nations with excessive import restrictions.[118]

Thus, throughout the Uruguay Round period, key issue-areas, including tariffs, non-tariff measures, natural resource-based products, tropical products, textiles and clothing, agriculture, subsidies, intellectual property, investments, and dispute settlement, entailing both economic and political considerations, needed to be addressed. One central issue was whether to adopt a specific "formula" to eliminate tariffs—that is, to establish agreed-upon tariff cuts across the board for all countries. The Punta del Este Declaration had failed to resolve this issue, and the language adopted regarding tariffs at the time reflected its failure. It stated, "Negotiations shall aim, by appropriate methods, to reduce or, as appropriate, eliminate tariffs including the reduction or elimination of high tariffs and tariff escalation."[119] The developing countries, given their weaker position in trade negotiations, proposed a formula approach, while the larger, industrialized countries, especially the United States, with greater leverage in trade negotiations, proposed instead item by-item bargaining in individual sectors. The medium powers—for example, the Nordic countries—offered a mixed approach, in which a formula would be used in high-tariff sectors and an item-by-item bargaining approach in low-tariff sectors.[120] Realizing that no comprehensive agreement could be achieved, both developed and developing countries agreed, at least temporarily, to pursue further negotiations along the lines of the MFN principle.

The Punta del Este Conference also failed to adopt any specific policy regarding non-tariff measures (NTMs). The declaration merely stated that the "negotiations shall aim to reduce or eliminate non-tariff measures, including quantitative restrictions, without prejudice to any action to be taken in fulfillment of the rollback commitment."[121]

Thus, while there were no significant disagreements in principle regarding overall commitments to GATT objectives and non-tariff measures, the specific approach to be taken proved controversial. For example, the European Community insisted on delinking NTMs from tariff negotiations, particularly with respect to the agricultural sector, while Australia and New Zealand proposed a formula approach for NTMs. A large number of developing countries, led by India and Brazil (especially the Latin American countries in the midst of attempting to solve their foreign debt problems), argued that under the unpropitious circumstances they could do no more than commit to adhering to GATT principles and avoid reversals, leaving wider agreements for further negotiations in the future.[122]

Particularly controversial and politically sensitive were the issues surrounding natural resource-based products—that is, raw materials and semifinished goods produced from them. The Punta del Este Declaration in 1986 promised that "negotiations shall aim to achieve the fullest liberalization of trade in resource-based products, including their processed and semi-processed forms. The negotiations shall aim to reduce or eliminate tariff and non-tariff measures, including tariff escalation."[123] However, as pointed out in earlier chapters, national control over natural resources constitutes the most essential ingredient of national sovereignty, and, not surprisingly, most governments throughout the Uruguay Round showed extreme reluctance to engage in serious negotiations in this regard. Developing, especially African, countries, whose trade earnings are largely derived from raw materials exports, found negotiations for liberalization hardly beneficial to their interests and directly challenging to their national sovereignty. The developed countries, on the other hand, saw a close relationship between negotiations on liberalization and secure access to supplies. The OPEC oil crises in the 1970s had amply demonstrated the close relationship between trade and access. The Uruguay Round produced no significant agreements regarding natural resource–based products.

Closely related to natural resources were environmental issues. Environmentalist groups, also referred to as the "Greens," viewed the application of GATT principles to natural resources as inimical to global environmental well-being. Trade liberalization, they argued, would accelerate extractive activities and would further damage the land, water, and air, as when chemicals are increasingly used in agriculture and mining and production pollutes the atmosphere and spreads toxicity on land (see also Chapter 10). GATT rules (Article XX [b]) provided that certain standards and protective measures devised "to protect human, animal or plant life and health" are permissible, but this provision was limited primarily to food and health safety in exported agricultural products and did not address environmental concerns. The Punta del Este Declaration said little on environmental and conservation issues. In fact, its provisions regarding agriculture promised to "minimiz[e] the adverse effects that sanitary and phytosanitary regulation and barriers can have on trade in agriculture, taking into account the relevant international agreements."[124]

Neither the developed nor the developing countries would agree to make concessions in agricultural trade without concrete guarantees for reciprocity. Indeed, food can be seen as a security issue for many states. The European Community and developing countries, reflecting their strongly protectionist position in favor of agricultural interests, opposed wide liberalization schemes in this sector, despite their desire to improve international trade relations. The European Community insisted on defending its **common agricultural policy (CAP)** for the protection of EC farmers. Japan and South Korea refused to lower limits on food imports—especially in the case of Japan, which rejected any proposals to remove barriers on rice imports. Rice is a cruical cultural symbol in addition to being a food staple.

The United States, for its part, insisted on maintaining its preferential status sanctioned in a waiver clause in the original GATT treaty for the protection of its farmers, particularly in such products as cereal, meat, dairy products, sugar, and cotton. Since the Truman administration, Washington had argued that agricultural protection, including export subsidies, was necessary as a countervailing measure against similar policies by trade partners. Thus, when in 1987 the Reagan administration suddenly proposed to eliminate, over a ten-year period, all agricultural subsidies affecting trade, most countries were surprised, since the administration, despite its calls for liberalization, in fact "presided over a profusion of U.S. trade restrictions, including new quotas on European steel and Japanese automobiles, as well as controls on imported machine tools, lumber, and computer memory devices."[125] Some even argued that the Reagan administration's proposal was not to be taken seriously, as it was intended for domestic political purposes.[126]

Developing (LDE) countries, whose principal objective was to gain greater access to developed markets, believed that the Uruguay Round negotiations had not provided a mechanism for economic improvement; the developed countries, while insisting that developing countries assume greater GATT obligations, had failed to agree on comprehensive tariff and NTM reductions in areas most critical to LDE interests.[127] By the late 1980s, however, Third-World solidarity had weakened because of disillusionment with nationalistic import substitution strategies, the failure of the North-South dialogue, and the international debt crisis.[128] In the 1990s, the development gap between AIEs and LDE widened so as to render such cooperation at least politically impractical, and the divisions during the Uruguay Round negotiations reflected their failure to present a united front. Further, in the 1980s, in part because of the failure of the Tokyo and Uruguay Rounds, interest in regional trade arrangements (discussed in Chapter 6) increased, with greater reliance on intra-regional trade liberalization, while maintaining relatively high trade barriers vis-a-vis outsiders and extra-regional competitors.[129]

What gains, then, were derived from the GATT-Uruguay Round negotiations? In analyzing multilateral treaty negotiations, it is necessary to distinguish between, on the one hand, negotiations as a forum for symbolic consensus and public pronouncements for domestic and international public consumption and, on the other hand, negotiations for the development of international rules and instruments of applicable policies and enforceable obligations.[130] The former, though important for the exchange of ideas and positions, produce few concrete solutions or specific policies, while the latter often prove controversial because of fears about loss of political sovereignty and genuine economic considerations. The Uruguay Round negotiations certainly served symbolic purposes, rendered more conspicuous because GATT and its successor, WTO, lack explicit enforcement mechanisms, relying instead on the consensus and compliance of signatory states. However, not all signatory states are equal, and, in an international environment in which some countries possess greater leverage in negotiations, trade principles, such as reciprocity, may hinder rather than promote cooperation. As one observer has noted, nations "abide by the rules when it suits them; otherwise realpolitik takes over."[131] However, while the numerous GATT rounds have served mainly political and public relations purposes, these negotiations nevertheless have contributed to the development of international standards with respect to trade practices. This seems to have been particularly true in GATT's dispute settlement system, designed to rule on whether GATT principles had been violated in specific cases.

In the formative stages well into the 1960s, GATT's dispute settlement procedures were used only sporadically. In the 1970s, however, as its formal processes developed, especially during the Tokyo Round, the number of disputes submitted to GATT increased. It is estimated that between 1947 and 1986, 233 cases were referred,[132] and by 1995, when GATT was succeeded by WTO, that number had reached approximately 300 cases.[133] For the period 1947–1986, a large majority (229 cases, or 98.3 percent) of the cases brought before GATT involved developed countries, and thirty-five cases alone (or 15 percent of the total) were between the United States and the EC.[134] The developed countries were complainants in 179 cases (76.8 percent) and respondents in 205 cases (or 88 percent). Only twenty-four (or 13 percent) of these complaints were against developing countries. The developed countries were involved in 75 cases (or 32.2 percent of the total 233) during the 1946–1986 period, and they were complainants in fifty cases, forty-seven (or 94 percent) of which were complaints against developed countries.[135] A considerable number of the cases submitted to GATT dispute settlement between 1947 and 1986 involved agricultural products, followed by the industrial sector. Of the 100 cases in the agricultural sector, twenty-eight complaints were against the European Community, and seventeen cases were against the United States. By contrast, fifteen cases in the industrial sector were against the United States, four against the EC.[136]

Another measure of the GATT-Uruguay Round's success is the degree of economic growth experienced under its system. Several studies have evaluated the impact of the Uruguay Round on world economic growth and have concluded that, despite the shortcomings in the system, measured in dollar value, the impact has been substantial, ranging from $212 billion to $510 billion, or from 1 percent to 5 percent growth in world income. For developing countries, estimates of income growth range from $86 billion to $122 billion.[137] For some economies, the gains were marked, as in the cases of Malaysia and Thailand, where Uruguay Round trade liberalization contributed 8.8 percent and 10.7 percent (the highest in percentage terms), respectively, to their GDPs in real income gains. For the Philippines and Indonesia, the figures were 4.2 percent and 2 percent, respectively. For developed countries, the gains were considerably lower, due largely to the fact that, as previously noted, for the larger economies, trade constitutes a smaller proportion of national income. Gains from trade for the European Union was 0.7 percent of GDP; for Japan, 0.6 percent; and, for the United States, 0.4 percent. For most of Latin America, the figure was about 1.6 percent of GDP, and, for the Middle East and North Africa, 0.2 percent. In the case of sub-Saharan Africa, unfortunately, that figure was −.5 percent, indicating loss in trade-generated income.[138]

With the exception of the figures for sub-Saharan Africa, these growth rates are certainly impressive; yet they represent aggregate data and ignore a number of critical questions about the contribution of international trade to domestic social and economic well-being. One such question is "who wins, who loses" from trade?[139] The Indonesian economic and political crisis in 1998 indicated that an increase in "income gains" does not automatically translate into gains for the population as a whole. The impact of trade gains (or deficits) varies from one group to the next. Expansion of trade may benefit the urban economy, or a national leadership clique, with little contribution to the rural sectors or population masses. Likewise, an increase in the exports of a certain manufactured good may be beneficial to a corporation in terms of profit, but not necessarily for the employees in terms of income or emotional well-being.[140]

Furthermore, feminist critics have argued that the acceleration in the globalization of trade and liberalization appears to have widened the inequality gap between men and women and to have contributed to social disintegration and environmental degradation. At the WIDE: World in Development/Europe annual conference in

Jarvanpaa, Finland, participants emphasized the need to link the structure of international trade with new international structures of accountability.[141] With greater deregulation of economies, it was feared that employees—men and women, in the developed and developing countries—would increasingly find themselves in a position of either accepting deplorable working conditions with declining living standards or being unemployed altogether.

Throughout its existence, GATT, as the world's primary multilateral arrangement for the management of international trade, failed to institute measures linking social well being with trade issues. Instead, it maintained that international organizations, such as the International Labor Organization (ILO), are better equipped to address employee and social issues. While the ILO charter provides a number of essential guarantees—for example, freedom of association and the right to collective bargaining—trade liberalization at the national and local levels can undermine the legal force of such standards, as the power of states and MNCs weakens international standard-setting instruments. The International Confederation of Free Trade Unions (ICFTU) has insisted on the inclusion of a "social clause" and labor standards in the charter of the World Trade Organization, GATT's successor.[142] Failure to address such problems can have serious consequences for communities, as in the case of Guatemala, where nearly 80 percent of families live in poverty. Guatemalan *maquila* women workers in the Guatemalan-, Korean-, or U.S.-owned clothing industry—including such brand names as Esprit, Bloomingdales, Eddie Bauer, and Haggar—demanded better working conditions and an increase in their $3.00-per-day pay. In the mid-1990s, when some workers became engaged in pro-union activities at the RCA *maquila,* they were reportedly killed (or "disappeared") or subjected to egregious human rights violations—a serious problem in Central American countries since at least the 1980s.[143] Whether the World Trade Organization shows a greater inclination to attend to such problems remains to be seen, but a lack of enforcement capabilities seriously weakens its potential for reform.

In the final phase of the Uruguay Round (October 1993), the participants accepted a comprehensive liberalization agreement, the Final Act of the Uruguay Round, signed at Marrakesh, Morocco, in April 1994 and entered into effect in July 1994. The signatories hoped to expand international trade to include raw materials, textiles, services, and intellectual property rights, such as copyrights and patents. However, the most fundamental change the 1994 Final Act made was the legal termination of the original GATT (now referred to as GATT-1947) and the creation of the *World Trade Organization* (WTO) to administer GATT agreements.

The World Trade Organization is a permanent institution for continuing international trade negotiations and administering signatories' compliance, similar to the institutional framework of the IMF and the World Bank. The WTO strengthens the international trade system, and, in a sense, it is the first major response to less developed states' demands for greater participation in the world trading community. The WTO has formalized the loose GATT system of periodic negotiation rounds into an ongoing consultative body, complete with a quasi-legislative biennial Ministerial Conference (based on the principle of "one country, one vote"—Tonga's vote equals Japan's, Tuvalu's equals the United States'), a Secretariat, and a General Council (with membership of each state able to act on recommendations from other specialized councils), along with quasi-judicial panels and other mechanisms to set standards and address disputes.[144] The WTO refines and expands the occasions for nearly continuous communication among members on important trade questions, as demonstrated in bilateral U.S.-Japanese talks in preparing for WTO sessions.

Philosophically, the WTO agreement emphasizes key principles related to liberalizing trade. First is the familiar notion of "most favored nation" (MFN), meaning that concessions granted to traders of one country must match those accorded to those of other states. For countries in which trade is "politicized," for example, as Washington sometimes tries to use trade to reward or penalize favored or disfavored nations, this can be a troubling principle (in 1996, because of controversies about yearly renewal of China's MFN status, the U.S. Congress, in fact, did away with MFN as a term in its trade legislation, speaking instead of general trade preferences). The second principle is that of "transparency," meaning that trade rules, regulations, and policies—even on controversial issues such as subsidies and dumping—should be published publicly and based on objective criteria. Along the lines of transparency, there even seems to be a preference for tariffs vs. non-tariff barriers to trade, such as quotas, domestic taxes, and regulations, since tariffs at least are straightforward and measurable. Reciprocity is the third main principle, meaning that each member government aims for an overall balance between its own obligations and the benefits it derives from others under the agreement. In fact, reciprocal benefits are the reason states are expected to stay in the WTO and abide by its provisions, even if the provisions cannot be enforced directly or if the countries lose on a specific

WTO Weather Report
Source: The Economist, April 29, 1995, p. 79.

dispute, since governments will want to maintain at least a certain minimum reputation for reliability. Reliability is probably an even greater asset in commercial relations than in security agreements, since business leaders will not risk capital on untrustworthy partners, though, the larger a country's economic power, the greater its attractiveness, even if it does not display complete reliability. Finally, "national treatment" is an important GATT/WTO consideration related to the question of tariff vs. non-tariff barriers. National treatment means the type of regulations and charges imposed on imports after they arrive across the border—inside the customer state. The treaty states that national treatment of such imported products or services should be no less favorable than, but not necessarily exactly the same as, that of comparable domestic products.[145]

In contrast to GATT, the World Trade Organization somewhat restricts individual states'—including the major powers'—ability to block action, and it establishes a clearer timetable and process for resolving and adjudicating disputes and claims. While based on essentially the same free trade philosophy, the WTO also is broader in scope than its predecessor, expanding its rules beyond merchandise trade to cover one of the fastest growing segments of international commerce—that is, trade in services, such as banking, tourism, education, insurance, telecommunications, and data processing, as well as intellectual property (patents, production licenses, copyrights).[146] The Marrakesh negotiations placed these issues under the guidelines of the General Agreement on Trade in Services (GATS),[147] thereby institutionalizing "sectoral negotiations."[148] In the area of agricultural goods, for example, signatories are required to lower tariffs by 36 percent and subsidized exports by 21 percent; textile quotas are expected to be eliminated by 2004.

Further, WTO membership is more comprehensive than was that of GATT, with 128 initial members and many additional applicants. Thus, there is potential for lively and contentious debate within the WTO, as, for example, when major service industries in the North—such as health care providers—seek to compete on an even keel with local service providers in less developed states, or as southern service providers—such as low-wage data entry and computer software firms—seek a bigger share of the business of developed country industries.[149]

Many of the policy disagreements are expected to be ironed out by conflict resolution mechanisms built into the WTO treaty. They consist mainly of international panels (Dispute Settlement Panels, DSPs) set up by the Dispute Settlement Body (DSB) to review specific trade issues and complaints (see Box 5.2). The DSPs, composed of governmental and nongovernmental experts, can hold hearings and issue binding decisions under the treaty. Their decisions can be appealed to a standing Appellate Body, composed of legal and trade experts. It is still not fully clear, and precedent alone can determine, whether these bodies will strongly impinge on national governments' or regional blocs' (for example, the EU) decision-making prerogatives. Also, the DSB, panels, and Appellate Body (limited to issues of law and legal interpretation) may or may not display the type of "judicial activism," taking on new issues, that has been displayed in national supreme courts.[150]

Despite this institutional improvement over GATT, however, the WTO may be seen as lacking in sufficient enforcement capacity. The only enforcement action authorized is for the aggrieved party to obtain DSB permission to sanction the other party through withdrawal of its own trade concessions in the same market sector. No other third party is obliged to follow these sanctions; since small and weak states lack the economic clout to make such penalties hurt, the overall effect of WTO dispute resolution is diluted unless major powers agree to abide by the same sanctions.

BOX 5.2

WTO DISPUTE RESOLUTION MECHANISMS

Consultation and Dispute Settlement are key functions of the GATT. They work alike for small and large countries, providing objective and enforceable adjudication of disputes, based either on the obligations of the Agreement or on the expectations which arise out of membership of the GATT. The GATT and other Agreements comprising the WTO comprise in some respects a code of rules. A breech of the rules is sufficient to establish a *prima facie* case of *impairment or nullification* of the rights of other members of the Agreement giving rise to a right to some form of remedy such as compensation or the suspension of equivalent concessions or obligations (if approved by the Council). In such case the breech of the rules alone creates the presumption of an impairment of rights and the party alleged to have breached the rules carries the burden of rebuttal.

. . . The WTO Agreement on Dispute Settlement is explicit that a *"Mutually acceptable solution"* to a dispute, which is at least consistent with the rules, is always preferable to a dispute procedure. The new agreement codifies this emphasis by making explicit provisions for *consultations*, ***mediation*** and (voluntary) ***arbitration*** of disputes.

The key changes in the Agreement will result in more speedy and more binding dispute procedures.

Dispute Panels: parties to a dispute may no longer block the appointment of a panel or the adoption of a panel report. Under the WTO a complaining party is *entitled* to the appointment of a panel once the dispute reaches a certain stage without resolution and, to prevent delay over the terms of reference, the panels are given standard *terms of reference.*

Decisions: the *adoption* of the recommendations of the panel may not be blocked by the parties to a dispute. Reports may be rejected only by a consensus against their recommendations in the Dispute Settlement Body.

Appeals: the main check on a panel report is now an *appeal* to independent, expert review.

Timing: the process has been given a specific timetable in an attempt to ensure speedy review and conclusion. Panels have been given specific *working procedures* in accordance with this timetable.

Article IV of The Agreement Establishing the WTO provides for the General Council of the WTO to convene as a *Dispute Settlement Body* to oversee all disputes arising from the obligations and expectations created by all of the WTO Agreements. . . .

The Agreement provides for enforcement of decision to involve suspension of the rights of infringing members *across sectors* (e.g., goods for services) if necessary. . . .

The first step in the dispute process is *consultation* between the parties . . . , possibly followed by WTO *mediation.* Most disputes never go further than this stage.

If, following consultation, the dispute has not been resolved the parties may *notify the dispute* to the Dispute Settlement Body and either party may seek the appointment of a *Panel* to report on the dispute.

The WTO is said to have a number of strengths that can facilitate greater integration and harmonization of international trade policies. Members are expected to be more actively and routinely involved in multilateral negotiations, and, since the scope of trade regulations has expanded, the impact of these regulations on domestic economies will be greater and potentially controversial. WTO trade policies will influence various industries, including telecommunications, film, music, investments, and insurance, with implications for "national language, culture, and the very character of society."[151] Further, since the WTO is expected to have the same level of institutionalization as the IMF and the World Bank, it will be better integrated with them to enhance their ability to coordinate global economic policies. Finally, the WTO has made an effort to strengthen its dispute settlement function. In one of its first international dispute settlement decisions, in January 1996, the WTO determined that U.S. clean air legislation unfairly discriminated against foreign (Venezuelan and Brazilian) oil refineries wishing to market products in the United States. Its three judge panel (from Finland, Hong Kong, and New Zealand) ordered the United States to modify its rules.[152] Whether WTO can enforce such decisions, however, remains unclear. States' refusal to comply certainly would weaken the institution.

Thus, despite its developing power, the WTO contains certain weaknesses. Member compliance with the rules and regulations is still voluntary, reflecting the political reality of the international system that consists of sovereign nation-states. Economic nationalism and neo-mercantilist strategies to protect domestic economies can have serious

BOX 5.2 (concluded)

WTO DISPUTE RESOLUTION MECHANISMS

The WTO panel *procedures* are more detailed and precise than those of the GATT, including the possible review of *Panel reports* by an *appellate body.*

In some circumstances, where a party does not implement a Panel's findings against it, the Dispute Settlement Body may authorize retaliation in the form of an equivalent *suspension of the contractual rights* of the Party found at fault. The Agreement is explicit on the proportionality and temporary nature of a suspension of rights.

Through the mid-1990s, the first WTO dispute resolution decisions and reports were issued, including those appellate decisions adopted by the WTO General Council:

REPORTS OF APPELLATE BODY

1. United States—Standards for Reformulated and Conventional Gasoline, complaints by Venezuela and Brazil. This ruling went against the United States for refusing to accept the records of unregulated foreign corporations concerning the historic emission test levels of their refined gasoline products. The US is expected to modify its environmental regulations to satisfy this judgment. The US Environmental Protection Agency moved to delay implementation until after the 1996 presidential elections for reasons of potential political embarrassment.
2. Japan—Taxes on Alcoholic Beverages, complaints by the European Union, Canada, and the United States, centering on differential taxation of domestic versus imported liquor. The Appellate Body ruled such taxation a violation of GATT as a non-tariff trade barrier. No remedial action by Japan in modifying its tax code reported to date.

DISPUTE PANEL REPORTS

3. Brazil—Measures Affecting Desiccated Coconut, complaint by the Philippines. Panel rejected the claim that the countervailing duty imposed by Brazil was a violation of GATT rules.

Additional pending cases before panels included Costa Rica's claim of excessive US restrictions on imports of cotton and artificial fibers; India's similar claim about US restrictions on woven shirts and blouses; Latin and US complaints against EU restrictions on bananas; US complaints about EU restrictions against meat and meat product (hormone) imports; US complaints about Canadian restrictions on imported periodicals and reading material; and US complaints against Japanese restrictions on photographic film and paper. Three additional requests for panels and some 27 consultations on dispute settlement were also in progress in 1997.

Sources: World Trade Organization. "Settling Disputes: The WTO's 'most individual contribution'." On-line http://www.wto.org/wto/dispute/dsu.htm. January 1997. Minyard, Alan D. "The World Trade Organization: History, Structure, and Analysis." On-line. http://www2.netdoor.com/~aminyrd/.

consequences for the future of the organization. Particularly crucial is the compliance of the leading countries, such as the United States, the EU, and Japan. The 1980s witnessed substantial increases in noncompliance with GATT rules, especially by the United States, the EU, and Canada.[153] In fact, the United States has threatened to withdraw from the WTO if the latter passes "three adverse, unfair rulings" against the United States within five years. Others, in turn, more emphatically the developing countries, have insisted on placing their own issues on the WTO agenda, including immigration, financing, corporate law, political stability, foreign debt, and poverty. While the WTO's expanded agenda and stronger institutional framework are improvements over its predecessor, it is threatened by divergent interests and objectives—especially if protectionism becomes a more serious problem than it has been thus far. The WTO cannot withstand heavy nationalist pressures, but countries also lose face by refusing to comply with international rulings.

Clearly, the potential is there for WTO treatment of issues ranging from harmonizing antitrust legislation to evaluating environmental pollution standards, but there is no assurance of effective action.[154] From the initial set of cases brought to the conflict resolution mechanisms, it appears that the WTO will be a vehicle both for LDEs to bring complaints against major powers for shutting them out of the import market and for major powers and trade blocs to struggle with each other over many of the same concerns. It is also clear that states, particularly major powers, found to have violated treaty provisions may or may not comply with the rulings. The leading hegemonic powers, however, have a vested interest in the survival of the WTO and GATT principles and, hence, are likely to comply at least often enough to keep the system credible.

CONCLUSION

A country's ability to compete successfully in trade relations requires a dynamic domestic economy, yet scholars and governments disagree on how to achieve economic growth. Issues of balance of trade and balance of payments involve economic but also political considerations, and they are of central importance for effective economic management. Governments possess a number of policy instruments for the management of trade relations. These include tariff and non-tariff barriers, such as quotas, subsidies, and regulations. One of the prerequisites for a dynamic economy, laissez-faire liberals argue, is a political system that does not interfere in the economic activities of the business community. The government creates a legal and regulatory environment conducive to free market competition and free trade. Based on comparative advantages, competition in a free market itself encourages trade expansion, which in turn stimulates economic growth. At the most, international organizations such as GATT and the WTO are needed to regulate trade behavior while lowering trade barriers across borders. Given the rapid changes in telecommunications technology and the virtual globalization of economic relations, liberals believe, the greater is the freedom to trade and the greater the opportunities to develop international cooperation and to eliminate conflict.

Dependencia theorists, however, maintain that, in sharp contrast to liberals' assumption of perfect free market competition, one of the key characteristics of the world economy is unequal distribution of wealth. Economic inequalities, historical experiences (such as colonialism), and an unstable domestic political climate leave poorer countries in a much weaker position vis-a-vis their wealthier counterparts and necessitate government intervention in domestic economic and foreign trade activities. A disproportionate share of world trade takes place among the industrialized countries. Trade between the advanced industrializing economies and the less developed economies, while growing slowly, lags behind. The principle of comparative advantage leads to commodity specialization and dependence on foreign markets. Accordingly, disadvantaged governments cannot rely on "market competition" but have to use the available means, including various tariff and non-tariff policies, to protect their economies. Somewhat along similar lines, scholars advocating *strategic alliances* argue that for various reasons not all countries can be equally competitive in world markets. Contrary to the theory of comparative advantage, international trade relations are not based on exchanges based on specific advantages but, rather, on technology gaps, economies of scale, and intra-industry trade networks.

Patterns of changing international trade relations have included the geographic distribution of trade, the composition of commodities traded, the established rules or terms of trade, and the role of technological development. These changes also have involved increased trade in services as well as within industries. Such competition has not been "free," since some countries started well ahead of others and possessed powerful governments able to step in during rule-making negotiations. Governments opt for free trade or protectionism because they stand to gain politically, and in so doing they play a central role in protecting and promoting specific competitive industries. They subsidize corporate R&D, provide tax and other incentives to encourage development, and facilitate corporate transnational activities by supporting various service sectors—for example, transportation.

The question remains as to who wins or loses from international trade, and trade under various conditions. Aggregate data suggest that the world economy as a whole and many individual economies and citizens gain from trade; yet the persisting disparities in income levels between the developed and developing countries indicate that trade alone cannot provide the means for a more equitable distribution of income and resources. This is true not only across international borders, but also within countries. Whether the WTO can transform itself from passive management to more active management of trade among nations with links to social well-being within nations remains to be seen.

Chapter Summary

Trade among nations has been an important part of world history, and the modern globalization of international economic activities has reemphasized the importance of interdependent trade relations.

Trade has been a cause of international cooperation and conflict. According to the classical liberal view, free trade is essential for the promotion of economic development and growth, but also for greater international cooperation.

Protectionists argue that the unequal distribution of wealth and natural resources renders poorer countries more vulnerable to world market pressures. Inequalities and market imperfections compel governments to interfere in trade relations to protect their respective domestic economies and to address problems of unemployment and imbalances in trade and balance of payments.

Each government strives to maintain a healthy balance between the nation's *credits* (exports, or money coming in) and *debits* (imports, or money going out). The nation's balance-of-payments equilibrium is generally viewed as indicative of a healthy economy.

Governments use a number of policy instruments to address trade imbalances. The two most commonly used are tariffs and quotas, although some countries are also accused of "dumping" practices and "non-tariff barriers" such as regulations.

Trade can be based on the principle of either absolute advantage or comparative advantage. In the case of the former, a country possesses certain natural resources and trades them with another country for resources at prices lower than if produced domestically. On the other hand, comparative advantage is when a country produces certain goods more efficiently than another country and, therefore, focuses its energies and resources on its most efficient production and trades excess production for higher value abroad.

Some scholars have rejected these views as too simplistic. The global relocation of production in search of cheaper labor, various trade and financial strategic alliances, transnational intra-industry trade—all facilitated by the advent of information telecommunications technologies—have led to *strategic trade theories*. Governments play an active role in trade relations by encouraging competitive industries, such as subsidizing research and development in the rapidly changing computer industry.

Government interference in trade for domestic purposes usually involves issues of reciprocity, employment protection, wage protection, diversification of economy, national security considerations, protection for infant industries, and revenue raising.

To check the negative consequences of protectionist policies, multilateral institutions, such as the General Agreement on Tariffs and Trade (GATT), have established formal rules and standards. They are premised on the belief that international cooperation reduces trade barriers and promotes structural stability. The Group of Eight (or G-8), comprised of eight advanced industrial states, is a forum for multilateral economic negotiations.

In 1994, the Final Act of the Uruguay Round terminated the original GATT and established the World Trade Organization (WTO), a permanent institution for continuing international trade negotiations and administration of compliance. There is little doubt that the WTO, though a vehicle for LDE views, will be dominated by three major economic powers in the world economy: the United States, the EU, and Japan.

Trade activities may contribute to economic gains in the developing countries, but it may also be necessary to establish closer policy linkages between the promotion of trade and the promotion of social well-being.

Points of Contention

What problems do international trade relations create for governments in the industrialized and developing countries?

To what extent have government efforts to address problems of unequal market competition among the industrialized economies been successful? among the developing countries? in relations between industrialized and developing countries?

Why do governments opt for free trade?

What are some of the problems in protectionism? in the *dependencia* theory? in the strategic trade theory?

To what extent do the patterns in international trade reflect conditions in your community?

Do you think less developed states are justified in blocking foregin imports? In insisting on lower barriers to their exports? In asking for development aid?

How successful was GATT in the multilateral management of trade? What are some of the advantages of, and deficiencies in, the WTO?

To what extent should the WTO develop linkages between international trade and national social well-being? Do you expect WTO to be able to settle trade disputes?

What are some of the advantages and disadvantages of trade relations based on technologically advanced communications systems?

Can you identify ten electronic consumer goods in your house or on campus that have no imported parts?

Notes

1. See, for example, David B. Yoffie and Benjamin Gomes-Casseres, *International Trade and Competition*, 2d ed. (New York: McGraw-Hill, 1994), 361–65; Donald Barry, with Mark O. Dickerson and James Gaisford, eds., *Toward a*

North American Community? (Boulder, CO: Westview Press, 1995); Hans J. Michelmann and Panayotis Soldatos, eds., *European Integration: Theories and Approaches* (Lanham, MD: University Press of America, 1994); Loukas Tsoukalis, *The New European Economy: The Politics and Economics of Integration,* rev. 2d ed. (Oxford: Oxford University Press, 1993).

2. UNCTAD, *Handbook of International Trade and Development Statistics,* 1994, pp. 2–3; World Trade Organization, *WTO Focus,* no. 28, March 1998, p. 1.
3. Robert Gilpin, *The Political Economy of International Relations* (Princeton: Princeton University Press, 1987), p. 31. See also Robert O. Keohane and Joseph S. Nye, *Power and Interdependence* (Boston: Little, Brown, 1977); Robert D. Putman and Nicholas Bayne, Hanging Together: *Cooperation and Conflict in the Seven-Power Summits* (Cambridge: Harvard University Press, 1987).
4. L. Rangarajan, "The Politics of International Trade," in Susan Strange, ed., *Paths to International Political Economy* (London: Allen and Unwin, 1984), pp. 127–128.
5. Robert A. Isaak, *International Political Economy: Managing World Economic Change* (Englewood Cliffs, NJ: Prentice Hall, 1991); Stephen Gill and David Law, *The Global Political Economy* (Baltimore: Johns Hopkins University Press, 1988); Paul Knox and John Agnew, *The Geography of the World Economy* (London: Hodder and Stoughton, 1989); Klaus Knorr, *The Power of Nations: The Political Economy of International Relations* (New York: Basic Books, 1975); John H. Jackson, *The World Trading System: Law and Policy of International Economic Relations* (Cambridge: MIT Press, 1989); Eric Roll, *A History of Economic Thought,* 5th ed. (London: Faber and Faber, 1992).
6. For a classic argument on center-periphery relations, see Johan Galtung, "A Structural Theory of Imperialism," *Journal of Peace Research* 2 (1971), pp. 81–98.
7. Michael Hart, "Searching for New Paradigms: Trade Policy Lessons from Recent and More Ancient History," in Barry, ed., *Toward a North American Community?* p. 37.
8. *The Economist,* "The State of the Nation-State," December 22, 1990, as quoted in *Ibid.,* pp. 43–44.
9. Roll, *A History of Economic Thought,* pp. 146–147; see also Mark Blaug, *Economic Theory in Retrospect,* 4th ed. (Cambridge: Cambridge University Press, 1992).
10. Milton H. Spencer, *Contemporary Economics,* 2d ed. (New York: Worth 1974), p. 562.
11. Steven Husted and Michael Melvin, *International Economics,* 2d ed. (New York: HarperCollins, 1993), pp. 288–289.
12. Robert S. Walters and David H. Blake, *The Politics of Global Economic Relations,* 4th ed. (Englewood Cliffs, NJ: Prentice Hall, 1992), pp. 29–30.
13. *The Economist,* August 12, 1995, pp. 88–89.
14. Patrick A. Messerlin, "Trade Policies in France," in Dominick Salvatore, ed., *National Trade Policies* (New York: Greenwood Press, 1992), p. 159.
15. Regarding interest group politics in the United States, see K. L. Schlozman and John T. Tierney, *Organized Interests and American Democracy* (New York: Harper and Row, 1986). See also Raymond A. Bauer, Ithiel de Sola Pool, and Lewis A. Dexter, *American Business and Public Policy: The Politics* (New York: Atherton Press, 1963); and Ronald Rogowski, *Commerce and Coalitions: How Trade Affects Domestic Political Alignments* (Princeton: Princeton University Press, 1989).
16. Rambod Behboodi, *Industrial Subsidies and Friction in World Trade: Trade Policy or Trade Politics?* (London: Routledge, 1994), p. 37.
17. The authors would like to thank the anonymous reviewers for stressing this point.
18. See Jagdish N. Bhagwati, ed., *International Trade,* 2d ed. (Cambridge: MIT Press, 1987); Michael Porter, *The Competitive Advantage of Nations* (New York: Free Press, 1990); Herman M. Schwartz, *States Versus Markets: History, Geography, and the Development of International Political Economy* (New York: St. Martin's Press, 1994).
19. See, for example, Paul R. Krugman, ed., *Strategic Trade Policy and the New International Economics* (Cambridge: MIT Press, 1986).
20. Fernando Henrique Cardoso and Enzo Faletto, *Dependency and Development in Latin America* (Berkeley: University of California Press, 1979); *Challenge to the South: The Report of the South Commission* [Nyerere Commission Report] (Oxford: Oxford University Press, 1990). See also Stephan Haggard, *Pathways from the Periphery* (Ithaca: Cornell University Press, 1990).
21. Paul Krugman, "Introduction: New Thinking About Trade Policy," in Krugman, ed., *Strategic Trade Policy,* p. 12.
22. *Ibid.*
23. *Ibid.* See also Paul R. Krugman, "Increasing Returns, Monopolistic Competition, and International Trade," in Bhagwati, ed., *International Trade,* pp. 129–140.
24. Krugman, "Introduction," p. 9.
25. The theory of strategic trade emphasizes the view that, as trade became more important in international political/economic relations, it virtually transformed the very nature of trade itself. Since the Second World War, a large share of the world trade has involved transnational exchanges, not based on specific advantages for countries exporting certain goods *per se* but, rather, primarily based on "arbitrary or temporary advantages resulting from economies of scale or shifting leads in close technological races." *Ibid.,* p. 7.
26. See James A. Brander, "Rationales for Strategic Trade and Industrial Policy," in Krugman, ed., *Strategic Trade Policy,* pp. 31–32; David P. Rapkin and Jonathan R. Strand, "Is

International Competitiveness a Meaningful Concept?" in C. Roe Goddard, John T. Passé-Smith, and John G. Conklin, eds., *International Political Economy: State-Market Relations in the Changing Global Order* (Boulder, CO: Lynne Rienner, 1996), pp. 109–129; Robert Z. Lawrence and Charles L. Schultze, eds., *An American Trade Strategy—Options for the 1990s* (Washington, DC: The Brookings Institution, 1990).

27 Randall M. Fort, *Economic Espionage: Problems and Prospects* (Washington, DC: Consortium for the Study of Intelligence, 1993); John V. Granger, *Technology and International Relations* (San Francisco: E. H. Freeman and Company, 1979).

28. Bradner, "Rationales for Strategic Trade and Industrial Policy," p. 33.

29. *Ibid.,* p. 43.

30. On subsidies and trade tensions, see Behboodi, *Industrial Subsidies and Friction in World Trade: passim* (London: Routledge, 1994).

31. Gene M. Grossman, "Strategic Export Promotion: A Critique," in Krugman, ed., *Strategic Trade Policy,* p. 63.

32. See Rangarajan, "The Politics of International Trade," in Strange, ed., *Paths to International Political Economy,* pp. 128–136.

33. *Ibid.,* p. 130.

34. *Ibid.*

35. *WTO Focus,* no. 28, March 1998, p. 2.

36. *Ibid.,* p. 6.

37. *Economic Report of the President, 1998* (Washington, DC: Government Printing Office, 1998), p. 217.

38. Thomas E. Skidmore and Peter H. Smith, *Modern Latin America,* 3d ed. (New York: Oxford University Press, 1992), p. 114.

39. Paul R. Krugman and Maurice Obstfeld, *International Economics: Theory and Policy,* 2d ed. (New York: HarperCollins, 1991), pp. 138–139; *Economic Report of the President,* 1998, p. 218.

40. Krugman and Obstfeld, *International Economics,* pp. 138–41.

41. At the same time, the United States had to contend with difficult economic issues at home, including substantial increases in the government's budget deficit—$290.4 billion in FY1992 and $254.7 billion in FY1993, accounting for about 21 percent of $1.38 trillion and $1.41 trillion budget, respectively—and a federal debt of $3.97 trillion in 1992, $4.35 trillion in 1993, and $4.64 trillion in 1994, requiring $292.3 billion, $292.5 billion, and $296.3 billion in interest payments, respectively. In comparison, Germany's budget deficit was 73.1 billion DMarks in 1992; France's 263.5 billion francs in 1992, and Japan's 89 billion yen in 1993. Meanwhile, in Europe high unemployment levels (over 10 percent in France, England, and Italy), slow economic growth, and Germany's reunification caused serious economic difficulties. These figures suggest that the economies of the industrialized world are experiencing domestic economic pressures to find ways to improve their economic well-being and to address national budget and trade imbalances. OECD, *Economic Outlook* [various years].

42. IMF, *Direction of Trade Statistics Yearbook 1995,* pp. 2–3; *The Economist,* May 17, 1997, p. 115; *Economic Report of the President, 1998,* p. 401.

43. UNCTAD, *Handbook of International Trade Statistics, 1994,* p. 26.

44. IMF, *Direction of Trade Statistics 1996,* p. 3.

45. *Ibid.,* p. 73.

46. *Economic Report of the President, 1998,* p. 401.

47. Stephen D. Cohen, "United States–Japan Trade Relations," *Political Science Quarterly 37,* 4 (1990), p. 124.

48. In the first three quarters of 1997, the U.S. trade deficit with Japan stood at $56 billion. *Economic Report of the President, 1998,* p. 401.

49. *The Economist,* May 17, 1997, p. 115.

50. *The Economist,* March 12, 1994, pp. 72–73.

51. *The Economist,* March 2, 1996, p. 33.

52. Because of the balanced trade relations, observers expect Europe's trade ties with "emerging Asia" to be free of similar strains in U.S.-Japan relations. Contrary to expectations after the collapse of communism in Eastern Europe, EU companies continued to look toward Asia for trade, which, in the mid 1990s, expanded faster than their trade with Eastern Europe. *Ibid.,* pp. 33–34.

53. UNCTAD, *Handbook of International Trade and Development Statistics, 1994,* p. 88.

54. See David Colman and Deborah Roberts, "The Common Agricultural Policy," in Mike J. Artis and Norman Lee, eds., *The Economics of the European Union: Policy and Analysis* (Oxford: Oxford University Press, 1994), pp. 92–118.

55. UNDP, *Human Development Report 1997* (New York: Oxford University Press, 1997), p. 148.

56. World Bank, *World Tables 1995* (Baltimore: Johns Hopkins University Press, 1995).

57. Stephen D. Krasner, *Structural Conflict: The Third World against Global Liberalism* (Berkeley: University of California Press, 1985); Stephen Gill and David Law, *The Global Political Economy* (Baltimore: Johns Hopkins University Press, 1988).

58. Arl P. Sauvant, *The Group of 77: Evolution, Structure, Organization* (New York: Oceana Publications, 1981).

59. *Nyerere Commission Report,* pp. 62–63.

60. UNCTAD, *Handbook of International Trade and Development Statistics 1994,* p. 24.

61. *Ibid.*

62. *Ibid.*

63. *Nyerere Commission Report,* pp. 97–99.
64. IMF, *Direction of Trade Statistics Yearbook 1996,* pp. 32–35.
65. *Ibid.,* pp. 55, 60.
66. *Ibid.,* p. 27.
67. *Ibid.,* p. 52.
68. Moshtak Parker, "No Longer Taboo," *Middle East* no. 221 (March 1993), pp. 35–38.
69. Stephen D. Krasner, "State Power and the Structure of International Trade," *World Politics* 28, 3 (April 1976): pp. 317–347.
70. Susan Strange, *States and Markets,* 2d ed. (London: Pinter, 1994).
71. Behboodi, *Industrial Subsidies and Friction in World Trade, passim.*
72. Susan Strange, *The Retreat of the State: The Diffusion of Power in the World Economy* (Cambridge: Cambridge University Press, 1996).
73. Krasner, "State Power," pp. 317–347, *passim.*
74. *Ibid.,* p. 319.
75. *Ibid.,* pp. 321–322.
76. *Ibid.,* pp. 322–323.
77. *Ibid.,* pp. 325–330.
78. *Ibid.,* p. 319.
79. Spencer, *Contemporary Economics,* p. 568; Michael J. Trebilcock and Robert Howse, *The Regulation of International Trade* (London: Routledge, 1995), pp. 6–11. See also Jagdish N. Bhagwati, *Protectionism* (Cambridge: MIT Press, 1988); Forrest H. Capie, ed., *Protectionism in the World Economy* (Aldershot, England: Edward Elgar, 1992); Tim Lang and Colin Hines, *The New Protectionism: Protecting the Future against Free Trade* (New York: The New Press, 1993).
80. Trebilcock and Howse, *Regulation of International Trade,* p. 7.
81. *Ibid.,* pp. 7–8.
82. Spencer, *Contemporary Economics,* p. 570.
83. Further, critics of wage protectionism contend that labor alone does not produce marketed products but that labor is one of several resources found in a country. Rather, successful production and marketing involve effective management, technical know-how, access to various forms of advanced technology, and capital. See *Ibid.*
84. *Ibid.,* p. 569.
85. *Ibid.*
86. *Ibid.*
87. See, for example, T. H. Moran, *Multinational Corporations and the Politics of Dependence: Copper in Chile* (Princeton: Princeton University Press, 1974).
88. Spencer, *Contemporary Economics,* pp. 569–570.
89. Trebilcock and Howse, *Regulation of International Trade,* p. 10.
90. The G-8 members are Britain, Canada, France, Germany, Italy, Japan, Russia, and the United States.
91. World Trade Organization, *GATT Activities: 1994–1995* (Geneva, Switzerland: GATT/WTO), p. 201.
92. Gilbert R. Winham, *The Evolution of International Trade Agreements* (Toronto: University of Toronto Press, 1992), pp. 46–52.
93. MFN has been relatively routinely awarded, but in U.S.-China relations it has continued to be a political issue, with threats by Washington to reconsider or withdraw, as some in Congress push for greater pressure on human rights concerns or for greater preferences to China's rival, Taiwan. Patrick E. Tyler, "China Welcomes U.S. Trade Policy," *The New York Times,* May 28, 1994, p. A1; Charles J. Brown and Charles Graybow, "Trade and Human Rights: Cutting the Gordian Knot," *The Christian Science Monitor,* June 16, 1994, p. 19.
94. Winham, *Evolution of International Trade Agreements,* pp. 46–47.
95. *Ibid.,* p. 125.
96. *Ibid.*
97. See Richard Sherman, "Symmetry Rules in International Trade Policy Negotiations," paper presented to the Annual Meeting of the American Political Science Association, 1995.
98. Winham, *The Evolution of International Trade Agreements,* p. 51.
99. Conklin, "From GATT to the World Trade Organization," p. 384.
100. Thomas D. Lairson and David Skidmore, *International Political Economy: The Struggle for Power and Wealth* (Orlando: Harcourt Brace Jovanovich, 1993), p. 64.
101. Winham, *The Evolution of International Trade Agreements,* pp. 54–55.
102. Geographical distribution of UN membership: 1945—Western Europe 8 (16%), Eastern Europe 6 (12%), Americas 22 (43%), Africa 4 (8%), Asia 9 (17%), Australia and Pacific 2 (4%); 1991—Western Europe 20 (12%), Eastern Europe 13 (8%), Americas 35 (21%), Africa 51 (31%), Asia 38 (23%), Australia and Pacific 9 (5%). Peter R. Baehr and Leon Gordenker, *The United Nations in the 1990s* (New York: St. Martin's Press, 1991), p. 44.
103. GA Res. 1514 (XV) (Dec. 14, 1960). For a discussion of the growing strength of the developing countries within the UN framework, see Simon Payaslian, "The United Nations and the Developing Countries in the 1990s," *University of Detroit Mercy Law Review* 73, 3 (Spring 1996): 525–549; Richard A. Falk, Samuel S. Kim, and Saul H. Mendlovitz, eds., *The United Nations and a Just World Order* (Boulder, CO: Westview Press, 1991); David A. Kay, *The New Nations in the United Nations 1960–1967* (New York: Columbia University Press, 1970).
104. GA Res. 1995, 19 UC GAOR Supp. 15, UN Doc. 1/5815 (1965). See also Report of the Second Committee, UN Doc. A/9946, 28 (Dec. 9, 1974); GA Res. 3281 (XXIX)

(Dec. 12, 1974); UNCTAD Res. 45 (III), UN Doc. TD/180 (May 18, 1972).

105. The Sixth Special Session of the UN General Assembly on Raw Materials and Development adopted the Declaration on the Establishment of a New International Economic Order, GA Res. 3201 (S-VI) (May 1, 1974); GA Res. 3203 (S-VI) (May 1, 1974); GA Res. 3362 (S-VI) (Sep. 16, 1975).
106. Kay, *New Nations in the United Nations;* Luard, *A History of the United Nations;* Arl P. Sauvant, *The Group of 77: Evolution, Structure, Organization* (New York: Oceana Publications, 1981); A. W. Singham and Shirley Hune, *Non-Alignment in an Age of Alignments* (London: Zed Books, 1986).
107. John H. Jackson, *The World Trading System: Law and Policy of International Economic Relations* (Cambridge: MIT Press, 1989), 275–276.
108. Winham, *The Evolution of International Trade Agreements,* pp. 54–55; John H. Jackson and William J. Davey, *Legal Problems of International Economic Relations,* 2d ed. (St. Paul: West, 1986), p. 326.
109. Jackson, *The World Trading System,* p. 276.
110. See, for example, Gunnar Sjöstedt and Bengt Sundelius, eds., *Free Trade—Managed Trade? Perspectives on a Realistic International Trade Order* (Boulder, CO: Westview Press, 1986).
111. Joan Edelman Spero, *The Politics of International Economic Relations* (New York: St. Martin's Press, 1990), p. 370.
112. The United States proposed greater liberalization, including relaxation of the EC's CAP restrictions, but neither the EC nor the Japanese were willing to modify their agriculture trade policies. *Ibid.*
113. John Croome, *Reshaping the World Trading System: A History of the Uruguay Round* (Geneva, Switzerland: World Trade Organization, 1995), pp. 6–8.
114. *Ibid.,* p. 10.
115. *Ibid.,* p. 28.
116. Conklin, "From GATT to the World Trade Organization," p. 385.
117. See the text in Croome, *Reshaping the World Trading System,* pp. 382–392.
118. *Ibid.,* p. 41.
119. Text in *Ibid.,* pp. 382–92.
120. *Ibid.,* pp. 43–48.
121. Text in *Ibid.,* pp. 382–92.
122. *Ibid.,* pp. 51–52.
123. Text in *Ibid.,* pp. 382–92.
124. *Ibid.*
125. Pietro S. Nivola, "Commercializing Foreign Policy? American Trade Policy, Then and Now," *Brookings Review* (Spring 1997), p. 38.
126. Croome, *Reshaping the World Trading System,* p. 114.
127. See J. M. Finger and A. Olechowski, *The Uruguay Round: A Handbook for the Multilateral Trade Negotiations* (Washington, DC: The World Bank, 1987); I. Goldin and O. Knudsen, eds., *Agricultural Trade Liberalization: Implications for Developing Countries* (Paris: OECD and the World Bank, 1990); W. Martin and L. A. Winters, eds., *The Uruguay Round and the Developing Countries* (Washington, DC: The World Bank, 1995).
128. T. N. Srinivasan, *Developing Countries and the Multilateral Trading System: From the GATT to the Uruguay Round and the Future* (Boulder, CO: Westview Press, 1998), p. 26.
129. *Ibid.,* pp. 4, 59–64.
130. John H. Jackson, *Restructuring the GATT System* (New York: Council on Foreign Relations, 1990), p. 48.
131. Srinivasan, *Developing Countries,* p. 13.
132. John H. Jackson, *The World Trading System: Law and Policy of International Economic Relations* (Cambridge: MIT Press, 1989), pp. 98–99.
133. World Trade Organization, *GATT Activities* [various years].
134. The United States was involved in 125 cases, as complainant in seventy-seven cases (33 percent of the total 233) and as respondent in forty-eight cases (20.6 percent of the total). The European Community was the complainant in twenty-six cases (11.2 percent of the total) and respondent in forty-two cases (18.0 percent of the total). Jackson, *World Trading System,* p. 99.
135. Among them, advanced industrializing economies (AIEs) were complainants in fifteen cases (6.4 percent of the total) and respondents in fourteen cases (6.0 percent). The figures for less developed economies were thirty-five (15.0 percent) and thirteen (5.6 percent), respectively. *Ibid.,* p. 99.
136. *Ibid.,* p. 100.
137. See Raed Safadi and Sam Laird, "The Uruguay Round Agreements: Impact on Developing Countries," *World Development* 24, 7 (July 1996), pp. 1223–1224; Srinivasan, *Developing Countries and the Multilateral Trading System,* pp. 46–47.
138. See Table 5.5 in Srinivasan, *Developing Countries and the Multilateral Trading System,* p. 47.
139. Mehrene Larudee, "Trade Policy: Who Wins, Who Loses?" in Gerald Epstein, Julie Graham, and Jessica Nembhard, eds., *Creating a New World Economy: Forces of Change and Plans for Action* (Philadelphia: Temple University Press, 1993), pp. 47–63.
140. Pressures of international competitiveness may require speeding up the assembly line, or laying off workers, with serious negative consequences for individuals and families. Such problems range from loss of self-esteem to depression to alcoholism to domestic violence. See, for example, Norman T. Feather, *The Psychological Impact of Unemployment* (New York: Springer-Verlag, 1990).
141. Women's International Network, "Trade Traps and Gender Gaps: Women Unveiling the Market," *WIN News* 24, 1

(Winter 1998): 83. "Dawn" (Development Alternatives with Women) is WIDE's counterpart in the South.

142. Angela Hale, "Trade Liberalization and Women Workers," *Ecologist* 27, 3 (May–June 1997), pp. 87–89.
143. Arnie Alpert and Judy Elliott, "Maquila Menace: Guatemalan Women Defy Their Brutal Bosses," *Dollars & Sense,* no. 202 (Nov.–Dec. 1995), pp. 28–32.
144. Alan D. Minyard, "The World Trade Organization: History, Structure, and Analysis," unpublished paper, Mississippi State University, Internet, January 1997, p. 6.
145. "WTO Key Principles," *Guide to WTO,* Internet, January 1997.
146. World Bank Group, "Trade Issues," *Questions About the World Bank Group,* Internet, January 1997.
147. WTO, *GATT Activities, 1994–1995,* pp. 27–32.
148. Conklin, "From GATT to the World Trade Organization," p. 387.
149. Among the service trade provisions in WTO are calls for "most favored nation treatment," meaning that countries must afford a service trade partner provisions no less favorable than those extended to any other service supplying countries; "transparency," meaning that governments must publicly reveal regulations affecting foreign service providers in their country; "economic integration," which allows for the formation of service trading blocs on similar terms to other regional trade blocs; and "recognition," i.e., governments cannot discriminate in recognizing the licenses of potential service providers from abroad. See "Trade in Services," *Guide to WTO,* Internet, January 1997.
150. Appellate decisions are reported back to the DSB, with 30 days allotted for rejection; otherwise, the decision stands.
151. Conklin, "From GATT to the World Trade Organization," p. 394.
152. David E. Sanger, "World Trade Group Orders U.S. to Alter Clean Air Act," *The New York Times,* January 18, 1996, pp. D1, D6.
153. Conklin, "From GATT to the World Trade Organization," p. 396; Jackson, *Restructuring the GATT System, passim.*
154. "The Emerging WTO System and Perspectives from East Asia," Symposium, Ann Arbor: The University of Michigan, August 1996, *Joint U.S.-Korea Academic Studies,* 7 (1997), pp. 1–5; Minyard, "The World Trade Organization," pp. 6–7.

CHAPTER SIX

THE POLITICS OF REGIONAL INTEGRATION

Bilateral and multilateral arrangements for cooperation are essential to the successful workings of international economic relations. With the expansion of international electronic transactions and transportation in general, nations can now develop wider and faster communication networks and achieve greater international **integration** and cooperation in the global political economy. One example of a more comprehensive approach to regional **integration** has been the European Community, established after WWII. Since then, it has evolved into a more integrated regional system, the European Union, with transboundary financial and institutional arrangements, as anticipated by the theories of functionalism and neo-functionalism.

In recent years, collective tendencies toward integration have been more pronounced through the formation of loosely organized "communities" and **free trade areas (FTAs)** at the regional level. Regional integrative trade areas with various levels of activity include, the **North American Free Trade Agreement (NAFTA)** among Canada, the United States, and Mexico; the *Asia-Pacific Economic Co-operation (APEC),* which consists of the United States, Canada, Japan, China, Taiwan, Mexico, Malaysia, and a number of other Asia-Pacific countries; *Mercosur,* a customs union including Argentina, Brazil, Paraguay, and Uruguay; the *Andean Group* of six countries (Ecuador, Chile, Colombia, Peru, Bolivia, and Venezuela; the *Arab Cooperation Council (ACC),* comprised of Egypt, Jordan, Iraq, and Yemen; the *Arab Maghrib Union (AMU),* made up of Algeria, Libya, Mauritania, Morocco, and Tunisia; the *Economic and Social Commission for Western Asia (ESCWA),* consisting of thirteen Middle Eastern countries; the *East African Common Community (EACC),* comprised of Kenya, Tanzania, and Uganda; and the *Southern African Development Community (SADC),* comprised of twelve countries "stretching from the Cape to Kilimanjaro" (see Map 6.1).[1] The results of such efforts have been mixed. In the Latin American experience, for example, the Latin American Free Trade Area (LAFTA), the Latin American Integration Association (ALADI), and the Central American Common Market (CACM) of the 1960s (a prior era of integrative activity) failed to establish effective institutions, while others, such as the G-3 (the Cantadora Group, including Mexico, Colombia, and Venezuela, to address the Central American conflicts throughout the 1980s), were formed to deal with regional tensions but may in the future evolve into free trade areas.[2]

These regional groupings to a large extent are based on cultural similarities,[3] but domestic political, economic, and regional market considerations have prominence in determining their success or failure.[4] One of the problems with regional trade groups is the failure to develop intra-regional structures for "mutual complementarity." Where members have similarly weak economies, they have too little to offer in trade and insufficient cash and market capacity to afford many imports. Regional groups centered on a single large economy, such as South Africa in SADC and the United States in NAFTA, may prove to be more successful, since one strong economy or large market offers opportunities for expansion and production growth for the smaller and poorer partners.

Currently, there are additional proposals for free trade areas and trade integration in other regions as well. The Association of South-East Asian Nations (ASEAN) has accepted a proposal to establish an FTA by 2003; NAFTA plans to include Chile and perhaps other South American states in a hemispheric FTA; the South Asian Preferential Trade Area may be emerging; the Czech Republic,

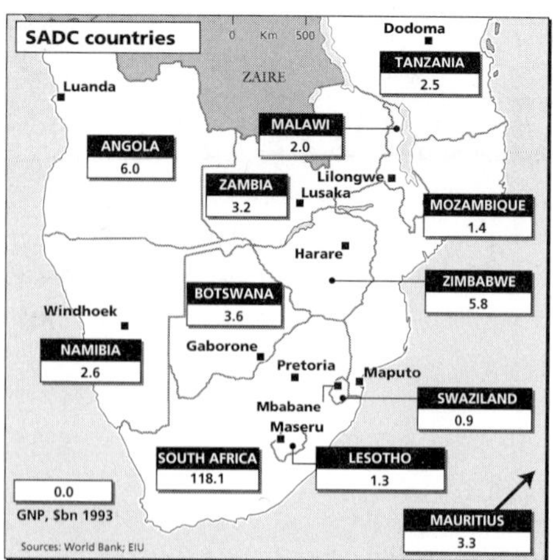

MAP 6.1
Source: The Economist, September 2, 1995, p. 35.

Slovenia, Hungary, Poland, and Slovakia have agreed to form a Central European Free Trade Area; and the EU has plans to extend free trade agreements to Eastern European and North African countries. Also being floated is the idea to establish an EU–North American "Atlantic" trade area, as advocated by some German and Canadian officials.[5]

Such regional arrangements increasingly are not exclusively for purposes of trade. They also encompass a mixture of issues and policies pertaining to domestic political stability and legitimacy, national security, and nationalism. Conflict settlement mechanisms ranging from courts (EU) to mediation and arbitration panels (NAFTA) also are sometimes built into the agreements to handle disputes over such issues as dumping, pollution, tax policy, or even human rights. Critics of these trends range from globalists, who fear that regional groupings will erect trade barriers against each other, to "antiglobalists," who fear that greater integration might lead to global supra-national governance, to nationalists, who fear that expanding integrationist schemes might create regional free trade areas at the expense of national interests and sovereignty.

INTERNATIONAL REGIONAL INTEGRATION: SOME CONCEPTS AND CONSIDERATIONS

That some nations are more powerful than others, and that national economic and military power is often used by one nation to impose compliance with its objectives by another, have been central features of relations among nations since time immemorial; yet, in parallel with this predominant *realpolitik* conception of international politics, nations also routinely cooperate. International cooperation appears in the form of participation in worldwide multilateral institutions, such as the United Nations and the World Trade Organization (WTO) but also in regional arrangements, such as the European Union, NAFTA, and the Arab Maghrib Union. These arrangements stem from a sense of shared regional identity and consensus with respect to values, objectives, and the means to realize them through various relations, including finance and trade. As discussed in Chapter 2, the *functionalist, neo-functionalist,* and *interdependence theories* maintain that international cooperation, based on incremental institutional adjustments, can lead to the development of transnational organizations and can provide mechanisms for multilateral collaboration in various sectors of economy, eventually diluting the realpolitik structures and values in international affairs. The principal objective in such cooperation, as envisioned by these integrationist theories, is the prevention of wars through the removal of mercantilist propensities of the nation-state. Added to this collaborative theme is the liberal conception of healthy free trade, reviewed in Chapter 5.

The process of regional integration, as experienced in the European Union, for example, rests on the willingness of nations and national leaders to engage in "*joint decisions* or to *delegate* the decision-making process to new central organs," thereby entrusting traditionally national powers in certain policy areas to multilateral regional structures.[6] The degree of regional integration depends on the level of regional institutionalization of economic activities, public administration, and political processes. Thus, the European Union is said to be the most advanced region in terms of integration, as it has developed regionwide political institutions in addition to monetary union; others are less institutionalized and therefore less integrated. In some cases, as in Latin America, an institutional framework for regional integration exists—note, for example, the widening role of the Inter-American Commission on Human Rights and the Inter-American Court of Human Rights in reviewing human rights violations under former Latin military regimes of the 1980s[7]—and, in recent years, there has been a greater effort to deepen regional integration, especially in the area of economic activities (finance, trade), which may in turn lead to integration of political processes (legislatures, courts) in the future.

Given the strength gained by regionalism in various parts of the world during the past two decades, some analysts argue that regionalism has assumed a far more powerful force in international relations than has globalization. Some, in fact, view regionalism as laying the foundation for a region-centric world political economy, as the three major economic centers—the European Union dominated by Germany, the Western Hemisphere by the United States, and Asia by Japan—compete for world supremacy. Hazel Johnson, for example, argues that regional arrangements, rather than globalization, more directly affect people's standards of living and that "*regionalization* will shift the balance of economic power away from the United States and toward Europe and Asia."[8] Johnson contends that, as Japan creates its "new empire" in Asia, and Germany dominates the European economies, it becomes necessary for American policymakers to pay closer attention to regional development in the Western Hemisphere, so as not "to lose economic ground to those parts of the world that better understand the concept of regionalization."[9] Construed as such, regionalism involves more than financial and trade relations; it also provides an opportunity for the regional power to institutionalize and consolidate its sphere of influence.

Regional agreements remain subsystems within the overall global scheme of things, however, while the processes of globalization become the predominant mode of international financial and trade relations dominated by the wealthier industrialized countries (the FIEs), as presented in Chapters 4 and 5. Indeed, critics would point out that most of the existing regional arrangements in the developing world were formed to counter the dominant economic position of the FIEs. Regionalism as such has been concerned primarily with economic development through the instruments of free trade areas and the creation of customs unions and common markets. As resources are more easily transferred and as intra-industry trade increases, it becomes necessary to harmonize economic policies,[10] yet international trade and related activities must be based on certain standards for the socioeconomic well-being of workers and families, as well as for the protection of the environment, made difficult especially if integration involves unequal partners.[11]

FTAs, Customs Unions, and Common Markets

Global free trade is not likely to become a reality in the foreseeable future; however, regional free trade arrangements among nations are common and continue to proliferate. Such agreements have typically taken three forms: free trade areas, customs unions, and common markets, which represent, in that order, increasing levels of economic integration.[12] A free trade area (FTA) is a regional multilateral arrangement whereby members agree to eliminate tariffs among themselves. Trading partners agree to impose no tariffs or quotas on one another, but they are free to impose such restrictions on nonmembers. One example was the European Free Trade Association (EFTA), created in 1960, including Austria, Great Britain, Sweden, Norway, Denmark, Switzerland, and Portugal, as a response to the success at that time of the European Economic Community (EEC), composed of Benelux, France, Germany, and Italy.[13] A **customs union,** on the other hand, is an FTA in which trading partners agree to eliminate trade barriers, such as tariffs and quotas, among themselves *and* to impose common tariffs, such as a common external tariff (CET) on imports from nonmembers. In a **common market,** trading partners agree to lift all tariffs or quotas among themselves, impose common barriers (for example, CETs) on nonmembers, *and* substantially reduce or completely eliminate national restrictions on the movement of labor and capital among themselves. The European Common Market, established in 1958, which became the EEC, EC, and finally EU, has been the best example of the emergence of a common market.[14]

Of the three models, the common market is the most advanced level of economic integration based on trade relations. It fosters greater efficiency in the allocation of members' resources, as expected by the theory of comparative advantage reviewed in Chapter 5, and creates a larger market for participants. This in turn allows their companies to take advantage of economies of scale through large-scale production, thus lowering costs of production and marketing per unit. The common market has certain disadvantages as well. It imposes common trade barriers between the members and nonmembers, potentially limiting opportunities for trade between the two. In addition, such regional integration strategies tend to benefit "more developed members with the overall effect of increasing the existing gap between them and the less developed members of the integration process."[15]

Studies indicate that free trade areas have substantially increased intra-regional trade, without necessarily raising tariffs on outsiders. In the case of the European Community, for example, while intra-regional trade accounted for about 55 percent of its total trade in the 1960s, by the mid-1990s that figure had risen to 70 percent (see Figure 6.1), and the EC continued to negotiate the lowering of external trade barriers during the GATT rounds.[16] However, issues related to regional trade are far more complicated than suggested by such numbers. One issue with which existing FTAs are grappling are the "rules of origin" of manufactured products. Governments use the

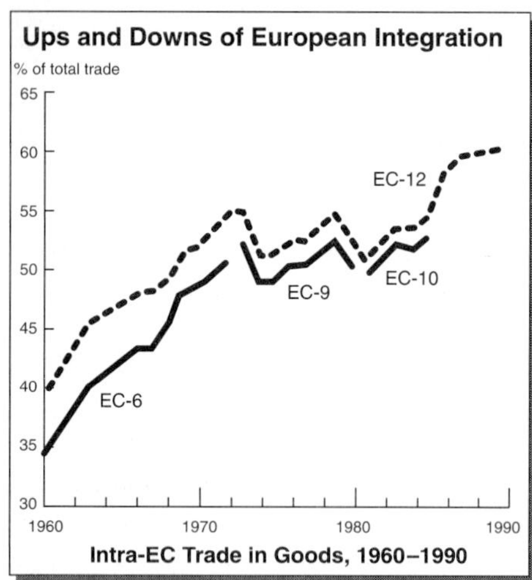

FIGURE 6.1
Source: Loukas Tsoukalis, The New European Economy: The Politics and Economics of Intergration (rev. 2d ed. Oxford University Press, 1993.)

rule of origin principle to determine whether a tariff should be added to an imported product. Should a car made in Canada with some French parts be considered Canadian? If it should, then it could be imported to the United States, under NAFTA, without a tariff. In a globalized economy, with vast transnational production networks, such rules are politically and symbolically meaningful, especially, for example, to labor unions. In the early 1990s, disagreements over the content-origin of Hondas made in Canada caused tensions between the United States and Canada. The latter argued that all U.S.-made parts should be counted for tariff purposes; the United States maintained that only the U.S.-made components of the U.S. parts should be counted.[17]

In addition to such technical considerations, critics of regional FTAs contend that their proliferation may lead to greater fragmentation of an already unruly and unstable global political economy, as well as to greater resistance to global trade liberalization as intended under the GATT-World Trade Organization. Proponents of regional FTAs, however, maintain that the contrary is true: regional FTAs develop a piecemeal approach to internal and global economic liberalization, strengthen intra-regional free trade relations based on common markets, and develop confidence-building mechanisms and mutual learning processes to enhance the long-term security and stability of the World Trade Organization. Countries such as Mexico moving toward greater internal economic liberalization while joining NAFTA, it is argued, will most likely continue to liberalize and open their economies and, hence, strengthen the competitive free trade process under WTO.[18]

Stages of Economic Integration

Regional or global economic integration involves a number of stages, each requiring a degree of harmonization of national economic policies, a complicated and potentially painful process. The first stage requires multilateral cooperation and negotiations to establish a free trade area. Existing tariffs and quotas are gradually reduced and then totally eliminated. The trading partners next create a customs union with no internal barriers to trade but maintain an external barrier against nonmembers. The common market stage entails the free movement of goods, labor, and services. In the next stage, the members create a monetary union, linking their separate currencies in terms of exchange rates and beginning to harmonize taxation policies. The total institutionalization of a common currency, with the attendant merging of fiscal and monetary policies and central banking, is the final stage toward full economic integration. Throughout the integration process, decision making institutions with varying powers may be formed. The North American Free Trade Agreement is currently in the first stage of creating a free trade area. The European Union, on the other hand, is in the process of creating an economic and monetary union. The EU created a customs union in 1968 and an internal common market in 1992.[19]

Some of the current issues involved with respect to regional integration include whether the EU's deepening economic integration will also lead to political union and encompass defense and security policy—there is already a move to a common foreign policy on certain issues, and hesitant moves on the security front, as in evolving common rules for weapons exports. Analysts express skepticism regarding the prospect of a United States of Europe, although an expanded and redefined NATO and the use of the *Western European Union* and the *Organization for Security and Cooperation in Europe* for security cooperation for the post–Cold War era remain viable options. NAFTA, however, is likely to remain a regional cooperation and trade organization without necessarily experiencing a deepening of political integration. Canada, for one, appears to be keenly interested in trade, especially in the U.S. market, but has shown little interest in closer political relations with the U.S. or Mexico. Not only has the United States not expressed any interest in further integration but the Hispanic immigration issue may lead to serious conflicts between Washington and Mexico City.

Ethnonationalism in North America, as elsewhere—including its more violent forms, such as neo-Nazi and neo-fascist movements—can destabilize and dissolve regional cooperative measures. The issue of Quebec's independence from Canada also looms as a question on this score.

Regional integration and FTAs may enhance policymakers' effectiveness in cultivating broader consensus and new regional ways of doing things, yet regional groupings, like so many aspects of the emerging global economy, present a direct challenge to national sovereignty and national interests (see Box 6.1). Nevertheless, some governments in developing countries have used regional integration arrangements to counter multinational corporations' (MNCs') financial and negotiating power, as well as to integrate markets for their local industries. From the perspective of Peruvian, Brazilian, or Nigerian nationalists, nothing has posed as much of a direct threat to national sovereignty as the MNCs. Since developing countries individually have failed to deal effectively with MNCs, integration has appeared to be a means of mustering some collective strength. For example, the Andean Group, created in 1969, established new international arrangements to strengthen its members' bargaining position with MNCs in the region. To that end, the Foreign Investment Code of the Andean Pact created strategies for regional coordination of foreign investments, while prohibiting intraregional competitive bidding. The pact required MNCs to share ownership with local enterprises, and it established an administrative agency to regulate technology transfer.[20] Further, its common external tariff and Decision No. 24, regulating investments within the region, restricted MNC transactions. By the late 1970s, however, the Andean Group faced internal tensions as some of its members, especially Chile, demanded reductions in or the total elimination of restrictions on MNCs. Neither did the group

BOX 6.1

REGIONAL INTEGRATION IN AFRICA

Shortly after gaining independence from European colonialism in the 1950s and 1960s, African countries sought to "delink" themselves from the U.S.- and European-dominated world political economy. Accordingly, they opted for "national self-reliance," on one hand, and "collective self-reliance," on the other. The latter strategy involved regional or subregional integration schemes along the lines of the European Community. African integration plans included the *East African Community (EAC),* comprised of Kenya, Tanzania, and Uganda; the *Economic Community of West African States (ECOWAS),* which consisted of sixteen member states (Benin, Burkina Faso, Cape Verde, Gambia, Ghana, Guinea, Guinea-Bissau, Côte d'Ivoire, Liberia, Mali, Mauritania, Niger, Nigeria, Senegal, Sierra Leone, and Togo); the *Economic Community of West Africa (CEAO),* comprised of Burkina Faso, Côte d'Ivoire, Mali, Mauritania, Niger, and Senegal; and the *Southern African Development Coordination Conference (SADCC),* whose member states include Angola, Botsawana, Lesotho, Malawi, Mozambique, Tanzania, Swaziland, Zambia, and Zimbabwe.

Each integration plan sought to lower international customs barriers to trade and transfer of capital, goods, services, and people among member states. Members also agreed to harmonize their external tariffs and policies for various economic sectors (agriculture, industry, finance). A number of factors, however, rendered such attempts inoperative or even led to their demise. These included insufficient capital and industrial capabilities, limited market capacity, internal competition with respect to national economic development, and unwillingness on the part of individual political leaders to surrender their personal authority and government sovereignty to a regional organization. EAC, for example, could not survive the emergence of Idi Amin's dictatorial regime in Uganda, and by the mid-1970s it was dissolved. The *Customs Union of West Africa (UDAO)* and the *Customs Union of West African States (UDEAO)* met a similar fate. Thus, as Chazan and associates have argued, the European laissez-faire assumptions undergirding African regional integration schemes, founded on customs unions, proved unrealistic (at best) within the context of African economic development. Instead, Chazan and associates propose more functionally limited intergovernmental cooperative strategies, such as "joint provision of services."

Despite these failures, however, observers and government officials have been optimistic that SADCC will be more successful than other African integration plans. Equally optimistically, the Organization of African Unity (OAU) has formally accepted the *Lagos Plan* to create an *African Common Market* by the year 2000.

Source: Naomi Chazan, Robert Mortimer, John Ravenhill, and Donald Rothchild, *Politics and Society in Contemporary Africa,* 2d ed. (Boulder, CO: Lynne Rienner, 1992), pp. 275–287, *passim.* See also Ibrahim A. Gambari, *Political and Comparative Dimensions of Regional Integration: The Case of ECOWAS* (London: Humanities Press, 1991).

guarantee economic growth by instituting regional control over MNC subsidiaries.[21]

REGIONAL INTEGRATION, TRADE RELATIONS, AND BLOCS

The New Europe: The European Union

The ratification of the Maastricht Treaty in 1993 established the European Union (EU), formerly known as the European Community (EC). In the 1990s, the integration and institutionalization of the EU's customs union and internal market have involved not only political issues of state sovereignty, a common concern for nations involved, but also greater intergovernmental institutional integration and "harmonization of policies to promote the free movement of goods, services, labor, and capital"[22] (see Box 6.2). The European Union has sought greater economic integration and development of the Economic and Monetary Union (EMU), as discussed in Chapter 4, and has included regional policymaking institutions, such as the European Parliament, the European Council, and the European Court, involved in decisions ranging from trade and finance to human rights. Its regional military security, however, remains mainly under the North Atlantic Treaty Organization (NATO) umbrella (including the U.S. and Canada) and the consultative Western European Union, as established after the Second World War.

Currently, the EU population is approximately 340 million, about 100 million larger than that of the United States, 200 million larger than Japan's, and 310 million larger than Canada's. By 1991, the EU was by far the world's largest trading area, with a gross domestic product (GDP) of over $6 trillion, equal to the GDP of the United States and Canada combined. After the creation of NAFTA in 1994, which has a combined total GDP of about $7 trillion, the EU became the world's second largest trading area. The fifteen EU countries conduct approximately $4 trillion worth of business per year, and they account for nearly 30 percent of the world's total GDP[23]

BOX 6.2

HISTORY OF THE EUROPEAN UNION

Unlike the other regional economic blocs, such as NAFTA, the founders of the EU intended it to become supra-national in nature, following the creation of the European Coal and Steel Community (ECSC) in 1951. Initially, the European Community consisted of three European Communities—the ECSC, the European Economic Community (EEC), and the European Atomic Energy Community (EAEC). A French inspired 1951 plan for a European Defence Community (EDC) was aborted when France itself balked at integrating its military forces with Germany.

In the early 1950s, the Schuman Plan led to the signing of the Treaty of Paris (1951), and the establishment of the ECSE. The Treaty of Rome in 1957, the basis of the EEC, signed by the original six states, sought to reduce and eventually to eliminate tariff and non-tariff trade barriers among the signatory states. The Treaty of Rome also established a customs union based on a common tariff barrier against nonmember states. The original six members eliminated tariff barriers by 1968; however, because of political and economic considerations, non-tariff barriers and the development of an internal market proved to be a more difficult task.

The creation of the internal market and closer financial integration also has led to a debate about creating an Economic and Monetary Union (EMU) based on a common currency. Proponents of EMU have argued that a common market requires a "comparatively level playing field," which can be facilitated by centrally directed interest rates and currency values. A common currency arrangement would be required legally and legitimately for greater market integration. While for various reasons, including nationalism, history, language and culture, the EU member states are not engaged in any serious discussion regarding a United States of Europe, the creation of the internal market in 1992 has convinced most national leaders that a common currency is required, at least as a mechanism to resolve international discrepancies in interest rates and inflation rates.

Initially, and to some extent even today, although the member states sought greater economic integration, they disagreed over and expressed serious reservations concerning "the value of economic union versus financial harmonization and over which should come first." They were concerned that such a multilateral arrangement would mean surrendering some degree of national political and economic sovereignty to supra-national regional institutions, with no guarantees for political or economic stability.

After the Second World War, the European Union evolved within the context of the Cold War, and it emerged as a

BOX 6.2 (concluded)

HISTORY OF THE EUROPEAN UNION

politically and economically powerful and competitive player in the global political economy as the Cold War closed. The architects of the post-WWII world order viewed stable international trade relations within ideologically delineated blocs as an essential component of stable political-military alliances. In the 1960s, but especially after the collapse of the Bretton Woods system in the early 1970s, trans-Atlantic frictions and intra-EC stagnation also reflected the weakening of the North Atlantic community and its political and military alliance.

In the late 1960s and 1970s, the *United Europe* envisioned by some of the founders of the EC, built on federalist and functionalist foundations, had become a victim of global economic instability and the inability of European institutions collectively to ameliorate the political problems associated with inflation, recession, and unemployment. In part to stave off Asian and U.S. competition in a high technology world, in 1986, the EC members signed the Single European Act, which promised to eliminate all barriers to the movement of people, capital, and goods. In the mid-1980s, the international political and economic climate had so changed that, as one observer notes, "terms such as 'Euro-pessimism' and 'Euro-sclerosis'" were suddenly removed from the lexicon of European politics. Stronger regional unity in the European Community reemerged as a viable and even necessary goal to enhance each member's competitiveness in the rapidly globalizing markets, as economic conditions continued to improve. With the signing of the Maastricht Treaty in January 1992, EU members created the free internal market in January 1993. Although some non-tariff barriers remained, the EU had already established a powerful presence beyond Europe as an independent actor in international organizations such as the United Nations, the Group of 8, and GATT/WTO. Creation of a common Euro-currency, while expected to facilitate unity, also could create strains of unemployment or recession as individual economies no longer stabilize themselves through adjusting interest or exchange rates.

Sources: See Loukas Tsoukalis, *The New European Economy: The Politics and Economics of Integration,* rev. 2d ed. (Oxford University Press, 1993), pp. 1–16; Gretchen M. MacMillan, "Managing Economic Convergence in the European Union," in Donald Barry, with Mark O. Dickerson and James Gaisford, eds., *Toward a North American Community?* (Boulder, CO: Westview Press, 1995), pp. 232–241; Martin Feldstein, "Europe's New Challenge to America," *New York Times,* May 7, 1998, p. A31.

(see Table 6.1). The EU's share of world trade—including world exports and intra-EU trade—continued to increase by an annual average of 5 percent, from 36 percent in the early 1980s to 41 percent in the early 1990s. Direct investment in the European Union also increased from $12.2 billion in 1985 to $72.2 billion in 1990, surpassing that of the United States. Significantly, these improvements can partly be attributed to the fact that the EU is home to the majority of G-8 countries and some of the world's largest companies.[24] However, in order to develop greater integration encompassing a wider geographical area, such as all of Europe, the respective governments—individually and collectively—would have to address their domestic economic problems, especially unemployment (see Box 6.3).[25]

Economists have developed theories of the sequences by which regional integration extends from one area to the next. With the end of the Cold War, sequential integration clearly was fostered between Western and Eastern Europe, particularly with the model of Germany's reunification, paid for by high tax investments by western Germany, on the expectation of great economic payoffs. However, it is argued that, if sequential West-East integration and freer trade do not take place in a timely enough fashion, the Central and Eastern European countries (CEECs) may be tempted to develop and attract viable industries behind protectionist walls of their own. CEECs are concerned that the EU may delay further integration until satisfied that reforms in the East reduce potential costs to support agriculture (EU's CAP, which promises to buy up surpluses and stabilize prices); clean up the environment from previously polluting industries; lower government spending (structural reform); and promote democracy, stability, and human rights. Unable to wait for a step-by-step process, CEECs may respond by offering incentives to North American and Asian industries to come and enjoy protection against EU firms. Such fragmentation would be potentially inefficient and, if history is a lesson, dangerous for Europe as a whole.[26]

Moreover, if sequential agreements involve only certain privileged, or "advanced," Eastern states, such as Hungary, Czech Republic, and Poland, they set up competitive discord and jealousy in the East. Jealousy is further extended to the

TABLE 6.1

Growth in the Value of World Merchandise Trade by Region, 1990–1997 (Billion Dollars and Percentage)

Exports						Imports				
Value	Annual Percentage Change					Value	Annual Percentage Change			
1997	1990–1995	1995	1996	1997		1997	1990–1995	1995	1996	1997
5,295	7.5	20.0	4.0	3.0	World	5,435	7.5	19.5	4.5	3.0
904	8.5	14.5	6.5	9.5	North America	1,100	8.0	11.0	6.0	10.5
280	9.0	22.0	12.0	11.0	Latin America	319	14.5	11.5	12.5	17.5
110	14.0	31.0	21.0	14.5	Mexico	113	12.5	210.5	225.5	22.5
170	7.0	17.5	7.5	9.0	Other Latin America	207	15.5	25.0	6.5	15.0
2,269	6.0	23.0	3.5	21.0	Western Europe	2,236	5.5	22.5	2.5	21.0
2,100	6.5	23.5	3.5	21.0	European Union (15)	2,045	5.5	22.0	2.0	21.0
179	7.0	27.0	7.5	4.0	Transition economies	192	5.0	26.0	15.5	7.5
89	7.5	26.5	5.5	6.5	Central and Eastern Europe	115	11.5	28.0	16.5	4.0
120	0.5	13.5	11.5	3.0	Africa	127	5.5	21.5	21.0	5.0
30	3.5	10.5	2.5	6.0	South Africa	32	10.5	30.5	21.5	5.0
163	1.5	13.5	14.0	0.0	Middle East	144	6.0	14.0	6.0	1.5
1,380	12.0	18.0	0.5	5.5	Asia	1,317	12.0	23.0	5.0	0.0
421	9.0	11.5	27.5	2.5	Japan	338	7.5	22.0	4.0	23.0
183	19.0	23.0	1.5	21.0	China	142	20.0	14.0	5.0	2.5
548	14.0	23.0	3.0	3.0	Six East Asian traders[a]	581	15.0	26.0	3.5	0.0

Source: World Trade Organization, *Focus,* no. 28 (March 1998), p. 3.
[a]Hong Kong, China; the Republic of Korea; Malaysia; Singapore; Chinese Taipei, Taiwan, and Thailand

Islamic world, where Turkey, a NATO member, has been campaigning for years for EU membership and has been held back by concerns about Turkish economic needs, as well as Greek opposition and objections to Turkey's human rights and foreign policy record. For some former East bloc members, especially those located geographically close to Russia, such as Byelorus, there may be long-term economic benefits in renewed economic ties to Russia, itself a potentially huge market; yet, for security and political reasons and the lure of already developed Western economies, states such as Ukraine and the Baltic Republics also seek immediate EU and North American ties. Thus, the determination of which states will be allowed into either the EU or NATO and on what timetable has profound implications for stable relations across Europe and with Russia.[27]

In the early Cold War years, Washington strongly supported European integration as a bulwark against the Soviet Union. U.S.-EC relations during the late 1960s and early 1970s, however, was characterized as one "gyrat[ing] between insensitivity and hostility," while each sought to strengthen its position in the global political economy.

During the 1960s, economic growth in Europe and tariff reductions after the Kennedy Round left few barriers to U.S. and Canadian exports to and investments in the EU market, with the exception of agricultural products. In the early 1960s, however, U.S. influence in European politics in general and on EC market integration in particular declined, as trade conflicts intensified. The "notorious chicken war" of 1963–1964, for example, caused by the EC Common Agriculture Policy's restrictive trade barriers against farm imports to the EC, virtually destroyed the U.S. market share of the EC poultry market.[28]

In the 1970s, Washington repeatedly expressed its discontent with the adverse influence the more united Europe began to exert on its political and economic interests. Europe saw U.S. efforts to retain virtually absolute hegemonic strength in trans-Atlantic trade and other negotiations as "patronizing," while relations further deteriorated because of differences in foreign policy orientation, such as over Vietnam, the 1973 Arab-Israeli war, the Arab oil embargo, and trans-Atlantic and trans-Pacific trade relations.[29]

The Nixon administration ended U.S. support for multilateral arrangements in the European Community and for the integration process but maintained bilateral relations with each government. Many in Europe even suspected

BOX 6.3

EUROPEAN INTEGRATION: THE EU CAUTIOUSLY OPENS EAST DOOR

European Union leaders cautiously opened the door Saturday to membership for East European nations but set no firm entry date for any of them. In the draft of a communique to be issued ending a two-day EU summit, the 12 leaders called their "pre-accession" strategy for Eastern Europe an "essential contribution to overcoming the legacy of past divisions and promoting peace." The draft, a copy of which was obtained by The Associated Press, stipulates that the EU won't take in any newcomers until it has reformed its institutions in an intergovernmental conference scheduled to start in 1996. Key membership candidates in the East are Poland, Hungary, the Czech Republic, and Slovakia, followed at a distance by Romania and Bulgaria. Leaders of the six nations—which have signed broad economic and political accords with the EU—were invited to the final session of the European Union summit Saturday. In the draft statement, the EU leaders said they hoped to soon bring the three Baltic republics and Slovenia into the "pre-accession" strategy. German officials, whose government is pushing hard for the EU's eastward expansion, stressed the summit decision constituted no formal start to membership talks, only the beginning of ever closer political and economic links.

The East European strategy seeks to bring the eastern economies up to speed to join the EU some day. In doing so, the West Europeans also seek to help preserve pan-European stability. The East Europeans will be required to continue apace with market reforms and gradually adopt EU single market laws. There will be annual meetings of EU and Eastern European government leaders and more frequent ministerial meetings. For their part, the EU leaders agreed, the union will continue to open markets to the East and consult their neighbors before imposing punitive trade measures.

Poland and Hungary are widely seen to be ready for EU membership by the year 2000. The fact that the union has declined to give them a specific entry date now has been a source of irritation in Warsaw and Budapest. The EU leaders said they would back the strategy of preparing these countries for accession with "appropriate funds" earmarked over several years. However, no figures were mentioned. Instead, the EU will use existing development funds for East Europe. Turning to economic measures within the EU, the leaders pledged to create more jobs "given the still intolerably high level of unemployment." During the recent recession, the nations' jobless rate soared to nearly 11 percent, forcing more than 17 million people onto the unemployment lines. "The fight against unemployment will also in the future remain the paramount task of the European Union and its member states," the draft statement said. "The current recovery will help in dealing with this task. That recovery is not, however, in itself sufficient to solve the problems of employment and unemployment in Europe."

In recent weeks, the EU states have been unable to agree on a five-year accession fund of $8.57 billion to help the East Europeans prepare. Germany and the Netherlands favored this, but a French-led camp of southern members insisted on parallel funding of $6.7 billion in aid to the EU's neighbors in North Africa and the Middle East. The leaders called the Mediterranean a "priority area of strategic importance for the European Union." The summit also declared Malta and Cyprus—which have applied for EU membership—would be candidates "in the next phase of EU expansion."

The European Union leaders also aimed to conclude work on establishing a European police agency by the middle of next year. But their draft communique indicated they had been unable to compromise on issues, including sharing of information on criminals, to combat cross-border organized crime and drug trafficking.

Source: Associated Press, December 11, 1994.

U.S. motives in response to the oil embargo and price increases during the 1973 Middle East war, as the EC countries and Japan depended more heavily on increasingly expensive oil imports than did the United States.[30]

While relations between the two sides of the Atlantic improved somewhat during the Carter years, the advent of the Reagan administration resuscitated economic and political tensions, exacerbated by the administration's opposition to the construction of the Soviet Union–Western European oil pipeline. In fact, in the 1980s, the United States and the European Community were for all intents and purposes engaged in trade wars, particularly in the areas of steel and agriculture. Spain's and Portugal's admission to the EC in 1986 did not help matters, causing further decline in U.S. agricultural exports.

The reintensification of the Cold War and nuclear tensions during the Reagan administration also had negative consequences for U.S.-EU relations, as reflected in the different foreign policy approaches toward East-West and North-South relations. The Reagan administration opposed

European sales of advanced technology, with potential military applications, to the Soviet Union and other Communist governments. It also opposed European support for the Cantadora peace process to end the military conflicts in Central America. Such differences spilled over into U.S.-EC trade relations[31] and may have had serious political and economic repercussions, as European integration, especially under German leadership, increasingly challenged the U.S. hegemonic position.

The bulk of Canadian trade interests has continued to focus on the U.S. market, but Ottawa has paid increased attention to Europe.[32] By the early 1970s, Canadian-EC relations improved, as both sides highlighted the growing significance of their mutual benefits in trade, especially for Canada as its relations with the EC became closely identified with the "third option"—that is, greater diversification in Canadian trade relations while distancing from the United States. In the 1970s, Canadian-EC relations were further institutionalized, as Ottawa and Brussels exchanged diplomatic missions and senior-level trade officials continued to maintain close ties. While Canada was interested in an increasing share of the EC market for its exports, the EC not only sought to increase its own role in North America through bilateral and multilateral ties but also sought alternative sources of oil (during the OPEC crisis in the early 1970s) and raw materials in Canada. Canada-EC bilateral relations were finally formalized under the Canada-EC Framework Agreement for Commercial and Economic Cooperation, signed in 1976, to promote trade and investment.[33]

Mexico, another North American economic partner, entered into a similar agreement with Brussels in 1975, granting mutual most favored nation status and establishing a Mexico-EC committee to further develop trade relations. The EC appreciated close ties with Mexico because of the latter's importance in Latin American politics, as well as its constructive contributions to the North-South dialogue. Mexican-EC trade relations began to be formalized and institutionalized in earnest in the second half of the 1980s, when they exchanged diplomatic missions (1989) and worked toward ending the military conflicts in Central America. Mexican economic instability concerned both EU states and the United States, and it was a major topic at the 1995 G-7 economic summit.

In the meantime, the momentous changes and political upheavals taking place in Eastern Europe in the late 1980s required a reappraisal of U.S. and Canadian policies toward Europe. The Bush administration indicated that neither the United States nor North America could ignore these developments and their implications for relations with the European Community. In May 1989, Bush invited Europeans to a U.S.-European "partnership in world leadership." As the process of European integration moved toward a common internal market, creating a more deeply institutionalized integration, the United States sought to adjust its relations with the EC as well within a context of trans-Atlantic multilateralism.[34] Neither the Bush nor the Clinton administration could fail to appreciate the fact that the EU is poised to become North America's principal trade rival well into the twenty-first century. Further, future extension of the EU to other European countries would substantially increase not only its population but also the region's production and trade capacity, exceeding that of the United States by approximately 30 percent.[35]

The United States and the European Union remain the largest trading actors in the world, and the largest trading bloc partners. In recent years, bilateral trade between them has reached about $200 billion, whereby the European Union accounts for over 23 percent of U.S. exports, and the United States for about 18 percent of EU exports. Together they account for well over 30 percent of world trade. With respect to the composition of trade, the manufacturing sector accounts for over 80 percent and agriculture about 10 percent of U.S. exports to the EU, while the manufacturing sector accounts for 89 percent and agriculture for 5 percent of EU exports to the United States, rendering both mutually and equally interdependent as trade partners. Finally, EU-U.S. foreign direct investments (FDIs) increased as well, as discussed in Chapter 7.[36] The EU also remains the second largest (after the United States) trade and investment partner for Canada and Mexico, comprising about 12 percent of Canada's and 10 percent of Mexico's total world trade—mainly in raw materials, pulp, paper, and petroleum.[37]

Canadian and Mexican total trade with the EU has declined, however, since the late 1980s, while their trade with the United States has increased.[38] NAFTA is expected to result in even greater dependence on the U.S. market, as the latter absorbs a larger share of Mexican trade.[39]

The post–Cold War environment, and especially the creation of NAFTA, raises fundamental questions regarding the future of the EU–North American relations. For the United States, and to a lesser extent for Canada, the central issue is power and influence. The NATO context and trade interests clearly still afford much momentum for trans-Atlantic cooperation; yet the post–Cold War and post-Maastricht context of U.S.-EU relations underscores the potential for strong competition as well. Since the creation of NATO and the Treaty of Rome, a politically stable and militarily powerful European Community, including a potentially powerful West Germany, has been viewed as critical for the construction of an effective Western alliance. Through such mechanisms, the United States used its role as the provider of the security umbrella in Europe. In the post–Cold War era, however, bilateral relations based on trade partnership and political power derived from security arrangements can no longer be viewed in such simplistic terms. As Potter has noted, "The removal of major structural features such as the Cold War and the difficulties encountered in completing the Uruguay Round, have created a situation in which the broad, traditional expectations and images of Europe held by North American decisionmakers are no longer sustainable."[40] Still, though, it is difficult to imagine Washington wishing to materially and substantially weaken the economies of its closest political allies in the world.

North America

The North American Free Trade Agreement (NAFTA) was established in January 1994. While it is not clear what the future implications for the region will be, the fact that NAFTA has been created—as the first formal trilateral regional trade arrangement among the United States, Canada, and Mexico—is in itself a major development not only in the Western Hemisphere but also in the world political economy. It should be emphasized, however, that even more than the EU, NAFTA encompasses countries of uneven levels of political power, economic development, and export capacity (see Table 6.2). Motives for investment in NAFTA range from Canadian and Mexican interests in selling to the large U.S. market—to the potential of sales and cheaper production and raw materials cost for U.S. firms interested in Canada and Mexico. Viewed in optimistic terms, NAFTA has created opportunities for regional cooperation, especially as it "establishes a precedent for cooperation between developed and developing countries."[41] As such, NAFTA can be seen as a major achievement following the recent patterns of regional integration in the world economy, thus validating laissez-faire principles of international cooperation through trade liberalization.

On the other hand, a critical difference between the European Union and NAFTA is that, while the former may lead to greater economic but also to political integration, NAFTA proclaims no such objectives. It is mainly a regional arrangement for purposes of closer cooperation in trade, although some form of political and administrative integration within the broader **Organization of American States (OAS)** system may be conceivable in the future. The absence of a drive for an EU-style integration can to some degree be attributable to the very disproportionate levels of political and economic development and historical and cultural suspicions. Canada and Mexico have vacillated between cooperation and nationalism in their foreign policies toward the United States (see Box 6.4), as the latter's foreign policy toward its neighbors historically has been characterized by territorial and economic expansion.

Canada and Mexico view each other as "distant friends," both sharing borders with a superpower. Canada also has close relations with European countries and trade partners across the Atlantic, while Mexico maintains close ties with some Europeans (e.g. Germany and Volkswagen) and its southern neighbors throughout the hemisphere. The creation of NAFTA is a significant step toward strengthening North American relations, at least as an *economic community*. However, bilateral economic as well as security-related ties—Canada-U.S. and Mexico-U.S.—have a long history in the region. During the Cold War, the United States and Canada created bilateral security systems, including the North American Air Defense Command (NORAD), as a protective shield against a potential Soviet attack.[42] Mexico became a member of the

TABLE 6.2

NAFTA Among Equals? World Export Market Shares (Percent of World Exports of Goods and Services)

	1970–1979	1980–1989	1990–1994	1995	1996	1997[a]	1998[a]
Canada	4.0	3.7	3.4	3.4	3.4	3.5	3.5
Mexico	0.6	1.0	1.0	1.1	1.2	1.3	1.4
United States	12.4	12.2	13.1	12.6	12.8	13.2	13.2

Source: International Monetary Fund, *World Economic Outlook,* May 1997, Table 8, p. 41.
[a]Projections

BOX 6.4

HISTORICAL ROOTS OF NAFTA

The Americas as a region historically—ever since the British and Spanish colonies gained independence in the late eighteenth and early nineteenth centuries—have been interested in some form of regionalism and regional integration, as envisioned by Simon Bolivar's *Federation* and implied in the Monroe administration's Monroe Doctrine. However, in more modern times, North American regionalism emerged as a serious issue in the United States first in the National Governors Association (NGA) in 1979 and 1980, when the NGA created a commission to examine the feasibility of a North American Council to "provide a forum to allow representatives of all levels of government and the private sector from the three countries to discuss issues of mutual concern." NGA's concern, also expressed by members of Congress, the bureaucracies, political parties, and interest groups, was the need to address the increasing vulnerability of the U.S. economy, as underscored by the oil crises of the 1970s, to the vicissitudes of an increasingly unstable world political economy. The United States was concerned with its (actual or perceived) declining position in world politics because of its stagnant economy due to persistent balance-of-payments deficits and deteriorating production capacity. Canada and Mexico would be reliable sources of oil and gas.

Equally important, although at the time less conspicuous, were the growing differences with the EC in foreign policy orientation toward the rest of the world and global issues, as well as the growing sense of competition with the EC in international trade and monetary areas. U.S. policymakers viewed the creation of a regional trade bloc as a way of strengthening the U.S. economy and its ability to compete in foreign markets. Thus, North American regionalism and economic cooperation offered "a way of enhancing U.S. strength in the face of the perceived decline of U.S. power, emerging strains between Washington and its allies, and rising East-West tension." The then presidential candidate Ronald Reagan stated that "the key to our own future security may lie in both Mexico and Canada becoming much stronger countries than they are today."

U.S. policymakers were concerned regarding transboundary problems, including air and water pollution, but most emphatically immigration across the U.S.-Mexican border. Regional cooperation, they hoped, would rectify the situation. They hoped that through NAFTA U.S. companies would have greater access to cheap labor and natural resources. Advocates of NAFTA argued that economic growth in Mexico as a result of this agreement "would increase Mexican demand for American goods and services," while at the same time promoting stability in Mexico. They feared that the recent Mexican economic reforms and liberalization, together with mounting debts, would render Mexico politically and economically unstable if not reinforced by its northern neighbors. Stability in Mexico was essential to effectively address the issue of illegal immigration, since most immigrants are believed to cross the U.S. border to find better jobs and a higher standard of living.

Initially, Canada and Mexico expressed reluctance to join the U.S.-proposed regional arrangement. As part of his presidential campaign strategy, Reagan visited Mexican President Jose Lopez Portillo in Mexico City in July 1979 to present the case for the North American agreement, while his senior campaign aides met with members of Canadian Prime Minister Joe Clark's staff in Ottawa. Both neighbors' responses were negative. Mexican policymakers, including Lopez Portillo, maintained that the U.S. objective is

> . . . incompatible with Mexico's social and economic development objectives, since the great disparity among the levels of development of the three countries would mean that any benefit resulting from such a union would be distributed unevenly, thereby emphasizing existing differences, and with the additional risk of endangering Mexico's

Rio Treaty (1947) promoted by the United States under the auspices of the Organization of American States for similar reasons.

With a population of 360 million and a production capacity of $7 trillion in goods and services, NAFTA currently constitutes the largest free trade area in the world economy. NAFTA's principal objective, as the name implies, is the gradual reduction in tariffs among the three member states. It also provides for greater regulation of intellectual property rights, public services, energy, labor conditions, and the environment, as well as mechanisms for international dispute resolution, to develop a more stable legal setting for trade and investment relations. NAFTA's long-term goal is to promote economic growth and facilitate exports to other regions of the world, enabling "the three parties to decrease their respective debts and current account deficits in a way they cannot achieve through trade among themselves."[43] The gradual addition of Chile to membership could open the way for inclusion of other Latin American states.[44] As shown in Table 6.1, the recent years have witnessed increases in trade, especially as the U.S. share of world exports rose to 13 percent, the highest since 1970. North American merchandise exports increased by 9.5 percent in 1997,

BOX 6.4 (concluded)

HISTORICAL ROOTS OF NAFTA

> sovereign ability to decide on the application of its economic policies.

Similarly, Clark's successor, Prime Minister Pierre Trudeau, believed that Canada's interests "were unlikely to be enhanced by mechanisms for comprehensive trilateral economic cooperation." Also, Canadian and Mexican businesses expressed fears of being consumed by "the more powerful American competitors".

Although during the early 1980s both Canada and Mexico continued to oppose trilateralism as proposed by the United States, in August 1983 the Trudeau government indicated willingness to negotiate separate trade relations with the United States "on a sectoral basis." The Reagan administration welcomed this change in the Canadian position, and "by February of 1984, the two sides had identified a number of sectors for potential action." Although in the summer of 1984 negotiations encountered a number of difficulties "in balancing tradeoffs among the various sectors," they continued with the new aim of arranging a more comprehensive free trade agreement. The election of Canadian Prime Minister Brian Mulroney in September 1984 provided an opportunity to accelerate the negotiations and to improve relations with the Reagan administration. In March 1985, the bilateral Mulroney-Reagan Shermock Summit in Quebec City agreed to move forward with the free trade negotiations, and the two leaders signed the final text of the Canada-U.S. Free Trade Agreement (CUSFTA) on January 2, 1988 (effective on January 1, 1989).

In the mid-1980s, the Mexican government under President Miguel de la Madrid introduced economic reforms, especially privatization and trade liberalization policies. His successor, Carlos Salinas de Gortari, continued even further with these reforms, extending them to foreign trade and investment areas as well. These reforms replaced the import-substitution strategies of the 1960s and 1970s. Mexico's debt crisis and dropping oil revenues convinced the de la Madrid and Salinas administrations to concentrate on trade and investment liberalization as a means of reviving the country's economy. Mexico, thus, joined GATT in 1986 and, during the next five years, lowered its tariff from 100 percent to 20 percent; privatized some of the major industrial sectors, including banking, telecommunications, and transport; relaxed all licensing requirements; and reduced government subsidies.

Meanwhile, the composition of Mexican exports changed from mostly primary and modest secondary products, such as tobacco, liquor, and textiles, to manufactured goods, such as machinery and chemical compounds. However, the Mexican economy and development grew dependent on the manufacturing sectors and related markets in the United States, which in turn rendered the Mexican economy more vulnerable to trade and financial policies made in Washington. As a result, from the Mexican policymakers' perspective, participation in the free trade agreement with the United States and Canada was necessary to guarantee greater investments and capital from the United States and Canada, and greater access to the Canadian but especially U.S. markets. The latter alone account for about 75 percent of Mexico's total exports. Finally, in June 1990 Salinas and Bush agreed to work toward free trade negotiations. In September, Canada's Prime Minister Mulroney indicated Canada's interest in participating, and in February 1991 the three leaders announced their agreement to begin negotiations for a comprehensive trilateral free trade accord.

Source: See Donald Barry, "The Road to NAFTA," in Donald Barry, with Mark O. Dickerson and James Gaisford, eds., *Toward a North American Community?* (Boulder, CO: Westview Press, 1995), pp. 4–17, *passim.*

although imports increased as well: 21 percent from Western Europe, 21 percent from China, and 14 percent from Japan.[45]

Opponents of NAFTA have argued that, since the accord embraces a market-oriented approach to international economic relations and related domestic policies, it restricts the member governments' ability to direct their national economies toward greater economic equality and maximum employment, as well as to promote ecologically sound industrialization.[46] Whether these governments will develop effective institutions to "depoliticize" and resolve trade, labor, and immigration issues and regain public confidence remains to be seen. Several ethnic-economic protests, including the Chiapas uprising in Mexico, the Native American Oka crisis, the Quebec separatist movement in Canada, and the intensification of the anti-Washington militia movement (as illustrated by the terrorist bombing of the federal building in Oklahoma City), however, are suggestive of some of the serious challenges ahead. Both Canada and Mexico are aware of the fact that, for the United States, NAFTA simply represents a response to the Japanese and EU competition. Preservation of economic hegemony, as the Cold War era experience showed, also entails "active state intervention in defining social and economic welfare," and despite

NAFTA the state will "continue to be an important social actor."[47]

Because of political conflicts, potential economic crises, and the cross pressures of dealing with Europe and Asia, some observers have serious reservations regarding the future of North American integration. One analyst has cautioned that, in the absence of the Cold War,

> without the unifying pressure of East-West polarization, the member states of EU may increasingly feel it unnecessary to maintain a common front with North America on international security or trade issues, leading to the unraveling of the traditional transatlantic political-security nexus. This may in turn create a fertile environment for the politicization of transatlantic trade relations, and thus the very real possibility of bloc-to-bloc antagonism—a situation in which the smaller states in NAFTA, that is Canada and Mexico, could get sidewiped in a pattern of U.S.-EU conflict.[48]

This, in turn, could lead to the unraveling of NAFTA.

Latin America

The concept of regional unity in Latin America dates back to the 1820s, when Simon Bolivar advocated the creation of a confederation of the Americas. The First Congress of American States met in Panama in 1826, and subsequent conferences included the Congresses of Lima in 1847–1848, Santiago in 1856, Chile in 1856, Lima in 1864–1865, and Montevideo in 1888–1889. Their shared colonial experiences and independence and their need to establish economic and political parity vis-a-vis the great powers after independence provided the impetus for such regional efforts. Although Bolivar's vision for a united Latin America never materialized, the congresses he organized in the 1820s set precedents for future Latin regional conferences for more integrated Latin American multilateral arrangements.[49]

Throughout the nineteenth and early twentieth centuries, Latin American leaders adopted the traditional free trade philosophy of classical liberalism, since it had served the Europeans well. In the 1950s and 1960s, they sought to create free trade areas because of the challenges presented by both the dominant U.S. economy and the founding of the European Community; in emulating the European Community and free trade, they hoped to encourage rapid economic development and modernization. Accordingly, they established such institutions as the Latin American Free Trade Association (LAFTA) and the Caribbean Free Trade Association (CARIFTA).[50]

As in Africa, however, the European free-trade model produced less than satisfactory results for Latin America (see Box 6.5). Critics, especially *dependencia* theorists, charged that the international economic system, as dominated by the rich North, did not allow Latin Americans to achieve industrialization and development independently of the North's capital and technologies. The region also was beset (and to an extent remains so) by severe wealth inequalities and concentrated landholding patterns. Economic growth experienced through intra-regional trade benefited the MNCs, the wealthy elites, and the more powerful countries (for example, Venezuela) in comparison to workers, peasants in the smaller and poorer countries (for example, Peru). During the 1960s and 1970s, Latin American countries adopted economic nationalism, such as import substitution, and regional trade areas for "collective self-reliance" to stimulate national industrialization and economic development.[51] Rather than promoting mere trade, per se, regional integration became the vehicle for higher levels of industrialization, productivity, and national economic development. These considerations led to the creation of such regional integration schemes as the Central American Common Market (CACM) (1960) and the Andean Group (1969). CACM ultimately failed economically and was destroyed by wars.

After the failures in the 1970s and early 1980s, some of the Latin countries sought to reinvigorate their economies and regional organizations, and proposed to create modest new regional arrangements, primarily based on greater economic liberalization.[52] After the collapse of Communism and the disintegration of the Soviet bloc, in addition to the rapid economic growth experienced in East Asia's newly industrialized countries (NICs), Latin American leaders expressed greater interest in trade liberalization and regional multilateral cooperation based on laissez-faire and privatization, such as ALADI, the Andean Group, and Mercosur.[53] Since the second half of the 1980s, Latin American intra-regional exports have increased from 12.5 percent of the region's total world exports in 1985 to about 20 percent in 1996.[54] In July 1994, twenty-five South American and Caribbean countries formed the Association of Caribbean States, making this area the fourth largest trade group in the world.[55] Mercosur alone accounts for 50 percent of South America's GDP and nearly 40 percent of the region's foreign trade.[56] Barring major reversals, as in the 1980s and as a spin-off of the Asian crises of the 90s, Latin American economies could achieve greater regional integration in the coming century; whether that translates into greater economic equality within countries and greater

BOX 6.5

THREE GENERATIONS OF REGIONAL COOPERATION IN THE DEVELOPING COUNTRIES

THE FIRST GENERATION, 1950s–1960s.

Free trade areas in the developing world began to appear in the 1950s and 1960s in response to the creation of the European Community. The developing countries hoped to improve their economic welfare based on free trade and expected increases in productivity. They believed that regional cooperation through customs unions would stimulate economic growth, development, and modernization. The first generation thus sought—through such institutions as the Latin American Free Trade Association (LAFTA) and the Caribbean Free Trade Association (CARIFTA)—to adapt to the underdeveloped economic environment free trade and market liberalization as used in the industrialized North. These moves also fit with ideals of Third World solidarity.

THE SECOND GENERATION, 1960s–1970s.

By the late 1960s, however, it became obvious that the free-trade model had failed to improve their economic situation significantly, especially in trade and financial relations with the North. Thus, reliance on the free-trade model was particularly criticized by dependency theorists for at least three reasons. First, the economic growth registered under market integration and intra-regional trade enhanced the economic and political influence MNCs had on the national economies of member countries. Further, intra-regional trade benefited the wealthier and economically more powerful member countries. Finally, these critics saw the global capitalist political economy and the structural North-South relations within it as the primary cause of underdevelopment and the difficulties encountered in the developing countries' efforts toward development. To counter such obstacles, the developing countries opted for more statist and collective self-reliance strategies for purposes of economic development, industrialization, and greater independence from foreign capital. National policies reflecting their economic nationalism—mainly import substitution—thus replaced the free-trade approach as the principal means of national development and regional economic integration, and the architects of regional economic integration expected integration to buttress national policies of import substitution, as in Africa, Asia, but particularly Latin America. Thus, while the first generation viewed regional economic integration as a vehicle to stimulate productivity and growth, the second generation preferred to use such institutions as extensions of economic nationalist policies, as vehicles to achieve higher levels of industrialization for economic development. Developing countries emphasized national industrialization not only to increase employment but also to check the impact of MNCs on their economies. They became convinced that the structure of the world economy as created after WWII was itself a barrier to development. These considerations were critical in the formation of the Central American Common Market (CACM) and the Andean Group. Through such collective efforts, they hoped to present a united front in their negotiations regarding trade, aid, and security issues with the advanced industrialized countries.

THE THIRD GENERATION, 1980s–1990s.

The latter half of the 1970s and the 1980s left no room for the optimism expressed by the previous generation. The oil shocks of the 1970s, the international debt crises, and the worsening world economy created an international environment less conducive to regional cooperation, and almost all regional institutions decayed. In the late 1980s and early 1990s, the developing countries attempted to revive the existing regional organizations and in some cases proposed to create new ones. Two approaches emerged: (a) a return to economic reforms and trade liberalization involving bilateral and multilateral arrangements (ALADI, Andean Group) and, (b) regional multilateral cooperation on specifically defined projects (SADCC, Mercosur).

Sources: W. Andrew Axline, "Introduction," in Axline, *The Political Economy of Regional Cooperation,* pp. 1–4; Rolf J. Langhammer and Ulrich Hiemenz, *Regional Integration among Developing Countries: Obstacles and Options* (Tübingen, Germany: Mohr, 1990).

independence from the developed countries remains to be seen. While intra-regional exports currently account for 20 percent of the region's total world exports, exports to the developed economies have remained around 70 percent during the past decade.[57] The following brief discussion of the Andean Group demonstrates the difficulties involved in attempting to balance domestic, regional, and global pressures.

In 1969, Bolivia, Chile, Colombia, Ecuador, and Peru signed the Cartagena Agreement, establishing the Andean Group, also known as the Andean Common Market. Venezuela joined in November 1973, and Chile withdrew in October 1976. The founding members believed that a new international economic order and trade arrangements would improve the region's economic condition. The main objective was to enhance their ability to regulate and manage multinational corporations' behavior in the region. The Andean Group countries believed that regional integration would not only strengthen their bargaining position in relations with the developed world in the North and with MNCs, but also with major Latin American trading partners, such as Argentina, Brazil, and Mexico.[58]

The principal focus of Andean integration was trade liberalization through "procedural automaticity:" rather than negotiate reduction of tariffs on a yearly basis, the Cartagena Agreement provided for automatic tariff reductions of 10 percent each year for the next decade. In addition, the Andean Group promoted "industrial programming, harmonization of economic policies, and special treatment for less developed countries."[59]

The first four or five years of Andean integration were its more celebrated years. In the 1960s and 1970s, the international system was experiencing fundamental changes, as more former colonial territories in Africa and Asia were gaining independence. This global transformation created new opportunities for developing countries throughout Latin America, Asia, and Africa to put forth a new global agenda, and a number of international conferences proposed major restructuring of the world political economy. The Bandung Conference in 1955 establishing the Non-Aligned Movement, the Movement's strengthening in the 1960s, and the establishment of UNCTAD underscored the need for greater unity among developing countries and for concerted efforts to address the problems in North-South relations. These changes and the "relative economic progress of the region in the 1960s contributed to create a climate of confidence which brought local governments to believe that progress lay ahead if only they could put their act together."[60]

Also, economic nationalism in Peru, Chile, and Bolivia ironically proved conducive to the Andean integration. In Peru, for example, the Juan Velasco Alvaredo government, since its seizure of power in October 1968, had launched policies of economic nationalism involving the nationalization and appropriation of key industrial and financial sectors, including the nationalization of the International Petroleum Company. Andean integration offered a collective opportunity to protect domestic economies against external, particularly North American, challenges; as long as the objectives of the integration were compatible with domestic objectives of economic development, domestic elites gladly supported the integration process.[61]

By the mid-1970s, however, domestic and international conditions had changed. The OPEC oil embargo in 1973 had a detrimental effect on the economies of developing countries. Oil price increases hindered economic growth and plans for development in the Andean member economies, as in Latin America in general, and the resulting financial pressures impeded further programs for integration.[62] Moreover, OPEC member Venezuela's accession to membership of the Andean Group further complicated the situation, requiring readjustments and reviving debates on the group's rules and regulations regarding production, "sectoral programming," and intra-group relations.[63] Despite these difficulties, the Andean Group welcomed Venezuelan membership, and, for its part, Caracas strongly supported Andean integration because enormous increases in the nation's oil revenues also increased the available pool of capital for foreign investment. By the end of the 1970s, 45 percent of Venezuelan foreign investments were in the Andean region.[64]

During the same years, Chile's domestic crisis, following the U.S.-backed military coup against Salvator Allende (September 1973), jeopardized the Andean integration. The military government of General Agusto Pinochet, with U.S. economic advice, dismantled public social and economic programs and in their stead promoted market and "supply side" economics, considerably reducing the government's role in the economy. Pinochet's economic liberalization policies also included substantial reductions in tariffs and the relaxation of restrictions on foreign investments independently of the Andean Group. The Andean integration process began to falter when Chile demanded similar changes regarding the Common External Tariff (CET) to invite foreign corporations to the region. In the name of promoting greater integration, Chile demanded either the total elimination of the region's tariff protection or, at most, tariffs at levels of no higher than 45 percent. While this tariff cutting effort was compatible with Chile's domestic economic agenda to make the national economy accessible for outside investors, it undermined the protectionist components of the original Andean integration scheme. The ensuing conflict led to Chile's withdrawal from the group in October 1976.[65]

The renewed oil crisis of 1979 and the subsequent world recession in the early 1980s ended any serious hopes for the further deepening of the Andean integration. The economies of some Latin countries, such as Peru and Bolivia, were pulverized. Some governments, including the members of the Andean Group, were forced to borrow enormous sums from international banks and found themselves in total economic chaos. The financial collapse put political pressure on the leadership to pay closer attention to domestic economies and to seek domestic solutions for domestic problems rather than rely on multilateral integration arrangements.[66]

In the final analysis, the Andean Pact failed to achieve the same level of integration as the European Union because the economic conditions and the political climate did not permit member governments to comply with integration objectives. Bolivia, Peru, and Ecuador adopted economic development policies largely incompatible with regional integration and trade liberalization, and, by the mid-1980s, disagreements over industrial policies, tariffs, and rules governing foreign investments rendered the Andean Group impotent. In May 1987, the Quito Protocol sought to revive the group, but it changed the original rules of the game so drastically (for example, it eliminated the sectoral programs and the Common External Tariff) as to reduce the regional integration process to mere bilateral agreements. The 1989 Cartagena Manifesto restated the original agreement's requirement that all member states respect their integration commitments, and the Macchu Picchu Conference (May 1990) promised greater cooperation in national and regional economic policies, as well as in foreign debt negotiations. In fact, following the European model of regionalism, the Macchu Picchu Conference even promised to establish a common market and a directly elected Andean parliament. In December 1991, the Andean Group members signed the Acta de Barahona, followed by yet another agreement on the Common External Tariff in 1994. These agreements provided for the creation of a customs union and the removal of custom duties, as well as tariffs, on imports and raw materials.[67]

Despite these promising steps, however, there is little consensus regarding the future direction of the Andean integration system.[68] On the one hand, given that most efforts to develop regional integration in the developing world fail for similar domestic and international reasons, as Mace has pointed out, the fact that "the Andean Group still exists 25 years after its creation constitutes a certain measure of success."[69] Nevertheless, it is also clear that the Andean Group, faced with powerful international economic forces, has failed to achieve its original objectives of economic development and economic autonomy from the FIEs. "The Andean Group of the 1990s has little in common with the integration scheme established in 1969 whose main policy instruments had been completely abandoned for all practical purposes."[70]

East Asia

As the global trading system, once completely dominated by the U.S., completely eroded in the 1970s, East Asian countries also began to emphasize intra-regional trade with preferential investment and export policies among themselves to counter Western schemes. Japan and other East Asian countries hoped to devise some form of a regional multilateral system in East Asia parallel to existing regional and worldwide trading and financial systems, such as GATT and the Atlantic or European Community. They believed that such a regional arrangement was necessary, since they viewed the GATT-IMF-World Bank system as being dominated by the West. However, none of the countries, including Japan and China, yet had the capacity to emulate the United States as the major market for East Asian exports. Indeed, East Asian dependence on North American and European markets has persisted. A large share of East Asia's trade is with countries outside the region, and Asians tend to view such powerful and exclusive regional arrangements as the European Union and NAFTA as competition for their principal markets.[71]

One of the first proposals for a Pacific Free Trade Area was made by two Japanese scholars, Kiyoshi Kojima and Hiroshi Kurimoto, in 1965.[72] The Kojima-Kurimoto model sought to end all intra-regional tariffs and to lower non-tariff barriers. One organization to prepare at least a rudimentary structure for integration was the Pacific Basin Economic Council (PBEC), attempted in 1967 by multinational corporations. PBEC was supposed to have been based on membership first from the business community and later from interested governments. The close relationship between the two, it was hoped, would muster sufficient political support to begin regional economic cooperation and coordination of development strategies. Further, PBEC sought to expand the region's geographic boundaries to the southeastern rim of the Pacific and to extend membership to Mexican and Chilean companies. In the late 1970s, another and less comprehensive design by Saburo Okita, a Japanese analyst and later foreign minister, proposed to concentrate on developing common codes of conduct to regulate regional economic relations. Similarly, professors Hugh Patrick and Peter Drysdale proposed to establish a regional organization, the Organization of Pacific Trade and Development (OPTAD), to "draft codes of conduct to promote trade, investment, and foreign aid, and [provide] mechanisms for resolving regional trade disputes."[73]

Among the early organizations created in the 1960s was the Pacific Trade and Development Conference (PAFTAD, or PACTAD). Its first conference in 1968 proposed to begin negotiations for a Pacific free-trade area. Failing that, PACTAD proposed piecemeal strategies for economic development, including investment opportunities and encouragement of trade and technology transfer. More than a decade later, still another effort was made to form an Asia-Pacific economic organization, the Pacific Economic

Cooperation Council (PECC), in 1980. It also sought the membership of Latin American countries (for example, Chile, Mexico, and Peru), as well as China, Hong Kong, Taiwan, and Russia.[74]

Initially created for geo-political and security purposes in the wake of the Vietnam War, the Association of Southeast Asian Nations (ASEAN) gradually extended its interests in regional economic issues in the 1970s to encourage cooperation in investment and development, including some negligible reductions in tariffs among East Asian economies. Between 1977 and 1984, ASEAN invited the partnership of Japan, Australia, and New Zealand, expanding conferences, known as the ASEAN Post-Ministerial Conference (ASEAN-PMC), to include representatives from the United States, Japan, South Korea, Canada, Australia, and New Zealand, as well as the European Community.[75]

Thus, in the late 1980s and in the 1990s, the EU and NAFTA regional integration schemes caused considerable uneasiness, if not outright anxiety and apprehension, in East Asia, and provided a significant impetus for East Asian regional integration. With Asian economies built on a strong export emphasis, it was feared that a world trading system based on *regional* competition, especially if the EU and NAFTA discriminate against extra-regional trading partners, would allow at best minimum access to major markets and thus hinder East Asians' *national* economic development.

With these considerations in mind, in January 1992, the ASEAN Free-Trade Area (AFTA) was established to abolish tariffs on intra-regional trade during the next decade or so. More emphatically, it was intended to lure foreign investment "by promising that a foreign venture in any one ASEAN country will be able to export its output on a duty-free basis to all other members of ASEAN—a market totaling more than 300 million people."[76]

In 1990, also in response to the EC and NAFTA integration, Malaysia suggested yet another organization, the East Asian Economic Group (EAEG). This scheme would have refused membership to the United States and Australia. However, the proposal failed, although the subsequent creation of the ASEAN Free-Trade Area constituted an essential part of the design. In its stead, however, Asia-Pacific efforts produced the Asia Pacific Economic Cooperation (APEC), formed in 1989, as a major achievement in devising a regional order. Its founding members included the founding members of the PECC—the ASEAN members (Brunei, Indonesia, Thailand, Malaysia, the Philippines, and Singapore), the United States, Japan, Canada, Australia, New Zealand, South Korea, since 1991 China, Hong Kong, Taiwan (under the name Chinese Taipei), and since 1993 Papua New Guinea, Mexico, and Chile. The Seattle conference in 1993 promised a stronger APEC, and the meeting in Mogor, Indonesia in 1994 promised a free-trade region by the year 2020.[77] As with other multilateral regional efforts involving East Asian or Asia-Pacific integration and free-trade schemes, it is doubtful that APEC can deliver on all its promises. It has yet to define the concept of free trade within the context of the APEC model, and its inability to move beyond elementary definitions indicates the lack of political will—mainly due to domestic pressures—to develop closer trade relations.[78] It is difficult to tell whether the Asian economic crises of the late 1990s will make regional and trans-regional integration easier or more difficult. A number of Asian leaders, such as those in Malaysia, criticized the United States and the IMF for trying to dictate solutions to the region, and Washington in turn criticized them for failing to make both economic and political reforms.

Relatively lower levels of U.S. investment in East Asia have not helped the situation. For three decades after the Second World War, U.S. investments in the region were the primary source of investment capital and hard currency. While in the early 1950s and 1960s the United States and East Asian economies relied mostly on Europe for trade, East Asian intra-regional trade accelerated in the 1970s, and by the early 1980s approximately 60 percent of their total trade was within the region, exceeding the level of intra-regional trade in the European Community.[79] In the meantime, Japan emerged as one of the major economic powers in the world trading system, and the major source of investment capital for industrial development in a number of countries in the region, especially Indonesia, Thailand, and Malaysia.

However, Japan's role proved highly vulnerable when the currencies of these overblown economies collapsed in 1998. East Asian countries had experienced fundamental political, economic, and social changes, forcing domestic priorities on reluctant policymakers. As one scholar has pointed out, in such a climate "foreign policy could well become hostage to parochial domestic objectives, so that foreign policies could become less subtle and more amenable to compromise. The result could be domestic-driven and unintended heightened regional instability."[80]

The Asian economic crisis of 1997–1998 appears to have been a major setback for the future of such engagement, but it may also underscore the need for integration. Regional integration is not beyond the capabilities of these states.

Policymakers may take advantage of the absence of external threats and military tensions and devote their energies to the construction of regional institutions for economic development—the very dream of the "Bandung spirit." The current regional system, based on ASEAN, may facilitate further integration, and policymakers in the region at least appear to be interested in such schemes. In 1993, the ASEAN countries created the ASEAN Regional Forum (ARF) to develop a security arrangement.[81] As the ASEAN experience indicates, such concerns are not new in East Asia.

In the 1990s, the disintegration of the Soviet bloc and end of the Cold War brought other opportunities as well as challenges for East Asian integration. Former Cold War antagonists began to see each other as potential trading partners, export markets, and sources of investment. Thus, China improved relations with India, Vietnam, South Korea, and Mongolia. None, however, was so dramatic as the improvement of relations between the United States and Vietnam.[82] Other changes included Beijing's and Hanoi's membership in the UN, the IMF, the World Bank, the Asian Development Bank, and soon GATT.[83]

These changes are likely to produce additional schemes for regional and subregional economic cooperation, some deeply rooted in ancient regional identities. Robert Scalapino has labeled such networks of commercial activity as "natural economic territories" (NETs).[84] One is "Greater China," a potentially powerful financial-trade complex encompassing littoral China, Hong Kong (reincorporated into China), Taiwan, Vietnam, and Chinese capitalists throughout Southeast Asia. Other potential subregional economic networks in East Asia include (1) the Tyumen River complex, joining Russia, China, Korea, and the Sea of Japan; (2) the "Bohai Circle" linking China and South Korea; 3) the "Sijori Growth Triangle" linking Singapore, Malaysia, and Indonesia; and (5) the Mekong River area linking Thailand, Cambodia, Laos, and China's Yunnan province.[85] During the past decade or so, the governments of these countries have promoted regional cooperation as well as private initiatives as a means to achieve rapid economic development and inflows of foreign investments and and technologies.[86]

As in Western Europe, U.S. economic policies toward East Asian countries throughout the Cold War were intertwined with political and military strategies to contain Communist expansionism around the globe. This is where the Truman administration, the first U.S. administration to "militarize" containment,[87] fought the Korean War, the Eisenhower administration proclaimed the "domino theory," and the Kennedy, Johnson, and Nixon administrations fought the Vietnam War.

In the aftermath of the Cold War, however, the East Asian region is confronted with the dilemma of less U.S. security involvement, although naval forces and U.S. bases still operate in the area of Japan, Korea, and Taiwan. The collapse of the Soviet Union is said to have depreciated the region's geo-strategic value, yet Western policymakers are also paying close attention to China's possible emergence as a world power. Potential military tensions between mainland China and Taiwan across the strait is not totally inconceivable if the issue of the island's independence is placed on the agenda again. China also has territorial disputes in the rocky but potentially oil-rich Spratly Island group with a host of countries, including Vietnam, Malaysia, Indonesia, Taiwan, and the Philippines. Whether Korea can be reunified without bloodshed is another serious question, although the German reunification provides some optimism. North Korea's nuclear and military export policies are also matters of grave concern. In case of Asian military conflicts, the United States is likely to use the Gulf War model of multilateral engagement, which had been used previously in the Korean War. It remains to be seen whether Washington would include Beijing as a partner in such moves, as it did with Russia in Bosnia and Iraq, and whether U.S. economic interests in East Asia will decline. Normalization of U.S. relations with Vietnam, security ties to Japan, and the U.S. role in Asia Pacific Economic Cooperation (APEC) for purposes of trade and investment suggest that the United States is not prepared to disengage itself from the region.[88]

The Middle East

As noted in Chapter 2, Islam provides a religious and cultural basis for international cooperation and conflict, and the combination of Islamic and Arabic regional identity could rapidly move the Middle East toward greater economic integration. In the 1940s and 1950s, Arab leaders frequently referred to the desirability and necessity of Arab unity for regional economic and political strength, first to resist colonial powers and then against Israel. At the time, the chief theoretician of the Syrian socialist Ba'ath Party, Michel Aflaq, argued that "there was a single Arab nation, with the right to live in a single united state. It had been formed by a great historical experience, the creation of the Prophet Muhammad of the religion of Islam and the society which embodied it."[89] Over the years, the creation of the Arab League (first under British auspices), the Gulf Cooperation Council (GCC), the Organization of Arab

Petroleum Exporting Countries (OAPEC), and the UN Economic and Social Commission for Western Asia (ESCWA) to some extent reflected that vision of Arab unity. The functional scope and institutional depth of regional integration, however, has been limited. One of the major experiments to develop stronger integration was the short-lived unification of Syria and Egypt as the "United Arab Republic," from 1958 to 1961, headed by Gamal Abdel Nasser. As an expression of Arab independence from colonial domination and Communist threats, Nasser and his supporters in Egypt and Syria advocated a united Arab region, but serious disagreements and clashes of culture and national interests led to its quick demise.[90]

The Soviet collapse and the Israel-Palestine peace process (one of Israel's interests was a greater regional economic role) provided the impetus to redouble efforts at regional integration in the 1990s. The Middle East and North Africa Economic (MENA) Summit in Casablanca, Morocco, in 1994 was one of the first major steps toward that end. At a second summit in Amman, Jordan, in 1995, the participants agreed to establish a MENA Bank for Economic Cooperation and Development, headquartered at Cairo, Egypt; a Regional Tourism Board; a Regional Business Council; and the Economic Summit Executive Secretariat at Rabat, Morocco. The primary purpose was to encourage the development of the private sector, infrastructure, finance, trade, and tourism.[91] The 1996 MENA conference in Cairo, however, was less optimistic, given the difficulties in the peace process and Israel's restrictions on the Palestinian economy. Nevertheless, the participants, which by one count included 3,500 business and government officials from ninety countries, concluded $10 billion worth of agreements involving natural gas, medicine, "and even the sale of most of Egypt's state-owned Stella beer company."[92] As members of the ESCWA, the thirteen Arab countries (Bahrain, Egypt, Iraq, Jordan, Kuwait, Lebanon, Oman, Palestine, Qatar, Saudi Arabia, Syria, the United Arab Emirates (UAE), and Yemen) in the region have supported closer regional integration, but their success is likely to depend on oil prices in world markets, as ten of the thirteen members are oil-exporting countries. Some of them have relatively high per capita GDPs—for example, the UAE $18,500, Qatar $13,700, and Kuwait $12,900 in 1995. Their optimism in the mid-1990s reflected the region's economic growth by 2.8 percent in 1995 and the nearly 9 percent increase in oil prices, which increased the region's oil revenues from $71.8 billion in 1994 to $78.4 billion in 1995.[93] Prices plummeted, however, at the decade's end, threatening both the optimism and some of these receipts.

The ESCWA region's total value of exports increased from $96 billion in 1990 to an estimated $112 billion in 1995, but the export share of the Gulf states (Bahrain, Kuwait, Oman, Qatar, Saudi Arabia, and the UAE) also increased from 71 percent to 89.3 percent for the same period, Saudi Arabia accounting for nearly 50 percent of the exports by the Gulf states.[94] Intra-regional exports dropped, however, from 10.9 percent in 1990 to 4.2 percent in 1995, as did intra-regional imports from 9.1 pecent to 5.9 percent. The region's exports to other developing countries, however, increased from 29.3 percent of total exports in 1990 to about 37.8 percent in 1995.[95] A larger share (65 percent in 1995) of its imports were from the developed countries, mostly (33.9 percent) from the EU.[96] Imports from the United States accounted for 12.6 percent in 1990 and increased to 13.6 percent in 1995, while the figures for Japan dropped from 11 percent to 7.4 percent.[97]

While there have been some moves to diversify Middle Eastern economies, and certainly to invest oil earnings overseas, the region's dependence on oil and economic inequality among its members stand to jeopardize regional integration. A number of additional issues can impede further deepening of the integration process as well. While many Israelis see their advanced technologies as a potential engine for regional trade and modernization, the Israel-Palestine and Israeli-Syrian conflicts, if intensified, can, as before, raise the divisive regional tensions and pressures on states such as Lebanon, Jordan, Iraq, Egypt, and Saudi Arabia. Israel itself trades mostly outside the region. Equally divisive may be Arab relations with the West, particularly with the United States, especially if domestic pressures, such as heightened militancy by the Muslim Brotherhood, or renewed trouble with Iraq, Libya, or Syria threaten political stability. Egypt's reliance on U.S. aid and Saudi Arabia's permission to land U.S. forces in the country of the holy cities Mecca and Medina can potentially lead to serious crises in the region, as the bombing of the U.S. military compounds demonstrated. Finally, another issue is the question of regional leadership. The region's richest states—Saudi Arabia, Kuwait, the Gulf sheikhdoms—are among the weakest militarily. Saudi Arabia's role (similar to the centrality of South Africa in SADCC) can be crucial, but its ability to lead the region toward greater integration would ultimately depend on oil prices. Moreover, it is not likely that Egypt, Syria, Iraq, and even Jordan—though itself a monarchy—would easily accede to Saudi leadership. Thus, observers agree that greater regional economic integration in the Middle East requires domestic as well as international structural economic and political reforms, which heavily depend on the outcome of the Israeli-Palestinian peace process; the future of governmental succession and stability in key states such as Iraq, Syria, Egypt, and Israel; the nature of the relations among Middle Eastern countries (for example, with non-Arab powers such as Turkey and Iran) and in North Africa; and the region's relations with the East, the West, and the former USSR.[98]

The Former Soviet Bloc Countries

The collapse of the Soviet Union brought Russia and the former Soviet republics back into the international political economy as independent actors. The Central Asian republics, Kazakhstan, Kyrgyzstan, Tajikistan, Turkmenistan, and Uzbekistan, had been incorporated into the tsarist empire in the nineteenth century. Ukraine and the Caucasian republics of Armenia, Azerbeijan, and Georgia had been under Communist rule since the early 1920s, as the Bolsheviks consolidated power. The Baltic republics of Estonia, Latvia, and Lithuania were annexed during the Second World War, followed by the integration of East European countries into what became known during the Cold War as the Soviet bloc. The former Soviet bloc countries had no independent foreign trade policies with the outside world for more than fifty years and remained insulated from the capitalist world economy, although Hungary and to some extent Rumania sought to expand their relations with the West through experimental liberalization policies. Their economies were integrated into Moscow's Five-Year Plans as determined by the Kremlin and the Gosplan (State Planning Committee). The Communist Party held monopoly over all aspects of the Soviet economy, with little regard for local economic and environmental conditions. Soviet republics and allies were expected (similar to the functionalist and modernization theories espoused by the West) to transcend their ties to old traditions and differences in culture, religion, economy, and so forth and to cooperate with Moscow and among themselves toward the creation of the Communist society as envisioned by the political party elite in Moscow. The system's failure to democratize and to improve standards of living relative to the West eroded the legitimacy of the Communist Party and led to the open revival of nationalism. By the late 1980s, Gorbachev's *glasnost* and *perestroika* could not rein in the forces of nationalism and secession.[99]

Since independence, each successor state has had to compensate for its domestic economic inefficiencies, financial shortages, and for the twin scourges of unemployment and rampant pollution. One of the major challenges has been to guide the direction of the transition to some form of market or mixed economy, while maintaining economic, social, and political stability. The post-Soviet leaders are interested in trade and investment arrangements that include advanced industrial technology as well as foreign—namely, Western—partners in joint ventures for the local production of consumer goods and services. To that end, they have engaged in forming NETs to develop trade and financial links. In Russia and Central European and Asian successor states, government revenues and productive investments have been limited by ineffective tax collection and undeveloped banking systems. What lessons the former Soviet bloc countries can draw from, and what lessons their experiences provide for, the existing regional integration schemes, such as the EU, will undoubtedly be a hotly contested debate.[100]

At the regional level, the successor states have sought to reestablish ancient trade relations.[101] In Central Asia, the least developed area under Soviet rule, trade links date far back to the bygone centuries of the Silk Road, and, since the demise of the Soviet Union, economic, diplomatic, and even security ties among the Central Asian countries as well as with neighboring countries—for example, Turkmenistan and Iran, Kazakhstan and China, and Azerbaijan and Turkey—have developed fairly rapidly. Several factors contribute to their cooperative relationship. They share Turkic- and Persian-based languages, the religion of Islam, and the experience of exploitation and suppression under, and concurrent independence from, Moscow's rule.[102] The collapse of the Soviet Union made Islam a more powerful unifying force. Ethnoreligious affinities and shared historical experiences have facilitated the cultivation of economic ties in the region.[103] Some of the Islamic republics, particularly Azerbeijan, also enjoy very significant proven oil reserves and have attracted considerable Western investments. Russia itself, with 60 billion barrels of proved oil reserves, can join OPEC as the leading oil exporter in the world. However, whether Moscow will look with favor on Western governments and MNC oil companies setting up trade, transport, and distribution systems on Russia's doorstep remains to be seen.[104]

Despite recurrent ethnic disputes, in part fueled by unequal distribution of resources, the Caucasian republics have also experimented with similar efforts to revive ancient NETs. The Black Sea area has witnessed new efforts to create trade routes across the waters. In February 1992, the countries in the region—Armenia, Azerbaijan, Bulgaria, Georgia, Moldova, Romania, Russia, Turkey, and Ukraine—created the Black Sea Economic Cooperation

Region, to reduce trade barriers and encourage Western investments for economic development.[105] Territorial conflicts in the region, especially the Nagorno-Karabagh (Artsakh) conflict, however, have created a serious dilemma for some of the countries, such as landlocked Armenia.[106] While the latter welcomed the opportunity to participate in the regional cooperation with the hope of gaining access to the Black Sea, the Turkish-Azeri blockade led to the virtual shutdown of Armenia's (and Karabagh's) economy after independence.[107] Armenians, nevertheless, hoped to circumvent the blockade.

The emerging Caspian Sea Pact connecting Azerbaijan, Kazakhstan, Russia, and Turkmenistan for purposes of regional trade and cooperation in oil production is another example of post-Soviet regional economic cooperation, while the western, Baltic republics (Latvia, Lithuania, and Estonia) are likely to increase their economic ties with Poland and Germany.[108] Russia's role has been to intervene selectively to dampen or accelerate regional cooperation and conflicts and to maintain regional hegemony where possible. Ethnic Russians also experience fear as long-time residents of states now run by non-Russian majorities, with emerging ties to some of Russia's ancient enemies, such as Germany.

The Bering Sea region is also witnessing similar developments. The Kamchatka, Chukotka, and Magadan oblasts, Provideniye and Magadan, and the Petropavlovsk naval base are engaged with the U.S. and Canadian Pacific northwest in rapidly expanding economic relations, including direct airline services, joint ventures, and telecommunications networks.[109] Russians and the native peoples of the region view the Bering Sea NET as a revival of old regional economic and trade relations. Alaska and the Pacific Northwest were Russian colonial territories from the late 1700s to the mid-1800s. In 1867, Russia sold Alaska to the United States and directed its energies to develop the Amur and Ussuri regions, while trade between the western-northwestern United States with Siberian ports continued.[110]

Finally, Russia's far eastern regions—Primorsky krai, Khabarovsk krai, and Sakhalin oblast are in the early stages of developing transnational NETs with China, potentially extending to include their Korean and Japanese neighbors.[111] The region has enormous natural resources, a relatively large population, skilled labor, developed industries, and a transportation infrastructure, especially railroad networks, near to Pacific Rim industrial areas. The northern Pacific Rim is expected to attract foreign investors to develop and move toward closer integration that will benefit the local economies.[112] The skilled workforce in Khabarovsk, Komsomolsk-na-Amur, and Vladivostok—once the major manufacturing centers of the Soviet navy—electronic equipment, and aircraft may be used for joint ventures and conversion to consumer production.[113] Since 1992, the United States and Russia have been negotiating to establish a Pacific Rim air hub in Vladivostok to promote economic development and a free-trade region, while the oil industry, most prominently the MMM consortium, including Marathon Oil, Mitsui, McDermott International, and Royal Dutch Shell, are involved in the extraction of oil throughout the Sakhalin region.[114] As previously noted, one proposal for the region involves the Tyumen River complex, including China, Korea, Russia, and the Sea of Japan.[115] The region's raw materials and cheap labor, combined with Japanese and South Korean technology and capital, can create a vibrant North-East Asian economic community.[116] Expanding opportunities for European and U.S. FDIs may also provide opportunities to counterbalance Japan's and potentially China's quasi-hegemonic role in the Pacific Rim economies. One uncertainty for the continued development and expansion of such projects is the future of the market-oriented policies begun under Boris Yeltsin's government, but seriously threatened by economic meltdown in the late 1990s.

CONCLUSION

In contrast to the *realpolitik* assumptions of international affairs, the functionalist, neo-functionalist, and interdependence theories hold that cooperation among nations can be encouraged and institutionalized. Regional organizations serve as vehicles for multilateral cooperation in various areas of economy and then can expand to incorporate integrative political and security arrangements into the regional system. In the process, particularly if fostered by economic opportunity and democratic governments, they potentially channel nations' energies and resources into collaboration, thereby minimizing, if not eliminating, conditions and propensities that lead to conflicts and war.

Since the Second World War, a large number of countries have participated in regional integration schemes in the form of FTAs (free trade areas), customs unions, and common markets to stimulate national and regional trade and cooperation. At some level, regionalism has largely been a manifestation of geographic and cultural proximity. However, the inclination to join a regional group has tended to be in response to two general forces.

The first force was the global structure of power and economy as divided between industrialized and developing countries. For the former, regionalism was expected to enhance international competitiveness and world market shares. Regionalism in the form of the European Union intensified EU–North American competition in the advanced markets, and this competition also drew in Asian economies, as in the case of APEC.

Each region, however, has its own cultures, economic traditions, and dominant countries. The European Union is said to be a German-centered region, although the British, French, Italians, and Europe's smaller states would resent the geopolitical implications of such an arrangement. In response to EU integration, North America formed its own region, NAFTA—a partnership among highly unequal economies, which, despite considerable returns to Canada and Mexico, is dominated by the United States. Greater regional integration in Asia would appear to place Japan or ultimately China at the center of the regional economy, although the Asian crisis of 1997–1998 raised a host of questions regarding the viability of such a process.

Regionalism has been part of developing countries' overall effort to equalize the distribution of world political and economic power between themselves and the FIEs. Unable to counter the trade and financial policies of the governments and MNCs in industrialized countries, the developing countries opted for collective strength. Their record, however, has been mixed at best. While they have been somewhat successful in developing FTAs and customs unions, they have yet to achieve the degree of integration attained by the EU, although it is possible that the early decades of the new century will witness a more concerted effort toward greater institutionalization. This would require individual developing countries to form joint decision making institutions beyond mere trade and finance (perhaps on the order of a strengthened OPEC) but also to develop political institutions, such as regional courts and parliaments, harmonized policies regarding such issues as taxation, government spending and human rights, and to avoid the temptation of making separate deals with the industrialized world.

Such deepening of integration, however, is hindered by the second force influencing regional integration—namely, domestic political and economic considerations. Nations do not easily surrender their sovereignty to regional, supranational organizations. They are more likely to engage in regional integration schemes when domestic political and economic conditions require alternative policy strategies. Governments and companies tend to opt for greater regional cooperation when they expect political gains (expanding coalitions, solving unemployment problems), stronger competitiveness, and profits. Domestic and regional political and ethnic conflicts and wars also impede wider integration, although at times integration into large units can be seen as a cure for such conflicts; some saw the EU, a success story in Franco-German relations, as a long-term escape valve for Northern Ireland's conflicts, for example.

"Regionalization" construed as such, then, does not operate at the regional level alone. As experienced in the second half of the twentieth century, regionalism has been part of the globalization process, shaped and reshaped by the global economic conditions and geo-political power configurations. Regionalism connects the domestic with the global and vice versa; if it gains strength in the twenty-first century, as expected, it will remain delicately balanced between the forces of nationalism and globalization.

Chapter Summary

While the realist school of thought emphasizes the predominant role of conflict and war in international relations, the functionalist, neo-functionalist, and interdependence theories stress cooperation. They argue that international cooperation at the regional level needs to be cultivated through the institutionalization of integrative arrangements, in an incremental process, so as to develop lasting mechanisms necessary for regional peace and prosperity.

The building blocks for regional integration as experienced since the Second World War have been free-trade areas, customs unions, and common markets aimed at enlarging markets by removing barriers for the free movement of goods and people across national borders. Governments, supported by powerful interest groups, have adopted such policies to reverse economic stagnation, to address the problems of unemployment, and to enhance corporate competitiveness and profits.

In the late twentieth century, a number of regional economic groupings have emerged. The most important and successful regional integration scheme has been the European Union, which began to take shape in the 1950s. Currently, European market activities total about $4 trillion per year, and the region accounts for nearly 30 percent of the world's total GDP.

To enhance their competitive edge vis-a-vis the EU and East Asian economies, the United States, Canada, and Mexico created NAFTA in 1994. Unlike the EU, however, NAFTA is an economic arrangement, with little discussion to deepen it further into a political integration scheme. It is expected, however, that NAFTA will expand to include

Chile and other South American countries. The East Asian countries in the future may develop a similar regional economic bloc or blocs (some based on "natural economic territories"), but such a process in the region is in its earliest stages at best.

Regional economic blocs are also in their formative stages in AIE and LDE countries—in Latin America, the Middle East/North Africa, and Africa. Some of the former Soviet republics and Eastern European countries also have expressed interest in such arrangements.

However, development gaps remain between the FIEs and AIEs and especially the LDEs. In the world economy, the first group dominates financial and trade relations, while the last two remain peripheral, supplying raw material and cheap labor for the FIEs. The extent to which they can change the direction of their economies depends on domestic political and economic conditions, but, equally as important, it depends on the nature and structure of globalization. Trade among AIEs and LDEs constitutes a relatively low percentage of total world trade, as discussed in Chapter 5.

Regional integration schemes involve a series of tortuous stages. Experience since the Second World War suggests that integrative efforts are threatened by combinations of domestic economic and political considerations, market fluctuations, and political circumstances in the world political economy.

Points of Contention

How well do the functionalist and interdependence theories, as opposed to the realist theory of international relations capture the essence of international cooperation?

What are some of the assumptions underlying the stages of economic integration? How reliably does "spill over" work? Is "spill back" possible?

To what extent is it possible to view regionalism independently of globalization? What role does competition from other regions play in a region's integration?

What types of political and social conflicts are raised by free-trade areas (FTAs), customs unions, or common markets?

Can you think of alternative ways of achieving regional integration? Is integration more likely in good economic times or bad?

How does the integration of the European Union differ from the regional integration schemes in other areas, such as NAFTA and the Andean Group?

What are the challenges of regionalism to national sovereignty? How do they differ from the challenges of globalization?

How effective have the developing countries been in using regional integration to counter the economic advantages of the industrialized economies?

Notes

1. *The Economist,* September 2, 1995, p. 35.
2. Gustavo Vega Canovas, "Mexico, Latin America and the Group of Three in the Context of NAFTA," Donald Barry, with Mark O. Dickerson and James Gaisford, eds., *Toward a North American Community? Canada, the United States, and Mexico* (Boulder: Westview Press, 1995), p. 113.
3. Samuel P. Huntington, "Clash of Civilizations," *Foreign Affairs* 72, 3 (Summer 1993), p. 27.
4. Josef C. Brada and Jose A. Mendez, "Political and Economic Factors in Regional Economic Integration," *Kyklos* 46,2 (Summer 1993), pp. 183–201.
5. *The Economist,* September 16, 1995, pp. 23–27.
6. Leon N. Lindberg, *The Political Dynamics of European Economic Integration* (Stanford: Stanford University Press, 1963), p. 6.
7. Simon Payaslian, "The Inter-American Human Rights System: Charismatic Values and Regional Integration," *Journal of the Third World Spectrum* 4, 1 (Spring 1997), pp. 1–36. In the early 1990s, the Inter-American Commission conducted on-site observations and visits to the Dominican Republic, Guatemala, Haiti, Paraguay, and Peru and published reports on Chile, Cuba, El Salvador, Guatemala, Haiti, Nicaragua, Panama, Paraguay, and Suriname. Organization of American States, *Annual Report of the Inter-American Commission on Human Rights, 1989–1990,* OEA/ser., L/V/II.77, doc. 7, rev. 1, 1990; Organization of American States, *Annual Report of the Inter-American Commission on Human Rights, 1991,* OEA/ser., L/V/II.81, doc. 6, rev. 1, 1992. In the *Velásquez Rodrîguez* case, the Inter-American Court of Human Rights held the Honduran government responsible for the "disappearance" of Velásquez Rodrîguez and ordered the Honduran government to compensate his family. See Linda Drucker, "Governmental Liability for 'Disappearances': A Landmark Ruling by the Inter-American Court of Human Rights," *Stanford Journal of International Law* 25 (1988), pp. 289–322.
8. Hazel J. Johnson, *Dispelling the Myth of Globalization: The Case for Regionalization* (New York: Praeger, 1991), pp. 1–2.
9. *Ibid.,* p. 13.
10. Richard O. Cunningham and Anthony J. LaRocca, "Harmonization of Competition Policies in a Regional

Economic Integration," Symposium on Free Trade Areas: The Challenge and Promise of Fair vs. Free Trade, *Law and Policy in International Business* 27, 4 (Summer 1996), pp. 879–902.

11. Glen Atkinson, "Regional Integration in the Emerging Global Economy: The Case of NAFTA," *Social Science Journal* 35, 2 (April 1998), pp. 159–168; Kong Chu, "Regional Integration Efforts and Environmental Problems in the Third World," *Journal of Third World Studies* 13, 2 (Fall 1996), pp. 13–24.
12. Gordon Mace, "Consensus-Building in the Andean Integration System:1968–1985," in W. Andrew Axline, ed., *The Political Economy of Regional Cooperation: Comparative Case Studies* (London: Pinter, (1994), p. 43. See also Anthony Payne, "The Politics of Regional Cooperation in the Caribbean: The Case of CARICOM," in *Ibid.*, pp. 72–104.
13. Melton H. Spencer, *Contemporary Economics,* 2nd ed. (New York: Worth Publishers, 1974), p. 596. Jagdish N. Bhagwati, ed., *International Trade,* 2nd ed. (Cambridge: MIT Press, 1987).
14. *Ibid.*
15. Tariff theory deals with commodity-based tariffs (that is, discriminatory policy with respect to certain products) or geographically based tariffs (that is, discriminatory policy with respect to country of origin). FTA and customs union theories deal with the latter. The traditional or classical liberal theory of customs unions holds that, since free trade increases community welfare, lowering tariffs among trading partners stimulates free trade and economic growth. Various economic theories of trade regionalization, however, suggest mixed results for consumers and governments involved. A hypothetical model illustrates the dilemma in regional free-trade areas. Suppose two countries decide to eliminate tariffs on their goods but maintain tariffs on their other trade partners. On the one hand, their citizens gain from this arrangement because it creates more trade, as both countries import from each other products they used to import from others. On the other hand, some valuable trade is also excluded in the process because now the two countries import from each other goods they used to import from foreign but more efficient and perhaps even less expensive producers. This leads to higher prices for the consumers and loss of tariff revenues for the governments in both countries. Regional free-trade areas, however, have the advantage of geographical proximity and facility of developing closer trade ties than trade partners separated by thousands of miles. It remains to be seen whether highly advanced telecommunications satellites and computer systems, which are already bringing distant countries closer, will eventually be able to eliminate geographical distance as a factor in trade relations. Mace, "Consensus-Building in the Andean Integration System," p. 43; Richard Lipsey, "The Theory of Customs Unions: General Survey," in Bhagwati, ed., *International Trade,* p. 357; *The Economist,* September 16, 1995, p. 24.
16. Andre Sapir, "Regional Integration in Europe," *Economic Journal* 102 (November 1992), pp. 1491–1506.
17. *The Economist,* September 16, 1995, p. 24.
18. *Ibid.*, pp. 23–27.
19. Gretchen M. MacMillan, "Managing Economic Convergence in the European Union," in Barry, eds., *Toward a North American Community?* p. 228.
20. Stephen D. Krasner, *"Structural Conflict: The Third World against Global Liberalism,"* (Berkley: University of California Press, 1985), p. 181.
21. See Francisco Orrego Vicuña, "El Control de las Empresas Multinacionales," *Foro Internacional* (Mexico City), 14, 1 (July-September, 1973), pp. 109–128. Translated by Sylvia Modelski, In George Modelski, ed., *Transnational Corporations and World Order* (San Francisco: W.H. Freeman, 1979), pp. 300–302. See also Mace, "Consensus-Building in the Andean Integration System," in Axline, ed., *Political Economy of Regional Cooperation,* pp. 51–52.
22. MacMillan, "Managing Economic Convergence in the European Union," p. 227.
23. *Ibid.*, pp. 250–251.
24. Evan H. Potter, "The Impact of European Economic Integration on North America: Adjustment Versus Radical Change," in Barry, ed., *Toward a North American Community?* p. 253.
25. Alan Riding, "9 East Europe Nations to Join Round Table Talks," *The New York Times,* May 28, 1994, p. A4.
26. Philippe Martin, "A Sequential Approach to Regional Integration: The European Union and Central and Eastern Europe," Internet, November 1994.
27. Potter, "The Impact of European Economic Integration on North America," pp. 250–251.
28. See Gary Clyde Hufbauer and Jeffrey J. Schott, *North American Free Trade* (Washington, D.C.: Institute for International Economics, 1992); Potter, "The Impact of European Economic Integration on North America," p. 244.
29. Hufbauer and Schott, *North American Free Trade.*
30. Potter, "The Impact of European Economic Integration on North America," p. 244.
31. In the early phases of the European integration process, Canada's relations with the European Community *qua* community were negligible, and Canada clearly lacked the political leverage enjoyed by the United States. In the late 1960s, trade disputes at GATT negotiations between Canada and the EC concerning the latter's restrictive Common Agriculture Policy (CAP) underscored Canada's failure to establish more accessible trade routes to the EC via such multilateral forums. Bilateral trade relations further deteriorated as the EC reduced its tariffs on some

imports from its Mediterranean and African trade partners, while maintaining CAP restrictions. *Ibid.*, pp. 244–246.

32. See Charles Pentland, "Europe 1992 and the Canadian Response," in Fen Osler Hampson and Christopher J. Maule, eds., *Canada Among Nations, 1990–1991* (Ottawa: Carleton University Press, 1991); Fenny S. Demers and Michael Demers, "Europe 1992: Implications for North America," in the same volume.
33. Potter, "The Impact of European Economic Integration on North America," pp. 244–245.
34. *Ibid.*, pp. 246–248.
35. *Ibid.*, p. 251.
36. *Ibid.*
37. *Ibid.*
38. *Ibid.*
39. *Ibid.*
40. *Ibid.*, pp. 242–243.
41. Donald Barry, "Introduction," in Barry, ed., *Toward a North American Community?* p. xi.
42. *Ibid.*, p. 15.
43. *Ibid.*
44. Joachim Bamrud, "Setting the Agenda: From Miami to Brazil," *Latin Trade* (June 1997), p. 3A.
45. WTO, *Focus*, no. 28 (March 1998), p. 3.
46. For different perspectives, see Hufbauer and Schott, *North American Free Trade;* Mario F. Bognanno and Kathryn J. Ready, eds., *The North American Free Trade Agreement: Labor, Industry, and Government Perspectives* (Westport CT. : Praeger, 1993).
47. Gustavo del Castillo, "Convergent Paths Toward Integration: The Unequal Experiences of Canada and Mexico," in Barry, ed., *Toward a North American Community?* pp. 96–97.
48. Potter, "The Impact of European Economic Integration on North America," p. 242; Gilbert R. Winham and Heather A. Grant, "NAFTA: An Overview," in *Ibid.*, pp. 15–31; Kathryn J. Ready, "NAFTA: Labor, Industry, and Government Perspectives," in Bognanno and Ready, eds., *The North American Free Trade Agreement,* pp. 3–52.
49. For a general overview, see Inter-American Institute of International Legal Studies, *The Inter-American System* (Dobbs Ferry, NY: Oceana Publications, 1966).
50. "Inter-American Development Bank Predicts Renewed Push for Economic Integration in Latin America," IMF Survey, December 10, 1984, p. 369; "The Mercosur Countries are Potentially a Huge Market," *Business America,* March 23, 1993, p. 8; Laurie MacNamara, "Andean Region Makes Integration Effort," *Business America,* March 23, 1992, p. 5. See also J.W. Sloan, "Lafta in the 1960s: Obstacles to Progress," *International Development Review* XIV (1972), pp. 16–25; Miguel S. Wionczek, "The Rise and Decline of Latin American Integration," *Journal of Common Market Studies* IX (September 1970), pp. 49–67; Miguel S. Wionczek, ed., *Latin American Economic Integration: Experiences and Prospects* (New York: Praeger, 1966).
51. See, for example, Aldo Ferrer, "Self-Reliance for Self-Determination: The Challenge of Latin American Foreign Debt," in Alaf Gauhar, ed., *Regional Integration: The Latin American Experience* (London: Third World Foundation, 1985), pp. 88–97.
52. See, for example, Victor Bulmer-Thomas, "The Central American Common Market: From Closed to Open Regionalism," *World Development* 26, 2 (February 1998), pp. 313–322; Pablo Rodas-Martini, "Intra-Industry Trade and Revealed Comparative Advantage in the Central American Common Market," *World Development* 26, 2 (February 1998), pp. 337–344.
53. W. Andrew Axline, "Introduction," in Axline, ed., *The Political Economy of Regional Cooperation,* pp. 1–4.
54. United Nations, *World Economic and Social Survey, 1997,* Table A.15, p. 246.
55. "Latin American, Caribbean Nations Set Ties," *Facts on File,* 54, 2806 (September 8, 1994), pp. 630–631.
56. Roberta Maynard, "At Crossroads in Latin America," *Nation's Business* 84, 4 (April 1996), pp. 38–42.
57. *Ibid.*
58. MacNamara, "Andean Region Makes Integration Effort"; Mace, "Consensus-Building in the Andean Integration System, 1968–1985," in Axline, ed., *Political Economy of Regional Cooperation,* pp. 34–38.
59. Mace, "Consensus-Building in the Andean Integration System," pp. 42–43.
60. *Ibid.*, pp. 44–46.
61. *Ibid.*, pp. 46–50.
62. See Thomas E. Skidmore and Peter H. Smith, *Modern Latin America* (New York: Oxford University Press, 1984); Eliana Cardoso and Ann Helwege, *Latin America's Economy: Diversity, Trends, and Conflicts* (Cambridge: MIT Press, 1992).
63. Mace, "Consensus Building in the Andean Integration System," p. 50.
64. *Ibid.*, p. 52.
65. Venezuela and Peru vehemently opposed the elimination of tariff protection, since their industries required high tariffs to survive. Their governments had historically supported economic nationalism, industrialization, and import substitution strategies. Initially, Colombia was willing to support Chile's proposal, as long as a compromise would save the integration. However, since Chile did not appear to be in a compromising mood, Colombia changed its policy and refused to support Chile in further negotiations. Bolivia and Ecuador appeared to be interested in lower tariffs; the former supported Chile's proposals, since the level of their industrialization was insignificant. In the end, Chile completely withdrew from the Andean Group, and during the

rest of the 1970s the integration process stood still. *Ibid.*, pp. 53–56; R. Vargas-Hidalgo, "The Crisis of the Andean Pact: Lessons for Integration Among Developing Countries," *Journal of Common Market Studies* XVII, 3 (March 1979), pp. 219–222.

66. The situation was exacerbated by the border clashes between Peru and Ecuador in 1981, and the change in the leadership in Bolivia. The Andean Group almost expelled Bolivia after a military coup by General Garcia Meza. Although Bolivians reestablished civilian rule, they were clearly disillusioned with respect to the Andean integration process. Mace, "Consensus-Building in the Andean Integration System," pp. 56–57, 60.
67. Hernan Anzola, "NAFTA's Little Sister," *International Economy* 6, 2 (March-April 1992), pp. 32–33.
68. Mace, "Consensus-Building in the Andean Integration System," pp. 60–61.
69. *Ibid.*
70. *Ibid.*
71. Michael G. Plummer, "ASEAN and the Theory of Regional Economic Integration: A Survey," *ASEAN Economic Bulletin* 14, 2 (November 1997), pp. 202–214; Robert S. Ross, "Introduction: East Asia in Transition," in Robert S. Ross, ed., *East Asia in Transition: Toward a New Regional Order* (Armonk, NY. : M.E. Sharpe, 1995), p. xv; Robert Gilpin, "Economic Change and the Challenge of Uncertainty," pp. 3–20, in the same volume.
72. See Harry Harding, "International Order and Organization in the Asia-Pacific Region," in Ross, ed., *East Asia in Transition,* pp. 331–336.
73. *Ibid.*
74. *Ibid.*
75. *Ibid.*, pp. 331–336.
76. *Ibid.*, p. 348.
77. *Ibid.*, pp. 350–351.
78. See, for example, Barry Eichengreen, "Is There a Monetary Union in Asia's Future?" *Brookings Review* (Spring 1997), pp. 33–35.
79. Harding, "International Order and Organization in the Asia-Pacific Region," pp. 333–336.
80. Ross, "Introduction," p. xviii.
81. *Ibid.*, p. xix.
82. Danny Unger, "From Domino to Dominant: Thailand's Security Policies in the Twenty-First Century," in *Ibid.*, p. 240.
83. Harding, "International Order," p. 340.
84. Robert Scalapino used the term, *natural economic territories* to "describe the phenomenon of previously isolated but adjacent border regions reaching across international boundary lines to achieve collective economic gains from pooled capital, labor, and raw material markets." Robert Scalapino, "Northeast Asia—Prospects for Cooperation," *Pacific Review* 5, 2 (1992), pp. 101–102; Robert A. Scalapino, "The United States and Asia: Future Prospects," *Foreign Affairs* 70, 5 (Winter 1991–92), pp. 20–21. See also James Clay Moltz, "Breaking with Moscow: The Rise of Trade and Economic Activity in Former Soviet Border Regions," in Deborah Anne Palmieri, ed., *Russia and the NIS in the World Economy: East-West Investment, Financing, and Trade* (Westport, CT: Praeger, 1994), p. 98.
85. *Ibid.*, p. 340; Mark Valencia, "Economic Cooperation in Northeast Asia: The Proposed Tumen River Scheme," *Pacific Review* 4, 3 (1991), p. 263.
86. P.J. Rimmer, "Regional Economic Integration in Pacific Asia," *Environment and Planning* 26, 11 (November 1994), pp. 1731–1759.
87. James A. Nathan and James K. Oliver, *United States Foreign Policy and World Order,* 3d ed. (Boston: Little, Brown and Company, 1985).
88. Ramesh Thakur, "Asia-Pacific After the Cold War," and William T. Tow, "Regional Order in Asia-Pacific," in Ramesh Thakur and Carlyle A. Thayer, eds., *Reshaping Regional Relations: Asia-Pacific and the Former Soviet Union* (Boulder, CO: Westview Press, 1993), pp. 1–26, 261–284.
89. Albert Hourani, *A History of the Arab Peoples* (New York: Warner Books, 1991), pp. 404–405.
90. Amitai Etzioni, *Political Unification* (New York: Holt, Rinehart, 1965); see also, Malcom H. Kerr, *The Arab Cold War: Gamal' Abdul-Nasir and his Rivals, 1958–1970* 3rd ed. (London: Oxford University Press, 1971).
91. UN, Economic and Social Commission for Western Asia, *Survey of Economic and Social Developments in the ESCWA Region, 1995* (New York, United Nations, 1996), p. 30.
92. Eileen Alt Powell, The Associated Press, November 14, 1996.
93. *Survey of Economic and Social Developments,* p. 21.
94. *Ibid.*
95. *Ibid.*, p. 51. The region's exports to other developing countries changed slightly with the developed economies, from 55.7 percent to 55.9 percent for the same period.
96. *Ibid.*
97. *Ibid.*
98. Dirk Vandewalle, "The Middle East Peace Process and Regional Economic Integration," *Survival* 36, 4 (Winter 1994), pp. 21–34.
99. Moltz, "Breaking with Moscow," p. 98.
100. See, for example, Leslie Budd, "Regional Integration and Convergence and the Problems of Fiscal and Monetary Systems: Some Lessons from Eastern Europe," *Regional Studies* 31, 6 (August 1997), pp. 559–570.
101. Lee Kendall Metcalf, "The (Re)Emergence of Regional Economic Integration in the Former Soviet Union," *Political Research Quarterly* 50, 3 (September 1997), pp. 529–549.
102. Graham E. Fuller and Ian O. Lesser, *Turkey's New Geopolitics: From the Balkans to Western China* (Boulder, CO: Westview Press, 1993); Graham E. Fuller, *The Center*

of the Universe: The Geopolitics of Iran (Boulder, CO: Westview Press, 1991); Jo-Ann Gross, *Muslims in Central Asia: Expressions of Identity and Change* (Durham, NC: Duke University Press, 1992).

103. Moltz, "Breaking with Moscow," p. 99.
104. Edward N. Krapels, "The Commanding Heights: International Oil in a Changed World," *International Affairs* 69, 1 (1993), pp. 71–88.
105. Omer Faruk Genchkaya, "The Black Sea Economic Co-Operation Project: A Regional Challenge to European Integration," *International Social Science Journal* 45, 4 (November 1993), pp. 549–558.
106. See Levon Chorbajian, Patrick Donabedian, and Claude Mutafian, *The Caucasian Knot: The History and Geo-Politics of Nagorno-Karabagh* (London: Zed Books, 1994).
107. *The Economist,* April 10, 1993, p. 58.
108. Moltz, "Breaking with Moscow," p. 100.
109. Alaskan companies have established more than eighty joint ventures in Siberia. Caterpillar, for example, has secured contracts to sell advanced heavy machinery, while the Rural Alaskan Television Network broadcasts to the Chukotka and Magadan regions. See *Ibid.*, pp. 101–2.
110. *Ibid.* See also Yereth Rosen, "Alaskans Capitalize on Closeness to Russia," *The Christian Science Monitor,* May 11, 1992, p. 9.
111. Amos A. Jordan and Jane Khanna, "Economic Interdependence and Challenges to the Nation-State: The Emergence of Natural Economic Territories in the Asia-Pacific," *Journal of International Affairs* 48, 2 (Winter 1995), pp. 433–462.
112. Moltz, "Breaking with Moscow," p. 102.
113. *Ibid.*
114. "Royal Dutch Joins Group to Study Sakhalin Fields," *The New York Times,* October 1, 1992, p. D4.
115. Clayton Jones, "Asian Neighbors Plot New Hub," *The Christian Science Monitor,* May 19, 1992, p. 4; Lincoln Kaye, "A Very Special Zone," *Far Eastern Economic Review,* May 14, 1992, p. 32.
116. While in South Korea, Yeltsin stated that "Russia is boldly opening its Far Eastern frontiers. . . . A zone of regional economic cooperation with Northeast Asia and the northern half of the Pacific as a whole could be created." As quoted in Moltz, "Breaking with Moscow," pp. 105–106.

CHAPTER SEVEN

THE POLITICS OF MULTINATIONALISM AND CAPITAL FLOWS

In the mid-1990s, more than 10,000 large and small **multinational corporations (MNCs)** owned and operated more than 90,000 subsidiaries worldwide. The United States was the home for the 500 largest industrial corporations, followed by Japan (111), Great Britain (43), and Germany (32).[1] The fifteen major industrialized countries were the base, or "home" country, to 26,891 MNCs, accounting for 69 percent of the world's total 38,747.[2] Increasingly, MNCs from developing countries are also expanding their operations. Playing a central role in the globalization of the world economy, MNC production and intra- and inter-industry trade activities across international borders allow them easy access to wealth and resources in different regions of the world,[3] with considerable impact on national economies.[4] As the world political economy becomes increasingly interdependent, MNCs accumulate greater political power vis-à-vis individual governments[5] to the extent that, as economic historian Charles Kindleberger has claimed, "the nation-state is just about through as an economic unit . . . [as] the multinational corporation is evolving into the international one faster than national governments are girding themselves to produce adequate policies to meet it."[6] Or, at least, as noted in previous chapters, while the nation-state may not necessarily be on the verge of extinction as an economic entity, MNCs do pose an unparalleled challenge to its sovereignty.[7]

Through their operations, MNCs provide transnational mechanisms facilitating greater international cooperation and functional integration. MNC operations have increased substantially since the 1950s and 1960s; a considerable part—over 65 percent—of world foreign direct investments (FDIs) have taken place in Western economies. FDI in developing countries also increased, from $6.0 billion in the early 1970s, to $12.8 billion in the early 1980s, to nearly $70 billion in 1996.[8] In the 1990s, MNCs have provided a considerable portion of employment around the world and about 25 percent of total world output,[9] with a substantial share of the labor force (about 40 percent) of MNC foreign affiliates in developing countries with lower wages.[10]

The principal objective of most corporations is to minimize operating expenditures and maximize profits. MNCs prefer, therefore, to invest in countries with minimum regulatory and financial burdens, and governments in need of foreign capital and technology provide various tax incentives and public goods and services to attract such investment.

Globalization and global competition require vast communications networks to develop sufficiently integrated and uniform design, production, and marketing capabilities. For many years, Ford has produced what it calls the global car, the Ford Escort, and its various facilities are directly linked via worldwide interactive computer and video networks; cars are produced with parts from different countries and assembled at regional locations. MNCs use such production and investment opportunities to gain control over certain sectors of industry and local markets. Multinational corporations, such as General Electric and Gillette, operate on the belief that they are or could be the number one or two producer of a specific product on the global market, or they will sell that product line. Gillette company leaders proudly note their company's ability to shift production from one country to another to avoid wage increases or to meet market demands. Others, such as Unilever and Nestlé, try to maintain a balance between local tastes and global competitiveness.[11] Effective accumulation and use of knowledge are key to successful corporate management and competition, and MNCs increasingly have the advantage of using worldwide resources and talents. Dallas-based Texas Instruments established computer facilities in Bangalore, India; (Oregon) Beaverton-based Nike produces shoes in the Philippines; and Stockholm-based Electrolux moved into Italy to take advantage of local knowledge, tastes, and designs.[12]

At times, MNCs try to thwart pressures for greater local political or economic control over operations or for modification of national taxation policies by the host government.[13] Sometimes MNCs successfully manipulate the host to their advantage, but their record has been mixed. To counter MNCs' financial and negotiating power, individual governments and the international community, particularly moved by the experiences of developing countries, have developed various national and international codes of MNC behavior.

MULTINATIONAL CORPORATIONS AND MULTINATIONALISM: SOME CONCEPTS AND CONSIDERATIONS

Scholars have debated how to define and what to call multinational corporations. Some prefer to call them "multinational enterprises," others "transnational corporations," and still others "international corporations." For the purposes of this text, multinational corporations are defined as producers of goods and services based on implicit or explicit contractual arrangements extending over national boundaries and operating under more than one sovereign government.[14] This definition stresses some of the key characteristics of and considerations and controversies involving MNCs, including ownership, the role of employees as *producers,* the costs, a variety of *goods and services,* and the issue of national *sovereignty.*

One consideration relates to *ownership and labor. Ownership* refers to individuals who directly or indirectly control the corporation. With the rise of giant companies in the seventeenth century, but especially since the late 1800s, the nature of ownership experienced major transformations. Single family ownership and management of major international businesses was common into the twentieth century. The operation involved at least the more mature and business-oriented members of the family, and they extended their operations across continents, largely relying on each other for technical and market support. Members of the Lazard family, the Rothschilds, or the Fabers had confidence in and loyalty toward family members, and personal interest in the company, although they might also have paid homage to the states in which they lived or operated. Also, their employees closely identified with the family, working for the "Lazard House" or the "House of Rothschild." Such loyalty might have been rewarded with long-term job security. Even in the modern age of global MNCs, family-owned enterprises remain active, as in the case of some Asian firms, owned by "overseas Chinese" families, for example (see Table 7.1).

Increasingly, however, exclusive family ownership of large MNCs declined, and ownership became separated from management as family firms became public companies, in which outside investors bought shares of stock in the enterprise. Investors, regardless of family relations or country of origin, provided the capital for various enterprises around the world, and professional managers were delegated the responsibility of managing the firm, mobilizing and allocating resources, and assuring as much profit on investments as possible. The newly emerging arrangement substantially widened the pool of available capital, but it also made business operations less personal. No longer was employee loyalty a significant factor, except, perhaps, in such countries as Japan, with a modified system of "lifetime employment." For stock owners, managers came to be viewed as instruments for the accumulation of wealth; for managers, employees were potentially replaceable instruments of production or resource extraction (in Nazi Germany, of course, this reached a psychotic extreme with the use of slave labor and the use of death camps).

A related consideration is the *international division of labor* MNCs tend to perpetuate. Employees in the richer industrialized countries enjoy far better working conditions and wages and are generally engaged in more capital-intensive, high-tech-oriented employment than are employees in developing countries. Employees in Sweden and Germany earn on average about $24 an hour and in the United States, France, Britain, and Japan $15–$17 an hour. Their counterparts in the so-called middle-income developing countries, such as South Korea, earn between $2 and $4 per hour, while wages in poorer countries, such as China, Haiti, and Thailand, are less than $1 per hour. The poorer countries offer sufficient incentives for labor-intensive industries—involving assembly, for example—to attract MNC operations.[15]

Another controversy concerns the costs and benefits of MNC operations. Generally speaking, on the positive side, MNCs contribute to society's economic development and

TABLE 7.1
Overseas Chinese Families

	Base	Main company	Businesses
Cheng Yu-tung	Hong Kong	New World Development	Property, telecoms, infrastructure
Kwok Brothers	Hong Kong	Sun Hung Kai Properties	Property
Lee Shau Kee	Hong Kong	Henderson Land	Property, convention centers
Li Ka-shing	Hong Kong	Cheung Kong	Property, telecoms, ports, energy
Eka Tjipta Widjaja	Indonesia	Sinar Mas	Paper, timber, banking, food, chemicals, property
Liem Sioe Liong	Indonesia	Salim Group	Food, cement, property, consumer goods
Prajogo Pangestu	Indonesia	Barito	Timber, paper, cars
Lim Goh Tong	Malaysia	Genting	Casinos, mining, theme parks, hotels
Robert Kuok	Malaysia	Kerry	Sugar, property, media, hotels, drinks, food
Quek/Kwek family	Mal./Sing.	Hong Leong	Property, hotels, banking
Lucio Tan	Philippines	Fortune Tobacco	Brewing, tobacco, airlines, hotels, banking
Chang Yung-fa	Taiwan	Evergreen	Shipping, airlines
Tsai family	Taiwan	Cathay Life Insurance	Insurance, property
Yue-Che Wang	Taiwan	Formosa Plastics	PVC, petrochemicals, semiconductors
Sophonpanich family	Thailand	Bangkok Bank	Banking, insurance, stockbroking
Chearavanont family	Thailand	Charoen Pokphand	Agriculture, food, telecoms, aquaculture, property, beer
Lamsam family	Thailand	Thai Farmers Bank	Banking, trading, agribusiness, insurance

Source: The Economist, March 9, 1996.

provide opportunities for employment and growth. MNCs bring to a country, in the form of foreign direct investments (see Box 7.1), various types of technologies for infrastructural development and services not readily available in most societies. Proponents of classical laissez-faire liberalism, therefore, contend that host governments should provide MNCs as much freedom as possible to maximize the profitability of their operations, which in turn would bring greater wealth and prosperity to the host country. For example, Beijing, the seat of one of the few Communist regimes left in the post–Cold War world, has invited MNCs to China to stimulate economic modernization and growth.

However, there are also costs of MNC operations. Critics note that, contrary to laissez-faire perspectives, investment operations frequently lead to various problems in the home and host societies. Globalization has meant that corporations can easily abandon their existing plants and employees in search for greater cost-cutting, profit-maximizing opportunities elsewhere.[16] As an MNC establishes a branch in a host country, it begins to meddle in the host country's domestic political and economic affairs to secure the safety and profitability of operations. To achieve their objectives, MNCs have been using strategies ranging from simple lobbying to bribery of local officials, to "divide and conquer" techniques, and even to the mobilization of military forces to protect their interests. In fact, the initial process of MNC-host government negotiations to establish a branch in the first place may involve a combination of these strategies. Moreover, the end-products of MNC activities in the host country, it has been argued, are the exploitation and perpetuation of poverty rather than prosperity (for example, when an MNC exhausts local bank capital by soaking up available loans), along with dependence on foreign MNC leadership and decisions made at MNC headquarters. These issues have led to heated

BOX 7.1

FOREIGN DIRECT INVESTMENTS

Foreign investments are assets in one country acquired by companies or individuals from another country. Foreign investment is the instrument through which the MNC brings capital into another country, and the MNC is the single most important instrument for foreign investment. In 1993, MNCs invested about $232 billion worldwide, and, according to one estimate; by 2020 their investments are expected to increase at least fourfold. There are two general types of foreign investments: direct investments and portfolio investments. *Foreign direct investments (FDIs)* are investments by one company in another for the purpose of securing some control over and profits from that company. *Portfolio investments,* on the other hand, are purchases of shares (stocks) in another company for purposes of profit but not control. FDIs, the more important of the two, are direct investments by a company establishing subsidiaries, or licensing local companies, in another country. FDIs can play an important role in a society in which individual savings are low and which cannot provide the capital necessary for future investments at home. Foreign investments, then, provide the capital needed to stimulate the economy. FDIs may also be used to finance a balance-of-payments deficit in which domestic demand for foreign goods from one country exceeds exports to that country.

Sources: See Peter Hertner and Geoffrey Jones, eds. *Multinationals: Theory and History,* (Aldershot: Bower Publishing Co., 1986).; *The Economist,* "Multinationals," [survey] June 24, 1995, p. 6.

theoretical debates regarding the nature and impact of MNCs. The following section reviews some of the major theories of multinationalization.

THEORIES OF MULTINATIONALIZATION

In addition to the major theories of international political economy presented in Chapter 2, a number of "micro-level" theories are geared to explain corporate behavior and multinationalization.[17] The most obvious explanation is maximization of profit. (The laissez-faire and Marxist theories, as well as their theoretical derivatives, for example, agree that the primary motive for corporate activities and expansion is profit.) To that end, corporations often are organized to integrate and coordinate "interdependent activities linked by flows of intermediate products."[18] Corporations internally and vertically extend their operations to integrate various segments of production processes, to avoid the costs and uncertainties associated with the external and imperfect market. That is, rather than trade with other producers and suppliers, the corporation minimizes the costs involved in market transactions and produces the parts and products itself in various advantageous locations.[19] Cost cutting considerations also work in the opposite direction, however, driving some MNCs, as in the auto industry, to give up their own production units and purchase parts or subassemblies from outside sources, a process known as "outsourcing."

A number of factors are involved in calculus of multinationalization. Locational considerations lead to multinationalization, as a company expands its operations overseas for reasons of geographical location and access to natural and human resources. In this respect, technological advancements, especially telecommunications technologies, have significantly contributed to multinationalization. Regarding public policy, the home and host country's domestic legal and political environment (for example, lack of strict regulatory policies), taxation, and social and economic conditions are critical in determining whether and the extent to which a company locates abroad. A politically stable country, with an educated but reasonably priced workforce that can provide a flexible legal environment with minimal constraints on export and import activities attracts MNCs.[20] Organizationally, a company's leaders have to be internationally oriented, rather than parochial, and the organization must possess the command and communication structure necessary for direct and effective communication and management between the company headquarters and affiliates abroad.

According to Hymer, corporations also internationalize their operations to enhance their *market power.*[21] A corporation first expands its operations in the home economy and seeks to maximize its domestic market share through monopolistic and oligopolistic practices, such as acquisitions and mergers. If successful these practices allow a firm to dictate prices. One of the main characteristics of domestic markets, however, is that they have certain limitations in terms of geography, size, and demography. Corporations overcome these constraints by investing in foreign markets, often with similar monopolistic and oligopolistic strategies. They establish production facilities in countries that can provide market structures amenable to corporate sales and concentration of power, as well as provide cheap labor so as to minimize costs of production, thus leading to international division of labor.[22]

In the early stages of the industrial revolution, the primary mode of international division of labor concentrated on the control and extraction of raw materials from the developing countries to fuel industrialization in the first industrialized economies (FIEs), while trade in manufactured goods also increased. The late nineteenth and early twentieth centuries saw the continued expansion of industrial production in as well as trade among the FIEs, but it also included trade of manufactured and agricultural goods between the FIEs (as the "core") and the developing countries (the "periphery"). As the Marxists and *dependencia* theorists have argued, however, the periphery continued to provide cheap raw materials and agricultural produce for the FIEs, while the core advanced toward greater industrial and technological development, leading to the current world structure characterized by unequal economic development.[23]

In the 1970s, an increasing number of analysts, including Fröbel, Henrichs and Kreye, and Palloix, argued that the older theories regarding international division of labor are no longer adequate, since MNCs have increased their direct investments in manufacturing facilities in the developing countries, giving rise to new industrial centers around the world, such as the new industrialized countries (NICs) of Taiwan and South Korea.[24] As a result, there has emerged a "new international division of labor" no longer limited to extraction of raw materials for the FIEs but also involving the production of manufactured goods in developing countries, leading to globalized production. This new development has encouraged greater industrialization and modernization in a number of developing countries, referred to as advanced industrializing economies (AIEs). Previously considered peripheral, now they are among the more advanced economies, with higher levels of GDPs and a wider industrial base.

Critics of the "new international division of labor" theory have argued that internationalization of MNC operations involves more than mere pursuit of cheap labor. Other considerations—such as home and host government policies and host market capacity—also contribute to internationalization. Companies thus widen their operations *horizontally* as they compete internationally for larger market shares in both developed and developing countries. MNCs also *vertically* expand their operations to other countries in which resources are located to minimize production or transportation costs.[25]

The *monopolistic theory* of multinationalization, proposed by Charles Kindleberger, contends that theories stressing MNC access to cheap labor and markets do not adequately explain why companies in host countries fail to benefit from such advantages.[26] Kindleberger maintains that U.S.- or Europe-based MNCs expand horizontally and vertically because they command control over certain "monopolistic advantages" that local companies in host countries lack. These may include more advanced technology, management and training skills, marketing skills, and the ability to produce new products and components. Marketing skills have contributed significantly to U.S. corporate successes in goods and services ranging from life insurance to pharmaceuticals to farm machinery to retailing in European and Asian markets for most of this century. Monopolistic expansion across national borders leads to horizontal integration, while external economies of scale lead to vertical integration.

The *product life cycle theory,* as advanced by Raymond Vernon, Mark Casson, and others, holds that continuous innovation in MNC products and the management of uncertainty and price-warfare in the market are the fundamental ingredients for long-term success. As most products have a short life span, companies must integrate new technologies to "update" their products or run the risk of becoming obsolete.[27] The product life cycle consists of five phases: introduction, growth or development, maturity, decline, and obsolescence.[28] Historically, the first phase has invariably taken place in the advanced industrial countries, affording them the advantages of monopoly over new technologies and markets in the world economy. On growth and maturity of the product and consolidation of the domestic market, corporations transfer their operations to other countries to take advantage of market and labor opportunities, as the previously mentioned theories also have stressed. Thus, successful companies overcome markets' geographical constraints in two ways: technological innovations or upgrades to avoid product obsolescence, or by convincing buyers that they need new models.[29] The best examples are the auto and the computer industries. The former has virtually invented a tradition of introducing new models each year, now modified and emulated by Microsoft and others in the computer industry, as seen in the wide publicity given to "Windows 95," "Windows 98," and so forth. Technological innovation, and its creative marketing, thus, become essential for competitiveness and for company survival.[30]

Critics have pointed out that, while the product life cycle theory may explain some MNC decisions to set up foreign subsidiaries, it fails to explain the complex nature of MNC operations in the globalized world economy.[31] For example, it does not adequately explain why a large share of the FDIs are among the FIEs; nor does it explain why U.S. and European FDIs in the developing world have disproportionately concentrated in a small number of developing countries. It also fails to explain the increase in European and Japanese FDIs in the United States.[32] Further, the product life cycle theory assumes that product initiation and innovation occur only in the FIEs and spread outward to developing countries, therefore failing to take into account that in a globalized production system subsidiaries in some advanced developing countries (such as the NICs) also may be sources of product initiation and innovation.[33] Given that the theory focuses primarily on manufacturing production, it also ignores the internationalization of services.[34] In fact, Vernon has noted that, as MNCs develop global networks of production subsidiaries, the product life cycle model increasingly fails to explain FDI flows between the United States and other FIEs, as well as those between the FIEs and developing countries.[35]

Finally, John Dunning's *eclectic paradigm* of international production incorporates several theoretical models to develop a more comprehensive explanatory framework. Dunning identified three conditions necessary for a corporation to internationalize its operations. The first involves *ownership-specific advantages* over competitors. These include tangible and intangible assets, such as product innovation, organizational and marketing skills, technical know-how, experience, and technological capabilities (for example, in production and marketing). These advantages enhance the competitive edge of the older corporations vis-à-vis new competitors and virtually accord it monopoly power.[36]

The second of Dunning's determining factors consists of *internalization-incentive advantages.* Internationalization of operations requires a certain degree of security and stability in operations. Accordingly, corporations seek to avoid costs and risks associated with the imperfect market and to internalize operational and market activities by extending their own network of operation to other countries (hence, vertical and horizontal integration) rather than licensing local firms to do the production or marketing. In so doing, an internationalizing corporation hopes to avoid the uncertainties and costs involved in the search for suppliers and labor, to avoid government barriers (for example, tariffs and quotas) to marketing, and to maintain control over the use of its own technology and greater flexibility in pricing as market competition may require.[37]

The third principal ingredient in Dunning's model consists of *location-specific variables.* When a corporation can mobilize the previously noted advantages, it must possess — or anticipate—certain locational advantages to determine where to set up shop. Influencing decisions with respect to location may be a combination of such factors as labor, access to natural resources, transnational transportation and communication costs, availability of a large host market, availability of infrastructure, accommodative government policies, and overall economic or political environment.[38] Wherever possible, locational decisions are made with an eye toward enhancing the diversification of operations and marketing so as to avoid dependence on a single country, a single labor force, or a single market.[39]

Dunning's eclectic paradigm has a number of advantages. Its greatest merit is in its ability to draw together the various theories of MNCs that separately lacked theoretical coherence. Moreover, the theoretical framework is not necessarily ideologically driven.[40] Laissez-faire theorists would praise the paradigm for underscoring the freedom in MNC decisions to locate and relocate their foreign plants. They would argue, however, that the eclectic paradigm fails to consider liberalism and market perfection as the most essential contributing factors to MNC and economic growth. In fact, laissez-faire theorists would criticize Dunning for his integration of Marx's theories of ownership and what is referred to now as internalization advantages and innovation.

On the other hand, Marxists might contend that the paradigm pays insufficient attention to class relationships and to the extent to which MNCs exert their dominant power over the poorer economies and workers. They would agree more with the international division of labor and monopolistic theories and their implications for markets and labor.

Mercantilist, or neo-statist, theorists would criticize these paradigms for failing to consider adequately the power of the state and state-advantages in cooperating with MNCs. It is, after all, the host government that decides whether or not foreign corporations may set up a plant or office within its jurisdiction. What incentives does the host state—leaders and bureaucracies—have in permitting foreign MNCs to establish branches on its territory?

From the perspective of Islam, these theories, even when they address issues of economy and power in corporate-state and corporate-society relations, fail to consider religion as a contributing factor to internalization and locational advantages. As such, they appear too Eurocentric or

U.S.-centric in their formulations. The ideal Islamic firm is expected to maximize its as well as society's welfare, not only through competition and profit but also through the moral obligations of charity and compassion. The firm is expected to produce only those goods that contribute to the general welfare of the community, regardless of profit considerations.[41] High-pressure marketing, with sexually explicit and glitzy advertising, would be strongly condemned, for example. These are clearly idealistic constructs. However, the expansion of international activities by corporations from Muslim societies in the 1980s and 1990s has underscored the growing relationship between such corporations and the presence of Muslim communities in host countries. The proliferation of Middle Eastern and Asian owned stores—as seen in major Western cities, for example—has brought a range of products from canned food to music through transnational distribution networks, yet the shop owners also have encountered local resentment and have been accused of cultural intolerance. To what extent do modern theories of multinationalization account for such factors of conflict?

Perhaps the most severe criticism of these paradigms would come from the feminist perspective. Feminists might criticize these theories of multinationalization as virtually ignoring gender equity as a factor. These models say little regarding the relationship between the globalization of production and "the gendering of the workforce." The international division of labor theory focuses primarily on the nature of division of labor between the FIEs and the developing AIE and LDE countries, but it does not consider division of labor between men and women— as, for example, in differential pay scales or "glass ceilings" limiting job advancement and promotions.[42] While the other theories consider such issues as corporate-state relations, they fail to account for the impact of such relations on women as wage earners and as family members, with great institutional (or structural) inequalities that translate into lower wages, less education, physical abuse, lack of child care, birth control restrictions, and subordination to men.[43]

THE RISE AND REACH OF MNCs AND FOREIGN DIRECT INVESTMENTS

Business historians trace the origins of modern multinational corporations to the international affairs of medieval banks. MNCs rose in the seventeenth and eighteenth centuries, during a period of national industrial and economic growth as the nation-state was consolidating power over territory, population, and economy, and firms eventually served as instruments of colonial expansion abroad. Governments and companies operated through mutually supportive mercantilist strategies. Companies emphasized "command-and-control management" in the hands of a small elite and production and distribution processes in foreign investments in mining and marketing activities, which employed thousands of workers in highly centralized and rigidly hierarchical organizational settings.[44] The international trading companies of the seventeenth and eighteenth centuries, such as the Dutch and British East India Companies and the Hudson's Bay Company, were the predecessors of twenty-first-century MNCs.[45]

By the second half of the nineteenth century, major companies had established manufacturing and mining facilities and had become significant players in the world political economy. While prior to the First World War European MNCs dominated the world economy, U.S. companies grew at a rapid pace during the period between the 1880s and 1920s and, after the Second World War, emerged far more powerful than their European counterparts. Truly global MNCs, however, did not emerge until the 1950s and 1960s, with the advent of advanced communication technology. By the early 1970s, Japanese, South Korean, Brazilian, German, and French MNCs began to challenge the preeminent position U.S. companies had held since WWII, setting the stage for the subsequent global competition.[46]

Before the First World War in 1914, multinational corporations had established large networks of extraction and distribution facilities outside of their home countries (see Box 7.2). MNCs from the most advanced countries—Great Britain, the United States, Germany, and France—accounted for about 87 percent of foreign investments worldwide. Approximately 63 percent of their investments were in the developing countries, mostly in Latin America and Asia.[47] Two patterns in MNC activity emerged by 1914. The first consisted of investments to furnish the home economy with raw materials. Generally, the host countries were less developed—at the time, "colonial territories"—but were endowed with vast natural resource reserves. MNC activities mostly (that is, nearly 85 percent immediately before the outbreak of WWI) involved the development of local infrastructure, such as railroads, utilities, and ports, to facilitate communication and the transportation of personnel, goods, and services between the home and host countries. The other type of MNC operations was market-oriented,

BOX 7.2

THE ORIGINS OF FIRMS FROM VARIOUS MAJOR POWERS

Countries that have long and intensive involvement in international operations are likely to become involved in such operations more frequently. The Europeans gradually surpassed the Asians in distant explorations because the former enhanced and more effectively used navigation technology, which ironically was originally imported from East Asia. By the seventeenth and eighteenth centuries, the combination of navigation and military technologies was a powerful mix in the hands of increasingly internationally oriented European leaders. Modern worldwide exploration dates back to the Portuguese and Spanish conquerors in the fifteenth century and later the Dutch. By the early eighteenth century, the British, due to some extent to their location but largely because of geo-political competition, had followed suit. However, the British became involved with greater zeal and energy because they had the added advantage of industrialization, which helped London use industrial technology for navigation and military purposes. Thus, Britain could expand and consolidate its worldwide empire. The British were also the first to introduce "chartered companies," the predecessor of the modern multinational corporation. British companies were involved in various sectors, including the extraction of resources (minerals and crops), transportation and utilities, and banking and commerce. In the 1860s and 1870s, such British giants as Unilever (and its Dutch partners), Courtaulds, Dunlop, Pilkington, Imperial Chemical Industries, British Petroleum, and Burmah Oil began to expand their production activities, processing and packaging, in other regions of the world, extending from the Americas to Asia to Africa.

The French empire, like its British counterpart, facilitated the expansion of French companies in new investment ventures and markets throughout the world. The empire created vast financial networks to provide capital for industrial development and expansion. By the late 1890s, French multinational companies had considerable investments in neighboring European countries, such as Germany, as well as in tsarist Russia, the Ottoman empire and the rest of Asia, Africa, the Pacific area, and the Caribbean. French corporate expansion intensified briefly at the turn of the century and after the First World War, but the Great Depression and the devastation caused by the Second World War postponed its development until after the war.

Major German corporations emerged during the years of economic unification after 1833 under the *Zollverein* system, and, with the unification of Germany under Chancellor Otto von Bismarck, German economic expansion and industrialization accelerated. Both Bismarck and his contemporary German business leaders showed international aspirations. They sought to make Germany a major player in European and global geo-politics and, in the 1880s, in competition with the British and the French, began to acquire colonial territories abroad in Africa and the Pacific. The state and corporations, thus, worked closely to expand the German empire. At the same time, as factories increased their output, companies developed better integrated organizational managerial systems from production to marketing. They were, in fact, better-managed corporate institutions than their British and French counterparts and, unlike the British, cultivated close relations between university training and corporations. Soon, led by some of the major companies, such as Siemens and Bayer, companies also established large cartels (or syndicates, trusts) to set prices and production limits and to regulate first domestic and then international distribution and marketing policies. Siemens and AEG had established themselves in South America; German locomotive companies were built in Italy and Russia; Mannesmann Tube factories were built in Britain, Austria-Hungary, and Italy and held substantial investments in the United States. The Deutsche Bank, the Commerzbank, and the Dresdner Bank worked closely with and played a major role in the financing and development of major companies. They mobilized savings and capital for corporate investments at home and abroad.

In addition to these major economies, some of the smaller countries also witnessed the emergence of their MNCs in the late nineteenth century. Italy's Pirelli had facilities in Britain, Spain, and as far away as Argentina. Swiss MNCs—such as CIBA and Geigy (chemical products), Brown Boveri (electrical products), Hoffman La Roche (medical products), and Nestlé and the Anglo-Swiss Condensed Milk Company—had investments throughout Europe and the United States.

In crucial areas, however, the British and French fell behind in the global competition with the United States. British companies' overseas operations reflected their family firm–oriented

involving investments in manufacturing and market distribution. Such activities, however, were found mainly in the more industrialized countries or countries in the process of rapid industrial growth, such as Russia.[48]

The case of the United States is particularly instructive, as illustrated by the Gillette Company's experience presented in Box 7.3. New inventions patents in the United States were fewer than 1,000 in the 1840s. By the late

BOX 7.2 (concluded)

THE ORIGINS OF FIRMS FROM VARIOUS MAJOR POWERS

structure at home. In the United States, on the other hand, the vast land required wider production and distribution capabilities and, therefore, more structured managerial hierarchies. Thus, while the British companies internationalized, their managerial apparatus was ill-suited for globalization; when the U.S. companies internationalized, their managerial infrastructure and experience were already in place. U.S. company leaders placed a greater emphasis on large-scale organizational planning, efficiency, and short- and long-term forecasting techniques to design not only their products but also their own internal production facilities and institutional management procedures. In the United States, near the end of the nineteenth century, company and community leaders established major universities, such as the Massachusetts Institute of Technology, to develop a cadre of highly trained technicians with varied expertise in engineering (machinery, electric, chemical) and business management. In Britain, such formal training in management or technical expertise did not fully develop until well into the 1950s.

As in the European experience, U.S. corporations expanded their operations first in the domestic market and then increasingly became international. Unlike their European counterparts, however, companies in the United States had a vast domestic market for the rapid accumulation of profits but also experienced the necessary structural evolution and adaptation to large markets. Since colonial times, scarcity of labor relative to land and capital compelled corporations to develop technological techniques and innovations to compensate for such scarcities with as much efficiency as possible. Major U.S. corporations, such as Singer, developed the institutional knowledge and administrative structure ready to be exported to foreign countries at the first opportunity to expand their investments in potential markets (such as in Europe) and production of resources (as in the developing world).

In Asia as well, some of today's multinational corporations, such as Korea's Samsung and the Japanese Mitsui trading company, the *sogo shosha,* have a long history, some dating back to the seventeenth century. With traditions of Confucianism, Japan's corporate and political leaders placed great emphasis on education and economic and military strength. Under the Tokugawa shogunate (1603–1868), the Japanese had already laid the foundations for close networks between business and government. However, the shoguns' inability to defend Japan against Western military technology and trade led to revolution against the Tokugawa dynasty and to the Meiji Restoration. In the early Meiji period (1868–1912), Japanese leaders decisively moved to strengthen the country's infrastructure, education, and technology to compete more successfully with the West. As in the United States, they adopted educational policies developing greater integration with businesses for rapid and efficient industrialization.

The Japanese infrastructural and technological development included massive expansion of the communications system throughout the central business districts and an emerging, powerful shipping industry under the Mitsubishi Company. As with European empires, the Meiji supported and used navigational capabilities to expand their territorial control—over Taiwan and the Korean peninsula, for example. As in the British case, Japanese companies were far more family-based than those of the French or Germans. However, unlike the British, but very much like German and U.S. companies, the Japanese family-based firms established close family partnerships, leading to huge conglomerates, or *zaibatsu,* in addition to government-corporate relationships. Government-business partnerships also enabled major Japanese companies to establish joint ventures with foreign companies, as in the case of Sumitomo, Mitsui, Mitsubishi Electric, American-Japan Sheet Glass, and Dunlop Rubber (Far East). These joint ventures led to the emergence of Japanese multinational corporations, even prior to World War II.

Sources: See Dennis M.P. McCarthy, *International Business History: A Contextual and Case Approach* (Westport, CT: Praeger, 1994), pp. 38–53, 217–219; Peter Hertner and Geoffrey Jones, eds., *Multinationals: Theory and History* (Aldershot UK: Gower, 1986), pp. 6–9; L. Franko, *The European Multinationals* (London, 1976), pp. 8–10; J.M. Stopford, "The Origins of the British-Based Multinational Manufacturing Enterprises," *Business History Review* (1974), pp. 303–335.

1850s, that number had increased to 5,000, to over 20,000 in the 1860s, to 40,000 by the late 1890s, and to about 70,000 by 1914 before the First World War. By then, as Table 7.2 shows, the United States had clearly established its predominance in the area of technological advancement. Among the four major Western economies, U.S. inventions accounted for 13.2 percent in 1800, 22.5 percent in 1850, 37.7 percent in 1900, and 46 percent in 1914.

MNC PROFILES: THE GILLETTE COMPANY

THE GILLETTE COMPANY

OVERVIEW

Is Warren Buffett a blade man, or does he use a shaver? Either way, The Gillette Company (of which Buffett's Berkshire Hathaway owns about 9%) has what he needs. Boston-based Gillette is the world's #1 maker of shaving supplies, offering razors and shavers for men and women. Buffett can also use Gillette's Paper Mate or Parker pens to jot down a shopping list of products (building sales and enhancing shareholder value), which might include an Oral-B toothbrush and dental floss, Right Guard deodorant, White Rain shampoo, Duracell batteries, and Braun shavers and appliances. If he makes a mistake, he can fix it with Liquid Paper correction fluid.

And big as it is stateside, Gillette is even bigger abroad: Almost two-thirds of sales are made overseas. The company meets its goal of maintaining the #1 or #2 spot in each of its markets by buying complementary companies and implementing vigorous research and development operations (it spends more than 2% of its sales on research). Gillette's newest introduction, perhaps the holy grail of smooth shaving, is the Mach3 triple-bladed razor.

WHEN

In 1895 King Gillette, a salesman for Baltimore Seal, originated the idea of a disposable razor blade while shaving with a dull straight razor at his home in Brookline, Massachusetts. For the next six years, Gillette developed his idea yet could find no backers. Finally, in 1901 MIT machinist William Nickerson joined Gillette and perfected the safety razor. With the financial support of some wealthy friends, the two men formed the Gillette Safety Razor Company in Boston.

Gillette put his safety razor on the market in 1903 but sold only 51 sets. The good news spread fast, however, and the next year Gillette Safety Razor sold 90,844 sets. Gillette established his first overseas operation in London in 1905. Five years later Gillette sold most of his interest in the business (he remained president of the company until 1931) to pursue his utopian corporate theories, which he had first described in his 1894 book *The Human Drift.*

Gillette Safety Razor sold shaving kits to the US government during WWI. In the 1920s the company distributed free razors through such outlets as banks (via the "Shave and Save" plan) and boxes of Wrigley's gum. The tactic brought millions of new customers. During the Depression, Gillette Safety Razor began sponsoring major sporting events. Its many sponsorships became known as the "Cavalcade of Sports" and carried its advertising worldwide.

The company began diversifying in 1948 by purchasing Toni (home permanent kits), which became the Personal Care Division in 1971. In the 1950s Gillette adopted its present name, introduced Foamy (shaving cream, 1953), and bought Paper Mate (pens, 1955).

During the 1960s and 1970s, the company expanded its product line further by introducing Right Guard (deodorant, 1960), Trac II (twin-blade razors, 1971), Cricket (disposable lighters, 1972; sold to Swedish Match, 1984), Good News (disposable razors, 1975), and Eraser Mate (erasable pens, 1979). It also acquired Braun (electric shavers and appliances, 1967) and Liquid Paper (1979). In 1984 Gillette branched into dental care products with the purchase of Oral-B.

Flat sales and profits led to a takeover bid two years later by financier Ron Perelman. Gillette's 1989–1990 purchase of the UK's Swedish Match (Wilkinson Sword razors) was derailed in 1991–1992 as both governments opposed the high market shares the acquisition would have given Gillette.

Alfred Zeien took over as CEO in 1991 and gave each Gillette business the goal of seizing or maintaining the #1 spot in its market. The company continued to expand its product base through the 1990s and found success in foreign markets. Gillette bought the Parker pen business in 1993. By 1996, 41% of sales came from products that had not existed five years before. Gillette also made acquisitions, but only in sectors where it could operate as the #1 or #2 player. That year the company acquired #1 battery maker Duracell.

In 1997 new products included a two-bowl-system food processor, a next-generation instant ear thermometer, and an electric shaver designed for younger men. After six years of preparation, an investment of roughly $1 billion, and much secrecy, in 1998 Gillette unveiled the triple-bladed Mach3 razor in an effort to maintain its overwhelming share (over 70%) of the US disposable razor and blade market. Duracell introduced its new Ultra alkaline batteries that year, which it claims can last 50% longer than regular batteries.

WHO

Chairman and CEO: Alfred M. Zeien, age 68, $3,416,667 pay
VC and Chief Legal Officer: Joseph E. Mullaney, age 64, $770,000 pay
President and COO: Michael C. Hawley, age 60, $1,358,333 pay
EVP, Gillette North Atlantic Group: Robert G. King, age 52, $723,750 pay
EVP, Diversified Group: Jacques Lagarde, age 59, $360,000 pay
EVP, Duracell North Atlantic Group: Edward F. DeGraan, age 54
EVP, International Group: Jorgen Wedel, age 49
SVP Finance and CFO: Charles W. Cramb, age 51
SVP and General Counsel: John M. Coleman, age 48
SVP Personnel and Administration: Robert E. DiCenso
Auditors: KPMG Peat Marwick LLP

WHERE

HQ: Prudential Tower Bldg., Boston, MA 02199
Phone: 617-421-7000 **Fax:** 617-421-7123
Web site: http://www.gillette.com

The Gillette Company sells its products in more than 200 countries and territories and manufactures them at 64 locations in 26 countries.

1997 Sales & Operating Income

	Sales $ mil.	Sales % of total	Operating Income $ mil.	Operating Income % of total
US	3,682	37	899	38
Western Europe	2,966	29	718	30
Latin America	1,219	12	309	13
Other regions	2,195	22	455	19
Adjustment	—	—	(57)	—
Total	**10,062**	**100**	**2,324**	**100**

WHAT

1997 Sales & Operating Income

	Sales $ mil.	Sales % of total	Operating Income $ mil.	Operating Income % of total
Blades & razors	2,881	29	1,186	51
Duracell products	2,478	25	526	22
Braun products	1,744	17	304	13
Toiletries & cosmetics	1,410	14	124	5
Stationery products	924	9	156	6
Oral-B	624	6	85	3
Other	1	—	—	—
Adjustments	—	—	(57)	—
Total	**10,062**	**100**	**2,324**	**100**

Selected Brand Names

Advantage
Atra
Braun
Dry Idea
Duracell
Good News
Gripper
Liquid Paper
Mach3
Oral-B
Paper Mate
Parker
Pro Plus
Right Guard
Satin Care
Sensor
Soft & Dri
Trac II
Ultra Floss
Waterman
White Rain

KEY COMPETITORS

American Safety Razor
BIC
Bristol-Myers Squibb
Colgate-Palmolive
Johnson & Johnson
Moulinex
Perrigo
Pfizer
Philips Electronics
Procter & Gamble
Ralston Purina
Rayovac
Remington Products
SmithKline Beecham
Sunbeam
Unilever
Warner-Lambert

HOW MUCH

NYSE symbol: G FYE: December 31	Annual Growth	1988	1989	1990	1991	1992	1993	1994	1995	1996	1997
Sales ($ mil.)	12.2%	3,581	3,819	4,345	4,684	5,163	5,411	6,070	6,795	9,698	10,062
Net income ($ mil.)	20.4%	269	285	368	427	513	288	698	824	949	1,427
Income as % of sales	—	7.5%	7.5%	8.5%	9.1%	9.9%	5.3%	11.5%	12.1%	9.8%	14.2%
Earnings per share ($)	16.8%	0.31	0.34	0.40	0.49	0.58	0.25	0.82	0.95	0.83	1.25
Stock price - FY high ($)	—	6.13	6.22	8.16	14.03	15.31	15.94	19.13	27.69	38.88	53.19
Stock price - FY low ($)	—	3.64	4.13	5.44	7.05	10.97	11.84	14.44	17.69	24.13	36.00
Stock price - FY close ($)	31.9%	4.16	6.14	7.84	14.03	14.22	14.91	18.72	26.06	38.88	50.22
P/E - high	—	20	18	20	29	26	64	23	29	47	43
P/E - low	—	12	12	14	14	19	47	18	19	29	29
Dividends per share ($)	16.1%	0.11	0.12	0.14	0.15	0.18	0.21	0.25	0.29	0.35	0.42
Book value per share ($)	—	(0.11)	0.09	0.33	1.29	1.66	1.62	2.22	2.76	3.98	4.25
Employees	4.5%	29,600	30,400	30,400	31,200	30,900	33,400	32,800	33,500	44,100	44,000

STOCK PRICE HISTORY

HIGH/LOW/CLOSE

1997 FISCAL YEAR-END

Debt ratio: 23.4%
Return on equity: 29.9%
Cash (mil.): $105
Current ratio: 1.78
Long-term debt (mil.): $1,476
No. of shares (mil.): 1,121
Dividends
Yield: 0.8%
Payout: 33.6%
Market value (mil.): $56,294

Source: Reprint with permission from Hoover's Online, www.hoovers.com

TABLE 7.2
Major Inventions, Discoveries, and Innovations by Country, 1750–1950 (as a Percentage of Total)

	Total	Britain (%)	France (%)	Germany (%)	USA (%)	Others (%)
1750–1775	30	46.7	16.7	3.3	10.0	23.3
1776–1800	68	42.6	32.4	5.9	13.2	5.9
1801–1825	95	44.2	22.1	10.5	12.6	10.5
1826–1850	129	28.7	22.5	17.8	22.5	8.5
1851–1875	163	17.8	20.9	23.9	25.2	12.3
1876–1900	204	14.2	17.2	19.1	37.7	11.8
1901–1914	87	16.1	8.0	17.2	46.0	12.7
1915–1939	146	13.0	4.1	13.0	58.6	11.3
1940–1950	34	2.9	0.0	6.7	82.4	8.8

Source: John H. Dunning, *Explaining International Production* (London: Unwin Hyman, 1988), p. 90.

Great Britain, on the other hand, declined continuously after the initial surge during the industrial revolution. While France and Germany also experienced increases in inventions during the first half of the nineteenth century, both were in the process of decline by the turn of the century. The U.S. (and, to a lesser extent, the French and German) comparative advantage was in such products as motor vehicles, electrical products, and chemicals—areas in which the British were falling behind.[49]

As Dunning reminds us, it is precisely such timely changes in a country's production and market structures for trade, symbolized by patent statistics, that are more indicative of *its competitiveness* in the world economy than its share of world trade per se. Structural adjustments to changing technological conditions develop and sustain fundamentally more stable and long-term dominance in world markets, while rapid growth in a country's share of world trade without the attendant structural adjustments are merely temporary competitive advantages soon displaced by competitors.[50]

The First World War disrupted normal international economic affairs and led to realignments in the globalwide MNC power structure. Political instability and changes in international boundaries caused major European firms to sell some of their investments and substantially reduced intra-European corporate operations. The Bolshevik Revolution in Russia and the fear of government expropriation (that is, **nationalization**) of privately owned companies virtually terminated MNC activities. The post-WWI world economy nevertheless recovered and witnessed an enormous expansion in MNC activities, with the exception of German MNCs, during the inter-war years, particularly among U.S. firms.[51]

The world economy witnessed rapid and unprecedented levels of MNC expansion immediately after the Second World War, which accelerated even more so during the following two decades. By the mid-1960s, the number of major MNCs' foreign subsidiaries had increased tenfold from that of the 1920s and sixfold from that of the immediate post-WWII period.[52] In 1969, there were about 7,276 parent MNCs headquartered in the fifteen major Western industrialized countries, and, by 1993, that number had reached 26,891.[53] Technological developments and national and international trade liberalization policies contributed to this proliferation. Expansion occurred in an extremely competitive environment, as more and more countries began to challenge U.S. corporate hegemony in world markets (see Table 7.3).

Increasingly, as new technologies and international production and service structures amplified MNC tendencies toward globalization, important differences became apparent in regional distribution of FDIs. A substantial portion of MNC expansion occurred in the Western industrialized societies. In the 1960s, when U.S. MNCs held nearly 50 percent of FDIs worldwide, the number of their affiliates increased from about 7,000 to well over 23,000, and the value of U.S. FDI increased from $32.8 billion in 1960 to $86 billion in 1971.[54] By the late 1960s, the United States accounted for nearly 69 percent of research and development (R&D) in the industrialized economies, while Britain accounted for 7.3 percent, Germany 6.3 percent, France 6 percent, and Japan 4.7 percent, a fact that increasingly

TABLE 7.3

The Top 100 MNCs Ranked by Foreign Assets, 1995 (Billions of Dollars and Number of Employees)

Ranking by					Assets		Sales		Employment		
Foreign Assets	Index[a]	Corporation	Economy	Industry[b]	Foreign	Total	Foreign	Total	Foreign	Total	Index[a]
1	17	Shell, Royal Dutch[c]	United Kingdom/ Netherlands	Oil, gas, coal, and related services	79.7	117.6	80.6	109.9	81,000	104,000	73.0
2	83	Ford Motor Company	United States	Automotive	69.2	238.5	41.9	137.1	103,334[c]	346,990	29.8
3	87	General Electric Company	United States	Electronics	69.2	228.0	17.1	70.0	72,000	222,000	29.1
4	22	Exxon Corporation	United States	Oil, gas, coal, and related services	66.7	91.3	96.9	121.8	44,000	82,000	68.8
5	86	General Motors	United States	Automotive	54.1	217.1	47.8	163.9	252,699	745,000	29.3
6	27	Volkswagen AG	Germany	Automotive	49.8	58.7	37.4	61.5	114,000	257,000	63.4
7	43	IBM	United States	Computers	41.7	80.3	45.1	71.9	112,944	225,347	54.9
8	78	Toyota Motor Corp.	Japan	Automotive	36.0	118.2	50.4	111.7	33,796	146,855	32.9
9	1	Nestlé SA	Switzerland	Food	33.2	38.2	47.8	48.7	213,637	220,172	94.0
10	71	Mitsubishi Corporation	Japan	Diversified	. . .[d]	79.3	51.0	124.9	3,859	9,241	39.5
11	18	Bayer AG	Germany	Chemicals	28.1	31.3	19.7	31.1	78,000	142,900	69.3
12	6	ABB Asea Brown Boveri Ltd.	United States Switzerland	Electrical equipment	27.2	32.1	29.4	33.7	196,937	209,637	88.6
13	66	Nissan Motor Co., Ltd.	Japan	Automotive	26.9	63.0	24.9	56.3	60,795[e]	139,856	43.5
14	40	Elf Aquitaine SA	France	Oil, gas, coal, and related services	26.9	49.4	27.8	42.5	40,650	85,500	55.8
15	32	Mobil Corporation	United States	Oil, gas, coal, and related services	26.0	42.1	48.4	73.4	26,300	50,400	60.0
16	70	Daimler-Benz AG	Germany	Automotive	26.0	66.3	45.6	72.1	68,907	310,993	41.5
17	8	Unilever[f]	United Kingdom/ Netherlands	Food	25.8	30.1	42.7	49.7	276,000	307,000	87.1
18	9	Philips Electronics N.V.	Netherlands	Electronics	25.2	32.7	38.4	40.1	221,000	265,100	85.4
19	10	Roche Holding AG	Switzerland	Pharmaceuticals	24.5	30.9	12.0	12.5	40,422	50,497	85.1
20	54	Fiat Spa	Italy	Automotive	24.4	59.1	26.3	40.6	95,930	248,180	48.2
21	59	Siemens AG	Germany	Electronics	24.0	57.7	35.5	62.0	162,000	373,000	47.4
22	33	Sony Corporation	Japan	Electronics	[e]	47.6	30.3	43.3	90,000	151,000	59.1
23	30	Alcatel Alsthom	France	Electronics	22.7	51.2	24.2	32.1	117,400	191,830	60.3

Continued

Source: UNCTAD, *World Investment Report 1997*, Table 1.7, pp. 29–30.

[a]The index of transnationality is calculated as the average of rations of foreign assets to total assets, foreign sales to total sales, and foreign employment to total employment.

[b]Industry classification for companies follows the United States Standard Industrial Classification as used by the United States Security Exchange Commission (SEC).

[c]Foreign sales are outside Europe, while foreign employment figures are outside the United Kingdom and the Netherlands.

[d]Data on foreign assets are either suppressed to avoid disclosure, or they are not available. In case of nonavailability, they are estimated on the basis of the ratio of foreign to total sales, foreign to total employment, and similar ratios for the transnationality index.

[e]Data on foreign assets are either suppressed to avoid disclosure, or they are not available. In case of nonavailability, they are estimated on the basis of the ratio of foreign to total sales, foreign to total employment, and similar ratios for the transnationality index.

[f]Foreign assets, sales, and employment figures are outside the United Kingdom and the Netherlands.

[g]Foreign assets, sales, and employment figures are outside the United Kingdom and Australia.

TABLE 7.3 (continued)

Ranking by					Assets		Sales		Employment		
Foreign Assets	Index[a]	Corporation	Economy	Industry[b]	Foreign	Total	Foreign	Total	Foreign	Total	Index[a]
24	53	Hoechst	Germany	Chemicals	21.9	36.7	13.4	36.3	100,035[e]	161,618	48.3
25	68	Renault SA	France	Automotive	21.2	44.6	19.1	36.8	40,066	139,950	42.7
26	62	Philip Morris	United States	Food/tobacco/ beverages	19.5	53.8	27.7	66.1	88,201	151,000	45.5
27	24	British Petroleum	United Kingdom	Oil, gas, coal, and related services	19.3	28.9	34.8	57.0	41,350	58,150	66.3
28	67	Du Pont (E.I.) De Nemours	United States	Chemicals	17.8	37.3	20.6	42.2	35,000	105,000	43.3
29	36	BASF AG	Germany	Chemicals	17.6	29.3	23.5	32.3	42,850	106,565	57.7
30	4	Seagram Company Ltd.	Canada	Beverages	17.5	21.4	9.5	9.7	14,447[e]	16,100	89.7
31	23	B.A.T. Industries Plc	United Kingdom	Tobacco	17.5	55.1	29.3	36.3	155,162	170,412	67.9
32	79	Mitsui & Co. Ltd.	Japan	Diversified	16.6	68.5	66.6	163.3	3,696[e]	11,378	32.5
33	28	Rhone-Poulenc SA	France	Chemicals/ pharmaceuticals	16.1	27.6	12.4	17.0	47,009	82,556	62.8
34	38	BMW	Germany	Automotive	15.6	28.5	22.5	32.2	52,416[e]	115,763	56.7
35	46	Honda Motor Co., Ltd	Japan	Automotive	15.5	33.7	23.5	39.6	50,937[e]	96,800	52.6
36	92	Itochu Corporation	Japan	Trading	15.1	72.0	45.1	186.6	2,649	9,994	23.9
37	29	TOTAL SA	France	Oil, gas, coal, and related services	15.0	28.4	19.6	27.2	30,215	53,536	60.5
38	34	Ciba-Geigy AG	Switzerland	Chemicals	14.9	26.5	7.5	17.5	63,674	84,077	58.2
39	81	Nissho Iwai Corporation	Japan	Trading	. . .[d]	47.2	29.5	89.1	2,103[e]	6,684	31.5
40	95	Hitachi, Ltd.	Japan	Electronics	14.7	102.7	20.5	94.7	80,000	331,673	20.0
41	16	News Corporation Ltd.	Australia	Media	14.5	24.1	9.0	10.3	22,062[e]	30,000	73.5
42	89	ENI Group	Italy	Oil, gas, coal, and related services	. . .[d]	55.9	12.4	37.3	15,713e	86,422	25.6
43	76	Chevron Corporation	United States	Oil, gas, coal, and related services	13.8	34.3	11.9	36.3	12,434	43,019	34.0
44	39	Dow Chemical Company	United States	Chemicals	13.5	23.6	11.2	20.2	22,185	39,500	56.2
45	91	Marubeni Corporation	Japan	Trading	13.4	71.0	42.8	144.9	2307[e]	9,533	24.2
46	51	Hewlett-Packard Company	United States	Computers	13.0	24.4	17.6	31.5	42,049	10,2300	50.0
47	61	Texaco Incorporated	United States	Oil, gas, coal, and related services	12.2	24.9	18.2	35.6	10,460	28,247	45.8
48	98	AT&T Corp.	United States	Telecommuni- cations	12.1	62.7	8.7	51.4	54,371[e]	300,000	18.1
49	48	Procter & Gamble Company	United States	Diversified	12.1	28.1	16.8	33.4	62,000	99,200	51.9
50	45	Robert Bosch GmbH	Germany	Automotive	. . .[d]	19.9	14.0	25.0	66,000	158,372	52.7
51	85	Sumitomo Corporation	Japan	Trading	12.0	50.7	58.4	152.5	. . .[e]	11,200[e]	29.5
52	56	Daewoo Corporation	Republic of Korea	Diversified	11.9	28.9	8.2	26.0	28,100	39,920	47.7
53	21	Saint-gobain SA	France	Construction	11.7	18.6	9.6	13.5	67,064	89,852	69.7

Continued

TABLE 7.3 (continued)

Ranking by					Assets		Sales		Employment		
Foreign Assets	Index[a]	Corporation	Economy	Industry[b]	Foreign	Total	Foreign	Total	Foreign	Total	Index[a]
54	3	Holderbank Financiere	Switzerland	Construction	11.5	12.5	6.5	7.0	40,473	43,923	92.1
55	14	Cable and Wireless Plc	United Kingdom	Telecommunications	11.2	13.8	5.9	8.5	30,466	39,636	75.6
56	77	Matusushita Electric	Japan	Electronics	11.1	75.6	28.9	64.1	107,530	265,538	33.5
57	69	Hanson Plc	United Kingdom	Construction	11.1	37.4	8.5	15.8	27,034[e]	65,000	41.6
58	7	Electrolux AB	Sweden	Electronics	10.7	12.4	15.0	16.3	97,351	112,300	88.3
59	15	Volvo AB	Sweden	Automotive	10.7	20.7	21.8	25.6	67,129	79,050	73.8
60	55	Xerox Corporation	United States	Machinery and equipment	10.4	26.0	9.2	16.6	40,717[e]	85,200	47.8
61	65	BCE Inc.	Canada	Telecommunications	10.2	28.4	10.7	18.1	46,000	121,000	44.4
62	82	Mitsubishi Motors Corp.	Japan	Automotive	10.2	27.7	7.8	33.0-	8,587[e]	28,383	30.3
63	74	International Paper	United States	Paper	10.1	24.0	5.5	19.8	30,068	81,500	35.6
64	2	Thomson Corporation	Canada	Publishing and printing	9.6	10.0	6.7	7.2	40,000	44,400	93.3
65	19	Grand Metropolitan Plc	United Kingdom	Food/beverages	9.5	17.5	11.4	12.6	45,978[e]	63,533	72.4
66	90	Amoco Corporaton	United States	Oil, gas, coal, and related services	9.1	29.8	6.7	31.0	8,872	42,689	24.3
67	35	Michelin	France	Mechanical rubber goods	8.7	14.2	10.9	13.2	35,091[e]	114,397	58.1
68	94	Nippon Steel Corporation	Japan	Metal	. . .[d]	42.0	5.6	27.5	8,203[e]	27,583	23.5
69	13	Glaxo Wellcome Plc	United Kingdom	Pharmaceuticals	8.4	13.2	11.1	12.1	40,392	54,359	76.5
70	88	Fujitsu Limited	Japan	Electronics	8.4	40.3	10.3	35.1	50,000	165,000	24.9
71	42	McDonald's Corporaton	United States	Recreation	8.2	15.4	5.3	9.8	125,000[e]	212,000	55.5
72	57	Motorola, Inc.	United States	Electronics	8.3	22.8	17.0	27.0	63,200	142,000	47.9
73	50	Johnson & Johnson	United States	Chemicals/ pharmaceuticals	8.2	17.9	9.7	18.8	44,300	82,300	50.3
74	5	Solvay SA	Belgium	Chemicals	. . .[d]	8.9	8.8	9.3	36,608	38,616	89.6
75	52	Canon Electronics Inc.	Japan	Computers	8.0	23.9	14.1	21.0	35,101	72,280	49.6
76	26	BTR Plc	United Kingdom	Chemicals	7.9	15.3	11.0	14.0	81,329[e]	125,065	65.0
77	80	BHP	Australia	Metals	7.8	21.8	4.4	12.7	12,900	48,500	32.3
78	12	Northern Telecom Ltd.	Canada	Telecommunications	7.7	9.4	9.2	10.7	42,689	63,715	78.4
79	84	Pepsico, Inc.	United States	Diversified	7.7	25.4	8.7	30.4	142,008[e]	480,000	29.6
80	31	Coca-Cola Company	United States	Beverages	7.5	15.0	12.7	18.0	19,238[e]	32,000	60.1
81	47	Rtz[g] Cra	United Kingdom/ Australia	Mining	7.3	15.8	4.7	9.3	31,616	51,492	52.5

Continued

TABLE 7.3 (concluded)

Ranking by					Assets		Sales		Employment		
Foreign Assets	Index[a]	Corporation	Economy	Industry[b]	Foreign	Total	Foreign	Total	Foreign	Total	Index[a]
82	20	Petrofina SA	Belgium	Oil, gas, coal, and related services	7.3	11.5	15.0	18.7	9,262	13,653	70.4
83	73	Mannesmann AG	Germany	Metals	7.2	15.8	7.6	22.3	42,000	122,684	37.9
84	58	Carrefour SA	France	Trading	7.2	13.1	11.2	29.5	51,200	102,900	47.6
85	11	SCA	Sweden	Paper	7.2	10.2	8.3	9.1	27,165	34,857	79.7
86	25	Pharmacia & Upjohn, Inc.	United States	Pharmaceuticals	7.2	11.5	4.7	6.9	22,893[e]	35,000	65.4
87	100	Chrysler Corporation	United States	Automotive	7.0	53.3	5.9	53.2	25,000	126,000	14.7
88	64	Petroleos De Venezuela	Venezuela	Diversified/trading	6.8	40.5	24.5	26.0	34,320	60,007	44.4
89	63	Groupe Danone SA	France	Food	6.7	19.0	8.6	16.2	32,770[e]	73,823	44.4
90	49	Sara Lee Corporation	United States	Food	6.7	12.4	7.1	17.7	91,439	149,085	51.7
91	72	American Home Products	United States	Pharmaceuticals	6.6	21.4	5.4	13.4	23,196	64,712	35.8
92	96	Toshiba Corporation	Japan	Electronics	6.5	51.8	12.7	47.7	36,437[e]	186,000	19.6
93	97	NEC Corporation	Japan	Electronics	6.3	43.8	11.3	41.1	21,059	15,2719	18.6
94	41	Thomson SA	France	Electronics	6.3	17.9	10.7	14.4	55,215	96,000	55.6
95	99	GTE Corporation	United States	Telecommunications	6.2	37.0	2.6	20.0	15,751[e]	106,000	14.9
96	93	Atlantic Richfield	United States	Oil, gas, coal, and related services	6.2	24.0	3.4	15.8	5,168[e]	22,000	23.5
97	37	ICI	United Kingdom	Chemicals	6.1	14.7	9.5	15.9	45,900	64,800	57.4
98	60	United Techologies	United States	Aerospace	6.0	16.0	10.3	22.8	99,700	170,600	47.0
99	75	RJR Nabisco Holding Corp.	United States	Food/tobacco	5.8	31.5	4.7	16.0	42,066	76,000	34.4
100	44	Pechiney SA	France	Metals	5.8	11.4	8.6	13.8	17,979	37,214	59.9

alarmed members of the European Community.[55] Most of MNC investments were in industrialized economies, and, by the late 1970s, 47.3 percent were in manufacturing, 23.6 percent were in petroleum industries, 5.2 percent in mining, and 23.9 percent in other industries.[56]

In the 1960s and 1970s, the developing countries received less than a third of the total MNC foreign direct investments worldwide. According to one estimate, 18 percent of foreign investments in the developing world were in Latin America, while Africa and Asia, mired in the turbulence of decolonization, received about 5.5 percent and the Middle East 3 percent. The major investors in these areas were the former colonial rulers, such as Belgium, Britain, France, Italy, the Netherlands, and Portugal—a pattern reflecting the strength of former colonial ties. As previously noted, MNCs concentrated their operations on extractive and public utility sectors in the developing countries. After the Second World War, however, the manufacturing sector began to expand as well, and by the mid-1970s the distribution of industries in the developing countries was as follows: 39.7 percent in the petroleum industries, 26.9 percent in manufacturing, 9.3 percent in mining, and 24.1 percent in other industries.[57]

Differences in production and marketing patterns among the industrialized economies became evident by the late 1980s and early 1990s. While U.S. MNCs were dominant in manufacturing, in information-telecommunications technologies, and in the service sector, Japanese and German MNCs concentrated on the information-telecommunications technologies, and British MNCs maintained a competitive advantage in financial services. Although international capital continued to grow, by the early 1980s the U.S. share of worldwide FDIs began to decline, while German and Japanese MNC shares increased.[58]

The picture in 1990 showed about $2 trillion of total global FDI, more than $460 billion of which was actually in the United States, since that country was both the world's largest market and most secure investment host. Total international portfolio investment—that is, excluding ownership of enterprises—by foreign investors was over $1.7 trillion in U.S. assets.[59] Five countries—the United States, Great Britain, Japan, Germany, and France—held approximately 75 percent of foreign direct investments worldwide (the United States came to hold about 32 percent, Great Britain 18 percent, Japan 11 percent, Germany 8 percent, and France 8 percent).[60] EU-U.S. foreign direct investments increased as well. By 1992, despite American worries about Japan's buying out the country, EU investors held over 50 percent of the FDI stocks in the United States, with Britain and the Netherlands leading the way, while 40 percent of U.S. investors' FDI stocks were in the EU. The combined total value of these investments exceeded $420 billion.[61]

Medium-power countries also had significant FDI holdings, but theirs, too, were largely in industrialized economies. In 1991, nearly $19.9 billion (or 20 percent) of Canada's total FDI, mostly in the manufacturing sector, was in the EU, a large share—61 percent, or $12.2 billion—invested in Great Britain. Between 1983 and 1990, the European Community's FDI in Canada increased from $13.4 billion (or 17.3 percent) to about $32 billion (or 23 percent). Thus, the EU became the second largest source of FDI in Canada after the United States. In fact, by 1993 the EU had replaced the United States as "the leading foreign investor (in terms of annual inflows, not total capital stock) in Canada."[62]

In the first half of the 1990s, FDI in the developing world expanded as well (see Figure 7.1). During the 1991–1993 period, net FDIs in developing countries totaled $134 billion—about two and a half times the average levels in the 1980s.[63] In 1993, FDI in developing countries was $70 billion, double the FDI levels of 1991,[64] and in 1995 that figure reached $90 billion, the highest levels yet.[65] On the positive side, these increases were indicative of greater opportunity for AIEs, along with MNCs' confidence in global markets, particularly as more countries liberalized their internal markets. Indeed, in 1995 over $167 billion of private capital flows, including portfolio investment, FDI, and private debt flows, went to developing economies.[66] On

FIGURE 7.1 Foreign Investment in Developed and Developing Economies

Source: IMF, *The Economist,* "Multinationals" [survey], June 24, 1995, p. 4.

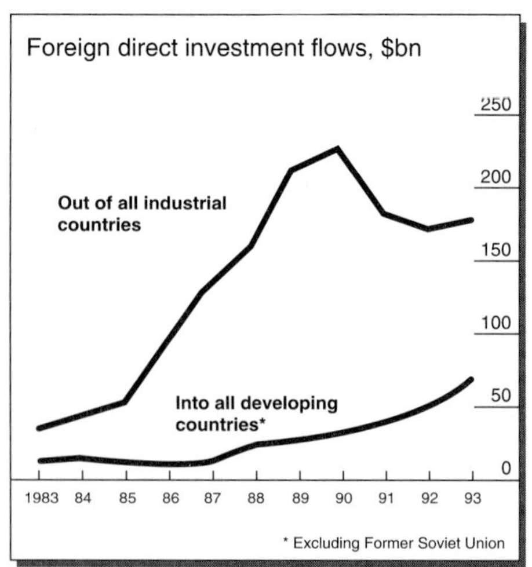

the other hand, only ten developing countries were the destination of over 75 percent of these investment flows. In 1996, nearly 67 percent of total direct investments were concentrated in southern and eastern Asia, and over 40 percent of the investments in this region were in China. Some of the countries in the region, most notably the NICs (Taiwan, South Korea, Hong Kong, and Singapore), have become sources of direct investments as well. However, their investments have been mostly in the developed economies.[67] Also in 1996, about 25 percent of total direct investments in the developing countries went to Latin America and the Caribbean, but only 5 percent to Africa, where perhaps it is needed the most.[68] It is also questionable whether MNCs assist or retard the development of indigenous industries in the developing countries.

Another significant development was the collapse of the Soviet Union and the emergence of new business opportunities in previously inaccessible Eastern European countries, especially in the service sector—banking, insurance, and advertising. FDI inflows to the region rose by 35 percent in 1993 and by another 5 percent (some $6 billion) in 1994. In 1995, these transitional economies accounted for 3 percent of total world FDI inflows ($13 billion) and $11 billion in 1996, involving nearly 55,000 foreign affiliates.[69] As in Asia, however, a large proportion (over 70 percent) of such investments were concentrated in a small group of transitional economies: Russia, Hungary, the Czech Republic, Poland, and Kazakhstan.[70]

The ever more competitive global environment has placed enormous pressures on MNCs to cultivate relations with faraway companies as producers and providers of various goods and services, even blurring the line between competitors. While thirty years ago a corporate manager was concerned only with the well-being of his or her company, now he or she will have to be concerned with other companies' well-being as well. Ironically, in order to be able to compete, MNCs must be willing to trade corporate secrets or create partnerships with other companies and cultivate mutual trust. The more serious challenge, however, appears to be for companies to cultivate trust between management and workers. During the 1980s, "downsizing"—corporate layoffs, firings, and plant closure—led to job insecurity, and workers' sense of loyalty to their employers diminished considerably.[71]

MNCs AND GLOBALIZATION

Multinational corporations have been the principal vehicles toward globalization of the international economy. As the discussion of MNCs has demonstrated, MNCs emerged during a period of national industrial and economic growth, and firms served as instruments of colonial expansion, as well as postcolonial readjustment. Governments and companies generally worked closely with each other toward mutually supportive objectives, but eras of nationalization and disputes occurred as well. MNCs emphasized "command-and-control management," and production and distribution processes involved huge facilities with assembly lines employing thousands of workers in a highly centralized and rigidly hierarchical organizational framework.[72] In the late twentieth century, however, globalization revealed major weaknesses in MNC structures and operations. Greater trade liberalization and market deregulation by governments widened the realm of MNC operations but also weakened the relationship between MNCs and governments, as MNCs opted for greater decentralization, spreading their management structures across continents within a vast maze of expansive communications networks.[73]

In line with modern management and production approaches, centralized command-and-control management gave way to "lean manufacturing," with fewer permanent employees and facilities, and "just-in-time production" with smaller inventories and computer-controlled production lines; MNCs began to show greater appreciation for local expertise and management as the latter served as cultural links between the company and the host society. Business experts argued that companies become more popular when they delegate greater responsibility to affiliates for production and distribution of the right goods and services in the right countries. Thus, General Electric established new headquarters in Asia, DuPont relocated its electronics section to Japan, Siemens transferred its air-traffic management to Britain, and Hyundai relocated its PC section to the United States. The German Volkswagon gained 65 percent of the car market in China along with a strong presence in Mexico, while Alcatel, a French telecommunications company, has overshadowed its competitors in telephones and related products. When German Chancellor Helmut Kohl visited China in 1993, he was instrumental in sealing contracts worth $4 billion for German companies, including Siemens' construction of a subway system in the Guangzhou province.[74]

With globalization, major and successful MNCs, such as Motorola, Coca-Cola, and PepsiCo, have adjusted their production and marketing operations and goods to satisfy local needs and tastes. *The Economist* states,

> People in the south of Japan like their Coca-Cola slightly sweeter than people in Tokyo, and the company obliges. PepsiCo was puzzled why one of its best-selling products "7-up" remained on the shelves in Shanghai until it discovered

that, in the local dialect, the phrase means "death through drinking." Even those pillars of American puritanism, IBM and Disney, have dropped their strict no-alcohol policy in France. Philip Morris has had to make local adjustments to its familiar advertising symbol, Marlboro man: in Hong Kong the advertisement focuses on the horse, because the man reminds locals of a coolie, and in Argentina the man was dropped entirely for a while, because cowboys were regarded as low-class wasters.[75]

Rapidly changing market and production structures have directly shaped the economic environment for workers as well. In the process of globalization, it became rather obvious that the traditional ways of doing things commercially, as inherited from "an age of high tariffs and high transport costs," had become too inefficient and expensive.[76] Since the late 1960s, MNCs in the industrialized societies have slashed the number of employees needed to run factories and related production facilities, as they tried to decentralize their operations into smaller and more manageable units. They gave local managers greater voice in decisions pertaining to local cultural tastes, as the previous quote illustrates. For example, Canon, one of the major Japanese office-equipment manufacturers, created a number of "mini-chief executives," each with its own set of responsibilities for production and marketing. Xerox and its affiliates—for example, Britain's Rank Xerox and Japan's Fuji Xerox—used to do almost all of their operations (product design, manufacturing, distribution). By the late 1980s and early 1990s, however, the need to compete more effectively and efficiently with other companies, such as Canon, led to the integration and standardization of its transnational operations while creating global product design and development groups. In the process of integration, according to *The Economist,* Xerox cut down the size of affiliated suppliers from 5,000 to 400.[77]

Strategic Alliances and Joint Ventures

MNCs also have created strategic alliances to take advantage of foreign markets, economies of scale, and local businesses' familiarity with local cultures and regulatory policies and practices. One recent phenomenon contributing to the further globalization of international economic activities by MNCs are their strategic integration

TABLE 7.4
Growth in Strategic Alliance Formation, 1980–1989 (Number and Percentage)

	1980–1984		1985–1989		
Industry/Region	**Number**	**Percent**	**Number**	**Percent**	**Percentage Change**
Automobiles	26	100	79	100	203
United States–Europe	10	39	24	30	140
United States–Japan	10	39	39	49	290
Europe–Japan	6	23	16	20	167
Biotechnology	108	100	198	100	83
United States–Europe	58	54	124	63	114
United States–Japan	45	42	54	27	20
Europe–Japan	5	4	20	10	300
Information technology	348	100	445	100	28
United States–Europe	158	45	256	58	62
United States–Japan	133	38	132	30	−0.8
Europe–Japan	57	16	57	13	———
New materials	63	100	115	100	83
United States–Europe	32	51	52	45	63
United States–Japan	16	25	40	35	150
Europe–Japan	15	24	23	20	53
Chemicals	103	100	80	100	−22
United States–Europe	54	52	31	39	−43
United States–Japan	28	27	35	44	25
Europe–Japan	21	20	14	17	−33

Source: UNCTAD, *World Investment Report 1994,* p. 139. The United Nations is the author of the original materials, and materials used with permission.

structures, devised to take advantage of low-cost production opportunities. Facilitated by the increase in international trade and domestic economic liberalization since the mid-1980s, worldwide economies of scale have encouraged competition but also oligopolistic arrangements between and within MNCs, restructuring the global political economy to manage production and marketing more effectively. Table 7.4 shows the magnitude of the increase in strategic alliances. As one UNCTAD report has noted, "alliances are common in many industries, but they are especially prevalent in information technology, biotechnology, automobiles and new materials industries . . . industries that are characterized by high entry costs, scale economies, rapidly changing technologies and substantial operating risks."[78] Strategic alliances and joint ventures to develop specific products multinationally (such as Europe's Airbus jetliners) enable companies of various sizes and with different resources to facilitate market entry and cooperation in R&D. Thus, GM competes but also allies with its Japanese counterpart, Toyota, as do Ford and Mazda, and Daimler-Chrysler and Mitsubishi.

Such arrangements are not limited to the major economies. By one estimate, there are 80,000 foreign joint ventures in China. Wal-Mart, for example, created an alliance with Thailand's Charoen Pokphand Group, which is one of the two largest investors in China, the other being Robert Kuok, a Malaysian Chinese.[79] Mitsubishi created an alliance with Indonesia's Lippo Group.[80]

Strategic alliances and **joint ventures** are not always between equal partners. They expand the influence of the major or parent MNC and put enormous pressures on the local company—as the junior partner—to prove, as quickly as possible, its ability to produce profits. In case of failure, the parent company transfers its operations to another country (see Box 7.4). Joint ventures also can increase costs and delay sales as each partner firm is given a piece of the product to develop. Such arrangements and the overall globalization of market and production structures have made it easier for MNCs to establish and to move parts of their operation or to export designs and production licenses to another country (although, as Enderwick has pointed out, MNCs also and more frequently use the *threat* of relocation rather than actually relocating). MNCs tend to be interested in

BOX 7.4

MNCs IN CHINA

China is now the largest recipient of FDI in the developing world, and the second largest in the world after the United States. Last year [1994] its economy as a whole grew by an estimated 11%, and its "special economic zones" in the south and along the coast much more quickly than that.

In this booming, bustling but worryingly unpredictable part of the world, the word on the lips of most multinational managers is "localisation." Locals are much more likely than foreigners to have the personal connections (known in China as "guanxi") so essential to doing business in the region. They also have the sort of insider's knowledge which saves them from making crass mistakes. The trouble with "localisation" is that good locals are difficult to come by. The Hong Kong labor market is one of the tightest in the world. On China's mainland, the dearth of managerial talent and technical skills that seems to be a common feature of communist and ex-communist countries was exacerbated by the cultural revolution, which thinned the ranks of people between 35 and 45.

Despite these problems, some companies are adopting a policy of "Chinese at any price", scouring the Chinese communities of the United States and Asia for suitable ethnic Chinese. The talk in Hong Kong is full of ABCs (American-born Chinese) and "returnees" (people who fled the People's Republic but are now returning as company men). The region is seeing the birth of a new sort of expatriate: an ethnic Chinese who has been educated in western business schools and spends his time moving from one lucrative posting to another. According to a local joke, in Hong Kong you hire the company, not the other way round.

Nevertheless, locals do not always go down well with the people they are supposed to impress. Mainlanders do not necessarily take to these "ABCs with their MBAs," particularly when they have little grasp of the local dialect. They like to negotiate with "grey hairs" rather than with people in their early 20s who still reek of Harvard Yard. Companies find that to clinch a serious deal with the Chinese authorities, they have to wheel out heavyweight senior company figures.

Source: "Multinationals," [survey] *The Economist,* June 24, 1995, pp. 12-13.

investing in or near their own regions as well. U.S. companies tend to invest in Central and South America, Japanese companies in Asian countries, and Europeans in Europe (increasingly including Eastern European countries) as regional cultural familiarity and geographic proximity strengthen their relations.[81]

Intra-Firm Trade

In the globalization of MNC operations, strategic alliances and joint ventures are complemented by the increasing **intra-firm trade**—that is, trade between the parent company and its affiliates and inter-affiliate trade worldwide. Table 7.5 presents the shares of parent and foreign affiliates' intra-firm exports and imports in four countries' total trade. In 1993, for example, intra-firm exports accounted for 34 percent of total French exports, and, in 1994, 38 percent of Swedish exports.[82]

The growth in intra-firm trade reflects the complexity of transnationally integrated production and service networks. What, in fact, has emerged by the 1990s is a global corporate system. Contrary to traditional views on FDI and trade as distinct processes, the growth in intra-firm trade indicates the close relationship between the two as part of the globalization process. Structurally, in addition to the geographical dispersion of parent-affiliates and affiliate-affiliate intra-firm trade relationships, the direction of that trade also must be considered; it also makes it easier for the parent company to restructure and to decentralize its home-affiliates operations so that the most essential components, which cannot be readily substituted, and technologically advanced end of the production, albeit with higher costs, remain in the home country, while the rest are devolved to affiliates for operations with minimum expenditures. MNCs tend to keep the capital- or technology-intensive sector in the Western advanced countries, while transferring the labor-intensive sector from high-wage, unionized regions (as in U.S. northern manufacturing cities) to low-wage, non- or weakly-unionized regions. As such, intra-firm trade has become the centerpiece for the restructuring of the international division of labor and labor competition.

Such divisions have certain advantages and disadvantages for countries. On the benefit side, the proliferation of affiliates and intra-firm trade create new opportunities for economic development and employment in both developed and developing countries. With added local-specific comparative advantages, a country or region can potentially become an important part of the global synchronization and production processes. Local affiliates benefit from technological innovations and grow more competitive in the domestic but also the international economy. However, the costs, especially for developing countries, include integration into an international division of labor that comparatively may suppress a country's pay scales and underutilize its human-resources potential. At the same time, integrative technological development in the industrial and financial centers heightens the vulnerability of national economies without sufficient indigenous capital and technologies to compensate for potential losses in international production and to absorb world market fluctuations.

TABLE 7.5
Intra-Firm Trade and Its Share in Total Trade, Various Countries and Years (Billions of Dollars and Percentages)

	Intra-Firm Exports		Intra-Firm Imports	
		Share in Country		Share in Country
Country	Value ($)	Exports (%)	Value ($)	Imports (%)
France				
1993	56	34	28	18
Japan				
1983	33	22	17	15
1993	92	25	33	14
Sweden				
1986	11	38	1	3
1994	22	38	4	9
United States				
1983	71	35	99	37
1993	169	36	259	43

Source: UNCTAD, *World Investment Report 1996,* note 3, p. 121.

Southern-Based MNCs

During the past two decades or so, MNCs from developing countries have made a greater effort to become globally competitive, and their home governments have supported their international expansion by reducing regulations on their operations. Their FDIs increased from an annual average of only $304 million in the 1970s to $33 billion in 1994,[83] and their share of total world FDI outflows rose from an annual average of a mere 0.3 percent in the 1970s to 10.1 percent for the 1990–1994 period (see Table 7.6). Despite this increase, however, the figures for the 1990s indicate that the share of MNCs from developing countries is low in comparison with that of MNCs based in the North. Southern-based MNCs' outward FDI stock totaled about $117 billion in 1993, no more than 5 percent of the worldwide total.[84] Table 7.7 lists the top thirty-one MNCs from developing countries. In comparison with northern-based MNCs, their total assets and sales remain quite low. Korean electronics giant Samsung's total assets, for example, the largest among them, were just over $50 billion in 1993, while those of U.S.-based General Electric were about $250 billion. Mexican-based Cemex S.A.'s total foreign assets, the largest in terms of foreign assets, were about $10 billion—that is, the equivalent of 90 percent of U.S.-based RJR Nabisco's foreign assets, the smallest among the world's top 100 MNCs.[85]

The largest share of domestic and foreign investments by southern-based MNCs is in the service sector (totaling nearly $120 billion in 1993), and some developing countries have taken the opportunity to diversify their holdings in areas ranging from construction and infrastructure to heavy equipment and electronics. Among the developing countries, Brazil is home to the largest number of MNCs (ten), followed by South Korea (nine), Taiwan and Hong Kong (seven each), Mexico (five), Malaysia (four), Singapore

TABLE 7.6

Average Annual FDI Outflows from Developing Economies and the World, 1970–1994 (Millions of Dollars)

Home Region/Economy	1970–1979	1980–1984	1985–1989	1990–1994
Developing region/economy, total	304	2,467	8,425	21,857
Africa	36	924	998	832
Nigeria	———	819	839	552
Latin America and the Caribbean of which	100	416	713	2,095
Brazil	90	236	212	734
Mexico	2	30	142	185
East, South and South-East Asia,[a] of which	149	895	5,816	18,507
China	———	90[b]	671	2,429
Hong Kong	———	355	1,968	10,245
Republic of Korea	10	73	157	1,271
Malaysia	75	245	231	904
Singapore	———	106	325	837
Taiwan Province of China	4	45	2,384	2,640
Thailand	5	2	49	171
West Asia	18	229	890	420
Kuwait	32[c]	141	438	598
World	27,705	49,523	136,381	215,502
Developing economies as percentage of world	0.3	5.0	6.2	10.1

Source: UNCTAD, *World Investment Report 1995,* Table I.11, p. 34. The United Nations is the author of the original materials, and materials used with permission.

[a]Includes the Pacific. The total FDI for the subregion for some years is less than the sum of economies listed below due to negative outflows.

[b]Annual average for 1982–1984

[c]Annual average for 1975–1979

TABLE 7.7

The Largest TNCs Based in Developing Economies, Ranked by Foreign Assets, 1993

Ranking by					Assets $(Millions)		Sales $(Millions)		Employment (Employees)		
Foreign Assets	Index	Corporation	Economy	Industry	Foreign	Total	Foreign	Total	Foreign	Total	(%)
1	8	Cemex S.A.	Mexico	Cement	3,603	8,018	949	2,897	5,171	18,395	35.3
2	10	Hutchison Whampoa Ltd.	Hong Kong	Diversified	2,743	8,375	815	3,202	9,046	22,489	32.8
3	17	Daewoo Group	Korea, Republic of	Electronics	. . .	44,352	. . .	30,893	64,000	156,000	26.6
4	40	Samsung Group	Korea, Republic of	Electronics	. . .	50,692	. . .	51,531	. . .	191,000	8.0
5	6	Jardine Matheson Holdiings Ltd.	Hong Kong	Diversified	. . .	9,799	5,510	8,424	. . .	220,000	38.8
6	45	Petroleo Brasileiro S/A–Petrobras	Brazil refining	Petroleum	. . .	20,178	1,037	15,263	17	51,228	4.9
7	36	Hyundai Motor Co.	Korea, Republic of and parts	Motor vehicles	1,105	8,983	1,439	10,544	979	42,306	9.4
8	16	Grupo Televisa S.A. de C.V.	Mexico	Media	948	3,442	208	1,925	. .	23,000	27.5
9	15	Souza Cruz S.A.	Brazil	Tobacco	770	1,040	262	3,721	. .	12,659	27.5
10	22	Genting Berhad	Malaysia	Diversified	752	1,541	101	744	. .	30,000	21.9
11	4	Dong Ah Construction Industrial Co	Korea, Republic of	Construction	706	2,935	858	1,895	6,366	12,097	40.6
12	19	Tatung Co. Ltd.	Taiwan Province of China	Electronics	703	3,836	806	3,121	8,564	27,254	25.2
13	37	New World Development Co. Ltd.	Hong Kong	Diversified	624	6,944	316	1,721	. .	28,000	9.3
14	25	Keppel Corporation Ltd.	Singapore	Diversified	565	6,948	134	946	2,500	10,707	15.2
15	28	LG Electronics Inc.	Korea, Republic of	Electronics	485	7,679	1,105	7,565	. .	58,8000	13.0
16	5	Acer	Taiwan Province of China	Electronics	467	1,909	1,116	2,010	2,579	6,348	40.2
17	12	Sirne Darby Berhad	Malaysia	Food	419	2,829	1,493	2,738	6,500	30,000	30.3
18	39	China Steel Corporation	Tainwan Province of China	Metals	. . .	6,215	476	2,355	6	9,601	8.8
19	14	CITIC Pacific Ltd.	Hong Kong	Diversified	366	3,438	599	1,386	1,455	4,500	28.7
20	32	San Miguel Corporation	Philippines	Food	359	1,984	198	2,234	2,386	32,832	11.4
21	13	The Hong Kong and Shanghai Hotels, Ltd.	Hong Kong	Hotel	339	2,019	43	217	3,048	5,921	29.3
22	31	Formosa Plastic	Taiwan Province of China	Chemicall	327	1,906	233	1,491	60	3,645	11.5
23	47	Yukong Ltd	Korea, Republic of	Pertroleum refining	. . .	6,412	300	6,901	4	5,898	3.1

Continued

TABLE 7.7 Concluded

The Largest TNCs Based in Developing Economies, Ranked by Foreign Assets, 1993

Ranking by					Assets $(Millions)		Sales $(Millions)		Employment (Employees)		
Foreign Assets	Index	Corportation	Economy	Industry	Foreign	Total	Foreign	Total	Foreign	Total	(%)
24	42	Empresas Ica Societad Controladora S.A.	Mexico	Construction	316	3,578	90	1,949	1,569	36,655	5.9
25	30	Wing On Intenational (Holdings) Ltd.	Hong Kong	Diversified	275	1,304	43	399	156	3,175	12.3
26	50	Chinese Petroleum	Taiwan Province of China	Petroleum refining	263	12,942	156	10,075	27	21,780	1.2
27	23	Compania Manufacturera de Papeles y Catones	Chile	Paper	242	2,077	285	755	1,132	9,325	20.5
28	3	Fraser & Neave Ltd.	Singapore	Diversified	232	2,065	412	823	4,332	6,323	43.3
29	26	Sadia Concordia S/A Industria e Comercio	Brazil	Food	211	1,037	425	1,714	30	32,473	15.1
30	44	Companhia Cervejaria Brahma	Brazil	Food	187	1,754	80	1,248	476	9,606	5.0
31	21	Malaysian International Shipping Co., Ltd. Industrial Co	Malaysia	Transport	137	1,758	331	639	286	2,837	23.2

Source: United Nations, *World Investment Report, 1995*, Table I.1, p. 30

(three), the Philippines (two), and India (one). Africa is not home to any of the top fifty developing world MNCs.[86]

Multinational Labor Organizations

The combination of expanding internationalization and globalization of economic relations and the rise of MNC's have contributed to the emergence of international trade union organizations, as well as international employers' associations. Some major international union confederations have included the International Confederation of Free Trade Unions (ICFTU), the World Federation of Trade Unions (WFTU), and the World Confederation of Labor (WCL). International trade unions have existed since the 1880s, but they gained in influence particularly after the Second World War as a response to MNCs' globalization.[87] In general, however, they have failed to adequately protect workers' interests. Labor unions have tried to combat MNC exploitation in the workplace and anti-labor influence in politics. In recent years, unions have criticized MNCs from the advanced industrialized countries for "exporting jobs" and pressuring for the lowest possible wages, yet corporations have maintained a high degree of latitude in such strategies.

Finally, globalization also has required greater involvement of international governmental organizations (IGOs). One of the oldest of IGOs is the International Labor Organization (ILO), established in 1919 under the auspices of the League of Nations. The ILO has developed international industrial standards, although, as with IGOs in general, the fact that it is comprised of states as members limits its ability to enforce legal obligations. The ILO cannot simply compel governments against their will to comply with international labor standards. The European Union has been more successful in setting international labor standards and codes for MNC conduct in the region.[88]

THE BLESSINGS AND CURSE OF MNC FOREIGN INVESTMENTS

The Blessings Proponents of MNC investments and operations in foreign countries hold that multinational corporations encourage economic development and growth through capital investment and transfer of new technology. Foreseeing such benefits, host governments offer various forms of tax relief and other incentives to attract them. In the industrialized world, major technologically advanced zones developed by MNCs include California's Silicon Valley in computer technology, Japan's Tsukaba Science City, and Taiwan's Hsinchu Science Park. MNCs, thus, create greater opportunities for local employment, education, product innovation, improved communication and transportation systems and infrastructural development, and integration into the world economy. For many countries, developing and developed, foreign capital is essential to correct their fiscal and trade imbalances, to pay their foreign debts.

MNC investments have increased rapidly during recent decades, despite the fluctuations in world markets. In 1980, U.S. FDI outward stock totaled $220 billion, Britain's $804 billion, Germany's $43 billion, France's $24 billion, and Japan's about $19 billion.[89] A decade later, U.S. FDI outward stock jumped to over $435 billion, and to about $706 billion in 1995. During the same period, Japanese FDIs increased to $205 billion and reached $306 billion in 1995. German FDI outward stock rose to $152 billion, and to $235 billion in 1995. French FDI was $110 billion in 1990 and $201 billion in 1995, while British FDIs increased from $231 billion in 1990 to $319 billion in 1995.[90]

FDI inward stock has experienced parallel increases. In 1980, the United States was the destination of a total of $83 billion in foreign FDIs; in 1990, that figure was $395 billion, and approximately $565 billion in 1995. Among the European Union countries, Britain continued to be the most favored FDI destination. Its FDI inward stock rose from $63 billion in 1980 to about $244 billion in 1995, as did Germany's from $37 billion in 1980 to $134 billion in 1995. In comparison, the figures for Japan were $3 billion and $18 billion, respectively.[91]

In addition to their dollar value, these figures also represent an increasing level of international cooperation as facilitated by the globalization of MNC operations and their transnational interactions. They provide a measure of the worldwide spread of investments, capital and technology transfers, and the employment opportunities created in developed and developing countries. According to UN estimates, MNCs employ about 73 million workers worldwide, 60 percent of whom work in parent companies located in the developed countries and 40 percent of whom work in MNC foreign affiliates. Women have discovered many new opportunities for employment in the process. Twelve million people (or a little over 16 percent of MNC employees) work for MNC affiliates in developing countries. In addition to workers directly employed, approximately 80 million workers are indirectly employed by MNC operations.[92]

MNCs create employment opportunities requiring varying degrees of modern technical expertise. Traditionally, corporations took their managers with them to head production and sales operations in the host country, while using local people for physical labor on the assembly lines.[93] With the advent of globalization, issues related to employment involve not only wages and benefits but also corporate management style and structure, including human resource development, "localization of management," and a more multicultural orientation within the higher echelons of the organization (see Box 7.5).[94] In China, for example, one of today's more dynamic economies, about 450,000 Chinese who have worked overseas have returned to manage MNCs.[95] Some MNCs, including PepsiCo, Hewlett-Packard, and Price Waterhouse, have established management training centers in Shanghai, China's historical financial center.[96]

Thus, laissez-faire theorists emphasize the advantages of MNC investments and operations and contend that both developed and developing economies stand to benefit from the liberalization of domestic and international economic activities and the removal of obstacles to MNC investments. The latter brings much needed capital—particularly to the developing countries—without which the North–South economic gap would be considerably wider. Moreover, they note, the failure of import-substitute industrialization (ISI), often led by state-owned or state-subsidized enterprises, as in Latin American countries in the 1960s and 1970s, underscored the inefficiencies in bloated public institutions and government operations. Developing economies, however, insulated behind protectionist policies, lacked both indigenous capital and technology, to the detriment of their standards of living.[97]

BOX 7.5

MULTICULTURALISM AND MNCs

Globalization has resulted in the recruitment of executives and managers from around the world and a greater emphasis on "multiculturalism." This has become particularly important, since the number of countries involved in the world's ten largest MNCs' stock trade has increased from fifty-eight to seventy. In 1996, the head of French cosmetics company L'Oreal was Lindsay Owen-Jones, a Welshman. U.S. food company Heinz was headed by Tony O'Reilly, an Irishman. Alexander J. Totman, a Scotsman, ran Ford. The head of German chemical company Schering was Guiseppe Vita, an Italian. Rajar Gupta, an Indian, headed one of the major U.S. consultancy firms, McKinsey. The head of Nestlé, a Swiss food company, was Helmut Maucher, a German. Further, MNCs today are increasingly dealing with stockholders from around the world. Avon, another cosmetics giant that has been doing well in emerging markets, especially in South America and East Asia, has established a "multicultural participation council," while one of the leading computer companies, Digital Equipment, sponsors multicultural events, such as "Hispanic Culture Week." Boston-based Gillette, one of the major companies in personal care products, offers courses in twenty-eight countries and transfers trainees to the United States, Britain and Singapore for eighteen months. McDonald's Hamburger University in Oak Brook, Illinois, offers courses for 250 students, nearly 50 percent of whom are from abroad, and uses a highly advanced translation system in twenty-two languages. In a more optimistic prognosis, one could argue that multiculturally oriented policies can perhaps in the long run contribute to greater peace or at least peaceful resolution of international and national conflicts.

However, these companies constitute a small minority. The leadership cadre of most MNCs remains closed to outsiders. This is true particularly of U.S. companies whose employees cannot speak other languages. A report by *The Economist* notes that

> companies have also been putting pressure on American business schools to become more international. That means recruiting staff and students from as many countries as possible, and offering courses that will help shake off the image of the "ugly American," unable to speak any foreign languages and utterly insensitive to cultural differences. Recruiters doing the rounds of business schools are particularly keen on hiring non-Americans who combine the advantage of an American business school education with an insider's knowledge of another culture.

It is estimated that, of the 500 leading U.S. companies in 1991, about 2.1 percent were headed by foreigners, the same proportion as in the late 1970s and early 1980s.

Source: See "Multinationals," [survey] *The Economist,* June 24, 1995, pp. 14–19. © 1995 The Economist Newspaper Group, Inc. Reprinted with permission. Further reproduction prohibited.

Another MNC contribution is that they can create opportunities for government-to-government cooperation. From a neo-functionalist perspective, for example, the growth in bilateral investment and taxation treaties since the 1950s has promoted investments but also international cooperation on a number of issues, including FDI entry, legal remedies, double taxation, information exchange, and international legal codes regulating international financial transactions. In the 1960s, about 100 bilateral investment treaties (BITs) were signed between developed and developing countries, and in the 1970s that number was over 200. In the 1980s, the number of BITs doubled to 400, and by 1996 it reached 1,160 (almost a 200 percent increase in less than a decade), pertaining to MNC investments in nearly 160 countries. In the 1980s, there were about fifty BITs among the developing countries; by 1996, the number had increased to 400.[98]

The Curse Despite the reputed benefits derived from MNC activities, critics contend that FDI-induced economic development exacerbates existing socioeconomic inequalities as MNCs drain jobs away from the relatively high-priced to relatively low-priced labor markets and undermine a host country's cultural, educational, and financial institutions. In the long run, MNCs also pose a serious challenge to the sovereignty of the nation-state.

Contrary to the laissez-faire view of MNCs as a modernizing, positive force, Marxist, *dependencia,* Islamic, and many feminist theorists tend to see MNCs as the byproducts and symbols of Western colonialism, as instruments of economic, political, and cultural domination and exploitation in a new form of "corporate colonialism."[99] For most countries, including developed economies, these issues can be particularly troubling, since the MNC has emerged as the second most important player in international political economy, next to the nation-state.

One central issue is flow of capital from the host countries to the MNC parent company. Although host governments generally welcome MNC investments, a major concern is the margin of profits remaining in the host country. Historically, the outflow of capital generally has far exceeded capital inflows into the host economy. To a large extent, MNCs have secured large shares of capital returns because of **transfer pricing**—that is, prices set for transactions between subdivisions within the MNC organization as opposed to market prices—and because host governments provide tax incentives to attract MNCs. MNC Subdivisions pay prices for components, raw materials, finished goods, loans, fees, and royalties transferred among themselves, and these prices are set by overinvoicing or underinvoicing, as determined by MNCs' needs to minimize the payment of tariffs and other expenditures, shifting profit from a

BOX 7.6

OBJECTIVES OF TRANSFER PRICING: SOME EMPIRICAL FINDINGS

Empirical studies reveal some interesting findings about the practices of U.S. companies in international transfer pricing. Researchers single out income tax minimization as the most important objective of transfer pricing. Still, other studies find that the influence of a given variable differs according to environments. For example, Jane Burns . . . surveyed 62 U.S. companies with subsidiaries in industrialized countries to identify the importance of 14 variables influencing transfer pricing decisions. Seung Kim and Stephen Miller . . . surveyed 342 U.S. companies with subsidiaries in eight developing countries to obtain the perceived importance of nine variables in transfer pricing decisions. According to Burns, the five most important influences on transfer pricing were: (1) market conditions in the foreign country, (2) competition in the foreign country, (3) reasonable profit for foreign affiliates, (4) U.S. federal income taxes, and (5) economic conditions in the foreign country. Kim & Miller found that the five most important objectives were: (a) profit repatriation restrictions within the host country, (b) exchange controls, (c) joint-venture constraints within the host country, (d) tariffs/customs duties within the host country, and (e) income tax liability within the host country.

Minimizing income tax ranked fourth highest in Burns' survey and fifth highest in Kim-Miller's survey. One problem with making a transfer pricing decision is that multiple objectives could conflict with each other. Therefore, multinational financial managers must understand transfer pricing objectives and their effect on transfer prices.

Sources: Suk H. Kim and Seung H. Kim, *Global Corporate Finance: Text and Cases* (Miami: Kolb, 1993), pp. 449–450. See also Jane O. Burns, "How the IRS Applies the Intercompany Pricing Rules of Section 482: A Corporate Survey," *Journal of Taxation* (May 1980), pp. 308–314; Seung H. Kim and Stephen W. Miller, "Constituents of the International Transfer Pricing Decision," *Columbia Journal of World Business* (Spring 1979), pp. 69–77.

high-taxation country to a low-taxation country.[100] Thus, one main objective of transfer pricing is to minimize taxes and duties MNCs pay in transboundary transactions. Indeed, MNCs often seek to avoid paying taxes altogether and opt for the informalization of some of their production and sales. Some empirical analyses, however, indicate that other factors are involved as well in transfer pricing decisions (see Box 7.6).[101]

It is extremely difficult to determine precisely how much governments lose to transfer pricing and unpaid MNC taxes. A 1990 study by the U.S. House of Representatives revealed that well over 50 percent of the forty major foreign companies in the United States had paid no taxes, with about $35 billion in annual government revenues lost by way of transfer pricing.[102] Analysts have found considerable empirical support for the argument that MNCs often are engaged in substantial transfer price manipulation. In the oil industry, for example, MNCs routinely underinvoice crude oil extraction and exports from oil exporting countries and overinvoice shipping charges.[103]

One of the most frequently heard criticisms of MNCs' foreign investments is their impact on host countries' labor conditions. In the mid-1980s, MNCs employed approximately 65 million workers worldwide, 22 million of whom were outside of MNCs' home countries. However, the geographic distribution of workers remains uneven; in some countries, MNCs directly employ as much as 50 percent of the labor force.[104] Jobs indirectly tied to MNC operations also are extensive, both in *capital-intensive* (technology-based) and *labor-intensive* (involving manual or physical labor) production. The former is concentrated primarily in the industrialized societies, the latter in the developing countries. MNCs have been criticized for the development of this international division of labor. Labor-intensive manufacturing and mining jobs constitute approximately 60–75 percent of MNC employment in the developing countries. Since MNCs often pay wages comparable to those in the host country, it is debatable whether this constitutes "exploitation" of labor. Over time there have been some improvements. During the second half of the 1980s, the average hourly wage in Mexico was less than a dollar, and in South Korea about $1.20. At that time, the average hourly wage in the United States was about $11.00, in West Germany $13.00, and in Japan $10.00. In 1994, Mexico's wages had increased to about $2.40, South Korea's $4.90, the United States' $17.00, Germany's $24.00, and Japan's $17.00.[105]

A third issue is the fact that, in order to minimize labor costs, MNCs frequently hire women employees, particularly in the area of clothing and electronics assembly.[106] There are serious inequalities in wages for comparable jobs, as well as in promotion to management levels. In most instances, women are employed in labor-intensive jobs, while male employees are in capital-intensive sectors. A major criticism is that, since MNCs accord higher priority to capital-intensive industries and production, women's contributions are neither appreciated nor compensated equally. They are simply classified as "unskilled labor." Nearly 80 percent of employees in **export-processing zones (EPZs)** are women, and women account for a significant proportion (for example, nearly 40 percent in Latin America) of the labor force in the informal sectors of MNC operations; the women are paid based on piece-work rather than hourly wages and with little or no protective regulations or fringe benefits.[107]

Further, MNCs use political influence and seek contractual arrangements with governments guaranteeing freedom in hiring and firing decisions. Unlike industrialized countries in which relatively strong labor laws have been in place since the 1930s, government-labor union relations in developing countries range from total government control to limited organizational autonomy to being prohibited by law. MNCs gravitate to countries, developed and developing, in which governments do not impose *de facto* or *de jure* "unionism." However, labor disputes, when they do occur, almost invariably assume nationalist overtones, because MNCs' decisions, while directly influencing employees' lives, are made in headquarters located in foreign countries. Governments unable to side with the workers to address grievances themselves are often viewed as conspiring against their own population in favor of foreign interests.

However, as the *dependencia* theorists argue, another set of issues remains and is related to the division of the world economy into the rich North and the poor South (discussed in greater detail in Chapter 9). As MNCs bind host economies into the global political economy,[108] the economic development they generate, even when contributing to host country wage increases and economic development, produces *economic dualism* and *economic dependency.* Economic dualism refers to the situation in which specific regions of a country, usually major cities or specifically designated economic zones, are the chief beneficiaries of economic development and modernization, while the rest of the country is kept in relative poverty, virtually excluded from the development process (see also Chapter 10).

An example of economic dualism is the proliferation of export-processing zones (also known as free trade zones, FTZs). EPZs are specific areas designated by the host government, where MNCs produce goods for export without taxation or the burden of governmental regulations, normally imposed on the national economy, but with the condition that 100 percent of goods assembled be exported. Since the 1960s, many countries have adopted this strategy to stimulate their economies, and by the early 1990s about 173 EPZs were operating in the developing world, employing nearly 4 million people.[109] Latin America and the Caribbean had eighty-five EPZs, with about 1.1 million employees; Asia (including the Middle East) and the Pacific region were home to fifty-seven EPZs, with 2.7 million workers; and Africa had thirty-one EPZs, employing about 230,650 workers. The largest number of EPZs were located in Mexico (twenty-three), followed by the Dominican Republic (eighteen), and Malaysia (ten); together the three provided employment to nearly 709,000 workers. China's seven EPZs, however, employed a total of 2.2 million workers, the largest EPZ employment in the developing countries.[110]

In East Asian countries, such as Singapore, South Korea and Taiwan, where EPZs had proliferated in the 1960s and 1970s, this "first generation" strategy was based on what one observer has called "the three T's: toys, textiles, and trash (for example, cheap shoes, hibachis, inflatable swimming pools) and so on."[111] Governments invited MNCs to set up shop in EPZs and to employ cheap labor, comprised mostly of poor women and even children eager to earn an income for their families. MNCs found these arrangements quite attractive: cheap labor provided workers to perform the physical, labor-intensive production, while MNCs avoided taxes on transactions and labor, as well as environmental regulations.[112] In the late 1980s and 1990s, East Asian (the "second generation") EPZs shifted to capital-intensive production, while labor-intensive production was transferred to Africa and Latin America.[113]

The EPZ strategy benefits host economies in a number of ways. MNCs absorb some of the unemployed, and those employed bring into their communities capital that otherwise would not be available. This new capital generated through EPZ employment enables the local population to purchase products made by and/or distributed through local entrepreneurs. Initially, domestic companies used EPZs also to become more familiar with the global markets and market standards, to improve their products and productivity, and to become more competitive in international trade, including trade with MNCs located in EPZs. Governments of newly industrialized countries (NICs), such as South Korea and Taiwan, encouraged exporting and distributed funds accordingly. By the mid-1970s and early 1980s, the NICs were not only already dealing in the "three T's sectors" but also had emerged as successful competitors in technologically advanced, capital-intensive products (cars, television, computers).[114]

However, not all areas benefited equally. Since the late 1960s, the Mexican government, with the support of the U.S. government and companies, imitated the Asian EPZ strategy to develop and introduce the Border Industrialization Program, extending various incentives to U.S. companies to build factories across the border. Factories, known as the *maquiladoras,* in the Mexican-U.S. border areas and their EPZs have been criticized as "exploitation and poverty zones." The initial plan promised better standards of living through economic development and employment, yet companies, seeking cheaper labor, often prefer to employ young women, and, as a result, their plants do not fully address local unemployment problems, since most males in the same households remain unemployed. In addition, *maquiladoras* factories generally pay about $1.00 an hour, which is better than having no income for the unemployed but is not sufficient to maintain a family. Assembly lines reportedly are set at a 25 percent faster pace than their counterparts in the United States,[115] and employees unable to keep pace are either fired or leave after a few years. Neither would their health and safety conditions meet U.S. standards. Companies using hazardous material in production and assembly processes reportedly either do not inform the employees of the dangers to their health or give false information. A report covering problems at a Kemet (Union Carbide) plant in the town of Matamoros states,

> In Ciudad Juarez we met a young man who told us he works with radioactive materials. The company, which manufactures smoke detectors, has told him that the radioactivity is minimal and that all he needs to do is use a small protector. This is an apparatus like a bracelet that is connected to a line over his head. As long as he wears this bracelet on his wrist, they told him, he will be completely safe. We made him see that they were lying to him. We told him of the risks he was running and he was very surprised.[116]

Women working in hazardous conditions with little or no regulation and accountability reportedly suffer serious health problems, giving birth to children with birth defects, as a number of cases in the Mallory Capacitors *maquila* appear to have demonstrated. However, companies have ignored women's concerns, and the women have not been able to force companies to improve working conditions. One *maquila* manager has noted that companies

> like to hire girls who don't have too much experience because they aren't spoiled. We shape them to our needs by appealing to their feminine sensibilities. Then you can trust they won't fly off the handle, making unrealistic demands or joining unions. We like to think of our company as a family where everyone knows their duties.[117]

In addition to the "dual economy" syndrome, *economic dependency* is also a problem for host, particularly developing, countries. Economic dependency results from the MNCs' heavy concentration of capital into specific sectors of a host country's economy, enabling MNCs to penetrate their communities, with serious implications for national sovereignty. While MNC-host government relations are, as a matter of daily routine, cooperative, there are inherent conflicts between their interests and objectives, as each seeks to promote and protect its own and its constituents' interests. Governments, as sovereign entities, insist on maintaining exclusive political control over their population and economy, yet they also have to promote economic growth and provide various public services. At the same time, however, heavy MNC involvement in the host country's economy can translate into enormous political influence in that country—especially to the extent that the host government cannot formulate and implement policies independently of MNCs. Decisions by an MNC's headquarters in a distant country to maximize profits for its investors and to promote the corporation's interests may not necessarily promote the interests of the host economy.

Economic nationalists argue that it is necessary for a country to develop its own institutions of knowledge, research and development capabilities, and inventions to maintain self-sustaining economic growth. In some cases, a contract between a developing country and a foreign company is viewed as a "sell out," and the public demands restitution. In India, for example, the elected nationalist government in the state of Maharashtra demanded in 1996 that Enron, a U.S. power company, renegotiate its $2.8 billion contract. Enron obliged, but without it the state could hardly generate the 540mw it needed—far short of the expected 2,200mw.[118] Indeed, MNC managers sometimes become frustrated when their advanced management or production techniques do not fit most country conditions.

These issues are directly related to the relative bargaining power of MNCs and host governments. As Dicken has put it, "the fundamental problem facing individual nation states is that each contains only part of any TNC's [transnational corporations] operations. This is so whether the TNC is foreign or domestic."[119] This fragmentation allows greater flexibility for the MNCs and limits the host government's ability to bargain. One observer has noted,

> Aurelio Peccei, a director of Fiat, once claimed that the multinational corporation was "the most powerful agent for the internationalization of society." Carl Gerstacker, sometime chairman of Dow Chemicals, confessed that he had "long dreamed of buying an island owned by no nation and of establishing the world headquarters of the Dow company on the truly neutral ground of such an island, beholden to no nation or society."[120]

THE REGULATION OF MULTINATIONAL CORPORATIONS

The previous discussion indicates that two general perspectives emerge with respect to multinational corporations and their impact on home and host countries. On the positive side, proponents of the classical liberal laissez-faire approach argue that MNCs make significant contributions, including economic development and efficiency, greater employment opportunities in communities, and the transfer and distribution of production and communications technologies and services (for instance, financial services), which host countries cannot obtain or develop locally. Accordingly, they argue, MNCs should operate in a free environment, unfettered by government regulations, to maximize both their profits and the well-being of host economies.[121] On the negative side, opponents contend that MNCs also bring with them numerous problems. These include political and even military interventions by MNCs' home governments (for example, U.S. interventions in Latin American countries, such as Nicaragua and Chile), increasing dependence on imported capital and technologies, bribery of political leaders, poverty, exploitation, and environmental degradation, while exacerbating local conflicts. Such difficulties, at least as viewed by host countries, challenge the host country's national sovereignty and prestige, and threaten local values and cultures. Above all, the presence of MNCs in a country shifts the balance of national power from the government to the companies, diminishing government responsiveness and accountability to the public.[122] To counter MNCs' financial and negotiating power, as well as to integrate the markets for their local industries, developing countries have used both regulation and regional integration arrangements.

Since the 1960s and 1970s, charges of political interventions and exploitation of labor in host countries have led to demands for greater national and international regulations or even nationalization of MNCs. International regulation involves a number of specific areas, such as competition, taxation, employment and industrial relations, and information regarding MNC operations. National regulations of MNCs range from customs controls for purposes of taxation to regulatory standards, to total nationalization.[123] International regulation has emerged under the Organization for Economic Cooperation and Development (OECD) for the industrialized countries and under the auspices of the United Nations for the developing countries. The proliferation in bilateral investment treaties was noted earlier. The following section looks at international codes of conduct.

The development of international codes of conduct delineating the parameters of MNC-host government relations and obligations has proven a difficult task, because the international system historically has lacked the legal and institutional bases for harmonization and standardization of such codes and regulations, as in the case of environmental concerns and the **Law of the Sea.**[124] In the 1920s, the League of Nations sought to institutionalize the legal protection of foreign investments and to address issues related to corporate taxation, and in the 1940s the Atlantic Charter and Lend-Lease Agreements between the U.S. and its allies (including the USSR) attempted to expand multilateral governmental and nongovernmental economic cooperation. These early efforts provided the basis for the United Nations to include principles of international cooperation in a chapter, entitled "International Economic and Social Cooperation," of the U.N. Charter.[125] However, a fundamental weakness in the regulatory structure is that it is premised on voluntary cooperation by MNCs, and it lacks enforcement mechanisms.

The United States and other Western governments, which generally support MNCs, have viewed international codes of MNC conduct, such as the OECD *Guidelines,* as establishing certain "rules of the game" beneficial to the interests of, and protecting relations between, MNCs and governments; Europeans, however, have paid closer attention to MNCs' social and economic obligations than have their U.S. counterparts. Developing countries have viewed international codes as instruments to address concerns about MNC economic and political power and to ensure some support from MNCs' home governments in compelling companies to accept certain responsibilities in the host countries, such as reinvesting a guaranteed percentage of profits.[126]

By the mid-1990s, regulatory regimes emerged under a number of organizations, including the International Chamber of Commerce, the International Labor Organization, the United Nations, the Organization for Economic Development and Cooperation (OECD), and the European Union. In 1977, the ILO enunciated a nonbinding *ILO Declaration of Principles Concerning Multinational Enterprises and Social Policy.* In the mid-1980s, the United Nations Center on Transnational Corporations (UNCTC) introduced *The United Nations Code of Conduct for Transnational Corporations,*[127] in an effort to establish universally applicable standards with respect to their activities in host countries and their relations with host governments and communities. Prodded mainly by developing countries, the UN code sought to restrict MNC activities in and interference into the political affairs of host countries and to protect national sovereignty. To that end, the developing countries demanded that the UN code be mandatory and legally binding. Changes in the world economy, however, led to rejection of such demands and to changes in the UN's and some developing countries' attitudes toward MNCs. While in the 1960s and 1970s the United Nations made greater efforts to check MNC operations in developing countries, in later years it has acted to promote greater cooperation between them.[128] For purposes of illustration in this section, it will suffice briefly to discuss one regulatory regime, the OECD *Guidelines,* currently in its formative stages.

In 1976, the OECD adopted the *Guidelines for Multinational Enterprises* (see Box 7.7). Although not legally binding, the OECD guidelines are important because most of the world's major MNCs and their investments are located in OECD countries and because the guidelines remain the most comprehensive document to date. One of their advantages is that they were written in the interest of both home and host countries.[129] The OECD guidelines consist of six sections, including sections on regulation of the disclosure of corporate information, MNC competition, financing and taxation, employment and industrial relations, and the uses and impact of science and technology. The general policies in the introduction of the guidelines well summarize the concerns of host and home countries. They pay special attention to the causes of potential conflicts between MNCs and governments in such areas as social and economic policies, industrial development, competition, and exploitation of resources. The guidelines seek greater cooperation between MNCs

BOX 7.7

OECD GUIDELINES FOR MNCS, 1976

General Policies

Enterprises should:

1. take fully into account established general policy objectives of the Member countries in which they operate;
2. in particular, give due consideration to those countries' aims and priorities with regard to economic and social progress, including industrial and regional development, the protection of the environment and consumer interests, the creation of employment opportunities, the promotion of innovation and the transfer of technology;
3. while observing their legal obligations concerning information, supply their entities with supplementary information the latter may need in order to meet requests by the authorities of the countries in which those entities are located for information relevant to the activities of those entities, taking into account legitimate requirements of business confidentiality;
4. favour close co-operation with the local community and business interests;
5. allow their component entities freedom to develop their activities and to exploit their competitive advantage in domestic and foreign markets, consistent with the need for specialization and sound commercial practice;
6. when filling responsible posts in each country of operation, take due account of individual qualifications without discrimination as to nationality, subject to particular national requirements in this respect;
7. not render—and they should not be solicited or expected to render—any bribe or other improper benefit, direct or indirect, to any public servant or holder of public office;
8. unless legally permissible, not make contributions to candidates for public office or to political parties or other political organizations;
9. abstain from any improper involvement in local political activities.

Source: International Investment and Multinational Enterprises. Copyright OECD. (1979).

and local businesses. They are premised on the belief that MNCs' investments must benefit local communities rather than simply generate profits exclusively for MNCs. The guidelines also seek to limit MNCs' influence in local political affairs and policymaking processes by prohibiting illegal contributions and bribes to candidates and political parties.

Like other legal instruments regulating MNC-host government relations, the OECD guidelines are premised on international principles of mutual respect and reciprocity aimed at avoiding tensions and conflicts. Not surprisingly, however, various controversies surround international codes of conduct. One controversy involves the question of whether such codes should be voluntary (not legally binding) or obligatory (legally binding). MNCs are neither sovereign states nor public international organizations. As such, they lack the legal authority to be directly involved in international standard-setting (that is, code-creating) processes. Codes and guidelines, therefore, do not, in and of themselves, constitute international law. At the same time, however, state parties (participant signatories) and nonparty states affected by MNC activities do possess the domestic authority to enforce international standards at home, and state practices may transform codes of MNC conduct into treaties or customary international law. Where states adopt internationally set codes and guidelines as part of their domestic law, they may be directly applied by domestic courts and enforceable as domestic law.[130]

To some limited extent, efforts to regulate MNCs have paid off, although initially MNCs vehemently opposed the establishment of international codes. MNCs gradually have become more self-conscious about their image around the world. They have developed specific internal codes of conduct with respect to employment practices (such as child labor), environmental issues, and their association with host governments. Some have signed the International Chamber of Commerce's Business Charter for Sustainable Development and have created permanent "ethics officers" to monitor the company's conduct. Digital, Compaq, and IBM have introduced stricter environmental standards, and oil companies such as British Petroleum and Arco have agreed to build environmentally safe schools and airports if given permission to drill for oil in Siberia and Alaska.[131] These were partly in response to two major disasters—the Union

Carbide accident in Bhopal, India, in 1984 and the Exxon oil spill in Valdez, Alaska, in 1989—both of which resulted in high-profile court cases and put, even if briefly, some pressure on companies to pay more attention to the environmental and health hazards their operations pose to local communities. In the Union Carbide incident, the UC plant at Bhopal leaked 5 tons of methyl isocyanate (extremely poisonous) gas and almost instantaneously killed more than 3,000 people and permanently injured 50,000. This was perhaps the worst industrial accident ever recorded in history. In the case of Exxon, the tanker oil spill, dumping 11 million gallons of North Slope crude oil into the Prince William Sound waters, poisoned 700 miles of Alaska's shoreline and sealife. The cost to repair the damage was estimated at the time be from $2.5 billion to $5 billion.[132]

As one way to strengthen their bargaining position toward MNCs, countries have sought regional cooperation, one advantage being that agreements such as customs unions and free trade areas create larger markets, giving MNCs greater incentives to invest in the region. To gain access to a larger market created under regional cooperation, MNCs are more inclined to acquiesce to FDI terms and conditions that, in individual countries with smaller markets, they otherwise might not accept.[133] However, MNCs also have opposed regional control over their investments and properties, and regional integration as a vehicle of control over MNC operations has not proven very successful, since MNCs can move their investments to other, less restrictive regions. Developing countries, regardless of their efforts to control MNC operations, remain economically dependent on them.[134]

The Foreign Investment Code of the Andean Pact, for example, created strategies for regional coordination of foreign investments, while prohibiting intra-region competitive bidding. The pact required multinational corporations to share ownership with local enterprises, and it established an administrative agency to regulate technology transfer.[135] Further, its common external tariff and Decision No. 24, which regulates investments within the region, restricted MNC transactions.[136] As noted in Chapter 6, however, by the late 1970s the Andean Group was faced with internal tensions as some of its members, especially Chile, demanded reductions in or the total elimination of MNC restrictions.[137]

THE POLITICAL ECONOMY OF INTERNATIONAL TAXATION

One proposed strategy to combat problems such as the North–South, rich-poor gap and lost capital in host countries, is through **international taxation** of MNCs.[138] The concept of international taxation needs clarification. Analysts inaccurately use the term to refer to *national* taxation of transnational transactions by MNCs and individuals. Here the hyphenated form (that is, inter-national taxation) will be used to refer to national taxation on international transactions, while reserving the term *international taxation* to mean taxation administered by an international, multilateral agency, such as a World Development Fund as proposed in the late 1970s and early 1980s by the Brandt Commission.[139]

Opponents of taxation on MNCs argue that such schemes will invariably have negative consequences for international trade and living standards as they distort the market and hinder competition. They contend that higher taxes risk recession and directly and indirectly influence international investments and therefore jeopardize a country's ability to attract capital and to compete in global markets.[140]

MNCs operate in a complex web of national taxation systems, and it is important for the MNC management to assess each country's tax policies. Each government has its own views concerning domestic and foreign enterprises and taxation (see Box 7.8). Technically (for example, under international law), there are no limits on the level of taxes national governments can levy on MNC income.[141] In fact, as previously discussed, in order to attract MNCs, some governments are more than willing to create accommodative tax structures designed to provide interested MNCs with various forms of "tax havens" and loopholes.[142] Countries such as Bermuda, the Bahamas, and Vanuatu impose no income taxes, while others such as Switzerland and Liechtenstein have very low taxes.[143]

MNCs earn a substantial portion of their after-tax profits through their foreign subsidiaries, and their foreign earnings often are subject to taxation by both the host and home governments. Capital flows from foreign subsidiaries to the parent company constitute one of the most essential means for repatriation of MNC earnings abroad, and their volume in terms of profits represents the size of an MNC's worldwide investments. In the mid-1980s, for example, the foreign subsidiaries of U.S. multinationals earned $30 billion after-foreign-tax profits abroad, $11.8 billion of which was repatriated in dividends to their parent companies in the United States. That amount of capital flowing into the U.S. economy is important for the investors but also for the U.S. government for purposes of revenues (that is, taxation).[144]

Kim and Kim distinguish between direct and indirect taxes. Direct taxes involve income and capital gains

BOX 7.8

PRINCIPLES OF INTERNATIONAL TAXATION

A government levies taxes on MNCs based on two legally defined jurisdictional principles: *nationality* and *territoriality*. In the former case, a government claims jurisdiction over "all income earned by a citizen or a company incorporated in that country . . . because of the legal connection to that country" regardless of the territorial origin of their income. Profits earned by a Spanish citizen or a corporation in Malaysia is subject to taxation in Spain—and usually in Malaysia. The legal justification for such a tax is the *privileges of nationality*—as an "insurance policy"—a citizen or a company enjoys abroad. While working abroad, citizens are protected by their home governments under international law and retain their legal right to freely return to their home country. Similarly, a corporation enjoys the legal protection of its home government, as provided by national and international laws, against threats to property (for example, nationalization by host government). In *Cook v. Tait* (1924), for example, the U.S. Supreme Court decided that taxation of the taxpayer's income in foreign countries was not unconstitutional and did not violate international law. Such taxation was justified, the court argued, because the benefits of U.S. citizenship "extend beyond territorial boundaries. "With respect to the principle of *territoriality*, a government justifies taxation on businesses on grounds that operations and consumption in the country make it possible to generate profits. Government might choose to tax corporate investment income derived from dividends, interest, royalties, and rent.

In theory, and from a purely economic standpoint, an international taxation policy should be designed so as not to directly influence investment and consumption decisions. This principle of "tax-neutrality" is based on three standards. The first is *capital-export neutrality*, in which taxation has no bearing on an investor's decision whether to invest at home or abroad. For instance, if a German corporation is taxed 20 percent in Germany on its worldwide income, and its income from a subsidiary in Argentina is also taxed 20 percent in Argentina, such a taxation would be considered capital-export neutral because the German corporation would pay 20 percent tax on its income whether the investment were in Germany or in Argentina. Such an arrangement, it is assumed, will enable the German corporation to "make its investment decisions based on business factors rather than tax rates." The second standard is *capital-import neutrality*, in which a government taxes at the same rate for all corporations operating in its home market. If England exempts a Japanese corporation's income from English taxation, this would be based on the principle of capital-import neutrality; the Japanese firm might be taxed at the comparable rate as Japanese corporations in Japan. The third standard is *national neutrality* whereby the total returns on capital shared between the taxed corporation and the Treasury are the same whether the capital is invested at home or abroad and regardless of other taxes levied on that corporation abroad.

Source: See Richard L. Doernberg, *International Taxation*, 2d ed. (St. Paul: West, 1993), pp. 4–19, *passim*.

taxes—that is, taxes on such assets as stocks and bonds—although MNCs also pay property taxes, registration and contract taxes, sales and excise taxes, and so forth. Indirect taxes include value-added taxes, on each stage of production, and tariffs.[145] However, not all taxes are equally distributed across countries. Tax rates in the early 1990s on MNCs ranged from zero, as in the case of the Bahamas, to over 50 percent, as in the case of Norway (the U.S. came in at roughly 30 percent). As sources of revenues, corporate income taxes, for example, are not as essential for most industrialized countries as they are for developing countries. Per capita income in the latter does not provide governments sufficient revenues; as a result, they rely on taxes of MNCs for a larger share of their revenues.[146]

All countries have some form of national taxation on individual and corporate incomes operating at home and abroad as determined by domestic tax structures and bilateral treaties, and most countries use a combination of the three tax systems of neutrality, as discussed in Box 7.8. The problem of **double taxation** arises when one government claims authority to tax based on the residence (or citizenship) of the taxpayer, while the other claims authority to tax based on origin of income. Of course, a similar problem occurs when each claims a taxpayer as resident or when each claims authority to tax based on origin of income.[147] Thus, when the governments of trading partners decide to tax profits from trade, the result can be overlapping claims and double taxation. To avoid such problems, some degree of policy coordination is necessary, and governments try to avoid double taxation through bilateral taxation treaties or national laws. By 1996, for example, EU member countries had 740 double taxation treaties; 323 (44 percent) were with developed countries, 314 (42 percent) with developing countries, and 103 (14 percent) with Central and Eastern European countries.[148]

We have already discussed in Chapter 1 the complicated nature of international taxation, as in the case of California's "unitary tax system." When a government imposes taxes on foreign MNCs, it is difficult to force them to pay the full amount. Taxation systems in most countries raise a host of questions regarding the nature and level of taxes to be imposed. Who should be taxed (the parent company or its subsidiaries, or both)? Who in the government has ultimate jurisdiction over the taxation of foreign companies? In a federal system, such as in the United States, the national, state, and local governments can claim jurisdiction over taxation issues, while in other countries only the national government can tax. Should an MNC pay taxes to a government on its incomes from operations worldwide? Or should it pay taxes on incomes derived from that country only?[149] In the British Barclays Bank case, the bank's lawyers contended that a state—in this case, California—lacks the legal authority to tax the bank's profits in other countries and that such a state tax violated the federal government's exclusive authority to regulate international commerce. The bank's lawyers argued that California's taxation system was, in fact, double taxation. When challenged as such, an MNC's home government can, and often does, intervene diplomatically, or through compensation, to protect the company.[150] However, the host government ultimately has the authority to protect its own interests. When the Container Corporation and Shell Petroleum challenged California's unitary tax system before the U.S. Supreme Court, in both cases the court upheld that state's right to tax.[151]

Some economists believe that taxes distort the free workings of the domestic and global markets and retard international competitiveness. Opponents of taxation contend that high taxes result "in the relatively low rates of capital formation" while encouraging borrowing and debt.[152] High taxes divert capital resources from corporate income, they argue; and, discourage saving for future investments. Taxation proponents maintain that some revenues generated are used for "valid public purposes," even if taxation on certain industries leads to misallocation of resources.[153]

In addition to inter-national taxation, some analysts have proposed the institutionalization of some form of international taxation to assist the underclass around the world, especially in poorer developing countries.[154] Since WWII, official development assistance has rarely (and only by a small number of European and Middle Eastern countries) reached above 1.0 percent of individual donor country's GNP[155] (discussed in Chapter 11). Moreover, bilateral assistance programs throughout the Cold War were highly ideological in orientation and functioned as instruments of "national security interests," rather than necessarily providing assistance to the poor.[156] Thus, proponents of international taxation contend that it is necessary to supplement existing bilateral and multilateral foreign assistance for a more equitable distribution of resources among nations.

The issue of international taxation has been debated frequently in political and academic circles, and various strategies have been proposed. In 1980, the Brandt Commission, for example, advocated the development of an international tax on international trade and similar transactions to produce capital for economic development. To that end, it proposed a new World Development Fund under UN auspices to administer international taxation and distribution of development assistance funds.[157] A UN agency such as a World Development Fund, the commission argued, would improve the structure of the global financial system and "serve as a channel for such resources as may be raised on a universal and automatic basis," to secure a constant flow of development funds to the developing economies.[158] In a similar vein, in 1990 the Nyerere Commission proposed the establishment of a South Bank to finance various projects in developing countries.[159] One proponent of such international taxation has argued that a South Bank, in cooperation with a World Development Fund, operating within the UN framework, would institute a much needed mechanism for the distribution of resources through UN agencies.[160] Under such a multilateral arrangement, all MNC transboundary trade and transactions—whether on land, air, or sea, as well as electronic—would be subject to international taxation by the United Nations. The total volume of world manufacturing trade subject to international taxation would be over $3.0 trillion.[161]

Two central concerns have posed difficulties regarding international taxation. First, as targets of taxation, MNCs naturally oppose such strategies. They would argue that competition in the global economy is already a test of survival, and they need no additional burdens to jeopardize their income. Second, governments also would oppose such an internationally based system, since historically the nation-state has held exclusive authority to tax; certainly giving U.N. agencies that authority would be politically controversial. However, in the absence of such policies for the "fair" distribution of resources, and out of frustration with their inability to accommodate domestic public needs and demands, governments sometimes have resorted to extreme measures, including the nationalization of MNC properties, which in turn have led to bloodshed and installation of tyrannical rulers.

The Political Economy of Nationalization

Nothing in host government–MNC relations can be more controversial than government nationalization of holdings and subsidiaries. As previously noted, nationalization is the government seizure of private corporate property owned by domestic and foreign companies. Government nationalization occurs in a number of ways. One is *confiscation,* whereby the host government nationalizes an MNC's subsidiary without compensation. Another is *expropriation,* nationalization with some compensation.[162]

Nationalization became a particularly important issue in the 1950s and 1960s as former colonial territories gained independence from European colonial powers. As newly emerging governments sought to consolidate political and economic power, they also sought to assert or reassert their control over the "commanding heights" of the national economy, including communications, transportation and hydroelectric power facilities, banking institutions, extractive and manufacturing industries, and other economic assets deemed essential for national security and political and economic independence.

Examples of government nationalization of foreign-owned enterprises abound. The 1917 Bolshevik Revolution in the Soviet Union, the Mexican Revolution in the 1910s, and the Chinese Communist Revolution in 1949 led to the nationalization of virtually all foreign-owned properties. Similarly, Communist takeovers in Eastern European countries after the Second World War and Cuba's revolution resulted in nationalization. Not all nationalizations, however, are by Communist governments. Most have occurred in the developing world as an expression of nationalism in pursuit of independence from foreign economic and political domination. A sample of nationalizations in Latin America appears in Table 7.8.

The results of politically motivated nationalizations have varied, with both long-term successes and problems. Mao Tse-tung's Communist revolution in the People's Republic of China brought widespread confiscation of private holdings. However, the Chinese Communist revolution was partly an extension of an ongoing nationalist revolution against Western government and corporate interference in Chinese political and economic affairs since the early twentieth century. In 1951, Iran's nationalist leader, Mohammed Mossadegh, nationalized the Anglo-Iranian Oil Company (now British Petroleum) for a similar reason, but, unlike Mao's case, in 1953 the CIA helped overthrow the Mossadegh government. The shah was brought back to power and signed a new contract with the Anglo-Iranian Oil Company. Also in 1953, Guatemala's nationalist leader, Jacobo Arbenz Guzman, nationalized the properties of the U.S.-owned United Fruit Company ("Chiquita Banana"), but shortly thereafter the CIA overthrew Arbenz, and the newly installed government returned the nationalized properties to the company. Thus, one overriding reason governments in the developing countries nationalize MNC enterprises is to assert or reassert national economic and political independence and to fortify the country's sovereignty against foreign encroachments.[163]

A related reason a host government nationalizes a company is that when, because of domestic economic and political pressures, the government demands a more equitable distribution of profits (usually in the form of a certain percentage of MNC profits before repatriation), the MNC may refuse to negotiate. Such demands have included, for example, a "51 percent" equity participation, the appointment of local managers in the MNC's management hierarchy, the training of local technicians, and a sufficient contribution to the host community's economic development.[164] Some of these demands are more objectionable than others to MNCs. In 1971, the Guyanese government nationalized the Demerara Bauxite Company (Demba), a subsidiary of one of the largest Canadian-based MNCs, Alcan Aluminum, Ltd. The government had demanded equity share and greater control because the Guyanese public resented Demba's control over mining operations and its exploitation of the local population. By the late 1960s, Demba was the largest business enterprise in Guyana, accounting for 14 percent of the country's GDP, 10 percent of all government revenues, and nearly 50 percent of Guyana's exports.[165]

Another reason for nationalization is the MNC's alleged interference in the host country's political affairs. In Chile, between 1971 and 1973, the government of Social Democrat Salvador Allende Gossens nationalized the Kennecott and Anaconda properties in the copper industry, the Bethlehem Steel and Armco Steel subsidiaries, the International Telephone and Telegraph (ITT) subsidiary, the branches of Bank of America and the First National Bank, and the subsidiaries of Coca-Cola, DuPont, General Motors, and RCA. Although the Allende administration was not the first government to nationalize MNC investments in Chile,

TABLE 7.8
A Sample of Nationalalized U.S. Enterprises in Latin America, 1900–1970s

Year	Country	Enterprise	Claim	Year/Amount of Settlement
1900	Nicaragua	Timber	$1,048,154	1909 / $600,000
1917–1941	Mexico	Landholdings Railways	$561,800 $75,000,000	1930 /$225,468 1941 /$40,000,000
1937	Bolivia	Standard Oil	$3,000,000	1942 /$1,729,375
1958	Argentina	American & Foreign Power Co.	$60,000,000	1961 /$53,632,000
1959–1960	Cuba	Cattle ranches, sugar lands and mills, oil refineries, banks, manufacturing plants, public utilities, hotels.	$3,346,000,000	Pending
1962	Brazil	ITT subsidiary	$6,000,000–$10,000,000	1963 /$7,300,000
1968	Peru	International Petroleum Company (Exxon)	$120,000,000	1974 / $23,100,000 and $4,400,000 in interest
1970	Peru	ITT subsidiary	$18,500,000	1970 / $17,900,000
1970	Ecuador	ITT subsidiary	$5,000,000–$7,500,000	1971 / $600,000
1971	Chile	Bethlehem Steel subsidiary Armco Steel subsidiary	Negotiated	1971 / $31,000,000
		Bank of America and First National Bank branches	Negotiated	1971 / $5,000,000
		ITT subsidiaries	$153,000,000	1974 / $125,000,000
1974	Venezuela	Bethlehem Steel and U.S. Steel mining subsidiaries	Negotiated	1975 / $101,400,000
1974	Ecuador	Texaco, Gulf subsidiaries	Negotiated	1974 / $148,000,000
1975	Peru	Gulf Oil subsidiary Marcona iron Mines	$2,000,000 $167,000,000	1977 / $1,540,000 1976 / $61,400,000

Source: Paul E. Sigmund, *Multinationals in Latin America* © 1980 The Twentieth Century Fund, Inc. Reprinted by permission of the University of Wisconsin Press, 36–39.

by the time of his election in 1971, Chilean nationalist and anti-U.S. sentiments had reached new and explosive levels, and the expropriations in 1971 were in reaction to the long history of foreign (mainly U.S.) MNC and government interference in Chile's elections and political affairs in general. These companies virtually dominated the Chilean economy for decades, and the symbiotic relationship between the U.S. companies and the U.S. government strengthened the MNC's political position in that country. The MNCs lobbied Washington to protect their interests and to influence election outcomes in Chile in favor of pro-MNC candidates. Following Allende's visit to Cuba in September 1973, the CIA orchestrated a military coup to overthrow the Allende government (resulting in the president's death), and most of the expropriated properties were returned to the MNCs after General Augusto Pinochet Ugarte was installed in power.[166] At the time, Secretary of State Henry Kissinger was quoted as saying, "Why should the U.S. stand by and let a country go Communist merely because of the short sightedness of its people?"

Still another but less frequently cited reason for nationalization is an MNC's willingness and even preference to hand over its properties and operations to the host government. Since MNCs generally purchase insurance in parent countries to cover their investments abroad, some companies prefer nationalization by the host government when the benefits of nationalization "outweigh the benefits of continuing troubled business relations in a host country in which the business climate is growing increasingly hostile."[167] Staged nationalizations, of course, violate insurance contracts, and insurance claims may be denied, for example, by the Overseas Private Investment Corporation (OPIC), a US government program, if the expropriation was caused by the company's own misconduct. In the case of ITT, for example, OPIC denied insurance claims because testimony by some CIA officials and ITT representatives in congressional hearings revealed the company's involvement in Chilean presidential elections.[168]

Finally, another reason for nationalization is mainly punitive: a government seizes a company to punish the company owners. The French government nationalized the Renault Motor Company after the Second World War because the Renault family had collaborated with the Nazi-Vichy regime during the war.[169] There is little doubt that, under national and international legal norms, governments, whether in industrialized or developing countries, have reserved to themselves the right to nationalize foreign investments if they deem it necessary. International institutions, such as the United Nations, have at times lent moral, if not necessarily legal, support for nationalization. For example, "The Charter of Economic Rights and Duties of States," adopted by the UN General Assembly Resolution 3281 in 1974, provides that

> each State has the right . . . to nationalize, expropriate, or transfer ownership of foreign property, in which case appropriate compensation should be paid by the State adopting such measures, taking into account its relevant law and regulations and all circumstances the State considers pertinent. In any case where the question of compensation gives rise to a controversy, it shall be settled under the domestic law of the nationalizing State and by its tribunals. . . . G.A.Res. 3281 U.N. GAOR Supp. (No.31) 50, U.N. Doc. A/9631 (1974).

The momentum for nationalization survived into the early 1980s, but, as the economic nationalist sentiments—particularly the vehemently anti-MNC variant—in Africa, Asia, and Latin America subsided, governments and the United Nations began to adopt a more accommodative posture toward MNCs. An increasing number of governments responded to the economic crises—most emphatically to the foreign debt crisis—at the end of the 1980s and the early 1990s by relaxing some of their regulatory constraints to attract foreign investments, and they promised or introduced plans for privatization of large portions of their economies.

The Political Economy of Privatization

Privatization is the sale of a state-owned industry, or a portion of it, to private entrepreneurs or companies. Proponents of the public sector argue that state-owned enterprises promote the public good by stimulating the economy rather than promoting private gain and high profits. As previously noted, however, critics of state-ownership—most notably, proponents of laissez-faire capitalism—argue that such enterprises absorb substantial financial resources from the national economy, while perpetuating inefficient and uninnovative operations. In state economic enterprises (SEEs) (or state-owned enterprises) both managers and employees supposedly lack incentives to compete effectively in the rapidly changing global markets. By the mid-1980s, the financial deficits and cash drains caused by external borrowing and foreign debt to run state-owned enterprises accounted for a large share of many states' national budgets. Rather than risk further economic decline and political instability, some governments adopted alternative strategies to cure their financial problems. Privatization of state-owned enterprises was one such strategy.[170]

In some countries, as in Britain and France, privatization was done partly to relieve government expenditures and as a bonus to private investors. In the former Soviet Union, privatization was directly related to democratization. Pressures for democratization required that the ruling Communist Party elites relinquish monopoly over the political institutions but also over the state-owned enterprises as the stagnant economy failed to serve and satisfy the public. Between 1989 and 1991, as the Communist Parties in Eastern Europe and in the former Soviet republics fell, these countries commenced the tortuous process of privatization. Ironically, however, among the first wave of new private owners were the ex-Communists themselves, as they had access to both finances and strategic information. In some Latin American countries, such as Chile under the Pinochet regime, privatization was closely associated with military dictatorial rule, and in the 1980s privatization in the context of U.S.–Latin American relations bore a significant Cold War ideological and geopolitical component.

Not all countries experienced privatization in such an extreme manner as did the former Soviet Union. Raymond Vernon has argued that in most countries around the world privatization of government-owned enterprises has come in fits and starts and has not been the result of ideological zeal embracing laissez-faire capitalism as a panacea for all social and economic ills. Governments have been rather pragmatic in their divestitures of interests in some companies while strengthening their financial stakes in others. In the case of Italy, for instance, has Vernon noted,

> Most IRI [Istito per la Ricostruzione Industriali] divestitures . . . have consisted of sales to the public of noncontrolling interests in IRI companies, with the sales proceeds going to bolster IRI's financial position. The explicit purpose of these divestitures has been to strengthen the performance of the IRI group, not to reduce the aggregate role of state-owned enterprises.[171]

Privatization occurs in two general ways: (1) the sale of all or a percentage of state ownership rights to private companies or investors and (2) replacement of specific public sector activities and services by private companies. In practice, privatization may involve a combination of the two, with a series of contracts with private companies in various economic sectors ranging from the management of housing units, the management of prisons, and garbage collection to the total private ownership of transportation, communications, and utility companies. The choice of specific strategies by a government depends on the political power configuration among the interest groups, bureaucracies, and policymakers in the principal institutions, the economic imperatives as dictated by domestic and international financial conditions, debts, and the overall ideological and historical context of privatization. As one observer has noted, "If all goes well later, the politicians can share in the glory. If all goes poorly, the politicians can point the finger at others who, after all, had independent responsibility for handling the problems."[172]

International factors also play a critical role. The International Monetary Fund and the World Bank have insisted on significant "structural adjustments," including privatization as a condition for further economic support. In the 1980s, state-owned companies in some African countries, especially Nigeria, Senegal, Sudan, and Zaire, experienced enormous financial losses and failed to promote economic development and social welfare.[173] The World Bank encouraged privatization through its structural adjustment loan programs aimed at financing and providing technical assistance for policy reforms—that is, to adopt market-oriented, liberal economic policies. Similarly, the IMF has emphasized privatization and greater restrictions on government spending on employment and wages.[174]

However, most government policies have been, at best, inconsistent toward privatization. It is estimated that state economic enterprises account for about 10 percent of world GDP.[175] In the Third World, SEEs accounted for nearly 9 percent of GDP in the 1980s, employing approximately 47 percent of the manufacturing labor force, absorbing 27 percent of all investments in the manufacturing sector, but with deficits of about 5.5 percent of GDP.[176] Despite the political rhetoric, the privatization record in the 1990s also has been mixed. In Latin America, although the most debt-ridden economies began to experiment with privatization in the late 1980s, a decade later it appeared that governments were reluctant to limit their control over SEEs, even if they encouraged greater trade liberalization and political democratization as their militaries withdrew from power.[177] Indeed, by the mid-1990s, certain major Latin American economies had halted the trend toward privatization. In Mexico, the annual total value of privatization programs increased from $55 million in 1988 to $787 million in 1991, the peak year, followed by a decline to $91 million in 1992.[178] Rather than withdraw from the economy, the Venezuelan government expanded its involvement in response to persistent economic difficulties, especially as oil prices dropped. Instead, the state-owned oil company, Petróleos de Venezuela, established Interven, a subsidiary, to internationalize its operations and purchase foreign oil facilities, including Cities Services (CITGO) in the United States, Sweden's Nynas Petroleum, and Germany's Ruhr Oel.[179]

The same holds true for other regions as well. In the late 1980s in Africa and the Middle East, for example, governments began to discuss experimentation with privatization, since the postindependence economic structures were no longer sustainable, but in both regions little has been actually transferred to the private sector. The economies of most African countries were heavily shaped by colonial statist structures on independence, and the statist tradition, most emphatically in terms of SEEs, continues to this day, "making Africa," as Callaghy and Wilson have stated, "the most etatist region of the Third World."[180] In the 1970s and 1980s, there were more than 3,000 state-owned enterprises in sub-Saharan Africa, with various degrees of state ownership and contribution to national economies. During this period, Sudan's more than 130 SEEs accounted for

40 percent of the national GDP and Zambia's 114 SEEs for nearly 38 percent of GDP, while the same figures for Liberia were twenty-two and 6.8 percent, respectively.[181] Sub-Saharan African SEEs account for approximately 20 percent of the region's GDP. By 1995, privatization sales in sub-Saharan Africa totaled $1.4 billion (or 1.2 percent of the total $113 billion for the developing countries), providing little opportunity for foreign investments in the region, which in fact have declined since 1990.[182]

Privatization has been uneven in the Middle Eastern countries, as well. Egypt's 391 SEEs accounted for 20 percent of GDP,[183] as did Tunisia's 400 SEEs.[184] On the other hand, Iraq's 400 SEEs, including the state-owned oil companies, accounted for 75 percent of GDP, and Algeria's seventy SEEs accounted for 25–30 percent of GDP, as compared with Syria's 6 percent.[185] In the 1990s, most of the major industries remained state-run operations, although some countries, especially Egypt, Jordan, and Israel, have relaxed regulatory policies for FDIs. During the 1989–1993 period, the region's total value of FDI from privatization was about $325 million, accounting for 5.5 percent of the region's FDIs, or about 2.7 percent of total FDIs from privatization in the developing world.[186]

In the industrialized world, in the mid-1980s, the French government privatized more than sixty government-owned industrial, banking, and insurance companies. However, few other countries attracted as much attention with respect to privatization as did Britain in the 1980s during the government of Margaret Thatcher. Staunch proponents of traditional laissez-faire, Thatcherites sought to limit the role of government in the economy and used privatization to address the country's economic problems during the recession years and to raise government revenues. Accordingly, the British government privatized some or all of the shares of major industries it had nationalized since the Second World War. Among them were British Aerospace, Britoil, Jaguar Cars, and Rolls-Royce. Government revenues from these sales increased from £377 million in 1980, to £2.6 billion in 1985, to £7.1 billion in 1989. The sales ranged from cases in which the British government sold shares in small increments (about 5 to 7 percent) per fiscal year, as in British Petroleum, to the sale of 100 percent of ownership, as in British Telecom, British Gas, and Rolls-Royce.[187]

While privatization is said to enhance corporate efficiency and international competitiveness, a number of costs are associated with it. Although time is needed to arrive at more definitive conclusions, by the second half of the 1990s it appeared that privatization led to neither reliably greater efficiency nor competitiveness. In the developing countries, a major source of resistance to wholesale privatization has been the fear that weakening state control would invite neo-colonialism and foreign domination. Many nationalist groups view privatization, especially as proposed by the IMF/World Bank and Western experts, as an instrument of reconquest "under the guise of economic reform, with privatization as the Trojan horse"[188]—hence, for example, the purchase of Argentina's YPF-Dock Sud Refinery (petroleum and petrochemicals company) by British Gas in 1993,[189] a decade after Argentina's devastating defeat in the Falklands/Malvinas War over the islands colonized by the British in the 1830s.

Some governments have sold only profitable companies to the private sector, and as such privatization was nothing more than a change in management and a source of revenues for a particular fiscal year. In some cases, the government simply handed the companies over to private owners, and even promised to continue financial support. In Peru, for example, when the Fujimori government introduced its major privatization programs, it promised not to profit from the sale of SEEs to investors but, rather, to reinvest the revenues in the newly privatized companies.[190] This meant that, while before privatization taxpayers were paying for enterprises run by government agencies with at least some degree of public accountability, after privatization taxpayers continued to pay for enterprises now owned by private, even foreign investors, but without public accountability. Governments often claim that privatization eases the financial burden on the public budget, but this is not always the case.[191]

In addition, given pressures to downsize and streamline production, privatization has not necessarily improved unemployment levels. Therefore, government welfare programs can become necessary to support those thrown out of work. Despite the inefficiency of Soviet state owned industries, Russian privatization appears to have led to ownership by cliques of former Communist officials, gangster organizations, and elite entrepreneurs, with few new indigenous products coming to market, enterprises allowed to stagnate, and hundreds of thousands of workers idled or unpaid.

CONCLUSION

In cooperation with home and host governments and facilitated by worldwide telecommunications technologies, MNCs have accelerated the process of globalization of the international economy. Globalization has required

MNCs to adjust their production and marketing operations to meet local needs and tastes, and to become heavily involved in joint ventures and strategic alliances to take advantage of foreign markets. Over the years, their operations have exhibited a number of advantages and disadvantages for host countries. MNC investments and operations in foreign countries encourage economic development and growth. Accordingly, host governments offer various forms of tax and other incentives to attract MNCs. MNCs bring capital, technical expertise, and new (and otherwise unavailable) technologies to a host country, particularly less developed countries, and encourage modernization and greater integration into the world economy. MNCs also create employment opportunities for regions with high unemployment levels.

On the negative side, *dependencia* theorists, statists, and nationalists view MNCs as the by-products and symbols of Western domination and exploitation. As such, MNCs not only have emerged as one of the most important types of actors in world politics but also as direct challengers to the sovereignty of nation-states. Host governments have not been very effective in dealing with such MNC practices as transfer pricing. While MNCs do provide employment opportunities, and while they are often regulated and taxed, they also lead to international division of labor, with well-paying, capital-intensive jobs found primarily in the industrialized economies, and low-paying, labor-intensive jobs mostly in the developing world. Further, the economic development they generate often results in economic dependency of and economic dualism in the host country in the form of export-processing zones or free trade zones, including *maquilas*-style, exploitative production facilities.

Besides the grand theories of IPE, a number of theories of corporate multinationalization attempt to explain corporate behavior and the reasons coporations internationalize their operations. Some theories, such as the market power theory, the international division of labor theory, and the monopolistic theory, support the *dependencia* contention that MNCs from the industrialized countries transfer their operations to the poorer, developing countries to monopolize or exploit the local markets and labor. The product life cycle theory, on the other hand, places less emphasis on power relations and, instead, focuses on the effective and efficient use of technology and innovation to expand market shares. The eclectic paradigm seeks to integrate these different approaches into a more coherent explanation. Despite their differences, these theories agree that the primary motive or the ultimate objective of the corporation is to maximize profit, a proposition criticized by Islam and socialism as benefiting private interests rather than the overall society. Feminists argue that these theories fail to consider gender equity, victimization, and empowerment and, in so doing, ignore a key dimension in international production and corporate behavior.

Globalization has enabled MNCs to relocate their operations from one country to another in search of more lax regulatory and tax environments, particularly in less developed countries where physical labor jobs are needed. For employees, globalization has led to major changes in the traditional ways of doing things, as MNCs have sought greater efficiency and flexibility. Globalization of MNCs has led to the creation of international trade union organizations, as well as international governmental organizations (IGOs) to encourage the development of international regulatory regimes and standards. One of the major weaknesses in this international regulatory regime, however, is the absence of effective enforcement mechanisms. Globalization also has led to proposals to establish tax policies for better distribution of the wealth generated by MNC transnational activities.

Few other issues have been the subject of such vigorous debates as the threat MNCs pose to national sovereignty and society. For some decades, governments in developing countries nationalized MNCs as a way of controlling corporate influence in domestic politics. Nationalization, however, while important symbolically, failed to solve their economic problems, and in recent years the trend has been reversed. Whether globalization of MNCs will improve global standards of living is uncertain. It is clear, however, that in the emerging years of the twenty-first century people continue to view them with awe and suspicion.

Chapter Summary

Globalwide MNC investments and production have expanded considerably since WWII, totalling more than 10,000 MNCs, with 90,000 subsidiaries worldwide. Globalization of MNC operations has led to intense competition, which in turn necessitates worldwide telecommunications networks for the integration and standardization of production and marketing.

The rise of MNCs has created a number of challenges regarding the nature of and relationship among ownership, management, and employees. This is true especially since family ownership of MNCs has declined; ownership has become separated from management as family companies have become public companies, enabling outside investors to buy shares.

Nothing, however, has been as controversial as MNC's impact on national sovereignty. Some countries—for example, in the industrialized West—have clearly benefited from MNC activities and investments. In fact, the principal beneficiaries of MNCs' worldwide operations and FDIs have been the Western industrialized economies.

On the positive side, MNCs create opportunities for economic development and employment for regions that otherwise would clearly lack such opportunities. However, MNCs have not established a reputation as vehicles for the even distribution of economic growth.

As profit-oriented entities, MNCs seek to minimize their expenditures and to maximize their gains; they prefer to invest in countries with the fewest regulatory and financial constraint. While governments in need of foreign capital and technology provide various tax incentives, public goods and services, in the absence of competition, MNC investments in local economic sectors enable them to monopolize those sectors in the host society. Since most major MNCs are from the Western industrialized countries, they are viewed as the by-products and symbols of Western colonialism, as instruments of domination and exploitation.

One controversial issue between MNCs and host governments has been transfer pricing (prices set for transactions between subdivisions within the MNC organization rather than market prices). MNCs almost guarantee large shares of capital returns from host economies because of transfer pricing, in addition to the various incentives provided by host governments to attract MNCs.

In the developing world, while MNCs have generated economic progress, they have also created economic dualism and dependency. Specific regions of a host country benefited more than others; some have been designated as economic zones highly favorable to MNC operations. MNCs and host governments have been praised and criticized for encouraging EPZs. Criticism often centers on exploitation of women and children. Furthermore, particularly troubling have been major social and environmental disasters such as the Union Carbide gas leak in Bhopal, India, and the Exxon oil spill in Valdez, Alaska.

Finally, MNCs have frequently interfered in the domestic politics of host countries. Such interference has included the overthrow of democratically elected governments and support of dictatorial regimes.

MNC interference in domestic politics, exploitation of employees, and generation of environmental and health hazards have put pressure on international organizations to regulate MNC behavior. The regulatory regime that has emerged over the years includes the ILO, the OECD, the United Nations, and the International Chamber of Commerce. In addition to regulation, some observers also have advocated international taxation of MNC transactions and profits. They hold that the globalization of international economic relations and of MNC operations requires global-wide mechanisms for a more just distribution of international resources.

MNCs and some governments oppose such strategies since they would risk losing even a greater degree of their autonomy. Instead of surrendering their national sovereignty to such international/multilateral schemes, some governments have opted for more nationalistic policies, such as the nationalization of MNC properties. International and domestic economic pressures in the 1980s and 1990s, however, led governments to choose privatization over nationalization as a way of stimulating economic growth.

Points of Contention

What are some of the advantages and disadvantages of MNC operations for host countries? Can you identify some advantages and disadvantages in your own community?

What impact does globalization of MNCs have on corporate-employee relations? How would you characterize that relationship?

Would you say that since WWII MNCs have generally contributed to greater cooperation in international relations? To a better distribution of wealth?

Which theory of multinationalization do you believe best captures the essence of MNC behavior?

Should international regulatory regimes have greater authority over MNCs? Are the OECD guidelines necessary? Have the guidelines and codes made a difference?

Should MNCs be permitted to move their operations freely from one country to another?

To what extent should governments regulate MNC activities?

Under what circumstances, *if at all,* do you believe that nationalization of an MNC's properties by the host government is justified?

Should the United Nations create a World Development Fund to institute international taxation of MNCs?

Since MNCs claim no exclusive loyalty to any particular country, should there be any national regulations on them in the first place?

To what extent do you agree with Charles Kindleberger's claim that "the nation-state is just about through as an economic unit"? Do MNCs pose such a total challenge to the role of the nation-state?

Notes

1. Frederic S. Pearson and J. Martin Rochester, *International Relations: The Global Condition in the Late Twentieth Century,* 3d ed. (New York: McGraw-Hill, 1992), p. 468.
2. U.N., *World Investment Report 1996,* Table IV.1, p. 96.
3. Peter Dicken, *Global Shift: The Internationalization of Economic Activity,* 2d ed. (New York: The Guilford Press, 1992), p. 47.
4. See David C. Korten, *When Corporations Rule the World* (West Hartford: Kumarian Press, 1995); Richard J. Barnet and John Cavanagh, *Global Dreams: Imperial Corporations and the New World Order* (New York: Touchstone Books, 1994); Richard J. Barnet and Ronald E. Muller, *Global Reach* (New York: Simon and Schuster, 1975); Forest L. Grieves, ed., *Transnationalism in World Politics and Business* (New York: Pergamon Press, 1979); George Modelski, ed., *Transnational Corporations and World Order* (San Francisco: W. H. Freeman, 1979); Raymond Vernon, *Sovereignty at Bay: The Multinational Spread of U.S. Enterprises* (New York: Basic Books, 1971); Richard Robinson, *The Internationalization of Business* (New York: Dryden Press, 1984); Alejandro Portes, Manuel Castells, and Lauren A. Benton, eds., *The Informal Economy* (Baltimore: Johns Hopkins University Press, 1989); J. J. Thomas, *Informal Economic Activity* (Ann Arbor: University of Michigan Press, 1992).
5. Robert O. Keohane and Joseph S. Nye, Jr., eds., *Transnational Relations and World Politics* (Cambridge: Harvard University Press, 1972); Robert Gilpin, *U.S. Power and the Multinational Corporation: The Political Economy of Foreign Direct Investment* (New York: Basic Books, 1975); Vernon, *Sovereignty at Bay.*
6. Charles P. Kindleberger, *American Business Abroad: Six Lectures on Direct Investment* (New Haven: Yale University Press, 1969), pp. 207–210. See also David Leyton-Brown, "The Nation-State and Multinational Enterprise: Erosion or Assertion," in Robert O. Matthews, et al., eds., *International Conflict and Conflict Management* (Scarborough, Ontario, Canada: Prentice-Hall, 1984), p. 330.
7. See, for example, Vernon, *Sovereignty at Bay.*
8. U.N., *World Economic and Social Survey,* 1997, p. 55.
9. Dicken, *Global Shift,* p. 48.
10. *The Economist,* April 2, 1994, p. 69; UNCTAD, *World Investment Report 1994* (New York: United Nations, 1994), p. 177. MNCs never established a reputation as vehicles for even distribution of economic growth, especially when they claim they are losing money. In the early 1990s, for example, major companies, such as Boeing, Caterpillar, Dayton-Hudson, DuPont, Texas Instruments, the Dutch Philips, Japan's Matsushita, and Germany's Daimler-Benz, reported enormous losses. Citicorp, the largest U.S.-based bank, lost $457 million in a single year, General Motors $23.5 billion, and IBM $8.1 billion. The figures are for 1991, 1992, 1993, respectively. "Multinationals," [survey] *The Economist,* June 24, 1995, p. 3.
11. "Multinationals," [survey] *The Economist,* June 24, 1995, p. 20.
12. Ibid., p. 21.
13. Edward M. Graham, "Strategic Management and Transnational Firm Behavior: A Formal Approach," in Christos N. Pitelis and Roger Sugden, eds., *The Nature of the Transnational Firm* (London: Routledge, 1991), pp. 160–161.
14. Mira Wilkins, "Defining a Firm: History and Theory," in Peter Hertner and Geoffrey Jones, eds., *Multinationals: Theory and History* (Aldershot, U.K.: Gower, 1986), p. 81.
15. *The Economist,* April 2, 1994, p. 69.
16. Barry Bluestone and Bennett Harrison, *The Deindustrialization of America: Plant Closings, Community Abandonment, and the Dismantling of Basic Industry* (New York: Basic Books, 1982).
17. For a useful survey of theories of MNCs, see Pitelis and Sugden, eds., *The Nature of the Transnational Firm.*
18. P. J. Buckley and M. Casson, *The Future of the Multinational Enterprise* (London: Macmillan, 1976), p. 36, quoted in Roger Sugden, "The Importance of Distributional Considerations," in Pitelis and Sugden, eds., *The Nature of the Transnational Firm,* pp. 168–169.
19. One of the most visible trends in multinationalization in recent decades has been the transformation of industrial structures from FDIs in import-substitution to the expansion of the "multi-divisional form of affiliates" of MNCs and intra-firm trade by way of greater integration of production facilities among affiliates worldwide—hence, the genuine *globalization* of MNC operations. By the closing decades of the twentieth century, the growing significance of such considerations has led to the expansion of intra-firm and intra-industry trade, which in turn has made the availability of communications technology even more essential. Despite the controversial nature of MNC involvement in host countries' internal affairs, the growth of MNC transnational integration has occurred in large part because of greater liberalization of government policy. See John H. Dunning, *Explaining International Production* (London: Unwin Hyman, 1988), pp. 83–84; 102–103.
20. John H. Dunning, *Explaining International Production* (London: Unwin Hyman, 1988), p. 106.
21. Stephen H. Hymer, *The International Operations of National Firms: Study of Foreign Direct Investment* (Cambridge, MA: MIT Press, 1976). See also John Cantwell, "A Survey of Theories of International Production," in Pitelis and Sugden, eds., *The Nature of the Transnational Firm,* pp. 16–63.
22. The theory of market power, and international division of labor as its component, as developed by Hymer, was further developed by Fröbel, Henrichs and Kreye, and Christian Palloix, who referred to it as the "new international division of labor." This theory placed a special emphasis on the corporate search for cheap labor to minimize production costs as the determining factor in the internationalization of

corporate operations. In Hymer's and the others' formulation, the corporation is an active agent, engaged in systematically planned strategies to control labor supplies, and the market with the objective of minimizing uncertainties. This view differed from the classical liberal theory of the passive corporation operating in a perfect market. Stephen H. Hymer, *The Multinational Corporation: A Radical Approach* (Cambridge: Cambridge University Press, 1979); Cantwell, "A Survey of Theories of International Production," in Pitelis and Sugden, eds., *The Nature of the Transnational Firm,* pp. 21–22; Folker Fröbel, Jürgen Henrichs, and Otto Kreye, *New International Division of Labor* (Cambridge: Cambridge University Press, 1980); Christian Palloix, "The Self-Expansion of Capital on a World Scale," *Review of Radical Political Economics* 9, 2 (1977): pp. 1–28.

23. Jeffrey Henderson, *The Globalization of High Technology Production* (London: Routledge, 1989), pp. 16–24.
24. Frederic C. Deyo, ed., *The Political Economy of the New Asian Industrialism* (Ithaca: Cornell University Press, 1987).
25. Dicken, *Global Shift,* pp. 125–126.
26. Kindleberger, *American Business Abroad.*
27. Vernon, *Sovereignty at Bay.*
28. See Rolando Polli and Victor Cook, "Validity of the Product Life Cycle," *Journal of Business* 42, 4 (October 1969); pp. 385–400. See also the useful diagram on the product life cycle, Figure 4.7, in Dicken, *Global Shift,* p. 111.
29. See Mark Casson, ed., *The Growth of International Business* (London: Allen and Unwin, 1983).
30. Focusing on U.S. companies, Vernon noted that the decision to establish manufacturing subsidiaries abroad was influenced by a number of factors, including capturing a share of the local market, bypassing trade barriers, offsetting threats by local or outside competitors, and lowering production costs. Expansion of operations by one company, however, triggers a similar response by competitors, who also seek to avoid problems of limited markets and product obsolescence. Competition, therefore, leads to intra-industry oligopolistic tendencies, as each company attempts to minimize its production costs and to maximize its innovation capacity relative to the capabilities of its competitors. Raymond Vernon, "The Location of Economic Activity," in John H. Dunning, ed., *Economic Analysis and the Multinational Enterprise* (London: Allen and Unwin, 1974), pp. 89–114; Dicken, *Global Shift,* pp. 112–13.
31. Cantwell, "A Survey of Theories of International Production," in Pitelis and Sugden, eds., *The Nature of the Transnational Firm,* pp. 37–57, *passim.*
32. See, for example, Kiyoshi Kojima, *Direct Foreign Investment: A Japanese Model of Multinational Business Operation* (London: Croom Helm, 1978).
33. See Dicken, *Global Shift,* pp. 141–142.
34. Susan Strange, *States and Markets,* 2d ed. (London: Pinter, 1994), p. 77.
35. Raymond Vernon, "The Product Cycle Hypothesis in a New International Environment," *Oxford Bulletin of Economics and Statistics* 41 (1979), pp. 255–268.
36. Multinationalization of operations creates greater opportunities as the corporation takes advantage of "geographic differences in factor endowments" as well as minimizing financial and political risks. Dunning, *Explaining International Production,* pp. 25–26.
37. *Ibid.,* pp. 26–31.
38. *Ibid.*
39. As Dunning has noted, "the greater the product or geographical diversification practised by an MNE, the greater the proportion of *O* [ownership-specific] advantages attributable to internalization gains (or more correctly the capitalization of such gains) is likely to be." *Ibid.,* p. 28.
40. Dunning's name is usually associated, as Susan Strange has noted, with "business historians on the right." Strange, *States and Markets,* p. 15. Dunning's eclectic paradigm, however, can be gainfully employed in "rightist" and "leftist" analysis.
41. Farhad Nomani and Ali Rahnema, *Islamic Economic Systems* (London: Zed Books, 1994), pp. 91–98.
42. See Ruth Pearson, "Industrialization and Women's Subordination: A Reappraisal," and Helen I. Safa, "Gender Inequality and Women's Wage Labour: A Theoretical and Empirical Analysis," in Valentine M. Moghadam, ed., *Patriarchy and Economic Development: Women's Positions at the End of the Twentieth Century* (Oxford: Clarendon Press, 1996), pp. 169–183; 184–219.
43. See Rita S. Gallin, "State, Gender, and the Organization of Business in Rural Taiwan," and Valentine M. Moghadam, "Development Strategies, State Policies, and the Status of Women: A Comparative Assessment of Iran, Turkey, and Tunisia," in Moghadam, ed., *Patriarchy and Economic Development,* pp. 220–240, 241–268.
44. Hertner and Jones, "Multinationals," in Hertner and Jones, eds., *Multinationals,* p. 4.
45. *Ibid.,* p. 1.
46. *Ibid.,* p. 2.
47. John H. Dunning, John A. Cantwell, and T. A. B. Corley, "The Theory of International Production: Some Historical Antecedents," in Hertner and Jones, eds., *Multinationals,* p. 27.
48. *Ibid.*
49. Dunning, *Explaining International Production,* pp. 89–91.
50. *Ibid.,* pp. 89–92.
51. The number of new overseas subsidiaries created by major Western manufacturing MNCs increased from about twenty-five in 1919 to as much as seventy per year in the early 1920s worldwide. Subsidiaries of U.S. firms increased from twelve to nearly thirty, British from eight to fifteen, and continental Europe from five to twenty-five. The U.S. share of the capital stock worldwide increased from 18.5 percent in 1914 to nearly 28 percent in 1928. About

60 percent of the technological innovations, as indicated by patent applications, occurred in the United States. British patent applications dropped to 12.5 percent, French applications to 8.5 percent, and German applications to 13 percent. Significantly, the United States also became the principal beneficiary of international patent registers. British patents in the United States increased from 1,288 in 1919 to 1,347 in 1939, French patents from 363 to 634, German from 131 to 2,480, and Japanese from fifty-six to fifty-seven. These innovations primarily focused on machinery and electrical equipments for television, radar, and jet engines, as well as pharmaceutical and various consumer products. During this period, companies developed more efficient production and standardization (Ford's Model T, for example) capabilities to minimize costs and use sophisticated promotion and sales techniques. All industrialized economies, however, experienced a sharp decline during the depression years in the 1930s and during the Second World War. See Dicken, *Global Shift,* pp. 49–52; Dunning, *Explaining International Production,* pp. 76–77, 91–93.

52. Dicken, *Global Shift,* p. 51.
53. *World Investment Report 1996,* p. 96.
54. Joan Edelman Spero, *The Politics of International Economic Relations* (New York: St. Martin's Press, 1990), p. 91.
55. Dunning, *Explaining International Production,* pp. 93–94.
56. United Nations Department of Economic and Social Affairs, *Multinational Corporations in World Development* (New York: United Nations, 1973), pp. 4–23, in Modelski, ed., *Transnational Corporations and World Order,* p. 21.
57. U.S. and British MNCs were primarily engaged in manufacturing (40 percent) and in extractive industries (30 percent). Japanese MNC's concentrated on trade to secure access to foreign markets and extractive industries to secure a continuous supply of resources (for example, oil). Over 80 percent of German MNC's foreign direct investments were in manufacturing and high-technology products (chemicals, transport, and electrical products). German investments in extractive industries were limited to approximately 5 percent in mining and 3 percent in petroleum. The service industries—for example, banking, tourism, and consultation—also gained prominence in MNC foreign investments. The number of U.S. bank affiliates overseas rose from 303 in 1965 to 1,009 in 1972. That year alone, U.S. banks established 106 foreign branches, British banks 192 branches, German banks 103, French banks 91, and Japanese banks 25. *Ibid.,* pp. 19, 21–23.
58. A number of indicators reflected this global structural change. For example, while in the early 1960s 292 (or 60 percent) of the world's 483 major industries were U.S. MNCs, by the mid-1980s the number had dropped to 213 (or 44 percent). In contrast, the number of Japanese MNCs increased from twenty-nine (or 6 percent) to seventy-nine (or 16 percent). At the same time, larger shares of foreign direct investments flowed to the Western industrialized economies. In the early 1960s, approximately 32 percent of worldwide FDIs were in Western Europe and the United States; in the early 1970s the figures rose to 38 percent, in the late 1970s to 47 percent, and by the mid-1980s to 59 percent. In addition, in the second half of the 1970s, the United States accounted for 49.5 percent of R&D in the industrialized economies (a substantial drop from the previous decade), Germany accounted for 11.9 percent, and Japan 13.6 percent; despite the greater concentration of MNC investments in the industrialized economies, some of the newly industrializing countries (NICs), including Mexico and Brazil, also experienced a rapid growth in patent registration. Dunning, *Explaining International Production,* pp. 82, 93–94.
59. John T. Rourke, *International Politics on the World Stage,* 4th ed. (Guilford, CT: Dushkin Publishing Group, 1993), p. 442.
60. "Multinationals," [survey] *The Economist,* June 24, 1995, p. 12. In addition, well over $50 billion of Canada-EU investments created strong interdependence between Canada and the EU. In 1991, nearly $19.9 billion (or 20 percent) of Canada's total foreign direct investment, mostly in the manufacturing sector, was in the EU, a large share—61 percent, or $12.2 billion—invested in Great Britain. Between 1983 and 1990, the European Community's FDI in Canada increased from $13.4 billion (or 17.3 percent) to about $32 billion (or 23 percent) of total inward investment stock. Thus, the EU became the second largest source of FDI in Canada after the United States. See Evan H. Potter, "The Impact of European Economic Integration on North America: Adjustment Versus Radical Change," in Donald Barry, with Mark O. Dickerson and James Gaisford, eds., *Toward a North American Community?* (Boulder, CO: Westview Press, 1995), p. 253.
61. Evan H. Potter, "The Impact of European Economic Integration on North America: Adjustment Versus Radical Change," in Barry, et al., eds., *Toward a North American Community?* p. 253.
62. *Ibid.*
63. *IMF Survey,* March 6, 1995, p. 67.
64. "Multinationals," [survey] *The Economist,* June 24, 1995, p. 12.
65. Total FDIs in Latin America reached $14 billion in 1992 and $13 billion in 1993—two to three times higher levels than in the 1980s. Asia was the recipient of about $66 billion during 1991–1993, constituting approximately 50 percent of all FDIs in the developing countries. East Asia (including China, Indonesia, Malaysia, the Philippines, and Thailand) received nearly $146 billion in FDIs during the 1986–1994 period. Japanese FDIs accounted for 18 percent, U.S. 11 percent, and Europe 10 percent of FDIs in the region during this period. Nearly 50 percent of FDIs in the region flowed from the new industrializing economies, including South Korea, Taiwan, Hong Kong, and Singapore. China, by far the largest recipient, received 40 percent of total FDIs in Asia. The former Warsaw Pact

countries of Eastern Europe received about 10 percent of total FDIs to developing countries. In 1994, the Czech Republic and Hungary, for example, received $749 million and $1.1 billion, respectively. In 1996, Hungary was expected to receive $1.7 billion. See *IMF Survey,* March 6, 1995, p. 67; *The Economist,* March 16, 1996, p. 78; *The Economist,* March 2, 1996, pp. 34, 100.

66. *The Economist,* March 16, 1996, p. 78.
67. U.N., *World Economic and Social Survey, 1997: Trends and Policies in the World Economy,* p. 55.
68. *Ibid.*, p. 56.
69. *World Investment Report 1995,* p. 17. *U.N., World Economic and Social Survey, 1997,* p. 53.
70. U.N., *World Economic and Social Survey, 1997,* pp. 53–54.
71. "Multinationals," [survey] *The Economist,* June 24, 1995, p. 13.
72. *Ibid.*, p. 4.
73. *Ibid.*
74. *Ibid.*, p. 10; *The Economist,* March 2, 1996, p. 34.
75. "Multinationals," [survey] *The Economist,* June 24, 1995, p. 10.
76. *Ibid.*, p. 4.
77. *Ibid.*, pp. 4–6.
78. *World Investment Report 1994,* p. 140.
79. "Business in Asia," [survey] *The Economist,* March 9, 1996, pp. 1–2.
80. "Multinationals," [survey] *The Economist,* June 24, 1995, p. 13.
81. *Ibid.*, p. 10.
82. In 1983 and 1993, intra-firm exports were 22 percent and 25 percent, respectively, of Japan's total exports and 35 percent and 36 percent of U.S. exports for the same years. UNCTAD, *World Investment Report 1996,* p. 121.
83. *World Investment Report 1995,* p. 29.
84. *Ibid.*, p. 33.
85. *Ibid.*, pp. 29–30.
86. *Ibid.*, pp. 32–33. Just five countries have accounted for the bulk of outgoing FDI from the South: China, Hong Kong, Singapore, South Korea, and Taiwan; these states may become foreign investment competitors for world markets in the coming century. Telecommunications technologies (computer e-mail services, teleconferences via satellite systems, and so on) enable each company to integrate the branches across continents and to develop plans for a particular project while maintaining the desirable degree of flexibility. At the same time, such geographic and structural subdivisions are also helpful for fiscal and tax purposes. Thus, MNCs weakened the decision-making authority of some of their national headquarters in an effort to combine their transnational operations within *a global* structure. "Multinationals," [survey] *The Economist,* June 24, 1995, pp. 5, 17.
87. Greg J. Bamber and Russell D. Lansbury, "Studying International and Comparative Industrial Relations," in Greg J. Bamber and Russell D. Lansbury, eds., *International and Comparative Industrial Relations* (Sydney: Unwin Hyman, 1987), pp. 3–9.
88. *Ibid.*
89. *World Investment Report 1996,* Annex Table 4, p. 245.
90. *Ibid.*
91. *Ibid.*, Annex Table 3, p. 239.
92. *World Investment Report 1994,* pp. 163–164.
93. "Multinationals," [survey] *The Economist,* June 24, 1995, pp. 110–113.
94. See *World Investment Report 1994,* pp. 238–240.
95. "Multinationals," [survey] *The Economist,* June 24, 1995, pp. 110–113.
96. *World Investment Report 1994,* pp. 238–240; "Multinationals," [survey] *The Economist,* June 24, 1995, pp. 110–113.
97. Raymond Vernon, ed., *The Promise of Privatization: A Challenge for American Foreign Policy* (New York: Council on Foreign Relations, 1988), p. 11.
98. *World Investment Report 1996,* pp. 147–148.
99. Jerry Mander, "Corporate Colonialism," *Resurgence* (September-October 1996), p. 1. Internet.
100. Graham Bannock, R. E. Baxter, and Evan Davis, *Dictionary of Economics,* 5th ed. (London: Penguin Books, 1992), p. 427; Suk H. Kim and Seung H. Kim, *Global Corporate Finance: Text and Cases* (Miami: Kolb, 1993), p. 445.
101. MNCs' decisions with respect to transfer pricing are influenced by a host of conditions and policies, including market conditions and competition in host countries, the extent of profitability of the venture, profit repatriation and restrictions within the host country, and the home country's tax structure. Bannock, Baxter, and Davis, *Dictionary of Economics,* p. 427; Kim and Kim, *Global Corporate Finance,* p. 445.
102. Dicken, *Global Shift,* p. 391.
103. The losses to the local economy may be even greater when one considers the various tax and financial incentives and lax regulatory environment national- and subnational-level governments provide for MNCs. These practices are common in both Western industrialized and developing countries. The U.S. national and state governments have provided considerable financial support for Japanese and German MNCs to build their factories in the United States. East Asian countries, such as Taiwan and China, have established a number of EPZs (export-processing zones) to attract foreign investments. Under such contracts, the host governments often agree to subsidize a portion or all of the construction of the infrastructure. See Dicken, *Global Shift,* p. 391; G. P. Jenkins and B. D. Wright, "Taxation of Income of Multinational Corporations: The Case of the United States Petroleum Industry," *Review of Economics and Statistics* 57, 1 (1975), pp. 1–11; Lorraine Eden, "The Microeconomics of Transfer Pricing," in Alan M. Rugman and Lorraine Eden, eds., *Multinational and Transfer Pricing* (New York: St. Martin's Press, 1985).
104. Dicken, *Global Shift,* pp. 400–401.
105. See Rachael Kamel, *The Global Factory: Analysis and Action for a New Economic Era* (Philadelphia: American Friends

Service Committee, 1990), p. 10; *The Economist,* April 2, 1994, p. 69.

106. Women constitute about 50 percent of the workforce in developed countries, a large majority of whom work in the service sector. *World Investment Report 1994,* p. 203.

107. *World Investment Report* 1994, p. 203. Critics note that MNC wages reflect to a large extent the generally male-oriented institutional view that "women's work is simply not as important as men's." Kamel, *Global Factory,* pp. 6–7. One explanation for lower wages is that women cannot make full commitment to their employers because of home and child-bearing responsibilities. Another explanation is that women are by nature supposedly docile and can more easily endure the tedious work on the assembly line. Significantly, therefore, MNCs view women as being "less likely than men to rebel and form labor unions." A related issue is that, when MNCs pay *higher* wages than local businesses, MNCs are viewed as appropriating "workers from domestic firms and possibly [threatening] their survival." Because of their financial strength, MNCs attract some of the host country's best and brightest for managerial and white-collar positions. This results in hiring employees from some of the best firms in the host country instead of the unemployed. See Dicken, *Global Shift,* p. 404; Kamel, *Global Factory,* p. 11.

108. Dicken, *Global Shift,* p. 420.

109. *World Investment Report 1994,* Table IV.11, p. 190.

110. *Ibid.*

111. Herman M. Schwartz, *State Versus Markets: History, Geography, and the Development of International Political Economy* (New York: St. Martin's Press, 1994), pp. 274–275.

112. *Ibid.*

113. *World Investment Report 1994,* p. 191.

114. Schwartz, *State Versus Markets,* pp. 274–275.

115. Kamel, *Global Factory,* p. 40.

116. *Ibid.*

117. *Ibid.,* p. 41.

118. *The Economist,* March 9, 1996 [survey], p. 9.

119. Dicken, *Global Shift,* p. 417.

120. "Multinationals," [survey] *The Economist,* June 24, 1995, p. 6.

121. *The Economist,* April 2, 1994, p. 69.

122. Edward M. Graham, "Strategic Management and Transnational Firm Behavior: A Formal Approach," in Pitelis and Sugden, eds., *The Nature of the Transnational Firm,* pp. 160–161.

123. John H. Jackson and William J. Davey, *Legal Problems of International Economic Relations,* 2d ed. (St. Paul: West, 1986), pp. 1058–1062.

124. See, for example, Clyde Sanger, *Ordering the Oceans: The Making of the Law of the Sea* (Toronto: University of Toronto Press, 1987).

125. John M. Kline, *International Codes and Multinational Business: Setting Guidelines for International Business Operations* (Westport: Quorum Books, 1985), pp. 10–11.

126. *Ibid.,* p. 4.

127. UN Center on Transnational Corporations, *The United Nations Code of Conduct on Transnational Corporations* (New York: United Nations, 1986).

128. "Multinationals," [survey] *The Economist,* June 24, 1995, p. 15.

129. Jackson and Davey, *Legal Problems of International Economic Relations,* p. 1057.

130. Hans W. Baade, "The Legal Effects of Codes of Conduct for Multinational Enterprises" in Norbert Horn, ed., *Legal Problems of Codes of Conduct for Multinational Enterprises* (Antwerp, the Netherlands; Hingham, MA: Kelwer-Deveuter, 1980), pp. 37–38. See also Jackson and Davey, *Legal Problems of International Economic Relations,* pp. 1051–1053.

131. "Multinationals," [survey] *The Economist,* June 24, 1995, p. 15.

132. Janet Lowe, *The Secret Empire: How 25 Multinationals Rule the World* (Homewood, IL: Business One Irwin, 1992), pp. 12–13.

133. United Nations Department of Economic and Social Affairs, *Report of the Group of Eminent Persons on the Impact of Multinational Corporations on Development and on International Relations* (New York: United Nations, 1974), pp. 25–57.

134. Francisco Orrego Vicuña, "El Control de las Empresas Multinacionales," in Modelski, ed., *Transnational Corporations and World Order,* pp. 300–302.

135. Krasner, *Structural Conflict,* p. 181.

136. Francisco Orrego Vicuña, "El Control de las Empresas Multinacionales," *Foro Internacional* (Mexico City), 14, 1 (July-September, 1973), pp. 109–128. Translated by Sylvia Modelski, in Modelski, ed., *Transnational Corporations and World Order,* pp. 300–302.

137. Gordon Mace, "Consensus-Building in the Andean Integration System: 1968–1985," W. Andrew Axline, ed., *The Political Economy of Regional Cooperation: Comparative Case Studies* (London: Pinter, 1994), pp. 51–52.

138. See Simon Payaslian, "The United Nations and the Developing Countries in the 1990s," *University of Detroit Mercy Law Review* 73, 3 (Spring 1996), pp. 525–549; Ruben P. Mendez, *International Public Finance: A New Perspective on Global Relations* (New York: Oxford University Press, 1992), pp. 213–231.

139. See *North-South: A Program for Survival. Report of the Independent Commission on International Development Issues* (Cambridge: MIT Press, 1980), p. 124 [hereinafter referred to as *Brandt Commission Report*].

140. Jackson and Davey, *Legal Problems of International Economic Relations,* p. 1105.

141. *Ibid.,* pp. 1101–1103.

142. Gary Clyde Hufbauer, *U.S. Taxation of International Income: Blueprint for Reform* (Washington, DC: Institute for International Economics, 1992).

143. Kim and Kim, *Global Corporate Finance,* p. 438.
144. Jemes R. Hines, Jr., and R. Glenn Hubbard, "Coming Home to America: Dividend Repatriations by U.S. Multinationals," in Assaf Razin and Joel Slemrod, eds., *Taxation in the Global Economy* (Chicago: The University of Chicago Press, 1990), p. 161.
145. Kim and Kim, *Global Corporate Finance,* pp. 430–431.
146. *Tariffs* are taxes levied on imported goods. In recent years, however, tariffs for purposes *of revenues* have been relatively insignificant. Governments in developed economies usually impose high tariffs when they seek to protect domestic industries, but they no longer rely on such taxes for their finances. Indeed, only in a small number of developing countries did tariffs *qua taxes* constitute a significant portion of government revenues. In the 1980s, for example, they accounted for 68 percent of government revenues in Gambia and about 53 percent in Benin. But, in Jamaica and Brazil, they accounted for no more than 4 percent. *Value-added taxes,* to give another example, are a type of sales tax levied at various stages of production and sale of goods. But the value-added tax is preferred "to avoid the compounding effect of sales taxes." For instance, when an appliance store owner buys a Magnavox television set for $1,000 from Philips Electronics, the manufacturer, and sells it for $1,700, the value-added tax is levied on the $700 added to the manufacturer's price. *Withholding taxes,* usually instituted and amended by bilateral taxation treaties, are taxes withheld from payments to foreigners. Withholding taxes are a host government's taxes on international investors' dividends and interests payments, but unlike income taxes they are collected prior to actually receiving the profits. The push toward greater trade liberalization in the 1990s will undoubtedly lead to the lowering of taxes on most, if not all, international transfers and transactions. See Roger H. Gordon and James Levinsohn, "The Linkages Between Domestic Taxes and Border Taxes," in Razin and Slemrod, *Taxation in the Global Economy,* p. 394; Kim and Kim, *Global Corporate Finance,* p. 430.
147. Richard L. Doernberg, *International Taxation,* 2d ed. (St. Paul: West , 1993), p. 2–3.
148. *World Investment Report 1996,* Table V.5, p. 149.
149. *The Economist,* April 2, 1994, p. 74.
150. *Ibid.,* p. 74.
151. Kim and Kim, *Global Corporate Finance,* pp. 428–430.
152. *Global Competition: The New Reality: The Report of the President's Commission on Industrial Competitiveness,* Vol. II (1985), pp. 120–125, excerpt in Jackson and Davey, *Legal Problems of International Economic Relations,* pp. 1103–1105.
153. Regarding the U.S. tax system, for example, Charles Hulten writes that

    Four general aspects of the U.S. tax system contribute to misallocation of capital among competing uses. First, corporate equity income is taxed twice while income from owner-occupied housing and municipal bonds is excluded from income taxation. Second, arbitrary capital cost recovery schemes and tax credits are used in place of neutral depreciation methods. Third, the tax system is not indexed for inflation; and fourth, gains and losses are treated asymmetrically.

    In the United States, technology-intensive manufacturing industries carry a higher tax burden than other manufacturing industries. According to one study, the manufacturing sector is usually taxed considerably more heavily than others—that is, approximately 46 percent, while commerce is taxed about 30 percent, and other industries 11 percent. See Jackson and Davey, *Legal Problems of International Economic Relations,* p. 1105.
154. Payaslian, "The United Nations and the Developing Countries in the 1990s"; Mendez, *International Public Finance,* pp. 213–231.
155. *Nyerere Commission Report,* p. 64.
156. Simon Payaslian, *U.S. Foreign Economic and Military Aid: The Reagan and Bush Administrations* (Lanham, MD: University Press of America, 1996); Cynthia Brown, ed., With Friends Like These (New York: Pantheon Books 1985); Daniel Pipes and Adam Garfinkle, eds., *Friendly Tyrants: An American Dilemma* (New York: St. Martin's Press, 1991); Noam Chomsky and Edward S. Herman, *The Political Economy of Human Rights: The Washington Connection and Third World Fascism* (Boston: South End Press, 1979); Michael T. Klare and Cynthia Arnson, *Supplying Repression* (Washington, DC: Institute for Policy Studies, 1981); Lars Schoultz, *Human Rights and United States Policy Toward Latin America* (Princeton: Princeton University Press, 1981).
157. *Brandt Commission Report,* p. 124.
158. *Ibid.,* pp. 139, 244, 291. See also Susan Strange, "Reaction to Brandt: Popular Acclaim and Academic Attack," *International Studies Quarterly* 25, 2 (June 1981), pp. 328–342.
159. *Nyerere Commission Report,* p. 171.
160. Payaslian, "The United Nations and the Developing Countries in the 1990s."
161. Dicken, *Global Shift,* p. 30.
162. Other terms used to refer to nationalization include *requisition, liquidation, and indigenization.* See Adeoye A. Akinsanya, *The Expropriation of Multinational Property in the Third World* (New York: Praeger, 1980), pp. 3–4.
163. But not all government seizures of companies have occurred in the developing or Communist countries. The British Labour Party believed that government control over the "commanding heights" economic sectors was necessary to manage the national economy effectively. Accordingly, it nationalized the Bank of England, the coal industry, and the airline industry in 1946; electricity in 1947; transportation and energy in 1948; and the steel industry in 1949. The last consolidated under the British Steel Corporation in 1967, controlled over 90 percent of British

steel production. Jeffrey A. Hart, *Rival Capitalists: International Competitiveness in the United States, Japan, and Western Europe* (Ithaca: Cornell University Press, 1992), pp. 150–154; Raymond Vernon, ed., *The Promise of Privatization: A Challenge for American Foreign Policy* (New York: Council on Foreign Relations, 1988), pp. 27–29.

164. Akinsanya, *Expropriation of Multinational Property in the Third World,* pp. 78–106.
165. Michael Morris, Ferid G. Lavipour, and Karl P. Sauvant, "The Politics of Nationalization: Guyana vs. Alcan," in Karl P. Sauvant and Ferid G. Lavipour, eds., *Controlling Multinational Enterprises* (Boulder, CO: Westview Press, 1976), p. 120, as cited in Akinsanya, *Expropriation of Multinational Property in the Third World,* pp. 141–145.
166. Paul E. Sigmund, *Multinational in Latin America: The Politics of Nationalization* (Madison: University of Wisconsin Press and the Twentieth Century Fund, 1980); Gary W. Wynia, *The Politics of Latin American Development,* 3d ed. (Cambridge: Cambridge University Press, 1990).
167. Akinsanya, *Expropriation of Multinational Property in the Third World,* p. 82.
168. *Ibid.,* p. 82.
169. Daniel T. Jones, *Maturity and Crisis in the European Car Industry* (Brighton, England: Sussex European Research Center, 1981), p. 36.
170. See Bannock, Baxter, and Davis, *Dictionary of Economics,* pp. 341–342; Vernon, *Promise of Privatization,* pp. 1–16.
171. Vernon, *Promise of Privatization,* pp. 1–16. The development of the EU common currency, however, could increase pressures against large state budgets, public spending, and public ownership.
172. John T. Tierney, "Government Corporations and Managing the Public's Business," *Political Science Quarterly* 99, 1 (1984), p. 78, quoted in Yair Aharoni, "The United Kingdom: Transforming Attitudes," in Vernon, ed., *The Promise of Privatization,* p. 39.
173. *Ibid.,* p. 263.
174. Similarly, development assistance donor states became increasingly reluctant to provide support for economies that, at least from the donors' standpoint, needed fundamental structural reforms. Greater privatization since the late 1980s has increased opportunities for foreign direct investments. In the area of infrastructural development (utilities, telecommunications, transport), for example, revenues from privatization in the developing countries totaled about $44 billion for the 1988–1995 period, and FDIs accounted for 51.1 percent of total revenues. In telecommunications, FDIs' share was about $14.3 billion, or 67 percent of the total $21.3 billion. *World Investment Report* 1996, Table I.10, p. 25. Overall, between 1988 and 1994, revenues from privatization in developing countries totaled $112 billion. World Bank, *World Debt Tables* 1996, Vol. I: *Analysis and Summary,* p. 119. See also Thomas M. Callaghy and Ernest J. Wilson III, "Africa: Policy, Reality or Ritual?" in Vernon, ed., *The Promise of Privatization,* pp. 179–186.
175. Callaghy and Wilson, "Africa: Policy, Reality or Ritual?" in Vernon, ed., *The Promise of Privatization,* pp. 183–184.
176. Alan Richards and John Waterbury, *A Political Economy of the Middle East: State, Class, and Economic Development* (Boulder, CO: Westview Press, 1990), p. 192.
177. The governments of Argentina, Brazil, Chile, Mexico, and Venezuela promised to launch privatization programs to reinvigorate their economies and to attract foreign direct investment as a way of dealing with their foreign debts. By 1995, Mexico had privatized about $20 billion of SEE assets, Argentina $16 billion, and Brazil $6 billion. Privatization encouraged FDIs from large MNCs, and the number of affiliates rose from 138 to 151 during the 1990– 1993 period, while the number of SEEs dropped from 105 to seventy-two. Argentina was by far the strongest supporter of privatization. In 1990, privatization accounted for 35 percent of FDI inflows, and by 1993 that figure had increased to 41.7 percent. *World Development Report 1995,* p. 70, Table II.4, p. 71.
178. *Ibid.* In Chile, revenues from privatization totaled $115 million, or 9 percent of FDI inflows in 1989, but virtually ceased in the 1990s. In Venezuela, in the 1970s, SEEs accounted for about 4 percent of total GDP and 7.5 percent of nonoil GDP.
179. Janet Kelly de Escobar, "Venezuela: Letting in the Market," in Vernon, ed., *The Promise of Privatization,* pp. 63, 78.
180. See Callaghy and Wilson, "Africa: Policy, Reality or Ritual?" in Vernon, ed., *The Promise of Privatization,* pp. 183–184.
181. *Ibid.*
182. *World Investment Report 1995,* p. 85.
183. Richards and Waterbury, *A Political Economy of the Middle East,* p. 197.
184. Iliya Harik, "Privatization and Development in Tunisia," in Iliya Harik and Denis J. Sullivan, eds., *Privatization and Liberalization in the Middle East* (Bloomington: Indiana University Press, 1992), p. 212.
185. Richards and Waterbury, *A Political Economy of the Middle East,* pp. 199, 201–202.
186. *World Investment Report 1995,* Table I.6, p. 18.
187. Vernon, *The Promise of Privatization,* pp. 1–16; Yair Aharoni, "The United Kingdom: Transforming Attitudes," in Vernon, ed., *The Promise of Privatization,* pp. 24–26.
188. Vernon, *The Promise of Privatization,* p. 189.
189. World Bank, *World Debt Tables 1996,* p. 124.
190. *Ibid.,* p. 119.
191. In Britain, for example, the Thatcher government's claims notwithstanding, government total outlays (GTOs) increased, from 40.9 percent of GDP in 1979 to about 44 percent of GDP in the mid-1980s and mid-1990s. *OECD Economic Outlook,* June 1996, Annex Table 28, p. A31.

CHAPTER EIGHT

THE POLITICS OF GLOBALIZED SCIENCE AND TECHNOLOGY

It is a fact of modern (and even "postmodern") life that technology in its various forms is necessary for economic development, and telecommunications technologies have accelerated the globalization of international relations. The globalization of the world political economy in its various manifestations, as discussed in the preceding chapters, would not have occurred without the scientific and technological and accompanying structural changes experienced at least since the emergence of the modern nation-state in the sixteenth and seventeenth centuries. Science and technology (S&T) are said to be inherently transnational, integral to the internationalization of production and capital by the multinational corporation (MNC), particularly through telecommunications technologies, and to the influence the MNC exerts on state domestic and foreign policies, as discussed in the preceding chapter.[1]

From the nation-state perspective, the centrality of science and technology in modern political economy poses a serious dilemma. On the one hand, science and technology are the foundations for the structures of national industrial production, capital, and information capabilities, all of which contribute to national economic and military power and security,[2] yet, in facilitating the internationalization of economic relations,[3] they also challenge the sovereignty of the nation-state. Indeed for centuries, even before the Age of Enlightenment, mercantilists and neostatists have viewed such challenges as a serious threat to the security of the state, while the state has used instruments of co-optation and coercion to gain and sustain the support of the scientific community. Science and technology may inherently be transnational, but scientists are not; in major research universities, think-tanks, and small shops, funds are essential for experimentation and innovation, and the state often justifies its expenditures as necessary for national security. The Reagan administration's Strategic Defense Initiative (SDI), more commonly referred to as the "star wars" program, was a case in point.[4] Washington's interest in funding Russia's nuclear scientists so that they are not tempted to sell their services abroad to nuclear weapons programs is another example.

S&T give rise to serious dilemmas from the global perspective as well, contributing to international cooperation[5] but also to arms races, environmental degradation (as well as potential safeguards), and the destruction of human lives. Scientists in the United States, Europe, Japan, and Russia in recent years have been engaged in various aspects of research and development (R&D) in the area of supercollider (particle smasher) technologies. One of the most ambitious international scientific programs has been the construction of the $15 billion Large Hadron Collider, scheduled to begin operation in 2004 under the auspices of the European Laboratory for Particle Research (CERN), headquartered in Geneva, an international consortium of nineteen European nations. Despite the international cooperation which makes CERN useful to scientists throughout the world, however, the competition among the major industrialized countries to conquer the next frontier in supercollider technology has been intense, since the commercial and military ramifications of such technologies are enormous.[6]

While military technology strengthens national security, the spread of such technology—especially the proliferation of nuclear weapons—may lead to international instability and, in worst case scenarios, to a nuclear holocaust annihilating humankind. As nations develop more advanced and expanding nuclear capabilities, even if for "peaceful purposes," it becomes more difficult to predict whether government leaders and technicians in control of such technologies will also possess the intellectual and institutional means to prevent intentional or accidental mass destruction; the disasters at Three Mile Island (Middletown, Pennsylvania) and Chernobyl (near Kiev, Ukraine), in March 1979 and April 1986, respectively, to mention only two, have raised serious concerns.[7] The availability of nuclear weapons arsenals continues to pose a serious threat to human lives, despite the ending of the Cold War, as the tensions between India and Pakistan have demonstrated.

THEORETICAL AND HISTORICAL DIMENSIONS OF SCIENCE AND TECHNOLOGY

Science and Technology as Concepts

Most people have an intuitive understanding of what science and technology are; here it will be useful to provide a loose definition, although a detailed discussion of the ingredients of both is well beyond the purview of this text. *Science* can be defined as a body of verifiable and falsifiable knowledge derived from replicable observations and experiments that attempt to identify, describe, explain, and predict the structures of the physical world and human behavior.[8] Strictly speaking, the branch of science that deals with the physical world is referred to as "natural sciences," or "physical sciences," while the branch dealing with human behavior and social structures is referred to as "social sciences." The line between the two is not as clear-cut as these labels suggest, however, and universities in recent years have placed a greater emphasis on interdisciplinary and multidisciplinary approaches to education. Neither is science (natural or social) a purely objective construct, as it reflects social and cultural values, the organizational framework within which research is conducted, and the historically or politically defined objectives science is expected to pursue. The scholars in Joan Rothschild's anthology, *Machina Ex Dea,* for example, have noted that, since science has traditionally been viewed as a male discipline, the historiography of science and technology has been androcentric, providing little information on women's role in the development of S&T and the impact of S&T on women in the workplace and society.[9]

Thomas Kuhn, in his classic work entitled *The Structure of Scientific Revolutions,* has argued that the scientific paradigm is a sociological construct developed by scientists who conduct their research within the structures of power, while the scientific community, operating within the dominant paradigm of its time, delineates the acceptable parameters of "normal science" characterized by incremental problem solving. Scientific revolutions against the dominant paradigm occur, however, as the accumulation of "anomalies"—that is, natural occurrences or phenomena that defy "the paradigm-induced expectations that govern normal science"—leads to deviation from "normal science," finally replacing the dominant paradigm with a new one.[10]

Technology is the concrete and practical application and the tangible product of science and, in turn, facilitates further scientific developments.[11] In fact, as Granger has noted, it is the effective use of this symbiotic relationship between science and technology "that characterizes the technologically advanced industries and nations."[12] As in science, "normal technology" advances through the incremental application of innovative techniques in product development and the routine adaptation of production processes and machinery to technological innovations. And, similar to the scientific paradigm, certain periods of history are dominated by a particular "technological paradigm,"[13] such as the "age of steam" or the "computer era," which shapes the social and economic organization of society and the attending "structures of production, finance, knowledge, and security."[14] There comes a time, however, as in science, when more radical technological innovations challenge and eventually replace the dominant technology and, in so doing, transform the existing structures and give rise to a new technological system.[15]

Science and Technology in Politics and Policy

The preceding chapters emphasized that economics cannot be separated from politics; the same holds true for the relationship between S&T and politics. As key economic components, science and technology coexist with politics in symbiotic and mutually complementary but sometimes mutually threatening, relationships. Historically, most societies have one way or another developed some form of S&T complexes to promote and protect the interests of the political and economic elites. That practice continues to this day; in more modern times, governments have the added pressures for elections and employment. Governments support S&T for a number of reasons. Ancient Chinese, Greek, and Arab empires married scientific discoveries to military conquests in ruling vast domains. In the age of mercantilism, the European monarchs encouraged and financially supported S&T as an instrument of state policy for the interest of the state and for warfare and competition. Henry the Navigator, king of Portugal (1433–1460), was a staunch supporter of science and brought together in his academy at Sagres cartographers, cosmographers, mathematicians, and other technicians to encourage navigation technology. His efforts launched the new age of ocean-going explorations and captured the imagination of scientists and sailors in Spain, England, and France. As discussed in Chapter 3, that century witnessed maritime explorations of the globe by Vasco da Gama, Columbus, and Magellan.[16] In the process, Portugal and Spain emerged, at least temporarily, as major global powers conquering vast continents from Africa to Asia and to the Americas. Less than a century later, the Dutch, the British, and the French followed, using more advanced military and navigation technologies. Echoes of such scientific involvement in the "Age of Exploration" can be seen today as scientists ride the space shuttles.

At times, however, scientists and political authorities collide, especially when the latter's interests are threatened. In the 1540s, famous Polish astronomer Nicolaus Copernicus' scientific studies and, later, in the 1620s, the equally famous Italian astronomer Galileo's publications attacking the Ptolemaic paradigm of the universe elicited the ire of religious authorities.[17] Copernicus and Galileo contended that, contrary to the Ptolemaic conception of the universe, the earth was not at the center of the universe and all things celestial did not revolve around humans. Giordano Bruno, another Italian astronomer, was burned by the Inquisition in 1600 for being engaged in such "heresies."[18]

Leaders of modern states, however, gradually realized that it was not easy or necessarily desirable to suppress scientific research and the advance of technology. In fact, despite the strains technology at times places on social and political institutions, as when twentieth-century scientists clone sheep, governments have, particularly since the advent of the industrial revolution, shown greater appreciation for and determination to use science and technological inventions to enhance the competitiveness of the national economy and national security capabilities. Science served the interests of the state, and particularly often military interests, and the state actively encouraged industrial research and development. In some cases, the state virtually forced the population to become more technology-conscious in order to propel society toward greater industrialization and modernization. In the 1860s and 1870s, the Meiji Restoration in Japan transformed that country from a primarily feudal, agricultural society to a rapidly expanding modern industrial power. Japan's military victory in the Russo-Japanese War (1905) was to a large extent attributable to Japan's industrial and technological prowess, as Russia lagged behind.[19] Also in the 1860s and 1870s, Otto von Bismarck was successful in rapidly industrializing the Prussian/German economy and "modernizing" the military capability of the second German Reich.[20] Germany's industrial base—including its infrastructural development, most emphatically its railroad networks (like the construction of the Roman roads centuries ago)—defeated France in the Franco-Prussian War (1870) and subsequently more firmly secured Germany's status as a global power.

In the late twentieth century, two sets of issues have emerged with respect to state policy toward S&T.[21] One involves the extent to which the state should fund industrial research and development. State funding may be in the form of direct subsidies, tax incentives or relief, and purchases. States use such policy instruments for a number of reasons—to reinvigorate a sluggish economy, to create jobs, and to support political allies and constituents. At the same time, however, foreign competitors may view state subsidies as non-tariff barriers (NTBs) for domestic companies to protect their markets. In the 1980s and 1990s, the European Union, the United States, and Japan repeatedly accused each other of engaging in such practices to enhance the international competitiveness of their domestic firms and to seal off their markets against foreign competitors.

Another set of issues pertains to the state's power and its allocative functions.[22] State funding for R&D is in essence allocation or reallocation of budgetary resources in a highly political process, as interest groups and state bureaucracies compete for support. The outcome reflects the competitors' political strengths or weaknesses, as measured in the dollar amounts allocated to them.[23] In the process, the more powerful groups also determine the nation's priorities in S&T and set the agenda for S&T policy in specific industrial sectors (chemistry, nuclear physics, communications, medicine), but also for the broader priorities in education and human resource development. Thus, the state, acting through its network of bureaucracies, is not a passive conveyor of resources but, rather, an active participant, channeling its resources into existing S&T programs that promise to sustain its strength and into emerging S&T frontiers that promise to enhance its power and prestige in society and in international political economy.

In virtually all societies, from the ancient times of the pharaohs to those of the modern kings, prime ministers, and presidents, the state and supportive powerful groups have sought to dominate "the knowledge structure" through the "use of whatever kinds of power they have, including coercive and legal power, to reinforce their privileged position."[24] As Susan Strange has pointed out, the ability to do so has become particularly crucial in recent years, since the "knowledge structure" has been changing far more rapidly than the structures of finance, production, and security.[25] If mismanaged, state power and allocation of a disproportionate share of resources on certain programs deemed essential by the elite can have disastrous consequences for the economy and, rather than strengthening the elite's privileged position, can actually lead to the loss of governmental legitimacy and collapse. The latter was experienced by the Communist elite in the former Soviet Union, in part because of its unsustainable expenditures on the military and defense-related S&T at the expense of consumer goods. In the United States, the Pentagon funded local economies across the country that grew too dependent on Cold War programs to develop their own locally sustainable economic base. The post–Cold War economic difficulties experienced by the city of New London, Connecticut, for example, painfully demonstrated the link between power and technology. *The Economist* best captured New London's problem: "once the heart of the world's nuclear-submarine industry and now a windswept clutter of vacant sites and boarded-up buildings. . . ."[26]

Technology, like almost everything else in life, is a double-edged sword. Acquisition and use of technology in a vast range of areas—from the steam engine, to the mechanization of meat-packing, to the mechanization of the kitchen, to the advent of the airplane and the automobile—raised nations' optimism and self-confidence in their ability to secure progress for a "better future,"[27] but they also created a sense of insecurity and pessimism due to destructive potential. Few would question that technology has made life longer and easier for vast numbers of people in advanced countries but also that multitudes have been left out or even harmed in the process; for the first time in history, as well, technology has made it possible for the human race to destroy itself entirely, and despoil its habitat.

Since the rise of the modern nation-state, countries with greater resources and organizational capacity have attained technological—and, by extension, military—advantages over others, and this process has continued to this day. As the industrial revolution and the subsequent emergence of the first industrialized economies (FIEs) created a wide gap between them and the predominantly agricultural developing world, so have the new technologies in various economic sectors led to a new division of the modern and postmodern international political economy between technology-rich and technology-poor economies.

Technology's contribution to economic growth and development has been widely acknowledged, although there has been little consensus on the optimal mix of variables (technology, capital, labor, government policy, culture) and on how technology should be used to achieve a human-friendly society. Laissez-faire liberalism stressed minimal government intervention and maximal economic freedom to advance S&T. Adam Smith criticized mercantilism because he viewed such restrictions on free economic activity as constricting the innovative and productive potential of manufacturers. Moreover, he argued, greater technological improvements in manufacturing lead to lower prices of goods, as "a much smaller quantity of labour becomes requisite for executing any particular piece of work."[28] Society would, therefore, attain economic growth through technological progress. More recently, in their empirical analysis of economic growth in the Group of Five countries (France, former West Germany, Japan, the United Kingdom, and the United States) during the 1957–1985 period, Baskin and Lau found that technical progress, relative to capital and labor, was "by far the most important source of economic growth."[29]

Technology as an engine for development also has elicited much criticism. Though Marxist states, such as the Soviet Union, tended to worship science and technology, even to the detriment of the environment, Karl Marx himself viewed science and technology as integral parts of capitalist development. Marx argued that technology, as a human invention, serves the interests of the capitalist (bourgeois) class as a tool for the exploitation of workers.[30] As industries reach a higher stage of development, in the long run, the integration of technology and machinery into new production processes pits workers against machines and then replaces workers with machines. Writing in the 1890s, Thorstein Veblen severely criticized the misuse and abuse of technological and industrial progress by the "leisure class," as he witnessed it in the United States, as wasting a community's resources through habits of "conspicuous consumption" and "pecuniary emulation."[31] E. P. Thompson, in his major work *The Making of the English Working Class,* contended that technological "progress" and industrialization in England impoverished the skilled trades, dulled human creativity, and sowed deep class divisions in society.[32] Others have similarly criticized industrial technology and scientific management ("Taylorism") as "deskilling" and alienating the worker and allowing greater centralization of production and, therefore, greater control over the worker,[33] while automation and robotics technologies directly and indirectly contribute to unemployment.[34] Technology, critics argue, thus becomes a source of power in the workplace and throughout society, and it replaces genuine human contact and humane reciprocity with human isolation and impersonal relationships via communication systems.[35] Such concerns give rise to skepticism, as in Charles Chaplain's classic 1920s film "Modern Times," and to discontent, the "Unibomber" case in the 1990s being a more extreme manifestation of hostility toward technology in the United States.

Five Phases of Technological Evolution

Since the advent of the industrial revolution, five major technological phases, each begun with a "technological revolution," have led the world economy into the modern age. Each technological revolution led to changes in the related organization of production and marketing facilities; the diffusion of the new technology throughout society changed the workplace, the home, and habits and tastes. At the national level, technological innovations contributed to the economic development and growth of some regions, as in the northern United States after the Civil War, while other regions, such as the American South, because of geography, investment decisions, and politics, remained agricultural and/or stagnated. At the international level, nations in command of the new technologies became world economic and military powers, and two among them, Britain and the United States, even emerged as world hegemons. Despite differences in the specific dates scholars use to delineate these phases, there is a general consensus—using the cyclical and "long wave" models of Kuznets, Jevons (whose "solar theory" was presented in Box 2.4), Kondratieff, and others—that the past two centuries can be divided into distinct phases, each about fifteen to twenty years (Kuznets) or fifty to sixty years (Kondratieff) long, as evidenced by fluctuations in economic growth and contraction. Using Carlota Perez's concept of "technological styles"[36] or paradigms, Tylecote has identified five phases in the past two centuries, with the following approximate dates (see Table 8.1):

- Water style, 1780s–1830s;
- Steam transport style, 1840s–1870s
- Steel and electricity style, 1880s–1910s
- Fordist style, 1920s–1970s
- Microelectronics and biotechnology style, 1980s-present[37]

According to Tylecote, the transition from one technological paradigm to the next was encouraged by "the appearance of new key *factors of production* which are: a) clearly very cheap, by past standards, and tending to get cheaper, and b) potentially all-pervasive."[38] Each phase was preceded by certain technological innovations in the extraction and application of resources, improved mechanical performance, and the generation of power, which in turn lowered prices and set the stage for the emerging technological paradigm.[39] In each phase, the diffusion of the dominant technology brought about various degrees of change in the organization and methods of production, but, as in Kuhn's "anomalies," each "technological style" contained within itself certain deficiencies that the new "technological style" was expected to resolve.

The *water style (1780s–1830s) phase* was based on the improvement and development of navigable river networks and canals. The use of water to generate power in England was spurred by the proliferation of manufacturing, while transportation costs, especially land transportation, remained prohibitively high, and human labor no longer provided a sufficient and efficient source of energy. Improvements in navigation and ship-building technology in the previous decades had slowly lowered the costs of water transportation, making transport over rivers more attractive than land transportation.[40] An important point not to overlook with respect to the significance of transportation is that these newly industrializing economies *were producing* goods and therefore required better transportation technology and systems to accommodate their expanding economic activities. Governments often financed such major projects for political and military purposes as well.[41]

In addition to transportation, water was also used as a source of power with the improved waterwheel and the invention of the steam engine. Since the latter was more expensive and inefficient, manufacturers initially preferred upgrading the waterwheel. Of course, the use of the waterwheel was not new; it had been used for centuries, but its structure had been more suitable for agricultural purposes. Its use for industrial power required greater durability, a problem solved by advances in ironmaking. Ironmaking technology, first using Abraham Darby's coke-smelting process in the early 1700s, had already spread by midcentury, followed by Henry Cort's improvements in the 1780s.[42] Particularly significant for the "water style" economic development was John Smeaton's contribution, in the 1750s, to the construction of a new waterwheel, replacing the wooden structure by cast iron in the axle, gears, rims, and bucket boards,

TABLE 8.1
Five Phases of Technological Revolution and World Leaders

Phase I 1780s–1830s	Phase II 1840s–1870s	Phase III 1880s–1910s	Phase IV 1920s–1970s	Phase V 1980s–present
Technologies				
water and steam power	steam and railways	steel	electronics	telecommunications
cotton textiles	iron and steel	electricity	synthetic materials	information technology
iron		chemicals	petrochemicals	
			automobiles	
			airplanes	
World Leaders				
Britain	**Britain**	**Britain**	Britain	Britain
France	**France**	**France**	France	France
Belgium	Belgium	Belgium	Belgium	Belgium
	United States	**United States**	**United States**	**United States**
	Germany	Germany	Germany	**Germany**
		Japan	Japan	**Japan**
		Switzerland	Switzerland	Switzerland
		Netherlands	Netherlands	Netherlands
			Sweden	Sweden

Source: Adapted from Andrew Tylecote, *The Long Wave in the World Economy* (London: Routledge, 1991), p. 68; Peter Dicken, *Global Shift: The Internationalization of Economic Activity*, 2d ed. (New York: The Guilford Press, 1992), p. 99. Boldfaced countries indicate the leading technological powers.

thereby enhancing the durability of the machinery and lowering the maintenance costs.[43] This was soon followed by James Watt's invention, in 1774, of the first useful steam engine, which, with gradual improvements in industrial application, afforded manufacturers greater choice in location.[44]

These developments improved production and commerce in textiles and clothing and machinery, and they attracted much capital from banks, which devised their own innovative techniques in financing investments and credit. Moreover, in every country where industrialization appeared, landowners, merchants, and manufacturers also secured government backing to encourage the new economic system.[45] Private and public funding was devoted to establish institutions for technical training, such as the French Ecole Polythechnique in 1794 and Ecole Centrale des Arts et Manufactures in 1829. In the United States, the University of Virginia was set up for a similar reason. Governments became interested in the emerging industrialization for a number of reasons, including the procurement of military uniforms and more sophisticated weapons and ships, manufactured by the use of the new technologies.[46] During this phase, Britain, already well positioned as an imperial power, further strengthened its position toward its competitors— especially France and to a lesser extent Belgium— and emerged as the leading economic and naval power.[47]

The second technological revolution, the *steam transport style (1840s–1870s)* phase, brought the development of railways based on steam power. Tylecote notes that, although the use of waterways and water power was a major improvement over land transportation and was relatively less expensive, manufacturers continued to search for ways to lower transportation costs and to minimize their dependence on geographical location.[48]

The railway offered several advantages over river transportation. It could transport large quantities of goods speedily on land in all directions across different terrains and climates. Manufacturers, thus, increasingly used the railway and had the added advantage of choosing between it and water transport.[49] However, the diffusion of the railway had a historically unparalleled impact on society. While well into the 1820s and the crystallization of the "water style" technological system modes of transportation used by manufacturers were intertwined with agricultural economies, the railway distinctively separated manufacturing and agricultural regions of society. Railways were built first and foremost to serve industrial interests, and transport for agriculture was only a by-product of that process, although the latter benefited as well.[50]

By midcentury, the railway enabled manufacturers to expand operations beyond their immediate regions, an expansion made possible by drawing on the increasing stock of available capital and credit from a similarly expanding banking system throughout the country. The banks sought to minimize their risk as much as possible by extending credit to those families and manufacturers who had a credible financial standing and the prospect for good returns on their investment. In some cases, the major financial houses, such as the Haute Banque of the Rothschilds and the Crédit Mobilier of the Péreire Brothers, competed vigorously to control the railways in France and elsewhere.[51]

Further, as in the "water style" system, governments seized the opportunity created by the railway to strengthen their administrative and military apparatus and to solve economic problems. In Belgium, for example, after independence from Holland in 1830, the government was confronted with the task of reviving the economy and lowering unemployment, and the construction of railways was a means to address both.[52] The extension of the railway played an important role in the formation of the new German and Italian states, as it enhanced the new state's instruments of communication and control.[53] It also enhanced accessibility to markets. Manufacturers and merchants throughout Europe lobbied their governments for a share of the railway network, and by the mid-nineteenth century thousands of miles of lines, including politically motivated *lignes électorales,* were opened across the continent. Where profitability was assured, as in most earlier industrialized regions in Britain and the northeastern United States, private capital followed the railways; where the risks for investors were higher, as in later industrialized parts of France, Germany, and the United States, government subsidies were required.[54] Accordingly, it was possible for and in the interest of the manufacturing classes in Britain to embrace the laissez-faire ideology advocated by Adam Smith some fifty years earlier, while the other European states, especially Germany, clung to well-versed mercantilist practices for a more systematic state organization and administration of the economy.

The impact of steam power[55] and railway, combined with the internal combustion engine, the nascent telegraph, and advanced gun and explosives technologies (for example, the invention of dynamite in 1866), began to shape military technology by the mid-nineteenth century,[56] as seen in the American Civil War. Britain's early industrialization and lead in the new technologies gave it technical and military advantages over its neighbors, especially in the area of naval supremacy.[57] By the middle of the century, Britain was clearly the world hegemonic power, having compensated for its loss in capital and prestige in the United States by colonizing nations throughout the world, especially India and—after the Opium Wars (1839–42; 1856–1858), when British military superiority was clearly demonstrated, parts of China. In 1860, with Britain constituting no more than 2 percent of the world's population, British

> energy consumption from modern sources (coal, lignite, oil) in 1860 was five times that of either the United States or Prussia/Germany, six times that of France, and 155 times that of Russia! It alone was responsible for one-fifth of the world's commerce, but for two-fifths of the trade in manufactured goods. Over one-third of the world's merchant marine flew under the British flag, and that share was steadily increasing.[58]

The principal technological revolutions during the third phase, the *steel and electricity style (1880s–1910s) phase,* involved improvements in metallurgy and steel production, the use of electricity, and inventions in chemical engineering, followed by the gradual development of the automobile and the airplane. Steel was already available for industrial and rail use by the 1850s; however, it was too expensive in comparison with pig iron, and further refinements were necessary before it could be used mass-scale for industrial and transportation purposes. Further improvements were made by Gilchrist-Thomas in the 1870s, and within a decade the price of steel dropped, which led to its widespread use in transportation and factories. In the United States, Andrew Carnegie used the Bessemer process to make steel rails and lowered the cost of production from nearly $107 per ton in 1870 to $48 in 1878, to $30 in the late 1880s, and to $12 in the late 1890s.[59]

Experimentation with electromagnetism had been conducted as early as the 1830s. In the 1870s, with the invention of Gramme's dynamo and the electric motor in Belgium, its use for public and industrial purposes spread rapidly. Within a decade, electric power began to replace water and steam power in industries. In the 1890s, factories used electric generators to distribute power throughout operations. Advances in electromagnetic field use during this period also included the X-ray technology developed by Madame Curie and Roentgen and the radio transmission technology by Marconi, leading to the communications revolution in the twentieth century. The internal combustion engine, used in cars and airplanes, was developed in the latter half of the nineteenth century, and it set the stage for the transportation revolution in the twentieth century.[60]

Chemical engineering at this time concentrated mainly on the refinement of raw materials, such as oil, for industrial use. Standard Oil developed its refining plants in the 1880s and reduced the cost of production of kerosene from 1.5¢ per gallon in 1882 to 0.54¢ in 1884, and to 0.45¢ in 1885.[61] Chemical engineering in general and oil in particular gained in importance as the shipbuilding industries, including warships, shifted from coal to oil as energy source, with enormous geo-political implications for the world political economy in the twentieth century.

Technological innovations in the case of electricity differed from the water and steam innovations in another important respect. In contrast to the preceding two phases, in which Britain was the primary source of technological innovations, technological changes in the 1870s and the early 1880s occurred in different countries: in addition to Belgian Gramme's electric motor in the early 1870s, Bell invented the telephone in the United States in the mid-1870s, Swan and Edison invented the filament lamp in Britain and the United States, respectively, in the late 1870s, while Siemens and Halske built the electric railway in Germany in 1881.[62] It appeared that Britain was losing the technological edge it enjoyed for more than a century over other European countries and the United States.

Also unlike the previous phases, during this period an Asian power, Japan, emerged, with its own expanding industrial structure, poised to challenge European dominance in East Asia. The competition for world market shares and cheap raw materials intensified, as demonstrated by the colonial "scramble for Africa," while the United States emerged as the leader in almost all areas of new technologies, with expanding interests in Latin America and across the Atlantic and the Pacific.[63] The opening of the Suez Canal in 1869, linking the Mediterranean to the Red Sea and the Indian Ocean, symbolized the European technological and military preponderance in the Mediterranean-Asian world, while the opening of the Panama Canal in 1915 symbolized American preponderance in the Atlantic-Pacific realm.

This phase also witnessed another significant change. Innovations in the areas of electricity and chemical engineering differed from the previous technological styles shifting from basically trial-and-error experimentation with familiar sources of energy—for example, water—to more complex theories and methods acquired in universities. Countries with institutional capacity and the human and capital resources to train new generations of scientists appeared to possess, as Charles Kindleberger argued, monopolistic advantages.

One of the principal characteristics of the fourth technological revolution, the *Fordist style (1920s–1970s) phase,* was the spread of mass production of various durable and nondurable consumer goods—electrical products, petrochemicals, synthetic materials—but most significantly automotive products, catapulting the United States into world hegemony.[64] By the 1890s, the assembly line, with its sequential system of separate functions, had been in use in the poultry industry—for example, in the slaughterhouses in the United States—for more than three decades, but it had tended to function as a simple conveyor.[65] The production technologies developed during the "steel and electricity" period were refined to use existing, and increasingly less expensive, sources of energy (especially oil) in turn to generate power for larger and more sophisticated factory operations. The emerging factory was comprised of an entire panoply of precision tools, machines, and sheet metal presses to produce precisely calibrated and interchangeable parts. These developments and their potential utility were appreciated by Frederick Winslow Taylor, as he formulated his scientific theory of management for the production of mass consumer goods. Thus, when Henry Ford adopted the assembly-line method in 1913–1914, a combination of theories in scientific management and production technologies was already in place.[66]

The Ford Motor Company integrated the new technologies of production into the assembly line, designed and coordinated within the company structure. This was soon adopted by Ford's competitors, General Motors and Chrysler, and their combined power eventually eliminated other competitors from the market, creating an oligopolistic "Big Three" system. At its giant River Rouge complex, Ford sought to control the entire production process, from iron ore shipped in via the Great Lakes to the final assembly of finished steel parts. Ford had stressed the utility of the "universal car," but it was General Motors that was particularly successful in marketing strategies. The *Fordist* factory system, as used by the automobile industry, changed the organization of production from a "unitary" to a "multidivisional" structure.[67] The unitary structure was possible while the ownership and management of the firm was a family affair, and a single management structure could govern the process of production, finance, and marketing. As Ford, General Motors, and Chrysler expanded their domestic and international operations, these functions were divided into separate units to enhance management and efficiency, or to foster the image of distinct product lines. Having developed his new factory system at home, Ford became increasingly and intensely interested in developing a network of international operations to secure the continuous flow of raw materials—

for example, rubber—and access to foreign markets.[68] Indeed, both Ford and General Motors became heavily involved even in the Nazi German wartime economy through subsidiaries.

Technological advances in communications, such as the telegraph and the telephone, and transportation, such as the airplane and supertanker also had a direct influence on the production structure. Lowered communication and transportation[69] costs made it easier for corporate managers to communicate with their subsidiaries across continents and to ship their goods to and from markets. They also contributed to a high degree of centralized control over production processes at home and abroad, to an extent unimaginable by the managers of the old British and Dutch East India companies.[70] As large corporations became multinational, financial institutions such as banks expanded their operations to keep pace. Such expansion, however, could not have been organizationally feasible without the new communications technologies, which set the stage for the next phase of the technological revolution in microelectronics.

The major technological changes during this phase, from the automobile to the airplane, were primarily centered in the United States, which during the Second World War had become the "arsenal of democracy" by shifting its auto and aircraft techologies to weapons. While the European competitors were in the process of recovering from the Second World War and subsequently became mired in colonial struggles, the expansion of U.S. corporations and the concomitant financial and communications networks strengthened the American position in world trade and finance. As discussed in Chapter 3, however, in the 1960s and 1970s, the world leadership group in technology widened, especially as Germany and Japan challenged U.S. hegemony. Symbolizing the change, the U.S. automotive Big Three became the "global Big Five" with Daimler Benz's purchase of Chrysler in 1998. At the same time, while the United States and the other industrialized economies were registering major successes in S&T, the technological gap between them and the developing countries, most of which gained independence during this period, widened even further, especially as synthetic materials lessened the industrialized countries' dependence on raw materials imports.

Tylecote has pointed out that, despite the successes of Fordist production, one of its limitations was the problem of "*control* mechanisation: the substitution of machines for the human brain in the direction and supervision of the productive process"—that is, artificial, or machine, intelligence.[71] These problems are addressed in the fifth technological revolution.

The fifth phase, *microelectronics and biotechnology style, 1980s–present,* involves information (or communications) technologies—computers, satellites, cellular and integrated digital networks, faxes, and fiber optics—and technologies in genetic engineering. Concurrent with developments in microelectronics technology, which supplied complex electric circuits on tiny reproducible silicone chips, were advances in biotechnology, particularly in genetic—that is "techniques for the manipulation, alteration and synthesis of the genetic material in cells in such a way that the functioning of the cell is modified."[72] In 1973, taking advantage of advances in biology and microelectronics technology, Boyer and Cohen were able to isolate and manipulate DNA. The application of advanced biotechnology to agricultural production, the management of waste and pollution, and health sciences in general is expected to bring enormous advantages to developed and developing economies.[73]

Electronics technologies, including the integrated circuit in 1961 and the microprocessor a decade later, contributed to the miniaturization and popularization of the computer in the 1980s. In the formative stage in the 1950s, computers were large and expensive "mainframe computers" used mostly by governments and major companies for management purposes— for example, payroll. They had limited information-processing and interconnectivity capabilities. In the late 1960s and early 1970s, small computer terminals, consisting of the "box" and the monitor, were developed, and included such features as interactivity, computer-aided design (CAD) capability, and digitalization.[74] As each new feature lowered the costs of increasingly miniaturized products, their diffusion followed the familiar pattern as experienced with the previous technologies. Computers were initially used by firms for purposes of enhanced productivity. Quickly, however, computer technology reached consumer markets, even before many people had a sense of how to use them, and, by the mid-1980s, small desktop units, known as "personal computers" (PCs), were set to become as widespread as household appliances and telephones were after the 1940s.

These changes bore enormous implications for the workplace and society at large. "The new telecommunications technologies," write Henderson and Castells, "are the electronic highways of the informational age, equivalent to the role played by railway systems in the process of industrialization."[75] They are "space-shrinking technologies," revolutionizing the way information is communicated and people and goods are transported across oceans and continents.[76] The telecom satellite Intelsat I's carrying capacity, for example, increased exponentially in the 1980s; Intelsat IV could transmit 6,000 phone conversations, Intelsat V 12,000, and its later model nearly 120,000. A future model is expected to transmit over 700,000 conversations simultaneously.[77] The globalization of international political economy is precisely the product of such technologies, which enable MNCs, governments, public and private institutions, and millions of individuals to communicate instantaneously across geographically distant areas.[78]

As in the previous technological styles, the corporate search for avenues to maximize profit and to lower production costs was the principal motive in the transition to and the crystallization of the new telecommunications technologies in the 1980s and 1990s. There was, however, one critical difference. The earlier technological revolutions shifted the primary mode of production from agriculture to industrialization and, in so doing, caused major demographic shifts from the rural to the urban areas where the new factories were located. The railroad contributed to this shift, as well as quickened the pace of the movement of goods and people. Despite these changes, however, a large human labor force was still necessary to operate the factories. The microelectronics paradigm, in contrast, provides corporations with a greater choice between employing human labor and using automation, and between centralizing and dispersing design, production, and marketing facilities.

Computer technology for mass production advanced rapidly and led to the development of robotics and the automation and programming of the assembly line. This shifted the demand from laborers to programmers, from assemblers to computer repair experts, with the potential loss of mass production jobs. Once robotics were installed, the costs of production involved mostly maintenance and upgrades. Moreover, computers facilitate a high degree of corporate flexibility—favoring centralization or decentralization, allowing for "on time" assembly without large parts inventories, advantages (and also some vulnerabilities, such as the inability to withstand long strikes or work stopages by parts suppliers)—which were rarely found in the previous periods.

The situation has significant implications for human labor. In addition to their intelligence and flexibility, humans bring their entire social-psychological baggage to the workplace, and they can be demanding. For the firm, human employment entails not only wages but also a widening array of benefits (health coverage, vacation time, retirement pensions, etc.). Automation, while requiring service and maintenance, would minimize, if not totally remove, these social burdens from the corporate balance sheet. Robots, unlike humans, do not organize labor unions. In the 1980s and 1990s, the major industries restructured and downsized their organizations, eliminating what they viewed as "excess productive capacity."[79] As noted in Chapter 1, when the Group of Seven (G-7) jobs conference was held in Detroit in March 1994, there were an estimated 120 million registered unemployed, most of whom had lost their jobs because of corporate downsizing. The increase in employment in the rest of the 1990s was found mostly in the service sector, with considerably lower wages and less job security.

However, technology's impact on labor can vary. Some Japanese companies reportedly have discovered that humans cannot effectively be eliminated from many production processes. Adaptation to unanticipated needs and quick model changeovers appear easier for humans than for robots. Information technology may indeed provide greater opportunities for people to work from home and become independant contractors. Women are beginning to make greater inroads through the computer into the corporate and business world. One study has found that currently 47 percent of female and 41 percent of male business owners have on-line subscriptions; 51 percent of female and 40 percent of male business owners regularly use the Internet; 22 percent of female and 14 percent of male business owners use the Internet for business-related research; 9 percent of female and 3 percent of male business owners use the Internet for business deals and contracts.[80] However, it is estimated that, of the 1,686 major technology companies, only 5.6 percent are owned by women.[81]

The recent technological advances have further widened the gap between the first industrialized economies (FIEs) and the developing countries. The major technological powers in this "information age" have been the United States, Japan, and Germany, although the other industrialized countries have kept pace as well. The former Soviet bloc countries, along with India and China, are in the process of "catching up" with the West, while most of the developing countries continue to lag behind in this age of modern information technology. Only a small number of developing countries—such as the Asian NICs, Argentina, Brazil, Chile, Mexico, Israel, and South Africa—have developed advanced telecommunications systems, and within some of these societies it is primarily the upper classes that have access to such technologies.

NEW TYPES OF TECHNOLOGY: CHALLENGES FOR NATIONAL AND MULTILATERAL POLICY

Technological development involves highly specialized knowledge and skills ranging from extraction of natural resources, to exploration, production, and marketing of soaps and cars, to technologies of space exploration. Discoveries involve the replacement of old products and production processes with new and remodeled ones, delivering better performance, cheaper costs, and new styles, but also running the risk of environmental degradation and depletion of natural resources. Such changes have implications not only for international trade relations and MNC competition in global markets but also for national policy with respect to agricultural, environmental, health, and defense sectors.

Beyond its practical uses, however, technology also provides intangible advantages, such as international prestige, hence part of the interest in possessing nuclear weapons. The extent of technological innovation a country generates is viewed as an indication of its geo-economic and political position, including its military capabilities in the world political economy.[82] Governments are expected to formulate economically and strategically sound *national* tech nology and industrial policies to promote their scientific and economic interests. The extent to which a government should intervene to protect technology for national economic and military interests is a highly controversial question for the twenty-first century, just as it was in earlier times, reflecting the tension between mercantilist and laissez-faire views.

Scientific and technological advances, particularly as used for commercial and defense purposes, also have led to the phenomenon of international spillovers, whereby scientific inventions and technologies of production emanate from the country of origin to other countries by way of technology transfers (such as through licensed overseas production), the proliferation of free trade areas, and so on.[83] MNC operations and their use of advanced technologies worldwide facilitate the transfer and spread of some of the latest technologies. The originating, or home, government, however, is presented with a dilemma: it supports and subsidizes home-based MNCs' research and development to strengthen the nation's economy and employment and to enhance its competitiveness in international markets; however, at the same time, the very scientific and technological achievements desired for competitiveness cannot be completely contained within the national borders.[84] Where international spillovers occur based on bilateral or multilateral agreements or MNC–host government contracts, technology strengthens transnational cooperation, but the source country loses, via exports and foreign direct investments, some degree of its competitive advantage and control over the use of the devices involved. Obversely, the recipient country might not gain full use of the new technology, which often is controlled by the contracting MNC.[85] However, know-how is difficult to contain, patents are not always iron-clad, and rules on the use of new processes cannot always be enforced.

International spillovers become a particularly pressing problem when they occur through economic or industrial espionage—that is, the secret acquisition of industry-specific information to gain market advantages vis-à-vis competitors. Economic espionage has been around since time immemorial. In more modern times, it has involved pirating business and industrial know-how, including blueprints and "insider information," to learn the "trade secrets." The secret importation of business and industrial knowledge is commonly done by businesses themselves, but various government bureaucracies facilitate and even encourage such espionage activities.[86] In the aftermath of the Cold War, economic espionage has emerged as one of the more salient concerns for individual government bureaucracies, such as the U.S., Russian, and French intelligence services.[87]

Historically, industrial intelligence involved a number of activities, including support for diplomatic negotiations regarding economic agreements, the monitoring of foreign legal and illegal operations at home and abroad, the monitoring of changes in business- and national security–related technological developments, and counterintelligence operations to identify and neutralize foreign intelligence activities in one's own country. As Laqueur reminds us, "The instructions Moses gave to his spies about Canaan predominantly concerned economic information, such as the quality of the land. The travelers who went to China in the Middle Ages to study the silk industry's secrets were engaging in technology transfer."[88] During the Cold War, Soviet bloc intelligence units were involved in stealing economic and military scientific and technological R&D information from the West, and the West developed various counterintelligence programs, such as the FBI's Developing Espionage and Counterintelligence Awareness (DECA), to combat such threats to national economic and military security.[89] As an aspect of their economic policies, especially in the post–Cold War era, governments have supported private businesses through economic intelligence and espionage.

The sense of U.S. economic decline since the early 1970s compelled Washington to address the espionage problem, and the Soviet collapse in the early 1990s afforded an opportunity to debate a readjustment in the role of the intelligence community (see Box 8.1).[90] The United States used its intelligence capabilities, as developed during the Cold War, to regain its competitive edge vis-à-vis Japan and the European Union. During the 1994 auto trade negotiations in Geneva, for example, the Japanese government reportedly complained that the CIA was eavesdropping on Japanese government and industry representatives to provide market information to U.S. Trade Representative Mickey Kantor.[91] Similarly, particular attention has been paid to French and Israeli intelligence activities spying on U.S. companies.[92]

Another challenging issue in the spread of technology is the so-called brain drain, whereby educated and skilled citizens leave their homeland for more advanced training, better jobs, and a better life in another country. For most of the early part of this century, brain drain was an issue among industrialized economies, particularly as highly educated and skilled European professionals migrated to the United States, Canada, and the wealthier Middle Eastern states. In recent decades, increasingly large numbers of skilled workers have migrated from developing

BOX 8.1

ECONOMIC ESPIONAGE: A POST–COLD WAR "PEACE DIVIDEND"?

On the banks of London's River Thames, a vast gleaming building being built for Britain's MI6 overseas spy agency is concrete evidence that the espionage business is still thriving seven years after the Cold War ended.

With Russia and Britain plunged into the worst East–West espionage row since the 1989 fall of the Berlin Wall, after Moscow accused nine British diplomats of espionage and ordered them out, intelligence experts say spying is vital in a volatile world.

The fictional gentlemen with their large hats and dead letterboxes who inhabit the spy novels of John Le Carre have largely been replaced by people operating floppy disks.

"The West is worried about the political situation inside Russia. It used to be extremely stable politically," said Margot Light, international relations expert at the London School of Economics.

"We are also worried about not only whether Russia is fulfilling the terms of arms control agreements, but also in case some of the material that is being dismantled is actually being smuggled out," Light added.

Despite friendly overtures, high-profile state visits and help with Russia's transition to a free-market economy, the West is still troubled by Moscow's capacity for unpredictable decisions.

Diplomats say the West is keen to establish who is really in control in the Kremlin and in the armed forces as the popularity of the ailing Boris Yeltsin sinks.

Several hundred British businesses have set up in the new free-market Russia, giving London what it feels is a legitimate concern in the future of the country. Russia's relations with nations such as China and Iran are also of keen interest.

Now that the Iron Curtain has parted, Russia shows no signs of bringing its own spies in from the cold.

Stella Rimington, head of Britain's MI5 domestic intelligence service, said last year there had been a recent upsurge in spying by Russia on other countries.

Intelligence experts say the Russian emphasis has shifted slightly to industrial espionage and trying to get hold of material and ideas without paying for them.

Russian expert Martin McCauley said that before the fall of communism, almost any information gleaned from the Soviet Union was regarded as espionage.

But he said there was now a fine line between gathering legitimate information and spying.

"There is a lot of money laundering in Moscow. It is the task of the British embassy to discover if any of this dirty money is going through England. There is also gun running and drug smuggling. This is all legitimate intelligence gathering. What's the difference between intelligence and espionage? It is in many ways just qualitative," McCauley said.

Russia is by no means the main target of the spies of the 1990s.

Argentina's 1982 invasion of the Falkland Islands and Iraq's 1990 invasion of Kuwait gave sharp reminders of the costly consequences when information gathering fails.

"At the end of the day, good intelligence—meaning effective espionage—saves lives and money. Only when it fails do we see the headlines," wrote thriller writer and former journalist Frederick Forsyth.

Source: Jill Serjeant, Reuter-London, May 7, 1996.

countries and the former Soviet republics to Europe, the United States, and Canada. Governments generally attempt to maintain certain checks on the outflow of skilled and educated employees, as the building of the Berlin Wall in 1961 demonstrated, but the demolition of that wall in 1989 also demonstrated governments' inability to so tightly control their borders as to prevent the movement of people and ideas across national borders.

Research and Development (R&D)

Governments morally and financially support and subsidize public and private R&D because technological advances are considered necessary for a strong economy, national security, and international competitiveness. Governments support technology to create new employment opportunities (albeit eliminating others) for the public and to increase tax revenues through economic growth. Despite the close relationship between government and contractors (for example, General Dynamics and the U.S. Department of Defense), in the globalized world economy it has become nearly impossible for a company to monopolize a technological niche; sophisticated electronics and engineering systems lead to the rapid dissemination of information and distribution of products—that is, international spillovers. Indeed, in the case of military technology, international arms transfers, in the form of military sales and military assistance programs, result in the transfer of technologies strategically essential for national security.

In Western economies, government investment involves public institutions and laboratories engaged in R&D directly for the government and private enterprises engaged in R&D subsidized by the government. In some developing countries, however, especially in Communist societies such as China, Cuba, North Korea, and Vietnam, governments tend to control all aspects of R&D.

Governments invest particularly in "strategic" technologies related to commerce and national defense, including aerospace.[93] As Granger has observed,

> in general, governments invest in R&D when important public benefits are perceived but individual firms are unable to balance the business benefits of the innovation with the various costs and risks entailed. . . . The source of investment funds, for government, is not as directly dependent on returns from previous investments as is the case in private industry. Thus competitive risks may exist in principle, in the sense that international political competition is often implicit, but they are entirely different from private sector R&D risks.[94]

Public subsidies provide insurance against private firms' financial losses with the expectation that the financial benefits trickle down to the consumer. Whether that actually occurs is debatable, however.

Also, in some economic sectors the government is the primary or only consumer of scientific and technological innovations, as for most defense technologies, although they may be classified as "dual-use" technologies applicable to commercial purposes as well. The market for nuclear energy and weapons technology worldwide is tightly controlled by a small number of governments, even where commercial and "peaceful uses" of nuclear energy have been encouraged, such as in Canada's "CANDU" nuclear reactors. Concern has grown that private groups, firms, or individuals might sell nuclear weapons for profits, as in the disrupted economies of the former Soviet bloc.

Government expenditures for national technology policies and scientific and technological R&D exert considerable influence on the national economy; such programs touch on the full spectrum of economic policy areas, including budgetary policies, industrial and labor policies, social welfare programs, defense and trade policies, and so forth.[95] Thus, governments encourage public and private R&D not only to develop new military and commercial technologies per se but also to stimulate different economic sectors, to expand employment opportunities, and to enhance competitive capabilities at home and abroad. Despite the importance of government expenditures, however, the primary source of [R&D] funding has been the private sector. Ironically, while the Japanese structure of overall political economy is said to be statist, private funds constitute a larger share of national R&D in Japan than in the United States.[96] Japan's science-technology policies have proved to be quite successful, as its ability to compete in international markets in the 1980s and early 1990s demonstrated. One crucial element was the public and private sectors' collaboration to closely monitor foreign and multinational companies' and nations' technological and economic performance to identify market opportunities worldwide. The central institution entrusted to lead this task has been the Ministry of International Trade and Industry (MITI). Effective monitoring of technological developments abroad has demanded considerable financial and competent human resources with technical expertise, as well as advanced, high-speed information retrieval systems.[97]

Figure 8.1 and Table 8.2 illustrate the trends in expenditures on science and technology by governments of the

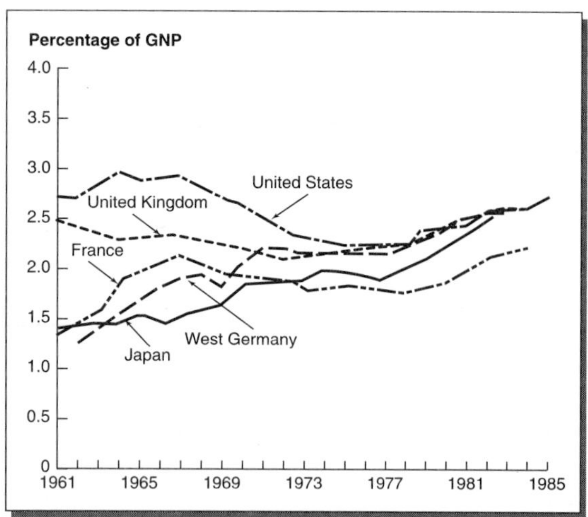

FIGURE 8.1 R&D Spending by Major Powers, 1960s to 1980s. *Source:* David C. Mowery and Nathan Rosenberg, *Technology and the Pursuit of Economic Growth* (Cambridge: Cambridge University Press, 1989), p. 208.

industrialized countries since the early 1960s. In the 1970s and 1980s, all major countries, but particularly the former West Germany and Japan, accelerated their R&D programs. In fact, when defense-related R&D expenditures are excluded, U.S. investments in R&D, while still the world's largest, actually declined relative to those of the other industrialized countries as a percent of GNP. Total British, German, and U.S. R&D expenditure percentages declined in the 1990s. Technologies such as robotics enabled Japanese automobile companies to develop and produce a new model in "one-half as much time" as their U.S. counterparts by the 1980s. Of course management approaches and determination also entered into such developments alongside technological discoveries themselves.[98] Japanese companies have been effective in adopting new home-grown and foreign technologies for purposes of commercialization, especially in the area of consumer electronics. While, for example, the United States led R&D in the development of the transistor, Japan led the "large-scale

TABLE 8.2

Government Funding of R & D, 1989–1993 in Millions of Current Home Currency (Percent of Government Budget)

Country	1989	1990	1991	1992	1993
Britain (£)					
Nondefense	2,616.7	2,778.9	2,785.7	2,979.1	3,097.4
Defense	2,021.4	2,154.7	2,208.8	2,065.2	2,289.2
Total	4,638.1	4,933.6	4,994.5	5,044.3	5,386.6
	(2.8%)	(2.6%)	(2.3%)	(2.1%)	(2.1%)
France (FF)					
Nondefense	52,730.0	55,385.0	59,523.1	58,225.3	59,922.6
Defense	31,000.0	37,000.0	33,600.0	30,756.3	30,189.5
Total	83,730.0	92,385.0	93,123.1	88,981.6	90,112.1
	(3.4%)	(3.5%)	(3.3%)	(2.9%)	(3.6%)
Germany (DM)					
Nondefense	20,612.8	21,734.3	26,215.0	27,982.3	28,810.1
Defense	3,023.4	3,384.2	3,234.5	3,120.6	2,670.5
Total	23,636.2	25,118.5	29,449.5	31,102.9	31,480.6
	(3.8%)	(3.7%)	(3.7%)	(3.2%)	(3.1%)
Japan (Y)					
Nondefense	1,722,131.0	1,816,603.0	1,907,586.0	2,007,687.0	2,129,090.0
Defense	93,068.0	104,268.0	115,045.0	126,989.0	137,175.0
Total	1,815,199.0	1,920,871.0	2,022,631.0	2,134,676.0	2,266,265.0
	(3.1%)	(3.3%)	(3.5%)	(3.7%)	(3.9%)
United States ($)					
Nondefense	21,450.0	23,856.0	26,569.0	28,315.0	28,635.0
Defense	40,665.0	39,925.0	39,328.0	40,083.0	41,249.0
Total	62,115.0	63,781.0	65,897.0	68,398.0	69,884.0
	(5.5%)	(5.3%)	(5.0%)	(4.9%)	(4.9%)

Source: OECD, *Basic Science and Technology Statistics,* Copyright OECD, (1995). Table 18, passim. Data for government budgets from *World Tables 1995.*

commercialization of transistor technology for the radio."[99] Similarly, although the United States developed and initially dominated the market for color television, in the 1980s Japan began to capture an increasingly larger share of the market, successfully challenging the U.S. position. The technological sophistication required for the design, manufacture and commercialization of the video cassette recorder (VCR) in the 1980s was primarily Japanese in skill if not in origin. During the 1980s, Japan emerged as one of the leading countries in many areas involving the most advanced technologies available in computers and memory chips, fiber optics, and various computer-based machine tools.[100]

Despite these successes, however, Japanese science and technology continue to be in a "catch-up with the United States" mode. U.S. companies emerged as quite competitive in the latest high resolution T.V. technology. The Japanese government was successful in encouraging inter-firm collaboration and in backing "winners" precisely because none of the participants' R&D was itself sufficient to culminate in significant technological breakthroughs. Accordingly, each firm preferred to cooperate in R&D exchanges in order to catch up with the United States, while attempting to strengthen its own R&D capabilities to be the first to conquer the next technological frontier at home and in international markets.[101]

While advanced economies such as the U.S. and Japan competed vigorously among themselves, the technological gap between the industrialized and developing countries widened even more precipitously in the 1980s and 1990s, with the advent of globalization of the world economy and the computer age. Figures 8.2 and 8.3 clearly demonstrate that gap. Most developing countries appropriate little over 0.5 percent of their national income on R&D, while industrialized countries spend between 2 and 3 percent.[102] In the early 1970s, Western industrialized countries were home to 55.4 percent of the world's total scientists and engineers. In addition, 32 percent were located in the former Soviet bloc countries. Thus, 87.4 percent of the world's R&D scientists and engineers were in the North, while merely 12.6 percent were in the developing countries. The North's expenditures on R&D were even more impressive, accounting for 97.1 percent of the world's total.[103] During the latter part of the 1970s, the total annual R&D spending in developing countries surged from $5 billion in 1975 to $20 billion in 1980 (from 4.2 percent to 10 percent, respectively), but it became stagnant again throughout the 1980s (as seen in Figure 8.4). Among the developing countries, the NICs,[104] nevertheless, experienced rapid economic growth based on "technology-intensive industries of telecommunications equipment and electrical machinery,"[105] as their R&D spending grew from $1.5 billion in 1980 to nearly $20 billion in 1990.[106]

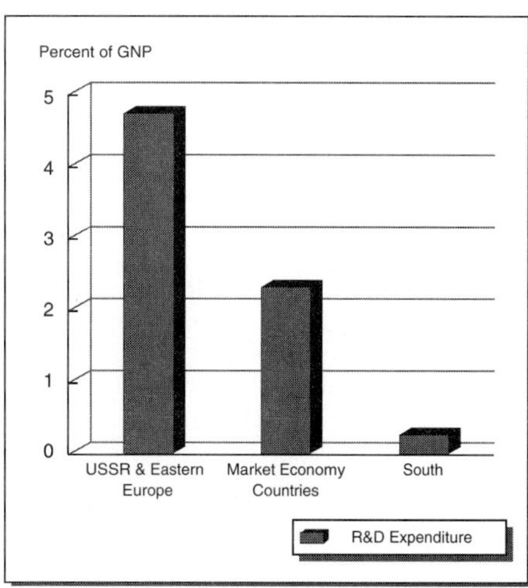

FIGURE 8.2 Expenditure on R & D as a percent of GNP in the North and in the South.
(*Source: UNESCO, Statistical Yearbook 1989.* Nyerere Commission Report, *Challenge to the South: The Report of the South Commission* (Oxford: Oxford University Press, 1990), p. 40.)

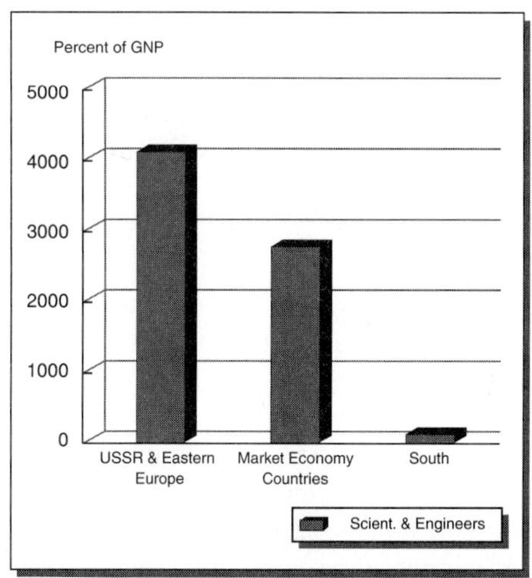

FIGURE 8.3 Numbers of Scientists and Engineers Per Million Population in the North and in the South.
(*Source:* UNESCO, *Statistical Yearbook 1989.* Nyerere Commission Report, *Challenge to the South: The Report of the South Commission* (Oxford: Oxford University Press, 1990), p. 40. Note, though, that India is said to have the largest number of trained scientists and engineers of any state in the world.)

Developing countries realize the challenge posed by the rapidly changing international political economy and the unequal distribution of scientific and technological

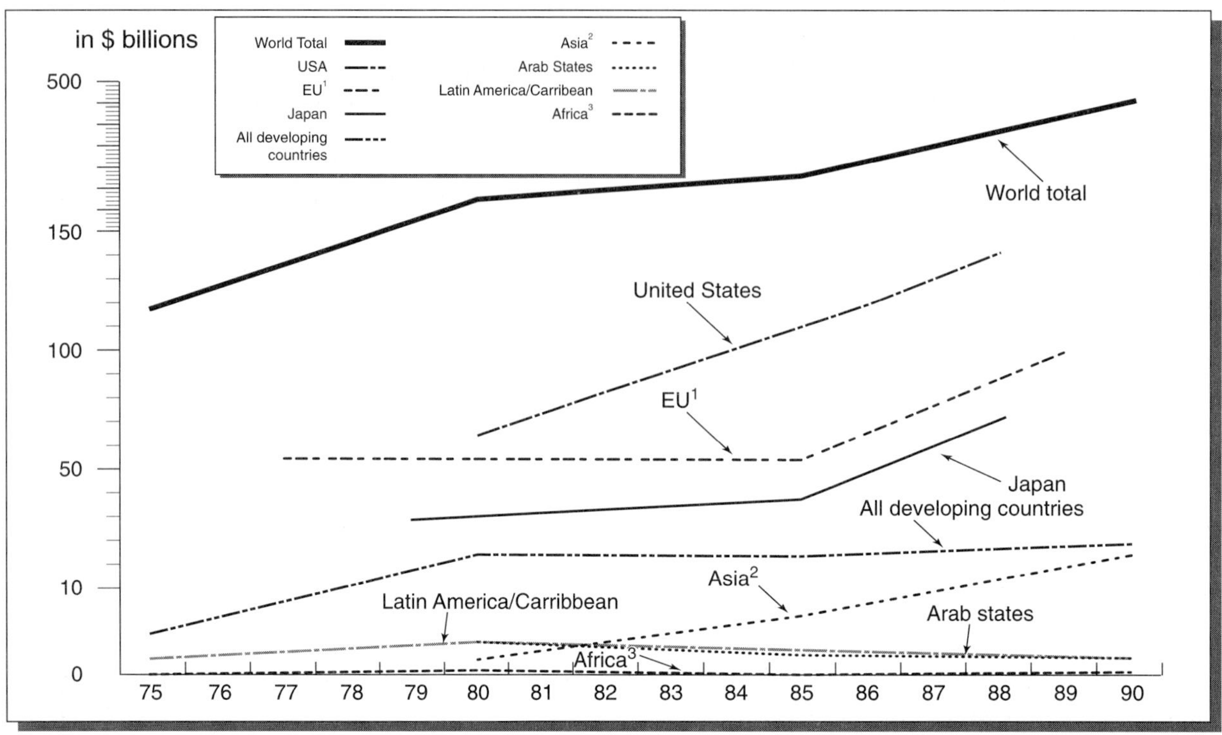

1 The 12 states of the then European Community in 1990
2 Without Arab states and Japan
3 Without Arab states

FIGURE 8.4 Worldwide Research and Development Spending 1975–90.
(*Source:* Ingomar Hauchler and Paul M. Kennedy, eds., *Global Trends: The World Almanac of Development and Peace* New York: The Continuum Publishing Group, 1994), p. 365.

capability. Along the lines *of dependencia* theory, they emphasize the need to make greater investments in indigenous R&D.[107] Many economists and environmentalists also have recommended more labor-intensive environmentally "sustainable" and locally "appropriate" technologies requiring less costly inputs of resources and capital, as well as simpler lifestyles requiring less consumerism to sustain local economies.[108]

In 1990, the Nyerere Commission on North–South issues argued that immediately after gaining independence from colonial rule the leadership in developing countries ignored issues related to national science and technology policy and relied on the industrialized West for political and economic reasons. As a result, developing countries failed to "train an adequate number of qualified scientists to whom countries could turn for advice on the scientific problems that are bound to arise when scientific knowledge is applied in practice."[109] They used R&D to improve agricultural production, water management systems, fertilizers, and pest control. The Green Revolution, for example—pioneered by western scientists working in the Philippines—increased agricultural output and improved "national food security."[110] Some developing countries were engaged in technological ventures in the production of iron, steel, hydropower, and petroleum and in redesigning and remanufacturing machinery via adapted technologies to enhance domestic and international competitiveness. However, in virtually all cases, the technologies and the required capital to finance them were imported from abroad, partly necessitated by the "disinvestment" of capital from newly independent former colonies by their former rulers. The lack of emphasis on science and technology, the Nyerere Commission noted, also generated a sense of intellectual inferiority in these areas, leading to the myth that the cultures and traditions found in the South somehow hinder scientific and technological developments, "despite the fact that experience has conclusively shown that science and technology can be

BOX 8.2

FACTORS CONTRIBUTING TO BRAIN DRAIN FROM DEVELOPING COUNTRIES TO THE UNITED STATES

Country of origin with

1. A large population
2. A pro-Western, capitalistic outlook
3. Speakers of English, rather than any other European language
4. Unstable economic conditions
5. A long history of well-established higher education
6. A colonial legacy that has not been too culturally dominant

Source: Bernard I. Logan, "The Reverse Transfer of Technology from Sub-Saharan Africa to the United States," *Journal of Modern African Studies 25,* 4 (1987), p. 603.

learned in a predictable manner by all people, irrespective of culture or country."[111]

As previously mentioned, the concept of "brain drain" refers to the flight of human capital, such as scientists, engineers, and doctors from one country to another. (The often interchangeably used "reverse transfer of technology" refers more specifically to brain drain from the less developed countries to the Western industrialized ones.[112]) While brain drain has been part of human history for centuries (indeed, the history of human migration is the history of brain drain), more salient issues in recent years have involved the migration of skilled labor from Europe to North America, particularly to the United States, from the developing to the industrialized countries, and, finally, from the former Soviet bloc to the West. After the post-WWII economic reconstruction had ended, the Western industrialized economies experienced rapid economic development and growth in the 1950s and 1960s, but they also experienced shortages in skilled labor.[113]

The primary concern with respect to the brain drain phenomenon is that, as educated and trained scientists and engineers leave a society, they take with them the knowledge and training needed for local communities' productivity, the very bases for economic development and growth.[114] In the developing world, policymakers have expressed serious concerns that their current and future scientists graduating from local or foreign universities move to other countries. Observers generally agree on the actual causes of brain drain (see Box 8.2), but they also agree that it is virtually impossible to state with mathematical precision the extent and effects of such losses on a society. They agree that, at least in the case of developing countries in which indigenous technology is much needed, the emigration of highly trained scientists and engineers at the very least "handicaps" economic development based on local resources. One observer has noted that the globalization of communications and mass media technologies contributes significantly to the brain drain, as "the prosperity gap [becomes] broadly visible and awaken[s] migration motives. The One World growing together spurs the international mobility of people while the revolutionization of transport makes it easier."[115] On the other hand, such networking also helps replace technical know-how through foreign sources, as useful information becomes available on line and in scholarly publications. However, this is not likely to be the most advanced forms of technology.

Brain drain is not a problem of developing countries alone. It was a serious problem for the former Soviet Union, so much so that Moscow tried to tax emigrants as they left, trying to charge them for their education and training. Soviet emigration policy historically restricted professional foreign travel, but during Gorbachev's *glasnost* a large number of scientists left the country. As previously mentioned, in less than three years, the number of scientists and engineers dropped by 300,000, as they left for temporary and permanent positions abroad. The former Soviet Academy of Sciences alone lost nearly 500 of its best scientists. Over 50 percent of scientists in Moscow have expressed an interest in going abroad on temporary contracts and 6 percent in permanently emigrating to the West, particularly to the United States.[116] Another favored destination, especially for Jewish scientists, has been Israel. In recent years, however, Israel's economy has faced enormous difficulties in absorbing the influx of scientists, and many immigrants have ended up with jobs (such as private security guards) unrelated to their education.[117]

In some cases, the home government finances a set number of students for education and training abroad with the explicit agreement or tacit understanding that after the student obtains an advanced degree he or she will return to the homeland to contribute to the economic advancement of the country. Not all students return, however (see Box 8.3). The Scientific and Industrial Research Council of India, for example, has estimated that between 1963 and 1967 emigration of highly trained professionals and technicians from India rose by 109 percent. Between 1970 and 1975, more than 1,453,240 Indians emigrated from the country, 62,231 of whom had secured employment abroad.[118]

Economic stagnation and lack of job opportunities have led to emigration from sub-Saharan African countries as well. Between 1980 and 1985, approximately 3,452 sub-Saharan African professionals and skilled workers took permanent residence in the United States, and, in the mid-1980s, they accounted for 41 percent of the total 8,490 African professionals claiming permanent residence in the United States.[119]

Emigration from developing countries to the industrialized West is often viewed as exacerbating existing international inequalities, to the detriment of the developing countries. As brain drain continuously extracts skilled human capital from the developing countries to the industrialized West, it perpetuates the international division of labor. While enhancing the West's capital-intensive industrial base, brain drain leaves the developing economies dependent on foreign capital and technology, limiting the potential pool of employment to available unskilled and cheap labor.

Critics of the brain drain thesis, on the other hand, contend that the problem is not brain drain but, rather, "brain overflow," in which the migrants constitute the *surplus* educated and skilled talent in the home country.[120] This situation develops in countries where the labor market cannot absorb all of the graduates, and some remain unemployed.[121] For years, for example, in order to offset social unrest, Egypt promised a job to all university graduates (a very large number of students). This frequently meant "make-work" positions shuffling paper in bloated government bureaucracies. Corporate hiring of or government subsidies for such labor can lead to a highly inefficient labor market and economy. Accordingly, many high- technology trade deals, especially for expensive military hardware, now have "offset" provisions written in, requiring local assembly and "countertrade" purchases to provide jobs for skilled personnel. Therefore, this line of argument goes, it may also be preferable for unemployed scientists to emigrate freely from the country of origin to find employment opportunities elsewhere before they become frustrated enough to rebel. The international community benefits from such migration because as a whole it achieves greater economic efficiency, while the host country, with amenities of higher standards of living, benefits from the immigration of trained scientists by the talent they bring, but also because it has to spend less on training. Emigration of unemployed skilled labor also functions as a safety valve by relieving domestic pressures on society and institutions, thereby averting political upheavals, and by providing some return of funds sent back to help the emigrant's family.[122]

Be that as it may, the loss of such human capital weakens the labor exporting economies and renders their economies and their technological development more dependent on outside expertise. The shortage of human capital exacerbates problems associated with economic underdevelopment in the developing world, which, as Askari and Cummings have argued, "*could* be at least partly alleviated by the return of citizens or former citizens to their country of origin. . . ."[123]

There also have been cases in which countries have successfully adopted and adapted foreign technologies to their national and local economic needs while at the same time reversing the direction of brain drain. South Korea is a case in point. In 1966, the Korean Ministry of Science and Technology and the U.S. National Academy of Sciences established the Korean Institute for Science and Technology (KIST) to stimulate an indigenous technological foundation for economic development. Comprised of scientists, engineers, economists, and other specialists, KIST was given the responsibility to collect information on the technological capabilities of various industrial sectors in society and to prepare specific proposals to strengthen their competence. The following are some examples of KIST recommendations as presented by Granger:

- To establish accurately the state of the art of the technology currently employed
- To establish the increase in sectoral productivity necessary to meet the estimated future market demand starting from the present industrial base
- To establish the improvement in quality and uniformity of the product necessary to meet the anticipated demands, and the price increase per unit of production that could be justified by such improvements
- To establish the availability of adequate supplies of necessary raw materials and the steps necessary to meet any shortfalls
- To determine the necessary training or reeducation of personnel at all levels required to achieve the desired production growth

BOX 8.3

MIDDLE EASTERN BRAIN DRAIN

Since the early 1950s, an increasing number of highly educated people have emigrated from the Middle East to the United States, Canada, Latin America, and Australia, resulting in serious brain drain. Between 1953 and 1973, more than 114,000 individuals emigrated from six countries (Egypt, Iran, Iraq, Jordan, Lebanon, and Syria) to establish permanent residence in the United States. While in 1953 immigrants from these Middle Eastern countries constituted 0.67 percent (1,142) of all immigrants (170,434) to the United States, by 1973 that figure had reached 2.97 percent (11,866) of all immigrants (400,063).

The following data show the occupations of Middle Eastern immigrants from the six countries to the United States in 1973. They include professionals, managers, and skilled workers in various areas—teachers, engineers, medical doctors, and scientists. In addition, the number of Middle Eastern students emigrating to the United States on temporary student visas increased from 1,934 (or 5.46 percent of total foreign students) in 1960 to 6,465 (or 71.3 percent) in 1973. In 1974, well over 45 percent of them studied engineering, 12.4 percent studied humanities, 11.9 percent studied physical sciences, 11.5 percent were in business administration, and the rest were in social sciences (9.2 percent), medical sciences (4.3 percent), education (2.7 percent), and agriculture (1.8 percent).

In the 1970s and 1980s, labor migration *within* the Middle East, particularly to the oil-producing countries, increased as well. During the civil war in Lebanon, more than 265,000 left the country, 47 percent of whom went to other Arab states and 53 percent to the West. In 1975, nearly 2 million foreigners worked in the Gulf states (Saudi Arabia, Qatar, Oman, Iraq, Kuwait, and the United Arab Emirates), 1.36 million (or 68 percent) of whom were from other Arab states (Egypt, Syria, Jordan, Yemeni Arab Republic, and Sudan), and the rest were from the West and Asian countries (Bangladesh, India, Korea, Pakistan, Sri Lanka, and Thailand). In 1980, that number had increased to 3 million, 1.95 million (or 65 percent) immigrating from the other Arab states. In the case of Egypt, for example, more than 1.25 million Egyptians emigrated to Iraq in the 1980s during the Iran-Iraq War. Their numbers in the Gulf states increased from 200,000 in 1973 to about 2.9 million. Sudan experienced a similar loss. In 1975, nearly 46,000 Sudanese emigrated to other Arab countries; by the mid-1980s, that number had reached 350,000. By the late 1980s and early 1990s, more than 4 million foreign workers were in the Gulf states.

Middle East Immigrants to the United States by Occupation, 1973
(percent)

Country	Professional, Technical, and Related Workers	Managers, Officials, and Proprietors	Skilled Workers, Craftsmen, Foremen, and Related Workers	Housewives, Children, and No Occupation
Egypt	25.7	2.3	6.6	55.8
Iran	27.8	5.4	5.9	49.5
Iraq	13.5	4.1	14.1	56.7
Jordan	10.5	5.3	9.0	61.1
Lebanon	9.6	4.6	13.1	59.7
Syria	16.2	4.1	18.4	51.3
All immigrants	10.2	2.3	10.1	60.9

Source: Hussein G. Askari and John Thomas Cummings, "The Middle East and the United States: A Problem of 'Brain Drain,'" *International Journal of Middle East Studies* 8 (1977), Table 9, p. 72; Gil Feiler, "Arab Labor Mobility in the Middle East in a Period of Economic Recession, 1982–1987," *Middle East Contemporary Survey* XI (1987), pp. 300–301.

- To quantify the requirement for additional capital investment necessary for the expansion of production[124]

Based on these analyses, KIST assisted the Ministry of Science and Technology and individual sectors of industries to determine which technology would be necessary for what purposes. Further, in the policy implementation process, the Korean government recruited from abroad Korean nationals with specific expertise to manage and administer the application of imported technology.[125]

BOX 8.4

AFRICA ON THE INTERNET

ABIDJAN (Reuter) – African states hoping to leapfrog into the new age of technology are lining up to join a $15 million U.S. initiative to help connect them on the Internet.

In West Africa, the scramble for Internet access has spread from Sierra Leone, which is at the bottom of the world ranking of nations in terms of development, to relatively prosperous Ivory Coast, U.S. officials and industry analysts say.

Experts from U.S. aid agency USAID, NASA, the U.S. Navy, the State Department and the private sector have begun country-by-country configuration and installation of Internet services in some 20 selected states under the so-called Leland initiative.

Internet use in Africa is currently limited by the lack of local gateways or nodes located within African countries and the prohibitive cost of dialing to nodes abroad.

The U.S. scheme will help ease the cost of installing local gateways in Africa that will cut communications costs for users.

"Basically it will involve equipment, training, personnel and subsidies satellite links for a three-year period to create a national gateway for Cote d'Ivoire," U.S. embassy spokesman Thomas Hart said of the Ivorian scheme, which is typical.

"The initial visits to the countries have been made and in the case of Cote d'Ivoire visits by State Department and USAID specialists were taken in May and again in July," Hart said.

South Africa is alone in having several private companies offering Internet access. The Paris-based airline communications company SITA offers a CompuServe node in most cities in Africa for local dialup but at a cost of about $28 an hour.

Africa Online, owned by Boston-based International Wireless, has started a service in Kenya, which is being exploited by the country's well-organised tour industry.

Sierra Leone's state-owned telephone company SIERRATEL said this week it would be in a position to offer a full Internet service later this year in the country devastated by five years of civil war. The scheme falls under the U.S. initiative.

Critics have questioned the rush for the Internet by governments with more pressing needs, such as water and health services for their people, for whom the telephone is a luxury.

But policymakers in Washington, backed by Vice President Al Gore, see the Internet in Africa as a means of advancing democracy and enhancing the environment for free enterprise.

Named after congressman Mickey Leland who died in a plane crash in Ethiopia in 1989, the five-year U.S. program will provide 20 or so African countries with access to the Internet and connections to the Global Information Infrastructure.

Source: John Chiahemen, *Reuters/Variety,* August 2, 1996.

The past two decades have witnessed major efforts to overcome technological gaps through greater international cooperation among developing countries, whose leaders accepted the fact that "the use of technology itself cannot be undertaken in a blind or *ad hoc* fashion. Whatever countries or groups employ modern technology as a tool of industrial development, must themselves elaborate technological strategies."[126] Accordingly, they established the Third World Academy of Sciences in 1983, which in turn sponsored the creation of the Third World Network of Scientific Organizations. The Third World Academy of Sciences became a forum for internationally recognized scientists from developing countries to encourage R&D for economic development based on advanced technologies in a wide range of areas, from fiber optics and biotechnology to robotics and pest control. Another objective of the Third World Academy of Sciences is to promote greater cooperation between scientists and engineers who have emigrated to the industrialized countries and their counterparts in the developing world. Furthermore, in 1989, the Summit of the Non-Aligned Movement proposed the creation of more than twenty "centers of science, high technology, and environment in different parts" of the developing world for the same purpose. One of the first serious efforts to achieve these goals was the creation of India's Center for Science and Technology of the Non-Aligned and Other Developing Countries.[127] Whether these institutions will be successful in narrowing the North–South technological gap remains to be seen (see Box 8.4). Equally important is the question of whether narrowing the technological gap will necessarily improve the political and economic conditions for the ordinary citizen in developing countries.

The experience of the former Soviet Union clearly indicates that scientific and technological achievements cannot in and of themselves create a politically and economically salubrious environment for a country's population. For years the former Soviet Union enjoyed world leadership in science and engineering, with the largest proportionate expenditure on R&D among the major industrialized countries (see Table 8.3). In 1988, prior to its

TABLE 8.3
Selected R & D Indicators for Russia and Other Major Nations

Nation	Scientist and engineers	Scientist and engineers per million of population	R & D expenditures per gross national product (percent)
United States[a]	806,200	3.317	2.6
Japan[b]	614,854	5.029	2.8
United Kingdom	101,400[c]	1.782[d]	2.2[e]
France (1987)	109,400	1.973	2.3
West Germany (1987)	165,614	2.724	2.8
U.S.S.R. (1988)	1,522,200	5.387	6.2
Russia (1989)	1,385,300[f]	9.398[g]	NA

[a]Dates for columns 1, 2, and 3 are 1987, 1987, and 1988 respectively.

[b]Dates for columns 1, 2, and 3 are 1988, 1988, and 1987 respectively.

[c]1987, from U.S. National Science Foundation. *International Science and Technology Data Update: 1991.* Washington, NSF, 1991. p. 43.

[d]1987, calculated from column 1 and a United Kingdom 1987 population of 56,890,000 from UNESCO *Statistical Yearbook: 1989.* France. UNESO, 1989 pp.1–10.

[e]1988, from *International Science and Technology Data Update: 1991.* op cit., p. 3.

[f]From Russian Academy of Sciences. Analytical Center for Problems of Socio-Economy and Science-Technology Development. *Science in Russia Today and Tomorrow: Part II.* Moscow, Mar. 1991. p. 21.

[g]Calculated from column 1 and a Russian 1989 population of 147,400,000 from *The World Almanc and Book of Facts, 1992.* New York, Newspaper Enterprises Association, Inc., 1991. p. 810.

Source: William C. Boesman, "Science and Technology in the Former Soviet Union: Capabilities and Needs," in Richard F. Kaufman and John P. Hardt, eds., for the Joint Economic Committee, Congress of the United States, *The Former Soviet Union in Transition* (Armonk: M.E. Sharpe, 1993), p. 615. Reprinted by permission from M.E. Sharpe, Inc., Armonk, NY 10504.

disintegration, the Soviet Union had more than 1.5 million scientists and engineers (or 5,387 per million of population), while its main competitor, the United States, had 806,200 (or 3,317 per million of population), and Japan had 614,854 (or 5,029 per million of population). The former Soviet Union's R&D expenditures totaled 6.2 percent per gross national product; that of the United States was 2.6 percent. Between 1988 and 1991, however, nearly 300,000 scientists and engineers left the Soviet Union, dropping the total to about 1.2 million.[128]

A major problem in Soviet R&D programs was the unequal distribution of resources, greatly favoring the military and space program. The military funded over 50 percent of R&D by the Soviet Academy of Sciences, the leading scientific institution in the country, and the Soviet government devoted nearly 75 percent of its budget to military R&D. This resulted in an uneven development of technology: military-related, including space, technologies became "world class," but civilian and commercial technologies, especially in the area of advanced communications, electronics, and computers, remained at relatively primitive levels. The Soviet Union became a military superpower and a major exporter of military hardware, but it lacked the ability to compete in world consumer markets.[129] The economic and nationalities crises in the 1980s and the Kremlin's inability to adjust the national political economy and local political demands to the rapidly changing global economy led to the country's systemic collapse.

In an ever more interdependent global economy, the spillover effects of transfer and diffusion of new technologies from one country to another cannot be easily prevented, as other countries can easily copy technologies; attempts to withhold them from the market run the risk of lagging behind in global competition. The dilemma for individual nations is that technology, despite the country of origin (like the "global Ford" discussed in the previous chapter), can no longer be viewed as *belonging to a nation.* While scientists and technicians may continue to remain loyal to their countries, and while patents and copyrights still technically apply, globalization increasingly requires

TABLE 8.4
Military Technological Revolutions: Selected Innovations in Warfare

Field/Name	Innovation	Date
Cavalry	Stirrups	Fifth century
Infantry	Pikes and longbows	Early Fourteenth century
Artillery	Cannon	Early Fifteenth century
Naval warfare	Ship-borne cannon	Early Sixteenth century
Napoleonic	Mass armies	Late Eighteenth century
Land warfare	Rifle, rail, telegraph	Mid–end Nineteenth century
Steamship	Engine and armor	Late Nineteenth century
Land and air	Tank, aircraft, radio	Early–mid Twentieth century
Nuclear	Fission, fusion, missiles	Mid Twentieth century

Source: The Economist, "Defence Technology," June 10, 1995 [survey], p. 6. Used here with minor modifications.

modification of the public's view of science and technology from a national to a global enterprise, which in turn may require more multilateral "academies of sciences" (such as the Third World Academy) worldwide, as well as more intellectual property negotiations to prevent pirating.

Dual (Civilian-Military) Technologies

The major transformations taking place in information technologies have had enormous ramifications for military technology as well. The close relationship between science and military in history has been previously noted (see also Table 8.4). Historically, technologies of commerce and technologies of war have been highly compatible and mutually complementary. The compass played as critical a role in enhancing navigation capabilities for the expansion of international trade as for the expansion of imperial military power. The telegraph, radio, radar, television, and laser technologies are *dual-use systems.* Modern military command, control, and communications and integrated intelligence (C3I) systems (to survey and control battlefield activity) and the various surveillance and data fusion structures[130] established in civilian airports and nuclear plants (for example, see Box 8.5), all rely on highly sophisticated information technologies of the type used by giant companies for daily communications, as well as by children playing Nintendo. Dual-use technologies now include advanced information and telecommunications systems and their components, such as digital computers and fiber optics.[131]

A central issue regarding these technologies is whether commercial devices, such as computers, which can be used for military purposes, should be released for transfer abroad. Dual technology transfers are viewed as ultimately threatening national security, both in the stricter military sense and in wider economic terms. Proponents of tight controls contend that their military applications and transfer abroad may prove detrimental to national security.

According to one estimate, by the late 1980s the U.S. government required export licenses for nearly 40 percent of manufactured goods.[132] The United States also enlisted the cooperation of allies by requiring that they apply for export licenses if they in turn sell products purchased from the United States to a third party. Over the years, perhaps exaggerating the strategic concerns, Washington

> seized Apple computers bound for Eastern Europe on the grounds that they could be useful in military applications; berated the Japanese for permitting the export of medium-sized trucks to Vietnam, since they could be used as mobile missile launching platforms; and threatened to restrict the distribution of photos taken by privately owned earth satellites.[133]

Growing global technological interdependence and expanding trade relations, however, make it difficult for governments to maintain such controls. One difficulty is whether it is possible to determine precisely what constitutes "sensitive" items. Allies and friendly governments also seek "the spin-off benefits of an active military design and production program" for their domestic commercial economies.[134] It is doubtful that a "protectionist" approach to dual-use technology transfers would find much political support in the business community in the 1990s and the twenty-first century, as it would hinder normal transactions and adversely affect competitiveness in world trade.

Indeed, recent trends indicate that governments are more than willing to eliminate as many regulatory policies as possible and actually to hand over—that is, privatize—previously state-owned operations, even when sensitive

BOX 8.5

NUCLEAR DETECTION GEAR IS BEING TESTED BY CUSTOMS SERVICE AT SOME ENTRY SITES

WASHINGTON—The U.S. Customs Service has installed nuclear detection devices at various points of entry in a demonstration project to test the government's ability to stop nuclear smuggling.

Although U.S. officals know of no specific threat, "we are trying to get ahead of the curve here," said Connie Fenchel, chief of strategic investigations for the Customs agency. The uneasiness is generated by concerns that nuclear materials in the former Soviet Union states may not be as well-guarded as the U.S. would like. " It flows from the fact that there have been nuclear seizures in Europe," Ms. Fenchel said.

She wouldn't disclose the location of the test sites, but she did say the project focuses on the importation, rather than the exportation, of nuclear materials.

The test project began in January when the devices were installed at what Ms. Fenchel described as a major international airport with an extremely active port of entry. She declined to name the airport, but she indicated it was chosen because of the wide variety of flights arriving there.

The project is testing four types of detection devices:

- Small radiation pagers for finding radiation materials on individuals.
- Fixed-site X-ray equipment with radiation detection capability for examining luggage.
- Mobile X-ray devices with radiation detection capacity for searching bulk cargo.
- Large, fixed-site detectors for examining container cargo and trucks.

Athough no nuclear smugglers have been caught, the devices have proved their effectiveness by detecting legitimate nuclear material, including that found in people who have received radiation treatment for cancer.

Even if no smugglers are caught, the test project may be continued as a permanent program because of its deterrent effect. Ms. Fenchel said some determination may be made by next January.

"Though there is no specific threat, the fact that nuclear material may be smuggled is enough for us to take some steps," she said, "We don't want to overreact, but we don't want to ignore the potential of a nuclear smuggling incident."

Source: Wall Street Journal, July 2, 1996, p. A14. Reprinted by permission of Wall Street Journal,

technologies are involved. The U.S. government's apparently growing willingness to privatize portions of the National Aeronautics and Space Administration's (NASA) space program is a case in point. NASA, that citadel and supreme symbol of national technological prowess, was established in 1961 in response to the launching of the Soviet space program. Throughout the Cold War, Washington viewed its space program as an integral component of U.S. military capability in competition with the Soviet Union. The space program, whose annual budget reached $3.2 billion, was more than a mere scientific venture to explore the universe; its military dimension was illustrated by the Reagan administration's proposed strategic defense initiative (SDI, or "star wars") program.[135] NASA funding also was used to support Russian collaboration in the international space station in the late 1990s,to the displeasure of some Russian nationalists.

Nothing has captured world markets and the imagination of millions of consumers as the electronics industry,[136] another form of dual-use technology. Electronics have virtually transformed our lives to the point at which it is almost impossible to imagine life without such technologies and accompanying amenities. The semiconductor industry has been one of the fastest growing industries in the past three decades, with applications ranging from microwave ovens to VCRs and the enormous proliferation of personal computers. These devices also now profoundly affect every aspect of international military and economic relations.

In the 1950s, when semiconductors were first introduced, the United States held a virtual monopoly over their production, along with that of integrated circuits and microprocessors; the U.S. dominance in the market continued well into the early 1980s. By the late 1980s, however, Japan held about 42 percent of the world's total production, while the U.S. share dropped to 26 percent. Europe accounted for 12 percent, with Germany accounting for 31 percent of Europe's total production, France 19 percent, and Britain 16 percent. In addition, East and Southeast Asian countries (Hong Kong, Malaysia, the Philippines, South Korea, Taiwan, and Thailand) also emerged as chief producers of such technologies.[137]

Competition in semiconductors trade, thus, became a major issue in the trade disputes between the United States and Japan.[138] In the late 1980s and early 1990s, Japan consistently registered huge trade surpluses (for example, $19 billion in 1989), while the United States and Europe had deficits of about $5.5 billion.[139] These numbers, however, fail to give the total picture, for the semiconductors' "war of supremacy" involves a great deal more than the mere volume and monetary value of exports and imports. Highly advanced technologies require a number of essential factors to develop and expand. As previously discussed, along with many domestic and international political, legal, and economic environments, sufficient financial and human resources for R&D are necessary, as are sophisticated marketing capabilities. Finally, the role of government and the nature of its relations with corporations and research institutions (for example, universities, privately funded think-tanks) also are critical. The ability to compete in such technical areas, then, is the product of varied factors.

SCIENCE AND TECHNOLOGY: INTERNATIONAL COOPERATION AND CONFLICT

The role of science and technology and growing interdependence in the world political economy can be viewed as an opportunity for greater cooperation among nations, but these trends, plus the growing competition over discoveries and markets, also contribute to international tensions.[140] Technology is the central component of global interdependence. As a source of cooperation, technologies in the areas of transportation (autos and airplanes) and telecommunications (computers and satellite networks) provide worldwide linkage and bring together people from different countries with different languages and cultures. Such technologies have facilitated a degree of transnational interconnectedness and interaction unparalleled in human history. Most countries are members of multilateral organizations involved in regulation and development of technologies in navigation, deep-water fishing, communicable diseases, and so forth.[141] Such transnational arrangements provide opportunities for international contact and negotiations to address social and economic problems that cannot be solved by individual governments alone. As discussed in Chapter 2, in earlier times the development of such technical cooperative institutions was termed "functionalism." It was assumed that technical cooperation would reduce petty rivalries among states as they concentrated on regulating navigation, health, and other areas of public policy.[142] Ultimately, however, it became clear that, despite the joint conquest of diseases such as smallpox, there is conflict even on such seemingly innocuous issues as when the World Health Organization (WHO) quarantines a country's ports for cholera, thus impeding its economy.

Global interdependence and technology, however, affect different societies differently, and they have serious ramifications for national sovereignty and security. Wide gaps in commercial and military technological capabilities lead to international resentments and tensions, as they create the potential or, at minimum, the perception or misperception of economic and military dominance by one over another. Some countries have accumulated huge arsenals of sophisticated weapons, while others lack the technological means to defend themselves against such a threat. Even among the countries that possess nuclear weapons, for example, the technological know-how for verification and related mutual confidence-building measures is not equal. During the Cold War, the latter situation led to disputes not only between the two superpowers, the United States and the Soviet Union, but also among the Western NATO countries, such as France and the United States, and between them and Third World leaders such as India. India indeed developed its own nuclear capabilities while criticizing the nuclear powers for not disarming, and Pakistan predictably soon followed suit.

Moreover, technology can threaten political stability as it introduces new and different ways of doing and thinking about things. Newly marketed products turn individuals into *consumers,* challenge their traditional values and place as "members of the community," and undermine the relationship between the community and the leadership. Technology disturbs a community's sense of cultural, social, and economic balance, and the fear of political upheavals causes political and community leaders to resist technology-induced changes, especially those from abroad, unless they can control technology immediately on its introduction. As noted earlier, the church vehemently resisted research and technologies that it feared would undermine its position in society and would upset the social order. In modern times, however, such conservative institutions, from Rome to Riyadh, have learned to use technology to their advantage while still attempting to limit its effects. Islamic states, such as Iran and Saudi Arabia, have embraced technology where it is judged useful for economic development. Yet certain technologies, such as those involved with information and communication, still potentially threaten governments, portending loss of control and the importation of dangerous or "corrupting" ideas. For years the USSR tried to limit public and even professional access to computers, faxes, and copying machines for this reason, restrictions which, of course, hurt Soviet technological development by cutting people off from the outside world.

Technology and International Cooperation

Most of the everyday transactions among the world's governments and among corporations are peaceful and routine. In turn, technology itself is regulated and used as "public goods" for the public interest. Examples of international cooperation involving technology have over the years included telecommunications (see Box 8.6) and international postal services, weather and earthquake warning systems, aviation and maritime safety, and defense-related areas,[143] such as the "hotline" between Moscow and Washington established immediately after the Cuban missile crisis in 1962.[144] The growth in Internet services at the turn of the twenty-first century represents both opportunity for small countries to participate in global commerce and controversy as they link those countries to easier marketing by the advanced economies such as the United States.

Public or intergovernmental, bilateral or multilateral, cooperation in various areas of science and technology also has increased through universal and regional organizations, such as the United Nations, as well as numerous international regimes. The UN Intergovernmental Committee for Science and Technology for Development and the International Telecommunication Union are two examples of such cooperation. Modern technology has enabled nations and firms to transcend geographic and, to a significant extent, even cultural barriers, enhancing opportunities for international cooperation and collaboration. Such relations have included private (MNCs, NGOs, individuals) and public institutions engaged in a wide range of commercial and developmental activities. An increasing number of multinational corporations have been involved in collaborative endeavors with foreign MNCs in R&D for product development, manufacturing, and marketing.

BOX 8.6

TELEGLOBE INC. ASSERTS ITS PRESENCE IN LATIN AMERICA WITH NEW GLOBEINTERNET™ SERVICE—GUATEMALA WILL NOW HAVE ACCESS TO INTERNET

Montreal [CNW].

Teleglobe International, a subsidiary of Teleglobe Inc., recently signed an agreement with Empresa Guatemalteca de Communicaciones (Guatel), the national telecommunications carrier of Guatemala, to link its network with Internet facilities in the U.S. via the Globeinternet™ service. This marks the first time Internet access is provided in Guatemala and will assure the country's increased participation in the global economy. Teleglobe International plans to offer the service to other Latin American countries this year as well.

Globeinternet™ provides intercontinental connectivity for overseas service providers wishing to gain access to Internet hosts and servers in North America, which are hooked up with similar facilities throughout the world.

"Teleglobe is positioning itself as a major Internet service provider, thanks to its capacity to aggregate flows of traffic through its superior network facilities," explained Robert Collet, Teleglobe International's Vice-President, Data Services. "Most Internet users want faster access to the Internet. Because our services are aimed at International Service Providers (ISP) only, we are able to overcome congestion problems. Therefore, our customers benefit from faster access," continued Collet.

In addition, Internet access service is provided by Teleglobe's network to other countries such as France, Sweden, Kuwait and Armenia.

Globeinternet™ advantages include greater availability, quicker access, competitive pricing and top-quality links. Customers can also expect monitoring 24 hours a day, seven days a week.

Teleglobe is recognized as a world leader in the field of intercontinental telecommunications. It operates a network of cables and satellites that reaches nearly 240 countries and territories, meeting the global connectivity needs of established and emerging carriers from around the world, as well as those of cable network operators and broadcasters. Teleglobe Inc. is listed on the Montreal Exchange, the Toronto Stock Exchange and the Vancouver Stock Exchange under the symbol "TGO."

Source: Reuters Toronto Bureau, full text of press release from Canada NewsWire, June 26, 1996. Copyright Reuters Limited 1998.

These have included, General Motors and Toyota in the automobile industry and National Steel of the U.S. and Nippon Kokan of Japan in the steel industry.[145]

International cooperation in scientific research and technological development has been necessary to address worldwide health, social, and economic problems affecting large numbers of people across national borders and regions. In some areas, public and private sectors have required similar collaboration to establish international standards for the transnational use of technology, as in maintaining pharmaceutical dosages and purity. As early as 1946, the UN Educational, Scientific and Cultural Organization (UNESCO) began to promote literacy, training, and skills for economic development. In the 1950s, important breakthroughs in the exploration of Antarctica were made multilaterally during the International Geophysical Year. In 1979, the UN Conference on Science and Technology for Development created the Intergovernmental Committee for Science and Technology for Development and, under the UN Secretariat, the Center for Science and Technology for Development.[146] The UN Food and Agricultural Organization (FAO) sponsors research in areas of agriculture and nutrition, while the World Health Organization (WHO) promotes research in health-related areas. The International Atomic Energy Agency, also under the auspices of the United Nations, promotes R&D in and the peaceful use of atomic energy. The International Council of Scientific Unions, an NGO established in 1918, encourages the coordination of worldwide multidisciplinary scientific research and technological development programs.[147]

Multilateral efforts to establish standards for transnational uses of technology, which began with the Danube River authority and the International Postal Union, have come to include the International Telecommunication Union (ITU), the World Meteorological Organization (WMO), the International Civil Aviation Organization (ICAO), the International Bureau for the Protection of Industrial Property, the International Bureau of Weights and Measures, and the Council for International Organizations of Medical Sciences. The ITU is one of the oldest of such organizations; it regulates international electronic (for example, radio) frequencies. The International Civil Aviation Organization develops systems for civil air traffic control.[148]

While some have criticized the ideological-political dominance of some countries over others (East–West or North–South tensions), they have also realized that certain issues—nuclear proliferation and environmental degradation, for example—cannot be addressed through bilateral means and are not necessarily based on any ideological orientation. An Exxon oil spill, a Chernobyl-style nuclear release, or a Union Carbide poisonous gas leak can occur anywhere, in rich and poor, in capitalist and socialist, in democratic and authoritarian countries. Needless to say, while encouraging much needed multilateral collaboration in important areas of the human global community, not all international efforts have met with success. Some nations have expressed dissatisfaction with the slow pace of multilateral arrangements and have opted for bilateral treaties. MNC and multilateral international cooperation in science and technology has become an integral part of the globalization of international political economy, sometimes referred to as "techno-globalism"[149] (see Box 8.7).

Technology and International Conflict

In addition to creating mechanisms and opportunities for international cooperation, however, on the negative side, technology and international competition—particularly for geopolitical objectives and military superiority—may fuel international tensions and lead to outright military engagements and mass destruction. The competition between Spain and England for naval supremacy in the Atlantic created intense hostility between the two great powers. By 1588, when the Spanish Armada began its voyage to attack England, the latter's considerably improved shipbuilding and weapons technologies already afforded military superiority. Spanish galleons, much heavier, slower, and more difficult to maneuver because of their flat bottoms, relied on heavy, short-range cannons. British warships, on the other hand, were better designed, used deeper keels, and were easily maneuverable, with more accurate long-range *culverins.* Unlike the rapidly changing technology of the second half of the twentieth century, however, historically major technological revolutionary changes occurred slowly. The chemical technology used for the gunpowder in Europe in the seventeenth century or in nineteenth century United States was quite similar to that used by the Chinese in the thirteenth century.[150]

Nevertheless, the proliferation of "military engineers" in the fifteenth through seventeenth centuries, reflecting the mercantilist political economy at the time, gradually institutionalized state-technology complexes (today's military-industrial-educational complexes) and increased the pace of science and technology R&D. The mercantilist state protected the scientific community, and the latter advanced the interests of the state. Among the world-famous European

BOX 8.7

THREE MEANINGS OF "TECHNO-GLOBALISM"

The innovation process is increasingly taking place on a global scale. Archibugi and Michie[a] have identified three major forms of globalisation of technology. . . .

a) Global exploitation of technology
First, the *global exploitation of technology* includes the use by firms of patents and other intellectual property rights to protect their inventions and block competitors as they prepare their entrance into foreign markets to license their technology to local producers. This large and growing phenomenon (6 percent growth rate a year) is due both to the practice of extending protection to more countries (three to four countries on average) and to actual growth in the number of patented inventions.

b) Global technological cooperation
Second, the amount of *international cooperation* in firms' innovative efforts points to the pooling of resources in different countries, due to the search for complementarities in firms' technological and marketing strategies. It may involve not only the generation of innovations but also their application, diffusion and adaptation to local markets. According to the database on inter-firm cooperation agreements developed by MERIT by Hagedoorn and Schankeread,[b] there has been an average annual increase of 6 percent in the number of international technology agreements between the first and the second half of the 1980s. International collaborations are revealed also in the rapid growth of patents with inventors from more than one country. . . . The number of US patents with at least one American and one foreign inventor grew from 90 in [1980] to 1,500 in 1993.

c) Global generation of technology
Third, *global generation of technology* is found within single multinational firms when innovation is the result of efforts undertaken in laboratories and plants situated abroad. . . . An indicator of this tendency is provided by the share of patents granted to foreign subsidiaries of multinational firms. Recent studies . . . have shown that these accounted for less than 4 percent of total patents in the period 1981–1986, with 1 per cent annual growth between the early and late 1980s.

Source: Daniele Archibugi and Mario Pianta, "Innovation Surveys and Patents as Technology Indicators: The State of the Art," in *Innovation, Patents, and Technological Strategies,* pp. 36–37. Copyright OECD. (1996).

[a]Daniele Archibugi and J. Michie, "The Globalization of Technology: A New Taxonomy," *Cambridge Journal of Economics* 19, 1 (1995), pp. 121–140.

[b]J. Hagedoorn and J. Schankeraad, "Strategic Technology Partnering and International Corporate Strategies," in K. Hughes, ed., *European Competitiveness* (Cambridge: Cambridge University Press, 1993), pp. 60–86.

military engineers at the time were Federigo Giambelli, Albrecht Dürer, Pedro Navarro, Niccoló Tartaglia, Leonardo da Vinci, Vannoccio Biringuccio, Simon Stevin, and Otto von Guericke. They were soldier-inventors, scientists, theoreticians, architects, and artists engaged in empirically based scientific and technological experiments and projects in a wide range of military sciences, including fortification, navigation, catapults and ballistic theories, and explosives, all at the service of the state. Much like Henry the Navigator's science academy at Sagres, state-technology complexes emerged in major European countries as governments appreciated the value of military research and training academies, and conscription of national standing armies replaced foreign mercenaries. A scientific society, including Galileo among its members, was established in Rome in 1603; England founded the Royal Society for the Promotion of Natural Knowledge in 1663; France established its Académe Royale des Sciences in 1666 and the Ecole Polytechnique in 1794; and one of the first science academies in Berlin was created in 1700.[151] Science and technology thus strengthened the mercantilist state as colonial competition intensified.

Some observers believe that technology has diminished the sovereignty of nation-states and has rendered the current international system based on the nation-state obsolete.[152] Technology and the international economic interdependence it generated, at least during the past two centuries, have made the nation-state vulnerable to economic arm-twisting and blockades, as well as short notice military attack by ballistic missiles and air raids. In the meantime, sophisticated transnational communications systems (shortwave radios, movies, television, cassette players, VCRs, satellite dishes, and the Internet on personal computers) have made public opinion more vulnerable to outside political and ideological influences and manipulation. National sovereignty is challenged not only by the rise of multinational corporations as discussed in the previous chapter but also by the very advances in science and technology which corporations and governments have fostered.

TABLE 8.5
Expenditures on Industrial and Scientific Research in Major North Atlantic Countries, 1961

	Total expenditure		Government expenditure	
	Millions of dollars	Percent of of national income	Millions of dollars	Percent of budget
United States	14,039	3.3	9,218	11.3
Britain	1,775	2.8	1,078	6.2
West Germany	966	1.6	529	4.7
France	700	1.5	546	3.6

Source: EFTA Reporter, April 5, 1965, in William R. Kintner and Robert L. Pfaltzgraff, Jr., "The Prospects for Western Science and Technology," in Robert L. Pfaltzgraff, Jr., ed., *Politics and the International System* (Philadelphia: J.B. Lippincott, 1969), p. 255.

Twentieth-century tensions culminated in the various phases of the U.S.-Soviet arms race, fueled by advances in and mutual "missile envy" of nuclear weapons technologies.[153] The Soviet Union responded to the Truman administration's use of the atomic bomb on Hiroshima and Nagasaki in August 1945 by quickly developing and testing its own atomic bomb in 1949. In response, the following year the Truman administration adopted NSC-68 (the National Security Council policy document), which advocated the acceleration of U.S. military buildup, with an estimated cost of about $40 billion (in 1950 dollars) for the defense budget (this in part resulted in the fusion, or hydrogen, bomb in 1952). In a similar vein, the United States responded to the Soviet Union's technological advancements in the 1950s, as symbolized by the launching of the first *Sputnik* satellite in 1957, by stressing the importance of education and R&D. The U.S. Congress and the Eisenhower administration began to spend more on the G.I. Bill for veterans and passed the National Defense Education Act of 1958 to fund training of new generations of scientists and to expand the pool of highly skilled personnel. For example, Table 8.5 shows the relative size of expenditures on R&D during the first year of the Kennedy administration. The U.S.-Soviet arms race continued for more than four decades, with an estimated $4 trillion expended by Washington on nuclear weapons alone; these expenditures, which can be termed wasteful or necessary, depending on one's point of view, reflected the action-reaction process inherent in competition for military superiority.[154] Such action-reaction patterns also have been seen in the spending patterns of Israel and its neighbors, as well as China, India, and Pakistan.

In the post–Cold War era, the growing importance of international trade and foreign investments in the world economy gradually placed civilian technology at the center of international competition and made the question of leadership—one key indicator being a country's scientific R&D and technological capabilities—in the world political economy a central issue, particularly as pertaining to the intensification of global competition among such major industrialized economies as the United States, Germany, and Japan. As the use of communications technology in its various forms became widespread, the protection of producers and markets emerged as a major issue in trade relations. For example, to protect its technological advantages vis-à-vis advanced competitors and developing countries, the United States insisted on including intellectual property rights (for example, patents, copyrights) and trade in counterfeit goods in the Punta del Este Declaration of 1986 and the Uruguay Round, and it has maintained that position in the World Trade Organization. Most developing countries showed no more than a lukewarm interest in this issue and viewed concerns related to it "as matters of internal policy and national sovereignty."[155] Less advanced states naturally wished to weaken patent or copyright limitations that restrict access to new technology. Developing countries argued that the Uruguay Round had no jurisdiction on these matters, which more properly fell within the World Intellectual Property Organization.[156] Smaller developed countries were concerned that restrictive trade rules in the name of protecting intellectual property rights would instead justify protectionist policies contrary to GATT principles. These disagreements are likely to persist as technological changes continue to afford greater advantages to some countries and while WTO—like its predecessor, GATT—lacks international mechanisms to enforce rules and principles with respect to intellectual property rights.

CONCLUSION

Technology serves as a vehicle for cooperation among nations, but it is also a source of conflict. The proliferation of vast, "space-shrinking" telecommunications and transportation networks has established instantaneous communication for people across continents. Since the rise of the modern nation-state, the symbiotic relationship between politics and technology has remained a fundamental characteristic of international political economy. The theory and the history of science and technology influence and are in turn influenced by the political environment in which they operate. As such, neither science nor technology is said to be advanced solely for the enhancement of human knowledge and understanding. Laissez-faire economists argue that S&T by firms can be used for purposes of profit and, in the long run, for the betterment of human life. The greater the freedom granted to the scientific community, they argue, the greater the likelihood that inventors and entrepreneurs will be motivated to contribute to society's well-being.

However, as the history of the evolution of "technological styles" before and since the industrial revolution has demonstrated, in none of the phases was technology disengaged from politics, and it was never possible to avoid all potential negative effects of technological break-throughs. Governments funded, used, and restricted access to S&T for economic and political reasons, and the state-technology relationship has become particularly pronounced as the state's role has expanded in domestic and international political economy, especially during the Cold War. Over the years, major issues regarding the nature of the relationship between technology and both international political economy and the natural environment have involved not only the relationship between governments and R&D but also the uneven international distribution of technological power.

Communications technologies encouraged multilateral cooperation in an ever widening circle, as information flowed across borders with unprecedented speed and facility, yet the technological gap between the first industrialized economies (FIEs) and the developing countries made the use of available advanced technologies for globalwide economic development more difficult and conflictual. Despite some advances among NICs and the "trickle down" of technology through assistance programs, transfers, and MNC multicountry operations, it would be unrealistic to assume that the more technologically advanced countries will simply surrender their dominance to bring about a more technologically egalitarian world economy. The prevailing environment of intense competition for larger shares of global markets and resources is hardly conducive to international cooperation between technology-rich and technology-poor countries. Within this context, highly advanced technologies—particularly dual-use technologies—and the use of industrial espionage in the competition to secure them could, as throughout history, prove to be the catalyst for greater international conflicts.

Chapter Summary

Science and technology (S&T) are essential aspects of economic development and modernization and are necessary components of the globalization process. Science is based on accumulated knowledge derived from observations and experiments. It seeks to identify, describe, explain, and predict the structures of the physical world and human behavior. Technology is the application of science to solve concrete problems, and in the process it also contributes to further scientific developments. S&T and politics are frequently and closely related, as governments support S&T to encourage economic growth, to enhance national competitiveness, and to prepare for warfare.

Since the industrial revolution, five phases in the evolution of technological styles can be identified: the water style, 1780s–1830s; the steam transport style, 1840s–1870s; the steel and electricity style, 1880s–1910s; the Fordist style, 1920s–1970s; and the microelectronics and biotechnology style, 1980s–present. Industries shifted from one style to the next to minimize production costs; as communications technologies spread, companies used them to develop automated assembly lines for purposes of restructuring and downsizing—that is, eliminating what they considered expensive labor.

Technology, thus, leads to positive and negative consequences. Acceleration in the globalization of communications technologies may have contributed to prodemocracy revolutions against repressive regimes but also to the spread of military technologies and weapons of mass destruction. For developing countries, the brain drain has become a serious concern, as new generations of trained and skilled workers, frustrated by the lack of opportunities, leave their home countries for better jobs and standards of living abroad.

Industrial espionage and technology transfer, especially dual-use technologies, pose a dilemma, since such technologies can be essential for competition in the market but also can be acquired for civilian and military purposes—a problem compounded by the growing trend toward the privatization of state-owned companies.

Technology can facilitate international cooperation, but it can also be a source of conflict. Global interdependence encourages cooperation, as through transportation and telecommunications by providing worldwide communications and bringing together people of diverse cultures, involving numerous international organizations. Technology also poses a serious challenge to national sovereignty and security, and the competition to acquire better and advanced technologies for purposes of market competition and military superiority can have deleterious effects on societies and the public's sense of security.

Points of Contention

How is the relationship between science and technology characterized in this chapter? Would classical laissez-faire economists favor such a relationship? Would environmentalists? What do you think?

What are the advantages and disadvantages of technological advancement? Can you identify some of each, based on your own daily experience or in your own town?

What problems or benefits do science and technology pose for national sovereignty?

How do science and technology contribute to international cooperation? to international conflict? Should governments continue to subsidize R&D for technological developments by MNCs? Should scientific inquiry into areas such as atomic energy or cloning be restricted?

What are the arguments for and against expanding the role of government intelligence organizations engaged in economic espionage? Would you support such an expansive role?

Would you consider brain drain as a reverse international spillover? What are the issues involved with respect to technology transfer to the developing countries?

What are the problems associated with dual technologies? How might such problems be solved?

How would you characterize the competition among the industrialized countries for the technological edge? How have developing countries responded to the challenge? To what extent have they been successful?

Who among the major industrialized economies do you think has won the war for technological supremacy? Is such a war winnable? Does the Internet represent a benefit or a curse?

Notes

1. UN Center on Transnational Corporations, *Transnational Corporations and Technology Transfer: Effects and Policy Issues* (New York: United Nations, 1987); Gerald Sussman and John A. Lent, *Transnational Communications: Wiring the Third World* (Newbury Park: Sage, 1991).
2. Susan Strange, *States and Markets,* 2d ed. (London: Pinter, 1994), pp. 133–135.
3. Peter Dicken, *Global Shift: The Internationalization of Economic Activity,* 2d ed. (New York: The Guilford Press, 1992), p. 98. As Dicken has correctly noted, however, one cannot overstress the point that technology per se does not, in and of itself, "cause" structural transformation in internationalization and globalization processes. Rather, technology is created and used by individuals and organizations for their economic and political objectives.
4. Donald R. Baucom, *The Origins of SDI: 1944–1983* (Lawrence: University Press of Kansas, 1992); Stephen J. Cimbala, ed., *The Technology, Strategy, and Politics of SDI* (Boulder, CO: Westview Press, 1987).
5. International cooperation and participation in foreign projects is not new. One of the earliest scientific exchanges between the U.S. and Russian governments occurred in the late 1780s, when the Washington administration sent "vocabularies" of the Indian Delaware and Shawnee languages to Russia at the request of Catherine II to assist in the compilation of her *Universal Dictionary.* In a letter, Washington recognized the significance of such scientific cooperation for more peaceful relations among nations:

   > To know the affinity of tongues seems to be one step towards promoting the affinity of nations. Would to god, the harmony of nations was an object that lay nearest to the hearts of Sovereigns; and that the incentives to peace (of which commerce and faculty of understanding each other are not the most inconsiderable) might be daily increased! Should the present or any other efforts of mine to procure information respecting the different dialects of the Aborigines in America, serve to reflect a ray of light on the obscure subject of language in general, I shall be highly gratified.

   Nikolai N. Bolkhovitinov, *Russia and the American Revolution,* trans. C. Jay Smith (Tallahassee: The Diplomatic Press, 1976), pp. 108–109. George Washington to Marquis de Lafayette, January 10, 1788. *Writings of George Washington,* xxix, pp. 373–375, as quoted in *Ibid.*, p. 109.
6. The U.S. Department of Energy was expected to contribute about $450 million and the National Science Foundation $250 million for the CERN supercollider project. Malcolm W. Browne, "German Budget Trims Put Research at Risk,"

The New York Times, August 6, 1996; *Ibid.,* April 2, 1996 (NYT online). Robert C. Crown, "European Supercollider: U.S. Physicists Eye Europe for Particle Research," *The Christian Science Monitor,* January 4, 1994, pp. 1, 18; U.S. Congress, House Committee on Science, Space, and Technology, Subcommittee on Science, *Termination of the Superconducting Super Collider Project,* 103 Con., 2nd sess, March 15, 1994 (Washington, DC: The Government Printing Office, 1994).

7. G.M. Ballard, ed., *Nuclear Safety after Three Mile Island and Chernobyl* (London: Elsevier Applied Science, 1988); Joseph V. Rees, *Hostages of Each Other: The Transformation of Nuclear Safety since Three Mile Island* (Chicago: University of Chicago Press, 1994); David R. Marples, *The Social Impact of the Chernobyl Disaster* (Edmonton: University of Alberta Press, 1988).
8. The literature on the philosophy and sociology of scientific knowledge is vast. Some of the most fascinating debates on the growth of scientific knowledge can be found in Imre Lakatos and Alan Musgrave, eds., *Criticism and the Growth of Knowledge* (Cambridge: Cambridge University Press, 1970). See also Thomas S. Kuhn, *The Structure of Scientific Revolutions,* 2d enl. ed. (Chicago: University of Chicago Press, 1970); Kuhn, *The Copernican Revolution* (Cambridge: Harvard University Press, 1974). On the problems of the sociological approach, induction, and verification, see Karl Popper, *The Logic of Scientific Discovery* (New York: Harper Torchbooks, 1968); Popper, *Realism and the Aim of Science* (Totowa, NJ: Rowman and Littlefield, 1983); Popper, *Conjectures and Refutations* (New York: Harper Torchbooks, 1965); Popper, *Objective Knowledge* (Oxford: The Clarendon Press, 1979). Popper contends that falsification, rather than verification, of hypotheses can generate real scientific knowledge. On various theoretical approaches to scientific knowledge, see Frederick Suppe, ed., *The Structure of Scientific Theory,* 2d ed. (Urbana: University of Illinois Press, 1977). The papers in Suppe's volume deal with traditional approaches. For a more radical approach, see Paul Feyerabend, *Against Method,* rev. ed. (London: Verso, 1988); Feyerabend, *Farewell to Reason* (London: Verso, 1987). On developments in the social sciences, see Karl W. Deutsch, Andrei S. Markovits, and John Platt, eds., *Advances in the Social Sciences: 1900–1980* (Lanham, MD: University Press of America, 1986). On technology and international relations, see, for example, John V. Granger, *Technology and International Relations* (San Francisco: E.H. Freeman and Company, 1979). On the application of scientific methods to the study of foreign policy and international relations, see J. David Singer, ed., *The Correlates of War, I: Research Origins and Rationale* (New York: The Free Press, 1979); James N. Rosenau, *The Scientific Study of Foreign Policy,* rev. enl. ed. (New York: Nichols, 1980).
9. Joan Rothschild, ed., *Machina ex Dea: Feminist Perspective on Technology* (New York: Pergamon Press, 1983).
10. Kuhn, *The Structure of Scientific Revolutions,* pp. 52–65. See the debate on "normal science" in Lakatos and Musgrave, eds., *Criticism and the Growth of Knowledge,* especially the papers by John Watkins, "Against 'Normal Science,'" pp. 25–37; and Karl Popper, "Normal Science and Its Dangers," pp. 51–58.
11. Not all science is necessarily relevant to technology, and at times there is little practical "interaction between science and technical change." Rather, interest in science can be "cultural" or "ideological." See Norman Clark, *The Political Economy of Science and Technology* (Oxford: Basic Blackwell, 1985), pp. 38–39.
12. Granger, *Technology and International Relations,* p. 10.
13. See Carlota Perez, "Structural Change and Assimilation of New Technologies in the Economic Social Systems," *Futures* (October 1983), pp. 357–375; Perez, "Microelectronics, Long Waves and World Structural Change: New Perspectives for Developing Countries," *World Development* 13, 3 (1985), pp. 441–463.
14. Strange, *States and Markets, passim.*
15. The contributions of a number of analysts in this area are particularly worth noting. See Andrew Tylecote, *The Long Wave in the World Economy* (London: Routledge, 1991); Christopher Freeman, ed., *Long Waves in the World Economy* (London: Butterworth, 1983); Freeman, ed., *Design, Innovation and Long Cycles in Economic Development* (London: Pinter, 1986); Freeman, "The Challenge of New Technologies," in OECD, *Interdependence and Cooperation in Tomorrow's World* (Paris: OECD, 1987); Giovanni Dosi, Christopher Freeman, Richard Nelson, and Luc Soete, eds., *Technical Change and Economic Theory* (London: Pinter, 1988).
16. Carlo M. Cipolla, *Guns, Sails, and Empires: Technological Innovation and the Early Phases of European Expansion* (New York: Minerva Press, 1965).
17. *Ibid.,* pp. 31–32.
18. Herbert Butterfield, *The Origins of Modern Science* (New York: Macmillan, 1951), pp. 42–87. In controversies concerning sources of electricity and methods to cope with dangers of the lightning, the Church publicly chastised Benjamin Franklin and insisted that the "correct" way was to ring the church bells to drive away the evil spirits. This proved not only physically dangerous to the church bell ringers but also politically dangerous to scientists engaged in such research. In long debates regarding related controversies, one day John Pringle, president of the British Royal Society and personal physician to King George III, finally replied that "he will always to the limit of his strength fulfill the desires of His Majesty, but he is not in a position to change the laws of nature, nor the operation of their forces." The king summarily dismissed Pringle both as His Majesty's Personal Physician and the president of the Royal Society. Bolkhovitinov, *Russia and the American Revolution,* pp. 95–96.

19. Bruce Cummings, "The Origins and Development of the Northeast Asian Political Economy: Industrial Sectors, Product Cycles, and Political Consequences," in Frederic C. Deyo, ed., *The Political Economy of the New Asian Industrialism* (Ithaca: Cornell University Press, 1987), pp. 51–52; Margaret S. Miller, *Economic Development of Russia, 1905–1914,* 2d ed. (New York: A.M. Kelly, 1967); David Walder, *The Short Victorious War: The Russo-Japanese Conflict* (London: Hutchinson, 1974); Denis Warner and Peggy Warner, *The Tide at Sunrise: A History of the Russo-Japanese War* (New York: Charterhouse, 1974); Richard Charques, *The Twilight of Imperial Russia* (London: Oxford University Press, 1958).
20. Fritz Stern, *Gold and Iron: Bismarck, Bleichröder, and the Building of the German Empire* (New York: Vintage Books, 1977).
21. See Clark, *The Political Economy of Science and Technology,* pp. 4–5.
22. *Ibid.*
23. Aaron Wildavsky, *The New Politics of the Budgetary Process* (Glenview, IL: Scott, Foresman and Company, 1988); Steven Parker, "Budgeting as an Expression of Power," in Jack Rabin and Thomas D. Lynch, eds., *Handbook on Public Budgeting and Financial Management* (New York: Marcell Dekker, 1983).
24. Strange, *States and Markets,* p. 128.
25. *Ibid.*, p. 136.
26. *The Economist,* June 13, 1998, pp. 27–28. Economic historians disagree on the determinants of the magnitude of state intervention in national political economy for purposes of technological development and economic growth. Alexander Gerschenkron, for example, has argued that state intervention in industrialization and economic development has been greater in the later industrialized economies because the technological gap and the need for capital to overcome that gap were greater. It was therefore left to the state to muster the necessary material and human resources to steer the nation toward development. Pollard, on the other hand, has contended that all societies have experienced expansion of state activism, "giving rise to the concept of 'organized capitalism,' and affecting the conditions into which the later comers had to insert themselves." Alexander Gerschenkron, *Economic Backwardness in Historical Perspective* (Cambridge: Belknap Press of Harvard University Press, 1966). See Pollard, *Peaceful Conquest,* pp. 220–221.
27. Siegfried Giedion, *Mechanization Takes Command* (New York: W.W. Norton, 1969).
28. Adam Smith, *The Wealth of Nations* (London: Penguin Books, 1982), p. 350.
29. Michael J. Boskin and Lawrence J. Lau, "Capital, Technology, and Economic Growth," in Nathan Rosenberg, Ralph Landau, and David C. Mowery, eds., *Technology and the Wealth of Nations* (Stanford: Stanford University Press, 1992), pp. 17–55.
30. Karl Marx, *Grundrisse: Foundations of the Critique of Political Economy,* trans. Martin Nicolaus (Harmondsworth, U.K.: Penguin Books, 1973).
31. Thorstein Veblen, *Theory of the Leisure Class* (Harmondsworth, U.K.: Penguin Books, 1979).
32. E.P. Thompson, *The Making of the English Working Class* (Harmondsworth, U.K.: Penguin Books, 1968).
33. See, for example, Jon M. Shepard, *Automation and Alienation: A Study of Office and Factory Workers* (Cambridge: MIT Press, 1971); Harry Braverman, *Labor and Monopoly Capital: The Degradation of Work in the Twentieth Century* (New York: Monthly Review Press, 1974); Erich Fromm, *The Sane Society* (New York: Rinehart, 1955); Herbert Marcuse, *One-Dimensional Man* (Boston: Beacon Press, 1991); John Kenneth Galbraith, *The New Industrial State* (Harmondsworth, U.K.: Penguin, 1972).
34. For a useful historical background on technology and industrial unemployment, see Rudi Volti, *Society and Technological Change* (New York: St. Martin's Press, 1988).
35. Ursula Franklin, *The Real World of Technology* (Concord: Anansi Press, 1992), pp. 48–51.
36. The concept of "technological style" was introduced by Perez, "Structural Change and Assimilation of New Technologies in the Economic Social Systems," pp. 357–375; Perez, "Microelectronics, Long Waves and World Structural Change," pp. 441–463. See also Tylecote, *The Long Wave in the World Economy,* pp. 18–24.
37. See Ch. 2 in Tylecote, *The Long Wave in the World Economy,* pp. 36–70. Dicken uses the Kondratieff "long waves." Dicken, *Global Shift,* pp. 99–100.
38. Tylecote, *The Long Wave in the World Economy,* p. 36.
39. *Ibid.*, p. 19.
40. *Ibid.*, pp. 37–38.
41. In the early 1800s, several canals were built including in France the "Canal Monsieur" (completed in 1832) to transport coal to Alsace, another connecting the Rhône River to the Rhine, and the Saint-Quentin Canal, built between 1803 and 1810. In Germany, the Fehrbellin Canal was constructed in 1766, the Bromberg connecting the Oder and the Vistula rivers in 1774, and the Klodnitz connecting the coalfields of Upper Silesia with the Oder River in 1806. In Belgium, of the nearly 1,000 miles of navigable waterways, about 280 miles were canals by 1830. Increasingly, however, tolls were added on water transportation, although the Congress of Vienna adopted a treaty in 1831 pledging free passage. Sidney Pollard, *Peaceful Conquest: The Industrialization of Europe 1760–1970* (Oxford: Oxford University Press, 1981), pp. 4–7; 127–128.
42. *Ibid.*, p. 12.
43. Tylecote, *The Long Wave in the World Economy,* pp. 37–48.
44. Pollard, *Peaceful Conquest,* p. 13. By the mid-1780s, Tylecote notes, "The water style took shape, technically; and by

the same date the organisational requirements—the development of hierarchical factory management, and the attitudes to match—had, more or less, been met." Tylecote, *The Long Wave in the World Economy,* p. 44.

45. *Ibid.*, pp. 37–48.
46. A. G. Kenwood and A. L. Lougheed, *The Growth of the International Economy, 1820–1990* (London: Routledge, 1992), pp. 9–11.
47. Ronald Hyam, *Britain's Imperial Century, 1815–1914,* 2d ed. (London: Macmillan, 1993).
48. In some areas in England, the use of horse-drawn tramways on rails made of cast iron was common, but, like the wooden waterwheel in the previous phase, they lacked sufficient carrying capacity and durability for the routine transport of heavy loads and were not efficient. In the first decades of the 1800s, experiments with and improvements in the design of steam locomotives by Trevithick (1805), Stephenson (1818), and Birkinshaw (1821) had proved successful, as demonstrated by the first runs between Stockton and Darlington in 1825, and between Liverpool and Manchester in 1830. Pollard, *Peaceful Conquest,* p. 23; Tylecote, *The Long Wave in the World Economy,* pp. 45–46.
49. Tylecote, *The Long Wave in the World Economy,* pp. 45–47.
50. Pollard, *Peaceful Conquest,* p. 31.
51. Pollard, *Peaceful Conquest,* pp. 37, 132.
52. *Ibid.*, p. 89.
53. Charles Tilly, *Coercion, Capital, and European States,* AD 990–1992 (Cambridge: Blackwell 1992).
54. Pollard, *Peaceful Conquest,* pp. 129–130.
55. In the United States, the use of steam engines for industrial purposes "doubled between 1860 and 1880, and it doubled again between 1880 and 1900." Nathan Rosenberg and L. E. Birdzell, *How the West Grew Rich: The Economic Transformation of the Industrial World* (New York: Basic Books, 1986), p. 213.
56. Eric J. Hobsbawm, *The Age of Capital,* 1848–1875 (New York: Meridian Book, 1979), p. 83.
57. Paul M. Kennedy, *The Rise and Fall of British Naval Mastery* (London: Ashfield Press, 1983).
58. Paul Kennedy, *The Rise and Fall of Major Powers* (New York: Random House, 1987), p. 151.
59. Peter Temin, *Iron and Steel in Nineteenth-Century America* (Cambridge: MIT Press, 1964), p. 284; Rosenberg and Birdzeli, *How the West Grew Rich,* p. 213.
60. Rosenberg and Birdzell, *How the West Grew Rich,* p. 214.
61. *Ibid.*, p. 213.
62. Tylecote, *The Long Wave in the World Economy,* pp. 50–51.
63. Walter LaFeber, *The American Age: U.S. Foreign Policy at Home and Abroad, 1750 to the Present,* 2d ed. (New York: W. W. Norton, 1994).
64. Mark Rupert, *Producing Hegemony: The Politics of Mass Production and American Global Power* (Cambridge: Cambridge University Press, 1995).
65. Tylecote, *The Long Wave in the World Economy,* p. 52.
66. Rupert, *Producing Hegemony,* pp. 59–63.
67. Tylecote, *The Long Wave in the World Economy,* p. 62.
68. In 1938, the German consul awarded Ford the Order of the Golden Eagle, the highest decoration the Third Reich "could award to foreigners (only three others had received this award, among whom was Mussolini)." Rupert, *Producing Hegemony,* pp. 144–146.
69. William N. Parker, *Europe, America, and the Wider World: Essays on the Economic History of Western Capitalism, I: Europe and the World Economy* (Cambridge: Cambridge University Press, 1984), pp. 156–157.
70. Prior to the telegraph and the telephone, pockets of financial centers proliferated to meet local investment and production demands. However, these banking and investment operations were inefficient and slow, and they lacked the capacity to transmit uniform and reliable information regarding stocks and commodity markets. The widespread use of the telephone by the 1940s increased the pace and quality of communication. The telephone was soon supplemented by other and more sophisticated inventions, which spurred global communications technologies, including the early stages of satellite technologies. In 1965, for example, the first (Intelsat I) satellite was introduced and stationed above the Atlantic Ocean, transmitting more than 200 phone conversations simultaneously. Dicken, *Global Shift,* p. 106.
71. Tylecote follows Coombs' analysis of the three stages of industrial development and the characteristics of labor: transformation mechanization, transfer mechanization, and control mechanization. R.W. Coombs, "Long Waves and Labour Process Change," in Christopher Freeman, ed., *Long Waves in the World Economy* (London: Butterworth, 1983), discussed in Tylecote, *The Long Wave in the World Economy,* pp. 54–55.
72. Margaret Sharp, ed., *Europe and the New Technologies* (London: Pinter, 1983), quoted in Tylecote, The Long Wave in the World Economy, pp. 60–61.
73. Tylecote, *The Long Wave in the World Economy,* p. 61.
74. *Ibid.*, p. 57.
75. Manuel Castells and Jeffery Henderson, "Techno-Economic Restructuring, Socio-Political Processes and Spatial Transformation: A Global Perspective," in Jeffery Henderson and Manuel Castells, eds., *Global Restructuring and Territorial Development* (London: Sage, 1987), p. 6.
76. Dicken, *Global Shift,* pp. 102–103.
77. Dicken, *Global Shift,* p. 106.
78. One central problem currently in microelectronic technology is that while "the conventional cable is universally available . . . [it] is woefully limited in its capacity; microwave transmission, for example, via satellite, is available, but is still expensive and restricted compared to fibre optics, which is potentially 'the answer' but requires huge 'infrastructural' investment." This became particularly apparent

with the rapid proliferation of PCs. Tylecote, *The Long Wave in the World Economy,* pp. 56–57.

79. Barry Bluestone and Bennett Harrison, *The Deindustrialization of America: Plant Closings, Community Abandonment, and the Dismantling of Basic Industry* (New York: Basic Books, 1982).
80. "Women Entrepreneurs Embrace New Information Technology," *WIN News* 24, 1 (Winter 1998), p. 79; Donna Allen, "What's the New Communications Technology Doing for Women?" *Media Report to Women* 24, 3 (Summer 1996), p. 11.
81. While sex discrimination has become less visible, at the same time the corporate environment has led to the "invisible-woman syndrome," whereby women's ideas in major business decision-making processes are usually ignored. Steve Hamm, "Why Women Are So Invisible," *Business Week,* August 18, 1997, p. 136. See also Dale Spender, "The Position of Women in Information Technology—or Who Got There First and with What Consequences?" *Current Sociology* 45, 2 (April 1997), pp. 135–147.
82. Granger, *Technology and International Relations,* pp. 10–12.
83. *Ibid.*, p. 18.
84. Douglas Irwin and Peter Klenow, "Learning-by-Doing Spillovers in the Semiconductor Industry," *Journal of Political Economy* (December 1994); see *The Economist,* March 18, 1995, p. 78.
85. New patents continue to be owned mainly by the advanced industrialized economies.
86. Peter Schweizer, *Friendly Spies* (New York: Atlantic Monthly Press, 1993).
87. See Randall M. Fort, *Economic Espionage: Problems and Prospects* (Washington, DC: Consortium for the Study of Intelligence, 1993).
88. Walter Laqueur, *A World of Secrets: The Uses and Limits of Intelligence* (New York: Basic Books, 1985), p. 38.
89. Fort, *Economic Espionage,* p. 3.
90. *Ibid.*
91. *The Wall Street Journal,* October 18, 1995, p. A17. The Bush administration, which since the 1940s was the first to view the world from a post–Cold War perspective, emphasized competitiveness in the world economy and defined the inability of U.S. companies to compete in global markets as a "national security threat." In a 1991 memo, Deputy Secretary of State Lawrence Eagleburger wrote that "U.S. competitiveness in the global economy must become one of the pillars of U.S. foreign policy and of our projection of strength and influence." Also in 1991, in an article entitled "Intelligence for a New World Order," Stansfield Turner, the former director of the CIA, wrote that

    > the preeminent threat to U.S. national security now lies in the economic sphere. . . . We must, then, redefine "national security" by assigning economic strength greater prominence. . . . If economic strength should now be recognized as a vital component of national security, parallel with military power, why should America be concerned about stealing and employing economic secrets?

    In a similar vein, in 1993 Secretary of State Warren Christopher maintained that "one of the first pillars of foreign policy is that it serve the economic needs of the United States." Quoted in Fort, *Economic Espionage,* pp. 4-5.
92. *Ibid.,* p. 3.
93. Other areas include agriculture and health care. See Granger, *Technology and International Relations,* p. 16.
94. *Ibid.*
95. *Ibid.*, pp. 38–40.
96. See, for example, Daniel I. Okimoto, "Political Inclusivity: The Domestic Structure of Trade," in Takashi Inoguchi and Daniel I. Okimoto, eds., *The Political Economy of Japan: The Changing International Context,* vol. 2 (Stanford: Stanford University Press, 1988), pp. 305–344. In the early 1980s, for example, the Japanese government funded approximately 22.2 percent of the national R&D, including grants-in-aid for state and private universities, while during the same period the U.S. government financed 46 percent, including defense-related R&D. As in post-WWII Western Europe, Japan also enjoyed the luxury of allocating minimum expenditures—that is, about 1 percent of GNP as required under Article 9 of the "MacArthur Constitution"—for national defense under the U.S. "security umbrella," which enabled the Japanese to concentrate their energies on consumer technologies. Mowery and Rosenberg, *Technology and the Pursuit of Economic Growth,* p. 221.
97. Another key factor in Japan's national technology policy was the role of the national government in funding and coordinating inter-company collaborative ventures in scientific research and marketing strategies. Beginning in the 1960s, the Japanese government encouraged the formation of Engineering Research Associations (ERAs), whereby collaborative efforts concentrated on clearly defined areas of R&D and specific technologies. During the next decade, these strategies, better funded and organized, led to the rapid expansion of Japanese MNCs operations, especially in the area of electronics and computers (for example, the Very Large Scale Integrated Circuit, VLSI, in the late 1970s). *Ibid.*, pp. 222–223.
98. *Ibid.*, pp. 207–208.
99. *Ibid.*, p. 219.
100. *Ibid.*, p. 220. Subsequently, the United States gained the competitive edge in high-resolution T.V. and silicon chips.
101. *Ibid.*, pp. 224–225.
102. *Challenge to the South: The Report of the South Commission* [Nyerere Commission Report] (Oxford: Oxford University Press, 1990), pp. 110–111.
103. S.K. Roy Chowdhry and P.R. Shukla, eds., *Encylopaedia of Economic Development,* vol. 7, *Development, Industrialization, and Technology* (New Delhi: Akashdeep, 1991), pp. 174–175.

104. NICs include the "four dragons" of East Asia: Hong Kong, Singapore, South Korea, and Taiwan. More recently, Brazil and Mexico have been included among them as well.
105. Mowery and Rosenberg, *Technology and the Pursuit of Economic Growth,* pp. 208–209.
106. Ingomar Hauchler and Paul M. Kennedy, eds., *Global Trends: The World Almanac of Development and Peace* (New York: Continuum Press, 1994), p. 365.
107. Nyerere Commission Report, *Challenge to the South,* pp. 15–16. See also Pradip K. Ghosh, ed., *Appropriate Technology in Third World Development* (Westport: Greenwood Press, 1984).
108. There also have been heated debates about whether international spillovers and technology transfers expedite the recipient country's economic development and enhance its manufacturing and production capabilities. A study by Coe and Helpman indicated that R&D expenditures in the G-7 countries led to production increases not only in their own countries but also in foreign countries. In each industrialized country, a 1 percent increase in its R&D stock raised its TFP (total factor productivity) by 0.23 percent, although the smaller economies benefited relatively less, 0.08%. R&D spending in the G-7 countries also benefited foreign economies. The largest percentage of spillovers came from the highest spender on R&D, the United States. "Every 1% rise in [the U.S. R&D] stock lifted TFP in the other 21 countries by an average of 0.04%." In a related study, Coe, Helpman, and Hoffmaister argued that poorer countries throughout the developing world also gain from R&D spillovers from the industrialized economies. While the latter generate little R&D in "strategic" and competitive technologies, they nevertheless benefit from Western R&D. During the period 1985–1990, for example, "a 1% rise in America's R&D stock increased the TFP of the 77 [developing countries] by an average of 0.04%. In some countries the benefits were much greater: Singapore's TFP was boosted by 0.22%." Foreign economies benefit from R&D spillovers through international trade. As developing countries import from the industrialized North, they not only import technologically advanced products but soon duplicate the technology developed by foreign companies. Furthermore, international trade compels some of them to develop efficient technologies themselves to compete in their own domestic markets. David Coe and Elhanan Helpman, "International R&D Spillovers," *European Economic Review;* David Coe, Elhanan Helpman, and Alexander Hoffmaister, "North–South R&D Spillovers," Center for Economic Policy Research, Discussion Paper No. 1133, February 1995, as discussed in *The Economist,* March 18, 1995, p. 78.
109. Nyerere Commission Report, *Challenge to the South,* pp. 39–45.
110. *Ibid.,* p. 41.
111. *Ibid.,* p. 42.
112. Bernard I. Logan, "The Reverse Transfer of Technology from Sub-Saharan Africa to the United States," *Journal of Modern African Studies* 25, 4 (1987), pp. 598–600.
113. Governments heavily invested in various higher education and training programs, such as the G.I. Bill and the National Defense Education Act of 1958 in the United States. In the meantime, however, Europeans viewed the brain drain from Europe to the United States as a serious problem. By the mid- to late-1970s governments in the industrialized West began to reap the benefits of their investments and the pool of highly trained and qualified labor had expanded. While the outflow of some of the best scientists from Britain continued, the immigration to Britain of educated individuals from the Commonwealth countries continued as well. Barbara Rhode, "Brain Drain, Brain Gain, Brain Waste: Reflections on the Emigration of Highly Educated and Scientific Personnel from Eastern Europe," in Russell King, ed., *The New Geography of European Migrations* (London: Belhaven Press, 1993), p. 234.
114. Rhode, "Brain Drain, Brain Gain, Brain Waste," p. 229; "Brain Drain Out of Africa," *New Scientist,* May 30, 1992; N. Ayoubi, "The Egyptian Brain Drain," *Journal of Middle East Studies* 15 (1983); Logan, "The Reverse Transfer of Technology," pp. 597–612.
115. Hauchler and Kennedy, *Global Trends,* p. 130.
116. William C. Boesman, "Science and Technology in the Former Soviet Union: Capabilities and Needs," in Richard F. Kaufman and John P. Hardt, eds., for the Joint Economic Committee, Congress of the United States, *The Former Soviet Union in Transition* (Armonk, NY: M. E. Sharpe, 1993), pp. 620–621.
117. Governments invest enormous sums of their national budget for various educational and postgraduate training programs to develop human resources and to improve the economic foundations and quality of life in their countries. They realize that a diverse pool of educated and skilled scientific talent is a necessary, if not sufficient, condition for economic development. As the skilled migrants leave, however, for the government the loss is especially great, as it loses both the money invested in their education and the potential revenues from various (income, sales) taxes generated by their incomes. Theodore W. Schultz, "Investment in Human Capital," *American Economic Review* 51 (March 1961), pp. 1–17; E. F. Denison, *The Sources of Economic Growth in the United States,* Supplementary paper No. 13, Committee for Economic Development, New York, 1962; "Education, Economic Growth, and Gaps in Information," *Journal of Political Economy* 70 (October 1962); Rhode, "Brain Drain, Brain Gain, Brain Waste," pp. 230–231.
118. In the case of the Philippines, in the mid-1970s, nearly 21 percent of "locally trained" medical doctors and 11 percent of engineers emigrated to an industrialized country. Logan, "The Reverse Transfer of Technology," pp. 602–603.

119. *Ibid.*, p. 608, Table 3.
120. Rhode, "Brain Drain, Brain Gain, Brain Waste," p. 231; G. Baldwin, "Brain Drain or Brain Overflow?" *Foreign Affairs* 48, 2 (1970): pp. 358–372.
121. J. Bhagwati and K. Hamada, "The Brain Drain, International Integration of Markets for Professionals and Unemployment: A Theoretical Analysis," *Journal of Development Economics* 1, 1 (1974): pp. 19–42; R. Dore, *The Diploma Disease* (London: Allen and Unwin, 1976).
122. Rhode, "Brain Drain, Brain Gain, Brain Waste," pp. 230–232.
123. Hussein G. Askari and John Thomas Cummings, "The Middle East and the United States: A Problem of 'Brain Drain,'" *International Journal of Middle East Studies* 8 (1977), p. 66.
124. Granger, *Technology and International Relations,* pp. 117–120.
125. *Ibid.*, p. 118.
126. Chowdhry and Shukla, eds., *Encylopaedia of Economic Development,* vol. 7, *Development, Industrialization, and Technology,* p. 177.
127. Nyerere Commission Report, *Challenge to the South,* p. 193.
128. Boesman, "Science and Technology in the Former Soviet Union," pp. 610–611.
129. *Ibid.*, p. 611.
130. W. Seth Carus, "Military Technology and the Arms Trade: Changes and Their Impact," *Annals of the American Academy of Political and Social Science* 535 (September 1994), pp. 163–174.
131. Frank Barnaby and Marlies ter Borg, eds., *Emerging Technologies and Military Doctrine: A Political Assessment* (New York: St. Martin's Press, 1986).
132. Dennis Pirages, *Global Technopolitics: The International Politics of Technology and Resources* (Pacific Grove, CA: Brooks/Cole, 1988), pp. 184–185.
133. *Ibid.*, p. 185.
134. Granger, *Technology and International Relations,* pp. 75–77.
135. See, for example, "Star in the Descendant," *The Economist,* September 29, 1990, pp. 95–98.
136. See also Dicken, *Global Shift,* p. 311.
137. A critical area of the computer and semiconductor industries is the production of the so-called dynamic random access memories (DRAMs). Here, too, until the mid-1970s, the United States had a monopoly, but by the late 1980s Japan had captured the largest share (well over 70 percent), as the U.S. share declined to 20 percent. European countries, however, held even a smaller share of production, while East and Southeast Asia's share surpassed that of Europe. *Ibid.*, pp. 310–313.
138. On U.S. and Japanese R&D in the technology of superconductivity, see *The Economist,* April 29, 1995, p. 97. See also Simon Foner and Terry P. Orlando, "Superconductors: The Long Road Ahead," in Albert H. Teich, ed., *Technology and the Future,* 5th ed. (New York: St. Martin's Press, 1990), pp. 334–349.
139. Dicken, *Global Shift,* pp. 311–313.
140. Kenneth H. Keller, "Science and Technology," *Foreign Affairs* 69 (Fall 1990), pp. 123–138.
141. Granger, *Technology and International Relations,* pp. 5–6.
142. David Mitrany, *A Working Peace System* (Chicago: Quadrangle Books, 1966); Mitrany, *The Functional Theory of Politics* (New York: St. Martin's Press, 1977).
143. See, for example, Stephen D. Krasner, *Structural Conflict: The Third World Against Global Liberalism* (Berkeley: University of California Press, 1985); Krasner, ed., *International Regimes* (Ithaca: Cornell University Press, 1983); Oran R. Young, *International Cooperation: Building Regimes for Natural Resources and the Environment* (Ithaca: Cornell University Press, 1989); Kenneth A. Oye, ed., *Cooperation Under Anarchy* (Princeton: Princeton University Press, 1986).
144. Richard Smoke, *National Security and the Nuclear Dilemma* (Reading, MA: Addison-Wesley, 1984), p. 138.
145. Mowery and Rosenberg, *Technology and the Pursuit of Economic Growth,* pp. 246–247.
146. Bennett, *International Organizations.*
147. Granger, *Technology and International Relations,* pp. 42–43.
148. *Ibid.*
149. Daniele Archibugi and Mario Pianta, "Innovation Surveys and Patents as Technology Indicators: The State of the Art," in OECD, *Innovation, Patents, and Technological Strategies* (Paris: Organization for Economic Cooperation and Development, 1996), p. 36.
150. Bernard Brodie and Fawn M. Brodie, *From Crossbow to H-Bomb,* rev. ed. (Bloomington: Indiana University Press, 1973), pp. 15–16, 66–67.
151. *Ibid.*, pp. 68–74, 88.
152. John H. Herz, *International Politics in the Atomic Age* (New York: Columbia University Press, 1959).
153. Helen Caldicott, *Missile Envy: The Arms Race and Nuclear War,* rev. ed. (Toronto: Bantam Books, 1986).
154. Fred Halliday, *The Making of the Second Cold War,* 2d ed. (London: Verso, 1986).
155. John Croome, *Reshaping the World Trading System: A History of the Uruguay Round* (Geneva: World Trade Organization, 1995), p. 119.
156. *Ibid.*, pp. 130–131.

PART III

IPE IN A DIVIDED GLOBAL SYSTEM

©Mariella Furrer/SABA

INTERNATIONAL COMPETITIVENESS AND THE INDUSTRIALIZED WORLD: THE UNITED STATES, EUROPE, AND JAPAN

In the early 1980s, international economic competitiveness became a major issue in the world economy and, a decade later, virtually replaced the superpower ideological competition after the collapse of the former Soviet Union. The debate with respect to international competitiveness became particularly contentious in the United States, where, as a global superpower, the stakes were high; the nation's relative decline as a world economic leader closely related to its ability to compete in world markets. However, international competitiveness should not be construed as mere economic or market capabilities. In the globalized world political economy, government and corporate relations across borders and continents are highly complex, entailing both cooperation and competition, as seen in international trade and financial relations, discussed in previous chapters. Unlike the narrower conception of competitiveness referring to competition among companies, a central issue regarding national competitiveness involves the overall health of the national economy, and technological rank in an increasingly globalized and complex world economy.[1]

Accordingly, the issue of competitiveness raises a host of questions regarding the role of government in society, the role of multinational and domestic corporations, labor unions, educational institutions, and research and development (R&D) facilities. In capitalist economies, such as the United States, the role of government in shaping economic and industrial policy can be highly controversial and political. Laissez-faire capitalism requires that the government abstain from direct and heavy involvement in the economy, yet, for over two decades, the relative loss of market competitiveness to Japan and Europe, the closing of factories in the historically major industrial cities, the transfer of jobs abroad, and the diminishing rates of job security all placed enormous pressures on the U.S. government and corporations to address the issue of competitiveness for economic and political reasons.

Competitiveness also raises questions about the role and impact labor unions have on major industries deemed essential for international competitiveness. In the United States, as in other industrialized countries grappling with issues of globalization and competitiveness, opponents have blamed trade unions and their demands (for example, high wages, pensions) as the primary contributing factor to trade deficits, declining productivity, and therefore loss of national competitiveness in world markets. Supporters of organized labor, however, have argued that there is no such relationship between unionization and loss of competitiveness: the United States has become less competitive in both unionized and nonunionized sectors, including electronics industries,[2] while in specialized auto markets the United States has been quite competitive with union labor.

Indeed, the debate on international competitiveness has been intensely political since the 1980s. This politicization of the concept of "competitiveness" has so obfuscated its meaning that the term can be misleading and ill-suited as a guide for foreign economic policymaking.[3] In fact, international competitiveness has assumed the characteristics of "world Olympics." It has become a political symbol, a sort of political slogan, like "world class," at the expense of reasonable economic debate on sound policies.[4] As such, the concept bears close similarity to the concept of *power* in international relations. In current IPE parlance, the concept of *competitiveness* has essentially become the equivalent of the traditional concept of *balance of power,* which was also used by political and economic leaders to protect and promote their own interests. Contrary to arguments that the term *competitiveness* has become meaningless, however, and despite the fact that it is often used and abused for economic and political self-interest,[5] the fact remains that whether a nation's productive and market capabilities increase or decrease is indicative of its ability to compete and survive economically, as shifts in international economic and technological competitiveness also shift the international balance of power, including military power.

CONCEPTUALIZING INTERNATIONAL COMPETITION

Competitiveness as an Economic Concept

Loosely defined, the concepts of "international competition" and "competitiveness" refer to a nation's ability to produce and sell its own products while maintaining a relatively larger share of export markets than its competitors' in world economy. During the Reagan administration, the President's Commission on Industrial Competitiveness defined competitiveness as "the degree to which a nation can, under free and fair market conditions, produce goods and services that meet the test of international markets while simultaneously maintaining or expanding the real income of its citizens."[6] A nation's ability to compete successfully in the world economy requires certain—albeit not always clearly defined—properties, or "factor endowments," such as knowledge, capital, natural resources, and infrastructure.[7] These in turn must be effectively used to develop and mobilize key areas of the economy in which the nation possesses comparative advantages: (1) sufficient productive capacity and productive growth, (2) relatively high savings and investment rates, (3) strong financial and institutional bases for highly advanced R&D, and (4) a sufficient technically skilled human resource base.[8] The evolution of the technological styles, as discussed in Chapter 8, suggests that an economy today must develop a number of industries for successful economic competition. These would include microelectronics, biotechnology, telecommunications, robotics and machine tools, and computers and software,[9] although as of yet unpredictable new technologies and products may also emerge.

It may be argued that the emergence, or reemergence, of Germany and Japan as major international economic centers since the 1970s has not necessarily diminished the U.S. gobal hegemonic position but, rather has returned the world economy to a state of "normality" disrupted by the Second World War, making the United States once more a "normal" power. The validity of this argument, however, does not lessen the significance of competitiveness as a matter of political economy. The U.S. relative decline in trade vis-à-vis Japan and the U.S. wage structure shaped the political debate regarding competitiveness. As Thurow points out, in the 1950s,

> what were high-wage products from the Japanese perspective were low-wage products in West Germany. What were high-wage products in West Germany were low-wage products in America. As a result, imports from West Germany or Japan were not seen as threatening the good jobs that Americans wanted. Conversely, America's exports did not threaten good jobs in West Germany or Japan. The United States exported agricultural products that they could not grow, raw materials that they did not have, and high-tech products, such as civilian jet airliners, that they could not build.[10]

The United States was not *merely* competitive; it was *the global economic superpower*. Its subsequent declining position reflected the seismic shift from being the world's largest creditor to becoming the largest debtor in 1985.[11] This structural transformation in the global political economy caused tensions among the major powers, which, with the passing of the U.S.-Soviet superpower military rivalry in 1990, were preparing for the potential intensification of economic rivalry in the next century.[12]

The intensification of the struggle for economic survival has reflected the transformations in the structures of the international political economy. Thurow argues that the world economy in the twentieth century was based on "niche competition," and the nature of international competition was a "win-win" situation. In other words, competitors found an industrial-technological niche with comparative advantage vis-a-vis others, and each side, finding its niche of successful production or specialization, was better off. The twenty-first century, on the other hand, he predicts, will witness a "head-to-head"—that is, zero-sum—competition, whereby countries unable to find a technological niche for themselves in the global economy will lag behind.

International competitiveness, however, even when aggressively pursued, is not necessarily predicated on win-or-lose conflicts; it may also lead to international cooperation. Major corporations as well as governments engage in various strategic joint production and market ventures across international borders. An example is the European Airbus Industries, owned by British, French, German, and Spanish interests, initially created to end the U.S. monopoly in that industry. Airbus Industries increased its market share to 20 percent, and was expected to capture about 30 percent of world markets by the end of the 1990s.[13]

However, more for political reasons than good economic policy, some politicians emphasize the conflictual, war-like situation in international competitiveness. In the case of the United States, for example, imports constitute about 14 percent of the American gross domestic product (GDP),[14] but the political debates waged concerning the trade deficit and competitiveness in recent elections have so misused and abused these terms as to confound the real economic significance of competition. The politically motivated application of the concept to domestic and foreign economic policies can have deleterious consequences for the national economy.

Competitiveness as a Political Concept and as Balance of Power

It is, in fact, mere truism to state that the concept of competitiveness is exploited for political purposes. In the United States, political and public opinion leaders, relying on demagoguery rather than serious debate, use the term *competitiveness* to make an issue or a policy more acceptable to the public and to justify policies they support in election seasons. Ideologically more conservative commentators stress the need to become more competitive and propose "less government" and cutbacks in government programs and corporate "fat," while liberals propose greater government involvement for the same goal. Ornstein has put it aptly:

> We want to be competitive in everything. We are sports fans. We watch horse races and political contests. The notion of appealing to patriotism by suggesting that it's us against them does get juices flowing. We can take an issue of that sort and make it all things to all people. We can talk about competitiveness in education and not necessarily make it the onerous burden for students or teachers of working longer. Instead Democrats can talk about increasing federal involvement in education and frame it in terms of competitiveness. In the same way, by framing in terms of competitiveness, Republicans can talk about unleashing industry without having to take the flak of being for big business. To whatever degree it can be cloaked as a patriotic issue that nobody can be against; everybody can gain some benefits from it.[15]

In a classic article, Ernst Haas argued that policymakers historically have used the concept of "balance of power" to mean whatever suited their political interests.[16] Some believed the struggle for the balance of power was a central feature of international relations, the driving force behind major powers' competition for power and wealth. Throughout the nineteenth and the early part of the twentieth centuries, for example, British, French, German, and Russian imperial policies were propelled by geo-strategic and economic considerations, and each viewed the others' territorial or diplomatic gains as a diminution of its own power relative to them. Political leaders perceived another power's ability to expand and maintain colonial territories as being indicative of national competitiveness, and they justified their own imperial policies accordingly.

Haas identified a number of meanings policymakers and commentators attach to the term *balance of power*.[17] The way in which the concept was used and for what purpose, according to Haas, was determined by one's ideological orientation. Opponents of the balance of power, such as Woodrow Wilson (of the *idealist,* or *moralist,* school), found it unacceptable as a foreign policy strategy, although Wilson indulged in power balancing in the European and Latin American contexts; proponents, mostly belonging to the Realpolitik school, emphasized its importance for international stability and peace. When political leaders used the concept of balance of power to *describe* the international system and relations among nations, they often meant distribution of power. Inequalities in the distribution of power among major powers caused disturbances in the international system, as the weaker sought to achieve or to reestablish a sense of parity. But the term was also used for *propaganda* purposes; balance of power became "no more than a convenient catchword to focus individual aspirations into a generally acceptable mold; and there can be no doubt that at certain times the concept of balance was an extremely popular one, whether it was used for policymaking or not."[18]

As with the term balance of power, nations use the concept of competitiveness "to estimate the trajectory of their own and other countries as they ascend, decline, or maintain their position in a hierarchically structured international system."[19] Nations and their leaders strive to maintain or enhance their relative position in that system, and the extent to which each meets the various social, economic, technological, and political challenges posed by international competition determines whether it succeeds or not. Competitiveness as such serves as a *guide* for foreign policymaking and accordingly prescribes certain "rules of survival." Paul Kennedy introduced his controversial book, *The Rise and Fall of Great Powers,* as follows:

> The relative strengths of the leading nations in world affairs never remain constant, principally because of the uneven rate of growth among different societies and of the technological and organizational breakthroughs which bring a greater advantage to one society than to another. . . . [T]here is detectable causal relationship between the shifts which have occurred over time

> in the general economic and productive balances and the position occupied by individual Powers in the international system. The move in trade flows from the Mediterranean to the Atlantic and northwestern Europe from the sixteenth century onward, or the redistribution in the shares of world manufacturing output away from western Europe in the decades after 1890, are good examples here. In both cases, the economic shifts heralded the rise of new Great Powers which would one day have a decisive impact upon the military/territorial order. This is why the move in the global productive balances toward the "Pacific rim" which has taken place over the past few decades cannot be of interest merely to economists alone.[20]

During the past two decades, especially after the Cold War, the United States expended enormous efforts to reassert its international competitiveness toward European and Asian countries, especially Germany and Japan. Politicians, corporate and union leaders, and others believed that another nation's ability to expand and control increasing shares of the world markets—as in the case of the auto industry, for example—was evidence of national competitiveness. Leaders in developing countries, such as Brazil and India, likewise have seen economic and technological prowess as a means of gaining international status and security.

The term *competitiveness* also has served as an *analytical concept.* It has provided the conceptual basis for economic theories of international relations, involving such uses as "econopower," "hegemony," and "equilibrium"—for example, the frequently heard "level playing field" argument in U.S.-Japan trade practices. As with geo-political balances of power, international competitiveness has increasingly assumed "natural (or universal) law" and "historical law" qualities, as indicated by the previous quote from Kennedy.

Critics of the concept of competitiveness, such as Paul Krugman, contend that it is meaningless, and that excessive concern regarding competitiveness is a "dangerous obsession," which may result in poorly conceived economic policies, international tensions, and trade wars.[21] As such, the term is often used for propaganda purposes, and competitiveness becomes, to repeat Haas, a "convenient catchword to focus individual aspirations into a generally acceptable mold. . . ."[22] Japanese leaders, indeed, are quick to point out that in the 1960s Washington criticized Japan for shoddy products and failure to export enough; today the criticism is precisely reversed.

Proponents of the Realpolitik school of thought emphasize the zero-sum (win-lose) nature of international competition and the importance of national trade strategies in generating both international influence and economic well-being. Prestowitz writes:

> But what about the kind of trade typified by the recent Saudi Arabian order for $6 billion of new airplanes? Why were the Europeans so upset and President Clinton so happy when the Saudis announced that U.S. producers would win all the orders? Both the Europeans and the Americans make warplanes, and this order means that the United States will gain jobs and income that Europe might have had but lost. This was largely a zero-sum trade situation. . . .[23]

"The real world," Thurow asserts, "is in a perpetual state of dynamic disequilibrium,"[24] and nations seek, through competitiveness, to achieve or reestablish a sense of parity.

THEORIES OF INTERNATIONAL COMPETITIVENESS

The debate regarding international economic competition in the 1980s led to a number of theories stressing different aspects of national attributes as the key to successful competitiveness. Some observers argued that, in addition to a nation's tangible and quantifiable attributes as mentioned above, its culture and ideological orientation toward industrialization and economic development also exert a significant impact on its ability to compete. The extent to which a society functions based on cummunitarian or individualistic principles; its degree of cultural homogeneity and value consensus; the nature and role of its social organizations, education, and political-economic institutions; the extent and purpose of governmental involvement in its economic affairs—all are directly related to the nation's competitiveness. For example, while the United States historically has maintained a relatively more liberal open attitude toward economic affairs, other governments, such as Japan's, have been more actively engaged and have operated with a more communitarian culture, hence the traditional banking and retailing networks that seem so closed and inefficient to Western eyes. Ideological approaches to national economic competitiveness vary from one political system to another, and, while there are numerous theories of international competition and competitiveness, as presented in Chapter 2, here we focus on three: statist theory, culturalist theories, and macroeconomic theories.

Statist Theory

A variant of the mercantilist theory presented in Chapter 2, statist theory views the government as the most powerful entity in society. The state is the central and sovereign actor, with its own set of interests in domestic and international economic relations, and is the driving force in economic development and competition, along the lines of the East Asian model of capitalism. Statist theory believes that the more centralized governments, such as Japan, can better enhance the competitiveness of their economies with greater effectiveness than their decentralized counterparts, such as the United States and Canada.[25]

Through various state institutions and policy strategies, the state promotes industrialization and technological advancement to strengthen the nation's economic position in the international political economy. Government cooperation with corporations to coordinate such policies as production and marketing motor vehicles, semiconductors, and computers is believed to be a necessary, even if undesirable, aspect of international competitiveness in the early twenty-first century. The government of Japan, for example, has a deep tradition in coordinating economic strategies. As Johnson has pointed out,

> the Meiji-era goal was the *fukoku-kyōhei* (rich country, strong military) of the late nineteenth and early twentieth centuries. This was followed during the 1930's and 1940's by the goals of depression recovery, war preparation, war production, and postwar recovery. From 1955, and explicitly since the Income-doubling Plan of 1960, the goal has been high-speed growth, sometimes expressed as "overtake Europe and America" (*Ōbei ni oikose*).[26]

Since the 1950s and 1960s, Tokyo has maintained a developmental approach, with planned strategies to enable Japanese firms to compete effectively in world markets.[27] The Ministry of International Trade and Industry (MITI), for example, is one of the principal government institutions involved in planning market strategies in cooperation with Japanese corporations. The U.S. government, on the other hand, has been more market-oriented, with greater emphasis on the regulation of firms' *market* behavior. Some observers have attributed U.S. firms' diminishing market shares to the inability of the government and corporations to cooperate and coordinate in the market. On the other hand, although the Japanese state "possessed the policy instruments necessary to reallocate resources across industries, while the U.S. state did not," Japan's severe recession in the late 1990s brought the government's ability to drive and stabilize the economy into question.[28] Concomitantly the corporate push for mergers, acquisitions, and larger units to compete internationally perhaps promotes a more uniform global business culture, with governments acquiescing in the process.

Statist theory, then, sees national competitiveness as a goal to be pursued not by corporations alone depending on the ebb and flow of market demands but through specifically designed strategies led and coordinated by the government in cooperation with corporations. As Hart has noted, state-societal arrangements—that is, "the manner in which state and civil societies are organized and institutionally linked"—involve government but also key business and labor organizations and propel society toward greater international competitiveness.[29]

Culturalist Theories

Other scholars argue that national culture is the principal determinant of economic competitiveness, as a society's cultural values shape and are shaped by the needs of the community's physical "survival, . . . justice, economy, self-fulfillment or self-respect" in the national and international environments.[30] Cultural world views, or "ontologies," enable the community to address a wide variety of internal and external social, political, and economic issues, such as productivity, income distribution, employment, demographic factors, wars, immigration, MNCs, and international competition.[31] Two major ontologies are *individualism* and *communitarianism.* An individualistic culture is "an atomistic conception of society, one in which the individual is the ultimate source of value and meaning."[32] It places a great emphasis on individual initiatives, such as scientific exploration, technological inventions, entrepreneurship, and private property, as a manifestation of one's successful survival. In addition, other essential components of individualism include market competition to meet the individual consumer's needs and desires (albeit mainly through pluralist structures),[33] a limited role for government, concepts of individual rights, and "scientific specialization and fragmentation."[34] The last component implies that society's progress is based on the individual's ability to compete freely and to contribute to the generation of scientific knowledge for the good of the *individual* first and, only by extension, of society as a whole. While some Western observers may view this individualistic ideology as the embodiment of all desirable qualities in a culture, critics see it as conducive to fragmentation, "straining society's adaptability" to major changes and challenges in the domestic and international environments.[35] Persistent poverty and the existence of an "under-class," for example, have in part been blamed on an overemphasis on individualism in some of the West's richest and most vibrant societies.

A communitarian culture, on the other hand, views society as a single "organic," rather than atomistic, entity, "the sum of its individuals and requiring explicit definition of its needs and priorities."[36] The individual expresses his or her identity through his or her position in the community and his or her needs and desires through the needs and desires of the community. As in Islam, each individual plays a well-defined and structured role in the society and economy. The greater the fulfillment of the community's—the neighborhood's and country's—needs and demands, the greater the fulfillment and honor of the individual. The state, along with corporations and labor unions, are accorded their own central role in the process to guarantee, in the hierarchical order of things, equality of result, a general consensus with respect to national values and expectations, and *holism*—that is, the harmonious workings of various interdependent institutions toward the betterment of the commonweal. Ezra Vogel maintains that "countries with a coherent communitarian ideology have been able to best adapt to this international competitive economic system."[37] According to the findings presented by Vogel and his colleagues, communitarian societies, such as Japan, South Korea, and Taiwan, have been far more successful in meeting the challenges of international competitiveness than have their Western individualist-oriented counterparts, especially the United States and Britain (see Table 9.1).

Communitarianism is not a guarantee of success, however. Islamic societies in the Middle East, as well as other communitarian societies, such as China and India, while having made significant economic progress, lag behind other countries for a number of other reasons—for example, their large or diverse population, lack of investment capital, and history of colonial exploitation. According to Krieger, British political culture symbolized democratic stability based on a balanced compromise between the push and pulls of individualism and communitarianism. Individualism enabled Britain to emerge as the first major industrial economy, while communitarianism sustained the coherence and, hence, the legitimacy of the system.[38] The internal tensions—for example, between the agricultural and manufacturing sectors, the demands for expanded franchise and participation—were resolved through systemic adjustments and readjustments, while the country emerged as a global hegemonic economic and military power in the eighteenth and nineteenth centuries. Britain did not withstand the transformations in the world political economy, however, and in the 1940s and 1950s it withdrew from its colonial holdings around the world. The advent of globalization, especially the turbulent international environment in the 1970s and the Thatcherite (and neo-individualist) response to it in the 1980s, did not greatly improve the situation.[39] Britain remained competitive on its own in a few economic sectors, but the European Union may be the key to the country's future viability.

In addition to the role of the state and the culture of individualism or communitarianism, other factors are also involved in enhancing a nation's international competitive-

TABLE 9.1
Ideology and Competitiveness

	Annual compound growth rate of real GNP per capita 1965–1984 (percent)		**Percentage point change in export share of world market (less oil exports) 1965–1984**		**Average share of investment in GNP 1965–1984 (percent)**	
	Rank	Number	Rank	Number	Rank	Number
Japan	3	5.27	1	4.4	1	29.0
Korea	1	7.22	2	1.5	3	22.9
Taiwan	2	6.78	3	1.4	5	19.4
Germany	6	2.66	7	21.0	2	23.3
France	5	2.90	6	20.6	4	21.0
Brazil	4	3.44	4	0.6	8	17.5
United States	8	2.02	8	24.0	9	15.4
United Kingdom	9	1.74	8	24.0	7	17.7
Mexico	7	2.33	5	20.2	6	18.1

Source: Translated and reprinted by permission of Harvard Business School Press. From *Ideology and National Competitiveness* by George C. Lodge and Erza F. Vogel, eds., Boston, MA 1987.

ness. Macroeconomic theories have made a significant contribution in this regard.

Macroeconomic Theories

Macroeconomic theories examine strictly economic, rather than cultural or institutional, conditions to explain international competitiveness. Laissez-faire economists look at such quantitative indicators as market prices and demand, rates of savings and investment, and foreign currency exchange rates,[40] determined, as postulated by the comparative advantage theory, by the "invisible hand" of market competition (see Chapter 2). According to this view, distortions in the market render an economy less competitive. For example, protectionist policies to insulate local markets against foreign competitors lead to higher prices, jeopardizing a nation's competitive potential in world markets.[41]

Levels of savings and investment are closely related to competitiveness as well. Economic growth generates higher levels of capital for savings and investment, keeping capital costs lower; that is, the greater the national propensity to save, the greater the ability to invest, which in turn provides a stronger competitive base. Table 9.2 presents the household savings rates as a percentage of disposable household income in the five major advanced industrialized countries since the late 1970s, and Table 9.3 shows their private savings, investment rates, and profit shares. Since the late 1970s, all five countries have witnessed a decline in their household savings rates, but those of the United States, as a consumer society, have remained the lowest. Despite the overall decline, the savings rates in France, Germany, and Japan have been higher than in Britain and the United States. In part cultural views may affect such differences and traditions.

The rate of corporate saving is closely related to the rate of investment, and the distribution of profits between savings and investment is crucial to overall capital accumulation and economic development. As indicated in Table 9.3, that distribution varied among the countries, led by Japan, whose disproportionately high savings rate reflected its economic growth and industrial output. In contrast to the culturalist theory, in all five countries, household savings constituted a smaller proportion of investment.[42] In the case of Japan, however, corporations kept a higher share of profits, reflecting the more tightly knit ownership structure among corporations and banks—that is, the East Asian–Japanese model (see Chapter 2). In the United States and the United Kingdom, the looser ownership structure, the Anglo-American model, led to broader distribution of dividends. It is estimated that, in Japan, individual ownership of shares accounted for 20 percent of total shares in 1987, while in the United States that figure was 65 percent.[43]

These simple calculations are not meant to prescribe a specific set of habits and tastes in order to improve savings and investment capacities in any one country. They indicate that a sort of economic culture may exist, based on history of inflation and recession, or based on ideology and custom (for example, communitarianism and individualism, Laissez-faire or government intervention), which condition the propensity to save or consume. However, mere savings and investments *per se* do not assure international competitiveness. Competitiveness is also comprised of various tangible and intangible factors, ranging from country size to domestic productivity and international prestige.

In the early 1980s, Hofheinz and Calder argued that East Asia's high savings rates were crucial for the region's economic competitiveness.[44] While most East Asian economies, including Japan and the newly industrialized countries (NICs), performed well and registered enormous successes in the 1980s and the first half of the 1990s, the savings and investment hypothesis fails to explain the region's economic slowdown and accompanying crisis in the second half of the 1990s. Structural factors at the domestic and global level, including the structures of production, finance, knowledge,

TABLE 9.2

Household Savings Rates, 1978–1996 (Percentage of Disposable Household Income)

	1978	1980	1982	1984	1986	1988	1990	1992	1994	1996[a]
Britain	10.9	13.4	11.3	11.1	8.7	5.6	8.1	12.2	9.6	10.1
France	20.4	17.6	17.3	14.5	12.9	11.0	12.5	13.6	13.6	13.9
Germany	12.1	12.8	12.7	11.4	12.3	12.8	13.8	12.8	11.6	11.7
Japan	20.8	17.9	16.7	15.8	15.6	13.0	12.1	13.1	12.8	13.1
United States	7.3	8.4	9.0	8.6	6.4	5.3	5.2	5.7	4.2	4.8

[a] Projected

Source: OECD Economic Outlook, June 1996, p. A29.

TABLE 9.3
Private Savings and Investment as a Percentage of GNP and Profit Shares in Selected OECD Countries

	1971–1980		1981–1990		Profit shares[a]		
Country/Sector	**Savings**	**Investment**	**Savings**	**Investment**	**1973**	**1980**	**1990**
United States							
Total	19.1	17.3	19.4	16.9	28.8	32.1	37.2
Households	10.7	7.5	10.3	7.0			
Corporate	8.4	9.8	9.1	9.9			
Japan							
Total	30.4	28.2	26.2	23.6	50.1	42.0	43.4
Households	17.9	10.3	14.9	7.5			
Corporate	12.6	17.9	11.3	16.1			
Germany							
Total	20.4	19.5	20.8	17.6	40.8	42.0	31.9
Households	8.7	———	7.9	———			
Corporate	11.8	———	12.9	———			
France							
Total	22.2	21.8	18.8	17.6	35.1	30.4	38.8
Households	13.6	10.0	9.8	7.4			
Corporate	8.6	11.8	9.0	9.9			
United Kingdom							
Total	15.3	15.7	15.5	15.7	31.8	31.3	36.2
Households	6.1	3.9	5.9	4.9			
Corporate	9.2	11.8	9.6	10.8			

Source: National Accounts Copyright OECD [various issues], *Historical Statistics* Copyright OECD [various issues]. In UN Conference on Trade and Development, *Trade and Development Report,* 1997 (New York: United Nations, 1997), Tables 42 and 43, pp. 107–108. The United Nations is the author of the original materials, and materials used with permission.

[a]Gross operating surplus as a percentage of gross value added in industry, transport, and communication

and security, as discussed by Strange, and the way in which a nation manages its affairs within these structures also determine its competitiveness. That the United States and Britain have lower savings rates should not be construed as a weakening of their competitiveness; however, a combination of variables in addition to savings and investment, such as declining productivity growth and chronic trade and budget deficits, may render their economies less competitive.[45] It may be that a hegemonic state tends to save less and consume more to maintain its dominant position in international trade and the world political economy in general.

Currency exchange rates also are said to enhance a country's economic competitiveness. According to this view, a country can rectify its trade imbalances by adjusting the currency rates. In the 1980s, the Reagan administration adopted this approach to address the trade deficit problem, devaluing the dollar in relation to currencies with more favorable trade standing.[46] The extent to which a currency's exchange rate and interest rates seriously enhance long-term competitiveness is debatable, however, even if there are instances of correlation between a lower exchange value and an increase in exports. During the Reagan administration, the U.S. trade deficit did not improve, even as increases in the interest rate attracted foreign investment.[47] The slight improvement in the U.S. motor vehicle trade deficit in the early 1990s might be attributable to the lower value of the dollar relative to the Japanese yen, but the key to enduring competitiveness would be enhanced productivity and better-quality products suited for appropriate markets. Some of these issues are discussed in the following section.

Thus, while useful in illuminating some aspects of international competitiveness, these macroeconomics theories in and of themselves are not sufficient to explain international competitiveness, nor are they necessarily useful in practice for purposes of economic policy. Such explanations appear over simplified as one takes into consideration the globalized networks of MNC production in high- and low-wage countries.[48] However, despite their shortcomings, a combination of these theories and the theories presented in Chapter 2 provides the intellectual tools necessary for a general understanding of competitiveness.

STRATEGIC INDUSTRIES AND THE PURSUIT OF THE COMPETITIVE EDGE

Historically very few countries have had the geographic, social, and economic advantages to emerge as competitive in the global political economy. According to some observers, international competitiveness does not mean being competitive in all areas but, rather, in *strategically* select industries that enable firms from one country to capture a relatively large share of the market in another. *Strategic competitiveness,* nevertheless, requires vast human and financial resources and infrastructural capabilities to manufacture technologically advanced and internationally competitive products for intensely competitive world markets.[49] It is well beyond the purview of this chapter to present and discuss an exhaustive list of all strategic industries. Such a list, however, would certainly include important industries such as transportation, metals and composite materials, medical technology, microelectronics, telecommunications, robotics, civil aviation, space technology, and various aspects of computers.[50] Box 7.3 in Chapter 7 showed the leading MNCs ranked by foreign assets in 1995. Suffice it here to note that 30 percent of the MNCs listed were U.S.-based, six of them among the top twenty, followed by Japan's 18 percent, three of which were among the top twenty. The major industries represented on that list included oil, gas, and coal; automotive; electronics; food; chemicals and pharmaceuticals; and computers.

For purposes of illustration, here we focus on a small sample of key industries—the steel industry, motor vehicles, semiconductors, computers, and medical technology—followed by the service sector, and base our discussion on two indices, production shares and export shares, which together indicate with some accuracy the overall level of the major industrialized nations' economic competitiveness in world markets.

Productivity and Production Shares

Before discussing production shares, however, and to avoid confusion it is useful to define productivity. *Productivity* is "the ratio of output to one or more inputs."[51] Productivity growth increases when output is greater than input; productivity growth drops when output is less than input:

> Economic growth can be achieved through increases in the quantity of inputs or productivity growth. Increases in labor, capital, and material inputs impose costs on society such as leisure time, lower current time, lower current consumption (because of increased investment), and lower reserves of natural resources. Productivity growth represents increases in output not attributable to increases in factor inputs. Therefore, productivity growth is the primary measure of changes in the efficiency of the economy. Without productivity growth there are few means of permanently raising the well-being of the average worker. Given finite resources, a lack of productivity growth would mean that economic changes would largely reflect shifts in the distribution of resources and wealth across the population.[52]

Several factors can contribute to productivity growth, including a greater pool of skilled workers, the effective use of managerial skills, effective application of technology, economic openness, investments in human capital, and technological change.[53] Productivity growth is a key ingredient in international competitiveness; it is essential for a nation's ability to meet the tests and tastes of global markets, as well as for the growth of real incomes.[54] It reflects a nation's successful application of all resources at its disposal, though measurement can mask employment problems, as when large numbers of workers are dismissed and greater demands are made of those remaining, all in the name of productivity. In the globalized world economy, productivity growth must be viewed in relative terms; one nation's rate of productivity growth "must compare favorably with those of major foreign competitors."[55]

Salgado's study on productivity growth found that, from 1973 to 1995 average annual growth rates of real GDP in the United States dropped to 2.3 percent and labor productivity to 0.8 percent. Salgado argued that the decline in output growth was closely correlated with the decline in labor productivity growth. Several factors contributed to the slowdown, including lower levels of capital accumulation, transition from manufacturing to the services sector, failure by some industries to benefit from the technological advances, and capital obsolescence due to structural changes and government regulations.[56] Allen has pointed to the failure of American companies to make full use of the information technology to enhance productivity growth. The widespread use of computers and greater investments in information technology were expected to increase productivity growth while leading to decline in employment levels. Allen notes, however, that recent studies show little relationship between investment in information technology and productivity growth, including employment levels. Some companies increased both employment and labor productivity, while others downsized and lost labor productivity. The use of information technology should have enhanced productivity growth and reduced labor. According to Allen, one explanation for this underutility may be that companies invest in a new technology as its use becomes less restrictive and less expensive (see also Chapter 8). Thus, in the early stages of diffusion, "monopoly rights or incomplete information," coupled with relatively high cost, may discourage high rates of investment in the new technology.[57]

Table 9.4 shows the annual percent change in hourly earnings, productivity, and unit labor costs in manufacturing. Most glaring in the table are the lower levels of hourly earnings rates and the negative shifts in labor costs after 1993, while productivity growth, with few exceptions, registered positive results. During the period between 1989 and 1996, both the United States and Germany consistently had positive productive growth, although German productivity growth rate was also consistently (and in 1994 considerably) higher than that of the United States.

Contrary to the negative forecasts prevalent in the 1980s and the early 1990s of the total loss of U.S. competitive edge, some studies indicated that this was not necessarily the case, as the United States, Japan, and the other advanced economies developed their own comparative advantages in different sectors, ranging from technology-intensive industries, such as information technologies, chemicals, and pharmaceuticals, to labor-intensive industries, such as natural resources and lumber.[58] These findings have underscored the point that productivity is closely related to comparative advantage and international trade relations.

As discussed in previous chapters, Britain began to experience a precipitous decline in its global power during the early decades of the twentieth century, and its declining productivity levels, especially in comparison with those of the other major powers, directly contributed to the empire's diminishing competitiveness (see raw production figures in Table 9.5). Even before the Second World War was over, British manufacturing production levels had been surpassed by all major powers except France, itself a declining empire. In the aircraft industry, for example, after the Second World War, the United States took British inventions (e.g., radar) and produced and commercialized them faster than the British. As a result, while the U.S. aircraft industry created opportunities for jobs and better standards of living in the United States, it eliminated opportunities for similar growth in Britain.[59] Three decades later, however, the United States began to experience its own relative decline, as a united European Community, including Britain, began to challenge U.S. production and market shares worldwide.[60] The competition in the steel industry is illustrative.

The Steel Industry The steel industry has long been considered an indispensable component of both economic (industrial) power and international competitiveness. Steel is considered one of the most important indicators of a country's power potential in the industrial era, since it is used for both consumer goods and military hardware. Although other materials are now used for such products as well, it is no coincidence that the major producers of steel are also the major industrialized and military powers. World production of steel rose from 313 million metric tons in the mid-1950s to 800 million metric tons in 1994.[61] By the mid-1980s, the U.S. share of world production had begun to shrink, declining from 37 percent in 1956 to 11.1 percent in 1985 (see Figure 9.1),[62] and stabilizing at about 12.5 percent in the mid-1990s.[63]

Meanwhile, as shown in Figure 9.1, Europe's share of world steel production increased from 28 percent in 1956 to 30 percent in 1960, but thereafter it declined to about 20 percent in the mid-1980s.[64] The picture improved slightly in the early 1990s, from 17.8 percent in 1992 to 19.2 percent in 1994.[65] Germany, the largest producer of steel in Europe, produced about 5–6 percent of world production in the early 1990s, while the British and French shares stood at about 2.5 percent each.[66] Japan's share of world steel production also rose in the post-WWII reconstruction period, from about 5 percent in the mid-1950s to nearly 18 percent in the 1970s and 1980s, at about 150 million metric tons per year.[67] By the early 1990s, however, its share had dropped from 14 percent (121 million metric tons) in 1990 to 13.5 percent (108 million metric tons) in 1994.[68]

The drops in production had serious consequences for jobs in the steel industry and standards of living in communities dependent on it. For example, between 1974 and 1988, U.S. employment in this sector declined precipitously from 478,00 to 170,000 (see Figure 9.2),[69] and, as expected by the productivity growth argument, although production increased in the early 1990s, the level of employment continued to fall, from 164,000 in 1990 to 126,000 in 1994.[70] Employment in the European and Japanese steel industries also declined. In Britain, it dropped from about 280,000 in the late 1960s to about 50,000 in the 1980s, and, in France, from 150,000–160,000 in the early 1970s to 50,000 in the mid-1980s. The decline in employment in the German and Japanese steel industries was not as severe as in Britain and the United States, but overall these losses contributed to chronic unemployment, especially in the European Union.

On the one hand, it can be argued that steel is no longer as relevant to post industrial economic growth as it had been in the age of railroads and Fordist production

TABLE 9.4

Advanced Economies: Hourly Earnings, Productivity, and Unit Labor Costs in Manufacturing, 1979–1998 (1997 and 1998 Projections)

	Average 1979–1988	1989	1990	1991	1992	1993	1994	1995	1996	1997	1998
Hourly Earnings											
Advanced economies	8.1	6.4	6.2	6.2	5.5	3.1	3.1	3.7	3.7	3.2	3.7
Major industrial countries	7.2	5.1	5.8	6.1	5.2	3.3	2.8	3.6	3.3	2.8	3.4
United States	6.4	3.3	4.7	5.3	4.4	2.4	2.8	3.6	3.6	2.9	3.5
Japan	3.9	6.7	6.5	5.9	4.6	2.6	2.7	2.5	1.7	1.3	3.1
Germany[a]	5.3	4.2	5.7	7.3	9.6	6.8	2.0	4.2	3.2	2.3	3.0
France	9.8	4.8	4.8	5.4	4.6	3.3	3.7	2.5	2.6	2.9	3.2
Italy	14.6	9.7	8.5	9.7	7.2	5.0	2.1	6.3	5.3	4.3	4.0
United Kingdom	11.0	9.0	9.0	8.0	5.1	4.3	4.4	5.1	3.7	4.3	4.9
Canada	6.5	5.3	5.2	4.7	3.5	2.1	1.6	1.4	3.2	3.0	1.9
Other advanced economies	12.5	12.7	8.3	6.4	6.8	2.1	4.4	4.4	5.8	4.9	4.9
Various groupings											
Industrial countries	7.5	5.5	6.1	6.3	5.4	3.4	2.9	3.6	3.4	2.9	3.4
European Union	9.6	7.2	7.2	7.6	7.0	5.0	3.2	4.3	3.7	3.5	3.7
Newly industrialized Asian economies	11.8	29.7	9.4	2.1	8.0	−5.4	6.2	4.7	8.6	6.9	7.5
Productivity											
Advanced economies	3.2	3.5	1.9	1.8	2.4	1.5	4.6	3.6	3.0	2.5	2.5
Major industrial countries	3.0	2.9	2.2	2.1	2.4	1.6	4.6	3.6	3.0	2.5	2.5
United States	2.5	1.8	1.8	2.5	3.4	2.1	3.2	3.3	4.0	2.6	2.3
Japan	3.2	4.5	2.8	1.5	−3.7	−1.6	3.5	4.9	3.9	2.7	3.4
Germany[a]	2.8	3.1	3.5	2.9	4.0	3.3	8.7	4.0	4.2	3.0	3.0
France	4.2	5.1	1.5	1.3	4.2	−0.2	8.9	3.0	2.0	3.4	2.4
Italy	4.5	3.0	1.4	1.3	3.9	1.9	5.6	6.9	−1.1	1.7	1.8
United Kingdom	3.7	4.4	2.2	2.1	4.3	4.7	4.4	1.9	−0.3	0.9	2.4
Canada	1.4	0.5	3.3	1.0	4.3	3.1	3.8	−0.9	0.9	1.0	1.1

Continued

[a]Data through 1991 apply to West Germany only

Source: IMF, *World Economic Outlook, May 1997* (Washington, DC: IMF, 1997), Table A10, p. 144.

TABLE 9.4 (concluded)

Advanced Economies: Hourly Earnings, Productivity, and Unit Labor Costs in Manufacturing, 1979–1998 (1997 and 1998 Projections)

	Average 1979–1988	1989	1990	1991	1992	1993	1994	1995	1996	1997	1998
Other advanced economies	3.8	6.2	0.6	0.4	2.3	1.1	4.9	3.9	2.9	2.8	2.5
Various groupings											
Industrial countries	3.1	3.1	1.9	2.9	2.4	1.9	4.8	3.6	2.9	2.5	2.4
European Union	3.8	4.3	1.9	2.0	3.7	3.0	7.1	3.9	1.5	2.4	2.3
Newly industrialized Asian economies	6.2	13.1	—	−4.4	1.3	−6.9	2.4	5.3	5.1	3.7	4.0
Unit Labor Costs											
Advanced economies	4.8	2.9	4.3	4.3	3.1	1.5	−1.5	0.1	0.7	0.6	1.1
Major industrial countries	4.1	2.1	3.5	4.0	2.8	−1.7	1.7	—	0.3	0.3	0.9
United States	3.8	1.5	2.9	2.7	0.9	0.3	−0.4	0.3	−0.3	0.3	1.2
Japan	0.7	2.0	3.5	4.3	8.6	4.3	−0.7	−2.3	−2.1	−1.4	−0.4
Germany[a]	2.5	1.0	2.1	4.2	5.4	3.4	−6.2	0.2	−1.0	−0.7	—
France	5.3	−0.3	3.3	4.0	0.3	3.6	−4.8	−0.5	0.6	−0.5	0.7
Italy	9.6	6.5	7.1	5.3	3.2	3.0	−3.3	−0.6	6.4	2.5	2.1
United Kingdom	7.0	4.4	6.7	5.7	0.7	−0.4	—	3.1	4.0	3.4	2.4
Canada	5.0	−4.8	1.8	3.7	−0.8	−1.0	−2.1	2.2	2.3	2.0	0.8
Other advanced economies	3.1	6.1	7.5	5.6	4.1	1.0	−0.6	0.3	2.5	1.8	2.0
Various groupings											
Industrial countries	4.3	2.3	4.0	4.2	3.0	1.5	−1.7	0.1	0.6	0.5	1.0
European Union	5.6	2.8	5.3	5.6	3.2	2.0	−3.5	0.5	2.2	1.1	1.4
Newly industrialized Asian economies	4.3	13.6	8.4	5.1	4.8	1.3	2.2	−1.5	2.2	2.2	2.4

TABLE 9.5
Annual Indices of Manafacturing Production, 1913–1938 (1913=100)

	World	United States	Germany	UK	France	USSR	Italy	Japan
1913	100.0	100.0	100.0	100.0	100.0	100.0	100.0	100.0
1920	93.2	122.2	59.0	92.6	70.4	12.8	95.2	176.0
1921	81.1	98.0	74.7	55.1	61.4	23.2	98.4	167.1
1922	99.5	125.8	81.8	73.5	87.8	28.9	108.1	197.9
1923	104.5	141.4	55.4	79.1	95.2	35.4	119.3	206.4
1924	111.0	133.2	81.8	87.8	117.9	47.5	140.7	223.3
1925	120.7	148.0	94.9	86.3	114.3	70.2	156.8	221.8
1926	126.5	156.1	90.9	78.8	129.8	100.3	162.8	264.9
1927	134.5	154.5	122.1	96.0	115.6	114.5	161.2	270.0
1928	141.8	162.8	118.3	95.1	134.4	143.5	175.2	300.2
1929	153.3	180.8	117.3	100.3	142.7	181.4	181.0	324.0
1930	137.5	148.0	101.6	91.3	139.9	235.5	164.0	294.9
1931	122.5	121.6	85.1	82.4	122.6	293.9	145.1	288.1
1932	108.4	93.7	70.2	82.5	105.4	326.1	123.3	309.1
1933	121.7	111.8	79.4	83.3	119.8	363.2	133.2	360.7
1934	136.4	121.6	101.8	100.2	111.4	437.0	134.7	413.5
1935	154.5	140.3	116.7	107.9	109.1	533.7	162.2	457.8
1936	178.1	171.0	127.5	119.1	116.3	693.3	169.2	483.9
1937	195.8	185.8	138.1	127.8	123.8	772.2	194.5	551.0
1938	182.7	143.0	149.3	117.6	114.6	857.3	195.2	552.0

Sources: League of Nations, *World Economic Survey* (Geneva: League of Nations, 1945), Table III, p. 134. Table 28 in Paul Kennedy, *The Rise and Fall of Major Powers* (New York: Random House, 1987), p. 299. The United Nations is the author of the original materials, and materials used with permission.

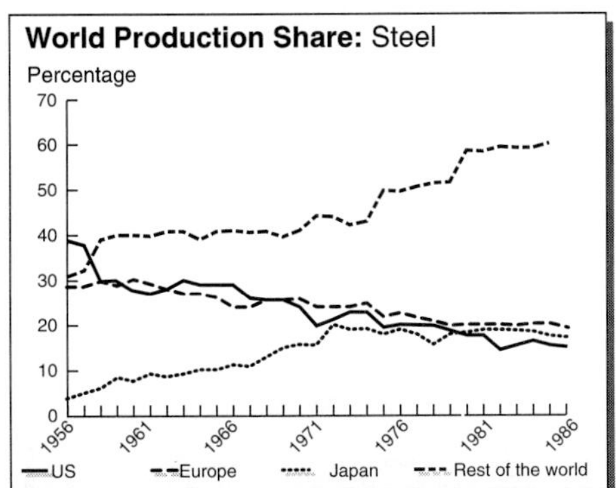

FIGURE 9.1 Steel Production
Source: American Iron and Steel Institute, Annual Statistical Report (Washington, D.C., various years), in Jeffrey A. Hart, *Rival Capitalists: International Competitiveness in the United States, Japan, and Western Europe* (Ithaca: Cornell University Press, 1992), p. 13.

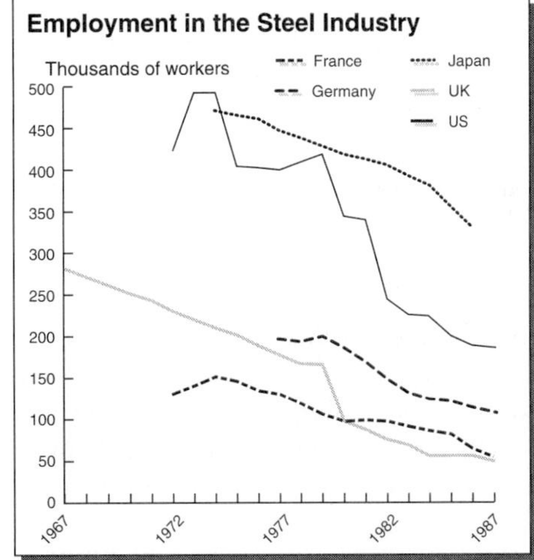

FIGURE 9.2 Employment in the Steel Industry
Source: Jeffrey A. Hart, *Rival Capitalists: International Competitiveness in the United States, Japan, and Western Europe* (Ithaca: Cornell University Press, 1992), p. 16.

structures. At the same time, however, it is also true that, despite the technological changes, steel, along with a host of other "industrial" and strategic materials, remains an essential commodity for manufacturing, for both civilian and military purposes.[71] In the long run, the employment difficulties experienced in this sector may be seen as related to the transition during the past two decades from manufacturing-based to service-based employment and the structural transformations brought about by corporate mergers and technological changes.

The Motor Vehicles Industry In addition to the high-technology milieu of semiconductors and computers, nothing has so intensely captivated the spirit of international competitiveness as the auto industry, which is, of course, related to the steel industry. The technological advances and intense competition for world markets in this sector in recent decades have been received by the public as the epitome of national competitiveness. Most other major U.S. industries, for example, such as computers, do not have the same emotional pull as the auto industry. GM's convertible Chevy and Ford's Mustang have a long-held sentimental value cultivated through years of TV commercials and Hollywood films. The computer industry has not had sufficient time yet to cultivate such an emotional bond. GM and Ford continue to be viewed as national icons of "Americanness," even when in reality they have many international partners and products. A country's production and marketing capabilities for motor vehicles (cars, vans, light and heavy trucks, buses) bear nameplates as symbols of national competitiveness and pride when successful, or lead to soul-searching, resentment, and outright hostility toward competitors and foreigners when challenged—as demonstrated by some members of the U.S. Congress smashing Toyotas in front of the Capitol.

Of course, competitiveness and nationalism do not become serious issues when markets are expanding, production levels are high, and people, even semi-skilled workers, have relatively high-paying jobs. They do become serious political problems, however, when jobs are adversely affected by changes in structures of production and in the distribution of domestic and international resources, as experienced by the Western economies in the 1970s and 1980s. Total world production of motor vehicles increased at an average of about 5 percent per year between the mid-1950s and the mid-1990s, from about 14 million vehicles in 1959 to nearly 50 million in the early 1990s.[72] At the same time, the U.S. share of world production fell from nearly 70 percent in the mid-1950s to about 25 percent in the 1980s and early 1990s. The U.S. share in passenger car production declined by about two-thirds after the 1970s. Meanwhile, Europe's share rose from approximately 20 percent in 1950 to 50 percent in the 1960s, but by the mid-1970s dropped back to about 32 percent. However, while Europe as a region had surpassed the United States, each European country still lagged behind the United States and Japan. Britain, for example, fell completely out of the domestic auto business, as its companies closed, merged, or were bought out by foreign corporations.

As seen in Figure 9.3, Japan's share of world production in motor vehicles increased from about 1 percent in the 1950s to about 21 percent in the mid-1970s, and to about 28 percent in the 1980s. Although by the early 1980s Japan's share of production had surpassed the United States', in the early 1990s its share receded to about 22 percent, as other nearby Asian states, such as South Korea, emerged as viable, cost-cutting producers. Japan and the U.S. continued to vie for the production lead throughout the 1990s.

The motor vehicle industry is an essential economic sector of the industrialized and industrializing economies, and direct and indirect employment levels play an important role in their overall economic well-being. In the United States in the 1980s, for example, an estimated 6.7 million employees were directly and indirectly employed by the motor vehicle and related automotive industries, comprising 6.2 percent of nonagricultural employment. Foreign competition, restructuring of production (for example, informalization, outsourcing, and automation), and declining levels of production and sales in the 1980s severely affected employment as thousands were laid off. Employment dropped from 304,000 in the second half of the 1970s to 194,000 in the early 1980s, although by the mid-1980s, employment figures rebounded to about 250,000. According to some observers, the increase in the mid-1980s was the result of

FIGURE 9.3 World Production Share
Source: Motor Vehicle Manufacturers Association, *Motor Vehicle Facts and Figures* (Detroit, various years), in Jeffrey A. Hart, *Rival Capitalists: International Competitiveness in the United States, Japan, and Western Europe* (Ithaca: Cornell University Press, 1992), p. 13.

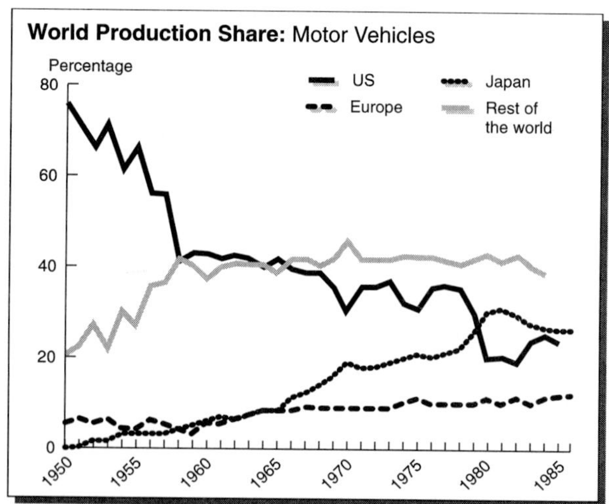

overall improved economy but also the result of the U.S.-Japan Voluntary Export Restraints (VERs) agreement. Further increases in the 1990s have mainly been due to American predominance in "specialty vehicles," such as sport utility minivans and light trucks. It is clear, however, that, among the five major economies, as Figure 9.4 shows, the United States experienced the most erratic fluctuations in employment levels in this industry.[73] The future technological challenge will come from alternate fuel vehicles, modular production techniques, and policy decisions in the area of public transportation.

The Semiconductor Industry The "high-technology" semiconductor (microchip) industry suffered a similar fate in Europe and the United States (see Figure 9.5). In the 1970s and 1980s, world production of semiconductors rose at about 18.8 percent per year, with Europe's share of the world production ranging from 15 to 20 percent. By the late 1980s, however, its share had steadily declined, hovering near 10 percent. The United States experienced nearly as great a drop. In the mid-1970s, the United States was the uncontested leader in the world semiconductor business, at about 70 percent of the world's production; a decade later, with Japan's upsurge, that figure had dropped to 40 percent. Japan's share increased from an annual average of about 27 percent in the early 1970s to nearly 50 percent in the mid-1980s. The United States recovered a degree of competitiveness in this field as well vis-à-vis Japan in the 1990s, suggesting that basic industries may in fact benefit from increased cross-national competition.[74]

Among the East Asian manufacturers, it was not Japan but South Korea that registered the highest rate of increase during the late 1980s and early 1990s. In the mid-1980s, the South Korean semiconductor production rate was about \$600 million per year; by 1992, that figure had climbed to \$3.3 billion—a 450 percent growth. By 1993, Samsung had emerged as the world's largest producer of DRAMs (dynamic random access memories), at 25 percent share of the world market.[75]

The manufacture of semiconductors requires huge investments in skilled human and sophisticated technical resources. The costs of building and operating manufacturing plants and R&D are extremely high, and they have become more expensive with time. In 1990, a DRAM manufacturing plant cost about \$400 million; by 1994, the cost had risen to over \$1 billion. However, competitiveness also requires that prices remain accessible. In the case of the U.S. semiconductor industry, between 1980 and 1992, companies spent an average 12 percent of revenues per year on R&D and 14 percent on advanced equipment, above the average of most other industries,[76] yet competition kept prices low,[77] as companies minimized their expenditures through inter-firm cost sharing, strategic alliances and partnerships, and layoffs.

In the 1970s and early 1980s, the industrialized countries experienced major increases in jobs in this sector.

FIGURE 9.4 Employment in the Motor Vehicles Industry
Source: Jeffrey A. Hart, *Rival Capitalists: International Competitiveness in the United States, Japan, and Western Europe* (Ithaca: Cornell University Press, 1992), p. 16.

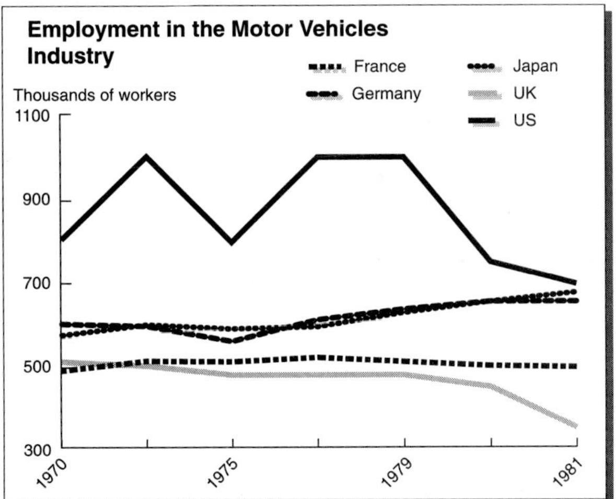

FIGURE 9.5 World Production Share
Source: Jeffrey A. Hart, *Rival Capitalists: International Competitiveness in the United States, Japan, and Western Europe* (Ithaca: Cornell University Press, 1992), p. 13.

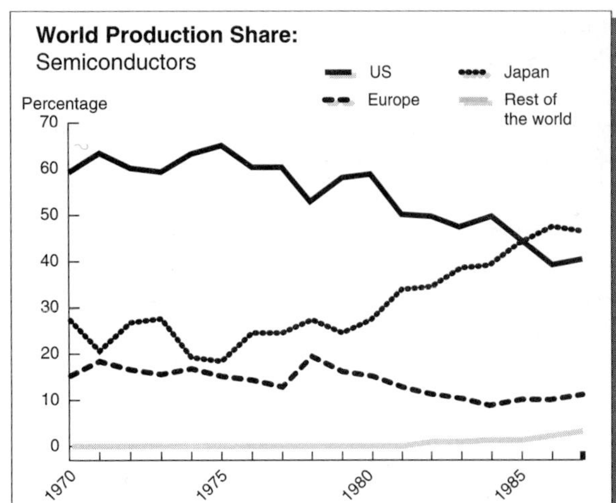

Employment in Japan's overall electronics industry rose from 948,000 in 1982 to 1,212,000 in 1986.[78] In France and Germany, employment in the semiconductor industry increased from 130,000 to 200,000, and from 108,000 to 153,000, respectively;[79] in Britain, it dropped from 182,000 to 164,000. By the early 1990s, as the productivity growth thesis suggests, largely due to improved efficiency in production, employment declined rapidly, despite increased sales. In 1987, for example, total U.S. employment in this sector was 546,000, but by 1992 that figure had dropped to 496,000 and to 479,000 in 1993.[80]

While it may seem obvious, it should be emphasized that high productivity growth and production levels alone cannot make a nation competitive. A nation can produce at high levels while reducing employment, but, if the produced goods are not marketable at home and abroad, high levels of production can hardly make that country competitive. Its ability to export on a sustained basis is an essential part of the process. However, theorists disagree on the direction (or cause and effect) of the production-export relationship. For example, laissez-faire capitalist theorists, emphasizing supply and demand, believe that increases in exports (that is, demand) lead to increases in production (supply). The market determines the quality and quantity of production. Marxist and world system theorists, on the other hand, argue that it is surplus production that fuels exports in search of markets abroad and that an MNC's international competitiveness is determined by its ability to exploit human and natural resources and to control greater shares of the world market. However, it may increasingly be the case that, as more companies adopt automation, increases in production, exports, and trade surpluses no longer contribute to national economic well-being. Automation and related technological progress in production may enhance competitiveness and productivity growth, but a disproportionately large share of the economic rewards derived from competitiveness may be confined to a small group of investors and managers. Culture may enter here as well; traditionally the salary gap between executives and workers in the United States has been substantially greater than in Japan, for example, and the Japanese have been more likely to keep workers employed rather than to "downsize." Price competition has put increased pressure on Japanese firms to abandon some of these traditions, however.

Export Shares

Exports have increasingly become an important part of the world economy, and a nation's export activity signifies its international competitiveness. The United States clearly dominated the world export share for over a decade after the Second World War. In the late 1960s, its share began to decline relative to European and Asian economies as they recovered from the war's devastation and rebuilt their factories, markets, finances, and infrastructure. As seen in Table 9.6, however, the U.S. share of world exports in goods and services has remained dominant, despite the increases in German and Japanese shares. Germany narrowed the gap somewhat in the 1970s and, along with Japan, in the first half of the 1990s, but their share consistently declined thereafter. Among the other European economies, both the British and French shares in world exports also shrank consistently during the last two decades of the twentieth century, although Britain recovered slightly in 1996. Only Italy experienced continuous growth, from 4.4 percent in the 1970s to 5.0 percent in 1996.[81]

Two points must be stressed here with respect to the export figures presented in Table 9.6. First, while the numbers are important, they must be viewed within the context of overall trade balances. As discussed in Chapter 5, the United States has consistently registered trade deficits for the past two decades, while Germany and Japan have had huge trade surpluses. Second, not all economies rely equally on exports. In 1992, U.S. and Japanese exports of goods and services comprised 10 percent of their national GDPs, German and British 24 percent, and French 23 percent.[82]

As for various high-technology export sectors, such as motor vehicles, computers, semiconductors, and medical technology, international competition has grown particularly intense. The following section briefly reviews these sectors.

Motor Vehicles According to market projections, the domestic market for passenger cars in the United States appears to be saturated, and it is expected to grow no more than 2 percent for the next decade. Traditionally, the gargantuan domestic market afforded the U.S. auto companies the luxury of concentrating their product lines, sales, and marketing energies at home. Exports appeared desirable but not essential. Intensification of worldwide operations and markets, however, placed enormous pressures on companies to strengthen their competitive position at home and abroad, especially as foreign companies began to invest heavily in the United States, and as U.S. companies' shares of the domestic and world markets shrank,[83] as indicated by the substantial increase in the U.S. motor vehicles trade deficit since the late 1980s. In 1993, U.S. vehicle exports totaled about $20 billion and, in 1994, about $22 billion. Imports increased from $63 billion to $66 billion for the same years, raising the trade

TABLE 9.6
Selected Economies: World Export Market Shares, 1970-1998
(Percentage of World Exports of Goods and Services)

	1970–1979	1980–1989	1990–1994	1995	1996	Projections 1997	Projections 1998
United States	12.4	12.2	13.1	12.6	12.8	13.2	13.2
Japan	6.3	7.9	8.1	7.9	7.2	6.8	6.7
Germany	10.3	9.7	10.3	9.8	9.4	8.8	8.7
France	7.0	6.6	6.4	5.9	5.7	5.4	5.4
Italy	4.4	4.4	4.9	4.8	5.0	4.8	4.7
United Kingdom	6.0	5.6	5.3	5.0	5.1	5.2	5.1

Source: IMF, *World Economic Outlook, May 1997,* Table 8, p. 41.

deficit from $43 billion to $44 billion.[84] Canada, the destination of 58 percent of American auto exports, was the largest market, importing 750,611 vehicles from the United States, with a total value of $11.1 billion in 1994.

As Table 9.7 illustrates, U.S. vehicle imports increased far more rapidly. In a single decade (1966–1976), imports quadrupled, and they doubled during the next decade. In the mid-1990s, the United States imported at least three times as many motor vehicles as it exported. Canada, the largest market for U.S. exports, and Japan have been the two primary suppliers of passenger cars to the U.S. market since the late 1960s.[85] In the late 1960s, Canada briefly became the number one exporter of passenger cars to the United States,[86] but, since the mid-1970s, Japan has dominated the U.S. market.[87]

Japanese motor vehicle exports also continued to challenge the United States and the EU in most countries around the world, with Toyota's foreign sales of $41.1 billion in 1993. Table 9.8 presents data for 1994 exports of passenger cars to illustrate the magnitude of the gap among major industrialized economies' international competitiveness in this industry. In some regions, such as Europe, competition was intense, but, in other areas, such as the Middle East, Japanese exports continued to dominate.[88]

Computers The computer industry has been one of the fastest growing economic sectors in the past two decades, led by more than 100 computer companies worldwide. In 1992, the top 100 companies registered over $318 billion in sales, with U.S. computer manufacturers holding the largest share, 61 percent, of the world market, followed by Japan's 25 percent, 2 percent lower than in previous years. U.S. and European firms, especially the latter, have concentrated on computer software, peripherals (printers, graphics), and services. In 1991, for example, they received 46 percent and 58 percent, respectively, of their total revenues from software. Their Japanese and East Asian counterparts, on the other hand, have focused primarily on computer hardware and equipment.[89]

However, in the computer industry as well, the U.S. position no longer seems secure. While in 1982 the United States led the world in total computer production at about $32 billion, followed by Europe's $18 billion, by the early 1990s Europe had clearly emerged as the leading computer producer worldwide. In 1992, Europe produced about $70 billion worth of computers, the United States $50 billion. Europe's computer exports data, however, which are usually about 20 percent of EU-produced computers, did not reflect Euro production capability, as the major markets are within the EU itself. In 1982, the United States exported nearly $9 billion worth of computers, followed by Europe's $5 billion. A decade later, U.S. computer exports increased to $26 billion, while Europe's remained around $15 billion (see Figure 9.6). The Japanese computer industry proved more successful in exports. In 1982, it ranked third in computer exports at about $3 billion. A decade later, its computer exports had increased 21 percent per year, making Japan the second largest exporter, with a total export value of $25 billion, slightly lower than the United States'.[90]

Despite the increase in U.S. production, the United States continued to register trade deficits in the 1990s. In 1989, the total value of U.S. computer exports was $22.4 billion and imports $21.7 billion, leaving a trade surplus of $0.7 billion. By the mid-1990s, however, the trade deficit increased to $17 billion,[91] a substantial portion with Japan and the East Asian NICs.[92] Japan was the single largest supplier of computers to the U.S. market and, together with the East Asian NICs as a region, accounted for 70 percent of all computer imports to the United States in 1993.[93] Total employment in the U.S. computer industry dropped from nearly 290,000 in 1987 to 190,000 in 1994.[94]

TABLE 9.7
Motor Vehicle Trade, 1966–1994 (Number of Units)

	1966	1970	1976	1980	1986	1990	1994
Britain							
Import	69,476	168,293	561,269	936,810	1,194,180	1,279,856	1,069,603[b]
Export	721,968	862,726	683,899	481,027	245,626	510,326	718,241
Balance	*+652,492*	*+694,433*	*+122,630*	*−455,783*	*−948,554*	*−769,530*	*−351,362*
France							
Import	201,252	327,561	695,933	790,129	1,161,272	1,550,960	1,379,340
Export	787,434	1,525,422	2,085,974	2,218,950	1,994,124	2,315,948	2,428,530
Balance	*+586,182*	*+1,197,861*	*+1,390,041*	*+1,428,821*	*+832,852*	*+764,988*	*+1,049,190*
Germany							
Import	359,876	682,734	883,165	1,075,688	1,379,125	1,959,203	1,774,695
Export	1,637,424	2,103,948	2,043,220	2,084,254	2,693,739	2,765,645	2,410,297
Balance	*+1,277,548*	*+1,421,214*	*+1,160,055*	*+1,008,566*	*+1,314,614*	*+806,442*	*+635,602*
Japan							
Import	15,754	19,552	41,028	47,917	74,262	252,841	310,608
Export	255,734	1,086,776	3,709,608	5,966,961	6,604,923	5,831,212	4,460,292
Balance	*+239,980*	*+1,067,224*	*+3,668,580*	*+5,919,044*	*+6,530,661*	*+5,578,371*	*+4,149,684*
United States							
Import	594,566[a]	2,167,091	2,701,292	3,459,800	6,042,638	4,710,610	4,804,652
Export	256,529	379,089	880,778	807,169	881,583	953,065	1,293,185
Balance	*−338,037*	*−1,788,002*	*−1,820,514*	*−2,652,631*	*−5,161,055*	*−3,757,545*	*−3,511,467*

Source: American Automobile Manufacturers Association, *World Motor Vehicle Data,* 1996.
[a] 1965
[b] 1993

Semiconductors International competition in the semiconductor industry has been equally intense, and the semiconductor market, especially that of the EU, has been aptly characterized as a "battleground for competition among the global semiconductor giants."[95] The United States clearly retains the largest share of the EU semiconductor market, followed by the EU, Japan, and South Korea.

Since the late 1980s, worldwide semiconductor exports have grown rapidly, but in this case, too, the U.S. trade deficit has increased. In 1989, the total value of U.S. semiconductor exports was $9.5 billion, which increased to about $16 billion in the mid-1990s, but the U.S. trade deficit in this sector was about $3.8 billion.[96] Most of the increases in sales were in North America and Pacific Asia, and the latter remained the United States' largest semiconductor trading partner, accounting for well over 50 percent of U.S. semiconductor imports and exports.[97] Canada and Mexico were the second largest destinations for U.S. semiconductors ($2.1 billion, or 18 percent), followed by the European Union ($1.6 billion, or 14 percent).

The largest share of the U.S. trade deficit was with Japan, at about $3.4 billion,[98] accounting for 28 percent of U.S. semiconductor imports, and the deficit increased to $3.7 billion in 1993. Semiconductor imports from the East Asian NICs accounted for about 45 percent ($6.9 billion) of U.S. semiconductor imports in 1992, a deficit of $1 billion. The "four tigers" (Hong Kong, Singapore, South Korea, and Taiwan), China, and Malaysia together registered the highest levels of growth in the first half of the 1990s, by nearly 23 percent in a single year (for example, in 1993).[99]

In 1991, the U.S.-Japan Semiconductor Arrangement raised expectations that foreign companies would gain at least 20 percent of Japan's domestic market share; while the following year they captured 20.2 percent, it fell to 19.1 percent in 1993.[100] For the rest of the 1990s, Japan and the United States were locked in competition for global leadership in the semiconductor industry. The economic crisis in 1997–1998 strengthened the U.S. dollar relative to the yen and made East Asian goods more attractive to consumers in the United States and Europe. While this threatened to enlarge the U.S. trade deficit further, failure to reverse the East Asian economic slowdown may in the long run have serious repercussions for Japan's and the NICs' position in international competition, as the rapid

TABLE 9.8
Passenger Car Exports and the Competitive Edge, 1994 (in Units)

	To Europe			To Middle East			To Latin America		
	Germany	France	Britain	Saudi Arabia	Israel	UAE	Argentina	Brazil	Chile
Britain	103,857	91,999	———	669	843	na	1,631	153	407
France	297,865	———	356,273	1,388	15,264	na	33,535	5,053	10,156
Germany	———	257,712	246,537	2,913	11,655	3,999	3,190	11,757	5, 750
Japan	287,885	37,070	124,586	52,258	34,398	24,087	7,600	15,750	12,534
United States	39,568	6,083	27,748	18,587	11,044	6,653	5,179	15,839	4,071

	To North America			To Asia			To Africa		
	Canada	Mexico	United States	Japan	China	Malaysia	South Africa	Nigeria	Morocco
Britain	776	1	29,855	25,541	56	350	136	12	20
France	1,751	128	2,570	7,011	8,445	3,655	na	4,908	7,619
Germany	14,667	873	194,328	109,219	35,707	4,383	2,638	498	689
Japan	105,268	na	1,441,858	———	46,681	31,482	9,144	1,559	560
United States	559,513	36,569	———	100,400	6,397	17	267	566	65

Source: Adapted from American Automobile Manufacturers Association, *World Motor Vehicle Data, 1996.*

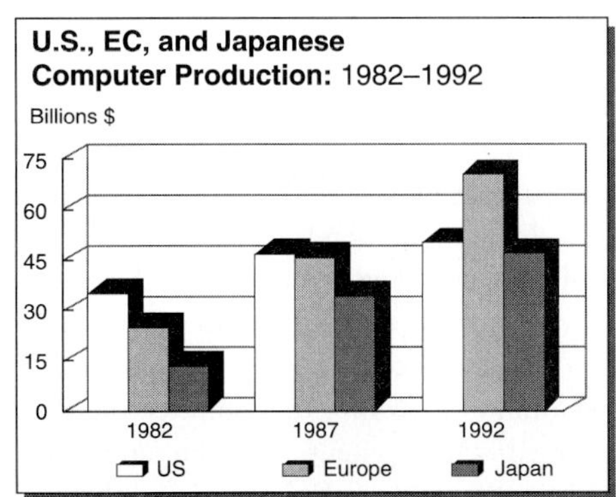

FIGURE 9.6 U.S., EC, and Japanese Computer Production 1982–199
Source: U.S. Industrial Outlook 1994, p. (26) 4.

technological changes require greater human and financial resources for investment in R&D and marketing.

No single European country was among the major U.S. trading partners in the semiconductor industry in the 1990s. The total value of EU semiconductor exports to the United States was $934 million, accounting for a mere 6.1 percent of the total U.S. semiconductor imports in 1992,[101] although the semiconductor market expanded by 14 percent, and production in overall electronics grew by about 5 percent in 1993.[102] That year marked a turning point in semiconductor market share for the EU, as East Asian markets performed better than the EU for the first time. Since the late 1980s, Japan and South Korea have considerably increased their semiconductor trade relations with the EU economies.[103]

Germany remains the strongest economy and, hence, the largest market in the EU, totaling about $4 billion per year in the 1990s, although German reunification was estimated to have resulted in nearly a 2 percent drop in economic growth in 1993.[104] Britain, however, is the largest market in Europe for U.S. semiconductors, expanding by nearly 15 percent in 1993 alone.[105] The British semiconductor market overall grew by 31 percent, with a total value of $4 billion in the early 1990s. The French and Italian semiconductor markets remain relatively smaller, valued at $1.5 billion and $1.3 billion, respectively.[106]

Medical Technology Despite the lack of attention paid to medical technology in public debates on international competitiveness, it is nevertheless as vast and important an industry as motor vehicles and computers. It includes medical equipment, such as advanced X-ray equipment, computer-tomography (C.T.) scanners, and surgical appliances, as well as pharmaceuticals. The pharmaceutical industry alone has been one of the most profitable and increasingly competitive businesses because of the rapidly changing bio-technologies and R&D; competition in this area has been dominated for years by the world's top pharmaceutical companies, such as Merck, Johnson & Johnson, Dow Chemical, DuPont, Glaxo, Funai, Ciba-Geigy, and Hoechst.[107]

Historically, the U.S. medical technology industry has fared better than the auto industry, in part because its competitive position in this sector has changed little since the 1940s. The United States has dominated this field, and it remains one of the major "strategic industry" sectors consistently registering trade surpluses. In the mid-1990s, when the U.S. semiconductor industry had a trade deficit of about $3.5 billion, the medical and dental equipment manufacturers generated a $3.5 billion trade surplus.[108]

In the mid-1980s, total world production of pharmaceuticals was $80 billion. The United States had the largest share at about 34 percent, followed by Japan's 24 percent. Among the European countries, Germany held 10 percent of the world total, Britain 6 percent, France 3 percent, and Italy 2 percent.[109] By the early 1990s, the United States was supplying 52 percent of the global market in medical equipment and about 50 percent of the pharmaceutical industry, including medicinals and botanicals, diagnostics, and biologicals.[110] International joint ventures and partnerships also emerged.

Despite Japan's protectionist policies restricting medical equipment imports (domestic producers maintain over 70 percent of the domestic market), in 1992 Japan was the largest consumer, importing about 13 percent ($988 million) of U.S. medical equipment and 14 percent ($963 million) of pharmaceuticals. In 1993, Japan's share of 21.9 percent ($1.02 billion) was the second largest after Germany in importing U.S. medical instruments and supplies.[111] Since the early 1980s, U.S. manufacturers have held about 21 percent of the Japanese market, and, as in the auto industry, limited access remains a major issue between the two countries, despite international agreements, such as the 1993 "Framework for a New Economic Partnership" and the Market-Oriented Sector-Selective Medical Device and Pharmaceutical (MOSS Med/Pharm) agreement to lower barriers.[112]

During the early 1990s, Canadian and Mexican imports of U.S. medical equipment accounted for 18 percent of United States total medical and dental equipment exports; Canadian imports alone accounted for 12 percent, the second largest market[113] (see Table 9.9). The combined value of their imports of U.S. pharmaceuticals was nearly $1 billion, or 15 percent, the second largest after the EU.[114] Under NAFTA, both Mexico and Canada are expected to become major partners for the United States in the manufacture and trade of medical equipment. In fact, between 1989 and 1993, U.S. exports to its southern neighbor increased from $63 million to $165 million. The Clinton administration hoped that NAFTA would lead to the creation of an approximately $32.7 billion market for medical equipment, "surpassing the EU as the world's largest market."[115]

During this period the European Union imported 40 percent of the U.S. world total medical and dental equipment exports[116] and about 50 percent (the highest) of all U.S. pharmaceutical exports, as it had been doing for years. In 1992, for example, the total value of U.S. pharmaceutical exports was $6.8 billion, $3.3 billion (or 48 percent) of which were imported by the EU. U.S. medical equipment manufacturers supplied 31 percent of the European Union's nearly $12 billion import market and were expected to increase their share at an annual average of 7 to 8 percent through the late 1990s. Among the EU countries, Germany's share of these imports was 10.8 percent (or $822 million), France's 6.1 percent ($465 million), and Britain's 5.9 percent (or $453 million).[117]

The United States, in turn, imported $4.67 billion worth of medical instruments and supplies from abroad in 1993. The major exporter to the United States was the EU, totaling $2.1 billion, or 44.7 percent, of U.S. imports that year. Germany held the largest share—24.7 percent—of the total U.S. imports, at a dollar value of $1.2 billion, Britain 5.1 percent ($239 million), and France 5.0 percent ($232 million). The top five exporters of medical equipment to the United States in 1993 also included Mexico, at about 10.8 percent (or $504 million), making that country the third largest supplier of medical equipment.[118] In the early 1990s, the EU was the largest exporter of pharmaceutical to the United States. In fact, in 1992 four of the five largest pharmaceutical exporters were European, including Britain (15.6 percent), Germany (14.6 percent), Switzerland (12.8 percent), and Ireland (6.9 percent). Japan was fourth, at a total value of $685 million (or 11.5 percent).[119]

In addition, these major competitors have opened up new arenas in certain regions. The disintegration of the Soviet bloc, for example, is most likely to lead to fierce competition—especially between the United States and Germany—in Central and Eastern Europe, as well as in the former Soviet republics.

TABLE 9.9
Medical Instruments and Supplies, 1992 (In Millions of Dollars/Percent Share)

	U.S. exports to		U.S. imports from	
	$ Value	Share (%)	$ Value	Share (%)
Canada/Mexico	1,335	17.5	660	14.2
EU	3,110	40.7	2,083	44.7
Japan	988	12.9	1,023	21.9
East Asia NICs	599	7.9	386	8.3
South America	337	4.4	12	0.3
Other	1,263	16.6	501	10.7
World total	7,632	100.0	4,665	100.0

Top Five Countries	U.S. exports to $ Value	Share (%)		U.S. imports from $Value	Share (%)
Japan	988	12.9	Germany	1,152	24.7
Canada	911	11.9	Japan	1,023	21.9
Germany	822	10.8	Mexico	504	10.8
France	465	6.1	UK	239	5.1
UK	453	5.9	France	232	5.0

Source: U.S. Industrial Outlook 1994, p. (44) 3; U.S. Department of Commerce: Bureau of the Census; International Trade Administration. Reprinted from the U.S. Industrial Outlook 1994.

The Service Sector and Postindustrial Competitiveness

The technological changes in telecommunications and transportation, as discussed in the preceding chapter, transformed the world economy, especially the FIEs, from the Fordist style of manufacturing to the microelectronic style. This, in turn, facilitated the rapid globalization of a wide variety of industries in the service, or tertiary, sector that increasingly became critical for trade and competitiveness in general, particularly as jobs in manufacturing declined. The following categories of industries comprise the service sector: hotels, tourism, and restaurants; communications and transportation; wholesale and retail trade; professional, financial, and insurance services; and cultural and personal services, including education, health, and recreation.

Unlike manufactured goods, which can be traded and stored for long distances and periods, most services are locationally determined in that both production and consumption occur at the same place.[120] Moreover, unlike in manufacturing and microelectronic technology, in which the FIEs are clearly the dominant economies, the **service economy** in the AIEs, and to a lesser extent in the LDEs, accounts for a greater share of their GDPs than do manufacturing and advanced technologies. However, the service sector in the developing countries is characterized primarily by low-technology, labor-intensive services, such as hotels and restaurants. In contrast, the FIEs dominate the technologically more advanced service sectors, such as professional services, consulting, finance, training and marketing, and this technological capability gives them uncontested advantages.

Increases in MNC manufacturing and other production activities since the Second World War, particularly during the past three decades, created new demands for such services worldwide, and various industries within the service sector from the advanced economies expanded their operations accordingly, considerably accelerating the competition among them in the service sector as well. The essential ingredient in the technology-intensive services is information. As Dicken has pointed out, in the internationalization of financial services, for example,

> *information is both the process and the product of financial services.* Their raw materials are information: about markets, risks, exchange rates, returns on investment, creditworthiness. Their products are also information: the result of adding value

> to these informational inputs. A particularly significant piece of added value is embodied in the speed with which financial service firms can perform transactions and the global extent over which such transactions can be made.[121]

The widespread use of computers and telecommunications technologies has substantially lowered information-transmitting and -processing costs, and corporations have invested heavily in information technologies. In the mid-1980s, for example, satellite telephone calls were used for nearly half of all international financial transactions.[122]

There are several factors contributing to a country's competitiveness in international financial services, including "the volume of international currency clearings, the size of the Eurocurrency market, foreign financial assets, and headquarters of the large international banks."[123]

There are also intangible qualities to competitiveness that are more difficult to quantify and measure. These include the history of a country's economic development, the organizational experiences a firm gains (the "learning curve") during that period, and the international credibility and prestige a firm commands in world markets. Thus, the two major centers of international finance, London and New York, continue to "occupy the apex of the international financial centre hierarchy."[124] In the mid-1980s, for instance, "there were only 76 foreign banking institutions in Tokyo compared with well over 400 in London and around 300 in New York . . . [and] the daily turnover on the London foreign exchange market was almost as large as the turnover in New York and Tokyo put together."[125] Both London and New York have historically provided the financial service sectors a politically, though not always economically, stable environment, thereby accumulating decades of international confidence and credibility for global operations and investments. Moreover, it may be that, from the corporate perspective, the fact that London and New York survived the Wall Street market crash of October 1987, the international debt crisis of the 1980s, and the Mexican economic crisis of 1994–1995 provides sufficient cause for confidence in the financial structures of both systems. The extent to which Japan can save its banks and facilitate East Asian recovery from the region's economic crisis of 1997–1998 may determine the degree of international confidence in and competitiveness of Tokyo.

For purposes of illustration, the following paragraphs briefly look at an often neglected service sector: the international travel industry.[126] In addition to the relationship between MNC operations and the accelerated pace of international financial activity through the globalization of telecommunications, another aspect of globalization is the growth of international travel, encouraged by faster and more advanced transnational communications and transportation (for example, high-capacity Boeing 747 and new cruise ships). As in the case of trade in goods, the fluctuations in international travel are also determined by export and import demands—that is, competitiveness in prices and fluctuations in exchange rates.[127]

Between 1970 and 1995, total world international travel receipts—that is, from "exports" (trade in goods and services) to tourists—increased from $19.2 billion to $361.9 billion. Estimates of total travel receipts for 1996 ranged from $389.4 billion to $432 billion.[128] Total revenues from tourism were $3.6 trillion, employing about 255 million people in travel/tourism services and related services in "government travel services, construction of tourism facilities and manufacturing of goods consumed by tourists."[129] In economic terms, international travel is significant in that it represents a combination of service industries—for example, transportation, hotel, and restaurant—with enormous advantages for the manufacturing sector as well. International travel also has cultural significance; as more people travel beyond their national borders, travel and tourism promote greater familiarity among distant peoples—tangible and intangible gains not accurately captured by dollar value.[130]

As in other areas of international economic relations, the developed countries received a large proportion (about 73 percent) of total world travel receipts in the mid-1990s, and 60 percent of tourists were from the developed countries, although the developing and former Soviet bloc countries have increased their share as well (especially China).[131] In terms of competitiveness among the leading developed countries in this sector, the United States ranked first in the share of total world "exports" ($66.7 billion) to tourists, followed by France ($24.8 billion) (see Table 9.10). The data also indicate that the gap between the two leading countries has widened considerably. While in 1980 the total receipts by the United States were $1.6 billion greater than those of Italy (which ranked second in that year), in 1994 the total U.S. receipts were about $42 billion more than those of France. The U.S. international competitive advantage is best captured by the fact that, in a single decade, total U.S. FDIs in services abroad increased from $66.3 billion in 1980 to $194.5 billion in 1990, and they more than doubled ($410.7 billion) in 1996.[132]

Germany's and Switzerland's ranks in tourism "exports" improved slightly, while Spain's and the United Kingdom's remained the same. Japan, on the other hand, was not among the top twenty, although its position also improved

TABLE 9.10

International Tourist Receipts of the Top Ten Leading Exporting Countries, 1980 & 1994[a]

Country[b]	Receipts in 1980 (millions $)	Rank in 1980	Receipts in 1994 (millions $)	Percent share of total $56.34 billion[c] 1980	Percent share of total $187.78 billion[c] 1994
United States	10,590	1	66,740	18.8	35.5
France	8,257	3	24,796	14.7	13.2
Italy	8,959	2	23,906	16.0	12.7
Spain	6,958	4	21,629	12.4	11.3
United Kingdom	6,916	5	15,233	12.3	8.1
Germany	5,000	7	14,002	8.8	7.5
Austria	6,489	6	13,102	11.5	7.0
Switzerland	3,171	9	8,359	5.7	4.5
Hong Kong	1,217	17	8,239	—	—
China	617	29	7,323	—	—
				100.2	99.8

Source: UN, *World Economic and Social Survey, 1997: Trends and Policies in the World Economy* (New York: United Nations, 1997), Table X.2, p. 187. Based on IMF and WTO data. The United Nations is the author of the original materials used with permission.

[a] "Export" refers to trade in goods and services to tourists.

[b] Ranking in descending order by amount of receipts in 1994

[c] Total amount includes the United States and the seven European countries. Authors' own calculation. Percentages do not add up to 100 percent due to rounding.

from 28th rank in 1980 to 22nd in 1994.[133] Japan, however, may benefit in the long run from the increase in international travel in East Asia since the 1980s.[134]

Significantly, among the seven leading Western countries in Table 9.10, the U.S. share increased substantially, while the share of every European country declined. In addition, in 1994 alone, Canadians took 54 million holiday trips to the United States; most travelers were age fifty-five to sixty-four, largely due to "their higher income and increased leisure."[135] The U.S. share of world travel receipts also rose from 12 percent in 1970 to 19.3 percent in 1995, largely due to the depreciation of the dollar relative to the major European currencies.[136] Dollar depreciation, while making the United States more attractive to foreigners, may also have been one reason for the decline in U.S. tourism to the European Union.[137] Within the EU, 75 percent of tourists, especially attracted to the coastal regions on the Mediterranean, were from the member countries.

In addition to the proliferation of communications and transportation technologies per se, several factors contributed to the growth of international travel and tourism during the past two decades. The fact that a large share of world travel was among the developed economies suggests that higher income levels and access to credit (for example, credit cards) played a significant role. Lower travel costs, relative to earlier periods, and shorter travel time across oceans and continents also were contributing factors. Travel cost is influenced by foreign exchange and inflation rates, however, resulting in wider tourism fluctuations. Extended holidays and vacations—for example, seven weeks in the Netherlands, two weeks in the United States—were important as well. Some government relaxation of travel restrictions, particularly the EU regional integration, and deregulation of the airline industry are said to have had a considerable impact on international tourism. Moreover, intra-EU travel also benefited from the completion of the Channel Tunnel between France and England and infrastructural development—for example, the high-speed rail.[138] In the United States, supporters of the travel industry argued that the U.S. government should more actively promote the industry abroad.[139]

Certain costs are associated with this growth, however. As increased travel and tourism heighten international competition, the large hotel MNCs, such as the U.S.-based Holiday Inn, Hilton International, Sheraton Hotels; the French-based Club Mediterranée and Novotel; and the British-based Trust Houses Forte, further expand their operations and drive out local hotels and travel- and tourism-related businesses. The giant MNCs bring their enormous capital and management and marketing expertise to compete with the local tourism businesses, which in most cases, as in Britain, France, and Italy, are small and often family-run operations, such as *pensiones* or "bed and breakfasts" (B&B) with little formal collective organization. In Italy, for example, an estimated 90 percent of the hotel business falls under this category.[140] For the traveler, the local businesses have advantages of charm, while the major MNCs provide "the comforts of home."

Further, their operations have oligopolistic tendencies. Some multinational hotel chains are directly affiliated with the airline industry. For example, until the 1980s, TWA owned Hilton International, and Pan American owned Inter-Continental Hotels. In 1980, Japan Airlines owned or operated seven, and had marketing contracts with 48, hotels abroad. In other cases, airlines, such as British Airways, Lufthansa, and Alitalia, held portfolio investment shares in hotel industries.[141] The French Nouvelles Frontieres, which was first set up as a travel agency in 1968, in the mid-1990s owned its own airline and hotels, as well as a language school.[142]

Finally, increasing competition in this area underscores the role of the host government. Where traditional areas with heavy tourism traffic are "overexploited," certain governmental regulations and services may be necessary to preserve the sites and the quality of life, water, and air.[143] Where new areas are promoted, the host government becomes directly involved in the planning process. These issues raise serious questions with respect to the host government's ability to negotiate with the major MNCs, especially where the local businesses, as in most developing countries, lack the capital and technical wherewithal to compete with the MNCs.[144] The result may be mixed (as discussed in Chapter 7). Opening the local economy to international travel and tourism invigorates the local economy, as it injects new capital into the local formal and informal sectors, encourages infrastructural development, and creates jobs. On the negative side, however, the host government provides tax incentives to, and relaxes regulations on, the tourist industries, and it contracts development programs (roads, utilities), with enormous economic and cultural costs for the local population. Such policies lead to inflationary pressures, cause environmental degradation, and may even require the displacement of local neighborhoods—problems that engender "love-hate" sentiments toward the service industries. Thus, as in the other areas of international competitiveness, while competitiveness in tourism may be in the interest of the U.S. and European travel MNCs, its impact on the developed and developing economies may have positive and negative consequences.

International competitiveness is not limited to the high-technology–high-economy products and services discussed in this section. In the realm of dolls, toys, and children's games, the U.S. domestic market is dominated primarily—that is, 75 percent—by imports, although the United States slightly improved its position in international markets in the early 1990s. However, in these sectors, too, as with the auto and computer industries, toys "imported" from overseas are not necessarily made totally overseas but contain parts exported abroad for assembly by U.S. subsidiaries. For example, Mattel manufactures products in Mexico that contain 70 percent U.S.-made parts.[145] In recent years, U.S. exports in the toys sector rose 9 percent ($755 million), and in 1993 production reached its highest levels in the fifteen years. That year, the five largest markets for U.S. exports were Canada, accounting for 24 percent of the total, Mexico at 15 percent, Britain at 9 percent, Japan at 5 percent, and Germany at 4 percent.[146] The dollar value of U.S. toy imports has been around $7.5 billion, and it was expected to increase in the second half of the 1990s. The major suppliers were China, accounting for 38 percent of the total, Japan at 34 percent, Taiwan at 6 percent, Mexico at 5 percent, and Malaysia at 3 percent.[147] Some of this trade also consists of counterfeit copies of major manufacturer designs.

A nation's production and export shares of world markets give an estimation of its competitive position in the international political economy. Combined with other economic indices, such as GNP, household savings, expenditures on R&D, and balances of trade and of payments, as discussed earlier, they offer sufficient tangible data to determine the extent to which a nation is, can remain, or potentially can become a successful competitor. Various theories, such as statist and culturalist theories, provide alternative perspectives to explain nations' successes and failures. It is necessary to keep in mind, however, as the globalization theory contends, that competition is also based on international cooperation. Government policies toward trade relations determine the extent of imports and exports companies under its jurisdiction can have. Strong protectionist policies can deny market access to foreign firms and eliminate imports; lack of government support for exports may weaken the competitive position; nationalization of foreign companies can end foreign investments. However, for various domestic and international reasons, governments usually cooperate and incorporate a combination of both laissez-faire free trade and protectionist or regulatory measures into their trade policies.

Prior to the Second World War, governments relied on tariffs to protect their economies. Increasing liberalization of international trade since the 1950s and 1960s has accelerated trade and stimulated competition, as has privatization in the developed and developing countries since the 1980s. In the 1990s, the EU tariff on motor vehicles, for example, stood at a little over 10 percent and the U.S. tariff about 3 percent, while Japan has suspended its tariffs. Such policies toward liberalization and privatization are the result of international cooperation in multilateral fora such as GATT and WTO, as discussed in Chapter 5. Where liberalization has failed, particularly in employment issues, governments have adopted bilateral arrangements, such as voluntary exports restraints, like those between the United States and Japan, to set specific limits on imports.

Governments also cooperate by allowing foreign companies to establish production and sales facilities in their domestic markets and transnational strategic alliances between foreign- and home-based companies. GM has had joint ventures with Isuzu in Japan, with Toyota in the United States, and with Suzuki in Canada. Ford developed joint ventures with Mazda and Yamaha. Ford and Volkswagon have had joint ventures in Argentina and Brazil. Daimler-Chrysler has had similar arrangements with Mitsubishi. Korean-based Daewoo has sold its cars in the United States under GM's name and Kia under Ford's name.[148]

Marxist and Gramscian critics see such transnational cooperation as an oligopolistic globalization of international economy. They point out that these worldwide networks of transnational production provide a strong basis for cooperation among a small group of capitalist elites in a small group of nations, the core, to perpetuate their hegemonic domination over the peripheral classes within their own countries and abroad.[149] International cooperation among the core countries and the power structures they create, as manifested by government-corporate cooperation, shape economies, polities, and cultures—all geared toward the legitimation of the capitalist world system, directly affecting millions of lives in the developed and developing countries.

INTERNATIONAL COMPETITIVENESS AND EMPLOYMENT

In addition to the calculus of which is the most powerful and most influential nation in the world, the pursuit of international competitiveness, as the previous discussion on specific industries indicated, virtually has transformed the workplace for millions of people worldwide, leading to a "postindustrial era" in the international political economy. Employment in manufacturing industries declined in the United States and the European Union, although in Japan it remained more stable at about 35 percent. Between 1970 and 1993, industrial employment fell from 40 percent to 30 percent of total employment in the EU and from 35 percent to 24 percent in the United States. In the same period, employment in the service sector increased from 40 percent to 65 percent in the EU, from 60 percent to nearly 75 percent in the United States, and from 40 percent to 60 percent in Japan.[150]

Unemployment, thus, became a major issue in the industrialized economies, especially in the EU.[151] Most of the newer jobs available have been in the lower-paying segment of the service sector or have involved relatively few highly trained specialists.[152] Companies have argued that the dictates of international competitiveness require restructuring and outsourcing of manufacturing industries to reduce labor costs. Companies prefer to hire cheaper employees or free-lance consultants, and have used "early retirement" buyouts as one way to reduce salary commitments.

As a result, one area that has been adversely affected is organized labor. In order to strengthen their competitive position, companies shed some of their financial burdens by challenging, in their respective industries, trade unions' bargaining positions as established since the early decades of the twentieth century. In the 1950s and 1960s, the number of unionized employees increased rapidly, and by 1970 about 45 percent of total wage and salary earners were members of trade unions in Britain, approximately 35 percent in Germany, 37 percent in Japan, and nearly 25 percent in the United States and France. By the early 1990s, with the exception of Germany, these figures had plunged substantially. In the U.S. private sector, the figure was about 11 percent and, together with the public sector, about 15–16 percent. In France, the percentage of unionized labor fell to less than 10 percent (mostly in the public sector), in Japan to 30 percent, and in Britain to 42 percent.[153]

Globalization of production on the one hand and the shift to the service sector on the other make it difficult for unions to organize and retain members, giving corporations greater strategic maneuverability in dealing with unions.[154] As one expert has noted, the unions can be strong in manufacturing plants, where there is a high concentration of workers and where the jobs they perform require heavy and usually dangerous physical labor. It is far more difficult for unions to mobilize and organize sales clerks and receptionists dispersed throughout vast geographical areas and working in small numbers.[155] Nevertheless, younger, more aggressive trade union leaders began to emerge in the 1990s, with an eye on renewed organizing campaigns in various service and manufacturing fields.

CONCLUSION

Competitiveness in the world economy is an essential part of maintaining a healthy economy at home. International competitiveness has come to symbolize national achievement, as indicated by productivity growth rates and export shares. It is argued that, in general, countries with larger world-market shares of technologically advanced strategic industries, such as motor vehicles, superconductors, computers, and medical technology (as well as others, such as aerospace), register trade surpluses, produce more in order to meet market demands worldwide, and, thus, can have greater employment opportunities and higher standards of living.

There are disagreements, however, with respect to the actual ingredients for successful competitiveness. Statist theorists maintain that the key component is the role the state plays in coordinating industrial policies, especially in the strategically important sectors. Cultural theorists contend that national competitiveness involves not only the nature and role of the state but also a full spectrum of cultural-ideological elements, ranging from individualism to communitarianism. Others emphasize macroeconomic factors, such as a nation's propensity to save, market demand levels, and currency exchange rates. Environmentalists question whether competition is the way to a livable future.

This debate has not been limited to academic circles. It has been an intensely debated political issue as well, leading some to argue that the meaning of the term *competitiveness* has been so politicized as to render it meaningless. Perhaps most damaging to the public debate in this respect has been the way politicians and analysts have used it for propaganda purposes to sell their policies to the public. As an economic concept, however, the term has survived by retaining at least some more concrete meaning and quantifiable measures. The difficulty in quantifying and measuring a country's international competitiveness, and thereby its "power," is that in essence competitiveness admittedly involves more than mere indices of manufacturing and trade shares; it also involves the tangible and intangible components of a society, such as its size, education level, motivation level, leadership skills, culture, and ideology. It is generally agreed that the most productive economies with the highest volumes of marketable goods and services also generally dominate global decision making on policies ranging from the environment to security and defense.

Chapter Summary

International economic competitiveness became a major political issue in the world economy in the 1980s and the 1990s, replacing East–West ideological competition after the collapse of the former Soviet Union. International competition and competitiveness are a nation's ability to produce and sell its own products and to maintain a relatively larger share of export markets than its competitors.

To be competitive, a country must have such "factor endowments" as accessibility to knowledge, capital, natural resources, and infrastructure; sufficient local productive capacity and productive growth; relatively high savings and investment rates; strong financial and institutional bases for highly advanced R&D; and a sufficient technically skilled human resource base.

Contrary to the view of international competitiveness as a zero-sum situation, international competitiveness may also be premised on international cooperation, as major corporations and governments engage in joint production and market ventures. Politicization of international competitiveness, similar to use of the traditional concept of balance of power by political and economic leaders to protect and promote their own self-interests, can adversely affect the national economy.

Statist theories of international competition see the government as the central actor in society and the driving force in economic development and international economic relations. They contend that the more centralized governments are in a better position to strengthen the competitiveness of their economies than are the decentralized governments.

Culturalist theories, such as individualism and communitarianism, emphasize the role of national culture as the principal determinant of economic competitiveness. Individualism views the person and his or her tastes and interests as central to domestic and international market activities, while communitarianism sees the individual's interests through the interests of the community. Unlike the limited role assigned to the state in individualistic cultures, the state has a central role in communitarianism.

Macroeconomic theorists examine strictly economic conditions to explain international competitiveness. They examine market prices and demand, rates of savings and investment, and foreign currency exchange rates, with great emphasis on the "invisible hand" of market competition.

In recent years, observers have paid greater attention to strategically significant industries that are competitive in world markets. These include high-technology products in transportation, metals and composite materials, medical technology, microelectronics, telecommunications, robotics, civil aviation, space technology, and computers.

In a globalized world economy, a country's productivity rate and its production and export shares are key determinants of its competitiveness. The United States has slipped in some economic sectors but has risen in others.

Ultimately, the globalization of international competition has a tremendous impact on the workplace for millions of people worldwide. As nations attempt to win the competitive edge, companies resort to restructuring and outsourcing manufacturing industries, in search of cheaper labor and as a way to meet the challenge of international competition. In the process, employment in traditionally middle-class jobs suffers, as does organized labor, leading to some decline in standards of living.

Points of Contention

What are some of the key determinants of international competitiveness? How does your campus community contribute to national competitiveness?

How is the concept of "international competitiveness" related to the concept of "balance of power"?

What were the critical changes in international political economy that increased the saliency of international competitiveness in the 1980s and 1990s? Which theory of international competitiveness do you find a more valid explanation for these changes?

How does the statist theory differ from the culturalist and macroeconomic theories? What aspects of these theories are applicable to the industries in your community?

What reasons are given for the success of communitarian societies in the world economy? To what extent are these arguments valid?

Which among the strategic industries discussed in the chapter do you believe are most important for you and your community? How would changes through restructuring and outsourcing in the local industries affect the economy?

What are some of the advantages and disadvantages of the service sector, as in the case of international travel and tourism, with respect to local economic growth?

What are some of the consequences of corporate emphasis on competitiveness? How has organized labor fared in your community?

Notes

1. David P. Rapkin and Jonathan R. Strand, "Is International Competitiveness a Meaningful Concept?" in C. Roe Goddard, John T. Passé-Smith, and John G. Conklin, eds., *International Political Economy: State-Market Relations in the Changing Global Order* (Boulder, CO: Lynne Rienner, 1996), p. 115.
2. Lawrence Mishel and Paula B. Voos, "Unions and American Economic Competitiveness," in Lawrence Mishel and Paula B. Voos, eds., *Unions and Economic Competitiveness* (Armonk, N.Y.: Economic Policy Institute and M.E. Sharpe, 1992), pp. 1–4.
3. Paul Krugman, "Competitiveness: A Dangerous Obsession," *Foreign Affairs* 73, 2 (1994), pp. 28–44. The concept of "productivity" is vague. It is often used to mean squeezing more hours and products out of fewer workers. Social costs are not generally calculated.
4. Rapkin and Strand, "Is International Competitiveness a Meaningful Concept?" pp. 110–111.
5. International competitiveness has become a major objective for industrialized nations' foreign policies, but there is little agreement among politicians and commentators as to what constitutes competitiveness. *Ibid.*, pp. 109–129.
6. *Global Competition: The New Reality,* Report of the President's Commission on Industrial Competitiveness, vol. 2 (Washington, DC: U.S. Government Printing Office, 1985), p. 6, as quoted in Jeffrey A. Hart, *Rival Capitalists: International Competitiveness in the United States, Japan, and Western Europe* (Ithaca: Cornell University Press, 1992), p. 5.
7. Michael Porter, *The Competitive Advantage of Nations* (New York: The Free Press, 1990); Rapkin and Strand, "Is International Competitiveness a Meaningful Concept?" p. 112.
8. *Ibid.*
9. Lester Thurow, "A New Economic Game," in Goddard, Passé-Smith, and Conklin, eds., *International Political Economy,* p. 132.
10. Thurow, "A New Economic Game," p. 131.
11. *The Economist,* August 16, 1986, p. 74.
12. Thurow, "A New Economic Game," pp. 131–132.
13. According to Thurow, the Japanese Mitsubishi and the German Daimler Benz-Deutsche Bank held a secret meeting in March 1990 to coordinate their industrial strategies. Thurow, "A New Economic Game," p. 134.
14. "According to the U.S. Department of Commerce, if one divides manufacturing output by manufacturing employment, every $45 billion in extra output represents one million jobs. Production of current imports would absorb more than 5 million of those 15 million underemployed and

unemployed people." Lester C. Thurow, "Microchips, Not Potato Chips," *Foreign Affairs* 73, 4 (July/August 1994), p. 190.

15. K. H. Keene, P. G. Kirk, Jr., N. Ornstein, E. J. Rollins, and J. H. Makin. "The Meaning of Competitiveness," in C. E. Barfield and J. H. Makin, eds., *Trade Policy and U.S. Competitiveness* (Washington, DC: American Enterprise Institute, 1987), p. 131, as quoted in Rapkin and Strand, "Is International Competitiveness a Meaningful Concept?" pp. 117–118.
16. Ernst B. Haas, "The Balance of Power: Prescription, Concept, or Propaganda," *World Politics* V (1953), pp. 442–477.
17. *Ibid.*
18. The term *balance of power* has also served as an *analytical concept,* and since the eighteenth and nineteenth centuries it has been a central component in the construction of Realpolitik theory of international relations. As such, they have used it to mean "power politics," "hegemony," power "equilibrium," and so forth in the Hobbesian view of the state of nature in which *world politics* is defined as struggle for power. Accepted as natural, balance of power assumes "natural (or universal) law" and "historical law" qualities as distinguished from "motivations of governments." Political leaders also use the principles undergirding the balance of power approach as a *guide* to foreign policymaking. The guiding principles prescribe a specific set of responses to foreign policy issues and crises; as such, they constitute "rules of survival." *Ibid.*
19. Rapkin and Strand, "Is International Competitiveness a Meaningful Concept?" p. 118.
20. Paul Kennedy, *The Rise and Fall of Major Powers: Economic Change and Military Conflict from 1500 to 2000:* (New York: Random house, 1987), pp. xv–xvi, xxii.
21. Krugman, "Competitiveness: A Dangerous Obsession," pp. 28–44; Rapkin and Strand, "Is International Competitiveness a Meaningful Concept?" p. 111. See the debate on competitiveness, Clyde V. Prestowitz, Jr., "Playing to Win," Thurow, "Microchips, Not Potato Chips," Rudolph Scharping, "Rule-Based Competition," Stephen S. Cohen, "Speaking Freely," Benn Steil, "Careless Arithmetic," and Krugman's reply to his critics, "Proving My Point," *Foreign Affairs* 73, 4 (July/August 1994), pp. 186–203.
22. Haas, "The Balance of Power," pp. 442–477.
23. Prestowitz, "Playing to Win," p. 187.
24. Thurow, "Microchips, Not Potato Chips," p. 190.
25. Hart, *Rival Capitalists,* pp. 31–32.
26. Chalmers Johnson, *MITI and the Japanese Miracle* (Stanford: Stanford University Press, 1982), p. 20.
27. *Ibid.*
28. *Ibid.*, p. 32.
29. Hart, *Rival Capitalists,* p. 2.
30. George C. Lodge, "Introduction," in George C. Lodge and Ezra F. Vogel, eds., *Ideology and National Competitiveness* (Boston: Harvard Business School Press, 1987), p. 3.
31. *Ibid.*
32. *Ibid.*, p. 9.
33. Pluralist theories of national competitiveness emphasize the network of interest groups operating in a system. According to this view, national economic policy is the product of intense competition among numerous interest groups as they lobby policymaking institutions. National competitiveness is determined by the extent to which the domestic social and political environment is conducive to interest group competition and the extent to which policymaking institutions are accessible and responsive to interest group needs and demands.
34. Lodge, "Introduction," pp. 10–13.
35. *Ibid.*, p. 13.
36. *Ibid.*, p. 10.
37. Ezra F. Vogel, "Conclusion," in Lodge and Vogel, eds., *Ideology and National Competitiveness,* p. 305.
38. Joel Krieger, "The United Kingdom: Symbiosis or Division," in Lodge and Vogel, eds., *Ideology and National Competitiveness,* pp. 29–53.
39. *Ibid.*
40. *Hart, Rival Capitalists,* pp. 27–31.
41. *Ibid.*
42. UN, Conference on Trade and Development, *Trade and Development Report, 1997* (New York: United Nations, 1997), p. 106.
43. *Ibid.*
44. Roy Hofheinz, Jr., and Kent E. Calder, *The Eastasia Edge* (New York: Basic Books, 1982).
45. Hart, Rival Capitalists, pp. 29–30. U.S. household wealth dropped by 8 percent in real terms in the early 1990s, Britain's by 15 percent. *The Economist,* February 9, 1991, p. 69.
46. Hart, *Rival Capitalists,* p. 30.
47. *Ibid.*
48. *Ibid.*, p. 29.
49. *Ibid.*, p. 6.
50. Thurow has identified seven such industries: "microelectronics, biotechnology, the new materials-science industries, telecommunications, civilian aviation, robotics and machine tools, and computers and softwares." See Thurow, "A New Economic Game," p. 132.
51. U.S. Department of Labor, Bureau of Labor Statistics, *Labor Composition and U.S. Productivity Growth, 1948–90,* Bulletin 2426 (Washington, DC: U.S. Government Printing Office, 1993), p. 1.
52. *Ibid.*
53. See Sebastian Edwards, "Openness, Productivity and Growth," *Economic Journal* 108 (March 1998), pp. 383–398. Richard I. D. Harris and Mary Trainor,

"Productivity Growth in the UK regions, 1968–1991," *Oxford Bulletin of Economics and Statistics* 59, 4 (Nov. 1997), pp. 485–509.

54. Rapkin and Strand, "Is International Competitiveness a Meaningful Concept," p. 114.
55. A. J. Lenz, *Beyond Blue Economic Horizons: U.S. Trade Performance and U.S. International Competitiveness in the 1990s* (New York: Praeger, 1991), p. 17, in *Ibid.*
56. Ranil Salgado, "Productivity Growth in Canada and the United States," *Finance and Development* 34, 4 (December 1997), pp. 26–29.
57. Donald S. Allen, "Where's the Productivity Growth?" *Federal Reserve Bank of St. Louis Review* 79, 2 (March–April 1997), pp. 15–25.
58. See, for example, William J. Baumol and Kenneth McLennan, eds., *Productivity Growth and U.S. Competitiveness* (Oxford: Oxford University Press, 1985); William J. Baumol, Sue Anne Batey Blackman, and Edward N. Wolff, *Productivity and American Leadership: The Long View* (Cambridge: MIT Press, 1989); Bela Balassa, *Comparative Advantage, Trade Policy and Economic Development* (New York: Harvester Wheatsheaf, 1989). For a more theoretical and technical discussion on productivity and growth, see Peter Diamond, ed., *Growth/Productivity/Unemployment* (Cambridge: MIT Press, 1990).
59. Prestowitz, "Playing to Win," p. 188.
60. In 1960 the United States held 25.9 percent share of gross world product, in 1970 23.0 percent, and in 1980 21.5 percent. The EEC held 26.0 percent, 24.7 percent, and 22.5 percent for the same years, while Japan's share increased from 4.5 percent, to 7.7 percent, to 9.0 percent. See Kennedy, *The Rise and Fall of Major Powers,* p. 436.
61. The figure for 1985 was 793 million metric tons, for 1989, 865 million metric tons, and for 1990, 850 million metric tons. American Iron and Steel Institute (AISI), Annual Statistical Report, 1994, p. 4.
62. In the early 1970s, the United States produced on average about 151 million metric tons per year, but that figure dropped to about 90 million metric tons in the mid-1980s. Hart, *Rival Capitalists,* pp. 12–14.
63. In the early 1990s, U.S. production rose to about 98–100 million metric tons, increasing the U.S. share of world production from 11.1 percent in 1985. AISI, *Annual Statistical Report,* 1994, p. 4.
64. Hart, *Rival Capitalists,* p. 14.
65. The European Union produced about 150 million metric tons in 1990, 146 million in 1992 and 1993, and 153 million in 1994.
66. AISI, *Annual Statistical Report, 1994,* pp. 108–10. The figures for France declined slightly from 21.9 million (2.58 percent) to 19.9 million metric tons (2.49) in 1990 and 1994, respectively. Britain's production also dropped from 19.7 million metric tons in 1990 to 17.9 million in 1992 but increased to 19.1 million metric tons in 1994. Its share of world production remained stable on average at about 2.3 percent.
67. Hart, *Rival Capitalists,* p. 14.
68. AISI, *Annual Statistical Report, 1994,* p. 110.
69. Hart, *Rival Capitalists,* p. 15.
70. AISI, *Annual Statistical Report, 1994,* p. 15.
71. See, for example, Kenneth A. Kessel, *Strategic Materials: U.S. Alternatives* (Washington, DC: National Defense University Press, 1990).
72. It rose from 29 million in 1969 to 40 million in 1979.
73. In Britain, the loss of jobs was equally great; between 1972 and 1985, employment dropped from 184,000 to 78,000. In the case of France, between 1970 and 1981, employment levels remained relatively stable at about 500,000. Germany's increased from 600,000 to nearly 690,000, after a brief drop in the mid-1970s. Japan's rose from about 570,000 in 1970 to over 700,000 in 1981. Hart, *Rival Capitalists,* Figure 6, p. 16.
74. *Ibid.*, p. 15.
75. *U.S. Industrial Outlook 1994,* p. (15) 8. In the early 1990s, however, overall production levels in semiconductor manufacturing declined, and companies canceled or completely shut down some of their production due to the economic slowdown in 1990–1992. Even in East Asian economies, whose production levels were relatively high, investment in this sector dropped; for example, in Japan it fell by 29 percent in 1992. Production levels for the rest of the 1990s were expected to increase somewhat, as companies again increased their R&D investments. Ibid., p. (15) 3.
76. *Ibid.*
77. *Ibid.*
78. Hart, *Rival Capitalists,* pp. 14–17.
79. Data include monolithic and hybrid integrated circuits. See *Ibid.*, p. 17.
80. *U.S. Industrial Outlook 1994,* p. (15) 1.
81. In terms of absolute dollar value, in 1992 the United States led the industrialized economies in merchandise exports, at about $450 billion, followed by Germany's $440 billion. Japan exported $350 billion worth of goods, France about $250 billion, and Britain $200 billion. In the early 1990s, the United States also was clearly the top exporter of services, such as finance and insurance services, totaling $150 billion. The figure for its closest competitor, France, was a little over $80 billion. The total value of services exported by Germany and Italy was $60 billion, by Britain about $58 billion, by Japan $50 billion, and by Canada nearly $20 billion. *U.S. Industrial Outlook 1994,* p. (15) 1.
82. OECD, *OECD Economic Outlook,* June 1996.
83. In 1993, BMW and Mercedes-Benz announced plans for production plants in the United States in the mid-1990s, as did the South Korean Kio Motors to develop a "West Coast sales network." *U.S. Industrial Outlook 1994,* p. (35) 2.

84. *Ibid.*, p. (35) 14.
85. American Automobile Manufacturers Association (AAMA), *World Motor Vehicle Data, 1996,* p. 280.
86. Canada's passenger car exports to the United States increased from 691,146 to 825,590 between 1969 and 1976.
87. Japan's share of exports to the United States and Canada increased from 0.7 percent in 1956 to 40.39 percent in 1976, and 56.3 percent in 1986 (peak year). Thereafter, it fell to 41.1 percent in 1991 and to 39.4 percent in 1994. This decline occurred in other regions as well for all motor vehicle types. In Asia, Japan's exports dropped from 744,461 in 1993 to 594,335 in 1994; in the Middle East, from 379,652 to 275,480; and in Europe from 1,280,989 to 1,053,095. Estimates for the rest of the 1990s suggest that Japan is not likely to recover soon from this decline, especially if the Asian economic crisis is prolonged. As of this writing, it is possible that Japan's weakening competitiveness combined with the economic crisis will cast its domestic economy into a vicious cycle of decline and diminishing public confidence. *Ibid.*, p. 49.
88. Globalization of MNC production structures in the automobile industry makes it difficult for governments to address such imbalances in international trade, as MNCs assemble their parts in several countries. In the early 1990s, in trade negotiations with the European Union, for example, the Japanese government agreed to reduce Japanese exports to that market through the end of this decade. However, the agreement had no provisions regarding Japanese motor vehicles produced in other countries, and Japanese subsidiaries in the United States, such as Mazda in Michigan, exported more than 10,000 vehicles to the EU markets. Although similar agreements with the United States have somewhat eased the trade deficit, Japanese exports continue to penetrate the EU market, the United States, and most markets. *Ibid.*, pp. 50, 276.
89. *U.S. Industrial Outlook 1994,* p. (26) 4.
90. *Ibid.*
91. *Ibid.*, p. (26) 1.
92. In 1992, the United States exported $2.9 billion worth of computers to Japan but imported $11.2 billion. In 1993, imports rose to $11.6 billion.
93. *U.S. Industrial Outlook 1994,* p. (26) 5.
94. *Ibid.*, p. (26) 3.
95. *Ibid.*, pp. (15) 6–7.
96. *Ibid.*, p. (15) 3.
97. *Ibid.*
98. Japan's semiconductor exports to the United States were $4.3 billion, while U.S. semiconductor exports to Japan totaled less than $1 billion (about $911 million, or 7.9 percent).
99. *Ibid.*, p. (15) 7.
100. The North American share of the East Asian market increased from 29 percent in 1987 to 39 percent in 1992, while Japan's share dropped from 47 percent to 34 percent. The United States retains the largest share of the computer microcomponents market in the region. Semiconductor sales in North America rose by 18.6 percent in 1993, exceeding Japan for the first time in years, and, for the rest of the 1990s, the North American market became even stronger. Canada exported $1.7 billion worth of semiconductors to the United States. It has been argued that the overall improvement was the result of the tariffs imposed by the U.S. government on $300 million exports annually to the U.S. market. Also, the Japanese computer—particularly the chip—industry sustained heavy losses, and, even when sales recovered in the late 1980s, prices had dropped. From 1985 to 1987, Japanese chip sales increased by 30 percent, but falling prices meant lower profits, by one estimate to the tune of a 40 percent drop. In the late 1980s and early 1990s, Japanese chip exports accounted for 30 percent of Japan's total chip production, nearly 33 percent exported to the U.S. markets, and 50 percent to East Asian countries to be assembled in products shipped to the United States. Among the top five destinations for U.S. semiconductor exports in 1992, Canada imported $1.6 billion worth of U.S. semiconductors, accounting for 13.7 percent (the largest share) of the total U.S. semiconductor exports. The figures for Malaysia were $1.5 billion (13 percent), Singapore $1.3 billion (11.7 percent), Taiwan $1.1 billion (9.6 percent), and Japan $911 billion (8 percent). The total value of Malaysia's and South Korea's exports to the United States was $1.98 billion (or 13 percent) each and Singapore's $1.3 billion (or 8.2 percent of all semiconductor exports to the United States). *The Economist,* October 31, 1987, pp. 60, 62; *U.S. Industrial Outlook 1994,* pp. (15) 6–9.
101. *U.S. Industrial Outlook 1994,* p. (15) 6.
102. *Ibid.*, p. (15) 6.
103. *Ibid.*, pp. (15) 6–7.
104. *Ibid.*, p. (15) 7.
105. *Ibid.*
106. These figures are particularly revealing when compared with the Japanese semiconductor market, valued at $23 billion in 1993. It has been noted, however, that "Japanese households are quickly reaching the saturation point with VCRs, TVs, camcorders, [and] stereo systems [and] Japanese consumer electronics firms have been unable to develop new products with the same explosive sales potential" as in the 1980s. The stronger yen in the early 1990s is also said to be a factor in the overall drop in the Japanese demand for semiconductors; in 1993, production dropped by 12 percent, the first drop since the late 1970s. *U.S. Industrial Outlook 1994,* p. (15) 7.
107. Thurow, "Microchips, Not Potato Chips," pp. 190–191.
108. *Ibid.*, p. (44) 3.
109. *The Economist,* July 18, 1987, p. 61.

110. *U.S. Industrial Outlook 1994,* p. (43) 1.
111. *Ibid.* Japan also imported $963 million worth of U.S. pharmaceutical products.
112. *Ibid.,* p. (44) 4.
113. *Ibid.,* p. (44) 3.
114. *Ibid.*
115. *Ibid.,* p. (44) 4.
116. That is, $3.11 billion worth of medical equipment from the United States. *Ibid.,* p. (44) 3.
117. *Ibid.*
118. *Ibid.*
119. *Ibid.*
120. Dicken, *Global Shift,* pp. 41-42.
121. *Ibid.,* p. 360. Emphasis in original.
122. T. F. Huertas, "U.S. Multinational Banking: History and Prospects," in G. Jones, ed., *Banks as Multinationals* (London: Routledge, 1990), 263, in *Ibid.,* p. 361.
123. *Ibid.,* p. 374.
124. *Ibid.,* p. 375.
125. Dicken, *Global Shift,* p. 375.
126. This section relies heavily on UN, *World Economic and Social Survey, 1997: Trends and Policies in the World Economy* (New York: United Nations, 1997), pp. 181–197.
127. Fariborz Moshirian, "Determinant of International Trade Flows in Travel and Passenger Services," *Economic Record* 69 (September 1993), pp. 239–252.
128. The UN figures are based on data for 110 countries from the IMF *Balance of Payments Statistics Yearbook* (various years). The figure $423 billion is from the World Tourism Organization, "which has a wider coverage of developing and transition [that is, former Soviet bloc] economies." See UN, *World Economic and Social Survey, 1997,* p. 181.
129. United Nations, *World Economic and Social Survey, 1997,* Table X.1, p. 184. On definition and measurement considerations, see pp. 182–183.
130. Sharone Parnes, "Peace Talks Bringing Hope for Travel Boom: Mideast Tourism Begins Historic Cooperation," *Advertising Age,* January 17, 1994, p. I2.
131. UN, *World Economic and Social Survey, 1997,* pp. 184–185.
132. *Economic Report of the President Transmitted to the Congress, February 1998* (Washington, DC: U.S. Government Printing Office, 1998), Table 7–3, p. 255.
133. UN, *World Economic and Social Survey,* 1997, p. 187.
134. Michael Mecham, "Pacific Travel Grows in Atlantic's Shadow," *Aviation Week & Space Technology* 141, 20 (November 14, 1994), p. 31.
135. Warren Clark, "Trading Travellers: International Travel Trends," *Canadian Social Trends* 45 (Summer 1997), pp. 2–5.
136. UN, *World Economic and Social Survey,* 1997, p. 185.
137. UN, *World Economic and Social Survey,* 1997, p. 186; Janet Meyers, "Mapping a Marketing Solution," *Advertising Age,* November 2, 1992, pp. S1–3.
138. UN, *World Economic and Social Survey, 1997,* pp. 186, 193–195.
139. Meyers, "Mapping a Marketing Solution."
140. UN, *World Economic and Social Survey, 1997,* p. 196.
141. John H. Dunning, *Explaining International Production* (London: Unwin Hyman, 1988), pp. 242–247.
142. CPC International (Corn Products Co.), a U.S.-based food company, to give another example, whose sales earned $67 billion in 1993, spent nearly $1 billion that year to purchase the German Pfanni potato company, Israel's Telma soup company, Brazil's Vitamilho, and Chile's JB sauce company. CPC International already owned, among others, Knorr (soup), Hallmann's and Best Foods (mayonnaise and salad dressing), and Skippy (peanut butter). Amy Feldman, "Have Distribution, Will Travel," *Forbes* (June 20, 1994), pp. 44–45; Bruce Crumley, "Frontieres Sells Its 'Democracy' Over Opulence: Leisure Travel Marketer Brings Cruises, Hotels Within Reach," *Advertising Age* (January 15, 1996), p. 110.
143. See, for example, "Vaccines for International Travel Satellite Videoconference," *Morbidity and Mortality Weekly Report* 45, 4 (February 2, 1996), p. 92.
144. With the rapid growth of the service sector, there has also been a greater awareness of the need to harmonize international standards. In 1998, the International Standards Organization (ISO) organized a series of multilateral meetings on different areas of the service sector and trade in services. WTO, *Focus,* 27 (February 1998), p. 6. The World Health Organization also monitors health-related requirements (for example, vaccination) for international travelers. WHO, "WHO Issues Vaccination Requirements for 1994 International Travel," *Public Health Reports* 109, 4 (July-August 1994), p. 591.
145. *Ibid.,* p. (37)18.
146. *Ibid.*
147. While in the 1980s U.S. shipments had declined by an average of 2.5 percent, in the early 1990s these figures registered increases of up to 7.6 percent per year, from $3.68 billion in 1987 to $4.31 billion in 1991 to an estimated $4.95 billion in 1994. *Ibid.,* pp. (37) 17–19.
148. Dicken, *Global Shift,* pp. 286–293.
149. See, for example, Robert W. Cox, "Social Forces, States and World Orders," *Millennium* 10 (1981), pp. 125–155.
150. *The Economist,* July 1, 1995, p. 54.
151. IMF, *World Economic Outlook, May 1997* (Washington, DC: IMF, 1997), Table 2, p. 18.
152. *The Economist,* June 10, 1995, p. 18.
153. *The Economist,* July 1, 1995, p. 54; Mishel and Voos, eds., *Unions and Economic Competitiveness,* p. 19.
154. UN, Conference on Trade and Development, *World Investment Report, 1994* (New York: United Nations, 1994), pp. 254–260.
155. *The Economist,* July 1, 1995, p. 54.

CHAPTER TEN

THE POLITICAL ECONOMY OF NORTH–SOUTH CONFLICT AND COOPERATION: A CLOSER LOOK AT FIE, AIE, AND LDE RELATIONS

The previous chapters discussed the historical evolution of the modern international political economy and the various causes that created and perpetuated the wide gap between the economies of industrialized and developing countries, including the advanced industrializing economies (AIEs). This gap—that is, the vast structural inequalities in financial, technological, and military capabilities—remains at the heart of North–South relations. While most regions in the North have experienced phases of prosperity since the 1950s, and while some southern states have advanced, the economies of vast regions in the South have remained underdeveloped and stagnant (see Figure 10.1).

In the early 1960s, the South's per capita GDP was about 9 percent of the North's. In the early 1970s, that figure dropped to 7.4 percent and by the late 1980s to 6.1 percent. Between 1960 and 1987, sub-Saharan Africa's ratio (excluding South Africa) fell from 6.9 percent to 3.5 percent, Latin America's (including the Caribbean economies) from 22.2 percent to 12.5 percent, and Asia–Southeast Asia's from 5.3 percent to 3.8 percent. Only the oil-producing Middle Eastern countries experienced improvement during this period, from 18.9 percent to 27.8 percent, while nonoil-producing countries' dropped from 15.2 percent to 11.8 percent of the North's per capita GDP.[1] Table 10.1 shows the regional differences in the UN Human Development Index (HDI), meant to rate economies on a variety of welfare factors, such as life expectancy and violence for industrialized and developing countries in 1994.[2]

Such inequalities in North–South relations have their historical roots in the legacy of Western colonialism and have involved serious lingering conflicts since the end of colonialism. Despite the conflicts, however, North–South relations also have involved cooperation in various policy areas. For example, during the Cold War, the U.S. national security priorities in regional defense policies led to a

FIGURE 10.1

*At constant 1980–1982 prices and exchange rates.

Sources: World Bank and OECD Secretariat estimates. OECD, *Twenty-Five Years of Development Cooperation, 1985 Report: A Review* (Paris: Organization for Economic Cooperation and Development, 1985), Chart XII-1, p. 266.

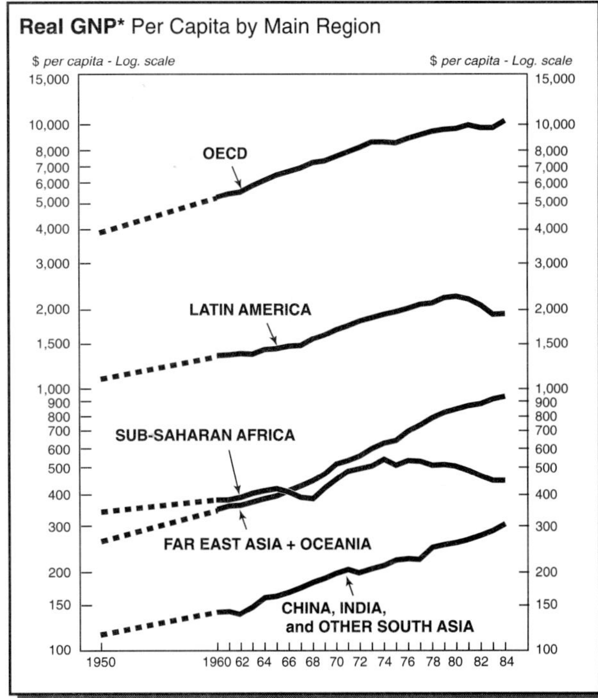

TABLE 10.1

Human Development Index, 1994

	Life Expectancy at Birth (years) 1994	Adult Literacy Rate (%) 1994	Combined First-, Second- and Third-Level Gross Enrollment Ratio (%) 1994	Real GDP per Capita (ppp$) 1994	Adjusted Real GDP per Capita (ppp$) 1994	Life Expectancy Index	Education Index	GDP Index	Human Development Index (HDI Value) 1994
All developing countries	61.8	69.7	56	2.904	2.904	0.61	0.65	0.46	0.576
Least developed	50.4	48.1	36	965	965	0.42	0.44	0.14	0.336
Sub-Saharan Africa	50.0	55.9	42	1,377	1,377	0.42	0.51	0.21	0.380
Industrial countries	74.1	98.5	83	15,986	6,037	0.82	0.93	0.98	0.911
World	63.2	77.1	60	5,798	5,798	0.64	0.71	0.94	0.764

Source: UNDP, *Human Development Report 1997* (New York: Oxford University Press, 1997), pp.146–148. The HDI value is on a scale of 0 (worst) to 1 (best) HDI achievement. The United Nations is the author of the original materials, and the materials are used with permission.

number of security and economic programs, such as the Alliance for Progress for the Western Hemisphere; cooperation in geo-strategically based economic programs overlapped with cooperation in areas of economic development and trade. The collapse of the Soviet Union increased hopes for the termination of decades of hostilities and suspicion in the developing world and for greater North–South cooperation.

However, certain conflicts could not be mitigated by the ending of the Cold War alone. The history of colonization and enormous financial problems, such as the debt crisis, encountered in more recent times have been a source of much North–South tension. As noted in Chapter 2, *dependencia* theorists argue that the world economic system as dominated by the capitalist West is to be blamed for much of the South's social, economic, and political problems and that trends toward increased interdependence and globalization perpetuate Northern domination, now in the form of neocolonialism. On the other hand, the liberalization and expansion of the world economy and international trade relations in the late 1980s and 1990s have raised expectations for greater cooperation, as anticipated by theories of liberalism. From the South's perspective, however, trade liberalization was not necessarily voluntary; most countries had exhausted alternative strategies to combat their social-economic ills and dependence on the North, with little success.[3] The deteriorating living standards and the debt crisis in the 1970s and 1980s strengthened the position of international institutions, such as the International Monetary Fund (IMF) and the World Bank as dominated by the West, as well as the bargaining position of MNCs and private international banks. Neither have development assistance programs proved entirely successful in alleviating poverty conditions (to be discussed in Chapter 11). The role of international institutions and MNCs was examined in previous chapters. The following section discusses the sources of North–South conflict under two general headings: the legacy of colonialism and efforts at nation-building in the aftermath of decolonization and the world-economic system within which the South operates.

SOURCES OF NORTH-SOUTH CONFLICT

The Colonial Legacy and Nation-Building

As discussed in preceding chapters (see Chapter 3), the industrial powers in the West (also referred to as the core countries) used the vast human and natural resources found in the South (the periphery) to develop their own domestic industrial base and to expand their colonial spheres of influence and market capabilities abroad. Colonialism led to the development of specific local economies (for example, supplies of raw materials) geared to benefit the colonial powers rather than the local populations. Production and transportation networks were developed to supply goods and workers, some as slaves, for the Western countries as quickly and cheaply as possible. "Development" in the South, thus, was viewed as development for the North, and the relationship between the two was based primarily on unequal distribution of wealth and power—a situation that prevails even today through net transfer of capital repatriated by MNC debt interest repayment from South to North and the "brain drain" discussed in earlier chapters.

For centuries, colonial administrative, financial, and military structures enabled the old and new colonial powers—Spain, Portugal, Britain, France, and later Japan, Germany, and the United States—to dominate the Southern countries' institutions, politics, and economies. In fact, domination by the old colonial powers appeared in military capability even as late as in 1982, during the British-Argentine War over the Malvinas/Falkland Islands, British territories since the 1830s. From the South's perspective, U.S. support for Britain in that war demonstrated the extent to which the old and new powers share similar objectives and *modus operandi.*

In the aftermath of decolonization, the developing countries (in Latin America well into the late nineteenth century, African and Asian countries a century later) began the tortuous process of nation- and state-building, often handicapped by the sudden withdrawal of Northern capital and direct and indirect military interventions. In Asia, Africa, and the Middle East, the political leaders of newly emerging states had to create a sense of national unity based on a national culture, while bridging the deep conflicts between their citizens and the government, on the one hand, and among different local ethnic and religious groups with equally deep mutual suspicions on the other. National revolutions for independence combined with superpower involvement at times escalated the local conflicts into full-fledged wars, as in Vietnam, Laos, Cambodia, and Angola, for three more decades after the major powers had concluded their wars in Europe. The end of the superpower Cold War seemed to lessen the impetus toward international war in the Third World but left open the gates for domestic violent conflicts, as in Rwanda, Zaire, Sudan, Liberia, and Somalia, creating opportunities for outside intervention.

The World-Economic System

Another source of North–South tensions has been the "world-economic system"—that is, the world political economy viewed as a single global market shaped by a small number of major capitalist countries, in the form of the OECD or G-8, and the multilateral organizations, such as the IMF, World Bank, and GATT, dominated by them. As noted in Chapters 2 and 3, the early and incremental evolution of the Western capitalist economies from agricultural to industrial and technologically advanced status over a period of more than a century placed them in a highly advantageous position toward the South. The colonial and postcolonial financial and administrative apparatus led to the development of what has become known as the capitalist world-economic system. While the financial crisis during the Great Depression of the 1920s and 1930s and the subsequent world war marked the end of the European-dominated world-economic system, in its stead the new U.S.-dominated system emerged with a new set of financial institutions—that is, the Bretton Woods system—and MNCs. Thus, when African and Asian countries became formally independent in the 1950s and 1960s, the new world capitalist system, as refashioned by the United States, with a set of free trade norms, was already in place.

Western governments and multinational corporations continued to influence events and policies in the developing countries after decolonization, and to date the latter, still largely sources of raw materials and cheap labor, have not had sufficient time to consolidate their political and economic institutions, which, according to the *dependencia* theory, remain vulnerable to formal and informal manipulations by the North. It is this dependency and what critics see as an exploitative relationship that remains one of the major sources of North–South, or core-periphery, conflict.[4] Even the introduction of higher technologies—such as computers and cell phones—is thus viewed as a means to further tie the South to Northern powers.[5] The emergence of a number of AIEs with centers of trade and rapid economic development, as in the case of the Asian "tigers" (South Korea, Taiwan, Hong Kong, and Singapore), indicated a potential for greater autonomy, but the extent to which autonomy can be sustained will depend on these states' ability to overcome such economic crises as experienced in the late 1990s.

The world-economic system created after the Second World War proved particularly contentious, since the principles of laissez-faire capitalism and free trade were not a viable option for most developing states. The process of decolonization and the various social and economic ills associated with capital shortages made nation- and state-building and economic development nearly impossible tasks for national leaders, even with the best of intentions. Many such leaders viewed the West, especially the United States, as neo-colonial powers exploiting the South under the guise of free trade principles. As a result, the South's reaction manifested itself in various forms, including nationalist and anticolonial movements, such as Nasserism in Egypt, Pan-Arabism, the Nonalignment Movement, Pan-Africanism, militant Islam, and variants of Marxism in a number of African, Asian, and Latin American countries. The policies adopted included wholesale nationalization of industries, regional integration attempts, and efforts to build strong national military capability, which pitted these movements against the interests of the North. For example, the creation of the Group of 77 (G-77) in 1964 at a UN Conference on Trade and Development (UNCTAD) and the adoption of the Declaration on the Establishment of a New International Economic Order (NIEO) a year later were not received well by staunch proponents of laissez-faire capitalism, particularly in the United States.

Such ideological movements and collective efforts, however, failed to ameliorate problems of specialization in certain primary commodities, such as tobacco, coffee, sugarcane, and fruits, all subject to uncertain market fluctuations. And, when governments in developing countries sought diversification through industrialization, they were again dependent on Northern markets, capital, and technology. The extent to which developing economies could accumulate wealth depended on political and economic conditions in the North. Exports were essential for the economies of (particularly smaller) developing countries because of their small domestic markets, but, contrary to the theory of *comparative advantage,* commodity specialization to capture a share of the North's markets only deepened their dependence.

More optimistically, since the mid-1980s, newly emerging stock markets have developed in a number of advanced developing countries, such as Brazil, Malaysia, and Taiwan, providing greater incentives for the development of export-oriented economies at a time when the world-economy was directed toward trade liberalization and privatization. This encouraged international investors and currency speculators to become more involved in international market activities and to expand their pool of foreign assets, but here, too, investments flowed to a small number of economically strong Southern economies—that is the AIEs. As mentioned in Chapter 7, in 1995, for example, ten developing countries received over 75 percent of the total

$167 billion in private capital flows, including FDIs.[6] In the mid-1990s, about 67 percent of FDI inflows to the developing countries went to southern and East Asia, over 40 percent of which went to China. Nearly 25 percent of the total FDIs in the developing countries went to Latin America and the Caribbean, while Africa received only 5 percent.[7] A number of East Asian countries, such as Taiwan, South Korea, Hong Kong, and Singapore, are now sources of FDIs, their investments are primarily in the developed economies.[8]

North–South inequalities were further exacerbated by the OAPEC (Organization of Arab Petroleum Exporting Countries) oil embargo in 1973 and the second "oil shock" of the late 1970s, leading to a decade of spiraling global inflation, as banks scrambled to lend out their surplus "petro-dollars," followed by a severe debt crisis in the 1980s. High oil prices resulted in high levels of inflation, unemployment, trade deficits, and overall economic stagnation, which hit poorer southern states particularly hard. As a result, many developing countries failed to pay the interest to foreign lenders.

Frustrated with the difficulties encountered in combatting dependency, underdevelopment, and unemployment, leaders in the developing countries sought multilateral avenues to strengthen South-South cooperation. The Nyerere (or the South) Commission's report, published in 1990, heavily emphasized the need for new South-South cooperative arrangements in the 1990s.[9] Despite impediments to regional integration as experienced in Latin America and Africa in the 1960s and 1970s, some governments opted for Southern trading communities, like Mercosur in South America and SADC in southern Africa. Whether these regional schemes will be successful in the long run is not clear, but there seems to be little opportunity for southern influence at the global level. For example, the UN World Summit for Social Development (the Copenhagen Summit), held in March 1995, whose primary object was to address problems of poverty, unemployment, and social disintegration around the world, produced little agreement with respect to such issues. In fact, the Western governments, largely because of their own budgetary concerns and because of the corruption associated with some of the aid programs, vehemently opposed proposals even to modestly increase foreign aid to the South.[10]

Within the context of the world-economic system, at the heart of the matter, the Nyerere Commission argued, is the need for permanent international structures not only to secure greater South-South cooperation but also to develop "a fairer system of global relationships through negotiations with the North."[11] The developing countries lack political or diplomatic clout of any significance in the world financial and trade arrangements because of their weaker economic base—for example, the developing countries account for no more than 10 percent of world trade. This is reflected in the structural arrangements of the IMF and the World Bank, in which decision making is controlled by the major powers through the weighted voting system. Voting power is distributed among member states according to their capital contribution to the IMF and the World Bank, enabling the first industrialized countries (FIEs), led by the United States, to dominate the decision-making process. The developing countries have advocated procedural reforms to institute the one-nation, one-vote principle, but the U.S. response has been lukewarm at best.[12] In the UN General Assembly, where each member state has one vote, regardless of contribution, the growing number of developing countries since the 1950s has enabled them to exert greater influence in shaping the organization's agenda. As the developing countries viewed Western, particularly U.S., dominance in the IMF and the World Bank as inimical to their interests, so did the Western states view the increasing power of the developing countries in the United Nations as inimical to their interests. The United States and Britain criticized the UN General Assembly for adopting what they perceived as socialist-, Marxist-, and, hence, Soviet-oriented programs, such as the New International Economic Order in 1974.[13] For two years, 1977–1979, the United States withdrew from the International Labor Organization (ILO) because it viewed the policy reforms advocated by the developing countries regarding labor, social, and economic issues as Soviet-Marxist inspired. For a similar reason, the United States and Britain withdrew from the UN Educational, Scientific, and Cultural Organization (UNESCO) in 1985.[14]

The Nyerere Commission proposed the creation of a "South Bank" specifically designed to pool financial resources to promote investments for all developing countries.[15] Many developing states saw the establishment of the World Trade Organization (WTO) in 1995 as a potential mechanism to redress this imbalance. However, the verdict on the overall pattern of WTO decisions and dispute settlement remains uncertain, since the North still exercises great power.

THE COLD WAR & NORTH–SOUTH CONFLICTS

The East–West rivalry from 1945–1989 was multifaceted, and, as discussed in the next section, it also was conducive to bilateral and multilateral cooperation in various areas centered on each superpower and ideologically aligned developing countries. One of the major issues of controversy in superpowers' relations with the developing countries was the arms race and the proliferation of arms throughout the developing regions. The arms buildup, driven partly for commercial gains and partly for strategic alliances in the developing world during the Cold War, was a contributing factor to conflicts in explosive regions such as the Middle East, East and Southeast Asia, and Africa.[16] The ongoing wars and conflicts between Israel and its Arab neighbors; the Korean and Vietnam wars and subsequent Vietnam-Cambodia wars; and the civil wars and bloodshed in Angola, Mozambique, and Nigeria all involved massive military hardware of various degrees of destructive capabilities, supplied mainly by European countries, the United States, China, and the Soviet bloc. Tables 10.2 and 10.3 present the data for arms exports and imports, and, as can be seen, the cost of arms represented a substantial drain on Third World economies, though actual economic and military defense effects are still debated.[17]

In some regions, particularly in Africa and the Middle East, the arms race and the East–West rivalry further exacerbated regional rivalries. The easy availability of arms fueled territorial, ethnic and nationalist fighting, creating greater demands for more weapons, leading to a vicious cycle. According to one estimate, more than 10 million people were killed in the developing world between the end of the Second World War and the early 1980s.[18] A large share, approximately 80 percent, of their weapons were supplied by the United States and the Soviet Union, followed by the three major European suppliers—France, Britain and Italy—as well as China and Czechoslovakia.[19] In wars such as the decade long Iran-Iraq war of the 1980s, a number of these suppliers sent arms simultaneously to *both* sides. In some instances, arms exports did not strictly substitute for direct military involvement: in the Korean, Vietnam, and Afghanistan wars, one of the superpowers, or powers such as China, and France, were directly involved in the military conflicts; in others, such as Angola and Nicaragua, the major powers supported and trained "proxy warriors" (such as the Cubans in Angola and the "Contras" in Nicaragua) in the fighting; in other wars, the powers supplied the military hardware and technical support.[20]

As African countries gained independence in the 1960s, for some African nationalist and socialist leaders, the Soviet Union served as a model for the development of a centrally planned national economy, and a source of arms and goods to resist the West. The West viewed Soviet supported "liberation movements" in the region as a threat to its investments, and Western powers directly and indirectly intervened to protect them, as in the Congo, and Angola.[21] Some African countries, notably Kenya, Angola, Somalia, Ethiopia, and Mozambique, became battlegrounds for the East–West as well as local rivalries, with enormous human and financial costs to the local population. In the Angolan civil war in the mid-1970s, the United States along with South African forces, backed one faction, while the Soviet Union and Cuban forces supported another, with Washington mainly interested in making things costly for Moscow. South African forces, with U.S. backing, launched major offensives against guerrillas in Namibia (then Southwest Africa) and Angola and against African National Congress forces in Mozambique and Lesotho. Meanwhile, local leaders, such as the Congo's (Zaire's) Mobutu sese Seku, took advantage of major-power competition to consolidate backing for their regimes.[22]

The East–West rivalry was even more intense in the Middle East. As in Africa, the withdrawal of European powers from the region created political opportunities for local leaders at a time when the two superpowers were consolidating their spheres of influence. The Arab-Israeli conflict and the Palestinian question, nationalist and revolutionary movements against the monarchies since the 1950s, and extremist socialist and Islamic movements created deep divisions and rendered the region vulnerable to outside influences from the 1940s onward. The United States tried to balance strong ties with Israel, Saudi Arabia, Turkey, the Shah's Iran, Jordan, Lebanon, and the pro-West Gulf states, while the Soviet Union was successful, albeit briefly, in Syria, Yemen, Iraq, and Egypt, even as Egyptian leaders, as well as those of Iraq, at different periods shifted alliances or alignments between East and West. For ambitious nationalist leaders, such as Egypt's President Gamal Abdel Nasser, throwing off the last vestiges of colonial domination, which stretched back to the building of the Suez Canal in the 1860s and even earlier, was the primary goal. Moreover, Arab states viewed U.S. support for Israel as an unwelcome intervention in their regional affairs, which fueled intense anti-U.S. sentiments, particularly among the more radical nationalist groups after the 1967 and 1973 wars. These groups threatened pro-Western leaders, who in turn responded by strengthening their military with support from the West. Neither was the Soviet Union very successful in its efforts to attract mass support among the Arab populations, even with its proclaimed support for Arab nationalism. Arabs viewed Soviet intentions and atheistic Marxism with suspicion and as an

TABLE 10.2

Amount of Exports of Major Conventional Weapons by the United States and USSR, 1953–1989 (In Millions of Dollars)

	1953[a]	1957	1961	1965	1967	1971	1975	1977	1979	1981	1983	1985	1987	1989
United States	210	240	230	440	260	1,179	2,343	4,826	2,063	6,155	6,289	4,114	6,328	3,465
USSR	120	170	280	200	680	1,515	2,160	2,156	3,678	8,480	8,038	9,106	10,936	8,862

Source: Stockholm International Peace Research Institute (SIPRI), *Yearbook of World Armaments and Disarmament; Tables of the Volume of the Trade in Major Conventional Weapons* (Oxford University Press, various years).

[a]Figures for the 1950s and 1960s are at constant 1968 prices, for the 1970s at constant 1975 prices, and for the 1980s at constant 1985 prices.

TABLE 10.3

Amount of Imports of Major Conventional Weapons by Area, 1953–1989 (In Millions of Dollars)

	1953[a]	1957	1961	1965	1967	1971	1975	1977	1979	1981	1983	1985	1987	1989
Middle East	60	230	110	260	600	1,758	3,527	5,190	3,354	9,386	12,211	10,086	13,523	4,436
Africa	20	10	50	240	190	326	1,172	2,307	1,808	5,158	3,491	3,805	3,468	1,217
Far East	170	170	130	150	120	419	640	653	2,051	2,981	2,591	3,633	3,254	3,932
Central America	10	5	90	10	5	47	137	60	75	776	1,122	731	564	287
South America	60	90	140	50	60	222	630	826	949	3,215	2,896	1,219	1,661	1,077

Source: SIPRI, *Yearbook of World Armaments and Disarmament; Tables of the Volume of the Trade in Major Conventional Weapons* (Oxford University Press, various years).

[a]Figures for the 1950s and 1960s are at constant 1968 prices, for the 1970s at constant 1975 prices, and for the 1980s at constant 1985 prices.

external involvement in the region. The Soviet invasion of Afghanistan in December 1979 merely confirmed these suspicions. Nevertheless, as in other regions, the East–West rivalry polarized various ethnic and religious communities in the region, as some of them aligned themselves with either the United States or the Soviet Union, creating additional layers of conflict and tension within each society. Amid this environment of profound mutual suspicion and intrigue, caught in action-reaction dynamics, the Middle East became one of the most militarized regions in the world by the 1990s.

In Latin America, the U.S. hemispheric hegemony had been established long before the Second World War. During the Cold War, the United States defined its relations with Latin countries as part of the global strategy to contain local revolutions, especially after Fidel Castro's emergence and radicalization in Cuba after 1958, and Soviet expansionism.[23] Moscow historically viewed the Western Hemisphere as too far removed from its immediate geo-political and economic interests and, until the Cuban Revolution of 1959, exerted little influence of any regional significance, except developing closer relations with local Communist parties. As in Asia and Africa, however, socialism in Europe and the Russian Revolution had inspired Marxist revolutionaries throughout Latin America, and the Marxist-Leninist Communist International (Comintern) in the 1920s found opportunities to influence the region's newly organized Communist parties, popular among workers and landless peasants.[24]

In Latin America, as elsewhere, Washington justified its covert operations and military interventions in support of dictatorial regimes, such as Nicaragua's Somoza family, and to overthrow leftist regimes, such as Castro's, as preventing Soviet or Marxist penetration in the Western Hemisphere on grounds of national security. These national security policies sometimes failed, however, as in the case of the Bay of Pigs invasion in April 1961, and Washington usually found its geo-political (security) and economic (corporate) interests at odds with local democratic forces. It opposed local grass-roots-level movements, such as *liberation theology,* led by Catholic priests, worked to overthrow democratically elected leaders, such as President Salvator Allende of Chile in 1973, and backed ruthless Argentine military rulers at least until the Falkland-Malvinas war in 1982. The U.S. involvement in Central America and the Caribbean in the 1980s and 1990s to "roll back communism," as in Grenada and Nicaragua, and to fight the "war on drugs"—arresting Panama's leader, Manuel Noriega, even as reports of CIA involvement with drug traffickers surfaced—only heightened Latin Americans' resentment toward the U.S. government and corporations.

The East–West rivalry in Asia manifested itself in far more complicated forms and with a far greater destructive force than in Latin America. The Chinese civil war between Chiang Kai-shek's Kuomintang (KMT) and Mao Tse-tung's Communist Party in the 1930s and 1940s, the Korean War (1950–1953) and the division of the peninsula on the 38th parallel, and the traumatic Vietnam War, first with French participation (1946–1954) and then American (1961–1973), including Soviet and Chinese roles, exhibited some of the worst symptoms of the East–West, North–South conflicts at the local, regional, and international levels. Although immediately after the Second World War the United States and the Soviet Union were preoccupied with the military, economic, and political situation in the European theater and the Middle East, they could not neglect the rapidly deteriorating situation in Asia, as revolutions and anticolonial nationalist movements, as well as China's emergence as a major power, and Japan's regional role demanded a reconfiguration of the power structure throughout the region.

To appreciate the local, regional, and global complexities involved in such conflicts, one must view the East–West rivalry within the context of North–South conflicts, and vice versa. The Cold War was prolonged because of the superpowers' geo-political ambitions and because of the prevalent political conditions and opportunities in the Third World amid struggles for decolonization. Whether governments learned any lessons from the Cold War experience is not clear. However, on a more optimistic note, it can be argued that, since both the United States and Russia have by now gained greater familiarity with the cultural, political and economic conditions in countries in which they were engaged, they can perhaps more effectively use that knowledge to promote greater international, regional, and local cooperation as a post–Cold War "peace dividend." As there have been opportunities for North–South conflicts during the past fifty years, so have there been opportunities for cooperation, and the North can build new structures on the existing ones. The following section looks at some of the dimensions of North–South cooperation.

OPPORTUNITIES FOR NORTH–SOUTH COOPERATION

The previous sections demonstrated in broad strokes the nature of the challenges encountered in international relations. Despite the difficulties, however, and often because of the difficulties, governments do cooperate. It has been easier to attain global cooperation on economic than security issues, in organizations like WTO, perhaps because there is less perceived risk to government regimes. Multilateral cooperation consists mainly of regional level arrangements, such as OAS, APEC, NAFTA, and the African Lomé Convention, and bilateral cooperation focusing on specific issues. The degree and methods of cooperation between nations[25] depend on the political needs of government leaders and the economic interests of corporations on a wide range of issues, from national security, to the "war on drugs," to the promotion of economic development, to the protection of human rights and the environment, to the provision of better social and welfare programs. The growing trends toward globalization of international transactions by way of rapid transportation and telecommunications systems have facilitated vast networks of international cooperation. As expected by the functionalist and globalization theories, such transactions for international cooperation, with their concomitant spillover effects for development,[26] and the globalization of the international political economy[27] have led to the integration and worldwide restructuring of production and manufacturing.[28] Meanwhile, it has also been the case, as expected by imperialist and dependencia theorists, that these developments tending toward cooperation have been far more salient in the North (most prominently, the European Community) than in the South. Governments in developing countries have been influenced by the North's domination of the "global structures," particularly during the Cold War, imposing its priorities on the South. This section focuses on security alliances and economic cooperation.

Security Alliances and Alignments

Governments engage in bilateral and multilateral military alliances (formal treaties) to pursue a specific set of common goals based on a number of considerations, including security, economic benefits, and prestige. The preceding discussion of the Cold War indicated that the major FIE powers frequently were involved in geo-political and economic competition in the developing countries. Such competition involved North–South bilateral and multilateral security alliances centered on the superpowers but also included efforts by leaders of developing countries to gain resources for their own regional struggles—for example, Pakistan's partnership with the United States as a means of gaining armaments vis-a-vis India during the Cold War.

U.S.–Latin American security arrangements and cooperation provide a further example. Immediately after the Second World War, the major hemispheric security alliance that was centered on the United States was the Inter-American Treaty for Reciprocal Assistance, or the Rio Treaty, formed in 1947 by its twenty or so member states. Together with the OAS Inter-American Committee on Peaceful Settlement, the Rio Treaty symbolized hemispheric cooperation and presented a united front against extra-hemispheric threats—especially the Soviet Union and communism.[29] Although the Soviet Union had no such alliances in Latin America, it did gain a foothold in Cuba after the Cuban Revolution, albeit at the expense of floating Cuba's economy in the face of a U.S. embargo. Attempting to provide Cuba with defense against the United States, Moscow's deployment of nuclear missiles on the island brought the world to the brink of a nuclear war in 1962. For its part, the United States was successful in mobilizing political, if virtually symbolic, support among Latin American countries under the Rio Treaty during the Cuban missile crisis. Another instance of OAS authorization of inter-American forces was the invasion of the Dominican Republic in 1965 to complete the ouster, in 1963, of a duly elected democratic president, Juan Bosch, which involved 1,743 Latin American troops from six countries and 11,000 U.S. troops. There was little doubt that the invasion was a U.S. operation and that the presence of Latin American troops merely provided a semblance of legal legitimacy under the Rio Treaty.

The United States sought to replicate NATO- and Rio-type regional security arrangements in other regions as well. In the 1950s, the Eisenhower administration's "pactomania" led to the creation of the Southeast Asia Treaty Organization (SEATO), the ANZUS defense treaty with Australia and New Zealand, and the "Baghdad Pact," subsequently the Central Treaty Organization (CENTO), in the Middle East. North–South security cooperation involved bilateral military agreements and treaties. As the Eisenhower administration developed multilateral regional security arrangements, it also sought "mutual security" pacts to strengthen the anti-Soviet containment policy with countries deemed geo-strategically important, as in mutual defense pacts with Japan, Taiwan, and South Korea, to contain both Soviet and Chinese power in East Asia. Bilateral arrangements over the years facilitated the transfer of U.S. military assistance, including such programs as the International Military Education and Training (IMET) Program, providing training to tens of thousands of military personnel. The United States used military assistance and various forms of economic and development assistance programs to support pro-U.S. governments throughout the world." A conservative estimate puts the total dollar amount spent on U.S. "security assistance" between 1946 and 1992, when the Cold War ended, at $150 billion.[30] During the Reagan administration's Cold War in Central America, El Salvador alone received nearly $2 billion worth of military support between 1983 and 1987.[31]

Given the economic and political stakes, North–South economic relations have often required at minimum the projection of military power to discourage potential disruptions in supply of natural resources and corporate seizures. In its *Congressional Presentation for Security Assistance Program* (FY1989), the U.S. Department of Defense stressed the need to contain political instability as follows:

> Successful efforts to avert and contain low intensity conflict help provide for the United States:
> - a free and growing international market for U.S. goods and services;
> - a stable international financial system;
> - secure access to strategic raw materials and to irreplaceable foreign military facilities;
> - and the broad political, economic and security cooperation of friends and allies around the world.[32]

Accordingly, it proposed congressional passage of security assistance programs totaling $8.3 billion for fiscal year 1989.[33]

Generally, direct means of protecting access to regions and sea communication networks have involved North–South bilateral military agreements for permission to station military facilities; in some cases maintenance of military facilities in a developing country represented remnants of traditional colonialism, as in the case of the U.S. navy's continued control of the Guantanamo base ("the oldest U.S. military base on foreign soil") in Cuba, the "number one enemy" of the United States in the Western Hemisphere.[34] Over the years, the United States has maintained numerous such facilities in the region: on the Bahamian island of Andros, the U.S. navy has operated the AUTEC (Atlantic Undersea Test and Evaluation Center) for tests in antisubmarine warfare; the U.S. navy's SONUS (Sound Surveillance System) has been the central station integrating a vast network of substations throughout the region for the purpose of worldwide marine surveillance operations to detect submarine movements; and the U.S. Southern Command (SOUTHCOM), a central agency of the Department of Defense, has been stationed in the Panama Canal Zone and has engaged in various inter-American military training and assistance programs, (it may have to move with the expiration of the Canal lease in 1999).

For developing countries, cooperation with major powers, such as the United States, entails a number of advantages, as well as costs. The government of a developing country opts for a security alliance with a major power because the latter can provide the military hardware necessary to keep that government in power. Also, the civilian economic and political elites find it necessary to guarantee the backing of a major power in case of domestic or regional opposition. Another reason for engaging in security alliances is international and domestic prestige; governments of some developing countries view security treaties with a superpower as a vote of confidence in their own leadership, competence, and devotion to national security. Unfortunately for the United States, however, policymakers in Washington often realize too late that arming allies to the teeth buys neither assured military strength nor stability, as illustrated by the fall of pro-U.S. regimes in Iran and Zaire/Congo in 1979 and 1997, respectively. For developing country leaders, too close an embrace with dominant major powers also can lead to interference in domestic affairs and the resentment of regional neighbors.

One of the foreign policy dilemmas for countries (in the North and the South) that were heavily involved in Cold War politics has been on what basis and around what issues to cooperate in the post-Cold War system. For over four decades, the Cold War provided people worldwide with an "geo-political compass" in relations with the superpowers. Developing states, however, were always more preoccupied with regional issues and economic development concerns than with East–West ideologies. For the United States, as the remaining global superpower, the central question in the post–Cold War era, when Cold War ideological and geo-political considerations are no longer operative, is how to secure the cooperation of developing countries under its hegemony in the world political economy. For the developing countries, the challenge is equally serious: they can no longer serve as "friendly governments" in a Cold War–style competition to secure economic and military assistance from the competing powers. They must rely on their own resources and leadership skills to demonstrate their ability to perform certain marketable functions in the global economy.

It was, therefore, no accident that developing countries' move toward market and trade liberalization coincided with the Cold War's decline and collapse. When the domestic costs for developing countries exceeded the benefits from security cooperation, some even demanded the revocation of base rights and the withdrawal of military personnel from their territories, as in the case of the Subic and Clark bases in the Philippines, and the controversial Panama Canal Treaty of 1977, under which the United States agreed to withdraw from the Canal Zone.[35]

As anticipated by the functionalists, the Cold War security arrangements also spilled over into other areas in North–South cooperation, as in the U.S.-Peruvian cooperation in the "war on drugs."[36] In October 1982, when the Reagan administration declared war on drugs, new institutional mechanisms were required (see Box 10.1).[37] In 1988, the United States signed bilateral agreements with twenty-eight countries in the Western Hemisphere, including Peru, to begin aerial herbicide Tebuthiuron (Spike) spraying. The U.S.-Peruvian agreement provided for an initial herbicide campaign over 100 to 250 hectares of coca fields,[38] throughout the Upper Huallaga Valley a strategy that proved quite controversial. Critics charged that, in addition to failing to stop the drug flow, the sprays caused environmental damage and jeopardized the health of Peruvians, civilians and revolutionaries alike. Although Peru's president eventually canceled the aerial sprays,[39] such projects provided opportunities for North–South cooperation but also were used by those who wanted to keep military spending high.

Economic Cooperation

For developing countries, the East-West rivalry during the Cold War was of secondary importance at best, but in order to gain Washington's support, cooperation with the United States had to be couched within the context of the East–West rivalry. The principal issue on the developing countries' agenda concerned economic development to address the problems of poverty and unemployment. North–South economic cooperation was an important aspect of economic development, if only because most (over 65 percent) of less developed countries (LDC) trade and investment relations were with the North.

The rationale for the West's support of economic development was similar to that of the Marshall Plan for Europe: since poverty and unemployment would create conditions favorable to communism, it was necessary to establish strong foundations for economic development and friendly regimes to defeat the ideological attraction of communism. However, in fact, both the United States and the Soviet Union extended economic support to developing countries supportive of their Cold War policies and not necessarily to address issues of poverty and unemployment (or even of ideological purity—as in Soviet support of states such as Egypt, which jailed communists). While North–South cooperation occurred in the area of economic development, the primary motive was not economic development itself. Nothing illustrates this point better than the Kennedy administration's Alliance for Progress program for Latin America.

The Kennedy administration introduced the Alliance for Progress program to assist Latin countries' economic development and "nation-building," largely in response to criticism that Washington extended $17 billion worth of economic aid to Europe through the Marshall Plan, while ignoring its southern neighbors, who also contributed to the defeat of Nazism and fascism in Europe. However, the primary impetus for the Alliance plan was provided by the Cuban Revolution and Castro's rapid shift to pro-Soviet communism and "continental revolutionism." Nathan and Oliver have pointed out that the principal objective of the Alliance was counterrevolutionary in orientation. It sought to promote economic development and alleviate poverty but with a number of conditions implied or attached: the program required that aid recipients purchase U.S. goods and services, check the spread of Castro's influence in the hemisphere, and not allow political and economic reforms to jeopardize political stability. To combat potential threats to stability, the Alliance was accompanied by training programs for Latin American military personnel in counterinsurgency operations "at Fort Bragg, North Carolina, home of the Green Berets, and in the Jungle Warfare School in the American-controlled Panama Canal Zone."[40]

The United States and the other Western industrialized countries also engage in developing economic cooperation for additional reasons, including, as discussed in previous chapters, securing cheap labor for companies, and promoting MNC investments and trade relations. Some regions of the world, however, assume greater geo-economic and, hence, geo-strategic and security significance than others. This is not to suggest, as some claim, that the United States depends so heavily on a specific region's trade or natural resources that it will use military force to intervene whenever it perceives a threat to its interests.[41] Interventions came more predictably when it appears that access to a key region might be denied or threatened. In the 1970s, for example, political unrest in Zaire resulted in disruptions of the cobalt supply and price increase of 700 percent[42]—a concern not only to the United States but also to its European allies.

BOX 10.1

THE "WAR ON DRUGS" AND NORTH–SOUTH COOPERATION: THE UNITED STATES AND PERU

In the 1980s, the U.S. Drug Enforcement Agency (DEA) conducted joint investigations with police agencies in Peru. It trained and equipped Peruvian law enforcement agencies, and the State Department and the DEA created "elite drug enforcement units composed of local police." The DEA trained them, appointed their supervisors, supervised their hiring, and funded their operations. For example, one such elite enforcement unit was Peru's Mobile Rural Patrol Unit (UMOPAR). The Reagan and Alan Garcia administrations adopted two major policies in their war on drugs: eradication and interdiction, which covered the region of Tingo Maria, the Upper Huallaga Valley, and which involved research, training, the development of infrastructure and sanitation services. It was largely financed and supervised by the State Department. The United States gave about $15 million in loans and $3 million in grants for a five-year period, while the Peruvian government spent $8.5 million.

Interdiction involved about 450 workers for the Special Project for the Control and Eradication of Coca in the Upper Huallaga (CORAH) and the Upper Huallaga Area Development Project (PEAH), financed by the U.S. Agency for International Development (AID). Under this program, coca growers were paid about $300 to destroy 1 hectare of coca. This policy failed, however, largely because coca traffickers could offer more than five times the government price. Coca growers refused to give up their lucrative enterprise. Another effort, "Operation Condor," involved air raids (targeting traffickers and their laboratories and airstrips) by joint U.S.-Peruvian officials, including Peru's 500 UMOPAR antidrug police, the *Guardia Civil,* the Investigative Police, the military, the U.S. State Department, U.S. pilots, DEA officials, and Evergreen Air, a private company. This operation also proved futile. Neither was "Operation Snowcap," introduced in 1989, successful. One obstacle was the presence of the Shining Path rebels in the Upper Huallaga Valley. Because of Shining Path's guerrilla activities, the police and the military resisted both U.S. and their government's calls for greater involvement in the war on drugs in regions under guerrillas' control.

One reason why Garcia cooperated was that the drug industry was mostly restricted to a small number of growers, so that it had not yet become a significant portion of Peru's middle-class economy, nor did it command a major portion of the Peruvian national economy, as in Bolivia. Another reason was that Garcia sought to eliminate government corruption, including corruption in his political party, the American Popular Revolutionary Alliance (APRA). He also hoped that the war on drugs would provide an opportunity to free Peru from the constant threat of revolution. Concomitantly, cooperation on the drugs issue would enable his government to maintain good relations with Washington at a time when the latter pursued aggressive policies against Marxist-Communist movements in the Western Hemisphere. U.S. aid to Peru was an important factor in Garcia's decision to make such a major commitment to the war on drugs, and he agreed to the U.S. aerial herbicide-spraying programs a short time before the U.S. Congress considered foreign aid bills.

Sources: Simon Payaslian, "The Formation of Dyadic Decision Regimes," paper presented at the International Studies Association annual meeting, Vancouver, B.C., March 1991; Steven Wisotsky, *Beyond the War on Drugs* (Buffalo: Prometheus Books, 1990), pp. 49–53; Cynthia McClintock, "The War on Drugs: the Peruvian Case," *Journal of Inter-American Studies and World Affairs* 30, 2 & 3 (Summer/Fall 1988), pp.130–136; Ethan A. Nadelmann, "The DEA in Latin America: Dealing with Institutionalized Corruption," *Journal of Inter-American Studies and World Affairs* 29, 4 (Winter 1987–88), pp. 3–4; Richard B. Craig, "Illicit Drug Traffic: Implications for South American Source Countries," *Journal of Inter-American Studies and World Affairs* 29, 2 (Summer 1987), p. 20; Louis W. Goodman and Johanna S.R. Mendelson, "The Threat of New Missions," in Louis W. Goodman, et al., eds., *The Military and Democracy* (Lexington, MA: Lexington Books, 1990), p. 193.

Regional roles in North–South relations have remained relatively constant: demand for natural resources and corporate investments constituted the primary bases for North–South economic cooperation before the Cold War, and it continues to do so after the Cold War, as in Washington's developing relations with oil-rich former Soviet Central Asian republics.

In recent years, the U.S. Army War College Strategic Studies Group has identified a number of key resources as the "most strategic materials," including chromium, platinum metals, tin, manganese, aluminum, titanium, cobalt, tantalum, nickel, mercury, and tungsten.[43] Western industrialized societies have imported a substantial share of these materials from the developing countries. For example, the

United States, a country relatively well endowed with natural resources, has imported 73 percent of its chromium supply from South Africa, Zimbabwe, Yugoslavia, and Turkey; 92 percent of platinum metals group supply from South Africa, Britain, and the former Soviet Union; 100 percent of its manganese supply from South Africa, France, and Brazil; 97 percent of its bauxite and aluminium supply from Australia, Jamaica, Guinea, and Suriname; 96 percent of its cobalt supply from Zaire, Zambia, Canada, and Norway; 92 percent of its tantalum supply from Thailand, Brazil, Malaysia, and Australia; and 100 percent of its columbium supply (used to manufacture alloys for the aerospace industry—for example, F-100 jet engines) from Brazil, Canada, and Thailand.[44] Numerous treaties are involved in securing cooperation to gain access to such raw materials.

Although North–South economic cooperation for the acquisition of natural resources may be viewed as exploitation of human and land resources, as the *dependencia* school does, such arrangements were developed with the cooperation of the leadership in developing countries. Access to natural resources entails major projects requiring formal contracts and informal contacts to secure the production, processing, and transport of materials. Disruptions in these processes can have a devastating impact on an industrialized nation's economy and, at times, as in the 1973 oil embargo, on the world economy. However, by the mid-1990s, the West had restructured its domestic and international energy resource policies to become less vulnerable to disruptions. The same cannot be said for most developing countries, whose economies remain as vulnerable as ever to fluctuations in prices and exchange rates—indeed, they also remain vulnerable to changes in energy and fuel prices. For developing countries, despite concerns regarding dependence, economic cooperation with governments and MNCs in the industrialized North has become an essential part of economic life, albeit within a framework of a capitalist world economy.

The EU and the Lomé Conventions The EU's relations with some developing countries has differed at least in one important respect from U.S. policy (except perhaps regarding Puerto Rico): some EU members had colonial territories after the Second World War, and they continued their close economic ties with them even after decolonization. In addition to development assistance programs (discussed in Chapter 11), the EU members established a number of trade agreements—as in the case of the two Yaoundé Conventions in 1963 and 1969–1975 between themselves and eighteen former French and Belgian colonies in Africa, as well as the Arusha Agreement with Kenya, Tanzania, and Uganda.[45] British membership in the European Common Market in 1975 required new or similar agreements with the British Commonwealth states, and in 1975 the first in a series of five-year term Lomé Conventions was signed between the EU members and forty-six African, Caribbean, and Pacific (ACP) countries (Lomé II 1979–1984, Lomé III 1984–1989, and Lomé IV for a ten-year-term 1989–1999, to be reviewed in 2000).

The Lomé Conventions established various preferential trade and development assistance programs and, in doing so, sought to address some of the major problems identified by the *dependencia* theorists. In the area of trade, the EU countries agreed to lower tariff barriers for products from the ACP countries, and the latter agreed to maintain most favored nation treatment for EU products. Innovative export price stability mechanisms, known as the Stabex and the Sysmin systems, were introduced with the purpose of absorbing the impact of world market fluctuations on ACP export earnings (that are heavily dependent on primary products, such as agricultural and raw materials). Under the Stabex system, Lomé IV identified nearly fifty such products, and the EU countries pledged 1.5 billion ECU to "compensate a country to the extent that its export earnings from a covered commodity fall below a reference level based on the six prior years."[46] Under the Sysmin system, the EU pledged 480 million ECU for the first half of the 1990s. The Lomé Conventions also identified various areas for development assistance and technical cooperation including the environment, agriculture, manufacturing, and telecommunications.

Post–Cold War Cooperation The end of the Cold War has not fundamentally changed economic conditions, but the recent shift to greater trade liberalization, particularly by the large "emerging markets," such as India and Brazil, has increased North–South trade and investment opportunities. According to one estimate, private investment in emerging markets has increased consistently since the early 1990s, totaling about $180 billion in 1995 and a record $244 billion in 1996.[47] Cooperation in trade also has been intensified, with widening networks of multilateral arrangements. In 1996, negotiations started to develop closer ties between the Southeast Asian and the North American free trade areas. Members of the ASEAN group (Brunei, Indonesia, Malaysia, the Philippines, Singapore, Thailand, and Vietnam)[48] and NAFTA (the United States, Canada, and Mexico) have expressed hopes for region-to-region cooperation, and further negotiations are expected. The Asia Pacific Economic Cooperation (APEC) ministerial conference in Christchurch, New Zealand, produced some specific plans and targets.[49] APEC's eighteen members have agreed to pursue trade and investment liberalization trade by the year 2020, and, according to Chris Butler, chair of APEC's Committee on Trade & Investment (CTI), "APEC has already produced results for its members."[50] APEC and similar arrangements are expected to complement the North–South dispute settlement mechanisms within "the global commercial watchdog, the World Trade Organization (WTO)."[51]

In addition, North–South cooperation in recent years has involved "fair trade" issues—that is, North–South trade relations designed to help developing economies benefit more from international trade with the North. International conferences on free trade among advanced economies have paid closer attention to fair trade, also known as "alternative trade."[52] Proponents of fair trade promote goods from developing countries in Northern markets while emphasizing improved working conditions, and the elimination of child labor, long hours, and so on. For instance, meeting in London in November 1996, the World Federation of Sporting Goods Industries (comprised of major brand names such as Nike, Reebok, and Adidas) accepted the challenge from various organizations, including UNICEF, to develop plans for production without abuses of child labor and low-wage workers in the developing world. According to the International Labor Organization, approximately 250 million children, mostly under the age of fourteen are working in developing countries. At a World Trade Organization conference in Singapore, members agreed to support more humane working conditions, to uphold internationally recognized core labor standards, and not to exploit child labor (in many countries, children bring home income important to the family—issues especially important in the informal economy as discussed in Chapter 12). Significantly, the developing countries, suspecting that the West would use the adoption of such international labor standards as a justification for more protectionist policies, demanded that the WTO pressure the advanced industrialized countries to leave their markets open to Third World exports.[53]

Nongovernmental organizations (NGOs), such as the Ford Foundation, Christian Aid, and Oxfam, have been particularly active in the advocacy of fair trade in Europe and the United States. In the United States, the Ford Foundation has reportedly provided the American Fair Trade Association with grants totaling about $75,000 toward the publication of a directory of North American fairtrade organizations and stores, entitled "Sweatshops or Fair Trade? Now You Have a Choice!" While in the United States and Canada fair trade sales are about $40 million, in Western Europe fair trade stores have proliferated, with total annual sales of up to $500 million. Efforts are underway in Europe and the United States to expand fairtrade markets in various areas of consumer goods.[54]

Cooperation in these areas may improve the future of North–South relations, especially if such relations are predicated on more equal terms, taking both importers' and exporters' interests into account. Other such trends include the Southern insistence on "offsetting" and "countertrade" provisions in agreements to purchase expensive northern goods, such as arms; on provisions for the return purchase of Southern products; and on provisions for more production in Southern factories. As should be obvious, not all issues are easily amenable to cooperation, precisely because interests vary, at times with seemingly irreconcilable differences. For example, environmental issues have required considerable energy to sustain North–South cooperation.

Environmental Issues

As the threat posed by environmental degradation to the physical survival of the "global village" became more obvious after the first "Earth Days" in the 1970s, concerns regarding auto and factory emissions and air and water pollution in the cities, deforestation, ozone depletion, and global warming placed the issue on the global agenda. In 1972, the United Nations established the UN Conference on Human Environment at Stockholm and, a decade later, in 1983, the World Commission on Environment and Development, the Brundtland Commission (named after its chair, Mrs. Gro Harlem Brundtland, then head of the Labor Party in Norway), to address growing environmental concerns worldwide. The UN General Assembly adopted the Brundtland Commission report, entitled *Our Common Future,* in New York on October 29, 1987—ironically, the day of the Wall Street market crash.[55] Reaction to the Brundtland Report was mixed. On the one hand, the report legitimized environmental-ecological problems as a global issue. Developed and developing country NGOs, some of which had closely worked with the Brundtland Commission and UN agencies in this area, welcomed this heightened attention to the environment;

yet, the commission's proposals proved controversial. Matthias Finger has observed,

> In the report, the causes of today's global environmental problems were identified as exclusively social and political: unsatisfied needs, "in particular the needs of the world's poor" and "limitations imposed by the state of technology and social organization on the environment's ability to meet present and future needs." Some of these elements, identified as causes of today's environmental problems, were also seen by the Brundtland Commission as solutions, i.e., in particular science and technology, economic growth in an open-market economy, and western-style management, especially resource management and risk management.[56]

In confirming the need to combat environmental degradation at the global level, the Brundtland Report also highlighted the tension between economic development and environmental considerations—a conflict that has become an integral dimension of the relationship between the FIEs in the North and the AIEs and LDEs in the South. In the 1990s, UN-sponsored world conferences on the environment, such as the Earth Summit in 1992, provided opportunities for North–South cooperation, articulating principles of environmentally "sustainable development," but failed to address the conflicts and the sense in the South that the North was asking for cleanups before the South had even experienced economic development.

The primary factor contributing to the decline in world environmental quality has been the spread of industrialization since the industrial revolution in the late 1700s and early 1800s and the subsequent acceleration in extraction of natural resources (for example, mining and oil drilling), the proliferation of factories, the transportation of resources from mines to factories, and the emission of pollution (for example, carbon dioxide, and various chemical compounds) from factories and autos, particularly troubling in the former Soviet bloc countries, Latin American, and the United States (see Figure 10.2).[57] While in the 1850s world emission of carbon dioxide (CO_2) from fossil fuel combustion was 1 million tons per year, a century later that figure was 1.5 million tons. Within a decade, it reached about 6 million tons and continued to increase unabated to about 23 million tons in the late 1980s (see Figure 10.3). The rapid and massive increase in world emission of chlorofluorocarbons (CFCs), CO_2, and nitrous oxide (N_2O) into the atmosphere damages the earth's ozone layer and is thought to cause global warming, or the greenhouse effect. Environmental-ecological degradation is not limited to air, however. Ships and supertankers alone dump 1,000 tons of sulfuric acid and various chemicals into the oceans of the world per day.[58]

The implications of environmental abuse for human survival are clear, involving rapid deforestation; a decline in air, water, and food quality; acid rain; rising sea levels; floods; and overall destruction of infrastructure are essential for the daily life (see Box 10.2). The fact that this environmental destruction has been occurring simultaneously with rapid growth in world population, now about 6 billion, nearly 50 percent of whom live in the coastal areas, severely tests the human ability to adapt and to survive.

These environmental problems and the solutions to them are particularly complicated by the very nature of the international political system. The flow of air and water pollution transcends international boundaries and makes it virtually impossible for individual governments acting alone to contain it. As a result, in recent years, multilateral

FIGURE 10.2

Source: Enquete-Kommission 1990, in Ingomar Hauchler and Paul M. Kennedy, eds., *Global Trends* (New York: Continuum, 1994), Fig. 5, p. 281.

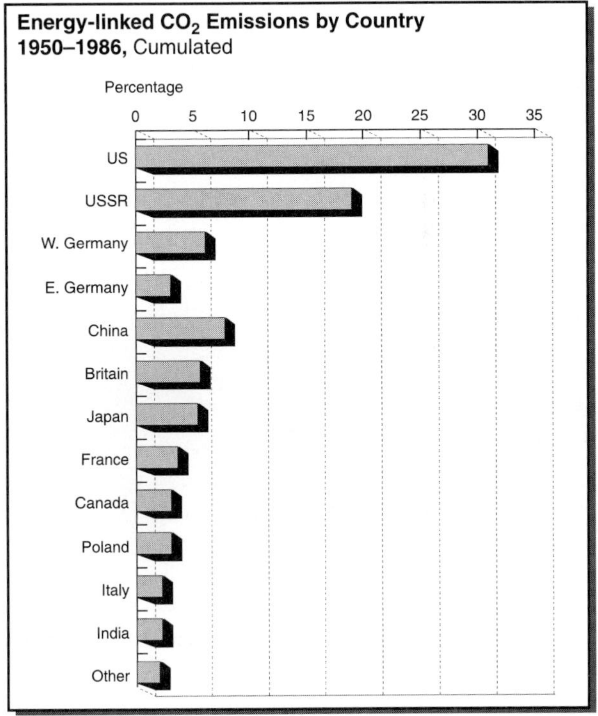

negotiations have attempted to set certain international standards and to coordinate environmental policies, yet, different states have different interests and priorities, with varying definitions of the sources of environmental problems and the solutions to them. Also, states do not all share the costs of environmental degradation equally. The Western industrialized countries consume a disproportionately large share of the world's resources, but they are also sufficiently powerful to shape the global agenda and influence environmental policies in international forums. They also possess most of the capital and technology necessary to combat environmental degradation.

The developing countries, however, are faced with a serious dilemma. On the one hand, they view the rising international standards in this area as "green imperialism" and an obstacle to their own national economic development.[59] They argue that the environmental issue was not on the global agenda and international environmental standards did not exist when the industrialized countries were reaping the benefits of rampant industrialization, labeled as "progress," during the past 170 years or so, as their factories and mining operations polluted vast areas from one continent to another. Having achieved a comfortable degree of industrial and technological superiority over the rest of the world, they assert, now the industrialized states seek to impose environmental standards to frustrate efforts by the developing countries to achieve a similar degree of industrialization and economic growth. Within the context of global politics, these issues and considerations have caused serious North–South tensions, but they have also underscored the need to cooperate. The failure to set and implement environmental policies simply results in increasingly severe environmental problems, with catastrophic consequences for people. In the 1980s, in order to balance their trade and budgets and to ease their foreign debt burden, developing countries, from Brazil to the Philippines to the Ivory Coast, launched massive programs to increase the extraction of natural resources, including timber; their policies resulted in the destruction not only of forests, as in the Amazon, but also of communities, as people were removed from their homes to clear the way for the bulldozers.

FIGURE 10.3

Source: Ingomar Hauchler and Paul M. Kennedy, eds., *Global Trends* (New York: Continuum, 1994), Fig. 5, p. 281.

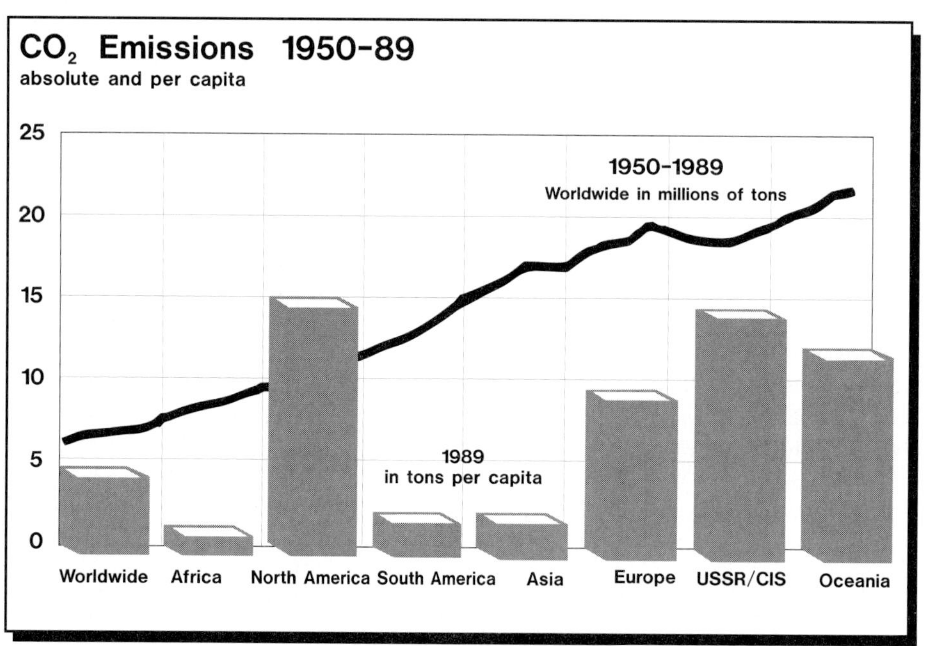

BOX 10.2

THE INTERNATIONAL POLITICS OF AMAZON DEFORESTATION

RIO DE JANEIRO, Brazil—After years of Brazilian government claims that stricter environmental laws had slowed destruction of the Amazon rain forest, newly issued figures show that deforestation has actually increased sharply since the 1992 Earth Summit was held here, with fires and logging consuming rain forests the size of Denmark in just a few years. The data, which covered deforestation from 1991 to 1994, appeared to support assertions by environmental groups that the drop-off in deforestation by 1991 was caused more by an economic downturn in Brazil than by any significant government action to reduce the destruction. It also put an end to government claims that deforestation had continued to decline in the years since the Earth Summit, when 118 nations gathered for the largest environmental conference ever held, and Brazil enjoyed the public relations windfall of seemingly having gained control over deforestation. "I think in the mind of many people, the burning of the Amazon rain forest had a beginning, a middle and an end," said Stephan Schwartzman, a senior scientist at the Environmental Defense Fund. The new data, he said, contradicted that impression. "The burning of the Amazon is not over. It's getting worse." The data show that deforestation rose 34 percent, from 4,296 square miles in the 1990–91 burning season to 5,750 square miles a year by 1994. Analysis of the data for 1995, which have not yet been released, is expected to show a yet greater increase in deforestation, since the number and location of fires detected last year showed many raging in virgin rain forests, said Philip M. Fearnside, an ecology professor at the National Institute for Research in the Amazon, in Manaus.

As it issued the updated figures on deforestation, the Brazilian government announced a series of measures to crack down on illegal logging of mahogany and virola, and increased to 80 percent from 50 percent the share of property that landowners in the Amazon must preserve as tropical forest. The measures came shortly before a meeting this week in Bonn, where representatives from the Group of Seven industrialized nations are gathering to evaluate a $280 million fund for pilot projects to save the Amazon. So far, only $10 million of the total has been spent, Bruce Beehler, from the U.S. State Department's ecology office, said by telephone from Bonn. By next year, industrialized nations will have to decide whether to extend the authorization and perhaps increase the fund, for which Brazil had originally sought $1.5 billion.

By the eve of the Bonn meeting, the government environmental agency responsible for overseeing the extraction of timber from the Amazon had found irregularities leading to the cancellation or suspension of 62 percent of the 1,200 authorizations for cutting mahogany and virola, said Paulo Beninca, director of natural and renewable resources at the federal environmental agency. The next step, he added, will be enforcement in the field. As for enforcing the newly increased rain forest preserves, Beninca said the agency would rely on more sophisticated equipment and draw on information available through other government agencies rather than hire more inspectors. The number of inspectors available to monitor illegal burning in the rain forest remains low, with about 80 inspectors covering 2 million square miles. The measures won praise from environmentalists, though many said they could gauge their importance only after seeing how seriously they would be enforced over time.

"Our worry is that this emergency action will die down as soon as the attention wanes," said Joao Paulo Capobianco, executive secretary of the Socio-Environmental Institute, a private group. "Government action in the Amazon has to be permanent." Thomas Lovejoy, the Smithsonian Institution's counselor for biodiversity and environmental affairs, said he was convinced that President Fernando Henrique Cardoso of Brazil was "very serious" about tackling destruction of the tropical rain forest. "These two are pretty forceful measures," Lovejoy said. "There's a depth of commitment that's greater than any we've seen before."

Others appeared concerned by the timing of the measures and the release of the data. In addition to this week's meeting in Bonn, the government will also take part in a weeklong commemoration of the Amazon in New York at the end of the month, when its record in the Amazon and the demarcation of Indian lands is likely to come under scrutiny. "What's unfortunate is that President Cardoso once again appears to be playing to the international gallery," said Schwartzman, who works in Washington and Brasilia. "He took these steps when he did in order to avoid any problems in Bonn, and to put a good face on the government participation in the Amazon."

Source: Diana Jean Schemo, "Burning of Amazon Picks Up Pace, with Vast Areas Lost," *The New York Times,* September 12, 1996, p. A3.

Despite various interpretations and labeling, whether viewed from the laissez-faire, Marxist, *dependencia,* or other perspectives, issues such as environmental degradation are transnational and, by their very nature, require bilateral and multilateral cooperation. It is estimated, for example, that if China with its massive population and existing air pollution, ever fully joins the automotive economy, the increase in atmospheric emissions could be a global nightmare (unless, of course, expensive new clean fuel technologies also become widely and cheaply available).

DEVELOPING COUNTRIES AND STRATEGIES FOR ECONOMIC DEVELOPMENT

From the South's perspective, the post-WWII international economic order, built on Western laissez-faire liberalism, had proved an unrealistic formula for economic development even before WWII. In Latin America, for example, the Great Depression gave rise to a host of questions regarding the applicability of laissez-faire capitalism to local conditions. The international economic environment in the 1930s and 1940s was hardly conducive to economic development and growth, least of all for *independent* development. Protectionist policies in the industrialized countries, shortages of capital, and the fact that immediately after the Second World War the North went its own way regardless of the South's grievances, led Latin American and the newly independent African and Asian countries to search for indigenous strategies for economic development. Initially, most developing countries stressed **import-substitution industrialization (ISI)**—that is, producing manufactured goods previously imported and nurturing local industries, often behind tariff walls—as the best available option for economic development. The East Asian NICs (Taiwan, South Korea, Hong Kong, and Singapore), however, quickly shifted from ISI to **export-led strategies** premised on a combination of statist strategies and free trade as the best course to stimulate economic growth and rapid development. A small number of countries, such as China and Tanzania, sought total **self-reliance.**

However, no single model or strategy, whether implemented in the developed or developing countries, can provide a viable blueprint for successful economic development. Strategies for structural reforms and even revolutions, such as the Chinese Communist revolution in 1949 and the Islamic revolution in Iran in 1978, often have their intellectual orientation rooted in theories and principles, as identified in the paradigms of political economy. The intellectual predilection to opt for a specific strategy, however, is also a reaction to social, economic, and political conditions in society, shaped by the history of national and international political economy. Thus, for example, the Chinese Communist leadership under Mao Tse-tung adopted the self-reliance strategy in reaction to a century of European colonialism, as did the Islamic revolution under Ayatollah Khomeini in adopting an Islamic strategy in reaction to a long history of Western domination and corruption in Iran.

Among the three strategies noted above, the export-led strategy has been the most successful, but export-led economies, by definition, are more immediately vulnerable to market fluctuations, as Asia's growing economic difficulties in the second half of the 1990s have underscored. In the early 1980s, the NICs consisted exclusively of the East Asian countries, but by the early 1990s the club of NICs included some Latin American countries as well, especially Argentina, Brazil, Mexico, Chile, and Costa Rica. It has been argued that these Latin states have "graduated" from the South proper; yet, there is little indication that they have overcome their development problems—namely, dependence on the markets, finances, and technologies of the North. Further, export-led policies have produced uneven domestic development and relatively high consumer prices. Regardless of the strategies adopted for economic development, the oil shocks of the 1970s and the ensuing global inflation, recession, and stagnation reminded the South that efforts to undo their dependent relationships with the North had not fully succeeded.

Import-Substitution Industrialization (ISI)

During the 1950s and 1960s, Latin American countries adopted the ISI strategy based on the principles of economic nationalism (such as protective tariffs for infant industries) to stimulate rapid industrialization and economic development.[60] For most of the nineteenth century and the first half of the twentieth, European, especially British, and U.S. MNCs had maintained extensive investments in Latin American economies in agriculture, mining, and finance. These multinationals had shaped the development of infrastructures, manufacturing, and the overall socioeconomic structures to serve their own interests and those of the political and economic elites supporting them. The Great Depression, however, convinced Latin American leaders that fundamental changes were necessary in the national economic structures and that rapid development required indigenous industrial strength.

In Brazil, for example, proto-fascist dictator Getúlio Vargas in the 1930s and 1940s, his successors in the 1950s, and the military generals who seized power in 1964 sought to industrialize Brazil's economy and enhance its position at home and abroad.[61] Once in power, the military created a dictatorial regime: it prohibited all opposition to its rule, including labor strikes, and unleashed, in the name of national security, the police and "death squads" against unarmed citizens, intellectuals, university professors and students, and artists accused of holding opinions against the state and, therefore, of being "Communist sympathizers." A strong government was necessary, the generals argued, to stabilize the economy and to stimulate investments in Brazil. The military *junta,* for their part, invested heavily in developing production facilities in steel, arms, petrochemicals, hydroelectric power, and communications. For a while, the economy did improve, and it achieved an annual growth in the national product of 11 percent in the early 1970s. The generals boasted of having ushered in a new "Brazilian era," a "Brazilian miracle." That miracle was short-lived, however, as the oil crises in the 1970s, inflation, and heavy borrowing from foreign banks to finance the ambitious economic development programs again brought Brazil face to face with economic chaos reminiscent of the 1930s. Increases in oil prices and subsequent increases in interest rates in the early 1980s caused economic slowdown and recession (some would call it depression), while Brazil borrowed billions to avert total economic collapse. Brazil's international debt mushroomed from about $40 billion in the late 1970s to nearly $100 billion in 1983. The Brazilian miracle dissipated, and in 1985 the military finally admitted defeat and agreed to surrender power to civilian leaders.

The Brazilian experience was repeated in most Latin American and other developing countries that experimented with ISI. Despite its erstwhile contribution to industrial and economic growth in the 1960s and 1970s, the import-substitution strategy led to serious financial problems, beginning in the second half of the 1970s. Injection of foreign finance in the late 1970s and early 1980s initially alleviated some of the economic difficulties, but, because of hyperinflation, income derived from exports did not fulfill projected returns on investments. These developing countries could not, due to limited domestic capacity and the limited returns from external markets, sustain industrialization based on foreign finance. In Africa and Asia, political instability after decolonization doomed ISI, while in Latin America the assumed return to financial-economic normality after the huge investments in industrialization and economic development in the 1960s and 1970s failed to materialize in the 1980s. By then, it had become amply clear to developing countries that the original objective of ISI—that is, to end **dependent development**—remained beyond their reach.[62]

Moreover, the ISI strategy, in order to be effective, required importation of expensive machinery, equipment, and raw materials to sustain projected development programs and to extend industrialization into different economic areas as necessary. Instead of overcoming foreign dependence, ISI programs paradoxically led to greater dependence; "any alteration in external prices or the slightest problem of foreign financing would cause serious difficulties, such as shortages and rising prices of essential consumer goods, the restriction of imports of raw materials and the consequent effect on productive capacity of delaying imports of machinery and equipment."[63]

Under ISI, the role of the state expanded considerably as well. As expected by the neo-mercantilist and neo-statist theories, ISI placed the state directly at the center of national industrial and financial activity, most notably in financing enormous projects for infrastructural development, such as communication, transportation, and energy, and in allocating resources for social and health services and educational programs. This expansive statist role, based on the promise of rapid industrialization, created a ravenous appetite for more capital, increasingly accommodated by foreign banks. While developing countries were borrowing heavily, however, their export markets entered a downward cycle amid world inflationary and recessionary pressures. As projected returns on investments did not materialize and exports stagnated, the tax base contracted, revenues declined, and the bloated state could no longer sustain itself. Budget deficits mounted, as did foreign debt, making states virtually dependent on decisions made in New York, London, and Paris. ISI had failed to create fundamental bases for local industrial and technological structures independently of foreign government and business support.[64]

ISI and related protectionist policies, aimed at encouraging domestic industries, also failed to keep out foreign MNCs, as the MNCs learned to manipulate tariffs and similar regulatory policies and established production and assembly plants within developing countries, usually with the tacit approval of sympathetic leaders. While

MNC-induced domestic production seemed attractive initially, by the late 1970s it had also led to expensive ventures in the importation of machinery and equipment and investments in infrastructural development, necessitating constant foreign financing.[65]

The problems created by ISI led to national soul-searching and experimentation with alternative approaches in the 1970s and 1980s. Chile, Peru, and Argentina first opted for statist-socialist policies, relying on expansion of the state's role. Chile's short-lived socialist Allende government, Peru's SINAMOS (National System for the Support of Social Mobilization), and Argentina's Peronistas (named after Juan Peron, Argentina's equivalent of Brazil's Vargas) sought a general reorientation of their national economies and emphasized policies that involved the nationalization of foreign companies, the creation of state-sponsored economic organizations, and the integration of various economic and industrial sectors as a way of strengthening their national economies against international market pressures.[66] Having failed with these policies as well, and under pressure from Northern creditors, by the 1980s each country had introduced liberalization policies to attract foreign investment. Pinochet's military government in Chile after 1973, the Garcia government in Peru, and Argentina's Alfonsin and Menem governments in the 1980s rolled back their predecessors' statist-socialist policies and encouraged liberalization and privatization.

This should not be construed as unlimited liberalization and total elimination of government regulations. Along with liberalization, governments have maintained a certain balance between privatization to encourage foreign investments and state regulation to maintain their influence and patronage. In early 1997, for instance, the Brazilian government announced that a consortium headed by the Brazilian Votorantim group and South African Anglo-American Corporation would bid at a privatization auction for a 45 percent share (3 billion reals, or $2.83 billion) of state-owned mining giant Vale do Rio Doce.[67] However, the government also set certain restrictions: for example, each company was permitted to buy no more than 10 percent share in any consortium bidding for the mining company. The stakes were high, as the consortium included ties with some of the major mining companies in the world, such as Japan's Mitsui, Australia's WMC, Ltd (Western Mining Corp.), and Brazil's own major metals and mining group, Caemi.[68] Whether this promises a better alternative to ISI remains to be seen.

It is debatable whether changes in economic strategy have improved living standards to any appreciable degree, however. In 1980, after three decades of ISI, Brazil's per capita GNP was $2,190, Mexico's $2,640, and Argentina's $2,890, while South Korea's was $2,330, and the United States' was $12,830.[69] Although a decade later Latin American states had improved, in comparison with the East Asian NICs they had not been especially successful. In 1990, Mexico's per capita GNP had actually declined to $2,580; Brazil's per capita GNP had reached $2,790; and Argentina's had reached $3,290; however, South Korea's had reached $5,770. Only by the mid-1990s did Argentina's per capita GNP increase to $7,220, substantially narrowing the gap with South Korea's $7,660. Brazil's was $2,930, and Mexico's was $3,610.[70]

Export-Led Strategies

The enormous economic growth experienced by the Asian NICs (Hong Kong, Singapore, South Korea, and Taiwan) sets them apart from the rest of the South. Lacking large domestic markets, since the mid-1960s these countries have pursued export-oriented economic development, with high domestic savings and modest consumption. Initially, post-WWII U.S. economic assistance and access to the U.S. market, the markets generated by Korean and Vietnam wars, and Japan's notable successes provided the financial strength and a model for rapid economic development. In the mid-1950s, South Korea and Taiwan had adopted the familiar policy of import-substitution industrialization, while the United States, to contain Communism, gave them billions of dollars in economic and military assistance. By the mid-1970s, the United States had pumped over $13 billion in economic and military aid into Korea and $5.6 billion aid into Taiwan, in addition to taking on military responsibilities for both countries. U.S. economic aid accounted for about 80 percent of Taiwan's imports, for example, while foreign savings, in U.S. aid dollars, constituted 40 percent of its GDP in the aggregate.[71] In the 1950s, the combination of ISI programs (protected by high tariffs), infrastructural development, and vast amounts of U.S. economic aid proved effective.

The NIC's export-led economic expansion in the 1960s was the continuation of economic growth experienced during the inter-war years while still under Japanese imperial rule (Taiwan from 1895, and Korea from 1910 to World War II). Between 1910 and 1940, as Japan's industrial sector expanded and GNP grew at an annual rate of about 3.4 percent, so did Korea's and Taiwan's manufacturing sector and GNP. In Korea, for example, manufacturing grew at an average of 10 percent per year and GNP at 3.6 percent.[72] Because of increasing integration into the Japanese industrial structure, the region also benefited from Japan's evolution from the production of textiles in the late nineteenth century, to heavy industry between the 1920s and 1960s, to high-technology industries in the 1970s and 1980s. In the process, Korea and Taiwan served as "receptacles for declining Japanese industries."[73] As Japan's economy shifted to the production and export of iron and steel, Korea's and Taiwan's exports in agricultural commodities, such as rice and sugar, increased. As Japan moved to high-technology industries, Korea and Taiwan increased their production and export of heavy industries.

Contrary to the orthodox laissez-faire approach, an integral part of this process was the role of the state as the central actor. State intervention in all, including economic, spheres of life, traditionally the norm in Asian political culture, continued after the Second World War. Unlike Latin America's relatively more ad hoc approach to ISI, however, East Asian governments made a concerted effort, in cooperation with the major corporations, to develop strategic sectors of their economies. Unlike their Latin counterparts, East Asians' ISI did not last long; by the mid-1960s, the Asians had begun to establish export processing zones (EPZs) (Taiwan opened Asia's first EPZ in 1965 at Kaohsiung) to encourage foreign investments, and, by the end of the decade, East Asia had shifted to export-led strategies in a number of key industries, including steel, shipbuilding, and autos.[74]

Based on an annual GNP growth rate of about 10 percent, with even higher rates in capital-intensive manufacturing, economic growth was so rapid that in a single generation East Asians converted their economic base from predominantly agricultural and small manufacturing to high-technology manufacturing. Soon, contrary to observers' predictions that further industrialization in Korea and Taiwan would fail because of their limited domestic markets, the shift to export-led strategies began to pay off. By the mid-1970s, the manufacturing sector had grown from 11 percent to 30 percent in Korea, with a parallel growth in Taiwan, while domestic capital constituted 30 percent of the GDP. In the meantime, as Japan moved toward high-technology areas in computers and electronics, Korea and Taiwan began to "deepen" their export-led industrialization, first in supertanker shipbuilding and chemical and auto plants and subsequently in light electronics industries.

Foreign investment contributed substantially to the NICs' and the region's overall economic activities. In Taiwan, for example, foreign investment in the first half of 1994 rose by 49 percent, to $640 million. This increase also occurred in other countries in the region: foreign investment in manufacturing in Malaysia doubled, to $3.9 billion; in Indonesia, it increased by 23 percent, to $5.3 billion; and in China it rose by 55 percent, to $14.7 billion.[75] In the late 1990s, the Chinese system was tested by the integration of Hong Kong (see Box 10.3). In the mid-1980s, as the industrialized world recovered from the oil shocks and the recession, products from the East Asian economies flooded the Western, particularly U.S., markets; by the early 1990s, high-technology industrialization in the area of computers and telecommunications in East Asian economies had so deepened that the initial importance of EPZs and similar industrial zones began to disappear.[76]

This rapid progress was generally achieved through strong state involvement in the economic activities, on Japan's model stressing MITI-style (Ministry of International Trade and Industry) administrative guidance through a combination of *keiretsu,* major banks, and bureaucracy, followed by their own national (that is, Korean and Taiwanese) system of state-business institutional arrangements.[77] By the mid-1950s, as in Japan, Taiwan and Korea also had developed major conglomerates (often owning firms in various economic and industrial sectors) built on elite familial, state, and business interlocking *keiretsu* structures. In Taiwan, the major conglomerates included the Tatung Group, comprised of companies in electric appliances, communications, construction, and publishing; Formosa Plastics; Far Eastern Textiles; Taiwan Cement; and Yue Loong Motors. In South Korea, the major *keiretsu*-style groups, called *chaebol* in Korean, included Samsung, with over twenty companies producing consumer goods; Hyundai, comprised of more than ten companies; Daewoo, consisting of about twenty companies involved in electronics, machinery, finance, and trade; and the so-called Lucky Group, which consisted of companies as diverse as the Bando Trading Company and the Honam oil refineries, as well as companies in petrochemicals, electronics, metals, and insurance.[78] Major corporate conglomerates proved, despite occasional political scandals, to be as effective in their competition in world markets as any of their U.S. or European competitors.

As in Latin America, the Cold War was also an important factor. In both Taiwan and South Korea, U.S. economic and military support to contain Communism in East Asia provided them the opportunity to strengthen their political institutions, as the ruling interlocking political and economic elites dominated both political and

BOX 10.3

CAPITALIST HONG KONG IN COMMUNIST CHINA: ONE COUNTRY, TWO SYSTEMS?

One of the major questions concerning Hong Kong is its future under Chinese rule. For the past century, the city-state had been under British colonial administration under a treaty with China providing for the reunification of Hong Kong in 1997. The British maintained a laissez-faire economy while suppressing local rule in Hong Kong for decades; in fact, that city remained the only place in the world where capitalism resembled what the classical liberals had envisioned, and London liberalized the political system as well during the 1990s. In 1997, however, reunification with China raised a host of questions regarding the city's future status. On the one hand, it is argued that the Chinese Communist Party could not maintain such a capitalist economy for long and that after the British withdrawal Beijing would impose its Communist political-economic structure in order to integrate Hong Kong into the national economy. According to this argument, Hong Kong could not survive the ideological contradictions, and, if the Communist Party's response to the prodemocracy movement in Tiananmen Square in 1989 was an indication of things to come, Beijing was ill-prepared to sustain such ideological disparities. This view has, since the early 1990s, led to massive emigration and capital flight from Hong Kong by wealthy business owners seeking new and safer havens in London, Vancouver, Los Angeles, and elsewhere.

Others, on the other hand, are less anxious. They have argued that, despite its professed ideology, Beijing would prefer to maintain Hong Kong as a capitalist enclave because of its share of wealth and investments. The Communist leaders would not sacrifice such a rich source of income for ideology. After all, this argument insists, the Communist ideology has not prevented Beijing from opening its economy to foreign investors and from strengthening its economic ties with capitalist states. Rather than impose the Communist system, Beijing would maintain a "one country, two systems" policy, as it has with Taiwan since the Communist Revolution in 1949, political rhetoric and symbolic military maneuvers notwithstanding.

As a microcosm of the world-economic system, post-1997 Hong Kong will demonstrate whether a Communist system can maintain a capitalist structure in order to strengthen its linkages with the process of globalization or will reject globalization altogether and stress the sovereign prerogatives of the nation-state. The collapse of the Soviet Union and more directly China's own modernization efforts in the 1980s indicate that the latter is not a viable option in the current international political economy. In the balance also is the extent to which Hong Kong's open political system and free press would be tolerated or repressed.

Source: For useful summaries of the history of Chinese domestic politics policy, see John K. Fairbank, *The United States and China,* 4th ed. (Cambridge: Harvard University Press, 1979), and Harry Harding, ed., *China's Foreign Relations in the 1980* (New Haven: Yale University Press, 1984). On Hong Kong's reunification and economy, see Ming Chan K. and Gerard A. Postiglione, eds., *The Hong Kong Reader: Passage to Chinese Sovereignty* (Armonk, NY: M.E. Sharpe, 1996), and Michael J. Enright, Edith E. Scott, and David Dodwell, *The Hong Kong Advantage* (Hong Kong and New York: Oxford University Press, 1997). On issues related to democratization and human rights, see Yu Ping, "Will Hong Kong be Successfully Integrated into China? A Human Rights Perspective," *Vanderbilt Journal of Transnational Law* 30, 4 (Oct. 1997), pp. 675–699.

economic spheres. Between 1947 and 1949, after his escape from mainland China to Taiwan with his wealth and entourage, Chiang Kai-shek declared martial law and established a one-party dictatorial regime, in effect well into the mid-1980s. Similarly, in Korea first Syngman Rhee and then Park Chung Hee maintained a rigidly bureaucratic and highly authoritarian regime, with little opportunity for the formation of opposition, with exception of the sporadic student demonstrations.[79]

Organized labor remained weak, despite the relatively more liberal labor laws introduced after the early 1980s,[80] some observers have attributed East Asian economic growth to the absence of effective labor opposition to cost-saving policies and innovations.[81] Labor strikes were limited in Japan and in the NICs. The unions, while formally representing the employees, in fact lacked political power.[82] In Taiwan, as in Brazil under Vargas and as in Chile under Pinochet, the ruling Kuomintang (KMT) Party, through the Chinese Federation of Labor (CFL), controlled the unions, their leaders, and their activities.[83] In South Korea, the Korean Central Intelligence Agency (KCIA) directly controlled the Federation of Korean Trade Unions. In Singapore, the government maintained tight controls over the National Trade Union Congress (NTUC).[84]

East Asian "Tigers" success in achieving high rates of growth, capital-intensive industrialization, and overall modernization led, by the mid-1990s, to the conclusion that the NICs had been "graduated" from the South, now each with its own programs for foreign assistance, as demonstrated by Seoul's extension of humanitarian assistance of $70,000 to Mongolia in May 1996 to help that country fight the huge fires that destroyed millions of hectares of land.[85] Measured in terms of personal income, the East Asian NICs registered major successes. In the 1950s, South Korea's per capita GNP was $146 and Taiwan's $224 (in 1974 dollars). In comparison, Nigeria's was $150 and Kenya's $129. In the 1980s, after two decades of export-led growth, South Korea's and Taiwan's per capita GNP reached about $6,000, Hong Kong's $4,432, and Singapore's $4,298,[86] while Nigeria's and Kenya's were $670 and $380, respectively. By 1993, a widening gap appeared; South Korea's per capita GNP was about $7600, Taiwan's a little over $10,000, and Singapore's $19,000, while Nigeria's (despite its oil) was $310 and Kenya's $270.[87]

The economic crisis in the late 1990s could not but shake public confidence, however. References to the "Brazilian miracle" and the "Mexican miracle" in the early 1970s were quickly discarded as the two countries confronted enormous economic and political challenges in the 1970s and 1980s. It remains to be seen whether the "East Asian miracle" is more resilient; the Indonesian political crisis, which included urban rioting in 1998 did not give much cause for optimism Yet democratic reforms in South Korea and Taiwan's relative stability indicated continued regional vitality as well.

Self-Reliance

In addition to the import-substitution industrialization and export-oriented strategies, a relatively small number of countries, on independence from colonial rule, pursued a policy of self-reliance, or autarky, explicitly delinking their economies from the global economic environment in hopes of minimizing their vulnerability to external pressures. As stressed by *dependencia* theory, over a century of European imperialism had hindered indigenous autonomous economic development. To remove externally imposed obstacles, and contrary to a growing trend toward global interdependence, countries such as China and Tanzania for a time embraced self-reliance. Cuba, faced with a U.S. embargo, and South Africa, similary sanctioned by the U.N. also exercised various degrees of self-reliance. Indeed, during the "Cultural Revolution" of the 1960s, China severed nearly all its diplomatic ties with other countries. By the late 1970s and throughout the 1980s, however, the forces of globalization had become too powerful for isolated attempts at national self-reliance. The evolution of China's economic position was discussed in Chapter 1. Suffice it to note that the Maoist, more radical Communist-nationalist route, in total opposition to Western capitalism, proved a major failure, with enormous human cost and economic difficulties. Maoists' ill-conceived agricultural and industrial policies, not unlike the Stalinist approach in the Soviet Union, led to famines and the dislocation of millions of people. Whether economic development justifies the attendant repressive measures is a moral question, but these failures led to a reassessment of self-reliance policies and eventually to their termination.

Still, it is instructive to examine these efforts, for they also spawned some degree of progress in basic living conditions, such as health care and education. Tanzania, for example, experimented with nonaligned socialism and self-reliance, with an emphasis on rural development rather than industrialization. President Julius Nyerere's *ujamaa* (familyhood), enunciated in the Arusha Declaration in February 1967, aimed at developing communal village socialism, based on local resources, with minimal dependence on foreign resources.[88] Nyerere's authoritarian personal rule resembled neither Stalin's nor Mao's dictatorial regime, although Zanzibar nationalists would argue otherwise; however, by the late 1970s *ujamaa*, too, deprived of foreign capital, proved a failure.

As the national platform of Tanzania's only party, the Tanganyikan African National Union (TANU), the Arusha Declaration encapsulated Nyerere's ideology and policy guidelines for the national economy. Nyerere sought to create a Tanzanian economy based on "African socialism," as opposed to orthodox Marxist "scientific socialism." The primary purpose of the Arusha Declaration was to grant the government the legal and moral authority to control the "commanding heights" of the economy by nationalizing "the major means of production and exchange . . . such things as land, forests, minerals, water, oil and electricity, news media, banks, insurance, import and export trade," and so forth.[89] It heralded Tanzania's self-reliance via socialist development.[90] The policy guidelines stressed rural development as the most reliable approach, given Tanzania's lack of necessary financial and industrial resources for industrialization, which would have required dependence on foreign capital and technology. To prevent such a potentiality, in the domestic realm, TANU's political authority expanded with the fusion of its institutions and the various economic and government organizations, as it asserted its political supremacy with every step of national cultural, political, and economic integration.[91] In foreign relations, TANU maintained diplomatic and economic ties with countries in the West and the East, but it limited its trade, technical, and military relations to a small number of nonaligned (for example, China) and smaller European countries such as Sweden.

Tanzania's philosophy of self-reliance was, at some abstract level, certainly attractive, especially as it stressed sustainable rural development and social improvements. In practice, however, strictly in economic and political terms the experiment failed; in the mid-1980s, one observer noted, "Far from becoming a self-reliant nation, Tanzania has entered a vicious cycle of dependence."[92] In the area of trade, for example, with few marketable products after the early 1970s, the country consistently registered a trade deficit, reaching well over $1 billion in 1993, placing Tanzania, on average, among the four (along with Lesotho, Mali, and Mozambique) worst performers in sub-Saharan Africa; despite Nyerere's claims to nonalignment and African regionalism, Tanzania's total value of imports from the United States exceeded imports from African countries.

Improvements, albeit minor, occurred after Nyerere withdrew from power in 1985. His successor, Ali Hassan Mwinyi, in office after November 1985, placed greater emphasis on economic development than on the principles of the Arusha Declaration. As in Latin American and Asian countries, Tanzania has opted for expansion of trade and financial relations with the capitalist world. However, agriculture, where nearly 90 percent of the labor force works, remains Tanzania's principal economic sector, and manufacturing has not increased.[93]

The experiences of Tanzania and most developing countries indicate that, despite their ideological predilections and national preferences as demonstrated by their strategies, they reaped the "worst of both worlds," failing to attract the support of wealthier partners, yet also failing to delink themselves from the globalization process of the world capitalist system. Export-oriented countries, such as the NICs, fared better than those pursuing ISI and self-reliance strategies. It would be wrong, however, to consider even NICs as having "graduated" from the South and from their dependency relations with the industrialized states. Export-oriented economies are, by definition, dependent on importing markets and on investment finances, the diminution or disappearance of which, as in Japan's recession of the 1990s, could wreak havoc on their economies. Despite the ending of the Cold War, they also continue to rely on U.S. military support for their security.[94] Neither has the recent shift to market-oriented liberalization, as witnessed in Latin America, ended the South's dependence on the West's technology and capital. To the contrary, the latter's dominance continues to grow, now within the post–Cold War context of multipolar globalized competition.

DEVELOPMENT, DEBT, AND DEMOCRATIZATION

Dependent Development

Over the past two centuries, the evolution of the global political economy has created the North–South dependency relationship, whereby the South, the periphery, grew dependent on the North, the core, as a source of capital and technology.[95] The capitalist world system emerged, dominated by the industrialized North, while different sectors in the South performed various functions based on the needs of the North. *Dependencia* theorists argue that the division of the world-economy into the rich North and the poor South, while oversimplified, is key to understanding the nature of the South's current political and economic problems.

In addition to the issues previously discussed, dependent development also has contributed to the phenomenon of **economic dualism,** in which regions, particularly major cities within a country such as Brazil, India, and China, and the urban political and economic elites gain from their government's relations with the North and develop and modernize, while the urban slum dwellers and the rest of the country remain neglected. Two points are worth mentioning here: first, the urban economic development that does take place remains dependent on the capital and technology largely from the North; second, the neglect with respect to economic conditions in various localities is not accidental, but rather generally is the result of a number of factors, including the government's decision to concentrate on "strategic" areas of the national economy, as defined by the urban financial and commercial elites in cooperation with their Northern counterparts.

Despite the greater significance attached to urban economies and governments' priorities with respect to industrialization and economic development, the agricultural sector, especially in Africa and Asia, remains an essential source of livelihood for millions of people and is particularly affected by women's labor. Historically, however, agricultural economy has been closely associated with colonial domination, when the economies throughout the developing world served as sources of primary commodities for the industrializing North. In Latin American countries, for example, as late as the 1930s, the landed agricultural elite, with the backing of their trade partners in the industrialized countries, could command enormous political and economic power. The growing emphasis on ISI strategies, however, shifted the balance of domestic power from the agricultural elite to the newly emerging urban commercial and manufacturing groups, with their own ties to the financial and manufacturing centers in the North. In a form of "internal colonialism," the urban elite increasingly viewed the agricultural sector as a source of cheap labor, as "industrialization required a 'draining' of agriculture for resources (cheap food, raw materials, foreign exchange), land, and capital (taxation)."[96] Neglect, combined with internal colonialism, bred resentment and anti-government movements, such as the Shining Path in Peru and the Zapatista movement in Mexico, demanding greater governmental attention to the plight of the rural poor. However, even when governments did pay attention, as in India's "Green Revolution," they generally introduced policies favoring the large landowning elites, more technologically advanced farmers, and huge agribusinesses and MNCs. Rather than address the problems of poverty, food scarcity, landlessness, exploitation, and unemployment, many governments tended to encourage commercialization and mechanization to become better integrated into the global food market and to increase their revenues and foreign capital, further exacerbating the farming and domestic nutritional situation. As a result, thousands migrated annually from the rural areas to the cities in search of jobs and economic opportunities.

The combination of concentrated capital and the industries in cities and the commercialization of agriculture in the rural areas has created a serious dilemma for governments in the developing countries. The failure of ISI programs to develop a strong national industrial base has led to the international debt crisis and to pressures by the International Monetary Fund, the World Bank, and aid donors to implement structural adjustment austerity programs to cut fiscal expenditures. Structural adjustment has also led to economic liberalization and privatization of previously state-owned enterprises, which in turn has led to increased foreign investments in privatized companies. At the same time, however, migration to the cities has increased demands for more social and welfare programs, affordable food, housing, schools, and hospitals, at the very time that state budgets are being cut—a politically explosive brew.

The International Debt Crisis

For decades, the largest share of foreign finances to developing countries came from private sources—that is, multinational corporations and banks. Initially, these private funds were comprised of foreign direct investments (FDIs) by companies; in the 1970s and 1980s, the composition changed as multinational banks, exceeding both FDIs and public funds, became the primary funding source to the developing countries. About thirty multinational banks from the industrialized countries were involved. Fueled by the growth of "petro-dollar" accounts deposited in Western banks, private credits from multinational banks to Latin America increased from $246 million per year in the mid-1960s to over $12.3 billion in the mid-1970s. This pattern was repeated in Asia and Africa, although Latin America was the recipient of a disproportionate share (about 80 percent) of multinational funds.[97] Banks chose to lend mainly to upper- or middle-income developing countries, such as Latin America (for example, Argentina, Brazil, Mexico, and Venezuela), while a relatively larger number of African countries in the low-income category (for example, Mozambique, Ethiopia, Tanzania, and Uganda) were not deemed "creditworthy" by international banks.

Multinational bank loans injected much needed capital into the economies of developing countries, capital to invest in their own economies but also to import needed goods. One serious problem, however, involved the costs of borrowing. Interest rates fluctuated between 8.2 percent and 19.9 percent during the inflation-ridden 1970s and 1980s.[98] Variable interest rates in the industrialized lending economies rendered the economic environment in the borrowing states less predictable and budget planning more difficult, if not impossible.[99] This led to the paradoxical situation in which the more the developing countries borrowed, the less net cash was available to invest and import, and in which net capital flows went from the poorer South to the richer North in the form of interest on debt. The costs of debt servicing had become too expensive to sustain the economies, and they would have to borrow even more *"merely to sustain a constant level of net transfer."*[100]

By the early 1980s, the key development problem was the debt crisis. The debt crisis of the 1980s, the worst financial crisis since the Great Depression, can be traced back to the two "oil shocks" in the 1970s, which led the Southern economies to recession, inflation, and unemployment. As previously noted, international banks' excess of "petro-dollars" stimulated excessive lending to countries in dire need of capital. Since most of the borrowing economies possessed little industrial and market capabilities, they could not produce enough and, therefore, could not export in sufficient volume to repay foreign banks (in the 1980s, the South's total exports accounted for about 10 percent of total world trade).[101] At the same time, their governments had for years promised economic development to meet public needs and demands for better standards of living. As in the case of Mexico, the borrowed dollars were for investments in the future of their countries—for roads, electrification, housing, business, and overall development—and they accepted the loans with that promise to their people, as long as the international banks were willing to lend. In fact, the debt crisis virtually exploded onto the international agenda in 1982, when Argentina, during the Falkland/Malvinas Islands War, and Mexico suspended payments; throughout the 1980s, the fear that the debt crisis could destablize the world banking system lingered on. According to one estimate, the amount involved for U.S. banks was between 150 and 200 percent of their capital, mostly concentrated in Latin America.[102]

Based on previous experiences with such Third World movements as the Group of 77, some analysts expected debtor countries to exert "debtor power" in international quarters to reform the international financial system; in the 1980s and 1990s, no such movement emerged, however. This was in part because the East Asian NICs, which pursued export-oriented strategies rather than ISI strategies, were not as severely affected by the debt crisis as were the Latin American economies. Further, in most cases, international banks dealt separately with individual debtor countries. As a result, the South, no longer unified by the decolonization experience, failed to present a common program to bargain more effectively with Northern governments, MNCs, and banks. Moreover, China's marketization and "red capitalism" and, most unexpectedly, the rapid collapse of the Soviet Union further depleted the anti-West and socialist ideological cohesion that had given rise to the "united fronts" in the 1960s and 1970s.

Thus, short of a major international reconfiguration of financial and political relations in the global political economy, which is not expected to occur in the foreseeable future, some economists recommend that Third World, but especially Latin American, governments (because of the experience in the 1980s) launch development policies for full employment and sustained growth, rather than short-term "debt crisis management."[103] However, the very processes of defining and formulating economic development policies is highly political; government belt tightening deprives citizens of the very improvements—for example, health care and affordable food—they had come to expect. Nevertheless, despite the threat of popular uprisings, most developing countries have leaned toward market liberalization in the 1990s.

In some respects, the extent of economic hardship brought about by the debt crisis was similar to that of the Great Depression of the 1930s but, as Griffith-Jones and Sunkel have pointed out, with a very critical difference. The depression occurred at a time when most Third World societies were primarily agrarian, with relatively minor concentrations of population in urban regions. By the 1980s, however, major urban centers had developed, with high population density and economic-industrial centers. Griffith-Jones and Sunkel have identified four key external and internal factors that contributed to the Latin American debt crisis in the 1980s:

1. The tendency in Latin America toward exhaustion of the process of industrialization through import-substitution, which began to prevail toward the end of the 1960s
2. The oil crisis of 1973 and the consequent substantial increases in the relative price of oil
3. The limitations and general characteristics of the public international financial system
4. The reconstitution and rapid expansion of a new international private financial market after the mid-1960s[104]

Latin American governments maintained huge public programs for development and subsidies, increasing the budget deficits to as much as 14 percent, as in the case of Mexico. Financial mismanagement combined with artificially low interest rates and rampant inflation led to capital flight, as investors and speculators placed their capital in foreign banks and investments rather than risk devaluation at home. As a result, dollars needed at home to finance imports and foreign debts were no longer available.[105]

The deteriorating situation in employment reflected the overall impact felt by the debt crisis, as demonstrated by some of the Latin countries. In the case of Argentina, for example, the unemployment level rose from 2 percent in 1979 to 4 percent in 1984. During the same years, Brazil's increased from 6.4 percent to 7.5 percent, Colombia's from 8.9 percent to 13.5 percent, Mexico's from 5.7 percent to 6.3 percent, Peru's from 6.5 percent to 10.9 percent, Uruguay's from 8.3 percent to 14.5 percent, and Venezuela's from 5.8 percent to 13.9 percent.[106] Each of these countries experienced rising external debt for this period. Argentina's rose $19 billion to $48 billion, Brazil's from $58.9 billion to $101.8 billion, Colombia's from $5.1 billion to $10.8 billion, Mexico's from $39.6 billion to $95.9 billion, Peru's from $9.3 billion to $13.5 billion, Uruguay's from $1.6 billion to $4.7 billion, and Venezuela's from $23.0 billion to $34.0 billion.[107] By 1984, Latin America's total external debt was about $360 billion, with servicing requirements of over 35 percent of exports.[108]

Such financial difficulties, and the uncertainties they created, led international bankers to reassess their lending practices, eventually leading to a sharp decline in loans to countries deemed too risky. This decline in loans, however, coincided with rising loan servicing costs and declining commodity prices. According to one estimate, "between 1981 and 1983 net capital inflows to Latin America [fell] by US$33.3 billion, while net payments of profit and interest grew by US$6.8 billion; as a result, net transfer of resources declined by US$40 billion in these two years to a level of—US$30 billion in 1983."[109]

In the case of sub-Saharan Africa, the debt crisis differed in that the large majority of African countries did not owe to Western commercial banks but to Western governments. African debt accumulated through government loans, including economic assistance (mostly development aid) programs. As in the rest of the developing world, however, the problem was the allocation of funds and the implementation of development aid programs. Some food aid, for example, was hoarded and sold by African government officials to merchants, thereby undercutting local farmers.

East Asian countries, such as South Korea and Thailand, with stricter controls on capital (controls which, however, did not preclude corrupt business practices and vast accumulation of personal wealth by some leaders, such as Indonesia's Suharto), were not as severely affected by international factors, indicating that their national macroeconomic policies to manage domestic finances proved important in controlling the extent and impact of capital inflows and outflows. Some analysts have argued that the East Asian experience points to an important, if often ignored, dimension of the debt crisis: the impact of foreign debt does not necessarily have to be completely negative, as its effective management can contribute to economic growth. One analysis identifies three necessary elements of success in this respect:

1. Flows of capital (both into and out of the country) were regulated.
2. Foreign inflows entered an economy in which the state had a clear "vision" of a development strategy, and in which, directly or indirectly, it played an important role in investment.
3. Deliberate policies were pursued by the state to orient market forces, such as in international trade and international capital markets, toward sustained growth in specific productive sectors.[110]

Efforts to address the debt crisis involved initial governmental and bank responses in the industrialized countries, led primarily by the U.S. Treasury Department and the Federal Reserve Board, as in the Mexican financial crisis of 1982. Various international governmental and commercial agencies and banks coordinated financial plans with developing countries to facilitate and in some cases, to reschedule debt repayment. The IMF played a key role in decisions determining whether a country could receive new loans, based on the general rule of thumb that borrowing countries had to meet certain conditions (see Chapter 4). As with all structural adjustment programs, borrowing countries were expected to control their budgets by shedding various public programs and by limiting the role of government in economic activities. For the debtor countries, meeting IMF conditions was a necessary but onerous condition for obtaining the capital needed for their economies and for maintaining a credit reputation for the future as members of capital markets.[111]

By 1985, developing countries were expressing frustration, arguing that, despite their adherence to IMF conditions and efforts to negotiate terms of repayment, their economies had not appreciably improved. This troubled them, particularly since the industrialized economies appeared to have recovered from the recession of the early 1980s. In response to their pressures, then U.S. Secretary of the Treasury James Baker proposed a new plan to combat the debt problem. Following the IMF strategy, the Baker Plan viewed the debt crisis as a long-term structural problem, rather than a problem of mere short-term liquidity. Accordingly, the Baker Plan called for deep structural adjustments and the liberalization of trade and foreign investments, along with the privatization of state enterprises. The plan also proposed that banks make new loans totaling $20 billion over the next three years, which constituted about 12.5 percent of the $250 billion in total bank claims. Multilateral banks, such as the World Bank and the Inter-American Development Bank, were to increase their lending levels by $10 billion during the next three years as well. The plan sought to balance both commercial and public banking involvement in coordinating the recovery from the debt crisis.[112]

Although the second half of the 1980s witnessed a transition to liberalization as proposed by the Baker Plan, plummeting oil prices (by as much as 50 percent in 1986) rendered the plan ineffective. For some debtor countries, such as Mexico, Nigeria, and Venezuela, their oil exports had constituted over 75 percent of their foreign earnings in the early 1980s. Mexico, for example, lost nearly $6 billion in oil-export earnings per year.[113] Developing economies experienced yet another severe recession in the second half of the 1980s, and political unrest in the Philippines, Mexico, and Venezuela underscored the need for a more viable strategy than that proposed by the Baker Plan.[114] Critics charged that the plan had put too much emphasis on strengthening the position of the banks, with little regard to the economic hardship experienced by people in the developing countries. The IMF and Baker Plan proposed fiscal restraints and privatization, when, in fact, the unemployed and the poor—that is, the majority of the population—in the developing countries needed more and better public programs, requiring greater, not less, government involvement.

The Brady Plan, introduced in March 1989 by the Bush administration's Secretary of the Treasury Nicholas Brady, was more palatable, if not successful. It emphasized voluntary debt reduction through reliance primarily on market forces while new lending to debtor countries continued. Although the plan initially contained certain flaws,[115] soon after the Brady Plan was enunciated, a number of countries, including Mexico, Venezuela and the Philippines, agreed to debt reduction. Some innovative approaches, such as "debt-equity" and "debt for nature" swaps, were launched, allowing debt to be forgiven in return for shares in companies, environmental policy improvements, and other socially beneficial projects. In Mexico's case, for example, the agreement eliminated nearly $15 billion from the outstanding loans of $50 billion. Also, the IMF, the World Bank, and the Japanese Export-Import Bank offered loans totaling $5 billion.[116] Mexico's economy grew and inflation was checked, while foreign capital inflows and investments increased. The confidence gained in the Mexican economy at home and abroad further improved the economy in the early 1990s, although the "peso crisis" shook that progress, and the Clinton administration had to propose a bailout loan guarantee plan.

In 1992–1993, there were hopes that the debt crisis had finally run its course and the affected economies would begin the process of recovery, as in Brazil (see Box 10.4). The threat of an international banking and financial collapse receded, as the debt owed to the major banks declined from 194 percent of capital in 1982 to about 63 percent. While in the 1980s the average economic growth rate for Latin countries had dropped, in the early 1990s these states registered an annual growth rate of about 3.2 percent—normal by most standards; inflation remained a problem, however, especially in Brazil, where it was as high as 20 percent *per month*. As governments embraced trade liberalization and privatization, foreign investors began to return in strength to Latin America. However, by 1998 confidence again eroded as the Asian and Russian economic crises seemed about to spread to Latin America, and the IFM's terms for an $18 billion Brazilian bailout proved extremely difficult for the Brazilian Congress to swallow.

Debt reduction plans have been proposed for other regions as well with equal, if not greater, political saliency. In the case of Egypt, for example, the second highest recipient of U.S. foreign economic and military aid, in 1991 the governments and banks of the major industrialized countries forgave 50 percent of their claims. Observers agree that this "was a reward for sending troops to the front lines in the Gulf War."[117] The same amount was forgiven in the case of Poland, rewarded for being a staunch supporter of the tilt toward the West in the former Communist Eastern European bloc, but also conceivably because of the large number of Polish voters in the United States.[118] In the 1990s, the major international debt crisis, which may become far more severe than any experienced in the 1980s, was that of the former Soviet republics. Russia alone had a debt of about $80 billion, although most of this was owed to foreign governments or multilateral agencies, rather than to private banks. Whether economic liberalization and political democratization work hand in hand, as proposed by the laissez-faire school, remains to be seen.

Toward Democratization?

During the past decade or so, as the Brazilian example demonstrated, there has been a growing trend not only toward economic but also political liberalization, largely in reaction to the economic and political crises in the 1970s

BOX 10.4

1996 WARNINGS: BRAZIL ECONOMY IS BOOMING, BUT SOME PROBLEMS LOOM

RIO DE JANEIRO, Brazil—It is among workers earning the barest of incomes that the benefits of the Real Plan, Brazil's two-year-old economic reform program, are most keenly felt. Without the triple-digit inflation of the past, their salaries have a newfound value, measured in an explosion of sales in consumer appliances. Over the last three years, the number of households with color television sets has grown 21.4 percent. Households with freezers have increased more than 40 percent. Along with the surge of sales to low-income consumers, who make up the vast majority of the Brazilian work force, has come a flood of investment from foreign companies. Propelled by the $2.4 billion privatization of Light, Rio de Janeiro state's electric utility, direct foreign investment through the end of July reached $4.96 billion, surpassing the combined total of the previous three years.

But despite the hard-won monetary stability, economists are warning there could be danger ahead. The achievements, they say, may well fall apart unless President Fernando Henrique Cardoso moves more quickly to revamp the traditionally statist economy and spur growth by easing the government demand on money. "The Real Plan had the right start, but now it needs to correct the fiscal mix so it can lower interest rates, loosen monetary policy and get growth," said Sebastian Edwards, a former World Bank economist and author of *Crisis and Reform in Latin America: From Despair to Hope* (1995, Oxford University Press).

Still, investors' eagerness to establish a presence here seems undeterred. Interest in a series of coming privatizations, including Eletrobras, Telebras and Vale do Rio Doce, giants of the electric, telecommunications and mining sectors, is expected to be strong among foreign—including American—investors. The prospects are alluring: About 80 percent of all households still lack telephones, for instance. "I think the majority of companies are going ahead and making investments right now," said John E. Mein, executive vice president of the American Chamber of Commerce branch in Sao Paulo. "Companies are coming in and positioning themselves so they're already in the market."

But economists both here and abroad are concerned by Cardoso's slowness in tackling the structural changes that would ease the government demand on money. They want to see swifter progress in cutting the 1.5 million-employee civil service sector, reforming the social security system, and shutting down the corruption-ridden state banks, many of which, along with private banks, are in serious trouble.

The private banks have been bailed out with $13 billion, of which $4.6 billion has been paid back so far, at a pace somewhat ahead of schedule. A bailout package for the state-run banks is expected to cost the federal government another $8 billion and will encourage, though not require, states to liquidate or privatize the troubled banks, which are frequently used as a political tool by governors and other local power brokers.

It has taken time for Cardoso, who was elected with the largest majority of any Brazilian president, to realize that despite his popularity he would have to deal with a Congress where traditions of financial and political horse-trading remain strong—particularly since many of the changes he has wanted to make require changes in the constitution. In addition, the economic changes appear to be taking a back seat to Cardoso's intention, announced late last year, to seek a constitutional amendment that would allow him to run for re-election. "President Cardoso is trying to balance a political agenda where the bitter medicine is given out in small doses, but if you give antibiotics or any medicine in small doses it may not be effective," Edwards said. While the lapses of Brazil as it moves toward reform are common to other Latin countries, investor enthusiasm for the market here makes the fiscal problems less apparent, economists warn. The administration's failure to tighten spending has led to shrinking growth, despite the investment boom. Unemployment in the Sao Paulo region recently hit 16 percent, and the economy is expected to grow only 2.6 percent this year, according to figures released by the Brazilian Institute of Geography and Statistics.

IBCA Ltd., Europe's largest credit rating agency, gave Brazil a B+ rating for the second consecutive year, reflecting monetary stability on the one hand and lack of fiscal discipline on the other. In particular, the company said, the ratio of Brazil's international reserves to outstanding government securities dropped to 40 percent from 65 percent over 18 months, undermining investor confidence and leaving the country vulnerable to a sudden flight of currency. In addition, IBCA noted, the Brazilian Constitution hampers fiscal responsibility with, for example, its guarantee of lifetime employment for civil servants, regardless of performance or government need. "To anybody from outside, this is a fun country, but it's volatile," said Rudiger Dornbush, an economics professor at the Massachusetts Institute of Technology. "There is no question in the world that enthusiasm about Brazil is warranted. You just want to make sure you don't get caught in a trap. . . ."

BOX 10.4 (concluded)

1996 WARNINGS: BRAZIL ECONOMY IS BOOMING, BUT SOME PROBLEMS LOOM

Dornbush was among the first international experts to sound fresh warnings, noting last June that Brazil was not taking the steps necessary to ensure long-term growth and stability. With projections for growth shrinking since his initial pronouncement, Dornbush said the failure to lighten the demands on the federal budget, and Brazil's roller-coaster economic history, ought to leave investors insecure—wondering, for example, whether a cash crunch would lead to laws to block the repatriation of capital. Instead, investors appear to be betting that the team running Brazil today—considered by many the most competent in memory—ultimately will not founder. Just this week, McDonald's announced plans to invest $500 million to open a new fast-food restaurant every five days through the end of the century, increasing its outlets in Brazil from 200 to 530. . . .

Government demand for money has kept interest rates at 26 percent a year—down by half from a year ago, but still prohibitive. Consumer borrowing rates can run a murderous 1,000 percent above inflation, and despite booming sales in sectors like appliances, consumer sales overall are declining. In the Madureira Shopping Center outside Rio, Marcelo do Espirito Santo Ferreira, 39, a telecommunications technician, considered buying a home computer he could use to supplement his income. In cash, its price was $2,000; paid for in 12 monthly installments, the cost rose to $3,700. "The government has to explain this to people," Ferreira said, adding that he planned to save the $2,000 to buy the computer in one lump sum.

In an interview in Brasilia, Pedro Malan, the finance minister, acknowledged that the government needed to shrink its size and role, but complained that critics underestimated the importance of controlling inflation, which he called "the most unjust and cruel" tax, disproportionately striking the poor. In addition, he agreed with critics who contend that Brazil has to move quickly to raise the education level of its work force if it is to compete in world markets in the long run. The average schooling of a Brazilian worker is four years, far behind Argentina's eight years and South Korea's 11 years, he noted. "I don't think the plan could blow up," Malan said. "It's a question of cost, time and speed. . . ."

The Brazilian-owned Blockbuster Video franchise is in for the long haul. It opened its first store in March 1995, invested $25 million last year and plans to have 170 outlets by the end of the century. The surge in the sales of televisions and videocassette recorders, unexpected when the franchise opened, had proved a surprising and welcome boon, said Luis Mario Bilenky, president of Blockbuster Video in Brazil. "Despite the economic difficulties Brazil is going through," he said, "you're still talking about an enormous country of 150 million people and a market with an incredible potential for growth."

Source: Diane Jean Schemo, "Brazil's Economic Samba," *The New York Times,* September 7, 1996, pp. 35, 37.

and 1980s. The end of the Cold War has increased expectations for greater democratization. The economic crises of the 1980s diminished what little political legitimacy autocratic, particularly military, governments commanded among their citizens. The deterioration of the nation's economic base and the international debt crises certainly hurt some people more than others, but the general environment of financial and political insecurity they created was hardly conducive to political stability and democratization. Thus, the withdrawal of the military and autocrats from politics in Latin America, parts of Asia, and Africa was, in essence, a political adjustment to the changing circumstances.[119]

A distinction must be made, however, between democracies that, over a long period, have developed relatively deep and stable political institutions and democratic/constitutional traditions and those that lack such historical development. In the former case, as in Chile, democratic institutions were already in place before the military coup of 1973 brought General Pinochet's brutal military dictatorship to power. The political "adjustment" after the military's withdrawal from power in 1990–1991 meant the country would return to its democratic institutions and begin the difficult process of redemocratization (Pinochet himself remained in charge of the armed forces). The main challenge was to revitalize the dormant political institutions, reinstitute public trust, and rechannel economic resources for an equitable economic base; accounting for past human rights violations was usually not as high a priority (with some exceptions such as Gen. Pinochet's arrest in Britain in 1998).

In other countries, however, such as Brazil, Argentina, and Peru, the lack of democratic institutions and the traditional preponderance of the military's power in politics meant that the task involved more than mere "adjustment." Instead, it required serious efforts toward democracy-building, the redefinition of the rules of the political and economic game, and a readjustment from the "national security" environment of the Cold War. It required the development of institutional capacity to sustain a healthy balance between external factors, such as MNC investments, U.S. military involvement, the IMF, and the World Bank and *their* priorities, on the one hand, and the domestic needs for better economic performance and social justice on the other. In fact, the enormity of the task, because of both domestic and international pressures, raises serious questions about whether democratization can be achieved. Even in Mexico, where since the 1911 revolution the military has refrained from direct intervention in politics, the dominant political party, Partido Revolucionario Institucional (PRI), has shown only grudging interest in democratic reforms, despite the serious challenges in recent elections to the party's monopoly. Political-economic elites appear content with the status quo, especially if the international financial and corporate communities lend support.

It is clear that democratization per se is meaningless when serious systemic economic problems plague a country, as they do in much of the developing world and, indeed, in much of the North. Despite its relatively improved standing in the international economy, Brazil's internal economic inequalities have yet to be resolved. A UN study on Latin American development indicated that during the 1990s, the richest 20 percent control 65 percent of national income; the poorest 50 percent control no more than 12 percent of income. The richest 10 percent earn thirty times as much as the poorest 40 percent. Indeed, Brazil ranked "last in terms of wealth distribution, behind Panama, Peru, Botswana and Kenya,"[120] a situation that breeds social conflict and resentment (see Box 10.5).

CONCLUSION

North–South relations have been one of the central issues in the international political economy. The divisions within and between the two regions, which began to take shape after the industrial revolution, became increasingly apparent as the FIEs used the financial, technological, and military advantages secured in the process of industrialization directly to colonize the developing regions and indirectly to dominate the world political economy. The U.S. hegemonic position after the Second World War was established through bilateral relations, as well as through multilateral institutions, such as the IMF and the World Bank. From the Marxist and *dependencia* perspectives, the U.S. strategy of containment, as implemented in collaboration with some developing countries and against others, and the multilateral institutions served as instruments of control and domination, which in turn perpetuated the structural inequalities in financial, technological, and military capabilities. Nevertheless, capital investments by North Americans, Europeans, Japanese, and others in the North brought new wealth and development options to the South. While some countries, such as the NICs, have attained a relatively high degree of economic growth and development, recurring economic and political problems have hindered greater independence from the structures of world political economy dominated by the FIEs.

This chapter has identified two principal sources of conflict between the FIEs on the one hand and the AIEs and LDEs on the other. These are the legacy of colonialism and the internecine conflicts fueled by the Cold War as the newly independent countries in Africa, Asia, and the Middle East were in the process of nation-building. Neither could the Latin American countries, which had gained independence by the 1820s, insulate themselves from the Cold War. On the contrary, despite lingering anticolonial resentment and suspicions of "Yankee imperialism," the deeply entrenched political, economic, and military institutions, with very few exceptions, found it in their interest to cooperate with the United States in the containment strategy, especially after the Cuban revolution in 1959.

Despite the tensions, the developed and developing countries also cooperated through bilateral and multilateral relations on an ever increasing number of issues, including formal military security alliances and informal alignments, as well as development programs as established by the Lomé Conventions. Through such cooperation, leaders of developing countries secured the military hardware and capital to strengthen their position against perceived or potential regional or internal threats and to enhance their prestige.

In the post–Cold War period, market competitiveness has replaced the Cold War containment strategy as a basis for cooperation. The governments in the developing countries have sought various avenues to address old issues of colonial domination and postcolonial dependence, as well as the new challenges of economic development and modernization. Regardless of the adopted policies—import-substitution

BOX 10.5

THE POLITICAL ECONOMY OF RACE AND DEMOCRATIZATION IN BRAZIL

In November 1695, Zumbi dos Palmares, warrior-leader of a 100-year-old breakaway group of rebel slaves in Brazil's interior, died in an ambush. Now, more than a century after Brazil abolished slavery, many blacks complain they are still treated as second-class citizens, packed into shantytowns, picked on by the police and paid less than whites. To mark the 300th anniversary of Zumbi's death Nov. 20, activists hope to muster 100,000 people for an unprecedented display of black protest in a march on capital Brasilia. "We want Zumbi's struggle to continue today," Vicente da Silva, president of the powerful Unified Labor Confederation and one of only a handful of prominent Brazilian blacks, said. "When Nelson Mandela was here he said he felt at home," columnist Verissimo wrote in Jornal do Brasil newspaper recently. "He was being nice. . . . He might also have been saying he felt he was in a disguised South Africa." Despite their march plans, activists recognize there is no groundswell of Brazilian black militancy to match October's Million Man March by blacks in Washington.

Official figures say blacks or people with black ancestors account for 44 percent of a total population of 150 million. Black groups say the figure is nearer 60 percent because many Brazilians are loathe to admit their African ancestry. They also argue there has been no Brazilian Martin Luther King, Malcolm X nor even a Louis Farrakhan to provide leadership because racism is widely considered a non-issue. "The myth that we live in a racial democracy has been used to delude us," said dreadlocked teacher Jonatas Conceicao in the port city of Salvador in Bahia state, where millions of Africans were herded from galley ships into slavery.

Many Brazilians speak with pride of their nation as a "racial democracy," a melting pot of cultures. The fact that blacks' average income is half that of whites is treated as a result of Brazil's acutely uneven distribution of wealth and is considered a social issue, not a racial one. There have been some changes in recent years. In elections last year, two black women were elected for the first time to the Senate. It is no longer common for black women to straighten their hair with hot irons and the African spirit-based religion of Candomble is making a comeback. But white remains the color of power in Brazil.

In Salvador, where 80 percent of the population is black and posters of Nelson Mandela and Bob Marley hang from open windows in the restored colonial center, there has never been an elected black mayor. "Salvador is the blackest city in Brazil and the most racist," said Vivaldo Bemvindo, a boiler-room operator who, like Conceicao, is a director of black self-help group Ile Aiye, which is known for its parades in Salvador's vibrant Carnival accompanied by 5,000 dancers, all of them black.

Next year a separate group will be opened for white revellers. Behind the scenes, Ile Aiye is advising local schools on including Zumbi in history lessons and runs a blacks-only school of its own in a house in one of Salvador's many slums. In a classroom hung with imported U.S. posters of Africa emblazoned with captions like "The Beginning," voluntary staff teach 100 children reading, writing and arithmetic as well as the religions, languages and legends of their forefathers. "This school is different because here you will learn about your culture, your religion, your origins," teacher Maria de Lourdes Ciqueira told a couple of dozen under 12-year-olds fidgeting in the afternoon heat. Such segregation is uncommon in Brazil but much needed, Bemvindo said. "The more you open up to whites . . . the more you deny racism exists in Brazil."

Despite plans one day for a Black Party, the immediate future for Brazil's black activists seems to lie with conventional politics. Having helped several black candidates win local elections, Luiz Alberto Silva dos Santos, coordinator of the Unified Black Movement (MNU) comprising several black groups, got enough votes last year to act as a stand-in for federal deputies from Bahia. If two of those deputies win local mayoral elections, as they are expected to do, Santos will join about ten blacks in the lower house and become the first black rights campaigner to represent Brazil's blackest state. He said his priorities were reform of school curricula to include African history and other topics of relevance to black students, official recognition of Afro-Brazilian religions and abolition of Brazil's military police force to end widespread impunity for killers of young blacks. "White Brazilians don't admit they are racist," Santos said. "It's up to us blacks to bring this conflict to a head so it can be addressed."

Source: William Schomberg, November 8, 1995, Reuter (On Line).

industrialization, export-led growth, or self-reliance—with the exception of a small number of countries, they have not fully succeeded in addressing the problem of dependent development. In the aftermath of the Cold War, one "peace dividend" for the developing countries could have been wider opportunities for new experiments with different combinations of development strategies. Although the Iranian Islamic model as another strategy was noted earlier in the chapter, unlike the other strategies, it has not been adopted by most other Islamic and non-Islamic countries. The Mexican and the East Asian economic crises in the 1990s have raised serious questions whether their "miracles" can provide the AIEs and LDEs with a useful model for economic growth and development within the existing structures of global markets and finance, especially when some problems, such as environmental issues, require greater domestic and international structural and serious multilateral negotiation. It remains to be seen whether international organizations, such as the UN, the IMF, the World Bank, and GATT-WTO, can serve as more effective instruments for North–South cooperation than they had been during the Cold War.

Chapter Summary

North–South relations—that is, relations among the first industrialized economies (FIEs), advanced industrializing economies (AIEs), and the less developed economies (LDEs)—have involved serious conflicts since the advent of modern international political economy and colonialism. Economic, technological, and military inequalities have been the principal characteristics of that relationship, and the gap has continued to widen.

The two primary sources of North–South conflict have been (1) the legacy of colonialism and efforts at nation-building in the aftermath of decolonization and (2) the world economic system. Colonialism led to the structural division of the world political economy into wealthy and poor or dependent societies, and the world capitalist system limited the options of former colonies in the nation-building process.

During the Cold War, the tensions were exacerbated by East–West ideological and military conflicts, as the United States and the Soviet Union sought to widen their spheres of influence across the globe. In the meantime, leaders in developing countries gaining independence from colonial rule attempted to strengthen their position at home by relying on neutralist or alliance policies as well as on the economic and military support they could secure from the superpowers.

Within the context of the colonial legacy and the world economic system, developing countries also experimented with different strategies for economic development: import-substitution industrialization (ISI), export-led strategies, and self-reliance. Leaders in developing countries attempting to diversify their economies through industrialization and technology found their efforts constrained by depen-dence on the North's markets, capital, and technology, and the two oil shocks and the international debt crisis in the 1970s and 1980s led to the abandonment of ISI and a shift toward greater liberalization.

Among the three strategies discussed in the chapter, the export-led strategy, as experienced by the East Asian economies, is said to be the most successful, although its success may have been attributable more to the geopolitical circumstances during the Cold War than to the export-led policies per se. While in the 1980s and the first half of the 1990s the economic growth in East Asian NICs was often referred to as the "East Asian miracle," the second half of the 1990s witnessed a sobering deterioration in their economies, and realization of their continued dependence on global and regional markets.

A small number of countries that experimented with self-reliance soon realized that that option was no longer tenable in an increasingly interdependent global political economy. Specialization in primary commodities kept the economies of the developing countries dependent on their markets in the developed countries, and therefore vulnerable to decisions made in and market fluctuations in the North.

In the 1980s and 1990s, most developing countries adopted the principles of structural adjustment and privatization—that is, economic liberalization—especially as supported by the West, the World Bank, and the IMF. According to classical liberalism, economic liberalization and political liberalization are mutually complementary, and the recent trend in the military withdrawal from power can be viewed as a confirmation of that hypothesis. Cuts in various public services and welfare programs as economies are attempting to recover from the financial and debt crises of the 1970s and 1980s can lead to social and political upheavals, however, as the Mexican and Indonesian cases have demonstrated. Debt crises have tended to be handled by multilateral and bilateral informal and voluntary arrangements to combine debt rescheduling or debt swapping with promised economic reforms and new loans.

Points of Contention

To what extent can the end of the Cold War and the trend toward economic liberalization enhance opportunities for cooperation among the FIEs, AIEs, and LDEs?

How has the colonial experience been a lingering source of North–South conflict? How did postcolonial efforts at nation-building in developing countries contribute to that conflict? What impact did the Cold War have on the nation-building process?

Which development strategies are more amenable greater to North–South or South–South cooperation?

To what extent can (or should) the export-led strategies of the East Asian "four tigers" (or NICs) be replicated in Africa and Latin America? What does the Brazilian experience suggest in this respect?

What are the problems associated with commodity specialization? How successful were the strategies adopted by developing countries in the 1950s and 1960s, or later, in combatting such problems? To what extent does economic liberalization offer a viable alternative to those strategies?

How successful were the Baker and the Brady plans?

How does free trade differ from fair trade? Which is preferable?

What is meant by "green imperialism," and why is it viewed as a source of North–South conflict? Can the strategies used by developing countries to combat economic dependence also address "green imperialism"?

To what extent can economic liberalization and political liberalization be mutually supportive in the developing countries in the 1990s? To what extent is democratization required for economic development?

Notes

1. Harry Magdoff, *Globalization: To What End?* (New York: Monthly Review Press, 1992), pp. 26–35.
2. The HDI is a composite index representing the level of human development in a country. It consists of measures for quality of life and standard of living, as well as education. For a more detailed description of the HDI data and methodology, see UNDP, *Human Development Report* 1997 (New York: Oxford University Press, 1997).
3. See *Challenge to the South: The Report of the South Commission* (Oxford: Oxford University Press, 1990) (hereinafter referred to as the *Nyerere Commission Report*).
4. Immanuel Wallerstein, "Class-Formation in the Capitalist World-Economy," *Politics and Society* 5, 3 (1975); Ronald H. Chilcote, *Theories of Comparative Politics* (Boulder, CO: Westview Press, 1981).
5. Gerald Epstein, Julie Graham, and Jessica Nembhard, eds., *Creating a New World Economy: Forces of Change and Plans for Action* (Philadelphia: Temple University Press, 1993); Stephen D. Krasner, *Structural Conflict: The Third World Against Global Liberalism* (Berkeley: University of California Press, 1985); Susan Strange, ed., *Paths to International Political Economy* (London: Allen and Unwin, 1984).
6. *The Economist,* March 16, 1996, p. 78.
7. *Ibid,* p. 56.
8. UN, *World Economic and Social Survey, 1997,* p. 55.
9. *Nyerere Commission Report,* pp. 206–210.
10. Simon Payaslian, "The United Nations and the Developing Countries in the 1990s," *The University of Detroit Mercy Law Review* 73, 3 (Spring 1996), pp. 525–549.
11. *Nyerere Commission Report,* pp. 206–210.
12. Krasner, *Structural Conflict.*
13. UN General Assembly, *Declaration on the Establishment of a New International Economic Order,* GA Res. 3201 (May 1, 1974); GA Res. 3203 (May 1, 1974); GA Res. 3362 (September 16, 1975).
14. Krasner, *Structural Conflict,* p. 80.
15. *Ibid.*
16. Frederic S. Pearson, *The Global Spread of Arms: Political Economy of International Security* (Boulder, CO: Westview Press, 1994).
17. A major concern were the exorbitant military expenditures that exceeded all expenditures on economic development and welfare. In the 1970s, for example, official development aid was no more than $20 billion. Military expenditures also reflected the states' priorities and the amount of manpower and research energies consumed (in the East and the West, in the North and the South) for military preparedness or actual military engagements. While the largest concentration of military hardware, including nuclear weapons, was in Europe between the NATO and Warsaw Pact forces and their economies felt the burden of military expenditures, the fact remained that most of the world could ill-afford to spend billions of dollars on weapons while their citizens suffered high rates of unemployment, infant mortality, malnutrition, and illiteracy. See *North–South: A Program for Survival: Report of the Independent Commission on International Development Issues* (Cambridge: MIT Press, 1980), p. 117 (hereinafter referred to as the Brandt Commission Report). See also Michael Brzoska and Frederic S. Pearson, "Development in the Global Supply of Arms: Opportunity and Motivation," in Robert E. Harkavy and Stephanie G. Neuman, eds., *The Arms Trade: Problems and Prospects in the Post–Cold War World.* Special issue of *The Annals of the American Academy of Political and Social Sciences* 535 (September 1994), p. 59; Robert E. Harkavy, "The Changing International System and the Arms Trade," in Harkavy and Neuman, eds., *The Arms Trade,* p. 20. Some importers (for example, Nigeria, Somalia, Uganda, China, Iraq, Jordan, and Pakistan) acquired weapons from both blocs while maintaining closer

relations with one or the other; and most importers successfully played off one superpower against the other.

18. Brandt Commission Report, p. 120.
19. *Ibid.*
20. In addition to arms transfers, covert intervention, involving intelligence agencies, was another serious problem in North–South relations, often justified by the major powers as defensive measures against their opponents. Such interventions came in various forms and were motivated by geopolitical (for example, dominance over the Panama and Suez canals, the Indian Ocean) and economic objectives (for example, oil in the Middle East, corporate interests in Latin America). See, for example, James A. Nathan and James K. Oliver, *United States Foreign Policy and World Order,* 3d ed. (Boston: Little, Brown and Company, 1985); Joseph Gerson and Bruce Birchard, eds., *The Sun Never Sets: Confronting the Network of Foreign U.S. Military Bases* (Boston: South End Press, 1991); Colin S. Gray, *The Geopolitics of Super Power* (Lexington: The University of Kentucky Press, 1988).
21. According to one estimate, in 1982 Western financial investment in South African strategic and mineral resources totaled about $25 billion, and the U.S. share accounted for $14 billion. Paul Cammack, David Pool, and William Tordoff, *Third World Politics: A Comparative Introduction* (Baltimore: Johns Hopkins University Press, 1988), pp. 216–217.
22. In Kenya, in the early 1960s the Kenyan African National Union (KANU), the leading political party, was torn by divisions between pro-Soviet and pro-U.S. factions led by Oginga Odinga and Tom Moya, respectively. Zaki Laïdi, *The Superpowers and Africa: The Constraints of a Rivalry, 1960–1990,* trans. Patricia Baudoin (Chicago: University of Chicago Press, 1990), pp. 7–16, and *passim.*
23. Thomas A. Skidmore and Peter H. Smith, *Modern Latin America* (New York: Oxford University Press, 1984), pp. 264–265.
24. In the 1930s and 1940s, Moscow provided some financial and organizational support but the Communist parties failed to overthrow a single Latin America government. After the Cuban Revolution, Moscow for the first time found an ally in the Western Hemisphere, although the revolution was neither Communist in its origin nor Moscow-sponsored. Also, with the exception of a honeymoon period between 1960 and 1963, a period that included the Bay of Pigs invasion in April 1961 and the Cuban Missile Crisis in October 1962, too many ideological and strategic differences surfaced between Havana and Moscow for Cuba to be considered a reliable Soviet "satellite." Castro and Che Guevara insisted on active support for "continental revolutionism" to mobilize guerrilla forces in every Latin American country, such as the *Fuerzas Armados de Liberación Nacional (FALN)* and the *Movimiento de la Izquierla Revolucionaia (MIR)* in Venezuela. Moscow, on the other hand, preferred "peaceful transition to socialism" and stable state-to-state relations for purposes of trade and spurned Castro's "revolutionism" as mere opportunism and a reckless provocation to the U.S. From Castro's and revolutionaries' point of view, Moscow's refusal to support such movements was the equivalent of U.S. efforts to destroy them; both East and West, it appeared, were in collusion against South-inspired changes in the status quo. See Rollie E. Poppino, *International Communism in Latin America: A History of the Movement, 1917–1963* (New York: Free Press of Glencoe, 1964), pp. 67–68; Thomas A. Skidmore and Peter H. Smith, *Modern Latin America* (New York: Oxford University Press, 1984); F. Parkinson, *Latin America, the Cold War and World Powers, 1945–1973: A Study in Diplomatic History* (Beverly Hills: Sage, 1974), pp. 186, 219; G. Pope Atkins, *Latin America in the International Political System* (New York: Free Press, 1977); Robert J. Alexander, *Communism in Latin America* (New Brunswick: Rutgers University Press, 1957).
25. Robert Axelrod and Robert O. Keohane, "Achieving Cooperation Under Anarchy," in Kenneth A. Oye, ed., *Cooperation Under Anarchy* (Princeton: Princeton University Press, 1986), p. 226.
26. James E. Dougherty and Robert L. Pfaltzgraff, *Contending Theories of International Relations,* 3d ed. (New York: Harper and Row, 1990).
27. Peter Dicken, *Global Shift: the Internationalization of Economic Activity,* 2d ed. (New York: the Guilford Press, 1992), p. 3.
28. *Ibid.*
29. Lars Schoultz, *National Security and United States Policy Toward Latin America* (Princeton: Princeton University Press, 1987), pp. 179–180.
30. *U.S. Overseas Loans and Grants,* July 1, 1945–September 30, 1992, p. 4.
31. See Simon Payaslian, *U.S. Foreign Economic and Military Aid: The Reagan and Bush Administrations* (Lanham, MD: University Press of America, 1996), p. 25.
32. *Congressional Presentation for Security Assistance Programs, FY1989* (Washington, DC: U.S. Government Printing Office, 1988), p. 7.
33. *Ibid.,* p. 15.
34. Schoultz, *National Security and United States Policy Toward Latin America,* p. 163.
35. See Ronald Reagan, "The Canal as Opportunity: A New Relations with Latin America," Orbis (Fall 1977): pp. 547–563.
36. Simon Payaslian, "The Formation of Dyadic Decision Regimes," paper presented at the annual meeting of the International Studies Association, Vancouver, B.C., Canada, March 1991.

37. Including the State Department, DEA, FBI, IRS, Coast Guard, Customs Service, Immigration and Naturalization Service, and National Institute on Drug Abuse. See also James Van Wert, "The US State Department's Narcotics Control Policy in the Americas," *Journal of Inter-American Studies and World Affairs* 30, 2 & 3 (Summer/Fall 1988), p. 7.
38. Cynthia McClintock, "The War on Drugs: The Peruvian Case," *Journal of Inter-American Studies and World Affairs,* 30, 2 & 3 (Summer/Fall 1988), pp. 130–133.
39. *Ibid.,* pp. 134–135.
40. James A. Nathan and James K. Oliver, *United States Foreign Policy and World Order,* 3d ed. (Boston: Little, Brown and Company, 1985), pp. 248–249.
41. Schoultz, *National Security and United States Policy Toward Latin America,* pp. 144–145.
42. *Ibid.*, p. 148.
43. Kenneth A. Kessel, *Strategic Materials: U.S. Alternatives* (Washington, DC: National Defense University Press, 1990); U.S. Department of the Interior, *Minerals Commodity Summaries* (Washington, DC: U.S. Government Printing Office, 1987).
44. *Ibid.*
45. George A. Bermann, Roger J. Goebel, William J. Davey, and Eleanor M. Fox, *Cases and Materials on European Community Law* (St. Paul: West, 1993), p. 948.
46. *Ibid.*, p. 949.
47. The Inter American Development Bank.
48. Burma was expected to become a full member of the ASEAN by 1998. June 22, 1996, Reuters (On Line). However, human rights violations continued. In May 1996, the Association accepted China and Russia as full dialogue partners. May 15, 1996, Reuters (On Line).
49. APEC includes Australia, Brunei, Canada, Chile, China, Hong Kong, Indonesia, Japan, Malaysia, Mexico, New Zealand, Papua New Guinea, the Philippines, Singapore, South Korea, Taiwan, Thailand, and the United States.
50. Chris Johnson, April 23, 1996, Reuter (On Line).
51. *Ibid.*
52. Paul Lewis, "Trade Aiding Third-World Laborers Scores Modest Gains," *The New York Times,* December 25, 1996 (On Line).
53. *Ibid.*
54. *Ibid.*
55. Matthias Finger, "Environmental NGOs in the UNCED Process," in Thomas Princen and Matthias Finger, *Environmental NGOs in World Politics: Linking the Local and the Global* (London: Routledge, 1994), pp. 187–188.
56. *Ibid.*, p. 189.
57. See also Gareth Porter and Janet Welsh Brown, *Global Environmental Politics* (Boulder, CO: Westview Press, 1991).
58. *Ibid.*, p. 9.
59. *Ibid.*, p. 127.
60. See, for example, Aldo Ferrer, "Self-Reliance for Self-Determination: The Challenge of Latin American Foreign Debt," in Alaf Gauhar, ed., *Regional Integration: The Latin American Experience* (London: Third World Foundation, 1985), pp. 88–97.
61. Thomas E. Skidmore, *Politics in Brazil, 1930–1964: An Experiment in Democracy* (London: Oxford University Press, 1967).
62. Stephany Griffith-Jones and Osvaldo Sunkel, *Debt and Development Crises in Latin America: The End of an Illusion* (Oxford: Clarendon Press, 1986), pp. 20–21.
63. *Ibid.*, pp. 21–22.
64. *Ibid.*, pp. 24–26.
65. *Ibid.*, pp. 22–23.
66. Gary W. Wynia, *The Politics of Latin American Development,* 3d ed. (Cambridge: Cambridge University Press, 1990), pp. 275–278.
67. March 24, 1997, Reuters Limited (On Line).
68. *Ibid.* Brazil's liberalization has involved other and technologically more sophisticated areas as well. In June 1996, Brazil and New Zealand signed an aviation agreement, linking both countries across the vast oceans, and further negotiations were on the way for agreements in sea transportation. Bilateral trade between Brazil and New Zealand totaled about $87.5 million in 1995. A large share of Brazil's exports were in paper, while over 50 percent of New Zealand's were dairy products. The 1996 agreement was expected to promote tourism between the two countries. June 18, 1996, Reuters (On Line).
69. World Bank, *World Tables 1995,* p. 4.
70. *Ibid.*, pp. 3–5.
71. Bruce Cumings, "The Origins and Development of the Northeast Asian Political Economy," in Frederic C. Deyo, ed. *The Political Economy of the New Asian Industrialism,* (Ithaca: Cornell University Press, 1987), pp. 69–70.
72. *Ibid.*, pp. 44–45.
73. *Ibid.*, p. 46.
74. Stephen Haggard and Tun-jen Cheng, "State and Capital in the East Asian NICs," in Deyo, ed. *The Political Economy of the New Asian Industrialism,* p. 92; Steve Chan, *East Asian Dynamism: Growth, Order, and Security in the Pacific Region* (Boulder, CO: Westview Press, 1993).
75. August 15, 1994, "Foreign Capital Is Streaming into Asian Markets," Gene Koretz, McGraw-Hill, Inc. (On Line).
76. Haggard and Cheng, "State and Capital in the East Asian NICs," p. 93.
77. *Ibid.*, p. 56.
78. Chalmers Johnson, "Political Institutions and Economic Performance," in Frederic C. Deyo, ed., *The Political Economy of the New Asian Industrialism,* pp. 160–162.

79. In contrast, Latin American ISI strategies, geared more toward the domestic markets to insulate themselves from external pressures, viewed industrialization as a means for wider distribution of political patronage, increasing domestic purchasing power, and integration of labor unions into the political process. Labor unions were at times repressed in some Latin American countries, such as Brazil and Chile. See Frederic C. Deyo, "State and Labor: Modes of Political Exclusion in East Asian Development," in Deyo, ed., *The Political Economy of the New Asian Industrialism,* p. 183.
80. *Ibid.*, pp. 190–200.
81. *Ibid.*, p. 183.
82. Johnson, "Political Institutions and Economic Performance," pp. 149–151.
83. Deyo, "State and Labor in East Asia," pp. 183–190; Johnson, "Political Institutions and Economic Performance," pp. 149–151.
84. Deyo, "State and Labor in East Asia," pp. 183–190; Johnson, "Political Institutions and Economic Performance," pp. 149–151.
85. May 1, 1996, Reuters (On-Line).
86. Johnson, "Political Institutions and Economic Performance," p. 136.
87. World Bank, *World Tables 1995* (Baltimore: Johns Hopkins University Press, 1995).
88. See Goran Hyden, *Beyond Ujamaa in Tanzania* (Berkeley: University of California Press, 1980), pp. 96–97.
89. Rodger Yeager, *Tanzania: An African Experiment* (Boulder, CO: Westview Press, 1982), p. 60.
90. Hyden, *Beyond Ujamaa in Tanzania,* pp. 96–97.
91. Yeager, *Tanzania,* p. 60.
92. Joel D. Barkan, "Comparing Politics and Public Policy in Kenya and Tanzania," in Joel D. Barkan, ed., *Politics and Public Policy in Kenya and Tanzania* (New York: Praeger, 1984), p. 33.
93. Manufacturing declined continuously in the 1970s and 1980s (from 10 percent in 1975 to 3.5 percent in 1991). In 1975, Tanzania's imports from African countries totaled $88 million, but $96 million from the United States. Between 1978 and 1983, those figures were $163 million and $297 million, respectively. During the same period, Tanzania's exports to Africa totaled $315 million, and to the United States $150 million, indicating a trade surplus of $152 million with African countries, but over $140 million trade deficit with the United States. Further, Tanzania's overall economic performance declined in the 1970s and 1980s. Its gross domestic product (GDP) dropped throughout the 1970s and did not improve until the late 1980s. Per capita GDP declined from $278 in 1975 to about $235 in 1985. Since the second half of the 1980s, however, it has relatively but consistently improved, reaching about $600 in the early 1990s. UN Economic Commission for Africa, *Foreign Trade Statistics for Africa, Summary Tables* (New York: United Nations, 1986), Table 2, p. 4, Table 7, pp. 36, 44; UN Industrial Development Organization, *Industry and Development: Global Report 1991/1992* (Vienna: UN Industrial Development Orga-nization, 1991), p. A-95.
94. Cumings, "Northeast Asian Political Economy," p. 77.
95. See Immanuel Wallerstein, *The Modern World System I* (New York: Academic Press, 1974); Wallerstein, *The Modern World System II* (New York: Academic Press, 1980).
96. Paul Knox and John Agnew, *The Geography of the World Economy* (London: Hodder and Stoughton, 1989), pp. 277–279.
97. Griffith-Jones and Sunkel, *Debt and Development Crises in Latin America,* pp. 60–61.
98. *Ibid.*, pp. 60–61.
99. *Ibid.*, pp. 77–79.
100. *Ibid.*
101. *Ibid.*, pp. 69–70.
102. William R. Cline, *International Economic Policy in the 1990s* (Cambridge: MIT Press, 1994), p. 113.
103. *Ibid.*, pp. 4–5.
104. Griffith-Jones and Sunkel, *Debt and Development Crises in Latin America,* p. 19.
105. Cline, *International Economic Policy in the 1990s,* p. 115.
106. Griffith-Jones and Sunkel, *Debt and Development Crises in Latin America,* p. 10.
107. *Ibid.*, p. 16.
108. *Ibid.*, p. 14.
109. *Ibid.*, p. 101.
110. *Ibid.*, p. 109.
111. Cline, *International Economic Policy in the 1990s,* p. 117.
112. *Ibid.*, pp. 118–120.
113. *Ibid.*, p. 121.
114. *Ibid.*, p. 123.
115. For example, note the difficulty in balancing market-oriented policies on the one hand and government and bank interventions for debt reduction on the other. There was also a contradiction in proposing new lending and debt reduction. *Ibid.*, p. 123.
116. Prior to the (tentative) agreement in principle, the treasury bill rate was as high as 55 percent, and after the agreement it dropped to 34 percent and to 25 percent after the signing of the actual debt agreement. *Ibid.*, p. 124.
117. *Ibid.*, p. 137.
118. *Ibid.*
119. See, for example, Stephan Haggard and Robert R. Kaufman, *The Political Economy of Democratic Transitions* (Princeton: Princeton University Press, 1995), p. 8.
120. June 17, 1996, Reuters (On Line).

CHAPTER ELEVEN

THE POLITICS OF DEVELOPMENT ASSISTANCE

Economic development is a central concern for governments in the developing and developed countries. As the previous chapters have indicated, nations engage in trade and develop financial and various other mutually beneficial arrangements to encourage economic development and growth. Development assistance, or aid, is expected to contribute to that process, although for most of the twentieth century the precise nature of the relationship between development assistance and economic development has been debated among different schools of thought in IPE, particularly within the context of North–South relations. The previous chapters identified a number of political and socioeconomic problems in the developing world, and Chapter 10 discussed some of the issues involved in North–South relations. This chapter focuses on North–South aid relations, commonly referred to as **official development assistance (ODA).**

The Development Assistance Committee (DAC) of the Organization for Economic Cooperation and Development (OECD) has defined official development assistance as "flows to developing countries and multilateral institutions *provided by official agencies,*" which engage in such transactions primarily to promote economic development and whose aid contains at least 25 percent concessionality, or reduced interest and a "grant element."[1] ODA may include bilateral or multilateral arrangements for the transfer of a combination of financial, technical, and human resources for—at least in theory—the purpose of economic development. Thus, the terms *ODA, assistance,* and *aid* refer to grants and loans (at concessional interest rates). *Bilateral aid* is direct country-to-country aid; *multilateral aid,* on the other hand, is transferred through an international agency, such as the World Bank, involved in development projects. Donor governments use **tied aid,** with certain conditions attached to aid, such as requiring the recipients to use aid loans and grants toward the purchase of products from the donor country, and **untied aid,** whereby no such explicit strings are attached.

Ideally, development assistance is said to express a nation's moral conviction to assist less fortunate nations in improving their standard of living. The widening economic gap between the first industrialized economies (FIEs) and the developing countries, as discussed in Chapter 10, necessitates international efforts to rectify global structural inequalities. Development assistance can be viewed as a moral responsibility, even a legal obligation under international norms of behavior, on the part of the wealthier countries as members of the same human community, to provide a certain level of assistance to countries that, for various historical and geographical reasons, lack similarly advanced levels of economic development. However, nations seldom behave in a purely altruistic fashion. Donors' motives vary, as do recipients' in accepting foreign assistance, and political and commercial interests are an integral part of dollar flows via ODA programs. The first section of this chapter discusses theories of foreign assistance.[2] These include the Realist approach, the theory of imperialism, the moralist school, and bureaucratic-incrementalist theories of budgetary politics. The chapter then examines bilateral and multilateral assistance, the trends in development assistance, and their consequences in recipient developing countries, with special attention to the relationship between development assistance and technology transfer, development management, and one of the most controversial issues—human rights.

THEORIES OF FOREIGN ASSISTANCE

Cooperation among nations is said to serve a number of purposes, and the protection of national security reigns supreme among them. Beyond denoting the physical survival of the nation, however, "national security" is not easily definable. In the "anarchical" and hostile international system, the *Realist* school of thought argues, the protection of national security requires active and vigilant engagement, which entails military power but also sufficient financial capability to lubricate bonds of friendship. Construed as such, development assistance is meant to buy cooperation and to bolster friendly governments. The primary objective of foreign assistance, according to this argument, is not to express some abstract idealism of humanitarian aspirations but the projection of national power, as aid is a component, at times a very essential component, of national security policy.[3] According to this theory, for example, the goal of the U.S. Latin American aid program of the 1960s, the Alliance for Progress, was to strengthen relations with friendly Latin American governments in the cause of containment against Soviet expansionism in the Western Hemisphere. By the same token, the goal of Moscow's economic and military support for Premier Fidel Castro in Cuba was to undermine that strategy, as its support for President Gamal Abdel Nasser in Egypt was meant to challenge the U.S. containment policy in the Middle East.

In a similar vein, the *imperialist* or *dependencia* theories of development assistance contend that rich, and particularly the powerful, capitalist states also use assistance to influence the domestic and foreign affairs of the recipient country. According to this argument, foreign assistance enables the donor country to co-opt the local elites in recipient countries for commercial and national security purposes, on the one hand, and to develop, through inter-elite networks, international financial and production structures to exploit the aid recipient country's natural and human resources. As such, development assistance serves as an instrument for the preservation and expansion of a wealthier country's power over the poorer, a system that perpetuates dependency.[4]

Moralists (or idealists), however, strongly disagree with the previously mentioned views and argue that development assistance should be essentially a humanitarian gesture, reflecting values of "humane internationalism."[5] This view holds that wealthier nations have a moral obligation to cultivate greater North–South cooperation and to respond to the social and economic developmental needs of the South. Religious principles, such as charitable contributions to the needy, and the promotion of peace among nations have provided the moral basis for international philanthropy and foreign aid. As far back as the early nineteenth century, British Christian missionary organizations, such as the London Missionary Society, supported social and economic programs—for example, schools, hospitals, and orphanages—as the British empire expanded. In the twentieth century, Islamic and Jewish societies have provided similar assistance. Moralists point out that development assistance programs promote mutually supportive and beneficial relations along with economic development and international human rights, law, and order.[6] This view concedes, however, that it is unrealistic to pursue a utopian vision of global egalitarianism. Equality as such has not been achieved within national communities or even within smaller units of the human community, but, moralists contend, provided in sufficient volume and used effectively and humanely, development assistance should remove from communities the scourge of poverty and unemployment and promote economic and social development that is both economically and morally sustainable.

In addition to these theories, development assistance, as a public policy, is also the product of *domestic politics* involving public opinion, interest groups (for example, ethnic groups), and governmental institutions, such as legislatures and bureaucracies, directly involved in policymaking processes, each promoting "the national interest" through its own political agenda.[7] A country's ODA level as a percentage of its governmental budget may be the result of a combination of these influences. In the case of the United States, for example, one quantitatively based study found that, in addition to geo-political and humanitarian considerations, *budgetary considerations* and *incrementalism* (the inertia of spending relatively the same ways from year to year) were among the most important factors that shaped foreign economic and military aid policies during the Reagan and Bush administrations.[8]

These theories suggest a number of objectives pursued by donors in the international political economy. These include a combination of humanitarian objectives, geo-political and ideological considerations, commercial interests, environmental concerns, and various factors in domestic politics. Humanitarian objectives, combined with the optimism of the period immediately after the Second World War, reflected the high level of confidence of the leadership in the Western industrialized countries, particularly the United States as the most powerful country, expressed in international cooperation to rebuild the war-torn economies of Europe. The Marshall Plan, worth $17 billion in aid, symbolized this confidence in the ability of foreign aid to reconstruct a new world, but the Marshall Plan, combined with the Truman administration's Point Four Program, also represented the administration's geo-strategic priorities to contain Soviet expansion in Western Europe. The economic programs were soon complemented by military programs in the form of the North Atlantic Treaty Organization (NATO). Increasingly, the rapid expansion of the Cold War throughout the developing world also necessitated, especially as viewed from Washington, similar aid programs to contain the spread of Communism in other regions. By the mid-1950s, U.S. objectives in providing foreign assistance to other countries had already begun to place a greater emphasis on Cold War priorities than on humanitarian considerations. Over the years, the geographical distribution of U.S. aid reflected its geo-political objectives: in the early 1950s for Taiwan and South Korea and in the 1960s for South Vietnam to contain Communism in East Asia, in the 1970s for Israel and Egypt to make peace and protect oil interests, and in the 1980s for Central American governments supportive of the U.S. effort to overthrow the Sandinista government in Nicaragua.

Geo-political considerations also governed aid programs by European governments. They supported the U.S. policy of containment, but they also had extensive political and commercial relations with their former colonies. Development aid provided a means to maintain their influence in developing regions. This has been true particularly in the case of France, whose aid programs, including technical assistance by engineers, educators and administrators, sought to retain some degree of control over the former African colonies and to promote French culture and institutions. Nevertheless, the humanitarian component in European aid appears to have been more pronounced in recent years, particularly by such countries as Denmark, the Netherlands, Norway, and Sweden.

Commercial interests also influence foreign aid policies. In the past two decades, powerful business interests and the pursuit of international competitiveness have replaced whatever moral/idealistic bases development assistance programs had in the post-WWII reconstruction period, and governments have used aid dollars to promote exports and FDIs by constituent companies. As a result, by the mid-1990s, ODA was serving the interests of donor countries' companies, particularly in the case of bilateral aid programs. In 1977, for example, the British government under Labour Prime Minister James Callaghan established the Aid and Trade Provision (ATP), in conjunction with the Department of Trade and Industry, to not only facilitate corporate export contracts in foreign markets but also as a way of addressing rising unemployment levels at home. The Conservative government of Margaret Thatcher, despite its ideological opposition to government intervention in the market, continued to support ATP for the same reason. The close ties between the business community and the Department of Trade and Industry rendered the British official aid agency, the Overseas Development Administration, impotent, although it legally possessed the authority to oversee and evaluate aid projects. Thus, for example, when the contract for the Pergau dam project in Malaysia was secured by British companies, ATP provisions subsidized, as official development assistance, the interested companies, including weapons deals, when, in fact, Malaysia, because of its relatively high standard of living, would not usually have been eligible for such aid.[9]

Japan also has frequently used aid for commercial interests. Japanese aid, which has grown to equal or surpass U.S. ODA levels, focuses on neighboring Asian countries but also has extended to other regions. The Overseas Economic Cooperation Fund (OECF), Japan's main ODA agency, has drawn criticism from other Western governments for financing and supporting Japanese exports. In the 1980s, because of Japan's enormous trade surplus, the U.S. and European governments demanded that Tokyo increase its multilateral contributions.

Thus, contrary to the moralist/idealist view, since its emergence as worldwide policy by the industrialized countries, development assistance has become too complicated to serve strictly humanitarian purposes. Development assistance certainly facilitates international cooperation and helps people, but the aim of that co-operation is not necessarily only to help poor people in poor countries to improve their standard of living. Development assistance is not above politics. It is intertwined with domestic and external political considerations and commercial interests.

THE ERA OF INTERNATIONAL OPTIMISM AND INSTITUTION-BUILDING, 1945–1970s

Economic assistance emerged as an important issue in the 1950s and 1960s as the major powers in the industrialized West, particularly influenced by the rationale of the Truman Doctrine and the Marshall Plan, used bilateral and multilateral foreign aid programs to prevent the spread of Communism in former colonies throughout the developing world. At the same time, based on the Western experience since the industrial revolution and based on the tenets of classical liberalism and modernization theory, Western leaders believed that development assistance would accelerate the pace of economic growth in the developing world, while enhancing opportunities for international economic cooperation between the West and the developing countries. By the late 1950s and early 1960s, the success of the Marshall Plan in Western Europe, itself a beneficiary of foreign assistance for postwar reconstruction, raised hopes that similar efforts could lead to more stable political systems and wider markets in the developing world as well. Thus, following the experience of creating multilateral economic networks, such as the Bretton Woods system in the 1940s, efforts were made to devise similar multilateral arrangements, along with bilateral country-to-country programs, for development assistance. The 1960s witnessed enormous proliferation and institutionalization of development aid programs (see Table 11.1). It soon became apparent, however, that these efforts alone could not assure that development assistance would be used effectively and efficiently.

Beginning in the 1950s, the Soviet Union also used foreign assistance as an instrument of foreign policy. Although some high-profile Soviet aid projects, most notably the Aswan High Dam in Egypt, drew Third World support, due to economic limitations, Soviet aid [levels] never equaled those of Western nations. During the second half of the 1960s, for example, while members of the Aid India Consortium supplied over 90 percent of India's foreign assistance, the Soviet Union (along with the East bloc countries) provided no more than 8 percent.[10] Its assistance programs were mainly in the public and heavy industrial areas, including the Bhilai and Bokaro steel plants, the coal mining facilities in Durgapur, and oil refineries in Barauni and Koyali.[11]

Arab countries also gradually introduced assistance programs. In 1961, the government of Kuwait established the Kuwait Fund for Arab Economic Development, initially designed exclusively for Arab countries but, after the mid-1970s, extended to other developing states as well. In the meantime, other Arab development assistance programs, such as the Arab Bank for Economic Development in Africa, Islamic Development Bank, and the Saudi Fund for Development, were inaugurated. In 1976 OPEC created its own Special Fund (headquartered in Vienna) for development assistance,[12] and by the end of the decade, additional Arab funds had been established, including the Abu Dhabi Fund and the Arab Fund for Economic and Social Development, collectively referred to as the Arab/OPEC Aid Agencies.

Nongovernmental organizations (NGOs) have made significant contributions to economic development as well. In 1958, the World Council of Churches adopted a resolution, subsequently submitted to the United Nations, stating that each developed country should aim at distributing 1 percent of its national income to the developing countries. NGOs have included a vast array of foundations established by major industrialists and financiers. For example, the Ford Foundation was instrumental in founding the Uttar Pradesh agricultural university and the Institute of Management in India, as was the Rockefeller Foundation in financing the Indian Council of Medical Research and the Central Rice Research Institute in India.[13]

In the meantime, however, it became patently obvious that bilateral and multilateral efforts were not significantly improving the lot of most people in the developing countries. Critics of official organizations and bureaucracies administering multilateral and bilateral aid—for example, the various World Bank agencies, the EU Directorate General for Development, the U.S. Agency for International Development, and the British Overseas Development Administration—charged that aid administration was poorly managed and often plagued with corruption. Western "donor" bureaucracies, whose august headquarters in some of the world's wealthiest cities (Geneva, Paris, New York) consumed a large part of their budgets, employed officials and staff lacking sufficient knowledge and field experience to formulate useful policies. Some of the projects they financed—ranging from sending frostbite medicine to the world's hottest countries and 110-volt refrigerators to countries using a 220-volt system, to the construction of gargantuan hydroelectric power facilities that required the removal of thousands of local people from their homes—either missed the mark entirely or served special interests in recipient and donor countries rather than the people most in need of real aid. For their part,

TABLE 11.1

The Proliferation and Institutionalization of Foreign Aid

Country	Period	Aid Institutions
Britain	1940s	Parliament reorganized the Colonial Development and Welfare Act and adopted the Overseas Resources Development Act, establishing the Colonial Development Corporation.
	1964	Parliament created the Ministry of Overseas Development (ODM), integrating all of the responsibilities in the area of foreign assistance.
France	1946	Fonds d'Investissement économique et social des territories d'outre-mer (FIDES) was established.
	1961	Ministry for Cooperation was created with the responsibility of distributing foreign assistance to the newly independent developing countries.
Germany	1961	Ministry for Economic Cooperation was established, with responsibilities in the area of technical assistance.
	1972	The ministry emerged as Germany's central ministry for all foreign bilateral and multilateral assistance programs.
Japan	1961	The Overseas Economic Cooperation Fund (OEFC) was founded for aid to the developing countries.
	1974	The Overseas Technical Cooperation Agency (OTCA) was integrated into the Japan International Cooperation Agency (JICA).
Switzerland	1961	Programs introduced for economic cooperation for technical assistance and development in the developing countries.
	1977	Directorate for Development Cooperation and Humanitarian Aid was established at the Department of Foreign Affairs, as well as the Federal Office for External Economic Affairs at the Department of Public Economics.
Belgium	1962	Office for Development Cooperation (ODC) was created and later integrated into the General Agency for Development Cooperation (AGCD).
Denmark	1962	Secretariat within the Ministry of Foreign Affairs established to administer financial and technical aid programs.
	1971	The secretariat became an independent department within the foreign ministry renamed the Danish International Development Agency (DANIDA).
Norway	1962	The Norwegian Agency for International Development (NORAD) was created as a directorate in the Ministry of Foreign Affairs.
	1983	A separate Ministry of Development Cooperation was created, integrating NORAD, the foreign ministry's aid office, and the NORIMPOD import office.
Netherlands	1963	The office of Secretary of State was established in the Ministry of Foreign Affairs for foreign assistance.
	1964	The Directorate-General for International Cooperation was founded.
	1965	The Minister for Development Cooperation was founded.
Sweden	1962	The Agency for International Assistance (AIA) was created.
	1965	AIA was succeeded by the Swedish International Development Authority (SIDA) under the Ministry of Foreign Affairs.
Canada	1960	External Aid Office (EAO) was established.
	1968	EAO reorganized as the Canadian International Development Agency (CIDA).
United States	1947	Marshall Plan for Europe.
	1952	Mutual Security Act established aid programs to strengthen Korea and Taiwan (Republic of China) against communism and the Soviet threat.
	1954	Congress instituted the food aid program known as P.L. 480.
	1961	Foreign Assistance Act was adopted, reorganizing the International Cooperation Administration and the Development Loan Fund under the newly created U.S. Agency for International Development (USAID).

Source: OECD, *Twenty-Five Years of Development Co-Operation, 1985 Report: A Review* (Paris: Organization for Economic Co-Operation and Development, 1985), pp. 69–70.

government leaders and officials in recipient countries sometimes accumulated enormous wealth funded through aid programs, with little benefit to the people.[14] As a result, observers in both developed and developing countries have looked with great suspicion at Western aid and its objectives.

As former colonies gained independence in the 1950s and 1960s and as their numbers increased at the UN General Assembly and associated agencies, various groups in the developing world called for a new international economic order (NIEO) and more concerted efforts, with fewer strings attached, to rectify the imbalances in the world economic system. From their perspective, the West's development assistance represented a new form of colonialism, whereby Western governments subsidized multinational corporations and financed brutal military leaders to promote and protect Western economic and political interests at the expense of the local population, marginalized with little to gain from billions of dollars spent on ODA. As Ryrie has pointed out, in the 1960s and 1970s, the Western countries initially exhibited a conciliatory attitude toward such demands and complaints. They increased ODA levels, encouraged, albeit reluctantly and with much consternation, the establishment of the UN Conference on Trade, Aid, and Development (1964), and they directly or indirectly engaged in the so-called North–South dialogue.[15] By the late 1970s and early 1980s, however, the differences between the industrialized West, particularly the United States and Britain, and the Third World proved too contentious and apparently irreconcilable.

NATIONALISM, POLITICAL CYNICISM, AND OPPOSITION TO AID, 1980s–1990s

By the mid-1970s, there was cause for optimism that more than two decades of institution-building in the area of bilateral and multilateral aid had established ODA as an essential component of the world political economy. The world ODA level had increased from about $8.2 billion in the mid-1950s to over $25 billion in the late 1960s, and to nearly $35 billion in the 1970s. Indeed in the 1980s, it increased to over $40 billion[16] and to nearly $60 billion in the early 1990s.[17]

The initial optimism of the first two decades, when the major international institutions were established, and public confidence in development assistance programs to induce rapid economic improvement disappeared in the 1980s, however, and ODA levels by the major contributors, such as the United States, declined. Some observers attributed that decline to "donor-fatigue," implying that donor countries had grown tired of constantly providing assistance to the poorer countries. In fact, far more fundamental factors in domestic and international political economy contributed to the overall decline in ODA levels. The world recession in the 1970s, and especially the international debt crisis experienced by a large number of developing countries in the 1980s, raised serious questions regarding the efficacy of such programs. Further, as the industrialized economies themselves began to experience serious problems of inflation, recession, and unemployment, the public mood increasingly and at times vehemently opposed "hand outs" to other states. Because of domestic budgetary pressures in the 1980s and the collapse of the Soviet Union by 1992, donor governments, particularly the United States, showed little interest in once more increasing aid levels.

In addition, as a result of the Cold War's end, some aid dollars, particularly in the case of Germany, were redirected either domestically or toward the newly independent countries of the former Soviet empire. These shifts in regional emphasis, accompanied by budgetary cuts, gave rise to concerns that aid levels to former recipient, particularly African, countries would drop even further in the 1990s. To a large extent, such fears were well founded. While the ODA dollar amount increased, overall ODA levels as a percentage of total resource flows to developing countries declined from 42.1 percent in 1985 to 33.0 percent in 1993. Bilateral disbursements dropped from 31.7 percent to 23.3 percent for the same years, as did multilateral disbursements, from 10.4 percent to 9.7 percent. In their stead, private flows, particularly in the form of direct investments, increased from 38.5 percent to 56.1 percent of total resource flows to the developing countries for the same years (see Table 11.2).[18]

BILATERAL ASSISTANCE

The 1 percent goal proposed by the World Council of Churches has proved overly optimistic and elusive, based on the ODA performance of the vast majority of donor countries. By the late 1960s, the 0.5 percent level of donor's GNP appeared to be more realistic and was established as an internationally acceptable objective formally adopted by the United Nations. A 0.7 percent goal was set in the 1970s. Since then, however, only a very small number of countries have actually increased their aid to these levels, and since the mid-1980s the trend indicates an overall decline, as seen in Tables 11.3 and 11.4.

In March 1995, the UN World Summit for Social Development at Copenhagen proposed to end poverty,

TABLE 11.2

Total Net Receipts of ODA by Region, 1960–1994 (as Percentage of Total World ODA)

Region	1960–1961	1970–1971	1978–1979	1983–1984	1988–1989	1993–1994
Sub-Saharan Africa	9.0	18.7	26.0	30.8	39.4	36.6
Asia	44.8	47.1	26.0	29.5	32.7	30.2
North Africa and Middle East	26.7	11.2	19.0	23.5	12.4	14.0
Latin America	9.9	16.0	11.3	11.0	11.2	11.0
Oceania	na	4.2	5.5	3.4	3.3	2.8
Southern Europe	9.3	2.8	3.0	1.8	1.1	5.3

Source: OECD, *Development Co-Operation, 1995 Report* (Paris: Organization for Economic Co-Operation and Development, 1996), Table 36, pp. A61–A62; OECD, *Twenty-Five Years of Development Co-Operation, 1985 Report: A Review* (Paris: Organization for Economic Co-Operation and Development, 1985), Table III-10, pp. 121–122.

unemployment, and social disintegration around the world.[19] The summit adopted a global agenda for the next decade based on Ten Commitments, including commitments "to create an economic, political, social, cultural and legal environment that will enable people to achieve social development," to "[eradicate] poverty in the world, through decisive national actions and international cooperation, as an ethical, social, political and economic imperative of humankind," and "to promoting the goal of full employment as a basic priority of our economic and social policies, and to [enable] all men and women to attain secure and sustainable livelihoods through freely chosen productive employment and work."[20] To that end, the Copenhagen Declaration urged donor countries to allocate 0.7 percent of their GNP to foreign economic aid and to cancel the debt of poor countries. Further, donor countries were expected to earmark 20 percent of their aid specifically for social programs, and recipients were expected to spend 20 percent of their national budget on such programs (the so-called 20/20 provision). However, there was little consensus among the participants regarding these proposals, which remain voluntary.[21] Only a small number of countries (Scandinavian and Islamic) have maintained aid levels approaching or exceeding the 0.7 percent target.

North–South Aid

In general, there is little support for foreign aid programs in most advanced countries, and most policymakers prefer to ignore the issue as much as possible. Of the major European countries, France has maintained its annual aid volume above the 0.5 percent level (Table 11.4), generally about 2 percent of the government's annual budget, making that country one of the highest contributors among the Development Assistance Committee countries. While in total dollar value British aid increased from about $900 million in the mid-1970s to over $3.0 billion in the early 1990s, as a percentage of GNP, it in fact dropped from 0.51 percent to about 0.31 percent for the same period, and this drop reflected in Britain's share of the total DAC ODA level.[22]

Sub-Saharan Africa and the poorer Asian countries remain the largest recipients of European ODA. French ODA has been concentrated in the former, francophone colonies in sub-Saharan Africa. In the early 1970s, about 71 percent of France's total annual $1.2 billion ODA went to Africa (47.5 percent to sub-Saharan Africa and 23.6 percent to North Africa), and in the early 1990s sub-Saharan Africa received 55 percent of the French annual total of nearly $9.0 billion ODA.[23] During the past two decades, the major recipients have been Algeria, New Caledonia, Morocco, French Polynesia, Côte d'Ivoire, Cameroon, and Egypt.[24] French ODA programs have focused primarily on education, as well as agricultural and industrial production. While this appears humanitarian in orientation, economic interests constituted an important element, as nearly 40 percent of its ODA in the early 1990s was tied aid, requiring procurement from French private or state-owned companies.[25]

The major recipients of German bilateral aid since the early 1970s have included China, Egypt, India, Indonesia, Israel, and Turkey. Well into the late 1980s, sub-Saharan Africa as a region received the highest level of German ODA, but the region's share declined substantially in the early 1990s, from nearly 60 percent of total German aid in the late 1980s to little over 36 percent in 1994.[26] Instead,

TABLE 11.3

Total ODA Disbursements by Individual DAC Countries, 1960–1994[a]

DAC Countries	$ Million								% Share of Total DAC		
	1960	1965	1970	1975	1980	1985	1990	1994	1973–1974	1983–1984	1993–1994
Australia	59	119	212	552	667	749	955	1,088	2.3	2.8	1.8
Austria	[b]	11	11	79	178	248	394	655	0.6	0.6	1.0
Belgium	101	102	120	378	595	440	889	726	2.4	1.7	1.3
Canada	65	97	337	880	1,075	1,631	2,470	2,250	4.5	5.6	4.0
Denmark	5	13	59	205	481	440	1,171	1,446	1.5	1.5	2.4
Finland	—	2	7	48	111	211	846	290	0.3	0.6	0.6
France	823	752	971	2,093	4,162	3,995	9,380	8,466	11.5	10.8	14.2
Germany	224	456	599	1,689	3,567	2,942	6,320	6,818	12.8	10.9	11.9
Italy	77	60	147	182	683	1,098	3,395	2,705	2.3	3.6	5.0
Japan	105	244	458	1,148	3,353	3,797	9,069	13,239	16.4	14.7	21.2
Netherlands	35	70	196	608	1,630	1,136	2,592	2,517	3.7	4.5	4.4
Norway	5	11	37	184	486	574	1,205	1,137	0.9	2.0	1.9
Sweden	7	38	117	566	962	840	2,012	1,819	2.8	2.7	3.1
Switzerland	4	12	30	104	253	302	750	982	0.9	1.1	1.5
United Kingdom	407	472	482	904	1,854	1,530	2,647	3,197	8.2	5.5	5.3
United States	2,760	4,023	3,153	4,161	7,138	9,403	11,366	9,927	28.6	30.6	17.4

Source: Data for total distribution by individual countries for 1960, 1965, 1970, 1975, 1980: OECD, *Twenty-Five Years of Development Co-Operation, 1985 Report: A Review* (Paris: Organization for Economic Co-Operation and Development, 1985), Table 25, p. 334; Year 1985: OECD, *Development Co-Operation, 1988 Report* (Paris: Organization for Economic Co-Operation and Development, 1991), Tables 47–52, pp. 234–245; Year 1990: OECD, *Development Co-Operation, 1991 Report* (Paris: Organization for Economic Cooperation and Development, 1991), Table 1, p. 171; Year 1994: OECD, *Development Co-Operation, 1995 Report* (Paris: Organization for Economic Cooperation and Development, 1996), Table 13, pp. A21–A22. Data for % share of total DAC from 1995 Report, Table 9, p. A16.

[a] Includes total bilateral ODA (grants and development lending and capital), concessional amounts, and contributions to multilateral organizations

[b] $100,000 or less

TABLE 11.4
Total ODA Disbursements by Individual DAC Countries, 1960–1994[a] (as Percentage of GNP)

DAC Countries	1960	1965	1970	1975	1980	1985	1990	1994
Australia	0.37	0.53	0.62	0.65	0.48	0.48	0.34	0.35
Austria	0.00	0.11	0.07	0.21	0.23	0.38	0.25	0.33
Belgium	0.88	0.60	0.46	0.60	0.50	0.55	0.45	0.32
Canada	0.16	0.19	0.41	0.54	0.43	0.49	0.44	0.43
Denmark	0.09	0.13	0.37	0.55	0.74	0.80	0.93	1.03
Finland	0.00	0.02	0.06	0.17	0.22	0.40	0.64	0.31
France	1.35	0.76	0.69	0.62	0.63	0.78	0.79	0.64
Germany	0.31	0.40	0.32	0.40	0.44	0.47	0.42	0.34
Italy	0.22	0.10	0.15	0.10	0.17	0.26	0.32	0.27
Japan	0.24	0.27	0.23	0.23	0.32	0.29	0.31	0.29
Netherlands	0.31	0.36	0.62	0.74	0.97	0.91	0.94	0.76
Norway	0.11	0.16	0.33	0.65	0.87	1.01	1.17	1.05
Sweden	0.05	0.19	0.35	0.78	0.78	0.86	0.90	0.96
Switzerland	0.04	0.09	0.14	0.18	0.24	0.31	0.31	0.36
United Kingdom	0.56	0.47	0.39	0.38	0.35	0.33	0.27	0.31
United States	0.54	0.58	0.32	0.27	0.27	0.24	0.21	0.15

Source: Data for 1960, 1965, 1970, 1975, 1980: OECD, *Twenty-Five Years of Development Co-Operation, 1985 Report: A Review* (Paris: Organization for Economic Co-Operation and Development, 1985), Table 26, p. 335; Year 1985: OECD, *Development Co-Operation, 1988 Report* (Paris: Organization for Economic Cooperation and Development, 1985), Tables 47–52, pp. 234–245; Year 1990; OECD, *Development Co-Operation, 1991 Report* (Paris: Organization for Economic Cooperation and Development, 1991), Table 1, p. 171; Year 1994: OECD, *Development Co-Operation, 1995 Report* (Paris: Organization for Economic Cooperation and Development, 1996), Table 13, pp. A21–A22.

[a]Includes total bilateral ODA (grants and development lending and capital), concessional amounts, and contributions to multilateral organizations

German aid to Indonesia, the Middle East, and the former states of Yugoslavia increased. Latin America's share of German ODA also rose from 11.5 percent in 1983–1984 to 13.8 percent in the early 1990s,[27] mostly for debt relief, agricultural and industrial production, economic infrastructure, and education. Similar to France, German tied aid constituted about 39 percent of ODA.

Sub-Saharan Africa has received the largest share of total British ODA as well, followed by south and central Asia, although both regions have experienced cuts in their share. Sub-Saharan Africa's share was nearly 38 percent in 1983–1984 and as high as 53 percent in the late 1980s. In the early 1990s, its share declined to 48 percent and to 46.6 percent by 1994.[28] South and central Asia's share of British ODA declined as well, from about 40 percent in the early 1980s to 22 percent by the mid-1990s. While Latin America's share increased somewhat, from an average of 6.7 percent in 1979–1980 to nearly 10 percent by 1994, the Middle East, North Africa, and Southern Europe experienced substantial increases, from 6.1 percent in the early 1980s to 14 percent in 1993–1994.

India, as the former "jewel" in the British empire, has received by far the largest share of British ODA. In the early 1970s, it accounted for 20 percent, followed by Kenya's 4 percent. By the early 1980s, however, India's share had declined to 12 percent and to about 4 percent by 1994, while aid to Bangladesh, Tanzania, and Kenya fluctuated between 5 and 2 percent in the 1980s. In the early 1990s, the states of the former Yugoslavia also began to receive aid, accounting for an average of 3.2 percent in 1993–1994, second only after India's 4 percent. Nearly 36 percent of British ODA is tied aid, and its aid programs have focused on energy resources, agricultural and industrial production, and education.

Although in 1970 the UN General Assembly declared the 1970s the Second UN Development Decade and set the target of 0.7 percent of each donor's GNP for ODA by the mid-1970s, only two countries—the Netherlands and Sweden—met the challenge at 0.74 percent and 0.78 percent, respectively, although the dollar value of ODA from each at about $600 million for 1975 paled beside U.S. aid worth $4.2 billion for the same year. In fact, unlike the United States and the other major European powers, the smaller European countries in the 1970s supported calls by the developing countries for a new international economic order (NIEO). By 1980, Denmark and Norway also increased their ODA levels above the 0.7 percent level, or $481 million and $486 million, respectively, and thereafter these four countries maintained their ODA contributions well above the 0.7 percent target. Although in dollar value their contributions were substantially lower than those of the major economies of Japan, Germany, and the United States, these smaller and medium-sized countries have been the front runners among the Western industrialized nations, and their ODA contributions have reached and in some years even passed the 1.0 percent level.[29]

As the United States enjoyed a clear hegemonic position in international political economy, it has traditionally promoted development assistance and shouldered the related responsibilities of providing financial and technical support. In the mid-1990s, the United States extended some form of foreign assistance to nearly 120 countries, totaling an annual average of about $11 billion. The convergence of U.S. geopolitical and commercial interests, on the one hand, and its economic and military supremacy on the other enabled the United States to shoulder the bulk of post-WWII aid responsibilities.

While in the 1950s and early 1960s U.S. bilateral aid policy seemed to work, largely based on the experience in Western Europe and to some extent in bolstering Taiwan and South Korea, its failure to achieve success in Vietnam raised a host of questions about the effectiveness of economic and military assistance. In the late 1970s, the revolutions against the U.S.-supported governments in Iran and Nicaragua further intensified the debate regarding the utility of foreign aid as an instrument of foreign policy. Given the fact that politicians and public opinion leaders had presented foreign economic aid as promoting friendship, it was difficult for the American public to understand why some developing countries exhibited hostility toward the United States. Public opinion with respect to foreign aid has thus vacillated between supporting specific humanitarian objectives, as after natural disasters, and opposition to its use for "political" purposes.[30] In general, the annual U.S. ODA level has been about 1 percent of the government budget and, in recent years, about 0.15 percent of GNP, the lowest among the DAC countries. The U.S. share of total DAC ODA has declined from 28.6 percent in the early 1970s to 17.4 percent in 1994, placing it second after Japan's 21.2 percent.[31] (Table 11.3).

In the early 1970s, the major U.S. aid recipients were India (13.9 percent), South Vietnam (10.5 percent), Indonesia (7.8 percent), and Pakistan (5.0 percent).[32] After the oil crisis in 1973, however, the focus of U.S. aid policy changed to the Middle East, followed by sub-Saharan Africa and Latin America. In the late 1970s, nearly 40 percent of total U.S. ODA went to the Middle East and North Africa, and, after a brief drop in the late 1980s (34 percent), total ODA hovered around 40 percent in the 1990s, with Israel and Egypt receiving the largest share.[33] The high levels of assistance to the two countries was seen as a reward for peace negotiations, which culminated in the Camp David Accords in 1978 and the Israeli-Egyptian Peace Treaty of 1979.[34] For the Carter administration, peaceful relations between Israel and Egypt were taking the region a step closer to stability, thus preventing potential disruptions in oil supplies and the expansion of Soviet influence. Throughout the 1980s and 1990s, despite fluctuations in U.S. aid levels, Israel and Egypt continued to receive the largest share, on average about 12 percent and 10 percent respectively. The next top three recipients in the mid-1990s were El Salvador (4.1 percent), Somalia (3.5 percent), and Haiti (2.6 percent).[35] The tied aid level of U.S. ODA has been relatively low, about 17 percent, or 27 percent with partially tied aid, with a large percentage (30 percent) of ODA in recent years going to debt relief programs.

While the U.S. share of DAC ODA declined, Japan's increased from nearly 15 percent in the early 1980s to over 21 percent in the mid-1990s, replacing the United States as the largest contributor of ODA among the industrialized countries (Table 11.3).[36] In the early 1990s, Japan's ODA level as percentage of GNP averaged at the 0.31 level, but it declined to 0.29 percent in 1994. As in the U.S. case, Japan's ODA has constituted a little over 1 percent of the government budget. Despite its reputation for linking aid to exports, Japan's tied aid levels are similar to those of the northern European countries, at about 12 percent of annual ODA in the early 1990s. About 27 percent of Japan's assistance has been in the area of economic infrastructure and transport and communications, with an equal amount in agricultural and industrial production.

Regionally, the largest share of Japan's ODA has been concentrated in South and East Asian countries; since the 1980s, East Asia's share has increased substantially, from about 29 percent in the late 1970s to 53 percent in 1992–1993.[37] China received about 10 percent of Japan's aid for 1993–94. Tokyo's aid to Asia dropped sharply, however, to 30.5 percent in 1993–1994, as the share of other regions increased.[38] The Middle East's, North Africa's, and Southern Europe's shares increased from 8.6 percent to over 20 percent, clearly reflecting Japan's expanding economic or market interests in those regions.[39] Sub-Saharan Africa's share increased from 10.1 percent in

1983–1984 to 13.7 percent in the mid-1990s, while Latin America received about 12 percent in the 90s.[40]

Like other donor countries, Japan also has used aid to reward friendly governments. In April 1997, after the Peruvian military ended the 126-day hostage crisis at the Japanese ambassador's residence, as a gesture of appreciation Japan announced an $11.5 million development aid package to improve Peru's health ($7.2 million) and energy ($4.3 million) facilities. Although the Japanese government complained that it had not been notified of the rescue operation in advance, the Japanese embassy expressed its gratitude to Peru's president, Alberto K. Fujimori, who is of Japanese descent, and stated that "with these donations the Japanese Government wants to give testimony to its decision to continue to help the development of Peru, after the hostage crisis, through programs to improve social infrastructure . . . [and] to express its intention to continue and strengthen the friendship and cooperation between the two countries."[41]

South–South Aid

In addition to the North–South aid relations previously discussed above, since the mid-1950s efforts have been made to promote South–South cooperation through assistance programs for various aspects of economic development. For developing countries, intra-South official development assistance symbolizes one such effort. The Bandung Conference of 1955 established the foundations for cooperation among the developing countries, and South–South bilateral and multilateral aid relations have become an important dimension of that cooperation. Over the years, intra-South ODA has also increased, albeit the actual dollar value pales in comparison with ODA levels by DAC countries. In the early 1960s total developed state ODA (by OECD countries) constituted nearly 88 percent of the world total; developing countries' share was 2.4 percent. By the early 1970s, their share increased to 5 percent, but it dropped to 2 percent in the second half of the 1970s and to less than 1 percent in the 1980s.[42] In 1985, the total dollar value of intra-South ODA was $3.3 billion, which increased to $6.0 billion in 1990. By 1994, however, it had dropped again to about $1 billion.[43] Countries in the developing world that have engaged in bilateral and multilateral assistance programs have included the OPEC/Arab countries, China, India, Cuba (despite its own severe needs), and increasingly NICs, such as Taiwan, South Korea, and Brazil. South–South bilateral ODA has been in the area of technical and infrastructural development, ranging from education and health services to the construction of stadiums and railways.

By the end of the 1970s, a number of Arab development assistance programs—for example, the Arab Bank for Economic Development in Africa, Islamic Development Bank, and the Saudi Fund for Development—had emerged,[44] and at that time OPEC/Arab aid constituted over 27 percent of total world ODA. In the 1980s, however, as oil prices dropped, so did individual country ODA levels (see Table 11.5).[45] In the early 1980s, the largest share of Arab aid went to Syria as the major Arab states, particularly Saudi Arabia, encouraged Syria to continue its stabilizing role in war-torn Lebanon.[46] During the Gulf War, there was a brief surge in Arab aid, especially by Kuwait and Saudi Arabia, to reward countries supporting the war effort. The total ODA level rose from $1.3 billion in 1989 to $6.16 billion in 1990. Egypt, for example, received $2.32 billion in Arab aid in 1990, as opposed to $73.9 million in 1987. For the Middle East as a whole, aid increased from $134.6 million in 1989 to $1.36 billion in 1990.[47]

Despite the relevant drop in Arab aid levels in recent years, a comparison of Tables 11.4 and 11.5 indicates that some of the Arab donor countries, especially Kuwait and Saudi Arabia, have been the largest aid-donor countries in the world.[48] While ODA levels (as percentage of GNP) by such major Western industrialized countries as the United States, Britain, and Germany have hardly passed the 0.5 percent level, Kuwaiti aid was 6.2 percent in 1970 and rose to 6.9 percent in 1975. Even during the decline in the 1980s, Kuwait's ODA level remained above 3.0 percent of GNP. Saudi Arabia's ODA level increased from 5.6 percent to 7.5 percent in 1975 and, as in the case of Kuwait, remained above 3.0 percent in the 1980s. Moralists might view inter-Arab aid as an expression of Islamic values predicated on the fundamental Quranic principle of charity. For a Christian perspective on aid, see Box 11.1. Note the ironic similarities between these religions and Marxist-*dependencia* theories in criticizing institutions like the I.M.F. On the other hand, *dependencia* theorists might also agree with some classical liberals that trade rather than charity is the preferable means of promoting development without dependence. They might differ, however, on whether trade preferences for the poor or simply "free trade" is the most desirable path to prosperity.

Among other donor developing countries, China, with its self-proclaimed leadership of the developing world and

TABLE 11.5

Concessional Assistance by Arab Countries, 1970–1990

Country	1970	1975	1980	1985	1990
	$ Million (as Percentage of GNP)				
Algeria	1	31	81	54	7
	(0.02)	(0.20)	(0.20)	(0.10)	(0.02)
Iraq	b	265	864	b	78
	b	(2.00)	(2.40)	(0.10)	b
Kuwait	148	910	1,140	771	1,295
	(6.20)	(6.90)	(3.50)	(3.20)	(5.10)
Libya	64	275	376	58	37
	(1.90)	(2.40)	(1.20)	(0.60)	(0.10)
Qatar	b	307	277	8	b
	b	(14.20)	(4.20)	(0.20)	b
Saudi Arabia	172	2,699	5,682	2,630	3,652
	(5.60)	(7.50)	(5.00)	(3.00)	(3.40)
UAE	b	929	1,118	122	888
	b	(11.70)	(4.10)	(0.50)	(2.60)

Source: OECD, *Development Co-Operation: 1994 Report* (Paris: Organization for Economic Cooperation and Development, 1995), Table 46, p. 11.
[a]Concessional aid amount is included here if loans consisted of at least 25 percent grant element.
[b]None or negligible

BOX 11.1

CHRISTIAN AID—"PENNIES FROM SEVEN"

For the first time since the World Bank and International Monetary Fund (IMF) were created at Bretton Woods 50 years ago, the Group of Seven nations (G7) have an opportunity for a thorough evaluation of the work of both institutions. At the instigation of the United States the roles of the Bank and Fund are to be discussed at the G7 Summit in Halifax, Canada, from June 16 to 18 [1995]. For half a century the World Bank and IMF have been the foundation of global economic regulation. Poor countries struggling under the burden of debt and starved of private investment urgently need international institutions which are capable of fostering global financial security and a redistribution of resources. Both the World Bank and the IMF must show themselves capable of reform if they are to meet such needs. This report, Pennies from Seven, highlights seven ways in which G7 can help the Third World. . . .

REPLACING LAST YEAR'S MODEL: *Recommendation:* the G7 summit should sanction a participatory, far-reaching review of the international financial system.

The world has changed almost beyond recognition in the 50 years since the international economic system led by the World Bank and the International Monetary Fund was set up. Nation-states have become more interdependent—less able to act in isolation on behalf of their citizens' interests. International trade has increased dramatically, and financial liberalisation has fostered a huge global capital market. The principles which inspired the foundation of the Bretton Woods institutions remain important, but the roles of both the World Bank and IMF need revaluation if we are to meet the challenge of effective regulation of the global economy in the 21st century. Christian Aid believes that the G7 Summit should set in place an open, participatory and far-reaching review of the international financial system, beginning with the World Bank and IMF. . . .

The Bank: a good idea unfulfilled. Given the continuing disparity in wealth between North and South, an institution such as the World Bank is still needed to channel funds to the poorest. The richest 20 per cent of the world's people have incomes at least 150 times that of the poorest 20 per cent. The Bretton Woods Commission suggested in July 1994 that private capital can take the place of development assistance but this idea is wildly optimistic. The market has no specific bias in favour of the poor, so commercial capital flows have been concentrated in a small number of better-off countries. Twelve countries account for 80 per cent of the money invested, and much of the investment is short term—of limited use for financing longer-term development needs. Ghana, which is seen as a World Bank

BOX 11.1 (continued)

CHRISTIAN AID—"PENNIES FROM SEVEN"

success story, has received almost no private capital flows. Any large international institution is bound to have its limitations, particularly in its ability to meet local needs on a small enough scale. But the World Bank is better equipped than individual aid donors to raise revenue on the capital markets. It also has the potential to avoid the narrow national self-interest which taints some government-to-government aid. . . . There is a need for an international institution with a global overview to identify the development problems which go beyond national boundaries—such as the debt crisis—and present solutions.

Focusing the Fund. The ultimate objective of the IMF—as with the World Bank—should be to improve the common good, with particular focus on the poorest. The Fund's role in pursuing monetary stability and economic growth must be seen in this context. The IMF's focus on the monetary system has left a bias towards reducing inflation while ignoring unemployment and other factors crucial to poverty reduction. Poorer countries in need of aid and debt relief should no longer be required to embrace the IMF's monetarist policies and fulfil its tough economic conditions. The Fund's Enhanced Structural Adjustment Facility should be transferred to the World Bank. Instead resources should be used to fund concessionary (low or interest-free) lending, and the IMF's outstanding debt should be reduced.

GOING WITH THE FLOWS: *Recommendation:* the G7 countries should substantially reduce the burden of debt.

Some economic problems cannot be solved nationally, and G7 leaders have a crucial role in addressing the international constraints to development. In their policy-based lending, the World Bank and IMF propose national remedies for what are essentially international problems. Encouraging a country to raise revenue by increasing commodity exports, for example, may make sense for that country's national economy but becomes a recipe for a disastrous price slump internationally when other countries are given similar advice. Such advice can only fail unless the G7 countries tackle the continuing debt crisis and unfair trade restrictions which hamper Third World recovery. To do this they need to come up with more resources. The shareholders of the Bretton Woods institutions have been too ready to accept resource constraints and advocate painful adjustment programmes in poorer countries to compensate for the shortfall, instead of arguing for adequate finance from the North.

A WORLD LOSING ITS BARINGS: *Recommendation:* the G7 countries should consider taxing currency speculation to finance aid spending.

The IMF could usefully bring some order to the international monetary system. In particular, it could tackle the increasing problem of currency speculation. The proposal for a tax on currency speculation has attracted increasing interest and support recently, and should be pursued. The latest figures show a sharp fall in the amount of aid provided by industrialised countries, down by nearly eight per cent. But the needs of the poorest countries remain as great as ever. Each day US$1 trillion changes hands via foreign currency transactions. Much of this is a necessary part of trade and investment, or simply the consequence of tourists going on holiday. But some of the transactions are purely speculative. They have no productive value and

as the most vocal proponent of cooperation among developing countries since the Bandung Conference, has been the largest non-OPEC/Arab donor of South–South aid. During the 1970s, its annual contributions averaged over $1 billion. In the early 1970s, Pakistan received the largest share of Chinese aid because of that country's conflicts with India, a traditional foe linked to Russia and often in geo-political conflict with China. In the early 1980s, however, China's ODA level declined considerably as domestic and foreign policy priorities changed from the Maoist brand of Communism to more commercialism and mixed capitalism. In 1981, Chinese ODA levels dropped to $148 million, or 0.05 percent of GNP; increased to about $360 million, or 0.12 percent in 1986;[49] but dropped again to an annual average of $120 million, or 0.03 percent, in the early 1990s.[50] The increase in 1986 was attributable to China's aid to multilateral agencies and new membership in the Asian Development Bank (ADB), where it held 7 percent of ADB's capital stock, the third largest. Other multilateral agencies receiving aid from Beijing that year included the African Development Bank ($12 million), the World Bank ($36 million), and various UN agencies, totaling $222 million, an enormous jump from the $31 million the previous year. Chinese bilateral aid did not experience a similar increase, however, and remained at $143 million.[51] The largest share (over 70 percent) of Chinese aid commitments went to sub-Saharan Africa, for economic reforms in Mauritania, a sports stadium in Zaire, and various food and fishing programs in Somalia, Mali, and Ivory Coast.[52] Beijing briefly and to a

BOX 11.1 (continued)

CHRISTIAN AID—"PENNIES FROM SEVEN"

they destabilise national economies. The most well known proposal for a levy on currency speculation is known as the Tobin Tax. In 1978 James Tobin proposed that a small tax, of about 0.5 per cent, be levied on all foreign exchange transactions. . . . The revenue from such a tax could be used to augment waning government aid spending. Money would be channelled through one or a collection of the international agencies. . . . Given the pressing need for concessionary aid flows, and the enormous potential revenue base of foreign currency transactions, G7 leaders should carefully consider proposals for a tax on foreign exchange. . . .

A VOICE FOR THE POOR: *Recommendation:* the G7 countries should make the World Bank and IMF more democratic and accountable.

The structures of both the World Bank and the International Monetary Fund are fundamentally undemocratic. Decision making is dominated by the industrialised countries. At present the G7 meetings have too great an influence on the decision-making process of the organisations. There is a danger that democratising the IMF and World Bank will reduce their power and the willingness of donors to provide finances. But both the principle and effect of this lack of democracy are too important to ignore. The tradition that the post of IMF Managing Director is reserved for a European, and that the President of the World Bank always comes from the USA, should be ended. Votes in both the Bank and Fund are allocated according to financial contribution. The allocation has become less democratic over the past 50 years, as the basic vote each country gets—regardless of income—has been reduced as a proportion of the whole. The basic vote as a proportion of overall allocation should immediately be returned to its original levels. This proportion should be increased until a time when there is one country one vote, rather than one dollar one vote.

A UNITED FRONT: *Recommendation:* the G7 countries should give the UN a wider economic remit.

Since 1947 the Bretton Woods institutions have officially been specialised agencies of the United Nations system. Under Article 70 of the United Nations Charter they are subject to supervision and guidance by the UN's Economic and Social Council (ECOSOC) and the General Assembly. But the World Bank and IMF insist on their independence. While the Bank and the Fund are able to address ECOSOC, participation in their meetings by the UN is much more limited. The Bank and Fund should be more accountable to the UN General Assembly and ECOSOC. Their representatives should submit annual reports and be prepared to appear for questioning. Ultimately there is a case for a forum broader than either the Bretton Woods institutions or the G7 to provide global leadership and wider international participation in economic policy. . . .

DEEDS AS WELL AS WORDS: *Recommendation:* the G7 countries should ensure that the World Bank meets its poverty reduction mandate.

At the Social Summit in Copenhagen the G7 nations, together with other governments of the world, agreed: "We commit ourselves to ensuring that when structural adjustment programmes are agreed to, they include social development goals, in particular eradicating poverty, promoting full and

limited extent sent aid to a few Latin American countries, such as war-torn Nicaragua and Bolivia, in the mid-1980s. Chinese aid was specialized primarily in the agricultural, transportation, and health sectors.

In addition to China, India has been another South–South donor. In the 1960s, the Indian government instituted the Indian Technical Co-Operation Program, extending technical support to African, Asian, and Latin American countries and, well into the late 1980s, providing at least $100 million in aid per year primarily to its smaller and poorer neighbors in the region, such as Bhutan, Bangladesh, and Vietnam. As part of its technical programs in the early 1980s, it sponsored approximately 1,500 students and trainees, and, in the 1981–1985 period, its average annual ODA level was about $137.4 million, or 0.07 percent of its GNP. As with the general world pattern, Indian ODA has declined to $110 million in the late 1980s; to $84 million, or 0.03 percent of GNP, for the years 1991–1992; and to $28 million, or 0.01 percent, in 1994. Bangladesh continued to be one of its major recipients; however, since the collapse of the Soviet Union, some of the former Soviet republics in Central Asia, such as Kazakhstan and Uzbekistan, have received Indian assistance as well.

Other and new ODA donor countries in the developing world include Israel and the NICs, but there appears to be no clear pattern of increase or decrease. Contrary to the world pattern of general decline, Korea's ODA level more

BOX 11.1 (concluded)

CHRISTIAN AID—"PENNIES FROM SEVEN"

productive employment and enhancing social integration." If G7 leaders are to make this pronouncement meaningful, they will have to encourage the World Bank and IMF to develop fundamentally different macro-economic advice. Structural adjustment programmes (SAPs) are the main macro-economic tool of the World Bank and IMF, and as such they have a significance far beyond the size of structural adjustment loans. All other lending and aid, whether from the Bank, governments or non-government organisations like Christian Aid, is allocated within the framework shaped by SAPs. . . .

Blind faith. The World Bank now acknowledges the relevance of many past criticisms from non-government organisations (NGOs) such as Christian Aid. In Copenhagen the Bank stressed the importance of protecting health and education spending. Great strides have been made within the Bank in the way it talks about poverty, the environment and the need for the people on the receiving end to participate in designing projects. There are also some welcome programme initiatives. But the more the World Bank talks about poverty reduction and sustainable development, the more the contradictions show through. There is mounting evidence that market mechanisms are not enough to reduce poverty or to produce sustainable growth. . . . Equity can only be achieved by targeted redistribution to the poor. World Bank assistance strategies for poor countries need to make explicit what the Bank's poverty reduction strategy for any given country is. The Bank needs to address the structural barriers which prevent the poor, particularly women, from sharing in economic growth. Where market structures are weak, removing a state monopoly is as likely to benefit a private oligopoly as to lead to increased economic output. What is needed is a far more pragmatic assessment of the relative strengths and weaknesses of both state and market. . . .

A POVERTY OF UNDERSTANDING: *Recommendation:* the role of the IMF should be restricted to exclude development lending.

The IMF's involvement in longer-term development lending has proved problematic, and development should be left to the World Bank. IMF financing should be restricted to low-conditionality cash provided for short-term balance of payments problems arising from external shocks. IMF lending is too short-term and its understanding of poverty reduction too limited to support development efforts.

CONCLUSION: TOWARDS THE 21st CENTURY

Christian Aid envisages a Fund which helps rich and poor countries alike to cope with balance of payments crises but does not insist on laying down an economic development path for almost every Third World nation. It envisages a Bank which provides resources for development on conditions that specify helping the poorest people. We do not believe the Bank should be tied to the coat tails of the IMF and to enforcing damaging structural adjustment. We envisage a Bank and Fund properly accountable to governments and the United Nations. Both should have a global perspective on economic problems and their solutions, and rich countries should bear their share of the burden.

Source: Excerpt from *Christian Aid,* June 1995. On-line.

than doubled from $65 million in 1990 to $140 million in 1994. Taiwan's, on the other hand, fluctuated rapidly. Its ODA level rose from $21 million, or 0.01 percent of GNP, in 1989 to $125 million, or 0.07 percent in 1991; declined to $61 million, or 0.03 percent, in 1993; and increased to $79 million, though still .03 percent, in 1994.[53] These erratic fluctuations in Taiwan's ODA can be explained in part by the fact that the island state, under enormous diplomatic pressure from mainland China, cannot participate in most multilateral organizations and its bilateral relations are easily influenced by political circumstances as dictated by other countries' bilateral relations with Beijing. Other states' aid potential has been affected by the global financial crisis of the late 1990s.

Despite the increases in South–South aid relations, South–South donors, much like the Western donors, also have failed to institute mechanisms for a more coordinated approach to development assistance policy. For example, although Arab aid donors adopted a number of formal declarations expressing their commitment to assist the developing countries in achieving greater international equality along the lines of the New International Economic Order,[54] and despite the fact that their aid levels as percentage of GNP often far exceeded those of Western donors, they also used aid programs for purposes of national objectives rather than to support economic development strictly for a more just distribution of resources.[55] The UN-sponsored Copenhagen Conference of 1995 failed to address this issue.

MULTILATERAL ASSISTANCE

Proponents of multilateral development assistance argue that assistance to developing countries is a shared responsibility for the common good across the globe. While bilateral assistance, they argue, can be subject to various political and economic pressures and arm-twisting between the donor and recipient governments, multilateral assistance would reflect collective effort independently of individual donors' domestic and foreign policy strategies. In bilateral aid, donor and recipient governments maintain control over their relationship and bargain over the volume and nature of assistance; in multilateral assistance, donor governments contribute a certain percentage of funds distributed by multilateral organizations.

Donor governments, thus, theoretically lose a certain degree of direct control over the distribution and uses of aid. Depending on domestic circumstances, at times (as in the 1980s and 90s in most of the industrialized West) governments have found it politically expedient to attack such multilateral organizations as infringement on national sovereignty. Generally, however, despite their loss of control, governments have, with exceptions such as U.S. footdragging on IMF contributions in 1998, supported and continued to replenish the treasuries of multilateral organizations and, through their voting power in such organizations, still exercise considerable influence over policies and spending patterns, even down to individual development projects.

The San Francisco conference in 1945, convened by fifty nations to create the United Nations, expressed interest in continuing the work of the Special Committee of the League of Nations on the Development of International Co-Operation in Economic and Social Affairs and established the Economic and Social Council (ECOSOC) as an integral institution within the United Nations for the purpose of promoting international cooperation in various areas of international relations. Soon, however, it became apparent that special agencies, in addition to the World Bank and the International Monetary Fund, were required specifically in the area of economic development. In 1948, the signatories to the Marshall Plan established the Organization for European Economic Co-Operation (OEEC), which in turn a year later created the Overseas Territories Committee (comprised of Belgium, Britain, France, the Netherlands, and Portugal) to survey the economic conditions and needs of the Overseas Territories (colonies). In 1957, the Rome Treaty created the European Economic Community and the European Development Fund for Overseas Countries and Territories. In December 1960, the Western countries agreed to reorganize the OEEC and replaced it by the Organization for Economic Co-Operation and Development (OECD). Within the OECD framework, they formed the Development Assistance Group (DAG) for the purpose of consultation and cooperation on assistance programs to the developing countries. The original DAG members included Belgium, Britain, Canada, France, West Germany, Italy, Portugal,[56] and the United States, joined by the Netherlands and Japan a few months later. In 1961, DAG was reorganized and replaced by the Development Assistance Committee (DAC), and during the next decade its membership expanded to include Norway in 1962, Denmark in 1963, Austria and Sweden in 1965, Australia in 1966, Switzerland in 1968, New Zealand in 1973, and Finland in 1975. However, well into the early 1980s, DAC remained a "collectivity of bilateral donors."[57]

Also in 1960, the World Bank created a new agency, the International Development Association (IDA), specifically for poorer developing countries that lacked the financial credit to borrow from the World Bank. The IDA supplies such countries with credits to be repaid over a period of thirty-five years with minimal interest rates (1 percent), which, in fact, renders the loan a grant. IDA programs are replenished every three years by donor countries.

In addition to multilateral efforts, other approaches to coordinate assistance programs for developing countries have been through consortia and regional development banks. In 1958, for example, the World Bank created the so-called India Consortium, consisting of the World Bank, Britain, Canada, Germany, Japan, and the United States, to address India's balance-of-payment problems. Two years later, a similar consortium was established for Pakistan,[58] and the OECD organized a consortium for Turkey in 1962.[59] In 1959, nineteen Latin American countries and the United States created the Inter-American Development Bank (IDB), with headquarters in Washington, DC.[60] In 1964, the African Development Bank was founded at Abidjan, Ivory Coast,[61] and in 1966 the Asian Development Bank at Manila, the Philippines.[62]

To date, the central organization with universal moral and legal legitimacy and obligations to be involved in multilateral assistance programs remains the United Nations. The various UN development programs illustrate the need to take into consideration the close relationship between economic assistance, North–South trade and related financial relations, and social and economic development in the developing countries. In 1948, the World Health Organization was created as a UN specialized agency. In 1964, the UN Conference on Trade and Development (UNCTAD) met at Geneva for the first time to devise programs that "provide, by means of international co-operation, appropriate solutions to the problems of world trade in the interest of all people and particularly to the urgent trade and development problems of the developing countries."[63]

At the United Nations, the Food and Agriculture Organization was founded in 1945, followed by the United Nations International Children's Emergency Fund (UNICEF), the United Nations Educational, Scientific and Cultural Organization (UNESCO) in 1946, and the Expanded Program of Technical Assistance in 1949. In 1960, the UN General Assembly adopted a resolution designating the 1960s as the United Nations Development Decade, with the twin objectives of achieving an economic growth rate of 5 percent in the developing countries by 1970 and increasing the flow of international aid amounts to 1 percent of the national income of the donor countries.[64] In 1963, the United Nations and FAO established the World Food Program to use food assistance in emergency relief operations but also to encourage economic development.[65] Continued efforts within these agencies as provided by the United Nations offered the institutional framework for maturing multilateral cooperation.

In 1965, the United Nations incorporated the UN Expanded Program of Technical Assistance and the UN Special Fund into a single institution, the UN Development Program (UNDP). By then, the number of Third World countries at the United Nations had drastically altered the Organization's composition and, to some extent, its agenda; programs such as the UNDP raised public expectations regarding the UN's ability to alleviate social and economic development issues in the developing world.

By the latter half of the 1960s, the developing countries had also established regional development banks, independently of the UN structure, as vehicles to meet their distinct regional needs. These included the Inter-American Development Bank (IDB), the African Development Bank (AfDB), and the Asian Development Bank (AsDB).

In the late 1960s, multilateral aid accounted for approximately 10 percent of the total world ODA, and, at that time, contrary to political leaders' public claims of commitment to international development, there was little hope that such recommendations as proposed by the Commission on International Development (or the Pearson Commission, named after its chairman Lester Pearson of Canada) for increasing the share to 20 percent would be taken seriously.[66] Nevertheless, by the late 1970s, multilateral aid accounted for about 30 percent of total aid, and in the early 1980s it constituted over 35 percent of total assistance to low-income countries.[67]

During the past two decades, however, while DAC contributions to a number of key multilateral development organizations shrank considerably, the global power structure in development assistance relations experienced some fundamental changes, both in terms of greater opportunities for international organizations and in terms of shifts in major power involvement. At the UN level, for example, the UNDP's share was 13.5 percent of total DAC contributions in the early 1970s, but it had declined to 6.8 percent by the mid-1980s.[68] As a result, UNDP's share of total aid to low-income countries decreased from 18.5 percent in the mid-1970s to 8.1 percent by the mid-1980s[69] and to 7.3 in the mid-1990s.[70] Despite this overall decline, budgetary pressures in the 1980s adversely affecting country-to-country aid left a greater proportion of development assistance responsibilities to multilateral agencies. The fluctuations in the following development aid figures are indicative of an increased role by regional agencies. In the early 1970s, development aid by the Inter-American Development Bank accounted for 16.1 percent of total concessional and non-concessional flows by multilateral agencies; although that figure dropped to 7.1 percent in 1980[71] and to 6.3 percent in the early 1990s, it had increased to 9 percent by the mid-1990s.[72] The African Development Bank's contribution increased from 0.78 percent in the mid-1970s to 1.53 percent in 1980, to 2.1 percent in the mid-1980s,[73] and to 7.4 percent in the mid-1990s.[74] The Asian Development Bank's share of contributions, which had declined from 4.9 percent in the mid-1970s to 3.8 percent in the early 1980s, rose to 5.2 percent in the mid-1980s[75] and to 9.2 percent in the mid-1990s.[76]

Furthermore, changes in aid relations between donor countries and multilateral organizations are also evident. For instance, while prior to the 1980s inter-American aid relations were viewed as the exclusive preserve of the United States, since the early 1980s other major industrialized countries, most notably Germany and Japan, have shown an increased interest in the Inter-American Development Bank. Japan's development assistance to the regional bank increased substantially, from $4.3 million, or

2.5 percent of total DAC contributions of $175.4 million, in the mid-1980s, to $137 million, or 55 percent of the DAC total of $251 million, by the mid-1990s, far exceeding the U.S. contribution, which dropped from $113 million, or 64.4 percent, to $60 million, or 24 percent, during the same period.[77]

The expanding role of international organizations bodes well for international cooperation, but their activities are fraught with political and financial problems. Operations by UNIDO, the UN Industrial Development Organization, headquartered in Vienna, illustrates some of the advantages and problems of international technical cooperation. Established by the UN General Assembly in November 1966, UNIDO's primary objective is to encourage industrial development in the developing world.[78] Its creation was part of the effort in the 1960s and 1970s by the developing countries, represented as the Group of 77 at the UN General Assembly, to develop a comprehensive plan with the necessary institutional mechanisms for the advancement of industrialization in their countries as the best means to combat poverty and unemployment and to secure greater economic independence. Framed within the context of the South's calls for a New International Economic Order, UNIDO was expected to be not only an institution for North–South cooperation but also a specific type of institution that would facilitate the transfer of technical assistance from the North to the developing countries without the attendant political and economic constraints of bilateral dependency or MNC intervention in local affairs. The Western nations, however, led by the United States, sought to disengage UNIDO's operations from the principles of international redistribution of wealth. They grudgingly accepted UNIDO as a vehicle for the development of technical cooperation but rejected the notion that it serve as yet another forum for aid demands.

Despite such political and ideological difficulties, UNIDO emerged as a specialized agency of the United Nations, with specific functions to promote industrialization in close cooperation with other UN agencies, such as ECOSOC and UNDP. The distribution of budget contributions by the major contributors to UNIDO's budget, following the UN budget system, were initially set as follows: the United States 25 percent, Japan 10.75 percent, post-Soviet Russia 10.1 percent, Germany 9.51 percent, France 6.31 percent, and Britain 4.82 percent. Nearly 60 percent of UNIDO's technical assistance operations are covered by the UNDP.[79] UNIDO's operational functions include

> assisting the developing countries in modernizing their industries; promoting selection, adaptation, transfer, and use of industrial technology; and organizing and supporting industrial training programs. Another aspect is rendering assistance in the field of the exploitation, conservation, and local transformation of natural resources in third world countries for the purpose of furthering their industrial development; providing pilot and demonstration plants; and assisting regional planning.[80]

While UNIDO operations extend to all developing regions, it places special emphasis on providing technical assistance to Africa and the least developing countries. It focuses primarily in three sectoral industrial areas: agriculturally based industries (food processing, leather, wood processing), engineering industries (metalworking and machine tools), and chemical industries (biotechnology, water management, medicine, organic chemicals).[81] In a 1995 resolution, UNIDO's mission was defined as follows:

> To serve as a global forum to exchange information, analysis and advice on industrial policies and institutions within the field of development; To provide integrated services to Governments, institutions and enterprises in recipient countries for the design and implementation of industrial policies, the development of selected industrial subsectors, private sector development, the development and transfer of clean technologies, industrial partnerships and investments, and development of human resources in line with the identified priorities of the Organization; [and] To function as a central coordinating agency within the United Nations system in the field of industry, for supporting the endeavors of developing countries to achieve sustainable development.[82]

Accordingly, Africa received 42.1 percent of technical cooperation services in 1995, Asia and the Pacific 29.2 percent, Latin America 11.3 percent, Europe and the post-Soviet republics 8.9 percent, and Arab states 8.6 percent. Sectoral distribution included investment and technology 29 percent, engineering and metallurgical industries 16 percent, chemical industries 21 percent, agricultural industries 11 percent, and related cross-sectoral support 23 percent. Distribution among newly approved technical cooperation projects included environment and energy 38 percent; innovation, productivity, and quality for international competitiveness 15 percent; industrial and information technology 15 percent; small and medium enterprises and networking 9 percent; Africa and LDCs integration of industry and agriculture 7 percent; rural industrial development 6 percent; and strategies and institution-building for global economic integration 5 percent.[83] Examples of UNIDO projects in the area of environment and energy include the use of advanced technologies to control mercury pollution in Ethiopia, Mozambique, Tanzania, and Zimbabwe; waste management in Ecuador; and the establishment of "national cleaner production centers" (NCPCs) in Brazil, China, the Czech Republic, India, Mexico, Slovakia, Tunisia, Tanzania, and Zimbabwe.[84]

In the area of global economic integration, the UNDP, Japan, South Korea, and Sweden have funded, through UNIDO, the coordination of industrial strategies worth $1.29 million in Vietnam, involving support for the private sector through the development of appropriate managerial skills, statistical information on manufacturing and industrial capacity, and uses of computer simulations of alternative industrial strategies.[85] Similar programs were implemented in a number of African countries (for example, Benin, Guinea, Mali, Niger, and Senegal), in Russia, in India, and in Mexico. In the area of technological innovation for international competitiveness, the UNDP-UNIDO spent $1.23 million in Saudi Arabia to develop the National Measurement and Calibration Laboratory, which also services the neighboring Gulf States—Bahrain, Kuwait, Oman, Qatar, and the United Arab Emirates—as members of the Gulf Cooperation Council.[86] Information technology programs with the support of more than a thousand experts were funded in 126 countries. Various technology transfer programs, including the preparation of a UNIDO Manual on Technology Transfer Negotiations, were introduced to develop new approaches to encourage foreign investments, as in Kenya, Uganda, India, Sri Lanka, and Ecuador. Special attention was paid to the former Soviet-bloc countries to facilitate their transition to market economies and integration into the global economy.[87]

This covers a wide area of activities, but dwindling funds raise serious questions with respect to the long-term viability of UNIDO programs. In the late 1970s, UNIDO's annual expenditure on technical cooperation was about $67 million, which increased to nearly $100 million in the mid-1980s and to $160 million by 1990 but declined to about $110 million in 1995.[88] Like the United Nations in general, since the 1980s UNIDO has witnessed serious budgetary difficulties as some of its contributors have fallen behind in their payments. By 1990, the United States owed $40 million, the largest debtor. Brazil owed $2.5 million, Argentina $1.4 million, Russia $1.3 million, and Iran $1.2 million. In 1995, the United States announced its withdrawal from UNIDO and refused to pay the debt owed to that organization. In 1995, UNIDO reported that its staff had been reduced from 1,174 in January 1994 to 965 by late 1995, as part of its organizational budgetary adjustment.[89]

Despite the enormous investments in such collective efforts, one OECD report has noted, "The results have been meager."[90] A number of difficulties can be identified vitiating the objectives and operations of some multilateral institutions. First, as previously noted, while a central assumption of multilateral assistance has been its independence from political considerations as experienced in bilateral aid, by the 1980s it had become clear that the multilateral agencies themselves were not above politics and had developed vested institutional interests. For some agency administrators, institutional survival as a principal objective relegated assistance to developing countries *per se* to a secondary consideration. Internal organizational politics, rather than recipients' needs, sometimes dictated distribution of aid. Second, donors have preferred different multilateral agencies for the transfer of their assistance. The major donors in the industrialized countries have preferred to work through the World Bank, with its weighted voting procedures. Others, particularly the smaller countries, have preferred the specialized UN agencies, while regional development banks have stressed the development priorities of their respective regions. Third, since donor governments have limited control over multilateral assistance, money flows to such agencies have been vulnerable to domestic political pressures, particularly in times of economic downturn, as in the early 1980s and the 1990s.[91]

The decline of the United States as the central player in such institutions has led Washington to place greater emphasis on "burden-sharing," which also has meant the diffusion of responsibility for coordination of aid programs at a critical juncture in the evolution of the institutions. Having developed the structural mechanisms for multilateral assistance from the 1950s to the 1970s, largely based on American initiatives, the world missed an opportunity in the 1980s to build and develop aid collaboration. As the world hegemon, the United States unexpectedly launched an ideological attack on such institutions during and after the 1980s. Whether the increasingly expansive role of Japan in multilateral assistance programs will continue and produce a new hegemon or new competition among donors in the twenty-first century remains to be seen. Japan agreed to forgive the debt of several African states in 1997, but had more trouble passing its aid budgets with its own economic downturn. The data and the analysis presented in this section suggest major changes in leadership and a general decline in multilateral development assistance. The question is whether the interests of multilateral agencies will converge to produce more coherent and better coordinated future development assistance programs.

ISSUES AND CONSEQUENCES

A central consideration of development assistance is whether and to what extent such assistance has improved the standard of living in recipient countries. Aid policies in various forms have been in place for more than forty years; therefore, analysts can determine with some confidence whether such policies have been successful in alleviating economic and social problems. Measuring the success or failure of assistance programs is a controversial issue, however. Proponents of laissez-faire economics emphasize the role of the private sector in promoting social and economic development, and they advocate a limited role for the government. At most, they argue, development assistance should focus on a small number of variables, such as education/literacy and health services as the principal domain of government responsibilities. More collectively oriented theorists use a more expansive definition and include numerous issue-areas, ranging from environmentally and ecologically sound water and air policies, i.e., so-called "sustainable development" techniques involving renewable forms of energy, to a more equitable distribution of financial resources, to the development of more grassroots-level, communitarian democracy. Others point to gender issues and advocate a greater role for development assistance in promoting the rights of women as an essential dimension of social and economic development.

Whether donor and recipient governments are seriously concerned with and take such issues into consideration is subject to debate, however. Governments tend to accord highest priority to political stability, law, and order, and address issues of poverty and unemployment when such problems might jeopardize political legitimacy and threaten stability. Improvements in living standards often take place within the confines of development policies promoting economic development for the elites, on the one hand, and protecting the political fortunes of the government on the other. As discussed in previous chapters, the colonial legacy, government neglect of social and economic problems, and marginalization of most of the developing countries in the world political economy, especially in trade and such technological areas as telecommunications, have hindered the full development of many countries.

For purposes of comparison, per capita GNP in the Western advanced industrialized economies increased by over 130 percent between the 1960s and 1990s. While in the 1960s per capita GNP in the developing world was approximately 17 percent of that of the industrialized economies, by the mid-1990s it had dropped to 15 percent. Among the developing regions, conditions in sub-Saharan Africa have been most troubling. As was shown in Table 11.2, sub-Saharan Africa has been the largest recipient of total world ODA since the early 1980s. In the 1960s and 1970s, its share of total ODA rose from 9.0 percent to 26.0 percent and in the 1980s to nearly 40 percent, yet per capita GNP in the region increased by no more than 1 percent per year on average in the 1960s and 1970s, and that figure declined to 0.8 percent in the 1980s and early 1990s, a situation further exacerbated by the region's population increase from an average of 2.6 percent per year to over 3 percent. In other words, aid benefits to Africa have been overwhelmed by social problems, including AIDs. African development experiences vary, however. Although Mozambique remained one of the poorest countries in the world, for example, with a per capita GNP of no more than $60, Sudan's per capita GNP increased from $390 in 1960 (constant in 1981 dollars) to $430 in the early 1980s. Its life expectancy rose from thirty-eight years to forty-seven years, child mortality declined from forty per thousand (aged one to four years) to nineteen, and the country's literacy rate increased from 13 percent of population to 32 percent. Tanzania's per capita GNP increased from $190 to $260 for the same period. Its life expectancy increased from forty years to fifty, child mortality declined from thirty-one to eighteen, and the literacy rate increased from 10 percent to nearly 80 percent. Kenya's per capita GNP climbed from $240 to $370. Life expectancy in that country rose from forty-six years to fifty-seven years, child mortality dropped from twenty-one to fourteen, and the literacy rate increased from 20 percent to 47 percent.

As laudable as such successes were, they should not blind observers to the fact that these countries were, in reality, struggling to catch up with the wealthier and more advanced societies in the North. There is little indication that African countries, as well as most countries in the developing world, have established a sufficient basis for sustainable growth independently of the North's ODA programs and economic and political relations in general. The economic decline experienced in the 1980s and 1990s has demonstrated their limited ability to achieve that primary objective. By 1993, Sudan's per capita GNP had slipped to about $239, Tanzania's to $108, and Kenya's to $266.[92] During the period 1980–1992, war-ravaged Mozambique registered a −3.6 percent average annual growth, Ethiopia −1.9 percent, Tanzania 0 percent, and Kenya a mere 0.2 percent.[93] Neither were other sub-Saharan African countries successful. Despite the fact that the region received the largest share of total world ODA in the 1980s and 1990s, then, most countries experienced a similar decline in economic growth, leading some to skepticism about aid programs and others to the conclusion that aid levels simply were insufficient or inappropriate to meet regional needs.[94]

In Asia, the picture has been somewhat brighter, but mainly because the economies of a small number of countries, particularly the "four tigers" (Hong Kong, South Korea, Singapore, and Taiwan), were, at least for a time, so successful. In the 1960s and the early 1970s, the region was by far the largest recipient of total world ODA levels. In the early 1960s, while Africa received 9 percent of total ODA, Asia received nearly 45 percent. A decade later, ODA to Africa accounted for nearly 19 percent of total ODA, but over 47 percent went to Asia. Having strengthened its position against Communism in Western Europe by the mid-1950s, the United States turned its attention to Asia, especially after the collapse of the U.S.-supported Chiang Kai-shek regime in mainland China and after the Korean War. Also, an increasingly large amount of aid was given to the regimes in South Vietnam to prevent another "loss" of a friendly government to Communism.

A brief comparison of South Korea's and India's economic performance might shed some light on the relationship between aid and economic development. After the termination of the U.S.–South Korea "Mutual Security Act" (1952–1961), South Korea continued to receive over 6 percent (third highest) of total U.S. ODA in the early 1960s, as well as 4.5 percent (fifth highest) in the early 1970s. Two other DAC countries, Denmark and Sweden, also contributed ODA dollars to Seoul, 7.4 percent and 6.3 percent, respectively. Overall, South Korea received between about 3.5 and 4.5 percent (fourth highest) of total world bilateral ODA by DAC countries in the 1960s and 1970s.[95] By the early 1980s, Seoul had "graduated" from Western aid programs and had emerged as a major competitor in trade relations. Its per capita GNP rose from $360 (in constant 1981 dollars) in 1950 to $1,670 in 1982[96] and to $7,670 by 1993.[97] During the 1980–1992 period, its average annual growth rate was about 8.5 percent.[98] Concomitantly, life expectancy increased from fifty-three years in 1960 to fifty-nine in 1970, to sixty-seven in 1980,[99] and to seventy-one years in 1992.[100] Infant mortality dropped from fifty-one (per thousand) in 1970 to thirteen in 1992, while the literacy rate rose from 71 percent of population in 1960 to over 95 percent by the early 1990s.[101]

On the other hand, India, which also received some of the highest levels of total world (including DAC) ODA for more than two decades after its independence in 1948, and particularly as it engaged in a territorial rivalry with China, was not as fortunate in improving its overall economic condition, although economic growth and efforts to promote infrastructural modernization indicate improvements in recent years. In the early 1960s, India received 16.8 percent of total world ODA and 11.5 percent of total DAC development assistance, by far the largest share.[102] Although by the early 1970s India's share had dropped somewhat to 14 percent of total world ODA, it remained the recipient of the highest level. By the early 1980s, India's share of total world ODA had dropped substantially, to 6.3 percent, but it still remained the highest recipient, followed by Egypt (5.5 percent) and Bangladesh (4.7 percent). Although India's share of total world and DAC aid continued to drop,[103] it remained among the top three recipients of total ODA in the early 1990s.[104]

Despite the high level of aid, India did not experience a level of economic growth comparable to South Korea's. In the 1950s, India's average annual GNP growth rate was 3.9, which rose to 4 percent in the 1960s but dropped to 3.4 percent in the 1970s; in terms of per capita GNP, that meant a drop from 2.0 percent to 1.0 percent. With its vast and growing population, India's per capita GNP increased modestly from $150 in 1950 to $210 in 1970 and to $240 in 1982 (in constant 1981 dollars). In contrast, South Korea's per capita GNP increased from $360 in 1950 to $1,670 in 1982. In the mid-1990s, India's per capita GNP was about $300, while South Korea's reached $7,670. Life expectancy in India increased from forty-two years in 1960 to fifty-five years in 1983 and to sixty-one years in the early 1990s, representing substantial progress. Between 1970 and 1992, the infant mortality rate dropped from 137 (per thousand live births) to seventy-nine, and literacy rose from 28 percent in 1960 to 33 percent in 1970, to 36 percent in 1983, to 52 percent in 1990.[105]

Aside from comparatively modest population pressure, the critical element propelling the South Korean economy toward greater economic development and modernization is believed to be defining the role of government. Joseph Stiglitz, chairman of the U.S. Council of Economic Advisers, pointed out that the primary difference between the experiences of the two countries was that, during the past thirty years or so, the South Korean government has encouraged effective strategies for market-oriented development in cooperation with companies rather than adopting socialist-oriented, rigid planning, as in the case of India.[106] Nevertheless, the extent of governmental intervention in the economy actually has been relatively comparable in both countries, but with an important difference, as Clive Hamilton put it aptly: "The difference is that in South Korea, government intervention is used to discipline private businesses, whereas in India government economic management is not insulated from particular sectional interests and serves to pamper domestic industry rather than forcing it to be efficient."[107] Although neither Stiglitz nor Hamilton was referring directly to the relationship between development assistance and economic growth, their argument is relevant to the extent that they highlight the role and style of government management of the national economy.

This points to an important and inescapable fact of political life, that government involvement in the economy, as a determinant of the success or failure of development assistance, ultimately entails the management of various trade-offs among various and intricately interrelated local and institutional customs, traditions, values, and priorities. Studies on management of development assistance have found that, while small-scale community projects successfully met local needs, the expansion of the same projects into government programs met failure. Implementation at the local level was more manageable and it attracted dedicated individuals more familiar with the needs of the community; therefore, the projects were more effective and efficient. The Indian national government, on the other hand, attempted to implement similar projects throughout the country—a process involving vast networks of bureaucracies, each with its own interests and rather rigid rules and regulations.[108]

The following section discusses the relationship between development assistance, development management, and technology transfer and development assistance and human rights. These dimensions of foreign aid have elements of both international cooperation and conflict.

Development Assistance, Development Management, and Technology Transfer

In the 1950s and 1960s, government bureaucracies that engaged in foreign aid administration lacked sufficient management experience, and most personnel had little direct knowledge of the social and political terrain in which they were expected to operate. "Competence" is difficult to define, even under ideal circumstances, but lack of competence is a problem made worse by the cultural gaps and clashes between the donor and the recipient of foreign assistance. As previously noted, by the mid-1960s new agencies had been established whose primary task was to develop expertise in specific areas of ODA policies and administration. Training acquired in Western universities and hands-on experience earned in domestic policy institutions in Washington, London, and Paris were not easily transferrable to the developing countries, however, although the European powers, because of their colonial experience, possessed greater diplomatic knowledge and institutional memory than their U.S. counterparts. This is not to suggest that public administration in the Western countries was necessarily superior to public administration in developing countries, but the social, economic, and political environment and institutions in the developing countries differed from those of the donor countries, where the purposes and programs of foreign aid were determined. Lack of familiarity, coupled with misdirected and ill-conceived political objectives, meant ineffective administration at best and, in some cases, led to disaster for the local population, as in Vietnam.

As a result, while in the 1950s and 1960s donor governments stressed nation- and institution-building, by the late 1970s the focus changed to "processes and procedures, to ways of doing things, reflecting the fact that whether aid works or fails depends upon a very broad context of policies, institutions and other resources."[109] Aid agencies learned through exchanges and training how to cooperate with local officials; their geographical subdivisions accumulated sufficient expertise in recipient countries to be able to determine the amount of funds and the type of development assistance necessary for effective implementation. Field missions acquired greater autonomy in local decision making and coordination between donor and recipient governments in their sector of expertise. Similarly, multilateral agencies, such as the World Bank and the UNDP, developed networks of specialized field agencies, facilitating international donor-recipient cooperation. Problems in management continue to plague aid implementation, however. As one report has noted, aid agencies cannot possess all of the technical expertise they would like to have and need. They therefore depend on outside consultants. "At times of economic recession, consultants come knocking on the doors of aid agencies, hoping for extra work, regardless of their particular fields of demonstrated competence. . . . Very few agencies, multilateral and bilateral alike, have solved the problem of how to maintain adequate and objective performance records, or of how to develop a discriminating recruitment process."[110]

Far less visible than war and peace issues in foreign policy, foreign aid management for effective economic development is nevertheless crucial for people's lives. It refers to the administrative machinery of distribution and management approaches of development assistance. It was hoped, for example, that innovations like Bangladesh's Grameen Bank, which has lent over $2.1 billion in small "microloans" of about $100 directly to over two million people for small enterprises, would jump-start local economies throughout the poorest countries. Evaluations have been mixed, however. A large percentage of such loans have helped women, for example, but interest rates have been relatively high and the overall impact uncertain, partly because of difficulties in collecting data.[111]

Development assistance programs also involve the controversial issue of technology transfer in the form of technical expertise, brain power, and technological hardware. Modeled after the Marshall Plan, the transfer of management and administrative technologies to the developing countries since the 1950s and 1960s assumed, at least in theory, that effective methods of public administration, systematic planning, and rational problem-solving methods would address local issues and solve social and economic problems in the Third World.[112] Western experts in public administration traveled back and forth to train people in administrative planning in developing countries, while students from the latter studied public administration in Western countries. However, donor-recipient relations were not purely technical and, as in the case of the Alliance for Progress, involved geo-political and ideological considerations.[113]

Despite these shortcomings, donor-recipient technical cooperation within DAC ODA programs increased from approximately 13 percent in the mid-1960s to about 30 percent in the 1980s, involving nearly 80,000 experts, teachers, and volunteers from donor to recipient countries in 1983, as well as 90,000 people, financed by donor countries, from the developing countries to acquire training in the donor countries.[114] The three major DAC contributors in technical cooperation in the 1980s were France, Germany, and the United States. In 1985, the dollar value of each was $2.6 billion, $2.1 billion, and $1.9 billion, respectively,[115] sponsoring and subsidizing thousands of students and trainees.[116] Together, DAC countries spent $10.9 billion. Other major donors were Japan ($878 million), Britain ($657 million), Italy ($648 million), and the Netherlands ($552 million).[117] In 1994, France spent $2.2 billion in technical cooperation, Germany and Japan $2.1 billion, and the United States $2.8 billion. Total DAC expenditure for technical cooperation for that year was $12.9 billion.[118]

Despite these efforts and the enormous sums they represented, by the late 1960s and early 1970s evaluations concluded that the U.S. Agency for International Development's (USAID) emphasis on development management and technology transfer had failed. The same held true for other Western donor countries. Too much emphasis supposedly had been placed on institution-building and rational administration as defined by Western values, while little attention was paid to the local human and cultural dimension in developing countries. Western concepts of separation of powers and separation between the public and private spheres were removed from the social, economic, and political realities of the developing countries. Western donor countries also realized that the creation of aid agencies and ministries alone would not be sufficient to make aid more effective. Technical aspects of development assistance required not only more money but also more expertise in various areas of relevant technologies from agriculture to health services to industrialization. In the early 1980s, a report on Finland's aid program, for example,

> referred to the need to strengthen FINNDA's management capacity for administering a fast-growing programme. In this connection it welcomed the recent steps taken to develop and implement new guidelines for the identification, preparation, appraisal, implementation and evaluation of projects. The Committee suggested the situation might be further assisted by a strengthening of Finland aid administration overseas in order to improve project monitoring and control.[119]

USAID, the agency responsible for the management of U.S. development assistance since its creation by the Foreign Assistance Act of 1961, has worked with more than 100 countries in Latin America, Africa, Asia, and the Middle East. It channeled billions of dollars in aid and managed financial and technical assistance in the form of U.S. government contracts with private and public firms at home and overseas, nongovernmental organizations, and universities. Increasing volume and complications of financial and technical support underscored the need for the institutionalization of effective management. Since its establishment, USAID has spent about 25 percent of its budget on improving the management of its projects and programs.[120]

With the globalization of world economic activities and rapid communications, public opinion in donor countries has become more aware of difficulties in and, therefore, more cynical toward the conduct of foreign aid programs. Especially in times of domestic economic pressures, the public demands cuts in aid dollars, greater accountability, and efficiency in the implementation of aid. As previously noted, foreign aid does not have the same constituency base as domestic programs. It is therefore more vulnerable to political pressures, especially when a donor country's economy is on a downward swing, people are unemployed, and there are no pressing national security concerns. Such domestic pressures can have serious repercussions for the management of foreign development assistance. Management costs usually consume about 5 to 10 percent of aid budgets. In areas of technologically more advanced projects—in telecommunications, for example—administrative costs can be as high as 25 to 30 percent. Cuts in such areas can render administration of programs less effective, which in turn would give rise to questions regarding the desirability of programs that fail to meet expectations. Thus, proponents of development assistance contend that institutional capability is essential for the success of development programs and that effective management requires money.

Development Assistance and Human Rights

Efforts by donors to link the allocation of foreign assistance to recipient governments' human rights performance is a relatively recent phenomenon in foreign policy, first instituted by the U.S. Congress in the early 1970s and implemented by the Carter administration in the second half of the 1970s.[121] In the late 1960s, some members of the U.S. Congress introduced measures to disassociate U.S. foreign aid from geo-political considerations and emphasized humanitarian and moral responsibilities as the primary justification for foreign aid. For example, Senator J. William Fulbright wrote,

> The obligation of the rich to help the poor is recognized . . . by every major religion, by every formal system of ethics, and by individuals who claim no moral code beyond a simple sense of human decency. Unless national borders are regarded as the limits of human loyalty and compassion as well as of political authority, the obligation of the rich to the poor clearly encompasses an obligation on the part of the rich nations to poor nations.[122]

Congressional hearings addressed this issue, and Congress subsequently instituted a human rights–foreign aid linkage. An amendment known as Section 32 of the Foreign Assistance Act of 1973 stated that "it is the sense of Congress that the President should deny any economic or military assistance to the government of any foreign country which practices the internment or imprisonment of that country's citizens for political purposes."[123] This was followed by a number of statutory provisions throughout the 1970s attempting to strengthen the human rights–foreign aid linkage. Congress required that the State Department submit annual human rights reports, today known as the *Country Reports on Human Rights Practices,* approved by the president, prior to allocation of foreign assistance.[124]

Whether such reforms have been successful or not has been the subject of heated debate since then. Some quantitatively based studies have found little consistency in the implementation of the human rights–foreign aid linkage. Others have found no relationship between a recipient's human rights performance and U.S. allocation of aid. Still others have found some relationship between economic aid and humanitarian concerns, such as the alleviation of poverty in aid recipient countries, but no relationship between human rights performance and military aid.[125] One study found that domestic factors—for example, the "prestige press" (*The New York Times* and *Washington Post*), bureaucracies, and incremental budgeting—were as important in foreign aid decisions as external determinants, such as poverty, ideology, and geo-political issues.[126]

However, geo-political and alliance considerations remained important enough to warrant enormous sums of dollars to contain Communism and to gain access to regions critical to U.S. economic interests. In the 1980s, among the Middle Eastern countries, for example, Israel alone received an annual average of $3.0 billion in "security assistance," the highest of all U.S. aid recipients worldwide, followed by Egypt's $2.0 billion and Turkey's $750 million.[127] This pattern continued into the Bush and Clinton administrations, although Turkey's share declined somewhat. In Central America, the Reagan administration sought to undermine the Sandinista government in Nicaragua and to eliminate revolutionary movements hostile to U.S. interests in the region. Thus, the administration increased economic aid to Nicaragua's neighbors. El Salvador went from $114 million in 1981 to $434 million in 1985; its military aid rose from $35.5 million to $136 million for the same years. Honduras received $36 million in 1981 in economic aid and about $230 million in 1985. Military aid to that country increased from $8.9 million in 1981 to $67.4 million in 1985.[128]

Since the Truman Doctrine in 1947 U.S. administrations have allocated billions of dollars to Turkey because of its geo-strategic position bordering on the Soviet Union.

In the 1960s and early 1970s, U.S. economic and military aid totaled about $3.3 billion, despite Turkey's egregious human rights violations. During the Reagan administration, security assistance to Turkey increased from $403 million in 1982 to $875 million in 1985. Improved relations with the Soviet Union during the administration's second term led to a brief decline, to $590 million in 1987 and to about $450 million in 1988 but Turkish aid increased again during the Bush administration, to over $800 million in 1991 and over $500 million in 1992, with an annual average of nearly $600 million during the 1989–1992 period.[129]

Table 11.6 presents data for a small, random sample of countries that received some form of U.S. economic or military aid during the Bush and Clinton administrations. During the Bush administration, Bolivia, Peru, Mozambique, and Zimbabwe each received over $100 million in economic aid, despite their poor human rights performance (especially Peru's). While over 50 percent of the listed countries experienced cuts in the level of economic aid received during the Clinton administration, all of them, with the exception of Malawi, saw their military aid levels decline—clearly the product of the end of the Cold War, as the bureaucracies involved could no longer justify some of these programs as a containment policy. In the case of some countries, the cuts were substantial. Economic aid to Bolivia declined from $182.8 million in 1992 to little over $106 million in 1994, and military aid dropped from $25.9 million to $3.4 million.[130] Economic aid to Indonesia dropped from $45.6 million in 1992 to $24.4 million in 1994; while that country had received $2.3 million worth of military aid in the early 1990s, it received no such aid in 1994, as Congressional criticism of its human rights record mounted. Other countries whose aid levels were reduced sharply included Mexico, Morocco, Mozambique, Togo, Tunisia, and Zimbabwe. While Burma (Myanmar), with one of the worst human rights records, received no aid in 1992 and 1994, aid to Sudan, with an equally nefarious human rights record, increased from $24.3 million to $66.3 million, possibly because of its position in the Arab world.

For some Central American countries, the anti-narcotics component of U.S. assistance was substantial. In 1992, economic aid to Colombia totaled $24 million, $23.4 million (or 98 percent) of which was to support Washington's "war on drugs." That country was one of the very few whose level of military aid, $49.3 million, was higher than economic aid, although its human rights performance was poor. In 1994, both aid levels declined, but the anti-drug component remained high, $20 million (or 93 percent) out of the total $21.6 million (with a very questionable record of success in reducing the drug trade).

The cuts in U.S. aid were the result of domestic budgetary considerations, the absence of Cold War priorities, and in some cases the recipients' human rights performance. It is clear, however, that there are inconsistencies in U.S. policy with respect to the human rights–foreign aid linkage. Despite these difficulties, however, the U.S. Congress and the Carter administration in the 1970s should be credited for at least raising human rights considerations as a legitimate foreign policy concern.

Similar foreign aid–human rights linkages were subsequently adopted by other Western governments as well. In the late 1970s, some members of the Canadian Parliament, for example, advocated a reduction in foreign assistance to governments with poor human rights records.[131] They, along with public commentators and interest groups, emphasized that development assistance be extended to governments "earnestly engaged in eradicating poverty *and* protecting human rights."[132] In 1986, the Special Joint Committee of Parliament on Canada's International Relations issued the Hockin-Simard report, emphasizing the need to institutionalize foreign aid–human rights linkages, a proposal supported in another official publication, the Winegard Report by the House of Commons Standing Committee on External Affairs and International Trade.[133] In the early 1980s, the governments of Guatemala, Guyana, Haiti, Honduras, Pakistan, Sri Lanka, and Uganda, to name a few, were identified as oppressive regimes, and the Canadian International Development Agency (CIDA) was advised to terminate assistance programs to these countries. As in the United States, the human rights priorities changed with the government in office. While the Liberal government of Prime Minister Joe Clark in the late 1970s, like the Carter administration, stressed the importance of human rights as an integral component of Canadian foreign policy, the Conservative Mulroney government in the 1980s, like the Reagan administration, more or less ignored the issue or defined its human rights objectives so as to render it nugatory.

Observers noted that, in most cases, as students of *realpolitik* would predict, Canada terminated aid programs to countries in which it had no significant strategic or commercial interests, as in Guatemala, or alternatively it took no action favorable to human rights, as in Pakistan and Indonesia.[134] In the case of Chile, Canadian aid programs continued and even increased after General Pinochet's

TABLE 11.6

Human Rights and U.S. Foreign Economic and Military Aid (Millions of Current Dollars)

		Bush Administration, 1992		Clinton Administration, 1994	
Country	Human Rights[a] Performance	Economic Aid	Military Aid	Economic Aid	Military Aid
Algeria	2.62	2.6	0.2	0.0	0.1
Argentina	1.81	1.9	1.3	3.0	0.1
Bolivia	2.60	182.8	25.9	106.1	3.4
Burkina Faso	2.98	11.7	0.0	12.6	0.0
Burma (Myanmar)	4.66	0.0	0.0	0.0	0.0
Burundi	2.88	15.5	0.2	52.8	0.0
Cameroon	3.10	25.8	0.4	3.9	0.1
Chile	2.14	5.4	0.4	6.1	0.1
Colombia	3.83	24.0	49.3	21.6	8.6
Dominican Republic	1.93	22.2	2.0	90.8	0.6
Ecuador	1.81	27.6	3.1	19.4	0.5
Guatemala	4.17	61.8	0.2	67.8	[b]
Haiti	4.29	51.0	0.0	106.0	0.0
Honduras	2.93	89.3	6.4	47.3	0.5
Indonesia	4.31	45.6	2.3	24.4	0.0
Jordan	2.52	29.4	20.6	46.9	9.8
Kenya	3.76	32.9	0.9	48.4	0.3
Madagascar	2.29	46.4	0.2	33.3	0.0
Malawi	3.21	54.4	0.1	54.6	0.1
Mexico	3.29	40.3	0.6	11.4	0.2
Morocco	2.62	91.1	23.2	43.0	0.5
Mozambique	3.43	146.5	0.2	74.7	0.0
Niger	3.64	34.0	1.0	26.7	0.2
Peru	4.05	123.0	0.1	156.1	0.0
Senegal	3.50	55.0	5.7	35.5	0.5
Sri Lanka	4.40	79.6	0.2	56.8	0.1
Sudan	4.67	24.3	0.0	66.3	0.0
Togo	2.76	16.1	0.0	6.0	0.0
Tunisia	2.74	20.0	11.3	3.2	0.5
Zimbabwe	2.86	101.2	0.7	40.3	0.2

Source: On recipient human rights performance and the Bush administration, see Simon Payaslian, *U.S. Foreign Economic and Military Aid: The Reagan and Bush Administrations* (Lanham, MD: University Press of America, 1996). For a detailed discussion on operationalization of human rights, see *Ibid.*, ch. 4. Aid figures are from USAID, *U.S. Overseas Loans and Grants* (Washington DC: GPO, 1995).

[a]Human rights performance score (for 1990) based on a scale of 1 to 5, where 1 indicates best human rights performance, and 5 worst.

[b]Indicates less than $50,000

military overthrow of the democratically elected Allende government in 1973. In Guyana, on the other hand, the Canadian government suspended credit toward newsprint purchases when it realized that "newsprint was not reaching the opposition press and Canada was thus indirectly contributing to a climate in Guyana of denial of political and civil rights."[135] Similarly, in 1985, the Canadian government suspended aid to the Mahaweli River project in Sri Lanka because of the latter's repressive government and discriminatory practices. At the same time, however, largely because of Canadian commercial interests, Indonesia remained one of the major recipients of Canadian aid, in spite of that government's reportedly genocidal policy in East Timor. It also certified an IMF loan of $1.07 billion to the *apartheid* regime in South Africa.[136]

The same trend appeared in Western European countries as well. In 1978, the British Labour government of James Callaghan stated its intention to strengthen human rights–foreign aid linkages. This effort was terminated by the Conservative Margaret Thatcher government in 1979, however, and there is little indication that, in the 1990s, London has been more interested in pursuing such a policy. The Netherlands and Norway have had a stronger human rights policy since the early 1980s, at the same time that their ODA levels increased. Japan, likewise, came to add human rights conditionality to its aid programs, as in Myanmar and Indonesia. Japan's Prime Ministers Noboru Takeshita and Kiichi Miyazawa publicly announced their intentions to insist on human rights improvements in both countries after the 1989 Tiananmen Square massacre in Beijing. Relations with China, however, continue to illustrate the cross pressures and difficulties of linking either trade or aid to human rights performance. For Washington, Tokyo, and other key capitals, the allure of the "China market" and strategic importance of the world's largest country make it extremely difficult and even dangerous to break relations or impose sanctions.

CONCLUSION

Development assistance has been an important part of international political economy since the Second World War. In the 1950s and 1960s, the creation of vast international bilateral and multilateral aid networks, modeled largely after the Marshall Plan, gave rise to expectations that North–South cooperation would lead to greater improvements in the standards of living in the developing world. Increased efforts during those decades were not sustained, however, and by the early 1970s aid levels had relatively declined. Most developing countries did experience improvements in their literacy, life expectancy, and infant mortality rates, yet, in comparison with the developed world, the North–South gap in social and economic development continued to widen, giving rise to doubts about the viability of aid as a developmental policy.

While some countries, such as South Korea and Taiwan, "graduated" from Western foreign aid programs and emerged as major competitors in world trade, most developing economies failed to develop a strong national economic-industrial base. Declining formal aid levels have led them to turn to experimentation with various programs, supported by the World Bank, UNDP and UNIDO, including micro-loans and greater involvement by the private sector. Such multilateral organizations' efforts have certainly enhanced the international environment for greater international cooperation, but declining financial support of these institutions does not bode well for the future of multilateral assistance. The Realist and imperialist (and neo-colonialist) theories of foreign aid seem to be closer than moralists to the hard political and economic facts of global economic competition, especially when one takes into consideration the weak relationship between foreign assistance and human rights.

Chapter Summary

Official development assistance (ODA) is a key component of North–South cooperation. It includes tied and untied, bilateral and multilateral assistance, mainly from the developed to the developing countries, but increasingly from the wealthier or more ambitious developing countries as well.

Donors' motives vary, ranging from geo-political considerations to humanitarian concerns and bureaucratic objectives. According to the Realist school, the primary purpose of foreign assistance is to support friendly governments for geo-strategic reasons. Proponents of humanitarianism (moralists or idealists) see foreign assistance as a way of helping people in poorer countries, while theorists of imperialism contend that foreign assistance is a mechanism used by the more powerful states to dominate the developing economies. Theorists of bureaucratic politics maintain that foreign assistance is ultimately the product of domestic politics and is shaped by the relationship between interest groups and bureaucracies.

During the Cold War, foreign aid programs, such as the Marshall Plan and the Alliance for Progress, were used to combat Communism in the developing world.

Since the 1980s, especially after the collapse of the former Soviet Union, there has been a noticeable decline in bilateral and multilateral foreign aid levels. That decline has been attributed to "donor-fatigue," the world recession of the 1970s and early 1980s, and chronic unemployment and financial problems. By the 1990s, the public mood in donor countries had shifted against foreign aid.

Among the four major European countries (Britain, France, Germany, and Italy), France alone has maintained its annual aid volume above the 0.5 percent level. Since the UN General Assembly set the target of 0.7 percent of each donor's GNP for ODA by the mid-1970s, only four Western countries—Denmark, Norway, the Netherlands, and Sweden—plus an Islamic donor group maintained that support level. In recent years, Japan became the largest ODA donor among the industrialized countries, but its own financial woes threatened that rank.

South–South aid—especially by the wealthier Arab states, such as Saudi Arabia—increased in the 1970s. Despite a move recent decline, Arab aid has been the highest in the world, with much of it going to poorer Islamic states. Some of the other major or proportionally significant ODA contributors have included the former Soviet Union, China, India, Cuba, and increasingly the NICs.

International organizations involved in multilateral aid include the World Bank and the various specialized agencies of the United Nations, as well as regional banks, such as the Inter-American Development Bank, the Inter-African Development Bank, and the Asian Development Bank.

Whether development assistance has transformed the recipient economies to any appreciable degree is debatable. The "successes" registered in most countries are incremental only. The case of sub-Saharan African countries raises serious questions regarding ODA as a viable instrument to address problems of poverty and underdevelopment. Where countries have been successful, as in the case of the "four tigers," it is clear that a great deal more was involved in the effort than merely ODA levels.

Foreign aid also has been controversial in areas of technology transfer. Governments and businesses are reluctant to aid other countries and competitors. In the area of human rights, the issue has been one of providing economic and military support to friendly governments that are frequently engaged in egregious violations of their citizens' rights. Public pressure since the 1970s has led to the institutionalization of greater controls on the distribution of foreign aid, but whether they have been successful remains an issue.

Points of Contention

As a government official, would you prefer to give bilateral or multilateral aid? Would you prefer to receive bilateral or multilateral aid?

Which is a more valid argument for foreign aid, geopolitical or humanitarian considerations? To what extent would you say aid is an instrument of imperialism? Can you identify any interest groups in your community that would be interested in influencing foreign aid decisions?

How successful was the Marshall Plan in Europe? How successful has foreign aid been in the developing countries? What were the similarities and differences?

What factors have contributed to the decline in foreign aid levels in recent years? Were fears that in the post–Cold War era sub-Saharan Africa would receive lower levels of aid justified?

The Copenhagen Declaration (1995) urged donor countries to allocate about 0.7 percent of their GNP to foreign economic aid. Is that a realistic target? What about other such targets at Copenhagen?

What are some of the benefits of South–South aid? What are the difficulties?

What are some of the advantages and disadvantages of multilateral assistance as provided by international organizations, such as the U.N. Industrial Development Organization?

Should there be a linkage between development assistance and human rights performance?

Notes

1. OECD, *Twenty-Five Years of Development Co-Operation, 1985 Report: A Review* (Paris: Organization for Economic Co-Operation and Development, 1985), p. 171.
2. This section on theories of foreign assistance draws on material presented in Simon Payaslian, *U.S. Foreign Economic and Military Aid: The Reagan and Bush Administrations* (Lanham, MD: University Press of America, 1996), pp. 1–9.
3. Hans Morgenthau, "A Political Theory of Foreign Aid," *American Political Science Review* 56, 2 (June 1962), pp. 301–309; Kenneth N. Waltz, *Theory of International Politics* (New York: Random House, 1979); Earl Conteh-Morgan, *American Foreign Aid and Global Power Projection* (Aldershot, UK: Dartmouth, 1990).
4. See Roger C. Riddell, *Foreign Aid Reconsidered* (Baltimore: The Johns Hopkins University Press, 1987); Cynthia

Brown, ed., *With Friends Like These* (New York: Pantheon Books, 1985); Noam Chomsky and Edward S. Herman, *The Political Economy of Human Rights: The Washington Connection and Third World Fascism* (Boston: South End Press, 1979); Theresa Hayter and Catharine Watson, *Aid: Rhetoric and Reality* (London: Pluto Press, 1985); Teresa Hayter, *Aid as Imperialism* (Middlesex, England: Penguin Books, 1971).

5. Olav Stokke, ed., *Western Middle Powers and Global Poverty* (Uppsala, Sweden: Scandinavian Institute of African Studies, 1989), pp. 10–12.
6. David Halloran Lumsdaine, *Moral Vision in International Politics: The Foreign Aid Regime, 1949–1989* (Princeton: Princeton University Press, 1993); Victor Ferkiss, "Foreign Aid: Moral Aspects and Political Aspects," in Kenneth W. Thompson, ed., *Moral Dimensions of American Foreign Policy* (New Brunswick, NJ: Transaction Books, 1984), p. 202.
7. On bureaucratic politics and foreign policy, see, for example, David C. Kozak and James M. Keagle, eds., *Bureaucratic Politics and National Security: Theory and Practice* (Boulder, CO: Lynne Rienner, 1988); Graham T. Allison, *Essence of Decision* (Boston: Little, Brown and Company, 1971); Morton Halperin, *Bureaucratic Politics and Foreign Policy* (Washington, DC: Brookings Institute, 1974). For the relationship between bureaucratic politics and foreign aid, see Judith Tendler, *Inside Foreign Aid* (Baltimore: The Johns Hopkins University Press, 1975).
8. Payaslian, *U.S. Foreign Economic and Military Aid,* pp. 57–72, 80–101.
9. William Ryrie, *First World, Third World* (London: Macmillan Press, 1995), pp. 15–16.
10. Vasant Sukhatme, "Assistance to India," in Anne O. Krueger, Constantine Michalopoulos, and Vernon W. Ruttan, eds., *Aid and Development* (Baltimore: The Johns Hopkins University Press, 1989), p. 205.
11. *Ibid.*, p. 208.
12. OECD, *Twenty-Five Years of Development Co-Operation, 1985,* p. 80.
13. Sukhatme, "Assistance to India," p. 208.
14. On various aspects of aid mismanagement and corruption, see Graham Hancock, *Lords of Poverty* (London: Macmillan, 1989).
15. Ryrie, *First World, Third World,* p. 20.
16. At 1983 prices and exchange rates. OECD, *Twenty-Five Years of Development Co-Operation, 1985,* Chart III-1, p. 94.
17. OECD, *Development Co-Operation, 1994 Report* (Paris: Organization for Economic Co-operation and Development, 1995), Table 1, pp. A1–A2.
18. *Ibid.*, p. A2.
19. Simon Payaslian, "The United Nations and the Developing Countries in the 1990s," *University of Detroit Mercy Law Review* 73, 3 (Spring 1996), pp. 525–549.
20. "Declaration and Programme of Action of the World Summit for Social Development," Report of the Main Committee, A\CONF.166\L.3; A/CONF.166/L.3/Add.2 (March 6–12, 1995).
21. Payaslian, "The United Nations and the Developing Countries in the 1990s," pp. 525–549.
22. German aid level, third in its share of total DAC ODA in the 1970s and 1980s, averaged about 0.47 percent in the early 1980s but dropped to 0.34 percent in 1994—in real dollar terms, over $6.5 billion in the first half of the 1990s. As a percentage of the governmental budget, however, it declined from 2.6 percent in the early 1980s to less than 2 percent by 1994. Italy's aid level rose to 0.17 percent ($683 million) in 1980 and to 0.42 percent in 1989, the highest ODA level by Italy. The average level for the first half of the 1990s was 0.31 percent of its GNP. In the early 1980s, nearly 60 percent of total Italian ODA went to sub-Saharan Africa, but that region's share decreased about 36 percent by 1994. In its stead, ODA levels to North Africa, the Middle East, and Southern Europe increased from 11.6 percent in the late 1980s to 38.0 percent in 1993–1994, as did Italian ODA levels to Latin American countries, from 9.1 percent in the early 1980s to 16.8 percent by 1994. The major recipients of Italian aid since the early 1970s have been Indonesia, Egypt, Ethiopia, Malta, Somalia, Tanzania, former Yugoslavia, and in recent years China, mostly in the areas of economic infrastructure, transport and communications, energy, and agricultural and industrial production. Italy's tied aid as percentage of ODA in the 1990s has exceeded 43 percent. OECD, *Development Co-Operation, 1995 Report,* Table 35, p. A60; Table 42, p. A75; and various years.
23. OECD, *Development Co-Operation, Report 1994,* Table 45, p. H20.
24. While in the early 1970s Egypt was not even among the top fifteen recipients, in the early 1980s it emerged as the fifteenth, and it shared the third highest (4.5 percent of French ODA) spot with New Caledonia in 1993–1994.
25. OECD, *Development Co-Operation, 1994 Report,* Table 30, p. F4.
26. OECD, *Development Co-Operation, 1995 Report,* and various years.
27. *Ibid.*
28. OECD, *Development Co-Operation* [various years].
29. Olav Stokke, ed., *Western Middle Powers and Global Poverty,* p. 9.
30. See, for example, Eugene R. Wittkopf, *Faces of Internationalism: Public Opinion and American Foreign Policy* (Durham: Duke University Press, 1990), pp. 70–76, 151–153. See also *Economic Report of the President, 1997,* Box 7-3, p. 265.
31. This decline also reflected the substantial drop in the level of foreign aid as percentage of GNP. The annual average for the 1956–1960 period was $2.3 billion, or 0.49 percent of

GNP, which increased to $3.5 billion, or 0.58 percent of GNP, in the 1960s. It dropped to 0.27 percent in the early 1980s and to 0.15 percent in 1994. The dollar value of U.S. aid increased from $7.1 billion in 1980 to $9.4 billion in 1985 and to $11.4 billion in 1990, but it dropped to $9.9 billion in 1994. OECD, *Development Co-Operation* [various years].

32. *Ibid.* [various years].
33. OECD, *Development Co-Operation, 1995 Report,* and [various years]; U.S. Agency for International Development, *U.S. Overseas Loans and Grants* (Washington, DC: U.S. Government Printing Office, various years).
34. See Deborah J. Gerner, *One Land, Two Peoples: The Conflict over Palestine* (Boulder, CO: Westview Press, 1994).
35. OECD, *Development Co-Operation, 1995 Report,* and [various years].
36. During the first two decades after WWII, Japan's aid level fluctuated erratically from year to year, ranging from 0.89 percent of GNP in 1958 (its highest level) to 0.14 percent in 1962. The average level of aid was $360 million, or 0.27 percent of GNP, for the 1965–1970 period; $881 million, or 0.23 percent of GNP, for 1971–1975, $2.2 billion, or 0.25 percent of GNP, for 1976–1980; and $3.6 billion, or 0.31 percent of GNP, for 1981–1985. OECD, *Twenty-Five Years of Development Co-Operation, 1985 Report: A Review,* Table 26, p. 335.
37. OECD, *Development Co-Operation* [various years].
38. In the early 1970s, the top three recipients—with a combined total of approximately 60 percent—were Indonesia (almost 30 percent), South Korea (nearly 20 percent), and India (over 10 percent). *Ibid.* [various years].
39. *Ibid.* [various years].
40. OECD, *Development Co-Operation, 1995 Report.*
41. *The New York Times,* April 29, 1997, p. A4. Ironically, in seizing the embassy, the Tupac Amaru Revolutionary Movement demanded not only the release of its members from prison but also the eradication of poverty in Peru and Japan's "meddling" in Peruvian affairs.
42. OECD, *Twenty-Five Years of Development Co-Operation, 1985 Report: A Review,* Table III-1, p. 93.
43. OECD, *Development Co-Operation, 1994 Report.*
44. OECD, *Twenty-Five Years of Development Co-Operation, 1985 Report: A Review,* p. 80.
45. Kuwaiti aid dropped from $1.14 billion in 1980 to $771 million in 1985, Qatar's from $277 million to $8 million, and Saudi Arabia's from $5.68 billion to $2.63 billion for the same years.
46. The top five also included Jordan (with a combined total of $1.3 billion for both years), followed by Bahrain ($363 million), Yemen ($384 million), and Sudan ($479 million). Total ODA dropped from $2.9 billion in 1987 to $1.9 billion in 1988.
47. OECD, *Development Co-Operation, 1987 Report* (Paris: Organization for Economic Co-Operation and Development, 1988), Table 46, pp. 228–229.
48. Donald Bobiash, *South–South Aid: How Developing Countries Help Each Other* (New York: St. Martin's Press, 1992), p. 15.
49. OECD, *Development Co-Operation, 1987 Report,* Table X-8, p. 158.
50. OECD, *Development Co-Operation, 1994 Report,* Table VI-1, p. 111.
51. *Ibid.,* p. 157.
52. *Ibid.*
53. OECD, *Development Co-Operation, 1995 Report* (Paris: Organization for Economic Cooperation and Development, 1996), Table 43, pp. 117–119, p. A86.
54. Bobiash, *South–South Aid,* p. 15.
55. See, for example, Shireen Hunter, *OPEC and the Third World* (London: Croom Helm, 1984).
56. Portugal withdrew from DAC in 1974 but rejoined in 1991.
57. OECD, *Twenty-Five Years of Development Co-Operation, 1985 Report: A Review,* pp. 140–145.
58. *Ibid.,* pp. 67–68.
59. *Ibid.,* p. 70.
60. *Ibid.,* p. 67.
61. *Ibid.,* p. 71.
62. *Ibid.,* p. 72.
63. *Ibid.,* p. 71.
64. *Ibid.,* p. 68.
65. *Ibid.,* p. 70.
66. *Ibid.,* p. 139.
67. Forty-five percent for China and the South Asian subcontinent and 43 percent for sub-Saharan Africa.
68. OECD, *Twenty-Five Years of Development Co-Operation, 1985 Report: A Review,* Table IV-1 and 2, pp. 142–143.
69. *Ibid.*
70. OECD, *Development Co-Operation, 1994 Report,* Table 24, p. D4.
71. OECD, *Twenty-Five Years of Development Co-Operation, 1985 Report: A Review,* Table IV-1 and 2, pp. 142–143.
72. OECD, *Development Co-Operation, 1994 Report,* Table 24, p. D4.
73. OECD, *Twenty-Five Years of Development Co-Operation, 1985 Report: A Review,* Table IV-1 and 2, pp. 142–143.
74. OECD, *Development Co-Operation, 1994 Report,* Table 24, p. D4.
75. OECD, *Twenty-Five Years of Development Co-Operation, 1985 Report: A Review,* Table IV-1 and 2, pp. 142–143.
76. OECD, *Development Co-Operation, 1994 Report,* Table 24, p. D4.
77. Alan Rix, *Japan's Foreign Aid Challenge: Policy Reform and Aid Leadership* (London: Routledge, 1993). On Japan's

foreign aid policies, see Ministry of Foreign Affairs, Economic Co-Operation Bureau, *Japan's ODA Annual Report 1995* (Tokyo: Association for Promotion of International Cooperation, 1996).

78. Youry Lambert, *The United Nations Industrial Development Organization* (Westport: Praeger, 1993).
79. *Ibid.*, p. 116.
80. *Ibid.*, p. 65.
81. UNIDO, *Annual Report 1995,* IDB.16/10-PBC.12/10, October 1996, p. 5.
82. *Ibid.*, p. 7.
83. *Ibid.*, pp. 10–11.
84. *Ibid.*, p. 16.
85. *Ibid.*
86. *Ibid.*, p. 21.
87. *Ibid.*, pp. 52–53.
88. *Ibid.*, p. 9.
89. *Ibid.*, p. 7.
90. OECD, *Twenty-Five Years of Development Co-Operation, 1985 Report: A Review,* p. 145.
91. *Ibid.*
92. OECD, *Development Co-Operation, 1994 Report,* Table 39, p. H8.
93. World Bank, *World Development Report 1994* (Oxford: Oxford University Press, 1994), p. 162.
94. *Ibid.*, p. 162.
95. OECD, *Twenty-Five Years of Development Co-Operation, 1985 Report: A Review,* Table III-11, p. 123.
96. *Ibid.*
97. OECD, *Development Co-Operation, 1994 Report,* Table 47, p. J3.
98. World Bank, *World Development Report 1994,* Table 1, p. 162.
99. OECD, *Twenty-Five Years of Development Co-Operation, 1985 Report: A Review,* Table XII, p. 270.
100. World Bank, *World Development Report 1994,* Table 1, p. 162.
101. In the meantime, South Korea introduced its own development assistance programs administered by the Korean International Cooperation Agency (KOICA) and the Economic Development Cooperation Fund (EDCF). In 1994, South Korea's total ODA level was $140 million (or about 0.04 percent of GNP). OECD, *Development Co-Operation, 1995 Report,* p. 119.
102. During the same period, all of sub-Saharan Africa's share was 9 percent of total world ODA, Latin America's 9.9 percent.
103. From 11.5 percent in 1970–1971 to 3 percent in 1982–1983, surpassed by Egypt (4.4 percent) and Israel (4 percent). OECD, *Twenty-Five Years of Development Co-Operation, 1985 Report: A Review,* Tables III-10 and III-11, pp. 121–123.
104. In the early 1990s, its share of world total development assistance declined further, to 5.6 percent in 1991 and to 3.9 percent by 1994, a drop of 3.3 percent between 1984 and 1994. World Bank, *World Development Report 1994,* Table 19, p. 198; OECD, *Development Co-Operation, 1995 Report,* Table 36, p. A61.
105. OECD, *Twenty-Five Years of Development Co-Operation, 1985 Report: A Review;* World Bank, *World Development Report 1994,* Table 27, p. 214.
106. Joseph E. Stiglitz, "The Role of Government in Economic Development," in Michael Bruno and Boris Pleskovic, eds., *Annual World Bank Conference on Development Economics, 1996* (Washington, DC: World Bank, 1997), p. 11.
107. Clive Hamilton, "Can the Rest of Asia Emulate NICs?" in Charles K. Wilber and Kenneth P. Jameson, eds., *The Political Economy of Development and Underdevelopment,* 5th ed. (New York: McGraw-Hill, 1992), p. 427.
108. David F. Pyle, "From Project to Program: Structural Constraints Associated with Expansion," NASPAA Working Paper No. 3, Washington: National Association of Schools of Public Affairs and Administration, discussed in Dennis A. Rondinelli, *Development Administration and U.S. Foreign Aid Policy* (Boulder, CO: Lynne Rienner, 1987), p. 121.
109. OECD, *Twenty-Five Years of Development Co-Operation, 1985 Report: A Review,* pp. 179–180.
110. *Ibid.*, p. 184.
111. Barbara Crossette, "U.N. Report Raises Questions About Small Loans to the Poor," *New York Times* (September 3, 1998), p. A8.
112. Rondinelli, *Development Administration and U.S. Foreign Aid Policy,* pp. 23–26.
113. In the 1950s, USAID, the United Nations, and the Ford Foundation devoted over $250 million for this purpose. USAID facilitated the development of public administration programs and related institutions in Brazil, Ecuador, El Salvador, South Korea, Mexico, Pakistan, Peru, the Philippines, Thailand, and Vietnam. In the meantime, more than 7,000 students from developing countries studied public administration in American universities. Moreover, as the name Mutual Security Act implied, aid also involved the transfer of military matériel and technical support. Economic development assistance went hand in hand with military assistance. The U.S. experience in Vietnam, however, raised serious questions regarding the political feasibility of such involvement.
114. OECD, *Twenty-Five Years of Development Co-Operation, 1985 Report: A Review,* p. 189.
115. At 1992 prices and exchange rates.
116. In 1985, France sponsored and subsidized 14,220 students and trainees, Germany 12,846, and the United States 13,790. OECD, *Development Co-Operation, 1994 Report,* Tables 33–34, pp. G2–G3.

117. *Ibid.*
118. In current prices and exchange rates.
119. OECD, *Twenty-Five Years of Development Co-Operation, 1985 Report: A Review,* p. 182.
120. Rondinelli, *Development Administration and U.S. Foreign Aid Policy,* p. 3.
121. See David P. Forsythe, *Human Rights and U.S. Foreign Policy: Congress Reconsidered* (Gainesville: University Press of Florida, 1988); Forsythe, *Human Rights and World Politics,* rev. 2d ed. (Lincoln: University of Nebraska Press, 1989).
122. J. William Fulbright, *The Arrogance of Power* (New York: Vintage Books, 1966), pp. 223–224.
123. Quoted in Mark L. Schneider, "A New Administration's New Policy: The Rise to Power of Human Rights," in Peter G. Brown and Douglas MacLean, eds., *Human Rights and U.S. Foreign Policy* (Lexington: Lexington Books, 1979), p. 7.
124. Cohen, Roberta, "Human Rights Decision-Making in the Executive Branch: Some Proposals for a Coordinated Strategy," in Donald P. Kommers and Gilburt D. Loescher, eds., *Human Rights and American Foreign Policy* (South Bend, IN: University of Notre Dame Press, 1979), pp. 179–180.
125. See, for example, David Carleton and Michael Stohl, "The Foreign Policy of Human Rights: Rhetoric and Reality from Jimmy Carter to Ronald Reagan," *Human Rights Quarterly* 7 (May 1985), pp. 205–229; David Carleton and Michael Stohl, "The Role of Human Rights in U.S. Foreign Assistance Policy: A Critique and Reappraisal," *American Journal of Political Science* 31 (1987), pp. 1002–1018; David L. Cingranelli and Thomas E. Pasquarello, "Human Rights and the Distribution of U.S. Foreign Aid to Latin American Countries," *American Journal of Political Science* 29 (1985), pp. 539–563; R. D. McKinlay and R. Little, "A Foreign Policy Model of U.S. Bilateral Aid Allocation," *World Politics* 33 (1977), pp. 58–86; R. D. McKinlay and R. Little, "The US Aid Relationship: A Test of Recipient Need and the Donor Interest Models," *Political Studies* 27 (1979), pp. 236–250; Steven C. Poe, "Human Rights and U.S. Foreign Aid: A Review of Quantitative Studies and Suggestions for Future Research," *Human Rights Quarterly* 12 (1990), pp. 499–512; Steven C. Poe, "Human Rights and the Allocation of U.S. Military Assistance," *Journal of Peace Research* 28 (1991), pp. 205–216.
126. Payaslian, *U.S. Foreign Economic and Military Aid,* pp. 50–72.
127. *Congressional Quarterly Almanac* (various years).
128. U.S. Agency for International Development, *U.S. Overseas Loans and Grants* (Washington, DC: U.S. Government Printing Office, various years).
129. Payaslian, *U.S. Foreign Economic and Military Aid,* p. xvi.
130. *Ibid.,* p. 27. Economic aid to Cameroon dropped from $25.8 million to $3.9 million, and to Honduras from $89.3 million to $47.3 million. Military aid to Honduras also declined from $6.4 million to less than a million. During the Reagan administration and the reintensification of the Cold War in Central America, U.S. economic aid to Honduras had increased from $36.4 million in 1981 to $229.0 million in 1985, and military aid from $8.9 million to $67.4 million.
131. T. A. Keenleyside, "Canadian Aid and Human Rights: Forging a Link," in Irving Brecher, ed., *Human Rights, Development and Foreign Policy: Canadian Perspective* (Halifax: The Institute for Research on Public Policy, 1989), pp. 330–333.
132. *Ibid.,* p. 330.
133. *Ibid.*
134. *Ibid.,* p. 340.
135. *Ibid.,* p. 346.
136. Rhoda E. Howard, "Civil-Political Rights and Canadian Development Assistance," in Brecher, ed., *Human Rights, Development and Foreign Policy,* pp. 358–359.

CHAPTER TWELVE

THE GLOBALIZATION OF INFORMAL ECONOMIES AND THE INFORMALIZATION OF THE INTERNATIONAL POLITICAL ECONOMY

The previous chapters noted the rapid expansion of electronic financial and commercial relations, which has led to the integration of national economies into a world economy. This integration has facilitated the globalization of various formal economic sectors, such as banking and manufacturing. At the same time, however, integration also has led to the internationalization of the informal aspects of national economies, which generally do not appear in national and international accounts. This chapter looks at some of the dimensions of the informal economy.

Although no comprehensive definition is attempted here, the informal economy can be defined as unregulated economic and financial transactions and activities not registered in national accounts.[1] Informalization is the process of transferring a share of economic activity from the formal to the informal sector. While the informal economy has a long history, scholars began to pay greater attention to it in the second half of the twentieth century, first in the developing countries and the former Soviet Union, and beginning in the 1970s in Western economies, when largely because of the recession, activities related to the informal labor market and tax evasion played an expanded role. The "hidden economy" in England, Germany's *Schwarzarbeit,* the *travail noir* in France, Argentina's *morocho,* and the *lavoro nero* in Italy[2] are variously labeled as "underground economy," "black economy," "shadow economy," and "unofficial economy."[3] Each label refers to specific differences in various categories of the informal economy. In this chapter, the term "informal economy" is used, subsuming the different dimensions under this single concept.[4]

UNREGULATED ECONOMIES AS SOURCES OF CONFLICT AND COOPERATION

During the past three decades, globalization has expanded the informal domain of various economic and market activities, and the world economy has experienced greater informalization as exchanges spill across national boundaries. In the 1970s, it was estimated that the size of the American informal economy ranged from about 3.4 percent of GNP to 16 percent, and, in the 1980s, from 5 percent to 30 percent of GNP. Among European countries, the estimated range was about 5–15 percent, and up to 50 percent of GNP in the case of Italy.[5] In developing countries, the size of the informal economy in Peru, for example, is estimated at 50–60 percent of GNP, in Argentina 40 percent, in India 20–50 percent, in Egypt 16–43 percent, in Yemen 70 percent, in Tanzania and Ghana about 32 percent, and in Taiwan 14–40 percent.[6]

Economists disagree as to precisely what constitutes the informal economy. Some informal domestic and transnational activities are illegal and escape regulation by authorities, but they reflect social and economic power structures and influence the national income, even though they "fail to adhere to the established institutional rules or are denied their protection."[7] A small sample of informal but institutionalized activities include household services, unofficial or unrecorded employment in the service sector, undocumented or illegal migrant labor, tax evasion, state corruption, organized crime, smuggling, and capital flight, each with its own degree of illegality and offense to public morality.

Other equally criminal but not institutionalized activities—for example, the age-old problem of mugging and the new phenomenon of car-jacking—are not included here because there is no reason to believe that they are as yet "institutionalized," with direct relations to the social and political institutions—unless, for example, they are related to organized crime or the drug trade.[8]

A number of reasons can be identified for the development of the informal economy, although these causes differ to some extent in the industrialized and developing economies.[9] In general, they include reactions to taxation, regulation, prohibition, corruption, international competition, industrialization, and world economic crises, which together lead to the creation of incentives and invisible economic and political structures of informal economic activity.[10] For example, when government taxation or regulation appear excessive, unjustified, wasteful, or just an inconvenience, individuals and companies may seek avenues to evade them, as in the black market that grew up in reaction to the American "Prohibition" of alcoholic beverages early in the twentieth century.[11] Strategies to evade taxes and regulations range from the under-reporting of income to international smuggling and "money laundering" operations.

All governments tolerate a certain level of corruption among their officials and inside their bureaucracies. The most common form of government corruption is bribery, used to secure state contracts, free passage of goods through the customs, "zoning ordinances and building permits, investment licenses, import and foreign exchange permits, allocation of consumption, investment and infrastructure goods that are in short supply, and a host of others."[12] In some states, payments may be informally required to assure access to the "right people" to conduct business and may even constitute traditional cultural practices. In addition, as the need to be competitive in the global market leads companies to secure less expensive labor for labor-intensive production, companies have been known to move parts of their operations underground.[13] Finally, another impetus for the development of the informal economy is economic hardship, such as in recessions and depressions, as people look for ways to compensate for lost income.[14]

By the mid-1990s, the informal economy had emerged as an integral component of national economies in the developed and developing countries. In the developing and transitional countries (the latter like Russia), conditions for the informal economy have been further exacerbated by a lack of economic diversification, insufficient investment capital and opportunities, an inadequate infrastructural base, an inadequate institutional capability for tax collecting, exploding rural-to-urban migration, lower levels of literacy and education, institutional barriers to the employment of women, and political instability.[15]

The informal economy involves professionals or "white collar," "blue collar," and "pink collar" (women) personnel in such sectors as household services and production, business operations, services, trade, and communications and transportation, as well as criminal activities involving extortion, drugs, prostitution, and smuggling. Institutions engaged in the informal economy range from major corporations, small businesses, politicians, and the self-employed to criminals and prisoners. The domestic structures of the informal economy are closely intertwined with international informal operations and financial transactions. Billions of dollars flow across international borders annually, through customs and via computers, involving transactions for illegal or unreported cash, goods, and services. For example, one Internal Revenue Service (IRS) report estimated that between $20 billion and $135 billion worth of such transactions occur each year between the United States and other countries. The IMF estimated that, during the period 1977–1983, approximately $300 billion net inflows were not registered in the national accounts of the home countries.[16]

The informal economy may have certain benefits as well as disadvantages for the national and international economy. Employment in the informal economy provides an additional source of income to families and individuals, improving their standard of living and affording various luxuries to those who desire them. Greater availability of spending capital in the hands of consumers increases demand and in turn stimulates the national economy. The informal economy "benefits" the consumer by providing goods at lower costs, through employing less expensive labor, by sidestepping taxes, and by avoiding licensing and insurance costs. By avoiding various government regulations, businesses can have greater flexibility in choosing their employees, their hours, their working conditions, and the quality of goods they produce.[17] For the wider society, the informal economy also functions as a shock absorber in times of economic contraction and unemployment by providing an additional layer of opportunities for employment and income, thereby absorbing potential social and political tensions.[18]

In international relations, informal economic relations provide opportunities for cooperation that otherwise would not be formally permitted, nor publicly admitted, by their respective governments. The relationship between mainland China (the People's Republic of China, PRC) and Taiwan (the Republic of China, ROC) is a case in point. For years after the Communist revolution overthrew the Chiang Kai-shek government and the latter's escaped to Taiwan, both Chinas, despite their acrimonious statements in public, maintained informal trade relations, mostly through Hong Kong. Formally, neither the PRC nor the ROC recognized the division, and each claimed to represent China. Mainland China insisted that all foreign governments and international organizations, including the United Nations, recognize only Beijing as China's government. International organizations, therefore, refer to Taiwan as the "Taiwan Province of China." Only in the mid-1990s, as Hong Kong's reunification with the PRC approached, did both begin negotiations for greater formal cooperation across the Taiwan Strait. In 1997, Taiwan introduced formal laws allowing the Kaohsiung export processing zone (EPZ) to formally import products from mainland China, although some informal trade already existed.[19]

Despite such advantages of the informal economy in domestic and international realms, the informal economy's negative consequences tend to outweigh the benefits. One obvious problem is that a large informal economy weakens the government's ability to manage national accounts and to use reliable data with respect to GNP, unemployment, inflation, and so on.[20] Tax evaders in the informal accounts do not contribute to national and local government budgets and social programs, such as social security and unemployment schemes.[21] The government therefore relies heavily on the tax-paying individuals, mostly the middle class, for a large share of its revenues. The growing burden of taxes causes increasing resentment among the middle class toward the government, whose taxation and regulatory policies increasingly come to be perceived as excessive.

For businesses, the disadvantages of operating within the informal economy include an unstable supply of employees and materials, lack of legal safeguards, as well as risks involving termination of operation by the state and potential penetration by organized crime. Continued operation requires bribes to officials and protection against organized crime. Organized labor also suffers in competition with undocumented low-paid workers, who in turn lack job protection and benefits packages. A combination of these disadvantages can make operating in the informal economy costly; as a result, most businesses, large and small, prefer to play by the rules of the formal economy.[22] Competition between the formal and informal sectors is particularly intense in the area of construction, services, small-scale production and repairs, and trade.[23] Business leaders sometimes complain about the advantages their competitors in the informal economy enjoy. Goods purchased formally have certain warranties and can usually be exchanged if defective. Such benefits are a fundamental component of regular market activity. In the informal market, on the other hand, no such guarantees exist, and goods sold are generally of inferior quality.[24]

Ultimately, whether one sees the informal economy as an advantage or a disadvantage depends on one's need and social and economic position in society. The overall impact of the informal economy, however, is that family and individual income fails to keep pace with expenses, employment opportunities in the formal economy are lost, and standards of living decline.[25]

It is important to bear in mind that both the formal and informal economies generally operate within a single national economic unit, but the relationship between the two realms of economic activity is not neatly separable. In fact, they are frequently linked through direct contacts within the private sector, as well as between the public and private sectors. In some countries in which public employment provides fringe benefits, as in the Middle East, public employees also hold a second job in the private sector, often with higher wages.[26] In the 1980s, some large corporations opted for the decentralization and informalization of their production to avoid what they viewed as regulatory burdens on their operations.[27] The informal sector is connected to the formal in other more mundane ways as well. Street vendors earning unreported informal income sell food to workers in factories in the formal economy. Sweatshop producers of shoes and clothes sell their products to firms in the formal economy, which in turn brings them to market. In the early 1970s, about 200 sweatshops operated in the apparel industry in New York City. A conservative estimate, excluding associated branches in New Jersey and neighboring areas, indicated that by the early 1980s that number had increased to 3,000, employing more than 50,000 mostly foreign workers, producing goods for New York City businesses. In New York City's construction industry, during the same period the proportion of unionized workers dropped to 67 percent, and one study of four blocks in Manhattan by the city's Department of Buildings found that 90 percent of all interior work was done without a legal building permit.[28] In Lima, Peru, about 40 percent of workers in the clothing industry and 30 percent in the construction industry in the informal sector provided material for the formal sector.[29] The picture is the same for a large number of sectors—footwear, taxi cabs, furniture, alterations—in which the informal sector provides undocumented services and finished products for businesses in the formal sector.

Despite these linkages, a number of differences between sectors should not be overlooked. The following sections look at some of the prevalent activities in the informal economy within the context of domestic and international political economy.

The Business of Household Services

Household services and production are economic activities performed mostly at home and mainly by women in virtually all industrialized and developing countries. In most national accounts, household labor and the work of homemakers go unreported unless an income statement is filed. Household activities range from the emotional energy, time, and physical labor spent on such activities as childrearing, to shopping for the family's food, to cleaning and laundering, to knitting and tailoring.[30] The Survey Research Center at the University of Michigan listed the following as household services: meal preparation and cleanup, cleaning and gardening, home repairs and hobbies, childcare, the helping and teaching of children, and medical care.[31] It is difficult to assign a price to such activities, and governments have made little effort to quantify and measure their contribution to social and economic development. Economic indicators published by official national and international institutions usually do not account for household activities, and the lack of any serious effort in this regard has led to charges of exploitation of women. "It may be," Ferber and Birnbaum write,

> that in the past some of the resistance to further work on this subject came from those who believed that the "invaluable" contribution of the homemaker would somehow be demeaned by being assigned a monetary value. It is likely, however, that our failure to assign a price for the services of the homemaker has tended to convey the impression that they are valueless rather than priceless.[32]

A controversial question in this issue is, who would pay whom? Nevertheless, a number of studies have experimented with the evaluation of housework to assign a monetary value. Estimates of annual value of housework vary from one study to another, depending on the period covered, the labor market in the country, and the definition of such work. One study, for example, estimated that the average annual value in 1972 was $13,392. Another study for the same year concluded that it was about $4,320; still another estimated $11,890 for 1974.[33]

Further, while children's assistance in housework and their market contribution (for example, tailoring, food sale) are difficult to document, especially if they do not operate at a single location, it is estimated that in countries such as Peru, between 9 and 18 percent of children, from the age of six, work full- or part-time jobs in the formal and informal economies, the latter sector not covered in official employment data. In the 1970s, when Uruguay launched its "monetarist," but politically and economically repressive, strategy to combat the recession, "90 percent of the population in Montevideo maintained its level of family earning due to the incorporation of more of its members into the labor force."[34] Wages for women, however, remained between about 50 percent and 66 percent of men's wages, a figure typical in the industrialized economies as well. Table 12.1 presents some of the estimated values of housework as a percentage of national income for a number of industrialized and developing countries. The figures are estimated measures of variation between the countries, and further improvements in statistics are necessary before these numbers can be used more confidently. They do, however, convey the economic significance of household contribution to national income.

Employment in the Expanding Informal Economy

Since the 1960s and 1970s, in most of the developing world economic development has been concentrated in urban or industrial centers. However, large numbers of people migrating from the rural regions to find jobs in cities were left unemployed and turned to informal sectors. Reports by the International Labor Organization estimate that the figures for informal sector employment range from 20 to over 60 percent of the urban labor force in developing countries (see Tables 12.2 and 12.3). In Lima, for example, in the 1980s nearly 40 percent of the labor force was engaged in the informal sector, including 7 percent comprised of homeworkers. The following estimates are from the Institute for Liberty and Democracy:

> In 1982, some 43 percent of all housing in Lima was built informally, providing shelter to 47 percent of the city's population. The replacement cost of this housing was calculated at US$8.3 billion. In commerce, over 91,000 street vendors supported an estimated 314,000 people and generated gross sales of US$322 million per year. . . . 39,000 other informal merchants built 274 street markets with an estimated value of US$41 million, supporting 125,000 people. In transport, informal entrepreneurs controlled over 90 percent of urban public buses. The 1984 replacement value of their fleet was estimated at US$620 million. The value of the related infrastructure (gas pumps, repair shops, etc.) was estimated at US$400 million.[35]

TABLE 12.1
Estimated Value of Housework Contribution to National Income

Country	Period Examined	Percentage of National Income
Belgium	1972	40
Britain	1956	42
Canada	1961–1971	37
Chile	1981	30
Denmark	1930–1946	17
Finland	1973	16
Germany	1953–1954	36
India	1970–1971	49
Pakistan	1975–1976	35
Sweden	1930	25
United States	1973	24
Venezuela	1982	37

Source: L. Goldschmidt-Clermont, *Unpaid Working in the Household* (Geneva: ILO, 1982), Appendix; L. Goldschmidt-Clermont, *Economic Evaluation of Unpaid Household Work: Africa, Asia, Latin America and Oceania* (Geneva: ILO, 1987), Appendix.
Note: Figures for developing countries refer to GDP; India's refers to NDP (net domestic product).

In the 1980s, the informal sector expanded in Latin American countries (Table 12.3). As the foreign debt crisis forced many of these countries to borrow heavily, their loans were used mostly to finance debts, providing little capital for investments in future development. As jobs in the formal sector disappeared, employment in the informal sector increased. According to an ILO report, "Employment in the urban informal sector rose at a cumulative

TABLE 12.2
Percentages of Working Population in Urban Informal Sector

Country (City)	Year	Percent
Africa		
Burkina	1986	73
Congo (Brazzaville)	1979	37
Djibouti	1980	20
Gambia (Bajul)	1975	42
Ghana (Kumasi)	1974	65
Ivory Coast	1975	44
Kenya (Nairobi)	1972	44
Niger	1976	65
Nigeria (Lagos)	1976	50
Senegal	1976	50
Togo (Lome)	1976	50
Asia		
India (Calcutta)	1971	45
Indonesia (Jakarta)	1976	45
Malaysia	1970	35
Pakistan	1972	69
Singapore	1970	23
Sri Lanka (Colombo)	1971	19
Thailand	1976	26

Source: J. Charmes, "A Critical Review of Concepts, Definitions and Studies in the Informal Sector," in D. Turnham, B. Salome, and A. Schwartz, eds., *The Informal Sector Revisited* (Paris: OECD Research Center, 1990); James J. Thomas, *Informal Economic Activity* (Herfordshire, England: Harvester Wheatsheaf, 1992), p. 67.

TABLE 12.3

Employment in the Informal Sector in Latin America, 1981 and 1985 (Percentage of Employed Labor Force)

Country	1981	1985
Argentina	14.3	24.0
Bolivia	44.0	63.0
Brazil	17.2	30.1
Chile	18.7	22.1
Colombia	25.1	29.2
Costa Rica	10.9	24.2
Honduras	32.7	44.7
Mexico	29.8	45.5
Panama	30.4	37.8
Paraguay	18.3	28.2
Peru	34.7	49.2
Uruguay	15.8	25.5
Venezuela	15.4	28.3

Source: James J. Thomas, *Informal Economic Activity* (Herfordshire, England: Harvester Wheatsheaf, 1992), p. 68.

annual of 6.6 percent between 1980 and 1985 (amounting to an increase of nearly 40 percent), while employment in manufacturing declined at a rate of 2.2 percent (a cumulative loss of over 10 percent). . . . The informal sector played a counter-cyclical role in Brazil, Mexico and Peru."[36]

If the case of Lima can be generalized to most of the developing world, a little over 4 percent of the formal sector, but nearly 13 percent of the informal, worked between sixty-one and eighty hours a week during the mid-1980s. The distribution of their monthly income levels showed great disparities. While 6.2 percent of employees in the formal sector earned the equivalent of $30 per month, about 19.5 percent earned that amount in the informal sector. Nearly 50 percent of the formal sector earned between $75 and $225 per month, as compared with 30 percent in the informal sector.

A main feature of the informal economy in both developing and advanced economies is multiple job-holding, which may involve violating laws and contracts, whereby incomes earned from the second job are not reported for taxation purposes. While estimates vary, multiple job-holding in Canada in the 1970s, for example, was estimated to be from 2 percent to 25 percent of employment in the formal economy, in France about 25 percent, in Italy from about 5 percent to as high as 69.8 percent in the 1970s and the early part of the 1980s, in West Germany 8 percent in the late 1970s, and in the United States from 5 percent to 25 percent in the 1970s.[37] In Italy in the early 1980s the number of people engaged in second employment in the overall economy increased by 2.5 million; in some urban areas, second employment increased to 20 percent of regular employment, 45 percent of which was in the household sector, including repairs, maintenance, and cleaning, and 27.3 percent in small workshops.[38] A large proportion of the second jobs are in the service sector, such as in tourism, catering, and the hotel and restaurant industries. In 1975, in Britain, 86 percent of second jobs were in the service sector, in Belgium 78 percent, in the Netherlands 76 percent, and in the United States 75 percent.[39] Unlike most European countries, however, there are no laws prohibiting "moonlighting" in the United States, and most second incomes probably are reported in national accounts.

While traditionally the majority of second job-holders have been men, since the 1960s, the number of women has increased drastically. In the case of the United States, for example, in the 1960s about 16 percent were women; by the early 1980s that number had increased to 30 percent.[40] Most people hold a second job "to make ends meet." In Italy, 70 percent of respondents to a survey indicated economic need, including earning extra cash for nonbasic needs, as the primary reason. In some cases, a second job improved the family income by as much as 35 percent.[41]

Migration

With the advent of industrialization and urbanization, illegal and internal migrations have fueled the informal economy, especially as easier global communications and transportation systems have led to rapid and unprecedented levels of migration from one country to another. This is not to suggest that immigration invariably results in the development of an informal economy. Immigrants tend to live in their own communities and, to some extent, generate their economic activities internal to the community. That does not in itself constitute an informal economy, however. *Illegal,* or *undocumented,* immigrants tend to work for lower wages than their counterparts in the formal economy, and their labor sustains the underdeveloped sectors in the economy. However, the structures of the informal economy (sweatshops, farms, gas stations) are already in place, whose operations and structural informalization are affected by the economic trends of the time. Immigrants "seize the opportunities represented by informalization," but, contrary to images in the media, "the opportunities are not necessarily created by immigrants."[42]

As with most other issues, migration is subject to various national rules and regulations and to the push and pull of political and economic circumstances. Similar to tax evasion, the stricter the laws to regulate migration, and the greater the economic or political hardship at home, the greater the inclination to migrate illegally. In the industrialized countries, "chain immigration"—members of family in the country of destination encouraging other members to migrate as well—brings people seeking employment and physical security in farm fields or factory towns and urban centers. In some developing and developed countries, migration is seasonal, with people leaving to build up an income and then returning across the border. This movement of labor can be legal, even contracted through government channels, or illegal, perhaps contracted by unscrupulous labor recruiters. Prior to the 1959 revolution, a large number of Haitians and Jamaicans regularly migrated to Cuba during the zafra, sugarcane harvest, probably not always under the best working conditions.[43] In Latin American and African countries, seasonal work continues to provide opportunities for employment. In parts of Africa and Asia, nomadic clans still herd their animals across borders.

Migration has certain advantages and disadvantages from the perspectives of both source and destination countries, as discussed in greater detail in Chapter 8. From the perspective of the source country, one advantage may be that, since those who wish to emigrate are dissatisfied with their living conditions, emigration serves as a "safety valve" and, hence, as a mechanism to diffuse potential threats to the political and economic elites. Emigration also removes some of the economic and political burden on the bureaucracies, especially in times of economic difficulties when unemployment increases, removing surplus labor and thereby reducing demands on social and welfare programs, which in turn releases capital for investments. From the perspective of the country of destination, immigration may bring in new talent and energy and economic renewal and vibrancy; clearly, this is more welcomed through legal than illegal channels, however. What is brain drain for the source country becomes brain gain for the adopted country.

However, there are also a number of disadvantages. Brain drain can be a serious problem for the source country, causing the loss not only of unskilled and unemployable labor but also of skilled labor, educated classes, and owners of capital. In the less tangible milieu, emigration may also diminish the political legitimacy of a country's institutions and leaders at home and its international prestige abroad. For the country of destination, immigration brings in different and unfamiliar cultures, and, as such, immigrants may be perceived as a threat to the local culture and the established order of things. Depending on the local labor market, immigrants may be viewed as adding new burdens to an already stagnant economy and overburdened government bureaucracies and as representing job competition for local citizens, trade unions, and ethnic groups.

Large-scale legal and illegal immigration is not a new phenomenon, and over the years certain cyclical patterns have been apparent. During the period of one century from the 1820s to the 1930s, the United States was the destination for approximately 37 million immigrants, 86.5 percent from Europe.[44] Europe itself experienced its own rising internal migration, especially to Belgium, Germany, France, Britain, and Switzerland. In the early twentieth century, about 800,000 immigrants (16 percent from Italy) sought jobs in the rapidly industrializing Germany. After the First and Second World Wars, German, British, and French governments encouraged immigration for postwar economic reconstruction. The French government signed agreements with a number of neighboring countries to invite foreign workers, and the number increased from 1.4 million immigrants in 1919 to 3 million in 1930. The depression years, however, saw rising hostility toward the foreign workers, and some of them were deported. After the Second World War, reconstruction again required immigrant labor, and Britain, France, and Germany again invited foreign workers. In the case of West Germany, which had received nearly 12 million refugees from what became East Germany immediately after the war, the number of "guest" workers from other European as well as Asian and African countries increased from about 10,000 in the mid-1950s to 2.3 million in the mid-1970s, contributing to an "economic miracle" for the Federal Republic. Social tensions surrounding the "guest workers," some who had lived their entire lives in Germany, rose markedly with neo-fascist and "skinhead" movements in the 1980s as well.

Today, it is estimated that more than 100 million people worldwide are living outside their native countries. Since the 1980s, the number of illegal immigrant workers to the Western countries has increased into the millions. In the United States, for example, that number ranges from 3 to 4 million. In the early 1970s and 1980s, for economic reasons but also because of the resurgence of nationalism and racism, public opinion turned against immigrants, and the Western governments adopted measures to reduce their numbers.

While unions sometimes complain that nonunion foreign workers flood the labor market and force wages down, some businesses in the agriculture and service sectors, which prefer nonunion workers at low wages, oppose government policies to restrict the immigration of foreign workers; increased government restrictions in the 1980s and 90s have led many foreign workers to disappear into the informal labor market, working for even lower wages than before. For example, in Miami, since the 1960s, Hispanic, especially Cuban, immigrants have provided a large share of both formal and informal labor in a number of areas. Many Cubans obviously "made it" in successful business and professional positions, yet, in Miami's garment industry, 85 percent of the workers are Hispanic women, most without union protection. In 1980, a survey by the U.S. Department of Labor found that 132 Miami businesses violated various labor laws, including $180 million in wages owed to 5,000 employees. A common violation was the illegal practice of home work (in the garment industry), which involved from 30 percent to 50 percent of garment production in Miami.[45]

The list of global migrants includes 36 million people in Asia and the Middle East, more than 23 million in Europe, more than 20 million in North America, 10 million in sub-Saharan Africa, 6 million in Latin America and the Caribbean, and 4 million in the Pacific. Among these totals, about 13 million were refugees from war and political oppression in the mid-1980s; by the early 1990s, refugee estimates had topped 19 million. An estimated 70 million people or more have been displaced by political conflicts since 1980. In addition, more than 70 million residents of the former Soviet Union also are now living outside their former homeland, adding to the previous migrant totals.

A very substantial proportion of immigrants go from one LDC to another, adding to the stresses and strains of economic development.[46] Thus, not all transnational migration is from the developing to the developed countries. Since the 1960s, oil-producing countries in the Middle East have been the destination of millions of immigrants, including many skilled workers and teachers, from neighboring Arab countries and increasingly from Asian Islamic countries (as Palestinians who previously had filled the positions came to be viewed as security risks). The Gulf states (Bahrain, Kuwait, Oman, Qatar, Saudi Arabia, and the UAE) were host to 660,000 foreign workers in 1970. That number increased to 1.25 million in the mid-1970s and to 6 million by the early 1980s. Approximately 3.2 million came from other Arab countries and the rest from Asia—the largest share, 1.7 million, from Pakistan.[47]

While the situation differs somewhat with internal migration, the issues with respect to economic problems pertaining to society and government policy are the same. Most internal migrants have little or no education. They migrate with the expectation of finding employment with higher wages in cities and better living conditions, away from and independent of the natural cycles of the agricultural economy. Droughts, floods, and similar natural calamities, agricultural modernization, and political violence (such as revolutions and wars), are incentives to move. Political violence, revolutions, and wars in this century, as in China, caused millions to migrate from the rural areas to the urban centers.[48] However, as in China in recent years, millions also migrated from the rural areas to the cities to profit from expanding urban economies.

Table 12.4 shows the differences between migrant workers and those with more than five years of residence in Bogotá, Colombia. Employment in the informal economy drops and formal employment rises as the length of residence increases. The data for employers indicate that not all rural migrants are poor; some of them become employers as well. Nevertheless, the data make it clear that people with more than five years of residence constitute a large proportion (nearly 87 percent) of the economically active population (EAP) in the city. Table 12.4 also compares the earnings of workers in the informal and formal sectors. The data show a clear relationship between informal employment and poverty. The earnings of about 90 percent of informal workers are less than the minimum wage of C$10,865 (or US$54) per month, while about 70 percent of those in the formal economy earn "the equivalent of more than two minimum wages."[49]

In the case of Mexico, the modernization and mechanization of agricultural production have caused en masse migration to the cities and to the United States. Mexican urban economies have increasingly become capital-intensive, with little opportunity for the unskilled. Where Mexican cities have failed to absorb the migrants into the labor force, U.S. agricultural regions, such as California's farms, have provided that opportunity.[50]

Rural to urban migration places various demands on the government at all levels of society. Effective policies to alleviate such pressures require larger government budgets to provide for housing, education, health, welfare, and, unemployment. In most developing countries, essential infrastructural development is necessary to provide electricity, water and sewerage systems, transportation, communications, and buildings to improve living conditions, yet governments are hardly in a position to finance such projects, even if they had the political will. At one extreme of the spectrum of policy choices, governments prefer to ignore this problem, because extensive government

TABLE 12.4

Labor Market by Length of Residence and Earnings in Bogotá, Colombia

Years of Residence	Informal Workers (%)	Formal Workers (%)	Employers (%)	Total (%)	As Percent of EAP
Less than one	70.3	27.3	2.4	100	2.4
One to two	56.2	42.9	0.9	100	4.3
Three to five	47.2	51.6	1.2	100	6.7
More than five	44.4	52.5	3.1	100	86.6
Earnings					
Below minimum wage	92.0	5.5	2.5	100	26.0
One to two minimum wages	33.0	66.1	0.9	100	48.1
More than two minimum wages	22.9	70.3	6.8	100	25.9

Source: National Department of Statistics (DANE), *National Survey of Households,* March 1984. Data presented by Mónica Lanzetta de Pardo and Gabriel Murillo Castaño, with Alvaro Triana Soto, "The Articulation of Formal and Informal Sectors in the Economy of Bogotá, Colombia," in Alejandro Portes, Manuel Castells, and Lauren A. Benton, eds., *The Informal Economy: Studies in Advanced and Less Developed Countries* (Baltimore: Johns Hopkins University Press, 1989), Tables 5.7 and 5.8, p. 101.

involvement would entail higher taxes on the middle and higher classes, inflationary pressures, and increased borrowing from foreign countries. International Monetary Fund (IMF) conditionality and austerity measures preclude a tilt to overly bloated bureaucracies and budgets. The World Bank has provided loans through its urban projects for improvements in squatter settlements; in the early 1980s, its loans totaled nearly $2 billion and, in the mid-1980s, $4 billion to twenty-eight countries for such projects.[51] At the other extreme end of options, governments may resort to the use of force, often with the support of the middle and upper classes, to evict and even imprison squatters, panhandlers, street children, and the homeless. Eviction is particularly common where new commercial developments, tourist attractions, and road construction are planned. As a result, unless migrants have relatives or friends willing to help them in their transition from rural life, they become "urban refugees" or live in shanty towns on the outskirts of cities. In the mid-1980s, nearly 600,000 people lived on the streets of Calcutta, bedding down in dense groups at night, while it is estimated that in Cairo more than 1 million people lived in cemeteries.[52] Under such conditions, just as in war-torn economies, the informal sector remains their only hope of earning a living.

A related phenomenon in the informal economy is child labor. Virtually all societies have laws prohibiting the employment of children for profit below a minimum age, yet minors are employed in all societies in violation of such laws. In some economic sectors, children are employed to compensate for the lack of sufficient adult labor and in others because the labor involved requires small bodies and fingers, such as in mining and weaving. However, in most cases, children are employed because they are less expensive and do not demand unions and pensions. The estimated total number of children employed under the age of fifteen in the 1970s was between 52 million and 150 million worldwide, but mostly in the developing economies. Still, in the developed countries, their estimated number was near 1.5 million.[53]

The "immorality" of child labor is complicated by the fact that, in poorer societies, children may bring home incomes that keep the family above the subsistence level. Is it better to enforce prohibitions against child labor and deprive those families of income or to allow such labor and to work for effective supervision of working conditions? Many would say that it is imperative that firms be forced to pay adults more, so that children can be children and obtain a proper education. Indeed, similar arguments have been heard in U.S. cities to account for the mushrooming of youths making sizeable incomes in drug trafficking and returning at least part of the money to their families. However, the staggering death tolls of urban youth, and the fact that the "really big" money in drugs is made by criminal syndicates, should alert people to the false benefits of child labor. The U.N. Convention on the Rights and Responsibilities of Children, opened for signature in the early 1990s, is meant in large part to address these economic and physical abuses.

Globalization, Telecommunications, and Tax Evasion: The Expanding Informal Domain

One of the new dimensions of the informal economy has involved the development of telecommunications technologies. The globalization of new technologies and methods of banking, trade, and communications and the instantaneous movement of capital have made regulation of such transactions ever more difficult. Off-shore banking is difficult to regulate, despite the existing banking laws as checks, credit cards, and electronic payments have expanded the *invisible* processes involved in the new global environment. Beepers, cellular phones, and the Internet have added other invisible dimensions to the widening informal economy, but their long-term impact is yet to be seen. Home, office, and international computer networking of complex electronic information on transactions now require far more sophisticated methods for recordkeeping than was possible to imagine even twenty years ago. In fact, recordkeeping itself has become invisible. In the electronic environment, Bose and Gunn write, "Unlike a classic manual fraud, you cannot detect a forged signature or see a changed amount."[54] Computer fraud, from hackers to email fraud and electronic bank robberies, already has become a serious problem in a new telecommunications informal economy, a problem costing millions of dollars yearly.

Unlike illegal immigrants, child labor, and exploitation in sweatshops, the high-technology aspects of the informal economy transcend traditional market structures and defy tracing and controls. Capital and services transmitted electronically through cyberspace, although amenable to quantification, are easily vulnerable to electronic fraud without detection. In the United States, about 300 banks have electronic branches on the Web. Sweden's S-E Banken, one of the country's largest banks, manages about 42,000 electronic transactions a day.[55] Further, off-shore banking practices, made easier via banking secrecy laws and global telecommunications, make it even more difficult to investigate and control transactions,[56] although investigation also can depend on the degree of influence exercised politically and economically by the "white collar" criminals involved in high tech fraud. This newly acquired flexibility explains the growth in off-shore banking. One study has pointed out that "in 1964 the Cayman Islands had two banks and no off-shore operations. By 1981 the Caymans had 360 branches of United States and other foreign banks, over 8,000 registered companies, and more telex machines per capita than any other country in the world."[57]

Businesses are often reluctant to make public reports of the level of fraud in their organizations "to avoid embarrassment, or because the fraud might reduce public confidence in their future activities."[58] Companies use such euphemisms as "stock shrinkage" to denote fraud, and national income accounts do not take such informal activities into consideration. One estimate in the 1970s indicated that, in Britain, "stock shrinkage" involved 2 to 5 percent of the actual value of stocks. In 1974 alone, the "invisible wage package" totaled an estimated £1.3 billion, or 1.8 percent of the GNP, and 12.7 percent of gross trading profits of companies.[59] In the mid-1980s, a survey by the American Bankers Association indicated that, out of 225 banks, over 60 percent admitted they were victims of computer fraud, mostly by insiders, amounting to millions of dollars.

Moreover, electronic banking and commerce have raised a host of questions regarding taxation and regulation for consumer protection against electronic fraud. The Electronic Commerce Policy Group of the Group of 7 (G-7) nations and the DG15 (the market directorate) of the European Commission have been examining the issue of electronic taxation and regulation. It is estimated that firms using the Internet for transactions will increase from 13 percent in 1997 to 60 percent in 1999. Britain's Chartered Institute of Taxation (CIT) has "warned that Britain could lose billions of pounds worth of tax revenue in trading over the Internet."[60] As a first step, it has been proposed that existing copyright laws be extended to cover transactions involving intellectual property items on the Internet. This would be followed by a "bit tax" on data relayed online, a proposal supported by the European Commission but opposed by the Clinton administration.[61] The latter instead has stressed the desirability of extending existing commerce taxes to cover electronic commerce on the Internet. A number of fundamental issues—privacy and taxing "free speech"—still must be addressed.

These issues raise questions as to how and by whom national and international regulatory and taxation policies should be implemented and enforced in cyberspace. Telecommunications enable companies to trade from anywhere in the world; it remains to be seen to what extent governments will compete in creating tax havens and informal sectors to attract enterprises to their shores. It also remains to be seen whether consumers stand to gain from this commercial revolution. For now, however, most governments are expected to increase taxes on consumption and labor, while avoiding cumbersome regulations, so as not to stifle high-technology industries, so critical to global competitiveness. Britain's financial services regulator, the Securities and Investments Board (SIB) has cautioned: "Anyone from anywhere in the world can offer anything for sale. Inevitably . . . there will be false bargains and frauds."[62] Frauds and tax evasion may force governments to return to the old system of taxing land property, a practice that has declined considerably in the twentieth century. In the United States, property taxes as a source of government revenue dropped from 60 percent in 1913 to 10 percent in the mid-1990s (see Figure 12.1).[63]

Thus, it was not surprising that tax evasion emerged as a serious economic problem in the industrialized countries in the 1970s, as governments tried to combat high levels of inflation and unemployment. At the time, it was noted that an increasing number of people and businesses with activities both at home and abroad were not paying taxes on at least part of their income. The total underreported income in the United States increased 51 percent from 1965 to 1969 and 48 percent from 1969 to 1973.[64] In 1976, the IRS estimated that between $13 billion and $17 billion were lost in federal income tax revenues, and in 1979 between $19 billion and $27 billion, almost the equivalent of the federal budget deficit for the year.[65] In the late 1980s, the unreported amount was about $50 billion and, in the early 1990s, nearly $63 billion. According to one estimate, the total tax gap of the underground income, including filers, nonfilers and corporations (excluding criminal transactions), was as high as $230 billion in the late 1980s and over $291 billion 1992.[66]

In comparison with other industrialized economies, in the United States and Germany, between 4 and 12 percent of GNP, as part of individual and corporate incomes, is not reported.[67] In Britain, tax-evaded income is about 3 percent of GNP.[68] Among the high tax rate Scandinavian countries, that figure is nearly 6 percent of Denmark's GNP and 4 to 6 percent in Sweden and Norway. In the countries of Southern Europe, it is even higher, above 20 percent of GNP.[69] The expanding informal sector in services is expected to further increase tax evasion during the rest of the 1990s, although the majority of citizens still pay their taxes and consider public services important.

To address the problem of the globalization of competition, Western governments have attempted to readjust their tax structures in favor of corporations. While prior to the 1940s federal taxes on corporations accounted for about 30 percent (larger than the share of personal tax) of federal revenues in the United States, by the mid-1990s that figure had dropped to 12 percent. In European countries, the tax rate on businesses dropped from nearly 50 percent in the early 1980s to 35 percent in the mid-1990s, while taxes on personal income increased.[70]

In less developed countries (LDCs), however, the tax structures are different, in that indirect (or hidden) and commerce taxes are far more important for government revenues. As a result, tax evasion in LDCs involves a different set of transactions and problems. Property taxes, for example, account for 1 to 5 percent of total government tax revenues and no more than 1 percent of GDP and, therefore, do not constitute an important source of government revenue. Tax avoidance in this case still occurs through undervaluation of property, and landowners easily manipulate the tax system to their advantage. There is, however, in the developing countries a greater reliance on import taxes, which makes smuggling more attractive.[71] According to one estimate, the value of smuggled goods to the Philippines from 1965 to 1975 was 29 percent of total imports. Smuggled goods accounted for nearly 32 percent of total Philippine imports from Japan, 29 percent from the EC, and 26 percent from the United States.[72]

In both developing and developed countries, a similar pattern emerges when one examines the relationship between political power structures and tax evasion. Politically and economically influential groups and their individual members—that is, the political and economic elite—are generally in a position to "manipulate the tax system in their interest."[73] In Latin American countries, for example, large landowners have historically dominated the political scene and, through it, have shaped the tax system.[74] As previously noted, and as described in Box 12.1, telecommunications technologies facilitating the globalization of the informal political economy have created an informal capital sector in cyberspace, and governments have been slow to respond to the tax violations in this sector, even as some Western governments—for example, Germany and the United States—have attempted to check the spread of electronic pornographic literature. Electronic commercial transactions

FIGURE 12.1 Workers Bear the Brunt: OECD Country Tax Revenues, 1965 and 1994.

Source: The Economist, May 31, 1997, p. 22. © 1997 The Economist Newspaper Group, Inc. Reprinted with permission. Further reproduction prohibited.

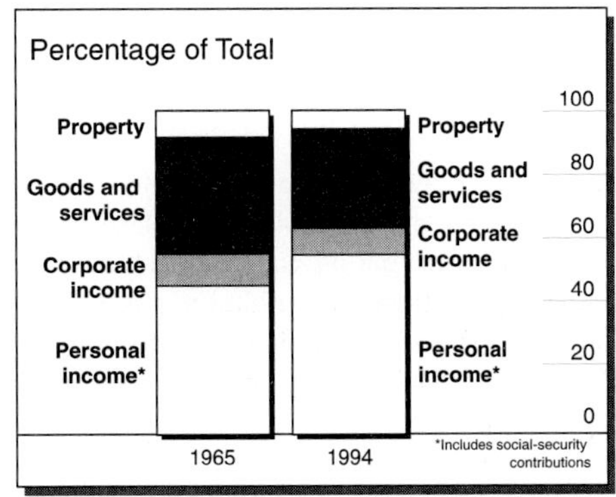

BOX 12.1

GLOBALIZATION AND DISAPPEARING TAX REVENUES

In an aptly entitled article, "Disappearing Taxes," *The Economist* has identified three reasons globalization is a tax problem. First, globalization allows corporations greater freedom to locate their modem-ready laptops anywhere taxes are low. While taxes are not the only consideration for location, the globalization of telecommunications capabilities leads to the intensification of competition among countries to lower taxes on company profits to attract foreign businesses to their shores. Second, globalization complicates the definition of "country of origin" for tax purposes. In addition to official tax incentives, the ability of companies to move production facilities to low-tax countries and to use sophisticated transfer-pricing methods further lowers their tax bills. *The Economist* explains: "By paying inflated prices for components imported from a subsidiary in a low-tax country, a firm can move its taxable profits to that country and so reduce its tax bill. Foreign subsidiaries of American companies report higher profit margins in low-tax countries than in high-tax ones. What a coincidence." Third, globalization also reduces the taxes on individual income. Since more and more people are earning their living abroad, their total income and savings are easier to hide from taxes.

Source: The New York Times, June 3, 1996, A4. "Surveys Rate Nigeria as Most Corrupt Nation for Business."

conducted on the Internet are not yet directly taxable, and firms are likely to capitalize on that.

Clearly, tax evasion has certain perceived advantages. One obvious one is that those who do not pay taxes keep a larger share of their income. A study of tax evasion in Belgium found that it enhanced the income distribution curve for the lower and upper classes.[75] Further, from companies' perspective, especially those engaged in international trade, tax avoidance also entails the avoidance of time-consuming bureaucratic red tape. Companies maintain that avoidance of such financially burdensome formal processes enables them to keep market prices low, or that they pass their profits on to their employees as wages and bonuses.

However, tax evasion also entails severe costs. Costs to government revenues and the loss in social programs have been mentioned. As one study has noted, the estimated $20 billion in lost tax revenues in the United States could have funded veterans' benefits.[76] For society at large, tax evasion results either in increased tax burdens on taxpayers complying with the tax laws or in diminished public services. In most societies, the burden of taxation is overwhelmingly on the middle class. As the Belgian study indicated, the lower classes do not possess sufficient income and resources to make a significant contribution to the state budget programs, while the upper classes possess the financial and political power to escape taxes with impunity. As Figure 12.1 showed, it remains for the middle-class workers to pay taxes to fund programs for the lower classes while compensating for the lost revenues from the upper classes. Between 1981 and 1994, the average tax rate on wages increased from 35 percent to 41 percent, and personal income taxes from these wages constitutes the largest share of government revenues.[77] It comes as no surprise, then, that the 1980s and 1990s witnessed mass "tax revolts" in the Western countries.

Added to the economic problem is the moral aspect of tax evasion. A presidential commission in the United States warned that tax evasion has adverse consequences for the "moral climate of our society."[78] In post-Communist Russia, the deterioration of the moral climate and the *mafiaization* of the political economy in recent years have resulted in the murder of twenty-six tax collectors, while "74 were injured in the course of their work; six were kidnapped, 41 had their homes burnt down."[79] Russia's inability to raise sufficient revenue from its new capitalist elite to pay its foreign debts jeopardizes the country's status with the I.M.F. and other important global institutions.

Figure 12.2 presents the relationship between tax evasion and dissatisfaction with government in the United States between 1973 and 1994, indicating a close correlation between the two variables. Dissatisfaction with government increased in the 1970s, as did unreported income as percentage of adjusted gross income (AGI). During the first part of the 1980s, both variables concurrently declined, increased in the late 1980s, and decreased again in the early 1990s.[80] Fiege has pointed out, "It seems that when taxpayers perceive their public representatives to be dishonest, and when they perceive a decline in the public

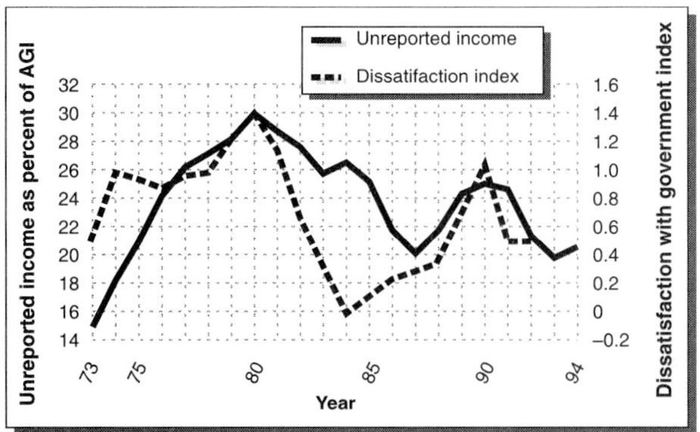

FIGURE 12.2 Unreported Income and Dissatisfaction with Government in the United States, 1973–1994.
Source: Edgar L. Feige, "Overseas Holdings of U.S. Currency and the Underground Economy," in Susan Pozo, ed., *Exploring the Underground Economy: Studies of Illegal and Unreported Activity* (Kalamazoo: W. E. Upjohn Institute for Employment Research, 1996), p. 56.

benefits obtained from their tax dollars, they are more likely to engage in tax evasion."[81]

One result of the invisibility of this type of fraud is that while such problems as illegal immigration, because of their visibility, become a major media and public issue as burdens on a weakening economy, electronic fraud and tax evasion, which could be far more burdensome on the economy and on governments' ability to balance budgets, do not assume the same degree of salience in public debates, precisely because they are not as visible. "Manual" bank robberies frequently appear in the news live via satellite; electronic bank robberies cannot be covered as such and are rarely reported. Detection and regulation of electronic fraud are a more complicated issue and require more sophisticated coverage, as well as a more-educated public.

The Criminal Sector

The informal economy also involves other criminal activities. Tax evasion and electronic fraud as criminal acts differ from such activities as prostitution and drug dealing in terms of public perception; although "white collar crime" is often labeled as "victimless," our analysis of tax evasion certainly shows that there are societal victims. The line of moral and legal demarcation between the two spheres of activities is not always clear, however. The criminal sector can be distinguished from the other sectors in the informal economy in that, in the legal sectors, "criminal activities take place in the production and/or distribution of goods and services that are themselves legal, whereas in the criminal sector the goods and services being produced are illegal"—for example, drugs and prostitution—although neither the use of drugs nor prostitution is totally illegal in every country.[82]

Two schools of thought have addressed the issue of crime. The *orthodox* school, along the lines of liberalism, holds that the developing countries are currently experiencing a historical evolution similar to that of the industrialized societies (for example, Britain and the United States) in the eighteenth and nineteenth centuries. Some studies have suggested a strong relationship between the degree of economic development, especially at the early stages, when there are many social dislocations, and crime rates.[83] The *dependency* school, however, contends that the parallels drawn between the northern and southern historical experiences are misleading, since for the South development and modernization have taken place after the experience of colonialism and within the global context of world capitalist economy, in which there was often massive "disinvestment" of capital from the former colonies as they were granted independence. During the era of colonialism, the colonial powers also used administrative and international law to define what constituted a crime, and colonial laws criminalized a given sector largely to extend colonial monopoly over that sector.[84] Illegal behavior pertaining to taxes (for example, tax evasion and tax avoidance), political corruption, and international organized crime are key components of the informal economy and international political economy, and dependency theorists see them as a product of the unequal and exploitative colonial and postcolonial systems. Orthodox theorists would answer that, no matter what the rationalization historically, the continued existence of these crimes saps the economic and moral health of the developing countries.

State Corruption

Prior to discoveries of the informal economy in the West, the concept of the informal, or second, economy was used by experts on the Soviet economy to describe the economic difficulties in the former Soviet Union—the role of the second economy to alleviate the hardships and its impact on the Soviet polity and public morale. Stealing from government bureaucracies and state organizations, including the *kolkhoz* collective farms, was a common practice in the Soviet second economy. In fact, stealing from the state was so commonplace that Soviets viewed it as an "implicit but integral part" of employment, without which the Soviet economy might have collapsed much sooner than it did.[85] In the early 1980s, Gregory Grossman wrote,

> It [stealing from the state] not only furnishes significant additional income in kind and in money to much of the public, conversely representing a major item of expense for the state, but also provides an important, often indispensable, basis for the second economy. The peasant steals fodder from the kolkhoz to maintain his animals, the worker steals material and tools with which to ply his trade "on the side," the physician steals medicines, the driver steals gasoline and the use of the official car to operate an unofficial taxi; and to all of them income from private activity on the side may be more important than the wage or salary they earn in their official jobs.[86]

For the Communist Party elite, stealing from the state involved the construction of a *dacha* (summer house) in resort areas, the purchase of an apartment, a company car, and international black market trade relations. The black market focused primarily on importation of superior-quality goods, ranging from dishwashers to television sets, from the West, for individual use or to be sold in stores exclusively for the political elite, behind the facade of state-ownership and the "classless society."[87]

Eventually, the inability of the economic and political structures to blend and balance the formal and informal sectors to improve the Soviet standard of living led to the dissolution of the empire in the early 1990s. In the aftermath of the Soviet collapse, many individuals and groups formerly engaged in state corruption became entrepreneurs, facilitating the transition to a market economy. Others, entrenched in national and international criminal networks, emerged in organized crime, making it extremely difficult to stabilize the economy. Among the lessons learned from the Soviet case was the fact that informal processes, despite their lure, could not sustain an economy.

Regarding government corruption, one study has argued that bribery and the sale of government goods add to the income of poorly paid government bureaucrats. Bribery, defined as "private taxation collected by public officials, who wield the effective monopoly from power invested in them to issue permits, licenses . . . for their private gain,"[88] acts as a lubricant for the invisible wheels of economy, enabling companies and individuals to conduct their businesses, bypassing burdensome government regulations.[89] Usually, corruption as such is not punished, because high-level bureaucratic leaders receive payments from low-ranking officials and vice versa. They realize that it is virtually impossible to maintain a family at official income levels. According to this argument, then, corruption contributes to the modernization of developing countries.

However, corruption also saps the resources of the national economy, and, in doing so, it prevents sustainable and equitable economic growth based on sound economic policies and democratic principles. Former Philippine dictator Ferdinand Marcos, as documented after his overthrow in 1986, during his twenty-year rule was rewarded by multinational corporations and foreign governments; in turn, he used "commissions" to establish power and patronage for "economic development." Walter points out that Marcos secretly funded a group of "associates," who maintained monopoly over the country's sugar industry, with a "profit" of about $1.15 billion during the 1975–1984 period. Marcos himself secretly owned copper and gold mining operations and held a monopoly over 40 percent of the country's telecommunications sector. In the 1970s, foreign banks extended billions of dollars worth of loans, and the country's foreign debt increased from $2 billion to $25 billion. Marcos reportedly received 15 percent of the total as a "reward" for his efforts to secure the loans. Westinghouse alone rewarded Marcos $80 million for its contract to construct a nuclear power plant in that country.[90]

A number of countries, including many potentially rich ones in the developing world, under leaders such as Congo/Zaire's former president, Mobutu Sese Seku, have been drained by similar corruption problems. Box 12.2 presents a "New York Times" description of corruption in a number of countries. With the exception of Russia, the top ten most corrupt countries are developing countries, while the ten least corrupt are from among the highly advanced. As a rough indicator of their relative levels of economic development, GNP per capita (in 1992 dollars) for the top ten corrupt countries ranged from $220 (Bangladesh) to $2,910 (Venezuela). The figures for the advanced economies ranged from $12,300 (New Zealand) to $36,080 (Switzerland). These data suggest a correlation between economic development and corruption, although the relationship is not necessarily perfect; indeed, prosperous Swiss banks "neglected" to return millions of dollars of confiscated Jewish wealth deposited there by the Nazis in World War II. U.S. GNP per capita is about $23,240, which is higher than six of the countries (New Zealand, Singapore, Australia, the Netherlands, Canada, and Finland) in the ten least corrupt group, but, as Box 12.2 indicates, the United States, a larger and more diverse nation, ranked 15th in corruption. Neither are Japan, with the second highest GNP per capita ($28,190) in the world, and Germany ($23,030) among the ten least corrupt. Obversely, not all LDCs have high rates of corruption.

BOX 12.2

NIGERIA RATED MOST CORRUPT NATION FOR BUSINESS IN 1996

Nigeria tops the list of countries that international business people consider the most corrupt, according to a ranking published Sunday by a Berlin-based independent organization, Transparency International. Fifty-four countries involved in international business are ranked by Transparency International in its second annual corruption index. The rankings are based on results from 10 surveys made by management and risk-analysis organizations as well as on information volunteered by representatives of international companies through the Internet. After Nigeria, business people ranked Pakistan, Kenya, Bangladesh, China, Cameroon, Venezuela, Russia, India and Indonesia as the most corrupt countries. The 10 least corrupt countries this year were New Zealand, Denmark, Sweden, Finland, Canada, Norway, Singapore, Switzerland, the Netherlands and Australia. The United States was judged the 15th-least-corrupt place, with a slightly worse reputation than Israel but better than Austria. The findings, stored and analyzed at Goettingen University in Germany, report perceptions of people in international business, mostly from industrialized nations, who deal regularly with foreign companies and governments.

Source: Thomas L. Friedman, *The New York Times,* December 8, 1996, E15. "Big Mac I."

Furthermore, since most developing countries lack a large set of welfare programs, fraud in this sector is relatively a minor part of the informal economy. Instead, government funds diverted through state-owned companies and through subsidies and credits to private businesses contribute to the larger proportion of the informal sector. According to a World Bank report, most governments in developing countries devote a large share of their expenditures to economic services—economic development, job creation, support for businesses, and funds to rectify regional imbalances. In the mid-1980s, the government of India spent 23 percent of its annual budget in this area; Mexico, Morocco, Pakistan, and Zimbabwe spent about 26 percent; Kenya spent 28 percent; Bangladesh spent 42 percent; and the Philippines spent 45 percent. In comparison, British and U.S. government expenditures in economic services totaled only about 9 percent. Thus, in the developing economies, the distribution of government funds, such as development project contracts and subsidies given to relatives and clients of top ministry officials, fuels the informal sector, while in the developed countries this sector generally is fueled through other channels, such as bribery and criminal syndicates.[91]

International Organized Crime

Organized crimes involve a vast range of activities too numerous to be discussed here in any appreciable detail. However, a number of areas are directly related to the international political economy. Here we focus on international organized crime.[92] Similar to debates regarding the impact of nuclear technology as rendering the nation-state "permeable," analysts have suggested that the tentacles of transnational organized crime in the 1980s and 1990s raise the specter of rendering the nation-state permeable to threats ranging from drugs to terrorism in the twenty-first century.[93]

One early form of organized crime involved *mafia* activities, as developed in southern Italy. When the traditional feudal structures began to disappear, the mafia, based on family crime syndicates, filled the political vacuum created by the absence of strong institutions, particularly in rural areas. With the subsequent emergence of the nation-state in the nineteenth century, mafia organizations already were in place, commanding sufficient loyalty among the local populous and, thus, were able to exert influence on the newly emerging political class and institutions. The symbiotic relationship as developed between the mafia, representing the ruling economic elite, and the politicians led to the creation of a powerful elite opposed to changes in the status quo and to social and economic reforms as proposed by unions, democrats, and Communists. This relationship between the mafia and conservative politicians has been sustained well into the late twentieth century, as seen by shocking revelations of high-level criminal-governmental conspiracies in post–World War II Italy (note, though, that no party, whether of the left or right, has been entirely immune to mafia contacts). Mafia operations rapidly spread first from the countryside to the cities and then across international borders, forming strong syndicates of organized smuggling, money laundering, prostitution, and drug running, encompassing both industrialized and developing countries.

In the nineteenth and twentieth centuries, some immigrants from Europe in New York, Boston, Chicago, and other big cities, seeking a quick route to American riches, engaged in various criminal activities, combined with political struggles for "turf," as the Irish did through Tammany Hall. In the early decades of the twentieth century, Sicilian mafia groups in New York formed the Unione Siciliana, which organized gambling and loansharking operations in a number of other cities. In 1917, the passage of the Eighteenth (Prohibition) Amendment prohibiting the production, sale, and consumption of alcohol, instead of eliminating drinking, led to the development of vast domestic and transnational illegal bootlegging operations and the intensification of inter-gang competition. In addition to Sicilians, Lupsha writes, the leadership of post-Prohibition "organized crime in the United States tended to be dominated by an Italian-American-Jewish coalition. . . . Charles 'Lucky' Luciano's group appeared paramount over all other so-called 'La Nostra' groups, and with its multi-ethnic leadership mix, it acted as the link connecting Jewish and Italian organized crime across the United States."[94] As more ethnic groups migrated from different regions, however, the predominance of the older ethnic syndicates was lost to Cuban, Mexican, South American, Asian, Russian, and Middle Eastern groups.

It is important to point out that such criminal behavior is not limited to mafia-type illegal organizations. Governments used similar operations as part of their foreign and domestic policies and intelligence operations, and the line between politics and crime can be blurred. In the nineteenth century, the British used opium as part of their colonial gunboat diplomacy to conquer China, which led to the Opium Wars of the 1830s and 1840s. In the United States, smuggling and drug operations have existed since colonial times. The Hancock family of Boston ran some of the most important smuggling operations in the colonies at the time. "This violated British law, but made them so popular among the colonists" that John Hancock became one of the leaders of the independence movement.[95] After the Second World War, American officials toyed with installing mafia bosses to rule southern Italy in order to forestall the Communists' coming to power. In the 1940s and 1950s, organized crime expanded with strong narcotics and gambling connections to Cuba, especially under the Batista regime, and, by the 1990s, a long history of U.S. governmental connections with illegal, often drug-connected operations in Latin America, the Caribbean, and Asia had been exposed.

After the Second World War, drug use and addiction in the United States and elsewhere increased substantially, and by the 1960s and 1970s it had become a serious social and economic scourge. Production and marketing of narcotic drugs stimulated rural economies that otherwise would not have been able to generate the same levels of income through agricultural production. In the meantime, the traditional local peasant economies, as in Bolivia, Colombia, parts of Lebanon, and the "golden triangle" of Southeast Asia, became heavily commercialized in drug production and integrated into the world economy.[96] Such a transition toward commercialization required infrastructural development, not only for production but also for export and import. It is highly unlikely that such infrastructures would develop without government—that is, police, armed forces, and bureaucracies—support, or at least complicity.[97]

In fact, it is not clear to what extent governments have been serious in combatting domestic and international commerce in drugs and in promoting antidrug education and treatment. Intermingling among organized crime, drugs, and politics has been an integral component of domestic economies and foreign policies. In Indochina in the 1940s and the early 1950s, the French were heavily engaged in the region's opium trade to gain local alliances against the anticolonial movements seeking independence from Paris. During the Vietnam War, the CIA financed and operated a similar program, and "the CIA-backed Chinese Kuomintang Army increased the Burmese hill-tribes' opium production tenfold—from 40 to 400 tons per annum by 1962. The opium from the Shan and Kachin states was loaded from mule caravans on to unmarked CIA Air America and Sea Supply Corporation aircraft, whence it was flown to be refined and exported from Bangkok and Hong Kong."[98] As debated in Congress, the CIA has been charged with—but denies—involvement in the peddling of drugs in largely African-American communities in major cities, such as Los Angeles, to finance allies in its anti-Communist Central American wars in the 1980s.[99]

While Washington has devised drug "interdiction" operations, spraying farmers' fields and offering financial support for alternative crops in drug-producing countries, international drug eradication efforts often have been half-hearted and contradictory and seemingly generated for symbolic and political-bureaucratic reasons.[100] On the drug "supply side," the production of coca, opium, and marijuana is a major industry in some societies, contributing considerable sums to the local rural economies, although, as with most other operations in the informal sector, it is difficult to present concrete data. On the "demand side," estimates of the annual income generated from drug sales in the United States in the 1970s ranged from $13 billion to $18 billion, about 1.2 to 1.6 percent of the national income. In the 1980s, total income from organized crime activities, such as drug selling, pornography, prostitution, illegal gambling, and loansharking, ranged from $22 billion, or about 2 percent of national income, to nearly $50 billion, or 4.4 percent, to $69 billion, or about 5 percent, per year.[101]

The globalization of organized crime operations and the international distribution of cocaine and other drugs have changed the worldwide structure of the informal sector. While prior to the 1960s the Italian and French "connections," extending from Palermo to New York, were the primary networks for smuggling drugs, during the past three decades Asian and Latin American drug production and smuggling have emerged as major competitors. As one observer has noted, perhaps this explains the relative decline of La Cosa Nostra in the United States and Europe.[102] Internationalization of drug operations also has changed the financial structures in some countries, as the expanding narco-dollar sector, in turn, has led to "the growing informalization of the financial sector."[103] Regarding the role of the drug industry in the Bolivian economy, for example, one observer noted that

> the cocaine boom has contributed to the "dollarization" of the Bolivian economy, swelling the currency black market. This has reinforced the informal market for credit. . . .
>
> Inflationary pressures during the period 1982–1985 produced demand for large amounts of circulating currency. Coca production and basic paste started to be paid in dollars. At the same time, peasant families saw dollars as a good means for protection of savings in the midst of galloping inflation. . . . Dollars became common currency in Bolivia, allowing the state to save on manufacture of paper money. The same process slowed down the excessive circulation of Bolivian pesos at a time when attempts were being made at containing inflation. Obsolescence followed the emission of paper money: in 1982 the highest denomination was one hundred pesos; by 1985, it was ten million.
>
> With such high levels of inflation, the circulation of dollars allowed the Bolivian economy to function.[104]

In fact, at the time it was estimated that 80 percent of the dollars in the Bolivian economy entered the country via the drug industry.[105]

Smuggling

Smuggling has a long history, at least as long as custom duties have been charged and borders patrolled. During the centuries of colonial competition for resources and markets, the Spanish, Portuguese, Dutch, British, and French empires used various smuggling strategies, including spices, spies, and weapons, to undermine others' monopolies in Asia, Africa, and the Americas. As Thomas has pointed out, "What has changed with time is the technology of smuggling, so the idea that it principally involves the individual hiding the odd bottle of whisky for personal use or small boats landing contraband on deserted beaches is long outdated."[106] This type of smuggling, however, has not disappeared completely. When the Canadian government raised taxes on cigarettes, smuggling across the U.S.-Canadian border became so pervasive that Ottawa eventually retreated.[107]

Smuggling in the twentieth century has been dominated by major companies using both modern technologies and modes of transportation and accounting to avoid taxes and customs duties. Containerization of ship cargoes, for example, has made it easier for import-export businesses to hide (in huge containers and in their accompanying invoices), undervalue, or overvalue goods, as dictated by the tax laws of the governments involved.[108] One indication of smuggling is found in the import-export data between two trading countries. Where the figures for one country's imports do not equal its trading partner's exports, the discrepancy to some extent may be attributable to error, but it also points to at least the suggestion that smuggling, and the diversion of goods to other countries, might be a factor.[109]

In the developing world, smuggling operations involve illegal products, such as drugs, but also legal agricultural and industrial products, as well as arms. Although Africa has not been an important source of illegal drugs, it has supplied other smuggled products. Poaching and smuggling of ivory for the East Asian and Western markets have come to public attention in recent years. This practice threatens the very survival of African elephants, with dire implications for the region's ecological well-being and tourist industry. In northern Cameroon, cattle smuggling is common among the Fulbe tribe. In Sierra Leone, diamond smuggling is a major industry, as are the Ghana-Ivory Coast-Togo and Nigeria-Dahomey cocoa-smuggling connections.[110]

In Asia, organized gangs and war lords have existed for centuries. In China, Japan, and Southeast Asia (Burma, Laos, Thailand, Vietnam), heroin production and smuggling became an important part of local economies, especially in the nineteenth and twentieth centuries with the advent of European colonialism. In Burma alone, smuggling activities have involved more than 500 metric tons of opium per year in recent years.[111] Operations of such magnitude by powerful, autonomous groups working near international borders in the mountains and countryside render government eradication programs virtually impotent, even if government officials had no financial and political ties to such groups. However, negotiations with certain of these groups appears to have produced agreements to control some of the traffic.

The Middle East also has been a major source of opium and cannabis for the Western markets. As in most major production operations, rich landlords have organized vast networks for production and smuggling of drugs, with the attendant bribes of local politicians and police. Before the Second World War, Iran, Lebanon, Syria, and Turkey were major producers of opium, with connections to Italian and French smuggling syndicates. Their operations, as a significant part of their local economies, continue to this day, although the political economy of oil and containment of the Soviet Union after the Second World War hid this issue under the heavy East–West ideological rhetoric. During the Lebanese civil war in the 1970s and 1980s, with the drug trade substituting for other legitimate forms of business,

> struggles for the huge profits from the drugs trade underlie a much greater proportion of the present fighting than is generally recognized: hashish is the country's major export crop, but heroin is catching up fast. High quality opium as well as hashish is transported in bulk from the Bekaa Valley by heavily armed Syrian and other syndicates. The profits provide both foreign exchange for Syria and weapons for warring Christian Phalangists and Palestinian groups alike. Tanks and patrolling sentries protect plantations of hashish in the Hermil Hills near the border with Syria.[112]

In South Asia, India and Afghanistan have remained among the largest producers of opium in the world, and increasingly showed up among the largest producers of heroin as well. These businesses gained political prominence in the late 1990s as Afghanistan's Taliban Islamic forces offered to crack down on narcotic farming in return for UN recognition as the legitimate Afghan government. While regionally Latin America is the principal source of foreign drugs to the United States, Asia is the principal source to Europe, with India as a primary transit route. According to one estimate, in 1983, 23 percent of the heroin imported by Britain originated in Pakistan and Afghanistan and was transferred through India. In 1985, that figure was 49 percent and, in 1986, 70 percent.[113]

Capital Flight

Another form of illegal or semilegal economy is the smuggling of funds from one country to another for lower taxes, secure banking, and safer investments in legal and illegal operations. Both legal and illegal capital flight pose a serious problem, particularly for the national economies of Russia and the poorer developing countries. Between the mid-1970s and mid-1980s, more than $200 billion left the developing countries for offshore assets.[114] Capital flight from Argentina totaled between $17.3 and $26 billion, from Brazil $12.5 to $18.7 billion, from the Philippines $3.7 to $5 billion, and from Venezuela $22.8 to $30.5 billion.[115] Mentioned earlier was the looting by a number of dictators. For example, Jean-Claude Duvalier of Haiti was estimated to have taken between $200 and $500 million when his government was overthrown in 1986. Anastasio Somosa, former ruler of Nicaragua, held an estimated $500 million in foreign investments when he was overthrown in 1979. Ethiopia's Emperor Haile Selassie had about $15 billion, Zaire's President Mobutu Sésé Séko $4 billion, and the Philippines' Ferdinand Marcos between $5 and $10 billion when he was overthrown in 1986.[116] The following quote regarding the papers uncovered by the government of Cory Aquino after the revolution indicates the extent of Ferdinand and Imelda Marcos' foreign assets and wealth:

> Papers left behind in Malacañang Palace gave helpful leads. There were 75 file cabinets of documents (not to mention three paper shredders apparently broken through overuse) containing information on Liechtenstein foundations, Netherlands Antilles corporations, Hong Kong moneychangers and coded Swiss accounts; there were statements relating to eight Swiss banks and 15 trusts, two with bond portfolios worth over $25 million, another two with cash of over $115 million and one with blue chip stocks and shares totalling some $65.5 million. . . . The Malacañang papers suggested that large sums were in Switzerland. Estimates for cash held in Swiss accounts begin at a modest $80 million and reach as high as $3 billion. . . . In addition to New York property, the Marcoses appear to have land in Texas worth $1.5 billion, as well as property in the United Kingdom administered through the Cayman Islands and valued over $4 million.[117]

Noting that the total value of the Marcoses' loot was as high as $10 billion, Walter added,

> It is sobering to realize that such figures represent several times the Philippine national budget, which for 1985 was $3.1 billion. Interesting too is that under the Constitution the annual salary of the President was $4,700, and that at the time the Marcoses fled the country, 70 per cent of Filipinos were living below the Philipino [sic] poverty standard, as opposed to 48 per cent in 1965 when Marcos became President.[118]

Capital flight also involves drug monies leaving the narco-markets via money-laundering operations. It is estimated that in one year (1981) alone, 86 percent of the formally reported $155.2 million worth of financial transactions to Panama involved drug-related activities.[119] This is hardly a success story, considering that annually $20 to $30 billion worth of drug-related international transactions take place in the Caribbean region alone. In 1985, it was estimated that "the volume of illicit currency through US financial institutions every year [is] $100 billion, of which $40–80 billion is attributed to drug money (compared to $4 billion in 1974)."[120] These "industries" have thrived in countries too poor or dependent on foreign capital to afford alternate viable legitimate business opportunities.

INTERNATIONAL MECHANISMS FOR CONTROL OF THE INFORMAL ECONOMY AND THE RESOLUTION OF POTENTIAL CONFLICTS

The informal economy has been a part of human history, and its structures and practices have evolved with the political and economic conditions of the times.[121] In recent years, partly because of the failure of individual governments to address the negative consequences of the informal economy, international organizations have made a greater effort to fill the policy void, usually, however, with little success. The United Nations itself generally has not been directly involved in this area and has virtually avoided hands-on intervention. Some agencies, such as the international police network, Interpol, have intervened, but governments generally have relied on the principle of sovereignty to deal with various aspects of the informal economy. This section discusses a number of unilateral, bilateral, and multilateral approaches.[122]

The Unilateral Track

Laws, such as the Acts of Enclosure, adopted by the British Parliament during the industrial revolution, contributed to the delineation of the legal and illegal, formal and informal spheres of economic activity. Prior to this law, it was accepted practice to allow peasants and the poor to "graze cattle on common land and collect manure, to collect wood for repairs and fuel, to cut peat and turf for fuel."[123] The Enclosure Acts changed the legal status of such activities, as common land, in economic terms what are referred to as a form of "collective goods" available to all, became property. As a result, the traditional practice of using common land became trespassing, wood collecting became theft, and the peasants and poor moved to expanding factory towns as labor. However, as Ditton has noted, the culture of using the factory as a "common land" did not entirely disappear. White-collar and blue-collar employees continued to take home whatever they could without being detected, which led company owners to introduce preventative measures, such as hiring security staff, conducting searches, and installing monitoring systems.[124] Passage of laws alone, therefore, cannot fully solve problems driven by economic incentives, temptation, and desperation.

As the world's major power and largest single economy, the United States has both more capability than other states to try to regulate the informal economy and a tradition of respecting privacy, which limits regulation. As a way of controlling illegal activities, governments today monitor domestic and international financial transactions. Under the Currency and Foreign Transactions Reporting Act of 1970 (CTR), for example, the U.S. federal government requires banks to report all (including telex) deposits over $10,000 in cash. As Walter has noted, however, this law has proved ineffective, especially with respect to off-shore banking, and it has been further weakened by the Right to Financial Privacy Act of 1978, which prohibits the exchange of financial information on bank clients between government agencies. Although the Treasury Department has granted greater authority to the U.S. Customs Service to inspect arriving and departing travelers, only a small number of departing travelers file CTR forms.[125]

In the 1980s, the U.S. government implemented a number of programs dealing directly with drug trafficking. In 1980, the U.S. Treasury and Justice Departments introduced *Operation Greenback* in Miami and, in 1984, *Operation Tracer* in Puerto Rico to investigate banks and clients showing irregular large transactions and to apprehend those engaged in criminal activities. Legal, administrative, and political complications led to failure, however, and, despite the occasional "drug bust," similar strategies neither stopped illegal transactions nor eradicated drug production at home or abroad as long as demand generated a lucrative market.

Neither have other governments been notably successful in these respects. The Canadian government, under the auspices of the Inspector-General of Banks, has required Canadian banks to pay close attention to unusual and large transactions, especially in their dealings with U.S. and Caribbean banks and customers. Since 1982, the Italian government has granted authority to local officials to investigate suspicious transactions, specifically to check mafia operations. In Britain, the government, under a number of such laws as the Forfeiture Act, has widened the scope of involvement by banks to report on financial irregularities.[126] These efforts have not produced encouraging results.

In the developing countries, governments are hardly in a better position. In the 1980s, a number of such countries also introduced plans to monitor domestic and international transactions. In 1985, the Indonesian government signed a contract with the Société Générale de Surveillance (SGS) of Geneva to investigate import-export certifications, payments of credit, and price checks on imports and exports to ensure that taxes are collected and customs duties are paid and to prevent illegal money-laundering transactions. Discoveries of huge unreported financial holdings by the ruling Suharto family in 1998 showed the hypocrisy of such efforts, however. Some African countries, including Angola, Nigeria, and Zaire, adopted similar regulatory policies. In Mexico, the largest foreign supplier of narcotics to the United States, the government and the ruling PRI Party, including the top leadership in enforcement agencies, have had close ties with the drug industry, as have government officials, including judges and police, in Colombia, Bolivia, and Peru. Some governments, such as Peru, Ecuador, and Brazil, have sought U.S. assistance in combatting the drug industry in their countries. Critics, however, have charged that governments in Latin America and the United States are using the "war on drugs" as a pretext to attack leftist movements challenging the status quo in the region. Moreover, they argue, in the absence of the Cold War, the war on drugs justifies military support and engagement. The fact remains that, where the potential for quick wealth exists, policies to control corruption, even if genuinely enforced, have not been very successful.[127]

The Bilateral Track

Since the 1970s and 1980s, bilateral efforts have sought to stop illegal activities involving capital flight and international organized crime, but the results have been mixed at best. The United States has signed a number of treaties with European, Asian, and Latin American governments to control the flow of illegal drugs and capital. In the 1970s, such treaties were signed, for example, with Canada, the Netherlands, Thailand, and Turkey. In the mid-1980s, under pressure by a number of governments to check the spread of international capital flight, the government of the Cayman Islands, one of the major centers of global off-shore banking with strict secrecy laws, agreed to cooperate with foreign governments to release confidential banking information; Switzerland also made similar ad hoc agreements. However, certain restrictions apply. Cayman treaties with the United States, for example, stipulate that records will be disclosed only if Washington can provide sufficient evidence of drug and other illegal activities, including tax evasion, related to the funds under investigation. Similar U.S. agreements were signed with the governments of Bermuda and the Bahamas. Other governments, however, refused to cooperate, partly because of the implication such treaties bear for national sovereignty and in part for the potential costs to their economies. The British Virgin Islands and Panama, for instance, repeatedly refused to collaborate with foreign governments in these areas.[128]

Critics have charged that major countries, such as the United States, use bilateral agreements to expand their legal jurisdiction beyond their borders as they attempt to solve their domestic problems. Regarding the failure of a U.S. tax treaty with the Netherlands Antilles, one observer noted that "the [U.S.] Treasury [Department] was playing macho about its efforts to make other jurisdictions play by U.S. rules on information sharing. . . . We have the sense that the various departments of the government—Treasury, the Securities and Exchange Commission, the State and Justice departments—have all sorts of aides racing around the world trying to impose regimes under which the U.S. can monitor and control capital moving into and out of the country."[129]

The Multilateral Track

In the late 1970s, as the issue of the informal economy was placed on the national agendas of the Western countries, the OECD responded by authorizing its Fiscal Affairs Committee (FAC) to examine the various problems involved, including tax evasion and related criminal activities. In its report, the FAC stressed the need to strengthen and to make more frequent use of international and multilateral conventions and methods to combat domestic and transnational tax evasion.

In the early 1980s, the Council of Europe assigned the Committee of Experts on Tax Law to look into the issue and to prepare a draft convention. The twenty-one-member council adopted a convention, entitled "The Draft Convention on Mutual Administrative Assistance in Tax Matters," in 1987. The convention provides for "automatic" mutual cooperation in the investigation of individual and corporate tax irregularities and the recovery of taxes, transnational access to tax accounts as well as sharing of tax information, and the authority "to confiscate property owned by a taxpayer who is a resident of another country even if the . . . case is still in dispute in his home country."[130]

This convention proved quite controversial. While its major proponents, the United States, Britain, France, and the Scandinavian countries, viewed it as a significant step toward greater cooperation in this area, other countries (Austria, Belgium, Ireland, Italy, Portugal, and Liechtenstein) either extended lukewarm support or expressed their strong opposition (Switzerland, Germany, and Luxembourg). The International Chamber of Commerce, an interested NGO, opposed the convention even more vehemently and warned that it risked "endanger[ing] the profitability and confidentiality of trans-border commercial dealings between companies."[131] It remains to be seen to what extent the unification of the European Union's monetary system will lead to greater harmonization of taxation and banking laws, and whether unification will lead to more effective mechanisms to prevent tax evasion and other international criminal activities.

Regarding multilateral efforts in the developing countries, it has been proposed that international financial organizations, particularly the International Monetary Fund, can assume a more active role in the area of monitoring international financial transactions. Rather than devise new institutions, it is argued, the IMF can use its technical competence and experience to institute various training and investigatory programs to monitor financial transactions worldwide. Moreover, the rationale for IMF involvement is that, because tax evasion, capital flight, fraud, illegal drugs, and various aspects of the informal economy cause or are symptoms of government economic mismanagement and maldistribution of resources between the rich and the poor, the IMF can be more directly and legitimately involved to check violations of domestic and international laws and standards. The organization's ability to impose its *conditionality rules* on governments in the 1980s and 1990s make the argument for an expansive role for the IMF more credible.

Critics, however, point to the fact that the IMF has opposed distributive and redistributive policies and has shown little concern for the problems associated with the maldistribution of resources between the rich and the poor, often a source of corruption. Further, they contend, the IMF's procapitalist and probusiness philosophy would lead to monitoring strategies more favorable to powerful MNCs and governments in the informal economy while further limiting the benefits of a minimum income and employment for the poor. We have already seen that it is debatable whether the informal economy helps or hurts the poorest classes in a society. In October 1979, for example, the Third European Regional Conference of the International Labor Organization passed a resolution to eliminate multiple job-holding.[132] One does not know what position the IMF and those wanting either to limit the informal economy or to make job opportunities more available to the working poor would take on such a resolution.

The UN Track

Some view the United Nations as the most representative organization to address the informal economy. Although the United Nations has taken steps to deal with some aspects of the informal economy, its efforts are in the formative stages, with no comprehensive international rules and standards or enforcement mechanisms. Rather, the UN has opted for an incremental, piecemeal standard setting approach. For example, in 1983, it introduced the Guidelines for International Cooperation to Combat International Tax Evasion and Avoidance. A year later, the UN General Assembly took steps to prepare a draft convention against illegal drugs. The draft convention, prepared by the UN Commission on Narcotic Drugs, was presented to the General Assembly in 1986. The convention stipulated greater cooperation among nations to take preventative measures against drug trafficking and money laundering. As with the Council of Europe's convention previously discussed, this one also stressed the need to share financial information between governments in order to trace and control illegal transactions. Also as with the Council of Europe's convention, the enforceability of UN conventions with respect to these issues is highly suspect. Governments' and the banking industry's cooperation with UN agencies in such areas cannot be assumed to develop overnight, and piecemeal methods would fail to impress on opium and cocaine producers to reveal or terminate their lucrative enterprises. Greater and more direct efforts toward the enforceability of UN strategies are vital, but are likely to be resisted by governments as a challenge to their sovereignty.

CONCLUSION

Whether the informal economy hinders or stimulates economic development and growth has been a controversial issue. Although some argue that the informal sector makes a significant contribution to economic development, the informal economy, especially the more technologically driven forces of globalization, has serious negative consequences for working-class people and taxpayers. Workers in both the formal and informal sectors contribute to the national economy, but those in the latter sector provide a cheaper pool of workers and cheaper goods for resale.[133] As such, the informal sector enables businesses in the formal sector to retain a greater share of their profits, augmenting their pool of investment capital. In the advanced industrial countries, the reliance on telecommunications technologies to maintain the competitive edge has thus far prevented any direct regulation and taxation of electronic transactions involving billions of dollars worth of electronic commerce, as well as fraud.

For developing economies, especially those with large international debts, expanding employment levels in the informal sector during the 1980s, as was seen in Table 12.3, provided a "safety valve" to alleviate unemployment pressures. In their turn, while in the past governments passed rules and regulations discouraging or even attempting to eliminate the informal economy as a waste of economic resources and a loss to government revenues, in recent years some governments have begun to encourage, or at least tolerate informal practices. With the tilt toward privatization and globalization, some governments have and related bureaucratic constraints than to address social and economic problems related to unemployment.[134]

Chapter Summary

The informal economy, defined as unregulated economic and financial transactions and activities not registered in national accounts, constitutes an important but opaque part of international political economy. Informalization is the process by which a share of an economic sector is transferred from the formal to the informal economy. With globalization, the world economy has witnessed an expansion of the informal economy in the traditional economic sectors (services), but also into new areas, especially telecommunications.

Informal sector activities include household services, unofficial employment in the service sector, undocumented or illegal migrant labor, tax evasion, state corruption, organized crime, smuggling, and capital flight. They involve professionals, and skilled and unskilled labor, in various economic sectors, including services and production, business operations, trade, communications, and transportation. Institutions engaged in the informal economy range from major corporations, small businesses, government agencies, and the self-employed to criminals and prisoners.

Reasons for the informal economy in the industrialized and developing economies include reactions to taxation, regulation, prohibition, corruption, international competition, industrialization, and world economic crises.

The informal economy benefits society in a number of ways. It provides individuals employment for extra income, goods at lower costs, while businesses gain greater flexibility in their operations based on less expensive labor. The informal economy also acts as a shock absorber in times of economic contraction and unemployment, absorbing potential social and political tensions. In addition, in international relations, informal economic relations provide opportunities for cooperation among governments.

The informal economy has many disadvantages as well. Informal economic activities render governments less effective in the management of national economies. Equally serious is the problem of tax evasion, whereby economic activities in the informal sectors deprive governments of revenue to fund national and local budgets and social programs, and impose heavier burdens on tax payers. Informalization has led to the fragmentation and "decollectivization" of labor, which in turn has weakened trade unions. Disadvantages for businesses operating within the informal economy include an unstable supply of employees and materials, risks involving confiscation by the state, and potential penetration by organized crime. In times of intense domestic and international competition or economic disruption, as well as competition between the formal and informal sectors, businesses nevertheless often resort to informalization to secure their profit margins.

While it is generally agreed that household activities contribute significantly to national economies, official economic indicators do not account for such activities. Critics argue that lack of official recognition of and lack of pay for housework is exploitation of women.

Migration, in the form of illegal immigrants or internal domestic migration, further expands the informal economy, as migrants work for low wages in sweatshops, farms, and enterprises unregulated by government. Nevertheless, in most cases, the informal sector remains their only hope of earning a living. A related problem concerns the prevalence of child labor.

A new phenomenon in the informal economy is the development of telecommunications technologies, which has facilitated the globalization of informal economies through new and more sophisticated methods of banking, trade, and communications and the instantaneous movement of capital, making regulation and taxation of such transactions more difficult.

State corruption is an old phenomenon, and the modern state is no exception. Governments usually do not act aggressively enough to prevent corruption (in the form of bribery, for example) because for officials it can be an important source of income, supplementing their official salaries. Moreover, some view corruption as desirable to lubricate the wheels of bureaucracy and as a way of encouraging economic development. Corruption, however, can be detrimental to the national economy and public morale, especially since people are aware that not only criminals but also politicians are frequently engaged in criminal activities, such as smuggling.

Globalization of the international political economy also has led to the internationalization of organized crime, as mafia-style operations have expanded from regional to worldwide operations. In the process, the structure of international organized crime also has changed, from the monopoly of a few syndicates to a large number of competitors from various regions of the world.

A number of approaches to control informal sector activities, especially by organized crime, are available. They involve unilateral, bilateral, and multilateral actions, including those of the United Nations; however, thus far, they have not been overly successful.

Points of Contention

Under what circumstances would employment in the informal economy be desirable, and under what circumstances would it be necessary?

Can you identify informal sectors in your community? What factors in your community would lead to the development of new informal sectors? How does globalization of the informal economy affect such activities in your community?

Should household labor—childbearing, shopping for the family's food, cleaning and laundering, knitting and tailoring, meal preparation, cleaning and gardening—be paid? To what extent and by whom?

Is it better to enforce prohibitions against child labor or to allow such labor and to work for effective supervision of working conditions?

How does illegal immigration contribute to the informal economy? How do informal or formal structures attract illegal immigrants?

How have globalization and telecommunications technologies expanded the informal economy? Should governments institute "bit taxes" on Internet transactions?

What are the effects of tax evasion on the national economy? Would you be willing to give up some privacy in your telephone or Internet communications to enforce antifraud laws?

If state corruption is said to contribute to overall national economic development, should it be purposely encouraged?

If poverty breeds temptation to engage in illicit operations, such as peasants growing narcotic crops for export, should massive aid programs be implemented to alleviate the underlying poverty? What are the pros and cons?

What mechanisms are available to address the problems associated with the informal economy? With international drug trafficking? How would you make those mechanisms more effective?

Notes

1. James J. Thomas, *Informal Economic Activity* (Ann Arbor: University of Michigan Press, 1992), p. 1.
2. Mark Tucker, "The Underground Economy in Australia," in Vito Tanzi, ed., *The Underground Economy in the United States and Abroad* (Lexington, MA: Lexington Books, 1982), p. 316.
3. See, for example, Tanzi, ed., *The Underground Economy in the United States and Abroad;* W. Gaertner and A. Wenig, eds., *The Economics of the Shadow Economy* (Berlin: Springer-Verlag, 1985); S. Alessandrini and B. Dallago, eds., *The Unofficial Economy* (Aldershot, UK: Gower, 1987); P. Barthelemy, *The Underground Economies: Tax Evasion and Information Distortion* (Cambridge: Cambridge University Press, 1989); S. N. Acharya, *Aspects of the Black Economy in India* (New Delhi: Ministry of Finance, 1985).
4. See also "Introduction," in *Alejandro Portes, Manuel Castells,* and Lauren A. Benton, eds., *The Informal Economy: Studies in Advanced and Less Developed Countries* (Baltimore: Johns Hopkins University Press, 1989), p. 3.
5. Harry I. Greenfield, *Invisible, Outlawed, and Untaxed: America's Underground Economy* (Westport, CT: Praeger,

1993), 94; Ingo Walter, *The Secret Money Market* (New York: Harper and Row, 1990), p. 19–22.
6. Greenfield, *Invisible, Outlawed, and Untaxed,* p. 100; Alan Richards and John Waterbury, *A Political Economy of the Middle East: State, Class, and Economic Development* (Boulder, CO: Westview Press, 1990), p. 270; Walter, *The Secret Money Market,* pp. 19–22.
7. Edgar L. Feige, quoted in Alejandro Portes, "The Informal Economy: Perspectives from Latin America," in Susan Pozo, ed., *Exploring the Underground Economy: Studies of Illegal and Unreported Activity* (Kalamazoo: W. E. Upjohn Institute for Employment Research, 1996), p. 147.
8. See, for example, Greenfield, *Invisible, Outlawed, and Untaxed,* pp. 2–5.
9. Walter, *The Secret Money Market,* pp. 14–17.
10. Carl P. Simon and Ann D. White, *Beating the System: The Underground Economy* (Boston: Auburn House, 1982), pp. 17–18.
11. See also Ingemar Hansson, "The Underground Economy in a High Tax Country: The Case of Sweden," in Tanzi, ed., *The Underground Economy in the United States and Abroad,* pp. 233–234.
12. Walter, *Secret Money Market,* p. 17.
13. Manuel Castells and Alejandro Portes, "World Underneath: The Origins, Dynamics, and Effects of the Informal Economy," in Portes, Castells, and Benton, eds., *The Informal Economy,* pp. 28–29.
14. *Economic Report of the President, 1991* (Washington, DC: GPO, 1991), p. 322.
15. Greenfield, *Invisible, Outlawed, and Untaxed,* p. 101.
16. Walter, *Secret Money Market,* pp. 24–27.
17. Bruno Dallago, *The Irregular Economy: The "Underground" Economy and the "Black" Labor Market* (Aldershot, UK: Dartmouth, 1990), p. 157.
18. Raffaele De Grazia, "Clandestine Employment: A Problem of Our Time," in Tanzi, ed., *The Underground Economy in the United States and Abroad,* p. 36.
19. Jessie Cheng, "Imports from Mainland to Go Directly into Kaohsiung Zone," *Free China Journal,* July 25, 1997, p. 8.
20. David J. Pyle, *Tax Evasion and the Black Economy* (London: Macmillan Press, 1989), p. 130.
21. *Ibid.,* p. 131.
22. Dallago, *The Irregular Economy,* p. 158.
23. Thomas, *Informal Economic Activity,* p. 181.
24. Dallago, *The Irregular Economy,* p. 161.
25. Castells and Portes, "World Underneath," in Portes, Castells, and Benton, eds., *The Informal Economy,* pp. 29–31.
26. Richards and Waterbury, *A Political Economy of the Middle East,* pp. 271–272.
27. Castells and Portes, "World Underneath," in Portes, Castells, and Benton, eds., *The Informal Economy,* p. 26.
28. Saskia Sassen-Koob, "New York City's Informal Economy," in Portes, Castells, and Benton, eds., *The Informal Economy,* pp. 65–66.
29. Thomas, *Informal Economic Activity,* p. 80.
30. *Ibid.,* p. 13.
31. M. Murphy, "Comparative Estimates of the Value of Housework in the United States for 1976," *Review of Income and Wealth* 28 (1982), pp. 29–43.
32. Quote in Thomas, *Informal Economic Activity,* p. 13.
33. *Ibid.,* p. 23.
34. Juan Carlos Fortuna and Suzana Prates, "Informal Sector Versus Informalized Labor Relations in Uruguay," in Portes, Castells, and Benton, eds., *The Informal Economy,* p. 81.
35. Portes, "The Informal Economy," in Pozo, ed., *Exploring the Underground Economy,* p. 156.
36. ILO, *World Employment Review,* 1988, p. 27, quoted in Thomas, *Informal Economic Activity,* pp. 81–82.
37. Dallago, *The Irregular Economy,* pp. 61–63.
38. *Ibid.,* pp. 63–64.
39. *Ibid.,* p. 69.
40. *Ibid.*
41. *Ibid.*
42. Sassen-Koob, "New York City's Informal Economy," in Portes, Castells, and Benton, eds., *The Informal Economy,* pp. 60–61.
43. Dallago, *The Irregular Economy,* p. 90.
44. Thomas, *Informal Economic Activity,* p. 183.
45. Alex Stepick, "Miami's Two Informal Sectors," in Portes, Castells, and Benton, eds., *The Informal Economy,* pp. 117–118.
46. Sharon Stanton Russell, "International Migration: Implications for the World Bank," *HRO Working Papers,* no. 54 (May 1995), Internet, p. 3; *Making Peace Work: Lessons for the International Development Community,* Conference Report (Washington, DC: Overseas Development Council, May 1996), p. 6.
47. Thomas, *Informal Economic Activity,* p. 246.
48. *Ibid.,* p. 93.
49. Mónica Lanzetta de Pardo and Gabriel Murillo Castaño, with Alvaro Triana Soto, "The Articulation of Formal and Informal Sectors in the Economy of Bogotá, Colombia," in Portes, Castells, and Benton, eds., *The Informal Economy,* p. 101.
50. Dallago, *The Irregular Economy,* pp. 90–92.
51. P. Nientied and J. van der Linden, "Approaches to Low-Income Housing in the Third World," in J. Gugler, ed., *The Urbanization of the Third World* (Oxford: Oxford University Press, 1988), p. 139.
52. Thomas, *Informal Economic Activity,* p. 96.
53. Dallago, *The Irregular Economy,* p. 99. See also J. Power, *Western Europe's Migrant Workers,* The Minority Rights

Group Report No. 28, London, as mentioned in Thomas, *Informal Economic Activity,* p. 184.

54. M. Bose and C. Gunn, *Fraud* (London: Unwin, 1989), p. 167.
55. Geoffrey Nairn, "Sweden, an Ideal Market," *Financial Times,* July 2, 1997, p. 4.
56. Walter, *Secret Money Market,* pp. 30–44.
57. Quoted in Thomas, *Informal Economic Activity,* p. 224, n13.
58. M. Levi, *Regulating Fraud: White Collar Crime and the Criminal Process* (London: Tavistock, 1987); Thomas, *Informal Economic Activity,* pp. 218–219.
59. Thomas, *Informal Economic Activity,* pp. 219, 221.
60. Nuala Moran, "Now It's Time for Action," *Financial Times,* July 2, 1997, p. 6.
61. *Ibid.,* p. 6; *The Economist,* May 31, 1997, p. 23.
62. Moran, "Now It's Time for Action," p. 6.
63. *The Economist,* May 31, 1997, p. 23.
64. Simon and White, *Beating the System,* Table A1-1, p. 26.
65. *Ibid.,* pp. xv, 20.
66. Greenfield, *Invisible, Outlawed, and Untaxed,* pp. 42–44.
67. One IRS study estimated that, in a single year in the 1970s, tax losses amounted to between $100 and $135 billion in individual and corporate income taxes. Vito Tanzi, "Underground Economy and Tax Evasion in the United States: Estimates and Implications," in Tanzi, ed., *The Underground Economy in the United States and Abroad,* p. 72.
68. See the various estimates discussed by Pyle, *Tax Evasion and the Black Economy,* pp. 61, 76.
69. M. Estellie Smith, ed., *Perspectives on the Informal Economy* (Lanham, MD: University Press of America, 1990), pp. 242–243.
70. *The Economist,* May 31, 1997, p. 23.
71. Thomas, *Informal Economic Activity,* pp. 227–228.
72. B. P. Alano, "Import Smuggling in the Philippines: An Economic Analysis," *Journal of Philippine Development* 11 (1984), pp. 157–190, as noted in Thomas, *Informal Economic Activity,* pp. 241–42.
73. Thomas, *Informal Economic Activity,* p. 231.
74. M. H. Best, "Political Power and Tax Revenues in Central America," *Journal of Development Economics* 71 (1976), pp. 49–82.
75. Simon and White, *Beating the System,* p. 20.
76. *Ibid.*
77. *The Economist,* May 31, 1997, p. 23.
78. Simon and White, *Beating the System,* p. 20.
79. *The Economist,* May 31, 1997, p. 21.
80. Edgar L. Feige, "Overseas Holdings of U.S. Currency and the Underground Economy," in Pozo, ed., *Exploring the Underground Economy,* p. 56.
81. *Ibid.*
82. Thomas, *Informal Economic Activity,* p. 259.
83. *Ibid.,* pp. 294–95. See also G. Rahav and S. Jaamdar, "Development and Crime: A Cross-National Study," *Development and Change* 13 (1982), pp. 447–462; M. B. Clinard and D. J. Abbott, *Crime in Developing Countries: A Comparative Perspective* (Cambridge: Cambridge University Press, 1973).
84. Thomas, *Informal Economic Activity,* pp. 295–296; C. Sumner, ed., *Crime, Justice and Underdevelopment* (London: Heinemann, 1982), pp. 1–39.
85. Gregory Grossman, "The Second Economy in the USSR," in Tanzi, ed., *The Underground Economy in the United States and Abroad,* p. 249.
86. *Ibid.*
87. *Ibid.,* pp. 257–259.
88. Thomas, *Informal Economic Activity,* p. 249. R. L. Chugh and J. S. Uppal, *Black Economy in India* (New Delhi: McGraw-Hill, 1986), p. 71.
89. Nathaniel Leff, "Economic Development Through Bureaucratic Corruption," *American Behavioral Scientist* (1964), pp. 8–14; Andrei Shleifer and Robert W. Vishney, "Corruption," *Quarterly Journal of Economics* (August 1993), pp. 599–617.
90. Walter, *Secret Money Market,* pp. 73–74.
91. Thomas, *Informal Economic Activity,* p. 227.
92. Louise I. Shelley, "Transnational Organized Crime: An Imminent Threat to the Nation-State?" *Journal of International Affairs* 48, 2 (Winter 1995), pp. 463–489.
93. *Ibid.*
94. P. A. Lupsha, "Organized Crime in the United States," in R. J. Kelly, ed., *Organized Crime: A Global Perspective* (Totowa, NJ: Rowan and Littlefield, 1983), p. 51, quoted in Thomas, *Informal Economic Activity,* p. 265.
95. *Ibid.,* p. 264.
96. José Blanes Jiménez, "Cocaine, Informality, and the Urban Economy in La Paz, Bolivia," in Portes, Castells, and Benton, eds., *The Informal Economy,* pp. 135–137.
97. *Ibid.,* p. 137.
98. B. Whitaker, *The Global Connection: The Crisis of Drug Addiction* (London: Jonathan Cape, 1987), pp. 333–334, quoted in Thomas, *Informal Economic Activity,* p. 299. See also Alfred McCoy, *The Politics of Heroin in Southeast Asia* (New York: Harper and Row, 1972); Jonathan Marshall, *Drug Wars: Corruption, Counterinsurgency and Covert Operations in the Third World* (Berkeley: Cohan and Cohen, 1991).
99. For a summary of this controversial issue, see Peter Dale Scott and Jonathan Marshall, *Cocaine Politics: Drugs, Armies, and the CIA in Central America* (Berkeley: University of California Press, 1991). In addition to interviews and media sources, Scott and Marshall also use the "Kerry Report," Sen. John Kerry (Mass.), Senate Subcommittee on Terrorism, Narcotics, and International Operations of the Committee

on Foreign Relations, Report, *Drugs, Law Enforcement and Foreign Policy*, 1989.

100. Steven Wisotsky, *Beyond the War on Drugs* (Buffalo: Prometheus Books, 1990).
101. Thomas, *Informal Economic Activity*, p. 285; Greenfield, *Invisible, Outlawed, and Untaxed*, p. 53.
102. Thomas, *Informal Economic Activity*, pp. 271–272.
103. José Blanes Jiménez, "Cocaine, Informality, and the Urban Economy in La Paz, Bolivia," p. 145.
104. *Ibid.*, p. 145.
105. *Ibid.*
106. Thomas, *Informal Economic Activity*, p. 241.
107. *The Economist*, May 31, 1997, p. 23.
108. Thomas, *Informal Economic Activity*, p. 241.
109. *Ibid.*, p. 254.
110. *Ibid.*, p. 297.
111. *Ibid.*, p. 298.
112. Whitaker, *The Global Connection*, pp. 72–73.
113. Walter, *The Secret Money Market*, p. 262.
114. *Ibid.*, p. 56.
115. R. Cumbry and R. Levich, "On the Definition and Magnitude of Recent Capital Flight," in D. R. Lessard and J. Williamson, eds., *Capital Flight and Third World Debt* (Washington, DC: Institute for International Economics, 1987), pp. 32–34; Thomas, *Informal Economic Activity*, pp. 241–242.
116. Walter, *Secret Money Market*, pp. 71–72.
117. *Ibid.*, p. 73.
118. *Ibid.*, pp. 72–73.
119. *Ibid.*, p. 243.
120. Ingo Walter, *Secret Money: The World of International Financial Secrecy* (Lexington, MA: Lexington Books, 1985), p. 136.
121. S. Henry, *The Hidden Economy: The Context and Control of Borderline Crime* (London: Martin Robertson, 1978).
122. See Walter's *The Secret Money Market* and *Secret Money*.
123. J. Ditton, *Part-Time Crime*, mentioned in Thomas, *Informal Economic Activity*, p. 205.
124. *Ibid.*, p. 205.
125. Walter, *The Secret Money Market*, p. 243.
126. *Ibid.*, pp. 262–263.
127. *Ibid.*
128. *Ibid.*, pp. 271–273, *passim.*
129. *Ibid.*, p. 275.
130. *Ibid.*, p. 293.
131. Axel Krause, "European Tax Pact Adopted," *International Herald Tribune*, Junc 27, 1987, quoted in *Ibid.*, p. 294.
132. Raffaele De Grazia, "Clandestine Employment: A Problem of Our Time," in Tanzi, ed., *The Underground Economy in the United States and Abroad*, pp. 41, 44.
133. Thomas, *Informal Economic Activity*, p. 81.
134. *Ibid.*, p. 82.

CHAPTER THIRTEEN

THE FUTURE OF THE INTERNATIONAL POLITICAL ECONOMY

Some economists have argued that the globalization process we have described throughout this book is something of a myth, serving the interests of politicians, analysts, bankers, and company c.e.o.'s. Clearly, a single global market does not yet prevail across industries and economic sectors. Regional and national markets still predominate.[1] Yet, despite the occasional exaggeration, the further deepening of globalization is likely be a fundamental characteristic of the international political economy in the early twenty-first century. Two powerful and frequently conflictual forces will continue to contend in international economics: the nation-state, which is identified with a specific, territorially delineated legal and administrative jurisdiction, and the multinational corporation (MNC), which, despite the reality of its home country base, increasingly transcends territorial constraints. Entering into the mixture as well are intergovernmental and non-governmental organizations (IGOs and NGOs).

The globalization process might be seen as a new phase in the history of the world political economy, in which nation-states continue to compete and to cooperate among themselves as before but also are compelled to compete and to cooperate with MNCs and other transnational actors as well. The globalization of production and financial networks and new "space-shrinking" communication and transportation technologies enable MNCs to influence developed and developing economies. MNCs use technological innovations to structure and restructure the processes of production to minimize costs and maximize profits; in doing so, they shape the domestic and international context of employment (although small enterprises continue to employ the most people in many countries), with enormous implications for North–South relations, dependency, informalization, gender equity, environmental degradation, and the general economic well-being of individuals and societies. Viewed from different perspectives, state intervention in economic affairs might be seen as hindering economic growth and development, exacerbating social and economic problems, and leading to international conflicts. Alternatively, it might be viewed as central to economic development, to social justice and greater cooperation. Serious questions remain, therefore, for the next century.

Within the context of the European Union, for example, as the most successful regional integration scheme, will citizens in France, Italy, Scandinavia, and elsewhere in Europe tolerate the social costs involved in adopting relatively uniform and stringent fiscal policy standards, lessening governmental social safety nets in the form of unemployment and pension support payments, and redefining the role of government in directing the economy (the traditional French term is *dirigisme*)? Will the British public, and those of the smaller Western European countries, accept the idea of losing control of their own money supplies and merging their treasuries with those of their partner states, potentially falling under German dominance? Will the complications of maintaining a common fiscal and tax policy complicate the planned admission of new states to the union, states with struggling economies and cultural differences, such as Poland, the Czech Republic, and perhaps, someday, Turkey? Will the Euro currency, backed by one of the largest advanced technological and industrial markets in the world, compete successfully against the dollar and yen for the dominance of international money markets? What will happen to the traditional European "social-market" economic culture, combining elements of capitalism and socialism?

THEORY AND PREDICTION

Entailed in such questions are the main issues for the future of the global economy:

- The issue of hegemony and which currency, if any, would stabilize global commerce as the "currency of choice"
- The culmination of the integration trend, seen in various regions, whereby separate states and cultures merge functions or their entire economies to form larger markets and trading communities
- Issues of economic centers and peripheries, which encompass the future of less developed countries as trade partners, labor markets, or resource suppliers
- The future of government intervention in regulating domestic and international markets and adopting policies designed to stimulate or support certain industries or economic sectors, while cushioning the public against inflation and recession
- The issue of global economic management—including the underlying philosophies governing trade, capital and labor flows, aid and development—through institutions such as the World Trade Organization (WTO), the International Monetary Fund (IMF), the World Bank, and regional development banks

These issues themselves are interrelated and conflict with each other in certain fundamental ways. For example, the integration trend could ease or impede the global management challenge. The more regions are closed off from the rest of the world in special trade and commercial relations, the less they are bound by common norms and rules with the rest of the international community. While free trade areas (FTAs) and customs unions, such as NAFTA, are recognized with special status under WTO rules, trade preferences for states within special trading areas can undermine the principle of "reciprocity" in lowering global trade barriers, whereby concessions granted among individual states or groups of states apply to all. Some experts have begun to debate a possible "Trans-Atlantic Free Trade Area" (TAFTA), to include both the EU and NAFTA, but they disagree on whether such a bloc would further or fracture development of common WTO principles. One problem, at least initially, would be that not all trade sectors would be covered in TAFTA—it would be very difficult to include a North American and European agricultural and textile trade agreement, given persistent disagreements between the two regions on these matters; therefore, TAFTA could fall short of WTO recognition as a full-fledged FTA and would have difficulty establishing exclusive benefits for its members.[2]

Traditions of hegemony also can complicate center-periphery relations. While the United States, its European allies, and Japan vie for hegemonic leadership, they also frequently collaborate to provide overall stability to the international economic system in terms of trade, currency, and investment markets. For example, they have been close partners in deciding when and to what extent to aid the struggling Russian economy. Conceivably, then, there will be no single future hegemon but a working group of dominant states, on the order of an economic security council, already embodied in the Group of seven or eight advanced industrial powers, which meet annually in well-publicized summits. The problem, however, is the still undefined roles of previously peripheral economic powers in such a hegemonic system, and particularly the roles of China and Russia, two very large emerging or "transitional" producers and markets. These particular states, coming from Marxist traditions, have until now conveniently been largely ignored in hammering out rules and policies for the IMF, World Bank, and WTO. It will no longer be possible to ignore them, and their "economic cultures,"—that is, the traditions that characterize their political and economic philosophies (see Chapter 2)—which may conflict with those of the G-7 as they enter the councils of power in a capitalist global economic management regime. There was much soul searching during the 1990s, for example, about the terms under which China and Russia would be allowed into the WTO. What degree of allowed protectionism, governmental subsidies, or one-way trade privileges, of the type sometimes granted to less developed states, would be allowed? China argued for these preferences as a "backward" economy, and the United States steadfastly refused them, citing instead China's dynamic economic growth rates and questionable practices regarding patents and copyrights. A good deal of "confidence building" or trust would be required to bridge the gaps. Inevitably, they would be bridged, but the terms of entry would play a crucial role in determining the future of economic hegemony and center-periphery relations.

Of course, China and Russia are not the only emerging or peripheral states to be allowed into the councils of economic management and consultation. Such large regional powers or "big emerging markets" as Brazil, India, Israel, South Africa, Turkey, and the Asian old and new "tigers" (Singapore, Indonesia, Malaysia, South Korea, and Taiwan) must somehow be accommodated, if not integrated among their regional neighbors. Struggling states with potential economic clout, such as Mexico, the Philippines, Nigeria, Pakistan, Iran, Thailand, Egypt, and Iraq, also must be made to value the benefits of a global economy. It is no longer possible to build a hegemonic system in the North and treat the South as an inferior class of dependencies, for the South will be armed, populous, and increasingly frustrated. Power hierarchies will always exist, but the developing countries will demand negotiations and better terms of trade whenever they can, as in the WTO and the 1998 meeting of the Group of 22—the advanced states and emerging markets—in Washington to debate the global financial crisis of the late 90s.

There are also cultural and political conflicts between parts of the North and South, as between Iran and the United States, which complicate the development of common economic principles and ventures. For the major Western economies, it used to be rather convenient to leave the "radicals" to the Soviet Union for economic ties, especially since the Egyptian, Cuban, and Vietnamese economies, along with those of Eastern Europe and Afghanistan, constituted a drag on Moscow's resources. Now that there is no Marxist bloc hegemon, those who looked to Moscow for their economic security have had to adapt quickly. When left to their own devices, Iraq, Cuba, Syria, Angola, India, Vietnam, and other former Soviet clients have found opportunities to trade with and encourage the investments of Northern economic firms. The question is whether Northern governments, and particularly hegemonic states such as the United States, will allow such commercial relations to flourish. They have done so with the largest Marxist state, China, for reasons of market fascination and security incentives. In certain cases, smaller oil-rich radical states, such as Libya and Angola, established strong ties to Western companies and leading European and Asian governments; however, it remains to be seen whether small leftist, radical, or militant states (North Korea and Cuba, for example) will offer incentives to warm relations with Washington. One reason it appears easier to cooperate in economic than in security realms is the sense that if someone cheats or fails to abide by economic agreements it is generally not a life and death matter.[3]

Will the responsibility for developing workable trade and commercial ties to various peripheral states devolve on individual Northern economic powers, or will they be somehow coordinated jointly by the Group of Seven or OECD? As in the traditional practice of assigning protectorates and mandates to major powers, some contend that it makes sense for the United States to be mainly responsible for cultivating Central and South American economies, for France to have that role in much of Africa, for Japan and China to stake out economic relations with other Asian states, and for Russia to move into parts of the Middle East, Central Asia, or South Asia. However, the major powers still cast suspicious eyes on each other in terms of marking out regional spheres of influence, for example, Europeans resent Washington's efforts to punish those who trade with Cuba—and less developed countries (LDCs) are suspicious of persistent dependency on one or a few big patrons. Washington does not want to be shut out completely from potentially lucrative deals over basic natural resources in the Middle East or Central Asia, for example; neither do Europe and Japan want to be excluded from the Americas or the Middle East. Japan's resource dependencies dictate its strategy of self-interested involvement in key regions, while its potential vulnerabilities dictate continued collaboration with giant powers, such as the United States. Powers such as Russia also appear to lack the economic clout and productivity needed for full fledged regional dominance.

We remain in an economic system of mixed incentives, many of which have changed little over the past three centuries. As argued by the mercantilist theory, states still vie for economic advantage over others; for access to needed resources, clients, and allies; for larger markets in which to sell their wares; and for relatively cheap labor. At the same time, revolutionary changes have occurred, with more transnational business and social ties, and emerging stock markets with millions more participants from all over the world, ranging from small investors to mammoth funds and conglomerates on programmed "buy-sell" routines, as facilitated by an overarching information explosion in the computer era. Thereby, states as well as nonstate actors (intergovernmental and nongovernmental organizations, private dealers, and interest groups, such as trade unions) also vie for influence, for access to, and for control of both capital and information. The international economy runs on the work of MNCs in dozens of countries and in multiple international joint ventures; on the work of financial centers in New York, London, Tokyo, and Zurich; on the work of women in countless homes and farms in Latin America, the Middle East, and Africa; and on the trade of smugglers operating in and near zones of poverty and of wealth throughout the world. The international economy is a vast network, with divergent actors and interests. As such, it is increasingly difficult but crucially important to predict where the economy is headed, under what conditions, and under whose leadership.

Because there are so many actors and interests, the international political economy defies control by any single bloc or organization. For example, one of the unresolved questions for the future is the degree to which capitalism can survive without a guaranteed supply of low-wage labor. Much of the controversy surrounding free trade zones, at least as they have been defined so far, is that they tend to favor the free movement of capital over the free movement of workers, yet there are pressures to import cheaper laborers for production and service jobs or to export jobs to other locations, where labor markets are cheaper. Part of companies' definition of *productivity* is to produce more per hour of labor employed and to produce more per unit of pay and other costs. Thus, there is considerable downward pressure on wages and employment, balanced by trade union and worker organizational efforts and by the scarcity of highly qualified labor, and service labor, and the inflated value of "labor" in certain sectors, such as sports and entertainment. Economists have detected a tendency for major investors to favor states with *skilled and educated* labor, not necessarily merely cheap labor. The substitution of robots and automated production somewhat diminishes the need for unskilled workers, but even states that have pioneered in these fields, such as Japan, have reverted to human labor in some circumstances, given the relative inflexibility of mechanized production lines. Thus, unless public education and training are improved, many will be left behind in the global economy.

Labor conflicts spill, often forcefully, into the political arena, pitting groups seeking the state's cooperation in lessening union power against those seeking the state's cooperation in validating union rights. Like the end of the nineteenth century, the close of the twentieth century has seen the game turn against organized labor in many parts of the world, but, just as labor rose on the impetus of the Great Depression at midcentury, there are possibilities that new economic crises and cyclical economic trends will reverse the fortunes of labor and management yet again. It has now nearly become a cliché that the nature of work itself is changing rapidly. Although many still engage in heavy manual labor, the vast "service" sector and computers have meant that workers shift to information processing and can work from remote locations, including their own homes. Sometimes this means that workers who would have been company employees in past decades now are "freelance" contractors, operating in both formal and informal economies (see Ch. 12), selling their services by the job to firms needing certain tasks performed, but without employee benefits packages and pensions. Trade unions have begun to show interest in organizing the service sector, but the diversity of locations and conditions of employment, and the fact that workers more frequently change careers complicate that effort.

One ominous sign for labor relations is chronic unemployment levels, seen particularly in Western Europe and the former Soviet Union, which impede government efforts to reduce spending, while diminishing tax revenues and heightening ethnic tensions among native and immigrant communities. Ugly scenes of antiforeign repression and xenophobia appear in many parts of the world. These range from outright violence to the denial of rights to citizenship, education or health care for migrant or foreign workers. Americans' love/hate relationship with migrant and illegal Latino immigrants, as well as Asian sweatshops in New York and California, testify to the attraction for, yet revulsion at, low-paid foreign workers. Social critics have called for a principle of "economic justice," requiring a firm to manufacture at least a portion of the product it sells to low-income customers in the neighborhood of those customers, yet such principles are given little credence by those interested in the benefits of the free market. Cultural clashes and ethnic violence are fueled partly by the competition for scarce jobs and for labor to do unwanted work. Labor migration, job placement, and production of highly marketable products, then, appear to be among the great challenges to order in the future international economy, and both free marketeers and government interventionists can agree on the general need for such order.

Thus, the resolution of problems in the five key issue areas are crucial not only to prospects for global prosperity but also for global peace and security. In an age when ideological differences have diminished, when cultural differences are emphasized, and when economic linkages have mushroomed, the key to peace appears to reside with states' and nationalities' achieving enough autonomy and sufficient income to satisfy social needs and population demands—which include aspects of both economic well-being and physical security. Governments will be challenged both politically and economically to devise ways of keeping social peace and guaranteeing minority rights while fostering gainful employment and livable incomes.

This represents a fundamental challenge to the international system as we have known it, particularly because so many forces seem arrayed against the geographical borders that were handed down to states from the colonial past. Information and capital, refugees and migrants, contraband and pollution now flow across borders relatively uncontrollably. It has been argued that "economic zones" of commerce, such as the Texas–Northern Mexico or the Washington State and British Columbia areas, will have their equivalents all over the world and will become more important economically than formal nation-states. Environmentalists also question whether the "consumer societies" which characterize the modern "developed" economy are conducive to survival on a planet with finite resources.

The myth of territorial integrity has been strongly entrenched in the international system at least since the seventeenth century, with the presumption that wholesale changes of borders, such as those drawn along commercial, ethnic, or religious lines, would be destabilizing and threatening to states around the world—as in Africa, for example. The economic, ecological, and social disasters witnessed over the past thirty years in African civil wars—as in Nigeria and Liberia in the west and in Somalia, Ethiopia, and Sudan in the east—testify to the unresolved questions of territorial division and social autonomy. Can economies progress without social peace? Will that peace require the redrawing of borders or the rewriting of constitutions? Is peace possible until economic realities improve? Does peace require "justice" and the redistribution of wealth? These crucial questions have yet to be faced either by world or regional powers, who conveniently tend to ignore disrupted areas of Africa and the Caucases of Central Asia, until the scenes of carnage and chaos are too unbearable.

FUTURE HEGEMONY?

The rules of international order generally have been set after great cataclysmic wars, such as the Napoleonic wars of the nineteenth century and the world wars of the twentieth century. In each case, a dominant state or a coalition set the norms for international law, international organizations, and the international economy. The Concert of Powers system in the nineteenth century was an attempt by conservative powers to prevent revolutions of the type witnessed in France, as well as to preserve the dominance of monarchies. The system gradually disintegrated. The League of Nations and United Nations systems of the twentieth century were set mainly through British and American influence, to prevent the previous war's recurrence by subduing former rival powers (the losers), at least for a period, and by addressing the social roots of the war, such as disrupted trade and massive inflation or depressions. In each case, we could speak of a hegemon, or a coalition around a hegemon, defining the new order and backing it with both military and financial commitments.

In the case of the most recent hegemon, the United States, these commitments were quite apparent in a willingness to station troops abroad after World War II, to provide rather generous foreign assistance programs, to campaign for freer trade, and to back global and regional organizations. Americans, along with their British colleagues, were aiming to consolidate liberal open trade principles, because they benefited from access to foreign markets and because trade disruptions were judged to undermine peace and prosperity. As the hegemon, the United States was even willing to provide foreign debtor states with debt forgiveness or with the means to pay off debts and avoid bankruptcy, so that they could continue to function in the newly reconstructed and free-trade-oriented system.

Although the United States, as we have seen in previous chapters, declined as a hegemonic power after 1970, it is not clear that it *cannot* continue to play the hegemonic role in most matters. When the hegemon is itself a major debtor, however, as happened to the United States in the 1980s with reliance on foreign capital to balance its budgetary and balance-of-payments deficits (deficits themselves generated largely by military spending), it is hardly in a position to continue "bankrolling" the world. If Americans were willing to tax themselves more heavily and to devote a greater proportion of their federal budget to foreign financing, perhaps at the expense of military spending or domestic programs, they probably could sustain their dominant global role in regulating and fostering the international economy. Indeed, through payments to financial organs such as the IMF and World Bank, and the proportional voting power such contributions bring, Washington can wield tremendous influence (ironically Washington delayed those payments in the late 1990s for fear of losing control to these organizations); simply witness its dictation of the choice of UN Secretary General in 1996, for example, based on the threat to continue to withhold its UN assessments if it did not get its way (it got its way but withheld payments anyway). As Helen Milner has argued, the increasing U.S. debt in and of itself is not an indication of decline in U.S. world power.[4]

At the same time, however, according to Miguel de Oliver, the U.S. desire to create NAFTA was "the manifestation of the increasing protectionism of a declining hegemon as the NAFTA primarily represents an economic barrier to other core states" while "allow[ing] for the procurement of the resources necessary in an attempt by the declining hegemon to maintain faltering comparative advantage."[5] Furthermore, at least in the 1980s and 1990s, the American public seemed weary of paying for global responsibilities, as the deferred payment of UN and IMF assessments and slashed allocations to foreign aid and the State Department budget indicated. This was partly because of political pique at events and issues not always ideologically and politically palatable for Americans in multilateral organizations and partly because of economic stringency, which diminished the political acceptability of foreign assistance or international financing.

As indicated in earlier chapters, a hegemon is, by nature, required to pay for the functioning of the international economy, because it gains from that economy in the form of purchases and influence, while other states depend on the hegemon's willingness to import goods—hence the high consumption levels. If the hegemon will not pay, it cannot remain hegemonic, though there is no guarantee that if it does pay it will rule in all cases. However, in the absence of a responsible hegemon, as such theorists as Charles Kindleberger have argued, the international economy itself may not remain stable. Kindleberger saw the roots of the Great Depression of the 1930s in Britain's inability and America's unwillingness to continue financing the growing external debt of countries involved in international trade. As noted by Schwartz,

> for a short time in the mid-1920s, US willingness to finance current account deficits elsewhere averted a contraction of global trade because of these imbalances. In particular, US lending helped the UK act as a market of last resort for its empire, then a huge part of the world economy. When the US became unwilling, or, like the British by the middle of the 1920s, unable to continue this finance on a global scale, a disastrous contraction of world trade ensued. Nations sought international payments balance through currency devaluation, exclusive tariffs, and bilateral exchanges, and the value of world trade fell by nearly two-thirds.
>
> Similarly, most [primary product economies] and developed economies emerged from the crises of the 1970s with large external imbalances and high levels of foreign debt. . . . During the 1980s the US again acted as a lender of last resort, particularly by supporting the IMF as it coerced new lending from developed country banks. But this lending fell far short of that needed to cover the enlarged current account deficits of LDCs. . . . Instead, unlike the 1920s, the US provided "lender of last resort" financing by expanding *imports* from debtor countries. In turn the US financed its own ballooning current account deficit by borrowing from Japan and Germany, who acted as lenders of last resort respectively for the US and European debtors.
>
> Just as with Britain in the late 1920s, however, the US can no longer continue acting as a market of last resort; the US is now a net debtor and must run a trade *surplus* [increase exports over imports] to finance its debts. If the US were willing to continue eroding its asset position and lenders were willing to finance this debt buildup, global balance could be achieved without any contraction of trade. But Japan and Germany, for different reasons, are both unwilling and unable to continue to finance the US deficit.[6]

While Washington still appears willing to pay for the military upkeep of strategic positions, such as those associated with Persian Gulf oil and other key resources, and to take on occasional peacekeeping or humanitarian relief operations, its reluctance to relieve international debt burdens and its backing of "conditionalities"—that is, stringent demands for budgetary reform in return for international assistance through the IMF and other multilateral bodies—signal a diminished hegemonic role. In this sense, efforts to dominate the international economy should not be confused with full hegemony, with all the attendant responsibilities. The United States may push its influence in the short term with such demands, and these demands may even make economic sense in individual cases (on a "micro" level), but in terms of "hegemonic stability theory," through a tight monetary policy, Washington reduces its own influence on a global scale and conceivably threatens the growth of the international economy, while exacerbating social ills.

The relationship between hegemony and the health of international trade seems more complicated than implied by Kindleberger, however. One careful study of this relationship, for example, revealed that high levels of international trade were most strongly associated with *declining* hegemony and with *moderate* levels of "concentration" in the international system—that is, the skewing of economic and political power and assets into relatively few hands.[7] Thus, as the twenty-first century and new millennium is ushered in amid the eroding U.S. hegemony, and a modicum of G-7 (or G-9, if one looks to the participation of Russia and China) collaboration, there is a prospect for continued vibrant international trade and prosperity. Certainly, global stock markets, even in politically threatened locations, such as Hong Kong, enjoyed a remarkably long general upward rise during the 1990s, despite the uncertainties of global hegemony. The markets fell sharply late in the decade, however, on the basis of global financial and monetary difficulties, which impeded both trade and profits. Therefore, one would want to know the limits of upward prospects—that is, the point at which the decline of hegemony and concentration, or other factors might lead to a breakdown of trade through lack of liquidity or a too thin spread of buying power along with the accumulation of unpayable debts.

In a comparison of the 1920s with the 1980s and 1990s, the hegemony question is viewed in the context of what many see as recurring cycles—cycles of boom and bust, inflation and depression, and war and peace in the international political economy. Indeed, "world system" theorists, premised on Marxist-Leninist views,[8] posit a close connection between cycles of increased and decreased power and economic concentration, on the one hand, and warfare in world politics on the other. These theorists tend to see the situation at the turn of the twenty-first century as portending crises and renewed global warfare by, say 2020, since it is the "end of a long wave that included the great post-war boom of the 1950s and 1960s and the slowdown of the 1970s and 1980s."[9] It is argued that, in earlier periods, when such declining hegemons as Britain were challenged by rising powers, such as Germany and Japan, world war resulted. The potential for such cataclysmic conflict is seen recurring with the rise of competitive hegemonic powers (U.S., China, Europe, Japan, Russia) in the early twenty-first century. However, the experience of the United States, overtaking Britain peacefully by the early 1900s, indicates that, if powers share similar cultural or political outlooks, hegemonic competition need not produce war.

Indeed, the growing shared democratic outlooks among the major economic powers, perhaps with the exception of China and Russia, may lead to peaceful transitions, and the United States in the 1990s was said to be increasingly engaged in global "democracy promotion," rather than the Cold War "national security" strategies that installed military regimes in the developing countries.[10] Optimistically speaking, international war seemed nearly to have vanished, in contrast to civil wars, during the 1990s.[11] However, it is possible that the overconfidence of the 1890s—that industrial and scientific progress would negate war and provide for the common welfare across the world—has its counterpart in 1990s overconfidence in the potential of the new global economy and the emergence of new democracies to foster peace and prosperity.

The prediction of recurrent trends and cycles is a controversial business; not every expert agrees that such cycles are regular and automatic. Historians tend to argue that each epoch, while an outgrowth of the past, has unique characteristics. Policy innovations, such as government interventions to preclude recessions, are meant as cyclical counterweights, just as dam- and dike-building along rivers is meant as a human stance against natural flood cycles. In hydrology, it has been learned that such interventions bear consequences, such as more devastating floods once the embankments are breached, as water explodes outward with greater force. By the same token, in economics or political science it is not yet clear that anticyclical policies and pro-democracy interventions are entirely effective in avoiding the worst consequences of economic downturns or hegemonic competition, or that they do not themselves entail undesired consequences. The debate continues between optimists who believe that human ingenuity can avert economic and military (including nuclear) disasters and skeptics more sanguine about what humans know and can do about social forces. Somewhere in the middle stand those who lament the fact that people may have stopped trying to use public policy to address political and economic problems amenable to solution if treated in a timely fashion.

INTEGRATION OR DISINTEGRATION?

One of the clear trends in the world political economy of the late twentieth century was that processes of both integration and disintegration were transpiring simultaneously in nearly every region. Integration entails the formation of larger political and economic units, often fashioned to liberalize trade and commerce through the creation of customs unions, free trade areas, and common markets (see Chapter 6). Disintegration occurred through the breakup of existing units into smaller, more autonomous regions, as in the former Soviet Union, Yugoslavia, and Czechoslovakia. The integration trend was driven largely by MNCs and political leaders seeking larger markets through cross-border production, sales, and technology transfer. The disintegration trend stems mainly from ethno-political groups' (nations, cultural, and religions communities) quest for security and self-government. Both trends, in their own ways, were carryovers from the nineteenth century, when nationalism spurred the breakup of large empires into nation-states and when the first experiments in customs unions occurred between such entities. Integration and disintegration can work at cross purposes as far as economic interests are concerned, since larger economic entities and economies of scale can be threatened by local autonomy campaigns, yet Germany and Italy themselves were formed in the nineteenth century by the joint influences of nationalism and commercial unification. There need not be a fatal conflict between political and economic goals.

Is it possible, then, to make sense of a world in which smaller, sometimes even suboptimally sized states separate from larger entities and yet in which larger entities are still being formed? Some analysts see the dissolution of larger entities and the explosion of inter-ethnic tensions as a symptom of disillusionment with the "downside" of modernity, with the harms caused by modern industrial society. Modernization since the seventeenth century has been characterized largely by a slow march of industry, urbanization, democracy, and nationalism. These have brought unprecedented material wealth to many people, but they have also brought disillusionment in the form of "poverty, child labor and the exploitation of women, class struggles, vicious authoritarianism, imperial conquests, and great inter-state wars,"[12] as well as pollution and resource depletion. The challenge of the modernization, or some would say "post-modern," process is to align industry, democracy, ecology and nationalism so that they produce benefits for more groups and so that fewer groups suffer exploitation. Some post-modernists despair of engineered solutions, however, even as scientists continue the search for answers and solutions to global problems.[13]

One possible way of reconciling integration and disintegration is in developing more flexible forms of integrated communities. Relatively unstructured consultative organizations and councils have sprung up in various regions to address fast-developing political and economic problems. The Asia-Pacific Economic Consultation (APEC) group of Pacific rim states appears to be one such evolving consultative, agenda-setting, and even rule-making body. In the Middle East, the Economic and Social Commission for Western Asia (ESCWA) may have a similar role. Evidently, NAFTA also is to be left as a loose free trade zone, rather than as a formal economic union of the Americas. Within large regions, subgroupings of states, or even of sub-national actors or areas, seem to spring up to test the waters of economic cooperation. For example, with at least a temporary retrenchment in American regional leadership, rival South American economic blocs emerged apart from NAFTA in the 1980s and 1990s. The four-nation Mercosur (shortened Spanish for Common Market of the South) group, led by Latin powers Argentina and Brazil, became the world's fourth largest single market, while others, such as Chile, the country slated for quick inclusion in NAFTA, moved closer to both Mercosur and the Andean Pact, along with bilateral accords with Canada and Mexico. Various European and Asian economic powers explored trade agreements with these Latin organizations, while segments of Central America also sought to organize themselves economically. A gradual coalition process appeared to be taking shape, whereby separate Latin trading communities would form, would explore mutual agreements and agreements with powers outside the region, and would move toward a form of Latin American or hemispheric free trade area. In the process, individual countries would keep their options open as much as possible to take part in various groups, at least until the U.S. leadership and sponsorship role in the hemisphere became clearer.[14]

Thus, some regions, such as Europe, said to be ripe for union and merger, may continue in that direction, especially if there is a large economic core of prosperous states attracting others to the union,[15] while other regions experience growing economic ties among culturally and politically distinct nations, which may require looser forms of integration or collaboration. Research has shown that, although such looser forms may promote freer trade, they also can be based on locally protectionist principles, and there is no general tendency for loose arrangements, such as the Latin regional trading arrangements (RTAs), to become more deeply integrated entities. Governments themselves also must define whether these arrangements will or will not promote overall principles of the General Agreement on Tariffs and Trade (GATT), such as trade liberalization and openness to new partners on a most favored nation (MFN) basis.[16]

As a case in point, several arguments and interests are offered as justifying a relatively integrated and structured East Asian trade community. These include more effective negotiation with or potential retaliation against other exclusive trade blocs; economies of scale through more cross-border collaboration; guaranteed access to Japanese markets; regional trade goods, such as electricity generation; the encouragement of further benefits, such as inter-regional labor mobility, foreign investment, and capital and technology flows; quicker movement toward global free trade, as small countries realize they must link up to larger regional communities rather than relying on most favored nation benefits from others' agreements; and a possible reduction of political tensions and security concerns, as in the multinational competition over the potential oil deposits of the Spratly Island areas in the South China Sea.[17]

However, there are also many compelling arguments against such a formal bloc, even as consultation takes place in such venues as APEC and the Association of Southeast Asian Nations (ASEAN). There is concern over a future competition between East Asia and other regional trade blocs, and an interest in cooperation rather than confrontation. It appears that the mutual suspicions of larger regional states and economies may persist enough to discourage disengagement from non-Asian trade ties and economic centers outside the region.

One central issue in this debate is the relationship of economic and security communities—that is, the continued perceived need for military commitments or alliances to reassure states against potentially hostile neighbors. As they form economic communities, major powers such as Japan and Germany have to debate whether to exclude or penalize their military partners, such as the United States; smaller states—for example, the Central and Eastern European countries (CEESs)—search within their respective regions for export markets and may view allies such as the United States, as economic partners and as potential power balancers to avoid total regional domination by the larger states. In balancing economic and security policy interests, governments like to retain options for ties to a variety of suppliers, protectors, and clients. Defining exact needs for military protection and alliances, however, may be increasingly difficult in a world in which economic competition is equally crucial. The ASEAN group, for example, began mainly as a consultative organization on Southeast Asian social and economic issues, such as population control, food and agriculture, and drug trafficking, but it has inherited security concerns as well, particularly as such issues as "exclusive economic zones" give rise to conflicts under the Law of the Sea treaty for access to offshore resources (including oil) in coastal territorial waters.

Thus, regional trade communities do not necessarily completely insulate a region from global connections. Indeed, they may even expand the region's negotiations with outside powers over topics as diverse as trade and security. It has been found that, although regional trade preferences and agreements generally raise the proportion of intra-regional trade, they have not isolated these regions from increased extra-regional trade. Regional and global economic integration, through the lowering of trade barriers, appear to proceed simultaneously, and although some individual states may be hurt in the process, as when European integration drastically cut trade access for former European colonies such as New Zealand, there is a general increase of prosperity.[18]

For less self-reliant and less prosperous regions, the local options are limited, and the lure of formal partnership with well-developed, even distant economic zones and military suppliers may be irresistible. Traditionally, for example, African extra-regional ties have been established with former colonial rulers and patrons—Belgium, Britain, France, Portugal, and Spain. As the latter merge into an EU economy, complete with a common foreign policy stance (at least formally, although with an as yet undeveloped common military policy), they are likely to generate more formal linkages between African RTAs and the EU—building from the old Lome Convention, which provided trade preferences to excolonies of the original six members of the European Common Market, as noted in Chapter 9. Thus, although an African regional customs union based on the existing subregional ones in western and southern Africa promises little immediate benefit in regional trade creation beyond what is available by bilateral agreements, efforts continue to build larger African trade organizations, if for no other reason than to establish firmer linkages to organizations such as the EU.[19]

Judging by the Western European experience, reduced trade barriers lead to initial industrial dispersion within a customs union, but longer-term effects seem to show a reconcentration of industry in central core member states, as the costs of intra-regional trade fall below a certain threshold.[20] In other words, within trading communities, locational benefits of establishing production, service, and distribution facilities across borders, such as transportation savings and lower wage costs, can be negated by the significantly lowered costs of shipping goods themselves or, in the future, of doing more business via computer.

Given the regionalization of trade communities and the gradual globalization of economic ties, many commentators assume that the globalized economy also promotes common norms and democratic reforms, opening societies to a freer flow of technology and ideas. However, China has sought to prove that economic reform and opening can take place without political liberalization. What are the implications of these contending forces of openness and autonomy, of liberalization and control? Box 13.1 contains a half-way facetious account of the pacifying effects of the "shrinking and linking" of the global economy through one "omnipresent" multinational firm, exporting what some see as a high point and others a low point of American culture.

In some ways, the account in Box 13.1 is analogous to the often repeated argument that war has never taken place between democracies—that is, while democracies become involved in war about as much as any other type of government, they seldom if ever raise swords against *each other*. There are various explanations for this "democratic peace" thesis, some dwelling on the lack of threat perception

BOX 13.1

IS A BIG MAC A HARBINGER OF PEACE?

So I've had this thesis for a long time and came here to Hamburger University at McDonald's headquarters to finally test it out. The thesis is this: No two countries that both have a McDonald's have ever fought a war against each other.

The McDonald's folks confirmed it for me. I feared the exception would be the Falklands war, but Argentina didn't get its first McDonald's until 1986, four years after that war with Britain. Civil wars don't count: McDonald's in Moscow delivered burgers to both sides in the fight between pro- and anti-Yeltsin forces in 1993.

Since Israel now has a kosher McDonald's, since Saudi Arabia's McDonald's closes five times a day for Muslim prayer, since Egypt has 18 McDonald's and Jordan is getting its first, the chances of a war between them are minimal. But watch out for that Syrian front. There are no Big Macs served in Damascus. India-Pakistan? I'm still worried. India, where 40 percent of the population is vegetarian, just opened the first beefless McDonald's (vegetable nuggets!), but Pakistan is still a Mac-free zone.

Obviously, I say all this tongue in cheek. But there was enough of a correlation for me to ask James Cantalupo, president of McDonald's International and its de facto secretary of state, what might be behind this Golden Arches Theory of Conflict Prevention—which stipulates that when a country reaches a certain level of economic development, when it has a middle class big enough to support a McDonald's, it becomes a McDonald's country, and people in McDonald's countries don't like to fight wars. They like to wait in line for burgers. Or as Cantalupo puts it: 'We focus our development on the more well-developed economies—those that are growing and those that are large—and the risks involved in being adventuresome (for those growing economies) are probably getting too great.'

In the 1950s and '60s, developing countries thought that having an aluminum factory and a U.N. seat was what made them real countries, but today many countries think they will have arrived only if they have their own McDonald's and Windows 95 in their own language. This year McDonald's went into its 100th country and for the first time it earned more revenue from McDonald's overseas than from McDonald's America. Said Cantalupo: "I feel these countries want McDonald's as a symbol of something—an economic maturity and that they are open to foreign investments. I don't think there is a country out there we haven't gotten inquiries from. I have a parade of ambassadors and trade representatives in here regularly to tell us about their country and why McDonald's would be good for the country."

The question raised by the McDonald's example is whether there is a tip-over point at which a country, by integrating with the global economy, opening itself up to foreign investment and empowering its customers, permanently restricts its capacity for troublemaking and promotes gradual democratization and widening peace. Francis Fukuyama, author of . . . "The End of History," argued to me that a country's getting its own McDonald's was probably not a good indicator of that tip-over point, because the level of per capita income needed in a country to host a McDonald's is too low. "I would not be surprised if in the next 10 years several of these McDonald's countries go to war with each other," he said.

Yes, there will be conflicts, but more inside countries than between them. True, the spread of McDonald's (a new one opens every three hours) is part of a worldwide phenomenon of countries integrating with the global economy and submitting to its rules, but this is not a smooth linear process. It produces a backlash inside countries from those who do not benefit from this globalization, who feel their traditional culture will be steamrolled by it and who fear that they won't eat the Big Mac, the Big Mac will eat them.

How well governments and global companies manage these frustrations will be the real determinant of whether economic development will lead to wider democratization and wider peace. Here again McDonald's is an intriguing pioneer. When the riots broke out in Los Angeles, one of the few commercial buildings not trashed was McDonald's.

Source: Thomas Friedman, *The New York Times News Service*, December 13, 1996.

among democracies and the difficulty of convincing populations to fight others very much like themselves. Others emphasize the correspondence of business and commercial interests among democracies. Skeptics note, however, that commercial ties between like-minded governments did not prevent World War I—Russia and Germany, ruled by family-related monarchs, had the highest mutual prewar trade relations in Europe and yet ended up deadly enemies.

Skeptics also claim that "democracy" is not a clearcut notion, and as the world gains more "democracies," by chance alone, the probability rises that they will fight over such issues as unresolved borders and access to resources.[21] Again, however, optimists argue that World War I era Germany, and certainly czarist Russia, were not pluralistic democracies and that democratic regimes would be more likely to refer mutual disputes to legal and diplomatic settlement processes, such as WTO, rather than to fight about them.

Friedman notes that some states and nations feel left out or threatened by the regionalization or globalization processes and that this also accounts for the continued disintegrative process. Integration promotes the definition and adoption of common rules and norms for conducting international economic exchange. This tends to break down some of the political barriers and cultural suspicions between separate states, but it does not eliminate them entirely. In U.S. history, despite the commercial pull of federation that replaced the looser eighteenth-century Articles of Confederation, economic and social gaps, such as slavery, between the North and South led to one of the world's bloodiest civil wars, a war that, although technically settled, has left many psychological scars visible to this day. Does the presence of McDonald's restaurants throughout the North and South preserve social peace in the United States, or are other forms of political accommodation still necessary? Is the same true for the world at large?

CENTER-PERIPHERY RELATIONS

While scholars speak of economic and military hegemons, certainly there is not a single prevailing political culture in the international economy. Segments of the globe subscribe to religious traditions, laws, and practices, as in Islam, Judaism, Buddhism, and Hinduism, while others are more politically secular. Some, as in Africa and Asia, stress collective responsibility, as distinguished from individualism in Western societies. How important these cultural differences will be in defining acceptable rules, norms of behavior, and practices in international economic relations remains to be seen. International economic cooperation requires institutional mechanisms, such as the World Trade Organization, and economic incentives to bridge cultural, political, and economic gaps. Some observers contend that nations must first address the "clash of civilizations"[22] in order to take further steps toward greater mutual understanding and accord.

While huge economic and technological gaps remain in North–South relations, the information age, with the proliferation of the Internet and satellite communications, has presented a more unified global information network than even a decade ago. Access to phones, faxes, and computers has grown, though it is still severely skewed in favor of the developed Northern states. Inevitably, however, it appears that this access will become more widespread across societies, perhaps rendering the traditional geo-political and culturally distinct understanding of international relations less relevant. Some contend that geo-politics is giving way to "infopolitics," with centers of power no longer confined within geographic boundaries but enjoying pervasive influence,[23] while enhancing people's awareness of social and economic problems in remote corners of the globe and enabling them to compare their plight with that of others. There is a good deal of potential for political instability and revolution in a system in which information is more equally available than is buying power.

During the Cold War, the two superpowers projected global economic and military power through tentacles of alliance, bases, treaties, and agreements extending thousands of miles and influencing events at great distances. The "info-age" promises to empower groups and economic enterprises, as well as governments, at least to the extent that each entity's base of operations could have multiple centers, offices or at least a formal presence, across many regions. This threatens to be a highly disorderly world, in contrast to early post–Cold War claims of a "new world order", especially given the uneven levels of economic development prevalent across regions. Factors such as "population explosion, floods of refugees, the exhaustion of natural resources and environmental degradation" all lead to relatively chaotic fragmentation,[24] yet optimists would note that such doomsday predictions have been wrong in the past and that the capacity of national leaders for innovative coordination could prove equal to the challenge of keeping economic order.

One key indicator of potential disorder in relations between the center and the periphery, and among states in the periphery, is the phenomenon of international migration. As noted in Chapter 12, more than 100 million people worldwide live outside their native countries. This in and of itself is not necessarily a destructive trend; people migrating in search of greater opportunity can bring tremendous new talent and energy with them. However, if the multitudes find no hospitable homeland and, instead, live in perpetual hardship, they constitute a massive and pervasive social problem.

Some countries, of course, encourage their citizens to go abroad either to study or to work in order to improve their skills and to send home support for their families, at least $71 billion in overseas "remittances" in 1990 alone. Some developing as well as developed countries, such as those with active petroleum industries, are very attractive to economic migrants. Once immigrants arrive in large numbers, they can fill important labor needs for the host state, but they also can become the target of significant ethnic and political hostility. The phenomenon of brain drain occurs as well, when those sent abroad for study stay in the wealthier developed states rather than return home to practice their skills, as discussed in Chapter 8.

The close connection between migration, poverty, and violence is seen in the fact that, during the 1980s, fifteen of the twenty poorest states in the world experienced significant political and social conflicts and massive refugee problems. "About half of all the low income countries in the world are either currently embroiled in conflict or are in the process of moving through the transition to peace."[25] This means that the already complicated task of economic development takes on new overtones when repairing wartorn societies and when addressing the needs of displaced people are considered, as shown in Box 13.2. On the bright side, a number of civil wars, such as those in Guatemala and other Central American countries, have ended in recent years, but the challenge of rebuilding viable economies remains.

In addition to war, tremendous population, or demographic, pressure is driving global crises and migration. Between 1970 and 1990, the working-age population of the developing world increased by 59 percent, while that of the developed states rose by only 23 percent. The challenge of employing these young people remains beyond the capability of most LDCs, and the corresponding projected working-age population increases for the 1990–2010 period are 41 percent for LDCs but only 9 percent for advanced economies.[26] President Clinton's search for contributors to a muli-billion dollar fund for Palestine in 1998 was meant to head off instabilities in Gaza and the West Bank territories which might jeopardize the fragile Arab-Israeli peace process.

Economists have applied numerous theoretical models to explain the initiation of migration, including "neo-classical" economic models stressing such factors as labor supply and demand in various countries (macro theory); micro-decision models of individuals deciding to move for the net personal payoffs; "new economics of migration," as groups decide to maximize family benefits and gain credit and capital abroad; "dual labor market theory," stressing the demand for low-wage workers in the formal and informal sectors in developed states; and world-economic system theory's emphasis on neo-colonial dependency and the influence of multinational firms in recruiting migrants and displacing native workers. The perpetuation of migration is attributed to such factors as networks among migrants providing information on supposed opportunities, institutions such as private and voluntary organizations that assist

BOX 13.2

PRIORITY TASKS FOR REBUILDING WARTORN SOCIETIES

- Provide civilian security: disarm military forces (including irregular forces), end impunity, and create effective, apolitical security forces. Restructuring police forces so that they serve citizens rather than engage in repression is a particularly high priority in postconflict environments.
- Ensure access to the basic means of survival: food, very basic health care, and shelter.
- Support reconciliation and confidence-building at the local level. Focus initially on effecting "functional accommodation"—that is, bringing people together out of common interest.
- Promote rural and urban economic revitalization; focus on creating jobs. This includes covering recurrent costs, such as civil servants' salaries.
- Address the needs of displaced and disaffected persons, including excombatants.
- Strengthen government so that it can fulfill key tasks. This does *not* imply a return to the status quo ante but generally involves significant reform of government institutions.
- Strengthen civil society so that it can effectively provide input into the government's decision-making process and fulfill a watchdog function.
- Create or strengthen the channels and mechanisms for resolving disputes and strengthening the rule of law: judicial reform, ombudsmen, civilian police force, human rights protection, and methods of adjudicating disputes over property rights.
- Develop mechanisms for dealing with the abuses of the past by all parties.

Source: Making Peace Work: Lessons for the International Development Community, Conference Report (Washington, DC: Overseas Development Council, May 1996).

migrants or those that recruit them (sometimes with patently false advertising), and the norms, expectations, and local conditions that pressure or induce people to move. Among these local conditions are environmental degradation and the depletion of agricultural lands and resources, as well as population growth and unequal distributions of wealth; in this sense, international migration can be seen as an extension of the internal migration patterns that for decades have moved people from rural to urban centers in search of greater opportunity.[27]

Migration is but one of the many stark and difficult choices facing the poverty-stricken masses in the developing world. Perhaps more typical and more difficult is the everyday tradeoff of decisions whether to spend scarce income on food versus on shoes or simple lifesaving needs, such as mosquito nets to protect against parasitic diseases and malaria, versus on kerosene fuel to boil water to protect against other lethal diseases. These tragically basic tradeoffs, on items costing as little as $10 or less, are the essence of life and death for most of the people on earth. Clearly, tremendous lifesaving potential comes from relatively low cost assistance programs providing such remedies as oral rehydration kits for diarrhea, swamp clearance projects, and childhood immunization shots. Even more revolutionary changes are possible through programs to provide employment, education, and purchasing power to people in distress, so that the conditions causing chronic poverty, rather than merely the symptoms, are alleviated.[28] Not all remedies are cheap, however, as the staggering challenge of providing relief from the worldwide AIDs epidemic testifies.

GOVERNMENT INTERVENTION

According to classical, laissez-faire liberalism, the international economic system operates on the basis of certain laws and principles—hence the belief in the efficiencies and benefits of free trade (see Chapters 2 and 5), yet one cannot neglect the facts of greater political and economic advantage for some than for others in that system. In the days of colonial empires, for example, it seemed "natural" for a relatively small state, such as Britain, to control massive distant territories and peoples, such as India. In that economic system, Indians essentially produced raw materials for processing into finished products in British factories and mills, products that were then re-exported to India for purchase. This was, obviously, a far sweeter system for the British than for the Indians. British economists of that day argued that the British empire was an efficient exchange system, bringing relatively high-quality products and "enlightenment" to remote areas of the world, but, to the people suffering low incomes under colonial rule, it was a game fixed to benefit the rich. Mohandas Gandhi finally organized Indian peasants to peacefully resist this exchange (through boycotts of British products and self-reliance) and campaigned for Indian independence. Similarly, today one's perspective on the benefits of "free trade" depends in part on who is gaining and losing in the game of global markets. The fact that total global production increases in such a system does not necessarily satisfy less developed or transitional economies, whose people lack the option of buying home-produced products and who remain exporters of mainly primary or primitive goods.

It appears that the future struggle in the global economy will be between the status quo views of those dominant in and benefiting from the system and the views of those who demand a larger share of production and income. The prevailing global economic philosophy, dictated largely by the dominant powers, will dictate the terms of this debate. Recently, that philosophy has stressed the notion that governments must strictly limit their domestic economic interventions in order to allow markets and entrepreneurs to flourish. The IMF and the World Bank, and the major powers holding the most votes on their ruling councils, have made international capital assistance—that is, bilateral or multilateral aid—dependent on satisfying various conditionality rules. The most serious has been the condition that aid-recipient governments slash their budgets and encourage privatization. While a number of Asian states have made tremendous industrial strides under such policies, conditions and cultures in Asia appear to differ significantly on such matters as consumption and savings from those in Latin America and Africa (see Ch. 10.).

Indeed, some critics see the laissez-faire philosophy as largely a myth. Even governments that articulate a policy of nonintervention often intervene selectively but on a massive scale to aid "strategic" and politically influential industries. One such industry is the armament industry. The governments of arms-producing states often attempt to nurture weapons manufacturers in order to preserve the capabilities of producing arms in wartime and to boost export profits. Arms generally are commissioned by government contract, and governments offer incentives and subsidies for new weapons research and development, as well as facilitate, through government offices and consultation with foreign military leaders, their sale overseas. Governments of major powers also often regulate the arms trade, hoping to prevent the latest advanced equipment from reaching enemies or troublesome groups abroad. In this sense government interests can diverge from corporate interests, since companies generally seek to sell equipment for profit wherever they can.[29] In recent years, with the shrinking of military budgets in many parts of the world and the general decline of military sales since the settlement of a series of wars in the 1980s, governments have encouraged the consolidation of defense industries. Rather than attempting to support four or five separate aerospace firms, for example, Washington and London have taken steps to encourage mergers and acquisitions. For example, when McDonnell-Douglas was denied the opportunity to compete for a new jet fighter contract for the early twenty-first century, it quickly announced a merger with Boeing, one of the companies selected to compete. Boeing needed McDonnell's extensive jet fighter experience, and the federal government had few antitrust objections to the formation of the world's largest aerospace firm.[30] Similar developments have been seen in automotive, petroleum, and other key industrial sectors, as previous government emphasis on anti-trust policy has been removed in the interest of global competitiveness (see Ch. 9).

Arms industries also are illustrative of the future in high-technology competition. Governments have a vested interest in encouraging technological breakthroughs, especially to avoid being caught short technologically in competition over military security and commercial sales. Indeed, global transactions, such as arms sales, have come to stress the exchange of technology even over the exchange of equipment.[31] States purchasing arms tend to demand "technology transfers" in the form of licenses to assemble the equipment or joint partnership in its development or modification or, as in countertrade agreements, in the form of commitments to purchase their own products in return for the arms sales. These agreements are designed to put skilled people to work in developing states and to justify politically the huge investment of public funds in purchasing arms abroad. While technology spreads, however, it tends to be at a pace which does not overturn existing power hierarchies and pecking orders.

It is likely, then, that the pattern of government involvement in arms production will be repeated in other forms of high-technology industry in the future. Although arms, by their nature, have a special place straddling both the security and commercial policy realms, all forms of high-technology production will gain some of this urgency, as discussed in Chapter 8. Technologies have many uses, and it will be difficult to predict which technologies will influence security concerns and strategies. Arms manufacturers are being encouraged to develop dual-use equipment and technologies for both civilian and military applications, and governments are likely to take fairly forceful positions on encouraging or discouraging corporate mergers, acquisitions, and reorganizations in various industrial fields to foster more competitive firms with greater access to investment capital and more international connections for marketing and technology acquisition. Whether a similar governmental willingness reemerges in many states to intervene to control the "business cycle" and to avert the boom and bust of inflation and recession remains to be seen.

MANAGEMENT OF THE GLOBAL ECONOMY

As difficult as it may be to manage domestic economies in the globalized world markets, it will be even more of a challenge for policymakers to manage the international economy. Again, like the nineteenth-century liberal theorists, some expect that the effects of free trade, combined with the information technology revolution, will provide a form of self-regulated harmony, as production and economic opportunities spread from continent to continent. This rosy view of the future, however, is by no means assured. If the past is any indicator, development trends will continue to be uneven, and certain regions will continue to lag behind. Controversies also will develop about interpreting the free-trade rules themselves, as in today's battles over whether governments are violating GATT rules by dumping goods on the market at artificially low prices, are conveniently ignoring international copyright provisions, or are negligently polluting the biosphere. Thus, there will continue to be a need for more effective policy coordination among states, for definitive regulations, and for the adjudication and enforcement of international norms and agreements.

Increasingly, it appears that the future of the global political economy will be played out in such institutions as the World Trade Organization. As discussed in Chapter 5, the WTO is expected to satisfy the less developed countries' calls for wider and more meaningful participation in world trade decisions and to function as a truly global mechanism for the development of international standards and dispute resolution.[32] Conflict-resolution mechanisms, such as the Dispute Settlement Body (DSB) and Dispute Settlement Panels (DSPs), established within the WTO are expected to address policy disagreements and to prevent trade conflicts.

The presence of such international institutions raises a host of questions with respect to national sovereignty or regional bloc autonomy in policy decisions, yet proponents of wider international activism argue that the WTO's enforcement capabilities are indeed limited and that, like other international organizations, this new system is based on consensual compliance with international norms of behavior, rather than coercion. Yet countries flaunting WTO rulings risk losing credibility as a reliable trade partner. Neither does the WTO necessarily address the serious issue of North–South inequalities. The WTO may enable developing countries to make their complaints regarding trade problems heard by major powers, but it cannot guarantee the resolution of issues. Still, the dispute mechanisims at least empower the weaker party to some extent by issuing decisions binding on the stronger parties. Whether the major industrial powers exhibit the political acumen to balance various and often diverging interests can be seen only after some years of experience with WTO. Nevertheless, for now the major powers appear to be interested in maintaining the GATT-WTO principles of trade liberalization and stability, despite tendencies toward politicization of trade, as in the linkage between most favored nation (MFN) and human rights regarding China.

Occasionally, waivers or special privileges are granted to meet the needs of certain WTO members, as in the Generalized System of Preferences, or preferential tariffs, allowed to developing countries by developed states on a nonreciprocal basis. These are designed to help "infant industries" in LDCs; the waiver of MFN principles in this regard was authorized at the Tokyo Round of GATT in 1971, recognizing the initiative of the UN Conference on Trade and Development (UNCTAD) from the 1960s. Other concessions to LDCs built into the WTO treaty include exemptions from some subsidy-reduction requirements and special attention to the needs of food-importing states in the agricultural sector, exemptions and time extensions on sanitary improvements, customs valuation, reduced technical barriers to trade, some flexibility on antidumping penalties, and delayed implementation of certain intellectual property rights provisions. LDCs also may require an LDC member on a dispute-resolution panel, and the Dispute Settlement Body is to take special note of LDC interests in conducting surveillance concerning the implementation of dispute-resolution agreements.[33]

Despite these concessions, it has been argued that the WTO system still favors the richer developed states in key areas, such as workers' rights. While the GATT treaty preamble refers to the objective of "full employment," the political reality has been a general tendency to export unemployment from the developed to less developed states, especially through de facto protectionism on products from low-wage states.[34] Wage rates are a hotly debated topic among WTO members, and the debate is not a simple one between laissez-faire liberals and Marxists. Labor unions and some leftists would agree with domestic employers in advocating the protection and exclusion of cut-wage products, but other business leaders (particularly those from MNCs) and some political liberals and conservatives would advocate the opportunity for LDCs to export their products, so that even low-wage earners can eat and build a better life. Clearly, this unresolved set of claims, based on contrasting notions of justice and equity, will test the WTO dispute-resolution mechanisms in the future.

As the erstwhile economic and security hegemon, the United States, since the Second World War, has generally favored the development of multilateral trade and commercial agreements, such as those of GATT and WTO, in the international system. In a sense, the United States has stood to gain from broad international agreements to legitimize, code, and enforce norms and rules favoring free trade and open markets. This commitment to multilateralism has been put to the test, as was seen in previous chapters, as Washington has seen its relative dominance in the global economy erode. Congressional leaders and others in the U.S. government and industry have seen dangers in being dragged into global organizations in which U.S. autonomy would be questioned and in which others would seek to limit Washington's freedom of action—for example, to keep out cheaply competitive foreign goods. Still, it is clear that for international cooperative regimes for the management of economic conflict to be effective, "they must represent a broad and sustainable consensus among the states of the international system. . . . Multilateral agreements more often than not are underpinned by great-power understandings. The conclusion of the GATT 1993 Uruguay Round . . . depended on prior EU-US agreement."[35] This means that the U.S. must continue to play a leading facilitative role and that a combination of multilateralism and bilateralism is necessary for international economic management to succeed.

Noted economist C. Fred Bergsten, for example, sees the fulfillment of GATT and the development of WTO as part of a twenty-first-century vision of global free trade, with healthy consequences for the spread of prosperity, in both the North and South. He notes the pledges of broad groupings of states—the European Union and Mediterranean countries (EUROMED), thirty-four

TABLE 13.1
Regional Free-Trade Arrangements' Share of World Trade, 1994

Grouping	Percentage
European Union	22.8
EUROMED	2.3
NAFTA	7.9
Mercosur	0.3
Free Trade Area of Americas (additional regional)	2.6
Asian Free Trade Association (AFTA)	1.3
Australia-New Zealand	0.1
APEC (additional regional)	23.7
Total	61.0

Source: C. Fred Bergsten, "Competitive Liberalization and Global Free Trade: A Vision for the Early 21st Century," *APEC Working Paper*, 96-15 (Washington, DC: Institute for International Economics, 1996), Internet, p. 2.

Western Hemisphere democracies (Free Trade Area of the Americas—FTAA), and the Asia Pacific Economic Cooperation (APEC) forum—to establish barrier-free trade in their regions by the first quarter of the twenty-first century. As seen in Table 13.1, he calculates that such groupings have already accounted for more than 60 percent of trade in the 1990s. This process, in which diverse countries from many parts of the world are joining, is termed "competitive liberalization." States, no matter what their prior economic philosophy—protectionist or liberal, individualistic or egalitarian—are obliged to attract global investment capital in the interdependent world economy. Only through negotiated mutual trade liberalization can they develop sufficient jobs, profits, and technology.

Bergsten sees the logic of such negotiations moving from regional to global arrangements, since the latter maximize the number of markets involved; however, regional arrangements persist because they are essentially easier and quicker to achieve. The system of competing regional trade blocs also allows for bargaining and mutual pressure, as when the announcement of an expansion plan for NAFTA spurred new separate Latin free-trade agreements to prepare for negotiations with the North, when the European Community reacted to U.S. free-trade initiatives with Israel and Canada by dropping its opposition to the Uruguay Round of GATT, and when the EU agreed to meet that round's deadlines when APEC in Asia set its own free-trade agenda. Thus, no major group wants to be left out of the bargain.[36]

Bergsten also sees threats implicit in the regional organizations of competitive liberalization. For example, he notes that, if TAFTA comes into existence across the Atlantic, the danger is that it will be seen as an exclusive "rich and white" trade club, once again excluding less affluent and nonwhite areas of the world, reversing progress made in the past two decades in integrating rich and poor states in Europe (the Mediterranean and the former Soviet bloc), Asia, and the Western Hemisphere (inclusion of Mexico and others with the United States and Canada). While others may see such integration as potentially perpetuating dependencies among the poor, he sees it as potentially eliminating the North–South conflict and raising LDC incomes.[37] There is also the danger that, in linking with neighbors, states may reduce their overall levels of public welfare and wage rates to lowest common denominators, rather than raising the lowest to higher levels. Bergsten argues that, since the 1980s, the United States has followed a policy of "full employment," creating more low-wage jobs to compete with foreign labor costs, while removing public support for the poor and allowing companies to downsize their employment rosters and benefits packages. By contrast, European leaders have continued to face chronic high unemployment levels but have maintained relatively high wage rates, generous vacations, and both company benefits and public assistance programs. Clearly, the pressure is on at the turn of the millennium for both Europeans and Americans to reconsider the implications of these policies.

CONCLUSION

Controversies about international economic management in the WTO and other bodies alert us to the importance of the economic perspectives—liberalism, globalism, nationalism, and Marxism—that were presented in this book. As the international economy becomes more of a polity—that is, a political community in which joint decision making, or "governance," takes place—people's contrasting views of what economics is about will be highlighted. Some contend that the system is naturally competitive, with stress on the fitness of individual entrepreneurs, firms, and states. Others see economics as a struggle over the distribution of resources and goods, and they advocate that more people share the wealth. In the heyday of Marxism, Soviet theorists argued that human rights, as defined in the West, were incomplete without the inclusion of "economic rights" and that denying people bread was just as damaging as denying them liberty. Echoes of this debate are still heard in U.S.-Chinese conflicts over human rights issues, although China has gone far toward opening its economy to market forces, even at the expense of social egalitarianism. Different cultural and political perspectives, as in Islam and feminism, condition people's interpretations of economic rights and responsibilities.

While analysts such as Bergsten see such potential obstacles to the benefits of free trade as protectionist dangers in a drumbeat of concern about environmentalism and unfair labor practices, others see the liberalization model as a rationale for a new form of "corporate colonialism." They fear that, by opening or exposing the economies of less developed states to MNC investment, new company dependencies will be formed. National governments supposedly then would fail to regulate and protect their own ecological environment, or to remedy the scourges of "poverty, landlessness, homelessness, violence, and alienation," which have poisoned people's views of the future—both in the developing world and in the big cities of the North. "We are now being asked to believe that the development processes that have further impoverished people and devastated the planet will lead to diametrically different and highly beneficial outcomes, if only they can be accelerated and applied everywhere, freely, without restriction: that is, when they are *globalized*."[38] Concern here is about a "casino economy," in which regulatory control over global corporate activity is eliminated and currencies no longer are controlled by national governments—that is, an economy ruled by currency speculators. As in other alarms throughout history, however, this appears to be an exaggeration of the problem; there may be room for regulation and reform within the liberalization, whether competitive or global; currency speculators may prove to be less important than governmental and inter-governmental financial bodies, and, indeed, there may be no way fully to restore national sovereignty and autonomy over currency matters. Too many dollars, yen, and ECUs circulate abroad in the modern world for state treasuries, even the most venerable one in London, to reassert total control.

In trying to explain international economic and political relations, some theorists who style themselves as "neo-realists" emphasize the basically "anarchical" state of international relations and the hierarchies of power that create a pecking order among states, i.e., the fact that there is no global government or set of regulators to moderate each state's self-interested competition with others for power and influence. The resulting "dog-eat-dog" world has states cooperating only for their own self interest and in limited and transitory ways, with leaders supposedly worried not only about their own gains, but the fact that others might be gaining relatively more than them (so called "absolute" vs. "relative" gains). Theorists styling themselves as "neo-liberals" or "liberal institutionalists," on the other hand, stress mainly absolute gains, which leave lots of room for joint gains, even uneven ones, through global cooperation in on-going institutions and regimes (like those institutions established in the Bretton-Woods and United Nations systems).[39] These two groups of theorists, corresponding roughly to some nationalists, Marxists, traditional liberals, and mercantilists on the one hand, and some globalists, modern commercial liberals, and world system thinkers on the other hand, have contrasting pessimistic and optimistic views about the future of international economic collaboration and institution building. For institutionalists, for example, with their emphasis on benefits of cooperation and interdependence among states, hegemony is not really necessary for economic progress since states will continue to see the benefits of maintaining global and regional regimes and institutions to handle problems such as trade and the environment. Institutionalists also would expect regimes to adapt to new demands and find new purposes, as in ASEAN becoming both a security and economic organization. Realists, on the other hand, have felt that most regimes and institutions were created mainly at the behest of the hegemonic power (the U.S. after World War II), and that with either hegemonic decline or the end of the cold war which had spurred Washington's commitments, these institutions and regimes will suffer and perhaps wither.[40]

Our look at the emerging global economy has revealed both optimism and pessimism, myths and realities, dangers and opportunities. Any future hegemonies would necessarily appear to be joint ones, and progress in trade liberalization and the effective management of the international economy would appear to require both patient bargaining and the removal of obstacles such as parochialism, nationalism, and exclusive regionalism, toward greater international cooperation. Consequences of unbridled "free markets" appear to make some form of government regulation and reform imperative, especially if core and periphery are to be bridged. The fascinating questions for the future of the international political economy are in the way varying philosophies of economics and social justice, as well as varying public and private interests, will be played out or reconciled in the emerging regional and global institutions. The results of this interplay will affect the lives of generations to come, and certainly of IPE students, in the most profound manner.

Many Americans awoke to the realities of the international economy when they suddenly experienced long gasoline lines during the oil boycott of the 1970s. Such shocks, one hopes, will not be necessary for people to pay closer attention to the contending forces and emerging collaboration in the international system in the new century.

Chapter Summary

Whether a new hegemonic leader, such as Japan, Germany, or the European Union, or a combination of them will replace the United States in the twenty-first century is one of the major questions in IPE in the 1990s. The answer will most certainly have serious ramifications for the U.S. economy and standard of living, but the transitional phase, if mismanaged, can, as during the decline of the British empire in the early 1900s, have severe consequences for the world economy as well. In an ever widening globalized system, the hegemonic leader or group of leaders plays a key role in maintaining international financial stability.

Regional integration for larger markets and trading communities may be a cause of inter-regional frictions, and thus ironically also lead to the fragmentation of the world economy. Within the context of globalization, however, regional integration is more likely to lead to greater international cooperation, as such economic regional entities as the EU expand their functions and boundaries to become more inclusive and negotiate with their counterparts elsewhere in the world.

Center-periphery relations within regions, as well as those between the North and the South, are expected to expand to encompass new trade partners, labor markets, and resource suppliers. Expanding trade and financial relations, however, do not necessarily guarantee the resolution of financial and trade disputes or of long-standing territorial, ethnic, and religious conflicts. National and international institutional arrangements are necessary for their management or resolution.

The role of government in regulating domestic and international markets and in encouraging strategic industries or economic sectors, while cushioning the public against inflation and recession in both developed and developing societies, will continue to be subject to controversy. The tilt in the 1980s and 1990s toward privatization diminishes governments' position in some respects and may prove beneficial for some groups in society. The failure to provide the general public with social and economic safety nets, however, may prove disastrous to citizens and governments alike, and might lead to a new cycle of government economic intervention.

The establishment of the World Trade Organization (WTO) has demonstrated that management of the global political economy in the twenty-first century will require more concerted efforts and greater participation—through such institutions. An ideologically more balanced approach than witnessed in the 1980s and 1990s to governing trade, capital and labor flows, and aid and development, combined with multilateral and bilateral bargaining and dispute-resolution mechanisms, will most likely enhance the management of international political economy.

The forces of philosophies, ideologies, and religions—capitalism, Marxism, nationalism, mercantilism, Christianity, Islam, Hinduism, and so forth—fluctuate, sometimes gaining in strength and popularity and at other times declining, but the effective management of cultural differences and economic linkages remains a key to international peace, with states, nationalities, and individuals achieving enough autonomy and sufficient income to satisfy social and economic needs and demands for economic well-being, physical security, and social justice.

Points of Contention

What are some of the issues involved regarding the future of the European Union? Is the EU the "wave of the future" as a model for other regions?

Will the emergence of new hegemonic leaders in the international political economy necessarily result in the demise of the United States as a hegemon? Is a single hegemon necessary for international economic stability?

What difficulties are involved in maintaining a world-economic system based on the principles of free trade?

What role are international institutions, such as the WTO, expected to play in international trade disputes? How effective do you think they will be? Who will benefit most?

To what extent is it possible to "assign" specific developing regions to individual industrialized countries as a means of encouraging closer economic relations and development? What role would groups in your community play in such a system?

What possible problems do you see in the formation of a "Trans-Atlantic Free Trade Area" (TAFTA)? Are such trends in regional integration incompatible with globalization? What other factors are involved?

What are some of the arguments for and against a more integrated and structured East Asian trade community? How would the smaller economies in the region view such a formal community?

What are the implications of the changing international economic environment for labor?

Ultimately, which (pessimist or optimist) view of the future of the world do you believe will be closer to reality in the twenty-first century?

Notes

1. Michael Veseth, *Selling Globalization: The Myth of the Global Economy* (Boulder, CO: Lynne Rienner, 1998). See also, James H. Mittelman, ed., *Globalization: Critical Reflections* (Boulder, CO: Lynne Rienner, 1996).
2. Brian Hindley, *Transatlantic Free Trade and Multilateralism*, Issues Paper No. 5 (London: British-North American Committee, April 1996), pp. 1–3.
3. Of course, much hinges on domestic interest groups and voting blocs that favor or oppose relations with so-called radical regimes. See Robert Axelrod and Robert O. Keohane, "Achieving Cooperation Under Anarchy: Strategies and Institutions," in David A. Baldwin, ed., *Neorealism and Neoliberalism: The Contemporary Debate* (New York: Columbia University Press, 1993), p. 92.
4. Helen Milner, "American Debt and World Power," *International Journal* 48, 3 (Summer 1993), pp. 527–560.
5. Miguel de Oliver, "The Hegemonic Cycle and Free Trade: The US and Mexico," *Political Geography* 12, 5 (September 1993), pp. 457–472.
6. Herman Schwartz, "Hegemony, International Debt and International Economic Instability," in Chronis Polychroniou, ed., *Issues and Perspectives in International Political Economy* (New York: Praeger, 1992); see also Charles P. Kindleberger, *The World in Depression, 1929–1939* (Berkeley: University of California Press, 1973).
7. "Concentrating on Hegemony: The Empirical Relationship Between International Trade and the Distribution of Power," December 29, 1996, Internet.
8. Lenin predicted wars of imperial conquest among capitalist powers at the outset of the twentieth century. While war came, it was also supported by socialist parties in most European states, contrary to the class consciousness Lenin would have predicted.
9. Christopher Chase-Dunn and Bruce Podobnik, "The Next War: World-System Cycles and Trends," *Journal of World-Systems Research* 1, 6 (1995), p.13, Internet. See also A.F.K. Organski and Jacek Kugler, *The War Ledger* (Chicago: University of Chicago Press, 1980).
10. William I. Robinson, *Promoting Polyarchy: Globalization, US Intervention, and Hegemony* (Cambridge: Cambridge University Press, 1996).
11. *SIPRI Yearbook 1996* (Oxford: Oxford University Press/Stockholm International Peace Research Institute, 1996), ch. 1.
12. Fred W. Riggs, "Ethnic Nationalism in the Para-Modern Context," paper presented to the Annual Meeting of the International Studies Association, June 1996, Internet, p. 2.
13. See John A. Vasquez, "The Post-Positivist Debate: Reconstructing Scientific Enquiry and International Relations Theory After Enlightenment's Fall," in Ken Booth and Steve Smith, eds., *International Relations Theory Today* (University Park, PA: Pennsylvania State University Press, 1995).
14. Larry Rohter, "Free Trade Goes South with or Without U.S.," *The New York Times,* January 6, 1997, p. A4.
15. See Karl W. Deutsch, *Political Community at the International Level* (Garden City, NY: Doubleday, 1959); Deutsch, *Nationalism and Social Communication* (Cambridge, MA: MIT Press, 1953); and Deutsch, et al., *Political Community and the North Atlantic Area* (Princeton: Princeton University Press, 1957).
16. Sareth Rajapatirana, "The Evolution of Trade Treaties and Trade Creation: Lessons for Latin America," paper presented at the Annual Regional Conference of the International Cooperative Alliance, Quito, Ecuador, August 1994.
17. World Bank, "Development Brief Number 27," January 1994.
18. Kym Anderson and Hege Northeim, "History, Geography and Regional Economic Integration," June 1993, Internet.
19. Paul Collier and Jan Willem Gunning, "Trade Policy and Regional Integration: Implications for the Relations Between Europe and Africa," July 1994, Internet.
20. Marius Brulhart and Johan Torsten Torstensson, "Regional Integration, Scale Economies and Industry Location in the European Union," July 1996, Internet.
21. On the democratic peace debate, see Bruce A. Russett, *Grasping the Democratic Peace* (Princeton: Princeton University Press, 1993); and Michael E. Brown, Sean M. Lynn-Jones, and Steven E. Miller, *Debating the Democratic Peace* (Cambridge, MA: MIT Press, 1996).
22. See Samuel P. Huntington's controversial article, "The Clash of Civilizations?" *Foreign Affairs* 72, 3 (Summer 1993), pp. 22–49. See also the articles by Fouad Ajami, Kishor Mahbubani, Robet L. Bartley, Liu Binyan, and Jeane J. Kirkpatrick in *Foreign Affairs* 72, 4 (September/October, 1993), pp. 2–26, in response to Huntington's essay.

23. Majid Tehranian, "Globalism and Its Discontents: Modernity and Postmodernity in a Fragmented World," *Report,* No. 8 (Spring 1995), Internet.
24. *Ibid.*
25. *Making Peace Work: Lessons for the International Development Community,* Conference Report (Washington, DC: Overseas Development Council, May 1996), p. 6.
26. *Ibid.,* pp. 4–5, 10.
27. *Ibid.,* pp. 7–8.
28. Nicholas D. Kristof, "Malaria Makes a Comeback and Is More Deadly Than Ever," *The New York Times,* January 8, 1997, pp. A1, A7; see also *Development Cooperation: Efforts and Policies of the Members of the DAC* (Washington, DC: Organization of Economic Cooperation and Development, Report, 1995).
29. See Keith Krause, *Arms and the State: Patterns of Military Production and Trade* (Cambridge, UK: Cambridge University Press, 1992); Herbert Wulf, ed., *Arms Industry Limited* (Oxford: Oxford University Press/Stockholm International Peace Research Institute, 1993).
30. Frederic S. Pearson, John Sislin, and Marie Olson, "Arms Trade, Economics of," *Encyclopedia of Violence, Peace, and Conflict* (San Diego: Academic Press, 1999 forthcoming).
31. William W. Keller, *Arm in Arm: The Political Economy of the Global Arms Trade* (New York: Basic Books, 1995), pp. 120–121; Frederic S. Pearson, *The Global Spread of Arms: Political Economy of International Security* (Boulder, CO: Westview Press, 1994); Barry Buzan and Eric Herring, eds., *The Arms Dynamic in World Politics* (Boulder, CO: Lynne Rienner, 1998).
32. Alan D. Minyard, "The World Trade Organization: History, Structure, and Analysis," unpublished paper, Mississippi State University, January 1997, Internet, p. 6.
33. "Developing Countries," *Guide to WTO,* January 1997, Internet.
34. "Worker's Rights," *Guide to WTO,* January 1997, Internet.
35. I. McLean, *Concise Oxford Dictionary of Politics* (Oxford: Oxford University Press, 1996), 328.
36. C. Fred Bergsten, "Competitive Liberalization and Global Free Trade: A Vision for the Early 21st Century," *APEC Working Paper,* 96-15 (Washington, DC: Institute for International Economics, 1996), Internet, pp. 4–5.
37. *Ibid.,* pp. 5–7.
38. Jerry Mander [*sic.*], "Corporate Colonialism," *Resurgence,* September–October 1996, Internet, p. 1.
39. See David A. Baldwin, ed., *Neorealism and Neoliberalism: The Contemporary Debate* (New York: Columbia University Press, 1993, part III.
40. Robert O. Keohane, "Institutional Theory and the Realist Challenge After the Cold War," in Baldwin, ed., *Neorealism and Neoliberalism,* pp. 284–91.

GLOSSARY

absolute advantage refers to a country's natural or acquired endowments that can provide another country with a set of goods or services for less than the latter can produce at home. (Ch. 2) *See also* Comparative advantage.

Asian Pacific Economic Cooperation (APEC) was formed in 1988 as a forum for trans-Pacific trade negotiations. It is composed of sixteen Pacific countries, including Australia, Brunei, Canada, China, Hong Kong, Indonesia, Japan, Malaysia, Mexico, South Korea, New Zealand, the Philippines, Singapore, Taiwan, Thailand, and the United States. Together APEC countries generate 50 percent of the world's trade and economic growth. (Chs. 1, 5)

Baker Plan (1985), by U.S. Secretary of the Treasury James Baker, was in response to the international debt crisis, particularly in Latin America, in the 1980s. It called for major structural adjustments and liberalization of trade and foreign investments, including privatization of state enterprises by the debt-ridden countries. (Ch. 10) *See also* Brady Plan.

balance of payments consists of the value of all of a country's transactions, including imports and exports of goods and services and the transfer of investments, currency, gold, and so on, with other countries. (Ch. 5)

balance of power refers to the geo-political configuration in international relations as indicated by the distribution of military capabilities among nations in a given period of time. By extension, it may also include economic and cultural dominance, as well as hegemonic leadership. (Chs. 1, 2, 5)

balance of trade is a country's total value of products exported minus its imports. *Balance of trade system,* more specifically, was the traditional mercantilist notion of economic strength as determined by the inflows of precious metals into the state treasury and the state's wealth accumulated through domestic protectionism and international expansion and conquest. (Chs. 2, 5)

Brady Plan (1989), by U.S. Secretary of the Treasury Nicholas Brady, replaced the Baker Plan. It emphasized voluntary debt reduction through reliance primarily on market forces while new lending to debtor countries continued. (Ch. 10) *See also* Baker Plan.

brain drain refers to the emigration by educated and skilled citizens from their homeland (usually developing countries) for more advanced training and better jobs in another (usually advanced industrialized) country. (Ch. 8)

capitalism as an economic philosophy advocates laissez-faire principles with an emphasis on private ownership of capital and production. It holds that the best approach to economic development, growth, and prosperity is through reliance on the "invisible hand" of market supply and demand, with minimal government intervention in economic activities. (Ch. 2) *See also* Classical liberalism *and* Laissez-faire.

classical liberalism, stressing limited government interference in the economy, seeks to eliminate "artificial" (that is, government-imposed) barriers to economic freedoms in production, consumption, competition, trade, and economic activity in general. It views freedom of economic activities by competitive units, private ownership of property, and engagement in domestic and international markets as "inalienable rights." (Ch. 2) *See also* Capitalism, Laissez-faire, *and* Liberal feminism.

common agricultural policy (CAP), in place since the 1950s, is a protectionist policy by the European Union for the union's agricultural interests against non-EU competitors. Has included agricultural suport programs. (Ch. 5)

common market is a free trade area in which trading partners agree to remove all tariffs or quotas among themselves, impose common barriers (for example, CETs) on nonmembers, and substantially reduce or completely eliminate national restrictions on the movement of labor and capital among themselves. (Chs. 5, 6) *See also* Customs union.

comparative advantage is a country's ability to produce certain goods efficiently relative to another country, even if that other country produces the goods more efficiently. The former, therefore, concentrates on the production of such goods for trade—hence, commodity specialization. (Ch. 2) *See also* Absolute advantage.

conditionality rules by the International Monetary Fund require loan recipients to adopt certain austerity (or *structural adjustment*) programs to reduce government expenditures and to introduce economic liberalization policies, including privatization of state-owned enterprises. (Ch. 4) *See also* Structural adjustment.

containment was the post-WWII U.S. policy of stopping the spread of Communism. First enunciated by the Truman administration with respect to security in Europe (for example, the Truman Doctrine, the Marshall Plan, and NATO), containment was subsequently extended to Asia and other parts of the world and became the overarching objective of U.S. foreign policy throughout the Cold War. (Ch. 3)

customs union is a free trade area in which trading partners agree to eliminate trade barriers, such as tariffs and quotas, among themselves. (Ch. 6) *See also* Common market.

dependencia theory contends that the economic discrepancies between the industrialized countries of the North (the core) and the developing countries in the South (the periphery) are the result of colonial and neo-colonial exploitation and domination by the former. It holds that early industrialization enabled the North to use advanced military technologies and colonial institutions to exploit the South's local resources, which were needed for industrialization and modernization, while impeding development in and for the South. (Ch. 2) *See also* Imperialism *and* World system.

dependent development refers to economic development in developing countries in which economic growth is dependent primarily on their ability to export raw materials and agricultural products to markets abroad, particularly to the Western industrialized economies. This situation leaves the economies of developing countries vulnerable to market fluctuations in the North. (Chs. 2, 10)

double taxation occurs in a number of ways. One is when an MNC is taxed by different levels of government in the host country. Another is when a government taxes MNCs' profits generated in other countries. Double taxation also occurs when one government claims authority to tax based on the residence (or citizenship) of the taxpayer, while another government claims authority to tax based on origin of income. (Ch. 7) *See also* International taxation *and* International taxation.

dual technologies are technologies that can be used for both civilian and military purposes. (Ch. 8)

dumping refers to the practice of selling a product in a foreign market at prices lower than those in the home market. (Ch. 5)

economic dualism is the division between urban and rural economies, in which the former are the center of economic activities while the latter remain underdeveloped. The key problem with this situation is that the urban political and economic elites gain from the government's relations with foreign governments and MNCs as cities develop and modernize. The rural areas, on the other hand, retain their traditional feudal structures, in some countries exacerbated by the introduction of advanced agricultural machinery, replacing human labor, which in turn leads to rural unemployment and massive migration to the cities (Ch. 10)

economic (or industrial) espionage refers to the secret acquisition of information by a company to gain market advantages against competitors. (Ch. 8)

economic nationalism, as in *mercantilism,* is government policy to institute trade barriers and various protectionist policies on imports to protect domestic industries. Such policies are usually adopted in times of unemployment and major economic dislocations, such as the Great Depression of the 1930s. (Ch. 2) *See also* Mercantilism *and* Kameralism.

European Union (EU), the successor to the European Community, was initially created under the Treaty of Rome in 1957. It currently consists of fifteen European countries (Austria, Belgium, Britain, Denmark, Finland, France, Germany, Greece, Ireland, Italy, Luxembourg, Netherlands, Portugal, Spain, and Sweden). The Maastricht Treaty on European Union (1992) moved the Community closer to developing a region-wide common European market with minimum barriers to internal trade. The EU also has been developing its own currency, the ECU. (Ch. 1)

export-led strategies are economic development policies that, due to a lack of large domestic markets, stress international competitiveness and the securing of markets abroad for the export of locally produced products. (Ch. 10)

export-processing zones (EPZs), also known as free trade zones (FTZs), are areas designated by the host government where MNCs produce goods for "export" without taxation or the burden of governmental regulations normally imposed on the national economy. (Ch. 7)

fixed exchange rates, the standard practice well into the early 1970s, refers to the value of a currency pegged to the price of another currency or exact ratios in relation to the cost of gold. Governments agree to set the official exchange rate at a specified level until such time as deemed necessary to readjust it. (Ch. 4)

floating exchange rates refers to the fluctuating exchange value of a currency as it appreciates or depreciates in relation to other currencies as determined by supply and demand in the foreign exchange markets. In *free (or clean) float exchange,* governments maintain a hands-off policy toward foreign exchange market fluctuations Under a *managed (or dirty) float* system, government policy determines foreign exchange rate. Presently all currencies of the industrialized economies operate under a managed float system. (Ch. 4)

foreign direct investments (FDIs) are investments by a parent company from one country to establish subsidiaries in another country. Unlike *portfolio investments,* in FDIs the parent company directly controls the operations of and profits from its subsidiaries. (Ch. 3) *See also* Portfolio investments.

foreign exchange rate is the price or value of one currency to purchase another currency. (Ch. 4)

free trade area (FTA) is a regional multilateral arrangement whereby members agree to eliminate tariffs among themselves. Trading partners agree to impose no tariffs or quotas on one other, but they are free to impose such restrictions on nonmembers. (Ch. 6) *See also* Customs union.

functionalism is a school of thought that contends that international collaboration on specific technical matters in the long run encourages greater cooperation among nations and eventually leads to a more stable and peaceful international system. (Ch. 2)

General Agreement on Tariffs and Trade (GATT) was created in 1947 to establish international rules for trade liberalization and to provide a forum for resolution of trade disputes. In 1994, GATT was succeeded by the World Trade Organization. (Ch. 1) *See also* World Trade Organization (WTO).

gross domestic product (GDP) represents the total value of all goods and services produced in a country. (Ch. 1)

gross national product (GNP) is the total value of all goods and services produced or exchanged in a country, including its inward and outward international economic activities. (Ch. 1)

Group of Seven (G-7) is an informal group of seven leading industrialized countries (Britain, Canada, France, Germany, Italy, Japan, and the United States). Its annual conferences, known as G-7 economic summits, are attended by the leaders of these countries to consult on economic and related issues. In the 1990s, post-Communist Russia as well as China have sought membership to the G-7 to indicate their international status as major economies. (Ch. 1)

hegemonic stability theory holds that the international system is dominated by a single hegemonic power as world leader, which creates structures of dominance and order. The presence of such a hegemon is said to be necessary to bring stability to an otherwise "anarchic" international system. (Ch. 2)

hegemony is the dominant position held by a single power in the world political economy for a long period of time. A hegemon usually emerges after a major war, and it subsequently establishes new international financial and political mechanisms and rules that enable it to consolidate power and perpetuate its dominance. (Ch. 2)

ijma refers to leading Muslim theologians' consensus on matters not clarified in the Quran and the Sunna. (Ch. 2)

imperialism refers to the control and domination a powerful country exercises over a weaker country or set of countries. Marxist-Leninist, *dependencia,* and capitalist world-system theorists view the relationship between the advanced capitalist governments and MNCs and the developing countries as exploitative, while the capitalist countries compete among themselves and divide the world into spheres of influence. (Ch. 2) *See also* Hegemony, Marxism-Leninism, *and* Dependencia.

import substitution industrialization (ISI) is an economic policy aimed at producing manufactured goods by domestic industries to replace imported products. This strategy is based on the principles of economic nationalism involving various protective measures, such as tariffs, to protect and develop local infant industries and to stimulate rapid industrialization and economic development. (Chs. 3, 10)

industrial targeting involves government-corporate strategies designed to promote, through various incentives, highly competitive and technology-intensive industries. This strategy was effectively used by the East Asian "four tigers" (Hong Kong, Singapore, South Korea, and Taiwan). (Ch. 3)

infant industries are newly emerging industries that need government protection in order to survive foreign competition. As they grow stronger in the domestic market, they expand their operations to international markets. (Ch. 3)

informal economy refers to unregulated economic and financial transactions and activities not registered in national accounts. (Ch. 12)

informalization refers to the process of transferring a share of economic activity from the formal to the informal sector. (Ch. 12)

interdependence refers to the interconnected nature of mutual economic dependence among states, characterized by reciprocal influences among them as well as other international actors. The term specifically underscores the mutually vulnerable nature of nation-states in the modern globalized international system. (Ch. 2)

international division of labor refers to the division of production operations among different countries, possibly leading to a spread of joint benefits, but also to situations where employees in the industrialized countries enjoy better working conditions and higher wages and are generally engaged in more capital-intensive employment than employees in developing countries. (Chs. 3, 7)

international governmental organizations (IGOs) are international organizations that consist exclusively of governments. (Ch. 1) *See also* Nongovernmental organizations (NGOs).

international labor competition, as instigated by the globalization of MNC production systems, involves the competition among workers in different regions and countries, especially between nonunion and low-wage labor versus its unionized and high-wage counterparts. (Ch. 7)

International Monetary Fund was established in 1944 as one of the principal institutions under the Bretton Woods system and as a UN specialized agency. Its purpose is to encourage international financial liquidity and cooperation. It provides capital for exchange rate stabilization and foreign trade. (Ch. 1) *See also* World Bank.

international political economy (IPE) refers to the relationship between politics and economics and its impact on global and domestic political, market, and production activities. (Ch. 1)

international regimes are multilateral arrangements for the collaboration and coordination of policies with respect to specific policy issue-areas. (Chs. 1, 2)

international spillovers refer to the international transfer of scientific inventions and technologies from the country of origin to other countries by way of MNC operations, development assistance in various technical cooperation programs, and military assistance. (Ch. 8) *See also* Functionalism, Ramification.

international taxation refers to taxation to be collected and administered by an international, multilateral agency, on international (civilian and military) trade and related transactions. Currently, no such taxation system exists but has been proposed as a way to address worldwide economic problems, such as poverty, hunger, homelessness, and unemployment. The Brandt Commission, for example, in 1980 proposed the creation of a World Development Fund for such a purpose. (Ch. 7) *See also* Inter-national taxation.

inter-national taxation refers to taxes levied by a government on international transactions and earnings of its citizens and parent companies operating abroad, as well as of foreign individuals and companies conducting business within its territory. (Ch. 7) *See also* International taxation.

intra-firm trade, in the globalization of MNC operations, is trade between the parent company and its affiliates as well as inter-affiliate trade, worldwide. (Ch. 7)

invisible hand refers to the market forces of supply and demand and market competition as the determining factors of value—that is, the prices of goods and services, labor wages, and so on. (Ch. 2) *See also* Classical liberalism *and* Laissez-faire.

joint ventures are combined operations by two or more companies to produce and market their products in a country. (Ch. 7) *See also* Strategic alliances.

kameralism is derived from the German word *kamer,* referring to the royal treasure chamber; kameralism refers to the administration of the royal treasury. As a form of mercantilist (or economic nationalist) policy, it emphasizes the use of natural resources, especially gold and silver, and all available physical labor to maximize national industrial production to strengthen the national economy. It stresses the production and consumption of domestic rather than foreign goods. (Ch. 2) *See also* Mercantilism *and* Import-substitution industrialization.

Keynesianism, named after British economist John Maynard Keynes, argues that, contrary to the laissez-faire principles of limited government and heavy reliance on the self-corrective market, governments in industrialized countries must be actively engaged, through instruments of fiscal and monetary policies, in directing the economy in order to address the problems of the Great Depression and to avert similar economic crises in the future. (Ch. 2)

laissez-faire is a capitalist doctrine emphasizing freedom of market activities. It assumes that the market is perfect and that therefore there is little or no need for governmental intervention. It argues that the *invisible hand* of market supply and demand is sufficient to maintain economic equilibrium and a balanced distribution of welfare. (Ch. 2) *See also* Classical liberalism *and* Capitalism.

liberal feminism emphasizes equality between men and women and advocates the elimination of masculine-feminine, superior-inferior dichotomous views of society and economic and political roles. As in the case of classical liberalism, but unlike *socialist* and *radical feminism,* liberal feminism argues that with some reforms the state can function as a neutral arbiter, based on liberal principles of equality and justice. (Ch. 2)

light industries are industries engaged in the production of consumer goods, as opposed to *heavy industries,* which produce industrial raw materials and machinery, including the machinery that produces consumer goods. (Ch. 3)

Marxism, as the various aspects of the theory of "class conflict" developed by Karl Marx have become known, criticizes capitalism as fundamentally exploitative because it is based on private property and competition for profit by capitalists who own the means of production. Marxism sees society as divided between the capitalists (the bourgeoisie) who own the means of production and the workers (the proletariat) who use their physical labor to earn a living. Capitalist economies are based on exploitative arrangements, as the bourgeoisie seek to maximize profits through the exploitation of others' labor. (Ch. 2)

Marxism-Leninism, as a theory of international political economy, holds that monopoly capitalism leads to the emergence of monopolistic operations in a few hands and to imperialism as capitalist countries compete for raw materials and spheres of influence. Lenin viewed imperialism as "the highest stage of capitalism," whereby capitalist societies attempt to ease domestic economic tensions through expansion and domination abroad. Capitalist monopolies eliminate competition in domestic markets, and imperialism attempts to eliminate competition in the global market. (Ch. 2)

mercantilism, as developed in Europe, seeks to strengthen the finances of the state through a balance-of-trade system, in which the government emphasizes imports of precious metals, such as gold and silver, into the country and sets strict controls (that is, protectionist policies) on trade activities to minimize the outflow of precious metals. The state, thus, encourages the development of newly emerging national industries and trade and relies heavily on protectionist measures to safeguard domestic industries against foreign competitors. In recent years, such policies have been referred to as neo-mercantilist. (Ch. 2) *See also* Kameralism.

most favored nation (MFN) means that trade concessions and privileges granted to one country must match the standard of those accorded to other countries. (Ch. 5)

multinational corporations (MNCs) are companies that produce goods and services based on implicit or explicit contractual arrangements or ownership extending over national boundaries and operating under more than one sovereign government. MNC operations involve the transnational management of production and marketing. (Ch. 7)

nationalization is a nationalist economic policy to expropriate foreign and domestic corporate properties. Socialist and developing governments have used nationalization (often with some compensation) to strengthen their economic and political position toward internal and external pressures. Usually a government resorts to nationalization if disagreements arise between the host government and the foreign company pertaining to such issues as the value of MNC-owned properties subject to taxation and the share of MNC profits to be reinvested in the host country. (Ch. 7) *See also* Privatization.

Nonalignment Movement was founded at the Bandung Conference in 1955 by more than twenty developing countries. The movement advocated the restructuring of the international system to end North-South economic inequalities, as well as to end the Cold War. The movement grew stronger after decolonization in the 1950s and 1960s, as the number of developing countries in the United Nations increased. (Ch. 3)

nongovernmental organizations (NGOs) are international private organizations. These include profit-oriented organizations, such as MNCs, and nonprofit organizations, such as the World Council of Churches. (Ch. 1) *See also* International governmental organizations (IGOs).

non-tariff barriers (NTBs) are various restrictions on the quality and quantity of foreign imported goods. NTBs include quotas, voluntary export restraints (VERs), safety and health regulations, intellectual property rights, and government subsidies for domestic producers. (Ch. 3)

North American Free Trade Agreement (NAFTA) is a treaty that went into effect in January 1994 to lower trade barriers among Canada, the United States, and Mexico and to more closely align their economies and markets. (Chs. 1, 5, 6)

North Atlantic Treaty Organization (NATO) was created as the military component of the U.S. containment policy, with Canada and Western Europe, as a defensive military alliance against any potential Soviet invasion of Western Europe. After the Cold War, some former Soviet bloc countries opted for membership, but the true function of NATO in the post–Cold War era remains highly ambiguous. (Ch. 1) *See also* Containment.

official development assistance (ODA) includes various economic aid programs provided through public bilateral and multilateral channels to developing countries to promote economic development. (Ch. 11)

Organization of Petroleum Exporting Countries (OPEC), created in 1960, is an international organization composed of thirteen developing countries that are major producers of oil. Its members include Algeria, Ecuador, Gabon, Indonesia, Iran, Iraq, Kuwait, Libya, Nigeria, Qatar, Saudi Arabia, the United Arab Emirates, and Venezuela. *Organization of Arab Petroleum Exporting Countries* (OAPEC) refers specifically to the Arab countries. (Ch. 1)

paradigms are "grand theories" or worldviews that seek to explain historical events and factual relationships between sets of units (or variables). In international political economy, a paradigm, such as *classical liberalism* or *Marxism,* attempts to explain domestic and foreign economic relations and provides certain theoretical guidelines to policymakers. (Ch. 2)

polyarchy in international political economy refers to the presence of multiple centers of competing power in the international system. (Ch. 3)

portfolio investments are acquisitions of shares (stocks) in company for purposes of profit. Unlike FDIs, however, portfolio investment does not imply control of the company. (Ch. 7) *See also* Foreign direct investments (FDIs).

privatization is the sale of a state-owned industry, or a portion of it, to private entrepreneurs or companies. (Chs. 3, 7) *See also* Nationalization.

protectionism is the regulation and taxation imposed on foreign goods to restrict their importation into a country. (Ch. 3) *See also* Quotas, Tariffs.

quotas are limits on the quantity of specific products imported. (Ch. 5) *See also* Protectionism.

Quran is the Holy Book of Islam. (Ch. 2)

radical feminism holds that social, political, and economic issues historically have been dominated by men, and male-dominated institutions have perpetuated male supremacy and the oppression of women. It argues that only through major restructuring of the current national and international institutions can male domination and women's oppression end. (Ch. 2) *See also* Liberal feminism *and* Socialist feminism.

ramification or **spill-over,** as proposed by the *functionalist* school after the Second World War, means that functional collaboration in one area leads to cooperation in other areas. As such, international peace can be achieved through piecemeal and incremental approaches, rather than through grand designs. (Ch. 2)

realism, or **realpolitik,** refers to the view of international relations as a constant "struggle for power" in a hostile, "anarchic" international system, in which nations struggle to survive and the strong dominate the weak. (Ch. 2) *See also* Hegemonic stability.

sanctions, such as embargoes, are punitive measures imposed unilaterally or multilaterally against a state said to act in violation of certain expectations, standards, and norms of behavior (Ch. 1)

self-reliance, or **autarky**, is a national economic policy that seeks to limit or even to terminate all economic ties with the global economic environment in hopes of minimizing national economic and political vulnerabilities to external pressures. (Ch. 10) *See also* Dependent development.

service economy consists of the production of services rather than the production of products per se. These include banking, communication, insurance, and education. During the 1980s, this sector grew rapidly in the industrialized societies, while employment in the traditional manufacturing and agricultural sectors declined. (Chs. 1, 9, 12)

socialism as a modern ideology emerged in the 1820s and 1830s in Europe as various movements (for example, the Chartists in England) advocated democratization and collectivism. Karl Marx and Frederic Engels argued that socialism would be the first step toward dismantling capitalist structures of exploitation, followed by communism, in which all private property and means of production—hence the market as the ultimate determinant of value—would be eliminated. (Ch. 2) *See also* Marxism *and* Socialist feminism.

socialist feminism underscores the economic, rather than cultural or institutional, domination of women by men. Socialist feminism primarily focuses on the relationship among production, reproduction, and the oppression of women. It argues that, historically, the emergence of the nation-state led to the marginalization of women and that the rise of capitalist industrialization led to divisions between commodity production and housework, while reproductive labor and housework were relegated to the *secondary economy*—hence the division of labor between the "personal" sphere (the home) and the "economic production" sphere (the workplace) along gender lines. (Ch. 2) *See also* Liberal feminism *and* Radical feminism.

sovereignty refers to the supremacy of state authority in all domestic and international matters in relation to all other entities within its territorial and administrative jurisdiction and in relation to all other external entities—for example, other governments and international organizations. (Ch. 3)

Special Drawing Rights (SDRs), established in 1969 by the Group of Ten within the International Monetary Fund, are equivalent to international currencies and are used largely to promote international trade. (Ch. 4)

strategic alliances are formed by MNCs to take advantage of foreign markets and local businesses' familiarity with local cultures and regulatory policies and practices. One of the most recent phenomena contributing to the further globalization of international economic activities by MNCs is their strategic integration structures, which are devised to take advantage of low-cost production opportunities. (Chs. 3, 7) *See also* Joint ventures.

structural adjustment refers to the implementation, by developing countries, of economic liberalization programs as required by the World Bank and the IMF. Structural adjustment programs usually involve reductions in government expenditures, the privatization of state-owned enterprises, and trade liberalization. (Ch. 4) *See also* Privatization.

sunna, in Islamic jurisprudence, consists of the Prophet Mohammed's words and deeds as legal precedent. (Ch. 2)

tariffs are taxes levied on imports. (Ch. 5) *See also* Inter-national taxation, Protectionism.

Taylorism is a method of industrial production management emphasizing systematic segmentation and time management of the work process on an assembly line. (Ch. 3)

tied aid refers to conditions attached to foreign aid requiring the recipients to use loans and grants toward the purchase of products from the donor country. **Untied aid,** on the other hand, involves no such strings. (Ch. 11)

transfer pricing involves prices set for transactions between subdivisions within an MNC organization, as opposed to market prices. (Ch. 7)

umma is the spiritual community of Muslim believers, regardless where they reside. (Ch. 2)

World Bank, also known as the International Bank for Reconstruction and Development (IBRD), was established in 1944 as one of the principal institutions under the Bretton Woods system and as a UN specialized agency. Its purpose is to provide capital for development programs. (Ch. 1) *See also* International Monetary Fund.

world system theory argues that, since the emergence of the nation-state and modern capitalism in the 1600s, the world economy has been dominated by capitalist structures, including a single global market; a small number of major, powerful capitalist countries that dominate the global market; and the division of the world system into core and periphery countries. (Ch. 2) *See also* Hegemony *and* Dependencia.

World Trade Organization (WTO) succeeded GATT in 1994 as a permanent institution providing a forum for international trade negotiations and the administration of compliance with the principles of trade liberalization. (Ch. 1) *See also* General Agreement on Tariffs and Trade.

zakat (charity-tax) is one of the five principles, or "pillars," of Islam. (Ch. 2)

SUGGESTED READINGS

Adams, J. D. R., and J. Whalley. *The International Taxation of Multinational Enterprises in the Developed Countries.* Westport: Greenwood Press, 1977.

Adams, William H. D., ed. *The Brain Drain.* London: Collier-Macmillan, 1968.

Ahmed, Akbar S., and Hastings Donnan, eds. *Islam, Globalization and Postmodernity.* London: Routledge, 1994.

Akinsanya, Adeoye A. *The Expropriation of Multinational Property in the Third World.* New York: Praeger, 1980.

Albert, Michel. *Capitalism vs. Capitalism.* New York: Four Wall Eight Windows, 1993.

Alessandrini, Sergio, and Bruno Dallago, eds. *The Unofficial Economy: Consequences and Perspectives in Different Economic Systems.* Aldershot, UK: Gower, 1987.

Aliber, Robert Z. *The Multinational Paradigm.* Cambridge: MIT Press, 1993.

Al-Omar, Fuad, and Mohammed Abdel-Haq. *Islamic Banking: Theory, Practice and Challenges.* Karachi, Pakistan: Oxford University Press, and London: Zed Books, 1996.

Amin, Samir. *Imperialism and Unequal Development.* Sussex, England: Harvester Press, 1978.

Amin, Samir. *Unequal Development: An Essay on the Social Formation of Peripheral Capitalism.* Sussex, England: Harvester Press, 1976.

Ansprenger, Franz. *The Dissolution of the Colonial Empires.* London: Routledge, 1981.

Artis, Mike J., and Norman Lee, eds. *The Economics of the European Union: Policy and Analysis.* Oxford: Oxford University Press, 1994.

Axline, W. Andrew, ed. *The Political Economy of Regional Cooperation: Comparative Case Studies.* London: Pinter 1994.

Ayubi, Nazih N. *Political Islam: Religion and Politics in the Arab World.* London: Routledge, 1991.

Ballard, G. M., ed. *Nuclear Safety After Three Mile Island and Chernobyl.* London: Elsevier Applied Science, 1988.

Bamber, Greg J., and Russell D. Lansbury, eds. *International and Comparative Industrial Relations.* Sydney, Australia: Unwin Hyman, 1987.

Barash, David P. *Introduction to Peace Studies.* Belmont,CA: Wadsworth, 1991.

Barnett, Richard J., and John Cavanagh. *Global Dreams: Imperial Corporations and the New World Order.* New York: Touchstone Books, 1994.

Barnett, Richard J., and Ronald E. Muller. *Global Reach.* New York: Simon and Schuster, 1975.

Barry, Donald, with Mark O. Dickerson and James Gaisford, eds. *Toward a North American Community?* Boulder, CO: Westview Press, 1995.

Baucom, Donald R. *The Origins of SDI: 1944–1983.* Lawrence: University Press of Kansas, 1992.

Becker, William H., and Samuel F. Wells, Jr., eds. *Economics and World Power: An Assessment of American Diplomacy Since 1789.* New York: Columbia University Press, 1984.

Behboodi, Rambod. *Industrial Subsidies and Friction in World Trade: Trade Policy or Trade Politics?* London: Routledge, 1994.

Beinin, Joel, and Zachary Lockman. *Workers on the Nile: Nationalism, Communism, Islam, and the Egyptian Working Class, 1882–1954.* Princeton, NJ: Princeton University Press, 1987.

Bergsten, C. Fred, and J. Williamson. *The Multiple Reserve Currency System: Evolution, Consequences, and Alternatives.* Washington, DC: Institute for International Economics, 1983.

Bermann, George A., Roger J. Goebel, William J. Davey, and Eleanor M. Fox. *Cases and Materials on European Community Law.* St. Paul: West, 1993.

Bernstein, Daniel. *Yen! Japan's New Financial Empire and Its Threat to America.* New York: Simon and Schuster, 1988.

Bhagwati, Jagdish N. *Protectionism.* Cambridge: MIT Press, 1988.

Bhagwati, Jagdish N., ed. *International Trade.* 2d ed. Cambridge: MIT Press, 1987.

Blake, David H., and Robert S. Walters. *The Politics of Global Economic Relations.* Englewood Cliffs, NJ: Prentice-Hall, 1992.

Blaug, Mark. *Economic Theory in Retrospect.* 4th ed. Cambridge: Cambridge University Press, 1992.

Blaut, James M. *The Colonizer's Model of the World.* New York: The Guilford Press, 1993.

Bloch, Fred. *Postindustrial Possibilities.* Berkeley: University of California Press, 1990.

Bluestone, Barry, and Bennett Harrison. *The Deindustrialization of America: Plant Closings, Community Abandonment, and the Dismantling of Basic Industry.* New York: Basic Books, 1982.

Blumberg, Rae Lesser. *Women, Development, and the Wealth of Nations: Making the Case for the Gender Variable.* Boulder, CO: Westview Press, 1992.

Bobiash, Donald. *South-South Aid: How Developing Countries Help Each Other.* New York: St. Martin's Press, 1992.

Bognanno, Mario F., and Kathryn J. Ready, eds. *The North American Free Trade Agreement: Labor, Industry, and Government Perspectives.* Westport, CT: Praeger, 1993.

Bordo, Michael, and Forrest Capie. *Monetary Regimes in Transition.* Cambridge: Cambridge University Press, 1994.

Boserup, Ester. *Women's Role in Economic Development.* New York: St. Martin's Press, 1970.

Brandt Commission Report. *North-South: A Program for Survival. Report of the Independent Commission on International Development Issues.* Cambridge: MIT Press, 1980.

Braverman, Harry. *Labor and Monopoly Capital: The Degradation of Work in the Twentieth Century.* New York: Monthly Review Press, 1974.

Bretton, Henry L. *The Power of Money: A Political-Economic Analysis with Special Emphasis on the American Political System.* Albany: State University of New York Press, 1980.

Brewer, Anthony. *Marxist Theories of Imperialism.* London: Routledge, 1980.

Brodie, Bernard, and Fawn M. Brodie. *From Crossbow to H-Bomb.* Rev. ed. Bloomington: Indiana University Press, 1973.

Brown, Cynthia, ed. *With Friends Like These.* New York: Pantheon Books, 1985.

Brown, Peter G., and Douglas MacLean, eds. *Human Rights and U.S. Foreign Policy.* Lexington, MA: Lexington Books, 1979.

Brown, Seyom. *New Forces, Old Forces, and the Future of World Politics.* Glenview, IL: Scott, Foresman, 1988.

Browne, Stephen. *Foreign Aid in Practice.* London: Pinter, 1990.

Browning, Robert. *The Byzantine Empire.* Rev. ed. Washington, DC: Catholic University of America Press, 1992.

Buckley, P. J., and M. Casson. *The Future of the Multinational Enterprise.* London: Macmillan, 1976.

Bull, Hedley. *The Anarchical Society: A Study of Order in World Politics.* New York: Columbia University Press, 1977.

Bull, Hedley, and Adam Watson, eds. *The Expansion of International Society.* Oxford: Clarendon Press, 1985.

Burt, A. L. *The British Empire and Commonwealth.* Boston: Heath, 1956.

Calleo, David P. *Beyond American Hegemony.* New York: Basic Books, 1987.

Campbell, Tim S., and William A. Kracaw. *Financial Institutions and Capital Markets.* New York: Harper Collins, 1994.

Capie, Forrest H., ed. *Protectionism in the World Economy.* Aldershot, England: Edward Elgar, 1992.

Caporaso, James A., and David P. Levine. *Theories of Political Economy.* New York: Cambridge University Press, 1992.

Carbaugh, Robert J. *International Economics.* 3d ed. Belmont, CA: Wadsworth, 1989.

Cardoso, Eliana, and Ann Helwege. *Latin America's Economy: Diversity, Trends, and Conflicts.* Cambridge: MIT Press, 1992.

Cardoso, Fernando Henrique, and Enzo Faletto. *Dependency and Development in Latin America.* Berkeley: University of California Press, 1979.

Carnoy, Martin, Manuel Castells, Stephen S. Cohen, and Fernando Henrique Cardoso. *The New Global Economy in the Information Age: Reflections on Our Changing World.* University Park: Pennsylvania State University Press, 1993.

Castells, Manuel. *The Informational City: Information Technology, Economic Restructuring, and the Urban-Regional Process.* Oxford: Basil Blackwell, 1989.

Chan, Steve. *East Asian Dynamism: Growth, Order, and Security in the Pacific Region.* Boulder, CO: Westview Press, 1993.

Chaney, Elsa M. *Supermadre: Women in Politics in Latin Amrica.* Austin: University of Texas Press, 1979.

Charlton, Sue Ellen, Jane Everett, and Kathleen Staudt, eds. *Women, the State, and Development.* Albany: State University of New York Press, 1989.

Chazan, Naomi, Robert Mortimer, John Ravenhill, and Donald Rothchild. *Politics and Society in Contemporary Africa.* 2d ed. Boulder, CO: Lynne Rienner 1992.

Chilcote, Ronald H. *Theories of Comparative Politics.* Boulder, CO: Westview Press, 1981.

Chomsky, Noam, and Edward S. Herman. *The Political Economy of Human Rights: The Washington Connection and Third World Fascism.* Boston: South End Press, 1979.

Chorbajian, Levon, Patrick Donabedian, and Claude Mutafian. *The Caucasian Knot: The History and Geo-Politics of Nagorno-Karabagh.* London: Zed Books, 1994.

Choudhury, Masudul Alam. *Islamic Economic Co-operation.* New York: St. Martin's Press, 1989.

Choudhury, Masudul Alam. *The Principles of Islamic Political Economy.* New York: St. Martin's Press, 1992.

Choudhury, Masudul Alam, and Uzir Abdul Malik. *The Foundations of Islamic Political Economy.* London: Macmillan, 1992.

Cimbala, Stephen J., ed. *The Technology, Strategy, and Politics of SDI.* Boulder, CO: Westview Press, 1987.

Cipolla, Carlo M. *Guns, Sails, and Empires: Technological Innovation and the Early Phases of European Expansion.* New York: Minerva Press, 1965.

Cipolla, Carlo M., ed. *The Fontana Economic History of Europe: The Emergence of Industrial Societies.* Glasgow: William Collins, 1973.

Clark, Norman. *The Political Economy of Science and Technology.* Oxford: Basic Blackwell, 1985.

Cleveland, William L. *A History of the Middle East.* Boulder, CO: Westview Press, 1994.

Cline, William R. *International Economic Policy in the 1990s.* Cambridge: MIT Press, 1994.

Cohen, Benjamin J. *The Question of Imperialism: The Political Economy of Dominance and Dependence.* New York: Basic Books, 1973.

Conteh-Morgan, Earl. *American Foreign Aid and Global Power Projection.* Aldershot, England: Dartmouth, 1990.

Costa, Dalla Mariarosa, and Giovanna F. Dalla Costa, eds. *Paying the Price: Women and the Politics of International Economic Strategy.* London: Zed Books, 1993.

Crane, George T., and Abla Amawi, eds. *The Theoretical Foundations of International Political Economy: A Reader.* New York: Oxford University Press, 1991.

Croome, John. *Reshaping the World Trading System: A History of the Uruguay Round.* Geneva: World Trade Organization, 1995.

Dallago, Bruno. *The Irregular Economy: The "Underground" Economy and the "Black" Labor Market.* Aldershot, England: Dartmouth, 1990.

Das, Dilip K., ed. *International Finance: Contemporary Issues.* London: Routledge, 1993.

Dasgupta, A. K. *Epochs of Economic Theory.* Oxford: Basil Blackwell, 1985.

Davis, Eric. *Challenging Colonialism: Bank Misr and Egyptian Industrialization, 1920–1941.* Princeton, NJ, Princeton University Press, 1983.

Dekmejian, R. Hrair. *Islam in Revolution: Fundamentalism in the Arab World.* Syracuse: Syracuse University Press, 1985.

Derian, Jean-Claude. *America's Struggle for Leadership in Technology.* Trans. by Severen Schaffer. Cambridge: MIT Press, 1990.

Destler, I. M. *American Trade Politics: System Under Stress.* Washington, DC: Institute for International Economics, 1986.

Deutsch, Karl W. *Nationalism and Social Communication.* Cambridge: MIT Press, 1953.

Deutsch, Karl W. *Political Community at the International Level.* Garden City, NY: Doubleday, 1959.

Deutsch, Karl W., Andrei S. Markovits, and John Platt, eds. *Advances in the Social Sciences: 1900–1980.* Lanham, MD: University Press of America, 1986.

Deutsch, Karl W., et al. *Political Community and the North Atlantic Area.* Princeton: Princeton University Press, 1957.

Deyo, Frederic C., ed. *The Political Economy of the New Asian Industrialism.* Ithaca: Cornell University Press, 1987.

Dicken, Peter. *Global Shift: The Internationalization of Economic Activity.* 2d ed. New York: The Guilford Press, 1992.

Dobb, Maurice. *Theory of Value and Distribution Since Adam Smith.* Cambridge: Cambridge University Press, 1973.

Doernberg, Richard L. *International Taxation.* 2d ed. St. Paul: West, 1993.

Donovan, Josephine. *Feminist Theory: The Intellectual Traditions of American Feminism.* Expanded ed. New York: Continuum, 1992.

Dosi, Giovanni, Christopher Freeman, Richard Nelson, and Luc Soete, eds. *Technical Change and Economic Theory.* London: Pinter, 1988.

Dougherty, James E., and Robert L. Pfaltzgraff. *Contending Theories of International Relations.* 3d ed. New York: Harper and Row, 1990.

Doyle, Michael W. *Empires.* Ithaca: Cornell University Press, 1986.

Drucker, Peter F. *The New Realities.* New York: Harper and Row, 1989.

Dunning, John H. *Explaining International Production.* London: Unwin Hyman, 1988.

Dunning, John H. *Multinationals, Technology, and Competitiveness.* London: Unwin Hyman, 1988.

Einzig, Paul. *Primitive Money in Its Ethnological, Historical and Economic Aspects.* London: Eyre and Spottiswoode, 1949.

Elliott, John H. *Imperial Spain, 1469–1716.* London: Penguin Books, 1990.

Enloe, Cynthia. *Bananas, Beaches and Bases: Making Feminist Sense of International Politics.* Berkeley: University of California Press, 1990.

Epstein, Gerald, Julie Graham, and Jessica Nembhard, eds. *Creating a New World Economy: Forces of Change and Plans for Action.* Philadelphia: Temple University Press, 1993.

Ernst, Dieter, and David O'Connor. *Technological Capabilities, New Technologies, and Newcomer Industrialization: An Agenda for the 1990s.* Paris: OECD Development Centre, 1990.

Esposito, John L., ed. *Islam and Development: Religion and Sociopolitical Change.* New York: Syracuse University Press, 1980.

Etzioni, Amitai. *Political Unification.* New York: Holt, Rinehart, 1965.

Fairbank, John K. *The United States and China.* 4th ed. Cambridge: Harvard University Press, 1979.

Feather, Norman T. *The Psychological Impact of Unemployment.* New York: Springer-Verlag, 1990.

Feige, Edgar L. *The Underground Economies: Tax Evasion and Information Distortion.* Cambridge: Cambridge University Press, 1988.

Feyerabend, Paul. *Against Method.* Rev. ed. London: Verso, 1988.

Feyerabend, Paul. *Farewell to Reason.* London: Verso, 1987.

Findlay, Allan M. *The Arab World.* London: Routledge, 1994.

Finger, J. M., and A. Olechowski. *The Uruguay Round: A Handbook for the Multilateral Trade Negotiations.* Washington, DC: The World Bank, 1987.

Forsythe, David P. *Human Rights and World Politics.* Rev. 2d ed. Lincoln: University of Nebraska Press, 1989.

Fort, Randall M. *Economic Espionage: Problems and Prospects.* Washington, DC: Consortium for the Study of Intelligence, 1993.

Frank, Andre Gunder. *Capitalism and Underdevelopment in Latin America.* New York: Monthly Review Press, 1969.

Franklin, Ursula. *The Real World of Technology.* Concord, MA: Anansi Press, 1992.

Freeman, Christopher, ed. *Design, Innovation and Long Cycles in Economic Development.* London: Pinter, 1986.

Freeman, Christopher, ed. *Long Waves in the World Economy.* London: Butterworth, 1983.

Freidberg, Aaron L. *The Wary Titan: Britain and the Experience of Relative Decline, 1895–1905.* Princeton: Princeton University Press, 1988.

Frieden, Jeffry A., and David A. Lake, eds. *International Political Economy: Perspectives on Global Power and Wealth.* 3d ed. New York: St. Martin's Press, 1995.

Fröbel, Folker, Jürgen Henrichs, and Otto Kreye. *New International Division of Labor.* Trans. by Pete Burgess. Cambridge: Cambridge University Press, 1980.

Fromm, Erich. *The Sane Society.* New York: Rinehart, 1955.

Frye, Marilyn. *The Politics of Reality: Essays in Feminist Theory.* Trumansburg, PA: Crossing Press, 1983.

Fuller, Graham E. *The Center of the Universe: The Geopolitics of Iran.* Boulder, CO: Westview Press, 1991.

Fuller, Graham E., and Ian O. Lesser. *Turkey's New Geopolitics: From the Balkans to Western China.* Boulder, CO: Westview Press, 1993.

Gabriel, Jurg Martin. *World Views and Theories of International Relations.* New York: St. Martin's Press, 1994.

Galbraith, John Kenneth. *The Great Crash, 1929.* Boston: Houghton Mifflin, 1988.

Galbraith, John Kenneth. *The New Industrial State.* Harmondsworth, UK: Penguin, 1972.

Gambari, Ibrahim A. *Political and Comparative Dimensions of Regional Integration: The Case of ECOWAS.* London: Humanities Press, 1991.

Gauhar, Alaf, ed. *Experience.* Lond

George, Susan. *A Fate W and the Poor.* Rev. ed.

Ghosh, Pradip K., ed. *Ap Development.* Westport, C

Gill, Stephen, ed. *Globalizatio lateralism.* Tokyo: United Natio

Gill, Stephen, ed. *Gramsci, Histori national Relations.* Cambridge: Ca 1993.

Gill, Stephen, and David Law. *The Glob* Baltimore: Johns Hopkins University Press,

Gilpin, Robert. *The Political Economy of Interna* Princeton: Princeton University Press, 1987.

Gilpin, Robert. *War and Change in World Politics.* C Cambridge University Press, 1981.

Goddard, C. Roe, John T. Passé-Smith, and John G. Conkli *International Political Economy: State-Market Relations in Changing Global Order.* Boulder, CO: Lynne Rienner 1996.

Goldin, I., and O. Knudsen, eds. *Agricultural Trade Liberalization: Implications for Developing Countries.* Paris: OECD and the World Bank, 1990.

Goldstein, Joshua S. *Long Cycles: Prosperity and War in the Modern Age.* New Haven: Yale University Press, 1988.

Granger, John V. *Technology and International Relations.* San Francisco: E.H. Freeman and Company, 1979.

Grant, Rebecca, and Kathleen Newland, eds. *Gender and International Relations.* Bloomington: Indiana University Press, 1991.

Gray, Colin S. *The Geopolitics of Super Power.* Lexington: University of Kentucky Press, 1988.

Greenfield, Harry I. *Invisible, Outlawed, and Untaxed: America's Underground Economy.* Westport, CT: Praeger, 1993.

Grieves, Forest L., ed. *Transnationalism in World Politics and Business.* New York: Pergamon Press, 1979.

Griffin, Keith. *Studies in Globalization and Economic Transitions.* Houndmills, UK: Macmillan, 1996.

...ansnational ...rence to Latin

...lobal View of Ethnopolitical ... United States Institute of Peace

...nd the Nation-State. Stanford: Stanford University ...64.

...rnst B. *The Uniting of Europe.* Stanford: Stanford University Press, 1958.

Haggard, Stephan. *Pathways from the Periphery.* Ithaca: Cornell University Press, 1990.

Haggard, Stephan, and Robert R. Kaufman. *The Political Economy of Democratic Transitions.* Princeton: Princeton University Press, 1995.

Halliday, Fred. *Iran: Dictatorship and Development.* Middlesex, England: Penguin Books, 1979.

Halliday, Fred. *The Making of the Second Cold War.* 2d ed. London: Verso, 1986.

Halperin, Morton. *Bureaucratic Politics and Foreign Policy.* Washington, DC: Brookings Institute, 1974.

Hamilton, Earl J. *American Treasure and the Price Revolution in Spain, 1501–1650.* Cambridge: Harvard University Press, 1934.

...npson, Fen Osler, and Christopher J. Maule, eds. *Canada ...ong Nations, 1990–1991.* Ottawa: Carleton University ...1991.

...ham. *Lords of Poverty.* London: Macmillan, 1989.

...nd Richard Jenkins. *The Myth of the Hidden ... a New Understanding of Informal Economic* ...ynes, UK: Open University Press, 1989.

.... Sullivan, eds. *Privatization and ...Middle East.* Bloomington: Indiana ...92.

...bert E., and Stephanie G. Neuman, eds. *The Arms ...: Problems and Prospects in the Post–Cold War World.* ...pecial issue of *The Annals of the American Academy of Political and Social Sciences,* vol. 535 (September 1994).

Hart, Jeffrey A. *Rival Capitalists: International Competitiveness in the United States, Japan, and Western Europe.* Ithaca: Cornell University Press, 1992.

Hayter, Teresa. *Aid as Imperialism.* Middlesex, England: Penguin Books, 1971.

Hayter, Theresa, and Catharine Watson. *Aid: Rhetoric and Reality.* London: Pluto Press, 1985.

Headrick, Daniel R. *The Tentacles of Progress: Technology Transfer in the Age of Imperialism, 1850–1940.* New York: Oxford University Press, 1988.

Headrick, Daniel R. *The Tools of Empire: Technology and European Imperialism in the Nineteenth Century.* New York: Oxford University Press, 1981.

Henderson, Jeffrey. *The Globalization of High Technology Production.* London: Routledge, 1989.

Herr, Hansjörg, Silke Tober, and Andreas Westphal, eds. *Macroeconomic Problems of Transformation: Stabilization Policies and Economic Reconstructuring.* Aldershot, UK: Edward Elgar, 1994.

Hershlag, Z. Y. *Introduction to the Modern Economic History of the Middle East.* Leiden, Netherlands: E.J. Brill, 1964.

Hertner, Peter, and Geoffrey Jones, eds. *Multinationals: Theory and History.* Aldershot, England: Gower, 1986.

Herz, John H. *International Politics in the Atomic Age.* New York: Columbia University Press, 1959.

Higgott, Richard A. *Political Development Theory: The Contemporary Debate.* London: Croom Helm, 1983.

Higgott, Richard, Richard Leaver, and John Ravenhill, eds. *Pacific Economic Relations in the 1990s: Cooperation or Conflict?* Boulder, CO: Lynne Rienner, 1993.

Hirsch, Fred. *Money International: Economics and Politics of World Money.* New York: Doubleday and Company, 1969.

Hobsbawm, Eric J. *Industry and Empire.* Harmondsworth, England: Penguin, 1969.

Hobsbawm, Eric J. *The Age of Capital, 1848–1875.* New York: Meridian, 1979.

Hobsbawm, Eric J. *The Age of Empire, 1875–1914.* New York: Vintage, 1987.

Hobsbawm, Eric J. *The Age of Revolution, 1789–1848.* New York: Mentor, 1962.

Hobson, John A. *Imperialism: A Study.* Ann Arbor: University of Michigan Press, 1972 [1902].

Hofheinz, Roy Jr., and Kent E. Calder. *The Eastasia Edge.* New York: Basic Books, 1982.

Hollander, Samuel. *Classical Economics.* New York: Basil Blackwell, 1987.

Hollist, W. Ladd, and F. Lamond Tullis, eds. *An International Political Economy.* Boulder, CO: Westview Press, 1985.

Horowitz, David, ed. *Corporations and the Cold War.* New York: Bertrand Russell Peace Foundation and Monthly Review Press, 1969.

Horowitz, Donald L. *Ethnic Groups in Conflict.* Berkeley: University of California Press, 1985.

Hourani, Albert. *A History of the Arab Peoples.* New York: Warner Books, 1991.

Hsiung, James C., ed. *Asia Pacific in the New World Politics.* Boulder, CO: Lynne Rienner, 1993.

Hufbauer, Gary Clyde. *U.S. Taxation of International Income: Blueprint for Reform.* Washington, DC: Institute for International Economics, 1992.

Hufbauer, Gary Clyde, and Howard F. Rosen. *Trade Policy for Troubled Industries.* Washington, DC: Institute for International Economics, 1986.

Hu *Tra* 1992.

Husted, Ste 2d ed. New

Hutchison, Terence *Knowledge.* Cambr

Huttenback, Robert A. York: Harper and Row, 19

Hyam, Ronald. *Britain's Imperia* London: Macmillan, 1993.

Hyden, Goran. *Beyond Ujamaa in Tan and an Uncaptured Peasantry.* Berkeley: U Press, 1980.

Hymer, Stephen H. *The International Operatio Firms: Study of Foreign Direct Investment.* Camb Press, 1976.

Hymer, Stephen H. *The Multinational Corporation: A Ra Approach.* Cambridge: Cambridge University Press, 1979.

Inoguchi, Takashi, and Daniel I. Okimoto, eds. *The Political Economy of Japan: The Changing International Context.* Vol. 2. Stanford: Stanford University Press, 1988.

Iqbar, Munawar, ed. *Distributive Justice and Need Fulfillment in an Islamic Economy.* Leicester, England: The Islamic Foundation, 1988.

Isaak, Robert A. *International Political Economy: Managing World Economic Change.* Englewood Cliffs, NJ: Prentice Hall, 1991.

Jackson, John H. *Restructuring the GATT System.* New York: Council on Foreign Relations, 1990.

Jackson, John H. *The World Trading System: Law and Policy of International Economic Relations.* Cambridge: MIT Press, 1989.

Jackson, John H., and William J. Davey. *Legal Problems of International Economic Relations.* 2d ed. St. Paul: West, 1986.

James, Harold. *International Monetary Cooperation Since Bretton Woods.* Washington, DC: International Monetary Fund, 1996.

Johnson, Chalmers. *MITI and the Japanese Miracle: The Growth of Industrial Policy.* Stanford: Stanford University Press, 1982.

Johnson, Hazel J. *Dispelling the Myth of Globalization: The Case for Regionalization.* New York: Praeger, 1991.

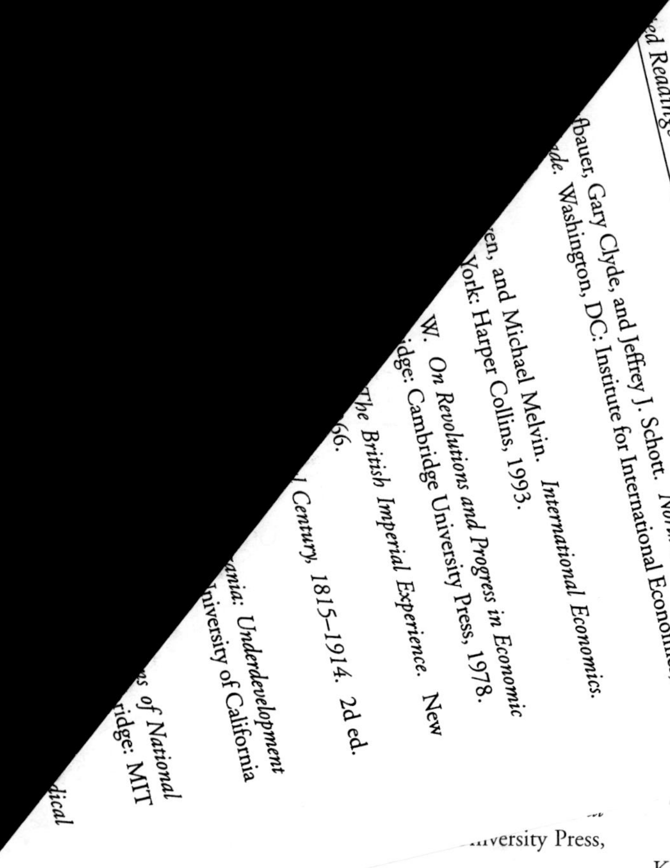

...iversity Press,

...ie, ed. *The Middle Eastern Economy: Studies in Economics and Economic History.* London: Frank Cass and Company, 1976.

Kegley, Charles W., Jr., and Eugene R. Wittkopf. *American Foreign Policy: Pattern and Process.* 4th ed. New York: St. Martin's Press, 1991.

Keller, William W. *Arm in Arm: The Political Economy of the Global Arms Trade.* New York: Basic Books, 1995.

Kennedy, Paul M. *The Rise and Fall of British Naval Mastery.* London: Ashfield Press, 1983.

Kennedy, Paul. *The Rise and Fall of Major Powers.* New York: Random House, 1987.

Kenwood, A. G., and A. L. Lougheed. *The Growth of the International Economy, 1820–1990.* London: Routledge, 1992.

Keohane, Robert O. *After Hegemony.* Princeton: Princeton University Press, 1984.

Keohane, Robert O., ed. *Neorealism and Its Critics.* New York: Columbia University Press, 1986.

...ert O., and Joseph S. Nye. *Power and Interdepen-* ...n: Little, Brown, 1977.

...ynard. *The General Theory of Employment, Interest,* ...n Diego: Harcourt Brace Jovanovich, 1953.

...d Nawaz. *Islamic and Other Economic Systems.* ...: Islamic Books, 1989.

...ung H. Kim. *Global Corporate Finance: Text* ... Kolb, 1993.

...P. *A Financial History of Western Europe.* ...ford University Press, 1993.

... *American Business Abroad: Six Lectures* ... New Haven: Yale University Press,

... *he World in Depression, 1929–1939.* ...lifornia Press, 1973.

...ussell, ed. *The New Geography of European Migrations.* London: Belhaven Press, 1993.

Klare, Michael T., and Cynthia Arnson. *Supplying Repression.* Washington, DC: Institute for Policy Studies, 1981.

Kline, John M. *International Codes and Multinational Business: Setting Guidelines for International Business Operations.* Westport CT: Quorum Books, 1985.

Knorr, Klaus. *The Power of Nations: The Political Economy of International Relations.* New York: Basic Books, 1975.

Knox, Paul, and John Agnew. *The Geography of the World Economy.* London: Hodder and Stoughton, 1989.

Kojima, Kiyoshi. *Direct Foreign Investment: A Japanese Model of Multinational Business Operation.* London: Croom Helm, 1978.

Kommers, Donald P., and Gilburt D. Loescher, eds. *Human Rights and American Foreign Policy.* South Bend, IN: University of Notre Dame Press, 1979.

Korten, David C. *When Corporations Rule the World.* West Hartford, CT: Kumarian Press, 1995.

Kozak, David C., and James M. Keagle, eds. *Bureaucratic Politics and National Security: Theory and Practice.* Boulder, CO: Lynne Rienner, 1988.

Krasner, Stephen D. *Structural Conflict: The Third World Against Global Liberalism.* Berkeley: University of California Press, 1985.

Krasner, Stephen D., ed. *International Regimes.* Ithaca: Cornell University Press, 1983.

Krause, Keith. *Arms and the State: Patterns of Military Production and Trade.* Cambridge: Cambridge University Press, 1992.

Kreinin, Mordechai E. *International Economics: A Policy Approach.* 4th ed. San Diego: Harcourt Brace Jovanovich, 1983.

Krueger, Anne O., Constantine Michalopoulos, and Vernon W. Ruttan, ed. *Aid and Development.* Baltimore: Johns Hopkins University Press, 1989.

Krugman, Paul R., ed. *Strategic Trade Policy and the New International Economics.* Cambridge: MIT Press, 1986.

Krugman, Paul R., and Maurice Obstfeld. *International Economics: Theory and Policy.* 2d ed. New York: HarperCollins, 1991.

Kuhn, Thomas S. *The Copernican Revolution.* Cambridge: Harvard University Press, 1974.

Kuhn, Thomas S. *The Structure of Scientific Revolutions.* 2d enl. ed. Chicago: University of Chicago Press, 1970.

Kunz, Diane B. *Butter and Guns: America's Cold War Economic Diplomacy.* New York: The Free Press, 1997.

Kuper, Leo. *Genocide: Its Political Use in the Twentieth Century.* New Haven, CT: Yale University Press, 1981.

LaFeber, Walter. *The American Age: U.S. Foreign Policy at Home and Abroad, 1750 to the Present.* 2d ed. New York: W.W. Norton, 1994.

Lairson, Thomas D., and David Skidmore. *International Political Economy: The Struggle for Power and Wealth.* Orlando: Harcourt Brace Jovanovich, 1993.

Lakatos, Imre, and Alan Musgrave, eds. *Criticism and the Growth of Knowledge.* Cambridge: Cambridge University Press, 1970.

Lambert, Youry. *The United Nations Industrial Development Organization.* Westport, CT: Praeger, 1993.

Lang, Tim, and Colin Hines. *The New Protectionism: Protecting the Future Against Free Trade.* New York: The New Press, 1993.

Lapidus, Ira M. *A History of Islamic Societies.* Cambridge: Cambridge University Press, 1988.

Laqueur, Walter. *A World of Secrets: The Uses and Limits of Intelligence.* New York: Basic Books, 1985.

Lawrence, Robert Z., and Charles L. Schultze, eds. *An American Trade Strategy—Options for the 1990s.* Washington, DC: The Brookings Institution, 1990.

Lichtheim, George. *Imperialism.* New York: Praeger, 1971.

Lindberg, Leon N. *The Political Dynamics of European Economic Integration.* Stanford: Stanford University Press, 1963.

Lips, Hilary. *Women, Men, and Power.* Mountain View, CA: Mayfield, 1991.

Little, Walter, and Eduardo Posada-Carbó, eds. *Political Corruption in Europe and Latin America.* London: Macmillan Press, 1996.

Lodge, George C., and Ezra F. Vogel, eds. *Ideology and National Competitiveness.* Boston: Harvard Business School Press, 1987.

Lowe, Janet. *The Secret Empire: How 25 Multinationals Rule the World.* Homewood, IL: Business One Irwin, 1992.

Luard, Evans. *The Globalization of Politics: The Changed Focus of Political Action in the Modern World.* Houndmills, England: Macmillan, 1990.

Lumsdaine, David Halloran. *Moral Vision in International Politics.* Princeton: Princeton University Press, 1993.

Lützler, Paul Michael, ed. *Europe After Maastricht: American and European Perspectives.* Providence, RI: Berghahn Books, 1994.

Madura, Jeff. *International Financial Management.* 2d ed. St. Paul: West, 1989.

Magdoff, Harry. *The Age of Imperialism.* New York: Monthly Review Press, 1969.

Mandlebaum, Michael. *The Fate of Nations: The Search for National Security in the Nineteenth and Twentieth Centuries.* New York: Cambridge University Press, 1988.

Marcuse, Herbert. *One-Dimensional Man.* Boston: Beacon Press, 1991.

Marples, David R. *The Social Impact of the Chernobyl Disaster.* Edmonton: University of Alberta Press, 1988.

Marshall, Jonathan. *Drug Wars: Corruption, Counterinsurgency and Covert Operations in the Third World.* Berkeley: Cohan and Cohen, 1991.

Martin, W., and L. A. Winters, eds. *The Uruguay Round and the Developing Countries.* Washington, DC: World Bank, 1995.

Marx, Karl. *Grundrisse.* Trans. by Martin Nicolaus. Harmondsworth, England: Penguin Books, 1973.

Mason, Edward S., and Robert E. Asher. *The World Bank Since Bretton Woods.* Washington, DC: Brookings Institution, 1973.

Matthews, Robert O., Arthur G. Rubinoff, and Janice Gross Stein, eds. *International Conflict and Conflict Management: Readings in World Politics.* Scarborough, Ontario, Canada: Prentice-Hall, 1984.

Maura, Juan Francisco. *Women in the Conquest of the Americas.* Trans. by John F. Deredita. New York: Peter Lang, 1997.

McCarthy, Dennis M. P. *International Business History: A Contextual and Case Approach.* Westport, CT: Praeger, 1994.

McCoy, Alfred. *The Politics of Heroin in Southeast Asia.* New York: Harper and Row, 1972.

Melson, Robert. *Revolution and Genocide: On the Origins of the Armenian Genocide and the Holocaust.* Chicago: University of Chicago Press, 1992.

Mendez, Ruben P. *International Public Finance: A New Perspective on Global Relations.* New York: Oxford University Press, 1992.

Michelmann, Hans J., and Panayotis Soldatos, eds. *European Integration: Theories and Approaches.* Lanham, MD: University Press of America, 1994.

Millett, Kate. *Sexual Politics.* Garden City, NY: Doubleday, 1970.

Millett, Kate. *The Politics of Cruelty.* New York: W.W. Norton, 1994.

Milner, Helen V. *Resisting Protectionism: Global Industries and the Politics of International Trade.* Princeton: Princeton University Press, 1988.

Mishel, Lawrence, and Paula B. Voos, eds. *Unions and Economic Competitiveness.* Armonk, NY: Economic Policy Institute and M.E. Sharpe, 1992.

Mitchell, Richard P. *The Society of the Muslim Brotherhood.* London: Oxford University Press, 1969.

Mitrany, David. *A Working Peace System.* Chicago: Quadrangle Books, 1966.

Mitrany, David. *The Functional Theory of Politics.* New York: St. Martin's Press, 1977.

Mittelman, James H. ed. *Globalization: Critical Reflections.* Boulder. CO: Lynne Rienner, 1996.

Modelski, George, ed. *Transnational Corporations and World Order.* San Francisco: W.H. Freeman, 1979.

Moghadam, Valentine M., ed., *Patriarchy and Economic Development: Women's Positions at the End of the Twentieth Century.* Oxford: Clarendon Press, 1996.

Monbiot, George. *Poisoned Arrows.* London: Michael Joseph, 1989.

Morgenthau, Hans J. *Politics Among Nations.* New York: Knopf, 1948.

Morse, Edward L. *Modernization and the Transformation of International Relations.* New York: The Free Press, 1976.

Mowery, David C., and Nathan Rosenberg. *Technology and the Pursuit of Economic Growth.* Cambridge: Cambridge University Press, 1989.

Murphy, Craig N., and Roger Tooze, eds. *The New International Political Economy.* Boulder, CO: Lynne Rienner, 1991.

Nash, June, and Maria Patricia Fernandez-Kelly, eds. *Women, Men and the International Division of Labor.* Albany: State University of New York Press, 1983.

Nathan, James A., and James K. Oliver. *United States Foreign Policy and World Order.* 3d ed. Boston: Little, Brown and Company, 1985.

Nomani, Farhad, and Ali Rahnema. *Islamic Economic Systems.* London: Zed Books, 1994.

Nye, Joseph S., Jr. *Bound to Lead: The Changing Nature of American Power.* New York: Basic Books, 1990.

O'Brien, Richard. *Global Financial Integration: The End of Geography.* London: The Royal Institute of International Affairs, 1992.

OECD. *Development Co-Operation: Efforts and Policies of the Members of the DAC.* Washington, DC: Organization for Economic Co-operation and Development, [various years].

OECD. *Innovation, Patents, and Technological Strategies.* Paris: Organization for Economic Co-operation and Development, 1996.

OECD. *Interdependence and Co-operation in Tomorrow's World.* Paris: OECD, 1987.

OECD. *Twenty-Five Years of Development Co-Operation, 1985 Report: A Review.* Paris: Organization for Economic Co-operation and Development, 1985.

Ostrogorsky, George. *History of the Byzantine State.* Rev. ed. New Brunswick, NJ: Rutgers University, 1969.

Oye, Kenneth A., ed. *Cooperation Under Anarchy.* Princeton: Princeton University Press, 1986.

Palmieri, Deborah Anne, ed. *Russia and the NIS in the World Economy: East-West Investment, Financing, and Trade.* Westport, CT: Praeger, 1994.

Paquet, Gilles, ed. *The Multinational Firm and the Nation-State.* Don Mills, Ontario: Collier-Macmillan Canada, 1972.

Parker, William N. *Europe, America, and the Wider World: Essays on the Economic History of Western Capitalism, I, Europe and the World Economy.* Cambridge: Cambridge University Press, 1984.

Parker, William N. *Europe, America, and the Wider World: Essays on the Economic History of Western Capitalism, II, America and the Wider World.* Cambridge: Cambridge University Press, 1991.

Parkinson, F. *Latin America, the Cold War and World Powers, 1945–1973: A Study in Diplomatic History.* Beverly Hills: Sage, 1974.

Parpart, Jane L. *Women and Development in Africa: Comparative Perspectives.* Lanham, MD: University Press of America, 1989.

Pastor, Manuel, Jr. *Inflation, Stabilization, and Debt: Macroeconomic Experiments in Peru and Bolivia.* Boulder, CO: Westview Press, 1992.

Patrick, Hugh T., and Ryuichiro Tachi, eds. *Japan and the United States Today: Exchange Rates, Macroeconomic Policies, and Finan--cial Market Innovations.* New York: Columbia University, 1986.

Payaslian, Simon. *U.S. Foreign Economic and Military Aid: The Reagan and Bush Administrations.* Lanham, MD: University Press of America, 1996.

Payer, Cheryl. *The Debt Trap: The International Monetary Fund and the Third World.* New York: Monthly Review Press, 1974.

Payer, Cheryl. *The World Bank: A Critical Analysis.* New York: Monthly Review Press, 1982.

Pearson, Frederic S. *The Global Spread of Arms: Political Economy of International Security.* Boulder, CO: Westview Press, 1994.

Peretz, Don. *The Middle East Today.* 5th ed. New York: Praeger, 1988.

Peterson, V. Spike, ed. *Gendered States: Feminist (Re)Visions of International Relations Theory.* Boulder, CO: Lynne Rienner, 1992.

Peterson, V. Spike, and Anne Sisson Runyan. *Global Gender Issues.* Boulder, CO: Westview Press, 1993.

Pfaltzgraff, Robert L., Jr., ed. *Politics and the International System.* Philadelphia: J.B. Lippincott, 1969.

Pinder, John. *European Community: The Building of a Union.* Oxford: Oxford University Press, 1991.

Pipes, Daniel, and Adam Garfinkle, eds. *Friendly Tyrants: An American Dilemma.* New York: St. Martin's Press, 1991.

Pirages, Dennis. *Global Technopolitics.* Pacific Grove, CA: Brooks/Cole, 1989.

Pirages, Dennis, and Christine Sylvester, eds. *Transformations in the Global Political Economy.* London: Macmillan, 1988.

Piscatori, James, ed. *Islamic Fundamentalisms and the Gulf Crisis.* Chicago: American Academy of Arts and Sciences, 1991.

Pitelis, Christos N., and Roger Sugden, eds. *The Nature of the Transnational Firm.* London: Routledge, 1991.

Polk, William R. *The Arab World Today.* Cambridge: Harvard University Press, 1991.

Pollard, Sidney. *Peaceful Conquest: The Industrialization of Europe 1760–1970.* Oxford: Oxford University Press, 1981.

Polychroniou, Chronis, ed. *Issues and Perspectives in International Political Economy.* New York: Praeger, 1992.

Popper, Karl. *Conjectures and Refutations.* New York: Harper Torchbooks, 1965.

Popper, Karl. *Objective Knowledge.* Oxford: The Clarendon Press, 1979.

Popper, Karl. *Realism and the Aim of Science.* Totowa, NJ: Rowman and Littlefield, 1983.

Popper, Karl. *The Logic of Scientific Discovery.* New York: Harper Torchbooks, 1968.

Poppino, Rollie E. *International Communism in Latin America: A History of the Movement, 1917–1963.* New York: Free Press of Glencoe, 1964.

Porter, Bernard. *The Lion's Share: A Short History of British Imperialism, 1850–1995.* 3d ed. London: Longman, 1996.

Porter, Gareth, and Janet Welsh Brown. *Global Environmental Politics.* Boulder, CO: Westview Press, 1991.

Porter, Michael. *The Competitive Advantage of Nations.* New York: The Free Press, 1990.

Portes, Alejandro, and John Walton. *Labor, Class, and the International System.* New York: Academic Press, 1981.

Portes, Alejandro, Manuel Castells, and Lauren A. Benton, eds. *The Informal Economy: Studies in Advanced and Less Developed Countries.* Baltimore: Johns Hopkins University Press, 1989.

Pozo, Susan, ed. *Exploring the Underground Economy: Studies of Illegal and Unreported Activity.* Kalamazoo: W.E. Upjohn Institute for Employment Research, 1996.

Princen, Thomas, and Matthias Finger. *Environmental NGOs in World Politics: Linking the Local and the Global.* London: Routledge, 1994.

Proctor, J. Harris, ed. *Islam and International Relations.* New York: Praeger, 1965.

Putman, Robert D., and Nicholas Bayne. *Hanging Together: Cooperation and Conflict in the Seven-Power Summits.* Cambridge: Harvard University Press, 1987.

Pyle, David J. *Tax Evasion and the Black Economy.* London: Macmillan Press, 1989.

Qadir, C. A. *Philosophy and Science in the Islamic World.* London: Routledge, 1988.

Razin, Assaf, and Joel Slemrod, eds. *Taxation in the Global Economy.* Chicago: University of Chicago Press, 1990.

Rees, Joseph V. *Hostages of Each Other: The Transformation of Nuclear Safety Since Three Mile Island.* Chicago: University of Chicago Press, 1994.

Reid, Gavin C. *Classical Economic Growth: An Analysis in the Tradition of Adam Smith.* New York: Basil Blackwell, 1989.

Renard, John. *Seven Doors to Islam: Spirituality and the Religious Life of Muslims.* Berkeley: University of California Press, 1996.

Rhodes, Robert I., ed. *Imperialism and Underdevelopment: A Reader.* New York: Monthly Review Press, 1970.

Rich, Bruce. *Mortgaging the Earth: The World Bank, Environmental Impoverishment, and the Crisis of Development.* Boston: Beacon Press, 1994.

Richards, Alan, and John Waterbury. *A Political Economy of the Middle East: State, Class, and Economic Development.* Boulder, CO: Westview Press, 1990.

Rix, Alan. *Japan's Foreign Aid Challenge: Policy Reform and Aid Leadership.* London: Routledge, 1993.

Robbins, Lionel. *Theory of Economic Policy.* London: Macmillan, 1952.

Robinson, Richard. *The Internationalization of Business.* New York: Dryden Press, 1984.

Robinson, William I. *Promoting Polyarchy: Globalization, US Intervention, and Hegemony.* Cambridge: Cambridge University Press, 1996.

Rodinson, Maxine. *Islam and Capitalism.* New York: Pantheon Books, 1974.

Rodney, Walter. *How Europe Underdeveloped Africa.* Washington, DC: Howard University Press, 1982.

Roll, Eric. *A History of Economic Thought.* 5th ed. London: Faber and Faber, 1992.

Rondinelli, Dennis A. *Development Administration and U.S. Foreign Aid Policy.* Boulder, CO: Lynne Rienner, 1987.

Rosenberg, Emily S. *Spreading the American Dream: American Economic and Cultural Expansion, 1890–1945.* New York: Hill and Wang, 1982.

Rosenberg, Nathan. *Technology and American Economic Growth.* New York: Harper and Row, 1972.

Rosenberg, Nathan, and L.E. Birdzell. *How the West Grew Rich: The Economic Transformation of the Industrial World.* New York: Basic Books, 1986.

Rosenberg, Nathan, Ralph Landau, and David C. Mowery, eds. *Technology and the Wealth of Nations.* Stanford: Stanford University Press, 1992.

Ross, Robert S., ed. *East Asia in Transition: Toward a New Regional Order.* Armonk, NY: M.E. Sharpe, 1995.

Rostow, Walt W. *Theories of Economic Growth from David Hume to the Present.* New York: Oxford University Press, 1990.

Rothermund, Dietmar. *The Global Impact of the Great Depression, 1929–1939.* London: Routledge, 1996.

Rothgeb, John M., Jr. *Defining Power: Influence and Force in the Contemporary International System.* New York: St. Martin's Press, 1993.

Rothschild, Joan, ed. *Machina ex Dea: Feminist Perspective on Technology.* New York: Pergamon Press, 1983.

Rugman, Alan M., and Lorraine Eden, eds. *Multinational and Transfer Pricing.* New York: St. Martin's Press, 1985.

Rupert, Mark. *Producing Hegemony: The Politics of Mass Production and American Global Power.* Cambridge: Cambridge University Press, 1995.

Rupesinghe, Kumar, Peter King, and Olga Vorkunova, eds. *Ethnicity and Conflict in a Post-Communist World: The Soviet Union, Eastern Europe and China.* New York: St. Martin's Press, 1992.

Russell, Sharon Stanton. *Making Peace Work: Lessons for the International Development Community.* Washington, DC: Overseas Development Council, May 1996.

Russett, Bruce A. *Grasping the Democratic Peace.* Princeton: Princeton University Press, 1993.

Ryan, Stephen. *Ethnic Conflict in International Relations.* Aldershot, UK: Dartmouth Publishing Co., 1990.

Ryrie, William. *First World, Third World.* London: Macmillan Press, 1995.

Sachs, Jeffrey D., ed. *Developing Country Debt and the World Economy.* Chicago: University of Chicago Press, 1989.

Saint-Etienne, Christian. *The Great Depression, 1929–1938: Lessons for the 1980s.* Stanford, CA: Hoover Institution Press, 1984.

Salvatore, Dominick, ed. *National Trade Policies.* New York: Greenwood Press, 1992.

Sanderson, Steven E., ed. *The Americas in the New International Division of Labor.* New York: Holmes and Meier, 1984.

Sanger, Clyde. *Ordering the Oceans: The Making of the Law of the Sea.* Toronto: University of Toronto Press, 1987.

Schelling, Thomas C. *Arms and Influence.* New Haven: Yale University Press, 1966.

Schoultz, Lars. *Human Rights and United States Policy Toward Latin America.* Princeton: Princeton University Press, 1981.

Schumpeter, Joseph A. *History of Economic Analysis.* London: George Allen and Unwin, 1954.

Schwartz, Herman M. *States Versus Markets: History, Geography, and the Development of International Political Economy.* New York: St. Martin's Press, 1994.

Schweizer, Peter. *Friendly Spies.* New York: Atlantic Monthly Press, 1993.

Scott, Peter Dale, and Jonathan Marshall. *Cocaine Politics: Drugs, Armies, and the CIA in Central America.* Berkeley: University of California Press, 1991.

Segrave, Kerry. *The Sexual Harassment of Women in the Workplace, 1600 to 1993.* Jefferson, NC: McFarland and Company, 1994.

Shelton, Judy. *Money Meltdown: Restoring Order in the Global Currency System.* New York: The Free Press, 1994.

Shepard, Jon M. *Automation and Alienation: A Study of Office and Factory Workers.* Cambridge: MIT Press, 1971.

Shillington, Kevin. *History of Africa.* London: Macmillan, 1989.

Shiva, Vandana. *Staying Alive: Women, Ecology, and Development.* London: Zed Press, 1988.

Sigmund, Paul E. *Multinational in Latin America: The Politics of Nationalization.* Madison: University of Wisconsin Press and the Twentieth Century Fund, 1980.

Simmel, Georg. *The Philosophy of Money.* Ed. by David Frisby. Trans. by Tom Bottomore and David Frisby. 2d enl. ed. London: Routledge, 1990.

Simmons, Andre. *Arab Foreign Aid.* London: Associated University Presses, 1981.

Simon, Carl P., and Ann D. White. *Beating the System: The Underground Economy.* Boston: Auburn House, 1982.

Singer, J. David, ed. *The Correlates of War, I, Research Origins and Rationale.* New York: The Free Press, 1979.

Singham, A. W., and Shirley Hune. *Non-Alignment in an Age of Alignments.* London: Zed Books, 1986.

Sjöstedt, Gunnar, and Bengt Sundelius, eds. *Free Trade—Managed Trade? Perspectives on a Realistic International Trade Order.* Boulder, CO: Westview Press, 1986.

Skidmore, Thomas E., and Peter H. Smith. *Modern Latin America.* 3rd ed. New York: Oxford University Press, 1992.

Smith, Adam. *The Wealth of Nations.* London: Penguin Books, 1982.

Smith, Anthony. *The Geopolitics of Information.* New York: Oxford University Press, 1980.

Smith, M. Estellie, ed. *Perspectives on the Informal Economy.* Lanham, MD: University Press of America, 1990.

Smoke, Richard. *National Security and the Nuclear Dilemma.* Reading, MA: Addison-Wesley, 1984.

South Commission. *Challenge to the South: The Report of the South Commission.* [Nyerere Commission Report]. Oxford: Oxford University Press, 1990.

Spencer, Milton H. *Contemporary Economics.* 2d ed. New York: Worth, 1974.

Spero, Joan Edelman. *The Politics of International Economic Relations.* New York: St. Martin's Press, 1990.

Srinivasan, T. N. *Developing Countries and the Multilateral Trading System: From the GATT to the Uruguay Round and the Future.* Boulder, CO: Westview Press, 1998.

Staley, Charles E. *A History of Economic Thought: From Aristotle to Arrow.* Cambridge: Blackwell, 1989.

Staniland, Martin. *What Is Political Economy?* New Haven: Yale University Press, 1985.

Stavenhagen, Rodoflo. *The Ethnic Question: Conflict, Development, and Human Rights.* Tokyo: United Nations University Press, 1990.

Stern, Fritz. *Gold and Iron: Bismarck, Bleichröder, and the Building of the German Empire.* New York: Vintage Books, 1977.

Stokke, Olav, ed. *Western Middle Powers and Global Poverty.* Uppsala, Sweden: Scandinavian Institute of African Studies, 1989.

Strange, Susan, ed. *Paths to International Political Economy.* London: Allen and Unwin, 1984.

Strange, Susan. *States and Markets.* 2d ed. London: Pinter, 1994.

Strange, Susan. *The Retreat of the State: The Diffusion of Power in the World Economy.* Cambridge: Cambridge University Press, 1996.

Sullivan, Michael P. *Power in Contemporary International Politics.* Columbia: University of South Carolina Press, 1990.

Suppe, Frederick, ed. *The Structure of Scientific Theory.* 2d ed. Urbana: University of Illinois Press, 1977.

Sussman, Gerald, and John A. Lent. *Transnational Communications: Wiring the Third World.* Newbury Park, CA: Sage, 1991.

Sweezy, Paul. *The Theory of Economic Development.* London: Dennis Dobson, 1946.

Tanzi, Vito, ed. *The Underground Economy in the United States and Abroad.* Lexington, MA: Lexington Books, 1982.

Tapscott, Don, and Art Caston. *Paradigm Shift: The New Promise of Information Technology.* New York: McGraw-Hill, 1993.

Taylor, A. J. P. *The Struggle for Mastery in Europe, 1848–1918.* Oxford: Oxford University Press, 1954.

Taylor, Peter J. *Political Geography: World-Economy, Nation-State and Locality.* 3d ed. London: Longman, 1993.

Teich, Albert H., ed. *Technology and the Future.* 5th ed. New York: St. Martin's Press, 1990.

Temin, Peter. *Did Monetary Forces Cause the Great Depression?* New York: Norton, 1976.

Temin, Peter. *Lessons from the Great Depression.* Cambridge: MIT Press, 1989

Tendler, Judith. *Inside Foreign Aid.* Baltimore: Johns Hopkins University Press, 1975.

Thakur, Ramesh, and Carlyle A. Thayer, eds. *Reshaping Regional Relations: Asia-Pacific and the Former Soviet Union.* Boulder, CO: Westview Press, 1993.

Thomas, James J. *Informal Economic Activity.* Ann Arbor: University of Michigan Press, 1992.

Thompson, Charles M., and Fred Mitchell Jones. *Economic Development of the United States.* New York: Macmillan, 1939.

Thompson, E. P. *The Making of the English Working Class.* Harmondsworth, England: Penguin Books, 1968.

Thompson, Kenneth W., ed. *Moral Dimensions of American Foreign Policy.* New Brunswick, NJ: Transaction Books, 1984.

Thweatt, William O., ed. *Classical Political Economy: A Survey of Recent Literature.* Boston: Kluwer Academic Publishers, 1988.

Tickner, J. Ann. *Gender in International Relations: Feminist Perspectives on Achieving Global Security.* New York: Columbia University Press, 1992.

Tilly, Charles. *Coercion, Capital, and European States, AD 990–1992.* Cambridge: Blackwell, 1992.

Trebilcock, Michael J., and Robert Howse. *The Regulation of International Trade.* London: Routledge, 1995.

Triffin, Robert. *Gold and the Dollar Crisis: The Future of Convertibility.* New Haven: Yale University Press, 1960.

Tsoukalis, Loukas. *The New European Economy: The Politics and Economics of Integration.* Rev. 2d ed. Oxford: Oxford University Press, 1993.

Tylecote, Andrew. *The Long Wave in the World Economy.* London: Routledge, 1991.

Tyson, Laura D'Andrea. *Who's Bashing Whom: Trade Conflicts in High Technology Industries.* Washington DC: Institute for International Economics, 1992.

United Nations. *World Economic and Social Survey, 1997: Trends and Policies in the World Economy.* New York: United Nations, 1997.

United Nations. Center on Transnational Corporations. *The United Nations Code of Conduct on Transnational Corporations.* New York: United Nations, 1986.

United Nations. Center on Transnational Corporations. *Transnational Corporations and Technology Transfer: Effects and Policy Issues.* New York: United Nations, 1987.

United Nations. Conference on Trade and Development. *World Investment Report.* New York: United Nations, [various years].

United Nations. Conference on Trade and Development. *Trade and Development Report, 1997.* New York: United Nations, 1997.

United Nations. Economic and Social Commission for Western Asia. *Survey of Economic and Social Developments in the ESCWA Region, 1995.* New York: United Nations, 1996.

United Nations Development Program. *Human Development Report 1997.* New York: Oxford University Press, 1997.

United States. *Economic Report of the President Transmitted to the Congress, February 1997.* Washington, DC: U.S. Government Printing Office, 1997.

United States. *Economic Report of the President Transmitted to the Congress, February 1998.* Washington, DC: U.S. Government Printing Office, 1998.

United States. Agency for International Development. *U.S. Overseas Loans and Grants.* Washington, DC: U.S. Government Printing Office, (various years)

United States. Congress. House Committee on Science, Space, and Technology. Subcommittee on Science. *Termination of the Superconducting Super Collider Project,* 103 Con., 2nd sess, March 15, 1994. Washington, DC: U.S. Government Printing Office, 1994.

United States. Congress. Senate Subcommittee on Terrorism, Narcotics, and International Operations of the Committee on Foreign Relations. *Drugs, Law Enforcement and Foreign Policy.* Washington, DC: U.S. Government Printing Office, 1989. "Kerry Report."

United States. Department of Labor, Bureau of Labor Statistics. *Labor Composition and U.S. Productivity Growth,1948–90.* Bulletin 2426. Washington, DC: U.S. Government Printing Office, 1993.

Usher, Abbott Payson. *The Early History of Deposit Banking in Mediterranean Europe.* New York: Russell and Russell, 1943.

Van de Laar, Aart. *The World Bank and the Poor.* The Hague: Martinus Nijhoff, 1980.

Van der Wee, Herman, ed. *The Great Depression Revisited.* The Hague: Martinus Nijhoff, 1972.

Vasiliev, A. A. *History of the Byzantine Empire.* 2 vols. Madison: University of Wisconsin Press, 1971.

Veblen, Thorstein. *Theory of the Leisure Class.* Harmondsworth, UK: Penguin Books, 1979.

Vernon, Raymond. *Sovereignty at Bay: The Multinational Spread of U.S. Enterprises.* New York: Basic Books, 1971.

Vernon, Raymond, ed. *The Promise of Privatization: A Challenge for American Foreign Policy.* New York: Council on Foreign Relations, 1988.

Veseth, Michael. *Selling Globlization: The Myth of the Global Economy.* Boulder, CO: Lynne Rienner, 1998.

Viljoen, Stephan. *Economic Systems in World History.* New York: Longman, 1974.

Volti, Rudi. *Society and Technological Change.* New York: St. Martin's Press, 1988.

Wallerstein, Immanuel. *The Capitalist World Economy.* Cambridge: Cambridge University Press, 1979.

Wallerstein, Immanuel. *The Modern World System I.* New York: Academic Press, 1974.

Wallerstein, Immanuel. *The Modern World System II.* New York: Academic Press, 1980.

Walter, Andrew. *World Power and World Money: The Role of Hegemony and International Monetary Order.* New York: Harvester Wheatsheaf, 1991.

Walter, Ingo. *Secret Money: The World of International Financial Secrecy.* Lexington, MA: Lexington Books, 1985.

Walter, Ingo. *The Secret Money Market.* New York: Harper and Row, 1990.

Walters, Robert S., and David H. Blake. *The Politics of Global Economic Relations.* 4th ed. Englewood Cliffs, NJ: Prentice Hall, 1992.

Waltz, Kenneth N. *Theory of International Politics.* Reading: Addison-Wesley, 1979.

Ward, Kathryn, ed. *Women Workers and Global Restructuring.* Ithaca: Cornell University Press, 1990.

Whitaker, B. *The Global Connection: The Crisis of Drug Addiction.* London: Jonathan Cape, 1987.

White, Rodney R. *North, South, and the Environmental Crisis.* Toronto: University of Toronto Press, 1993.

Wilber, Charles K., and Kenneth P. Jameson, eds. *The Political Economy of Development and Underdevelopment.* 5th ed. New York: McGraw-Hill, 1992.

Wilkins, Mira. *The Emergence of Multinational Enterprises: American Business Abroad from the Colonial Era to 1914.* Cambridge, MA: Harvard University Press, 1970.

Wilson, Rodney. *Economic Development in the Middle East.* London: Routledge, 1995.

Winham, Gilbert R. *The Evolution of International Trade Agreements.* Toronto: University of Toronto Press, 1992.

Wionczek, Miguel S., ed. *Latin American Economic Integration: Experiences and Prospects.* New York: Praeger, 1966.

Wisotsky, Steven. *Beyond the War on Drugs.* Buffalo: Prometheus Books, 1990.

Wolff, Richard D., and Stephen A. Resnick. *Economics: Marxian Versus Neoclassical.* Baltimore: Johns Hopkins University Press, 1987.

World Bank. *World Tables 1995.* Baltimore: Johns Hopkins University Press, 1995.

World Trade Organization. *GATT Activities* [various years].

Wynia, Gary W. *The Politics of Latin American Development.* 3d ed. Cambridge: Cambridge University Press, 1990.

Yamamura, Kozo, and Yasukichi Yasuba, eds. *The Political Economy of Japan: The Domestic Transformation.* Stanford: Stanford University Press, 1987.

Yeager, Leland B. *International Monetary Relations: Theory, History and Policy.* New York: Harper and Row, 1976.

Yoffie, David B., and Benjamin Gomes-Casseres. *International Trade and Competition.* 2d ed. New York: McGraw-Hill, 1994.

Young, Oran R. *International Cooperation: Building Regimes for Natural Resources and the Environment.* Ithaca: Cornell University Press, 1989.

NAME INDEX

SUBJECT INDEX